2010-2012 EDITION

IRENE C. FOUNTAS
GAY SU PINNELL

THE FOUNTAS AND PINNELL

LEVELED BOOK LIST K-8+

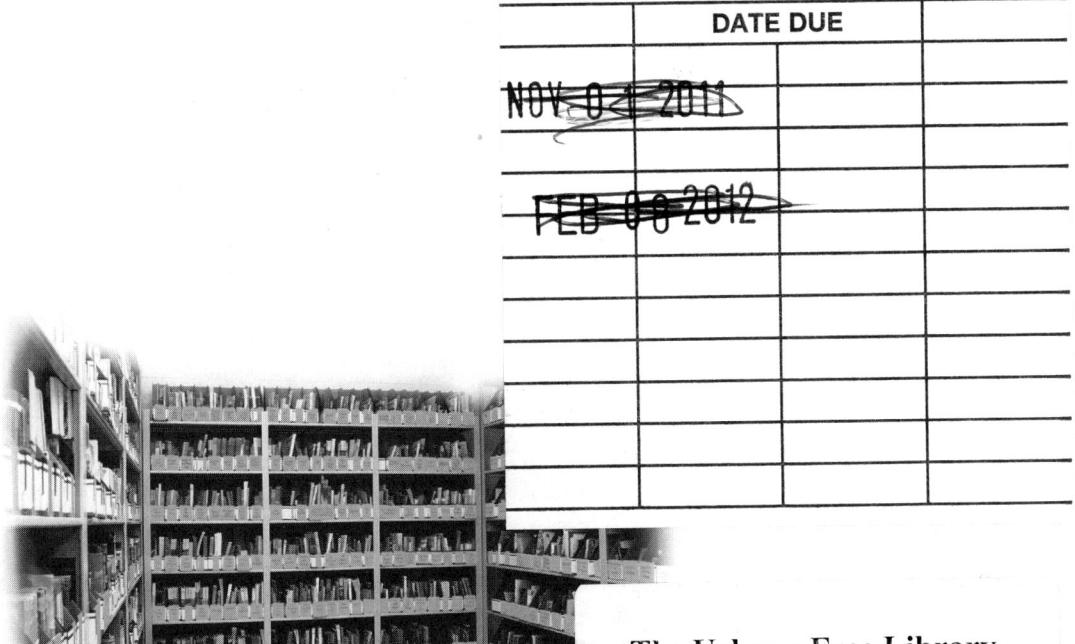

Heinemann
Portsmouth, NH

8111
6250

Heinemann
361 Hanover Street
Portsmouth, NH 03801-3912
www.heinemann.com

Offices and agents throughout the world

© 2009, 2006 by Irene C. Fountas and Gay Su Pinnell

Library of Congress Cataloging-in-Publication Data

Fountas, Irene C.
   The Fountas and Pinnell leveled book list K-8+ / Irene C. Fountas, Gay Su Pinnell.—2010–2012 ed.
   p. cm.
ISBN 978-0-325-02608-4 (alk. paper)
1. Reading (Elementary) 2. Reading (Middle school) 3. Children—Books and reading.
I. Pinnell, Gay Su. II. Title. III. Title: Leveled book list K-8.
   LB1573.F638 2009
   372.41—dc22

                       2008038718

Printed in the United States of America on acid-free paper
13 12 11 10 09 VP 1 2 3 4 5

We dedicate this extensive resource to our colleague

Carol Woodworth

with much fondness and deep appreciation.

TABLE OF CONTENTS

INTRODUCTION TO THE BOOK LIST   vii

EVALUATION RESPONSE FOR TEXT GRADIENT   xi

THE LIST
ORGANIZED ALPHABETICALLY BY **BOOK TITLE**   1

APPENDIX A
PUBLISHER AND DISTRIBUTOR INFORMATION   682

Introduction to the Book List

All teachers want their students to be successful, confident readers. This process begins with sensitive, responsive reading instruction; an understanding of how books support the "learning to read" process; and access to a sufficient quantity of high-quality books at appropriate instructional levels. In our books *Guided Reading: Good First Teaching for All Children* (Heinemann, 1996); *Guiding Readers and Writers: Teaching Comprehension, Genre, and Content Literacy* (Heinemann, 2001); and *Teaching for Comprehending and Fluency: Thinking, Talking, and Writing About Reading, K-8* (Heinemann, 2006), we describe a comprehensive language and literacy framework designed to help students develop a broad and integrated range of reading, writing, and language abilities.

Then in *Leveled Books K–8: Matching Texts to Readers for Effective Teaching* (Heinemann, 2006), we focus on the texts you will need to support a rich environment for literacy teaching and learning, beginning with a description of the most effective ways to use books in the classroom. That book also describes our gradient of leveled texts and its uses. We encourage the use of leveled books for instruction in guided reading and small-group literacy intervention lessons. Our levels will help you make good choices for students at various stages of reading development. For the specific characteristics of texts at each level and the competencies students need to acquire at each level, refer to our book, *The Continuum of Literacy Learning, K-8* (Heinemann, 2007).

This book—*The Fountas and Pinnell Leveled Book List, K–8*—is a reference resource of over 33,000 titles that have been through an in-depth analysis by teams of experts who are experienced in analyzing features of texts as well as in teaching guided reading. The list includes a wide variety of genres and formats, fiction and nonfiction. Of course, we can't possibly level every book published. As you get to know books at our levels, talk with colleagues about the books you have that are not yet part of this list and assign them a tentative level.

The leveling process is ongoing, including constant review and revision as books are used by teachers in the classroom. "Leveling" is not an exact science. A level is an approximation, not an absolute designation; not all books on a level are precisely alike. There are many variables to take into account in determining text difficulty. A text's demands and supports cannot be reduced to a mathematical formula. The concepts of "easier" and "harder" must always be understood in relation to the complex and interrelated text factors that we describe in *Leveled Books K–8*. What's more, myriad student factors have an impact on text readability as well. The readability of a text is influenced by the background knowledge required of the reader to understand the text, the reader's facility with word solving, the number of complex sentences embedded in the text, and so on. The specialized process of determining text difficulty is a challenge worthy of our time because the more we learn about texts, the better we understand their demands on the individual readers we teach—the first step in matching books to readers.

The most current book list can be found at *www.fountasandpinnellleveledbooks.com*. This online database version of the book list is updated monthly with hundreds of new titles as well as revisions to existing levels as they are needed. The web site also includes a wide variety of other professional development resources to support your work in the classroom, including video clips of teaching in guided reading.

Book collections continually evolve. You build your collection slowly over time as you test books with students. We hope our gradient and book list will help you select texts that are "just right" for your readers.

How to Use the Book List

The list is sorted alphabetically by book title. In the database, you can sort by level or series. The tabs along the page edge make it possible to quickly turn to the letter you want.

As you will see, there are six columns on each page. The contents of each column are described below.

❑ **Title:** The first column indicates the title of the book. Books are placed alphabetically by the first word of the title—unless it is *a, an,* or *the,* in which case the article follows the title. Titles beginning with a numeral are placed at the beginning of the list in order by number.

❑ **Level:** The second column indicates the level assigned to the book, from A to Z or Z+. We use the letter A to indicate the easiest books to read and the letter Z to identify the most challenging books. In addition, we have added titles recommended for high school, which are labeled Z+ and are integrated throughout the book. More detailed descriptions of the text features of each level can be found in *Leveled Books K–8.* Two other abbreviations are used in this column:

• *WB - Wordless Books:* Books without any words in them at all (books that tell a story only in pictures) are excellent for the development of oral language and so are included in our list. However, they are not "leveled" in the same sense that the other books in the list are leveled.

• *LB - Label Books:* These are books with only one word or a very short phrase on every page. As with Wordless Books, we find leveling these books inappropriate. We do not recommend label books for use in guided reading.

❑ **Genre:** The third column indicates the type of book, or genre. Genre is a term that means type of text. We have classified each book as one genre though you will find there are some books that have elements of more than one. With the wealth and variety of children's books available today, it is sometimes difficult to make a designation of genre for a particular text. A text may have some features of an informational text, such as describing a series of actions; but the characters in the illustrations may be animals talking or getting dressed like people. In this case, the text would be fantasy. In this list, if material in the text or illustrations has elements of fantasy, the book is classified as fantasy. In addition, there are many "hybrid texts" that combine elements of fiction and nonfiction; for example, a group of fictional children might visit a museum and learn a great deal about fossils. The text would be realistic fiction but would provide authentic information to the reader. Where any part of the text is fiction, we have designated it as fiction. You will want to analyze texts carefully, however, to take advantage of all the text characteristics and learning opportunities.

The following codes are used to indicate genre:

• *TL - Traditional Literature*
• *RF - Realistic Fiction*
• *HF - Historical Fiction*
• *SF - Science Fiction*
• *F - Fantasy*
• *B - Biography (includes autobiography and memoir)*
• *I - Information Book*

❑ **Words:** The fourth column provides the number of words appearing in the book. Note: "250+" indicates the book contains more than 250 words.

❑ **Author/Series:** The fifth column provides the name of the author or specific reading series.

❑ **Publisher/Distributor:** The sixth column indicates the publisher's or distributor's name. A list of addresses and phone numbers for each publisher or distributor of reading series and collections can be found in Appendix A. Trade books listed with the author's name are available from a variety of distributors.

Short Story Collection

❏ You'll notice that some books are marked with an * (asterisk). The asterisk indicates that the book is a collection of short stories. Some collections contain story books in which each story is completely independent of the others. In other collections, the stories are interrelated in some way, such as short biographies or a common character or theme. These can often be read out of order.

❏ **Graphic Text:** You will also notice a new category, marked with a # (pound sign). The pound sign indicates a graphic text, or a text that is written with illustrations and speech bubbles in a sequence.

The true test of any leveling system, of course, is using the texts with students over time. We have included a form on the following page, **Evaluation Response for Text Gradient,** to gather more information about the books on our list and to provide you the opportunity to suggest new books for leveling. We want teachers in many different geographic areas to test the books and provide feedback based on their use with students in guided reading. We invite you to send feedback to us at any time. As the online database and this book are revised, we will take your comments and suggestions into consideration.

Evaluation Response for Text Gradient

Directions: Since any text gradient is always in the process of construction as it is used with varying groups of children, we expect our list to change every year. We encourage you to try the levels with your students and to provide feedback based on your own experiences. Please suggest changes to existing book levels and suggest new books for the list. Please provide the information requested below.

Name: _____ Grade Level You Teach: _____

Telephone: ( ) _____ E-mail address: _____

Address (street, city, state): _____

Book Evaluated:

Book Title: _____

Level: A B C D E F G H I J K L M N O P Q R S T U V W X Y Z Z+

Author: _____

Publisher: _____

This book is:

_____ A book listed on the gradient that I have evaluated with my class.
(Complete SECTION A and make comments in SECTION C.)

_____ A book listed on the gradient that I am recommending as a benchmark for a level.
(Complete SECTION A and make comments in SECTION C.)

_____ A new book that I suggest adding to the collection.
(Complete SECTION B and make comments in SECTION C.)

SECTION A: (for an evaluation of a book currently included in the list)

Is it appropriately placed on the level (explain)? _____
To what level should the book be moved?

A   B   C   D   E   F   G   H   I   J   K   L   M   N   O   P   Q   R   S   T   U   V   W   X   Y   Z   Z+

Are there points of difficulty that make it harder than it seems? _____

_____

Is the text supportive in ways that might not be noticeable when examining the superficial characteristics?

_____

SECTION B: (for the recommendation of a new book) Indicate recommended level: _____

How does this book support readers at this level? _____

_____

What challenges does it offer? _____

_____

SECTION C: Please place additional comments on the back or on another sheet.

Mail or fax (603–431–7840) this form to:
Leveled Book List Suggestions
c/o Heinemann
361 Hanover Street
Portsmouth, NH 03801–3912

Book List

TITLE	LEVEL	GENRE	WORD COUNT	AUTHOR / SERIES	PUBLISHER / DISTRIBUTOR
1 Is for One	E	F	82	Bookshop	Mondo
1 Potato 2 Potato	N	I	250+	Literacy 2000	Rigby
1, 2, 3 in the Box	B	RF	23	Tarlow, Ellen	Scholastic
1, 2, Kangaroo	LB	F	54	Reading Corners	Pearson Learning Group
2 of Everything	I	RF	217	Talking Point Series	Pearson Learning Group
2, 4, 6, 8 Legs	C	I	57	Literacy by Design	Rigby
2, 4, 6, 8 Legs	C	I	57	On Our Way to English	Rigby
3,2,1... Lift Off!	K	RF	250+	Storyteller-Shooting Stars	Wright Group/McGraw Hill
3-2-1 Blast-Off	I	RF	291	Talking Point Series	Pearson Learning Group
3-D ABC: A Sculptural Alphabet	Q	I	368	Raczka, Bob	Millbrook Press
4 Kids in 5E & 1 Crazy Year	S	RF	250+	Schwartz, Virginia Frances	Holiday House
5 Novels	V	F	250+	Pinkwater, Daniel	Farrar, Straus and Giroux
7 Facts About the Weather	I	I	231	Leveled Readers Science	Houghton Mifflin Harcourt
7 Uses for Air	B	I	46	Independent Readers Science	Houghton Mifflin Harcourt
7 Ways to Get Energy	J	I	193	Independent Readers Science	Houghton Mifflin Harcourt
10 9 8 Polar Animals!	I	I	224	Counting Books	Capstone Press
10 Bravest Everyday Heroes, The	T	I	250+	The 10 Books	Franklin Watts
10 Cats	LB	RF	13	Leveled Readers Language Support	Houghton Mifflin Harcourt
10 Deadliest Plants, The	T	I	250+	The 10 Books	Franklin Watts
10 Greatest Accidental Inventions	T	I	250+	The 10 Books	Franklin Watts
10 Most Amazing Animal Movies, The	T	I	250+	The 10 Books	Franklin Watts
10 Most Wondrous Ancient Sites, The	V	I	250+	The 10 Books	Franklin Watts
10 Smartest Animals, The	T	I	250+	The 10 Books	Franklin Watts
12 Again	V	F	250+	Corbett, Sue	Penguin Group
*13 Ghosts: Strange But True Stories	X	F	250+	Osborne, Will	Scholastic
13th Floor, The	P	F	250+	Storyteller - Autumn Leaves	Wright Group/ McGraw Hill
13th Floor, The: A Ghost Story	U	F	250+	Fleischman, Sid	Bantam
15 Best Things About Being the New Kid, The	K	RF	585	Silly Millies	Millbrook Press
15 Facts about Atoms	S	I	654	Independent Readers Science	Houghton Mifflin Harcourt
15 Facts about Snakes	K	I	347	Rigby Focus	Rigby
15 Facts about Stars	W	I	1652	Independent Readers Science	Houghton Mifflin Harcourt
15 Facts about the Solar System	P	I	474	Independent Readers Science	Houghton Mifflin Harcourt
18th Emergency, The	R	RF	250+	Byars, Betsy	Bantam
20 Pennies	E	RF	212	Teacher's Choice Series	Pearson Learning Group
20,000 Leagues Under the Sea	Z+	F	250+	Verne, Jules	Scholastic
26 Fairmount Avenue	N	B	250+	DePaola, Tomie	Putnam/Penguin
33 Snowfish	Z+	RF	250+	Rapp, Adam	Candlewick Press
40 Nights to Knowing the Sky	Z	I	250+	Schaaf, Fred	Henry Holt & Co.
47	X	F	250+	Mosley, Walter	Little, Brown & Co.
52 Days by Camel: My Sahara Adventure	T	I	250+	Raskin, Lawrie	Annick Press
89th Kitten, The	O	RF	250+	Nilsson, Eleanor	Scholastic
97 Ways to Train a Dragon	P	F	250+	McMullan, Kate	Scholastic
100 Days	B	RF	16	Bebop Books	Lee & Low Books Inc.
100 Days and 99 Nights	P	RF	250	Madison, Alan	Little, Brown & Co.
100 Days of School	L	I	264	Harris, Trudy	Millbrook Press
100 Pets	J	RF	368	Gear Up!	Wright Group/McGraw Hill

TITLE	LEVEL	GENRE	WORD COUNT	AUTHOR / SERIES	PUBLISHER / DISTRIBUTOR
100 Years Ago	E	I	119	Learn to Read	Creative Teaching Press
100 Years Ago	H	I	135	Twig	Wright Group/McGraw Hill
100th Day of School, The	K	I	250+	Holidays and Celebrations	Picture Window Books
100th Day, The	G	RF	138	Maccarone, Grace	Scholastic
145th Street	Z+	RF	250+	Myers, Walter Dean	Laurel-Leaf Books
1,000 Reasons Never to Kiss a Boy	X	RF	250+	Freeman, Martha	Holiday House
1000 Facts about Space	X	I	250+	Beasant, Pam	Scholastic
1980s, The	R	I	1144	Leveled Readers Social Studies	Houghton Mifflin Harcourt
2095	P	SF	250+	Scieszka, Jon	Penguin Group
5010 Calling	O	SF	1496	Powell, J.	Stone Arch Books
20th Century African American Singers	U	B	2956	Reading Street	Pearson

Organized Alphabetically by Title
Storable Database at www.fountasandpinnellleveledbooks.com

* Collection of short stories
\# Graphic text

TITLE	LEVEL	GENRE	WORD COUNT	AUTHOR / SERIES	PUBLISHER / DISTRIBUTOR
A. Lincoln and Me	M	RF	250+	Borden, Louise	Scholastic
A.L.L to the Rescue	S	RF	1000	Leveled Readers/TX	Houghton Mifflin Harcourt
A-10 Thunderbolt, The	U	I	250+	Cross-Sections	Capstone Press
Abarat	Z	F	250+	Barker, Clive	HarperCollins
Abby	M	RF	250+	Hanel, Wolfram	North-South Books
Abby Takes a Stand	Q	HF	250+	McKissack, Patricia	Scholastic
ABC Bunny, The	H	F	161	Ga'g, Wanda	Scholastic
ABC I Like Me!	H	F	136	Carlson, Nancy	Puffin/Penguin
ABC Who's Got Me?	E	F	40	Instant Readers	Harcourt School Publishers
Abe Lincoln: Log Cabin To White House	Z	B	250+	North, Sterling	Random House
Abe Lincoln's Hat	M	B	250+	Brenner, Martha	Random House
Abel's Island	T	F	250+	Steig, William	Farrar, Straus and Giroux
Abigail Adams	S	B	250+	Amazing Americans	Wright Group/McGraw Hill
Abigail Adams	S	B	3710	History Maker Bios	Lerner Publications
Abigail Adams	W	I	3123	Leveled Readers	Houghton Mifflin Harcourt
Abigail Adams	W	I	3123	Leveled Readers/CA	Houghton Mifflin Harcourt
Abigail Adams	W	I	3123	Leveled Readers/TX	Houghton Mifflin Harcourt
Abigail Adams	Q	B	250+	Primary Source Readers	Teacher Created Materials
Abigail Adams, Patriot	U	B	2288	Leveled Readers Social Studies	Houghton Mifflin Harcourt
Abigail Adams: Girl of Colonial Days	R	B	250+	Wagoner, Jean Brown	Aladdin
Abominable Snowman, The	M	F	250+	Bookweb	Rigby
Aboriginal and Inuit Worlds	T	I	3,467	Take Two Books	Wright Group/McGraw Hill
About 100 Years Ago	I	I	250+	Yellow Umbrella Books	Red Brick Learning
About How Many?	M	I	250+	Early Connections	Benchmark Education
About Milk	N	I	670	Springboard	Wright Group/ McGraw Hill
About Pets	F	I	178	We Both Read	Treasure Bay
About the B'nai Bagels	T	RF	250+	Konigsburg, E. L.	Dell
About the Ocean	I	I	475	We Both Read	Treasure Bay
Above and Below	C	I	41	Location	Lerner Publishing
Above and Below	F	I	128	Sunshine	Wright Group/McGraw Hill
Above and Below	I	I	239	Where Words	Capstone Press
Abracadabra	L	RF	372	Reading Unlimited	Pearson Learning Group
Abracadabra	LB	F	14	Rigby Rocket	Rigby
Abracadabra Kid, The	X	B	250+	Fleischman, Sid	Beech Tree Books
Abracadabra!	C	RF	35	InfoTrek	ETA Cuisenaire
Abraham Lincoln	S	B	250+	Amazing Americans	Wright Group/McGraw Hill
Abraham Lincoln	P	B	250+	Early Biographies	Compass Point Books
Abraham Lincoln	M	B	235	Famous Americans	Capstone Press
Abraham Lincoln	N	B	214	First Biographies	Capstone Press
Abraham Lincoln	Q	B	250+	Gross, Ruth Belov	Scholastic
Abraham Lincoln	S	B	3783	History Maker Bios	Lerner Publications
Abraham Lincoln	T	B	250+	In Their Own Words	Scholastic
Abraham Lincoln	U	B	250+	Let Freedom Ring	Red Brick Learning
Abraham Lincoln	S	B	250+	Parin d'Aulaire, Ingri & Edgar	Bantam
Abraham Lincoln	Q	B	250+	Photo-Illustrated Biographies	Red Brick Learning
Abraham Lincoln	U	B	250+	Primary Source Readers	Teacher Created Materials
Abraham Lincoln	U	B	250+	Profiles of the Presidents	Compass Point Books
Abraham Lincoln: A Life of Respect	O	B	492	Pull Ahead Books	Lerner Publications
Abraham Lincoln: Defender of the Union	Y	B	250+	The Civil War	Carus Publishing Company
Abraham Lincoln: Lawyer, President, Emancipator	M	B	250+	Biographies	Picture Window Books
Abraham Lincoln: President of a Divided Country	O	B	250+	Greene, Carol	Children's Press

TITLE	LEVEL	GENRE	WORD COUNT	AUTHOR / SERIES	PUBLISHER / DISTRIBUTOR
Abraham Lincoln: Sixteenth President	R	B	250+	Getting to Know the U.S. Presidents	Children's Press
Abraham Lincoln: The Great Emancipator	R	B	250+	Stevenson, Augusta	Aladdin
Abraham's Battle: A Novel of Gettysburg	T	HF	250+	Banks, Sara Harrell	Atheneum
Absent Author, The	N	RF	250+	A to Z Mysteries	Random House
Absolutely Normal Chaos	V	RF	250+	Creech, Sharon	HarperTrophy
Absolutely Not!	E	F	199	Story Steps	Rigby
Absolutely True Diary of a Part-Time Indian, The	Z+	RF	250+	Alexie, Sherman	Little, Brown & Co.
Absolutely True Story, The: How I Visited Yellowstone Park With the Terrible Rupes	R	RF	250+	Roberts, Willo Davis	Aladdin
Abyssinian Cats	I	I	119	Cats	Capstone Press
Acceptable Time, An	X	F	250+	L'Engle, Madeleine	Laurel-Leaf Books
Accident in the Forest	M	RF	839	Springboard	Wright Group/McGraw Hill
Accident on the Bike Track	M	RF	712	Springboard	Wright Group/McGraw Hill
Accident Prone	P	RF	250+	Bookweb	Rigby
Accident, The	H	RF	313	Foundations	Wright Group/McGraw Hill
Accidental Angel (Secret Sisters)	P	RF	250+	Byrd, Sandra	WaterBrook Press
Accidents	D	RF	35	Visions	Wright Group/McGraw Hill
Accidents May Happen: Fifty Inventions Discovered	T	I	250+	Jones, Charlotte Foltz	Delacorte Press
Ace Reporter	L	RF	250+	Bookweb	Rigby
Ace: The Very Important Pig	R	F	250+	King-Smith, Dick	Alfred A. Knopf
Achilles	W	I	250+	World Mythology	Capstone Press
Achoo! The Most Interesting Book You'll Ever Read About Germs	R	I	250+	Romanek, Trudee	Scholastic
Acid Rain	Y	I	1702	Independent Readers Science	Houghton Mifflin Harcourt
Acid Rain	U	I	250+	Our Planet In Peril	Capstone Press
Acid Rain	L	I	368	Wonder World	Wright Group/McGraw Hill
A-Counting We Will Go	E	RF	191	Learn to Read	Creative Teaching Press
Across Five Aprils	Z	HF	250+	Hunt, Irene	Follett
Across Ice and Snow	J	I	138	Gear Up!	Wright Group/McGraw Hill
Across the Lines	W	HF	250+	Reeder, Carolyn	Avon Camelot
Across the Oregon Trail	T	HF	250+	Storyteller -Mountain Peaks	Wright Group/McGraw Hill
Across the Seasons	C	I	75	Early Connections	Benchmark Education
Across the Stream	F	F	94	Ginsburg, Mirra	Morrow
Across the Wide and Lonesome Prairie	U	HF	250+	My America	Scholastic
Act I, Act II, Act Normal	T	RF	250+	Weston, Martha	Roaring Book Press
Action Safety	O	I	250+	Bookweb	Rigby
Action: Defense	T	I	250+	Sails	Rigby
Active Volcanoes	N	I	572	Springboard	Wright Group/ McGraw Hill
Ad Break	P	RF	250+	Bookweb	Rigby
Adam Canfield of the Slash	U	RF	250+	Winerip, Michael	Candlewick Press
Adam Canfield Watch Your Back!	U	RF	250+	Winerip, Michael	Candlewick Press
Adam Joshua Capers: Halloween Monster	N	RF	250+	Smith, Janice Lee	HarperTrophy
*Adam Joshua Capers: Kid Next Door and Other Headaches, The	N	RF	250+	Smith, Janice Lee	HarperTrophy
*Adam Joshua Capers: Monster in the Third Dresser Drawer, The	N	RF	250+	Smith, Janice Lee	HarperTrophy
Adam Joshua Capers: Nelson in Love	N	RF	250+	Smith, Janice Lee	HarperTrophy
Adam Joshua Capers: Show-and-Tell War, The	N	RF	250+	Smith, Janice Lee	HarperTrophy
Adam Joshua Capers: Superkid!	N	RF	250+	Smith, Janice Lee	HarperTrophy
Adam Joshua Capers: Turkey Trouble	N	RF	250+	Smith, Janice Lee	HarperTrophy
Adam of the Road	W	HF	250+	Gray, Elizabeth Janet	Scholastic

* Collection of short stories
# Graphic text

TITLE	LEVEL	GENRE	WORD COUNT	AUTHOR / SERIES	PUBLISHER / DISTRIBUTOR
Adaptations to Land and Water	S	I	250+	Science Support Readers	Houghton Mifflin Harcourt
Add It Up	J	RF	311	Story Box	Wright Group/McGraw Hill
Add the Animals	D	I	74	Early Connections	Benchmark Education
Addie Meets Max	J	RF	250+	Robins, Joan	Harper & Row
Addie's Bad Day	J	RF	566	Robins, Joan	HarperTrophy
Addie's Dakota Winter	T	RF	250+	Lawlor, Laurie	Pocket Books
Adding Arctic Animals	I	I	120	Yellow Umbrella Books	Red Brick Learning
Adding It Up at the Zoo	G	I	250+	Yellow Umbrella Books	Red Brick Learning
Addition Annie	G	RF	30	Rookie Readers	Children's Press
Addy Learns a Lesson: A School Story	Q	HF	250+	The American Girls Collection	Pleasant Company
Addy Saves the Day: A Summer Story	Q	HF	250+	The American Girls Collection	Pleasant Company
Addy's Surprise: A Christmas Story	Q	HF	250+	The American Girls Collection	Pleasant Company
Adeline's Dream	T	HF	45612	From Many Peoples	Fitzhenry & Whiteside
Adios, Anna	N	RF	250+	Giff, Patricia Reilly	Bantam
Adios, Coyote	K	F	250+	Rigby Literacy	Rigby
Admiral Perry	T	B	2451	Independent Readers Social Studies	Houghton Mifflin Harcourt
Adventure at Sea	J	F	250+	Storyworlds	Heinemann Educational Books
Adventure in Alaska	O	I	250+	Kramer, S. A.	Random House
Adventure in the Purple Forest	I	F	214	Spaceboy	Literacy Footprints
Adventure to the New World	T	HF	5668	Reading Street	Pearson
Adventure Travel	T	I	250+	Boldprint	Steck-Vaughn
Adventure Vacations	M	I	250+	Rigby Literacy	Rigby
Adventurers, The	O	I	250+	Scooters	ETA Cuisenaire
Adventures in Matunaland	U	RF	8913	Reading Street	Pearson
Adventures of a Kite	L	F	33	Jellybeans	Rigby
*Adventures of Ali Baba Bernstein, The	O	RF	250+	Hurwitz, Johanna	Scholastic
Adventures of Audubon, The	U	B	250+	WorldScapes	ETA Cuisenaire
Adventures of Baby Bear, The	N	I	1173	Nature Babies	Fitzhenry & Whiteside
Adventures of Captain Underpants, The	P	F	250+	Pilkey, Dav	Scholastic
Adventures of Erik, The	O	B	956	Leveled Readers	Houghton Mifflin Harcourt
Adventures of Erik, The	O	B	956	Leveled Readers/CA	Houghton Mifflin Harcourt
Adventures of Erik, The	O	B	956	Leveled Readers/TX	Houghton Mifflin Harcourt
Adventures of George Washington, The	N	B	250+	Davidson, Margaret	Scholastic
Adventures of Granny Gatman, The	L	RF	250+	Meadows, Graham	Pearson Learning Group
Adventures of Huckleberry Finn, The	Z	HF	250+	Twain, Mark	Scholastic
#Adventures of Marco Polo, The	U	B	250+	Freedman, Russell	Scholastic
Adventures of Marco Polo, The	U	I	250+	Graphic Library	Capstone Press
Adventures of Max and Ned, The	N	F	250+	Little Celebrations	Pearson Learning Group
Adventures of Ratman	M	F	250+	Weiss, Ellen; Freidman, Mel	Random House
Adventures of Snail at School	J	F	250+	Stadler, John	HarperTrophy
Adventures of Sophie Bean, The: The Red Flyer Roller Coaster	K	RF	2600	Yevchak, Kathryn	Kaeden Books
Adventures of Spider, The	R	TL	250+	Arkhurst, Joyce C.	Scholastic
Adventures of the Buried Treasure, The	L	F	250+	McArthur, Nancy	Scholastic
Adventures of the Robber Pig	K	F	250+	Storyteller-Shooting Stars	Wright Group/McGraw Hill
Adventures of the Shark Lady	Q	I	250+	McGovern, Ann	Scholastic
Adventures of Tom Sawyer, The	Z	HF	250+	Twain, Mark	Scholastic
Adventures on Amelia Island: A Pirate, A Princess, and Buried Treasure	R	F	250+	Wood, Jane R.	Bluefish Bay Publishing
Advertisements	K	I	405	Rigby Flying Colors	Rigby
#Advertisements	U	I	250+	Sails	Rigby
Aeneid, The	Z+	TL	250+	Virgil	Penguin Group

* Collection of short stories
# Graphic text

TITLE	LEVEL	GENRE	WORD COUNT	AUTHOR / SERIES	PUBLISHER / DISTRIBUTOR
*Aesop & Company: With Scenes from His Legendary Life	O	TL	250+	Bader, Barbara	Houghton Mifflin Harcourt
Aesop's Fables	K	I	209	Vocabulary Readers	Houghton Mifflin Harcourt
Aesop's Fables	K	I	209	Vocabulary Readers/CA	Houghton Mifflin Harcourt
Afghanistan: A Question and Answer Book	P	I	250+	Questions and Answers: Countries	Capstone Press
Afraid	D	I	18	Feelings	Lerner Publishing
Africa	N	I	250+	Continents	Capstone Press
Africa	V	I	250+	Eyewitness Books	DK Publishing
Africa	N	I	442	Pull Ahead Books	Lerner Publications
African American Athletes	T	B	2426	Reading Street	Pearson
African Americans in History	K	I	250+	Literacy by Design	Rigby
African Animals	B	I	49	Belle River Readers	Belle River Readers, Inc.
African Art	J	I	194	Take Two Books	Wright Group/McGraw Hill
African Dance Drumbeat in Our Feet	L	RF	258	Bebop Books	Lee & Low Books Inc.
African Elephants	O	I	1410	Early Bird Nature Books	Lerner Publishing
African Elephants	K	I	333	Pull Ahead Books	Lerner Publications
African Giants	M	I	250+	World Quest Adventures	World Quest Learning
African Glasslands	P	I	1100	Time for Kids	Teacher Created Materials
African Hunting Dog, The	M	I	250+	Sunshine	Wright Group/McGraw Hill
African Nature Reserve, An	L	I	709	Leveled Readers	Houghton Mifflin Harcourt
African Nature Reserve, An	L	I	709	Leveled Readers/CA	Houghton Mifflin Harcourt
African Rhinos	K	I	425	Pull Ahead Books	Lerner Publications
African Safari	V	I	250+	PM Collection	Rigby
*African-American Scientists	O	B	250+	St. John, Jetty	Capstone Press
African-Americans in the Colonies	U	I	250+	We The People	Compass Point Books
African-Americans in the Old West	V	I	250+	Cornerstones of Freedom	Children's Press
African-Americans in the Thirteen Colonies	V	I	250+	Cornerstones of Freedom	Children's Press
Africans in America 1619-1865	T	I	250+	Coming to America	Capstone Press
Africa's Big Three	M	I	781	Big Cat	Pacific Learning
Africa's Changing Geography	U	I	2832	Reading Street	Pearson
After Goldilocks	E	F	44	Instant Readers	Harcourt School Publishers
After School	F	I	148	Explorations	Eleanor Curtain Publishing
After School	F	I	148	Explorations	Okapi Eductional Materials
After School	H	RF	199	Foundations	Wright Group/McGraw Hill
After School	D	I	107	Springboard	Wright Group/McGraw Hill
After School	D	I	58	Sunshine	Wright Group/McGraw Hill
After School Excitement	P	RF	1841	Reading Street	Pearson
After School Fun	D	RF	78	Nelson, May	Scholastic
After School Ghost Hunter	O	RF	250+	Klooz	Stone Arch Books
After the Crash	W	HF	2952	Leveled Readers	Houghton Mifflin Harcourt
After the Crash	W	HF	2952	Leveled Readers/CA	Houghton Mifflin Harcourt
After the Dancing Days	W	HF	250+	Rostkowski, Margaret I.	HarperTrophy
After the Earthquake	S	I	250+	Navigators Social Studies Series	Benchmark Education Company
After the Flood	G	RF	210	PM Extensions-Green	Rigby
After the Goat Man	R	RF	250+	Byars, Betsy	Puffin/Penguin
After the Rain	Z	RF	250+	Mazer, Norma Fox	Avon
After the Storm	G	I	130	Explorations	Eleanor Curtain Publishing
After the Storm	G	I	130	Explorations	Okapi Eductional Materials
After the War	W	HF	250+	Matas, Carol	Aladdin
Afternoon of the Elves	S	F	250+	Lisle, Janet Taylor	Scholastic
Afternoon on the Amazon	M	F	250+	Osborne, Mary Pope	Random House
Against the Odds	P	I	250+	Layden, Joe	Scholastic

* Collection of short stories
\# Graphic text

TITLE	LEVEL	GENRE	WORD COUNT	AUTHOR / SERIES	PUBLISHER / DISTRIBUTOR
Against the Odds	Q	I	250+	Orbit Collections	Pacific Learning
Against the Odds	R	I	250+	Wildcats	Wright Group/McGraw Hill
Against the Rules	R	RF	250+	Costello, Emily	Dell
Agent for the Stars	W	RF	2986	Leveled Readers	Houghton Mifflin Harcourt
Agent for the Stars	W	RF	2986	Leveled Readers/CA	Houghton Mifflin Harcourt
*Aggie and Ben: Three Stories	J	RF	250+	Ries, Lori	Charlesbridge
Aggressive In-Line Skating	M	I	250+	To the Extreme	Capstone Press
Aggressive In-Line Skating	R	I	250+	X-Sports	Capstone Press
Agnes Macphail: Canada's Champion of the Poor	U	B	2412	Independent Readers Social Studies	Houghton Mifflin Harcourt
Agnes Parker…Girl in Progress	T	RF	250+	O'Dell, Kathleen	Puffin Books
Agnes the Sheep	R	F	250+	Taylor, William	Bantam
Agua, Agua, Agua	H	TL	94	Little Celebrations	Pearson Learning Group
Ah Liang's Gift	J	RF	352	Sunshine	Wright Group/McGraw Hill
Ah, Treasure	F	F	19	Voyages	SRA/McGraw Hill
AH-64 Apache Helicopter, The	U	I	250+	Cross-Sections	Capstone Press
Ah-choo!	J	RF	291	Samuels, Aurora	Sadlier-Oxford
Ahyoka and the Talking Leaves	S	HF	250+	Roop, Peter & Connie	Beech Tree Books
Aim High: Astronaut Training	S	I	1227	Reading Street	Pearson
Aimee	Z+	RF	250+	Miller, Mary Beth	Penguin Group
Air Disasters	W	I	7870	Disasters Up Close	Lerner Publications
Air Raid - Pearl Harbor!: The Story of December 7, 1941	Z	I	250+	Taylor, Theodore	Scholastic
Air: A Resource Our World Depends On	V	I	250+	Managing Our Resources	Heinemann
Air: Outside, Inside, and All Around	M	I	250+	Amazing Science	Picture Window Books
Airborne	X	I	250+	iOpeners	Pearson Learning Group
Aircraft Adventures	O	I	250+	Tristars	Richard C. Owen
Aircraft Carriers	T	I	250+	Land and Sea	Capstone Press
Aircraft Carriers	G	I	124	Mighty Machines	Capstone Press
Aircraft Carriers	V	I	4961	Military Hardware in Action	Lerner Publications
Aircraft Carriers	N	I	414	Pull Ahead Books	Lerner Publications
Aircraft Carriers: The Nimitz Class	T	I	250+	War Machines	Capstone Press
Airedale Terriers	I	I	118	Dogs	Capstone Press
Airplane Adventures	S	I	250+	Dangerous Adventures	Red Brick Learning
Airplane, The	P	I	250+	Great Inventions	Red Brick Learning
Airplane, The	B	RF	21	Sunshine	Wright Group/McGraw Hill
Airplanes	F	I	60	Pebble Books	Capstone Press
Airplanes	M	I	250+	Transportation	Compass Point Books
Airport	I	I	116	Barton, Byron	HarperCollins
Ajeemah and His Son	S	HF	250+	Berry, James	HarperTrophy
*Akira to Zoltan: Twenty-Six Men Who Changed the World	S	B	250+	Chin-Lee, Cynthia	Charlesbridge
Aki's Special Gift	H	RF	240	Leveled Readers Language Support	Houghton Mifflin Harcourt
Aksum: Heart of Ancient Ethiopia	X	I	2568	Independent Readers Social Studies	Houghton Mifflin Harcourt
Al Capone Does My Shirts	X	HF	250+	Choldenko, Gennifer	Puffin Books
Al Gore: Fighting for a Greener Planet	U	B	6336	Gateway Biographies	Lerner Publications
Al Kalifa and the Nile	R	HF	250+	Bookweb	Rigby
Alabama	T	I	250+	Hello U.S.A.	Lerner Publications
Alabama	S	I	250+	Land of Liberty	Red Brick Learning
Alabama	R	I	250+	This Land Is Your Land	Compass Point Books
Aladdin & the Magic Lamp	J	TL	851	Traditional Tales	Pearson Learning Group
Alamo Journals, The	T	HF	250+	Power Up!	Steck-Vaughn

TITLE	LEVEL	GENRE	WORD COUNT	AUTHOR / SERIES	PUBLISHER / DISTRIBUTOR
Alamo Wars	W	RF	250+	Villareal Ray	Pinata Books
Alamo, The	P	I	673	Pull Ahead Books	Lerner Publications
Alas My Albatross Is Molting	T	I	250+	Literacy 2000	Rigby
Alaska	T	I	250+	Hello U.S.A.	Lerner Publications
Alaska	S	I	250+	Land of Liberty	Red Brick Learning
Alaska	R	I	250+	This Land Is Your Land	Compass Point Books
Alaska Natives	T	I	1390	Vocabulary Readers	Houghton Mifflin Harcourt
Alaska's Natives	T	I	1390	Vocabulary Readers/CA	Houghton Mifflin Harcourt
Alaska's Natural Resources	X	I	2811	Vocabulary Readers	Houghton Mifflin Harcourt
Alaska's Natural Resources	X	I	2811	Vocabulary Readers/CA	Houghton Mifflin Harcourt
Albatross, the Survivor	Q	I	250+	Sails	Rigby
Albert Einstein	P	B	250+	Early Biographies	Compass Point Books
Albert Einstein	N	B	189	First Biographies	Capstone Press
Albert Einstein	R	B	250+	Getting to Know the World's Greatest Inventors and Scientists	Children's Press
Albert Einstein	R	B	3418	History Maker Bios	Lerner Publications
Albert Einstein: A Biography	T	B	250+	Meltzer, Milton	Holiday House
Albert Einstein: Gentle Genuis	Y	B	250+	Science Readers	Teacher Created Materials
Albert the Albatross	I	F	191	Hoff, Syd	HarperCollins
Albert's Raccoon	K	F	250+	I Am Reading	Kingfisher
Albie's Secret	P	F	250+	Scooters	ETA Cuisenaire
Alcatraz	V	I	250+	Cornerstones of Freedom	Children's Press
Aldo and Abby	I	RF	235	Leveled Readers	Houghton Mifflin Harcourt
Aldo and Abby	I	RF	235	Leveled Readers/CA	Houghton Mifflin Harcourt
Aldo and Abby	I	RF	235	Leveled Readers/TX	Houghton Mifflin Harcourt
Aldo Applesauce	O	RF	250+	Hurwitz, Johanna	Morrow Junior Books
Aldo Ice Cream	O	RF	250+	Hurwitz, Johanna	Penguin Group
Aldo Peanut Butter	O	RF	250+	Hurwitz, Johanna	Penguin Group
Aleutian Islands, The	M	I	586	Gear Up!	Wright Group/ McGraw Hill
Alex and the Ironic Gentleman	Y	F	250+	Kress, Adrienne	Weinstein Books
Alex Rodriguez	P	B	1965	Amazing Athletes	Lerner Publications
Alex Rodriguez	T	B	250+	Sports Heroes	Red Brick Learning
Alexander and the Stallion	M	HF	434	Books for Young Learners	Richard C. Owen
Alexander and the Terrible, Horrible, No Good, Very Bad Day	M	RF	250+	Viorst, Judith	Scholastic
Alexander and the Wind-Up Mouse	L	F	250+	Lionni, Leo	Scholastic
Alexander Ant Cools Off	F	F	76	Little Books	Sadlier-Oxford
Alexander Graham Bell	Q	B	250+	Early Biographies	Compass Point Books
Alexander Graham Bell	N	B	250+	First Biographies	Red Brick Learning
Alexander Graham Bell	R	B	250+	Getting to Know the World's Greatest Inventors and Scientists	Children's Press
Alexander Graham Bell	K	B	412	Leveled Readers	Houghton Mifflin Harcourt
Alexander Graham Bell	K	B	412	Leveled Readers/CA	Houghton Mifflin Harcourt
Alexander Graham Bell	K	B	412	Leveled Readers/TX	Houghton Mifflin Harcourt
Alexander Graham Bell	N	B	1890	On My Own Biography	Lerner Publications
Alexander Graham Bell	P	B	250+	Photo-Illustrated Biographies	Red Brick Learning
Alexander Graham Bell	M	B	250+	Rosen Real Readers	Rosen Publishing Group
Alexander Graham Bell	X	B	250+	The Canadians	Fitzhenry & Whiteside
Alexander Graham Bell and the Telephone	P	B	250+	Windows on Literacy	National Geographic
Alexander Graham Bell, Teacher of the Deaf	Q	F	1930	Reading Street	Pearson
Alexander Graham Bell: An Inventive Life	U	B	250+	MacLeod, Elizabeth	Kids Can Press Ltd.
Alexander Hamilton	V	B	250+	Amazing Americans	Wright Group/ McGraw Hill
Alexander the Great	V	I	1355	Leveled Readers	Houghton Mifflin Harcourt
Alexander the Great	V	I	1355	Leveled Readers/CA	Houghton Mifflin Harcourt

* Collection of short stories
# Graphic text

TITLE	LEVEL	GENRE	WORD COUNT	AUTHOR / SERIES	PUBLISHER / DISTRIBUTOR
Alexander, Who's Not (Do you hear me? I mean it!) Going to Move	M	RF	250+	Viorst, Judith	Scholastic
Alfie the Apostrophe	N	F	250+	Donohue, Moira Rose	Scholastic
Alfie's Gift	L	F	250+	Literacy 2000	Rigby
Alfred	F	RF	54	Voyages	SRA/McGraw Hill
Alfred Kropp: The Thirteenth Skull	Z+	F	250+	Yancey, Rick	Bloomsbury Children's Books
Alfred the Curious	O	RF	250+	PM Collection	Rigby
Alfred Wegener: Uncovering Plate Tectonics	U	B	250+	Science Readers	Teacher Created Materials
Algonquin, The	V	I	3436	Leveled Readers Social Studies	Houghton Mifflin Harcourt
*Ali Baba Bernstein, Lost and Found	O	RF	250+	Hurwitz, Johanna	HarperCollins
Ali Baba: Fooling the Forty Thieves	U	TL	3643	Graphic Myths and Legends	Lerner Publications
Ali, Hassan and the Donkey	I	TL	250+	Storyworlds	Heinemann Educational Books
Alice in Rapture: Sort of	U	RF	250+	Naylor, Phyllis Reynolds	Aladdin
Alice in Wonderland	V	F	250+	Carroll, Lewis	Scholastic
Alice the Brave	U	RF	250+	Naylor, Phyllis Reynolds	Aladdin
Alice: Alice Alone	U	RF	250+	Naylor, Phyllis Reynolds	Simon & Schuster
Alice's Diary, Living With Diabetes	S	I	250+	Gibson, Marie	Pacific Learning
Alice's Funny Photo	L	RF	869	Sun Sprouts	ETA Cuisenaire
Alicia: The Clique Summer Collection	X	RF	250+	Harrison, Lisi	Little, Brown & Co.
Alida's Song	Y	RF	250+	Paulsen, Gary	Random House
Alien Abduction	O	SF	1694	Zucker, Jonny	Stone Arch Books
Alien at the Zoo	E	F	85	Sunshine	Wright Group/McGraw Hill
Alien Attack - Rex Jones	P	SF	1706	Zucker, Jonny	Stone Arch Books
Alien in the Classroom	N	F	250+	Keene, Carolyn	Pocket Books
Alien Plant and Animal Invaders	V	I	3318	Leveled Readers Science	Houghton Mifflin Harcourt
Alien Secrets	X	F	250+	Klause, Annette Curtis	Laurel-Leaf Books
Alien Vacation	F	F	105	Instant Readers	Harcourt School Publishers
Alien Visitors and Abductions	Z	I	250+	Unsolved Mysteries	Steck-Vaughn
Alien, The	H	F	177	Windmill Books	Rigby
Alien, the Giant, and Rocketman, The	Q	RF	250+	Bookshop	Mondo
Aliens	H	RF	232	Sails	Rigby
Aliens	Z	I	3842	The Unexplained	Lerner Publications
Aliens Ate My Homework	Q	F	250+	Coville, Bruce	Pocket Books
Aliens Don't Wear Braces	M	F	250+	Dadey, Debbie; Jones, Marcia Thornton	Scholastic
Aliens for Breakfast	M	F	250+	Etra, Jonathan; Spinner, Stephanie	Random House
Aliens for Dinner	M	F	250+	Spinner, Stephanie	Random House
Aliens for Lunch	M	F	250+	Spinner, Stephanie; Etra, Jonathan	Random House
Aliens on the Lawn	H	F	175	Windmill Books	Rigby
Ali's Story	H	RF	236	Sunshine	Wright Group/McGraw Hill
Alison Wendlebury	J	RF	250+	Literacy 2000	Rigby
Alison's Puppy	K	RF	250+	Bauer, Marion Dane	Hyperion
Alison's Wings	K	RF	250+	Bauer, Marion Dane	Hyperion
All Aboard!: Trains and Texas	S	I	250+	Literacy By Design	Rigby
All Aboard!: Trains and Texas	S	I	250+	On Our Way to English	Rigby
All About African Elephants	K	I	326	Leveled Literacy Intervention/ Blue System	Heinemann
All About Animal Babies	F	I	135	Leveled Literacy Intervention/ Green System	Heinemann
All About Ants	H	I	214	Rosen Real Readers	Rosen Publishing Group

TITLE	LEVEL	GENRE	WORD COUNT	AUTHOR / SERIES	PUBLISHER / DISTRIBUTOR
All About Apples	E	I	35	Rosen Real Readers	Rosen Publishing Group
All About Arthropods	U	I	250+	Orbit Chapter Books	Pacific Learning
All About Astronauts	N	I	580	Leveled Literacy Intervention/ Blue System	Heinemann
All About Bats	J	I	354	Leveled Literacy Intervention/ Blue System	Heinemann
All About Bats	J	I	296	Leveled Readers	Houghton Mifflin Harcourt
All About Bats	J	I	296	Leveled Readers/CA	Houghton Mifflin Harcourt
All About Bats	J	I	296	Leveled Readers/TX	Houghton Mifflin Harcourt
All About Bats	J	I	250+	Ready Readers	Modern Curriculum
All About Bears	N	I	250+	Voyages	SRA/McGraw Hill
All About Bicycles	L	I	250+	Sunshine	Wright Group/McGraw Hill
All About Bikes	O	I	250+	iOpeners	Pearson Learning Group
All About Boats	H	I	199	Leveled Literacy Intervention/ Green System	Heinemann
All About Bugs	F	I	143	Leveled Literacy Intervention/ Blue System	Heinemann
All About Cats and Kittens	N	I	250+	Neye, Emily	Grossett & Dunlap
All About Chile	K	I	271	Vocabulary Readers	Houghton Mifflin Harcourt
All About Chile	K	I	271	Vocabulary Readers/CA	Houghton Mifflin Harcourt
All About Chile	K	I	271	Vocabulary Readers/TX	Houghton Mifflin Harcourt
All About Chimps	H	I	218	Leveled Literacy Intervention/ Green System	Heinemann
All About Chocolate	M	I	479	Time for Kids	Teacher Created Materials
All About Codes	Q	I	250+	Riley, Gail Blasser	Steck-Vaughn
All About Danny	A	RF	33	Coulton, Mia	Maryruth Books
All About Deer	Q	I	250+	Arnosky, Jim	Scholastic
All About Dinosaurs	I	I	215	Leveled Literacy Intervention/ Blue System	Heinemann
All About Dinosaurs	C	I	34	Teacher's Choice Series	Pearson Learning Group
All About Dogs	L	I	551	Springboard	Wright Group/ McGraw Hill
All About Dolphins	J	I	242	Leveled Literacy Intervention/ Green System	Heinemann
All About Drums	M	I	250+	Rosen Real Readers	Rosen Publishing Group
All About Eggs	P	I	250+	Sunshine	Wright Group/McGraw Hill
All About Energy	W	I	250+	Science Readers	Teacher Created Materials
All About Fireflies	L	I	319	Leveled Readers	Houghton Mifflin Harcourt
All About Fireflies	L	I	319	Leveled Readers/CA	Houghton Mifflin Harcourt
All About Fireflies	L	I	319	Leveled Readers/TX	Houghton Mifflin Harcourt
All About Frogs	Q	I	250+	Arnosky, Jim	Scholastic
All About Grass	K	I	522	Vocabulary Readers/TX	Houghton Mifflin Harcourt
All About Hair	M	I	250+	Rigby Rocket	Rigby
All About Hair	S	I	250+	Take Two Books	Wright Group/McGraw Hill
All About Hamsters	R	I	1710	Vocabulary Readers	Houghton Mifflin Harcourt
All About Hamsters	R	I	1710	Vocabulary Readers/CA	Houghton Mifflin Harcourt
All About Hand-Blown Glass	N	I	454	Time for Kids	Teacher Created Materials
All About Honeybees	I	I	194	Leveled Literacy Intervention/ Green System	Heinemann
All About Light and Sound	W	I	250+	Science Readers	Teacher Created Materials
All About Manatees	Q	I	250+	Arnosky, Jim	Scholastic
All About Me	L	I	250+	iOpeners	Pearson Learning Group
All About Me	A	RF	32	Literacy by Design	Rigby
All About Me!	J	RF	250+	Pacific Literacy	Pacific Learning
All About Meat	K	I	367	Springboard	Wright Group/McGraw Hill

* Collection of short stories
\# Graphic text

TITLE	LEVEL	GENRE	WORD COUNT	AUTHOR / SERIES	PUBLISHER / DISTRIBUTOR
All About Mechanical Engineering	Y	I	250+	Science Readers	Teacher Created Materials
All About Mice	K	I	675	Vocabulary Readers	Houghton Mifflin Harcourt
All About Mice	K	I	548	Vocabulary Readers/CA	Houghton Mifflin Harcourt
All About Mice	K	I	548	Vocabulary Readers/TX	Houghton Mifflin Harcourt
All About Miss Miller	H	RF	168	InfoTrek	ETA Cuisenaire
All About Mitosis and Meiosis	Z	I	250+	Science Readers	Teacher Created Materials
All About Money	O	I	250+	Let's See	Compass Point Books
All About Owls	Q	I	250+	Arnosky, Jim	Scholastic
All About Penguins	C	I	97	Leveled Literacy Intervention/ Blue System	Heinemann
All About Pine Trees	L	I	822	Leveled Readers/TX	Houghton Mifflin Harcourt
All About Plants	L	I	250+	Home Connection Collection	Rigby
All About Potbellied Pigs	M	I	250+	Rigby Literacy	Rigby
All About Rattlesnakes	Q	I	250+	Aronsky, Jim	Scholastic
All About Redwood Trees	I	I	226	Leveled Literacy Intervention/ Blue System	Heinemann
All About Robots!	K	I	280	Leveled Literacy Intervention/ Blue System	Heinemann
All About Sam	Q	RF	250+	Lowry, Lois	Bantam
All About Schools	V	I	2084	Reading Street	Pearson
All About Seeds	Q	I	250+	Berger, Melvin	Scholastic
All About Sharks	Q	I	250+	Arnosky, Jim	Scholastic
All About Sharks	F	I	130	Leveled Literacy Intervention/ Blue System	Heinemann
All About Skyscrapers	M	I	492	Time for Kids	Teacher Created Materials
All About Sled Dogs	H	I	185	Leveled Literacy Intervention/ Blue System	Heinemann
All About Snakes	J	I	467	Gear Up!	Wright Group/McGraw Hill
All About Snakes	C	I	100	Leveled Literacy Intervention/ Blue System	Heinemann
All About Soccer	J	I	239	Nonfiction Set 7	Literacy Footprints
All About Spiders	H	I	146	Leveled Literacy Intervention/ Blue System	Heinemann
All About Stacy	L	RF	250+	Giff, Patricia Reilly	Bantam
All About Teeth	H	I	154	Healthy Teeth	Capstone Press
All About the Sonoran Desert	J	I	295	Leveled Literacy Intervention/ Blue System	Heinemann
All About Things People Do	K	I	250+	Rice, Melanie & Chris	Scholastic
All About Turtles	Q	I	250+	Arnosky, Jim	Scholastic
All About Volcanoes	N	I	557	Leveled Literacy Intervention/ Blue System	Heinemann
All About You	G	I	250+	Anholt, Catherine & Laurence	Scholastic
All Alone in the Universe	S	RF	250+	Perkins, Lynne Rae	Greenwillow
All Along the River	L	I	250+	Rookie Read About Science	Children's Press
All American Girl	Y	RF	250+	Cabot, Meg	HarperCollins
All Around Me I See	H	F	138	Steinberg, Laya	Dawn Publications
All Around Our Country	E	I	112	Hutchins, Jeannie	Scholastic
All Around the Cake	G	RF	159	InfoTrek	ETA Cuisenaire
All Around the United States: A Travel Adventure	R	RF	250+	Pair-It Books	Steck-Vaughn
All But Alice	U	RF	250+	Naylor, Phyllis Reynolds	Dell
All by Myself	H	RF	215	Cambridge Reading	Pearson Learning Group
All By Myself	E	RF	105	Foundations	Wright Group/McGraw Hill
All By Myself	E	F	157	Mayer, Mercer	Golden

TITLE	LEVEL	GENRE	WORD COUNT	AUTHOR / SERIES	PUBLISHER / DISTRIBUTOR
All By Myself	E	I	60	Shutterbug Books	Steck-Vaughn
All Charged Up!	R	I	250+	On Our Way to English	Rigby
All Clean	F	F	163	Sails	Rigby
All Creature Great and Small	Z+	RF	250+	Herriot, James	St. Martin's Paperbacks
All Dressed Up	B	RF	38	Visions	Wright Group/McGraw Hill
All Dressed Up	H	RF	137	Voyages	SRA/McGraw Hill
All Fall Down	B	F	23	Instant Readers	Harcourt School Publishers
All Fall Down	B	F	23	Rigby Rocket	Rigby
All Fall Down	L	I	206	Spyglass Books	Compass Point Books
All Fall Down	C	F	72	Wildsmith, Brian	Oxford University Press
All for the Better: A Story of El Barrio	R	RF	250+	Mohr, Nicholasa	Steck-Vaughn
All From a Bottle	N	F	250+	Phonics and Friends	Hampton-Brown
All I Did	E	RF	83	Instant Readers	Harcourt School Publishers
All in a Day	D	RF	78	Reading Street	Pearson
All in the Family	W	I	250+	InfoQuest	Rigby
All Is Well	R	HF	250+	Litchman, Kristin Embry	Bantam
All Join In	D	F	38	Literacy 2000	Rigby
All Kinds of Animals	O	I	250+	It's Science	Children's Press
All Kinds of Babies	B	I	71	Literacy by Design	Rigby
All Kinds of Babies	B	I	71	On Our Way to English	Rigby
All Kinds of Books	E	I	77	Canizares, Susan; Chessen, Betsey	Scholastic
All Kinds of Clothes	F	I	120	Yellow Umbrella Books	Red Brick Learning
All Kinds of Eyes	L	I	250+	Discovery World	Rigby
All Kinds of Eyes	I	I	128	Pacific Literacy	Pacific Learning
All Kinds of Families	E	I	86	Reading Street	Pearson
All Kinds of Farms	G	I	146	Yellow Umbrella Books	Red Brick Learning
All Kinds of Fish	D	F	37	Instant Readers	Harcourt School Publishers
All Kinds of Flowers	L	I	250+	Turner, Teresa	Steck-Vaughn
All Kinds of Food	D	RF	72	Carousel Readers	Pearson Learning Group
All Kinds of Food	D	I	72	Learn to Read	Creative Teaching Press
All Kinds of Homes	G	RF	116	Reading Street	Pearson
All Kinds of Kids	D	I	88	Rookie Readers	Children's Press
All Kinds of Maps	N	I	163	Windows on Literacy	National Geographic
All Kinds of Museums	N	I	250+	Sunshine	Wright Group/McGraw Hill
All Kinds of People: What Makes Us Different	J	I	250+	Spyglass Books	Compass Point Books
All Kinds of Rocks	G	RF	136	Instant Readers	Harcourt School Publishers
All Kinds of Shoes	B	I	63	Little Readers	Houghton Mifflin Harcourt
All Kinds of Things	B	I	24	Pacific Literacy	Pacific Learning
All Kinds of Wheels	E	I	76	Pair-It Books	Steck-Vaughn
All Mixed Up	G	F	105	Little Books	Sadlier-Oxford
All Night Long	E	RF	65	Visions	Wright Group/McGraw Hill
All of Me	B	RF	25	Literacy 2000	Rigby
All of the Above	U	RF	250+	Pearsall, Shelley	Scholastic
All or Nothing	L	TL	786	Rigby Flying Colors	Rigby
All Over Me!	LB	RF	24	Pair-It Books	Steck-Vaughn
All Over the World	E	RF	82	Jones, D.	Continental Press
All Pigs Are Beautiful	N	I	250+	King-Smith, Dick	Candlewick Press
All Pull Together	D	F	69	Home Connection Collection	Rigby
All Roads Lead to Rome	T	I	250+	WorldScapes	ETA Cuisenaire
All the Colors of the World	H	I	160	Gear Up!	Wright Group/McGraw Hill
All the World Loves a Puppet	P	I	250+	Lighthouse	Ginn & Co.
All the World's a Stage	O	I	250+	Literacy Tree	Rigby
All Through the Week with Cat and Dog	C	F	91	Learn to Read	Creative Teaching Press

* Collection of short stories
# Graphic text

TITLE	LEVEL	GENRE	WORD COUNT	AUTHOR / SERIES	PUBLISHER / DISTRIBUTOR
All Through the Year	F	I	261	Visions	Wright Group/McGraw Hill
All Tied Up	S	I	250+	WorldScapes	ETA Cuisenaire
All Together Now	J	F	250+	Jeram, Anita	Candlewick Press
All Tutus Should Be Pink	I	RF	243	Brownrigg, Sheri	Scholastic
All Wet!	B	I	28	Ready Readers	Pearson Learning Group
Allen Jay and the Underground Railroad	O	HF	250+	Brill, Marlene Targ	Carolrhoda Books
Allen Say, Writer and Artist	K	B	219	Leveled Readers Social Studies	Houghton Mifflin Harcourt
Alley Cat	C	RF	30	Books for Young Learners	Richard C. Owen
Alley of Shadows	T	F	250+	Brezenoff, Steve	Stone Arch Books
Allie Alligator Goes Shoe Shopping	D	F	77	Springboard	Wright Group/McGraw Hill
Allie Alligator Goes to See the King	G	F	305	Springboard	Wright Group/McGraw Hill
Allie Alligator's Adventure	I	F	435	Springboard	Wright Group/McGraw Hill
Allie Alligator's Knitting	H	F	339	Springboard	Wright Group/McGraw Hill
Allie Visits Crystal River	L	F	831	Springboard	Wright Group/McGraw Hill
Allie's Basketball Dream	K	RF	250+	Barber, Barbara E.; Ligasan, Darryl	Scholastic
Allie's Basketball Dream	K	RF	250+	Soar To Success	Houghton Mifflin Harcourt
Alligator Alley	M	RF	250+	Woodland Mysteries	Wright Group/McGraw Hill
Alligator Ann	B	F	15	Reading Street	Pearson
Alligator Baby	L	F	250+	Munsch, Robert	Scholastic
Alligator in the Bathtub	N	F	628	Leveled Readers	Houghton Mifflin Harcourt
Alligator Mouse and Other Disasters	K	F	250+	Voyages	SRA/McGraw Hill
Alligator Shoes	G	F	122	Dorros, Arthur	Dutton/Penguin
*Alligator Tails and Crocodile Cakes	J	F	250+	I Am Reading	Kingfisher
Alligator Tails and Crocodile Cakes	K	F	250+	Storyteller-Shooting Stars	Wright Group/McGraw Hill
Alligator, The	M	I	250+	Crewe, Sabrina	Steck-Vaughn
Alligators	O	I	1623	Early Bird Nature Books	Lerner Publications
Alligators	N	I	250+	World of Reptiles	Capstone Press
Alligators & Crocodiles	U	I	250+	The Untamed World	Steck-Vaughn
Alligators All Around	LB	F	59	Sendak, Maurice	HarperCollins
Alligators to Zebras	J	I	273	Springboard	Wright Group/McGraw Hill
All-of-a-Kind Family	Q	RF	250+	Taylor, Sydney	Bantam
Allosaurus	I	I	130	Dinosaur and Prehistoric Animals	Capstone Press
Allosaurus	N	I	250+	Discovering Dinosaurs	Capstone Press
All-Pro Biographies: Dan Marino	P	B	250+	Stewart, Mark	Children's Press
All-Pro Biographies: Gwen Torrence	P	B	250+	Stewart, Mark	Children's Press
All's Well That Ends Well	P	TL	250+	Storyteller - Autumn Leaves	Wright Group/ McGraw Hill
All-Star Fever	M	RF	250+	Christopher, Matt	Little, Brown & Co.
All-Star Pride	W	RF	250+	Orca Sports	Orca Book Publishers
Alma Flor Ada, Storyteller	F	B	75	Leveled Readers Language Support	Houghton Mifflin Harcourt
Alma Flor Ada: From a Family of Storytellers	G	B	75	Leveled Readers	Houghton Mifflin Harcourt
Almost Home	T	RF	250+	Baskin, Nora Raleigh	Little, Brown & Co.
Almost Starring Skinnybones	O	RF	250+	Park, Barbara	Random House
Almost to Freedom	R	F	1782	Nelson, Vaunda Micheaux	Carolrhoda Books
Almost Undone	T	RF	250+	Bookshop	Mondo
Alone and Together	H	RF	292	Early Connections	Benchmark Education
Alone in the Desert	T	I	250+	Drew, David	Rigby
Alone in the Storm	R	RF	250+	Leveled Readers Language Support	Houghton Mifflin Harcourt
Alone in the Wilderness!: Brennan Hawkins' Story of Survival	R	I	250+	True Tales of Survival	Capstone Press
Along Came a Spider	J	I	257	Vocabulary Readers	Houghton Mifflin Harcourt

TITLE	LEVEL	GENRE	WORD COUNT	AUTHOR / SERIES	PUBLISHER / DISTRIBUTOR
Along Came a Spider...	J	I	257	Vocabulary Readers/CA	Houghton Mifflin Harcourt
Along Came a Spider...	J	I	257	Vocabulary Readers/TX	Houghton Mifflin Harcourt
Along Came Greedy Cat	G	F	166	Pacific Literacy	Pacific Learning
Along Comes Jake	C	RF	86	Sunshine	Wright Group/McGraw Hill
Alphabet Book	WB	I	N/A	Springboard	Wright Group/McGraw Hill
Alphabet Game, The	H	F	272	Story Basket	Wright Group/McGraw Hill
Alphabet Race, The	C	F	7	Visions	Wright Group/McGraw Hill
Alphabet, The	R	I	250+	Literacy 2000	Rigby
Alroy's Very Nearly Clean Bedroom	O	RF	250+	SupaDoopers	Sundance
Althea Gibson, Sports Hero	R	I	1395	Vocabulary Readers	Houghton Mifflin Harcourt
Althea Gibson, Sports Hero	R	B	1395	Vocabulary Readers/CA	Houghton Mifflin Harcourt
Althea Gibson: An American Hero	O	B	250+	In Step Readers	Rigby
*Altogether, One at a Time	S	RF	250+	Konigsburg, E. L.	Simon & Schuster
Alvin Ailey	P	B	250+	Pinkney, Andrea Davis	Hyperion
Alvin Ailey, an American Dancer	N	B	326	Vocabulary Readers	Houghton Mifflin Harcourt
Alvin Ailey: Master of Dance	S	B	250+	Explore More	Wright Group/McGraw Hill
Always Be Safe	F	I	117	Rookie Readers	Children's Press
Always Elephant	M	TL	250+	Rigby Star Plus	Rigby
Always Elephant: A Traditional Tale	M	TL	250+	Rigby Literacy	Rigby
Always Learning	K	I	392	Leveled Readers	Houghton Mifflin Harcourt
Always Learning	K	I	392	Leveled Readers/CA	Houghton Mifflin Harcourt
Always Learning	K	I	392	Leveled Readers/TX	Houghton Mifflin Harcourt
Always My Dad	N	RF	250+	Wyeth, Sharon Dennis	Alfred A. Knopf
Alysha's Flat Tire	D	RF	108	Adams, Lorraine; Bruvold, Lynn	Eagle Crest Books
Am I Ready Now?	C	RF	41	Visions	Wright Group/McGraw Hill
Am I Scary?	K	I	250+	Scooters	ETA Cuisenaire
Amalia and the Grasshopper	K	RF	392	Tello, Jerry; Krupinski, Loretta	Scholastic
Amanda Joins the Circus	R	F	250+	Avi	Bantam
Amanda Miranda	Y	HF	250+	Peck, Richard	Penguin Group
*Amanda Pig and Her Big Brother Oliver	L	F	250+	Van Leeuwen, Jean	Puffin/Penguin
Amanda's Bear	G	F	154	Reading Corners	Pearson Learning Group
Amaze Us!	T	I	250+	Wildcats	Wright Group/McGraw Hill
Amazing People	X	I	250+	Boldprint	Steck-Vaughn
Amazing Adaptations	O	I	453	Independent Readers Science	Houghton Mifflin Harcourt
Amazing Adventures of Batbird, The	L	F	1252	Big Cat	Pacific Learning
Amazing Adventures of Ordinary Girl	P	RF	250+	Literacy by Design	Rigby
Amazing Amoeba, The	X	I	1290	Independent Readers Science	Houghton Mifflin Harcourt
Amazing Animal Adventures at the Poles	U	I	250+	Going Wild Series	Fitzhenry & Whiteside
Amazing Animal Adventures in Rivers	U	I	250+	Going Wild Series	Fitzhenry & Whiteside
Amazing Animal Adventures on Islands	U	I	250+	Going Wild	Fitzhenry & Whiteside
Amazing Animal Rescue Team, The	Q	I	250+	Blankenhorn, Rebecca	Steck-Vaughn
Amazing Animals	L	I	800	Reading Street	Pearson
Amazing Animals	F	I	125	Rookie Readers	Children's Press
Amazing Animals: From Performance to Preservation	T	I	250+	Explore More	Wright Group/McGraw Hill
Amazing Ant, The	M	I	250+	Story Box	Wright Group/McGraw Hill
Amazing Balina, The	P	TL	1000	Leveled Readers/TX	Houghton Mifflin Harcourt
Amazing Bats	L	I	250+	Simon, Seymour	Chronicle Books
Amazing Birds of Antarctica	O	I	759	Leveled Readers	Houghton Mifflin Harcourt
Amazing Birds of Antarctica	O	I	759	Leveled Readers/CA	Houghton Mifflin Harcourt
Amazing Birds of Antarctica	O	I	759	Leveled Readers/TX	Houghton Mifflin Harcourt
Amazing Birds of the Rain Forest	M	I	250+	Pair-It Books	Steck-Vaughn
*Amazing But True Sports Stories	Q	I	250+	Hollander, Phyllis & Zander	Scholastic
Amazing Ears	I	I	145	Gear Up!	Wright Group/McGraw Hill

* Collection of short stories
# Graphic text

TITLE	LEVEL	GENRE	WORD COUNT	AUTHOR / SERIES	PUBLISHER / DISTRIBUTOR
Amazing Earthworm, The	I	I	169	Leveled Readers Language Support	Houghton Mifflin Harcourt
Amazing Egg, The	J	I	220	Spyglass Books	Compass Point Books
Amazing Eggs	J	I	250+	Discovery World	Rigby
Amazing Fish, The	G	TL	167	Pair-It Books	Steck-Vaughn
Amazing Flight of Darius Frobisher	T	F	250+	Harley, Bill	Peachtree
Amazing Geography of the West, The	Q	I	1564	Reading Street	Pearson
Amazing Grace	L	RF	250+	Hoffman, Mary	Scholastic
Amazing Grain: The Wonders of Corn	Q	I	250+	Explorer Books-Pathfinder	National Geographic
Amazing Grain: The Wonders of Corn	P	I	250+	Explorer Books-Pioneer	National Geographic
Amazing Hands	K	I	250+	Rigby Literacy	Rigby
Amazing Humpback Whales	M	I	474	Springboard	Wright Group/McGraw Hill
Amazing Impossible Erie Canal, The	S	I	250+	Harness, Cheryl	Simon & Schuster
Amazing Journeys	P	I	250+	Literacy 2000	Rigby
Amazing Journeys: Following in History's Footsteps	S	I	250+	High Five Reading	Red Brick Learning
Amazing Lasers	M	I	250+	On Our Way to English	Rigby
Amazing Life of Benjamin Franklin, The	T	B	250+	Giblin, James Cross	Scholastic
Amazing Life of Daisy Ryan, The	Q	RF	4398	Take Two Books	Wright Group/ McGraw Hill
Amazing Lifetimes	N	I	250+	Explorations	Eleanor Curtain Publishing
Amazing Lifetimes	N	I	250+	Explorations	Okapi Educational Materials
Amazing Magic Tricks: Apprentice Level	R	I	250+	Magic Tricks	Capstone Press
Amazing Magic Tricks: Beginner Level	R	I	250+	Magic Tricks	Capstone Press
Amazing Magic Tricks: Expert Level	R	I	250+	Magic Tricks	Capstone Press
Amazing Magic Tricks: Master Level	R	I	250+	Magic Tricks	Capstone Press
Amazing Magnets	C	I	53	Twig	Wright Group/McGraw Hill
Amazing Maps	Q	I	250+	Wonder World	Wright Group/McGraw Hill
Amazing Maze, The	J	RF	334	Foundations	Wright Group/McGraw Hill
Amazing Medical Machines	W	I	250+	Connectors	Pacific Learning
Amazing Mr. Franklin, The	S	B	250+	Ashby, Ruth	Peachtree
Amazing Mr. Mulch, The	L	F	250+	Cambridge Reading	Pearson Learning Group
Amazing Mudskippers	L	I	450	Springboard	Wright Group/ McGraw Hill
Amazing Nests	I	I	270	Vocabulary Readers	Houghton Mifflin Harcourt
Amazing Nests	I	I	270	Vocabulary Readers/CA	Houghton Mifflin Harcourt
Amazing Nests	I	I	270	Vocabulary Readers/TX	Houghton Mifflin Harcourt
Amazing Octopus, The	L	I	346	Leveled Readers	Houghton Mifflin Harcourt
Amazing Octopus, The	L	I	346	Leveled Readers/CA	Houghton Mifflin Harcourt
Amazing Octopus, The	L	I	346	Leveled Readers/TX	Houghton Mifflin Harcourt
Amazing Paul Bunyan, The	M	TL	250+	Windows on Literacy	National Geographic
Amazing Plants	J	I	278	Explorations	Eleanor Curtain Publishing
Amazing Plants	J	I	278	Explorations	Okapi Educational Materials
Amazing Popple Seed, The	G	F	113	Read Alongs	Rigby
Amazing Race, The	A	RF	28	Smart Starts	Rigby
Amazing Rocks	T	I	1894	Leveled Readers Science	Houghton Mifflin Harcourt
Amazing Sea Lizards	K	I	318	Explorations	Eleanor Curtain Publishing
Amazing Sea Lizards	K	I	318	Explorations	Okapi Eductional Materials
Amazing Senses	P	I	250+	Scooters	ETA Cuisenaire
Amazing Silkworm, The	M	I	250+	Windows on Literacy	National Geographic
Amazing Skyscrapers	S	I	2047	Independent Readers Social Studies	Houghton Mifflin Harcourt
Amazing Soybean, The	O	I	250+	Orbit Chapter Books	Pacific Learning
Amazing Spiders	Q	I	250+	Eyewitness Juniors	Alfred A. Knopf
Amazing Story of Adolphus Tips, The	U	HF	250+	Morpurgo, Michael	Scholastic
Amazing Trains	L	I	482	Pair-It Books	Steck-Vaughn

TITLE	LEVEL	GENRE	WORD COUNT	AUTHOR / SERIES	PUBLISHER / DISTRIBUTOR
Amazing Tricks	K	I	250+	Storyteller-Shooting Stars	Wright Group/McGraw Hill
Amazing Whales	K	I	250+	Rigby Rocket	Rigby
Amazing World of Caves, The	Q	I	1335	Gear Up!	Wright Group/ McGraw Hill
Amazing, Incredible Idea Kit, The	Q	I	1931	Reading Street	Pearson
Amazon River, The	N	I	250+	Rookie Read-About Geography	Scholastic
Amazon, The	N	I	250+	Early Connections	Benchmark Education
Amber Brown Goes Fourth	O	RF	250+	Danziger, Paula	Scholastic
Amber Brown Is Feeling Blue	O	RF	250+	Danziger, Paula	Scholastic
Amber Brown Is Green With Envy	O	RF	250+	Danziger, Paula	Scholastic
Amber Brown Is Not a Crayon	N	RF	250+	Danziger, Paula	Scholastic
Amber Brown Sees Red	O	RF	250+	Danziger, Paula	Scholastic
Amber Brown Wants Extra Credit	O	RF	250+	Danziger, Paula	Scholastic
Amber Cat, The	P	RF	250+	McKay, Hilary	Simon & Schuster
Amber Spyglass, The	Z	F	250+	Pullman, Phillip	Alfred A. Knopf
Amber's Big Dog	E	RF	208	Rigby Rocket	Rigby
Ambulances	G	I	119	Mighty Machines	Capstone Press
Ambulances	K	I	379	Pull Ahead Books	Lerner Publications
Amelia Bedelia	L	F	250+	Parish, Peggy	HarperTrophy
Amelia Bedelia and the Baby	L	F	250+	Parish, Peggy	Harper & Row
Amelia Bedelia and the Surprise Shower	L	F	250+	Parish, Peggy	Harper & Row
Amelia Bedelia Goes Camping	L	F	250+	Parish, Peggy	Avon Camelot
Amelia Bedelia Helps Out	L	F	250+	Parish, Peggy	Avon Camelot
Amelia Bedelia Under Construction	L	F	250+	Parish, Herman	Scholastic
Amelia Bedelia's Family Album	L	F	250+	Parish, Peggy	Avon
Amelia Earhart	N	B	218	First Biographies	Capstone Press
Amelia Earhart	R	B	3465	History Maker Bios	Lerner Publications
Amelia Earhart	Q	B	250+	Literacy Tree	Rigby
Amelia Earhart	P	B	250+	Parlin, John	Bantam
Amelia Earhart	P	B	250+	Photo-Illustrated Biographies	Red Brick Learning
Amelia Earhart: Adventure in the Sky	O	B	250+	Pennypacker, Sara	Scholastic
Amelia Earhart: Challenging the Skies	S	B	250+	Sloate, Susan	Fawcett Columbine
Amelia Earhart: Courage in the Sky	S	B	250+	Kerby, Mona	Puffin/Penguin
Amelia Earhart: Flying for Adventure	S	B	250+	Wade, Mary Dodson	Millbrook Press
Amelia Earhart: Young Aviator	R	B	250+	Gormley, Beatrice	Aladdin
*Amelia to Zora: Twenty-Six Women Who Changed the World	S	B	250+	Chin-Lee, Cynthia	Charlesbridge
Amelia's Road	O	RF	250+	Soar To Success	Houghton Mifflin Harcourt
*America Street: A Multicultural Anthology of Stories	R	RF	250+	Mazer, Anne	Persea Books
America Votes: How Our President Is Elected	V	I	250+	Granfield, Linda	Kids Can Press
America: A Dream	R	HF	1620	Leveled Readers	Houghton Mifflin Harcourt
American Alligator, The	R	I	250+	Wildlife of North America	Red Brick Learning
American Army of Two, An	O	HF	1665	On My Own History	Lerner Publications
American Beavers	M	I	488	Springboard	Wright Group/McGraw Hill
American Beginnings: You're Right There!	P	HF	250+	Navigators Drama Series	Benchmark Education
American Bison	U	I	5159	Nature Watch Books	Lerner Publications
American Bison, The	R	I	250+	Wildlife of North America	Red Brick Learning
American Cities Countdown	R	I	250+	Explore More	Wright Group/McGraw Hill
*American Dragons: Twenty-Five Asian American Voices	Z	RF	250+	Yep, Laurence	HarperTrophy
American Dream, An	Q	HF	250+	Leveled Readers Language Support	Houghton Mifflin Harcourt
American Dream, The: Coming to the United States	M	I	423	Reading Street	Pearson

Organized Alphabetically by Title
Storable Database at www.fountasandpinnellleveledbooks.com

* Collection of short stories
# Graphic text

TITLE	LEVEL	GENRE	WORD COUNT	AUTHOR / SERIES	PUBLISHER / DISTRIBUTOR
*American Eyes: New Asian-American Short Stories for Young Adults	Z	RF	250+	Carlson, Lori M.	Ballantine Books
American Flag, The	S	I	250+	A True Book	Children's Press
American Flag, The	N	I	250+	American Symbols	Capstone Press
American Flag, The	Q	I	250+	Let's See	Compass Point Books
American Flag, The	P	I	700	Pull Ahead Books	Lerner Publications
American Fur Trade, The	V	I	2247	Leveled Readers	Houghton Mifflin Harcourt
American Fur Trade, The	V	I	2247	Leveled Readers/CA	Houghton Mifflin Harcourt
American Fur Trade, The	V	I	2200	Leveled Readers/TX	Houghton Mifflin Harcourt
American Heroes	M	I	189	Phonics Readers	Compass Point Books
American History Adds Up	T	I	250+	Navigators Math Series	Benchmark Education
American Indians in the 1800s	S	I	250+	Primary Source Readers	Teacher Created Materials
American Plague, An	Z	I	250+	Murphy, Jim	Clarion
American Revolution, The	T	I	250+	Bliven, Bruce, Jr.	Random House
American Revolution, The	V	I	250+	Carter, Alden R.	Franklin Watts
American Revolution, The	S	I	250+	Primary Source Readers	Teacher Created Materials
American Road Trip: Famous U.S. Highways	R	I	250+	Explore More	Wright Group/McGraw Hill
American Shorthair Cats	I	I	124	Cats	Capstone Press
American Tall Tales	T	TL	250+	Osborne, Mary Pope	Alfred A. Knopf
Americans of the Midwest: The Potawatomi	P	I	701	Leveled Readers Social Studies	Houghton Mifflin Harcourt
America's 13: The Original Colonies	W	I	250+	Literacy By Design	Rigby
America's Birthplace: Independence Hall	K	RF	249	Leveled Readers Social Studies	Houghton Mifflin Harcourt
America's City Parks	U	I	2811	Leveled Readers	Houghton Mifflin Harcourt
America's City Parks	U	I	2811	Leveled Readers/CA	Houghton Mifflin Harcourt
America's City Parks	U	I	2811	Leveled Readers/TX	Houghton Mifflin Harcourt
America's Deadliest Day: The Battle of Antietam	X	I	250+	Bloodiest Battles	Capstone Press
America's First City: Caral	X	I	2654	Independent Readers Social Studies	Houghton Mifflin Harcourt
America's First Firefighters	M	I	619	Leveled Readers	Houghton Mifflin Harcourt
America's First Firefighters	M	I	619	Leveled Readers/CA	Houghton Mifflin Harcourt
America's First Firefighters	M	I	619	Leveled Readers/TX	Houghton Mifflin Harcourt
America's First Traitor: Benedict Arnold Betrays the Colonies	S	I	250+	Headlines from History	Rosen Publishing Group
America's Forests and Woodlands	V	I	250+	Bookshop	Mondo
America's Most Wanted Fifth-Graders	R	RF	250+	Lawrence, Jan; Raskin, Linda	Scholastic
America's Mountains	W	I	250+	Bookshop	Mondo
America's Mountains: Guide to Plants and Animals	V	I	250+	Wallace, Marianne D.	Fulcrum Publishing
America's Prairies and Grasslands: Guide to Plants and Animals	V	I	250+	Wallace, Marianne D.	Fulcrum Publishing
America's Seashores: Guide to Plants and Animals	V	I	250+	Wallace, Marianne D.	Fulcrum Publishing
America's Urban Parks	U	I	2657	Leveled Readers	Houghton Mifflin Harcourt
America's Urban Parks	U	I	2657	Leveled Readers/CA	Houghton Mifflin Harcourt
America's Urban Parks	U	I	2657	Leveled Readers/TX	Houghton Mifflin Harcourt
Amigo	O	F	250+	Baylor, Byrd	Aladdin
Among the Betrayed	Z	SF	250+	Haddix, Margaret Peterson	Simon & Schuster
Among the Flowers	M	I	250+	Look Once Look Again	Creative Teaching Press
Among the Hidden	Z	SF	250+	Haddix, Margaret Peterson	Aladdin
Among the Volcanoes	Y	RF	250+	Castaneda, Omar S.	Bantam
Amos & Boris	O	F	250+	Steig, William	Farrar, Straus and Giroux
Amos and the Alien	R	F	250+	Paulsen, Gary	Bantam
Amos Binder, Secret Agent	R	F	250+	Paulsen, Gary	Bantam
Amos Fortune: Free Man	V	HF	250+	Yates, Elizabeth	Puffin/Penguin

* Collection of short stories
# Graphic text

TITLE	LEVEL	GENRE	WORD COUNT	AUTHOR / SERIES	PUBLISHER / DISTRIBUTOR
Amos Gets Famous	R	F	250+	Paulsen, Gary	Bantam
Amos Gets Married	R	F	250+	Paulsen, Gary	Bantam
Amos Goes Bananas	R	F	250+	Paulsen, Gary	Bantam
Amos's Killer Concert Caper	R	F	250+	Paulsen, Gary	Bantam
Amphibians	M	I	250+	Exploring the Animal Kingdom	Capstone Press
Amphibians	N	I	891	Rigby Flying Colors	Rigby
Amphibious Ships	T	I	250+	Land and Sea	Capstone Press
#Amulet, Book One: The Stonekeeper	Q	SF	250+	Kibuishi, Kazu	Scholastic
Amy Goes to School	D	RF	89	Literacy Tree	Rigby
Amy Loves the Snow	F	RF	127	Hoban, Julia	Scholastic
Amy Loves the Sun	F	RF	122	Hoban, Julia	Scholastic
Amy Loves the Wind	F	RF	116	Hoban, Julia	Scholastic
Amy's Airplane	E	RF	147	Leveled Readers	Houghton Mifflin Harcourt
Amy's Airplane	E	RF	147	Leveled Readers/CA	Houghton Mifflin Harcourt
Amy's Airplane	E	RF	147	Leveled Readers/TX	Houghton Mifflin Harcourt
Amy's True Prize	Q	HF	250+	The Little Women Journals	Avon
Amy's Water Wings	K	F	250+	Lighthouse	Rigby
An Wang: A Mind for Computers	R	B	3495	Leveled Readers Science	Houghton Mifflin Harcourt
Anacondas	M	I	250+	Snakes	Capstone Press
Anahita's Woven Riddle	Z	HF	250+	Sayres, Meghan Nuttail	Amulet Books
Anak the Brave	L	F	250+	Sunshine	Wright Group/McGraw Hill
Anansi Does the Impossible	O	TL	250+	Aardema, Verna	Simon & Schuster
Anansi the Spider: A Tale From the Ashanti	L	TL	250+	McDermott, Gerald	Scholastic
Anansi Weaves a Gift: An Ashanti Folktale from Ghana	K	TL	309	Gear Up!	Wright Group/ McGraw Hill
Anansi's Narrow Waist	I	TL	157	Little Celebrations	Pearson Learning Group
Anastasia Again!	Q	RF	250+	Lowry, Lois	Bantam
Anastasia at This Address	Q	RF	250+	Lowry, Lois	Bantam
Anastasia at Your Service	Q	RF	250+	Lowry, Lois	Bantam
Anastasia Has the Answers	Q	RF	250+	Lowry, Lois	Bantam
Anastasia Krupnik	Q	RF	250+	Lowry, Lois	Bantam
Anastasia on Her Own	Q	RF	250+	Lowry, Lois	Bantam
Anastasia, Absolutely	Q	RF	250+	Lowry, Lois	Bantam
Anastasia, Ask Your Analyst	Q	RF	250+	Lowry, Lois	Bantam
Anastasia's Chosen Career	Q	RF	250+	Lowry, Lois	Bantam
Anaxander: A Man of Glory	X	TL	250+	Reading Safari	Mondo
Ancient Baghdad: City at the Crossroads of Trade	W	I	1989	Leveled Readers	Houghton Mifflin Harcourt
Ancient China	W	I	250+	Early Civilizations	Capstone Press
Ancient China	Y	I	250+	Eyewitness Books	DK Publishing
Ancient China	S	I	250+	InfoQuest	Rigby
Ancient China	Y	I	2971	Vocabulary Readers	Houghton Mifflin Harcourt
Ancient China	Y	I	2971	Vocabulary Readers/CA	Houghton Mifflin Harcourt
Ancient Egypt	W	I	250+	Early Civilizations	Capstone Press
Ancient Egypt	Y	I	250+	Eyewitness Books	DK Publishing
Ancient Egypt	W	I	250+	Let's See	Compass Point Books
Ancient Egypt	U	I	250+	Make It Work!	World Book
Ancient Greece	W	I	250+	Early Civilizations	Capstone Press
Ancient Greece	Y	I	250+	Eyewitness Books	DK Publishing
Ancient Greece	S	I	250+	Journey Into Civilization	Chelsea House
Ancient Greece	W	I	250+	Let's See	Compass Point Books
Ancient Greece and Modern Culture	X	I	2559	Reading Street	Pearson
Ancient Greeks	Q	I	250+	Worldwise	Franklin Watts

* Collection of short stories
# Graphic text

TITLE	LEVEL	GENRE	WORD COUNT	AUTHOR / SERIES	PUBLISHER / DISTRIBUTOR
Ancient Heritage: The Arab-American Minority, An	Z	I	250+	Ashabranner, Brent	HarperCollins
Ancient Indochina	W	I	2456	Independent Readers Social Studies	Houghton Mifflin Harcourt
Ancient Inventions: Ahead of Their Time	T	I	250+	Pair-It Books	Steck-Vaughn
Ancient Life Along the Nile	W	I	3194	Reading Street	Pearson
Ancient Mesopotamia	W	I	250+	Let's See	Compass Point Books
Ancient Romans	Q	I	250+	Worldwise	Franklin Watts
Ancient Romans, The	U	I	2005	Leveled Readers	Houghton Mifflin Harcourt
Ancient Romans, The	U	I	2005	Leveled Readers/CA	Houghton Mifflin Harcourt
Ancient Rome	W	I	250+	Early Civilizations	Capstone Press
Ancient Rome	Y	I	250+	Eyewitness Books	DK Publishing
Ancient Rome	W	I	250+	Let's See	Compass Point Books
Ancient Wonders	S	I	2308	Take Two Books	Wright Group/ McGraw Hill
Ancient Worlds	T	I	250+	Boldprint	Steck-Vaughn
And Billy Went Out to Play	I	RF	227	Bookshop	Mondo
And Grandpa Sat on Friday	K	RF	250+	Voyages	SRA/McGraw Hill
And I Mean it Stanley	J	RF	184	Bonsall, Crosby	HarperCollins
And Justice for All	Y	I	250+	Power Up!	Steck-Vaughn
And Now for the Weather	T	I	250+	Bookweb	Rigby
. . . and Now Miguel	Z	RF	250+	Krumgold, Joseph	Scholastic
And One For All	V	RF	250+	Nelson, Theresa	Dell
And Still the Turtle Watched	Q	RF	250+	MacGill-Callahan, Sheila	Penguin Group
And the Teacher Got Mad	H	RF	109	City Kids	Rigby
And the Teacher Smiled	H	RF	86	City Kids	Rigby
And the Winner Is…	N	RF	250+	Storyteller Summer Skies	Wright Group/McGraw Hill
And Then It Was Sugar	N	RF	250+	Story Vines	Wright Group/McGraw Hill
And Then There Were Birds	L	TL	156	Books for Young Learners	Richard C. Owen
And Then What Happened, Paul Revere?	R	B	250+	Fritz, Jean	Bantam
And You Can Come Too	J	RF	224	Ohi, Ruth	Annick Press
Andi's Wool	H	I	107	Books for Young Learners	Richard C. Owen
Andrew Carnegie	R	B	250+	Amazing Americans	Wright Group/McGraw Hill
Andrew Carnegie	P	B	530	Leveled Readers Social Studies	Houghton Mifflin Harcourt
Andrew Carnegie: Builder of Libraries	P	B	250+	Community Builders	Children's Press
Andrew Carnegie: The Man Who Built Libraries	U	I	1621	Vocabulary Readers	Houghton Mifflin Harcourt
Andrew Carnegie: The Man Who Built Libraries	U	B	1621	Vocabulary Readers/CA	Houghton Mifflin Harcourt
Andrew Jackson	S	B	250+	Amazing Americans	Wright Group/McGraw Hill
Andrew Jackson	S	B	3691	History Maker Bios	Lerner Publications
Andrew Jackson	U	B	250+	Profiles of the Presidents	Compass Point Books
Andrew Jackson: Seventh President	R	B	250+	Getting to Know the U.S. Presidents	Children's Press
Andrew Johnson	U	B	250+	Profiles of the Presidents	Compass Point Books
Andrew Johnson: Seventeenth President	R	B	250+	Getting to Know the U.S. Presidents	Children's Press
Andrew's Angry Words	M	F	250+	Lachner, Dorothea	North-South Books
Andriana's Birthday	N	RF	250+	InfoTrek	ETA Cuisenaire
Androcles and the Lion	L	TL	250+	PM Tales and Plays-Silver	Rigby
Andy (That's My Name)	H	F	104	DePaola, Tomie	Aladdin
Andy and Tamika	N	RF	250+	Adler, David A.	Harcourt Trade
Andy Fox at School	E	F	198	Leveled Literacy Intervention/ Blue System	Heinemann
Andy Shane and the Pumpkin Trick	K	RF	250+	Jacobson, Jennifer Richard	Candlewick Press
Andy Shane and the Very Bossy Dolores Starbuckle	K	RF	250+	Jacobson, Jennifer Richard	Candlewick Press

TITLE	LEVEL	GENRE	WORD COUNT	AUTHOR / SERIES	PUBLISHER / DISTRIBUTOR
Andy Shane Is NOT in Love	K	RF	250+	Jacobson, Jennifer Richard	Candlewick Press
Angel and the Soldier Boy, The	WB	F	N/A	Collington, Peter	Alfred A. Knopf
Angel Child, Dragon Child	O	RF	250+	Surat, Michele Maria	Scholastic
Angel Factory, The	X	SF	250+	Blacker, Terence	Simon & Schuster
Angel for Solomon Singer, An	T	RF	250+	Rylant, Cynthia	Orchard Books
Angel Girl	U	HF	1391	Friedman, Laurie	Carolrhoda Books
Angel Island	U	I	250+	Bookshop	Mondo
Angel Island and the Land of Promise	V	I	2595	Independent Readers Social Studies	Houghton Mifflin Harcourt
Angel Park Hoopstars: Nothing But Net	O	RF	250+	Hughes, Dean	Alfred A. Knopf
Angel Park Hoopstars: Point Guard	O	RF	250+	Hughes, Dean	Alfred A. Knopf
Angel Park Soccer Stars: Backup Goalie	O	RF	250+	Hughes, Dean	Random House
Angel Park Soccer Stars: Defense!	O	RF	250+	Hughes, Dean	Alfred A. Knopf
Angel Park Soccer Stars: Psyched!	O	RF	250+	Hughes, Dean	Random House
Angel Park Soccer Stars: Total Soccer	O	RF	250+	Hughes, Dean	Alfred A. Knopf
Angel Park Soccer Stars: Victory Goal	O	RF	250+	Hughes, Dean	Alfred A. Knopf
Angelina Trueheart and the Fox	I	RF	228	Voyages	SRA/McGraw Hill
*Angels and Other Strangers	T	RF	250+	Paterson, Katherine	HarperTrophy
Angels Don't Know Karate	M	F	250+	Dadey, Debbie; Jones, Marcia Thornton	Scholastic
Angel's Mother's Boyfriend	O	RF	250+	Delton, Judy	Houghton Mifflin Harcourt
Angels on the Roof	Z	RF	250+	Moore, Martha	Bantam Doubleday Dell
Angry	D	I	14	Feelings	Lerner Publishing
*Angry Bull and Other Cases, The	O	RF	250+	Simon, Seymour	Avon
Angry Old Woman, The	E	F	126	Adventures in Reading	Pearson Learning Group
Angus and Sadie	P	F	250+	Voigt, Cynthia	HarperCollins
Angus and the Cat	I	F	250+	Flack, Marjorie	Viking/Penguin
Angus Thought He Was Big	G	F	58	Giant Step Readers	Educational Insights
Angus, Thongs and Full-Frontal Snogging: Confessions of Georgia Nicolson	Z	RF	250+	Rennison, Louise	HarperCollins
Anila's Journey	Z	HF	250+	Finn, Mary	Candlewick Press
Animal , Vegetable, or Mineral?	G	I	105	Dominie Factivity Series	Pearson Learning Group
Animal Actions	I	I	190	Home Connection Collection	Rigby
Animal Adventures	N	HF	250+	Wilder, Laura Ingalls	HarperTrophy
Animal Adventures	M	RF	250+	Navigators Fiction Series	Benchmark Education
Animal Advertisements	N	F	250+	Sails	Rigby
Animal Ancestors	O	I	964	Big Cat	Pacific Learning
Animal Antics: The Beast Jokes Ever!	O	F	1921	Make Me Laugh!	Lerner Publications
Animal Appetites	L	I	325	Gear Up!	Wright Group/ McGraw Hill
Animal Armor	I	I	155	Windows on Literacy	National Geographic
Animal Artists	B	I	32	Little Celebrations	Pearson Learning Group
Animal Babies	R	I	250+	Kalman, Bobbie	Crabtree
Animal Babies	B	I	114	Little Red Readers	Sundance
Animal Babies	C	I	75	Rigby Rocket	Rigby
Animal Babies	E	I	114	Rookie Readers	Children's Press
Animal Babies	C	I	63	Springboard	Wright Group/McGraw Hill
Animal Babies	F	I	131	Twig	Wright Group/McGraw Hill
Animal Babies	J	I	369	Vocabulary Readers	Houghton Mifflin Harcourt
Animal Babies	J	I	369	Vocabulary Readers/CA	Houghton Mifflin Harcourt
Animal Band, The	K	TL	250+	PM Tales and Plays-Purple	Rigby
Animal Behaviorists	P	B	250+	Navigators Biography Series	Benchmark Education
Animal Bodies	F	I	166	PM Science Readers	Rigby
Animal Builders	I	I	148	Little Celebrations	Pearson Learning Group
Animal Champions	M	I	250+	Explorations	Eleanor Curtain Publishing

* Collection of short stories
# Graphic text

TITLE	LEVEL	GENRE	WORD COUNT	AUTHOR / SERIES	PUBLISHER / DISTRIBUTOR
Animal Champions	M	I	250+	Explorations	Okapi Educational Materials
Animal Champions	O	I	250+	Jones, Teri Crawford	Pearson Learning Group
Animal Chatter	V	I	250+	High-Fliers	Pacific Learning
Animal Close-Ups	I	I	211	Explorations	Okapi Eductional Materials
Animal Close-Ups	I	I	211	Explorations	Eleanor Curtain Publishing
Animal Coats	L	I	250+	Rigby Rocket	Rigby
Animal Coats	B	I	48	Sails	Rigby
Animal Communication	N	I	250+	Cambridge Reading	Pearson Learning Group
Animal Communication	S	I	250+	Pair-It Books	Steck-Vaughn
Animal Communication	L	I	569	Rigby Flying Colors	Rigby
Animal Coverings	E	I	153	Early Connections	Benchmark Education
Animal Crackers	D	F	194	Bookshop	Mondo
Animal Dazzlers: The Role of Brilliant Colors in Nature	T	I	250+	Collard, Sneed B.	Franklin Watts
Animal Doctors	N	I	801	Leveled Readers	Houghton Mifflin Harcourt
Animal Doctors	N	I	801	Leveled Readers/CA	Houghton Mifflin Harcourt
Animal Doctors	N	I	801	Leveled Readers/TX	Houghton Mifflin Harcourt
Animal Ears	N	I	250+	Look Once Look Again	Creative Teaching Press
Animal Ears	I	I	250+	Yellow Umbrella Books	Red Brick Learning
Animal Eyes	M	I	250+	Look Once Look Again	Creative Teaching Press
Animal Farm	Z	F	250+	inZone Books	Hampton-Brown
Animal Farm	Z	F	250+	Orwell, George	Harcourt Trade
Animal Farm, An	H	I	233	Springboard	Wright Group/McGraw Hill
Animal Farmers	N	I	250+	Literacy Tree	Rigby
Animal Fathers	N	I	250+	Literacy 2000 Satellites	Rigby
Animal Feathers and Fur	M	I	250+	Look Once Look Again	Creative Teaching Press
Animal Feet	M	I	250+	Look Once Look Again	Creative Teaching Press
Animal Feet	I	I	166	Rigby Literacy	Rigby
Animal Feet	H	I	136	Rigby Star Quest	Rigby
Animal Fibers	I	I	440	Sunshine Science	Wright Group/McGraw Hill
Animal Files, The	T	I	250+	WorldScapes	ETA Cuisenaire
Animal Friends	N	I	250+	Literacy 2000	Rigby
Animal Giants	L	I	411	Yellow Umbrella Books	Red Brick Learning
Animal Graphs	F	I	139	PM Math Readers	Rigby
Animal Groups	I	I	265	Early Connections	Benchmark Education
Animal Habitats	B	I	73	Little Celebrations	Pearson Learning Group
Animal Habitats	B	I	73	Little Red Readers	Sundance
Animal Headgear	L	I	342	Sails	Rigby
Animal Helpers	K	I	250+	Literacy by Design	Rigby
Animal Helpers	F	I	151	PM Science Readers	Rigby
Animal Helpers	M	I	813	Reading Street	Pearson
Animal Heroes	U	I	250+	Connectors	Pacific Learning
Animal Heroes: True Rescue Stories	T	I	8566	Markle, Sandra	Millbrook Press
Animal Hiding Places	O	I	250+	Windows on Literacy	National Geographic
Animal Homes	R	I	250+	Boldprint	Steck-Vaughn
Animal Homes	B	I	48	Early Connections	Benchmark Education
Animal Homes	D	I	53	Instant Readers	Harcourt School Publishers
Animal Homes	E	I	170	Leveled Readers/CA	Houghton Mifflin Harcourt
Animal Homes	E	I	170	Leveled Readers/TX	Houghton Mifflin Harcourt
Animal Homes	B	I	48	Little Red Readers	Sundance
Animal Homes	A	I	35	On Our Way to English	Rigby
Animal Homes	K	I	193	Pair-It Books	Steck-Vaughn
Animal Homes	G	I	193	PM Plus Nonfiction	Rigby
Animal Hospital	K	I	250+	DK Readers	DK Publishing

TITLE	LEVEL	GENRE	WORD COUNT	AUTHOR / SERIES	PUBLISHER / DISTRIBUTOR
Animal Hospital	G	RF	193	Sunshine	Wright Group/McGraw Hill
Animal Hospital, The	B	I	24	Windows on Literacy	National Geographic
Animal Inventions	G	I	80	Sunshine	Wright Group/McGraw Hill
Animal Legs	B	I	37	Discovery World	Rigby
Animal Life Cycles	L	I	538	Science Support Readers	Houghton Mifflin Harcourt
Animal Lights	H	I	171	Sails	Rigby
Animal Look-Alikes	O	I	250+	iOpeners	Pearson Learning Group
Animal Messengers	I	I	116	Discovery Links	Newbridge
Animal Moms and Dads	E	I	121	Tarlow, Ellen	Scholastic
Animal Mothers and Babies	F	I	71	Time for Kids	Teacher Created Materials
Animal Mouths	M	I	250+	Look Once Look Again	Creative Teaching Press
Animal Mummies of Ancient Egpyt	W	I	2896	Independent Readers Social Studies	Houghton Mifflin Harcourt
Animal Mysteries	L	I	250+	Rigby Literacy	Rigby
Animal Neighbors	Q	I	250+	Orbit Double Takes	Pacific Learning
Animal Neighbors	I	I	250	Vocabulary Readers	Houghton Mifflin Harcourt
Animal Noises	D	I	56	Little Red Readers	Sundance
Animal Noses	M	I	250+	Look Once Look Again	Creative Teaching Press
Animal Opposites	E	I	57	Shutterbug Books	Steck-Vaughn
Animal Pals	E	I	111	Cherrington, Janelle	Scholastic
Animal Patterns	L	I	300	Finding Patterns	Capstone Press
Animal Patterns	F	I	130	Yellow Umbrella Books	Capstone Press
Animal Pets	L	I	250+	Sunshine	Wright Group/McGraw Hill
Animal Presents	A	F	35	Rigby Star	Rigby
Animal Race	B	F	48	Little Dinosaur	Literacy Footprints
Animal Records	K	I	250+	Windows on Literacy	National Geographic
Animal Reports	L	I	277	Little Red Readers	Sundance
Animal Scavengers	M	I	250+	Rigby Literacy	Rigby
Animal Sculpture	LB	I	24	Canizares, Susan; Chanko, Pamela	Scholastic
Animal Senses	M	I	250+	Cambridge Reading	Pearson Learning Group
Animal Senses	G	I	212	PM Science Readers	Rigby
Animal Senses	J	I	224	Spyglass Books	Compass Point Books
Animal Senses and Defenses	I	I	266	Shutterbug Books	Steck-Vaughn
Animal Senses: Sight and Hearing	T	I	250+	Sails	Rigby
Animal Senses: Smell, Taste, Touch	T	I	250+	Sails	Rigby
Animal Shapes	H	I	133	Rigby Focus	Rigby
Animal Shapes	D	I	14	Wildsmith, Brian	Oxford University Press
Animal Shelters	N	I	250+	Bookshop	Mondo
Animal Shelters	L	I	601	Reading Street	Pearson
Animal Shelters	H	I	193	Sun Sprouts	ETA Cuisenaire
Animal Show, The	B	F	30	Sails	Rigby
Animal Skeletons	G	I	91	Alphakids	Sundance
Animal Skeletons	E	I	131	Sails	Rigby
Animal Skin and Scales	N	I	250+	Look Once Look Again	Creative Teaching Press
Animal Sounds	C	I	21	Visions	Wright Group/McGraw Hill
*Animal Stories	Q	F	250+	King-Smith, Dick	Penguin Group
*Animal Stories by Young Writers	R	F	250+	Rubel, William; Mandel, Gerry	Tricycle Press
Animal Stretches	C	RF	35	Little Celebrations	Pearson Learning Group
Animal Symmetry	H	I	225	PM Math Readers	Rigby
Animal Tails	L	I	250+	Lighthouse	Rigby
Animal Tails	N	I	250+	Look Once Look Again	Creative Teaching Press
Animal Talk	A	I	45	Vocabulary Readers	Houghton Mifflin Harcourt
Animal Talk	A	I	45	Vocabulary Readers/CA	Houghton Mifflin Harcourt

* Collection of short stories
# Graphic text

TITLE	LEVEL	GENRE	WORD COUNT	AUTHOR / SERIES	PUBLISHER / DISTRIBUTOR
Animal Talk	A	I	45	Vocabulary Readers/TX	Houghton Mifflin Harcourt
Animal Teeth	H	I	98	Shutterbug Books	Steck-Vaughn
Animal Trackers, The	M	I	333	Independent Readers Science	Houghton Mifflin Harcourt
Animal Tracks	L	I	250+	Dorros, Arthur	Scholastic
Animal Tracks	D	I	152	Wonder World	Wright Group/McGraw Hill
Animal Tricks	D	RF	115	Jasper the Cat	Pioneer Valley
Animal Tricks	H	F	102	Wildsmith, Brian	Merrimak
Animal Walk, The	B	RF	39	Rigby Literacy	Rigby
Animal Workers	M	I	759	Rigby Flying Colors	Rigby
Animal Worlds	E	I	94	Early Connections	Benchmark Education
Animal Wrestlers, The	J	TL	338	Cambridge Reading	Pearson Learning Group
Animal, the Vegetable, and John D. Jones, The	R	RF	250+	Byars, Betsy	Bantam
Animals	D	I	70	Foundations	Wright Group/McGraw Hill
Animals	LB	I	14	Instant Readers	Harcourt School Publishers
Animals	I	I	294	Science Support Readers	Houghton Mifflin Harcourt
Animals	A	I	28	Smart Starts	Rigby
Animals	I	I	149	Time for Kids	Teacher Created Materials
Animals	D	I	88	Vocabulary Readers	Houghton Mifflin Harcourt
Animals	D	I	88	Vocabulary Readers/CA	Houghton Mifflin Harcourt
Animals	D	I	88	Vocabulary Readers/TX	Houghton Mifflin Harcourt
Animals and Air	M	I	250+	Sunshine	Wright Group/McGraw Hill
Animals and Human Culture	X	I	250+	Connectors	Pacific Learning
Animals and the Environment	I	I	252	Ecology	Lerner Publications
Animals and Their Babies	E	I	166	Early Connections	Benchmark Education
Animals and Their Teeth	K	I	510	Sunshine	Wright Group/McGraw Hill
Animals and Their Young	N	I	484	Kratky, Lada Josefa	Hampton-Brown
Animals and Us	C	RF	110	InfoTrek	ETA Cuisenaire
Animals Armed for Survival	M	I	250+	Literacy by Design	Rigby
Animals Around the World	J	I	240	Reading Street	Pearson
Animals at Night	I	I	215	First Start	Troll Associates
Animals at Night	D	I	161	Leveled Readers	Houghton Mifflin Harcourt
Animals at Night	L	I	520	Leveled Readers	Houghton Mifflin Harcourt
Animals at Night	D	I	161	Leveled Readers/CA	Houghton Mifflin Harcourt
Animals at Night	D	I	161	Leveled Readers/TX	Houghton Mifflin Harcourt
Animals at Night	C	I	35	Windows on Literacy	National Geographic
Animals at School	I	I	250+	Early Transitional, Set 1	Pioneer Valley
Animals at the Aquarium	H	I	257	Leveled Readers	Houghton Mifflin Harcourt
Animals at the Aquarium	H	I	257	Leveled Readers/CA	Houghton Mifflin Harcourt
Animals at the Aquarium	H	I	257	Leveled Readers/TX	Houghton Mifflin Harcourt
Animals at the Extremes	S	I	250+	Navigators Math Series	Benchmark Education Company
Animals at the Mall	D	F	39	Teacher's Choice Series	Pearson Learning Group
Animals at the Zoo	F	I	158	First Start	Troll Associates
Animals at Work	M	I	250+	Home Connection Collection	Rigby
Animals at Work	T	I	2814	Reading Street	Pearson
Animals Build	H	I	129	Discovery Links	Newbridge
Animals Building Homes	L	I	250+	Animal Behavior	Capstone Press
Animals Can	A	I	27	Little Readers	Houghton Mifflin Harcourt
Animals Can Change	B	I	54	Sails	Rigby
Animals Can Help	E	I	140	Sails	Rigby
Animals Communicating	M	I	250+	Animal Behavior	Capstone Press
Animals Eat	C	I	27	We Do Too Series	Pearson Learning Group
Animals Everywhere	D	I	50	Gear Up!	Wright Group/McGraw Hill
Animals' Eyes and Ears	K	I	411	Early Connections	Benchmark Education

TITLE	LEVEL	GENRE	WORD COUNT	AUTHOR / SERIES	PUBLISHER / DISTRIBUTOR
Animals Finding Food	L	I	250+	Animal Behavor	Capstone Press
Animals from Long Ago	G	I	141	Discovery Links	Newbridge
Animals from the Past	N	I	304	Independent Readers Science	Houghton Mifflin Harcourt
Animals Go Home	D	I	89	Literacy by Design	Rigby
Animals Go Home	D	I	89	On Our Way to English	Rigby
Animals Grow	I	I	152	Wonder World	Wright Group/McGraw Hill
Animals Grow and Change	I	I	122	Reading Street	Pearson
Animals Have Babies	C	I	42	We Do Too Series	Pearson Learning Group
Animals Have Homes	C	I	31	We Do Too Series	Pearson Learning Group
Animals Helping People	N	I	1017	Vocabulary Readers	Houghton Mifflin Harcourt
Animals Helping People	N	I	1017	Vocabulary Readers/CA	Houghton Mifflin Harcourt
Animals Helping People	N	I	1017	Vocabulary Readers/TX	Houghton Mifflin Harcourt
Animals Hide	D	I	55	Discovery Links	Newbridge
Animals Hide	B	I	64	Literacy by Design	Rigby
Animals Hide	B	I	64	On Our Way to English	Rigby
Animals Hide and Seek	C	I	56	Twig	Wright Group/McGraw Hill
Animals Hiding	B	I	61	Bookshop	Mondo
Animals' Homes	E	I	170	Leveled Readers	Houghton Mifflin Harcourt
Animals I Like to Feed	C	I	38	Little Red Readers	Sundance
Animals in a Human's World	T	I	2345	Reading Street	Pearson
Animals in Africa	B	I	47	In Step Readers	Rigby
Animals in Art	F	F	45	Pair-It Turn and Learn	Steck-Vaughn
Animals in Danger	M	I	250+	Pair-It Books	Steck-Vaughn
Animals in Danger	K	I	351	Yellow Umbrella Books	Red Brick Learning
Animals in Danger!	K	I	503	Vocabulary Readers	Houghton Mifflin Harcourt
Animals in Danger!	K	I	503	Vocabulary Readers/CA	Houghton Mifflin Harcourt
Animals in Danger!	K	I	503	Vocabulary Readers/TX	Houghton Mifflin Harcourt
Animals in Fall	F	I	100	All About Fall	Capstone Press
Animals in the City	D	I	72	Sails	Rigby
Animals in the Dark	P	I	250+	Simon, Seymour	Scholastic
Animals in the Desert	D	I	31	Carousel Readers	Pearson Learning Group
Animals in the Desert	B	I	30	Sails	Rigby
Animals in the Fall	E	I	34	Preparing for Winter	Capstone Press
Animals in the Grass	E	RF	42	Reading Street	Pearson
Animals in the Grasslands	B	I	37	Sails	Rigby
Animals in the Mountains	B	I	42	Sails	Rigby
Animals in the Rain Forest	C	I	33	Vocabulary Readers	Houghton Mifflin Harcourt
Animals in the Snow	C	I	79	Sails	Rigby
Animals in the Snow	A	I	20	Vocabulary Readers	Houghton Mifflin Harcourt
Animals in the Snow	A	I	20	Vocabulary Readers/CA	Houghton Mifflin Harcourt
Animals in the Sun	C	I	44	Reading Street	Pearson
Animals in the Water	C	I	84	Sails	Rigby
Animals in the Woods	A	I	15	Leveled Readers	Houghton Mifflin Harcourt
Animals in the Woods	A	I	15	Leveled Readers/CA	Houghton Mifflin Harcourt
Animals in Winter	H	I	138	All About Winter	Capstone Press
Animals in Winter	C	I	42	Rosen Real Readers	Rosen Publishing Group
Animals in Winter	L	I	250+	Soar To Success	Houghton Mifflin Harcourt
Animals Keep Warm	C	I	25	We Do Too Series	Pearson Learning Group
Animals Live Everywhere	H	I	250+	Phonics and Friends	Hampton-Brown
Animals Love the Fair	E	F	43	Literacy 2000	Rigby
Animals Make Noises	C	I	19	We Do Too Series	Pearson Learning Group
Animals Nearby	O	I	943	Leveled Readers Science	Houghton Mifflin Harcourt
Animals of Africa	K	I	286	Vocabulary Readers	Houghton Mifflin Harcourt
Animals of Africa	K	I	286	Vocabulary Readers/CA	Houghton Mifflin Harcourt

* Collection of short stories
# Graphic text

TITLE	LEVEL	GENRE	WORD COUNT	AUTHOR / SERIES	PUBLISHER / DISTRIBUTOR
Animals of Alaska	J	I	147	Rosen Real Readers	Rosen Publishing Group
Animals of Alaska	S	I	517	Vocabulary Readers	Houghton Mifflin Harcourt
Animals of Denali	Q	I	250+	Explorer Books-Pathfinder	National Geographic
Animals of Denali	P	I	250+	Explorer Books-Pioneer	National Geographic
Animals of Long Ago	N	I	250+	Ring, Susan	Scholastic
Animals of the African Grasslands	O	I	250+	Explorations	Eleanor Curtain Publishing
Animals of the African Grasslands	O	I	250+	Explorations	Okapi Educational Materials
Animals of the Amazon	R	I	683	Vocabulary Readers	Houghton Mifflin Harcourt
Animals of the Arctic and Antarctic	P	I	1242	Take Two Books	Wright Group/ McGraw Hill
Animals of the Ice and Snow	O	I	250+	Literacy 2000	Rigby
Animals of the Rainforest	B	I	30	Sails	Rigby
Animals of the Redwood Forest	S	I	1484	Leveled Readers	Houghton Mifflin Harcourt
Animals of the Redwood Forest	S	I	1484	Leveled Readers/CA	Houghton Mifflin Harcourt
Animals of the Redwood Forest	S	I	1484	Leveled Readers/TX	Houghton Mifflin Harcourt
Animals of the Savanna	M	I	250+	Rosen Real Readers	Rosen Publishing Group
Animals of the Sea	S	I	250+	Navigators Math Series	Benchmark Education
Animals of the Tropical Forest	M	I	250+	Rosen Real Readers	Rosen Publishing Group
Animals of the Tropical Rain Forest	M	I	250+	Sunshine	Wright Group/McGraw Hill
Animals of the Tundra	N	I	250+	Little Celebrations	Pearson Learning Group
Animals on Our Farm	F	I	162	PM Science Readers	Rigby
Animals on Show	F	I	165	PM Science Readers	Rigby
Animals on the Go	I	I	204	Green Light Readers	Harcourt
Animals on the Loose	M	F	642	Leveled Readers	Houghton Mifflin Harcourt
Animals on the Move	K	I	145	Planet Earth	Rigby
Animals on the Move	T	I	250+	PM Extensions	Rigby
Animals Play	C	I	27	We Do Too Series	Pearson Learning Group
Animals Raising Offspring	L	I	250+	Animal Behavior	Capstone Press
Animals Say	M	F	250+	Sails	Rigby
Animals Sleeping	L	I	250+	Animal Behavior	Capstone Press
Animals Sleeping	B	RF	61	Bookshop	Mondo
Animals Staying Safe	L	I	250+	Animal Behavior	Capstone Press
Animals Talk, Too	N	I	250+	Literacy 2000	Rigby
Animals that Build	F	I	137	Sails	Rigby
Animals that Burrow	P	I	250+	Woolley, M.; Pigdon, K.	Scholastic
Animals That Go Fast	A	I	83	Leveled Literacy Intervention/ Orange System	Heinemann
Animals That Live in the City	E	I	105	Springboard	Wright Group/McGraw Hill
Animals That Live in the Ocean	J	I	259	Springboard	Wright Group/McGraw Hill
Animals That Work	A	I	14	Foundations	Wright Group/McGraw Hill
Animals Then and Now	S	I	250+	Literacy By Design	Rigby
Animals Went to Bed, The	B	F	32	Smart Starts	Rigby
Animals With Backbones	M	I	177	Windows on Literacy	National Geographic
Animals With Wings	L	I	363	Leveled Literacy Intervention/ Blue System	Heinemann
Animals You Will Never Forget	R	I	250+	Pair-It Books	Steck-Vaughn
Animals, The	A	F	18	Sails	Rigby
Animated Illusions	S	I	250+	Sunshine	Wright Group/McGraw Hill
Animorphs	U	F	250+	Applegate, K. A.	Scholastic
Ankylosaurus	N	I	250+	Discovering Dinosaurs	Capstone Press
Anna Allen Faces the White Dragon	P	I	250+	Leveled Readers Language Support	Houghton Mifflin Harcourt
Anna and the King	V	HF	250+	Landon, Margaret	HarperTrophy
Anna Casey's Place in the World	U	RF	250+	Fogelin, Adrian	Peachtree
Anna Is Still Here	V	HF	250+	Vos, Ida	Puffin/Penguin

TITLE	LEVEL	GENRE	WORD COUNT	AUTHOR / SERIES	PUBLISHER / DISTRIBUTOR
Anna, Grandpa, and the Big Storm	N	RF	250+	Stevens, Carla	Penguin Group
Annabel	H	RF	251	Story Basket	Wright Group/McGraw Hill
Annabel the Actress Starring in Gorilla My Dreams	L	RF	250+	Conford, Ellen	Simon & Schuster
Annabelle Swift, Kindergartner	N	RF	250+	Schwartz, Amy	Orchard Books
Anna's Art Adventure	R	F	2066	Sortland, Bjorn	Carolrhoda Books
Anna's Beetle Surprise	R	RF	1489	Leveled Readers	Houghton Mifflin Harcourt
Anna's Beetle Surprise	R	RF	1489	Leveled Readers/CA	Houghton Mifflin Harcourt
Anna's Big Day	D	RF	73	Sun Sprouts	ETA Cuisenaire
Anna's Blizzard	R	HF	250+	Hart, Alison	Peachtree
Anna's First Day	E	RF	138	Joy Starters	Pearson Learning Group
Anna's Sandwich	C	RF	33	Windmill Books	Rigby
Anna's Tree	I	RF	213	Windmill Books	Rigby
Anne Bradstreet	R	B	548	Independent Readers Science	Houghton Mifflin Harcourt
Anne Frank	S	B	250+	Epstein, Rachel	Franklin Watts
Anne Frank Remembered: The Story of the Woman Who Helped Hide the Frank Family	Y	B	250+	Gies, Miep	Simon & Schuster
Anne Frank: Beyond the Diary	X	I	250+	Van der Rol, Ruud; Verhoeven, Rian	Puffin/Penguin
Anne Frank: Life in Hiding	W	B	250+	Hurwitz, Johanna	Avon
Anne Frank: The Diary of a Young Girl	Y	B	250+	Frank, Anne	Bantam
Anne Hutchinson	V	B	250+	Amazing Ameicans	Wright Group/McGraw Hill
Anne Hutchinson: Religious Reformer	V	B	250+	Let Freedom Ring	Capstone Press
Anne of Green Gables	V	RF	250+	Montgomery, L. M.	Scholastic
Anne Sullivan	J	B	255	Leveled Readers	Houghton Mifflin Harcourt
Anne Sullivan	J	B	255	Leveled Readers/CA	Houghton Mifflin Harcourt
Anne Sullivan	J	B	255	Leveled Readers/TX	Houghton Mifflin Harcourt
Annie and the Old One	O	RF	250+	Miles, Miska	Little, Brown & Co.
Annie Bananie Moves To Barry Avenue	L	RF	250+	Komaiko, Leah	Bantam
Annie John	Z	RF	250+	Kincaid, Jamaica	Farrar, Straus and Giroux
Annie Oakley	R	B	2962	History Maker Bios	Lerner Publications
Annie Oakley	R	B	250+	Wilson, Ellen	Aladdin
Annie's Ancient Discoveries	M	RF	250+	Pair-It Turn and Learn	Steck-Vaughn
Annie's Pet	J	RF	250+	Bank Street	Bantam
Annie's Pictures	L	RF	460	Leveled Readers/TX	Houghton Mifflin Harcourt
Annie's Secret Diary	M	RF	250+	Little Celebrations	Pearson Learning Group
Annika Sorenstam	P	B	1615	Amazing Athletes	Lerner Publications
Anno's USA	WB	I	N/A	Mitsumaso, Anna	Philomel/Penguin
Another Day, Another Challenge	L	RF	250+	Literacy 2000	Rigby
Another Life	X	RF	2480	Leveled Readers	Houghton Mifflin Harcourt
Another Life	X	RF	2480	Leveled Readers/CA	Houghton Mifflin Harcourt
Another Point of View	P	RF	250+	Wildcats	Wright Group/McGraw Hill
Another Sneeze Louise!	E	RF	69	Potts, Cheryl A.	Kaeden Books
Another View	X	RF	3334	Leveled Readers	Houghton Mifflin Harcourt
Another View	X	RF	3334	Leveled Readers/CA	Houghton Mifflin Harcourt
Another View	X	RF	3334	Leveled Readers/TX	Houghton Mifflin Harcourt
Ansel Adams, Photographer	R	B	1763	Leveled Readers Social Studies	Houghton Mifflin Harcourt
Answer the Phone, Fiona!	G	RF	119	Lighthouse	Rigby
Ant	O	I	250+	Chinery, Michael	Troll Associates
Ant and the Aphid, The	J	F	477	Gear Up!	Wright Group/McGraw Hill
Ant and the Chrysalis, The	K	TL	377	Springboard	Wright Group/McGraw Hill
Ant and the Dove, The	I	TL	222	Literacy by Design	Rigby
*Ant and the Dove, The	G	TL	173	New Way Blue	Steck-Vaughn
Ant and the Dove, The	I	TL	250+	PM Plus Story Books	Rigby

* Collection of short stories
# Graphic text

TITLE	LEVEL	GENRE	WORD COUNT	AUTHOR / SERIES	PUBLISHER / DISTRIBUTOR
Ant and the Dove, The	F	TL	196	Storyworlds	Heinemann Educational Publishers
Ant and the Grasshopper, The	I	TL	231	Aesop's Fables	Pearson Learning Group
Ant and the Grasshopper, The	L	TL	250+	Little Celebrations	Pearson Learning Group
Ant and the Grasshopper, The	J	TL	250+	PM Plus Story Books	Rigby
Ant and the Grasshopper, The	L	TL	664	Reading Street	Pearson
Ant and the Grasshopper, The	J	TL	250+	Story Steps	Rigby
Ant and the Grasshopper, The: A Play	I	TL	250+	Literacy Tree	Rigby
Ant Can't	C	F	131	Leveled Literacy Intervention/ Green System	Heinemann
Ant Cities	O	I	250+	Dorros, Arthur	HarperCollins
Ant City	J	RF	393	PM Collection	Rigby
Ant Life Sweet	Q	F	250+	Reading Safari	Mondo
Ant, The	D	F	48	Ray's Readers	Outside the Box
Ant, The	E	F	97	Ready Readers	Pearson Learning Group
Antarctic Adventure	T	I	250+	High-Fliers	Pacific Learning
Antarctic Adventure	R	RF	250+	Reading Expeditions	National Geographic
Antarctic Adventure, An	M	I	296	Vocabulary Readers	Houghton Mifflin Harcourt
Antarctic Animals	L	I	328	Vocabulary Readers	Houghton Mifflin Harcourt
Antarctic Animals	L	I	328	Vocabulary Readers/CA	Houghton Mifflin Harcourt
Antarctic Animals	L	I	328	Vocabulary Readers/TX	Houghton Mifflin Harcourt
Antarctic Diary	M	I	250+	Voyages	SRA/McGraw Hill
Antarctic Ocean, The	N	I	250+	Oceans	Capstone Press
Antarctic Penguins	N	I	250+	PM Animal Facts: Silver	Rigby
Antarctic Seals	N	I	250+	PM Animal Facts: Silver	Rigby
Antarctica	N	I	250+	Continents	Capstone Press
Antarctica	L	I	250+	Fowler, Allan	Scholastic
Antarctica	T	I	250+	Literacy 2000	Rigby
Antarctica	N	I	298	Pull Ahead Books	Lerner Publications
Antarctica	L	I	250+	Read-About Geography	Children's Press
Antarctica	L	RF	250+	Soar To Success	Houghton Mifflin Harcourt
Antarctica	J	I	239	Sun Sprouts	ETA Cuisenaire
Antarctica Adventure	S	I	250+	DK Readers	DK Publishing
Antarctica Land of Possibility	U	I	2026	Vocabulary Readers	Houghton Mifflin Harcourt
Antarctica, Land of Possibility	U	I	2026	Vocabulary Readers/CA	Houghton Mifflin Harcourt
Antarctica: Ice-Covered Continent	N	I	250+	Phonics and Friends	Hampton-Brown
Antarctica: Journey to the South Pole	X	I	250+	Myers, Walter Dean	Scholastic
Antarctica: Land of the Penguins	P	I	1315	Big Cat	Pacific Learning
Antarctica: The Frozen Continent	M	I	334	Reading Street	Pearson
Antarctica: The Last Great Wilderness	O	I	250+	Rigby Literacy	Rigby
Anteater's Tongue, The	F	F	137	Sails	Rigby
Anthony Burns: Defeat and Triumph of a Fugitive Slave	Y	B	250+	Hamilton, Virginia	Alfred A. Knopf
Anthony's New Glasses	H	RF	202	Adams, Lorraine; Bruvold, Lynn	Eagle Crest Books
Anthony's Unhappy Birthday	K	RF	560	Leveled Readers	Houghton Mifflin Harcourt
Anti-Bully Machine, The	O	F	250+	High-Fliers	Pacific Learning
Antietam: Day of Courage and Sacrifice	Y	I	250+	The Civil War	Carus Publishing Company
Antoine Lavoisier: Founder of Modern Chemistry	X	B	250+	Science Readers	Teacher Created Materials
Antonia Novello: Doctor for the Nation	K	B	204	Independent Readers Science	Houghton Mifflin Harcourt
Antonio's Music	J	B	250+	Emery, Joanna	Scholastic
Ants	H	I	96	Bugs, Bugs, Bugs	Red Brick Learning
Ants	B	I	16	Discovery Links	Newbridge
Ants	N	I	250+	Early Connections	Benchmark Education

TITLE	LEVEL	GENRE	WORD COUNT	AUTHOR / SERIES	PUBLISHER / DISTRIBUTOR
Ants	E	I	50	Insects	Capstone Press
Ants	N	I	250+	Nature's Friends	Compass Point Books
Ants	H	I	250+	Sunshine	Wright Group/McGraw Hill
Ants	G	I	94	Wonder World	Wright Group/McGraw Hill
Ants All Around	M	I	479	Gear Up!	Wright Group/ McGraw Hill
Ants and Grasshoppers, The	J	F	250+	The Wright Skills	Wright Group/McGraw Hill
Ants and the Grasshoppers, The	G	TL	144	New Way Blue	Steck-Vaughn
Ants and Their Nests	J	I	150	Animal Homes	Capstone Press
Ants Aren't Antisocial	S	I	250+	Action Packs	Rigby
Ants Everywhere	C	RF	24	Visions	Wright Group/McGraw Hill
Ants Go Home, The	B	F	60	Johns, Linda	Scholastic
Ants Go Marching, The	J	TL	250+	Traditional Songs	Picture Window Books
Ants Love Picnics, Too	B	F	27	Literacy 2000	Rigby
Ants of All Kinds	O	I	898	Vocabulary Readers	Houghton Mifflin Harcourt
Ants of All Kinds	O	I	898	Vocabulary Readers/CA	Houghton Mifflin Harcourt
Ants of All Kinds	O	I	898	Vocabulary Readers/TX	Houghton Mifflin Harcourt
Ants on a Log	E	RF	246	Leveled Literacy Intervention/ Blue System	Heinemann
Ants on a Picnic	C	F	35	Joy Readers	Pearson Learning Group
Ants, Ants, Ants	E	I	131	Sunshine	Wright Group/McGraw Hill
Ants, Aphids, and Caterpillars	S	I	1819	Vocabulary Readers	Houghton Mifflin Harcourt
Ants, Aphids, and Caterpillars	S	I	1819	Vocabulary Readers/CA	Houghton Mifflin Harcourt
Ants, The	B	RF	112	Leveled Literacy Intervention/ Blue System	Heinemann
Ants, The	B	F	30	Sails	Rigby
Any Small Goodness: A Novel of the Barrio	X	RF	250+	Johnston, Tony	Hampton-Brown
Anya's Camera	G	RF	214	PM Photo Stories	Rigby
Anybody Home?	U	I	250+	Boldprint	Steck-Vaughn
Anyone Can Have a Pet	K	RF	503	PM Plus Story Books	Rigby
Anywhere Everywhere Bus, The	K	F	250+	Home Connection Collection	Rigby
Apache Indian Community, An	O	I	250+	Rosen Real Readers	Rosen Publishing Group
Apache Indians, The	P	I	250+	Native Peoples	Red Brick Learning
Apache, The	R	I	250+	First Reports	Compass Point Books
Apache, The: Nomadic Hunters of the Southwest	S	I	250+	American Indian Nations	Capstone Press
Apaches, The	T	I	3966	Native American Stories	Lerner Publications
Apatosaurus	O	I	250+	A True Book	Children's Press
Aphrodite's Blessings	Z	TL	250+	McLaren, Clemence	Atheneum
Apollo	K	F	208	Gregoire, Caroline	Kane/Miller Book Publishers
Apollo Moon Rocks, The	R	I	1430	Leveled Readers	Houghton Mifflin Harcourt
Apollo Moon Rocks, The	R	I	1430	Leveled Readers/CA	Houghton Mifflin Harcourt
Apollo Moon Rocks, The	R	I	1430	Leveled Readers/TX	Houghton Mifflin Harcourt
Appaloosa Horse, The	R	I	250+	Horses	Capstone Press
Appetite for Detention	Z+	F	250+	Tanen, Sloane	Bloomsbury Children's Books
Apple Bird, The	WB	F	N/A	Wildsmith, Brian	Oxford University Press
Apple Farm, The	E	RF	95	Ready Readers	Pearson Learning Group
Apple Floats, An	D	I	35	Science	Outside the Box
Apple for Harriet Tubman, An	P	B	250+	Turner, Glennette Tiley	Albert Whitman & Co.
Apple Fractions	J	I	213	Rookie Read-About Math	Children's Press
Apple Harvest	F	I	93	All About Fall	Capstone Press
Apple Man, The	P	F	1094	Leveled Readers	Houghton Mifflin Harcourt
Apple Picking	B	RF	44	Bookshop	Mondo

* Collection of short stories
# Graphic text

TITLE	LEVEL	GENRE	WORD COUNT	AUTHOR / SERIES	PUBLISHER / DISTRIBUTOR
Apple Pie	B	I	51	Leveled Literacy Intervention/ Green System	Heinemann
Apple Pie Calzones and Other Cookie Recipes	S	I	250+	Fun Food for Cool Cooks	Capstone Press
Apple Pie Family, The	E	RF	72	Pair-It Books	Steck-Vaughn
Apple Pie Tree, The	K	I	250+	Zoe Hall	Scholastic
Apple Star, The	C	RF	33	First Stories	Pacific Learning
Apple Thief, The	G	F	62	Voyages	SRA/McGraw Hill
Apple Tree	I	RF	110	Book Bank	Wright Group/McGraw Hill
Apple Tree	G	RF	198	Literacy Tree	Rigby
Apple Tree Apple Tree	G	RF	340	Blocksma, Mary	Children's Press
Apple Tree Dilemma, The	R	RF	250+	Sails	Rigby
Apple Tree, The	J	I	160	Sunshine	Wright Group/McGraw Hill
Apple Trees	D	I	62	Pebble Books	Capstone Press
Apples	LB	I	23	Berger, Samantha; Chessen, Betsey	Scholastic
Apples	A	RF	25	Leveled Readers	Houghton Mifflin Harcourt
Apples	D	I	100	Leveled Readers	Houghton Mifflin Harcourt
Apples	D	I	100	Leveled Readers/CA	Houghton Mifflin Harcourt
Apples	A	RF	25	Leveled Readers/CA	Houghton Mifflin Harcourt
Apples	D	I	100	Leveled Readers/TX	Houghton Mifflin Harcourt
Apples	C	I	45	Williams, Deborah	Kaeden Books
Apples and More Apples	E	I	97	Pair-It Books	Steck-Vaughn
Apples and Pumpkins	I	RF	185	Rockwell, Ann	Scholastic
Apples for America	P	B	824	Leveled Readers	Houghton Mifflin Harcourt
Apples for Sale	J	RF	354	PM Math Readers	Rigby
Apples for Santa	I	F	265	Little Elf	Literacy Footprints
Apples for the Teacher	E	RF	203	Joy Starters	Pearson Learning Group
Apples for Tiffy	F	RF	169	PM Photo Stories	Rigby
Apples to Oregon	O	TL	250+	Hopkinson, Deborah & Carpenter, Nancy	Scholastic
Apples!	J	RF	503	Cambridge Reading	Pearson Learning Group
Appointment with Action	P	RF	250+	Wildcats	Wright Group/McGraw Hill
Apprenticeship of Lucas Whitaker, The	U	HF	250+	DeFelice, Cynthia	Avon
April Fool's Day Mystery, The	L	RF	1182	Rigby Flying Colors	Rigby
April Fool's Day Mystery, The	M	RF	250+	Soar To Success	Houghton Mifflin Harcourt
April Morning	X	HF	250+	Fast, Howard	Bantam
April Showers	C	I	86	Vocabulary Readers	Houghton Mifflin Harcourt
April Showers	C	I	86	Vocabulary Readers/CA	Houghton Mifflin Harcourt
April Who? April Fools!	I	RF	197	Sunshine	Wright Group/McGraw Hill
Apron Annie in the Garden	G	RF	153	Learn to Read	Creative Teaching Press
Apron Annie's Pies	G	RF	167	Learn to Read	Creative Teaching Press
Apsaalooke (Crow) Nation, The	P	I	250+	Native Peoples	Red Brick Learning
Aquarium, The	LB	I	24	KinderReaders	Rigby
Aquarium, The	LB	I	18	Kloes, Carol	Kaeden Books
Aquarium, The	A	I	29	Leveled Readers	Houghton Mifflin Harcourt
Aquarium, The	A	I	29	Leveled Readers/CA	Houghton Mifflin Harcourt
Arachne	M	TL	558	Sun Sprouts	ETA Cuisenaire
Arapaho, The: Hunters of the Great Plains	S	I	250+	American Indian Nations	Capstone Press
Arbor Day	Q	I	250+	Holiday Histories	Heinemann Library
Archaeological Adventures	T	I	250+	Explore More	Wright Group/McGraw Hill
Archaeologists Dig for Clues	P	I	250+	Duke, Kate	HarperCollins
Archaeology and the Ancient Past	T	I	250+	Reading Expeditions	National Geographic
Archipelagoes	O	I	250+	Earthforms	Capstone Press
Arctic	R	I	250+	The Heinle Reading Library	Thomson Learning

TITLE	LEVEL	GENRE	WORD COUNT	AUTHOR / SERIES	PUBLISHER / DISTRIBUTOR
Arctic and Antarctic	W	I	250+	Eyewitness Books	DK Publishing
Arctic Babies	P	I	250+	Darling, Kathy	Scholastic
Arctic Food Web, The	P	I	250+	Rigby Literacy	Rigby
Arctic Foxes	H	I	107	Polar Animals	Capstone Press
Arctic Hares	H	I	117	Polar Animals	Capstone Press
Arctic Investigations: Exploring the Frozen Ocean	T	I	250+	Young, Karen Romano	Steck-Vaughn
Arctic Journey	I	I	198	Sunshine	Wright Group/McGraw Hill
Arctic Life	M	I	250+	Robinson, F. R.	Steck-Vaughn
Arctic Ocean, The	N	I	250+	Oceans	Capstone Press
Arctic Tundra	N	I	250+	Habitats	Children's Press
Are All the Giants Dead?	V	F	250+	Norton, Mary	Harcourt Trade
Are Mountains Growing Taller? Questions and Answers About the Changing Earth	R	I	250+	Berger, Melvin & Gilda	Scholastic
Are Organized Sports Better for Kids Than Pickup Games?	U	I	250+	Bookshop	Mondo
Are They All the Same?	C	I	121	InfoTrek	ETA Cuisenaire
Are They Look-Alikes?	I	I	194	Independent Readers Science	Houghton Mifflin Harcourt
Are We Hurting the Earth?	K	I	363	Early Connections	Benchmark Education
Are We There Yet?	F	RF	127	Teacher's Choice Series	Pearson Learning Group
Are You a Ladybug?	F	I	116	Sunshine	Wright Group/McGraw Hill
Are You a Team Player?	S	I	1493	Vocabulary Readers	Houghton Mifflin Harcourt
Are You a Team Player?	S	I	1493	Vocabulary Readers/CA	Houghton Mifflin Harcourt
Are You Afraid of . . .?	B	I	18	Little Celebrations	Pearson Learning Group
Are You My Mommy?	F	F	112	Dijs, Carla	Simon & Schuster
Are You My Mother?	I	F	250+	Eastman, Philip D.	Random House
Are You the New Principal?	E	RF	120	Teacher's Choice Series	Pearson Learning Group
Are You There, Bear?	F	F	42	Maris, Ron	Greenwillow
Are You There, God? It's Me, Margaret.	T	RF	250+	Blume, Judy	Bantam
Are You There?	D	F	81	Sun Sprouts	ETA Cuisenaire
Argentina	O	I	2408	A Ticket to …	Carolrhoda Books
Argentina	P	I	2461	Country Explorers	Lerner Publications
Argentina: A Question and Answer Book	P	I	250+	Question and Answer Countries	Capstone Press
Arguments	K	F	398	Read Alongs	Rigby
Ariel of the Sea	U	F	250+	Calhoun, Dia	Winslow Press
Arizona	T	I	250+	Hello U.S.A.	Lerner Publications
Arizona	S	I	250+	Land of Liberty	Red Brick Learning
Arizona Cardinals, The	S	I	250+	Team Spirit	Norwood House Press
Arizona Diamondbacks, The	S	I	250+	Team Spirit	Norwood House Press
Ark, The	O	HF	250+	Geisert, Arthur	Houghton Mifflin Harcourt
Arkadians, The	W	F	250+	Alexander, Lloyd	Puffin/Penguin
Arkansas	T	I	250+	Hello U.S.A.	Lerner Publications
Arkansas	S	I	250+	Land of Liberty	Red Brick Learning
Arkansas	R	I	250+	This Land Is Your Land	Compass Point Books
Arky, the Dinosaur With Feathers	K	HF	529	PM Plus Story Books	Rigby
Arlington National Cemetery	V	I	250+	Cornerstones of Freedom	Children's Press
Armadillo	M	RF	134	Books for Young Learners	Richard C. Owen
Armadillo from Amarillo, The	N	F	800	Cherry, Lynne	Harcourt Brace
Armadillo, The	L	I	250+	Sunshine	Wright Group/McGraw Hill
Armadillo, The	R	I	250+	Wildlife of North America	Red Brick Learning
Armadillos	H	I	93	Desert Animals	Capstone Press
Armadillos	I	I	232	Sails	Rigby
Armando Asked, "Why?"	I	RF	250+	Ready Set Read	Steck-Vaughn
Armies of Ants	M	I	250+	Retan, Walter	Scholastic

* Collection of short stories
# Graphic text

TITLE	LEVEL	GENRE	WORD COUNT	AUTHOR / SERIES	PUBLISHER / DISTRIBUTOR
Armor	M	I	641	Sun Sprouts	ETA Cuisenaire
Armored Dinosaurs	P	I	909	Meet the Dinosaurs	Lerner Publications
Army Ants	P	I	2044	Animal Scavengers	Lerner Publishing
Army Ants	I	I	245	Sails	Rigby
Arnold Lobel: Words and Pictures Together	L	B	375	Leveled Readers	Houghton Mifflin Harcourt
Around and About	E	RF	209	Sun Sprouts	ETA Cuisenaire
Around and Around	B	I	72	PM Plus Nonfiction	Rigby
Around and Around	J	I	424	Sails	Rigby
Around My School	E	I	60	Exploring History & Geography	Rigby
Around the Neighborhood	E	I	74	Pair-It Books	Steck-Vaughn
Around the World	D	RF	57	Big Cat	Pacific Learning
Around the World	Q	I	1998	Take Two Books	Wright Group/ McGraw Hill
Around the World in a Hundred Years: From Henry the Navigator to Magellan	W	I	250+	Fritz, Jean	Putnam/Penguin
Around-the-World Lunch, The	K	RF	250+	Canetti, Yanitzia	Steck-Vaughn
Art Around the World	M	I	250+	Discovery World	Rigby
Art Around the World	J	I	239	Early Connections	Benchmark Education
Art Class, The	H	RF	240	Leveled Readers	Houghton Mifflin Harcourt
Art For You	B	I	21	Shutterbug Books	Steck-Vaughn
Art in Caves	R	I	806	Leveled Readers	Houghton Mifflin Harcourt
Art in Caves	R	I	806	Leveled Readers/CA	Houghton Mifflin Harcourt
Art in Caves	R	I	806	Leveled Readers/TX	Houghton Mifflin Harcourt
Art in Sub-Saharan Africa	W	I	2877	Independent Readers Social Studies	Houghton Mifflin Harcourt
Art in the Past	Q	I	250+	Rigby Star Quest	Rigby
Art Is a…	P	I	141	Raczka, Bob	Lerner Publications
Art Is All Around You	O	I	720	Vocabulary Readers	Houghton Mifflin Harcourt
Art Is All Around You	O	I	720	Vocabulary Readers/CA	Houghton Mifflin Harcourt
Art Lesson, The	M	B	246	DePaola, Tomie	Putnam/Penguin
Art of Makeup, The: Going Behind the Mask	T	I	1752	Reading Street	Pearson
Art Riddle Contest, The	Q	RF	250+	Medearis, Angela Shelf	Steck-Vaughn
Art Scene	V	I	250+	Boldprint	Steck-Vaughn
Art Show, The	K	RF	857	Leveled Readers/TX	Houghton Mifflin Harcourt
Artemis Fowl	Y	F	250+	Colfer, Eoin	Hyperion
Artemis Fowl: The Arctic Incident	Y	F	250+	Colfer, Eoin	Hyperion
#Artemis Fowl: The Graphic Novel	Y	F	250+	Colfer, Eoin & Donkin, Andrew	Hyperion
Artful Stories	P	I	250+	Rigby Literacy	Rigby
Arthropods Everywhere!	S	I	1304	Leveled Readers	Houghton Mifflin Harcourt
Arthropods Everywhere!	S	I	1304	Leveled Readers/CA	Houghton Mifflin Harcourt
Arthropods Everywhere!	S	I	1304	Leveled Readers/TX	Houghton Mifflin Harcourt
Arthropods Rule!	S	I	1337	Leveled Readers	Houghton Mifflin Harcourt
Arthropods Rule!	S	I	1337	Leveled Readers/CA	Houghton Mifflin Harcourt
Arthropods Rule!	S	I	1337	Leveled Readers/TX	Houghton Mifflin Harcourt
Arthur Accused!	M	F	250+	Brown, Marc	Little, Brown & Co.
Arthur and the Big Blow-Up	M	F	250+	Brown, Marc	Little, Brown & Co.
Arthur and the Cootie-Catcher	M	F	250+	Brown, Marc	Little, Brown & Co.
Arthur and the Crunch Cereal Contest	M	F	250+	Brown, Marc	Little, Brown & Co.
Arthur and the Forbidden City	R	F	250+	Besson, Luc	Harper Trophy
Arthur and the Lost Diary	M	F	250+	Brown, Marc	Little, Brown & Co.
Arthur and the Poetry Contest	M	F	250+	Brown, Marc	Little, Brown & Co.
Arthur and the Popularity Test	M	F	250+	Brown, Marc	Little, Brown & Co.
Arthur and the Scare-Your-Pants-Off Club	M	F	250+	Brown, Marc	Little, Brown & Co.
Arthur and the TL Contest	M	F	250+	Brown, Marc	Little, Brown & Co.
Arthur Goes To Camp	L	F	731	Brown, Marc	Little, Brown & Co.

* Collection of short stories
# Graphic text

TITLE	LEVEL	GENRE	WORD COUNT	AUTHOR / SERIES	PUBLISHER / DISTRIBUTOR
Arthur Lost and Found	L	F	250+	Brown, Marc	Little, Brown & Co.
Arthur Lost in the Museum	I	F	250+	Brown, Marc	Random House
Arthur Makes the Team	M	F	250+	Brown, Marc	Little, Brown & Co.
Arthur Meets the President	L	F	995	Brown, Marc	Little, Brown & Co.
Arthur Rocks with BINKY	M	F	250+	Brown, Marc	Little, Brown & Co.
Arthur Writes a Story	L	F	600	Brown, Marc	Little, Brown & Co.
Arthur, For the Very First Time	R	RF	250+	MacLachlan, Patricia	Bantam
Arthur's Baby	K	F	250+	Brown, Marc	Scholastic
Arthur's Back to School Day	K	F	250+	Hoban, Lillian	HarperTrophy
Arthur's Birthday	L	F	740	Brown, Marc	Little, Brown & Co.
Arthur's Camp-Out	K	F	250+	Hoban, Lillian	HarperTrophy
Arthur's Chicken Pox	L	F	801	Brown, Marc	Little, Brown & Co.
Arthur's Christmas Cookies	K	F	250+	Hoban, Lillian	HarperTrophy
Arthur's Eyes	K	F	250+	Brown, Marc	Scholastic
Arthur's Family Vacation	L	F	785	Brown, Marc	Little, Brown & Co.
Arthur's Fantastic Party	I	F	254	Big Cat	Pacific Learning
Arthur's First Sleepover	L	F	878	Brown, Marc	Little, Brown & Co.
Arthur's Funny Money	K	F	250+	Hoban, Lillian	HarperTrophy
Arthur's Great Big Valentine	K	F	250+	Hoban, Lillian	HarperTrophy
Arthur's Halloween Costume	K	F	250+	Hoban, Lillian	Harper Collins
Arthur's Honey Bear	K	F	250+	Hoban, Lillian	HarperCollins
Arthur's Loose Tooth	K	F	250+	Hoban, Lillian	HarperCollins
Arthur's Mystery Envelope	M	F	250+	Brown, Marc	Little, Brown & Co.
Arthur's New Puppy	L	F	969	Brown, Marc	Little, Brown & Co.
Arthur's Pen Pal	K	F	250+	Hoban, Lillian	HarperCollins
Arthur's Prize Reader	K	F	250+	Hoban, Lillian	HarperTrophy
Arthur's Teacher Trouble	L	F	809	Brown, Marc	Little, Brown & Co.
Arthur's Underwear	L	F	683	Brown, Marc	Little, Brown & Co.
Artist for the Revolution, An	W	HF	3095	Leveled Readers	Houghton Mifflin Harcourt
Artist for the Revolution, An	W	HF	3095	Leveled Readers/CA	Houghton Mifflin Harcourt
Artist for the Revolution, An	W	HF	3095	Leveled Readers/TX	Houghton Mifflin Harcourt
Artist in the Woods	G	F	228	Seedlings	Continental Press
Artist, The	F	F	83	Books for Young Learners	Richard C. Owen
Artists All Around You	M	I	862	Leveled Readers	Houghton Mifflin Harcourt
Artists All Around You	M	I	862	Leveled Readers/CA	Houghton Mifflin Harcourt
Artists All Around You	M	I	862	Leveled Readers/TX	Houghton Mifflin Harcourt
*Artists and Their Art	Q	I	250+	Medearis, Michael	Steck-Vaughn
Artists Are Everywhere	M	I	842	Leveled Readers	Houghton Mifflin Harcourt
Artists Are Everywhere	M	I	842	Leveled Readers/CA	Houghton Mifflin Harcourt
Artists Are Everywhere	M	I	842	Leveled Readers/TX	Houghton Mifflin Harcourt
Artists in Training	P	I	813	Vocabulary Readers	Houghton Mifflin Harcourt
Artists in Training	P	I	813	Vocabulary Readers/CA	Houghton Mifflin Harcourt
Artists in Training	P	I	813	Vocabulary Readers/TX	Houghton Mifflin Harcourt
Arturo's Baton	K	RF	250+	Hoff, Syd	Clarion Books
Arturo's Baton	L	RF	250+	Soar To Success	Houghton Mifflin Harcourt
As Fast as a Fox	D	RF	69	Ready Readers	Pearson Learning Group
As Heavy As	F	I	170	PM Math Readers	Rigby
As Long as Grass Should Grow and Water Flow	V	I	250+	Rigby Literacy	Rigby
As Still as a Statue	K	RF	783	Sun Sprouts	ETA Cuisenaire
As Time Goes By	N	I	250+	On Our Way to English	Rigby
Ashes for Gold	K	TL	250+	Folk Tales	Mondo
Ashes of Roses	Y	HF	250+	Auch, Mary Jane	Random House
Ashley's Elephant	J	F	250+	Zaretsky, Evan	Kaeden Books
Ashley's World Record	L	F	250+	Little Celebrations	Pearson Learning Group

* Collection of short stories
\# Graphic text

TITLE	LEVEL	GENRE	WORD COUNT	AUTHOR / SERIES	PUBLISHER / DISTRIBUTOR
Ashwater Experiment, The	U	RF	250+	Koss, Amy Goldman	Scholastic
Asia	N	I	250+	Continents	Capstone Press
Asia	N	I	460	Pull Ahead Books	Lerner Publications
Ask Einstein!	N	RF	250+	Orbit Chapter Books	Pacific Learning
Ask Mr. Bear	J	F	613	Flack, Marjorie	Macmillan
Ask Nicely	F	F	110	Literacy 2000	Rigby
Asleep	C	RF	26	Joy Readers	Pearson Learning Group
Asli's Story	S	I	250+	Jansen, Adrienne	Pacific Learning
Assassination at Sarajevo: The Spark That Started World War I	Y	I	250+	Snapshots in History	Compass Point Books
Assassination of Abraham Lincoln, The	V	B	250+	Cornerstones of Freedom	Children's Press
#Assassination of Abraham Lincoln, The	U	I	250+	Graphic Library	Capstone Press
Assassination of John F. Kennedy, The	V	B	250+	Cornerstones of Freedom	Children's Press
Assassination of Martin Luther King, Jr., The	V	B	250+	Cornerstones of Freedom	Children's Press
Assembly Line, The	M	I	501	Leveled Readers Social Studies	Houghton Mifflin Harcourt
Asteroid, The	M	F	752	PM Collection	Rigby
Asteroids	Q	I	250+	The Galaxy	Red Brick Learning
Asthma	K	I	250+	Health Matters	Capstone Press
Astronaut	B	I	22	Hoenecke, Karen	Kaeden Books
Astronaut Adventure	C	F	41	Phonics and Friends	Hampton-Brown
Astronaut, The	B	RF	30	Sunshine	Wright Group/McGraw Hill
Astronaut: Living in Space	L	I	250+	DK Readers	DK Publishing
Astronauts	M	I	250+	Community Helpers	Red Brick Learning
Astronauts	H	I	142	Exploring the Galaxy	Capstone Press
Astronauts	I	I	200	On Deck	Rigby
Astronauts	I	I	118	Phonics Readers	Compass Point Books
Astronauts	I	I	171	Wonder World	Wright Group/McGraw Hill
Astronauts and Cosmonauts	U	I	2882	Reading Street	Pearson
Astronauts at Work	N	I	250+	Explore Space!	Red Brick Learning
Astronauts in Space	J	I	135	Windows on Literacy	National Geographic
Astronauts Take Flight	Q	I	250+	iOpeners	Pearson Learning Group
Astronauts, The	F	F	112	Foundations	Wright Group/McGraw Hill
Astronomers	T	B	250+	Navigators Biography Series	Benchmark Education Company
Astronomers Through Time	S	B	250+	Science Readers	Teacher Created Materials
At 1600 Pennsylvania Avenue	O	I	250+	Wirth, Crystal	Scholastic
At Christmas	C	RF	26	Visions	Wright Group/McGraw Hill
At Grandma's House	E	RF	118	Handprints D, Set 1	Educators Publishing Service
At Grandma's House	D	RF	66	Teacher's Choice Series	Pearson Learning Group
At Her Majesty's Request: An African Princess in Victorian England	X	HF	250+	Myers, Walter Dean	Scholastic
At Home and at School	B	I	32	Leveled Readers Social Studies	Houghton Mifflin Harcourt
At Home Around the World	F	I	82	Rosen Real Readers	Rosen Publishing Group
At Home in Space	V	I	2547	Leveled Readers	Houghton Mifflin Harcourt
At Home on the Prairie	N	I	436	Vocabulary Readers	Houghton Mifflin Harcourt
At Last!	D	RF	41	Rigby Literacy	Rigby
At Last!	D	RF	65	Rigby Star	Rigby
At Lunchtime	I	I	461	Explorations	Eleanor Curtain Publishing
At Lunchtime	I	I	461	Explorations	Okapi Eductional Materials
At My Grandfather's	G	RF	63	City Stories	Rigby
At My House	A	I	40	On Our Way to English	Rigby
At My School	B	I	43	Little Books for Early Readers	University of Maine
At Night	D	RF	21	Literacy Tree	Rigby

TITLE	LEVEL	GENRE	WORD COUNT	AUTHOR / SERIES	PUBLISHER / DISTRIBUTOR
At Night	B	I	32	Sails	Rigby
At School	A	I	45	Leveled Literacy Intervention/ Orange System	Heinemann
At School	A	I	28	Little Books for Early Readers	University of Maine
At School	LB	I	12	Rise & Shine	Hampton-Brown
At School	B	I	63	Springboard	Wright Group/McGraw Hill
At School	B	I	23	Sunshine	Wright Group/McGraw Hill
At School	A	I	20	Vocabulary Readers	Houghton Mifflin Harcourt
At School	B	I	29	Vocabulary Readers	Houghton Mifflin Harcourt
At School	A	I	20	Vocabulary Readers/CA	Houghton Mifflin Harcourt
At School	G	I	250+	Yellow Umbrella Books	Red Brick Learning
At the Airport	B	I	42	Leveled Readers Social Studies	Houghton Mifflin Harcourt
At the Apple Farm	G	I	250+	Albanese, Rachel and Smith, Laura	Scholastic
At the Aquarium	B	I	45	Explorations	Eleanor Curtain Publishing
At the Aquarium	B	I	45	Explorations	Okapi Eductional Material
At the Aquarium	A	I	24	Leveled Readers	Houghton Mifflin Harcourt
At the Aquarium	A	I	24	Leveled Readers/CA	Houghton Mifflin Harcourt
At the Art Museum	M	I	250+	Rosen Real Readers	Rosen Publishing Group
At the Ballpark	H	RF	105	Sunshine	Wright Group/McGraw Hill
At the Barbershop	F	RF	179	Visions	Wright Group/McGraw Hill
At the Beach	B	I	30	Discovery Links	Newbridge
At the Beach	E	RF	114	InfoTrek	ETA Cuisenaire
At the Beach	G	RF	231	Leveled Literacy Intervention/ Blue System	Heinemann
At the Beach	B	I	74	Leveled Readers Emergent	Houghton Mifflin Harcourt
At the Beach	E	RF	43	Literacy 2000	Rigby
At the Beach	A	RF	32	Literacy by Design	Rigby
At the Beach	E	RF	85	Oxford Reading Tree	Oxford University Press
At the Beach	D	I	125	PM Science Readers	Rigby
At the Beach	LB	RF	15	Rigby Literacy	Rigby
At the Beach	C	I	74	Sun Sprouts	ETA Cuisenaire
At the Beach	A	I	15	Vocabulary Readers	Houghton Mifflin Harcourt
At the Beach	A	I	15	Vocabulary Readers/CA	Houghton Mifflin Harcourt
At the Car Wash	E	RF	143	Visions	Wright Group/McGraw Hill
At the Coal Mine	L	I	317	Rigby Focus	Rigby
At the Controls: Questioning Video and Computer Games	S	I	250+	Media Literacy	Capstone Press
At the Dentist	G	I	128	Healthy Teeth	Capstone Press
At the Doctor	J	I	250+	Story Starter	Wright Group/McGraw Hill
At the Edge of the Sea	M	I	693	Sunshine	Wright Group/McGraw Hill
At the End of the Day	L	RF	250+	Pacific Literacy	Pacific Learning
At the Fair	B	I	48	Leveled Literacy Intervention/ Blue System	Heinemann
At the Fair	A	RF	20	Leveled Readers	Houghton Mifflin Harcourt
At the Fair	A	RF	20	Leveled Readers/CA	Houghton Mifflin Harcourt
At the Fair	LB	I	14	Little Books for Early Readers	University of Maine
At the Fair	D	I	116	Little Red Readers	Sundance
At the Fair	C	RF	58	Rise & Shine	Hampton-Brown
At the Fair	C	F	76	Springboard	Wright Group/McGraw Hill
At the Fair	D	RF	175	Sunshine	Wright Group/McGraw Hill
At the Farm	B	I	60	Leveled Literacy Intervention/ Orange System	Heinemann
At the Farm	C	I	52	Little Red Readers	Sundance

* Collection of short stories
\# Graphic text

TITLE	LEVEL	GENRE	WORD COUNT	AUTHOR / SERIES	PUBLISHER / DISTRIBUTOR
At the Farm	M	I	250+	Look Once Look Again	Creative Teaching Press
At the Firehouse with Dad	H	RF	218	Bebop Books	Lee & Low Books Inc.
At the Game	G	F	85	City Stories	Rigby
At the Horse Show	D	I	24	Books for Young Learners	Richard C. Owen
At the Ice Cream Shop	C	I	35	Vocabulary Readers	Houghton Mifflin Harcourt
At the Lake	I	RF	176	Books for Young Learners	Richard C. Owen
At the Lake	C	RF	23	KinderReaders	Rigby
At the Library	F	F	31	Little Celebrations	Pearson Learning Group
At the Library	C	I	69	PM Starters	Rigby
At the Market	A	I	40	Leveled Literacy Intervention/ Orange System	Heinemann
At the Museum	B	RF	28	Ready Readers	Pearson Learning Group
At the Ocean	C	RF	26	Early Emergent	Pioneer Valley
At the Ocean	A	I	29	Little Books for Early Readers	University of Maine
At the Park	C	I	32	Bebop Books	Lee & Low Books Inc.
At the Park	F	RF	163	Early Connections	Benchmark Education
At the Park	C	RF	77	Handprints B	Educators Publishing Service
At the Park	C	I	40	Harry's Math Books	Outside the Box
At the Park	D	I	37	Hoenecke, Karen	Kaeden Books
At the Park	A	I	24	InfoTrek	ETA Cuisenaire
At the Park	A	I	48	Leveled Literacy Intervention/ Green System	Heinemann
At the Park	A	I	36	Leveled Readers	Houghton Mifflin Harcourt
At the Park	A	I	36	Leveled Readers/CA	Houghton Mifflin Harcourt
At the Park	A	I	36	Leveled Readers/TX	Houghton Mifflin Harcourt
At the Park	D	I	91	Little Red Readers	Sundance
At the Park	E	RF	29	Oxford Reading Tree	Oxford University Press
At the Park	LB	RF	14	Rigby Rocket	Rigby
At the Park	D	RF	74	Teacher's Choice Series	Pearson Learning Group
At the Park	F	I	127	Yellow Umbrella Books	Capstone Press
At the Pet Store	I	I	177	Foundations	Wright Group/McGraw Hill
At the Playground	G	I	151	Discovery Links	Newbridge
At the Playground	B	I	54	Little Books for Early Readers	University of Maine
At the Playground	C	I	86	Little Red Readers	Sundance
At the Playground	B	I	48	Rigby Flying Colors	Rigby
At the Playground	LB	I	25	Visions	Wright Group/McGraw Hill
At the Playground	LB	I	8	Windows on Literacy	National Geographic
At the Pond	A	I	40	Leveled Literacy Intervention/ Orange System	Heinemann
At the Pond	A	RF	25	Leveled Readers	Houghton Mifflin Harcourt
At the Pond	B	RF	51	Leveled Readers Science	Houghton Mifflin Harcourt
At the Pond	A	RF	25	Leveled Readers/CA	Houghton Mifflin Harcourt
At the Pond	A	RF	32	Literacy by Design	Rigby
At the Pond	M	I	250+	Look Once Look Again	Creative Teaching Press
At the Pond	E	I	55	Vocabulary Readers	Houghton Mifflin Harcourt
At the Pool	C	I	64	Foundations	Wright Group/McGraw Hill
At the Pool	F	RF	87	Oxford Reading Tree	Oxford University Press
At the Pool	A	I	29	Vocabulary Readers	Houghton Mifflin Harcourt
At the Post Office	H	RF	100	City Stories	Rigby
At the Powwow	J	RF	250+	Reading Street	Pearson
At the Races	S	I	250+	NASCAR Racing	Capstone Press
At the Root of It	Q	I	250+	iOpeners	Pearson Learning Group
At the Science Center	H	I	158	Discovery Links	Newbridge

* Collection of short stories
\# Graphic text

TITLE	LEVEL	GENRE	WORD COUNT	AUTHOR / SERIES	PUBLISHER / DISTRIBUTOR
At the Seashore	N	I	250+	Look Once Look Again	Creative Teaching Press
At the Seaside	E	RF	85	Oxford Reading Tree	Oxford University Press
At the Seaside	LB	I	16	Rigby Star	Rigby
At the Store	B	I	21	Read-More Books	Pearson Learning Group
At the Store	LB	I	14	Visions	Wright Group/McGraw Hill
At the Supermarket	C	RF	60	Little Readers	Houghton Mifflin Harcourt
At the Supermarket	C	I	60	Little Red Readers	Sundance
At the Supermarket	D	I	29	Read-More Books	Pearson Learning Group
At the Supermarket	A	RF	32	Springboard	Wright Group/McGraw Hill
At the Toy Store	C	I	35	PM Plus Nonfiction	Rigby
At the Toyshop	D	RF	41	Home Connection Collection	Rigby
At the Track	E	RF	122	Ready Readers	Pearson Learning Group
At the Truckstop	LB	RF	25	Kloes, Carol	Kaeden Books
At the Vet	D	RF	83	Leveled Readers	Houghton Mifflin Harcourt
At the Vet	A	RF	30	Rigby Rocket	Rigby
At the Water Hole	K	I	236	Foundations	Wright Group/McGraw Hill
At the Water Hole	D	I	70	Little Red Readers	Sundance
At the Wildlife Park	B	I	34	Little Red Readers	Sundance
At the Zoo	B	I	40	Early Connections	Benchmark Education
At the Zoo	B	RF	29	Kloes, Carol	Kaeden Books
At the Zoo	A	I	40	Leveled Literacy Intervention/ Orange System	Heinemann
At the Zoo	A	RF	20	Leveled Readers	Houghton Mifflin Harcourt
At the Zoo	B	I	40	Leveled Readers Emergent	Houghton Mifflin Harcourt
At the Zoo	A	RF	20	Leveled Readers/CA	Houghton Mifflin Harcourt
At the Zoo	D	RF	37	Little Celebrations	Pearson Learning Group
At the Zoo	B	RF	54	Little Readers	Houghton Mifflin Harcourt
At the Zoo	C	I	73	Little Red Readers	Sundance
At the Zoo	M	I	250+	Look Once Look Again	Creative Teaching Press
At the Zoo	B	I	40	PM Starters	Rigby
At the Zoo	D	RF	116	Predictable Storybooks	SRA/McGraw Hill
At the Zoo	C	I	88	Springboard	Wright Group/McGraw Hill
At the Zoo	G	F	206	Springboard	Wright Group/McGraw Hill
At the Zoo	E	I	54	Vocabulary Readers	Houghton Mifflin Harcourt
At Work	B	I	29	Bookshop	Mondo
At Work	C	I	29	Geist, Ellen	Scholastic
At Work	B	I	54	Independent Readers Social Studies	Houghton Mifflin Harcourt
Athena	V	I	1594	Vocabulary Readers	Houghton Mifflin Harcourt
Athena	V	I	1594	Vocabulary Readers/CA	Houghton Mifflin Harcourt
Athena	W	I	250+	World Mythology	Capstone Press
Athletic Shorts: Six Short Stories	Y	RF	250+	Crutcher, Chris	Harper Collins
Athur's Pet Business	L	F	878	Brown, Marc	Little, Brown & Co.
Atlanta Braves, The	S	I	4737	Team Spirit	Norwood House Press
Atlantic Ocean, The	N	I	250+	Oceans	Capstone Press
Atlantis	X	I	250+	The Unexplained	Capstone Press
Atlantis: The Lost City?	W	I	250+	DK Readers	DK Publishing
Atlas of Endangered Species	V	I	250+	Bookshop	Mondo
Atoms	V	I	250+	Simply Science	Compass Point Books
Atoms and Elements	Z	I	1392	Science Support Readers	Houghton Mifflin Harcourt
Attaboy, Sam	Q	RF	250+	Lowry, Lois	Bantam
Attack and Defense	Q	I	250+	Explorers	Wright Group/McGraw Hill
Attack Helicopters: The AH-64 Apaches	U	I	250+	War Planes	Capstone Press
Attack of the 50-Ft. Cupid	N	SF	250+	Benton, Jim	Aladdin Paperbacks

* Collection of short stories
# Graphic text

TITLE	LEVEL	GENRE	WORD COUNT	AUTHOR / SERIES	PUBLISHER / DISTRIBUTOR
Attack of the Giant Squirrel!	N	F	653	Leveled Readers	Houghton Mifflin Harcourt
Attack of the Paper Bats	T	F	605	Dahl, Michael	Stone Arch Books
Attack on Montreal	Y	I	250+	History for Young Canadians	Fitzhenry & Whiteside
Attack on Pearl Harbor, The: An Interactive History Adventure	V	HF	250+	You Choose Books	Capstone Press
Attack Submarines: The Seawolf Class	T	I	250+	War Machines	Capstone Press
Atul's Christmas Hamster	I	I	250+	Cambridge Reading	Pearson Learning Group
ATV Racing	S	I	250+	Motor Sports	Red Brick Learning
Aung San Suu Kyi	V	B	1980	Leveled Readers Social Studies	Houghton Mifflin Harcourt
Aunt Clara Brown: Official Pioneer	P	B	250+	Lowery, Linda	Lerner Publishing
Aunt Eater Loves a Mystery	J	F	250+	Cushman, Doug	HarperTrophy
Aunt Eater's Mystery Christmas	J	F	250+	Cushman, Doug	HarperTrophy
Aunt Eater's Mystery Vacation	J	F	250+	Cushman, Doug	HarperTrophy
Aunt Flossie's Hats (and Crab Cakes Later)	M	RF	250+	Howard, Elizabeth	Scholastic
Aunt Jessie	G	RF	114	Literacy 2000	Rigby
Aunt Louisa Is Coming for Lunch	G	RF	118	Windmill Books	Rigby
Aunt Maud's Mittens	H	F	200+	Landman, Yael	Scholastic
Aunt Tabitha's Gift	R	RF	250+	Sails	Rigby
Aunt Victoria's Monster	R	F	250+	Storyteller -Whispering Pines	Wright Group/McGraw Hill
Aunt Wilhelmina's Will	L	RF	250+	Voyages	SRA/McGraw Hill
Auntie Maria and the Cat	F	RF	215	Sunshine	Wright Group/McGraw Hill
Aunts	F	I	42	Families	Capstone Press
Aunts	D	I	49	Pebble Books	Capstone Press
Aunty Mo's Kids	I	RF	250+	Sails	Rigby
Austere Academy, The	V	F	250+	Snicket, Lemony	Scholastic
Austin and the Toyman	I	RF	250+	Reading Safari	Mondo
Australia	P	I	250+	A True Book	Children's Press
Australia	H	I	27	Chessen, Betsey; Chanko, Pamela	Scholastic
Australia	N	I	250+	Continents	Capstone Press
Australia	U	I	250+	Countries and Cultures	Red Brick Learning
Australia	O	I	250+	Countries of the World	Red Brick Learning
Australia	Q	I	250+	First Reports: Countries	Compass Point Books
Australia	N	I	336	Pull Ahead Books	Lerner Publications
Australia ABCs: A Book About the People and Places of Australia	Q	I	250+	Country ABCs	Picture Window Books
Australia in Colors	N	I	250+	World of Colors	Capstone Press
Australia's Deserts	Q	I	250+	Theme Sets	National Geographic
Australia's First People	X	I	2579	Vocabulary Readers	Houghton Mifflin Harcourt
Australia's First People	X	I	2579	Vocabulary Readers/CA	Houghton Mifflin Harcourt
Author on My Street, The	J	RF	260	Books for Young Learners	Richard C. Owen
Auto Mechanics	M	I	250+	Community Helpers	Red Brick Learning
Autobiography of Benjamin Franklin, The	Z+	B	250+	Franklin, Benjamin	Simon & Schuster
Autobiography of Miss Jane Pittman, The	Z+	HF	250+	Gaines, Ernest J.	Bantam Books
Automobile, The	P	I	250+	Great Inventions	Red Brick Learning
Automobiles and How They Work	Q	I	894	Time for Kids	Teacher Created Materials Publishing
Autumn	M	I	225	Pebble Books	Red Brick Learning
Autumn Leaves	LB	I	17	Preparing for Winter	Capstone Press
Autumn Leaves	G	RF	84	Voyages	SRA/McGraw Hill
Autumn Street	V	HF	250+	Lowry, Lois	Bantam
AV-8B Harrier Jump Jet, The	U	I	250+	Cross-Sections	Capstone Press
Avalanche!	L	I	250+	Rosen Real Readers	Rosen Publishing Group
Avalanches	W	I	250+	Disasters Up Close	Lerner Publications
Avalanches	M	I	668	Pull Ahead Books	Lerner Publications

TITLE	LEVEL	GENRE	WORD COUNT	AUTHOR / SERIES	PUBLISHER / DISTRIBUTOR
Avi	T	B	250+	Markham, Lois	Learning Works, The
Avion My Uncle Flew, The	Y	RF	250+	Fisher, Cyrus	Penguin Group
Avoiding Drugs	V	I	654	Pull Ahead Books	Lerner Publications
Awake and Dreaming	S	F	250+	Person, Kit	Puffin/Penguin
Award Day	G	RF	195	PM Stars	Rigby
*Awarding Greatness: Nobel, Caldecott, Pulitzer	Q	B	250+	High-Fliers	Pacific Learning
Away From Home	L	RF	250+	Literacy by Design	Rigby
Away Went the Hat	I	F	260	New Way Green	Steck-Vaughn
Awful Mess, The	H	RF	58	Rockwell, Anne	Four Winds
Awful Waffles	G	F	296	Williams, D. H.	Continental Press
Awfully Short for the Fourth Grade	Q	RF	250+	Woodruff, Elvira	Bantam
Awumpalema	L	TL	250+	Literacy 2000	Rigby
Awww	C	RF	35	Little Celebrations	Pearson Learning Group
Aye-Aye, The	J	I	150	Weird Animals	Capstone Press
A-Z Fascinating Facts About Animals	R	I	250+	Literacy 2000	Rigby
Aztec News, The	W	I	250+	The History News	Candlewick Press
Aztec People, The	L	I	236	Take Two Books	Wright Group/McGraw Hill
Aztec Warriors	T	I	250+	Warriors of History	Capstone Press
Aztec, Inca and Maya	Y	I	250+	Eyewitness Books	DK Publishing
Aztec, The	Q	I	250+	A True Book	Children's Press
Aztec, The	W	I	2193	Reading Street	Pearson
Aztecs, The	Y	I	2583	Leveled Readers	Houghton Mifflin Harcourt
Aztecs, The	Y	I	2583	Leveled Readers/CA	Houghton Mifflin Harcourt
Aztecs, The	Q	I	250+	Windows on Literacy	National Geographic
Aztecs, The: Rise and Fall of a Great Empire	W	I	250+	High Five Reading	Red Brick Learning

* Collection of short stories
# Graphic text

TITLE	LEVEL	GENRE	WORD COUNT	AUTHOR / SERIES	PUBLISHER / DISTRIBUTOR
B. B. King	U	B	2632	Leveled Readers/CA	Houghton Mifflin Harcourt
B. B. King	U	B	2632	Leveled Readers/TX	Houghton Mifflin Harcourt
B.B. King	U	B	2632	Leveled Readers	Houghton Mifflin Harcourt
B-2 Spirit Stealth Bomber, The	U	I	250+	Cross-Sections	Capstone Press
B-2 Spirit Stealth Bomber, The	U	I	250+	Cross-Sections	Capstone Press
Baa Baa Black Sheep	L	TL	250+	Trapani, Iza	Charlesbridge
Baba Nangko	P	F	250+	Voyages	SRA/McGraw Hill
Baba Yaga	K	TL	250+	Literacy 2000	Rigby
Baba Yaga: A Russian Folktale	N	TL	250+	Phinney, Margaret Y.	Mondo
Babe & Me	T	F	250+	Gutman, Dan	Harper Trophy
Babe Didrikson Zaharias: All-Around Athlete	N	B	1747	On My Own Biography	Lerner Publications
Babe Didrikson: Athlete of the Century	R	B	250+	Knudson, R. Rozanne	Bantam
Babe Ruth	Q	B	1176	Leveled Readers	Houghton Mifflin Harcourt
Babe Ruth	Q	B	1176	Leveled Readers/CA	Houghton Mifflin Harcourt
Babe Ruth	Q	B	1176	Leveled Readers/TX	Houghton Mifflin Harcourt
Babe Ruth: One of Baseball's Greatest	R	B	250+	Van Riper, Guernsey	Aladdin
Babe the Gallant Pig	R	F	250+	King-Smith, Dick	Random House
Babies	D	I	42	Canizares, Susan; Chanko, Pamela	Scholastic
Babies	A	I	35	On Our Way to English	Rigby
Babies in the Pouches	D	I	120	Sails	Rigby
Babies on the Move	LB	I	30	Canizares, Susan; Moreton, Daniel	Scholastic
Babies!	B	I	72	Literacy by Design	Rigby
Baboon Troops	M	I	250+	Sails	Rigby
Baby	A	RF	29	Instant Readers	Harcourt School Publishers
Baby	A	I	24	Leveled Literacy Intervention/ Orange System	Heinemann
Baby	A	I	28	Little Books for Early Readers	University of Maine
Baby	T	RF	250+	MacLachlan, Patricia	Language for Learning Assoc.
Baby	A	I	24	PM Plus Starters	Rigby
Baby Animal Zoo	O	I	250+	Martin, Ann M.	Scholastic
Baby Animals	M	I	250+	Berger, Melvin & Gilda	Scholastic
Baby Animals	D	I	41	Discovery Links	Newbridge
Baby Animals	D	I	78	Foundations	Wright Group/McGraw Hill
Baby Animals	B	I	44	Reading Corners	Pearson Learning Group
Baby Animals	E	I	109	Rigby Focus	Rigby
Baby Animals	B	I	89	Rigby Literacy	Rigby
Baby Animals	C	I	134	Rigby Star Quest	Rigby
Baby Animals	A	I	24	Vocabulary Readers	Houghton Mifflin Harcourt
Baby Animals at Home	C	I	64	Twig	Wright Group/McGraw Hill
Baby Animals Learn	C	I	52	Chanko, Pamela; Berger, Samantha	Scholastic
Baby Animals of the Rain Forest	J	I	294	Reading Street	Pearson
Baby Animals, The	A	I	55	Leveled Literacy Intervention/ Orange System	Heinemann
Baby at Our House, The	H	RF	93	Foundations	Wright Group/McGraw Hill
Baby Bear Climbs a Tree	F	F	147	PM Plus Story Books	Rigby
Baby Bear Goes Fishing	E	F	112	PM Story Books	Rigby
Baby Bear's Hiding Place	F	F	187	PM Plus Story Books	Rigby
Baby Bear's Present	F	F	206	PM Story Books	Rigby
Baby Bear's Ride	WB	F	N/A	Ready Readers	Pearson Learning Group
Baby Bear's Toys	A	F	35	Phonics and Friends	Hampton-Brown

* Collection of short stories
# Graphic text

TITLE	LEVEL	GENRE	WORD COUNT	AUTHOR / SERIES	PUBLISHER / DISTRIBUTOR
Baby Bird	G	F	251	Leveled Literacy Intervention/ Green System	Heinemann
Baby Birds	D	I	51	Pebble Books	Capstone Press
Baby Birds	E	I	181	Vocabulary Readers	Houghton Mifflin Harcourt
Baby Birds	E	I	181	Vocabulary Readers/CA	Houghton Mifflin Harcourt
Baby Birds	E	I	181	Vocabulary Readers/TX	Houghton Mifflin Harcourt
Baby Birds	D	I	37	Windows on Literacy	National Geographic
Baby Brother, The	I	RF	131	Voyages	SRA/McGraw Hill
Baby Can Ride	C	I	67	Leveled Readers Emergent	Houghton Mifflin Harcourt
Baby Cat	G	RF	194	Rigby Flying Colors	Rigby
Baby Chimp	A	RF	14	Twig	Wright Group/McGraw Hill
Baby Elephant	O	I	1414	Nature Babies	Fitzhenry & Whiteside
Baby Elephant Gets Lost	D	F	90	Foundations	Wright Group/McGraw Hill
Baby Elephant's New Bike	G	F	187	Foundations	Wright Group/McGraw Hill
Baby Elephant's Sneeze	F	F	78	Foundations	Wright Group/McGraw Hill
Baby Food	C	RF	21	Dunn, Tansy	Scholastic
Baby Food	L	RF	993	Rigby Gigglers	Rigby
Baby Fox	O	I	1407	Nature Babies	Fitzhenry & Whiteside
Baby Gets Dressed	LB	RF	16	Sunshine	Wright Group/McGraw Hill
Baby Grand, the Moon in July, and Me, The	P	RF	250+	Barnes, Joyce Annette	Penguin Group
Baby Grizzly	O	I	1517	Nature Babies	Fitzhenry & Whiteside
Baby Ground Squirrel	O	I	1495	Nature Babies	Fitzhenry & Whiteside
Baby Hippo	D	RF	117	PM Extensions-Yellow	Rigby
Baby in the Cart	C	RF	84	Foundations	Wright Group/McGraw Hill
Baby Island	P	RF	250+	Brink, Carol Ryrie	Simon & Schuster
Baby Kangaroo	B	F	46	Sails	Rigby
Baby Kangaroos	L	I	256	Leveled Readers	Houghton Mifflin Harcourt
Baby Kangaroos	L	I	256	Leveled Readers/CA	Houghton Mifflin Harcourt
Baby Kangaroos	L	I	256	Leveled Readers/TX	Houghton Mifflin Harcourt
Baby Koala	O	I	1437	Nature Babies	Fitzhenry & Whiteside
Baby Lamb's First Drink	C	F	64	PM Story Books	Rigby
Baby Lion	O	I	1436	Nature Babies	Fitzhenry & Whiteside
Baby Monkey	I	F	250+	Reading Unlimited	Pearson Learning Group
Baby Owl	O	I	1463	Nature Babies	Fitzhenry & Whiteside
Baby Owl	C	F	51	Sails	Rigby
Baby Owl Goes Away	E	F	151	Sails	Rigby
Baby Owl is Scared	G	F	226	Sails	Rigby
Baby Owls, The	C	RF	90	PM Extensions-Red	Rigby
Baby Panda	D	RF	97	PM Plus Story Books	Rigby
Baby Penguin	O	I	1118	Nature Babies	Fitzhenry & Whiteside
Baby Pictures	E	F	203	Leveled Literacy Intervention/ Green System	Heinemann
Baby Porcupine	O	I	1525	Nature Babies	Fitzhenry & Whiteside
Baby Says	LB	RF	26	Steptoe, John	Morrow
Baby Seal	O	I	1427	Nature Babies	Fitzhenry & Whiteside
Baby Shark, The	D	I	49	Windows on Literacy	National Geographic
Baby Sister for Frances, A	K	F	250+	Hoban, Lillian	Scholastic
Baby Skunk	A	RF	24	Handprints A	Educators Publishing Service
Baby Sloth	O	I	1445	Nature Babies	Fitzhenry & Whiteside
Baby Stegosaurus	J	F	717	Little Dinosaur	Literacy Footprints
Baby Talk	D	I	76	Joy Starters	Pearson Learning Group
Baby Tiger Cheats Cheetah	D	F	68	Reading Safari	Mondo
Baby Tiger's Blanket	J	F	712	Georgie Giraffe	Literacy Footprints

* Collection of short stories
# Graphic text

B

TITLE	LEVEL	GENRE	WORD COUNT	AUTHOR / SERIES	PUBLISHER / DISTRIBUTOR
Baby Turtle, The	H	I	122	Big Cat	Pacific Learning
Baby Wakes Up	C	RF	50	PM Plus Story Books	Rigby
Baby Whale Rescue: The True Story of J.J.	P	I	250+	Arnold, Caroline; Hewett, Richard	Troll Associates
Baby Whales Drink Milk	M	I	250+	Soar To Success	Houghton Mifflin Harcourt
Baby Writer	I	RF	182	Stepping Stones	Nelson/Michaels Assoc.
Baby, The	E	RF	60	Burningham, John	Crowell
Baby, The	A	I	40	Leveled Literacy Intervention/ Orange System	Heinemann
Baby's Birthday	D	RF	53	Literacy 2000	Rigby
Baby's Dinner	E	RF	26	Literacy 2000	Rigby
Baby-Sitter Burglaries, The	S	RF	250+	Keene, Carolyn	Pocket Books
Babysitter, The	H	RF	243	PM Extensions-Green	Rigby
Baby-Sitter, The	E	RF	69	Oxford Reading Tree	Oxford University Press
Baby-Sitters Club Mystery: Beware, Dawn!	O	RF	250+	Martin, Ann M.	Scholastic
Baby-Sitters Club Mystery: Claudia, Clue in the Photograph	O	RF	250+	Martin, Ann M.	Scholastic
Baby-Sitters Club Mystery: Claudia, Mystery at the Museum	O	RF	250+	Martin, Ann M.	Scholastic
Baby-Sitters Club Mystery: Claudia, Recipe for Danger	O	RF	250+	Martin, Ann M.	Scholastic
Baby-Sitters Club Mystery: Dawn, Disappearing Dogs	O	RF	250+	Martin, Ann M.	Scholastic
Baby-Sitters Club Mystery: Dawn, Halloween Mystery	O	RF	250+	Martin, Ann M.	Scholastic
Baby-Sitters Club Mystery: Dawn, Surfer Ghost	O	RF	250+	Martin, Ann M.	Scholastic
Baby-Sitters Club Mystery: Jessi, Jewel Thieves	O	RF	250+	Martin, Ann M.	Scholastic
Baby-Sitters Club Mystery: Kristy, Haunted Mansion	O	RF	250+	Martin, Ann M.	Scholastic
Baby-Sitters Club Mystery: Kristy, Missing Child	O	RF	250+	Martin, Ann M.	Scholastic
Baby-Sitters Club Mystery: Kristy, Missing Fortune	O	RF	250+	Martin, Ann M.	Scholastic
Baby-Sitters Club Mystery: Kristy, Vampires	O	RF	250+	Martin, Ann M.	Scholastic
Baby-Sitters Club Mystery: Mallory, Ghost Cat	O	RF	250+	Martin, Ann M.	Scholastic
Baby-Sitters Club Mystery: Mary Anne, Library Mystery	O	RF	250+	Martin, Ann M.	Scholastic
Baby-Sitters Club Mystery: Mary Anne, Secret in the Attic	O	RF	250+	Martin, Ann M.	Scholastic
Baby-Sitters Club Mystery: Mary Anne, Zoo Mystery	O	RF	250+	Martin, Ann M.	Scholastic
Baby-Sitters Club Mystery: Mystery at Claudia's House	O	RF	250+	Martin, Ann M.	Scholastic
Baby-Sitters Club Mystery: Stacey and the Mystery Money	O	RF	250+	Martin, Ann M.	Scholastic
Baby-Sitters Club Mystery: Stacey, Haunted Masquerade	O	RF	250+	Martin, Ann M.	Scholastic
Baby-Sitters Club Mystery: Stacey, Missing Ring	O	RF	250+	Martin, Ann M.	Scholastic
Baby-Sitters Club Mystery: Stacey, Mystery at the Empty House	O	RF	250+	Martin, Ann M.	Scholastic
Baby-Sitters Club Mystery: Stacey, Mystery at the Mall	O	RF	250+	Martin, Ann M.	Scholastic
Baby-Sitters Club Special Edition, The: Readers' Request	O	RF	250+	Martin, Ann M.	Scholastic
Baby-Sitters Club: Abby and the Best Kid Ever	O	RF	250+	Martin, Ann M.	Scholastic

* Collection of short stories
# Graphic text

TITLE	LEVEL	GENRE	WORD COUNT	AUTHOR / SERIES	PUBLISHER / DISTRIBUTOR
Baby-Sitters Club: Abby, the Bad Sport	O	RF	250+	Martin, Ann M.	Scholastic
Baby-Sitters Club: Claudia and the Bad Joke	O	RF	250+	Martin, Ann M.	Scholastic
Baby-Sitters Club: Claudia and the Little Liar	O	RF	250+	Martin, Ann M.	Scholastic
Baby-Sitters Club: Claudia and the New Girl	O	RF	250+	Martin, Ann M.	Scholastic
Baby-Sitters Club: Claudia and the Phantom Phone Calls	O	RF	250+	Martin, Ann M.	Scholastic
Baby-Sitters Club: Dawn and Too Many Sitters	O	RF	250+	Martin, Ann M.	Scholastic
Baby-Sitters Club: Dawn's Big Move	O	RF	250+	Martin, Ann M.	Scholastic
Baby-Sitters Club: Dawn's Wicked Stepsister	O	RF	250+	Martin, Ann M.	Scholastic
Baby-Sitters Club: Get Well Soon, Mallory	O	RF	250+	Martin, Ann M.	Scholastic
Baby-Sitters Club: Ghost at Dawn's House, The	O	RF	250+	Martin, Ann M.	Scholastic
Baby-Sitters Club: Good-bye Stacey, Good-bye	O	RF	250+	Martin, Ann M.	Scholastic
Baby-Sitters Club: Hello, Mallory	O	RF	250+	Martin, Ann M.	Scholastic
Baby-Sitters Club: Jessi and the Bad Baby-Sitter	O	RF	250+	Martin, Ann M.	Scholastic
Baby-Sitters Club: Jessi and the Superbrat	O	RF	250+	Martin, Ann M.	Scholastic
Baby-Sitters Club: Jessi Ramsey, Pet-sitter	O	RF	250+	Martin, Ann M.	Scholastic
Baby-Sitters Club: Kristy and the Snobs	O	RF	250+	Martin, Ann M.	Scholastic
Baby-Sitters Club: Kristy's Big Day	O	RF	250+	Martin, Ann M.	Scholastic
Baby-Sitters Club: Kristy's Great Idea	O	RF	250+	Martin, Ann M.	Scholastic
Baby-Sitters Club: Mary Anne and Camp BSC	O	RF	250+	Martin, Ann M.	Scholastic
Baby-Sitters Club: Mary Anne Saves the Day	O	RF	250+	Martin, Ann M.	Scholastic
Baby-Sitters Club: Welcome to the BSC, Abby	O	RF	250+	Martin, Ann M.	Scholastic
Baby-Sitter's Little Sister	O	RF	250+	Martin, Ann M.	Scholastic
Baby-Sitter's Little Sister : Karen's Accident	O	RF	250+	Martin, Ann M.	Scholastic
Baby-Sitter's Little Sister : Karen's Big Fight	O	RF	250+	Martin, Ann M.	Scholastic
Baby-Sitter's Little Sister : Karen's Big Sister	O	RF	250+	Martin, Ann M.	Scholastic
Baby-Sitter's Little Sister : Karen's Copycat	O	RF	250+	Martin, Ann M.	Scholastic
Baby-Sitter's Little Sister : Karen's Dinosaur	O	RF	250+	Martin, Ann M.	Scholastic
Baby-Sitter's Little Sister : Karen's Monsters	O	RF	250+	Martin, Ann M.	Scholastic
Baby-Sitter's Little Sister: Karen's Campout	O	RF	250+	Martin, Ann M.	Scholastic
Baby-Sitter's Little Sister: Karen's Mystery, Super Special	O	RF	250+	Martin, Ann M.	Scholastic
Baby-Sitter's Little Sister: Karen's Nanny	O	RF	250+	Martin, Ann M.	Scholastic
Baby-Sitter's Little Sister: Karen's Stepmother	O	RF	250+	Martin, Ann M.	Scholastic
Baby-Sitter's Little Sister: Karen's Two Families	O	RF	250+	Martin, Ann M.	Scholastic
Babysitting Activities: Fun with Kids of All Ages	S	I	250+	Babysitting	Capstone Press
Babysitting Basics: Caring for Kids	S	I	250+	Babysitting	Capstone Press
Babysitting Jobs: The Business of Babysitting	S	I	250+	Babysitting	Capstone Press
Babysitting Rules: A Guide for When You're in Charge	S	I	250+	Babysitting	Capstone Press
Babysitting Safety: Preventing Accidents and Injuries	S	I	250+	Babysitting	Capstone Press
Babysitting Skills: Traits and Training for Success	S	I	250+	Babysitting	Capstone Press
Baby-Snatcher	Z	RF	250+	Terris, Susan	Scholastic
Back and Forth	E	I	54	The Way Things Move	Capstone Press
Back Home	O	RF	250+	Pinkney, Gloria Jean	Penguin Group
Back of Beyond: A Story about Lewis and Clark, The	S	B	8408	Creative Minds Biographies	Lerner Publications
Back to School, Mallory!	O	RF	250+	Friedman, Laurie	Lerner Publications
Back to The Day Lincoln Was Shot!	S	I	250+	Gormley, Beatrice	Scholastic
Back to the Dentist	M	RF	199	City Kids	Rigby
Back to The Titanic!	S	F	250+	Gormley, Beatrice	Scholastic
Back to Year Zero	V	I	250+	WorldScapes	ETA Cuisenaire

* Collection of short stories
# Graphic text

TITLE	LEVEL	GENRE	WORD COUNT	AUTHOR / SERIES	PUBLISHER / DISTRIBUTOR
Backhoes	F	I	118	Mighty Machines	Capstone Press
Backstage	I	I	220	Twig	Wright Group/McGraw Hill
Backstage Pass	Q	I	250+	Bookweb	Rigby
Backup Goalie	P	RF	250+	Maddox, Jake	Stone Arch Books
Backward Bird Dog, The	R	F	250+	Wallace, Bill	Bantam
Backyard Angel	O	RF	250+	Delton, Judy	Houghton Mifflin Harcourt
Backyard Beasties: Jokes to Snake You Smile!	O	F	1571	Make Me Laugh!	Lerner Publications
Backyard Camp-Out	L	RF	628	Leveled Readers	Houghton Mifflin Harcourt
Backyard Hunter: The Praying Mantis	P	I	250+	Lavies, Bianca	Penguin Group
Backyard Zoo	G	I	167	Ready Readers	Pearson Learning Group
Bacon Saturday Mornings	K	RF	365	Books for Young Learners	Richard C. Owen
Bad Beginning, The	V	F	250+	Snicket, Lemony	HarperTrophy
Bad Boy, Billy	G	RF	129	Cambridge Reading	Pearson Learning Group
Bad Boy: A Memoir	Y	B	250+	Myers, Walter Dean	Harper Collins
Bad Dad List, The	M	RF	250+	Kenna, Anna	Pacific Learning
Bad Day for Ballet	N	RF	250+	Keene, Carolyn	Pocket Books
Bad Day for Benjamin, A	L	RF	250+	Reading Unlimited	Pearson Learning Group
Bad Day for Little Dinosaur, A	E	F	153	PM Stars	Rigby
Bad Day, The	D	RF	93	Teacher's Choice Series	Pearson Learning Group
Bad Dream, The	E	RF	88	Teacher's Choice Series	Pearson Learning Group
Bad Girls	U	RF	250+	Voigt, Cynthia	Scholastic
Bad Girls in Love	Z+	RF	250+	Voigt, Cynthia	Simon & Schuster
Bad Hair Day	E	RF	113	Teacher's Choice Series	Pearson Learning Group
Bad Luck of King Fred, The	O	F	250+	Literacy Tree	Rigby
Bad News, Good News	P	RF	250+	Storyteller - Autumn Leaves	Wright Group/ McGraw Hill
Bad Spell for the Worst Witch, A	P	F	250+	Murphy, Jill	Puffin/Penguin
Bad Weather, Good Weather	G	I	182	Springboard	Wright Group/McGraw Hill
Bad, Badder, Baddest	U	RF	250+	Voigt, Cynthia	Scholastic
Badger in the Basement	Q	RF	250+	Daniels, Lucy	Barron's Educational
Badgers: Active at Night	M	I	250+	The Wild World of Animals	Capstone Press
Badlands	R	F	250+	Orbit Chapter Books	Pacific Learning
Bad-Luck Day	J	RF	466	Leveled Literacy Intervention/ Green System	Heinemann
Bad-Luck Penny, The	L	F	250+	O'Connor, Jane	Grossett & Dunlap
Bad-News Report Card, The	K	RF	250+	Poydar Nancy	Holiday House
Bag of Coal, The	G	F	195	Storyworlds	Heinemann Educational Books
Bagels for Kids	O	I	250+	Pacific Literacy	Pacific Learning
Bags, Cans, Pots, and Pans	C	RF	56	Ready Readers	Pearson Learning Group
*Bake a Cake and Other Stories	C	RF	94	Story Steps	Rigby
Bake Sale Battle, The	N	RF	250+	Literacy by Design	Rigby
Bake Sale, The	K	RF	604	Leveled Readers	Houghton Mifflin Harcourt
Bake Sale, The	K	RF	604	Leveled Readers/CA	Houghton Mifflin Harcourt
Bake Sale, The	K	RF	604	Leveled Readers/TX	Houghton Mifflin Harcourt
Baked Beans	K	I	221	Lighthouse	Rigby
Baked Potatoes	D	RF	73	Book Bank	Wright Group/McGraw Hill
Baker, The	A	RF	25	Leveled Readers	Houghton Mifflin Harcourt
Baker, The	A	RF	25	Leveled Readers/CA	Houghton Mifflin Harcourt
Bakers	M	I	250+	Community Helpers	Red Brick Learning
Baking	D	I	27	Harry's Math Books	Outside the Box
Baking	A	F	35	Leveled Literacy Intervention/ Orange System	Heinemann
Baking a Cake	LB	I	7	Windows on Literacy	National Geographic
Baking Bread	L	I	426	How-To Series	Benchmark Education

TITLE	LEVEL	GENRE	WORD COUNT	AUTHOR / SERIES	PUBLISHER / DISTRIBUTOR
Baking Bread	F	I	70	Windows on Literacy	National Geographic
Baking Day	C	F	35	Windmill Books	Rigby
Balance	E	I	42	Simple Tools	Lerner Publishing
Balancing	C	I	46	Twig	Wright Group/McGraw Hill
Balcony Garden	G	I	258	Storyteller Nonfiction	Wright Group/McGraw Hill
Bald Bandit, The	N	RF	250+	A to Z Mysteries	Random House
Bald Eagle Free Again!, The	P	I	250+	Young Readers' Series	Barron's Educational
Bald Eagle Is Back, The	W	I	2691	Leveled Readers	Houghton Mifflin Harcourt
Bald Eagle, The	N	I	250+	A True Book	Children's Press
Bald Eagle, The	N	I	250+	American Symbols	Capstone Press
Bald Eagle, The	P	I	556	Pull Ahead Books	Lerner Publications
Bald Eagle, The	R	I	250+	Wildlife of North America	Red Brick Learning
Bald Eagles	Q	I	250+	Action Packs	Rigby
Bald Eagles	O	I	1941	Early Bird Nature Books	Lerner Publications
Bald Eagles	L	I	420	Leveled Readers	Houghton Mifflin Harcourt
Bald Eagles	L	I	420	Leveled Readers/CA	Houghton Mifflin Harcourt
Bald Eagles	L	I	420	Leveled Readers/TX	Houghton Mifflin Harcourt
Baleen	O	TL	250+	Book Blazers	ETA Cuisenaire
Balina	Q	TL	1000	Leveled Readers/TX	Houghton Mifflin Harcourt
Ball Book, The	E	I	342	Easy Stories	Norwood House Press
Ball Bounced, The	D	F	33	Tafuri, Nancy	Morrow
Ball Called Sam, A	E	RF	128	Rigby Star	Rigby
Ball Game	B	RF	16	Literacy 2000	Rigby
Ball Game, A	D	I	72	Carousel Readers	Pearson Learning Group
Ball Game, The	E	RF	45	Packard, David	Scholastic
Ball Games	B	RF	44	PM Starters	Rigby
Ball Games	B	F	77	Reading Safari	Mondo
Ball, The	C	RF	40	KinderReaders	Rigby
Ballad of Robin Hood, The	P	HF	250+	Literacy 2000	Rigby
Ballad of the Civil War, A	T	HF	250+	Stolz, Mary	HarperTrophy
Ballerina Girl	D	RF	77	My First Reader	Grolier Press
Ballet	L	I	413	Rigby Flying Colors	Rigby
Ballet Dance	S	I	250+	Dance	Capstone Press
Ballet of the Elephants	Q	I	250+	Schubert, Leda	Roaring Book Press
Balloon Fun	I	I	254	Springboard	Wright Group/McGraw Hill
Balloon Ride	A	F	32	Early Connections	Benchmark Education
Balloon Ride, The	F	F	245	Pearson, Mary E	Kaeden Books
Balloon Ride, The	B	RF	30	Sails	Rigby
Balloon, The	D	F	64	Carousel Readers	Pearson Learning Group
Ballooning Adventures	S	I	250+	Dangerous Adventures	Red Brick Learning
Balloons	B	I	55	Early Emergent	Pioneer Valley
Balloons	I	I	211	Independent Readers Science	Houghton Mifflin Harcourt
Balloons	M	I	57	iOpeners	Pearson Learning Group
Balloons	B	RF	57	PM Plus Starters	Rigby
Balloons	WB	RF	N/A	Rigby Literacy	Rigby
Balloons Go Pop!	C	RF	74	PM Stars	Rigby
Balloons!	D	F	56	Storyteller-First Snow	Wright Group/McGraw Hill
Balloons, The	B	RF	36	Sails	Rigby
Balloons, The	LB	RF	19	Sunshine	Wright Group/McGraw Hill
Ballroom Dancing	S	I	250+	Dance	Capstone Press
Balls	D	I	54	Rookie Readers	Children's Press
Balls	C	I	33	Windows on Literacy	National Geographic
Ballyhoo!	F	F	124	Story Basket	Wright Group/McGraw Hill
Baltimore Orioles, The	S	I	250+	Team Spirit	Norwood House Press

* Collection of short stories
# Graphic text

TITLE	LEVEL	GENRE	WORD COUNT	AUTHOR / SERIES	PUBLISHER / DISTRIBUTOR
Baltimore Ravens, The	S	I	250+	Team Spirit	Norwood House Press
Balto and the Great Race	P	RF	250+	Kimmel, Elizabeth Cody	Random House
Bambi: A Life in the Woods	T	F	250+	Salten, Felix	Aladdin
Bamboo Cutter's Daughter, The	T	TL	250+	WorldScapes	ETA Cuisenaire
Banana Belt, The	Q	I	3033	Take Two Books	Wright Group/ McGraw Hill
Banana Monster, The	D	F	54	Joy Readers	Pearson Learning Group
Banana Shake	C	RF	44	Book Bank	Wright Group/McGraw Hill
Banana Split Pizza and Other Snack Recipes	S	I	250+	Fun Food for Cool Cooks	Capstone Press
Banana Split Pizza and Other Snack Recipes	S	I	250+	Fun Food for Cool Cooks	Capstone Press
Banana-Berry Smoothies and Other Breakfast Recipes	S	I	250+	Fun Food for Cool Cooks	Capstone Press
Banana-Berry Smoothies and Other Breakfast Recipes	S	I	250+	Fun Food for Cool Cooks	Capstone Press
Bananas at My Table	B	I	48	Literacy by Design	Rigby
Bananas for Breakfast	H	F	250+	Rigby Rocket	Rigby
Bananas on My Table	B	I	48	On Our Way to English	Rigby
Band	F	I	87	On Deck	Rigby
Band of Bears, A	U	I	250+	Jean-Michel Cousteau Presents	London Town Press
Band of Brave Men, A	X	I	250+	iOpeners	Pearson Learning Group
Band, The	C	I	33	Sun Sprouts	ETA Cuisenaire
Band, The	C	RF	31	Voyages	SRA/McGraw Hill
Bandages	F	F	139	Moskowitz, Ellen	Kaeden Books
Bandit Moon	V	HF	250+	Fleischman, Sid	Dell Yearling
Bang	F	F	55	Literacy 2000	Rigby
Bang	Z+	RF	250+	Orca Soundings	Orca Book Publishers
Banished, The	W	F	250+	Levin, Betty	William Morrow
*Bank Robbery and Jack and the Beanstalk, The	L	TL	250+	New Way Literature	Steck-Vaughn
Bank Tellers	M	I	250+	Community Workers	Compass Point Books
Bank Tellers: Then and Now	N	I	250+	Primary Source Readers	Teacher Created Materials
Bar Graphs	K	I	345	Making Graphs	Capstone Press
Barb and Dingbat's Crybaby Hotline	Z+	RF	250+	Jennings, Patricks	Holiday House
Barbara Esbensen: Words into Pictures	R	B	1043	Leveled Readers	Houghton Mifflin Harcourt
Barbara McClintock	V	B	1926	Independent Readers Science	Houghton Mifflin Harcourt
Barbecue, The	LB	RF	14	Sunshine	Wright Group/McGraw Hill
Barbers	L	I	552	Pull Ahead Books	Lerner Publications
Bare Feet	B	RF	40	Visions	Wright Group/McGraw Hill
Barefoot: Escape on the Underground Railroad	S	HF	250+	Edwards, Pamela Duncan	HarperTrophy
Bargain for Frances, A	K	F	250+	Hoban, Russell	HarperTrophy
Bargains for Everyone	P	RF	1025	Leveled Readers	Houghton Mifflin Harcourt
Barker	E	RF	214	Rigby Rocket	Rigby
Barn Dance	C	F	47	Story Box	Wright Group/McGraw Hill
Barn Dance, The	B	RF	46	Leveled Readers Emergent	Houghton Mifflin Harcourt
Barn Party	K	F	250+	I Am Reading	Kingfisher
Barn Party	K	F	250+	Storyteller-Shooting Stars	Wright Group/McGraw Hill
Barn, The	T	RF	250+	Avi	Avon
Barnaby	C	RF	100	Sails	Rigby
Barnaby Bullfrog	F	F	121	Seedlings	Continental Press
Barnaby's Birthday	J	RF	214	Voyages	SRA/McGraw Hill
Barnaby's New House, The	G	RF	135	Literacy 2000	Rigby
Barney	P	RF	250+	Literacy 2000	Rigby
Barney Bear Gets Dressed	D	F	38	Learn to Read	Creative Teaching Press
Barney Bear, World Traveler	H	F	65	Learn to Read	Creative Teaching Press
Barney Owl	E	F	154	Rigby Flying Colors	Rigby
Barney's Horse	I	HF	250+	Hoff, Syd	HarperTrophy

TITLE	LEVEL	GENRE	WORD COUNT	AUTHOR / SERIES	PUBLISHER / DISTRIBUTOR
Barney's Lovely Lunch	K	RF	330	Windmill Books	Rigby
Barnyard Bandit, The	K	RF	371	Leveled Readers	Houghton Mifflin Harcourt
Barnyard Bandit, The	K	RF	371	Leveled Readers/CA	Houghton Mifflin Harcourt
Barnyard Bandit, The	K	RF	371	Leveled Readers/TX	Houghton Mifflin Harcourt
Barnyard Baseball	C	F	19	Pair-It Books	Steck-Vaughn
Barnyard Math with Farmer Fred	G	RF	139	Learn to Read	Creative Teaching Press
Barnyard Song	F	TL	196	PM Readalongs	Rigby
Baron: Rescue Dog	I	RF	120	Books for Young Learners	Richard C. Owen
Barracudas	H	I	83	Under the Sea	Capstone Press
Barrel in the Basement, The	R	F	250+	Wallace, Barbara Brooks	Aladdin
Barrel of Gold, A	K	F	251	Story Box	Wright Group/McGraw Hill
Barry and Bennie	H	F	251	Little Celebrations	Pearson Learning Group
Barry Bonds	P	B	1650	Amazing Athletes	Lerner Publications
Barry Bonds: Revised Edition	P	B	250+	Amazing Athletes	Lerner Publications
Bart's Amazing Charts	N	RF	250+	Ochiltree, Dianne	Scholastic
Baseball	P	I	250+	A True Book	Children's Press
Baseball	K	I	250+	On Deck	Rigby
Baseball	LB	RF	14	Sunshine	Wright Group/McGraw Hill
Baseball Ballerina	J	RF	250+	Cristaldi, Kathryn	Random House
Baseball Birthday Party, The	J	RF	250+	Prager, Annabelle	Random House
Baseball Blues	S	RF	1800	Leveled Readers/TX	Houghton Mifflin Harcourt
Baseball Boys	P	RF	1146	Leveled Readers	Houghton Mifflin Harcourt
Baseball Boys	P	RF	1146	Leveled Readers/CA	Houghton Mifflin Harcourt
Baseball Boys	P	RF	1146	Leveled Readers/TX	Houghton Mifflin Harcourt
Baseball Fever	O	RF	250+	Hurwitz, Johanna	William Morrow
Baseball Firsts	P	I	1059	Vocabulary Readers	Houghton Mifflin Harcourt
Baseball Firsts	P	I	1059	Vocabulary Readers/CA	Houghton Mifflin Harcourt
Baseball Flyhawk	Q	RF	250+	Christopher, Matt	Little, Brown & Co.
Baseball for Fun	S	I	250+	Sports for Fun	Compass Point Books
Baseball Friends	P	RF	1214	Leveled Readers	Houghton Mifflin Harcourt
Baseball Friends	P	RF	1214	Leveled Readers/CA	Houghton Mifflin Harcourt
Baseball Friends	P	RF	1214	Leveled Readers/TX	Houghton Mifflin Harcourt
Baseball Fun	E	RF	51	Geddes, Diana	Kaeden Books
Baseball Game, The	I	F	211	Foundations	Wright Group/McGraw Hill
Baseball Game, The	L	I	358	Leveled Readers	Houghton Mifflin Harcourt
Baseball Game, The	L	I	358	Leveled Readers/CA	Houghton Mifflin Harcourt
Baseball Game, The	L	I	358	Leveled Readers/TX	Houghton Mifflin Harcourt
Baseball Heroes	Q	B	1131	Reading Street	Pearson
Baseball Heroes, The	M	RF	250+	Woodland Mysteries	Wright Group/McGraw Hill
*Baseball in April and Other Stories	U	RF	250+	Soto, Gary	Harcourt Trade
Baseball in the Barrios	P	I	250+	Horenstein, Henry	Harcourt Trade
Baseball Math	N	I	250+	Early Connections	Benchmark Education
Baseball Megastars	O	I	250+	Weber, Bruce	Scholastic
Baseball Memories	S	RF	1800	Leveled Readers/TX	Houghton Mifflin Harcourt
Baseball Pals	Q	RF	250+	Christopher, Matt	Little, Brown & Co.
*Baseball Pitching Challenge and Other Cases, The	O	RF	250+	Simon, Seymour	Avon
Baseball Saved Us	O	HF	250+	Mochizuki, Ken	Scholastic
*Baseball's Best: Five True Stories	O	B	250+	Step into Reading	Random House
*Baseball's Greatest Pitchers	P	B	250+	Kramer, S. A.	Random House
Basesball Fever	I	RF	453	We Both Read	Treasure Bay
Basil's Night Out	J	F	471	Gear Up!	Wright Group/McGraw Hill
Basket Counts, The	R	RF	250+	Christopher, Matt	Little, Brown & Co.
Basket Full of Surprises, A	B	RF	43	Little Books	Sadlier-Oxford

Storable Database at www.fountasandpinnellleveledbooks.com

* Collection of short stories
\# Graphic text

TITLE	LEVEL	GENRE	WORD COUNT	AUTHOR / SERIES	PUBLISHER / DISTRIBUTOR
Basket of Beethoven	S	RF	250+	Currie, Susan	Fitzhenry & Whiteside
Basketball	K	I	250+	On Deck	Rigby
Basketball	I	I	159	Ready Readers	Pearson Learning Group
Basketball	C	RF	23	Visions	Wright Group/McGraw Hill
Basketball	B	I	20	Wonder World	Wright Group/McGraw Hill
Basketball Buddies	N	RF	250+	Boyz Rule!	Mondo
Basketball for Fun	S	I	250+	Sports for Fun	Compass Point Books
Basketball Game, The	L	RF	607	Leveled Readers Science	Houghton Mifflin Harcourt
Basketball Showdown	N	RF	250+	Girlz Rock!	Mondo
Basketball War	P	SF	1946	Zucker, Jonny	Stone Arch Books
Basset Hounds	I	I	152	Dogs	Capstone Press
Bat 6	Z	HF	250+	Wolff, Virginia Euwer	Scholastic
Bat and Parrot	B	F	46	Sails	Rigby
Bat Bones and Spider Stew	K	RF	250+	Poploff, Michelle	Bantam
Bat Boy & His Violin, The	Q	RF	250+	Curtis, Gavin	Scholastic
Bat Loves the Night	M	RF	250+	Read and Wonder	Candlewick Press
Bat, The	H	RF	256	Gear Up!	Wright Group/McGraw Hill
Bat-Chen Diaries, The	X	B	13802	Shahak, Bat-Chen	Kar-Ben Publishing
Bath Day for Brutus	K	RF	347	Little Red Readers	Sundance
Bath Eyes	F	RF	154	PM Photo Stories	Rigby
Bath for a Beagle	D	RF	102	First Start	Troll Associates
Bath for Patches, A	E	RF	89	Carousel Readers	Pearson Learning Group
Bath Time	B	I	44	Bebop Books	Lee & Low Books Inc.
Bath Time	B	I	33	InfoTrek	ETA Cuisenaire
Bath Time	C	I	23	Wonder World	Wright Group/McGraw Hill
Bath, The	LB	RF	14	Ready Readers	Pearson Learning Group
Bath, The	B	RF	28	Smart Starts	Rigby
Bathtub Beach	J	F	368	Leveled Readers	Houghton Mifflin Harcourt
Bathtub Beach	J	F	368	Leveled Readers/CA	Houghton Mifflin Harcourt
Bat-Poet, The	S	F	250+	Jarrell, Randall	HarperCollins
Bats	O	I	2473	Early Bird Nature Books	Lerner Publications
Bats	O	I	250+	Gibbons, Gail	Holiday House
Bats	O	I	250+	Holmes, Kevin J.	Red Brick Learning
Bats	P	I	250+	Literacy 2000	Rigby
Bats	O	I	250+	Nature's Friends	Compass Point Books
Bats	I	I	162	Phonics Readers	Compass Point Books
Bats	M	I	250+	PM Animal Facts: Gold	Rigby
Bats	J	I	250+	Wood, Lily	Scholastic
Bats about Bats!	N	I	250+	Storyteller Summer Skies	Wright Group/McGraw Hill
Bats and Burglars	N	RF	250+	First Flight	Fitzhenry & Whiteside
Bats at Bat	D	F	36	Pair-It Books	Steck-Vaughn
Bats in Blankets	H	I	182	Sails	Rigby
Bat's Night Out	L	RF	172	Books for Young Learners	Richard C. Owen
Bats on the Move	Q	I	865	Vocabulary Readers	Houghton Mifflin Harcourt
Bats on the Move	Q	I	865	Vocabulary Readers/CA	Houghton Mifflin Harcourt
Bats Out the Window	O	RF	250+	First Flight	Fitzhenry & Whiteside
Bats, Bats, Bats	E	I	33	Pair-It Books	Steck-Vaughn
Bats, Bats, Bats	D	I	29	Rosen Real Readers	Rosen Publishing Group
Bats, The	C	I	21	Twig	Wright Group/McGraw Hill
Bats: The Amazing Upside-Downers	S	I	250+	A First Book	Franklin Watts
Batter Up	G	RF	183	Adventures in Reading	Pearson Learning Group
Batter Up	C	I	8	Bebop Books	Lee & Low Books Inc.
Batter Up!	C	RF	39	Bookshop	Mondo
Batter Up!	P	RF	250+	Maddox, Jake	Stone Arch Books

TITLE	LEVEL	GENRE	WORD COUNT	AUTHOR / SERIES	PUBLISHER / DISTRIBUTOR
Batteries	G	I	105	Early Connections	Benchmark Education
Batteries, Bulbs and Wires	R	I	250+	Young Discoverers	Kingfisher
Batting Against the Odds	Q	B	250+	WorldScapes	ETA Cuisenaire
Battle for Iwo Jima, The	W	I	250+	Cornerstones of Freedom	Children's Press
Battle for Monmouth, The	S	I	1285	Vocabulary Readers	Houghton Mifflin Harcourt
Battle for Survival, The	P	I	250+	Sunshine	Wright Group/McGraw Hill
Battle for the Castle, The	P	F	250+	Winthrop, Elizabeth	Yearling
Battle of Bull Run, The: An Interactive History Adventure	V	HF	250+	You Choose Books	Capstone Press
Battle of Bunker Hill, The: An Interactive History Adventure	T	HF	250+	You Choose Books	Capstone Press
Battle of Chancellorsville, The	V	I	250+	Cornerstones of Freedom	Children's Press
Battle of Gettysburg, The: Turning Point of the Civil War	V	I	250+	Let Freedom Ring	Capstone Press
Battle of Lake Erie, The	Y	I	250+	History for Young Canadians	Fitzhenry & Whiteside
Battle of Leyte, The	U	I	974	Leveled Readers Social Studies	Houghton Mifflin Harcourt
Battle of Monmouth, The	S	I	1285	Vocabulary Readers/CA	Houghton Mifflin Harcourt
Battle of Monmouth, The	S	I	1285	Vocabulary Readers/TX	Houghton Mifflin Harcourt
Battle of the Alamo, The	V	I	250+	Cornerstones of Freedom	Children's Press
#Battle of the Alamo, The	U	I	250+	Graphic Library	Capstone Press
Battle of the Alamo, The: An Interactive History Adventure	V	HF	250+	You Choose Books	Capstone Press
Battle of the Bands	Z+	RF	250+	Orca Soundings	Orca Book Publishers
Battle of the Games	N	RF	250+	Boyz Rule!	Mondo
Battle of the Little Bighorn, The	V	I	250+	Cornerstones of Freedom	Children's Press
Battle of Words, A	O	RF	250+	Literacy 2000	Rigby
Battle of Yorktown, The	V	I	250+	Let Freedom Ring	Red Brick Learning
Battle Over Rain Forest Lands, The	U	I	250+	Reading Street	Pearson
Battlefield Support	V	I	4310	Military Hardware in Action	Lerner Publications
Battles at Sea	R	I	1386	Vocabulary Readers	Houghton Mifflin Harcourt
Battles at Sea	R	I	1386	Vocabulary Readers/CA	Houghton Mifflin Harcourt
Battles at Sea	R	I	1386	Vocabulary Readers/TX	Houghton Mifflin Harcourt
Battles of Lexington & Concord, The	T	I	250+	We The People	Compass Point Books
Battles of Lexington and Concord, The	V	I	250+	Let Freedom Ring	Red Brick Learning
Battles of the Civil War	U	I	250+	Primary Source Readers	Teacher Created Materials
Battles of the War of 1812, The	Y	I	250+	History for Young Canadians	Fitzhenry & Whiteside
Battleships	T	I	250+	Land and Sea	Capstone Press
Bay Run, The	C	RF	80	Foundations	Wright Group/McGraw Hill
B-day Box, The	Q	F	250+	Literacy by Design	Rigby
Be a Clown	C	I	29	The Candid Collection	Pearson Learning Group
Be a Good Friend!	J	I	250+	Spyglass Books	Compass Point Books
Be a Good Sport!	J	I	250+	Spyglass Books	Compass Point Books
Be a Perfect Person in Just Three Days!	N	RF	250+	Manes, Stephen	Dell
Be a Plant Scientist	L	I	250+	Take Two Books	Wright Group/McGraw Hill
Be Careful of Strangers	I	RF	362	Rigby Flying Colors	Rigby
Be Careful What You Wish For!	Q	TL	250+	Literacy by Design	Rigby
Be Careful!	D	F	133	Gear Up!	Wright Group/McGraw Hill
Be Careful, Matthew!	F	RF	80	Sunshine	Wright Group/McGraw Hill
Be Careful, Ogre!	I	F	192	Sun Sprouts	ETA Cuisenaire
Be Quiet	A	RF	25	Literacy 2000	Rigby
Be Quiet	B	RF	25	Smart Starts	Rigby
Be Quiet Parrot	J	F	405	Be Nice at School	Carolrhoda
Be Quiet!	E	RF	95	Rigby Star	Rigby
Be Ready at Eight	K	F	250+	Parish, Peggy	Simon & Schuster

Organized Alphabetically by Title
Storable Database at www.fountasandpinnellleveledbooks.com

* Collection of short stories
# Graphic text

TITLE	LEVEL	GENRE	WORD COUNT	AUTHOR / SERIES	PUBLISHER / DISTRIBUTOR
Be Safe on Your Bike	J	I	250+	Rosen Real Readers	Rosen Publishing Group
Be the Change: People Who Have Made a Difference	T	B	250+	Power Up!	Steck-Vaughn
Beach Boat, The	F	RF	168	PM Stars	Rigby
Beach Creatures	H	I	231	Pair-It Books	Steck-Vaughn
Beach Feet	D	RF	68	Books for Young Learners	Richard C. Owen
Beach House, The	F	RF	164	PM Plus Story Books	Rigby
Beach Riddles	K	F	467	Silly Millies	Millbrook Press
Beach, The	D	RF	38	Book Bank	Wright Group/McGraw Hill
Beach, The	J	RF	292	Leveled Readers	Houghton Mifflin Harcourt
Beach, The	J	RF	292	Leveled Readers/CA	Houghton Mifflin Harcourt
Beach, The	J	RF	292	Leveled Readers/TX	Houghton Mifflin Harcourt
Beach, The	LB	I	16	Little Celebrations	Pearson Learning Group
Beacons of Light: Lighthouses	O	I	250+	Gibbons, Gail	Scholastic
Beading for Fun!	S	I	250+	For Fun! Crafts	Compass Point Books
Beading: Bracelets, Barrettes, and Beyond	Q	I	250+	Crafts	Capstone Press
Beads	C	I	16	Instant Readers	Harcourt School Publishers
Beagle Brigade, The	N	I	250+	Literacy by Design	Rigby
Beagles	I	I	101	Dogs	Capstone Press
Beak Book, The	D	I	48	Chanko, Pamela	Scholastic
Beaks	G	I	125	Discovery Links	Newbridge
Beaks	H	I	100	Gear Up!	Wright Group/McGraw Hill
Beaks and Feet	J	I	234	Alphakids	Sundance
Bean	N	I	250+	Life Cycles	Creative Teaching Press
Bean Bag That Mom Made, The	I	RF	270	Tadpoles	Rigby
Beanbag	K	RF	250+	Literacy 2000	Rigby
Beanpole Billy	L	F	250+	Lighthouse	Ginn & Co.
Beans	F	I	89	Life Cycles	Lerner Publications
Beans	LB	I	35	Pebble Books	Capstone Press
Beans on the Roof	L	RF	250+	Byars, Betsy	Bantam
Beany (Not Beanhead)	M	RF	250+	Wojciechowski, Susan	Candlewick Press
Beany and the Dreaded Wedding	M	RF	250+	Wojciechowski, Susan	Candlewick Press
Beany and the Magic Crystal	M	RF	250+	Wojciechowski, Susan	Candlewick Press
Beany and the Meany	M	RF	250+	Wojciechowski, Susan	Candlewick Press
Beany Goes to Camp	M	RF	250+	Wojciechowski, Susan	Candlewick Press
Bear and the Bees, The	J	TL	250+	PM Plus Story Books	Rigby
Bear and the Trolls, The	L	TL	250+	PM Tales and Plays-Silver	Rigby
Bear at the Beach	K	F	250+	Carmichael, Clay	North-South Books
Bear Called Paddington, A	T	F	250+	Bond, Michael	Bantam
Bear Collection, The	N	I	250+	PM Collection	Rigby
Bear Cubs	J	I	408	Vocabulary Readers	Houghton Mifflin Harcourt
Bear Cubs	J	I	408	Vocabulary Readers/CA	Houghton Mifflin Harcourt
Bear Eats Fish, A	C	I	44	Windows on Literacy	National Geographic
Bear Escape, The	D	F	42	Pair-It Books	Steck-Vaughn
Bear Facts	E	I	41	Pair-It Books	Steck-Vaughn
Bear For Miguel, A	K	RF	250+	Alphin, Elaine Marie	HarperTrophy
Bear Goes to Town	K	F	250+	Browne, Anthony	Doubleday Books
Bear Hunt	F	RF	146	Lighthouse	Rigby
Bear in the Air	I	F	367	Sun Sprouts	ETA Cuisenaire
Bear in Trouble	I	F	439	Sails	Rigby
Bear Lived in a Cave, A	D	I	102	Little Red Readers	Sundance
Bear Man, The	J	TL	358	Reading Street	Pearson
Bear Needs a Place to Climb, A	B	I	49	Independent Readers Science	Houghton Mifflin Harcourt
Bear Needs a Place to Climb, A	B	I	49	Science Support Readers	Houghton Mifflin Harcourt

TITLE	LEVEL	GENRE	WORD COUNT	AUTHOR / SERIES	PUBLISHER / DISTRIBUTOR
Bear Shadow	J	F	489	Asch, Frank	Simon & Schuster
Bear Swims	E	F	151	Leveled Readers	Houghton Mifflin Harcourt
Bear Swims	E	F	151	Leveled Readers/CA	Houghton Mifflin Harcourt
Bear Swims	E	F	151	Leveled Readers/TX	Houghton Mifflin Harcourt
Bear That Heard Crying, The	P	HF	250+	Kinsey-Warnock, Natalie; Kinsey, Helen	Penguin Group
Bear That Wouldn't Growl, The	I	F	250+	Storyworlds	Heinemann Educational Books
Bear Wakes Up	B	F	76	First Stories	Pacific Learning
Bear, The	LB	I	17	Carousel Earlybirds	Pearson Learning Group
Bear, The	M	I	250+	Life Cycles	Steck-Vaughn
Bear, The: An American Folk Song	K	F	250+	Bookshop	Mondo
Bear's Birthday	I	F	432	Leveled Literacy Intervention/ Green System	Heinemann
Bearing Witness: Teaching About the Holocaust	Z+	I	250+	Greenbaum, Beth Aviv	Heinemann
Bears	O	I	250+	Holmes, Kevin J.	Red Brick Learning
Bears	D	F	56	Joy Readers	Pearson Learning Group
Bears	P	I	3286	Leveled Readers Science	Houghton Mifflin Harcourt
Bears	B	I	59	Storyteller Nonfiction	Wright Group/McGraw Hill
Bears and the Honey, The	D	F	86	Storyworlds	Heinemann Educational Publishers
Bears and the Magpie, The	G	F	205	PM Plus Story Books	Rigby
Bears and Their Dens	J	I	131	Animal Homes	Capstone Press
Bears Are Curious	J	I	250+	Milton, Joyce	Random House
Bear's Ball	A	F	32	Sun Sprouts	ETA Cuisenaire
Bear's Bargain	J	F	250+	Asch, Frank	Scholastic
Bear's Bicycle, The	I	F	185	McLeod, Emilie	Little, Brown & Co.
Bear's Christmas	M	F	250+	Berenstain, Stan & Jan	Random House
Bear's Diet	L	RF	652	PM Collection	Rigby
Bears Have Cubs	M	I	250+	Animals and Their Young	Compass Point Books
Bears' House, The	T	RF	250+	Sachs, Marilyn	Puffin/Penguin
Bears in the Night	D	F	108	Berenstain, Stan & Jan	Random House
Bear's Long, Brown Tail	H	TL	332	Leveled Readers	Houghton Mifflin Harcourt
Bear's Long, Brown Tail	H	TL	332	Leveled Readers/CA	Houghton Mifflin Harcourt
Bear's Long, Brown Tail	H	TL	332	Leveled Readers/TX	Houghton Mifflin Harcourt
Bears on Hemlock Mountain, The	M	RF	250+	Dalgliesh, Alice	Aladdin
Bears on Wheels	D	F	89	Berenstain, Stan & Jan	Random House
Bears' Picnic	M	F	250+	Berenstain, Stan & Jan	Random House
Bears' Picnic, The	D	F	61	Story Box	Wright Group/McGraw Hill
Bears Ride in Style, The	M	RF	735	Leveled Readers	Houghton Mifflin Harcourt
Bears Ride in Style, The	M	RF	735	Leveled Readers/CA	Houghton Mifflin Harcourt
Bears Ride in Style, The	M	RF	735	Leveled Readers/TX	Houghton Mifflin Harcourt
Bear's Tail	G	TL	292	Leveled Readers	Houghton Mifflin Harcourt
Bear's Tail	G	TL	292	Leveled Readers/CA	Houghton Mifflin Harcourt
Bear's Tail	G	TL	292	Leveled Readers/TX	Houghton Mifflin Harcourt
Bear's Tale, The	H	TL	155	Books for Young Learners	Richard C. Owen
Bears Through the Year	A	F	20	Leveled Readers	Houghton Mifflin Harcourt
Bears Through the Year	A	F	20	Leveled Readers/CA	Houghton Mifflin Harcourt
Bear's Year, A	J	I	213	Phonics Readers	Compass Point Books
Bears, Bears Everywhere	D	F	52	Rookie Readers	Children's Press
Bears, Bears, Bears	I	F	250+	Little Readers	Houghton Mifflin Harcourt
Bears, Bears, Bears	D	RF	76	Step-By-Step Series	Pearson Learning Group
Bears, Bears, Bears	E	F	250+	Story Steps	Rigby
Bears, Bears, Everywhere	E	F	67	Learn to Read	Creative Teaching Press

* Collection of short stories
# Graphic text

TITLE	LEVEL	GENRE	WORD COUNT	AUTHOR / SERIES	PUBLISHER / DISTRIBUTOR
Bears, The	A	F	30	Sails	Rigby
Bearstone	V	RF	250+	Hobbs, Will	Hearst
Beast	X	F	250+	Napoli, Donna Jo	Atheneum
Beast and the Halloween Horror	M	RF	250+	Giff, Patricia Reilly	Bantam
Beast Beneath the Stairs	T	F	584	Dahl, Michael	Stone Arch Books
Beast in Ms. Rooney's Room, The	M	RF	250+	Giff, Patricia Reilly	Bantam
Beast of Moogill, The	K	SF	596	Rigby Gigglers	Rigby
Beast, The	Z+	RF	250+	Myers, Walter Dean	Scholastic
Beat Goes On, The	Q	I	250+	Explorer Books-Pioneer	National Geographic
Beat Goes On, The	R	I	250+	Explorer Books-Pathfinder	National Geographic
Beat This	D	RF	79	Ready Readers	Pearson Learning Group
Beat, The: The Music Scene	U	I	250+	Boldprint	Steck-Vaughn
Beating Diabetes	S	I	250+	Orbit Double Takes	Pacific Learning
Beating the Cold	Q	I	250+	WorldScapes	ETA Cuisenaire
Beating the Drought	M	RF	250+	Orbit Chapter Books	Pacific Learning
Beating the Frost	O	RF	250+	Orbit Chapter Books	Pacific Learning
Beating the Heat	Q	I	883	Leveled Readers	Houghton Mifflin Harcourt
Beating the Heat	Q	I	883	Leveled Readers/CA	Houghton Mifflin Harcourt
Beating the Heat	Q	I	883	Leveled Readers/TX	Houghton Mifflin Harcourt
Beating the Heat, Desert Style	W	I	1874	Leveled Readers	Houghton Mifflin Harcourt
Beatles, The	R	B	250+	Venezia, Mike	Children's Press
Beatrix Potter	J	B	135	iOpeners	Pearson Learning Group
Beatrix Potter	K	B	314	Leveled Readers	Houghton Mifflin Harcourt
Beatrix Potter	K	B	314	Leveled Readers/CA	Houghton Mifflin Harcourt
Beatrix Potter	K	B	314	Leveled Readers/TX	Houghton Mifflin Harcourt
Beatrix Potter	O	B	250+	Wallner, Alexandra	Holiday House
Beauregard the Cat	M	RF	250+	Bookshop	Mondo
Beautiful Bugs	E	I	70	Fleming, Maria	Scholastic
Beautiful Flowers	B	I	28	Wonder World	Wright Group/McGraw Hill
Beautiful Land: A Story of the Oklahoma Land Rush	S	I	250+	Antle, Nancy	Penguin Group
Beautiful Pig	J	F	423	Read Alongs	Rigby
Beauty	V	RF	250+	Wallace, Bill	Holiday House
Beauty and the Beast	K	TL	250+	PM Tales and Plays-Gold	Rigby
Beauty and the Beast	K	TL	250+	Sunshine	Wright Group/McGraw Hill
Beauty, the Beast, and the Sisters: A Thrice-told Tale	T	TL	250+	Bookshop	Mondo
Beauty: A Retelling of the Story of Beauty and the Beast	X	F	250+	McKinley, Robin	Harper Trophy
Beaver Engineers	N	I	250+	Take Two Books	Wright Group/McGraw Hill
Beaver Tale, A	E	I	228	Twig	Wright Group/McGraw Hill
Beaver, The	M	I	250+	Crewe, Sabrina	Steck-Vaughn
Beavers	N	I	250+	Bookshop	Mondo
Beavers	I	I	218	Sails	Rigby
Beavers	H	I	119	Wetland Animals	Capstone Press
Beavers and Their Lodges	J	I	121	Animal Homes	Capstone Press
Beavers Beware!	K	I	250+	Bank Street	Bantam
Beaver's Photo	E	F	120	Springboard	Wright Group/McGraw Hill
Beaver's Tail, The	J	TL	250+	Rigby Rocket	Rigby
Because a Little Bug Went Ka-Choo	I	F	250+	Stone, Rosetta	Random House
Because Daddy Did My Hair	I	RF	214	Teacher's Choice Series	Pearson Learning Group
Because I'm Little	B	RF	51	Home Connection Collection	Rigby
Because of Walter	N	RF	250+	Action Packs	Rigby
Because of Winn-Dixie	R	RF	250+	DiCamillo, Kate	Candlewick Press

TITLE	LEVEL	GENRE	WORD COUNT	AUTHOR / SERIES	PUBLISHER / DISTRIBUTOR
Becky's Blue Butterfly	K	RF	664	Rigby Flying Colors	Rigby
Becky's Special Folder	I	RF	396	Rigby Flying Colors	Rigby
Becoming a Butterfly	J	I	178	Gear Up!	Wright Group/McGraw Hill
Becoming a Butterfly	H	I	83	Rosen Real Readers	Rosen Publishing Group
Becoming a Citizen	R	I	250+	A True Book	Children's Press
Becoming a Citizen	P	I	209	Vocabulary Readers	Houghton Mifflin Harcourt
Becoming a Pop Star	V	I	250+	10 Things You Need to Know About	Capstone Press
Becoming a Real Hero	T	B	1650	Leveled Readers	Houghton Mifflin Harcourt
Becoming Joe DiMaggio	T	HF	250+	Testa, Maria	Candlewick Press
Becoming Modern America	U	I	250+	Kids Discover Reading	Wright Group/McGraw Hill
Becoming Naomi Leon	V	RF	250+	Ryan, Pam Munoz	Scholastic
Bed for Paul, A	L	TL	606	Reading Street	Pearson
Bed Full of Cats, A	I	RF	250+	Green Light Readers	Harcourt
Bed Rest	E	I	34	Rhythm 'N' Rhyme Readers	Pearson Learning Group
Bedroom Makeover Crafts	P	I	4053	Ross, Kathy	Millbrook Press
Beds	C	I	44	Interaction	Rigby
Bedtime	C	RF	23	Books for Young Learners	Richard C. Owen
Bedtime	C	RF	83	PM Plus Story Books	Rigby
Bedtime at Aunt Carmen's	K	RF	250	Ready Readers	Pearson Learning Group
Bedtime for Bear	C	F	12	Instant Readers	Harcourt School Publishers
Bedtime for Bear	C	F	40	Rigby Rocket	Rigby
Bedtime for Carl	A	RF	24	Bonnell, Kris	Reading Reading Books
Bedtime for Frances	K	F	250+	Hoban, Russell	Scholastic
Bedtime for Paulette	G	RF	212	On Our Way to English	Rigby
Bedtime Fun	B	RF	46	Bebop Books	Lee & Low Books Inc.
Bedtime Story, A	K	RF	250+	Bookshop	Mondo
Bee in Your Ear, A	L	RF	250+	Orca Echoes	Orca Book Publishers
Bee My Valentine!	H	RF	250+	Cohen, Miriam	Bantam
Bee, The	M	I	250+	Crewe, Sabrina	Steck-Vaughn
Bee, The	C	RF	26	Story Box	Wright Group/McGraw Hill
Beekeeper, The	M	I	250+	Literacy 2000	Rigby
Beekeeper's Work, A	K	I	304	Reading Street	Pearson
Beeman Interview	N	F	250+	Sails	Rigby
Beeman, The	F	F	148	Sails	Rigby
Beep, Beep	F	F	51	Start to Read	School Zone
Beep, Beep, Beep	D	F	86	Foundations	Wright Group/McGraw Hill
Beeper Bakes	C	F	34	Brand New Readers	Candlewick Press
Beeper Counts	C	F	30	Brand New Readers	Candlewick Press
Beeper Flies	C	F	31	Brand New Readers	Candlewick Press
Beeper Paints	C	F	36	Brand New Readers	Candlewick Press
Bees	O	I	250+	A True Book	Children's Press
Bees	O	I	250+	Holmes, Kevin J.	Red Brick Learning
Bees	N	I	250+	Nature's Friends	Compass Point Books
Bees	N	I	250+	World of Insects	Capstone Press
Bees and Their Hives	J	I	112	Animal Homes	Capstone Press
Bees and Wasps	I	I	458	Sails	Rigby
Bees at Work	L	I	456	Leveled Readers	Houghton Mifflin Harcourt
Bees at Work	L	I	456	Leveled Readers/CA	Houghton Mifflin Harcourt
Bees at Work	L	I	456	Leveled Readers/TX	Houghton Mifflin Harcourt
Bee's Beautiful Garden	N	F	720	Leveled Readers	Houghton Mifflin Harcourt
Bee's Beautiful Garden	N	F	720	Leveled Readers/CA	Houghton Mifflin Harcourt
Bee's Beautiful Garden	N	F	720	Leveled Readers/TX	Houghton Mifflin Harcourt
Bees Buzzed, The	B	RF	41	Science	Outside the Box

* Collection of short stories
# Graphic text

TITLE	LEVEL	GENRE	WORD COUNT	AUTHOR / SERIES	PUBLISHER / DISTRIBUTOR
Bee's Home, A	K	I	127	Salem, Lynn	Continental Press
Bees in My Garden	E	I	104	Flying Colors	Rigby
Bee's Life, A	H	I	100	Time for Kids	Teacher Created Materials
Bees on Trees	H	F	250+	Sunshine	Wright Group/McGraw Hill
Beethoven Lives Upstairs	S	I	250+	Nichol, Barbara	Orchard Books
Beetles	H	I	115	Bugs, Bugs, Bugs!	Capstone Press
Beetles	D	I	39	Insects	Capstone Press
Beetles	N	I	250+	Minibeasts	Franklin Watts
Beetles	E	I	59	Sails	Rigby
Beetles	C	I	36	Science	Outside the Box
Beetles	Q	I	1242	Vocabulary Readers	Houghton Mifflin Harcourt
Beetles	Q	I	1242	Vocabulary Readers/CA	Houghton Mifflin Harcourt
Beetles, Lightly Toasted	Q	RF	250+	Naylor, Phyllis Reynolds	Bantam
Beezus & Ramona	O	RF	250+	Cleary, Beverly	Avon
Before I Go to School	B	I	71	Storyteller-First Snow	Wright Group/McGraw Hill
Before It Wriggles Away	O	B	250+	Meet the Author	Richard C. Owen
Before the First Flight	U	I	1718	Vocabulary Readers	Houghton Mifflin Harcourt
Before the First Flight	U	I	1718	Vocabulary Readers/CA	Houghton Mifflin Harcourt
Before the Fridge	G	I	88	Seedlings	Continental Press
Before the Talkies	K	RF	402	Leveled Readers	Houghton Mifflin Harcourt
Before the Talkies	K	RF	402	Leveled Readers/CA	Houghton Mifflin Harcourt
Before the Talkies	K	RF	402	Leveled Readers/TX	Houghton Mifflin Harcourt
Before the Top Stops	C	RF	51	InfoTrek	ETA Cuisenaire
Before They Were President	M	I	583	Vocabulary Readers	Houghton Mifflin Harcourt
Before They Were President	M	I	583	Vocabulary Readers/CA	Houghton Mifflin Harcourt
Beginning Knitting: Stitches with Style	Q	I	250+	Crafts	Capstone Press
Beginnings of Sports	R	I	250+	PM Nonfiction-Ruby	Rigby
Behind and in Front	C	I	48	Location	Lerner Publishing
Behind Castle Walls	T	I	250+	WorldScapes	ETA Cuisenaire
Behind Rebel Lines	T	HF	250+	Reit, Seymour	Harcourt Trade
Behind the Bedroom Wall	V	HF	250+	Williams, Laura E.	Milkweed Editions
Behind the Couch	N	F	250+	Gerstein, Mordicai	Hyperion
Behind the Rocks	E	RF	50	Wonder World	Wright Group/McGraw Hill
Behind the Scenes	R	I	250+	Literacy 2000	Rigby
Behind the Scenes	P	I	894	Vocabulary Readers	Houghton Mifflin Harcourt
Behind the Scenes	P	I	894	Vocabulary Readers/CA	Houghton Mifflin Harcourt
Behind the Scenes	P	I	894	Vocabulary Readers/TX	Houghton Mifflin Harcourt
Behind the Scenes at the Airport	R	I	250+	Explore More	Wright Group/McGraw Hill
Behind the Scenes at the Zoo	R	I	250+	Rigby Literacy	Rigby
Behind the Scenes with Sammy	N	I	250+	Little Celebrations	Pearson Learning Group
Behind the Secret Window: A Memoir of a Hidden Childhood During World War II	Y	B	250+	Toll, Nelly S.	Scholastic
Behind the Wheel	S	I	250+	NASCAR Racing	Capstone Press
Being a Bug Scout	S	I	250+	Navigators How-To Series	Benchmark Education Company
Being a Leader	E	I	101	Citizenship	Lerner Publishing
Being a Spider	N	I	694	Vocabulary Readers	Houghton Mifflin Harcourt
Being a Spider	N	I	694	Vocabulary Readers/CA	Houghton Mifflin Harcourt
Being an Astronaut	I	I	133	Reading Street	Pearson
Being Bee	T	RF	250+	Bateson, Catherine	Holiday House
Being Billy	R	RF	250+	PM Plus Chapter Books	Rigby
Being Danny's Dog	U	RF	250+	Naylor, Phyllis Reynolds	Aladdin
Being Fair	F	I	102	Citizenship	Lerner Publications

* Collection of short stories
\# Graphic text

TITLE	LEVEL	GENRE	WORD COUNT	AUTHOR / SERIES	PUBLISHER / DISTRIBUTOR
Being Famous	V	I	250+	10 Things You Need to Know About	Capstone Press
Being Friends	C	I	21	Rosen Real Readers	Rosen Publishing Group
Being Responsible	F	I	77	Citizenship	Lerner Publications
Belgian Horse, The	R	I	250+	Horses	Capstone Press
Bell of Atri	O	TL	250+	WorldScapes	ETA Cuisenaire
Bell on the Cat, The	I	TL	235	Sun Sprouts	ETA Cuisenaire
Bell, the Book, and the Spellbinder, The	S	F	250+	Strickland, Brad	Puffin/Penguin
Bella & Rosie Trick or Treat	E	F	129	Bella and Rosie Series	Literacy Footprints
Bella and Rosie Play Hide and Seek	D	F	118	Bella and Rosie Series	Pioneer Valley
Bella at Midnight	V	HF	250+	Stanley, Diane	Harper Trophy
Bella Is a Bad Dog	H	F	132	Bella and Rosie Series	Pioneer Valley
Bella's Baby Bird	K	RF	514	Gear Up!	Wright Group/McGraw Hill
Bella's Birthday	D	F	59	Bella and Rosie Series	Pioneer Valley
Bella's Picnic	F	RF	273	Rigby Flying Colors	Rigby
Bella's Ride	E	RF	181	Rigby Flying Colors	Rigby
Belle Prater's Boy	V	RF	250+	White, Ruth	Bantam
Below the Green Pond	N	I	250+	Read All About It	Steck-Vaughn
Below Zero	O	I	250+	WorldScapes	ETA Cuisenaire
Beltons' Imagination, The	Q	F	1505	Leveled Readers	Houghton Mifflin Harcourt
Beltons' Imagination, The	Q	F	1505	Leveled Readers/CA	Houghton Mifflin Harcourt
Beltons' Imagination, The	Q	F	1505	Leveled Readers/TX	Houghton Mifflin Harcourt
Ben & Becky in the Haunted House	J	F	734	We Both Read	Treasure Bay
Ben and Me	S	HF	250+	Lawson, Robert	Little, Brown & Co.
Ben and Sooty	H	RF	152	Leveled Readers/TX	Houghton Mifflin Harcourt
Ben and the Bear	I	F	250+	Riddell, Chris	Harper & Row
Ben and the Cold	C	RF	76	Sun Sprouts	ETA Cuisenaire
Ben and the Crab	G	RF	205	Sun Sprouts	ETA Cuisenaire
Ben at the Theme Park	F	RF	214	Sun Sprouts	ETA Cuisenaire
Ben Ate It	E	RF	130	Teacher's Choice Series	Pearson Learning Group
Ben Franklin Goes to Paris	R	I	1603	Vocabulary Readers	Houghton Mifflin Harcourt
Ben Franklin Goes to Paris	R	I	1603	Vocabulary Readers/CA	Houghton Mifflin Harcourt
Ben Franklin Goes to Paris	R	I	1603	Vocabulary Readers/TX	Houghton Mifflin Harcourt
Ben Franklin of Old Philadelphia	U	B	250+	Cousins, Margaret	Random House
Ben Franklin Remembers	P	B	493	Vocabulary Readers	Houghton Mifflin Harcourt
Ben Franklin, Founding Father	Q	I	1030	Vocabulary Readers	Houghton Mifflin Harcourt
Ben Franklin, Founding Father	Q	B	1030	Vocabulary Readers/CA	Houghton Mifflin Harcourt
Ben Franklin: A Man with Many Talents	O	B	250+	On Our Way to English	Rigby
Ben Franklin: Scientist	J	I	266	Leveled Readers Science	Houghton Mifflin Harcourt
Ben Franklin's Big Shock	N	I	1552	On My Own History	Lerner Publications
Ben Franklin's Fire Company	I	I	147	Leveled Readers Language Support	Houghton Mifflin Harcourt
Ben Lost a Tooth	E	I	31	iOpeners	Pearson Learning Group
Ben Runs	C	RF	66	Sun Sprouts	ETA Cuisenaire
Ben the Bold	C	RF	71	Literacy 2000	Rigby
Ben the Cat	D	F	124	Leveled Readers	Houghton Mifflin Harcourt
Ben the Cat	D	F	124	Leveled Readers/CA	Houghton Mifflin Harcourt
Ben the Cat	D	F	124	Leveled Readers/TX	Houghton Mifflin Harcourt
Bend and Stretch: Learning About Your Bones and Muscles	M	I	250+	Amazing Body	Picture Window Books
Bend, Stretch, and Leap	J	RF	250+	PM Plus Story Books	Rigby
Beneath Earth's Surface	O	I	250+	Rosen Real Readers	Rosen Publishing Group
Beneath the Waves	Q	I	250+	InfoQuest	Rigby
Benedict Arnold	V	B	250+	Let Freedom Ring	Capstone Press

Organized Alphabetically by Title
Storable Database at www.fountasandpinnellleveledbooks.com

* Collection of short stories
\# Graphic text

TITLE	LEVEL	GENRE	WORD COUNT	AUTHOR / SERIES	PUBLISHER / DISTRIBUTOR
Benedict Arnold	S	I	1225	Leveled Readers	Houghton Mifflin Harcourt
Benedict Arnold	S	I	1225	Leveled Readers/CA	Houghton Mifflin Harcourt
Benedict Arnold	S	I	1225	Leveled Readers/TX	Houghton Mifflin Harcourt
Benedict Arnold at Saratoga	Y	HF	2151	Leveled Readers	Houghton Mifflin Harcourt
#Benedict Arnold: American Hero and Traitor	T	B	250+	Graphic Library	Capstone Press
Benita's Plan	M	RF	250+	On Our Way to English	Rigby
Benito's Goal	Q	RF	250+	In Step Readers	Rigby
Benjamin Banneker	T	B	250+	Amazing Americans	Wright Group/McGraw Hill
Benjamin Banneker	P	B	250+	American Lives	Heinemann Educational Publishers
Benjamin Banneker	N	B	231	First Biographies	Capstone Press
Benjamin Banneker	S	B	3957	History Maker Bios	Lerner Publications
Benjamin Banneker: An American Scientist	K	B	374	Leveled Readers Science	Houghton Mifflin Harcourt
Benjamin Banneker: Pioneering Scientist	O	B	1870	On My Own Biography	Lerner Publications
Benjamin Franklin	U	B	250+	Amazing Americans	Wright Group/ McGraw Hill
Benjamin Franklin	N	B	250+	Biography	Benchmark Education
Benjamin Franklin	Q	B	250+	Early Biographies	Compass Point Books
Benjamin Franklin	S	B	3897	History Maker Bios	Lerner Publications
Benjamin Franklin	U	B	250+	Kent, Deborah	Scholastic
Benjamin Franklin	U	B	250+	Let Freedom Ring	Red Brick Learning
Benjamin Franklin	N	B	250+	Pebble Books	Capstone Press
Benjamin Franklin	Q	B	250+	Photo-Illustrated Biographies	Red Brick Learning
Benjamin Franklin	R	B	250+	Primary Source Readers	Teacher Created Materials
Benjamin Franklin: A Man with Many Jobs	O	B	250+	Greene, Carol	Children's Press
Benjamin Franklin: A Scientist by Nature	X	B	2095	Leveled Readers	Houghton Mifflin Harcourt
Benjamin Franklin: American Inventor	N	B	250+	Rosen Real Readers	Rosen Publishing Group
Benjamin Franklin: Writer, Inventor, Statesman	M	B	250+	Biographies	Picture Window Books
Benjamin Franklin: Young Printer	R	B	250+	Stevenson, Augusta	Aladdin
Benjamin Harrison	U	B	250+	Profiles of the Presidents	Compass Point Books
Benjamin Harrison: Twenty-third President	R	B	250+	Getting to Know the U.S. Presidents	Children's Press
Benji's Pup	I	RF	439	Evangeline Nicholas Collection	Wright Group/McGraw Hill
Bennie	A	RF	29	Ray's Readers	Outside the Box
Benny Bakes a Cake	I	RF	250+	Rice, Eve	Greenwillow
Benny's Baby Brother	E	RF	89	Start to Read	School Zone
Benny's School Trip	G	RF	217	Pair-It Books	Steck-Vaughn
Ben's Amazing Birthday	L	RF	250+	Cambridge Reading	Pearson Learning Group
Ben's Banana	C	F	60	Foundations	Wright Group/McGraw Hill
Ben's Bath	C	RF	56	Sun Sprouts	ETA Cuisenaire
Ben's Bike	J	RF	414	Sails	Rigby
Ben's Brilliant Birthday	D	RF	63	Rigby Rocket	Rigby
Ben's Colors	C	RF	75	Sun Sprouts	ETA Cuisenaire
Ben's Dad	E	RF	102	PM Story Books	Rigby
Ben's Dream	WB	F	N/A	Van Allsburg, Chris	Houghton Mifflin Harcourt
Ben's First Words	D	RF	49	Bonnell, Kris	Reading Reading Books
Ben's Fun Box	D	RF	63	New Way Red	Steck-Vaughn
Ben's Jigsaw Puzzle	D	RF	103	PM Stars	Rigby
Ben's New Trick	F	RF	219	Ready Readers	Pearson Learning Group
Ben's Pets	C	RF	30	Ready Readers	Pearson Learning Group
Ben's Red Car	B	RF	49	PM Starters	Rigby
Ben's Story	L	RF	1060	Rigby Flying Colors	Rigby
Ben's Teddy Bear	D	RF	68	PM Story Books	Rigby
Ben's Tooth	H	RF	197	PM Story Books	Rigby
Ben's Treasure Hunt	D	RF	72	PM Story Books	Rigby

* Collection of short stories
# Graphic text

TITLE	LEVEL	GENRE	WORD COUNT	AUTHOR / SERIES	PUBLISHER / DISTRIBUTOR
Ben's Tune	N	RF	250+	PM Collection	Rigby
*Beowulf	U	TL	250+	Literacy 2000	Rigby
Berenstain Bear Scouts and the Coughing Catfish	M	F	250+	Berenstain, Stan & Jan	Scholastic
Berenstain Bear Scouts, The: Ghost Versus Ghost	M	F	250+	Berenstain, Stan & Jan	Scholastic
Berenstain Bears and the Ghost of the Auto Graveyard, The	M	F	250+	Berenstain, Stan & Jan	Random House
Berenstain Bears and the Missing Honey	M	F	531	Berenstain, Stan & Jan	Random House
Berlin Wall, The	V	I	2050	Independent Readers Social Studies	Houghton Mifflin Harcourt
Berlioz the Bear	N	F	250+	Brett, Jan	Scholastic
Bermuda Triangle, The	U	I	250+	The Unexplained	Capstone Press
Bermuda Triangle, The	Z	I	250+	Unsolved Mysteries	Steck-Vaughn
Bernardo de Gálvez	W	B	1818	Leveled Readers	Houghton Mifflin Harcourt
Berry Cake, The	G	RF	171	PM Photo Stories	Rigby
Berta: A Remarkable Dog	N	RF	250+	Lottridge, Celia Barker	Groundwood Books
Bertie Beaver Goes to the City	C	F	100	Springboard	Wright Group/McGraw Hill
Bertie the Bear	I	F	250+	Allen, Pamela	Coward
Bert's Boat	E	RF	64	Rigby Star	Rigby
Bess and Bella	K	F	250+	Haas, Irene	Margaret K. McElderry Books
Bess in My Garden	E	I	104	Rigby Flying Colors	Rigby
Bessie Coleman	O	B	250+	Brager, Bruce	Scholastic
Bessie Coleman	N	B	257	First Biographies	Capstone Press
#Bessie Coleman: Daring Stunt Pilot	R	B	250+	Graphic Library	Capstone Press
Bessie Coleman: Daring to Fly	N	B	1706	On My Own Biography	Lerner Publications
Bessie Coleman: Queen of the Sky	K	B	229	Sunshine	Wright Group/McGraw Hill
Bessie's Bed	J	F	435	Silly Millies	Millbrook Press
Bess's Log Cabin Quilt	P	HF	250+	Love, D. Anne	Bantam
Best Friends	WB	RF	N/A	Books for Young Learners	Richard C. Owen
Best Bad Thing, The	T	RF	250+	Uchida, Yoshiko	Aladdin
Best Birthday Gift Ever, The	I	RF	249	Talking Point Series	Pearson Learning Group
Best Birthday Mole Ever Had, The	E	F	252	Ready Readers	Pearson Learning Group
Best Birthday Present, The	K	RF	250+	Literacy 2000	Rigby
Best Blackberries, The	J	RF	410	Springboard	Wright Group/McGraw Hill
Best Boat, The	J	I	690	Leveled Readers Science	Houghton Mifflin Harcourt
Best Book for Terry Lee, The	I	RF	250+	Literacy Tree	Rigby
Best Bread, The	F	RF	181	Adams, Lorraine; Bruvold, Lynn	Eagle Crest Books
Best Cake, The	F	RF	162	PM Story Books	Rigby
Best Car for Us, The	I	I	161	Windows on Literacy	National Geographic
Best Children in the World, The	F	F	148	Story Box	Wright Group/McGraw Hill
Best Class Trip, The	F	RF	214	Leveled Readers	Houghton Mifflin Harcourt
Best Clown in Town, The	L	RF	250+	Bradley, Tom	Pearson Learning Group
Best Dancer, The	F	RF	166	PM Photo Stories	Rigby
Best Detective, The	N	RF	250+	Keene, Carolyn	Pocket Books
Best Diver in the World, The	M	RF	250+	Sunshine	Wright Group/McGraw Hill
Best Dog in the Whole World, The	K	RF	250+	Sunshine	Wright Group/McGraw Hill
Best Enemies	P	RF	250+	Leverich, Kathleen	Beech Tree Books
Best Enemies Again	P	RF	250+	Leverich, Kathleen	Alfred A. Knopf
Best Enemies Forever	P	RF	250+	Leverich, Kathleen	William Morrow
Best Fish Ever, The	O	RF	884	Leveled Readers	Houghton Mifflin Harcourt
Best Foot Forward	X	RF	250+	Bauer, Joan	Speak
Best Friends	F	RF	255	Adams, Lorraine; Bruvold, Lynn	Eagle Crest Books

* Collection of short stories
# Graphic text

TITLE	LEVEL	GENRE	WORD COUNT	AUTHOR / SERIES	PUBLISHER / DISTRIBUTOR
Best Friends	B	I	28	Bebop Books	Lee & Low Books Inc.
Best Friends	E	RF	31	Fitros, Pamela	Kaeden Books
Best Friends	D	RF	15	Instant Readers	Harcourt School Publishers
Best Friends	F	HF	127	Learn to Read	Creative Teaching Press
Best Friends	D	RF	68	Little Readers	Houghton Mifflin Harcourt
Best Friends	E	RF	106	Real Kids Readers	Millbrook Press
Best Friends	C	I	43	Rosen Real Readers	Rosen Publishing Group
Best Friends	C	RF	34	Windows on Literacy	National Geographic
B-E-S-T Friends	L	RF	250+	Giff, Patricia Reilly	Bantam
Best Friends Don't Fight	M	RF	250+	Bookshop	Mondo
Best Friends for Frances	K	F	250+	Hoban, Russell	HarperTrophy
Best Friends for Never	X	RF	250+	Harrison, Lisi	Little, Brown & Co.
Best Ghost Stories Ever, The	Z	F	250+	Krovatin, Christopher	Scholastic
Best Guess, The	I	RF	241	Foundations	Wright Group/McGraw Hill
Best Hats, The	G	RF	201	PM Plus Story Books	Rigby
Best Job for Scooter, The	J	RF	580	Leveled Readers	Houghton Mifflin Harcourt
Best Little Monkeys in the World, The	J	F	250+	Standiford, Natalie	Random House
Best Nest	J	F	250+	Eastman, Philip D.	Random House
Best New Friends	G	RF	257	Leveled Literacy Intervention/ Green System	Heinemann
Best of Both Worlds	T	I	250+	WorldScapes	ETA Cuisenaire
Best Older Sister, The	L	RF	250+	Choi, Sook Nyul	Bantam
Best Part, The	K	RF	250+	PM Story Books-Silver	Rigby
Best Pet for Al, The	G	F	203	Literacy by Design	Rigby
Best Pet Yet, The	H	RF	472	Real Kids Readers	Millbrook Press
Best Pet, The	J	RF	250+	Lighthouse	Rigby
Best Pet, The	K	I	421	Sun Sprouts	ETA Cuisenaire
Best Place, The	C	F	77	Leveled Readers	Houghton Mifflin Harcourt
Best Place, The	C	RF	61	Literacy 2000	Rigby
Best Places, The	D	RF	68	Ready Readers	Pearson Learning Group
Best Present, The	G	RF	146	Rigby Literacy	Rigby
Best Ranger, The	K	RF	396	Leveled Readers	Houghton Mifflin Harcourt
Best School Year Ever, The	P	RF	250+	Robinson, Barbara	HarperTrophy
Best Student, The	J	RF	390	Leveled Readers	Houghton Mifflin Harcourt
Best Student, The	J	RF	390	Leveled Readers/CA	Houghton Mifflin Harcourt
Best Student, The	J	RF	390	Leveled Readers/TX	Houghton Mifflin Harcourt
Best Teacher in the World, The	K	RF	250+	Chardiet, Bernice	Scholastic
Best Thing About Food, The	F	I	132	Twig	Wright Group/McGraw Hill
Best Thing About Valentines, The	I	F	132	Hudson, Eleanor	Scholastic
Best Thing, The	G	I	108	Bebop Books	Lee & Low Books Inc.
Best Way to Play, The	K	I	250+	Cosby, Bill	Scholastic
Best Web of All, The	G	F	160	Gear Up!	Wright Group/McGraw Hill
Best Wishes	O	B	250+	Meet The Author	Richard C. Owen
Best Wishes for Eddie	M	RF	250+	Nayer, Judy	Pearson Learning Group
Best Worst Day, The	L	RF	250+	Graves, Bonnie	Hyperion
Best-Loved Doll, The	L	RF	250+	Caudill, Rebecca	Henry Holt & Co.
Beth's Bed	E	RF	81	Supersonics	Rigby
Beth's Snow Dancer	Q	HF	250+	The Little Women Journals	Avon
Betina and the Talent Show	M	RF	538	Leveled Readers/TX	Houghton Mifflin Harcourt
Betsy and Tacy Go Downtown	Q	HF	250+	Lovelace, Maud Hart	HarperTrophy
Betsy and Tacy Go Over the Big Hill	Q	HF	250+	Lovelace, Maud Hart	HarperTrophy
Betsy and Tacy: 60th Anniversary Edition	Q	HF	250+	Lovelace, Maud Hart	HarperTrophy
Betsy and the Boys	P	RF	250+	Haywood, Carolyn	Harcourt Trade
Betsy Ross	N	B	197	First Biographies	Capstone Press

B

* Collection of short stories
# Graphic text

TITLE	LEVEL	GENRE	WORD COUNT	AUTHOR / SERIES	PUBLISHER / DISTRIBUTOR
Betsy Ross	U	B	250+	Let Freedom Ring	Red Brick Learning
Betsy Ross	L	B	250+	Pebble Books	Red Brick Learning
Betsy Ross: Designer of Our Flag	R	B	250+	Weil, Ann	Aladdin
Betsy the Babysitter	F	RF	115	First Start	Troll Associates
Better Brown Stories, The	T	F	250+	Ahlberg, Allan	Penguin Group
Better Idea, A	J	RF	492	In Step Readers	Rigby
Better Life, A	T	RF	1066	Independent Readers Social Studies	Houghton Mifflin Harcourt
Better Look, A	H	I	106	Windows on Literacy	National Geographic
Better Plan, A	S	RF	2617	Leveled Readers	Houghton Mifflin Harcourt
Better Plan, A	S	RF	2617	Leveled Readers/CA	Houghton Mifflin Harcourt
Better Plan, A	S	RF	2617	Leveled Readers/TX	Houghton Mifflin Harcourt
Better Than TV	J	RF	250+	Miller, Sara Swan	Bantam
Betty Bee Wouldn't Budge	I	F	267	Pair-It Turn and Learn	Steck-Vaughn
*Between Earth and Sky: Legends of Native American Sacred Places	Z	TL	250+	Bruchac, Joseph	Voyager Books
Between the Dragon and the Eagle	W	HF	250+	Schneider, Mical	Carolrhoda Books
Between the Lines	U	B	250+	Rigby Literacy	Rigby
Between the Tides	E	I	52	Wonder World	Wright Group/McGraw Hill
Between the Wars	V	I	250+	Primary Source Readers	Teacher Created Materials
Between Two Worlds	T	I	250+	WorldScapes	ETA Cuisenaire
Between Two Worlds: A Story about Pearl Buck	S	B	7415	Creative Minds Biographies	Lerner Publications
Beware!	N	RF	250+	Orbit Chapter Books	Pacific Learning
Beware, Princess Elizabeth	Y	HF	250+	Meyer, Carolyn	Harcourt Trade
Beyond Belief	S	I	250+	Orbit Collections	Pacific Learning
*Beyond Belief	Z	I	250+	Steiger, Brad	Scholastic
Beyond Little Women: A Story About Louisa May Alcott	R	B	8360	Creative Minds Biographies	Carolrhoda Books
Beyond Providence	X	RF	250+	Schnur, Steven	Harcourt Brace
Beyond Reality	X	I	250+	Boldprint	Steck-Vaughn
Beyond the Beyond	Q	I	250+	Wildcats	Wright Group/McGraw Hill
Beyond the Black Hole	Q	SF	250+	Bookweb	Rigby
Beyond the Burning Lands	U	F	250+	Christopher, John	Aladdin
Beyond the Grave	Z	I	7190	The Unexplained	Lerner Publications
Beyond the Mango Tree	V	RF	250+	Zemser, Amy Bronwen	HarperTrophy
Beyond the Myth: The Story of Joan of Arc	Z	B	250+	Brooks, Polly Schoyer	Houghton Mifflin Harcourt
Beyond the Ordinary Camera	V	I	250+	Rigby Literacy	Rigby
Beyond the Western Sea, Book II: Lord Kirkle's Money	V	HF	250+	Avi	Avon Camelot
BFG, The	U	F	250+	Dahl, Roald	Penguin Group
Bibim Bap for Dinner	L	I	250+	Bebop Books	Lee & Low Books Inc.
Bicentennial Gift, The	T	RF	1906	Leveled Readers	Houghton Mifflin Harcourt
Bichons Frises	I	I	153	Dogs	Capstone Press
Bicycle Book, The	O	I	250+	PM Nonfiction-Emerald	Rigby
Bicycle for Rosaura, A	M	F	250+	Soar To Success	Houghton Mifflin Harcourt
Bicycle Man, The	P	RF	250+	Say, Allen	Houghton Mifflin Harcourt
Bicycle Patrol Officers	S	I	250+	Law Enforcement	Capstone Press
Bicycle Rider	O	B	250+	Scioscia, Mary	HarperTrophy
Bicycle, The	Q	I	250+	Great Inventions	Capstone Press
Bicycle, The	C	F	29	Story Box	Wright Group/McGraw Hill
Bicycles	M	I	250+	Windows on Literacy	National Geographic
Bicycles of the Past	M	I	250+	On Deck	Rigby
Bicycling Adventures	S	I	250+	Dangerous Adventures	Red Brick Learning
Biff's Aeroplane	E	RF	64	Oxford Reading Tree	Oxford University Press

* Collection of short stories
\# Graphic text

TITLE	LEVEL	GENRE	WORD COUNT	AUTHOR / SERIES	PUBLISHER / DISTRIBUTOR
Big Al	L	F	250+	Clements, Andrew	Scholastic
Big Al and Shrimpy	L	F	250+	Clements, Andrew	Aladddin Paperbacks
Big and Green	D	I	12	Wonder World	Wright Group/McGraw Hill
Big and Little	B	I	77	Adams, Lorraine; Bruvold, Lynn	Eagle Crest Books
Big and Little	LB	I	59	Berger, Samantha; Chanko, Pamela	Scholastic
Big and Little	B	F	40	Carousel Earlybirds	Pearson Learning Group
Big and Little	B	I	56	Early Connections	Benchmark Education
Big and Little	LB	I	21	Foundations	Wright Group/McGraw Hill
Big and Little	D	F	92	Joy Readers	Pearson Learning Group
Big and Little	LB	I	24	KinderReaders	Rigby
Big and Little	C	I	66	Little Readers	Houghton Mifflin Harcourt
Big and Little	B	I	68	PM Plus Starters	Rigby
Big and Little	B	I	38	Rigby Literacy	Rigby
Big and Little	B	I	55	Rigby Rocket	Rigby
Big and Little	B	RF	40	Storyteller	Wright Group/McGraw Hill
Big and Little	C	I	36	Sunshine	Wright Group/McGraw Hill
Big and Little	A	I	21	Time for Kids	Teacher Created Materials
Big and Little	WB	I	N/A	Vocabulary Readers	Houghton Mifflin Harcourt
Big and Little Dinosaurs	E	I	50	Planet Earth	Rigby
Big and Small: An Animal Opposites Book	K	I	250+	Animal Opposites	Capstone Press
Big Animals in the Sea	A	I	24	Sails	Rigby
Big Animals, Little Animals	D	I	133	Sails	Rigby
Big Babies	M	I	250+	Yellow Umbrella Books	Red Brick Learning
Big Bad Rex	I	I	176	Erickson, Betty	Continental Press
Big Bad Wolf, The	I	RF	250+	PM Plus Story Books	Rigby
Big Bad Wolf?	F	F	121	Rigby Rocket	Rigby
Big Balloon Festival, The	L	RF	625	PM Collection	Rigby
Big Balloon Race, The	K	RF	250+	Coerr, Eleanor	HarperTrophy
Big Barn, The	C	RF	81	Teacher's Choice Series	Pearson Learning Group
Big Barry Baker and the Bullies	J	RF	250+	Storyworlds	Heinemann Educational Books
Big Barry Baker in Big Trouble	J	RF	250+	Storyworlds	Heinemann Educational Books
Big Barry Baker on the Stage	J	RF	250+	Storyworlds	Heinemann Educational Books
Big Barry Baker's Parcel	J	RF	250+	Storyworlds	Heinemann Educational Books
Big Bear's Socks	E	F	75	Storyteller	Wright Group/McGraw Hill
Big Bed, The	I	RF	346	Pacific Literacy	Pacific Learning
Big Beet, The	L	F	250+	Ready Readers	Pearson Learning Group
Big Ben	E	RF	100	Real Kids Readers	Millbrook Press
Big Bend Treasure Hunt	S	I	250+	Literacy By Design	Rigby
Big Bend Treasure Hunt	S	I	250+	On Our Way to English	Rigby
Big Bird Relatives	L	I	449	Springboard	Wright Group/ McGraw Hill
Big Bird, The	D	RF	118	Reading Street	Pearson
Big Bird's Copycat Day	F	F	232	Lerner, Sharon	Random House
Big Black Bears	F	I	43	Rosen Real Readers	Rosen Publishing Group
Big Blue Sea, The	C	I	69	Scott, Janine	Scholastic
Big Blue Whale	N	RF	250+	Read and Wonder	Candlewick Press
Big Bo Peep	K	F	250+	Lighthouse	Ginn & Co.
Big Boo Bird, The	C	F	66	Joy Readers	Pearson Learning Group
Big Boots	I	RF	250+	Storyworlds	Heinemann Educational Books

* Collection of short stories
# Graphic text

TITLE	LEVEL	GENRE	WORD COUNT	AUTHOR / SERIES	PUBLISHER / DISTRIBUTOR
Big Box, The	D	F	81	Leveled Readers	Houghton Mifflin Harcourt
Big Box, The	H	RF	183	New Way Green	Steck-Vaughn
Big Box, The	E	RF	111	Real Kids Readers	Millbrook Press
Big Boy	O	TL	250+	Mollel, Tololwa M.	Houghton Mifflin Harcourt
Big Bradley	D	F	30	Ray's Readers	Outside the Box
Big Bridges	M	I	508	Vocabulary Readers	Houghton Mifflin Harcourt
Big Bridges	M	I	508	Vocabulary Readers/CA	Houghton Mifflin Harcourt
Big Bridges	M	I	508	Vocabulary Readers/TX	Houghton Mifflin Harcourt
Big Brother	C	I	49	Explorations	Eleanor Curtain Publishing
Big Brother	C	I	49	Explorations	Okapi Educational Materials
Big Brother at School	Q	SF	1938	Powell, J.	Stone Arch Books
Big Brown Bear	F	F	97	Green Light Readers	Harcourt
Big Bug, The	E	RF	81	Reading Street	Pearson
Big Bugs	M	I	250+	Simon, Seymour	Chronicle Books
Big Bulgy Fat Black Slugs	M	F	250+	Stepping Stones	Nelson/Michaels Assoc.
Big Cat Babies	I	I	282	Big Cat	Pacific Learning
Big Cat Trouble	N	RF	250+	World Quest Adventures	World Quest Learning
Big Cat, Little Cat	B	I	61	Rigby Focus	Rigby
Big Cat, The	D	RF	41	Ready Readers	Pearson Learning Group
Big Catch, The	K	RF	250+	Literacy 2000	Rigby
Big Catch, The	U	RF	250+	Reading Expeditions	National Geographic
Big Cats	S	I	250+	Boldprint	Steck-Vaughn
Big Cats	J	I	250+	Evans, Lynette	Scholastic
Big Cats	P	I	1189	Vocabulary Readers	Houghton Mifflin Harcourt
Big Cats	P	I	1189	Vocabulary Readers/CA	Houghton Mifflin Harcourt
Big Cats	P	I	1189	Vocabulary Readers/TX	Houghton Mifflin Harcourt
Big Cats Little Cats	I	I	210	Springboard	Wright Group/McGraw Hill
Big Change, A	I	RF	259	Reading Street	Pearson
Big Chase, The	A	F	14	Foundations	Wright Group/McGraw Hill
Big Chase, The	M	F	250+	SupaDoopers	Sundance
Big Chief of the Neverwoz, The	H	F	250+	Little Celebrations	Pearson Learning Group
Big City Life	H	I	133	Shutterbug Books	Steck-Vaughn
Big City, The	C	RF	93	Leveled Literacy Intervention/ Blue System	Heinemann
Big Crocodile, The	G	F	61	Little Celebrations	Pearson Learning Group
Big Day, A	E	RF	120	InfoTrek	ETA Cuisenaire
Big Dipper and You, The	Q	I	250+	Krupp, E. C.	Mulberry Books
Big Dipper, The	M	I	585	Leveled Readers Science	Houghton Mifflin Harcourt
Big Dog, Little Dog	I	F	265	Eastman, Philip D.	Random House
Big Ears	B	I	30	Sails	Rigby
Big Egg	E	F	103	Coxe, Molly	Random House
BIG Elephants	D	I	41	Rosen Real Readers	Rosen Publishing Group
Big Enough	C	RF	49	Visions	Wright Group/McGraw Hill
Big Family, The	H	RF	250+	Sunshine	Wright Group/McGraw Hill
Big Fat Worm, The	G	F	250+	Van Laan, Nancy	Random House
Big Fish Is Coming!, The	C	F	108	InfoTrek	ETA Cuisenaire
Big Fish Little Fish	K	TL	250+	Folk Tales	Wright Group/McGraw Hill
Big Fish, The	C	RF	82	Early Emergent	Pioneer Valley
Big Fish, The	N	RF	250+	Sunshine	Wright Group/McGraw Hill
Big Fish, The	I	RF	301	Yukish, Joe	Kaeden Books
Big Foot	X	I	4555	Monster Chronicles	Lerner Publications
Big Foot	X	I	250+	The Unexplained	Capstone Press
Big Friend, Little Friend	E	RF	56	Greenfield, Eloise	Houghton Mifflin Harcourt
Big Game, The	J	F	751	Little Dinosaur	Literacy Footprints

* Collection of short stories
# Graphic text

TITLE	LEVEL	GENRE	WORD COUNT	AUTHOR / SERIES	PUBLISHER / DISTRIBUTOR
Big Game, The	H	RF	69	Pacific Literacy	Pacific Learning
Big Giant, The	C	F	43	Sails	Rigby
Big Gold Mountain	N	RF	250+	Bookweb	Rigby
Big Green Caterpillar, The	J	RF	161	Literacy 2000	Rigby
Big Greg the Firefighter	D	RF	100	Springboard	Wright Group/McGraw Hill
Big Greg to the Rescue	K	RF	535	Springboard	Wright Group/McGraw Hill
Big Greg's Campaign	N	RF	250+	Springboard	Wright Group/ McGraw Hill
Big Greg's First Ski Lesson	K	RF	696	Springboard	Wright Group/McGraw Hill
Big Gust, The	N	F	650	Leveled Readers	Houghton Mifflin Harcourt
Big Helicopter, The	E	RF	125	PM Stars	Rigby
Big Hill, The	C	F	55	PM Plus Story Books	Rigby
Big Hill, The	D	F	19	Story Box	Wright Group/McGraw Hill
Big Hippo and Little Hippo	J	F	445	Sails	Rigby
Big Hole, The	E	RF	150	Developing Books	Pioneer Valley
Big Hole, The	B	RF	39	PM Stars	Rigby
Big House, Little Mouse	B	RF	37	Handprints B	Educators Publishing Service
Big Hungry Bear, The	I	F	148	Wood, Don & Audrey	Scholastic
Big Hungry Cat, The	D	RF	78	Bonnell, Kris	Reading Reading Books
Big Hunt, The	S	HF	2619	Leveled Readers	Houghton Mifflin Harcourt
Big Hunt, The	S	HF	2619	Leveled Readers/CA	Houghton Mifflin Harcourt
Big Hunt, The	S	HF	2619	Leveled Readers/TX	Houghton Mifflin Harcourt
Big Hush, The	I	RF	281	Story Box	Wright Group/McGraw Hill
Big Interview, The	R	RF	1397	Leveled Readers	Houghton Mifflin Harcourt
Big Interview, The	R	RF	1397	Leveled Readers/CA	Houghton Mifflin Harcourt
Big Interview, The	R	RF	1397	Leveled Readers/TX	Houghton Mifflin Harcourt
Big Iron Ranch	O	I	2134	In Step Readers	Rigby
Big Iron Ranch	O	I	250+	Literacy By Design	Rigby
Big Kick, The	C	RF	67	PM Story Books	Rigby
Big Laugh, A	F	RF	183	Sails	Rigby
Big Laugh, The	I	F	152	Sunshine	Wright Group/McGraw Hill
Big Lie, The: A True Story	T	B	250+	Leitner, Isabella	Scholastic
Big Lizard, Little Lizard	C	F	97	Leveled Literacy Intervention/ Blue System	Heinemann
Big Long Animal Song	C	F	29	Little Celebrations	Pearson Learning Group
Big Machines	E	I	66	Rookie Readers	Children's Press
Big Mama and Grandma Ghana	J	RF	250+	Medearis, A. Shelf	Scholastic
Big Mammals	B	I	42	Little Red Readers	Sundance
Big Max	J	F	250+	Platt, Kin	HarperTrophy
Big Mess, A	J	RF	250+	On Our Way to English	Rigby
Big Mess, The	I	F	167	Storyworlds	Heinemann Educational Books
Big Mix-Up, The	G	F	70	City Stories	Rigby
Big Monster is Running Away	C	F	41	Rigby Rocket	Rigby
Big Mouse, Little Mouse	I	F	370	Sails	Rigby
Big Mouths	B	I	37	Sails	Rigby
Big Move, A	E	RF	65	Reading Street	Pearson
Big Nap, The: A Chet Gecko Mystery	R	F	250+	Hale, Bruce	Harcourt, Inc.
Big Ned and the Eggs	L	TL	690	Sun Sprouts	ETA Cuisenaire
Big Noodle, The	D	F	110	Joy Starters	Pearson Learning Group
Big Nothing, The	Y	RF	250+	Fogelin, Adrian	Peachtree
Big or Little?	B	I	35	Bebop Books	Lee & Low Books Inc.
Big or Little?	D	I	64	Dominie Factivity Series	Pearson Learning Group
Big or Little?	I	RF	250+	Stinson, Kathy	Pearson Learning Group

* Collection of short stories
\# Graphic text

TITLE	LEVEL	GENRE	WORD COUNT	AUTHOR / SERIES	PUBLISHER / DISTRIBUTOR
Big or Small?	B	I	30	Yellow Umbrella Books	Red Brick Learning
Big Orange Splot, The	L	F	250+	Pinkwater, Daniel Manus	Scholastic
Big Pancake, The	I	TL	312	Storyworlds	Heinemann Educational Books
Big Picture, The	R	I	250+	Bennett, Mary	Pacific Learning
Big Pig and Little Pig	D	F	83	Green Light Readers	Harcourt
Big Pig, Little Pig	E	F	54	Little Celebrations	Pearson Learning Group
Big Prize, The	K	F	401	Adventures in Reading	Pearson Learning Group
Big Race, The	L	RF	250+	Home Connection Collection	Rigby
Big Race, The	N	F	250+	Pye, Trevor	Pacific Learning
Big Race, The	H	RF	250+	Start to Read	School Zone
Big Red and the Car Wash	G	F	250	Sails	Rigby
Big Red Apple, The	H	F	250+	Momentum Literacy Program	Troll Associates
Big Red Comes to Stay	F	RF	298	Sails	Rigby
Big Red Fire Engine	G	F	158	First Start	Troll Associates
Big Red Tomatoes	I	I	168	Windows on Literacy	National Geographic
Big Rigs	L	I	113	On Deck	Rigby
Big Rigs	L	I	488	Pull Ahead Books	Lerner Publications
Big Rigs	M	I	250+	Transportation	Compass Point Books
Big Rocks, Little Rocks	E	I	180	Early Connections	Benchmark Education
Big Rocks, Small Rocks	C	I	49	Dominie Factivity Series	Pearson Learning Group
Big Roundup, The	G	I	121	Wonder World	Wright Group/McGraw Hill
Big Sale, The	H	RF	486	Real Kids Readers	Millbrook Press
Big Sea Animals	B	I	79	PM Plus Starters	Rigby
Big Seed, The	E	RF	83	New Way	Steck-Vaughn
Big Shapes and Little Shapes	C	I	99	PM Math Readers	Rigby
Big Shrink, The	L	F	250+	Cambridge Reading	Pearson Learning Group
Big Sister	C	RF	44	Visions	Wright Group/McGraw Hill
Big Sky Country	T	RF	250+	Reading Expeditions	National Geographic
Big Smelly Bear	J	F	250+	Teckentrup, Britta	Scholastic
Big Sneeze, The	K	F	131	Brown, Ruth	Lothrop
Big Sneeze, The	D	F	112	Foundations	Wright Group/McGraw Hill
Big Snow, The	E	RF	150	Developing Books	Pioneer Valley
Big Snow, The	J	I	150	Early Connections	Benchmark Education
Big Snowball Fight	C	RF	15	Bebop Books	Lee & Low Books Inc.
Big Snowball, The	G	F	250	Storyworlds	Heinemann Educational Books
Big Spider	I	TL	250+	Rigby Star	Rigby
Big Spider, A	H	I	271	Sails	Rigby
Big Splash, The	B	F	33	Big Cat	Pacific Learning
Big Storm, The	Q	I	250+	Hiscock, Bruce	Aladdin
Big Storm, The	F	F	123	Leveled Literacy Intervention/ Green System	Heinemann
Big Surprise, The	H	RF	123	Pacific Literacy	Pacific Learning
Big Surprise, The	B	F	29	Storyworlds	Heinemann Educational Publishers
Big Tease, The	I	RF	250+	Story Box	Wright Group/McGraw Hill
Big Teeth, No Teeth	D	I	153	Sails	Rigby
Big Tennis Match, A	I	I	122	Vocabulary Readers	Houghton Mifflin Harcourt
Big Things	A	I	33	PM Starters	Rigby
Big Things	C	I	81	Sails	Rigby
Big Things	D	I	88	Springboard	Wright Group/McGraw Hill
Big Toe Robbery, The	N	F	250+	PM Collection	Rigby
Big Toe, The	E	F	123	Story Box	Wright Group/McGraw Hill

* Collection of short stories
\# Graphic text

TITLE	LEVEL	GENRE	WORD COUNT	AUTHOR / SERIES	PUBLISHER / DISTRIBUTOR
*Big Tree Gang, The	M	F	250+	Orca Echoes	Orca Book Publishers
Big Tug	D	F	80	Leveled Readers	Houghton Mifflin Harcourt
Big Wave, The	Q	RF	250+	Buck, Pearl S.	Scholastic
Big Wheel, The	M	HF	250+	Windows on Literacy	National Geographic
Big Yellow Castle, The	E	RF	135	PM Plus Story Books	Rigby
Big, Bad Cook, The	J	TL	250+	Literacy Tree	Rigby
Big, Big Box, A	B	RF	35	Ready Readers	Pearson Learning Group
Big, Big Trucks	H	I	162	Start to Read	School Zone
Big, Big Wall, The	E	F	92	Green Light Readers	Harcourt
Big, Bigger, Biggest	C	RF	32	Rigby Star Quest	Rigby
Big, Bigger, Biggest	LB	I	58	Shutterbug Books	Steck-Vaughn
Big, Bigger, Biggest	C	I	31	Windows on Literacy	National Geographic
Big, Brown Box, The	E	RF	93	Voyages	SRA/McGraw Hill
Big, Brown Pot, The	J	F	250+	Mahy, Margaret	Scholastic
Big, Fat, Wide Mouth	G	F	183	Story Box	Wright Group/McGraw Hill
Big, Hit, The	D	RF	120	PM Plus Story Books	Rigby
Big, Small, or Just Right?	C	F	40	Leveled Readers Language Support	Houghton Mifflin Harcourt
Bigfoot Backpacking Bonanza	Q	F	250+	Wiley & Grampa's Creature Features	Little, Brown & Co.
Bigfoot Doesn't Square Dance	M	F	250+	Dadey, Debbie; Jones, Marcia Thornton	Scholastic
Bigger and Bigger	C	I	49	Twig	Wright Group/McGraw Hill
Bigger Burger, A	I	RF	253	Story Box	Wright Group/McGraw Hill
Bigger or Smaller?	F	I	112	Sunshine	Wright Group/McGraw Hill
Bigger Than? Smaller Than?	D	I	123	Early Connections	Benchmark Education
Biggest Bear in the Woods, The	K	F	250+	Little Celebrations	Pearson Learning Group
Biggest Cake in the World, The	F	F	120	Pacific Literacy	Pacific Learning
Biggest Fish, The	I	RF	254	PM Story Books-Orange	Rigby
Biggest Klutz in Fifth Grade, The	V	RF	250+	Wallace, Bill	Simon & Schuster
Biggest Land Animal, The	J	I	376	Sails	Rigby
Biggest Pool of All, The	K	RF	250+	Sunshine	Wright Group/McGraw Hill
Biggest Pumpkin Ever, The	L	F	250+	Kroll, Steven	Scholastic
Biggest Sandwich Ever, The	E	F	87	Pair-It Books	Steck-Vaughn
Bigggest, Smallest, Fastest, Slowest	I	I	248	Literacy by Design	Rigby
Big-Hearted Monkey and the Crocodile, The	K	TL	250+	World Quest Adventures	World Quest Learning
Big-Hearted Monkey and the Lion, The	K	TL	250+	World Quest Adventures	World Quest Learning
Bighorn Sheep	C	I	107	Vocabulary Readers	Houghton Mifflin Harcourt
Bighorn Sheep	C	I	107	Vocabulary Readers/CA	Houghton Mifflin Harcourt
Bighorn Sheep, The	R	I	250+	Wildlife of North America	Red Brick Learning
Bike Daredevils	N	RF	250+	Boyz Rule!	Mondo
Bike For Alex, A	I	RF	250+	PM Plus Story Books	Rigby
Bike for Brad, A	K	RF	510	PM Story Books	Rigby
Bike for Russ, A	C	RF	37	Handprints B	Educators Publishing Service
Bike Lesson	I	F	250+	Berenstain, Stan & Jan	Random House
Bike Parade, The	LB	RF	16	Literacy 2000	Rigby
Bike Race, The	B	RF	48	Sails	Rigby
Bike Ride, The	D	RF	100	Emergent	Pioneer Valley
Bike Ride, The	D	RF	72	Leveled Readers Language Support	Houghton Mifflin Harcourt
Bike Ride, The	E	RF	118	Springboard	Wright Group/McGraw Hill
Bike That Spike Likes, The	E	RF	91	Ready Readers	Pearson Learning Group
Bike Trip, The	D	RF	60	Leveled Readers	Houghton Mifflin Harcourt

* Collection of short stories
# Graphic text

TITLE	LEVEL	GENRE	WORD COUNT	AUTHOR / SERIES	PUBLISHER / DISTRIBUTOR
Bike, The	LB	I	14	Twig	Wright Group/McGraw Hill
Biker City	T	F	4,274	Masters, Anthony	Stone Arch Books
Bikes	F	I	133	Discovery Links	Newbridge
Bikes	G	RF	156	Foundations	Wright Group/McGraw Hill
Bikes	D	I	45	Gear Up!	Wright Group/McGraw Hill
Bikes	D	I	62	Sails	Rigby
Bikes at Work	D	I	123	Sails	Rigby
Biking Safely	K	RF	250+	On Our Way to English	Rigby
Bill	I	RF	166	Sunshine	Wright Group/McGraw Hill
Bill and Ted at the Store	D	F	50	Joy Readers	Pearson Learning Group
Bill Clinton	T	B	3837	History Maker Bios	Lerner Publications
Bill Clinton: Forty-second President	R	B	250+	Getting to Know the U.S. Presidents	Children's Press
Bill Clinton: Forty-Second President of the U.S.	O	B	250+	Greene, Carol	Children's Press
Bill Cosby: The Changing Black Image	X	B	250+	Rosenberg, Robert	Millbrook Press
Bill Cosby's Little Bill: The Best Way to Play	L	F	250+	Cosby, Bill	Scholastic
Bill Gates	U	B	250+	Amazing Americans	Wright Group/McGraw Hill
Bill Gates: Helping People Use Computers	P	B	250+	Community Builders	Children's Press
Bill of Rights in Translation, The: What It Really Means	V	I	250+	Kids' Translations	Capstone Press
Bill of Rights, The	S	I	250+	A True Book	Children's Press
Bill of Rights, The	V	I	250+	Cornerstones of Freedom	Children's Press
Bill of Rights, The	O	I	364	Independent Readers Social Studies	Houghton Mifflin Harcourt
Bill Pickett, Rodeo King	V	B	3134	Leveled Readers	Houghton Mifflin Harcourt
Billie the Hippo	N	I	250+	Pacific Literacy	Pacific Learning
Billie's Book	F	I	110	Sunshine	Wright Group/McGraw Hill
Billions of Bugs	N	I	250+	On Our Way to English	Rigby
Bill's Baby	E	RF	41	Tadpoles	Rigby
Bill's Trip	E	RF	77	Dominie Phonics Reader	Pearson Learning Group
Billy at School	F	RF	163	PM Plus Story Books	Rigby
Billy Bones: Tales from the Secrets Closet	U	F	250+	Lincoln, Christopher	Little, Brown & Co.
Billy Can Count	D	RF	122	PM Plus Story Books	Rigby
Billy Goats Gruff	F	TL	381	Hunia, Fran	Ladybird Books
Billy Goats Gruff, The	I	TL	300	Sun Sprouts	ETA Cuisenaire
Billy Hooten: Owl Boy	Q	F	250+	Sniegoski, Thomas E.	Yearling
Billy Is Hiding	D	RF	97	PM Plus Story Books	Rigby
Billy Magee's New Car	J	RF	391	Foundations	Wright Group/McGraw Hill
Billy the Ghost and Me	L	F	250+	Greer, Gery; Ruddick, Bob	HarperTrophy
Billy, the Number Champ	J	RF	377	PM Math Readers	Rigby
Billy, the Pet Bird	H	RF	371	Leveled Readers/TX	Houghton Mifflin Harcourt
Billy's Pen	D	RF	166	Leveled Literacy Intervention/ Blue System	Heinemann
Billy's Box	G	F	207	Cambridge Reading	Pearson Learning Group
Billy's Sticker Book	I	RF	372	PM Math Readers	Rigby
Billy's Truck Diary	N	I	250+	Sunshine	Wright Group/McGraw Hill
Bingo	D	TL	179	PM Readalongs	Rigby
B-I-N-G-O	C	RF	41	Tiger Cub	Peguis
Bingo and the Bone	C	F	41	Storyworlds	Heinemann Educational Publishers
Bingo and the Ducks	E	RF	121	PM Stars	Rigby
Bingo Goes to School	F	RF	171	PM Plus Story Books	Rigby
Bingo Wants to Play	C	F	45	Storyworlds	Heinemann Educational Publishers

* Collection of short stories
\# Graphic text

TITLE	LEVEL	GENRE	WORD COUNT	AUTHOR / SERIES	PUBLISHER / DISTRIBUTOR
Bingo's Birthday	E	RF	116	PM Plus Story Books	Rigby
Bingo's Ice-Cream Cone	D	RF	88	PM Plus Story Books	Rigby
Binxie Gets Lost	L	F	819	Leveled Readers	Houghton Mifflin Harcourt
Binxie Gets Lost	L	F	819	Leveled Readers/CA	Houghton Mifflin Harcourt
Binxie Gets Lost	L	F	819	Leveled Readers/TX	Houghton Mifflin Harcourt
Biodiversity Hotspots	Y	I	250+	Independent Readers Science	Houghton Mifflin Harcourt
Biography of Benjamin Banneker, A	O	B	733	Gear Up!	Wright Group/ McGraw-Hill
Biography of Faith Ringgold, A	J	B	132	Vocabulary Readers	Houghton Mifflin Harcourt
Biomes	V	I	1420	Independent Readers Science	Houghton Mifflin Harcourt
Bionics	Y	I	250+	Cool Science	Lerner Publications
Biosphere, The	U	I	1845	Science Support Readers	Houghton Mifflin Harcourt
Birchbark House, The	T	HF	250+	Erdrich, Louise	Hyperion
Bird	V	I	250+	Eyewitness Books	DK Publishing
Bird and a Bug, A	F	RF	47	Windows on Literacy	National Geographic
Bird Barn, The	I	I	241	Foundations	Wright Group/McGraw Hill
Bird Beaks	I	I	180	Wonder World	Wright Group/McGraw Hill
Bird Behavior: Living Together	M	I	631	Sunshine	Wright Group/McGraw Hill
Bird Chain, The	M	F	250+	Voyages	SRA/McGraw Hill
Bird Eggs	F	I	50	Pebble Books	Capstone Press
Bird Fact File	M	I	792	Rigby Flying Colors	Rigby
Bird Families	F	I	60	Pebble Books	Capstone Press
Bird Feeder, The	D	I	55	Coulton, Mia	Kaeden Books
Bird Feeder, The	C	I	31	Storyteller-First Snow	Wright Group/McGraw Hill
Bird Feeder, The	C	RF	40	Sun Sprouts	ETA Cuisenaire
Bird Feeders, The	H	RF	311	Leveled Literacy Intervention/ Blue System	Heinemann
Bird Flies By, A	E	I	87	Windows on Literacy	National Geographic
Bird for You, A: Caring for Your Bird	M	I	250+	Pet Care	Picture Window Books
Bird Has Feathers, A	C	I	27	Science	Outside the Box
Bird Hotel	I	F	358	Sails	Rigby
Bird in the Basket, The	M	RF	250+	Beveridge, Barbara	Pacific Learning
Bird is a Bird, A	D	F	116	Sails	Rigby
Bird Lady, The	J	I	250+	Story Steps	Rigby
Bird Nests	C	I	48	Little Celebrations	Pearson Learning Group
Bird Nests	F	I	78	Pebble Books	Capstone Press
Bird on the Bus, A	E	RF	115	Leveled Readers	Houghton Mifflin Harcourt
Bird Race	I	TL	195	Leveled Readers	Houghton Mifflin Harcourt
Bird Song	I	F	99	Storyteller-Night Crickets	Wright Group/McGraw Hill
Bird Table, The	H	RF	166	Book Bank	Wright Group/McGraw Hill
Bird Talk: Kok, Kok	B	F	42	Little Celebrations	Pearson Learning Group
Bird That Could Think, The	I	F	250+	PM Plus Story Books	Rigby
Bird Watchers	L	I	250+	Storyteller-Lightning Bolts	Wright Group/McGraw Hill
Bird Watching	J	RF	475	PM Plus Story Books	Rigby
Bird, The	K	RF	852	Rigby Flying Colors	Rigby
Bird, The	A	F	30	Sails	Rigby
Birds	D	I	39	All About Pets	Red Brick Learning
Birds	F	I	54	Birds Series	Pearson Learning Group
Birds	M	I	68	Exploring the Animal Kingdom	Capstone Press
Birds	A	I	32	Leveled Literacy Intervention/ Orange System	Heinemann
Birds	F	I	50	Literacy 2000	Rigby
Birds	N	I	250+	Nature's Friends	Compass Point Books
Birds	B	I	18	Rigby Focus	Rigby
Birds	LB	I	12	Vocabulary Readers	Houghton Mifflin Harcourt

TITLE	LEVEL	GENRE	WORD COUNT	AUTHOR / SERIES	PUBLISHER / DISTRIBUTOR
Birds	F	I	68	Windows on Literacy	National Geographic
Birds and How They Grow	N	I	250+	National Geographic Society	National Geographic
Birds and Their Nests	J	I	175	Animal Homes	Capstone Press
Birds at My Barn, The	L	RF	230	Books for Young Learners	Richard C. Owen
Birds at My Feeder	R	I	250+	Kalman, Bobbie	Crabtree
Bird's Bad Day	C	F	36	Instant Readers	Harcourt School Publishers
Birds' Feet	C	I	86	Sails	Rigby
Birds in the Bushes: A Story About Margaret Morse Nice	R	B	8996	Creative Minds Biographies	Carolrhoda Books
Birds in Winter	D	I	34	Gear Up!	Wright Group/McGraw Hill
Birds Need Trees	D	I	63	Teacher's Choice Series	Pearson Learning Group
Birds' Nests	J	I	111	Wonder World	Wright Group/McGraw Hill
Birds of a Feather	N	RF	250+	Literacy 2000	Rigby
Birds of Flight	T	I	2158	Reading Street	Pearson
Birds of Prey	S	I	250+	Peterson Field Guides	Houghton Mifflin Harcourt
Birds of Prey	M	I	250+	Storyteller- Lightning Bolts	Wright Group/ McGraw Hill
Birds of Prey	O	I	250+	Woolley, M.; Pigdon, K.	Mondo
Birds of Prey in North America	U	I	2249	Vocabulary Readers	Houghton Mifflin Harcourt
Birds of Prey in North America	U	I	2249	Vocabulary Readers/CA	Houghton Mifflin Harcourt
Birds of Prey: A Look at Daytime Raptors	U	I	250+	Collard III, Sneed B.	Franklin Watts
Birds of the City	M	I	840	Sunshine	Wright Group/McGraw Hill
Birds on Stage	H	F	153	Romay, Saturnino	Scholastic
Birds That Can't Fly!	M	I	651	Reading Street	Pearson
Birds Under the Water	D	I	116	Sails	Rigby
Birds, Bees, and Sailing Ships	I	F	243	Sunshine	Wright Group/McGraw Hill
Bird's-Eye View	J	RF	393	PM Collection	Rigby
Bird's-Eye View, A	K	I	250+	People, Spaces & Places	Rand McNally
Bird's-Eye View, A	H	I	402	Sails	Rigby
Bird-Watcher	O	I	250+	Wonder World	Wright Group/McGraw Hill
Bird-Watching	S	I	250+	iOpeners	Pearson Learning Group
Birdwing	V	F	250+	Martin, Rafe	Scholastic
Birdwoman Interview	M	RF	250+	Sails	Rigby
Birman Cats	I	I	102	Cats	Capstone Press
Birth of Earth	U	I	250+	News Extra	Richard C. Owen
Birthday	N	RF	250+	Steptoe, John	Henry Holt & Co.
Birthday Balloons	F	RF	182	PM Extensions-Blue	Rigby
Birthday Balloons	D	F	104	Rigby Literacy	Rigby
Birthday Bear	D	F	91	Sun Sprouts	ETA Cuisenaire
Birthday Bike for Brimhall, A	K	RF	250+	Delton, Judy	Bantam
Birthday Bird, The	F	RF	82	Books for Young Learners	Richard C. Owen
Birthday Book	H	RF	93	Story Box	Wright Group/McGraw Hill
Birthday Buddy, The	M	RF	250+	Windows on Literacy	National Geographic
Birthday Bug, The	B	RF	53	Story Steps	Rigby
Birthday Cake	D	RF	27	Literacy 2000	Rigby
Birthday Cake for Ben, A	C	RF	59	PM Extensions-Red	Rigby
Birthday Cake, The	G	RF	107	Rigby Focus	Rigby
Birthday Cake, The	H	F	201	Story Box	Wright Group/McGraw Hill
Birthday Cake, The	LB	F	22	Sunshine	Wright Group/McGraw Hill
Birthday Candles	C	RF	52	Carousel Readers	Pearson Learning Group
Birthday Candles	F	RF	145	InfoTrek	ETA Cuisenaire
Birthday Car, The	E	RF	176	Fairy Tales and Folklore	Norwood House Press
Birthday Celebrations	E	I	111	Early Connections	Benchmark Education
Birthday Dig, The	R	F	1216	Leveled Readers	Houghton Mifflin Harcourt
Birthday Disaster	Q	RF	250+	Literacy 2000	Rigby

* Collection of short stories
\# Graphic text

TITLE	LEVEL	GENRE	WORD COUNT	AUTHOR / SERIES	PUBLISHER / DISTRIBUTOR
Birthday Dog	I	RF	250+	Sunshine	Wright Group/McGraw Hill
Birthday Flood, The	P	RF	250+	Storyteller	Wright Group/ McGraw Hill
Birthday for Frances, A	K	F	250+	Hoban, Russell	Scholastic
Birthday Girl, The	M	RF	250+	Orca Echoes	Orca Book Publishers
Birthday in the Woods, A	F	F	199	Salem, Lynn; Stewart, Josie	Continental Press
Birthday Invitation, The	L	RF	1075	Rigby Flying Colors	Rigby
Birthday Kitten, The	E	RF	149	PM Photo Stories	Rigby
Birthday Party for Cornelius, A	N	RF	250+	Leveled Readers Language Support	Houghton Mifflin Harcourt
Birthday Party, A	C	RF	47	Early Emergent	Pioneer Valley
Birthday Party, A	F	RF	109	Sunshine	Wright Group/McGraw Hill
Birthday Party, The	O	F	797	Leveled Readers	Houghton Mifflin Harcourt
Birthday Party, The	LB	I	16	Rise & Shine	Hampton-Brown
Birthday Party, The	LB	RF	15	Sunshine	Wright Group/McGraw Hill
Birthday Pinata, The	H	RF	128	Handprints D	Educators Publishing Service
Birthday Present for Mom, A	F	I	98	In Step Readers	Rigby
Birthday Present for Mom, A	J	RF	529	Rigby Flying Colors	Rigby
Birthday Present for Spaceboy, A	E	F	130	Spaceboy	Literacy Footprints
Birthday Present, The	E	F	86	Leveled Readers Language Support	Houghton Mifflin Harcourt
Birthday Presents	F	RF	162	PM Plus Story Books	Rigby
Birthday Room, The	V	RF	250+	Henkes, Kevin	William Morrow
Birthday Song, The	D	F	183	Leveled Literacy Intervention/ Blue System	Heinemann
Birthday Surprise	H	RF	265	Leveled Readers	Houghton Mifflin Harcourt
Birthday Surprise, A	H	RF	157	Developing Books, Set 2	Pioneer Valley
Birthday Surprise, The	H	RF	237	On Our Way to English	Rigby
*Birthday Surprises: Ten Great Stories to Unwrap	R	RF	250+	Hurwitz, Johanna	William Morrow
Birthday Wishes	L	RF	250+	Voyages	SRA/McGraw Hill
Birthday, A	C	F	39	New Way	Steck-Vaughn
Birthday, The	C	RF	30	Harry's Math Books	Outside the Box
Birthday, The	A	I	23	Little Books for Early Readers	University of Maine
Birthday, The	B	RF	36	Sails	Rigby
Birthdays	C	RF	59	Foundations	Wright Group/McGraw Hill
Birthdays	K	I	250+	Holidays and Celebrations	Picture Window Books
Birthdays	K	I	59	Purkis, Sallie	Nelson/Michaels Assoc.
Birthdays	I	I	147	Sunshine	Wright Group/McGraw Hill
Birthdays Around the World	M	I	250+	Early Connections	Benchmark Education
Birthdays Around the World	J	I	375	Leveled Readers	Houghton Mifflin Harcourt
Birthdays Around the World	J	I	375	Leveled Readers/CA	Houghton Mifflin Harcourt
Birthdays Around the World	J	I	375	Leveled Readers/TX	Houghton Mifflin Harcourt
Birthdays Around the World	N	I	795	Reading Street	Pearson
Birthdays Around the World	J	I	178	Vocabulary Readers	Houghton Mifflin Harcourt
Birthdays Around the World	J	I	178	Vocabulary Readers/CA	Houghton Mifflin Harcourt
Birthdays in Many Cultures	I	I	108	Life Around the World	Capstone Press
Bisa's First Gallop	J	RF	439	Springboard	Wright Group/McGraw Hill
Biscuit	F	RF	132	Capucilli, Alyssa Satin	HarperTrophy
Biscuit Finds a Friend	F	RF	114	Capucilli, Alyssa Satin	HarperTrophy
Biscuit Visits the Big City	F	RF	150	Capucilli, Alyssa Satin	Scholastic
Bison Are Back!, The	P	RF	743	Leveled Readers	Houghton Mifflin Harcourt
Bite of the Gold Bug, The: A Story of the Alaskan Gold Rush	S	I	250+	DeClements, Barthe	Penguin Group

* Collection of short stories
# Graphic text

TITLE	LEVEL	GENRE	WORD COUNT	AUTHOR / SERIES	PUBLISHER / DISTRIBUTOR
Black	B	I	26	Colors	Lerner Publications
Black and White	B	I	23	Reading Safari	Mondo
Black and White	D	I	77	Storyteller Nonfiction	Wright Group/McGraw Hill
Black and White	C	I	32	Voyages	SRA/McGraw Hill
Black Bear Cub	L	F	250+	Lind, Alan	Scholastic
Black Bear Rescue	Q	RF	250+	Reading Expeditions	National Geographic
Black Bears	E	I	50	Pebble Books	Capstone Press
Black Bears	Q	I	1272	Vocabulary Readers	Houghton Mifflin Harcourt
Black Bears	Q	I	1272	Vocabulary Readers/CA	Houghton Mifflin Harcourt
Black Bears	Q	I	1272	Vocabulary Readers/TX	Houghton Mifflin Harcourt
Black Beauty: The Greatest Horse Story Ever Told	S	RF	250+	DK Readers	DK Publishing
Black Boy	Z	RF	250+	Wright, Richard	HarperPerennial
Black Cat and Poodle Dog	J	F	334	Sails	Rigby
Black Cat Goes Away	J	F	403	Sails	Rigby
Black Cat Stays Out	I	F	302	Sails	Rigby
Black Diamond: Story of the Negro Baseball Leagues	W	I	250+	McKissack, Patricia & Fred	Scholastic
Black Eagles: African Americans in Aviation	X	B	250+	Haskins, Jim	Scholastic
Black Elk: A Man with a Vision	N	B	250+	Rookie Biographies	Children's Press
Black Gold	R	RF	250+	Henry, Marguerite	Aladdin
Black Gold	S	I	250+	Orbit Chapter books	Pacific Learning
Black Hearts in Battersea	V	HF	250+	Aiken, Joan	Houghton Mifflin Harcourt
*Black Heroes of the American Revolution	X	B	250+	Davis, Burke	Harcourt Trade
Black Holes	Q	I	250+	A True Book	Children's Press
Black Kitten, The	E	RF	115	Handprints C, Set 2	Educators Publishing Service
Black Pearl, The	X	RF	250+	O'Dell, Scott	Bantam
*Black Pioneers of Science and Invention	Y	B	250+	Haber, Louis	Harcourt Trade
Black Ships Before Troy: The Story of the Iliad	Y	F	250+	Sutcliff, Rosemary	Laurel-Leaf Books
Black Snowman, The	P	F	250+	Mendez, Phil	Scholastic
Black Stallion, The	T	RF	250+	Farley, Walter	Language for Learning Assoc.
Black Star, Bright Dawn	V	RF	250+	O'Dell, Scott	Ballantine Books
Black Storm Comin'	W	HF	250+	Wilson, Diane Lee	Aladdin
Black Swan's Breakfast	G	RF	147	Book Bank	Wright Group/McGraw Hill
Black Tooth the Pirate	G	RF	198	Take Two Books	Wright Group/McGraw Hill
Black Velvet Mystery, The	N	RF	250+	Keene, Carolyn	Pocket Books
Black: Seeing Black All Around Us	L	I	250+	Colors	Capstone Press
Black-and-White Ruffed Lemurs	H	I	94	Seedlings	Continental Press
Blackbeard's Last Stand	T	HF	250+	High-Fliers	Pacific Learning
Blackbeard's Sword: The Pirate King of the Carolinas	T	HF	2,565	O'Donnell, Liam	Stone Arch Books
Blackberries	D	F	107	PM Story Books	Rigby
Blackberries in the Dark	N	RF	250+	Jukes, Mavis	Alfred A. Knopf
Blackbird Diary	N	I	996	Rigby Flying Colors	Rigby
Blackbirds	L	I	250+	Sunshine	Wright Group/McGraw Hill
Blackbird's Nest	G	RF	71	Pacific Literacy	Pacific Learning
Blackboard Bear	J	F	117	Alexander, Martha	Penguin Group
Black-Eyed Susan	Q	HF	250+	Armstrong, Jennifer	Alfred A. Knopf
Blackfeet, The	R	I	250+	First Reports	Compass Point Books
Blackfeet, The: People of the Dark Moccasins	S	I	250+	American Indian Nations	Capstone Press
Blackout!	P	RF	250+	Bookweb	Rigby

* Collection of short stories
# Graphic text

TITLE	LEVEL	GENRE	WORD COUNT	AUTHOR / SERIES	PUBLISHER / DISTRIBUTOR
Blackwater Swamp	T	RF	250+	Wallace, Bill	Language for Learning Assoc.
Blair's Deer	K	RF	250+	Phonics and Friends	Hampton-Brown
Blanche Bruce of Mississippi	K	B	413	Leveled Readers Social Studies	Houghton Mifflin Harcourt
Blank Sheet of Paper, The	J	RF	379	Springboard	Wright Group/McGraw Hill
Blanket, The	E	RF	65	Burningham, John	Crowell
Blast Off with Ellen Ochoa!	M	B	250+	Greetings	Rigby
Blast Off!	N	I	250+	Home Connection Collection	Rigby
Blast Off!	F	I	95	Ready Readers	Pearson Learning Group
Blast to the Past	N	SF	250+	Orbit Chapter Books	Pacific Learning
Blat, the Alley Cat	H	F	300	Sails	Rigby
Blazer Drive	U	RF	250+	Orca Sports	Orca Book Publishers
Blazing a Cattle Trail	T	I	2747	Leveled Readers	Houghton Mifflin Harcourt
Blazing a Cattle Trail	T	I	2747	Leveled Readers/CA	Houghton Mifflin Harcourt
Blazing a Cattle Trail	T	I	2747	Leveled Readers/TX	Houghton Mifflin Harcourt
Bless Me, Ultima	Z	RF	250+	Anaya, Rudolfo	Warner Books
Blimps	O	I	250+	A True Book	Children's Press
Blind Men and the Elephant, The	K	TL	250+	Backstein, Karen	Scholastic
Blind Outlaw, The	P	RF	250+	Rounds, Glen	Scholastic
Blister	S	RF	250+	Shreve, Susan	Scholastic
Blizzard	S	HF	250+	Duey, Kathleen	Simon & Schuster
Blizzard of the Blue Moon	N	RF	250+	Osborne, Mary Pope	Scholastic
Blizzards	W	I	7777	Disasters Up Close	Lerner Publications
Blizzards	S	I	250+	Natural Disasters	Capstone Press
Blizzards	M	I	666	Pull Ahead Books	Lerner Publications
Blizzards	N	I	250+	Weather Update	Capstone Press
Blizzards!	M	HF	250+	Hopping, Lorraine Jean	Scholastic
Block Party, The	H	I	127	Learn to Read	Creative Teaching Press
Blocks	C	RF	60	Early Emergent	Pioneer Valley
Blood	T	I	250+	Theme Sets	National Geographic
Blood	J	I	241	Twig	Wright Group/McGraw Hill
Blood Is Thicker	Y	RF	250+	Langan, Paul & Blackwell, D.M.	Townsend Press
Blood on the River: James Town 1607	W	HF	250+	Carbone, Lisa	Scholastic
Bloodhounds	I	I	147	Dogs	Capstone Press
Bloodsuckers: Bats, Bugs and Other Bloodthirsty Creatures	W	I	250+	High Five Reading	Red Brick Learning
Bloomability	V	RF	250+	Creech, Sharon	HarperCollins
Blossom	J	F	225	Voyages	SRA/McGraw Hill
Blossom Promise, A	R	RF	250+	Byars, Betsy	Bantam
Blossoms and the Green Phantom, The	R	RF	250+	Byars, Betsy	Dell
Blossom's Babies	I	F	250+	Book Bus	Creative Edge
Blossoms Meet the Vulture Lady, The	R	RF	250+	Byars, Betsy	Bantam
Blow, Wind, Blow! And Other Stories	D	RF	114	Story Steps	Rigby
Blowing in the Wind	T	I	250+	Literacy 2000	Rigby
Blowing in the Wind	E	I	45	Shutterbug Books	Steck-Vaughn
Blown Away	U	RF	250+	Reading Expeditions	National Geographic
Blown Away: Forces of Nature	S	I	250+	Kids Discover Reading	Wright Group/McGraw Hill
Blubber	T	RF	250+	Blume, Judy	Bantam
Blue	C	F	51	Bonnell, Kris	Reading Reading Books
Blue	B	I	26	Colors	Lerner Publications
Blue Birthday, A	J	RF	250+	Literacy by Design	Rigby
Blue Bug and the Bullies	D	F	18	Poulet, Virginia	Children's Press
Blue Bug Goes to School	D	F	57	Poulet, Virginia	Children's Press
Blue Bug Goes to the Library	F	F	59	Poulet, Virginia	Children's Press

TITLE	LEVEL	GENRE	WORD COUNT	AUTHOR / SERIES	PUBLISHER / DISTRIBUTOR
Blue Bug's Book of Colors	E	F	49	Poulet, Virginia	Children's Press
Blue Bug's Vegetable Garden	D	F	27	Poulet, Virginia	Children's Press
Blue Day	C	RF	35	Literacy 2000	Rigby
Blue Door, The	X	HF	250+	Rinaldi, Ann	Scholastic
Blue Goo	I	F	65	Rigby Star	Rigby
Blue Gorph, The	P	F	250+	Scooters	ETA Cuisenaire
Blue Heron	W	RF	250+	Avi	Avon
Blue Highway	Z+	RF	250+	Tullson, Diane	Fitzhenry & Whiteside
*Blue Hill Meadows, The	M	RF	250+	Rylant, Cynthia	Harcourt Trade
Blue Ice	U	RF	250+	Salata, Estelle	Fitzhenry & Whiteside
Blue Jay, The	H	RF	173	Little Readers	Houghton Mifflin Harcourt
Blue Jay's Home	L	F	250+	Pair-It Turn and Learn	Steck-Vaughn
Blue Kangaroo, The	H	F	361	Leveled Readers	Houghton Mifflin Harcourt
Blue Layer, The	N	I	250+	Voyages	SRA/McGraw Hill
Blue Lollipops	G	RF	250	Stepping Stones	Nelson/Michaels Assoc.
Blue Mittens, The	I	RF	250+	Mann, Rachel	Scholastic
Blue Moon	T	RF	250+	Orca Soundings	Orca Book Publishers
Blue Moon Effect, The	Q	F	250+	Extreme Monsters	Penny Candy Press
Blue Morpho Butterflies	M	I	668	Springboard	Wright Group/ McGraw Hill
Blue Ribbon Blues	M	RF	250+	Spinelli, Jerry	Random House
Blue Stone, The: A Journey Through Life	R	F	250+	Liao, Jimmy	Little, Brown & Co.
Blue Sue	G	F	121	Ready Readers	Pearson Learning Group
Blue Sword, The	Y	F	250+	McKinley, Robin	Puffin/Penguin
Blue Whales	U	I	250+	The Untamed World	Steck-Vaughn
Blue Willow	V	RF	250+	Gates, Doris	Puffin/Penguin
Blue: Seeing Blue All Around Us	L	I	250+	Colors	Capstone Press
Blueberries for Sal	M	RF	250+	McCloskey, Robert	Scholastic
Blueberries from Maine	A	RF	28	Little Books for Early Readers	University of Maine
Blueberry Muffins	D	RF	191	Story Box	Wright Group/McGraw Hill
Bluebird Out My Window	L	RF	633	Leveled Readers Science	Houghton Mifflin Harcourt
Blue-Eyed Daisy, A	W	RF	250+	Rylant, Cynthia	Simon & Schuster
Blue-green Mystery, The	P	RF	1563	Gear Up!	Wright Group/ McGraw Hill
Bluish	S	RF	250+	Hamilton, Virginia	Scholastic
BMX Bikes	Q	I	250+	Wild Rides!	Capstone Press
BMX Billy	G	RF	93	Literacy 2000	Rigby
BMX Bully	P	RF	4609	Maddox, Jake	Stone Arch Books
BMX Freestyle	M	I	250+	Horsepower	Capstone Press
BMX Racing	M	I	250+	To the Extreme	Capstone Press
BMX Racing	S	I	250+	X-Sports	Capstone Press
BMX Winner, The	F	RF	219	Handprints D, Set 2	Educators Publishing Service
Bo and Peter	C	RF	44	Franco, Betsy	Scholastic
Bo Peep's Sheep	C	TL	39	Pair-It Books	Steck-Vaughn
Boa Constrictors	J	I	250+	Rain Forest Animals	Red Brick Learning
Boa Constrictors	M	I	250+	Snakes	Capstone Press
Board Rebel	P	RF	250+	Maddox, Jake	Stone Arch Books
Boards and More	I	RF	250+	Phonics Readers Plus	Steck-Vaughn
Boat	W	I	250+	Eyewitness Books	DK Publishing
Boat Race, The	J	F	366	Leveled Readers	Houghton Mifflin Harcourt
Boat Race, The	J	F	366	Leveled Readers/CA	Houghton Mifflin Harcourt
Boat Race, The	J	F	366	Leveled Readers/TX	Houghton Mifflin Harcourt
Boat Ride with Lillian Two Blossom	N	F	250+	Polacco, Patricia	Pilomel Books
Boat Ride, The	C	F	38	PM Stars	Rigby
Boat Rides	C	I	100	Vocabulary Readers	Houghton Mifflin Harcourt

* Collection of short stories
# Graphic text

TITLE	LEVEL	GENRE	WORD COUNT	AUTHOR / SERIES	PUBLISHER / DISTRIBUTOR
Boat Rides	C	I	100	Vocabulary Readers/CA	Houghton Mifflin Harcourt
Boat Trip, The	D	F	70	Carousel Earlybirds	Pearson Learning Group
Boat, The	LB	RF	14	Pacific Literacy	Pacific Learning
Boat, The	A	F	30	Sails	Rigby
Boat, The	A	RF	28	Sunshine	Wright Group/McGraw Hill
Boats	C	I	100	Pebble Books	Capstone Press
Boats	E	I	275	Rigby Flying Colors	Rigby
Boats	G	I	84	Rockwell, Anne	Penguin Group
Boats	G	I	260	Sails	Rigby
Boats	M	I	250+	Transportation	Compass Point Books
Boats	D	I	57	Twig	Wright Group/McGraw Hill
Boats Afloat	M	I	752	Sunshine	Wright Group/McGraw Hill
Boats of the Past	M	I	250+	On Deck	Rigby
Boats, Boats, Boats	D	I	44	My First Reader	Grolier Press
Boats, Boats, Boats	L	I	250+	Yellow Umbrella Books	Red Brick Learning
Bob	J	F	488	Pearson, Tracy Campbell	Farrar, Straus, and Giroux
Bob and Billy	I	F	434	Sails	Rigby
Bobbie and the Baby	C	RF	62	Literacy by Design	Rigby
Bobbie and the Baby	C	RF	62	Rigby Literacy	Rigby
Bobbie and the Kite	WB	RF	N/A	Rigby Literacy	Rigby
Bobbie and the Monster	B	RF	24	Rigby Literacy	Rigby
Bobbie and the Parade	C	RF	49	Rigby Literacy	Rigby
Bobbie and the Play	F	RF	164	Literacy By Design	Rigby
Bobbie and the Play	F	RF	164	Rigby Literacy	Rigby
Bobbie Goes on Vacation	F	RF	240	Rigby Literacy	Rigby
Bobbie's Airplane	E	RF	64	Oxford Reading Tree	Oxford University Press
Bobbie's New Coat	F	RF	189	Literacy By Design	Rigby
Bobbie's New Coat	F	RF	189	Rigby Literacy	Rigby
Bobby's New Apartment	M	RF	1350	Reading Street	Pearson
Bobby's Zoo	E	RF	54	Rookie Readers	Children's Press
Bobcat Tells a Tale	J	F	250+	Leveled Readers/TX	Houghton Mifflin Harcourt
Bobcats	O	I	1392	Early Bird Nature Books	Lerner Publications
Bobo's Magic Wishes	L	F	250+	Little Readers	Houghton Mifflin Harcourt
Body Battles	P	I	250+	Gelman, Rita G.	Scholastic
Body Beasts	R	I	250+	Explorer Books-Pathfinder	National Geographic
Body Beasts	P	I	250+	Explorer Books-Pioneer	National Geographic
Body Dictionary, A	S	I	250+	High-Fliers	Pacific Learning
Body Numbers	K	I	250+	Discovery World	Rigby
Body Parts Work Together	I	I	119	Instant Readers	Harcourt School Publishers
Body Systems	T	I	250+	The News	Richard C. Owen
Bogeymen Don't Play Football	M	F	250+	Dadey, Debbie; Jones, Marcia Thornton	Scholastic
Boggart and the Monster, The	U	F	250+	Cooper, Susan	Aladdin
Boggart, The	U	F	250+	Cooper, Susan	Simon & Schuster
Boggywooga	I	F	274	Sunshine	Wright Group/McGraw Hill
Bogle's Card	H	F	244	Sunshine	Wright Group/McGraw Hill
Bogle's Feet	I	F	280	Sunshine	Wright Group/McGraw Hill
Bokuden and the Bully	N	TL	1483	On My Own Folklore	Millbrook Press
Bolivia	Q	I	250+	First Reports: Countries	Compass Point Books
Bomb Detection Squads	S	I	250+	Law Enforcement	Capstone Press
Bomb, The	Z	HF	250+	Taylor, Theodore	Avon
Bombed House, The	T	HF	250+	Zucker, Jonny	Stone Arch Books
Bombers	J	I	105	Mighty Machines	Capstone Press
Bombers	V	I	4552	Military Hardware in Action	Lerner Publications

TITLE	LEVEL	GENRE	WORD COUNT	AUTHOR / SERIES	PUBLISHER / DISTRIBUTOR
Bommyknocker Tree, The	R	RF	250+	PM Extensions	Rigby
Bonanza Girl	T	HF	250+	Beatty, Patricia	Scholastic
Bon-Bon the Downtown Cow	K	F	838	Appleton-Smith, Laura	Flyleaf Publishing
Bone Dance	X	RF	250+	Brooks, Martha	Random House
Bone Detectives	W	I	1818	Reading Street	Pearson
Bone Museum, The	M	RF	250+	Sunshine	Wright Group/McGraw Hill
Bone Tree, The	N	F	250+	Voyages	SRA/McGraw Hill
Bone: Out From Boneville	W	F	250+	Smith, Jeff	Scholastic
Bone: The Dragonslayer	W	F	250+	Smith, Jeff	Scholastic
Bones	J	I	182	Rigby Focus	Rigby
Bones	C	I	56	Rigby Literacy	Rigby
Bones	L	I	545	Sun Sprouts	ETA Cuisenaire
Bones	T	I	250+	The News	Richard C. Owen
Bones	T	I	250+	Theme Sets	National Geographic
Bones for Lunch	K	F	221	Sunshine	Wright Group/McGraw Hill
Bones!	O	F	250+	High-Fliers	Pacific Learning
Bongos, Maracas, and Xylophones	I	I	210	Vocabulary Readers	Houghton Mifflin Harcourt
Bongos, Maracas, and Xylophones	I	I	210	Vocabulary Readers/CA	Houghton Mifflin Harcourt
Bongos, Maracas, and Xylophones	I	I	210	Vocabulary Readers/TX	Houghton Mifflin Harcourt
Bonnie on the Beach	H	RF	198	Little Readers	Houghton Mifflin Harcourt
Bony Back: The Adventure of Stegosaurus	N	I	250+	Dinosaur World	Picture Window Books
Bony-Legs	K	F	250+	Cole, Joanna	Scholastic
Boo!	B	RF	41	Handprints B	Educators Publishing Service
Boodil My Dog	Q	RF	250+	Lindenbaum, Pija	Henry Holt & Co.
Boogie-Woogie Man, The	D	F	101	Story Box	Wright Group/McGraw Hill
Boogly, The	E	F	61	Literacy 2000	Rigby
Boo-Hoo	E	F	149	Story Box	Wright Group/McGraw Hill
Book	X	I	250+	Eyewitness Books	DK Publishing
Book About Planets and Stars, A	R	I	250+	Reigot, Betty Polisar	Scholastic
Book About Your Skeleton, A	M	I	250+	Gross, Ruth Belov	Scholastic
Book Club, The	H	RF	247	Leveled Readers Language Support	Houghton Mifflin Harcourt
Book Making and Paper Making: Be Your Own Publisher	Q	I	250+	Crafts	Capstone Press
*Book of Black Heroes from A to Z	P	B	250+	Hudson, Wade; Wesley, Valerie Wilson	Scholastic
Book of Boats, A	H	I	106	Gear Up!	Wright Group/McGraw Hill
Book of Hours, A	O	I	250+	Cambridge Reading	Pearson Learning Group
Book of Monsters, The	P	I	250+	Sunshine	Wright Group/McGraw Hill
*Book of Monsters: Tales to Give You the Creeps	T	F	250+	Coville, Bruce	Scholastic
*Book of Spine Tinglers: Tales to Make You Shiver	T	F	250+	Coville, Bruce	Scholastic
Book of Story Beginnings, The	W	F	250+	Kladstrup, Kristin	Candlewick Press
Book of Three, The	U	F	250+	Alexander, Lloyd	Bantam
Book Steps	T	I	250+	Bookweb	Rigby
Book that Dripped Blood, The	T	F	835	Dahl, Michael	Stone Arch Books
Book Thief, The	Z+	HF	250+	Zusack, Markus	Alfred A. Knopf
Book Week	E	RF	71	Oxford Reading Tree	Oxford University Press
Booker T. Washington	N	B	250+	First Biographies	Steck-Vaughn
Booker T. Washington	N	B	1634	On My Own Biography	Lerner Publications
Booker T. Washington	P	B	250+	Photo-Illustrated Biographies	Red Brick Learning
Booker T. Washington: Educator and Leader	P	B	250+	Great African Americans	Capstone Press

* Collection of short stories
# Graphic text

TITLE	LEVEL	GENRE	WORD COUNT	AUTHOR / SERIES	PUBLISHER / DISTRIBUTOR
Books	C	RF	21	Beginning Literacy	Scholastic
Books	D	RF	145	Leveled Literacy Intervention/ Green System	Heinemann
Books	B	I	21	Smart Starts	Rigby
Books	B	RF	29	Sunshine	Wright Group/McGraw Hill
Books for Oliver	P	RF	250+	Bookshop	Mondo
Bookstore Cat	I	RF	207	Little Readers	Houghton Mifflin Harcourt
Bookworm Who Hatched, A	O	B	250+	Meet The Author	Richard C. Owen
Boom and Bust	Q	I	250+	Orbit Chapter Books	Pacific Learning
Boom Boom Bay!	D	RF	130	Phonics and Friends	Hampton-Brown
Boom!	N	I	250+	Gutner, Howard	Scholastic
Boomtowns of the West	S	I	250+	Kalman, Bobbie	Crabtree
Boonsville Bombers, The	N	RF	250+	Herzig, Alison	Puffin/Penguin
Booooo!	E	RF	90	Rigby Star	Rigby
Boot Balancers Wanted	O	F	250+	Sails	Rigby
Bootlace Soup	J	TL	250+	Voyages	SRA/McGraw Hill
Boots	C	RF	57	Schreiber, Anne; Doughty, Arbo	Scholastic
Boots and Shoes	D	F	68	Cooper, Anne	Kaeden Books
Boots and Shoes	B	I	74	Leveled Literacy Intervention/ Green System	Heinemann
Boots for the King	D	F	93	Sun Sprouts	ETA Cuisenaire
Boots for Toots	C	F	41	Pacific Literacy	Pacific Learning
Bootscooting	B	I	38	First Stories	Pacific Learning
Bootsie Barker Ballerina	K	F	250+	Bottner, Barbara	HarperTrophy
Boring Day, The	D	RF	81	Emergent Books	Pioneer Valley
Boring Old Bed	J	F	250+	Lighthouse	Rigby
Boring Old Bed	I	RF	211	Sunshine	Wright Group/McGraw Hill
Boris Bad Enough	G	F	167	Kraus, Robert	Simon & Schuster
Born Blue	Z+	RF	250+	Nolan, Han	Harcourt
Born to be a Butterfly	H	I	250+	DK Readers	DK Publishing
Born to Trot	R	RF	250+	Henry, Marguerite	Aladdin
Born Too Short	Z+	RF	250+	Elish, Dan	Simon & Schuster
Borning Room, The	Y	HF	250+	Fleischman, Paul	HarperCollins
Borreguita and the Coyote	O	TL	250+	Aardema, Verna	Scholastic
Borrowers, The	S	F	250+	Norton, Mary	Harcourt Trade
Boss	C	F	48	Foundations	Wright Group/McGraw Hill
Boss for a Day	I	RF	250+	DePaola, Tomie	Grossett & Dunlap
Boss, The	H	RF	281	Leveled Literacy Intervention/ Blue System	Heinemann
Bossy and Wag	D	F	63	Sun Sprouts	ETA Cuisenaire
Bossy Bettina	F	RF	97	Literacy 2000	Rigby
Bossy Pig, The	G	F	240	Leveled Literacy Intervention/ Green System	Heinemann
Boston Coffee Party, The	L	HF	250+	Rappaport, Doreen	HarperCollins
Boston Massacre, The	V	I	250+	Let Freedom Ring	Red Brick Learning
Boston Massacre, The: An Interactive History Adventure	T	HF	250+	You Choose Books	Capstone Press
Boston Massacre, The: Five Colonists Killed by British Soldiers	S	I	250+	Headlines from History	Rosen Publishing Group
Boston Red Sox, The	S	I	250+	Team Spirit	Norwood House Press
Boston Tea Party, The	V	I	250+	Cornerstones of Freedom	Children's Press
#Boston Tea Party, The	U	I	250+	Graphic Library	Capstone Press
Boston Tea Party, The	V	I	250+	Let Freedom Ring	Red Brick Learning
Boston Tea Party, The	T	I	250+	We The People	Compass Point Books

* Collection of short stories
# Graphic text

TITLE	LEVEL	GENRE	WORD COUNT	AUTHOR / SERIES	PUBLISHER / DISTRIBUTOR
Boston Tea Party, The: Angry Colonists Dump British Tea	S	I	250+	Headlines from History	Rosen Publishing Group
Boston Tea Party: Rebellion in the Colonies	T	I	250+	Adventures in Colonial America	Troll Associates
Both Sides of the Story	L	RF	701	Gear Up!	Wright Group/ McGraw Hill
Bot's Bits	G	F	99	Supersonics	Rigby
Botticelli	R	B	250+	Venezia, Mike	Children's Press
Bottle Garden, A	E	I	52	Wonder World	Wright Group/McGraw Hill
Bottle Mystery, The	M	I	250+	Sun Sprouts	ETA Cuisenaire
Bottlenose Dolphins	O	I	961	Leveled Readers	Houghton Mifflin Harcourt
Bottlenose Dolphins	O	I	961	Leveled Readers/CA	Houghton Mifflin Harcourt
Bottlenose Dolphins	O	I	961	Leveled Readers/TX	Houghton Mifflin Harcourt
Bottles, Boxes, and Bins	C	I	36	Twig	Wright Group/McGraw Hill
Bouncer Comes to Stay	I	RF	250+	Storyworlds	Heinemann Educational Books
Bouncy Balls	I	RF	389	InfoTrek	ETA Cuisenaire
Bound for Oregon	S	HF	250+	Van Leeuwen, Jean	Puffin Books
Bound for Rock Bottom	W	F	2705	Leveled Readers	Houghton Mifflin Harcourt
Bound for Rock Bottom	W	F	2705	Leveled Readers/CA	Houghton Mifflin Harcourt
*Bound for the North Star: True Stories of Fugitive Slaves	Z	B	250+	Fradin, Dennis Brindell	Houghton Mifflin Harcourt
Boundaries Washed Away	O	RF	250+	On Our Way to English	Rigby
Boundless Grace	M	RF	250+	Hoffman, Mary	Scholastic
Bouquet, The	A	RF	38	Carousel Earlybirds	Pearson Learning Group
Bow Down, Shadrach	R	RF	250+	Cowley, Joy	Wright Group/McGraw Hill
Bowhunting	S	I	250+	The Great Outdoors	Capstone Press
Bowling at Home	F	RF	151	PM Stars	Rigby
Bowling Buddies	N	RF	250+	Girlz Rock!	Mondo
Bowman's Store: A Journey to Myself	Z	B	250+	Bruchac, Joseph	Lee & Low Books Inc.
Box Can Be Many Things, A	E	RF	51	Rookie Readers	Children's Press
Box House, The	G	RF	194	Sails	Rigby
Box of Butterflies, A	K	RF	250+	Leveled Readers Language Support	Houghton Mifflin Harcourt
Box, A	D	I	118	Leveled Literacy Intervention/ Green System	Heinemann
Box, The	A	RF	31	First Stories	Pacific Learning
Box, The	C	RF	30	Leveled Readers Language Support	Houghton Mifflin Harcourt
Boxcar Children Return, The	O	RF	250+	Warner, Gertrude Chandler	Albert Whitman & Co.
Boxcar Children Special: The Mystery at Snowflake Inn	O	RF	250+	Warner, Gertrude Chandler	Albert Whitman & Co.
Boxcar Children Special: The Mystery at the Ballpark	O	RF	250+	Warner, Gertrude Chandler	Albert Whitman & Co.
Boxcar Children Special: The Mystery at the Fair	O	RF	250+	Warner, Gertrude Chandler	Albert Whitman & Co.
Boxcar Children Special: The Pilgrim Village Mystery	O	RF	250+	Warner, Gertrude Chandler	Albert Whitman & Co.
Boxcar Children: The Amusement Park Mystery	O	RF	250+	Warner, Gertrude Chandler	Albert Whitman & Co.
Boxcar Children: The Animal Shelter Mystery	O	RF	250+	Warner, Gertrude Chandler	Albert Whitman & Co.
Boxcar Children: The Basketball Mystery	O	RF	250+	Warner, Gertrude Chandler	Albert Whitman & Co.
Boxcar Children: Benny Uncovers a Mystery	O	RF	250+	Warner, Gertrude Chandler	Albert Whitman & Co.
Boxcar Children: Bicycle Mystery	O	RF	250+	Warner, Gertrude Chandler	Albert Whitman & Co.
Boxcar Children: The Black Pearl Mystery	O	RF	250+	Warner, Gertrude Chandler	Albert Whitman & Co.
Boxcar Children: Blue Bay Mystery	O	RF	250+	Warner, Gertrude Chandler	Albert Whitman & Co.
Boxcar Children: The Boxcar Children	O	RF	250+	Warner, Gertrude Chandler	Albert Whitman & Co.

* Collection of short stories
# Graphic text

TITLE	LEVEL	GENRE	WORD COUNT	AUTHOR / SERIES	PUBLISHER / DISTRIBUTOR
Boxcar Children: Bus Station Mystery	O	RF	250+	Warner, Gertrude Chandler	Albert Whitman & Co.
Boxcar Children: Caboose Mystery	O	RF	250+	Warner, Gertrude Chandler	Albert Whitman & Co.
Boxcar Children: The Camp-Out Mystery	O	RF	250+	Warner, Gertrude Chandler	Albert Whitman & Co.
Boxcar Children: The Canoe Trip Mystery	O	RF	250+	Warner, Gertrude Chandler	Albert Whitman & Co.
Boxcar Children: The Castle Mystery	O	RF	250+	Warner, Gertrude Chandler	Albert Whitman & Co.
Boxcar Children: The Cereal Box Mystery	O	RF	250+	Warner, Gertrude Chandler	Albert Whitman & Co.
Boxcar Children: The Chocolate Sundae Mystery	O	RF	250+	Warner, Gertrude Chandler	Albert Whitman & Co.
Boxcar Children: The Deserted Library Mystery	O	RF	250+	Warner, Gertrude Chandler	Albert Whitman & Co.
Boxcar Children: The Dinosaur Mystery	O	RF	250+	Warner, Gertrude Chandler	Albert Whitman & Co.
Boxcar Children: The Disappearing Friend Mystery	O	RF	250+	Warner, Gertrude Chandler	Albert Whitman & Co.
Boxcar Children: The Firehouse Mystery	O	RF	250+	Warner, Gertrude Chandler	Albert Whitman & Co.
Boxcar Children: The Ghost Ship Mystery	O	RF	250+	Warner, Gertrude Chandler	Albert Whitman & Co.
Boxcar Children: The Growling Bear Mystery	O	RF	250+	Warner, Gertrude Chandler	Albert Whitman & Co.
Boxcar Children: The Haunted Cabin Mystery	O	RF	250+	Warner, Gertrude Chandler	Albert Whitman & Co.
Boxcar Children: The Lighthouse Mystery	O	RF	250+	Warner, Gertrude Chandler	Albert Whitman & Co.
Boxcar Children: Mike's Mystery	O	RF	250+	Warner, Gertrude Chandler	Albert Whitman & Co.
Boxcar Children: Mountain Top Mystery	O	RF	250+	Warner, Gertrude Chandler	Albert Whitman & Co.
Boxcar Children: The Mystery at Snowflake Inn	O	RF	250+	Warner, Gertrude Chandler	Albert Whitman & Co.
Boxcar Children: The Mystery at the Alamo	O	RF	250+	Warner, Gertrude Chandler	Albert Whitman & Co.
Boxcar Children: The Mystery at the Ballpark	O	RF	250+	Warner, Gertrude Chandler	Albert Whitman & Co.
Boxcar Children: The Mystery at the Dog Show	O	RF	250+	Warner, Gertrude Chandler	Albert Whitman & Co.
Boxcar Children: Mystery at the Fair	O	RF	250+	Warner, Gertrude Chandler	Albert Whitman & Co.
Boxcar Children: Mystery Behind the Wall	O	RF	250+	Warner, Gertrude Chandler	Albert Whitman & Co.
Boxcar Children: The Mystery Bookstore	O	RF	250+	Warner, Gertrude Chandler	Albert Whitman & Co.
Boxcar Children: The Mystery Cruise	O	RF	250+	Warner, Gertrude Chandler	Albert Whitman & Co.
Boxcar Children: The Mystery Girl	O	RF	250+	Warner, Gertrude Chandler	Albert Whitman & Co.
Boxcar Children: The Mystery Horse	O	RF	250+	Warner, Gertrude Chandler	Albert Whitman & Co.
Boxcar Children: The Mystery in San Francisco	O	RF	250+	Warner, Gertrude Chandler	Albert Whitman & Co.
Boxcar Children: The Mystery in the Cave	O	RF	250+	Warner, Gertrude Chandler	Albert Whitman & Co.
Boxcar Children: The Mystery in the Old Attic	O	RF	250+	Warner, Gertrude Chandler	Albert Whitman & Co.
Boxcar Children: Mystery in the Sand	O	RF	250+	Warner, Gertrude Chandler	Albert Whitman & Co.
Boxcar Children: The Mystery in Washington, DC	O	RF	250+	Warner, Gertrude Chandler	Albert Whitman & Co.
Boxcar Children: Mystery of the Hidden Beach	O	RF	250+	Warner, Gertrude Chandler	Albert Whitman & Co.
Boxcar Children: The Mystery of the Lost Mine	O	RF	250+	Warner, Gertrude Chandler	Albert Whitman & Co.
Boxcar Children: The Mystery of the Lost Village	O	RF	250+	Warner, Gertrude Chandler	Albert Whitman & Co.
Boxcar Children: The Mystery of the Missing Cat	O	RF	250+	Warner, Gertrude Chandler	Albert Whitman & Co.
Boxcar Children: The Mystery of the Mixed-Up Zoo	O	RF	250+	Warner, Gertrude Chandler	Albert Whitman & Co.
Boxcar Children: The Mystery of the Stolen Boxcar	O	RF	250+	Warner, Gertrude Chandler	Albert Whitman & Co.
Boxcar Children: The Mystery of the Stolen Music	O	RF	250+	Warner, Gertrude Chandler	Albert Whitman & Co.
Boxcar Children: The Mystery on Stage	O	RF	250+	Warner, Gertrude Chandler	Albert Whitman & Co.
Boxcar Children: The Mystery on the Train	O	RF	250+	Warner, Gertrude Chandler	Albert Whitman & Co.
Boxcar Children: Mystery Ranch	O	RF	250+	Warner, Gertrude Chandler	Albert Whitman & Co.
Boxcar Children: The Outer Space Mystery	O	RF	250+	Warner, Gertrude Chandler	Albert Whitman & Co.
Boxcar Children: The Pizza Mystery	O	RF	250+	Warner, Gertrude Chandler	Albert Whitman & Co.
Boxcar Children: Schoolhouse Mystery	O	RF	250+	Warner, Gertrude Chandler	Albert Whitman & Co.
Boxcar Children: Snowbound Mystery	O	RF	250+	Warner, Gertrude Chandler	Albert Whitman & Co.

* Collection of short stories
\# Graphic text

Organized Alphabetically by Title
Storable Database at www.fountasandpinnellleveledbooks.com

TITLE	LEVEL	GENRE	WORD COUNT	AUTHOR / SERIES	PUBLISHER / DISTRIBUTOR
Boxcar Children: The Soccer Mystery	O	RF	250+	Warner, Gertrude Chandler	Albert Whitman & Co.
Boxcar Children: Surprise Island	O	RF	250+	Warner, Gertrude Chandler	Albert Whitman & Co.
Boxcar Children: The Box that Watch Found	O	RF	250+	Warner, Gertrude Chandler	Albert Whitman & Co.
Boxcar Children: The Creature in Ogopogo Lake	O	RF	250+	Warner, Gertrude Chandler	Albert Whitman & Co.
Boxcar Children: The Ghost in the First Row	O	RF	250+	Warner, Gertrude Chandler	Albert Whitman & Co.
Boxcar Children: The Giant Yo-Yo Mystery	O	RF	250+	Warner, Gertrude Chandler	Albert Whitman & Co.
Boxcar Children: The Rock 'n' Roll Mystery	O	RF	250+	Warner, Gertrude Chandler	Albert Whitman & Co.
Boxcar Children: The Seattle Puzzle	O	RF	250+	Warner, Gertrude Chandler	Albert Whitman & Co.
Boxcar Children: The Secret of the Mask	O	RF	250+	Warner, Gertrude Chandler	Albert Whitman & Co.
Boxcar Children: The Vanishing Passenger	O	RF	250+	Warner, Gertrude Chandler	Albert Whitman & Co.
Boxcar Children: The Woodshed Mystery	O	RF	250+	Warner, Gertrude Chandler	Albert Whitman & Co.
Boxcar Children: The Yellow House Mystery	O	RF	250+	Warner, Gertrude Chandler	Albert Whitman & Co.
Boxers	I	I	109	Dogs	Capstone Press
Boxes	A	RF	38	Davidson, Avelyn	Scholastic
Boxes	E	F	103	Foundations	Wright Group/McGraw Hill
Boxes	H	F	153	Literacy 2000	Rigby
Boxes of Fun	D	RF	95	Story Steps	Rigby
Boxes, Boxes, Boxes	E	RF	63	Stewart, Josie; Salem, Lynn	Continental Press
Boxes, Cans, and Balls	E	I	171	PM Math Readers	Rigby
Boy	T	B	250+	Dahl, Roald	Puffin/Penguin
Boy and His Donkey, A	K	F	250+	Literacy 2000	Rigby
Boy and the Elk Dogs, The	T	TL	1688	Leveled Readers	Houghton Mifflin Harcourt
Boy and the Goats, The	F	TL	346	Fairy Tales and Folklore	Norwood House Press
Boy and the Lion, The	H	TL	166	Aesop	Wright Group/McGraw Hill
Boy and the Wolf, The	I	TL	200	Book Bank	Wright Group/McGraw Hill
Boy Called Slow, A	S	B	250+	Bruchac, Joseph	Putnam/Penguin
Boy in the Doghouse, A	N	RF	250+	Duffey, Betsy	Simon & Schuster
Boy Named Beckoning: The True Story of Dr. Carlos Montezuma, Native American Hero, A	S	B	3611	Capaldi, Gina	Carolrhoda Books
Boy Named Boomer, A	K	B	250+	Esiason, Boomer	Scholastic
Boy of the Three-Year Nap, The	N	TL	250+	Soar To Success	Houghton Mifflin Harcourt
Boy Who Ate Dog Biscuits, The	N	RF	250+	Sachs, Betsy	Random House
Boy Who Cried Bigfoot, The	N	F	250+	The Zack Files	Grossett & Dunlap
Boy Who Cried Wolf, The	I	TL	136	Aesop	Wright Group/ McGraw Hill
Boy Who Cried Wolf, The	J	TL	460	Aesop's Fables	Pearson Learning Group
Boy Who Cried Wolf, The	L	TL	250+	Literacy Tree	Rigby
Boy Who Cried Wolf, The	J	TL	140	Littledale, Freya	Scholastic
Boy Who Cried Wolf, The	K	TL	250+	PM Tales and Plays-Purple	Rigby
Boy Who Cried Wolf, The	L	TL	970	Reading Street	Pearson
Boy Who Cried Wolf, The	D	TL	97	Storyworlds	Heinemann Educational Publishers
Boy Who Cried Wolf, The	H	TL	324	Sunshine	Wright Group/McGraw Hill
Boy Who Dared, The	Y	HF	250+	Bartoletti, Susan Campbell	Scholastic
Boy Who Lost His Face, The	R	RF	250+	Sachar, Louis	Alfred A. Knopf
Boy Who Owned the School, The	U	RF	250+	Paulsen, Gary	Bantam
Boy Who Reversed Himself, The	Y	SF	250+	Sleator, William	Puffin/Penguin
Boy Who Saved Baseball, The	U	RF	250+	Ritter, John H.	Penguin Group
Boy Who Saved Cleveland, The	Q	HF	250+	Giblin, James Cross	Henry Holt & Co.
Boy Who Spoke Dog, The	S	F	250+	Morgan, Clay	Puffin Books
Boy Who Stretched to the Sky, The	M	F	463	Book Bank	Wright Group/McGraw Hill
Boy Who Tried to Hide, The	I	TL	219	Storyteller-Night Crickets	Wright Group/McGraw Hill
Boy Who Turned Into a T.V. Set, The	L	F	250+	Manes, Stephen	Avon Camelot
Boy Who Went to the North Wind, The	L	TL	250+	Literacy 2000	Rigby

* Collection of short stories
\# Graphic text

B

TITLE	LEVEL	GENRE	WORD COUNT	AUTHOR / SERIES	PUBLISHER / DISTRIBUTOR
Boy, a Dog, and a Frog, A	WB	F	N/A	Mayer, Mercer	Dial/Penguin
Boyfriend Rules of Good Behavior, The	Y	RF	250+	Bateson, Catherine	Holiday House
Boys Against Girls	S	RF	250+	Naylor, Phyllis Reynolds	Bantam
Boys and Girls	D	RF	62	Williams, Deborah	Kaeden Books
Boys are Dogs	R	RF	250+	Margolis, Leslie	Bloomsbury Children's Books
Boys Start the War and the Girls Get Even, The	S	RF	250+	Naylor, Phyllis Reynolds	Bantam
*Boys Who Rocked the World: From King Tut to Tiger Woods	U	B	250+	Carlsmith, L.; Mann, B.; McCann, M. R.; & Strelow, E.	Beyond Words
*Boys Will Be	X	I	250+	Brooks, Bruce	Hyperion
Boy's Will, A	S	HF	250+	Haugaard, Erik Christian	Houghton Mifflin Harcourt
Bozo	H	RF	94	Wonder World	Wright Group/McGraw Hill
Bozo the Clone	N	SF	250+	The Zack Files	Grossett & Dunlap
Bracelet, The	R	HF	250+	Uchida, Yoshiko	Philomel/Penguin
Brachiosaurus	N	I	250+	Discovering Dinosaurs	Capstone Press
Brachiosaurus in the River	L	F	200	Wesley & The Dinosaurs	Wright Group/McGraw Hill
Brad and Butter Play Ball!	N	RF	250+	Hughes, Dean	William Morrow
Brad and His Brilliant Ideas	K	RF	826	Rigby Flying Colors	Rigby
Brad's Birthday Cake	H	RF	200	PM Stars	Rigby
Brady	V	HF	250+	Fritz, Jean	Puffin/Penguin
Braids	D	RF	24	Visions	Wright Group/McGraw Hill
Braids for Naya	G	RF	89	City Stories	Rigby
Brain	V	I	250+	You And Your Body	Troll Associates
Brain Block	M	F	250+	Rigby Gigglers	Rigby
Brain Drain	Q	I	250+	WorldScapes	ETA Cuisenaire
Brain Matter	T	I	250+	Sails	Rigby
Brain, The	Q	I	668	Time for Kids	Teacher Created Materials
Brain-in-a-Box	M	F	250+	Matthews, Steve	Sundance
*Brainstorm!: The Stories of Twenty American Kid Inventors	P	B	250+	Tucker, Tom	Farrar, Straus and Giroux
Brand New Butterfly, A	L	I	186	Literacy 2000	Rigby
Brand New Ideas	T	I	250+	The News	Richard C. Owen
Brandon's New School	F	RF	163	Developing Books, Set 3	Pioneer Valley
Brasilia	P	I	250+	Leveled Readers	Houghton Mifflin Harcourt
Brave As	P	RF	250+	Orbit Chapter Books	Pacific Learning
Brave Baby, The	I	TL	321	Big Cat	Pacific Learning
Brave Ben	K	RF	162	Literacy 2000	Rigby
Brave Bessie: Queen of the Skies	S	HF	1889	Reading Street	Pearson
Brave Dave and the Dragons	C	F	46	Reed, Janet	Scholastic
Brave Father Mouse	E	RF	92	PM Story Books	Rigby
Brave Irene	S	F	250+	Steig, William	Farrar, Straus and Giroux
Brave Little Monster	M	F	250+	Baker, Ken	Scholastic
Brave Little Mouse	I	F	249	Story Steps	Rigby
Brave Little Snail	D	RF	110	Rigby Flying Colors	Rigby
Brave Little Tailor, The	J	TL	250+	PM Tales and Plays Turquoise	Rigby
Brave Little Tailor, The: A German Folktale	O	TL	660	Leveled Readers	Houghton Mifflin Harcourt
Brave Maddie Egg	M	RF	250+	Standiford, Natalie	Random House
Brave Past, A	V	I	1931	Leveled Readers	Houghton Mifflin Harcourt
Brave Pilot, A	U	B	660	Vocabulary Readers	Houghton Mifflin Harcourt
Brave Settlers in a Strange Land	Q	I	1013	Reading Street	Pearson
Brave Taco	E	F	129	Leveled Literacy Intervention/Green System	Heinemann
Brave Thing to Do, A	K	RF	623	Gear Up!	Wright Group/McGraw Hill
Brave Triceratops	G	F	178	PM Story Books	Rigby

TITLE	LEVEL	GENRE	WORD COUNT	AUTHOR / SERIES	PUBLISHER / DISTRIBUTOR
Bravest Dog Ever, The: The True Story of Balto	L	I	250+	Standiford, Natalie	Random House
Bravo Amelia Bedelia!	L	F	250+	Parish, Herman	Avon
Brazil	P	I	250+	A True Book	Children's Press
Brazil	O	I	250+	Countries of the World	Red Brick Learning
Brazil	Q	I	250+	First Reports: Countries	Compass Point Books
Brazil: A Question and Answer Book	P	I	250+	Questions and Answers: Countries	Capstone Press
Bread	D	RF	69	Sunshine	Wright Group/McGraw Hill
Bread and Jam for Frances	K	F	250+	Hoban, Russell	Scholastic
Bread and Roses: How an Orphan Girl Helped American Women Win the Vote	R	HF	250+	Navigators Fiction Series	Benchmark Education
Bread for Life	O	I	250+	Orbit Chapter Books	Pacific Learning
Bread for the Ducks	D	RF	109	PM Plus Story Books	Rigby
Bread Song	Q	RF	250+	Bookshop	Mondo
Bread, Bread, Bread	F	I	95	Morris, Ann	Scholastic
Breadwinner, The	Z	RF	250+	Ellis, Deborah	Groundwood Books
Break with Charity, A: A Story About the Salem Witch Trials	X	HF	250+	Rinaldi, Ann	Harcourt Trade
Breakdancing	S	I	250+	Dance	Capstone Press
Breakfast	C	RF	35	Foundations	Wright Group/McGraw Hill
Breakfast	C	I	37	Little Books for Early Readers	University of Maine
Breakfast	D	RF	23	Voyages	SRA/McGraw Hill
Breakfast Around the World	S	I	1894	Leveled Readers Social Studies	Houghton Mifflin Harcourt
Breakfast Around the World	N	I	846	Time for Kids	Teacher Created Materials Publishing
Breakfast Around the World	J	I	101	Twig	Wright Group/McGraw Hill
Breakfast at the Farm	B	RF	56	Bookshop	Mondo
*Breakfast Bird and Other Animal Stories	M	F	250+	Bookshop	Mondo
Breakfast for Bears	I	F	477	Leveled Readers	Houghton Mifflin Harcourt
Breakfast for Pickles	C	RF	62	Pickles the Dog Series	Pioneer Valley
Breakfast in Bed	G	F	36	Tadpoles	Rigby
Breakfast in Bed	C	RF	10	Voyages	SRA/McGraw Hill
Breakfast in the Bathtub	D	RF	94	InfoTrek	ETA Cuisenaire
Breakfast in the Rainforest: A Visit with Mountain Gorillas	U	I	250+	Sobol, Richard	Candlewick Press
Breakfast on the Farm	D	I	73	Storyteller Nonfiction	Wright Group/McGraw Hill
Breakfast Time	G	F	250+	Bookshop	Mondo
Breakfast with John	C	RF	29	Books for Young Learners	Richard C. Owen
Breaking News	U	I	250+	News Extra	Richard C. Owen
Breath of Air, A	T	I	1356	Leveled Readers Science	Houghton Mifflin Harcourt
Breath of Fresh Air, A	P	RF	961	Leveled Readers	Houghton Mifflin Harcourt
Breath of the Dragon	P	RF	250+	Giles, Gail	Bantam
Breathe In, Breathe Out: Learning About Your Lungs	M	I	250+	Amazing Body	Picture Window Books
Breathing	L	I	106	Bookshop	Mondo
Breathing Under Water	C	I	39	Sunshine	Wright Group/McGraw Hill
Breathing Underwater	Z+	RF	250+	Flinn, Alex	HarperCollins
Breathing Underwater: Adventures in Chemistry	Y	RF	1752	Leveled Readers Science	Houghton Mifflin Harcourt
Bremen Town Band	J	TL	250+	Reading Safari	Mondo
Bremen Town Musicians	K	TL	567	Sun Sprouts	ETA Cuisenaire
Bremen-Town Musicians, The	K	TL	741	Gross, Ruth Belov	Scholastic
Brendan the Navigator: A History Mystery about the Discovery of America	R	I	250+	Fritz, Jean	Penguin Group
Brenda's Birthday	A	RF	18	Story Box	Wright Group/McGraw Hill

Organized Alphabetically by Title
Storable Database at www.fountasandpinnellleveledbooks.com

* Collection of short stories
\# Graphic text

TITLE	LEVEL	GENRE	WORD COUNT	AUTHOR / SERIES	PUBLISHER / DISTRIBUTOR
Brenda's Private Swing	K	RF	250+	Chardiet, Bernice; Maccarone, Grace	Scholastic
Brer Rabbit at the Well	I	TL	268	Leveled Readers	Houghton Mifflin Harcourt
Brer Rabbit at the Well	I	TL	268	Leveled Readers/CA	Houghton Mifflin Harcourt
Brer Rabbit at the Well	I	TL	268	Leveled Readers/TX	Houghton Mifflin Harcourt
Brett Favre	T	B	250+	Sports Heroes	Red Brick Learning
Brett Got Wet	C	RF	50	Gear Up!	Wright Group/McGraw Hill
Brewster Rooster	J	F	250+	Underwood, Barbara J.	Kaeden Books
Brian Fixit	H	RF	317	Springboard	Wright Group/McGraw Hill
Brian's Brilliant Career	P	RF	250+	Literacy 2000	Rigby
Brian's Song	Z	I	250+	Blinn, William	Bantam
Brian's Winter	R	RF	250+	Paulsen, Gary	Bantam
Bricks, Wood, and Stones	D	I	54	Windows on Literacy	National Geographic
Bridge Building: Bridge Designs and How They Work	V	I	250+	High Five Reading	Red Brick Learning
Bridge Is Too Small, The	H	RF	250+	Reading Safari	Mondo
Bridge of Grass, A	N	RF	715	Gear Up!	Wright Group/ McGraw Hill
Bridge to Terabithia	T	RF	250+	Paterson, Katherine	HarperTrophy
Bridge, The	M	I	250+	Cambridge Reading	Pearson Learning Group
Bridge, The	J	F	250+	Reading Safari	Mondo
Bridge, The	B	F	32	Story Box	Wright Group/McGraw Hill
Bridges	D	I	49	Canizares, Susan; Moreton, Daniel	Scholastic
Bridges	M	I	250+	Explorations	Eleanor Curtain Publishing
Bridges	M	I	250+	Explorations	Okapi Educational Materials
Bridges	Q	I	730	Gear Up!	Wright Group/ McGraw Hill
Bridges	R	I	250+	InfoTrek	ETA Cuisenaire
Bridges	E	I	137	Sails	Rigby
Bridges	D	RF	62	Seedlings	Continental Press
Bridges	N	I	250+	Wildcats	Wright Group/McGraw Hill
Bridges - Across the Gap	R	I	250+	Wonder World	Wright Group/McGraw Hill
Bridging Beyond	X	F	250+	Duble, Kathleen Benner	Penguin Group
Bridging the Gap	Q	I	250+	Orbit Chapter Books	Pacific Learning
Bridle the Wind	Y	RF	250+	Aiken, Joan	Harcourt
Bright Idea, A	X	I	250+	iOpeners	Pearson Learning Group
Bright Ideas	Q	I	250+	Explorers	Wright Group/McGraw Hill
Bright Ideas About Light	R	I	250+	In Step Readers	Rigby
Bright Lights and Shadowy Shapes	L	I	250+	Spyglass Books	Compass Point Books
Bright Paddles	P	HF	250+	Downi, Mary Alice	Fitzhenry & Whiteside
Bright Shadow	T	F	250+	Avi	Aladdin
Brighty of the Grand Canyon	R	RF	250+	Henry, Marguerite	Aladdin
Brigid Beware	L	RF	250+	Leverich, Kathleen	Random House
Brigid Bewitched	L	RF	250+	Leverich, Kathleen	Random House
Brigid the Bad	L	RF	250+	Leverich, Kathleen	Random House
Brilliant Blunders	T	I	250+	Connectors	Pacific Learning
Brilliant Bugologist, The	N	RF	250+	Orbit Chapter Books	Pacific Learning
Brilliant Mind, A	W	B	250+	WorldScapes	ETA Cuisenaire
Bring Me Your Horses	J	I	250+	Phonics and Friends	Hampton-Brown
Bringing the Rain to Kapiti Plain	J	TL	739	Aardema, Verna	Scholastic
Bringing the Sea Back Home	L	F	250+	Literacy 2000	Rigby
Bringing Up Baby Chimp	N	I	495	Independent Readers Science	Houghton Mifflin Harcourt
Brinker's Isle	T	RF	2475	Leveled Readers	Houghton Mifflin Harcourt
Bristol Motor Speedway	S	I	250+	NASCAR Racing	Capstone Press
Brith the Terrible	M	F	250+	Literacy 2000	Rigby

* Collection of short stories
# Graphic text

TITLE	LEVEL	GENRE	WORD COUNT	AUTHOR / SERIES	PUBLISHER / DISTRIBUTOR
British Redcoats	T	I	250+	Warriors of History	Capstone Press
Broad Stripes and Bright Stars	R	I	250+	Explorer Books-Pathfinder	National Geographic
Broad Stripes and Bright Stars	P	I	250+	Explorer Books-Pioneer	National Geographic
Broccoli Tapes, The	S	RF	250+	Slepian, Jan	Scholastic
Broken Blade, The	T	HF	250+	Durbin, William	Yearling
Broken Bones	J	I	250+	Sunshine	Wright Group/McGraw Hill
Broken Bridge, The	Z	RF	250+	Pullman, Philip	Alfred A. Knopf
Broken Clock, The	E	RF	174	Leveled Literacy Intervention/ Blue System	Heinemann
Broken Flower Pot, The	G	RF	203	PM Plus Story Books	Rigby
Broken Plate, The	I	RF	198	Foundations	Wright Group/McGraw Hill
Broken Window	G	RF	136	New Way Blue	Steck-Vaughn
*Broken Window and Other Cases, The	O	RF	250+	Simon, Seymour	Avon
Bronco Charlie and the Pony Express	U	B	1824	Leveled Readers	Houghton Mifflin Harcourt
Bronco Charlie and the Pony Express	M	HF	1867	On My Own History	Lerner Publications
Bronto's New House	H	F	342	Springboard	Wright Group/McGraw Hill
Brontosaurus, Beaver	I	F	130	Springboard	Wright Group/McGraw Hill
Bronx Masquerade	Z+	RF	250+	Grimes, Nikki	Dial Books
Bronze Bow, The	U	HF	250+	Speare, Elizabeth George	Houghton Mifflin Harcourt
Brooke and Her Crayons	H	RF	283	Leveled Readers	Houghton Mifflin Harcourt
Brookfield Days	N	HF	250+	Wilder, Laura Ingalls	HarperTrophy
Brooklyn Bridge, The	Q	I	1294	Vocabulary Readers	Houghton Mifflin Harcourt
Brooklyn Bridge, The	Q	I	1294	Vocabulary Readers/CA	Houghton Mifflin Harcourt
Brooklyn Bridge, The: Eighth Wonder of the World	Z	I	3473	Leveled Readers	Houghton Mifflin Harcourt
Brooklyn Dodgers, The	J	I	323	Vocabulary Readers	Houghton Mifflin Harcourt
Brooklyn Dodgers, The	J	I	323	Vocabulary Readers/CA	Houghton Mifflin Harcourt
Brooklyn Dodgers, The	J	I	323	Vocabulary Readers/TX	Houghton Mifflin Harcourt
Brother Love	E	RF	116	Rigby Rocket	Rigby
Brother to Shadows	Z	SF	250+	Norton, Andre	Avon
Brothers	F	I	63	Families	Capstone Press
Brothers	B	I	36	Pebble Books	Capstone Press
Brothers	E	I	65	Talk About Books	Pearson Learning Group
Brothers Are Forever	L	RF	536	Leveled Readers	Houghton Mifflin Harcourt
Brothers Grimm, The	X	B	2435	Leveled Readers	Houghton Mifflin Harcourt
Brothers Grimm, The	X	B	2435	Leveled Readers/CA	Houghton Mifflin Harcourt
Brothers in Arms	Z	RF	250+	Langan, Paul & Alirez, Ben	Townsend Press
Brown	B	I	26	Colors	Lerner Publications
Brown Bear Figures it Out!	K	F	250+	Phonics and Friends	Hampton-Brown
Brown Bear Gets in Shape	K	F	250+	I Am Reading	Kingfisher
Brown Bear, Brown Bear	C	F	185	Martin, Bill	Henry Holt & Co.
Brown Bears	O	I	1363	Early Bird Nature Books	Lerner Publications
Brown Bears	E	I	45	Pebble Books	Capstone Press
Brown Bears	K	I	250+	PM Animal Facts: Turquoise	Rigby
Brown Cow Frowned, The	F	F	102	Seedlings	Continental Press
Brown Mouse Gets Some Corn	F	F	158	PM Plus Story Books	Rigby
Brown Mouse Plays a Trick	F	F	155	PM Plus Story Books	Rigby
Brown Sunshine of Sawdust Valley	O	RF	250+	Henry, Marguerite	Aladdin
Brown: Seeing Brown All Around Us	L	I	250+	Colors	Capstone Press
Brownie	C	RF	38	Hooker, Karen	Continental Press
Brownie and Spottie	I	F	250+	Reading Safari	Mondo
Brownie Math	I	I	206	Rosen Real Readers	Rosen Publishing Group
Bruises	Z	RF	250+	De Vries, Anke	Bantam
Bruno's Birthday	E	RF	32	Literacy 2000	Rigby

* Collection of short stories
# Graphic text

TITLE	LEVEL	GENRE	WORD COUNT	AUTHOR / SERIES	PUBLISHER / DISTRIBUTOR
Brushes	E	I	109	Rigby Literacy	Rigby
Brushing Teeth	G	I	147	Healthy Teeth	Capstone Press
Brushing Well	D	I	42	Dental Health	Capstone Press
Brutus Learns to Fetch	F	RF	155	Little Red Readers	Sundance
Bryce Canyon National Park	O	I	250+	A True Book	Children's Press
Bubble Booth, The	I	RF	152	InfoTrek	ETA Cuisenaire
Bubble Gum	B	RF	21	Carousel Readers	Pearson Learning Group
Bubble Gum	H	RF	66	City Kids	Rigby
Bubble Gum Can Be Trouble	E	RF	147	Visions	Wright Group/McGraw Hill
Bubble Gum Contest, The	J	F	737	Spaceboy	Literacy Footprints
Bubbles	M	I	250+	Cambridge Reading	Pearson Learning Group
Bubbles	C	I	34	Discovery Links	Newbridge
Bubbles	B	I	48	Leveled Literacy Intervention/ Green System	Heinemann
Bubbles	I	RF	236	Leveled Readers Science	Houghton Mifflin Harcourt
Bubbles	C	RF	33	Literacy 2000	Rigby
Bubbles	C	RF	31	Sunshine	Wright Group/McGraw Hill
Bubbles Everywhere	C	I	41	Twig	Wright Group/McGraw Hill
Bubbles in the Sky	C	RF	57	PM Stars	Rigby
Bubbles on the Bus	I	RF	250+	The Story Basket	Wright Group/McGraw Hill
Bubbling Crocodile	K	F	250+	Pacific Literacy	Pacific Learning
Buck Leonard, Baseball Hero	Q	B	250+	Leveled Readers Language Support	Houghton Mifflin Harcourt
Buck Leonard, Baseball's Greatest Gentleman	R	B	1419	Leveled Readers	Houghton Mifflin Harcourt
Buck Stops Here, The	T	I	250+	Provensen, Alice	Harcourt Brace
Buckle My Shoe	C	RF	31	Sunshine	Wright Group/McGraw Hill
Buck's Way	L	F	359	Reading Street	Pearson
Bud on the Beach	E	RF	61	Rigby Star	Rigby
Bud the Mud Bug	D	F	72	Reading Street	Pearson
Bud, Not Buddy	U	RF	250+	Curtis, Christopher Paul	Random House
Buddha Boy	X	RF	250+	Koja, Kathe	Puffin/Penguin
Buddha's Diamonds, The	T	RF	250+	Marsden, Carolyn & Niem, Thay Phap	Candlewick Press
Buddies	F	F	177	Instant Readers	Harcourt School Publishers
Buddy	Q	RF	1522	Leveled Readers	Houghton Mifflin Harcourt
Buddy: The Puppy Place	N	RF	250+	Miles, Ellen	Scholastic
Buddy: The First Seeing Eye Dog	M	I	250+	Moore, Eva	Scholastic
Buddy's Bath	E	RF	131	Literacy by Design	Rigby
Budgie's Dream	J	F	250+	Story Starter	Wright Group/McGraw Hill
Buds and Blossoms: A Book About Flowers	M	I	250+	Growing Things	Picture Window Books
Buffalo Before Breakfast	M	F	250+	Osborne, Mary Pope	Random House
Buffalo Bill and the Pony Express	K	B	250+	Coerr, Eleanor	HarperTrophy
Buffalo Bill's Wild West Show	V	B	1750	Leveled Readers	Houghton Mifflin Harcourt
Buffalo Bills, The	S	I	250+	Team Spirit	Norwood House Press
Buffalo Gal	U	RF	250+	Wallace, Bill	Simon & Schuster
Buffalo Hunt	W	I	250+	Freedman, Russell	Holiday House
Buffalo Hunt	S	HF	2489	Leveled Readers	Houghton Mifflin Harcourt
Buffalo Hunt	S	HF	2489	Leveled Readers/CA	Houghton Mifflin Harcourt
Buffalo Hunt	S	HF	2489	Leveled Readers/TX	Houghton Mifflin Harcourt
Buffalo Soldiers and the Western Frontier	R	I	250+	On Deck	Rigby
Buffalo Woman	N	TL	250+	Goble, Paul	Aladdin
Buffalo, The	M	I	250+	Crewe, Sabrina	Steck-Vaughn
Buffalo's Homework	N	F	250+	Springboard	Wright Group/McGraw Hill
Buffy	B	F	28	Literacy 2000	Rigby

* Collection of short stories
# Graphic text

Storable Database at www.fountasandpinnellleveledbooks.com

TITLE	LEVEL	GENRE	WORD COUNT	AUTHOR / SERIES	PUBLISHER / DISTRIBUTOR
Buffy's Tricks	G	RF	97	Literacy 2000	Rigby
Bug Bus, The	K	F	250+	Sunshine	Wright Group/McGraw Hill
Bug Business	T	I	250+	Power Up!	Steck-Vaughn
Bug Off!	L	F	250+	Dussling, Jennifer	Grossett & Dunlap
Bug Parts	A	RF	17	Leveled Readers	Houghton Mifflin Harcourt
Bug Parts	A	RF	17	Leveled Readers/CA	Houghton Mifflin Harcourt
Bug Party	F	I	131	Twig	Wright Group/McGraw Hill
Bug School, The	C	F	66	Reading Safari	Mondo
Bug Watching	B	I	25	Twig	Wright Group/McGraw Hill
Bug, a Bear, and a Boy, A	F	F	250+	McPhail, David	Scholastic
Buggy Riddles	I	F	221	Little Books	Sadlier-Oxford
Bug-head and Me	M	RF	250+	Literacy By Design	Rigby
Bug-head and Me	M	RF	250+	Rigby Literacy	Rigby
Bugliest Bug, The	N	F	250+	Shields, Carol Diggory	Candlewick Press
Bugs	P	I	250+	Animals Are Amazing	Carus Publishing
Bugs	A	I	32	Handprints A	Educators Publishing Service
Bugs	O	I	250+	Parker, Nancy Winslow; Wright, Joan Richards	Mulberry Books
Bugs and Other Insects	O	I	250+	Kalman, Bobbie	Crabtree
*Bugs And Other Stories	F	RF	250+	Story Steps	Rigby
Bugs Are Insects	M	I	250+	Rockwell, Anne	Harper Collins
Bugs Beware!	T	I	250+	Literacy by Design	Rigby
Bugs Beware!	T	I	250+	On Our Way to English	Rigby
Bugs for Breakfast	F	F	158	PM Plus Story Books	Rigby
Bugs for Dinner	A	I	35	Leveled Readers	Houghton Mifflin Harcourt
Bugs for Dinner	A	I	35	Leveled Readers/CA	Houghton Mifflin Harcourt
Bugs for Lunch	J	RF	193	Facklam, Margery	Charlesbridge
Bugs in My Backyard	D	I	55	Bonnell, Kris	Reading Reading Books
Bugs in the Garden	B	RF	59	Literacy by Design	Rigby
Bugs on the Menu	M	I	250+	Sails	Rigby
Bugs!	R	I	250+	Boldprint	Steck-Vaughn
Bugs!	L	I	250+	Phonics and Friends	Hampton-Brown
Bugs!	C	F	32	Rookie Readers	Children's Press
Bugs!	A	I	20	Vocabulary Readers	Houghton Mifflin Harcourt
Bugs!	A	I	20	Vocabulary Readers/CA	Houghton Mifflin Harcourt
Bugs! Bugs! Bugs!	M	I	250+	DK Readers	DK Publishing
BugZ	S	F	250+	Power Up!	Steck-Vaughn
Build It Strong!	M	I	250+	First Science	Children's Press
Build Your Own Weather Station	I	I	250	Leveled Readers Science	Houghton Mifflin Harcourt
Build Your Own Web Site	X	I	250+	iOpeners	Pearson Learning Group
Build, Build, Build	M	I	470	Sunshine	Wright Group/McGraw Hill
Builder's Day, A	J	I	417	Springboard	Wright Group/McGraw Hill
Building	V	I	250+	Eyewitness Books	DK Publishing
Building a Case	N	I	379	Vocabulary Readers	Houghton Mifflin Harcourt
Building a Castle	L	I	250+	Early Connections	Benchmark Education
Building a Doghouse	M	I	250+	On Our Way to English	Rigby
Building a Dream	V	HF	250+	Reading Expeditions	National Geographic
Building a Dream: Mary Bethune's School	R	B	250+	Kelso, Richard	Steck-Vaughn
Building a House	H	I	83	Barton, Byron	Morrow
Building a House	G	I	197	PM Plus Nonfiction	Rigby
Building a Nest	N	I	512	Springboard	Wright Group/ McGraw Hill
Building a Road	I	I	106	Construction Zone	Capstone Press
Building a Skyscraper	J	I	110	Construction Zone	Capstone Press

* Collection of short stories
# Graphic text

TITLE	LEVEL	GENRE	WORD COUNT	AUTHOR / SERIES	PUBLISHER / DISTRIBUTOR
Building an Ice Hotel	U	I	250+	iOpeners	Pearson Learning Group
Building Beavers	K	I	407	Pull Ahead Books	Lerner Publications
Building Blocks	T	I	250+	WorldScapes	ETA Cuisenaire
Building Bridges	V	I	250+	iOpeners	Pearson Learning Group
Building Bridges	S	I	250+	Navigators Science Series	Benchmark Education
Building High	O	I	1510	Big Cat	Pacific Learning
Building Homes, Building Hope	O	I	250+	Sunshine	Wright Group/McGraw Hill
Building Lady Liberty	K	I	450	Leveled Readers Social Studies	Houghton Mifflin Harcourt
Building Shapes	G	I	30	Canizares, Susan; Berger, Samantha	Scholastic
Building Strong Bridges	M	I	250+	Twig	Wright Group/McGraw Hill
Building the Capital City	V	I	250+	Cornerstones of Freedom	Children's Press
Building the Hoover Dam	W	I	1878	Leveled Readers Science	Houghton Mifflin Harcourt
Building the Railroad	K	I	250+	Twig	Wright Group/McGraw Hill
Building Things	F	I	24	Sunshine	Wright Group/McGraw Hill
Building with Blocks	LB	RF	20	Sunshine	Wright Group/McGraw Hill
Buildings	C	I	61	Chessen, Betsey; Chanko, Pamela	Scholastic
Buildings	Q	I	250+	InfoTrek	ETA Cuisenaire
Buildings	F	I	85	Leveled Readers Science	Houghton Mifflin Harcourt
Buildings	G	I	327	Sails	Rigby
Buildings of Distinction: Exploring State Capitols	R	I	250+	Explore More	Wright Group/McGraw Hill
Buildings on My Street	F	RF	109	Foundations	Wright Group/McGraw Hill
Buildings That Go Up, Up, Up	I	I	133	Shutterbug Books	Steck-Vaughn
Built for Speed Aircraft	T	I	250+	Graham, Ian	Steck-Vaughn
Built Like That	S	I	250+	PM Plus Nonfiction	Rigby
Built to Last	U	I	250+	InfoQuest	Rigby
Built to Last: Famous Structures of the World	U	I	250+	Explore More	Wright Group/McGraw Hill
Bull Harris and the Purple Ooze	M	RF	250+	SupaDoopers	Sundance
Bull in a China Shop, A	K	F	250+	Literacy 2000	Rigby
Bull Rider	T	RF	250+	Orca Soundings	Orca Book Publishers
Bull Riding	N	RF	250+	Boyz Rule!	Mondo
Bull Run	Y	HF	250+	Fleischman, Paul	HarperCollins
Bull Shark	J	I	129	Sharks	Capstone Press
Bulldog George	K	RF	250+	Voyages	SRA/McGraw Hill
Bulldogs	R	I	250+	All About Dogs	Capstone Press
Bulldogs	I	I	133	Dogs	Capstone Press
Bulldozer, The	D	I	48	Sunshine	Wright Group/McGraw Hill
Bulldozers	F	I	94	Mighty Machines	Capstone Press
Bullies	V	I	250+	10 Things You Need to Know About	Capstone Press
Bull's Eye	Z+	RF	250+	Orca Soundings	Orca Book Publishers
Bull's-eye!	F	RF	87	Oxford Reading Tree	Oxford University Press
Bully Bear	F	F	139	Rigby Literacy	Rigby
Bully Bear	F	F	144	Rigby Star	Rigby
Bully Book, The: How to Deal with the Mean Crowd	S	I	250+	Power Up!	Steck-Vaughn
Bully Cat	I	F	324	Sails	Rigby
Bully Cat and Fat Cat	J	F	400	Sails	Rigby
Bully Cat and the Birds	G	F	158	Sails	Rigby
Bully Cat's Mistake	F	F	190	Sails	Rigby
Bully Dinosaur	E	F	118	Little Dinosaur	Literacy Footprints
Bully for You, Teddy Roosevelt!	X	B	250+	Fritz, Jean	Penguin Group

TITLE	LEVEL	GENRE	WORD COUNT	AUTHOR / SERIES	PUBLISHER / DISTRIBUTOR
Bully of Barkham Street	R	RF	250+	Stolz, Mary	HarperTrophy
Bully, The	Y	RF	250+	Langan, Paul	Townsend Press
Bully, The	L	RF	250+	PM Story Books	Rigby
Bumble Bear	F	F	89	Start to Read	School Zone
Bumble Bee	D	I	53	Pacific Literacy	Pacific Learning
Bumble Bee, The	E	RF	55	Szymanek, Susie	Kaeden Books
Bumble Bees	I	I	123	Bugs, Bugs, Bugs	Capstone Press
Bumble Bees	E	I	56	Insects	Capstone Press
Bumblebee Queen, The	M	I	250+	Sayre, April Pulley	Charlesbridge
Bumblebees	P	I	1958	Early Bird Nature Books	Lerner Publishing
Bump	F	I	217	Sun Sprouts	ETA Cuisenaire
Bump!	C	F	12	KinderReaders	Rigby
Bump, Bump, Bump	D	RF	51	Cat on the Mat	Oxford University Press
Bumper Cars, The	C	RF	94	PM Extensions-Red	Rigby
Bumper Cars, The	B	RF	36	Sails	Rigby
Bumpity, Bumpity, Bump	F	RF	62	Parker, Carol	Continental Press
Bumps in the Night	L	F	250+	Allard, Harry	Bantam
Bumpy Snowman, The	H	RF	334	Leveled Readers	Houghton Mifflin Harcourt
Bumpy Snowman, The	H	RF	334	Leveled Readers/CA	Houghton Mifflin Harcourt
Bumpy Snowman, The	H	RF	334	Leveled Readers/TX	Houghton Mifflin Harcourt
Bumpy the Frog	K	F	250+	Beers, Steven	Kaeden Books
Bun, The	I	TL	421	Storyteller-Moon Rising	Wright Group/McGraw Hill
Bundle Up!	B	RF	35	Science	Outside the Box
Bungee Hero	S	RF	4080	Bertagna, J.	Stone Arch Books
Bungy 70528	O	RF	250+	Belcher, Angie	Pacific Learning
Bunker's Cove	S	I	1125	Leveled Readers	Houghton Mifflin Harcourt
Bunnicula	Q	F	250+	Howe, James	Avon
Bunnicula Strikes Again!	Q	F	250+	Howe, James	Simon & Schuster
Bunnies in the Bathroom	Q	RF	250+	Baglio, Ben M.	Scholastic
Bunny and the Monster	F	F	161	Leveled Literacy Intervention/ Green System	Heinemann
Bunny Hop, The	I	F	250+	Slater, Teddy	Scholastic
Bunny Magic	I	RF	176	Books for Young Learners	Richard C. Owen
Bunny Opposites	LB	F	14	Pair-It Books	Steck-Vaughn
Bunny Runs Away	K	F	250+	Chardiet, Bernice; Maccarone, Grace	Scholastic
Bunny to Love, A	I	RF	444	Adams, Lorraine; Bruvold, Lynn	Eagle Crest Books
Bunny, Bunny	D	F	40	My First Reader	Grolier Press
Bunny's Recess	A	I	35	Little Books for Early Readers	University of Maine
Bunrakkit	K	F	250+	Sunshine	Wright Group/McGraw Hill
Burger Time	L	I	250+	Voyages	SRA/McGraw Hill
Burglar Next Door, The	I	RF	599	Rigby Flying Colors	Rigby
Burglars' Ball, The	N	F	250+	Wonder World	Wright Group/McGraw Hill
Buried Eye, The	M	F	250+	Woodland Mysteries	Wright Group/McGraw Hill
Buried in Ice: The Mystery of a Lost Arctic Expedition	U	I	250+	Beattie, Owen & Geiger, John	Scholastic
Buried Treasure	O	I	250+	Rigby Focus	Rigby
Buried Treasure	N	RF	1480	Take Two Books	Wright Group/McGraw Hill
Burly Reid	S	RF	250+	Sails	Rigby
Burn	Z+	RF	250+	Phillips, Suzanne	Little, Brown & Co.
Burning Questions of Bingo Brown, The	U	RF	250+	Byars, Betsy	Puffin/Penguin
Burning Secrets	S	F	250+	Brezenoff, Steve	Stone Arch Books
Burning Up: Losing Our Ozone Layer	R	I	250+	On Deck	Rigby
Burps, Boogers, and Bad Breath	K	I	246	Spyglass Books	Compass Point Books

* Collection of short stories
# Graphic text

TITLE	LEVEL	GENRE	WORD COUNT	AUTHOR / SERIES	PUBLISHER / DISTRIBUTOR
Burrows	E	I	51	Storyteller-Setting Sun	Wright Group/McGraw Hill
Burrows, Tunnels, and Chambers	N	I	250+	Sails	Rigby
Bus Driver	C	I	26	Work People Do	Lerner Publishing
Bus Driver's Birthday, The	G	RF	234	Springboard	Wright Group/McGraw Hill
Bus Ride, The	C	RF	52	Gear Up!	Wright Group/McGraw Hill
Bus Ride, The	C	F	164	Little Celebrations	Pearson Learning Group
Bus Ride, The	C	F	175	Reading Unlimited	Pearson Learning Group
Bus Ride, The	F	RF	99	Storyteller-Setting Sun	Wright Group/McGraw Hill
Bus Stop, The	G	RF	110	Hellen, Nancy	Orchard Books
Bus, The	C	I	46	Twig	Wright Group/McGraw Hill
Buses	K	I	403	Pull Ahead Books	Lerner Publications
Bush Bunyip, The	J	F	250+	Bookshop	Mondo
Bush Tucker	M	I	250+	Sunshine	Wright Group/McGraw Hill
Bushfire in the Koala Reserve	K	RF	250+	PM Plus Story Books	Rigby
Bushwhacker, The: A Civil War Adventure	V	HF	250+	Garrity, Jennifer Johnson	Peachtree
Business Basics	U	I	250+	In Step Readers	Rigby
Business Sense	W	I	3237	Vocabulary Readers	Houghton Mifflin Harcourt
Business Sense	W	I	3237	Vocabulary Readers/CA	Houghton Mifflin Harcourt
Business Sense	W	I	3237	Vocabulary Readers/TX	Houghton Mifflin Harcourt
Buster	M	F	250+	Bookshop	Mondo
Buster	C	I	36	Twig	Wright Group/McGraw Hill
*Buster and Phoebe: The Great Bone Game	K	F	250+	Bechtold, Lisze	Houghton Mifflin Harcourt
Buster and the Dance Contest	J	F	586	Brown, Marc	Little, Brown & Co.
Buster and the Giant Pumpkin	J	F	498	Brown, Marc	Little, Brown & Co.
Buster and the Great Swamp	J	F	615	Brown, Marc	Little, Brown & Co.
Buster Baxter, Cat Saver	M	F	250+	Brown, Marc	Little, Brown & Co.
Buster Catches a Wave	J	F	417	Brown, Marc	Little, Brown & Co.
Buster Changes His Luck	J	F	250+	Brown, Marc	Little, Brown & Co.
Buster Climbs the Walls	K	F	1093	Brown, Marc	Little, Brown & Co.
Buster Hits the Trail	K	F	250+	Brown, Marc	Little, Brown & Co.
Buster Hunts for Dinosaurs	J	F	506	Brown, Marc	Little, Brown & Co.
Buster Makes the Grade	M	F	250+	Brown, Marc	Little, Brown & Co.
Buster McCluster	E	F	71	Wonder World	Wright Group/McGraw Hill
Buster McCluster has Chicken Pox	E	RF	77	Wonder World	Wright Group/McGraw Hill
Buster on the Farm	J	F	589	Brown, Marc	Little, Brown & Co.
Buster on the Town	J	F	250+	Brown, Marc	Little, Brown & Co.
Buster Plays Along	K	F	250+	Brown, Marc	Little, Brown & Co.
Buster the Balloon	E	F	70	Mathtales	Mimosa
*Buster: The Very Shy Dog	K	F	250+	Bechtold, Lisze	Houghton Mifflin Harcourt
Buster's Dino Dilemma	M	F	250+	Brown, Marc	Little, Brown & Co.
Buster's Sugartime	J	F	642	Brown, Marc	Little, Brown & Co.
Busy Animals at Night	D	I	183	Leveled Readers	Houghton Mifflin Harcourt
Busy Animals at Night	D	I	183	Leveled Readers/CA	Houghton Mifflin Harcourt
Busy Animals at Night	D	I	183	Leveled Readers/TX	Houghton Mifflin Harcourt
Busy Ants	L	I	392	Pull Ahead Books	Lerner Publications
Busy Ants and the Lazy Ants, The	J	F	375	InfoTrek	ETA Cuisenaire
Busy Baby	J	RF	250+	Sunshine	Wright Group/McGraw Hill
Busy Beaver, A	I	I	323	Leveled Readers	Houghton Mifflin Harcourt
Busy Beaver, A	I	I	323	Leveled Readers/CA	Houghton Mifflin Harcourt
Busy Beaver, A	I	I	323	Leveled Readers/TX	Houghton Mifflin Harcourt
Busy Beavers	K	RF	80	Dabcovich, Lydia	Scholastic
Busy Beavers	I	I	123	Reading Street	Pearson
Busy Beavers, The	I	RF	362	PM Story Books-Orange	Rigby
Busy Bees	K	F	1137	InfoTrek	ETA Cuisenaire

* Collection of short stories
# Graphic text

TITLE	LEVEL	GENRE	WORD COUNT	AUTHOR / SERIES	PUBLISHER / DISTRIBUTOR
Busy Bees	L	I	417	Leveled Readers	Houghton Mifflin Harcourt
Busy Bees	M	I	514	Leveled Readers	Houghton Mifflin Harcourt
Busy Bees	L	I	417	Leveled Readers/CA	Houghton Mifflin Harcourt
Busy Bees	L	I	417	Leveled Readers/TX	Houghton Mifflin Harcourt
Busy Bees	K	I	177	Rosen Real Readers	Rosen Publishing Group
Busy Bees	LB	RF	12	Voyages	SRA/McGraw Hill
Busy Bird	LB	F	14	Pacific Literacy	Pacific Learning
Busy Body Book, The	O	I	250+	Rockwell, Lizzy	Scholastic
Busy Buzzers: Bees in Your Backyard	M	I	250+	Backyard Bugs	Picture Window Books
Busy Dad	A	RF	24	Mom and Dad Series	Pioneer Valley
Busy Fingers	H	RF	87	Bowie, C.W.	Charlesbridge
Busy Guy, A	K	RF	72	Rookie Readers	Children's Press
Busy Mosquito, The	C	F	112	Foundations	Wright Group/McGraw Hill
Busy People	C	RF	40	Little Celebrations	Pearson Learning Group
Busy Street	E	RF	67	Tadpoles	Rigby
Busy Toes	LB	RF	69	Bowie, C.W.	Charlesbridge
Busy Week, A	D	RF	49	Pair-It Books	Steck-Vaughn
Busy, Lively, Sleepy, and Quiet Pond, The	J	I	416	Reading Street	Pearson
*Busybody Nora	N	RF	250+	Hurwitz, Johanna	Penguin Group
But Granny Did!	D	RF	58	Voyages	SRA/McGraw Hill
But I Knew Better	H	RF	242	Home Connection Collection	Rigby
But I Want It!	J	RF	250+	On Our Way to English	Rigby
But I'll Be Back Again	V	B	250+	Rylant, Cynthia	Beech Tree Books
Butch, the Outdoor Cat	E	RF	65	Carousel Readers	Pearson Learning Group
Buttercup Moon	F	RF	61	Book Bank	Wright Group/McGraw Hill
Butterflies	I	I	94	Bugs, Bugs, Bugs	Capstone Press
Butterflies	O	I	250+	Holmes, Kevin J.	Red Brick Learning
Butterflies	E	I	47	Insects	Capstone Press
Butterflies	C	I	16	Instant Readers	Harcourt School Publishers
Butterflies	F	I	101	Life Cycles	Lerner Publications
Butterflies	O	I	250+	Nature's Friends	Compass Point Books
Butterflies	I	I	250+	Neye, Emily	Grosset & Dunlap
Butterflies	K	I	213	Nonfiction Set 7	Literacy Footprints
Butterflies	L	I	416	Reading Street	Pearson
Butterflies	E	I	79	Sails	Rigby
Butterflies	F	I	168	Vocabulary Readers	Houghton Mifflin Harcourt
Butterflies	F	I	168	Vocabulary Readers/CA	Houghton Mifflin Harcourt
Butterflies	F	I	168	Vocabulary Readers/TX	Houghton Mifflin Harcourt
Butterflies	N	I	250+	World of Insects	Capstone Press
Butterflies & Caterpillars	N	I	250+	Berger, Melvin & Gilda	Scholastic
Butterflies and Moths	L	I	250+	Early Connections	Benchmark Education
Butterflies and Moths	N	I	250+	Kalman, Bobbie	Crabtree
Butterflies in My Garden	G	RF	177	Bookshop	Mondo
Butterflies of the Sea	L	I	250+	Marine Life for Young Readers	Pearson Learning Group
Butterflies!	O	I	725	Leveled Readers	Houghton Mifflin Harcourt
Butterfly	G	I	84	Joy Starters	Pearson Learning Group
Butterfly and Me, The	F	RF	41	Reading Links	Steck-Vaughn
Butterfly and Moth	W	I	250+	Eyewitness Books	DK Publishing
Butterfly Colors	F	I	52	Pebble Books	Capstone Press
Butterfly Day	K	RF	250+	Pacific Literacy	Pacific Learning
Butterfly Eggs	F	I	57	Pebble Books	Capstone Press
Butterfly Farm Burglar, The	M	RF	250+	Woodland Mysteries	Wright Group/McGraw Hill
Butterfly House, The	D	RF	113	Rigby Flying Colors	Rigby
Butterfly Net, The	I	I	141	Storyteller	Wright Group/McGraw Hill

* Collection of short stories
# Graphic text

TITLE	LEVEL	GENRE	WORD COUNT	AUTHOR / SERIES	PUBLISHER / DISTRIBUTOR
Butterfly Pyramid, The	N	TL	250+	Story Vines	Wright Group/McGraw Hill
Butterfly Quilt, The	J	RF	313	Reading Street	Pearson
Butterfly Report, The	D	I	86	Rigby Flying Colors	Rigby
Butterfly Robber, The	I	F	293	Sails	Rigby
Butterfly Survival	K	I	329	Vocabulary Readers	Houghton Mifflin Harcourt
Butterfly Survival	K	I	329	Vocabulary Readers/CA	Houghton Mifflin Harcourt
Butterfly, The	M	I	250+	Crewe, Sabrina	Steck-Vaughn
Butterfly, The	C	I	21	Science	Outside the Box
Butterfly's Life, A	K	I	250+	Burke, Melissa Blackwell	Steck-Vaughn
Butterfly's Life, A	H	I	99	Time for Kids	Teacher Created Materials
Button Soup	K	RF	250+	Bank Street	Bantam
Buttons	C	RF	81	First Stories	Pacific Learning
Buttons Buttons	LB	I	26	Learn to Read	Creative Teaching Press
Buttons for General Washington	M	HF	250+	Roop, Peter & Connie	Carolrhoda Books
Buying and Building Airplanes	O	I	608	Gear Up!	Wright Group/ McGraw Hill
Buzby	J	F	250+	Hoban, Julia	HarperTrophy
Buzz and Bingo in the Fairy Tale Forest	N	F	774	Big Cat	Pacific Learning
Buzz and Bingo in the Starry Sky	N	SF	1271	Big Cat	Pacific Learning
Buzz Is Part of a Bee, A	E	RF	162	Rookie Readers	Children's Press
Buzz Said the Bee	G	F	62	Lewison, Wendy	Scholastic
Buzz, Buzz, Buzz	H	F	162	Barton, Byron	Macmillan
Buzzing Bee	LB	F	28	Rigby Star	Rigby
Buzzing Bees	LB	RF	69	Mathtales	Mimosa
Buzzing Bumblebees	K	I	440	Pull Ahead Books	Lerner Publications
Buzzing Flies	C	RF	45	Sunshine	Wright Group/McGraw Hill
Buzzing Rattlesnakes	K	I	323	Pull Ahead Books	Lerner Publications
Buzzy Fly	C	F	72	Gear Up!	Wright Group/McGraw Hill
Buzzzzzz Said the Bee	G	F	147	Lewison, Cheyette	Scholastic
By E-mail with Love	Q	RF	250+	Leveled Readers	Houghton Mifflin Harcourt
By Lakes and Rivers	N	I	250+	Animal Trackers	Crabtree
By Land, Sea and Air	N	I	250+	Explorations	Eleanor Curtain Publishing
By Land, Sea and Air	N	I	250+	Explorations	Okapi Educational Materials
By Myself or with My Friends	E	RF	200	Learn to Read	Creative Teaching Press
By Sea to America	S	HF	250+	Literacy By Design	Rigby
By the Great Horn Spoon!	V	HF	250+	Fleischman, Sid	Little, Brown & Co.
By the Sea	B	I	65	Leveled Readers	Houghton Mifflin Harcourt
By the Sea	B	I	65	Leveled Readers/CA	Houghton Mifflin Harcourt
By the Sea	I	I	251	PM Science Readers	Rigby
By the Seashore	N	I	250+	Animal Trackers	Crabtree
By the Shores of Silver Lake	Q	HF	250+	Wilder, Laura Ingalls	HarperTrophy
By the Stream	E	RF	73	Oxford Reading Tree	Oxford University Press
By the Tree	D	RF	75	Ready Readers	Pearson Learning Group
Bye, Bye, Bali Kai	U	RF	250+	Luger, Harriett	Harcourt Brace

* Collection of short stories
# Graphic text

TITLE	LEVEL	GENRE	WORD COUNT	AUTHOR / SERIES	PUBLISHER / DISTRIBUTOR
C and P Pies, The	I	RF	257	Take Two Books	Wright Group/McGraw Hill
C. W. Post: A Pioneer in His Time	X	B	2121	Leveled Readers	Houghton Mifflin Harcourt
C.A.L.I.F.O.R.N.I.A	P	I	859	Springboard	Wright Group/ McGraw-Hill
Cabbage Caterpillar	I	F	221	Sunshine	Wright Group/McGraw Hill
Cabbage Princess, The	K	TL	250+	Literacy 2000	Rigby
Cabin Faced West, The	R	HF	250+	Fritz, Jean	Bantam
Cabin in the Hills, The	J	RF	349	PM Collection	Rigby
Cabot: John Cabot and the Journey to North America	U	B	250+	Exploring the World	Compass Point Books
Cacti	J	I	305	Rigby Flying Colors	Rigby
Cactus Town	C	RF	43	Sunshine	Wright Group/McGraw Hill
Cactuses	K	I	237	Windows on Literacy	National Geographic
Caddie Woodlawn	R	HF	250+	Brink, Carol Ryrie	Bantam
Cafeteria Contest, The	O	RF	1286	Leveled Readers	Houghton Mifflin Harcourt
Cafeteria Contest, The	O	RF	1286	Leveled Readers/CA	Houghton Mifflin Harcourt
Cafeteria Contest, The	O	RF	1286	Leveled Readers/TX	Houghton Mifflin Harcourt
Cage, The	Z	B	250+	Sender, Ruth Minsky	Simon & Schuster
Cages	W	RF	250+	Kehret, Peg	Puffin Books
Cairo by Camel	U	I	250+	WorldScapes	ETA Cuisenaire
Cajun Country	S	I	2013	Leveled Readers Social Studies	Houghton Mifflin Harcourt
Cake for Mom, A	D	RF	63	Home Connection Collection	Rigby
Cake That Mack Ate, The	H	TL	189	Robart, Rose; Kovalski, Maryann	Little, Brown & Co.
Cake Walk	M	RF	250+	Books for Young Learners	Richard C. Owen
Cake, The	M	RF	250+	Read Alongs	Rigby
Cake, The	E	RF	250+	Story Steps	Rigby
Cake, The	C	I	40	Sun Sprouts	ETA Cuisenaire
Calamity Jane	N	B	2003	On My Own Folklore	Lerner Publications
Calamity Kate	Q	RF	250+	Deary, Terry	HarperTrophy
Calcium	Q	I	250+	A True Book	Children's Press
Caleb's Choice	S	HF	250+	Wisler, Clifton G.	Penguin Group
Calendar, The	N	I	180	Take Two Books	Wright Group/ McGraw Hill
Calendar's Trick, The	E	F	88	Reading Safari	Mondo
Calico Bush	W	HF	250+	Field, Rachel	Simon & Schuster
Calico Captive	S	HF	250+	Speare, Elizabeth George	Yearling
Calico Cat at School	G	F	86	Charles, Donald	Children's Press
Calico Cat at the Zoo	F	F	88	Charles, Donald	Children's Press
Calico Cat Meets Bookworm	G	F	90	Charles, Donald	Children's Press
Calico Cat's Rainbow	E	F	78	Charles, Donald	Children's Press
Calico the Cat	F	F	82	Charles, Donald	Children's Press
California	T	I	250+	Hello U.S.A.	Lerner Publications
California	S	I	250+	Land of Liberty	Red Brick Learning
California	Q	I	250+	One Nation	Capstone Press
California	T	I	250+	Sea To Shining Sea	Children's Press
California	T	I	250+	Theme Sets	National Geographic
California	R	I	250+	This Land Is Your Land	Compass Point Books
California Blue	Y	RF	250+	Klass, David	Scholastic
California Gold Rush, The	V	I	250+	Cornerstones of Freedom	Children's Press
California Gold Rush, The	V	I	250+	Let Freedom Ring	Red Brick Learning
California Gold Rush, The	T	I	250+	McNeer, May	Random House
California Gold Rush, The	U	I	250+	Pair-It Books	Steck-Vaughn
California Gold Rush, The	T	I	250+	We The People	Compass Point Books
California Gold Rush, The: A Letter Home	P	HF	392	Reading Street	Pearson
California Gold Rush, The: An Interactive History Adventure	T	HF	250+	You Choose Books	Capstone Press

* Collection of short stories
# Graphic text

TITLE	LEVEL	GENRE	WORD COUNT	AUTHOR / SERIES	PUBLISHER / DISTRIBUTOR
California or Bust!	N	HF	250+	Stamper, Judith	Scholastic
Call 911	C	I	22	Twig	Wright Group/McGraw Hill
Call It Courage	X	RF	250+	Sperry, Armstrong	Aladdin
Call Me Fizz	S	RF	250+	Scooters	ETA Cuisenaire
Call Me Francis Tucket	V	HF	250+	Paulsen, Gary	Yearling
Call Me Hope	W	RF	250+	Olson Gretchen	Little, Brown & Co.
Call Me Ruth	R	RF	250+	Sachs, Marilyn	Beech Tree Books
Call Mr. Vasquez, He'll Fix It!	K	I	250+	Our Neighborhood	Children's Press
Call of the Selkie	Q	RF	250+	Action Packs	Rigby
Call of the Wild	Y	RF	250+	London, Jack	Signet Classics
Call Waiting	Y	RF	250+	Stine, R. L.	Scholastic
Called To a Cause	R	B	250+	Power Up!	Steck-Vaughn
Called To a Cause	R	B	250+	Power Up!	Steck-Vaughn
Callie's Scrapbook	K	RF	687	InfoTrek	ETA Cuisenaire
Calvin Coolidge: Thirtieth President	R	B	250+	Getting to Know the U.S. Presidents	Children's Press
Calvin Coolidge	U	B	250+	Profiles of the Presidents	Compass Point Books
Cam in the Cave	J	RF	461	Sails	Rigby
Cam Jansen and the Chocolate Fudge Mystery	L	RF	250+	Adler, David A.	Puffin/Penguin
Cam Jansen and the Ghostly Mystery	L	RF	250+	Adler, David A.	Puffin/Penguin
Cam Jansen and the Mystery at the Haunted House	L	RF	250+	Adler, David A.	Puffin/Penguin
Cam Jansen and the Mystery at the Monkey House	L	RF	250+	Adler, David A.	Puffin/Penguin
Cam Jansen and the Mystery of Flight 54	L	RF	250+	Adler, David A.	Puffin/Penguin
Cam Jansen and the Mystery of the Babe Ruth Baseball	L	RF	250+	Adler, David A.	Puffin/Penguin
Cam Jansen and the Mystery of the Carnival Prize	L	RF	250+	Adler, David A.	Puffin/Penguin
Cam Jansen and the Mystery of the Circus Clown	L	RF	250+	Adler, David A.	Puffin/Penguin
Cam Jansen and the Mystery of the Dinosaur Bones	L	RF	250+	Adler, David A.	Puffin/Penguin
Cam Jansen and the Mystery of the Gold Coins	L	RF	250+	Adler, David A.	Puffin/Penguin
Cam Jansen and the Mystery of the Monkey House	L	RF	250+	Adler, David A.	Puffin/Penguin
Cam Jansen and the Mystery of the Monster Movie	L	RF	250+	Adler, David A.	Puffin/Penguin
Cam Jansen and the Mystery of the Stolen Corn Popper	L	RF	250+	Adler, David A.	Puffin/Penguin
Cam Jansen and the Mystery of the Stolen Diamonds	L	RF	250+	Adler, David A.	Puffin/Penguin
Cam Jansen and the Mystery of the Television Dog	L	RF	250+	Adler, David A.	Puffin/Penguin
Cam Jansen and the Mystery of the U.F.O.	L	RF	250+	Adler, David A.	Puffin/Penguin
Cam Jansen and the Scary Snake Mystery	L	RF	250+	Adler, David A.	Puffin/Penguin
Cam Jansen and the Secret Service Mystery	L	RF	250+	Adler, David A.	Scholastic
Cam Jansen and the Triceratops Pops Mystery	L	RF	250+	Adler, David A.	Puffin/Penguin
Cam the Camel	K	F	334	Leveled Readers	Houghton Mifflin Harcourt
Cam the Camel	K	F	334	Leveled Readers/CA	Houghton Mifflin Harcourt
Cam the Camel	K	F	334	Leveled Readers/TX	Houghton Mifflin Harcourt
Cam the Cow	B	F	32	Reading Street	Pearson
Cambodian New Year	M	I	395	Nonfiction Set 9	Literacy Footprints
Camel Ben	F	RF	32	Books for Young Learners	Richard C. Owen

TITLE	LEVEL	GENRE	WORD COUNT	AUTHOR / SERIES	PUBLISHER / DISTRIBUTOR
Camel Called Bump-Along, A	K	F	373	Evangeline Nicholas Collection	Wright Group/McGraw Hill
Camel Fair	Q	I	1394	Big Cat	Pacific Learning
Camels	H	I	108	Desert Animals	Capstone Press
Camels	H	I	123	Sails	Rigby
Camels and Their Cousins	L	I	250+	Storyteller Chapter Books	Wright Group/ McGraw Hill
Camel's Hump	I	TL	274	Leveled Readers	Houghton Mifflin Harcourt
Camel's Hump	I	TL	274	Leveled Readers/CA	Houghton Mifflin Harcourt
Camel's Hump	I	TL	274	Leveled Readers/TX	Houghton Mifflin Harcourt
Camels: Ships of the Desert	T	I	667	Vocabulary Readers	Houghton Mifflin Harcourt
Camera, The	Q	I	250+	Great Inventions	Capstone Press
Cameras on the Battlefield: Photos of War	W	I	250+	High Five Reading	Red Brick Learning
Camouflage	M	I	250+	Cambridge Reading	Pearson Learning Group
Camouflage	B	I	56	Nonfiction Set 2	Literacy Footprints
Camouflage	K	I	202	Rigby Focus	Rigby
Camouflage	H	I	154	Sunshine	Wright Group/McGraw Hill
Camp Big Paw	J	RF	250+	Cushman, Doug	HarperTrophy
Camp Can't: The Complicated Life of Claudia Cristina Cortez	S	RF	250+	Gallagher, Diana G.	Stone Arch Books
Camp Knock Knock	K	RF	250+	Duffey, Betsy	Bantam
Camp Knock Knock Mystery, The	K	RF	250+	Duffey, Betsy	Bantam
Camp Sink or Swim	M	RF	250+	Davis, Gibbs	Random House
Camp Wild	T	RF	250+	Orca Currents	Orca Book Publishers
C-A-M-P! Camp!	K	I	595	Vocabulary Readers	Houghton Mifflin Harcourt
C-A-M-P! Camp!	K	I	595	Vocabulary Readers/CA	Houghton Mifflin Harcourt
Campfire Mallory	O	RF	17381	Friedman, Laurie	Carolrhoda Books
Camping	C	RF	49	Foundations	Wright Group/McGraw Hill
Camping	D	RF	64	Hooker, Karen	Kaeden Books
Camping	F	RF	71	Leveled Readers	Houghton Mifflin Harcourt
Camping	B	RF	19	Literacy 2000	Rigby
Camping	I	I	200	Rigby Star Quest	Rigby
Camping	E	RF	76	Storyteller	Wright Group/McGraw Hill
Camping	E	RF	264	Sunshine	Wright Group/McGraw Hill
Camping	S	I	250+	The Great Outdoors	Capstone Press
Camping at School	L	RF	522	Gear Up!	Wright Group/ McGraw Hill
Camping Chaos	N	RF	250+	Girlz Rock!	Mondo
Camping In	K	RF	589	Springboard	Wright Group/McGraw Hill
Camping in the Woods	Q	I	250+	Sails	Rigby
Camping in the Yard	G	RF	171	Joy Starters	Pearson Learning Group
Camping Is Fun!	D	RF	86	Windows on Literacy	National Geographic
Camping Out	H	RF	218	Sun Sprouts	ETA Cuisenaire
Camping Out	E	RF	141	Visions	Wright Group/McGraw Hill
Camping Out	C	I	59	Vocabulary Readers	Houghton Mifflin Harcourt
Camping Out	C	I	59	Vocabulary Readers/CA	Houghton Mifflin Harcourt
Camping Outside	F	RF	95	Book Bank	Wright Group/McGraw Hill
Camping Trip, The	E	RF	71	Leveled Readers Language Support	Houghton Mifflin Harcourt
Camping Under the Stars	A	I	21	Vocabulary Readers	Houghton Mifflin Harcourt
Camping Under the Stars	A	I	21	Vocabulary Readers/CA	Houghton Mifflin Harcourt
Camping with Claudine	K	RF	250+	Literacy 2000	Rigby
Camping with Dad	J	RF	316	Sails	Rigby
Camping with Grandma	M	RF	250+	Reading Safari	Mondo
Camping with Our Dad	L	RF	250+	Sunshine	Wright Group/McGraw Hill
Campout, The	H	RF	298	Rigby Flying Colors	Rigby
Can a Cow Hop?	D	I	40	Ready Readers	Pearson Learning Group

* Collection of short stories
# Graphic text

C

TITLE	LEVEL	GENRE	WORD COUNT	AUTHOR / SERIES	PUBLISHER / DISTRIBUTOR
Can a Fox Wear Polka-Dotted Socks?	D	F	51	Dominie Readers	Pearson Learning Group
Can a Hippo Hop?	E	I	140	Tidd, Louise Vitellaro	Kaeden Books
Can Do, Jenny Archer	M	RF	250+	Conford, Ellen	Random House
Can Hank Sing?	F	F	83	Reading Street	Pearson
Can I Bring My Pterodactyl to School, Ms. Johnson?	M	F	250+	Grambling, Lois G.	Charlesbridge
Can I Have a Dinosaur?	L	RF	250+	Literacy 2000	Rigby
Can I Have a Lick?	C	RF	69	Carousel Readers	Pearson Learning Group
Can I Have a Pet?	A	RF	36	Bebop Books	Lee & Low Books Inc.
Can I Help?	F	F	250	Janovitz, Marilyn	North-South Books
Can I Play Outside?	H	RF	121	Literacy 2000	Rigby
Can I Play?	C	F	30	The Book Project	Sundance
Can It Rain Cats and Dogs?	R	I	250+	Berger, Melvin & Gilda	Scholastic
Can We Be Friends?	C	I	71	Bonnell, Kris	Reading Reading Books
Can We Do It?	E	RF	79	Reading Street	Pearson
Can We Go?	C	RF	25	Cherrington, Janelle	Scholastic
Can You Believe?: Hurricanes	Q	I	250+	Markle, Sandra	Scholastic
Can You Do This?	B	F	20	The Book Project	Sundance
Can You Eat a Fraction?	M	I	250+	Yellow Umbrella Books	Capstone Press
Can You Find a Pattern?	B	I	41	Gear Up!	Wright Group/McGraw Hill
Can You Find It?	B	I	34	Ready Readers	Pearson Learning Group
Can You Find the Pattern?	D	I	113	Visions	Wright Group/McGraw Hill
Can You Fly High, Wright Brothers?	O	B	250+	Berger, Melvin & Gilda	Scholastic
Can You Fly?	C	I	51	Foundations	Wright Group/McGraw Hill
Can You Guess?	G	I	185	InfoTrek	ETA Cuisenaire
Can You Guess?	K	I	196	Yellow Umbrella Books	Capstone Press
Can You Imagine?	O	B	250+	Meet The Author	Richard C. Owen
Can You Read a Map?	C	F	38	Learn to Read	Creative Teaching Press
Can You See An Insect?	J	I	171	Windows on Literacy	National Geographic
Can You See Me?	C	I	48	Foundations	Wright Group/McGraw Hill
Can You See Me?	B	I	72	Rigby Flying Colors	Rigby
Can You See the Eggs?	C	I	87	PM Starters	Rigby
Can You See the Wagon?	A	I	40	On Our Way to English	Rigby
Can You See?	B	F	30	Sails	Rigby
Can You Spot It?	E	RF	79	Reading Street	Pearson
Can You Top That?	H	RF	250+	Bebop Books	Lee & Low Books Inc.
Canada	H	I	68	Canizares, Susan; Berger, Samantha	Scholastic
Canada	O	I	250+	Countries of the World	Red Brick Learning
Canada	Q	I	250+	First Reports: Countries	Compass Point Books
Canada	L	I	331	Time for Kids	Teacher Created Materials
Canada ABCs: A Book About the People and Places of Canada	Q	I	250+	Country ABCs	Picture Window Books
Canada Celebrates Multiculturalism	T	I	250+	Kalman, Bobbie	Crabtree
Canada Geese Quilt, The	P	RF	250+	Kinsey-Warnock, Natalie	Bantam
Canada Under Siege	Y	I	250+	History for Young Canadians	Fitzhenry & Whiteside
Canada: A Question and Answer Book	P	I	250+	Questions and Answers: Countries	Capstone Press
Canada: The Culture	T	I	250+	Kalman, Bobbie	Crabtree
Canada: The Land	T	I	250+	Kalman, Bobbie	Crabtree
Canada: The People	T	I	250+	Kalman, Bobbie	Crabtree
Canal Boat Cat	J	F	250+	Storyworlds	Heinemann Educational Books
Canals	J	I	257	Sails	Rigby

* Collection of short stories
# Graphic text

TITLE	LEVEL	GENRE	WORD COUNT	AUTHOR / SERIES	PUBLISHER / DISTRIBUTOR
Canary Caper, The	N	RF	250+	A to Z Mysteries	Random House
Candle Making: Work with Wicks and Wax	Q	I	250+	Crafts	Capstone Press
Candlelight	G	RF	231	PM Story Books	Rigby
Candlelight Service	O	RF	250+	Literacy 2000	Rigby
Candles to Lasers	S	I	1164	Take Two Books	Wright Group/McGraw Hill
Candy Corn Contest, The	L	RF	250+	Giff, Patricia Reilly	Bantam
Candy Creations from the "Candy Queen"	N	I	250+	Bookshop	Mondo
Candy Store, The	I	RF	230	InfoTrek	ETA Cuisenaire
Candy, the Old Car	H	F	234	PM Plus Story Books	Rigby
Candyfloss	U	RF	250+	Wilson, Jacqueline	Roaring Book Press
Cannonball Chris	L	RF	250+	Marzollo, Jean	Random House
Canoe Diary	O	I	250+	Orbit Chapter Books	Pacific Learning
Canoeing	S	I	250+	The Great Outdoors	Red Brick Learning
Can't You Make Them Behave, King George?	R	I	250+	Fritz, Jean	Putnam/Penguin
Can't You See We're Reading?	D	RF	71	Stepping Stones	Nelson/Michaels Assoc.
Can't You Sleep, Little Bear?	L	F	250+	Waddell, Martin	Candlewick Press
Canyons	V	F	250+	Paulsen, Gary	Laurel-Leaf Books
Cape of Rushes, The	M	TL	250+	Cambridge Reading	Pearson Learning Group
Caper of the Crown Jewels, The	P	SF	250+	Secret Agent Jack Stalwart	Weinstein Books
Capitol, The	V	I	250+	Cornerstones of Freedom	Children's Press
Caps for Sale	K	F	675	Slobodkina, Esphyr	Harper & Row
Capsize!	P	RF	250+	Bookweb	Rigby
Captain Bluefin's Underwater Ride	J	I	250+	Phonics Readers Plus	Steck-Vaughn
Captain B's Boat	G	F	158	Sunshine	Wright Group/McGraw Hill
Captain Bumble	K	F	510	Story Box	Wright Group/McGraw Hill
Captain Cat	H	F	250+	Hoff, Syd	HarperTrophy
Captain Felonius	L	F	250+	Literacy 2000	Rigby
Captain Foot and the Treasure	I	F	282	InfoTrek	ETA Cuisenaire
Captain Gallant	M	SF	763	Springboard	Wright Group/McGraw Hill
Captain Grey	U	HF	250+	Avi	HarperTrophy
Captain Orinocos Onion	K	RF	250+	Voyages	SRA/McGraw Hill
Captain Pepper's Pets	L	F	250+	I Am Reading	Kingfisher
Captains Courageous	Z+	HF	250+	Kipling, Rudyard	Bantam Books
Captive or Free: Zoos in Debate	W	I	2516	Reading Street	Pearson
Capture of Detroit, The	Y	I	250+	History for Young Canadians	Fitzhenry & Whiteside
Captured Off Guard: The Attack on Pearl Harbor	T	HF	250+	Lemke, Donald	Stone Arch Books
Car	W	I	250+	Eyewitness Books	DK Publishing
Car Accident, The	F	RF	161	Foundations	Wright Group/McGraw Hill
Car Followed Us, A	D	RF	54	Books for Young Learners	Richard C. Owen
Car Ride, The	A	RF	41	Little Red Readers	Sundance
Car Trip, A	C	RF	64	PM Stars	Rigby
Car Trouble	L	RF	724	PM Collection	Rigby
Car Wash Kid	D	RF	55	Rookie Readers	Children's Press
Car Wash, The	G	RF	214	Handprints D	Educators Publishing Service
Car Wash, The	G	I	98	Windows on Literacy	National Geographic
Cara's Letters	R	RF	250+	PM Chapter Books	Rigby
Caravan Boy	X	HF	3258	Leveled Readers	Houghton Mifflin Harcourt
Cardboard Box, A	K	TL	250+	Ready to Read	Pacific Learning
Careers	G	I	121	Benger, Wendy	Kaeden Books
Careers-Day Surprise	Q	RF	2177	Take Two Books	Wright Group/ McGraw Hill
Careful Crocodile, The	I	HF	271	PM Story Books-Orange	Rigby
Cargo Cat	G	F	222	Sails	Rigby

* Collection of short stories
# Graphic text

TITLE	LEVEL	GENRE	WORD COUNT	AUTHOR / SERIES	PUBLISHER / DISTRIBUTOR
Caribbean Cats	M	RF	250+	Books for Young Learners	Richard C. Owen
Caribbean, The	M	I	349	Time for Kids	Teacher Created Materials
Caribou	H	I	120	Polar Animals	Capstone Press
Caribou (Reindeer)	N	I	250+	PM Animal Facts: Silver	Rigby
Caribou Journey, A	Q	I	250+	Miller, Debbie S.	Little, Brown & Co.
Caring	L	I	250+	Character Education	Red Brick Learning
Caring	C	I	47	Interaction	Rigby
Caring for Earth	P	I	250+	PM Extensions	Rigby
Caring for Earth	H	I	80	Windows on Literacy	National Geographic
Caring for Eggs and Babies	E	I	113	Sails	Rigby
Caring for Our Lizard	G	I	133	Learn to Read	Creative Teaching Press
Caring for Our Pets	C	I	74	Early Connections	Benchmark Education
Caring for Our World	N	I	250+	Rigby Star Quest	Rigby
Caring for Outdoor Places	M	I	1001	Rigby Flying Colors	Rigby
Caring for Your Bird	K	I	250+	Positively Pets	Capstone Press
Caring for Your Cat	L	I	250+	Positively Pets	Capstone Press
Caring for Your Dog	I	I	250+	All About Dogs	Literacy Footprints
Caring for Your Dog	L	I	250+	Positively Pets	Capstone Press
Caring for Your Ferret	K	I	250+	Positively Pets	Capstone Press
Caring for Your Fish	L	I	250+	Positively Pets	Capstone Press
Caring for Your Gerbil	K	I	250+	Positively Pets	Capstone Press
Caring for Your Guinea Pig	K	I	250+	Positively Pets	Capstone Press
Caring for Your Hamster	L	I	250+	Positively Pets	Capstone Press
Caring for Your Hermit Crab	L	I	250+	Positively Pets	Capstone Press
Caring for Your Horse	K	I	250+	Positively Pets	Capstone Press
Caring for Your Pet Bird	O	I	1360	Reading Street	Pearson
Caring For Your Pets: A Book About Veterinarians	I	I	175	Community Workers	Picture Window Books
Caring for Your Rabbit	L	I	250+	Positively Pets	Capstone Press
Caring for Your Snake	K	I	250+	Positively Pets	Capstone Press
Carl Goes Shopping	WB	F	N/A	Day, Alexandra	Green Tiger Press
Carl Goes to Daycare	WB	F	N/A	Day, Alexandra	Green Tiger Press
Carla Crow's Pie	I	F	288	Springboard	Wright Group/McGraw Hill
Carla Gets a Pet	I	RF	250+	Ready Readers	Pearson Learning Group
Carla's Big Splash	A	RF	19	Beckley, Kimberly	Kaeden Books
Carla's Bookcase	F	RF	198	On Our Way to English	Rigby
Carla's Breakfast	G	RF	225	Harper, Leslie	Kaeden Books
Carla's Corner	J	RF	646	Leveled Readers	Houghton Mifflin Harcourt
Carla's New Glasses	I	RF	207	Coulton, Mia	Kaeden Books
Carla's Ribbons	G	RF	212	Harper, Leslie	Kaeden Books
Carla's Talent Show	J	RF	388	Beckley, Kimberly	Kaeden Books
Carla's Wheels	I	RF	200	Story Box	Wright Group/McGraw Hill
Carlita Ropes the Twister	L	F	363	Pair-It Books	Steck-Vaughn
Carlo Watches the Boys	M	RF	1002	Leveled Readers	Houghton Mifflin Harcourt
Carlo Watches the Boys	M	RF	1002	Leveled Readers/CA	Houghton Mifflin Harcourt
Carlo Watches the Boys	M	RF	1002	Leveled Readers/TX	Houghton Mifflin Harcourt
Carlos and his Friends	M	RF	250+	Sunflower	Intercultural Center for Research in Education
Carlos Goes Camping	D	RF	99	In Step Readers	Rigby
Carlos Goes Camping	D	RF	99	Literacy by Design	Rigby
Carlos Picks a Pet	I	RF	427	Reading Street	Pearson
Carlos's Big Yawn	G	RF	228	Springboard	Wright Group/McGraw Hill
Carlota's Cooking Class	L	RF	250+	On Our Way to English	Rigby
Carl's Afternoon in the Park	WB	F	N/A	Day, Alexandra	Green Tiger Press

TITLE	LEVEL	GENRE	WORD COUNT	AUTHOR / SERIES	PUBLISHER / DISTRIBUTOR
Carl's Birthday	WB	F	N/A	Day, Alexandra	Green Tiger Press
Carl's High Jump	K	RF	250+	PM Plus Story Books	Rigby
Carly Patterson	P	B	1934	Amazing Athletes	Lerner Publications
Carmelita's Cabbage	H	F	240	Springboard	Wright Group/McGraw Hill
Carmen's Colors	LB	RF	14	Bebop Books	Lee & Low Books Inc.
Carmen's Star Party	J	RF	250+	Phonics and Friends	Hampton-Brown
Carnival	P	I	250+	Holidays and Festivals	Compass Point Books
Carnival Horse, The	K	RF	499	PM Plus Story Books	Rigby
Carnival King	T	HF	250+	High-Fliers	Pacific Learning
Carnival Time!	S	I	250+	WorldScapes	ETA Cuisenaire
Carnival, The	F	RF	82	Oxford Reading Tree	Oxford University Press
Carnivals Around the World	I	I	116	Lighthouse	Rigby
Carnivorous Carnival, The	V	F	250+	Snicket, Lemony	Scholastic
Carole: The Inside Story	R	RF	250+	Bryant, Bonnie	Skylark
Carolina Crow Girl	T	F	250+	Hobbs, Valerie	Puffin/Penguin
Carolina Panthers, The	S	I	250+	Team Spirit	Norwood House Press
Caroline's Treats	R	RF	1184	Leveled Readers	Houghton Mifflin Harcourt
Caroline's Treats	R	RF	1184	Leveled Readers/CA	Houghton Mifflin Harcourt
Caroline's Treats	R	RF	1184	Leveled Readers/TX	Houghton Mifflin Harcourt
Carpenters	M	I	250+	Community Helpers	Red Brick Learning
Carpenters	L	I	250+	Community Workers	Compass Point Books
Carpenters	M	I	477	Pull Ahead Books	Lerner Publications
Carpenter's Tools, A	D	I	63	Nonfiction Set 3	Literacy Footprints
Carrier-Based Jet Fighters: The F-14 Tomcats	V	I	250+	War Planes	Capstone Press
Carrot Seed, The	G	F	101	Krauss, Ruth	Harper & Row
Carrot Soup	H	TL	142	Literacy Tree	Rigby
Carrot, The	C	F	48	Leveled Readers Language Support	Houghton Mifflin Harcourt
Carrots	B	I	51	Pebble Books	Capstone Press
Carrots Don't Talk!	J	F	250+	Ready Readers	Pearson Learning Group
Carrots, Peas, and Beans	F	RF	142	Sunshine	Wright Group/McGraw Hill
Carry it All!	C	I	51	Little Celebrations	Pearson Learning Group
Carry Me	WB	I	N/A	Big Cat	Pacific Learning
Carry on, Mr. Bowditch	Y	B	250+	Latham, Jean Lee	Houghton Mifflin Harcourt
Carrying Babies	D	I	98	Sails	Rigby
Carrying the Load	T	I	250+	Connectors	Pacific Learning
Carry-Out Food	D	RF	56	Tadpoles	Rigby
Cars	LB	I	24	Big Cat	Pacific Learning
Cars	Q	I	250+	Early Connections	Benchmark Education
Cars	B	I	30	Little Readers	Houghton Mifflin Harcourt
Cars	C	I	30	Little Readers	Houghton Mifflin Harcourt
Cars	F	I	72	Rockwell, Anne	Dutton/Penguin
Cars	LB	I	18	Transportation	Capstone Press
Cars of the Past	M	I	182	On Deck	Rigby
Cars!	F	I	56	Independent Readers Social Studies	Houghton Mifflin Harcourt
Cartier: Jacques Cartier in Search of the Northwest Passage	U	B	250+	Exploring the World	Compass Point Books
Cartoonist, The	S	RF	250+	Byars, Betsy	Puffin/Penguin
Carved in Stone: Borglum and Mount Rushmore	W	I	2997	Leveled Readers	Houghton Mifflin Harcourt
Cascarones Are for Fun	M	I	534	Reading Street	Pearson
Case for Jenny Archer, A	M	RF	250+	Conford, Ellen	Random House
Case of Capital Intrigue, The	S	RF	250+	Keene, Carolyn	Pocket Books

* Collection of short stories
# Graphic text

TITLE	LEVEL	GENRE	WORD COUNT	AUTHOR / SERIES	PUBLISHER / DISTRIBUTOR
Case of Hermie the Missing Hamster, The	M	RF	250+	A Jigsaw Jones Mystery	Scholastic
Case of Jake's Escape, The	I	RF	962	Appleton-Smith, Laura	Flyleaf Publishing
Case of the Captured Queen	S	RF	250+	Keene, Carolyn	Pocket Books
Case of the Carnival Cash, The	R	RF	250+	Power Up!	Steck-Vaughn
Case of the Cat's Meow, The	K	RF	250+	Bonsall, Crosby	HarperTrophy
Case of the Christmas Snowman, The	M	RF	250+	A Jigsaw Jones Mystery	Scholastic
Case of the Clothing Culprit, The	R	F	2228	Leveled Readers	Houghton Mifflin Harcourt
Case of the Clothing Culprit, The	R	F	2228	Leveled Readers/CA	Houghton Mifflin Harcourt
Case of the Cool-Itch Kid, The	L	RF	250+	Giff, Patricia Reilly	Bantam
Case of the Dangerous Solution, The	S	RF	250+	Keene, Carolyn	Pocket Books
Case of the Diamond Dog Collar, The	S	RF	1385	Leveled Readers	Houghton Mifflin Harcourt
Case of the Diamond Dog Collar, The	S	RF	1385	Leveled Readers/CA	Houghton Mifflin Harcourt
Case of the Dirty Bird, The	O	RF	250+	Paulsen, Gary	Bantam
Case of the Disappearing Bones	N	RF	250+	SupaDoopers	Sundance
Case of the Disappearing Daughter, The	N	RF	3338	Damian Drooth Supersleuth	Stone Arch Books
Case of the Double Cross, The	K	RF	250+	Bonsall, Crosby	HarperTrophy
Case of the Dumb Bells, The	K	RF	250+	Bonsall, Crosby	HarperTrophy
Case of the Elevator Duck, The	M	RF	250+	Berends, Polly Berrien	Random House
Case of the Floating Crime, The	S	RF	250+	Keene, Carolyn	Pocket Books
Case of the Food Fight, The	M	RF	250+	A Jigsaw Jones Mystery	Scholastic
Case of the Furry Thing, The	G	RF	267	Ready Readers	Pearson Learning Group
Case of the Groaning Ghost, The	M	RF	250+	A Jigsaw Jones Mystery	Scholastic
Case of the Hungry Stranger, The	K	RF	1358	Bonsall, Crosby	HarperTrophy
Case of the Invisible Cat, The	Q	RF	250+	Parker, A. E.	Scholastic
Case of the Lion Dance	U	RF	250+	Yep, Laurence	HarperTrophy
Case of the Measled Cowboy, The	Q	F	250+	Erickson, John R.	Puffin/Penguin
Case of the Midnight Rustler, The	Q	F	250+	Erickson, John R.	Puffin/Penguin
Case of the Missing Cat, The	Q	F	250+	Erickson, John R.	Puffin/Penguin
Case of the Missing Cookie, The	M	F	873	Leveled Readers	Houghton Mifflin Harcourt
Case of the Missing Cookie, The	M	F	873	Leveled Readers/CA	Houghton Mifflin Harcourt
Case of the Missing Cutthroats, The	S	RF	250+	George, Jean Craighead	HarperTrophy
Case of the Missing Dog Collar, The	S	F	1385	Leveled Readers	Houghton Mifflin Harcourt
Case of the Missing Fish, The	I	RF	119	Reading Street	Pearson
Case of the Missing Grass, The	O	F	1041	Leveled Readers	Houghton Mifflin Harcourt
Case of the Missing Grass, The	O	F	1041	Leveled Readers/CA	Houghton Mifflin Harcourt
Case of the Missing Grass, The	R	I	1310	Leveled Readers/TX	Houghton Mifflin Harcourt
Case of the Missing Homework, The	H	RF	181	Literacy by Design	Rigby
Case of the Missing Iguana, The	P	RF	2374	Reading Street	Pearson
Case of the Missing Key, The	P	F	1198	Leveled Readers	Houghton Mifflin Harcourt
Case of the Missing Snacks, The	J	RF	454	Sunshine	Wright Group/McGraw Hill
Case of the Nervous Newsboy, The	N	RF	250+	Hildick, E. W.	Sundance
Case of the Pop Star's Wedding, The	N	RF	250+	Damian Drooth Supersleuth	Stone Arch Books
Case of the Sabotaged School Play, The	R	RF	250+	Singer, Marilyn	Bantam
Case of the Scaredy Cats, The	K	RF	250+	Bonsall, Crosby	HarperTrophy
Case of the Secret Valentine, The	M	RF	250+	A Jigsaw Jones Mystery	Scholastic
Case of the Smelly Water	R	RF	250+	Reading Expeditions	National Geographic
Case of the Smiling Shark, The	N	F	250+	High-Fliers	Pacific Learning
Case of the Snowboarding Superstar, The	M	RF	250+	A Jigsaw Jones Mystery	Scholastic
Case of the Spooky Sleepover, The	M	RF	250+	A Jigsaw Jones Mystery	Scholastic
Case of the Stolen Baseball Cards, The	M	RF	250+	A Jigsaw Jones Mystery	Scholastic
Case of the Talking Trousers, The	O	F	250+	High-Fliers	Pacific Learning
Case of the Twin Teddy Bears, The	S	RF	250+	Keene, Carolyn	Pocket Books
Case of the Two Masked Robbers, The	K	F	250+	Hoban, Lillian	HarperTrophy
Casey and the Nest	J	F	966	Georgie Giraffe	Literacy Footprints

C

TITLE	LEVEL	GENRE	WORD COUNT	AUTHOR / SERIES	PUBLISHER / DISTRIBUTOR
Casey Jones	N	B	1875	On My Own Folklore	Lerner Publications
Casey's Art Project	J	RF	417	Springboard	Wright Group/McGraw Hill
Casey's Case	Q	RF	250+	Literacy 2000	Rigby
Casey's Code	Q	RF	250+	Riley, Gail Blasser	Steck-Vaughn
Casey's Lamb	D	I	75	Literacy by Design	Rigby
Casey's Lamb	D	I	75	On Our Way to English	Rigby
Cass Becomes a Star	L	B	250+	Literacy 2000	Rigby
Cassandra's Sister	Y	HF	250+	Bennett, Veronica	Candlewick Press
Cassidy's Magic	S	F	250+	Literacy 2000	Rigby
Cassie Binegar	T	RF	250+	MacLachlan, Patricia	HarperTrophy
Cassie's Castle	L	RF	250+	Rigby Literacy	Rigby
Cast Your Vote	Q	RF	250+	Orbit Chapter Books	Pacific Learning
Casting Nets	I	I	107	Reading Street	Pearson
Castle	E	I	37	Exploring History & Geography	Rigby
Castle	X	I	250+	Eyewitness Books	DK Publishing
Castle	X	I	250+	Macaulay, David	Scholastic
Castle Corona, The	U	F	250+	Creech, Sharon	Harper Collins
Castle in the Attic, The	R	F	250+	Winthrop, Elizabeth	Bantam
Castle of Llyr, The	W	F	250+	Alexander, Lloyd	Dell
Castle Under Attack	K	F	250+	DK Readers	DK Publishing
Castle, The	H	RF	286	Storyworlds	Heinemann Educational Books
Castles	M	I	231	Big Cat	Pacific Learning
Castles	F	I	89	Nonfiction Set 4	Literacy Footprints
Castles	Q	I	250+	Tristars	Richard C. Owen
Castles in the Air	O	TL	250+	Literacy by Design	Rigby
Castles: Towers, Dungeons, Moats, and More	U	I	250+	High Five Reading	Red Brick Learning
Cat	V	I	250+	Eyewitness Books	DK Publishing
Cat and Dog	WB	F	N/A	Big Cat	Pacific Learning
Cat and Dog	C	F	71	Learn to Read	Creative Teaching Press
Cat and Dog	B	RF	41	Leveled Readers	Houghton Mifflin Harcourt
Cat and Dog	C	F	31	Sails	Rigby
Cat and Dog at School	F	F	101	Learn to Read	Creative Teaching Press
Cat and Dog Go Shopping	G	F	127	Learn to Read	Creative Teaching Press
Cat and Dog Go To Town	C	F	32	Reading Street	Pearson
Cat and Dog Make the Best, Biggest, Most Wonderful Cheese Sandwich	G	F	250+	Learn to Read	Creative Teaching Press
Cat and Dog Play Hide and Seek	B	F	27	Big Cat	Pacific Learning
Cat and Dog Talk	H	I	399	Sails	Rigby
Cat and Dog: The Super Snack	F	F	161	Learn to Read	Creative Teaching Press
Cat and Mouse	C	F	31	Brand New Readers	Candlewick Press
Cat and Mouse	B	F	75	PM Starters	Rigby
Cat and Rat	M	TL	250+	Young, Ed	Henry Holt & Co.
Cat and Rat Fall Out	J	TL	250+	Lighthouse	Rigby
Cat and the King, The	D	F	30	Literacy 2000	Rigby
Cat and the Mice, The	I	F	526	Book Bank	Wright Group/McGraw Hill
Cat at School?, A	D	RF	58	Independent Readers Social Studies	Houghton Mifflin Harcourt
Cat Ate My Gymsuit, The	U	RF	250+	Danziger, Paula	Putnam/Penguin
Cat Burglar of Pethaven Drive, The	N	F	250+	Literacy 2000	Rigby
Cat Burglar, The	M	RF	250+	Krailing, Tessa	Barron's Educational
Cat Called Tim, A	L	RF	250+	New Way Literature	Steck-Vaughn
Cat Called, The	B	F	18	Ray's Readers	Outside the Box
Cat Came Back, The	I	TL	250+	Little Celebrations	Pearson Learning Group

* Collection of short stories
# Graphic text

TITLE	LEVEL	GENRE	WORD COUNT	AUTHOR / SERIES	PUBLISHER / DISTRIBUTOR
Cat Came Back, The	B	TL	22	Ready Readers	Pearson Learning Group
Cat Chat	F	F	85	Ready Readers	Pearson Learning Group
Cat Concert	J	F	250+	Literacy 2000	Rigby
Cat Crazy	O	RF	250+	Baglio, Ben M.	Scholastic
Cat Culture	P	I	250+	Storyteller - Whispering Pines	Wright Group/ McGraw Hill
Cat for Keeps, A	L	RF	250+	Cambridge Reading	Pearson Learning Group
Cat for You, A: Caring for Your Cat	M	I	250+	Pet Care	Picture Window Books
Cat Games	E	F	229	Ziefert, Harriet	Puffin/Penguin
Cat Goes Fiddle-i-fee	F	TL	333	Galdone, Paul	Houghton Mifflin Harcourt
Cat in the Bag	E	RF	85	Rookie Reader	Children's Press
Cat in the Hat	J	F	250+	Seuss, Dr.	Random House
Cat in the Tree, A	F	F	79	Oxford Reading Tree	Oxford University Press
Cat Named Ben, A	D	F	131	Leveled Readers	Houghton Mifflin Harcourt
Cat Named Ben, A	D	F	131	Leveled Readers/CA	Houghton Mifflin Harcourt
Cat Named Ben, A	D	F	131	Leveled Readers/TX	Houghton Mifflin Harcourt
Cat on the Mat	B	F	37	Wildsmith, Brian	Oxford University Press
Cat on the Move	A	F	30	Phonics and Friends	Hampton-Brown
Cat on the Roof	H	RF	250+	Story Box	Wright Group/McGraw Hill
Cat Out of the Bag	O	F	250+	High-Fliers	Pacific Learning
Cat Party	B	F	37	Sails	Rigby
Cat Prints	C	RF	25	Pair-It Books	Steck-Vaughn
Cat Running	U	RF	250+	Snyder, Zilpha Keatley	Bantam
Cat Show, The	C	F	43	Sails	Rigby
Cat Tails	D	I	40	Books for Young Learners	Richard C. Owen
Cat Talk	N	I	250+	Orbit Chapter Books	Pacific Learning
Cat That Broke the Rules, The	G	F	192	Ready Readers	Pearson Learning Group
Cat That Sat, The	D	RF	66	Start to Read	School Zone
Cat Traps	D	F	93	Coxe, Molly	Random House
Cat Walk	R	F	250+	Stolz, Mary	Bantam
Cat Whispers	H	RF	250+	Rigby Literacy	Rigby
Cat Who Loved Red, The	D	F	63	Salem, Lynn; Stewart, Josie	Continental Press
Cat Who Went to Heaven, The	S	F	250+	Coatsworth, Elizabeth	Aladdin
Cat Who Wore a Pot on Her Head, The	N	F	250+	Slepian, Jan; Seidler, Ann	Scholastic
Cat with No Tail, The	I	TL	137	Books for Young Learners	Richard C. Owen
Cat with the Yellow Star: Coming of Age in Terezin, The	Z	B	250+	Rubin, Susan Goldman	Holiday House
Cat!	S	I	250+	Kroll, Virginia L.	Dawn Publications
Cat, The	A	I	40	InfoTrek	ETA Cuisenaire
Cat, The	A	I	28	Leveled Readers Science	Houghton Mifflin Harcourt
Cat, The	A	I	42	Little Books for Early Readers	University of Maine
Cat, The	C	RF	23	Smart Starts	Rigby
Catalyst	Z	RF	250+	Anderson, Laurie Halse	Penguin Group
Catastrophe!	Z	I	250+	Boldprint	Steck-Vaughn
Catch It!	E	F	73	Pair-It Turn and Learn	Steck-Vaughn
Catch It!	A	RF	25	Rigby Star	Rigby
Catch It, Marvin	E	RF	61	Windmill Books	Rigby
Catch Me If You Can!	F	F	180	Green Light Readers	Harcourt
Catch Me If You Can!: The Roadrunner	M	I	250+	Sunshine	Wright Group/McGraw Hill
Catch Me, Cat	C	F	131	Sails	Rigby
Catch That Ball!	F	RF	114	Reading Street	Pearson
Catch That Bus!	F	RF	119	Reading Street	Pearson
Catch That Cat!	LB	RF	16	Rookie Readers	Children's Press
Catch That Frog	E	F	131	Reading Unlimited	Pearson Learning Group
Catch That Pass!	Q	RF	250+	Christopher, Matt	Little, Brown & Co.

TITLE	LEVEL	GENRE	WORD COUNT	AUTHOR / SERIES	PUBLISHER / DISTRIBUTOR
Catch the Cookie	J	F	250+	Little Celebrations	Pearson Learning Group
Catcher With a Glass Arm	P	RF	250+	Christopher, Matt	Little, Brown & Co.
Catcher's Mask, The	M	RF	250+	Christopher, Matt	Little, Brown & Co.
Catching	B	I	35	Teacher's Choice Series	Pearson Learning Group
Catching Sunlight: A Book About Leaves	M	I	250+	Growing Things	Picture Window Books
Catching Air!	S	RF	250+	PM Chapter Books	Rigby
Catching Some Respect	T	RF	3009	Leveled Readers	Houghton Mifflin Harcourt
*Catching the Sun	M	TL	250+	Take Two Books	Wright Group/McGraw Hill
Catching the Wind	N	I	250+	iOpeners	Pearson Learning Group
Caterpillars	M	I	114	Bookshop	Mondo
Caterpillars	P	I	250+	Mini Pets	Steck-Vaughn
Caterpillars	N	I	250+	Minibeasts	Franklin Watts
Caterpillars	F	I	54	Pebble Books	Capstone Press
Caterpillar's Adventure	F	F	69	Story Box	Wright Group/McGraw Hill
Catherine the Counter	E	RF	86	Sunshine	Wright Group/McGraw Hill
Catherine, Called Birdy	X	HF	250+	Cushman, Karen	Clarion
Catnapper, The	J	F	398	Leveled Readers	Houghton Mifflin Harcourt
Catnapper, The	J	F	398	Leveled Readers/CA	Houghton Mifflin Harcourt
Catnapper, The	N	I	323	Leveled Readers/TX	Houghton Mifflin Harcourt
Cats	D	I	43	All About Pets	Red Brick Learning
Cats	A	I	21	Big Cat	Pacific Learning
Cats	O	I	1981	Early Bird Nature Books	Lerner Publishing
Cats	K	I	338	Nonfiction Set 9	Literacy Footprints
Cats	J	I	250+	PM Animal Facts: Orange	Rigby
Cats	A	I	24	Vocabulary Readers	Houghton Mifflin Harcourt
Cats	C	I	45	Williams, Deborah	Kaeden Books
Cats	I	I	137	Wonder World	Wright Group/McGraw Hill
Cats and Kids	F	I	136	Silly Millies	Millbrook Press
Cats and Kittens	F	I	44	Reading Unlimited	Pearson Learning Group
Cats and Mice	H	F	51	Gelman, Rita	Scholastic
*Cats and Other Stories	J	F	250+	Story Steps	Rigby
Cats' Burglar, The	K	F	250+	Parish, Peggy	Hearst
Cat's Day, A	B	I	23	Twig	Wright Group/McGraw Hill
Cat's Diary	M	F	250+	Sails	Rigby
Cat's Dream, A	A	F	20	Handprints A	Educators Publishing Service
Cats Everywhere	F	RF	51	Books for Young Learners	Richard C. Owen
Cats Have Kittens	M	I	250+	Animals and Their Young	Compass Point Books
Cats in Krasinski Square, The	V	HF	250+	Hesse, Karen	Scholastic
Cat's Meow, The	O	F	250+	Soto, Gary	Scholastic
Cats of the Night	K	RF	379	Book Bank	Wright Group/McGraw Hill
Cats on the Farm	H	I	71	Pebble Books	Red Brick Learning
Cat's Party	F	F	39	Sunshine	Wright Group/McGraw Hill
Cat's Surprise Party	I	F	376	Leveled Readers	Houghton Mifflin Harcourt
Cat's Trip	G	F	158	Ready Readers	Pearson Learning Group
Cat's Whiskers, A	I	I	250+	Windows on Literacy	National Geographic
Cats!	D	RF	50	Rookie Readers	Children's Press
Cats, Cats, Cats	Q	I	250+	Literacy 2000	Rigby
Cats, Cats, Cats	B	I	14	Pair-It Books	Steck-Vaughn
Cats, Cats, Cats	G	RF	217	Story Basket	Wright Group/McGraw Hill
Catten, The	K	F	769	Jellybeans	Rigby
Cattle	L	I	250+	PM Animal Facts: Purple	Rigby
Cattle Drive!	V	I	2940	Vocabulary Readers	Houghton Mifflin Harcourt
Cattle Drive!	V	I	2940	Vocabulary Readers/CA	Houghton Mifflin Harcourt

* Collection of short stories
# Graphic text

TITLE	LEVEL	GENRE	WORD COUNT	AUTHOR / SERIES	PUBLISHER / DISTRIBUTOR
Cattle Drive!	V	I	2940	Vocabulary Readers/TX	Houghton Mifflin Harcourt
Catwings	N	F	250+	Le Guin, Ursula K.	Scholastic
Catwings Return	N	F	250+	Le Guin, Ursula K.	Scholastic
Caty the Caterpillar	H	RF	175	Leveled Readers	Houghton Mifflin Harcourt
Caty the Caterpillar	H	RF	175	Leveled Readers/CA	Houghton Mifflin Harcourt
Caty the Caterpillar	H	RF	175	Leveled Readers/TX	Houghton Mifflin Harcourt
Caught by the Sea	N	RF	250+	Keating, Rosemary	Pacific Learning
Caught in a Flash	P	I	250+	Orbit Chapter Books	Pacific Learning
Caught in the Storm	H	RF	250+	Home Connection Collection	Rigby
Caught Out	S	I	250+	WorldScapes	ETA Cuisenaire
Causes of the Revolution	S	I	250+	Primary Source Readers	Teacher Created Materials
Cave Bear	N	I	250+	Extinct Monsters	Capstone Press
Cave Creatures	Q	I	872	Independent Readers Science	Houghton Mifflin Harcourt
Cave Dwellers	O	I	2005	Take Two Books	Wright Group/ McGraw-Hill
Cave In	S	HF	250+	Duey, Kathleen; Bale, Karen A.	Simon & Schuster
Cave of the Bookworms, The	T	F	250+	Dahl, Michael	Stone Arch Books
Cave, The	C	RF	67	Book Bank	Wright Group/McGraw Hill
Cave, The	T	F	250+	Book Blazers	ETA Cuisenaire
Caves	M	I	250+	Discovery World	Rigby
Caves	N	I	250+	Earthforms	Capstone Press
Caves	D	I	80	Sails	Rigby
Caves	G	I	79	Seedlings	Continental Press
Caves	I	I	155	Storyteller	Wright Group/McGraw Hill
Caves	P	I	1719	Take Two Books	Wright Group/ McGraw Hill
Caves	R	I	250+	The Wonders of Our World	Crabtree
Caves	R	I	250+	Wood, Jenny	Scholastic
Caves and Caverns	O	I	250+	Gibbons, Gail	Harcourt Trade
Caving Adventures	S	I	250+	Dangerous Adventures	Red Brick Learning
Cay, The	V	HF	250+	Taylor, Theodore	Avon
CD and the Giant Cat	V	SF	250+	Action Packs	Rigby
Cecil the Caterpillar	E	F	130	Lighthouse	Ginn & Co.
Cecil the Caterpillar	E	F	130	Lighthouse	Rigby
Ceiling of Stars, A	U	RF	250+	Creel, Ann Howard	Pleasant Company
Celebrate Art	M	I	228	Twig	Wright Group/McGraw Hill
Celebrating Chanukah: Eight Nights	J	I	188	Learn to Read	Creative Teaching Press
Celebrating Chinese New Year: Nick's New Year	J	I	142	Learn to Read	Creative Teaching Press
Celebrating Christmas: Christmas Decorations	J	I	165	Learn to Read	Creative Teaching Press
Celebrating Cinco de Mayo: Fiesta Time!	J	I	41	Learn to Read	Creative Teaching Press
Celebrating Easter: The Easter Egg Hunt	J	I	166	Learn to Read	Creative Teaching Press
Celebrating Father's Day: Father's Day Is for Special People	F	RF	115	Learn to Read	Creative Teaching Press
Celebrating Martin Luther King, Jr. Day: Dreaming of Change	J	I	152	Learn to Read	Creative Teaching Press
Celebrating Mother's Day: Mom's Memory Box	E	F	100	Learn to Read	Creative Teaching Press
Celebrating Patriotic Holidays: Honoring America	H	I	175	Learn to Read	Creative Teaching Press
Celebrating President's Day	H	I	181	Learn to Read	Creative Teaching Press
Celebrating Thanksgiving: Giving Thanks	F	I	145	Learn to Read	Creative Teaching Press
Celebrating the New Year	K	I	234	Take Two Books	Wright Group/ McGraw Hill
Celebrating Valentine's Day: My Special Valentines	F	RF	137	Learn to Read	Creative Teaching Press
Celebrations	G	I	37	Berger, Samantha; Moreton, Daniel	Scholastic
Celebrations	G	I	107	Storyteller-Moon Rising	Wright Group/McGraw Hill

C

* Collection of short stories
# Graphic text

Storable Database at www.fountasandpinnellleveledbooks.com

TITLE	LEVEL	GENRE	WORD COUNT	AUTHOR / SERIES	PUBLISHER / DISTRIBUTOR
Celebrations	L	I	199	Yellow Umbrella Books	Capstone Press
Celebrations Around the World	J	I	205	Early Connections	Benchmark Education
Celebrities That Care	S	I	250+	High-Fliers	Pacific Learning
Celery Stalks at Midnight, The	R	F	250+	Howe, James	Atheneum
Celeste's Harlem Renaissance	X	HF	250+	Tate, Eleanora	Little, Brown & Co.
Celia	K	RF	182	Leveled Readers	Houghton Mifflin Harcourt
Celia and Ali	I	RF	137	Leveled Readers Language Support	Houghton Mifflin Harcourt
Celia's Gift	M	RF	231	On Our Way To English	Rigby
Cell Scientists: Discovering How Cells Work	Y	B	250+	Science Readers	Teacher Created Materials
Cells	R	I	1649	Leveled Readers Science	Houghton Mifflin Harcourt
Cells	Y	I	1831	Science Support Readers	Houghton Mifflin Harcourt
Cells	J	I	96	Wonder World	Wright Group/McGraw Hill
Cement Tent	G	F	358	First Start	Troll Associates
Center Court Sting	R	RF	250+	Christopher, Matt	Little, Brown & Co.
*Centerburg Tales: More Adventures of Homer Price	Q	RF	250+	McCloskey, Robert	Puffin/Penguin
Centerfield Ballhawk	M	RF	250+	Christopher, Matt	Little, Brown & Co.
Centipede's New Shoes	D	F	78	Reading Safari	Mondo
Central Intelligence Agency, The: Stopping Terrorists	S	I	250+	Line of Duty	Capstone Press
Centuries of Horsepower: Horses at Work	T	I	250+	Explore More	Wright Group/McGraw Hill
Cephalopods	N	I	250+	Pacific Literacy	Pacific Learning
Cervantes, A Life of Adventure	W	I	2165	Vocabulary Readers	Houghton Mifflin Harcourt
Cervantes, A Life of Adventure	W	I	2165	Vocabulary Readers/CA	Houghton Mifflin Harcourt
Cervantes, A Life of Adventure	W	I	2165	Vocabulary Readers/TX	Houghton Mifflin Harcourt
Cesar Chavez	V	B	250+	Amazing Ameicans	Wright Group/McGraw Hill
Cesar Chavez	N	B	262	Biography	Benchmark Education
Cesar Chavez	Q	B	250+	Early Biographies	Compass Point Books
Cesar Chavez	M	B	262	Famous Americans	Capstone Press
Cesar Chavez	M	B	295	Independent Readers Social Studies	Houghton Mifflin Harcourt
Cesar Chavez	Y	B	2023	Leveled Readers	Houghton Mifflin Harcourt
Cesar Chavez	O	B	1890	On My Own Biography	Lerner Publications
Cesar Chavez	P	B	262	Photo-Illustrated Biographies	Red Brick Learning
Cesar Chavez	Y	B	250+	Rodriguez, Consuelo	Chelsea House
Cesar Chavez	M	B	250+	Rookie Biographies	Children's Press
Cesar Chavez: Fighter in the Field	T	B	250+	High Five Reading	Red Brick Learning
Cesar Chavez: The Farm Workers' Friend	N	B	250+	Literacy by Design	Rigby
Cesar Chavez: The Farm Workers' Friend	N	B	250+	On Our Way to English	Rigby
Cezar's Pollution Solution	P	RF	1270	Leveled Readers	Houghton Mifflin Harcourt
Cezar's Pollution Solution	P	RF	1270	Leveled Readers/CA	Houghton Mifflin Harcourt
Cezar's Pollution Solution	P	RF	1270	Leveled Readers/TX	Houghton Mifflin Harcourt
Chad and the Big Egg	F	F	204	Leveled Readers	Houghton Mifflin Harcourt
Chain of Giving, The	K	TL	250+	Rigby Rocket	Rigby
Chair for My Mother, A	M	RF	250+	Williams, Vera B.	Scholastic
Chairs, Chairs, Chairs!	E	I	70	Rookie Readers	Children's Press
Chalk Talk	C	I	69	Storyteller-First Snow	Wright Group/McGraw Hill
Chalkbox Kid, The	N	RF	250+	Bulla, Clyde Robert	Random House
Challenge at Second Base	Q	RF	250+	Christopher, Matt	Little, Brown & Co.
Challenge of Change, The	U	I	250+	WorldScapes	ETA Cuisenaire
Challenger Disaster, The	U	I	250+	Cornerstones of Freedom	Children's Press
Challenger, The: The Explosion on Liftoff	R	I	250+	Disaster!	Capstone Press
Challenges of Storm Chasing, The	S	I	1877	Reading Street	Pearson

* Collection of short stories
# Graphic text

TITLE	LEVEL	GENRE	WORD COUNT	AUTHOR / SERIES	PUBLISHER / DISTRIBUTOR
Chameleon	Z+	RF	250+	Smith, Charles R. Jr.	Candlewick Press
Chameleon Wore Chartreuse, The: A Chet Gecko Mystery	R	F	250+	Hale, Bruce	Harcourt, Inc.
Chameleons	D	RF	73	Reading Street	Pearson
Chameleons	I	I	289	Sails	Rigby
Chameleons	L	I	201	Twig	Wright Group/McGraw Hill
Chameleons Are Cool	M	I	250+	Read and Wonder	Candlewick Press
Chameleon's Colors	L	F	250+	Tashiro, Chisato	Scholastic
Chameleons of the Rain Forest	N	I	250+	Pacific Literacy	Pacific Learning
Champ	Q	RF	250+	Jones, Marcia	Scholastic
Champ	M	HF	1015	Leveled Readers	Houghton Mifflin Harcourt
Champ	M	HF	1015	Leveled Readers/CA	Houghton Mifflin Harcourt
Champ	M	HF	1015	Leveled Readers/TX	Houghton Mifflin Harcourt
Champ	I	RF	274	Story Box	Wright Group/McGraw Hill
Champ of Hoover Dam	M	HF	869	Leveled Readers	Houghton Mifflin Harcourt
Champ of Hoover Dam	M	HF	869	Leveled Readers/CA	Houghton Mifflin Harcourt
Champ of Hoover Dam	M	HF	869	Leveled Readers/TX	Houghton Mifflin Harcourt
Champion Billy Mills	P	B	725	Leveled Readers	Houghton Mifflin Harcourt
Champion of Change, A	S	B	1341	Leveled Readers	Houghton Mifflin Harcourt
Champion of Change, A	S	B	1341	Leveled Readers/CA	Houghton Mifflin Harcourt
Champion of Change, A	S	B	1341	Leveled Readers/TX	Houghton Mifflin Harcourt
Champions	C	I	13	Twig	Wright Group/McGraw Hill
Champions on Ice	S	I	1880	Leveled Readers	Houghton Mifflin Harcourt
Champions on Ice	S	I	1880	Leveled Readers/CA	Houghton Mifflin Harcourt
Champions on Ice	S	I	1880	Leveled Readers/TX	Houghton Mifflin Harcourt
Chan Li's Pot of Gold	T	HF	2705	Leveled Readers	Houghton Mifflin Harcourt
Chan Li's Pot of Gold	T	HF	2705	Leveled Readers/CA	Houghton Mifflin Harcourt
Chan Li's Pot of Gold	T	HF	2705	Leveled Readers/TX	Houghton Mifflin Harcourt
Chance to Dance, The	Q	B	250+	WorldScapes	ETA Cuisenaire
Chancey of the Maury River	S	F	250+	Amateau, Gigi	Candlewick Press
Chancy and the Grand Rascal	R	F	250+	Fleischman, Sid	Beech Tree Books
Change for Zoe, A	K	RF	250+	Home Connection Collection	Rigby
Change in Plans, A	L	F	250+	On Our Way to English	Rigby
Change in the Community	P	I	250+	PM Extensions	Rigby
Change the Locks	S	RF	250+	French, Simon	Scholastic
Changes	WB	I	N/A	Book Bank	Wright Group/McGraw Hill
Changes All Around Us	M	I	250+	Windows on Literacy	National Geographic
Changes Around Us	J	I	176	Instant Readers	Harcourt School Publishers
Changes for Addy: A Winter Story	Q	HF	250+	The American Girls Collection	Pleasant Company
Changes for Felicity: A Winter Story	Q	HF	250+	The American Girls Collection	Pleasant Company
Changes for Josefina: A Winter Story	Q	HF	250+	The American Girls Collection	Pleasant Company
Changes for Kirsten: A Winter Story	Q	HF	250+	The American Girls Collection	Pleasant Company
Changes for Molly: A Winter Story	Q	HF	250+	The American Girls Collection	Pleasant Company
Changes for Samantha: A Winter Story	Q	HF	250+	The American Girls Collection	Pleasant Company
Changes in Materials	J	I	441	Science Support Readers	Houghton Mifflin Harcourt
Changes in Seasons	I	I	250+	Phonics Readers Plus	Steck-Vaughn
Changes, Changes	WB	I	N/A	Hutchins, Pat	Aladdin
Changing and Growing	H	I	315	Sails	Rigby
Changing Caterpillar, The	G	I	56	Books for Young Learners	Richard C. Owen
Changing Colors	B	I	16	Pair-It Books	Steck-Vaughn
Changing Colors	M	I	247	Vocabulary Readers	Houghton Mifflin Harcourt
Changing Cultures	P	I	250+	PM Extensions	Rigby
Changing Earth	T	I	250+	The News	Richard C. Owen
Changing Earth, The	Q	I	250+	Exploring the Earth	Capstone Press

TITLE	LEVEL	GENRE	WORD COUNT	AUTHOR / SERIES	PUBLISHER / DISTRIBUTOR
Changing Earth, The	P	I	250+	iOpeners	Pearson Learning Group
Changing Land, The	I	I	64	Pacific Literacy	Pacific Learning
Changing Schools	F	RF	53	City Stories	Rigby
Changing Seasons	S	I	1936	Leveled Readers Science	Houghton Mifflin Harcourt
Changing Seasons	I	I	106	Shutterbug Books	Steck-Vaughn
Changing Shape	I	I	143	Rigby Literacy	Rigby
Changing Shape	J	I	250+	Rigby Star Quest	Rigby
Changing Shores	O	I	250+	iOpeners	Pearson Learning Group
Changing the Past	Y	SF	3387	Leveled Readers	Houghton Mifflin Harcourt
Changing the Past	Y	SF	3387	Leveled Readers/CA	Houghton Mifflin Harcourt
Changing the Rules	S	RF	1908	Leveled Readers	Houghton Mifflin Harcourt
Changing Times	Q	RF	250+	Treasured Horses Collection	Scholastic
Changing to Survive: Bird Adaptations	S	I	2536	Reading Street	Pearson
Changing Weather	G	I	145	Early Connections	Benchmark Education
Chang's Paper Pony	L	RF	250+	Coerr, Eleanor	HarperTrophy
Chano	H	RF	124	Literacy 2000	Rigby
Chaos in the Kitchen	K	F	250+	Home Connection Collection	Rigby
Characteristics of Matter	U	I	2036	Science Support Readers	Houghton Mifflin Harcourt
Charged Up: The Story of Electricity	Q	I	250+	Science Works	Picture Window Books
Chariot Race, The	Q	HF	1676	Take Two Books	Wright Group/ McGraw Hill
Charlemagne and the Holy Roman Empire	Y	B	3083	Leveled Readers Social Studies	Houghton Mifflin Harcourt
Charles	C	RF	48	Learn to Read	Creative Teaching Press
Charles Lindbergh	P	B	250+	Early Biographies	Compass Point Books
Charles Lindbergh	P	B	250+	Photo-Illustrated Biographies	Red Brick Learning
Charles M. Schulz	L	B	186	First Biographies	Red Brick Learning
Charley Skedaddle	U	HF	250+	Beatty, Patricia	Troll Associates
Charlie	L	F	250+	Literacy 2000	Rigby
Charlie and the Chocolate Factory	R	F	250+	Dahl, Roald	Bantam
Charlie and the Great Glass Elevator	R	F	250+	Dahl, Roald	Bantam
Charlie Best	J	F	250+	Voyages	SRA/McGraw Hill
Charlie Bone and the Invisible Boy	U	F	250+	Nimmo, Jenny	Orchard Books
Charlie Bone and the Time Twister	U	F	250+	Nimmo, Jenny	Orchard Books
Charlie Is a Chicken	P	RF	250+	Smith, Jane Denitz	HarperTrophy
Charlie Malarkey and the Singing Moose	R	F	250+	Kennedy, William & Brendan	Puffin/Penguin
Charlie Needs a Cloak	I	HF	187	DePaola, Tomie	Prentice-Hall
Charlie Strong and His Favourite Song	G	RF	120	Breakthrough	Longman/Bow
Charlie Takes a Shot	W	RF	2507	Leveled Readers	Houghton Mifflin Harcourt
Charlie the Bridesmaid	K	RF	250+	Rigby Literacy	Rigby
Charlie the Bridesmaid	K	RF	250+	Rigby Star	Rigby
Charlie, the Pancake Pirate	M	F	250+	Wonder World	Wright Group/McGraw Hill
Charlie's Black Hen	E	RF	89	Seedlings	Continental Press
Charlie's Great Race	K	RF	867	PM Plus Story Books	Rigby
Charlie's P.E. Gear	E	RF	102	Lighthouse	Rigby
Charlie's PE Kit	E	RF	114	Lighthouse	Ginn & Co.
Charlie's Story	W	RF	250+	Friel, Maeve	Peachtree
Charlotte Bobcats, The	S	I	250+	Team Spirit	Norwood House Press
Charlotte's Web	R	F	250+	White, E. B.	HarperTrophy
Charlotte's Web Page	P	RF	250+	Action Packs	Rigby
Charmed	Z+	RF	250+	Orca Soundings	Orca Book Publishers
Charters of Freedom	Y	I	2738	Independent Readers Social Studies	Houghton Mifflin Harcourt
Charters of Freedom, The	T	I	250+	Literacy by Design	Rigby
Charting Your Course	T	I	250+	iOpeners	Pearson Learning Group
Charts and Graphs	F	I	123	Shutterbug Books	Steck-Vaughn

* Collection of short stories
# Graphic text

TITLE	LEVEL	GENRE	WORD COUNT	AUTHOR / SERIES	PUBLISHER / DISTRIBUTOR
Chase, The	D	I	52	Bonnell, Kris	Reading Reading Books
Chase, The	F	F	85	Oxford Reading Tree	Oxford University Press
Chasing Redbird	V	RF	250+	Creech, Sharon	HarperCollins
Chasing Storms	R	I	1373	Leveled Readers	Houghton Mifflin Harcourt
Chasing Storms	R	I	1373	Leveled Readers/CA	Houghton Mifflin Harcourt
Chasing the Shadow	O	F	250+	The Adventures of Sam X	Stone Arch Books
Chasing the Train	P	HF	768	Leveled Readers	Houghton Mifflin Harcourt
Chasing Tornadoes	P	I	250+	Gold, Becky	Pearson Learning Group
Chasing Tornadoes!	P	I	250+	Rigby Literacy	Rigby
Chasing Vermeer	T	RF	250+	Balliett, Blue	Scholastic
Chat Room	W	RF	250+	Orca Currents	Orca Book Publishers
Chato and the Party Animals	Q	F	250+	Soto, Gary	Puffin Books
Chattering Chipmunks	K	I	341	Pull Ahead Books	Lerner Publications
Cheaper, Faster, Better	W	I	3253	Reading Street	Pearson
Cheat, The	W	RF	250+	Koss, Amy Goldman	Speak
Check it Out!	B	I	24	Little Celebrations	Pearson Learning Group
Check It Out!	M	RF	250+	Social Studies Connects	Kane Press
Check Out the Library	N	I	839	Vocabulary Readers	Houghton Mifflin Harcourt
Check Out the Library	N	I	839	Vocabulary Readers/CA	Houghton Mifflin Harcourt
Check Out the Library	N	I	839	Vocabulary Readers/TX	Houghton Mifflin Harcourt
Checkout!	P	I	250+	Bookweb	Rigby
Cheer All-Stars: Best of the Best	T	I	250+	Cheerleading	Capstone Press
Cheer Basics: Rules to Cheer By	S	I	250+	Cheerleading	Capstone Press
Cheer Challenge	P	RF	250+	Maddox, Jake	Stone Arch Books
Cheer Competitions: Impressing the Judges	T	I	250+	Cheerleading	Capstone Press
Cheer Essentials: Uniforms and Equipment	S	I	250+	Cheerleading	Capstone Press
Cheer Professionals: Cheer as a Career	T	I	250+	Cheerleading	Capstone Press
Cheer Skills: Beginning Tumbling and Stunting	S	I	250+	Cheerleading	Capstone Press
Cheer Spirit: Revving Up the Crowd	S	I	250+	Cheerleading	Capstone Press
Cheer Squad: Building Spirit and Getting Along	S	I	250+	Cheerleading	Capstone Press
Cheer Tryouts: Making the Cut	S	I	250+	Cheerleading	Capstone Press
Cheerful King, The	K	F	351	Little Books	Sadlier-Oxford
Cheerleaders, The	D	F	36	Reading Safari	Mondo
Cheerleading	F	I	56	On Deck	Rigby
Cheerleading for Fun!	S	I	250+	Activities for Fun	Compass Point Books
Cheers for the Cheetahs	N	RF	889	Reading Street	Pearson
Cheers, Chants, and Signs: Getting the Crowd Going	T	I	250+	Cheerleading	Capstone Press
Cheese, Please?	C	RF	62	Story Steps	Rigby
Cheesecake Cupcakes and Other Cake Recipes	S	I	250+	Fun Food for Cool Cooks	Capstone Press
Cheetah Conservation	R	I	250+	Storyteller -Whispering Pines	Wright Group/McGraw Hill
Cheetahs	I	I	139	African Animals	Capstone Press
Cheetahs	O	I	2085	Early Bird Nature Books	Lerner Publications
Cheetahs	G	RF	140	Seedlings	Continental Press
Chefs	L	I	250+	Community Workers	Compass Point Books
Chefs	J	I	239	On Deck	Rigby
Chemical Changes	V	I	983	Science Support Readers	Houghton Mifflin Harcourt
Chemical Compounds	Y	I	1404	Science Support Readers	Houghton Mifflin Harcourt
Chen's Christmas Tree	E	RF	166	Developing Books	Pioneer Valley
Cherokee Indians, The	P	I	250+	Native Peoples	Red Brick Learning
Cherokee Little People, The	I	TL	250+	Rigby Star	Rigby
Cherokee Little People, The: A Native American Tale	I	TL	250+	Rigby Literacy	Rigby
Cherokee, The	R	I	250+	First Reports	Compass Point Books

TITLE	LEVEL	GENRE	WORD COUNT	AUTHOR / SERIES	PUBLISHER / DISTRIBUTOR
Cherokee, The: Native Basket Weavers	R	I	250+	America's First Peoples	Capstone Press
Cherokees, The	T	I	4165	Native American Stories	Lerner Publications
Cherries and Cherry Pits	M	RF	250+	Williams, Vera B.	Houghton Mifflin Harcourt
Cherries, The	H	F	286	Leveled Literacy Intervention/ Green System	Heinemann
Cherry Blossom Cat	J	F	250+	Storyworlds	Heinemann Educational Books
Cherry Blossom Festival, The	S	I	250+	WorldScapes	ETA Cuisenaire
Cherry Blossoms Everywhere	M	I	370	Independent Readers Social Studies	Houghton Mifflin Harcourt
Cherry Tree, The	R	F	1684	Leveled Readers	Houghton Mifflin Harcourt
Cherry Tree, The	R	F	1684	Leveled Readers/CA	Houghton Mifflin Harcourt
Chesapeake Bay	R	I	1192	Leveled Readers Social Studies	Houghton Mifflin Harcourt
Chesapeake Bay Wetlands	P	I	1082	Time for Kids	Teacher Created Materials
Chester A. Arthur	U	B	250+	Profiles of the Presidents	Compass Point Books
Chester A. Arthur: Twenty-first President	R	B	250+	Getting to Know the U.S. Presidents	Children's Press
Chester Cricket's New Home	S	F	250+	Selden, George	Bantam
Chester Cricket's Pigeon Ride	S	F	250+	Selden, George	Bantam
Chester Greenwood's Big Idea	N	I	642	Leveled Literacy Intervention/ Blue System	Heinemann
Chester the Wizard	M	F	250+	Reading Unlimited	Pearson Learning Group
Chester The Worldly Pig	M	F	250+	Peet, Bill	Houghton Mifflin Harcourt
Chester's Good Idea	M	B	250+	Leveled Readers Language Support	Houghton Mifflin Harcourt
Chester's Way	M	F	250+	Henkes, Kevin	Scholastic
Chew, Chew, Chew	C	RF	24	Literacy 2000	Rigby
Cheyenne, The	P	I	250+	A New True Book	Children's Press
Cheyenne, The	R	I	250+	First Reports	Compass Point Books
Cheyenne, The: People of the Central Plains	S	I	250+	Theme Sets	National Geographic
Chicago American Giants, The	S	I	1058	Reading Street	Pearson
Chicago Bears, The	S	I	250+	Team Spirit	Norwood House Press
Chicago Bulls, The	S	I	250+	Team Spirit	Norwood House Press
Chicago Cubs, The	S	I	5128	Team Spirit	Norwood House Press
Chicago Defender and the Great Migration, The	Y	I	2694	Reading Street	Pearson
Chicago Fire, The	P	I	250+	Gutner, Howard	Scholastic
Chicago White Sox, The	S	I	4630	Team Spirit	Norwood House Press
Chicago Winds	K	I	173	Evangeline Nicholas Collection	Wright Group/McGraw Hill
Chick and the Duckling, The	D	F	112	Ginsburg, Mirra	Macmillan
Chick Catches Dinner	J	F	451	Sun Sprouts	ETA Cuisenaire
Chick Challenge	O	RF	250+	Baglio, Ben M.	Scholastic
Chick That Wouldn't Hatch, The	F	F	173	Green Light Readers	Harcourt
Chicken	M	I	250+	Life Cycles	Creative Teaching Press
Chicken and Egg Chores	C	RF	27	Little Books for Early Readers	University of Maine
Chicken and the Egg, The	E	I	68	Sun Sprouts	ETA Cuisenaire
Chicken Boy	W	RF	250+	Dowell, Frances O'Roark	Aladddin Paperbacks
Chicken Feed	E	RF	67	Joy Readers	Pearson Learning Group
Chicken Foot Farm	X	RF	250+	Estevis, Anne	Pinata Books
Chicken for Dinner	C	RF	27	Story Box	Wright Group/McGraw Hill
Chicken in the Middle of the Road	J	RF	250+	Bookshop	Mondo
Chicken Licken	I	TL	698	Big Cat	Pacific Learning
Chicken Licken	H	TL	171	Rigby Star	Rigby
Chicken Licken	I	TL	346	Sunshine	Wright Group/McGraw Hill
Chicken Licken	H	TL	233	Supersonics	Rigby

* Collection of short stories
\# Graphic text

TITLE	LEVEL	GENRE	WORD COUNT	AUTHOR / SERIES	PUBLISHER / DISTRIBUTOR
Chicken Little	E	TL	256	Leveled Literacy Intervention/ Blue System	Heinemann
Chicken Little	I	TL	250+	PM Traditional Tales-Orange	Rigby
Chicken Little	E	TL	107	Sunshine	Wright Group/McGraw Hill
Chicken Little	L	TL	587	Traditional Tales & More	Rigby
Chicken Pox	K	I	250+	Health Matters	Capstone Press
Chicken Pox	H	RF	220	Little Readers	Houghton Mifflin Harcourt
Chicken Soup	B	I	38	Fitros, Pamela	Kaeden Books
Chicken Soup with Rice	M	F	310	Sendak, Maurice	HarperCollins
Chicken Sunday	N	RF	250+	Polacco, Patricia	Scholastic
Chickens	D	I	23	Books for Young Learners	Richard C. Owen
Chickens	G	I	105	Bookshop	Mondo
Chickens	B	I	24	Pebble Books	Capstone Press
Chickens	L	I	250+	PM Animal Facts: Purple	Rigby
Chickens and Chicks	B	I	31	Animal Families	Lerner Publications
Chickens Are Here!, The	D	I	50	Vocabulary Readers	Houghton Mifflin Harcourt
Chickens Aren't the Only Ones	L	I	250+	Heller, Ruth	Scholastic
Chickens Have Chicks	M	I	250+	Animals and Their Young	Compass Point Books
Chickens on the Farm	G	I	59	Pebble Books	Capstone Press
Chickens on the Farm	F	I	68	Vocabulary Readers	Houghton Mifflin Harcourt
Chickens on Vacation	G	F	169	Seedlings	Continental Press
Chickerella	N	TL	250+	Auch, Mary Jane and Herm	Holiday House
Chick-in-a-Box	K	RF	250+	Voyages	SRA/McGraw Hill
Chick's Adventure	I	F	363	Sun Sprouts	ETA Cuisenaire
Chicks Are Hatching, The	D	F	81	Gilbert the Pig	Pioneer Valley
Chicks Don't Say Quack	D	F	86	Sun Sprouts	ETA Cuisenaire
Chick's Walk	A	F	14	Story Box	Wright Group/McGraw Hill
Chico	D	RF	86	Literacy by Design	Rigby
Chico	D	RF	86	On Our Way to English	Rigby
Chief Great Raven	N	TL	250+	Orbit Double Takes	Pacific Learning
Chief Joseph	S	B	3585	History Maker Bios	Lerner Publications
Chief Joseph	Y	B	2199	Leveled Readers	Houghton Mifflin Harcourt
Chief Joseph of the Nez Percé	P	B	250+	Photo-Illustrated Biographies	Red Brick Learning
Chief Justice John Marshall	U	B	250+	Bookshop	Mondo
Chief Seattle	T	B	250+	Amazing Americans	Wright Group/McGraw Hill
Chief Washakie	U	B	2073	Leveled Readers	Houghton Mifflin Harcourt
Chief Washakie	U	B	2073	Leveled Readers/CA	Houghton Mifflin Harcourt
Chief Washakie	U	B	2073	Leveled Readers/TX	Houghton Mifflin Harcourt
Chihuahuas	R	I	250+	All About Dogs	Capstone Press
Chihuahuas	I	I	158	Dogs	Capstone Press
Child Called "It", A	Z+	B	250+	Pelzer, Dave	Health Communications
Child in Prison Camp, A	X	HF	250+	Takashima, Shizuye	Tundra Books
Child of the Owl	W	RF	250+	Yep, Laurence	HarperTrophy
Child of the Wolves	U	RF	250+	Hall, Elizabeth	Bantam
Childhood in Pre-War Japan	V	I	1832	Reading Street	Pearson
Children	C	I	45	Pebble Books	Capstone Press
Children Around the World	M	I	250+	People, Spaces & Places	Rand McNally
Children Around the World	P	I	250+	Rigby Focus	Rigby
Children as Young Scientists	K	I	393	Early Connections	Benchmark Education
Children at Play	F	I	101	Little Red Readers	Sundance
Children of Ancient Greece	P	I	250+	Rosen Real Readers	Rosen Publishing Group
*Children of Christmas: Stories for the Season	R	RF	250+	Rylant, Cynthia	Orchard Books
Children of Clay: A Family of Pueblo Potters	S	I	250+	Swentzell, Rina	Lerner Publishing
Children of Green Knowe, The	T	F	250+	Boston, L. M.	Harcourt Trade

TITLE	LEVEL	GENRE	WORD COUNT	AUTHOR / SERIES	PUBLISHER / DISTRIBUTOR
Children of Sierra Leone, The	J	I	142	Books For Young Learners	Richard C. Owen
Children of the Dust Bowl	Y	I	250+	Stanley, Jerry	Crown
Children of the Earth and Sky	P	I	250+	Krensky, Stephen	Scholastic
Children of the Fire	P	HF	250+	Robinet, Harriette	Aladdin
Children of the Longhouse	S	HF	250+	Bruchac, Joseph	Penguin Group
Children of the River	X	RF	250+	Crew, Linda	Bantam
Children of the Sierra Madre, The	U	I	250+	Staub, Frank	Carolrhoda Books
Children of the Wild West	X	I	250+	Freedman, Russell	Clarion
Children's Clothing of the 1800's	S	I	250+	Historic Communities	Crabtree
Children's Farm, The	I	I	390	Explorations	Eleanor Curtain Publishing
Children's Farm, The	I	I	390	Explorations	Okapi Eductional Materials
Children's Forest, The	Q	I	250+	Explorer Books-Pathfinder	National Geographic
Children's Forest, The	P	I	250+	Explorer Books-Pioneer	National Geographic
Child's Day, A	T	I	250+	Historic Communities	Crabtree
Child's Day, A	C	RF	34	Sunshine	Wright Group/McGraw Hill
Child's Life in Korea, A	M	I	638	Reading Street	Pearson
Child's Portrait of Shakespeare, A	Q	B	250+	Burdett, Lois	Firefly Books
Childtimes: A Three-Generation Memoir	X	B	250+	Greenfield, Eloise; Little, Lessie Jones	HarperTrophy
Chile	Q	I	250+	First Reports: Countries	Compass Point Books
Chile Peppers	E	I	115	On Our Way to English	Rigby
Chili for Lindy	J	RF	250+	Leveled Readers Language Support	Houghton Mifflin Harcourt
Chili Pepper Pinata, The	H	RF	257	Story Box	Wright Group/McGraw Hill
Chill	U	RF	250+	Orca Soundings	Orca Book Publishers
Chill Wind	Z	RF	250+	McDonald, Janet	Farrar, Straus and Giroux
Chimp Communities	U	I	1618	Leveled Readers Science	Houghton Mifflin Harcourt
Chimpanzees	O	I	2307	Early Bird Nature Books	Lerner Publications
Chimpanzees	S	I	1605	Leveled Readers Science	Houghton Mifflin Harcourt
Chimpanzees	H	I	86	Rain Forest Animals	Capstone Press
Chimpanzees	I	I	200	Sails	Rigby
Chimpanzees	M	I	250+	The Wild World of Animals	Capstone Press
Chimpanzees of Happytown, The	M	F	250+	Andreae, Giles	Scholastic
China	O	I	2373	A Ticket to …	Carolrohoda Books
China	P	I	250+	A True Book	Children's Press
China	O	I	250+	Countries of the World	Red Brick Learning
China	Q	I	250+	First Reports: Countries	Compass Point Books
China	P	I	250+	Many Cultures, One World	Capstone Press
China	W	I	250+	Primary Source Readers	Teacher Created Materials
China	V	I	250+	Theme Sets	National Geographic
China ABCs: A Book About the People and Places of China	Q	I	250+	Country ABCs	Picture Window Books
China in Colors	N	I	250+	World of Colors	Capstone Press
China Teacup, The	M	F	250+	Voyages	SRA/McGraw Hill
China, America, and Me	T	I	2309	Reading Street	Pearson
China: A Question and Answer Book	P	I	250+	Questions and Answers: Countries	Capstone Press
China: Everyday Kids Now and Then	S	HF	250+	Reading Expeditions	National Geographic
China: Now and Then	T	I	1387	Reading Street	Pearson
China: The Culture	T	I	250+	Kalman, Bobbie	Crabtree
China: The Land	T	I	250+	Kalman, Bobbie	Crabtree
China: The People	T	I	250+	Kalman, Bobbie	Crabtree
Chinampa, The	K	RF	405	Take Two Books	Wright Group/McGraw Hill
China's Amazing Buildings	T	I	498	Vocabulary Readers	Houghton Mifflin Harcourt

* Collection of short stories
\# Graphic text

TITLE	LEVEL	GENRE	WORD COUNT	AUTHOR / SERIES	PUBLISHER / DISTRIBUTOR
China's Bravest Girl: The Legend of Hua Mu Lan	O	TL	250+	Chin, Charlie	Children's Press
China's Gifts to the World	Q	I	1352	Reading Street	Pearson
China's Huang River	S	I	2036	Independent Readers Social Studies	Houghton Mifflin Harcourt
Chinese Americans: An Imigration History	W	I	2660	Reading Street	Pearson
Chinese Foods and Recipes	P	I	250+	Rosen Real Readers	Rosen Publishing Group
Chinese Immigrants 1850-1900	T	I	250+	Coming to America	Capstone Press
Chinese Immigrants in America: An Interactive History Adventure	V	HF	250+	You Choose Books	Capstone Press
Chinese Immigration	V	I	250+	Theme Sets	National Geographic
Chinese Kites	LB	I	15	Twig	Wright Group/McGraw Hill
Chinese New Year	J	I	176	Holidays and Celebrations	Capstone Press
Chinese New Year	O	I	250+	Holidays and Festivals	Compass Point Books
Chinese New Year	N	I	1679	On My Own Holidays	Lerner Publications
Chinese New Year	D	I	33	Pacific Literacy	Pacific Learning
Chinese New Year	N	I	812	Springboard	Wright Group/McGraw Hill
Chinese New Year	F	I	79	Vocabulary Readers	Houghton Mifflin Harcourt
Chinese New Year, The	J	TL	250+	Cambridge Reading	Pearson Learning Group
Chin's Lunch	G	RF	188	On Our Way to English	Rigby
Chipmunk at Hollow Tree Lane	K	F	250+	Sherrow, Victoria	Scholastic
Chipmunks Do What Chipmunks Do	I	F	138	Leveled Readers/TX	Houghton Mifflin Harcourt
Chipmunk's New Home	I	F	300	Leveled Readers	Houghton Mifflin Harcourt
Chipmunk's New Home	I	F	300	Leveled Readers/CA	Houghton Mifflin Harcourt
Chipmunk's New Home	I	F	300	Leveled Readers/TX	Houghton Mifflin Harcourt
Chip's Dad	K	RF	250+	Rigby Literacy	Rigby
Chisholm Trail, The	V	I	250+	Cornerstones of Freedom	Children's Press
Chloe Doe	Z+	RF	250+	Phillips, Suzanne	Little, Brown & Co.
Chloe the Chameleon	F	F	250+	Warren, Celia	Scholastic
Chocolate	N	I	250+	What's For Lunch?	Children's Press
Chocolate	L	I	191	Windows on Literacy	National Geographic
Chocolate by Hershey: A Story about Milton S. Hershey	R	B	250+	Burford, Betty	Carolrhoda Books
Chocolate Cake, The	J	RF	250+	PM Plus Story Books	Rigby
Chocolate Cake, The	B	RF	23	Story Box	Wright Group/McGraw Hill
Chocolate Chip Cookies	LB	I	12	Preiss, Leah Palmer	Henry Holt & Co.
Chocolate Chip Cookies	B	I	32	Ready Readers	Pearson Learning Group
Chocolate Fever	O	F	250+	Smith, Robert	Bantam
Chocolate Flier, The	R	I	250+	Action Packs	Rigby
Chocolate Maker's Secrets, The	N	I	250+	Sun Sprouts	ETA Cuisenaire
Chocolate Touch, The	N	F	250+	Catling, Patrick Skene	Bantam
Chocolate Trail, The	N	I	250+	Rigby Focus	Rigby
Chocolate Tree, The	N	TL	2178	On My Own Folklore	Millbrook Press
Chocolate!	P	I	250+	Action Packs	Rigby
Chocolate, Chocolate, Chocolate	E	RF	106	Visions	Wright Group/McGraw Hill
Chocolate...Yum!	M	I	579	Springboard	Wright Group/McGraw Hill
Chocolate-Chip Muffins	J	RF	204	Sunshine	Wright Group/McGraw Hill
Chocolate-Covered Contest, The	S	RF	250+	Keene, Carolyn	Pocket Books
Choctaws, The	T	I	3586	Native American Stories	Lerner Publications
Choice for Sarah, A	K	RF	250+	PM Plus Story Books	Rigby
Chomp	L	I	250+	Berger, Melvin	Scholastic
Chook, Chook	E	RF	42	Sunshine	Wright Group/McGraw Hill
Choose Me!	H	F	204	Reading Corners	Pearson Learning Group
Choosing a Pet	A	I	31	Leveled Readers	Houghton Mifflin Harcourt

* Collection of short stories
# Graphic text

TITLE	LEVEL	GENRE	WORD COUNT	AUTHOR / SERIES	PUBLISHER / DISTRIBUTOR
Choosing a Pet	A	I	31	Leveled Readers/CA	Houghton Mifflin Harcourt
Choosing a Puppy	E	RF	158	PM Extensions-Yellow	Rigby
Choosing a Trip	L	I	672	Sun Sprouts	ETA Cuisenaire
Choosing Eyeglasses with Mrs. Koutris	J	I	299	Our Neighborhood	Children's Press
Choosing Up Sides	V	RF	250+	Ritter, John H.	Puffin/Penguin
Chop and Pop	F	I	99	Reading Safari	Mondo
Chop, Simmer, Season	LB	I	21	Brandenburg, Alexa	Harcourt Brace
Choppers	M	I	250+	Horsepower	Capstone Press
Choppers	W	I	5275	Motor Mania	Lerner Publications
Chopsticks	H	RF	222	On Our Way to English	Rigby
Chores	D	RF	50	Windows on Literacy	National Geographic
Chorus	F	I	77	On Deck	Rigby
Chorus of Frogs, A	U	I	250+	Wild Life Series	London Town Press
Christa McAuliffe	N	B	250+	Explore Space!	Capstone Press
Christa McAuliffe: Teacher in Space	W	B	250+	Naden, Corinne J.; Blue, Rose	Millbrook Press
Christina's Ghost	R	F	250+	Wright, Betty Ren	Bantam
Christmas	H	I	129	All About Winter	Capstone Press
Christmas	Q	I	250+	Celebrate!	Capstone Press
Christmas	F	I	106	Fiesta Holiday Series	Pearson Learning Group
Christmas	M	I	250+	Holidays and Celebrations	Picture Window Books
Christmas	J	I	133	Holidays and Celebrations	Capstone Press
Christmas	O	I	250+	Holidays and Festivals	Compass Point Books
Christmas	P	I	250+	Let's See	Compass Point Books
Christmas	LB	I	16	Smart Starts	Rigby
Christmas Around the World	N	I	1699	On My Own Holidays	Lerner Publications
Christmas at Wapos Bay	T	RF	250+	From Many Peoples	Fitzhenry & Whiteside
Christmas Carol, A	U	F	250+	Dickens, Charles	Scholastic
Christmas in Many Cultures	I	I	125	Life Around the World	Capstone Press
Christmas in the Big Woods	J	HF	250+	Wilder, Laura Ingalls	HarperCollins
Christmas in the Trenches	T	HF	250+	McCutcheon, John	Peachtree
Christmas Santa Almost Missed, The	G	F	158	First Start	Troll Associates
Christmas Shopping	E	RF	48	Literacy 2000	Rigby
Christmas Spurs, The	R	RF	250+	Wallace, Bill	Bantam
Christmas Surprise	G	RF	145	First Start	Troll Associates
Christmas Tree, The	F	RF	163	PM Story Books	Rigby
Christmas: Why We Celebrate It the Way We Do	P	I	250+	Hintz, Martin & Kate	Red Brick Learning
Christopher Columbus	M	B	250+	First Biographies	Red Brick Learning
Christopher Columbus	S	B	3543	History Maker Bios	Lerner Publications
Christopher Columbus	T	B	250+	In Their Own Words	Scholastic
Christopher Columbus	S	B	250+	Primary Source Readers	Teacher Created Materials
Christopher Columbus: A Great Explorer	O	B	250+	Greene, Carol	Children's Press
#Christopher Columbus: Famous Explorer	R	B	250+	Graphic Library	Capstone Press
Christopher Reeve: A Life Worth Living	Q	B	1518	Gear Up!	Wright Group/ McGraw Hill
Christopher Reeve: Still a Hero	R	B	250+	Leveled Readers Language Support	Houghton Mifflin Harcourt
Christophe's Story	Q	RF	250+	Cornwell, Nicki	Frances Lincoln
Christy's First Dive	J	RF	250+	Leveled Readers Language Support	Houghton Mifflin Harcourt
Chu Ju's House	W	RF	250+	Whelan, Gloria	Scholastic
Chug the Tractor	F	F	203	PM Story Books	Rigby
Chug, Chug, Chug!	F	RF	137	Reading Street	Pearson
Chumash, The	T	I	4147	Native American Stories	Lerner Publications
Chunk of Cheese, A	F	F	215	Leveled Readers	Houghton Mifflin Harcourt
Chunk of Cheese, A	F	F	215	Leveled Readers/CA	Houghton Mifflin Harcourt

* Collection of short stories
\# Graphic text

TITLE	LEVEL	GENRE	WORD COUNT	AUTHOR / SERIES	PUBLISHER / DISTRIBUTOR
Chunk of Cheese, A	F	F	215	Leveled Readers/TX	Houghton Mifflin Harcourt
Church	LB	I	17	Visions	Wright Group/McGraw Hill
Cicadas	J	I	87	Pebble Books	Red Brick Learning
Cincinnati Bengals, The	S	I	250+	Team Spirit	Norwood House Press
Cincinnati Reds, The	S	I	250+	Team Spirit	Norwood House Press
Cinco de Mayo	E	I	120	Fiesta Holiday Series	Pearson Learning Group
Cinco de Mayo	Q	I	250+	Holiday Histories	Heinemann Library
Cinco de Mayo	J	I	144	Holidays and Celebrations	Capstone Press
Cinco de Mayo	O	I	250+	Holidays and Festivals	Compass Point Books
Cinco de Mayo	N	I	1731	On My Own Holidays	Lerner Publications
Cinderella	J	TL	250+	Jumbled Tumbled Tales & Rhymes	Rigby
Cinderella	K	TL	250+	Once Upon a Time	Wright Group/McGraw Hill
Cinderella	K	TL	250+	PM Tales and Plays-Gold	Rigby
Cinderella	I	TL	580	Traditional Tales	Pearson Learning Group
Cinderella at the Ball	F	TL	269	Fairy Tales and Folklore	Norwood House Press
Cinderella Dressed in Yellow	E	F	81	Learn to Read	Creative Teaching Press
Cinderfella's Big Night and Other Fractured Fairy Tales	P	TL	250+	Action Packs	Rigby
Cindy and the Football Boots	M	RF	250+	Lighthouse	Ginn & Co.
Cinnabar and the Island of Shadows: The Fairy Chronicles	Q	F	11700	Sweet, J.H.	Sourcebooks
Circle	B	I	32	Shapes	Lerner Publications
Circle of Gold	R	RF	250+	Boyd, Candy Dawson	Bantam
Circle of Quiet, A	Z	B	250+	L'Engle, Madeleine	HarperCollins
Circle of Time, A	Y	RF	250+	Montes, Marisa	Harcourt Trade
Circle Unbroken, A	V	HF	250+	Leveled Readers Language Support	Houghton Mifflin Harcourt
Circles	C	I	56	Dominie Readers	Pearson Learning Group
Circles Around Town	J	I	253	Shapes Around Town	Capstone Press
Circles Everywhere	A	I	40	On Our Way to English	Rigby
Circles: Seeing Circles All Around Us	L	I	198	Shapes	Capstone Press
*Circuit, The	Z	HF	250+	Francisco, Jimenez	Scholastic
Circular Movement	E	I	43	The Way Things Move	Capstone Press
Circulatory System, The	S	I	250+	A True Book	Children's Press
Circulatory System, The	P	I	2175	Early Bird Body Systems	Lerner Publishing
Circulatory System, The	M	I	171	Human Body Systems	Red Brick Learning
Circus	B	I	20	Twig	Wright Group/McGraw Hill
Circus Book, The	I	I	250+	Reading Unlimited	Pearson Learning Group
Circus Clown, The	A	RF	31	Literacy 2000	Rigby
Circus Detective, The	R	RF	250+	Book Blazers	ETA Cuisenaire
Circus Fun	E	RF	280	Easy Stories	Norwood House Press
Circus Fun	G	RF	219	Momentum Literacy Program	Troll Associates
Circus Mystery, The	M	RF	250+	Woodland Mysteries	Wright Group/McGraw Hill
Circus Train, The	A	F	48	Little Red Readers	Sundance
Circus Tricks	H	I	236	Scooters	ETA Cuisenaire
Circus, The	WB	I	N/A	Carle, Eric	HarperCollins
Circus, The	LB	I	31	Literacy 2000	Rigby
Circus, The	D	RF	42	Wonder World	Wright Group/McGraw Hill
Cities Around the World	M	I	250+	Pair-It Books	Steck-Vaughn
Cities Below the Sea	O	I	250+	WorldScapes	ETA Cuisenaire
Cities of Splendor: The Facts and the Fables	R	TL	250+	Landscapes of Legend	Children's Press
Cities Then, Cities Now	M	I	406	Leveled Readers Social Studies	Houghton Mifflin Harcourt
Cities: The Building of America	Q	I	250+	Thompson, Gare	Children's Press

* Collection of short stories
# Graphic text

TITLE	LEVEL	GENRE	WORD COUNT	AUTHOR / SERIES	PUBLISHER / DISTRIBUTOR
Cities: Then and Now	O	I	250+	People, Spaces & Places	Rand McNally
Citizen's Movements	U	I	2079	Reading Street	Pearson
Citizens of the World	T	I	2642	Independent Readers Social Studies	Houghton Mifflin Harcourt
Citizenship	L	I	250+	Everyday Character Education	Capstone Press
City and Country	G	I	268	Vocabulary Readers	Houghton Mifflin Harcourt
City and Country	G	I	268	Vocabulary Readers/CA	Houghton Mifflin Harcourt
City and the Country, The	B	I	48	Leveled Readers Emergent	Houghton Mifflin Harcourt
City Animals	G	RF	102	Higgins, Malcom	Houghton Mifflin Harcourt
City Buildings	G	I	133	Discovery Links	Newbridge
City Buried in Time, A	U	I	1429	Vocabulary Readers	Houghton Mifflin Harcourt
City Buried in Time, A	U	I	1429	Vocabulary Readers/CA	Houghton Mifflin Harcourt
City Bus, The	B	RF	21	Visions	Wright Group/McGraw Hill
City by the Lake	N	I	250+	Early Connections	Benchmark Education
City Cat	J	F	250+	Storyworlds	Heinemann Educational Books
City Cat and the Country Cat, The	E	F	152	Ready Readers	Pearson Learning Group
City Divided, A	X	HF	250+	Power Up!	Steck-Vaughn
City Dog, Country Dog	H	RF	203	Literacy by Design	Rigby
City Friends, Country Friends	L	RF	908	Reading Street	Pearson
City Fun	F	RF	250+	Let's Play	Norwood House Press
City Garden, A	G	RF	77	City Stories	Rigby
City Garden, A	C	I	111	Leveled Readers	Houghton Mifflin Harcourt
City Garden, A	C	I	111	Leveled Readers/CA	Houghton Mifflin Harcourt
City Green	L	RF	250+	DiSalvo-Ryan, DyAnne	Scholastic
City in the Cliffs	Q	HF	1454	Leveled Readers	Houghton Mifflin Harcourt
City in the Cliffs	Q	HF	1454	Leveled Readers/CA	Houghton Mifflin Harcourt
City in the Cliffs	Q	HF	1454	Leveled Readers/TX	Houghton Mifflin Harcourt
City Life	C	I	32	Rosen Real Readers	Rosen Publishing Group
City Life and Country Life	E	F	66	Moriarty, Julie	Scholastic
City Life: Then and Now	T	I	2253	Reading Street	Pearson
City Lights	N	RF	250+	Orbit Double Takes	Pacific Learning
City Lights	LB	RF	16	Visions	Wright Group/McGraw Hill
City Mouse and Country Mouse	D	TL	87	Learn to Read	Creative Teaching Press
City Mouse and Country Mouse	I	TL	168	Reading Street	Pearson
City Mouse and the Country Mouse, The	K	TL	636	Leveled Literacy Intervention/Blue System	Heinemann
City Mouse-Country Mouse	J	TL	198	Wallner, John	Scholastic
City Noises	D	RF	37	Instant Readers	Harcourt School Publishers
City of Ember, The	W	F	250+	DuPrau, Jeanne	Random House
City of Gold & Lead, The	V	F	250+	Christopher, John	Aladdin
City of Ruins	X	SF	250+	Williams, Mark London	Candlewick Press
City of the Beasts	Z	F	250+	Allende, Isabel	Harper Trophy
City of the Inca	S	B	250+	WorldScapes	ETA Cuisenaire
City on a Lake, The	R	I	642	Vocabulary Readers	Houghton Mifflin Harcourt
City or Country	H	I	88	Pair-It Turn and Learn	Steck-Vaughn
City Park	N	I	250+	Habitats	Children's Press
City Park, A	I	RF	59	Leveled Readers	Houghton Mifflin Harcourt
City Parks	L	I	650	Vocabulary Readers/TX	Houghton Mifflin Harcourt
City Patterns	J	I	270	Finding Patterns	Capstone Press
City Scenes	E	RF	24	Pacific Literacy	Pacific Learning
City Senses	C	I	85	Twig	Wright Group/McGraw Hill
City Shapes	G	I	176	Yellow Umbrella Books	Red Brick Learning
City Sights	G	I	250+	Phonics and Friends	Hampton-Brown

* Collection of short stories
\# Graphic text

TITLE	LEVEL	GENRE	WORD COUNT	AUTHOR / SERIES	PUBLISHER / DISTRIBUTOR
City Sounds	G	RF	142	Marzollo, Jean	Scholastic
City Storm	E	I	180	Twig	Wright Group/McGraw Hill
City Through the Ages	U	I	250+	Steele, Philip	Troll Associates
City Transportation	L	I	459	Rigby Flying Colors	Rigby
City, The	C	I	98	Vocabulary Readers	Houghton Mifflin Harcourt
City, The	C	I	98	Vocabulary Readers/CA	Houghton Mifflin Harcourt
Civil Rights Marches	V	I	250+	Cornerstones of Freedom	Children's Press
Civil Rights Movement	U	I	250+	Primary Source Readers	Teacher Created Materials
Civil Rights Movement in America, The	V	I	250+	Cornerstones of Freedom	Children's Press
Civil Rights Movement, The	V	I	1916	Reading Street	Pearson
Civil War Is Coming	T	I	250+	Primary Source Readers	Teacher Created Materials
Civil War Leaders	T	B	250+	Primary Source Readers	Teacher Created Materials
Civil War on Sunday	M	F	250+	Osborne, Mary Pope	Random House
Civil War Spies	U	I	250+	Spies	Capstone Press
Civil War, The	V	I	250+	America Goes to War	Red Brick Learning
Civil War, The	T	I	250+	Reading Expeditions	National Geographic
Civilizations - Yesterday, Today	W	I	250+	Connectors	Pacific Learning
Claiming Georgia Tate	Z+	HF	250+	Amateau, Gigi	Candlewick Press
Clap for the Show	I	RF	250+	Phonics and Friends	Hampton-Brown
Clap Your Hands!	B	I	22	Pair-It Books	Steck-Vaughn
Clara and the Bookwagon	K	RF	250+	Levinson, Nancy Smiler	HarperTrophy
Clara and the Bossy	K	F	684	Ohi, Ruth	Annick Press
Clara Barton	N	B	203	First Biographies	Capstone Press
Clara Barton	S	B	3920	History Maker Bios	Lerner Publications
Clara Barton	M	B	320	Independent Readers Social Studies	Houghton Mifflin Harcourt
Clara Barton	P	B	250+	Photo-Illustrated Biographies	Red Brick Learning
Clara Barton: Angel of the Battlefield	M	B	250+	Rosen Real Readers	Rosen Publishing Group
Clara Barton: Founder of the American Red Cross	R	B	250+	Stevenson, Augusta	Aladdin
Clarence the Crocodile	L	F	250+	New Way Literature	Steck-Vaughn
Clarice Bean Spells Trouble	R	RF	250+	Child, Lauren	Scholastic
Clarice Bean, Don't Look Now	Q	RF	250+	Child, Lauren	Candlewick Press
Class Calender	H	I	81	Windows on Literacy	National Geographic
Class Clown	O	RF	250+	Hurwitz, Johanna	Scholastic
Class Photograph, The	J	RF	462	PM Math Readers	Rigby
Class Play with Ms. Vanilla, A	I	RF	234	Ehrlich, Fred	Puffin/Penguin
Class Play, The	J	RF	250+	Little Readers	Houghton Mifflin Harcourt
Class President	O	RF	250+	Hurwitz, Johanna	Scholastic
Class Rules	G	RF	143	Windows on Literacy	National Geographic
Class Teddy Bear	F	RF	106	Windows on Literacy	National Geographic
Class Trip from the Black Lagoon, The	N	F	250+	Black Lagoon Adventures	Scholastic
Class Trip to the Cave of Doom	Q	F	250+	McMullan, Kate	Grossett & Dunlap
Class, The	F	RF	93	Reading Street	Pearson
Classroom Animals	I	I	328	Explorations	Eleanor Curtain Publishing
Classroom Animals	I	I	328	Explorations	Okapi Eductional Materials
Classroom Caterpillars, The	H	RF	216	PM Plus Story Books	Rigby
Classroom Pets	K	I	250+	Literacy by Design	Rigby
Classroom Rules	F	I	190	On Our Way to English	Rigby
Claude Monet: Sunshine and Waterlilies	S	B	250+	Kelley, True	Grossett & Dunlap
Claudine's Concert	L	RF	250+	Literacy 2000	Rigby
Claws	I	I	228	Sails	Rigby
Clay	M	I	250+	Materials	Capstone Press
Clay Art	F	I	62	Chanko, Pamela; Chessen, Betsey	Scholastic

TITLE	LEVEL	GENRE	WORD COUNT	AUTHOR / SERIES	PUBLISHER / DISTRIBUTOR
Clay Creatures	I	I	213	Literacy by Design	Rigby
Clay Creatures	I	I	213	Rigby Literacy	Rigby
Clay Dog, The	L	HF	250+	Lighthouse	Rigby
Clay Marble, The	V	RF	250+	Ho, Minfong	Farrar, Straus and Giroux
Clay Things, Play Things	J	I	250+	Phonics Readers	Scholastic
Clay Today!	C	RF	37	Learn to Read	Creative Teaching Press
Clean Air	P	I	250+	Independent Readers Social Studies	Houghton Mifflin Harcourt
Clean and Clear	P	I	806	Independent Readers Social Studies	Houghton Mifflin Harcourt
Clean and Healthy	I	I	199	Rosen Real Readers	Rosen Publishing Group
Clean Beaches	I	I	155	Early Connections	Benchmark Education
Clean House for Mole and Mouse, A	H	F	201	Ziefert, Harriet	Scholastic
Clean Machine, The	L	RF	250+	Home Connection Collection	Rigby
Clean My Teeth!	C	F	51	Sails	Rigby
Clean Out the Fridge, Fred	I	F	250+	Popcorn	Sundance
Clean Up Your Room	B	RF	35	Visions	Wright Group/McGraw Hill
Clean Your Room, Tanya!	L	RF	250+	Scooters	ETA Cuisenaire
Cleaning Day	C	RF	26	Bebop Books	Lee & Low Books Inc.
Cleaning My Room	I	I	189	Early Connections	Benchmark Education
Cleaning Teeth	D	I	37	Wonder World	Wright Group/McGraw Hill
Cleaning Up	A	I	26	Early Connections	Benchmark Education
Cleaning Up the Park	H	I	153	Home Connection Collection	Rigby
Clean-Up Day	H	RF	179	Instant Readers	Harcourt School Publishers
Clean-Up Day	D	RF	72	Rigby Rocket	Rigby
Clean-Up Team, The	G	RF	159	InfoTrek	ETA Cuisenaire
Clean-Up Time	F	RF	226	Handprints D, Set 1	Educators Publishing Service
Clearing the Dust	V	HF	2327	Leveled Readers	Houghton Mifflin Harcourt
Clementine	L	TL	101	Traditional Songs	Picture Window Books
Cleopatra	T	B	250+	Ancient Egypt	Capstone Press
Cleopatra	X	B	250+	Green, Robert	Franklin Watts
Cleopatra	W	B	2055	Independent Readers Social Studies	Houghton Mifflin Harcourt
Cleopatra	T	B	250+	Stanley, Diane; Vennema, Peter	Mulberry Books
Cleopatra: Egypt's Last and Greatest Queen	Y	B	250+	Sterling Biographies	Sterling Publishing
Cleveland Browns, The	S	I	250+	Team Spirit	Norwood House Press
Cleveland Indians, The	S	I	250+	Team Spirit	Norwood House Press
Clever Ali	S	TL	250+	Farmer, Nancy	Orchard Books
Clever and Quirky Creatures	U	I	250+	Story Surfers	ETA Cuisenaire
Clever Animals	J	I	332	Vocabulary Readers/TX	Houghton Mifflin Harcourt
Clever Bird	K	F	250+	Little Celebrations	Pearson Learning Group
Clever Brown Mouse	G	F	199	PM Plus Story Books	Rigby
Clever Calculations	X	I	250+	WorldScapes	ETA Cuisenaire
Clever Chick	G	F	250+	Rigby Star	Rigby
Clever Coyote and Other Wild Dogs	L	I	250+	Storyteller Chapter Books	Wright Group/ McGraw Hill
Clever Fox	D	RF	114	PM Plus Story Books	Rigby
Clever Hamburger	K	F	560	Jellybeans	Rigby
Clever Happy Monkey	C	F	28	Joy Readers	Pearson Learning Group
Clever Jackals, The	H	TL	231	PM Stars	Rigby
Clever Joe	B	RF	53	Storyworlds	Heinemann Educational Publishers
Clever Little Bird	D	F	73	Storyteller-Setting Sun	Wright Group/McGraw Hill
Clever Lollipop	P	F	250+	King-Smith, Dick	Candlewick Press

* Collection of short stories
\# Graphic text

TITLE	LEVEL	GENRE	WORD COUNT	AUTHOR / SERIES	PUBLISHER / DISTRIBUTOR
Clever Mr. Brown	K	F	397	Story Box	Wright Group/McGraw Hill
Clever Penguins, The	G	I	174	PM Story Books	Rigby
Clever Raccoons	K	I	388	Pull Ahead Books	Lerner Publications
Clever Tortoise, The	H	TL	202	Cambridge Reading	Pearson Learning Group
Clever Trick, A	K	TL	674	Springboard	Wright Group/ McGraw Hill
Clever, Crow, The	H	TL	223	PM Plus Story Books	Rigby
Click	E	RF	41	Books for Young Learners	Richard C. Owen
Click!	G	RF	250+	Foundations	Wright Group/McGraw Hill
Click, Clack, Moo Cows That Type	M	F	250+	Cronin, Doreen	Scholastic
Click: A Story about George Eastman	R	B	5614	Creative Minds Biographies	Carolrhoda Books
Cliff Can't Come	F	RF	276	Leveled Readers	Houghton Mifflin Harcourt
Clifford Can	E	F	55	Blevins, Wiley	Scholastic
Clifford, the Big Red Dog	J	F	241	Bridwell, Norman	Scholastic
Clifford, the Firehouse Dog	J	F	250+	Bridwell, Norman	Scholastic
Clifford, the Small Red Puppy	J	F	499	Bridwell, Norman	Scholastic
Clifford's First Halloween	J	F	250+	Bridwell, Norman	Scholastic
Clifford's Good Deeds	J	F	250+	Bridwell, Norman	Scholastic
Clifford's Puppy Days	J	F	308	Bridwell, Norman	Scholastic
Climate	P	I	250+	Reading Expeditions	National Geographic
Climate Change in the Past	Y	I	2922	Leveled Readers	Houghton Mifflin Harcourt
Climate Change in the Past	Y	I	2922	Leveled Readers/CA	Houghton Mifflin Harcourt
Climbers	F	I	128	Sails	Rigby
Climbing	C	F	34	Literacy 2000	Rigby
Climbing	B	I	48	PM Starters	Rigby
Climbing Everest	W	I	250+	iOpeners	Pearson Learning Group
Climbing Mount Everest	R	I	250+	Windows On Literacy	National Geographic
Climbing the Continents: Everest, McKinley, Kilimanjaro	W	I	3847	Leveled Readers Social Studies	Houghton Mifflin Harcourt
Climbing to Success	S	I	250+	Explorer Books-Pathfinder	National Geographic
Climbing to Success	P	I	250+	Explorer Books-Pioneer	National Geographic
Climbing Tree Frogs	L	I	386	Pull Ahead Books	Lerner Publications
Clinging Sea Horses	L	I	356	Pull Ahead Books	Lerner Publications
Clique, The	X	RF	250+	Harrison, Lisi	Little, Brown & Co.
Cliques	V	F	250+	10 Things You Need to Know About	Capstone Press
Cloak of the Wind	O	HF	250+	Voyages in Time	Wright Group/McGraw Hill
Clock That Couldn't Tell Time, The	H	F	310	Carousel Readers	Pearson Learning Group
Clock Watch	B	I	76	Early Connections	Benchmark Education
Clocks and More Clocks	J	RF	374	Hutchins, Pat	Scholastic
Clockwork	Z	F	250+	Pullman, Philip	Scholastic
Close Call, A	M	RF	250+	Kenna, Anna	Pacific Learning
Close to Home: A Story of the Polio Epidemic	R	I	250+	Weaver, Lydia	Bantam
Close Up on Careers	T	I	250+	InfoQuest	Rigby
Close Your Eyes	E	RF	131	Foundations	Wright Group/McGraw Hill
Closer and Closer	LB	I	13	Twig	Wright Group/McGraw Hill
Closet in the Hall, The	D	F	84	Wonder World	Wright Group/McGraw Hill
Closet Under the Stairs, The	I	RF	214	Story Box	Wright Group/McGraw Hill
Cloth	G	I	90	Materials	Lerner Publications
Clothes	C	I	25	Interaction	Rigby
Clothes	F	I	103	Talk About Books	Pearson Learning Group
Clothes	D	RF	63	Voyages	SRA/McGraw Hill
Clothes	C	I	18	We Are Alike and Different	Lerner Publishing
Clothes	L	I	386	Wonder World	Wright Group/McGraw Hill
Clothes & Crafts in Ancient Egypt	T	I	250+	Balkwill, Richard	Dillon Press

* Collection of short stories
\# Graphic text

TITLE	LEVEL	GENRE	WORD COUNT	AUTHOR / SERIES	PUBLISHER / DISTRIBUTOR
Clothes & Crafts in Ancient Greece	T	I	250+	Steele, Philip	Dillon Press
Clothes & Crafts in Aztec Times	T	I	250+	Dawson, Imogen	Dillon Press
Clothes & Crafts in Roman Times	T	I	250+	Steele, Philip	Dillon Press
Clothes & Crafts in the Middle Ages	T	I	250+	Dawson, Imogen	Dillon Press
Clothes & Crafts in Victorian Times	T	I	250+	Steele, Philip	Dillon Press
Clothes Around the World	J	I	214	Vocabulary Readers	Houghton Mifflin Harcourt
Clothes in Many Cultures	I	I	79	Life Around the World	Capstone Press
Clothes That Help	I	I	252	Sails	Rigby
Clothing	C	I	23	Basic Human Needs	Lerner Publishing
Cloud Book, The	N	I	250+	DePaola, Tomie	Scholastic
Cloud Catcher	P	F	250+	Action Packs	Rigby
Cloud Forest	P	I	1313	Big Cat	Pacific Learning
Clouds	A	RF	47	Bookshop	Mondo
Clouds	D	RF	40	Costain, Meredith	Scholastic
Clouds	J	I	246	Early Connections	Benchmark Education
Clouds	L	I	345	Gear Up!	Wright Group/McGraw Hill
Clouds	C	I	67	Handprints C, Set 1	Educators Publishing Service
Clouds	J	I	204	Independent Readers Science	Houghton Mifflin Harcourt
Clouds	L	I	40	iOpeners	Pearson Learning Group
Clouds	C	RF	92	Leveled Literacy Intervention/ Green System	Heinemann
Clouds	N	I	250+	Literacy 2000	Rigby
Clouds	C	RF	44	Science	Outside the Box
Clouds	H	I	108	Sunshine	Wright Group/McGraw Hill
Clouds	H	I	132	Twig	Wright Group/McGraw Hill
Clouds	B	RF	42	Voyages	SRA/McGraw Hill
Clouds	I	I	249	Weather	Capstone Press
Clouds of Terror	L	HF	250+	Soar To Success	Houghton Mifflin Harcourt
Clouds of Terror	L	HF	250+	Welsh, Catherine A.	Carolrhoda Books
Clouds Tell the Weather	E	F	89	Bonnell, Kris	Reading Reading Books
Clouds, Rain, and Fog	K	I	488	Sunshine	Wright Group/McGraw Hill
Cloudy	B	I	27	Weather	Lerner Publications
Cloudy Day Sunny Day	E	RF	108	Green Light Readers	Harcourt
Cloudy Day, A	E	I	90	Weather	Lerner Publishing
Cloudy With a Chance of Meatballs	M	F	250+	Barrett, Judi	Atheneum
Clown	WB	I	N/A	Blake, Quentin	Henry Holt & Co.
Clown	C	RF	146	Sails	Rigby
Clown and Elephant	C	F	38	Story Box	Wright Group/McGraw Hill
Clown Around	F	F	67	Early Readers	Compass Point Books
Clown Face	LB	RF	14	Twig	Wright Group/McGraw Hill
Clown Fish	J	I	123	Under the Sea	Capstone Press
Clown in the Well, The	D	F	140	Story Box	Wright Group/McGraw Hill
Clown Is Sick	I	F	350	Sails	Rigby
Clown Paints His House	E	RF	143	Sails	Rigby
Clown, The	LB	I	31	First Stories	Pacific Learning
Clown, The	LB	I	13	Smart Starts	Rigby
Clown, The	LB	I	29	Urmston, Kathleen; Evans, Karen	Kaeden Books
Clowning Around	L	I	250+	Rigby Literacy	Rigby
Clowns	K	I	289	Rigby Flying Colors	Rigby
Clown's Clothes	B	RF	54	Sails	Rigby
Clown's Party	C	RF	115	Sails	Rigby
Clowns with Frowns Parade, The	I	F	291	Springboard	Wright Group/McGraw Hill

* Collection of short stories
# Graphic text

TITLE	LEVEL	GENRE	WORD COUNT	AUTHOR / SERIES	PUBLISHER / DISTRIBUTOR
Clubhouse, The	K	RF	659	PM Collection	Rigby
Cluck! Quack! Moo!	F	RF	209	Sun Sprouts	ETA Cuisenaire
Clucky	I	F	250+	PM Plus Story Books	Rigby
Clue at the Bottom of the Lake, The	Q	RF	250+	Gregory, Kristiana	Scholastic
Clue at the Zoo, The	L	RF	250+	Giff, Patricia Reilly	Bantam
Clue Club, The	M	RF	660	Leveled Readers	Houghton Mifflin Harcourt
Clue in the Castle, The	M	RF	250+	Woodland Mysteries	Wright Group/McGraw Hill
Clue in the Glue, The	N	RF	250+	Keene, Carolyn	Pocket Books
Clue of the Gold Doubloons, The	S	RF	250+	Keene, Carolyn	Pocket Books
Clue, Jr.: The Case of the Chocolate Fingerprints	O	RF	250+	Hinter, Parker C.	Scholastic
Clues in the Car Wash	O	RF	250+	Klooz	Stone Arch Books
Clues in the Woods	M	RF	250+	Parish, Peggy	Bantam
Clues to Crime	T	I	250+	The News	Richard C. Owen
Clumsy Clinton	M	RF	894	Springboard	Wright Group/McGraw Hill
Clyde Klutter's Room	I	F	146	Sunshine	Wright Group/McGraw Hill
Clyde the Otter	J	F	250+	Reading Safari	Mondo
Clyde Tombaugh and the Search for Planet X	N	B	250+	Wetterer, Margaret K.	Carolrhoda Books
Coach Amos	R	RF	250+	Paulsen, Gary	Bantam
Coach Kaputo	R	RF	1476	Leveled Readers	Houghton Mifflin Harcourt
Coach Kaputo	R	RF	1476	Leveled Readers/CA	Houghton Mifflin Harcourt
Coaches	L	I	547	Pull Ahead Books	Lerner Publications
Coal Miner's Son, A	U	RF	2652	Leveled Readers Science	Houghton Mifflin Harcourt
Coast to Coast	N	I	250+	People, Spaces & Places	Rand McNally
Coasts	J	I	273	Landforms	Lerner Publications
Coastwatcher, The	U	HF	250+	Weston, Elise	Peachtree
Coat Full of Bubbles, A	G	RF	72	Books for Young Learners	Richard C. Owen
Coats	A	I	32	Ray's Readers	Outside the Box
Cobber Dog and Old Mary	K	F	509	Springboard	Wright Group/McGraw Hill
Cobra Cat	J	F	250+	Storyworlds	Heinemann Educational Books
Cobra Strike	U	RF	250+	Orca Sports	Orca Book Publishers
Cobras	M	I	250+	Snakes	Capstone Press
Cobsdown Cat Case, The	L	RF	250+	Rigby Rocket	Rigby
Cobwebs, Elephants, and Stars	M	F	779	Sunshine	Wright Group/McGraw Hill
Cock-A-Doodle-Do	F	RF	160	Brandenberg, Franz	Greenwillow
Cocker Spaniels	I	I	146	Dogs	Capstone Press
Cockroach Cooties	O	RF	250+	Yep, Laurence	Hyperion
Cockroaches	P	I	2529	Early Bird Nature Books	Lerner Publishing
Cockroaches	I	I	60	Pebble Books	Red Brick Learning
Cockroaches	I	I	283	Sails	Rigby
Cockroaches	N	I	250+	World of Insects	Capstone Press
Coconut Lunches	J	RF	564	Sunshine	Wright Group/McGraw Hill
Coconut Seed or Fruit?	N	I	250+	iOpeners	Pearson Learning Group
Cocoons and Cases	C	I	59	Rigby Literacy	Rigby
Coco's Bell	H	RF	224	PM Plus Story Books	Rigby
Code Breakers	Q	RF	1520	Powell, J.	Stone Arch Books
Code in the Tree, The	F	RF	191	Leveled Readers	Houghton Mifflin Harcourt
Code in the Tree, The	F	RF	191	Leveled Readers/CA	Houghton Mifflin Harcourt
Code Talkers, The	W	I	2207	Reading Street	Pearson
Code that No One Broke, The	L	I	90	Independent Readers Social Studies	Houghton Mifflin Harcourt
Code, The: The 5 Secrets of Teen Success	U	I	250+	Asgedom, Mawi	Hampton-Brown
Codes and Signals	N	I	250+	Cambridge Reading	Pearson Learning Group

TITLE	LEVEL	GENRE	WORD COUNT	AUTHOR / SERIES	PUBLISHER / DISTRIBUTOR
Cody's Snake Tale	M	RF	250+	Windows on Literacy	National Geographic
Cogs in the Wheel	V	I	250+	InfoQuest	Rigby
Coin Magic	L	I	250+	How-To Series	Benchmark Education
Coins	A	I	32	On Our Way to English	Rigby
Cold and Hot	B	RF	24	Bebop Books	Lee & Low Books Inc.
Cold as Ice	T	RF	250+	Keene, Carolyn	Pocket Books
Cold Case: Dinosaurs	U	I	2718	Reading Street	Pearson
Cold Day, A	E	I	71	Pebble Books	Capstone Press
Cold Day, Hot Chocolate	E	RF	110	On Our Way to English	Rigby
Cold Day, The	F	RF	80	Oxford Reading Tree	Oxford University Press
Cold Place, A	B	I	43	Sails	Rigby
Cold Places	M	I	388	Sails	Rigby
Cold Shoulder Road	V	RF	250+	Aiken, Joan	Bantam
Cold War Leaders	U	B	250+	Primary Source Readers	Teacher Created Materials
Cold War Spies	X	I	250+	Spies	Capstone Press
Cold War, The	W	I	250+	Primary Source Readers	Teacher Created Materials
Cold, The	D	RF	96	Leveled Literacy Intervention/ Blue System	Heinemann
Coldest Places, The	H	I	224	PM Science Readers	Rigby
Colds	K	I	250+	Health Matters	Capstone Press
Cole, the Midwest Giant	M	F	977	Springboard	Wright Group/McGraw Hill
Colibri	W	RF	250+	Cameron, Ann	Farrar, Straus and Giroux
Colin Powell	S	B	4022	History Maker Bios	Lerner Publications
Colin Powell	K	B	250+	Welcome Books	Children's Press
Colin Powell, American Leader	H	B	77	Leveled Readers Social Studies	Houghton Mifflin Harcourt
Colin Powell: It Can Be Done!	U	B	250+	High Five Reading	Red Brick Learning
Colin Powell: Straight to the Top	S	B	250+	Blue, Rose; Naden, Corinne J.	Millbrook Press
Collecting Badges	J	I	250+	Stepping Stones	Nelson/Michaels Assoc.
Collecting Cones	I	I	127	Wonder World	Wright Group/McGraw Hill
Collecting Dreams	O	RF	2391	Reading Street	Pearson
Collecting Leaves	K	I	250+	Stepping Stones	Nelson/Michaels Assoc.
Collecting Shapes	J	I	250+	Stepping Stones	Nelson/Michaels Assoc.
Collecting Things Is Fun!	G	RF	134	Learn to Read	Creative Teaching Press
Collections	E	RF	54	Ballinger, Margaret; Gosset, Rachel	Scholastic
Collections	J	RF	250+	Voyages	SRA/McGraw Hill
Collies	I	I	120	Dogs	Capstone Press
Colonial Adventure, The	N	HF	1007	Reading Street	Pearson
Colonial Crafts	T	I	250+	Historic Communities	Crabtree
Colonial Families	K	I	250+	Rosen Real Readers	Rosen Publishing Group
Colonial Life	S	I	250+	A True Book	Children's Press
Colonial Life	S	I	250+	Historic Communities	Crabtree
Colonial New England	O	I	457	Reading Street	Pearson
Colonial Teachers	L	I	250+	Rosen Real Readers	Rosen Publishing Group
Colonial Times	T	I	250+	Navigators Social Studies Series	Benchmark Education Company
Colonial Times 1600-1700	T	I	250+	Masoff, Joy	Scholastic
Colonial Times from A to Z	T	I	250+	Kalman, Bobbie	Crabtree
Colonial Town, A: Williamsburg	T	I	250+	Historic Communities	Crabtree
Colonialism and Native Peoples	W	I	2595	Reading Street	Pearson
Colony of Massachusetts, The	T	I	250+	The Library of the Thirteen Colonies and The Lost Colony	Rosen Publishing Group
Colony of New York, The	T	I	250+	The Library of the Thirteen Colonies and The Lost Colony	Rosen Publishing Group

C

Organized Alphabetically by Title
Storable Database at www.fountasandpinnellleveledbooks.com

* Collection of short stories
\# Graphic text

TITLE	LEVEL	GENRE	WORD COUNT	AUTHOR / SERIES	PUBLISHER / DISTRIBUTOR
Colony of Pennsylvania, The	T	I	250+	The Library of the Thirteen Colonies and The Lost Colony	Rosen Publishing Group
Colony of Virginia, The	T	I	250+	The Library of the Thirteen Colonies and The Lost Colony	Rosen Publishing Group
Color	M	I	250+	Early Connections	Benchmark Education
Color	P	I	250+	Our Physical World	Capstone Press
Color Around Us	V	I	250+	PM Plus	Rigby
Color It My Way	G	RF	123	Story Steps	Rigby
Color Me Dark	V	HF	250+	Dear America	Scholastic
Color of His Own, A	I	F	239	Lionni, Leo	Scholastic
Color of Life, The	Q	B	250+	WorldScapes	ETA Cuisenaire
Color of Light, The	M	I	558	Leveled Readers Science	Houghton Mifflin Harcourt
Color Wizard, The	J	F	250+	Bank Street	Bantam
Colorado	T	I	250+	Hello U.S.A.	Lerner Publications
Colorado	S	I	250+	Land of Liberty	Red Brick Learning
Colorado	T	I	250+	Sea To Shining Sea	Children's Press
Colorado	R	I	250+	This Land Is Your Land	Compass Point Books
Colorado River, The	T	I	250+	Waterways of the World	Franklin Watts
Colorado Rockies, The	S	I	250+	Team Spirit	Norwood House Press
Colorful Animals	D	I	142	Sails	Rigby
Colorful Animals	M	I	250+	Sunshine	Wright Group/McGraw Hill
Colorful Facts	N	I	561	Leveled Readers Science	Houghton Mifflin Harcourt
Colorful Ghost, The	E	F	135	TOTTS	Tott Publications
Colorful Peacocks	L	I	333	Pull Ahead Books	Lerner Publications
Colors	A	I	20	Belle River Readers	Belle River Readers, Inc.
Colors	G	RF	118	Big Cat	Pacific Learning
Colors	F	I	198	Foundations	Wright Group/McGraw Hill
Colors	B	I	40	InfoTrek	ETA Cuisenaire
Colors	LB	I	9	Leveled Readers Language Support	Houghton Mifflin Harcourt
Colors	A	I	9	Little Red Readers	Sundance
Colors	B	I	38	Science	Outside the Box
Colors	LB	I	29	Shutterbug Books	Steck-Vaughn
Colors	A	I	16	Time for Kids	Teacher Created Materials
Colors	LB	I	6	Vocabulary Readers	Houghton Mifflin Harcourt
Colors Around Me	LB	I	7	Reading Street	Pearson
Colors at the Zoo	B	I	59	Little Books	Sadlier-Oxford
Colors in the City	LB	I	61	Urmston, Kathleen; Evans, Karen	Kaeden Books
Colors of Australia	P	I	250+	Colors of the World	Carolrhoda Books
Colors of Fall, The	A	I	26	Gear Up!	Wright Group/McGraw Hill
Colors of Germany	P	I	250+	Colors of the World	Carolrhoda Books
Colors of Ghana	P	I	250+	Colors of the World	Carolrhoda Books
Colors of Horses	E	I	49	Brand, Mona	Kaeden Books
Colors of India	P	I	250+	Colors of the World	Carolrhoda Books
Colors of Kenya	P	I	250+	Colors of the World	Carolrhoda Books
Colors of Leaves, The	I	F	561	Leveled Readers/TX	Houghton Mifflin Harcourt
Colors of Mexico	P	I	250+	Colors of the World	Carolrhoda Books
Colors of My Day, The	F	I	147	Learn to Read	Creative Teaching Press
Colours	LB	I	8	Pienkowski, Jan	Penguin Group
Columbia	U	I	250+	Countries and Cultures	Red Brick Learning
Columbian Exchange, The	Z	I	2956	Leveled Readers	Houghton Mifflin Harcourt
Columbian Exchange, The	Z	I	2956	Leveled Readers/CA	Houghton Mifflin Harcourt
Columbus and the Americas	S	I	250+	Reading Expeditions	National Geographic

C

TITLE	LEVEL	GENRE	WORD COUNT	AUTHOR / SERIES	PUBLISHER / DISTRIBUTOR
Columbus Day	Q	I	250+	Holiday Histories*	Heinemann Library
Columbus Day	N	I	2221	On My Own Holidays	Lerner Publications
Comanche Indians, The	P	I	250+	Native Peoples	Red Brick Learning
Comanche Warriors	T	I	250+	Warriors of History	Capstone Press
Combat Rescue Helicopters: The MH-53 Pave Lows	V	I	250+	War Planes	Capstone Press
Come	A	F	20	Sails	Rigby
Come and Have Fun	I	F	250+	Hurd, Edith Thacher	HarperCollins
Come and Have Fun	A	F	49	KinderReaders	Rigby
Come and Play	B	F	104	Bookshop	Mondo
Come and Play	B	F	34	Interaction	Rigby
Come and Play	B	RF	84	Rigby Flying Colors	Rigby
Come and Play	D	F	104	Story Steps	Rigby
Come and Play, Cats!	C	RF	45	Early Emergent	Pioneer Valley
Come and Play, Sarah!	D	RF	49	Sunshine	Wright Group/McGraw Hill
Come and See!	G	RF	134	Foundations	Wright Group/McGraw Hill
Come Back, Amelia Bedelia	L	F	250+	Parish, Peggy	Harper & Row
Come Back, Pip!	J	RF	355	PM Plus Story Books	Rigby
Come for a Swim!	D	F	107	Leveled Readers	Houghton Mifflin Harcourt
Come for a Swim!	D	F	107	Leveled Readers/CA	Houghton Mifflin Harcourt
Come for a Swim!	F	RF	129	Sunshine	Wright Group/McGraw Hill
Come Here Spinner!	K	F	250+	Foundations	Wright Group/McGraw Hill
Come Here, Puppy	B	F	56	Bella and Rosie Series	Literacy Footprints
Come Here, Puppy!	C	RF	39	Handprints B	Educators Publishing Service
Come Here, Tiger!	D	RF	62	Green Light Readers	Harcourt
Come in the Grass	A	F	24	Sails	Rigby
Come In!	B	F	20	The Book Project	Sundance
Come Meet Some Seals	I	I	118	Little Books	Sadlier-Oxford
Come Morning	V	HF	250+	Guccione, Leslie Davis	Lerner Publishing
Come On Down	K	I	250+	World Quest Adventures	World Quest Learning
Come On Up	A	F	16	KinderReaders	Rigby
Come On!	B	RF	22	Sunshine	Wright Group/McGraw Hill
Come On, Mom	D	RF	56	New Way	Steck-Vaughn
Come On, Tim	G	RF	198	PM Story Books	Rigby
Come Out and Play Little Mouse	H	F	198	Kraus, Robert	Morrow
Come Play With Me	D	RF	69	Leveled Readers	Houghton Mifflin Harcourt
Come Play With Me	C	F	36	Little Readers	Houghton Mifflin Harcourt
Come Sing, Jimmy Jo	V	RF	250+	Paterson, Katherine	Penguin Group
Come to Mexico	M	I	250+	Yellow Umbrella Books	Red Brick Learning
Come to My House	C	F	56	Joy Readers	Pearson Learning Group
Come to My House!	F	RF	131	Sunshine	Wright Group/McGraw Hill
Come to My Party	D	RF	84	Windows on Literacy	National Geographic
Come to Nicodemus	S	HF	1859	Leveled Readers	Houghton Mifflin Harcourt
Come to Nicodemus	S	HF	1859	Leveled Readers/CA	Houghton Mifflin Harcourt
Come to Nicodemus	S	HF	1859	Leveled Readers/TX	Houghton Mifflin Harcourt
Come to School, Dear Dragon	E	F	301	Dear Dragon	Norwood House Press
Come with Me	C	RF	25	Story Box	Wright Group/McGraw Hill
Come! Sit! Speak!	H	RF	57	Rookie Readers	Children's Press
Comeback Challenge, The	Q	RF	250+	Christopher, Matt	Little, Brown & Co.
Comeback Dog, The	O	RF	250+	Thomas, Jane Resh	Bantam
Comet Dust	U	I	2489	Leveled Readers	Houghton Mifflin Harcourt
Comet Dust	U	I	1671	Leveled Readers/CA	Houghton Mifflin Harcourt
Comet Dust	U	I	1671	Leveled Readers/TX	Houghton Mifflin Harcourt

* Collection of short stories
\# Graphic text

TITLE	LEVEL	GENRE	WORD COUNT	AUTHOR / SERIES	PUBLISHER / DISTRIBUTOR
Comets	U	I	250+	A First Book	Franklin Watts
Comets	S	I	250+	Sails	Rigby
Comets	Q	I	250+	The Galaxy	Red Brick Learning
Comets and Meteor Showers	Q	I	250+	A True Book	Children's Press
Comets, Asteroids, and Meteoroids	S	I	250+	Our Solar System	Compass Point Books
Comfort	Z+	RF	250+	Dean, Carolee	Houghton Mifflin Harcourt
Comic Books: From Superheroes to Manga	R	I	250+	High Five Reading	Red Brick Learning
Comic-Book Facts	T	I	250+	Power Up!	Steck-Vaughn
Coming Distractions: Questioning Movies	S	I	250+	Media Literacy	Capstone Press
Coming Home	U	HF	1920	Leveled Readers	Houghton Mifflin Harcourt
Coming to America	L	I	185	Vocabulary Readers	Houghton Mifflin Harcourt
Coming to Ellis Island	N	I	172	In Step Readers	Rigby
Commander Toad and the Big Black Hole	K	F	250+	Yolen, Jane	Putnam/Penguin
Commander Toad and the Dis-Asteroid	K	F	250+	Yolen, Jane	Putnam/Penguin
Commander Toad and the Intergalactic Spy	K	F	250+	Yolen, Jane	Putnam/Penguin
Commander Toad and the Planet of the Grapes	K	F	250+	Yolen, Jane	Putnam/Penguin
Commander Toad and the Space Pirates	K	F	250+	Yolen, Jane	Putnam/Penguin
Commander Toad and the Voyage Home	K	F	250+	Yolen, Jane	Putnam/Penguin
Commander Toad in Space	K	F	250+	Yolen, Jane	Scholastic
Communication	N	I	250+	Literacy 2000	Rigby
Communication Connection	S	I	250+	Kids Discover Reading	Wright Group/McGraw Hill
Communication in the U.S.A., Then & Now	P	I	739	Time for Kids	Teacher Created Materials
Communication Then and Now	P	I	250+	Lighthouse	Ginn & Co.
Communication Then and Now	I	I	123	Then and Now	Lerner Publications
Communities	D	I	42	Pebble Books	Capstone Press
Communities	E	I	59	Wonder World	Wright Group/McGraw Hill
Communities	I	I	42	Yellow Umbrella Books	Red Brick Learning
Communities Everywhere	P	I	250+	PM Extensions	Rigby
Community Garden, The	J	RF	419	Leveled Readers	Houghton Mifflin Harcourt
Community Garden, The	J	RF	419	Leveled Readers/CA	Houghton Mifflin Harcourt
Community Garden, The	J	RF	419	Leveled Readers/TX	Houghton Mifflin Harcourt
Community Helpers	J	I	301	Reading Street	Pearson
Community Jobs	I	I	207	Early Connections	Benchmark Education
Community Leaders: Then and Now	N	I	250+	Primary Source Readers	Teacher Created Materials
Community Service	F	I	80	On Deck	Rigby
Community Teamwork	O	I	1100	Vocabulary Readers/TX	Houghton Mifflin Harcourt
Commuter	M	I	343	Independent Readers Social Studies	Houghton Mifflin Harcourt
Composting	N	I	755	Vocabulary Readers	Houghton Mifflin Harcourt
Composting	N	I	755	Vocabulary Readers/CA	Houghton Mifflin Harcourt
Composting - Worms Tell All	P	I	250+	InfoTrek	ETA Cuisenaire
Computer Buttons	I	F	250+	Sunshine	Wright Group/McGraw Hill
Computer Error	L	F	250+	Rigby Literacy	Rigby
Computer Evidence	Q	I	250+	Forensic Crime Solvers	Capstone Press
Computer Game, The	E	RF	75	Literacy by Design	Rigby
Computer Game, The	E	RF	75	Rigby Literacy	Rigby
Computer Game, The	E	RF	85	Rigby Star	Rigby
Computer Keys	E	F	85	Reading Safari	Mondo
Computer Nut, The	R	SF	250+	Byars, Betsy	Bantam
Computer Pals	J	RF	365	InfoTrek	ETA Cuisenaire
Computer Pigs	M	F	250+	Reading Safari	Mondo
Computer Virus	M	RF	250+	Rigby Gigglers	Rigby
Computer, The	P	I	250+	Great Inventions	Red Brick Learning
Computer, The: Passport to the Digital Age	R	I	250+	On Deck	Rigby

* Collection of short stories
# Graphic text

TITLE	LEVEL	GENRE	WORD COUNT	AUTHOR / SERIES	PUBLISHER / DISTRIBUTOR
Computers and Movies	S	I	1271	Vocabulary Readers	Houghton Mifflin Harcourt
Computers and Movies	S	I	1271	Vocabulary Readers/CA	Houghton Mifflin Harcourt
Computers Are for Everyone	K	I	464	Sunshine	Wright Group/McGraw Hill
Computers Can Help	G	I	86	Shutterbug Books	Steck-Vaughn
Comsats and Phone Calls	P	I	487	Springboard	Wright Group/ McGraw Hill
Comstock Lode, The	U	I	2086	Leveled Readers Social Studies	Houghton Mifflin Harcourt
Conceived in Liberty: The Gettysburg Address	X	I	2069	Leveled Readers	Houghton Mifflin Harcourt
Concert Night	K	RF	250+	Literacy 2000	Rigby
Concert, The	B	I	49	Rigby Flying Colors	Rigby
Concrete	H	I	123	Books for Young Learners	Richard C. Owen
Concrete Jungle	L	RF	250+	Pacific Literacy	Pacific Learning
Concrete Mixers	G	I	110	Mighty Machines	Capstone Press
Concrete Mixers	L	I	510	Pull Ahead Books	Lerner Publications
Condoleezza Rice: Strength of Conviction	T	B	250+	Explore More	Wright Group/McGraw Hill
Condor Rescue	Q	RF	250+	Reading Expeditions	National Geographic
Cones	K	I	226	3-D Shapes	Capstone Press
Confederate Girl, A	U	I	250+	Diaries and Memoirs	Capstone Press
Confucius	X	B	250+	Primary Source Readers	Teacher Created Materials
Confucius, Teacher for a Troubled Time	X	I	2349	Leveled Readers	Houghton Mifflin Harcourt
Confucius, Teacher for a Troubled Time	X	I	2349	Leveled Readers/CA	Houghton Mifflin Harcourt
Confucius: The Golden Rule	Y	HF	250+	Russell Freedman	Scholastic
Congress	S	I	250+	A True Book	Children's Press
Congress and Parliament	W	I	1803	Leveled Readers Social Studies	Houghton Mifflin Harcourt
Congress of the United States, The	W	I	250+	American Civics	Red Brick Learning
Connecticut	T	I	250+	Hello U.S.A.	Lerner Publications
Connecticut	S	I	250+	Land of Liberty	Red Brick Learning
Connecticut	T	I	250+	Sea To Shining Sea	Children's Press
Connecticut	R	I	250+	This Land Is Your Land	Compass Point Books
Connecticut Colony, The	R	I	250+	The American Colonies	Capstone Press
Connecting to the Internet	O	I	250+	Rigby Literacy	Rigby
Connie's Dance	M	RF	361	Windmill Books	Rigby
Conquering England: The Battle of Hastings	X	I	250+	Bloodiest Battles	Capstone Press
Conquering Mount Everest	S	I	250+	Navigators Social Studies Series	Benchmark Education
Consideration	L	I	250+	Character Education	Red Brick Learning
Consideration	K	I	250+	Everyday Character Education	Capstone Press
Constantinople in the Center of the World	Z	I	2840	Independent Readers Social Studies	Houghton Mifflin Harcourt
Constellations	Q	I	250+	A True Book	Children's Press
Constellations	Q	I	250+	The Galaxy	Capstone Press
Constitution and the Bill of Rights, The	T	I	250+	Primary Source Readers	Teacher Created Materials
Constitution, The	S	I	250+	A True Book	Children's Press
Constitution, The	V	I	250+	Cornerstones of Freedom	Children's Press
Constitutional Convention, The	T	I	1267	Leveled Readers Social Studies	Houghton Mifflin Harcourt
Construction Alphabet Book, The	M	I	250+	Pallotta, Jerry	Charlesbridge
Construction Crews	J	I	115	Construction Zone	Capstone Press
Construction Tools	I	I	113	Construction Zone	Capstone Press
Construction Workers	M	I	250+	Community Helpers	Red Brick Learning
Contact	T	F	250+	Reading Safari	Mondo
Contemporary Age, The	R	I	250+	Journey Through History	Barron's Educational
Contender, The	Z+	RF	250+	Lipsyte, Robert	HarperTrophy
Contest, The	K	RF	250+	PM Plus Story Books	Rigby
Continents, The	M	I	250+	Spyglass Books	Compass Point Books
Controlling Traffic	V	I	250+	PM Collection	Rigby
Conversation Club, The	L	F	250+	Stanley, Diane	Aladdin

* Collection of short stories
\# Graphic text

TITLE	LEVEL	GENRE	WORD COUNT	AUTHOR / SERIES	PUBLISHER / DISTRIBUTOR
Coo Coo Caroo	G	F	57	Books for Young Learners	Richard C. Owen
Cook: Captain James Cook Charts the Pacific Ocean	U	B	250+	Exploring the World	Compass Point Books
Cookcamp, The	V	RF	250+	Paulsen, Gary	Bantam
Cookie Count!	M	I	250+	Early Connections	Benchmark Education
Cookie House, The	F	TL	310	Fairy Tales and Folklore	Norwood House Press
Cookie Jar, The	G	RF	106	Sunshine	Wright Group/McGraw Hill
Cookies	D	RF	18	Little Celebrations	Pearson Learning Group
Cookies	LB	I	15	Twig	Wright Group/McGraw Hill
Cookies for a Royal Snack	G	F	136	Dominie Math Stories	Pearson Learning Group
Cookies for Santa	H	F	217	Little Elf	Literacy Footprints
Cookies to Share	E	RF	45	Pair-It Books	Steck-Vaughn
Cookie's Week	F	RF	84	Ward, Cindy	Putnam/Penguin
Cooking	B	RF	30	Sails	Rigby
Cooking at School	G	RF	68	City Kids	Rigby
Cooking Catastrophe	N	RF	250+	Girlz Rock!	Mondo
Cooking Contest, The	K	RF	904	Early Connections	Benchmark Education
Cooking Dinner	G	I	86	Windows on Literacy	National Geographic
*Cooking Pot	L	TL	250+	Story Box	Wright Group/ McGraw Hill
Cooking Pot, The	I	TL	250+	Storyworlds	Heinemann Educational Books
Cooking Pot, The	F	F	132	Sunshine	Wright Group/McGraw Hill
Cooking Spaghetti	I	RF	150	City Kids	Rigby
Cooking Thanksgiving Dinner	E	RF	126	Early Emergent	Pioneer Valley
Cook-Out, The	E	RF	78	Oxford Reading Tree	Oxford University Press
Cool	L	RF	137	Books for Young Learners	Richard C. Owen
Cool Cat, A	O	RF	250+	Leveled Readers	Houghton Mifflin Harcourt
Cool Clive	M	RF	250+	High-Fliers	Pacific Learning
Cool Clive and the Bubble Trouble	M	RF	250+	High-Fliers	Pacific Learning
Cool Clive and the Little Pest	M	RF	250+	High-Fliers	Pacific Learning
Cool Crabs	H	I	258	Sails	Rigby
Cool Customs	K	I	250+	Spyglass Books	Compass Point Books
Cool in the Summer	E	I	63	Windows on Literacy	National Geographic
Cool Off	C	RF	37	Bookshop	Mondo
Cool School	O	F	250+	Sails	Rigby
Cool School, A	G	RF	138	City Stories	Rigby
Cool Tools	I	I	238	Sails	Rigby
Cool Tools	B	I	42	Shutterbug Books	Steck-Vaughn
Cool Tools	K	I	250+	Spyglass Books	Compass Point Books
Cool Treasure, The	N	RF	250+	Orbit Chapter Books	Pacific Learning
Coolest Rock, The	L	I	250+	Chanek, Sherilin	Hampton-Brown
Cooling Off	D	RF	104	Reading Corners	Pearson Learning Group
Cooped Up	K	RF	250+	Pacific Literacy	Pacific Learning
Cooperation	L	I	250+	Everyday Character Education	Capstone Press
Copán: City of the Maya	Z	I	3688	Leveled Readers	Houghton Mifflin Harcourt
Copper Lady, The	M	HF	250+	Ross, Alice & Kent	Carolrhoda Books
Copperheads	M	I	250+	Snakes	Capstone Press
Copycat	C	F	54	Story Box	Wright Group/McGraw Hill
Cora at Camp	M	RF	250+	Leveled Readers Language Support	Houghton Mifflin Harcourt
Cora at Camp Blue Waters	N	RF	772	Leveled Readers	Houghton Mifflin Harcourt
Coral	L	I	250+	Marine Life For Young Readers	Pearson Learning Group
Coral in Crisis	S	I	1272	Leveled Readers	Houghton Mifflin Harcourt
Coral in Crisis	S	I	1272	Leveled Readers/CA	Houghton Mifflin Harcourt

* Collection of short stories
# Graphic text

TITLE	LEVEL	GENRE	WORD COUNT	AUTHOR / SERIES	PUBLISHER / DISTRIBUTOR
Coral Reef	N	I	250+	Habitats	Children's Press
Coral Reef Diary	K	I	595	Explorations	Eleanor Curtain Publishing
Coral Reef Diary	K	I	595	Explorations	Okapi Eductional Materials
Coral Reef Hunters	N	I	250+	Soar To Success	Houghton Mifflin Harcourt
Coral Reef, A	I	I	153	Rigby Focus	Rigby
Coral Reef, The	L	I	250+	Books for Young Learners	Richard C. Owen
Coral Reef, The	H	I	186	Discovery Links	Newbridge
Coral Reef: Inside Australia's Great Barrier Reef	P	I	250+	Cambridge Reading	Pearson Learning Group
Coral Reefs	Q	I	250+	Explorer Books-Pathfinder	National Geographic
Coral Reefs	P	I	250+	Explorer Books-Pioneer	National Geographic
Coral Reefs	Q	I	250+	First Reports	Compass Point Books
Coral Reefs	P	I	250+	Gibbons, Gail	Holiday House
Coral Reefs	H	I	206	Leveled Readers	Houghton Mifflin Harcourt
Coral Reefs	H	I	206	Leveled Readers/CA	Houghton Mifflin Harcourt
Coral Reefs	H	I	206	Leveled Readers/TX	Houghton Mifflin Harcourt
Coral Reefs	I	I	266	Vocabulary Readers	Houghton Mifflin Harcourt
Coral Reefs	I	I	266	Vocabulary Readers/CA	Houghton Mifflin Harcourt
Coral Reefs	I	I	266	Vocabulary Readers/TX	Houghton Mifflin Harcourt
Coraline	W	F	250+	Gaiman, Neil	HarperCollins
Corals	G	I	51	Ocean Life	Capstone Press
Corals	K	I	133	Under the Sea	Capstone Press
Corduroy	K	F	250+	Freeman, Don	Scholastic
Coretta Scott King	R	B	3995	History Maker Bios	Lerner Publications
Coretta Scott King: Civil Rights Activist	P	B	250+	On Deck	Rigby
Corey's Christmas Wish	M	RF	250+	Pony Tails	Skylark
Cork	K	RF	473	Gear Up!	Wright Group/McGraw Hill
Corkscrew, The	Q	RF	250+	WorldScapes	ETA Cuisenaire
Cormorant, The	P	RF	250+	Tristars	Richard C. Owen
Corn	L	I	612	Rigby Flying Colors	Rigby
Corn	K	I	221	Windows on Literacy	National Geographic
Corn	L	I	401	Yellow Umbrella Books	Red Brick Learning
Corn Bread for Everyone!	J	RF	250+	On Our Way to English	Rigby
Corn for Sale	F	I	128	Literacy by Design	Rigby
Corn Husk Doll, The	K	RF	250+	Schiller, Melissa	Scholastic
Corn Is Maize: The Gift of the Indians	O	I	250+	Aliki	Steck-Vaughn
Corn That Kay Grew, The	D	RF	80	Windows on Literacy	National Geographic
Corn: An American Indian Gift	M	I	690	Pair-It Books	Steck-Vaughn
Corn: From Table to Table	H	I	171	Discovery Links	Newbridge
Cornelius Vanderbilt and the Railroad Industry	R	B	250+	On Deck	Rigby
Corner of the Universe, A	Y	RF	250+	Martin, Ann M.	Scholastic
Coronado and the Cities of Gold	Y	B	2051	Leveled Readers	Houghton Mifflin Harcourt
Coronado: Francisco Vasquez de Coronado Explores the Southwest	U	B	250+	Exploring the World	Compass Point Books
Coronado's Golden Quest	R	F	250+	Weisberg, Barbara	Steck-Vaughn
Corps of Discovery, The	S	I	1000	Leveled Readers/TX	Houghton Mifflin Harcourt
Corps of Discovery, The	Q	I	250+	Literacy by Design	Rigby
Corps of the Bare-Boned Plane, The	X	RF	250+	Horvath, Polly	Farrar Straus Giroux
Corrie's Important Decision	V	I	250+	Leveled Readers Language Support	Houghton Mifflin Harcourt
Corrie's Secret	W	I	1726	Leveled Readers	Houghton Mifflin Harcourt
Corvettes	T	I	250+	High Performance	Red Brick Learning
Cosmic Clock, The	Y	I	250+	High-Fliers	Pacific Learning
Cosmic Joker, The	Z	I	250+	Unsolved Mysteries	Steck-Vaughn
Costa Rica	O	I	2503	A Ticket to ...	Carolrohoda Books

* Collection of short stories
\# Graphic text

TITLE	LEVEL	GENRE	WORD COUNT	AUTHOR / SERIES	PUBLISHER / DISTRIBUTOR
Costa Rica	P	I	2216	Country Explorers	Lerner Publications
Costa Rica: A Question and Answer Book	P	I	250+	Question and Answer Countries	Capstone Press
Costume	W	I	250+	Eyewitness Books	DK Publishing
Costume Box, The	B	F	55	Leveled Readers	Houghton Mifflin Harcourt
Costume Box, The	B	F	55	Leveled Readers/CA	Houghton Mifflin Harcourt
Costume Parade, The	E	RF	57	Learn to Read	Creative Teaching Press
Costume Party	C	RF	64	Early Connections	Benchmark Education
Costume Party	A	RF	32	Joy Readers	Pearson Learning Group
Costume Party, The	J	RF	145	City Kids	Rigby
Costume Party, The	A	RF	35	Handprints A	Educators Publishing Service
Costume Party, The	M	F	577	Leveled Literacy Intervention/ Blue System	Heinemann
Costume Party, The	B	RF	15	Sunshine	Wright Group/McGraw Hill
Costume, The	A	RF	20	Leveled Readers	Houghton Mifflin Harcourt
Costume, The	A	RF	20	Leveled Readers/CA	Houghton Mifflin Harcourt
Costumes	C	RF	23	Oxford Reading Tree	Oxford University Press
Costumes	C	I	36	Pebble Books	Capstone Press
Costumes on Show	K	I	378	Rigby Flying Colors	Rigby
Cottle Street	N	RF	250+	Action Packs	Rigby
Cotton Comes From Plants	K	I	161	Windows on Literacy	National Geographic
Cotton Gin, The	R	I	250+	Theme Sets	National Geographic
Cotton Plant to Cotton Shirt	L	I	250+	Early Connections	Benchmark Education
Cottontail Rabbits	K	I	371	Pull Ahead Books	Lerner Publications
Couch was a Castle, The	H	F	138	Ohi, Ruth	Annick Press
Cougars	O	I	1475	Early Bird Nature Books	Lerner Publications
Cougars	R	I	250+	Predators in the Wild	Capstone Press
Could It Be?	J	RF	250+	Bank Street	Bantam
Could We Live on the Moon?	O	I	250+	iOpeners	Pearson Learning Group
Count and See	WB	I	N/A	Hoban, Tana	Macmillan
Count Karlstein	Y	F	250+	Pullman, Philip	Alfred A. Knopf
Count on Me!	Q	I	250+	Orbit Collections	Pacific Learning
Count on Your Body	K	I	250+	Rigby Literacy	Rigby
Count on Your Body	K	I	250+	Rigby Star Quest	Rigby
Count the Animals	LB	I	10	Windows on Literacy	National Geographic
Count to a Million	V	I	250+	Pallotta, Jerry	Scholastic
Count with Me	A	I	49	Little Books	Sadlier-Oxford
Count Your Chickens	G	I	123	Yellow Umbrella Books	Red Brick Learning
Count Your Money with the Polk Street School	M	RF	250+	Giff, Patricia Reilly	Bantam
Count Your Way Through Afghanistan	P	I	619	Count Your Way Books	Carolrhoda Books
Count Your Way Through Africa	P	I	1257	Count Your Way Books	Carolrhoda Books
Count Your Way Through Brazil	Q	I	1095	Count Your Way Books	Carolrhoda Books
Count Your Way Through China	P	I	967	Count Your Way Books	Carolrhoda Books
Count Your Way Through Egypt	P	I	828	Count Your Way Books	Carolrhoda Books
Count Your Way Through France	P	I	990	Count Your Way Books	Carolrhoda Books
Count Your Way Through Greece	P	I	1060	Count Your Way Books	Carolrhoda Books
Count Your Way Through India	P	I	1026	Count Your Way Books	Carolrhoda Books
Count Your Way Through Iran	P	I	700	Count Your Way Books	Carolrhoda Books
Count Your Way Through Ireland	P	I	1288	Count Your Way Books	Carolrhoda Books
Count Your Way Through Israel	Q	I	1086	Count Your Way Books	Carolrhoda Books
Count Your Way Through Italy	P	I	891	Count Your Way Books	Carolrhoda Books
Count Your Way Through Japan	P	I	749	Count Your Way Books	Carolrhoda Books
Count Your Way Through Kenya	P	I	544	Count Your Way Books	Carolrhoda Books
Count Your Way Through Korea	P	I	991	Count Your Way Books	Carolrhoda Books

C

* Collection of short stories
# Graphic text

TITLE	LEVEL	GENRE	WORD COUNT	AUTHOR / SERIES	PUBLISHER / DISTRIBUTOR
Count Your Way Through Mexico	P	I	1097	Count Your Way Books	Carolrhoda Books
Count Your Way Through Russia	P	I	507	Count Your Way Books	Carolrhoda Books
Count Your Way Through South Africa	P	I	700	Count Your Way Books	Carolrhoda Books
Count Your Way Through the Arab World	P	I	936	Count Your Way Books	Carolrhoda Books
Count Your Way Through Zimbabwe	P	I	618	Count Your Way Books	Carolrhoda Books
Count!	H	RF	70	Fleming, Denise	Scholastic
Countdown	G	F	70	Literacy Tree	Rigby
Countdown to a Space Shuttle Launch	W	I	250+	Literacy By Design	Rigby
Countdown to the Year 1000	P	F	250+	McMullan, Kate	Scholastic
Countdown: a play	J	F	250+	Story Box	Wright Group/McGraw Hill
Counterfeit Tackle, The	P	RF	250+	Christopher, Matt	Little, Brown & Co.
Countess Below the Stairs, A	Z+	HF	250+	Ibbotson, Eva	Speak
Countess Veronica	Q	RF	250+	Robinson, Nancy K.	Scholastic
Counting Around Town	D	RF	84	Early Connections	Benchmark Education
Counting Down	C	RF	93	PM Math Readers	Rigby
Counting Insects	K	I	230	Early Connections	Benchmark Education
Counting Many Ways	J	I	250+	Yellow Umbrella Books	Capstone Press
Counting Money	G	I	122	Early Connections	Benchmark Education
Counting Money	E	I	107	Money	Lerner Publishing
Counting My Collections	F	I	126	Early Connections	Benchmark Education
Counting One to Five	B	I	64	Early Connections	Benchmark Education
Counting Pets by Twos	I	I	234	Counting Books	Capstone Press
Counting Seeds	C	I	63	Early Connections	Benchmark Education
Counting Stars	F	I	144	Early Connections	Benchmark Education
Counting to 100	J	I	247	Gear Up!	Wright Group/McGraw Hill
Counting with Apollo	K	F	285	Gregoire, Caroline	Kane/Miller Book Publishers
Countries of the World	Q	I	250+	High-Fliers	Pacific Learning
Country Artist, The: A Story About Beatrix Potter	R	B	6783	Creative Minds Biographies	Carolrhoda Books
Country Fair	J	HF	250+	Wilder, Laura Ingalls	HarperCollins
Country Family	G	RF	262	Instant Readers	Harcourt School Publishers
Country Mouse and the Town Mouse, The	F	TL	200+	Reed, Janet	Scholastic
Courage	K	I	250+	Everyday Character Education	Capstone Press
Courage of Helen Keller, The	N	B	250+	Rosen Real Readers	Rosen Publishing Group
Courage of Sarah Noble, The	O	HF	250+	Dalgliesh, Alice	Aladdin
Courtney's Twos	C	RF	30	Harry's Math Books	Outside the Box
Cousin Kira	J	RF	250+	Sunshine	Wright Group/McGraw Hill
Cousins	F	I	56	Families	Capstone Press
Cousins	T	RF	250+	Hamilton, Virginia	Language for Learning Assoc.
Cousins	D	I	41	Pebble Books	Capstone Press
Cousins in the Castle	U	F	250+	Wallace, Barbara Brooks	Aladdin
Covers	E	RF	30	Little Celebrations	Pearson Learning Group
Cow	O	I	250+	Older, Jules	Charlesbridge
*Cow in the Garden and Other Stories, The	H	F	158	New Way Literature	Steck-Vaughn
Cow Jumped Over the Moon, The	C	F	33	Rigby Rocket	Rigby
*Cow of No Color, The: Riddle Stories and Justice Tales From Around the World	U	TL	250+	Jaffe, Nina; Zeitlin, Steve	Henry Holt & Co.
Cow Up a Tree	H	F	215	Read Alongs	Rigby
Cowboy	X	I	250+	Eyewitness Books	DK Publishing
Cowboy Days	N	HF	926	Reading Street	Pearson
Cowboy Jake	I	RF	174	Sunshine	Wright Group/McGraw Hill
Cowboy Trade, The	S	I	250+	Rounds, Glen	Holiday House

C

* Collection of short stories
# Graphic text

TITLE	LEVEL	GENRE	WORD COUNT	AUTHOR / SERIES	PUBLISHER / DISTRIBUTOR
Cowboy, The	C	RF	35	Step-By-Step Series	Pearson Learning Group
Cowboys	T	I	250+	Sandler, Martin W.	HarperTrophy
Cowboys of the Wild West	X	I	250+	Freedman, Russell	Clarion
Cowboys on a Ranch	H	I	210	On Our Way to English	Rigby
Cowhands and Cattle Trails	S	I	250+	Navigators Social Studies Series	Benchmark Education Company
Cowpokes and Desperadoes	O	RF	250+	Paulsen, Gary	Bantam
Cows and Calves	B	I	33	Animal Families	Lerner Publications
Cows Have Calves	M	I	250+	Animals and Their Young	Compass Point Books
Cows in the Garden	G	F	163	PM Story Books	Rigby
Cow's Lunch	L	RF	363	Leveled Readers	Houghton Mifflin Harcourt
Cow's Lunch	L	RF	363	Leveled Readers/CA	Houghton Mifflin Harcourt
Cow's Lunch	L	RF	363	Leveled Readers/TX	Houghton Mifflin Harcourt
Cows on the Farm	G	I	56	Pebble Books	Capstone Press
Coyote and the Rabbit	M	TL	1018	Leveled Readers/TX	Houghton Mifflin Harcourt
Coyote and the Rabbit, The	H	TL	243	Leveled Literacy Intervention/ Blue System	Heinemann
Coyote Girl	M	TL	250+	Cambridge Reading	Pearson Learning Group
*Coyote in Trouble	L	TL	250+	Beveridge, Barbara	Pacific Learning
*Coyote Not-So-Clever	N	TL	250+	Beveridge, Barbara	Pacific Learning
Coyote Plants a Peach Tree	I	TL	233	Books for Young Learners	Richard C. Owen
Coyote, Fox, and Wolf Tales	K	TL	250+	Storyteller- Lightning Bolts	Wright Group/McGraw Hill
Coyote, The	R	I	250+	Wildlife of North America	Red Brick Learning
Coyote: A Trickster Tale From the American Southwest	M	TL	400	McDermott, Gerald	Voyager Books
Coyotes	L	I	250+	Story Box	Wright Group/McGraw Hill
Crab at the Bottom of the Sea, The	H	TL	141	Literacy 2000	Rigby
Crab Hunt, The	G	RF	179	PM Photo Stories	Rigby
Crab Moon	N	RF	250+	Horowitz, Ruth	Candlewick Press
Crabbing Time	I	RF	75	Books for Young Learners	Richard C. Owen
Crabby Cat at School	E	F	142	Joy Starters	Pearson Learning Group
Crabby Cat's Exercise	D	F	65	Joy Starters	Pearson Learning Group
Crabby Cat's Party	D	F	99	Joy Starters	Pearson Learning Group
Crabby Cat's Shopping	C	F	39	Joy Starters	Pearson Learning Group
Crabs	E	I	46	Ocean Life	Capstone Press
Crabs	L	I	501	Sunshine	Wright Group/McGraw Hill
Crabs	H	I	111	Under the Sea	Capstone Press
Crabs	M	I	272	Wonder World	Wright Group/McGraw Hill
Crabs for Dinner	H	RF	231	Adams, Lorraine; Bruvold, Lynn	Eagle Crest Books
Crabs on a Rock	D	RF	77	Sun Sprouts	ETA Cuisenaire
Crabs, Shrimp & Lobsters	L	I	322	Marine Life For Young Readers	Pearson Learning Group
Cracked	T	RF	250+	Orca Currents	Orca Book Publishers
Cracker Jack, The	D	F	25	Sunshine	Wright Group/McGraw Hill
Cracker Jackson	T	RF	250+	Byars, Betsy	Puffin/Penguin
CrackerJack Halfback	Q	RF	250+	Christopher, Matt	Little, Brown & Co.
Cracking the Code	V	I	250+	High-Fliers	Pacific Learning
Cracking the Code	Z	I	3314	Leveled Readers Science	Houghton Mifflin Harcourt
Cracking the Code	V	I	250+	WorldScapes	ETA Cuisenaire
Cracking the German Code	W	I	2141	Reading Street	Pearson
Cracking the Wall: The Struggles of the Little Rock Nine	R	I	1403	On My Own History	Lerner Publications
Craft Makers	A	I	24	Early Connections	Benchmark Education
Craft Stick Project, The	L	RF	250+	On Our Way to English	Rigby

* Collection of short stories
# Graphic text

TITLE	LEVEL	GENRE	WORD COUNT	AUTHOR / SERIES	PUBLISHER / DISTRIBUTOR
Crafts	G	I	50	Chessen, Betsey; Chanko, Pamela	Scholastic
Crafts and Games Around the World	U	I	250+	iOpeners	Pearson Learning Group
Crafts for Kids Who Are Learning About Dinosaurs	P	I	3383	Ross, Kathy	Millbrook Press
Crafts for Kids Who Are Learning About Insects	P	I	3725	Ross, Kathy	Millbrook Press
Crafty Jackal	L	TL	250+	Folk Tales	Wright Group/McGraw Hill
Cranberries: Fruit of the Bogs	T	I	250+	Burns, Diane L.	Carolrhoda Books
Crane Wife, The	M	F	620	Pair-It Books	Steck-Vaughn
Cranes	I	I	228	Leveled Literacy Intervention/ Blue System	Heinemann
Cranes	G	I	105	Mighty Machines	Capstone Press
Cranes	L	I	454	Pull Ahead Books	Lerner Publications
Cranes	N	I	250+	Take Two Books	Wright Group/McGraw Hill
Cranky Old Magician, The	J	F	522	Rigby Gigglers	Rigby
Crash	A	RF	29	First Stories	Pacific Learning
Crash	V	RF	250+	Spinelli, Jerry	Alfred A. Knopf
Crawfish Hunt	N	RF	250+	Boyz Rule!	Mondo
Crawl, Caterpillar, Crawl!	C	RF	24	Pair-It Books	Steck-Vaughn
Crayfish	O	I	2507	Early Bird Nature Books	Lerner Publications
Crayfish Thief, The	O	RF	1875	Take Two Books	Wright Group/ McGraw Hill
Crayola Counting Book, The	G	I	102	Learn to Read	Creative Teaching Press
Crazy Cats	A	I	42	Little Books for Early Readers	University of Maine
Crazy Chewing Gum	K	RF	250+	Rigby Gigglers	Rigby
Crazy Critter's Cooking Convention, The	K	F	232	Springboard	Wright Group/McGraw Hill
Crazy Fish	T	RF	250+	Mazer, Norma Fox	Avon
Crazy Horse	S	I	515	Vocabulary Readers	Houghton Mifflin Harcourt
Crazy Lady!	U	RF	250+	Conly, Jane Leslie	HarperCollins
Crazy Miss Maisey's Alphabet Pets	K	F	250+	Storyteller- Lightning Bolts	Wright Group/McGraw Hill
Crazy Quilt, The	G	F	148	Little Celebrations	Pearson Learning Group
Crazy Quilt, The	G	F	148	Little Readers	Houghton Mifflin Harcourt
Crazy Wheels	I	I	215	Sails	Rigby
Creative Impulse	R	I	250+	Orbit Collections	Pacific Learning
Creativity	P	RF	250+	Steptoe, John	Clarion Books
Creature Chase - Rex Jones	P	F	1576	Zucker, Jonny	Stone Arch Books
Creature Features	E	RF	172	Windows on Literacy	National Geographic
Creature Features: Exploring Animal Characteristics	W	I	250+	Literacy By Design	Rigby
*Creature from Beneath the Ice and Other Cases, The	O	RF	250+	Simon, Seymour	Avon
Creature of Cassidy's Creek, The	N	RF	250+	PM Collection	Rigby
Creatures of the Dark	N	I	250+	Literacy 2000	Rigby
Creatures of the Deep	T	I	250+	Boldprint	Steck-Vaughn
Creatures of the Deep	O	I	842	Vocabulary Readers	Houghton Mifflin Harcourt
Creatures of the Deep	O	I	842	Vocabulary Readers/CA	Houghton Mifflin Harcourt
Creatures of the Extreme	T	I	250+	Connectors	Pacific Learning
Creatures of the Night	M	I	250+	Murdock & Ray	Mondo
Creatures of the Night	M	I	250+	Rigby Focus	Rigby
Creatures of the Reef	S	I	250+	Belcher, Angie	Pacific Learning
Creek, The	T	I	4374	Native American Stories	Lerner Publications
Creek, The: Farmers of the Southeast	S	I	250+	American Indian Nations	Capstone Press
Creep Show	L	F	250+	Dussling, Jennifer	Grossett & Dunlap
Creepiest, Crawliest Places	M	I	651	Leveled Readers	Houghton Mifflin Harcourt
Creepiest, Crawliest Places	M	I	651	Leveled Readers/CA	Houghton Mifflin Harcourt

* Collection of short stories
# Graphic text

TITLE	LEVEL	GENRE	WORD COUNT	AUTHOR / SERIES	PUBLISHER / DISTRIBUTOR
Creeping Bookends, The	T	F	250+	Dahl, Michael	Stone Arch Books
Creepy Castle	G	F	208	Storyworlds	Heinemann Educational Books
Creepy Caterpillar	E	F	118	Little Readers	Houghton Mifflin Harcourt
Creepy Crawlies	B	RF	38	Carousel Earlybirds	Pearson Learning Group
Creepy Crawlies	P	I	250+	Literacy 2000	Rigby
Creepy Crawlies	F	I	35	Voyages	SRA/McGraw Hill
Creepy Creatures	Q	I	250+	Explorers	Wright Group/McGraw Hill
Creepy Creatures (Goosebumps)	U	F	250+	Stine, R. L.	Scholastic
Creepy Customers	L	F	250+	I Am Reading	Kingfisher
Cricket Bat Mystery, The	I	RF	250+	Storyworlds	Heinemann Educational Books
*Cricket Boy and Other Stories, The	L	TL	250+	New Way Literature	Steck-Vaughn
Cricket in Times Square, The	S	F	250+	Selden, George	Bantam
Cricket Song, A	F	RF	54	Appleton-Smith, Laura	Flyleaf Publishing
Cricket the Dog	I	I	250+	All About Dogs	Literacy Footprints
Crickets	H	I	89	Bugs, Bugs, Bugs!	Red Brick Learning
Crickets	D	I	48	Insects	Capstone Press
Crickets on the Go	D	F	56	Little Celebrations	Pearson Learning Group
Crime at the Chat Café	S	RF	250+	Keene, Carolyn	Pocket Books
Crime Busters	W	I	250+	Boldprint	Steck-Vaughn
Crime for Christmas, A	S	RF	250+	Keene, Carolyn	Pocket Books
Crime in the Queen's Court	S	RF	250+	Keene, Carolyn	Pocket Books
Crime Scene Clues	X	I	250+	Independent Readers Science	Houghton Mifflin Harcourt
Crime Scene Investigators: Uncovering the Truth	S	I	250+	Line of Duty	Capstone Press
Crime Solvers	W	I	250+	Orbit Chapter Books	Pacific Learning
*Crinkum Crankum	M	F	250+	Pacific Literacy	Pacific Learning
Crispin: At the Edge of the World	W	HF	250+	Avi	Hyperion
Crispin: The Cross of Lead	W	HF	250+	Avi	Hyperion
Crispus Attucks: Black Leader of Colonial Patriots	R	B	250+	Millender, Dharathula H.	Aladdin
Critics in Hollywood	V	I	1799	Leveled Readers	Houghton Mifflin Harcourt
Critics in Hollywood	V	I	1799	Leveled Readers/CA	Houghton Mifflin Harcourt
Critics in Hollywood	V	I	1799	Leveled Readers/TX	Houghton Mifflin Harcourt
Critter Race	G	F	118	Reese, Bob	Children's Press
Crocheting for Fun!	S	I	250+	For Fun! Crafts	Compass Point Books
Crocodile and a Whale, A	E	RF	127	PM Plus Story Books	Rigby
Crocodile in the Garden, A	L	F	250+	Ready to Read	Pacific Learning
Crocodile in the Library, A	L	F	250+	Pacific Literacy	Pacific Learning
Crocodile Lake	K	F	322	Pacific Literacy	Pacific Learning
Crocodile Rescue	Q	RF	250+	Reading Expeditions	National Geographic
Crocodiles	P	I	2023	Animal Predators	Lerner Publishing
Crocodiles	L	I	250+	Sunshine	Wright Group/McGraw Hill
Crocodiles	N	I	250+	World of Reptiles	Capstone Press
Crocodiles Are Dangerous	J	I	217	Breakthrough	Longman Group UK
Crocodile's Bag	K	F	250+	Storyteller- Shooting Stars	Wright Group/McGraw Hill
Crocodile's Christmas Jandals, The	L	F	250+	Pacific Literacy	Pacific Learning
Crocodile's Smile	E	F	86	Seedlings	Continental Press
Crocodilians	O	I	250+	Literacy 2000	Rigby
Crocodilians	U	I	250+	Short, Joan; Bird, Bettina	Mondo
Crocodilians: Reminders of the Age of Dinosaurs	S	I	250+	A First Book	Franklin Watts
Crocs!	O	F	250+	Greenberg, David T.	Little, Brown & Co.

TITLE	LEVEL	GENRE	WORD COUNT	AUTHOR / SERIES	PUBLISHER / DISTRIBUTOR
Crosby Crocodile's Disguise	K	F	250+	LIteracy 2000	Rigby
Crossbow	T	RF	250+	Orca Currents	Orca Book Publishers
Cross-Country Cousins	O	RF	919	Leveled Readers	Houghton Mifflin Harcourt
Cross-Country Cousins	O	RF	919	Leveled Readers/CA	Houghton Mifflin Harcourt
Cross-Country Cousins	O	RF	919	Leveled Readers/TX	Houghton Mifflin Harcourt
Cross-Country Race	C	RF	33	Windmill Books	Rigby
Cross-Country Race, The	H	RF	246	PM Story Books	Rigby
Crossing Borders: Stories of Immigrants	T	I	250+	iOpeners	Pearson Learning Group
Crossing Jordan	X	RF	250+	Fogelin, Adrian	Peachtree
Crossing the Atlantic: One Family's Story	N	I	250+	iOpeners	Pearson Learning Group
Crossing the Creek	C	F	35	Learn to Read	Creative Teaching Press
Crossing the Ocean	K	I	374	Vocabulary Readers	Houghton Mifflin Harcourt
Crossing the Ocean	K	I	374	Vocabulary Readers/CA	Houghton Mifflin Harcourt
Crossing the Street	G	RF	142	City Stories	Rigby
Crow and the Pitcher, The	I	TL	265	Aesop's Fables	Pearson Learning Group
Crow Said No	K	F	250+	Haight, Angela B.	Kaeden Books
Crow, The	Y	F	250+	Croggon, Alison	Candlewick Press
*Crowded Dock and Other Cases, The	O	RF	250+	Simon, Seymour	Avon
Crowfoot	X	B	250+	The Canadians	Fitzhenry & Whiteside
Crow-Girl, The	S	RF	250+	Bredsdorff, Bodil	Farrar, Straus and Giroux
Cruise Control	T	RF	250+	Reading Safari	Mondo
Cruisers	T	I	250+	Land and Sea	Capstone Press
Cruising the Caribbean	U	I	250+	WorldScapes	ETA Cuisenaire
Crunch and Munch	K	I	535	Big Cat	Pacific Learning
Crunchy Munchy	G	F	189	Bookshop	Mondo
Crush	Z+	RF	250+	Orca Soundings	Orca Book Publishers
Cry of the Crow, The	S	RF	250+	George, Jean Craighead	HarperTrophy
*Crying Rocks and Other Cases, The	O	RF	250+	Simon, Seymour	Avon
Cryobiology	Y	I	6679	Cool Science	Lerner Publications
Crystal Cave, The	Z+	TL	250+	Stewart, Mary	HarperCollins
Crystal Doors Book I: Island Realm	W	F	250+	Moesta, Rebecca & Anderson, Kevin J.	Little, Brown & Co.
Crystal Doors Book II: Ocean Realm	W	F	250+	Moesta, Rebecca & Anderson, Kevin J.	Little, Brown & Co.
Crystal Doors Book III: Sky Realm	W	F	250+	Moesta, Rebecca & Anderson, Kevin J.	Little, Brown & Co.
Crystal Unicorn, The	N	RF	250+	PM Collection	Rigby
Crystals	L	I	661	Sun Sprouts	ETA Cuisenaire
Cuauhtemoc, the Last Aztec Ruler	S	B	1598	Leveled Readers Social Studies	Houghton Mifflin Harcourt
Cub in the Cupboard	Q	RF	250+	Baglio, Ben M.	Scholastic
Cub Saves the Day	H	RF	156	Leveled Readers	Houghton Mifflin Harcourt
Cub Saves the Day	H	RF	156	Leveled Readers/CA	Houghton Mifflin Harcourt
Cub Saves the Day	H	RF	156	Leveled Readers/TX	Houghton Mifflin Harcourt
Cuba	O	I	250+	Countries of the World	Red Brick Learning
Cuba	Q	I	250+	First Reports: Countries	Compass Point Books
Cuba 15	W	RF	250+	Osa, Nancy	Delacorte Press
Cuban Americans	U	I	1590	Reading Street	Pearson
Cubby's Gum	J	F	250+	Ready Readers	Pearson Learning Group
Cubes	K	I	252	3-D Shapes	Capstone Press
Cuckoo Bird, The	I	I	236	Sails	Rigby
Cuckoo Child, The	Q	F	250+	King-Smith, Dick	Hyperion
Cuckoo's Sacrifice, The: A Tale From the Yucatán	T	F	1900	Leveled Readers	Houghton Mifflin Harcourt
Culpepper's Canyon	O	RF	250+	Paulsen, Gary	Bantam

Organized Alphabetically by Title
Storable Database at www.fountasandpinnellleveledbooks.com

* Collection of short stories
\# Graphic text

TITLE	LEVEL	GENRE	WORD COUNT	AUTHOR / SERIES	PUBLISHER / DISTRIBUTOR
Cultural Clothes	P	I	1543	Take Two Books	Wright Group/ McGraw Hill
Cultural Games	L	I	373	Take Two Books	Wright Group/ McGraw Hill
Cultural Instruments	Q	I	1414	Take Two Books	Wright Group/ McGraw Hill
Culture Clash	Q	I	250+	Explorer Books-Pioneer	National Geographic
Culture Clash	R	I	250+	Explorer Books-Pathfinder	National Geographic
Cumberland Gap, The	S	I	1262	Leveled Readers Social Studies	Houghton Mifflin Harcourt
Cunning Creatures	K	I	250+	Home Connection Collection	Rigby
Cupboard Full of Summer, A	J	RF	234	Pacific Literacy	Pacific Learning
Cupcakes	E	F	68	Leveled Readers	Houghton Mifflin Harcourt
Cupcakes	J	RF	665	Rigby Flying Colors	Rigby
Cupids Don't Flip Hamburgers	M	F	250+	Dadey, Debbie; Jones, Marcia Thornton	Scholastic
Curious About Animals That Dig	D	I	82	Vocabulary Readers	Houghton Mifflin Harcourt
Curious About Animals that Dig	D	I	82	Vocabulary Readers/CA	Houghton Mifflin Harcourt
Curious About Playing Ball	A	I	25	Vocabulary Readers	Houghton Mifflin Harcourt
Curious About Playing Ball	A	I	25	Vocabulary Readers/CA	Houghton Mifflin Harcourt
Curious About School	B	I	65	Vocabulary Readers	Houghton Mifflin Harcourt
Curious About School	B	I	65	Vocabulary Readers/CA	Houghton Mifflin Harcourt
Curious About School	B	I	65	Vocabulary Readers/TX	Houghton Mifflin Harcourt
Curious About School Helpers	G	I	203	Vocabulary Readers	Houghton Mifflin Harcourt
Curious About School Helpers	G	I	203	Vocabulary Readers/CA	Houghton Mifflin Harcourt
Curious About the Animal Park	A	I	20	Vocabulary Readers	Houghton Mifflin Harcourt
Curious About the Animal Park	A	I	20	Vocabulary Readers/CA	Houghton Mifflin Harcourt
Curious About What Kids Can Do	D	I	124	Vocabulary Readers	Houghton Mifflin Harcourt
Curious About What Kids Can Do	D	I	124	Vocabulary Readers/CA	Houghton Mifflin Harcourt
Curious Cases	S	I	250+	Orbit Collections	Pacific Learning
Curious Cat	E	F	95	Little Celebrations	Pearson Learning Group
Curious George and the Animals	A	F	29	Leveled Readers	Houghton Mifflin Harcourt
Curious George and the Animals	A	F	29	Leveled Readers/CA	Houghton Mifflin Harcourt
Curious George and the Hungry Animals	A	F	23	Leveled Readers	Houghton Mifflin Harcourt
Curious George and the Hungry Animals	A	F	23	Leveled Readers/CA	Houghton Mifflin Harcourt
Curious George and the Newspapers	F	F	137	Leveled Readers	Houghton Mifflin Harcourt
Curious George and the Newspapers	F	F	137	Leveled Readers/CA	Houghton Mifflin Harcourt
Curious George at the Library	I	F	281	Leveled Readers	Houghton Mifflin Harcourt
Curious George at the Library	I	F	281	Leveled Readers/CA	Houghton Mifflin Harcourt
Curious George at the Library	I	F	281	Leveled Readers/TX	Houghton Mifflin Harcourt
Curious George Finds Out About School	C	F	51	Leveled Readers	Houghton Mifflin Harcourt
Curious George Finds Out About School	C	F	51	Leveled Readers/CA	Houghton Mifflin Harcourt
Curious George Finds Out About School	C	F	51	Leveled Readers/TX	Houghton Mifflin Harcourt
Curious George Goes for a Ride	B	F	35	Leveled Readers	Houghton Mifflin Harcourt
Curious George Goes for a Ride	B	F	35	Leveled Readers/CA	Houghton Mifflin Harcourt
Curious George Likes to Ride	B	F	44	Leveled Readers	Houghton Mifflin Harcourt
Curious George Likes to Ride	B	F	44	Leveled Readers/CA	Houghton Mifflin Harcourt
Curious George Rides a Bike	J	F	250+	Rey, Margaret	Scholastic
Curious George Visits Animal Friends	A	F	26	Leveled Readers	Houghton Mifflin Harcourt
Curious George Visits Animal Friends	A	F	26	Leveled Readers/CA	Houghton Mifflin Harcourt
Curious George Visits School	C	F	88	Leveled Readers	Houghton Mifflin Harcourt
Curious George Visits School	C	F	88	Leveled Readers/CA	Houghton Mifflin Harcourt
Curious George Visits School	C	F	88	Leveled Readers/TX	Houghton Mifflin Harcourt
Curious George Visits the Woods	E	F	91	Leveled Readers	Houghton Mifflin Harcourt
Curious George Visits the Woods	E	F	91	Leveled Readers/CA	Houghton Mifflin Harcourt
Curious George's Day at School	C	F	87	Leveled Readers	Houghton Mifflin Harcourt
Curious George's Day at School	C	F	87	Leveled Readers/CA	Houghton Mifflin Harcourt
Curious George's Day at School	C	F	87	Leveled Readers/TX	Houghton Mifflin Harcourt

C

* Collection of short stories
# Graphic text

TITLE	LEVEL	GENRE	WORD COUNT	AUTHOR / SERIES	PUBLISHER / DISTRIBUTOR
Curious Kat	P	RF	250+	Leveled Readers	Houghton Mifflin Harcourt
Curly and His Friends	LB	F	15	Rigby Literacy	Rigby
Curly and the Big Berry	D	F	94	Rigby Rocket	Rigby
Curly and the Cherries	WB	F	N/A	Rigby Literacy	Rigby
Curly and the Honey	F	F	113	Rigby Star	Rigby
Curly and the Log	C	F	38	Rigby Rocket	Rigby
Curly Finds a Home	B	F	30	Rigby Literacy	Rigby
Curly Is Hungry	B	F	41	Rigby Literacy	Rigby
Curly Is Hungry	B	F	41	Rigby Star	Rigby
Curly to the Rescue	E	F	107	Rigby Literacy	Rigby
Curly to the Rescue	E	F	127	Rigby Star	Rigby
Curlylocks and the Three Bears: A Play	F	TL	194	Rigby Literacy	Rigby
Current in Your Home, The	T	I	554	Leveled Readers Science	Houghton Mifflin Harcourt
Curse of Being Pharaoh, The	P	RF	250+	Orbit Chapter Books	Pacific Learning
#Curse of King Tut's Tomb, The	U	I	250+	Graphic Library	Capstone Press
*Curse of the Campfire Weenies and Other Warped and Creepy Tales, The	T	F	250+	Lubar, David	Tom Doherty
Curse of the Cobweb Queen, The	L	F	250+	Hayes, Geoffrey	Random House
Curse of the Kitty Litter	Q	F	250+	Wiley & Grampa's Creature Features	Little, Brown & Co.
Curse of the Squirrel, The	N	F	250+	Yep, Laurence	Random House
Curse of the Wendigo, The:	T	F	250+	Welvaert, Scott R.	Stone Arch Books
Curtains! A High School Musical Mystery	S	RF	250+	Dahl, Michael	Stone Arch Books
Cuss	U	HF	250+	Franklin, Kristine	Candlewick Press
Custard	E	RF	82	Wonder World	Wright Group/McGraw Hill
Custard's Cat Flap	F	F	198	Sails	Rigby
Custodians	M	I	250+	Community Helpers	Red Brick Learning
Custodians	K	I	304	Pull Ahead Books	Lerner Publications
Custom Cars	W	I	6333	Motor Mania	Lerner Publications
Customs Service	S	I	250+	Law Enforcement	Capstone Press
Cut	Z+	RF	250+	McCormick, Patricia	Scholastic
*Cut From the Same Cloth: American Women of Myth, Legend, and Tall Tale	T	TL	250+	San Souci, Robert D.	Puffin/Penguin
Cuts, Scrapes, Scabs, and Scars	S	I	250+	My Health	Franklin Watts
Cut-Throat Pirates - Rex Jones	P	F	1837	Zucker, Jonny	Stone Arch Books
Cutting and Sticking	K	RF	250+	Cambridge Reading	Pearson Learning Group
Cutting Machines	G	I	132	Sunshine	Wright Group/McGraw Hill
Cutting Our Food	B	I	40	Early Connections	Benchmark Education
Cuttlebone	L	I	429	Sun Sprouts	ETA Cuisenaire
Cyberpals: According to Kaley	S	RF	11817	Regan, Dian Curtis	Darby Creek Publishing
Cyberspace	S	SF	250+	Wildcats	Wright Group/McGraw Hill
Cybil War, The	S	RF	250+	Byars, Betsy	Scholastic
Cycle of Nature, A - Migrating Journeys	U	I	250+	Connectors	Pacific Learning
Cycles and Patterns in Space	P	I	2000	Science Support Readers	Houghton Mifflin Harcourt
Cyclops Doesn't Roller-Skate	M	F	250+	Dadey, Debbie; Jones, Marcia Thornton	Scholastic
Cylinders	K	I	237	3-D Shapes	Capstone Press
Cynthia Rylant, Author	J	B	137	Vocabulary Readers	Houghton Mifflin Harcourt
Cyril the Dragon	M	F	250+	Sun Sprouts	ETA Cuisenaire

* Collection of short stories
# Graphic text

TITLE	LEVEL	GENRE	WORD COUNT	AUTHOR / SERIES	PUBLISHER / DISTRIBUTOR
D.W.'s Guide to Perfect Manners	K	F	250+	Brown, Marc	Little, Brown & Co.
D.W.'s Guide to Preschool	J	F	250+	Brown, Marc	Little, Brown & Co.
Da Gama: Vasco da Gama Sails Around the Cape of Good Hope	U	B	250+	Exploring the World	Compass Point Books
Da Vinci	R	B	250+	Venezia, Mike	Children's Press
Da Wild, Da Crazy, Da Vinci	P	F	250+	Scieszka, Jon	Penguin Group
Dabble Duck	K	RF	250+	Ellis, Anne Leo	HarperTrophy
Dabbling in Dough	K	I	250+	Book Bank	Wright Group/McGraw Hill
Dachshunds	I	I	136	Dogs	Capstone Press
Dad	B	I	37	InfoTrek	ETA Cuisenaire
Dad	A	RF	24	Leveled Literacy Intervention/ Orange System	Heinemann
Dad	B	RF	21	Little Readers	Houghton Mifflin Harcourt
Dad	A	I	24	PM Starters	Rigby
Dad and Beth Clean Up	E	RF	113	Book Bus	Creative Edge
Dad and Fif Fan	D	RF	31	Reading Street	Pearson
Dad and I	A	RF	40	On Our Way to English	Rigby
Dad and I	C	RF	59	Rise & Shine	Hampton-Brown
Dad and the Bike Race	J	RF	416	Sails	Rigby
Dad and the Cake	I	F	308	Sails	Rigby
Dad and the Go-Cart	H	RF	317	Sails	Rigby
Dad and the Grizzly Bear	I	RF	274	Sails	Rigby
Dad and the Mosquito	I	RF	246	Sunshine	Wright Group/McGraw Hill
Dad and the Skateboard	F	RF	202	Sails	Rigby
Dad at the Beach	I	F	318	Sails	Rigby
Dad at the Fair	I	RF	345	Sails	Rigby
Dad at the Park	C	RF	117	Sails	Rigby
Dad Cooks Breakfast	H	RF	195	Windmill Books	Rigby
Dad Didn't Mind at All	F	RF	134	Literacy 2000	Rigby
Dad Goes Fishing	J	F	453	Sails	Rigby
Dad Goes to School	A	RF	43	Mom and Dad Series	Pioneer Valley
Dad Still Smiles	L	RF	212	Books for Young Learners	Richard C. Owen
Daddy Saved the Day	M	RF	250+	Greetings	Rigby
Daddy Works Out	D	RF	39	Visions	Wright Group/McGraw Hill
Dad's Bathtime	E	RF	114	Literacy Tree	Rigby
Dad's Bike	E	RF	52	Literacy 2000	Rigby
Dad's Dinner	E	RF	159	Sails	Rigby
Dad's Favorite Tie	A	RF	35	Bonnell, Kris	Reading Reading Books
Dad's Garden	Q	RF	1000	Leveled Readers/TX	Houghton Mifflin Harcourt
Dad's Garden	D	RF	25	Literacy 2000	Rigby
Dad's Hamburger	D	I	51	Bonnell, Kris	Reading Reading Books
Dad's Headache	F	RF	86	Sunshine	Wright Group/McGraw Hill
Dad's New Path	F	RF	218	Foundations	Wright Group/McGraw Hill
Dad's Pasta	L	RF	250+	Sails	Rigby
Dad's Phone	F	RF	142	Springboard	Wright Group/McGraw Hill
Dad's Pizza	D	RF	77	Windows on Literacy	National Geographic
Dad's Promise	L	RF	250+	Cambridge Reading	Pearson Learning Group
Dad's Ship	C	RF	42	PM Stars	Rigby
Dad's Shirt	F	RF	38	Joy Readers	Pearson Learning Group
Dad's Surprise	J	RF	202	Foundations	Wright Group/McGraw Hill
Dad's Turkey Sandwich	A	RF	26	Mom and Dad Series	Pioneer Valley
Daffodil Spring	M	I	456	Leveled Readers/TX	Houghton Mifflin Harcourt
Daffodils for You	D	RF	90	Adams, Lorraine; Bruvold, Lynn	Eagle Crest Books
Daily Life in a Plains Indian Village: 1868	U	I	250+	Terry, Michael Bad Hand	Clarion

D

TITLE	LEVEL	GENRE	WORD COUNT	AUTHOR / SERIES	PUBLISHER / DISTRIBUTOR
Daily Life of the Cherokee, The	N	I	647	Vocabulary Readers	Houghton Mifflin Harcourt
Daily Life of the Cherokee, The	N	I	647	Vocabulary Readers/CA	Houghton Mifflin Harcourt
Daily Life of the Cherokee, The	N	I	647	Vocabulary Readers/TX	Houghton Mifflin Harcourt
Daily Meow, The	M	F	250+	Sails	Rigby
Dairy	F	I	93	Food Groups	Lerner Publications
Dairy Group, The	H	I	97	The Food Guide Pyramid	Capstone Press
Daisy	J	RF	250+	Stepping Stones	Nelson/Michaels Assoc.
Daisy Divine, Dancing Dog	M	F	763	Leveled Readers	Houghton Mifflin Harcourt
Dalai Lama: A Life of Compassion, The	P	B	609	Pull Ahead Books	Lerner Publications
Dale Earnhardt	Q	B	250+	NASCAR Racing	Capstone Press
Dale Earnhardt Jr.	P	B	1843	Amazing Athletes	Lerner Publications
Dallas Cowboys, The	S	I	4427	Team Spirit	Norwood House Press
Dallas Mavericks, The	S	I	250+	Team Spirit	Norwood House Press
Dallas Shapes Up	T	RF	250+	On Our Way to English	Rigby
Dalmatians	I	I	132	Dogs	Capstone Press
Dalmatians	F	RF	70	Seedlings	Continental Press
Dalmations	E	I	70	Seedlings	Continental Press
Damage	Z+	RF	250+	Jenkins, A.M.	HarperCollins
Dame Shirley and the Gold Rush	R	B	250+	Rawls, Jim	Steck-Vaughn
Dan and Dan	E	RF	96	Real Kids Readers	Millbrook Press
Dan and His Brothers	C	RF	105	Leveled Readers	Houghton Mifflin Harcourt
Dan and His Brothers	C	RF	105	Leveled Readers/CA	Houghton Mifflin Harcourt
Dan Did It!	C	RF	28	Reading Street	Pearson
Dan Gets Dressed	B	RF	42	Story Box	Wright Group/McGraw Hill
Dan Goes Home	E	F	153	Story Basket	Wright Group/McGraw Hill
Dan the Dunce	J	TL	539	Tales from Hans Andersen	Wright Group/McGraw Hill
Dan the Flying Man	C	F	60	Story Box	Wright Group/McGraw Hill
Dance	W	I	250+	Eyewitness Books	DK Publishing
Dance Around the World	N	I	211	Gear Up!	Wright Group/McGraw Hill
Dance at Grandpa's	J	HF	250+	Wilder, Laura Ingalls	HarperCollins
Dance Day	M	RF	1392	Gear Up!	Wright Group/McGraw Hill
Dance for Fun!	S	I	250+	Activities for Fun	Compass Point Books
Dance My Dance	L	TL	250+	Foundations	Wright Group/McGraw Hill
Dance of the Swan: A Story about Anna Pavlova	S	B	8434	Creative Minds Biographies	Lerner Publications
Dance Team	S	I	250+	Dance	Capstone Press
Dance to the Beat	D	I	83	Big Cat	Pacific Learning
Dance Trap: The Complicated Life of Claudia Cristina Cortez	S	RF	250+	Gallagher, Diana G.	Stone Arch Books
Dance Wth Rosie	N	RF	250+	Giff, Patricia Reilly	Penguin Group
Dance, The	C	F	35	Learn to Read	Creative Teaching Press
Dances We Do, The	G	I	131	Twig	Wright Group/McGraw Hill
Dancin' Down	I	RF	193	Evangeline Nicholas Collection	Wright Group/McGraw Hill
Dancing	D	I	27	Canizares, Susan; Chessen, Betsey	Scholastic
Dancing	E	I	42	Instant Readers	Harcourt School Publishers
Dancing	C	RF	38	Visions	Wright Group/McGraw Hill
Dancing Around the World	T	I	250+	iOpeners	Pearson Learning Group
Dancing Around the World	I	I	210	Leveled Readers	Houghton Mifflin Harcourt
Dancing Around the World	I	I	210	Leveled Readers/CA	Houghton Mifflin Harcourt
Dancing Carl	U	RF	250+	Paulsen, Gary	Aladdin
Dancing Dinosaurs	E	F	45	Little Celebrations	Pearson Learning Group
Dancing Dragon, The	I	F	236	Bookshop	Mondo
Dancing Fly, The	F	F	108	Sunshine	Wright Group/McGraw Hill
Dancing Gingerbread	H	RF	236	PM Photo Stories	Rigby

* Collection of short stories
\# Graphic text

TITLE	LEVEL	GENRE	WORD COUNT	AUTHOR / SERIES	PUBLISHER / DISTRIBUTOR
Dancing in Soot	L	RF	250+	Cambridge Reading	Pearson Learning Group
Dancing in the Cadillac Light	T	HF	250+	Holt, Kimberly Willis	G.P. Putnam's Sons
Dancing Naked	Z+	RF	250+	Hrdlitschka, Shelley	Orca Book Publishers
Dancing on the Edge	Z	RF	250+	Nolan, Han	Harcourt School Publishers
Dancing Shoes	B	F	23	Literacy 2000	Rigby
Dancing to Freedom: The True Story of Mao's Last Dancer	S	B	250+	Cunxin, Li	Walker & Company
Dancing to the River	J	TL	250+	Cambridge Reading	Pearson Learning Group
Dancing with Jacques	P	HF	250+	Voyages in Time	Wright Group/McGraw Hill
Dancing with Katya	P	HF	250+	Chaconas, Dori	Peachtree
Dancing with Manatees	N	I	250+	McNulty, Faith	Scholastic
Dancing with the Indians	M	HF	250+	Medearis, Angela	Scholastic
Dandelion and Other Stories	H	F	250+	Story Steps	Rigby
Dandelion Year	H	I	136	Little Celebrations	Pearson Learning Group
Dandelion, The	E	RF	99	Sunshine	Wright Group/McGraw Hill
Dandelions	Q	I	1672	Early Bird Nature Books	Lerner Publications
Dandelions: Stars in the Grass	K	I	216	Posada, Mia	Carolrhoda Books
Danger	C	RF	66	Story Box	Wright Group/McGraw Hill
Danger at Sand Cave	N	HF	1505	On My Own History	Lerner Publications
Danger at the Breaker	N	HF	1871	On My Own History	Lerner Publications
Danger at Work	W	I	250+	Boldprint	Steck-Vaughn
Danger Guys	N	RF	250+	Abbott, Tony	HarperTrophy
Danger Guys Blast Off	N	RF	250+	Abbott, Tony	HarperTrophy
Danger Guys on Ice	N	RF	250+	Abbott, Tony	HarperTrophy
Danger in Quicksand Swamp	W	RF	250+	Wallace, Bill	Simon & Schuster
Danger in the Dark	W	F	250+	Dark Man	Ransom
Danger in the Parking Lot	J	RF	250+	PM Plus Story Books	Rigby
Danger on Ice	S	I	250+	Power Up!	Steck-Vaughn
Danger on Midnight River	O	RF	250+	Paulsen, Gary	Bantam
Danger on Panther Peak	R	RF	250+	Wallace, Bill	Pocket Books
Danger on Parade	T	RF	250+	Keene, Carolyn	Pocket Books
Danger! Children at Work	V	I	1784	Reading Street	Pearson
Danger, Landslides!	Q	I	250+	Leveled Readers Language Support	Houghton Mifflin Harcourt
Danger: Dynamite!	Q	HF	250+	Capeci, Anne	Peachtree
Danger: The World Is Getting Hot!	V	I	1483	Reading Street	Pearson
Dangerous Animals	R	I	250+	Explorers	Wright Group/McGraw Hill
*Dangerous Comet and Other Cases, The	O	RF	250+	Simon, Seymour	Avon
Dangerous Days of Daniel X, The	Y	F	250+	Patterson, James & Michael Ledwidge	Little, Brown & Co.
Dangerous Droughts	L	I	250+	Rosen Real Readers	Rosen Publishing Group
Dangerous Jobs	L	I	373	Sails	Rigby
Dangerous Mission of Emily Geiger, The	T	I	1273	Leveled Readers	Houghton Mifflin Harcourt
Dangerous Plants	F	I	115	Explorations	Eleanor Curtain Publishing
Dangerous Plants	F	I	115	Explorations	Okapi Eductional Materials
Dangerous Professions of the Past	O	I	250+	Rigby Focus	Rigby
Dangerous Trip, A	S	HF	1359	Leveled Readers	Houghton Mifflin Harcourt
Dangerous Trip, A	S	HF	1359	Leveled Readers/CA	Houghton Mifflin Harcourt
Dangerous Trip, A	S	HF	1359	Leveled Readers/TX	Houghton Mifflin Harcourt
Dangerous Waters	Q	I	250+	Leveled Readers	Houghton Mifflin Harcourt
Dangerous Waves	P	I	915	Vocabulary Readers	Houghton Mifflin Harcourt
Dangerous Waves	P	I	915	Vocabulary Readers/CA	Houghton Mifflin Harcourt
Dangerous Waves	P	I	915	Vocabulary Readers/TX	Houghton Mifflin Harcourt
Dangerous Wishes	U	F	250+	Sleator, William	Penguin Group

* Collection of short stories
# Graphic text

TITLE	LEVEL	GENRE	WORD COUNT	AUTHOR / SERIES	PUBLISHER / DISTRIBUTOR
Danica Patrick	P	B	2160	Amazing Athletes	Lerner Publications
Daniel	F	RF	161	Literacy 2000	Rigby
Daniel and the Great Bearded One	W	F	250+	Bookshop	Mondo
Daniel Boone	R	B	3586	History Maker Bios	Lerner Publications
Daniel Boone	N	B	1889	On My Own Biography	Lerner Publications
Daniel Boone: Frontier Scout	V	B	250+	Let Freedom Ring	Capstone Press
Daniel Boone: Man of the Forests	O	B	250+	Greene, Carol	Children's Press
Daniel Boone's Great Escape	T	B	250+	Spradlin, Michael P.	Walker & Company
Daniel Inouye: Hero from Hawaii	W	B	3114	Leveled Readers	Houghton Mifflin Harcourt
Daniel Inouye: Senator from Hawaii	P	B	799	Leveled Readers Social Studies	Houghton Mifflin Harcourt
Daniel's Basketball Team	E	RF	80	Carousel Readers	Pearson Learning Group
Daniel's Dog	K	RF	250+	Bogart, Jo Allen	Scholastic
Daniel's Duck	K	RF	250+	Bulla, Clyde Robert	HarperTrophy
Daniel's Pet	F	RF	76	Green Light Readers	Harcourt
Daniel's Story	Z	HF	250+	Matas, Carol	Scholastic
Danny and Abby Are Friends	E	RF	109	Coulton, Mia	Maryruth Books
Danny and Abby Play Hospital	E	F	60	Coulton, Mia	Maryruth Books
Danny and Abby Play Tag	E	F	74	Coulton, Mia	Maryruth Books
Danny and Bee's Book of Opposites	D	F	41	Coulton, Mia	Maryruth Books
Danny and Bee's Safety Rules	F	RF	106	Coulton, Mia	Maryruth Books
Danny and Dad Go Shopping	C	I	69	Coulton, Mia	Maryruth Books
Danny and the Bully	H	F	344	Coulton, Mia	Maryruth Books
Danny and the Dinosaur	J	F	250+	Hoff, Syd	Scholastic
Danny and the Dinosaur Go to Camp	H	F	250+	Hoff, Syd	HarperTrophy
Danny and the Four Seasons	C	RF	55	Coulton, Mia	Maryruth Books
Danny and the Little Worm	F	F	174	Coulton, Mia	Maryruth Books
Danny and the Monarch Butterfly	I	I	282	Coulton, Mia	Maryruth Books
Danny at the Car Wash	E	RF	124	Coulton, Mia	Maryruth Books
Danny Can Sort	C	I	42	Coulton, Mia	Maryruth Books
Danny Dragon Goes to the City	D	F	64	Reading Safari	Mondo
Danny Drives Too Fast	E	RF	160	Reading Safari	Mondo
Danny Gets Fit	E	RF	177	Coulton, Mia	Maryruth Books
Danny Goes for a Walk	C	F	50	Coulton, Mia	Maryruth Books
Danny Likes Red	B	RF	28	Coulton, Mia	Maryruth Books
Danny Likes to Help	D	F	60	Coulton, Mia	Maryruth Books
Danny Looks for Abby	E	RF	120	Coulton, Mia	Maryruth Books
Danny Paints a Picture	F	F	117	Coulton, Mia	Maryruth Books
Danny, Champion of the World	T	RF	250+	Dahl, Roald	Language for Learning Assoc.
Danny's Bee (the beginning)	LB	RF	5	Coulton, Mia	Maryruth Books
Danny's Big Adventure	K	F	250+	Coulton, Mia	Maryruth Books
Danny's Big Jump	L	RF	250+	Take Two Books	Wright Group/McGraw Hill
Danny's Castle	D	F	61	Coulton, Mia	Maryruth Books
Danny's Desert Rats	X	RF	250+	Naylor, Phyllis Reynolds	Aladdin
Danny's Dinner	G	F	142	Coulton, Mia	Maryruth Books
Danny's Dollars	D	RF	88	Reading Corners	Pearson Learning Group
Danny's Drums	F	F	109	Pair-It Turn and Learn	Steck-Vaughn
Danny's Favorite Shapes	F	F	95	Coulton, Mia	Maryruth Books
Danny's Five Senses	D	RF	52	Coulton, Mia	Maryruth Books
Danny's Groundhog Day	F	RF	126	Coulton, Mia	Maryruth Books
Danny's New Toy	E	RF	70	Coulton, Mia	Maryruth Books
Danny's Party	B	RF	21	Coulton, Mia	Maryruth Books
Danny's Timeline	D	F	73	Coulton, Mia	Maryruth Books
Danny's Window	C	RF	62	Coulton, Mia	Maryruth Books

* Collection of short stories
\# Graphic text

TITLE	LEVEL	GENRE	WORD COUNT	AUTHOR / SERIES	PUBLISHER / DISTRIBUTOR
Dan's Box	G	F	105	Cambridge Reading	Pearson Learning Group
Dan's Old Van	H	F	145	Supersonics	Rigby
Darby	T	HF	250+	Fuqua, Jonathon Scott	Candlewick Press
Darcy and Gran Don't Like Babies	K	RF	250+	Cutler, Jane	Scholastic
Darcy Devlin and the Mystery Boy	Q	RF	250+	PM Plus Chapter Books	Rigby
*Dare to Be Scared: Thirteen Stories to Chill and Thrill	V	F	250+	San Souci, Robert D.	Cricket Books
Daredevil Club	T	RF	250+	Orca Currents	Orca Book Publishers
Daredevils	Q	HF	250+	Capeci, Anne	Peachtree
Daring Escape of Ellen Craft, The	P	B	1893	On My Own History	Lerner Publications
Daring Rescue of Marlon the Swimming Pig, The	P	F	250+	Saunders, S.	Random House
Daring Riders of the Pony Express, The	U	I	1853	Vocabulary Readers	Houghton Mifflin Harcourt
Daring Riders of the Pony Express, The	U	I	1853	Vocabulary Readers/CA	Houghton Mifflin Harcourt
Dark and Full of Secrets	N	RF	250+	Carrick, Carol	Houghton Mifflin Harcourt
Dark and Stormy Night, A	G	F	160	Little Red Readers	Sundance
Dark Canoe, The	X	RF	29300	O'Dell, Scott	Sourcebooks
Dark Dreams of Hell, The	W	F	250+	Dark Man	Ransom
Dark Fire of Doom, The	W	F	250+	Dark Man	Ransom
Dark Glass, The	W	F	250+	Dark Man	Ransom
Dark Is Rising, The	X	F	250+	Cooper, Susan	Macmillan
Dark Never Hides, The	W	F	250+	Dark Man	Ransom
Dark Night, Sleepy Night	F	I	123	Ziefert, Harriet	Puffin/Penguin
Dark Side of Magic, The	W	F	250+	Dark Man	Ransom
Dark Side of the Creek, The	M	RF	250+	Sunshine	Wright Group/McGraw Hill
Dark Stairs	V	RF	250+	Byars, Betsy	Puffin/Penguin
Dark Waters of Time, The	W	F	250+	Dark Man	Ransom
Dark, Dark Tale, A	F	F	115	Brown, Ruth	Penguin Group
Darkness Before Dawn	Z+	RF	250+	Draper, Sharon M.	Simon & Schuster
Darkness into Light	S	I	1482	Reading Street	Pearson
Darkness Under the Water, The	Z	HF	250+	Kanell, Beth	Candlewick Press
*Dark-Thirty: Southern Tales of the Supernatural	R	F	250+	McKissack, Patricia C.	Alfred A. Knopf
Darlene and the Art Show	N	RF	963	Leveled Readers/TX	Houghton Mifflin Harcourt
Darren Dwayne DeBakery and His Amazing Inventions	R	F	250+	Pair-It Books	Steck-Vaughn
Darryl the Doorman	F	RF	85	City Stories	Rigby
Darwin Expedition, The	Z+	RF	250+	Orca Soundings	Orca Book Publishers
Dash of Science, A	W	I	250+	Literacy By Design	Rigby
Dash, the Young Meerkat	K	RF	250+	PM Plus Story Books	Rigby
Dashing Through the Snow: The Story of the Jr. Iditarod	U	I	250+	Bookshop	Mondo
Daughter of the Mountains	V	HF	250+	Rankin, Louise	Penguin Group
Daughter of the Sun	H	RF	210	Storyteller-Night Crickets	Wright Group/McGraw Hill
Daughter of Venice	X	HF	250+	Napoli, Donna Jo	Random House
Daughters of Liberty	S	B	1620	Independent Readers Social Studies	Houghton Mifflin Harcourt
David Beckham	P	B	250+	Amazing Athletes	Lerner Publications
David Beckham	O	B	928	Leveled Readers	Houghton Mifflin Harcourt
David Beckham	O	B	928	Leveled Readers/CA	Houghton Mifflin Harcourt
David Beckham	O	B	928	Leveled Readers/TX	Houghton Mifflin Harcourt
David Beckham Soccer Superstar	O	B	953	Leveled Readers/CA	Houghton Mifflin Harcourt
David Beckham Soccer Superstar	O	B	953	Leveled Readers/TX	Houghton Mifflin Harcourt
David Beckham, Soccer Superstar	O	B	953	Leveled Readers	Houghton Mifflin Harcourt

D

* Collection of short stories
# Graphic text

TITLE	LEVEL	GENRE	WORD COUNT	AUTHOR / SERIES	PUBLISHER / DISTRIBUTOR
David McCord: Poet	Q	B	407	Vocabulary Readers	Houghton Mifflin Harcourt
David Mortimore Baxter: Chicken!	P	RF	250+	Tayleur, Karen	Stone Arch Books
David Mortimore Baxter: Excuses!	P	RF	8776	Tayleur, Karen	Stone Arch Books
David Mortimore Baxter: Haunted!	P	RF	250+	Tayleur, Karen	Stone Arch Books
David Mortimore Baxter: Liar!	P	RF	9827	Tayleur, Karen	Stone Arch Books
David Mortimore Baxter: Manners!	P	RF	10673	Tayleur, Karen	Stone Arch Books
David Mortimore Baxter: Promises!	P	RF	10748	Tayleur, Karen	Stone Arch Books
David Mortimore Baxter: Secrets!	P	RF	10548	Tayleur, Karen	Stone Arch Books
David Mortimore Baxter: Spies!	P	RF	250+	Tayleur, Karen	Stone Arch Books
David Mortimore Baxter: The Truth!	P	RF	10667	Tayleur, Karen	Stone Arch Books
David Mortimore Baxter: Wild!	P	RF	250+	Tayleur, Karen	Stone Arch Books
David Ortiz	P	B	2023	Amazing Athletes	Lerner Publications
David Wiggles	F	RF	54	City Stories	Rigby
David's Cold	E	I	151	Little Celebrations	Pearson Learning Group
Davin	R	F	250+	Gordon, Dan; Gordon, Zaki	Bantam
DaVinci's Designs	V	B	1669	Reading Street	Pearson
Davis Buys a Dog	K	RF	299	Reading Street	Pearson
Davy Crockett	R	B	3885	History Maker Bios	Lerner Publications
Davy Crockett	P	B	250+	Photo-Illustrated Biographies	Red Brick Learning
Davy Crockett and the Wild Cat	H	F	148	Instant Readers	Harcourt School Publishers
Davy Crockett: Frontier Hero	V	B	2127	Leveled Readers	Houghton Mifflin Harcourt
Davy Crockett: His Life and Legend	S	B	250+	Power Up!	Steck-Vaughn
Dawn of Fear	X	HF	250+	Cooper, Susan	Simon & Schuster
Day and Night	G	I	115	Discovery Links	Newbridge
Day and Night	I	I	228	Gear Up!	Wright Group/McGraw Hill
Day and Night	M	TL	250+	Orbit Chapter Books	Pacific Learning
Day and Night	J	I	188	Patterns in Nature	Capstone Press
Day and Night	D	I	102	Rigby Rocket	Rigby
Day and Night	T	I	250+	The News	Richard C. Owen
Day and Night	D	I	102	Twig	Wright Group/McGraw Hill
Day at a Time, A	LB	I	27	Shutterbug Books	Steck-Vaughn
Day at Rainbow Lake, A	I	I	250+	Phonics Readers Plus	Steck-Vaughn
Day at School, A	A	F	15	Leveled Readers	Houghton Mifflin Harcourt
Day at School, A	A	I	21	Leveled Readers Emergent	Houghton Mifflin Harcourt
Day at School, A	A	F	15	Leveled Readers/CA	Houghton Mifflin Harcourt
Day at School, A	C	RF	38	Sunshine	Wright Group/McGraw Hill
Day at the Beach, A	E	RF	207	Rigby Flying Colors	Rigby
Day at the Fair, A	B	RF	42	Bebop Books	Lee & Low Books Inc.
Day at the Market, A	J	I	250+	Explorations	Eleanor Curtain Publishing
Day at the Market, A	J	I	250+	Explorations	Okapi Educational Materials
Day at the Park, A	C	RF	105	Leveled Literacy Intervention/ Green System	Heinemann
Day at the Pond, A	I	I	193	InfoTrek	ETA Cuisenaire
Day at the Races, A	H	RF	85	Bauer, Roger	Kaeden Books
Day at the Races, A	M	RF	250+	Michaels, Eric	Pearson Learning Group
Day at the Trout Farm, A	L	I	653	Rigby Flying Colors	Rigby
Day Buzzy Stopped Being Busy, The	G	F	147	First Start	Troll Associates
Day for J. J. and Me, A	M	RF	371	Evangeline Nicholas Collection	Wright Group/McGraw Hill
Day for Night	Q	I	947	Reading Street	Pearson
Day I Chose My Family, The	I	F	292	Springboard	Wright Group/McGraw Hill
Day I Had to Play with My Sister, The	G	RF	139	Bonsall, Crosby	HarperCollins
Day I Lost My Bus Pass, The	J	RF	131	City Kids	Rigby
Day I Tore My Shorts, The	I	RF	209	City Kids	Rigby

* Collection of short stories
# Graphic text

TITLE	LEVEL	GENRE	WORD COUNT	AUTHOR / SERIES	PUBLISHER / DISTRIBUTOR
Day in Japan, A	G	I	54	Moreton, Daniel; Berger, Samantha	Scholastic
Day in San Juan, A	M	I	621	Vocabulary Readers/CA	Houghton Mifflin Harcourt
Day in Space, A	L	SF	250+	Lord, Suzanne; Epstein, Jolie	Scholastic
Day in the Life of a Ballet Dancer, A	O	I	824	Time for Kids	Teacher Created Materials
Day in the Life of a Colonial Cabinetmaker, A	S	I	250+	The Library of Living and Working in Colonial Times	Rosen Publishing Group
Day in the Life of a Colonial Dressmaker, A	S	I	250+	The Library of Living and Working in Colonial Times	Rosen Publishing Group
Day in the Life of a Colonial Glassblower, A	S	I	250+	The Library of Living and Working in Colonial Times	Rosen Publishing Group
Day in the Life of a Colonial Sea Captain, A	S	I	250+	The Library of Living and Working in Colonial Times	Rosen Publishing Group
Day in the Life of a Colonial Soldier, A	S	I	250+	The Library of Living and Working in Colonial Times	Rosen Publishing Group
Day in the Life of a Colonial Surveyor, A	S	I	250+	The Library of Living and Working in Colonial Times	Rosen Publishing Group
Day in the Life of a Computer, A	K	I	250+	On Our Way to English	Rigby
Day in the Life of a Cowhand, A	N	I	803	Time for Kids	Teacher Created Materials Publishing
Day in the Life of a Firefighter, A	N	I	818	Time for Kids	Teacher Created Materials Publishing
Day in the Life of a Garbage Collector, A	K	I	250+	Community Helpers at Work	Capstone Press
Day in the Life of a Librarian, A	L	I	250+	Community Helpers at Work	Capstone Press
Day in the Life of a Vet, A	M	I	1215	Reading Street	Pearson
Day in the Life of a Zoo Keeper, A	L	I	250+	Community Helpers at Work	Capstone Press
Day in the Life of Peter and Eve, A	V	HF	1974	Reading Street	Pearson
Day in the Life of the Great Plains, A	Q	I	1287	Leveled Readers Social Studies	Houghton Mifflin Harcourt
Day in Town, A	K	RF	206	Story Box	Wright Group/McGraw Hill
Day It Rained Forever, The: A Story of the Johnstown Flood	S	I	250+	Gross, Virginia T.	Penguin Group
Day Jimmy's Boa Ate the Wash, The	K	F	250+	Noble, Trinka H.	Scholastic
Day Martin Luther King, Jr., Died, The	M	RF	250+	Story Vines	Wright Group/McGraw Hill
Day Martin Luther King, Jr., Was Shot, The	Y	B	250+	Haskins, Jim	Scholastic
Day Miss Francie Got Skunked, The	N	RF	250+	DeFord, Diane	Pearson Learning Group
Day No Pigs Would Die, A	Z	HF	250+	Peck, Robert Newton	Random House
Day of Ahmed's Secret, A	M	RF	250+	Heide, Florence Perry; Gilliland, Judith Heide	Scholastic
Day of Pleasure, A: Stories of a Boy Growing Up in Warsaw	W	B	250+	Singer, Isaac Bashevis	Farrar, Straus and Giroux
Day of the Blizzard	Q	I	250+	Moskin, Marietta	Scholastic
Day of the Dead	N	I	1630	On My Own Holidays	Lerner Publications
Day of the Dead, The	I	RF	250+	Greetings	Rigby
Day of the Dragon King	M	F	250+	Osborne, Mary Pope	Random House
Day of the Iguana	R	RF	250+	Winkler, Henry and Oliver, Lin	Grosset & Dunlap
Day of the Rain, The	L	F	250+	Cowley, Joy	Pearson Learning Group
Day of the Snow, The	L	F	250+	Cowley, Joy	Pearson Learning Group
Day of the Tornadoes	P	I	552	Vocabulary Readers	Houghton Mifflin Harcourt
Day of the Wind, The	L	F	250+	Cowley, Joy	Pearson Learning Group
Day Shopping, A	E	RF	157	Foundations	Wright Group/McGraw Hill
Day the Earth Shook, The	T	I	1889	Leveled Readers Science	Houghton Mifflin Harcourt
Day the Fifth Grade Disappeared, The	Q	F	250+	Fields, Terri	Scholastic
Day the Gorilla Came to School, The	I	RF	293	Sunshine	Wright Group/McGraw Hill
Day the Sky Fell Down, The	H	F	226	Lighthouse	Rigby

* Collection of short stories
# Graphic text

TITLE	LEVEL	GENRE	WORD COUNT	AUTHOR / SERIES	PUBLISHER / DISTRIBUTOR
Day the Sky Turned Green, The	M	F	250+	Reeves, Barbara	Pearson Learning Group
Day the Women Got the Vote, The: A Photo History of the Women's Rights Movement	Y	B	250+	Sullivan, George	Scholastic
Day to Remember, A	J	RF	280	Take Two Books	Wright Group/McGraw Hill
Day With a Mail Carrier, A	J	I	187	Welcome Books	Children's Press
Day With a Mechanic, A	J	I	147	Welcome Books	Children's Press
Day with Air Traffic Controllers, A	J	I	145	Welcome Books	Children's Press
Day with Aunt Eva, A	K	RF	509	Pair-It Turn and Learn	Steck-Vaughn
Day with Belugas, A	Q	I	250+	WorldScapes	ETA Cuisenaire
Day with Dad, A	L	RF	250+	Holmberg, Bo R.	Candlewick Press
Day with Emily Emeryboard	K	F	250+	Foundations	Wright Group/McGraw Hill
Day with Firefighters, A	H	I	171	Welcome Books	Children's Press
Day with My Dad, A	C	RF	88	Fiesta Series	Pearson Learning Group
Day with My Family, A	J	RF	250+	Parker, David	Scholastic
Day with Paramedics, A	F	I	147	Kottke, Jan	Scholastic
Day with the Dogs, A	M	RF	1037	Reading Street	Pearson
Day with the Mayor, A	N	RF	704	Leveled Readers Social Studies	Houghton Mifflin Harcourt
Day with Wilbur Robinson, A	N	RF	250+	Joyce, William	HarperTrophy
Day with Your Dog, A	C	I	32	Rosen Real Readers	Rosen Publishing Group
Day, A	F	I	109	Calendars	Lerner Publications
Day, A	H	I	134	The Calendar	Capstone Press
Day, Night	B	RF	42	Reading Safari	Mondo
Day, The	LB	F	12	Sails	Rigby
Days at the Beach	E	I	85	Sun Sprouts	ETA Cuisenaire
Days of Adventure	E	F	47	Bookshop	Mondo
Days of Courage: The Little Rock Story	R	I	250+	Kelso, Richard	Steck-Vaughn
Days of Decision: An Oral History of Conscientious Objectors in the Military During the Vietnam War	Z+	B	250+	Gioglio, Gerald R.	The Broken Rifle Press
Days of the Knights: A Tale of Castles and Battles	V	HF	250+	DK Readers	DK Publishing
Days of the Week	E	I	166	PM Math Readers	Rigby
Days of the Week, The	A	RF	54	InfoTrek	ETA Cuisenaire
Days to Remember	R	I	250+	iOpeners	Pearson Learning Group
*Days With Frog and Toad	K	F	250+	Lobel, Arnold	HarperTrophy
Dayton and the Happy Tree	M	RF	1237	Sunshine	Wright Group/McGraw Hill
Dazzle of Hummingbirds, A	U	I	250+	Wild Life Series	London Town Press
Dazzling Designs	R	I	250+	WorldScapes	ETA Cuisenaire
De Soto: Hernando de Soto Explores the Southeast	U	B	250+	Exploring the World	Compass Point Books
Dead Cool	Q	F	4627	Clover, Peter	Stone Arch Books
Dead Girls Don't Write Letters	W	RF	250+	Giles, Gail	Millbrook Press
Dead Letter	S	RF	250+	Byars, Betsy	Puffin/Penguin
Dead Man's Map	S	RF	250+	Peschke, M.	Stone Arch Books
Deadbolts and Dinkles	N	RF	250+	Tapp, Kathy Kennedy	Mondo
Dead-End Job	Z+	RF	250+	Orca Soundings	Orca Book Publishers
Deadliest Dinosaurs, The	P	I	1106	Meet the Dinosaurs	Lerner Publications
Deadly Doll, The	S	F	250+	Burke, J.	Stone Arch Books
Deadly Dungeon, The	N	RF	250+	A to Z Mysteries	Random House
Deadly Sea Creatures	N	I	1308	Take Two Books	Wright Group/McGraw Hill
Dealing with Dragons	U	F	250+	Wrede, Patricia	Harcourt
Dear America: Letters From Vietnam	Z+	I	250+	Edelman, Bernard	Pocket Books
Dear Benjamin Banneker	U	B	250+	Pinkney, Andrea Davis	Voyager Books
Dear Butterflies . . .	L	RF	414	Leveled Readers	Houghton Mifflin Harcourt

* Collection of short stories
# Graphic text

TITLE	LEVEL	GENRE	WORD COUNT	AUTHOR / SERIES	PUBLISHER / DISTRIBUTOR
Dear Cousin	W	HF	3804	Leveled Readers	Houghton Mifflin Harcourt
Dear Cousin	W	HF	3804	Leveled Readers/CA	Houghton Mifflin Harcourt
Dear Cousin	W	HF	3804	Leveled Readers/TX	Houghton Mifflin Harcourt
Dear Diary	M	RF	712	Leveled Readers/TX	Houghton Mifflin Harcourt
Dear Diary	N	RF	250+	Literacy 2000 Satellites	Rigby
Dear Dr. Bell…Your Friend, Helen Keller	W	B	250+	St. George, Judith	Scholastic
Dear Dragon Goes to the Library	E	F	250+	Dear Dragon	Norwood House Press
Dear Dragon's A Is for Apple	E	F	250+	Dear Dragon	Norwood House Press
Dear Dragon's Day with Father	F	F	250+	Dear Dragon	Norwood House Press
Dear Future	Q	RF	250+	Literacy 2000	Rigby
Dear Grandma	M	I	264	Storyteller Nonfiction	Wright Group/McGraw Hill
Dear Juno	M	RF	250+	Park, Soyung	Scholastic
Dear Levi: Letters from the Overland Trail	T	HF	250+	Woodruff, Elvira	Alfred A. Knopf
Dear Mabel!	H	RF	138	Little Celebrations	Pearson Learning Group
Dear Mr. Blueberry	L	F	250+	James, Simon	Aladddin Paperbacks
Dear Mr. Henshaw	Q	RF	250+	Cleary, Beverly	HarperCollins
Dear Mrs. Parks: A Dialogue with Today's Youth	V	I	250+	Parks, Rosa	Lee & Low Books Inc.
Dear Papa	S	HF	250+	Ylvisaker, Anne	Candlewick Press
Dear Pop	N	RF	250+	Wonder World	Wright Group/McGraw Hill
Dear Prime Minister	O	I	250+	Roberts, Chris	Fitzhenry & Whiteside
Dear Santa	B	F	50	Literacy 2000	Rigby
Dear Tom	H	RF	153	Wonder World	Wright Group/McGraw Hill
Dear Tooth Fairy	K	F	250+	Ruelle, Karen Gray	Holiday House
Dear Zoo	F	F	115	Campbell, Rod	Macmillan
Dearly, Nearly, Insincerely: What Is an Adverb?	O	I	362	Words Are CATegorical	Millbrook Press
Death Be Not Proud	Z+	B	250+	Gunther, John	HarperCollins
Death Mountain	U	RF	250+	Shahan, Sherry	Peachtree
Death of Issac Brock, The	Y	I	250+	History for Young Canadians	Fitzhenry & Whiteside
Death of Tecumseh, The	Y	I	250+	History for Young Canadians	Fitzhenry & Whiteside
Death Valley	S	HF	250+	Duey, Kathleen; Bale, Karen A.	Simon & Schuster
Death Valley	Q	I	1571	Vocabulary Readers	Houghton Mifflin Harcourt
Death Valley	Q	I	1571	Vocabulary Readers/CA	Houghton Mifflin Harcourt
Death Valley Desert	P	I	1097	Time for Kids	Teacher Created Materials
Death Wind	Z+	RF	250+	Orca Soundings	Orca Book Publishers
Death's Door	V	RF	250+	Byars, Betsy	Puffin/Penguin
Deathwatch	Z+	RF	250+	White, Robb	Bantam Doubleday Dell
Deborah Sampson, Soldier of the American Revolution	P	B	250+	Leveled Readers Language Support	Houghton Mifflin Harcourt
Deborah Sampson: Soldier of the Revolution	S	B	1207	Leveled Readers	Houghton Mifflin Harcourt
Debra's Dog	H	F	157	Tadpoles	Rigby
Deb's Secret Wish and Other Stories	H	F	250+	New Way Literature	Steck-Vaughn
December Secrets	L	RF	250+	Giff, Patricia Reilly	Bantam
Decision at Fort Laramie	W	HF	3450	Leveled Readers/CA	Houghton Mifflin Harcourt
Decision at Fort Laramie	W	HF	3450	Leveled Readers/TX	Houghton Mifflin Harcourt
Decisions at Fort Laramie	W	HF	3450	Leveled Readers	Houghton Mifflin Harcourt
Deck of Monsters, A	O	F	250+	Zucker, Jonny	Stone Arch Books
Declaration of Independence and Benjamin Franklin of Pennsylvania, The	R	B	250+	Framers of the Declaration of Independence	Rosen Publishing Group
Declaration of Independence and John Adams of Massachusetts, The	R	B	250+	Framers of the Declaration of Independence	Rosen Publishing Group
Declaration of Independence and Richard Henry Lee of Virginia, The	R	B	250+	Framers of the Declaration of Independence	Rosen Publishing Group
Declaration of Independence and Robert Livingston of New York, The	R	B	250+	Framers of the Declaration of Independence	Rosen Publishing Group

D

* Collection of short stories
# Graphic text

TITLE	LEVEL	GENRE	WORD COUNT	AUTHOR / SERIES	PUBLISHER / DISTRIBUTOR
Declaration of Independence and Roger Sherman of Connecticut, The	R	B	250+	Framers of the Declaration of Independence	Rosen Publishing Group
Declaration of Independence and Thomas Jefferson of Virginia, The	R	B	250+	Framers of the Declaration of Independence	Rosen Publishing Group
Declaration of Independence in Translation, The: What It Really Means	V	I	250+	Kids' Translations	Capstone Press
Declaration of Independence, The	S	I	250+	A True Book	Children's Press
Declaration of Independence, The	V	I	250+	Cornerstones of Freedom	Children's Press
Declaration of Independence, The	V	I	250+	Let Freedom Ring	Red Brick Learning
Declaration of Independence, The	Q	RF	250+	Mazer, Anne	Scholastic
Declaration of Independence, The	T	I	250+	Primary Source Readers	Teacher Created Materials
Declaration of Independence, The	T	I	250+	We The People	Compass Point Books
Declaring Independence	T	I	250+	Reading Expeditions	National Geographic
Dede and the Dinosaur	K	F	232	Cumpiano, Ina	Hampton-Brown
DeDe Takes Charge!	O	RF	250+	Hurwitz, Johanna	Morrow
Dee and Me	G	RF	189	Ready Readers	Pearson Learning Group
Deep Blue Lake, A	V	I	2270	Leveled Readers	Houghton Mifflin Harcourt
Deep Blue Sea, The	G	I	195	Wood, Audrey	Scholastic
Deep Diving Adventures	S	I	250+	Dangerous Adventures	Red Brick Learning
Deep Freeze	Q	I	250+	Explorer Books-Pathfinder	National Geographic
Deep Freeze	P	I	250+	Explorer Books-Pioneer	National Geographic
Deep in the Forest	WB	TL	N/A	Turkle, Brinton	Dutton/Penguin
Deep in the Jungle	S	I	250+	WorldScapes	ETA Cuisenaire
Deep in the Woods	E	RF	164	Carousel Readers	Pearson Learning Group
Deep Ocean, The	T	I	250+	Connectors	Pacific Learning
Deep Sea, The	G	I	152	Ready Readers	Pearson Learning Group
Deer	H	I	80	Woodland Animals	Capstone Press
Deer and the Crocodile, The	G	F	178	Literacy 2000	Rigby
Deer Family, The	K	I	412	Vocabulary Readers	Houghton Mifflin Harcourt
Deer Family, The	K	I	412	Vocabulary Readers/CA	Houghton Mifflin Harcourt
Deer Have Fawns	M	I	250+	Animals and Their Young	Compass Point Books
Deer Hunting	S	I	250+	The Great Outdoors	Capstone Press
Deer in the Wood, The	J	HF	250+	Wilder, Laura Ingalls	HarperCollins
Deer Report, The	J	RF	765	The Fawn	Pioneer Valley
Defenders, The	T	B	250+	McGovern, Ann	Language for Learning Assoc.
Defending Irene	U	RF	250+	Nitz, Kristen Wolden	Peachtree
Definitely Cool	X	RF	250+	Wilkinson, Brenda	Scholastic
Definitely Different	I	RF	102	Voyages	SRA/McGraw Hill
Definitely, Positively, Absolutely NO!	D	F	147	Story Basket	Wright Group/McGraw Hill
Delaware	T	I	250+	Hello U.S.A.	Lerner Publications
Delaware	S	I	250+	Land of Liberty	Red Brick Learning
Delaware	T	I	250+	Sea to Shining Sea	Children's Press
Delaware	R	I	250+	This Land Is Your Land	Compass Point Books
Delaware Colony, The	R	I	250+	The American Colonies	Capstone Press
Delaware People, The	P	I	250+	Native Peoples	Red Brick Learning
Delaware, The	T	I	4094	Native American Stories	Lerner Publications
Delivering Justice	U	B	250+	Haskins, Jim	Candlewick Press
Delivering Your Mail: A Book About Mail Carriers	H	I	120	Community Workers	Picture Window Books
Demanding Justice: A Story About Mary Ann Shadd Cary	R	B	8711	Creative Minds Biographies	Carolrhoda Books
Demeter and Persephone	T	TL	250+	Bookshop	Mondo
Demolition	J	I	118	Construction Zone	Capstone Press

* Collection of short stories
# Graphic text

TITLE	LEVEL	GENRE	WORD COUNT	AUTHOR / SERIES	PUBLISHER / DISTRIBUTOR
Demolition	V	I	250+	iOpeners	Pearson Learning Group
Demolition Derby Cars	Q	I	250+	Wild Rides!	Capstone Press
Den, The	B	RF	34	Rigby Star	Rigby
Denali National Park	K	I	390	Springboard	Wright Group/McGraw Hill
Denali National Park and Preserve	O	I	250+	A True Book	Children's Press
Dennis Tito: First Space Tourist	Q	I	250+	Rosen Real Readers	Rosen Publishing Group
Denny Davidson, Detective	M	F	250+	Tristars	Richard C. Owen
Dentist, The	G	I	201	PM Nonfiction-Blue	Rigby
Dentist, The	D	RF	77	Rigby Star	Rigby
Dentists	M	I	250+	Community Helpers	Red Brick Learning
Dentists	M	I	565	Pull Ahead Books	Lerner Publications
Dentist's Dream, A	O	RF	250+	Tristars	Richard C. Owen
Denver Broncos, The	S	I	250+	Team Spirit	Norwood House Press
Deputy Dan and the Bank Robbers	L	RF	250+	Rosenbloom, Joseph	Random House
Deputy Dan Gets His Man	L	RF	250+	Rosenbloom, Joseph	Random House
Derek Jeter	P	B	1955	Amazing Athletes	Lerner Publications
Derek Jeter	R	B	250+	Sports Heroes	Red Brick Learning
Desert	V	I	250+	Eyewitness Books	DK Publishing
Desert	F	I	96	Habitats	Lerner Publications
Desert	H	I	133	Reading Street	Pearson
Desert Animals	J	I	195	Rosen Real Readers	Rosen Publishing Group
Desert Animals	I	I	134	Spyglass Books	Compass Point Books
Desert Animals	P	I	250+	Theme Sets	National Geographic
Desert Animals	E	I	186	Vocabulary Readers	Houghton Mifflin Harcourt
Desert Animals	E	I	186	Vocabulary Readers/CA	Houghton Mifflin Harcourt
Desert Animals	E	I	186	Vocabulary Readers/TX	Houghton Mifflin Harcourt
Desert Birds	N	I	250+	A New True Book	Children's Press
Desert Climate	R	I	250+	Theme Sets	National Geographic
Desert Clowns	J	I	283	On Our Way to English	Rigby
Desert Dance	G	RF	184	Little Celebrations	Pearson Learning Group
Desert Day	C	I	23	Twig	Wright Group/McGraw Hill
Desert Friends	E	I	48	Ray's Readers	Outside the Box
Desert Giant: The World of the Saguaro Cactus	R	I	250+	Bash, Barbara	Scholastic
Desert Iguanas	K	I	381	Pull Ahead Books	Lerner Publications
Desert Life	K	I	129	Independent Readers Science	Houghton Mifflin Harcourt
Desert Life	J	I	230	Literacy by Design	Rigby
Desert Life	N	I	250+	Mann, Rachel	Scholastic
Desert Machine, The	K	I	202	Sunshine	Wright Group/McGraw Hill
Desert Pirates, The	R	F	250+	Masters, Anthony	Stone Arch Books
Desert Plants	N	I	250+	Life in the World's Biomes	Capstone Press
Desert Rain	K	I	214	Windows on Literacy	National Geographic
Desert Run, The	P	I	250+	Orbit Chapter Books	Pacific Learning
Desert Treasure	M	RF	250+	Pair-It Books	Steck-Vaughn
Desert, The	C	I	34	Carousel Readers	Pearson Learning Group
Desert, The	A	I	32	Literacy by Design	Rigby
Desert, The	A	I	32	On Our Way to English	Rigby
Desert: Inside Australia's Simpson Desert	P	I	250+	Cambridge Reading	Pearson Learning Group
Deserts	O	I	250+	A True Book	Children's Press
Deserts	K	I	212	Early Connections	Benchmark Education
Deserts	Q	I	250+	Ecosystems	Red Brick Learning
Deserts	I	I	154	Explorations	Eleanor Curtain Publishing
Deserts	I	I	154	Explorations	Okapi Eductional Materials
Deserts	Q	I	250+	First Reports	Compass Point Books
Deserts	O	I	250+	Gibbons, Gail	Holiday House

D

TITLE	LEVEL	GENRE	WORD COUNT	AUTHOR / SERIES	PUBLISHER / DISTRIBUTOR
Deserts	N	I	250+	Habitats of the World	Pearson Learning Group
Deserts	M	I	250+	PM Plus Nonfiction	Rigby
Deserts	R	I	250+	The Wonders of Our World	Crabtree
Deserts	S	I	250+	Theme Sets	National Geographic
Deserts Are Not Deserted	R	I	250+	WorldScapes	ETA Cuisenaire
Deserts of the World	Q	I	1288	Leveled Readers Science	Houghton Mifflin Harcourt
Designed for Living	P	I	250+	InfoQuest	Rigby
Designs	E	I	15	Little Celebrations	Pearson Learning Group
Desperate Journey	V	HF	250+	Murphy, Jim	Scholastic
Destination America: How Immigration Shaped Our Nation	T	I	250+	Explore More	Wright Group/McGraw Hill
Destination Disaster	P	RF	250+	Action Packs	Rigby
Destination Hawaii	T	I	250+	WorldScapes	ETA Cuisenaire
Destination Planet Blobb	N	F	250+	Sails	Rigby
Destination: Mars	Y	I	2966	Reading Street	Pearson
Destiny in the Dark	W	F	250+	Dark Man	Ransom
Destroyers	T	I	250+	Land and Sea	Capstone Press
Destroyers	J	I	84	Mighty Machines	Capstone Press
Destroyers: The Arleigh Burke Class	T	I	250+	War Machines	Capstone Press
Detective Business, The	J	F	590	Georgie Giraffe	Literacy Footprints
*Detective Dinosaur	J	F	250+	Skofield, James	HarperTrophy
Detective Dog	H	F	198	The Story Basket	Wright Group/McGraw Hill
Detective Dog and the Search for Cat	E	F	142	Learn to Read	Creative Teaching Press
Detective LaRue: Letters from the Investigation	N	F	250+	Teague, Mark	Scholastic
Detective Max	LB	RF	32	Pair-It Books	Steck-Vaughn
*Detective Stories	Z	RF	250+	Pullman, Philip	Kingfisher
Detective's Duel	O	RF	250+	Klooz	Stone Arch Books
Detectives of the Past	T	I	250+	WorldScapes	ETA Cuisenaire
Detective's Tools, A	O	I	797	Vocabulary Readers	Houghton Mifflin Harcourt
Detective's Tools, A	O	I	797	Vocabulary Readers/CA	Houghton Mifflin Harcourt
Detector Dog	O	I	250+	Bookweb	Rigby
Determined to Be First	S	B	250+	Rigby Literacy	Rigby
Detour for Emmy	Z+	RF	250+	Reynolds, Marilynn	Morning Glory Press
Detroit Pistons, The	S	I	4656	Team Spirit	Norwood House Press
Detroit Tigers, The	S	I	250+	Team Spirit	Norwood House Press
Devil's Arithmetic, The	Y	F	250+	Yolen, Jane	Puffin/Penguin
Devil's Bridge	R	RF	250+	DeFelice, Cynthia	Avon
Devil's Highway, The	T	HF	250+	Applegate, Stan	Peachtree
Dewberry and the Lost Chest of Paragon: The Fairy Chronicles	Q	F	13300	Sweet, J.H.	Sourcebooks
DeWitt and Lila Wallace: Charity for All	P	B	250+	Community Builders	Children's Press
Dex Is a Hero	S	SF	1492	Leveled Readers	Houghton Mifflin Harcourt
Dex Is a Hero	S	SF	1492	Leveled Readers/CA	Houghton Mifflin Harcourt
Dex Is a Hero	S	SF	1492	Leveled Readers/TX	Houghton Mifflin Harcourt
Diabetes	S	I	250+	My Health	Scholastic
Diamond Champs, The	P	RF	250+	Christopher, Matt	Little, Brown & Co.
Diamond Hunter	T	SF	250+	Sails	Rigby
Diamond of Doom, The	M	RF	250+	Woodland Mysteries	Wright Group/McGraw Hill
Dian Fossey and the Mountain Gorillas	N	B	1723	On My Own Biography	Lerner Publications
Diana	W	I	250+	World Mythology	Capstone Press
Diana Made Dinner	E	RF	81	Carousel Readers	Pearson Learning Group
Diana Princess of Wales	T	B	250+	Queens and Princesses	Capstone Press
Diary Disaster	N	RF	250+	Girlz Rock!	Mondo
Diary of a Dog	J	F	495	Sun Sprouts	ETA Cuisenaire

D

* Collection of short stories
# Graphic text

TITLE	LEVEL	GENRE	WORD COUNT	AUTHOR / SERIES	PUBLISHER / DISTRIBUTOR
Diary of a Honeybee	L	I	250+	Literacy 2000	Rigby
Diary of a Hurricane	S	RF	3402	Leveled Readers Science	Houghton Mifflin Harcourt
Diary of a Pioneer Boy	Q	HF	250+	Massie, Elizabeth	Steck-Vaughn
Diary of a Sunflower	L	I	250+	Story Steps	Rigby
Diary of Anne Frank, The	Y	B	250+	Frank, Anne	Pocket Books
Dia's Story Cloth: The Hmong People's Journey of Freedom	R	I	250+	Cha, Dia	Lee & Low Books Inc.
Dicey's Song	X	RF	250+	Voigt, Cynthia	Ballantine Books
Dick Whittington	L	TL	250+	PM Tales and Plays-Silver	Rigby
Dickens: His Work and His World	V	B	250+	Rosen, Michael	Candlewick Press
Dictionary About Maps, A	N	I	394	In Step Readers	Rigby
Dictionary of Animals	K	I	270	Literacy by Design	Rigby
Dictionary of Snake Facts, A	J	I	250+	Literacy by Design	Rigby
Dictionary of Space, A	H	I	181	On Our Way to English	Rigby
Did I Scare You?	H	RF	238	Sun Sprouts	ETA Cuisenaire
Did You Carry the Flag Today, Charley?	N	RF	250+	Caudill, Rebecca	Bantam
Did You Hear About Jake?	I	RF	383	Real Kids Readers	Millbrook Press
Did You Hear Wind Sing Your Name?	N	TL	182	Bookshop	Mondo
Did You Hear?	M	RF	250+	On Our Way to English	Rigby
Did You Know?	G	I	22	Learn to Read	Creative Teaching Press
Did You Know?	L	I	250+	Sunshine	Wright Group/McGraw Hill
Did You Say, "Fire"?	G	F	158	Pacific Literacy	Pacific Learning
Did You See Chip?	I	RF	250+	Yee, Wong Herbert	Scholastic
Diddle Diddle Dumpling	E	F	54	Seedlings	Continental Press
Diego Rivera	O	B	250+	First Biographies	Steck-Vaughn
Diego Rivera	R	B	250+	Venezia, Mike	Children's Press
Diego Rivera: An Artist's Life	L	B	250+	Pair-It Books	Steck-Vaughn
Diego's Moving Day	F	RF	192	On Our Way to English	Rigby
Different Beat, A	U	RF	250+	Boyd, Candy Dawson	Penguin Group
Different Dogs	C	I	38	Windows on Literacy	National Geographic
Different Dragons	P	RF	250+	Little, Jean	Penguin Group
Different Drawing, A	M	RF	705	Reading Street	Pearson
Different Faces from Different Places	I	I	148	Twig	Wright Group/McGraw Hill
Different Fish	E	I	40	Reading Street	Pearson
Different Foods, Different Cultures	O	I	250+	InfoTrek	ETA Cuisenaire
Different Homes Around the World	K	I	200	Rigby Literacy	Rigby
Different Kinds of Homes	C	I	44	Windows on Literacy	National Geographic
Different Places, Different Faces	Q	I	250+	InfoQuest	Rigby
Different Seasons	B	I	37	Leveled Readers Science	Houghton Mifflin Harcourt
Different Tune, A	G	F	86	Start to Read	School Zone
Difficult Day, The	J	RF	304	Read Alongs	Rigby
Difficult Origami	R	I	250+	Origami	Capstone Press
Dig	C	F	20	KinderReaders	Rigby
Dig Dig Digging	J	I	250+	Mayo, Margaret	Scholastic
Dig In	I	I	96	iOpeners	Pearson Learning Group
Dig, Dig	A	RF	12	Cat on the Mat	Oxford University Press
Digby	I	RF	250+	Little Readers	Houghton Mifflin Harcourt
*Digby and Kate	K	F	250+	Baker, Barbara	Puffin/Penguin
Digestive System, The	S	I	250+	A True Book	Children's Press
Digestive System, The	P	I	1957	Early Bird Body Systems	Lerner Publishing
Digestive System, The	L	I	173	Human Body Systems	Red Brick Learning
Digestive System, The	S	I	250+	Time for Kids	Teacher Created Materials
Digger Pig and the Turnip	G	TL	195	Green Light Readers	Harcourt
Digging Armadillos	K	I	366	Pull Ahead Books	Lerner Publications

TITLE	LEVEL	GENRE	WORD COUNT	AUTHOR / SERIES	PUBLISHER / DISTRIBUTOR
Digging Deep	T	I	250+	WorldScapes	ETA Cuisenaire
Digging Dinosaurs	P	I	250+	Nayer, Judy	Pearson Learning Group
Digging for Dinosaurs	P	I	250+	Lighthouse	Ginn & Co.
Digging into the Ice Age	S	RF	250+	Reading Expeditions	National Geographic
Digging into the Past	T	I	250+	Kids Discover Reading	Wright Group/McGraw Hill
Digging to China	H	F	108	Books for Young Learners	Richard C. Owen
Digging Tunnels	J	I	143	Construction Zone	Capstone Press
Digging Up Dinosaurs!	O	I	848	Vocabulary Readers	Houghton Mifflin Harcourt
Digging Up Dinosaurs!	O	I	848	Vocabulary Readers/CA	Houghton Mifflin Harcourt
Digging Up Secrets	Q	RF	250+	Reading Expeditions	National Geographic
Digging Up Tyrannosaurus Rex	P	I	250+	Horner, John; Lessem, Don	Crown
Dillon Dillon	S	RF	250+	Banks, Kate	Farrar, Straus and Giroux
Dilly Duck and Dally Duck	D	F	139	PM Plus Story Books	Rigby
Dimples Delight	M	RF	250+	Orca Echoes	Orca Book Publishers
Dine, The	T	I	1900	Reading Street	Pearson
Dingoes at Dinnertime	M	F	250+	Osborne, Mary Pope	Random House
Dinner	A	F	21	KinderReaders	Rigby
Dinner	E	RF	154	Rigby Flying Colors	Rigby
Dinner	B	F	30	Sails	Rigby
Dinner at Aunt Connie's House	Q	F	250+	Ringgold, Faith	Scholastic
Dinner by Five	F	RF	215	Ready Readers	Pearson Learning Group
Dinner for Maisy	H	RF	239	Leveled Literacy Intervention/ Green System	Heinemann
Dinner for Two Hundred	S	RF	2471	Leveled Readers	Houghton Mifflin Harcourt
Dinner for Two Hundred	S	RF	2471	Leveled Readers/CA	Houghton Mifflin Harcourt
Dinner for Two Hundred	S	RF	2471	Leveled Readers/TX	Houghton Mifflin Harcourt
Dinner Time	I	F	500	Gilbert the Pig	Pioneer Valley
Dinner Time	A	I	28	On Our Way to English	Rigby
Dinner Time	C	RF	37	Storyworlds	Heinemann Educational Publishers
Dinner!	LB	RF	19	Sunshine	Wright Group/McGraw Hill
Dino at the Park	E	RF	131	PM Photo Stories	Rigby
Dino Info	N	I	776	Springboard	Wright Group/McGraw Hill
Dino World	I	I	203	Sun Sprouts	ETA Cuisenaire
Dino-Dinners	P	I	250+	Manning, Mick and Granstrom, Brita	Holiday House
Dinosaur	M	I	250+	Cambridge Reading	Pearson Learning Group
Dinosaur	W	I	250+	Eyewitness Books	DK Publishing
Dinosaur	B	I	17	Science	Outside the Box
Dinosaur Alphabet Book, The	O	I	250+	Pallotta, Jerry	Charlesbridge
Dinosaur Babies	L	I	250+	Penner, Lucille Recht	Random House
Dinosaur Bones Don't Rot	I	I	147	Reading Street	Pearson
Dinosaur Breakout	T	F	250+	Silverthorne, Judith	Fitzhenry & Whiteside
Dinosaur Canyon	N	F	250+	In Step Readers	Rigby
Dinosaur Chase, The	I	HF	240	PM Story Books-Orange	Rigby
Dinosaur Connection, The	O	I	250+	Literacy Tree	Rigby
Dinosaur Dan	G	F	197	Springboard	Wright Group/McGraw Hill
Dinosaur Dance, The	B	F	52	Little Books	Sadlier-Oxford
Dinosaur Days	L	I	250+	Milton, Joyce	Random House
Dinosaur Days	K	RF	250+	Ready Readers	Pearson Learning Group
Dinosaur Detective	O	I	250+	Wildcats	Wright Group/McGraw Hill
Dinosaur Detectives	K	F	250+	Pacific Literacy	Pacific Learning
Dinosaur Detectives	L	I	328	Reading Street	Pearson
Dinosaur Dinners	K	I	250+	DK Readers	DK Publishing

Organized Alphabetically by Title
Storable Database at www.fountasandpinnellleveledbooks.com

* Collection of short stories
\# Graphic text

TITLE	LEVEL	GENRE	WORD COUNT	AUTHOR / SERIES	PUBLISHER / DISTRIBUTOR
Dinosaur Discoveries	S	I	250+	WorldScapes	ETA Cuisenaire
Dinosaur Discovery	I	I	250+	Story Steps	Rigby
Dinosaur Extremes	L	I	156	Windows on Literacy	National Geographic
Dinosaur Fan, The	F	F	125	Windmill Books	Rigby
Dinosaur Fossils	I	I	370	Vocabulary Readers	Houghton Mifflin Harcourt
Dinosaur Fossils	I	I	370	Vocabulary Readers/CA	Houghton Mifflin Harcourt
Dinosaur Fossils	I	I	370	Vocabulary Readers/TX	Houghton Mifflin Harcourt
Dinosaur Fun Facts	E	I	84	Pair-It Books	Steck-Vaughn
Dinosaur Girl	N	RF	250+	Literacy Tree	Rigby
Dinosaur Herds	H	I	101	Reading Street	Pearson
Dinosaur Hideout	T	RF	250+	Silverthorne, Judith	Fitzhenry & Whiteside
Dinosaur Hunt, The	G	RF	155	Rigby Literacy	Rigby
Dinosaur Hunt, The	G	F	131	Windmill Books	Rigby
Dinosaur Hunters	L	I	250+	McMullan, Kate	Random House
Dinosaur Hunting	N	I	579	Leveled Readers Science	Houghton Mifflin Harcourt
Dinosaur in Trouble	G	F	121	First Start	Troll Associates
Dinosaur Morning	J	I	225	The Story Basket	Wright Group/McGraw Hill
Dinosaur Named Sue, A	P	I	250+	Robinson, Fay	Scholastic
Dinosaur Nests	J	I	349	Sails	Rigby
Dinosaur on the Motorway	K	F	231	Wesley & the Dinosaurs	Wright Group/McGraw Hill
Dinosaur Party	B	F	27	Smart Starts	Rigby
Dinosaur Reports	L	I	324	Little Red Readers	Sundance
Dinosaur Roar!	LB	F	59	Strickland, Paul & Henrietta	Scholastic
Dinosaur Rock	A	F	28	Big Cat	Pacific Learning
Dinosaur Show and Tell	G	RF	212	Pair-It Books	Steck-Vaughn
Dinosaur Snack, A	D	F	74	Little Dinosaur	Literacy Footprints
Dinosaur Stakeout	T	F	250+	Silverthorne, Judith	Fitzhenry & Whiteside
Dinosaur Time	K	I	250+	Parish, Peggy	HarperTrophy
Dinosaur Times	D	RF	43	Sunshine	Wright Group/McGraw Hill
Dinosaur Who Lived in My Backyard, The	I	F	250+	Hennessy, Brendan G.	Scholastic
Dinosaur Zoo, The	J	F	250+	Literacy Tree	Rigby
Dinosaur, The	F	F	131	Joy Readers	Pearson Learning Group
Dinosaur, The	A	F	14	Sunshine	Wright Group/McGraw Hill
Dinosaurs	S	I	250+	Boldprint	Steck-Vaughn
Dinosaurs	K	I	193	Bookshop	Mondo
Dinosaurs	M	I	250+	Gibbons, Gail	Holiday House
Dinosaurs	E	I	37	Instant Readers	Harcourt School Publishers
Dinosaurs	F	I	115	Maccarone, Grace	Scholastic
Dinosaurs	R	RF	250+	PM Plus Chapter Books	Rigby
Dinosaurs	C	I	100	Sails	Rigby
Dinosaurs	H	I	117	Sunshine	Wright Group/McGraw Hill
Dinosaurs & Other Reptiles	I	I	123	Planet Earth	Rigby
Dinosaurs Before Dark	M	F	250+	Osborne, Mary Pope	Random House
Dinosaur's Cold, The	J	F	244	Literacy 2000	Rigby
Dinosaurs Dance	E	F	17	Rookie Readers	Children's Press
Dinosaurs Dancing	F	F	115	Learn to Read	Creative Teaching Press
Dinosaurs Galore	D	F	34	Eaton, Audrey; Kennedy, Jane	Continental Press
Dinosaurs on the Motorway	K	F	250+	Wesley & the Dinosaurs	Wright Group/McGraw Hill
Dinosaurs, Dinosaurs	G	I	96	Barton, Byron	HarperCollins
Dinosaurs: Giant Jigsaws	S	I	250+	Sails	Rigby
Diplodocus in the Garden, A	K	F	210	Wesley & the Dinosaurs	Wright Group/McGraw Hill
Diplodocus	N	I	250+	Discovering Dinosaurs	Red Brick Learning
Dipper and the Old Wreck	F	F	207	Storyworlds	Heinemann Educational Publishers

D

TITLE	LEVEL	GENRE	WORD COUNT	AUTHOR / SERIES	PUBLISHER / DISTRIBUTOR
Dipper Gets Stuck	F	F	200	Storyworlds	Heinemann Educational Publishers
Dipper in Danger	F	F	192	Storyworlds	Heinemann Educational Publishers
Dipper to the Rescue	F	F	216	Storyworlds	Heinemann Educational Publishers
Dippy Dinner Drippers, The	H	F	181	Sunshine	Wright Group/McGraw Hill
Dirt Bike Racer	S	RF	250+	Christopher, Matt	Little, Brown & Co.
Dirt Bike Runaway	S	RF	250+	Christopher, Matt	Little, Brown & Co.
Dirt Bikes	M	I	250+	Horsepower	Capstone Press
Dirt Bikes	Q	I	250+	Wild Rides!	Capstone Press
Dirt: The Scoop on Soil	M	I	250+	Amazing Science	Picture Window Books
Dirty and Wet Dogs	J	F	590	Bella and Rosie Series	Literacy Footprints
Dirty Beasts	O	F	250+	Dahl, Roald	Penguin Group
Dirty Dog	A	RF	19	Rigby Rocket	Rigby
Dirty Larry	D	RF	53	Rookie Readers	Children's Press
Dirty Mike	C	RF	54	InfoTrek	ETA Cuisenaire
Dirty Socks Don't Win Games	R	RF	250+	Marney, Dean	Scholastic
Disability Rights Movement, The	W	I	250+	Cornerstones of Freedom	Children's Press
Disappearing Acts	S	RF	250+	Byars, Betsy	Puffin/Penguin
Disappearing Bike Shop, The	Q	SF	250+	Woodruff, Elvira	Bantam
*Disappearing Cookies and Other Cases, The	O	RF	250+	Simon, Seymour	Avon
*Disappearing Ice Cream and Other Cases, The	O	RF	250+	Simon, Seymour	Avon
*Disappearing Snowball and Other Cases, The	O	RF	250+	Simon, Seymour	Avon
Disaster Around the Indian Ocean	P	I	990	Springboard	Wright Group/ McGraw Hill
Disaster in the Mountains!: Colby Coombs' Story of Survival	S	I	250+	True Tales of Survival	Capstone Press
Disaster of the Hindenburg, The: The Last Flight of the Greatest Airship Ever Built	Z	I	250+	Tanaka, Shelley	Scholastic
Disaster Plan	T	I	250+	Bookweb	Rigby
Disaster, The	R	RF	1309	Leveled Readers	Houghton Mifflin Harcourt
Disasters at Sea	W	I	8571	Disasters Up Close	Lerner Publications
Discover the Rain Forest	L	I	348	Yellow Umbrella Books	Red Brick Learning
Discovering Dinosaurs	M	F	335	Little Books	Sadlier-Oxford
Discovering Dinosaurs	K	I	211	Spyglass Books	Compass Point Books
Discovering Jupiter: The Amazing Collision in Space	T	I	250+	Berger, Melvin	Scholastic
Discovering Nature's Laws: A Story About Isaac Newton	T	B	8285	Creative Minds Biographies	Carolrhoda Books
Discovering the Past	S	I	250+	Literacy 2000	Rigby
Discovering the Titanic	O	I	250+	Trumbore, Cindy	Pearson Learning Group
Discovery in Egypt	S	RF	250+	Literacy By Design	Rigby
Discovery of the Americas, The	S	I	250+	Maestro, Betsy & Giulio	William Morrow
Discovery: Past, Present, Future	T	I	250+	Kids Discover Reading	Wright Group/McGraw Hill
Disease Detectives	U	I	250+	Connectors	Pacific Learning
Disease Detectives on the Case	V	I	250+	Explore More	Wright Group/McGraw Hill
Dishy-Washy	E	F	92	Story Basket	Wright Group/McGraw Hill
*Distant Stars and Other Cases, The	O	RF	250+	Simon, Seymour	Avon
Ditching School	J	RF	128	City Kids	Rigby
Dive In!	F	RF	133	Ready Readers	Pearson Learning Group
Dive to the Deep Ocean: Voyages of Exploration and Discovery	W	I	250+	Kovacs, Deborah	Steck-Vaughn
Dive!: My Adventures in the Deep Frontier	V	B	250+	Earle, Sylvia A.	Scholastic
Dive, The	K	RF	488	Leveled Readers	Houghton Mifflin Harcourt

* Collection of short stories
\# Graphic text

TITLE	LEVEL	GENRE	WORD COUNT	AUTHOR / SERIES	PUBLISHER / DISTRIBUTOR
Diver, The	B	RF	30	Sunshine	Wright Group/McGraw Hill
Divers' Dream	P	I	250+	Pacific Literacy	Pacific Learning
Divers of the Deep Sea	S	I	250+	Windows on Literacy	National Geographic
Divers, The	C	I	25	Wonder World	Wright Group/McGraw Hill
Divided Loyalties	T	HF	250+	Reading Expeditions	National Geographic
Dividing the Strawberries	E	I	93	In Step Readers	Rigby
Diving	G	RF	164	Story Box	Wright Group/McGraw Hill
Diving at the Pool	M	RF	519	PM Plus Story Books	Rigby
Diving Beetles: Underwater Insect Predators	T	I	2695	Insect World	Lerner Publications
Diving Deep	I	I	120	Gear Up!	Wright Group/McGraw Hill
Diving for Treasure	M	I	284	Books for Young Learners	Richard C. Owen
Dizzy Lizzy	E	RF	37	Literacy 2000	Rigby
Do Animals Have a Sixth Sense?	M	I	377	Reading Street	Pearson
Do Animals Live in Plants?	F	I	56	Instant Readers	Harcourt School Publishers
Do Bears Buzz?: A Book About Animal Sounds	M	I	250+	Animals All Around	Picture Window Books
Do Bed Bugs Bite?	N	I	250+	Why In the World?	Capstone Press
Do Bees Make Butter?: A Book About Things Animals Make	M	I	250+	Animals All Around	Picture Window Books
Do Cows Eat Cake?: A Book About What Animals Eat	M	I	250+	Animals All Around	Picture Window Books
Do Dogs Make Dessert?: A Book About How Animals Help Humans	M	I	250+	Animals All Around	Picture Window Books
Do Ducks Live in the Desert?: A Book About Where Animals Live	M	I	250+	Animals All Around	Picture Window Books
Do Elephants Talk?	Q	I	250+	Explorer Books-Pathfinder	National Geographic
Do Elephants Talk?	P	I	250+	Explorer Books-Pioneer	National Geographic
Do Frogs Have Fur?: A Book About Animal Coats and Coverings	M	I	250+	Animals All Around	Picture Window Books
Do Goldfish Gallop?: A Book About Animal Movement	M	I	250+	Animals All Around	Picture Window Books
Do I Have To?	Q	I	250+	Kids Talk	Picture Window Books
Do Ladybugs Go to School?	E	F	75	Visions	Wright Group/McGraw Hill
Do Not Open This Book!	F	F	134	Story Basket	Wright Group/McGraw Hill
Do Not Spill!	C	RF	79	Reading Street	Pearson
Do Not Touch	B	I	51	Reading Safari	Mondo
Do Parrots Have Pillows?: A Book About Where Animals Sleep	M	I	250+	Animals All Around	Picture Window Books
Do Penguins Have Puppies?: A Book About Animal Babies	M	I	250+	Animals All Around	Picture Window Books
Do Salamanders Spit?: A Book About How Animals Protect Themselves	M	I	250+	Animals All Around	Picture Window Books
Do Squirrels Swarm?: A Book About Animal Groups	M	I	250+	Animals All Around	Picture Window Books
Do Stars Have Points?	R	I	250+	Berger, Melvin & Gilda	Scholastic
Do That, Do This!	H	RF	151	Supersonics	Rigby
Do the Funky Pickle	U	RF	250+	Spinelli, Jerry	Scholastic
Do Tornadoes Really Twist?	S	I	250+	Berger, Melvin	Scholastic
Do We Have Enough?	A	RF	42	InfoTrek	ETA Cuisenaire
Do We Need It? Do We Want It?	G	I	111	Early Connections	Benchmark Education
Do Whales Have Wings?: A Book About Animal Bodies	M	I	250+	Animals All Around	Picture Window Books
Do You Know Me?	Q	RF	250+	Farmer, Nancy	Penguin Group
Do You Know the Monkey Man?	Y	RF	250+	Butler, Dori Hillestad	Peachtree

D

* Collection of short stories
# Graphic text

TITLE	LEVEL	GENRE	WORD COUNT	AUTHOR / SERIES	PUBLISHER / DISTRIBUTOR
Do You Know Where Your Water Has Been?: The Disgusting Story Behind What You're Drinking	S	I	250+	Sanitation Investigation	Capstone Press
Do You Know Why?	C	I	56	Little Celebrations	Pearson Learning Group
Do You Like Cats?	K	I	250+	Bank Street	Bantam
Do You Like Grapes?	B	RF	31	Science	Outside the Box
Do You Like My Pet?	A	F	35	Phonics and Friends	Hampton-Brown
Do You Read Me?	W	I	250+	24/7 Science Behind the Scenes	Scholastic
Do You Remember When?	D	RF	198	Visions	Wright Group/McGraw Hill
Do You See Mouse?	G	F	201	Crume, Marion	Ginn & Co.
Do You Want to be My Friend?	A	F	8	Carle, Eric	Penguin Group
Doaks of Montana, The	T	HF	2426	Reading Street	Pearson
Doctor	C	I	24	Work People Do	Lerner Publishing
Doctor Boondoggle	D	F	51	Story Box	Wright Group/McGraw Hill
Doctor DeSoto	N	F	250+	Steig, William	Scholastic
Doctor Foster	D	F	68	Seedlings	Continental Press
Doctor Has the Flu, The	H	RF	106	Ready Readers	Pearson Learning Group
Doctor Witch's Animal Hospital	L	F	250+	I Am Reading	Kingfisher
Doctor, The	G	I	179	PM Nonfiction-Blue	Rigby
Doctors	M	I	250+	Community Helpers	Red Brick Learning
Doctors	L	I	250+	Community Workers	Compass Point Books
Doctors	L	I	463	Pull Ahead Books	Lerner Publications
Doctor's Busy Day, A	L	I	250+	Rosen Real Readers	Rosen Publishing Group
Doctor's Office, The	K	I	272	Pebble Books	Capstone Press
Doctors: Then and Now	P	I	250+	Primary Source Readers	Teacher Created Materials
Does a Babysitter Know What to Do?	F	RF	177	Reading Street	Pearson
Does a Kangaroo Have a Mother Too?	F	I	214	Carle, Eric	Scholastic
Does a Penguin Have Fur?	D	RF	74	Rigby Literacy	Rigby
Does Third Grade Last Forever?	O	RF	250+	Schanback, Mindy	Troll Associates
Dog	V	I	250+	Eyewitness Books	DK Publishing
Dog	B	RF	37	Pacific Literacy	Pacific Learning
Dog and Cat	F	RF	62	My First Reader	Grolier Press
Dog and the Bone, The	E	TL	67	Leveled Readers	Houghton Mifflin Harcourt
Dog Called Bear, A	K	RF	438	PM Story Books	Rigby
Dog Called Kitty, A	R	RF	250+	Wallace, Bill	Pocket Books
Dog Called Mischief, A	D	RF	42	Cat on the Mat	Oxford University Press
Dog Control	T	RF	2354	Leveled Readers	Houghton Mifflin Harcourt
Dog Control	T	RF	2354	Leveled Readers/CA	Houghton Mifflin Harcourt
Dog Day!, A	LB	RF	21	Smart Starts	Rigby
Dog Family, The	J	I	250+	Story Steps	Rigby
Dog for a Day, A	M	RF	250+	High-Fliers	Pacific Learning
Dog for Each Day, A	G	RF	107	Rookie Readers	Children's Press
Dog for Mrs. Muddle Mud-Puddle, A	H	F	194	Story Box	Wright Group/McGraw Hill
Dog for You, A: Caring for Your Dog	M	I	250+	Pet Care	Picture Window Books
Dog From Outer Space, The	I	SF	250+	Lighthouse	Rigby
Dog Helpers	M	I	495	Vocabulary Readers	Houghton Mifflin Harcourt
Dog Helpers	M	I	495	Vocabulary Readers/CA	Houghton Mifflin Harcourt
Dog Helpers	J	I	495	Vocabulary Readers/TX	Houghton Mifflin Harcourt
Dog I Share, The	N	RF	250+	Orbit Chapter Books	Pacific Learning
Dog in the Freezer, The	W	F	250+	Mazer, Harry	Simon & Schuster
Dog Named Honey, A	F	I	46	iOpeners	Pearson Learning Group
Dog on Barkham Street, A	R	RF	250+	Stolz, Mary	HarperTrophy
Dog on the Loose	N	RF	250+	Girlz Rock!	Mondo
Dog on Vacation	B	F	69	First Stories	Pacific Learning

* Collection of short stories
\# Graphic text

TITLE	LEVEL	GENRE	WORD COUNT	AUTHOR / SERIES	PUBLISHER / DISTRIBUTOR
Dog Safety Rules	C	RF	91	InfoTrek	ETA Cuisenaire
Dog School	E	I	133	Explorations	Okapi Educational Materials
Dog School	E	RF	133	Explorations	Eleanor Curtain Publishing
Dog School	I	RF	224	Story Steps	Rigby
Dog School	LB	RF	11	TOTTS	Tott Publications
Dog Sense	W	RF	250+	Collard, Sneed B.	Peachtree
Dog Show, The	K	RF	250+	Cambridge Reading	Pearson Learning Group
Dog Show, The	F	I	131	Foundations	Wright Group/McGraw Hill
Dog Show, The	B	RF	35	Rigby Star	Rigby
Dog Sled Ride, The	I	RF	374	Adams, Lorraine; Bruvold, Lynn	Eagle Crest Books
Dog Tales	R	I	250+	Boldprint	Steck-Vaughn
Dog Talk	J	I	324	Leveled Readers	Houghton Mifflin Harcourt
Dog Talk	J	I	324	Leveled Readers/CA	Houghton Mifflin Harcourt
Dog Talk	J	I	324	Leveled Readers/TX	Houghton Mifflin Harcourt
Dog that Pitched a No-Hitter, The	L	F	250+	Christopher, Matt	Little, Brown & Co.
Dog that Stole Football Plays, The	L	F	250+	Christopher, Matt	Little, Brown & Co.
Dog that Stole Home, The	L	F	250+	Christopher, Matt	Little, Brown & Co.
Dog to Walk, A	E	RF	178	Developing Set 4	Pioneer Valley
Dog Walker	W	RF	250+	Orca Currents	Orca Book Publishers
Dog Walker, Inc.	P	RF	1640	Leveled Readers	Houghton Mifflin Harcourt
Dog Walker, Inc.	P	RF	1640	Leveled Readers/CA	Houghton Mifflin Harcourt
Dog Walker, Inc.	P	RF	1640	Leveled Readers/TX	Houghton Mifflin Harcourt
Dog Walker, The	D	RF	100+	Reed, Janet	Scholastic
Dog Went for a Walk	D	RF	51	Voyages	SRA/McGraw Hill
Dog Who Thought He Was Santa, The	R	F	250+	Wallace, Bill	Holiday House
Dog Who Wanted to Be a Tiger!, The	M	F	250+	Little Celebrations	Pearson Learning Group
Dog Years	R	RF	250+	Warner, Sally	Alfred A. Knopf
Dog, The	G	RF	56	Burningham, John	Crowell
Dog-Gone Hollywood	L	F	250+	Sharmat, Marjorie Weinman	Random House
Doggy Dare	O	RF	250+	Baglio, Ben M.	Scholastic
Doghouse Discounts	Q	RF	250+	In Step Readers	Rigby
Dogs	D	I	44	All About Pets	Red Brick Learning
Dogs	F	I	116	Foundations	Wright Group/McGraw Hill
Dogs	I	I	116	Hutchins, Pat	Wright Group/McGraw Hill
Dogs	B	I	79	Leveled Readers	Houghton Mifflin Harcourt
Dogs	B	I	79	Leveled Readers/CA	Houghton Mifflin Harcourt
Dogs	B	I	79	Leveled Readers/TX	Houghton Mifflin Harcourt
Dogs	B	RF	27	Levin, Amy	Scholastic
Dogs	J	I	250+	PM Animal Facts: Orange	Rigby
Dogs and Puppies	B	I	35	Animal Families	Lerner Publications
Dogs and Puppies	G	I	210	Dominie Factivity Series	Pearson Learning Group
Dogs Are My Favorite Things	J	RF	246	Bookshop	Mondo
Dogs at School	F	F	94	Books for Young Learners	Richard C. Owen
Dogs at Work	Q	I	250+	Explorer Books-Pathfinder	National Geographic
Dogs at Work	P	I	250	Explorer Books-Pioneer	National Geographic
Dogs at Work	J	I	250+	Little Readers	Houghton Mifflin Harcourt
Dogs at Work	I	I	153	Reading Street	Pearson
Dog's Best Friend, A	M	RF	647	Pair-It Books	Steck-Vaughn
Dog's Diary	M	F	250+	Sails	Rigby
Dogs, Dogs, Dogs	R	I	250+	Literacy 2000	Rigby
Dogs Don't Tell Jokes	O	RF	250+	Sachar, Louis	Alfred A. Knopf
Dog's Guide to Humans, The	M	F	250+	Bookweb	Rigby
Dogs Have Puppies	M	I	250+	Animals and Their Young	Compass Point Books
Dogs Learn Every Day	C	I	38	Vocabulary Readers	Houghton Mifflin Harcourt

* Collection of short stories
# Graphic text

Storable Database at www.fountasandpinnellleveledbooks.com

TITLE	LEVEL	GENRE	WORD COUNT	AUTHOR / SERIES	PUBLISHER / DISTRIBUTOR
Dog's Life, A	WB	I	N/A	Windows on Literacy	National Geographic
Dog's Life, A: The Autobiography of a Stray	S	F	250+	Martin, Ann M.	Scholastic
Dogs Love to Play Ball	I	F	159	Books for Young Learners	Richard C. Owen
Dogs on the Farm	I	I	85	Pebble Books	Red Brick Learning
Dog's Party	I	F	628	Leveled Readers	Houghton Mifflin Harcourt
Dogs That Help People	N	I	824	Leveled Readers	Houghton Mifflin Harcourt
Dogs That Help People	N	I	824	Leveled Readers/CA	Houghton Mifflin Harcourt
Dogs That Help People	M	I	824	Leveled Readers/TX	Houghton Mifflin Harcourt
Dogs to the Rescue	R	I	1154	Leveled Readers	Houghton Mifflin Harcourt
Dogs to the Rescue	R	I	1154	Leveled Readers/CA	Houghton Mifflin Harcourt
Dogs to the Rescue	R	I	1154	Leveled Readers/TX	Houghton Mifflin Harcourt
Dogs to the Rescue	H	I	105	Reading Street	Pearson
Dogs, Dogs, Dogs	H	I	183	Appleton-Smith, Laura	Flyleaf Publishing
Dogsong	V	RF	250+	Paulsen, Gary	Simon & Schuster
Dogstar	J	F	250+	Literacy 2000	Rigby
Dogwood Tree, The	J	I	363	Vocabulary Readers	Houghton Mifflin Harcourt
Dogwood Tree, The	J	I	363	Vocabulary Readers/CA	Houghton Mifflin Harcourt
Doing Jobs Together	F	RF	194	Early Connections	Benchmark Education
Doing My Job	H	I	188	Early Connections	Benchmark Education
Doing the Dishes	L	RF	136	City Kids	Rigby
Dollar, The	K	RF	169	Books for Young Learners	Richard C. Owen
Dolley Madison	N	B	197	First Biographies	Capstone Press
Dolley Madison	S	B	3435	History Maker Bios	Lerner Publications
Dolley Madison, First Lady	L	B	330	Leveled Readers Social Studies	Houghton Mifflin Harcourt
Dolley Madison: First Lady	U	B	250+	Let Freedom Ring	Capstone Press
Dolley Madison, First Lady	J	B	250+	Leveled Readers Social Studies	Houghton Mifflin Harcourt
Dollhouse Murders, The	S	RF	250+	Wright, Betty Ren	Scholastic
Doll's House, The	R	RF	250+	Godden, Rumer	Penguin Group
Dolly's Car	H	RF	192	Handprints C, Set 2	Educators Publishing Service
Dolores Huerta, Civil Rights Leader	U	B	1655	Leveled Readers Social Studies	Houghton Mifflin Harcourt
Dolphin	L	I	250+	Morris, Robert A.	HarperTrophy
Dolphin Adventure	P	RF	250+	Grover, Wayne	Beech Tree Books
Dolphin Caller, The	R	RF	250+	PM Chapter Books	Rigby
Dolphin on the Wall, The	K	RF	250+	PM Story Books-Silver	Rigby
Dolphin Rescue	Q	RF	250+	Reading Expeditions '	National Geographic
Dolphin Treasure	P	RF	250+	Grover, Wayne	Beech Tree Books
Dolphin, The	P	I	250+	Animal Close-Ups	Charlesbridge
Dolphins	K	I	111	Bookshop	Mondo
Dolphins	O	I	1474	Early Bird Nature Books	Lerner Publishing
Dolphins	O	I	250+	Holmes, Kevin J.	Red Brick Learning
Dolphins	N	I	250+	Kalman, Bobbie	Crabtree
Dolphins	I	I	44	Pebble Books	Red Brick Learning
Dolphins	Q	I	1073	Reading Street	Pearson
Dolphins	Q	I	250+	Storyteller - Raging Rivers	Wright Group/ McGraw Hill
Dolphins	U	I	250+	The Heinle Reading Library	Thomson Learning
Dolphins	I	I	91	Under the Sea	Capstone Press
Dolphins	J	I	111	Wonder World	Wright Group/McGraw Hill
Dolphins	N	I	250+	World of Mammals	Capstone Press
Dolphins at Daybreak	M	F	250+	Osborne, Mary Pope	Random House
Dolphin's First Day: The Story of a Bottlenose Dolphin	N	I	250+	Zoehfeld, Kathleen Weidnetz	Scholastic
Dolphins!	L	I	250+	Bokoske, Sharon	Random House
Dolphins, The	L	RF	721	PM Collection	Rigby

* Collection of short stories
# Graphic text

TITLE	LEVEL	GENRE	WORD COUNT	AUTHOR / SERIES	PUBLISHER / DISTRIBUTOR
Dome, The	T	SF	250+	Power Up!	Steck-Vaughn
Domes of Mars, The	U	SF	6559	Reading Street	Pearson
Dominic	R	F	250+	Steig, William	Farrar, Straus and Giroux
Dominican Republic, The: A Question and Answer Book	P	I	250+	Questions & Answers: Countries	Capstone Press
Dominic's Collections	L	RF	894	Rigby Gigglers	Rigby
Dominoes	P	I	250+	Games Around the World	Compass Point Books
Dom's Dragon	E	RF	176	Take Two Books	Wright Group/McGraw Hill
Dom's Handplant	L	RF	250+	Literacy 2000	Rigby
Don't Go in the Cellar	O	F	250+	Strong, Jeremy	Stone Arch Books
Don't Shoot! Chase R's Top Ten Reasons NOT to Move to the Country	V	RF	250+	Rosen, Michael J.	Candlewick Press
Donald Quixote	Q	RF	1300	Leveled Readers	Houghton Mifflin Harcourt
Donald Quixote	Q	RF	1300	Leveled Readers/CA	Houghton Mifflin Harcourt
Donald Quixote	Q	RF	1300	Leveled Readers/TX	Houghton Mifflin Harcourt
Donald's Garden	K	RF	250+	Reading Unlimited	Pearson Learning Group
Donavan's Word Jar	N	RF	250	DeGross, Monalisa	HarperCollins
Donkey	M	F	250+	Literacy 2000	Rigby
Donkey in the Lion's Skin, The	G	TL	56	Aesop	Wright Group/McGraw Hill
Donkey in the Lion's Skin, The	G	TL	213	PM Plus Story Books	Rigby
Donkey of Gallipoli, The	T	HF	250+	Greenwood, Mark	Candlewick Press
Donkey Rescue	M	RF	250+	Krailing, Tessa	Barron's Educational
Donkey Work	H	I	129	Wonder World	Wright Group/McGraw Hill
Donkeys	M	I	250+	Voyages	SRA/McGraw Hill
Donkey's Tale, The	J	TL	250+	Bank Street	Bantam
Donna O'Neeshuck Was Chased By Some Cows	L	RF	250+	Grossman, Bill	HarperTrophy
Donner Party, The	Q	HF	250+	Werther, Scott P.	Scholastic
Don't Be Late	D	F	111	Gibson, Akimi	Scholastic
Don't Be Late!	L	RF	250+	Cambridge Reading	Pearson Learning Group
Don't Be My Valentine: A Classroom Mystery	J	RF	250+	Lexau, Joan M.	HarperTrophy
Don't Be Silly	E	F	76	Teacher's Choice Series	Pearson Learning Group
Don't Bug Me!	T	RF	2224	Leveled Readers	Houghton Mifflin Harcourt
Don't Call Me Beanhead!	M	RF	250+	Wojciechowski, Susan	Candlewick Press
Don't Cut Down This Tree	G	F	129	Voyages	SRA/McGraw Hill
Don't Eat the Stick	I	F	250+	Sunshine	Wright Group/McGraw Hill
Don't Eat Too Much Turkey	J	TL	250+	Cohen, Miriam	Bantam
Don't Forget	E	RF	80	Literacy Tree	Rigby
Don't Forget Fun	L	RF	250+	Little Celebrations	Pearson Learning Group
Don't Forget the Bacon	M	RF	174	Hutchins, Pat	Puffin/Penguin
Don't Get Lost	E	RF	105	Emergent Set 4	Pioneer Valley
Don't Go Out	F	F	179	Take Two Books	Wright Group/McGraw Hill
Don't Interrupt!	I	RF	225	Windmill Books	Rigby
Don't Kid Yourself: Relatively Great (Family) Jokes!	O	F	2212	Make Me Laugh!	Lerner Publications
Don't Leave Anything Behind!	C	RF	26	Literacy 2000	Rigby
Don't Let Ted Have Bubble Gum!	I	RF	250+	Phonics Readers Plus	Steck-Vaughn
Don't Let the Cat Out!	F	RF	109	Independent Readers Social Studies	Houghton Mifflin Harcourt
Don't Let the Pigeon Stay Up Late!	K	F	193	Willems, Mo	Scholastic
Don't Look Down!	H	I	120	Storyteller	Wright Group/McGraw Hill
Don't Panic!	E	RF	122	Book Bank	Wright Group/McGraw Hill
Don't Panic!	T	F	250+	Power Up!	Steck-Vaughn
Don't Sit on My Lunch!	L	RF	250+	Klein, Abby	Scholastic
Don't Splash Me!	A	RF	24	Windmill Books	Wright Group/McGraw Hill

TITLE	LEVEL	GENRE	WORD COUNT	AUTHOR / SERIES	PUBLISHER / DISTRIBUTOR
*Don't Split the Pole: Tales of Down-Home Folk Wisdom	S	RF	250+	Tate, Eleanora E.	Bantam
Don't Stomp on That Bug	J	I	250+	Literacy by Design	Rigby
Don't Stomp on That Bug	I	I	250+	Rigby Literacy	Rigby
Don't Talk to Strangers	E	I	157	Rosen Real Readers	Rosen Publishing Group
Don't Tell!	G	RF	82	Little Books	Sadlier-Oxford
Don't Throw It Away	J	I	330	Springboard	Wright Group/McGraw Hill
Don't Throw It Away!	I	RF	235	InfoTrek	ETA Cuisenaire
Don't Throw It Away!	F	I	90	Wonder World	Wright Group/McGraw Hill
Don't Throw Your Spinach	I	RF	155	Story Box	Wright Group/McGraw Hill
Don't Touch	I	RF	250+	Kline, Suzy	Penguin Group
Don't Touch	I	I	177	Sails	Rigby
Don't Touch It, Lily	K	F	250+	Popcorn	Sundance
Don't Try This at Home	S	I	250+	Story Surfers	ETA Cuisenaire
Don't Wake the Baby	B	RF	18	Literacy 2000	Rigby
Don't Worry	J	RF	339	Literacy 2000	Rigby
Don't You Laugh at Me!	E	F	167	Sunshine	Wright Group/McGraw Hill
Doodler, The	T	RF	2012	Leveled Readers	Houghton Mifflin Harcourt
Doohickey and the Robot	O	F	250+	High-Fliers	Pacific Learning
Doomed Queen Anne	Z	HF	250+	Meyer, Carolyn	Harcourt Trade
Doomed to Disappear? Endangered Species	T	I	250+	Navigators Science Series	Benchmark Education Company
Doomsday Virus, The	U	SF	250+	Barlow, Steve	Stone Arch Books
Door in the Wall, The	U	HF	250+	De Angeli, Marguerite	Bantam
Door to Time, The	R	F	250+	Moore, Ulysses	Scholastic
Doorbell Rang, The	J	RF	283	Hutchins, Pat	Greenwillow
Doors	D	I	83	Sails	Rigby
Doorway to Darkness	T	SF	250+	Banks, John	Stone Arch Books
Dora's Decision	M	RF	250+	On Our Way to English	Rigby
Dora's Soapbox Car	J	RF	250+	On Our Way to English	Rigby
Dora's Time to Shine	O	RF	250+	Literacy by Design	Rigby
Doris Free	U	HF	250+	Bookshop	Mondo
Dorothea Dix: Social Reformer	U	B	250+	Let Freedom Ring	Capstone Press
Dorothea Lange	T	B	250+	Amazing Americans	Wright Group/McGraw Hill
Dory Story	M	F	588	Pallotta, Jerry	Charlesbridge
Dot, The	L	RF	250+	Reynolds, Peter H.	Candlewick Press
Dots, Dots, Dots	B	RF	25	Reading Street	Pearson
Dotty's Dots	I	RF	296	Reading Street	Pearson
Double Act	L	RF	1038	Rigby Flying Colors	Rigby
Double Danger	P	F	250+	Hager, Mandy	Pacific Learning
Double Dutch	E	RF	191	Visions	Wright Group/McGraw Hill
Double Life of Pocahontas, The	U	B	250+	Fritz, Jean	Language for Learning Assoc.
Double Play	V	RF	3662	Leveled Readers	Houghton Mifflin Harcourt
Double Play	V	RF	3662	Leveled Readers/CA	Houghton Mifflin Harcourt
Double Play	U	RF	4526	Reading Street	Pearson
Double Play at Short	Q	RF	250+	Christopher, Matt	Little, Brown & Co.
Double Switch	M	RF	250+	Orbit Chapter Books	Pacific Learning
Double the Animals	M	I	250+	Yellow Umbrella Books	Red Brick Learning
Double Trouble	Q	RF	250+	Leveled Readers Language Support	Houghton Mifflin Harcourt
Double Trouble	M	TL	250+	Literacy 2000	Rigby
Double Trouble	L	RF	890	Reading Street	Pearson
Double Trouble	L	RF	250+	Sunshine	Wright Group/McGraw Hill

TITLE	LEVEL	GENRE	WORD COUNT	AUTHOR / SERIES	PUBLISHER / DISTRIBUTOR
Dough Boy	Z+	RF	250+	Marino, Peter	Holiday House
Doughnut Danger	K	F	250+	I Am Reading	Kingfisher
Douglas Fir	N	I	250+	Habitats	Children's Press
Douglas Florian	K	B	250+	Leveled Readers Language Support	Houghton Mifflin Harcourt
Douglas Florian, Poet and Artist	M	B	484	Leveled Readers	Houghton Mifflin Harcourt
Douglas MacArthur	T	B	3624	History Maker Bios	Lerner Publications
Dove Dream	Z+	RF	250+	Rumbaut, Hendle	Houghton Mifflin Harcourt
Dove Isabeau	T	F	250+	Yolen, Jane	Harcourt Brace
Dovey Coe	U	RF	250+	Dowell, Frances O'Roark	Aladddin Paperbacks
Do-Whacky-Do	H	F	249	Read Alongs	Rigby
Down	Z+	RF	250+	Orca Soundings	Orca Book Publishers
Down at the Billabong	F	RF	93	Voyages	SRA/McGraw Hill
Down at the River	E	RF	51	Pacific Literacy	Pacific Learning
Down By the Bay	E	RF	121	Little Celebrations	Pearson Learning Group
Down by the Pond	F	I	131	Leveled Literacy Intervention/ Blue System	Heinemann
Down by the Pond	B	F	72	On Our Way to English	Rigby
Down by the Pond	I	I	118	Story Box	Wright Group/McGraw Hill
Down by the Sea	G	RF	173	PM Plus Story Books	Rigby
Down by the Stream	E	I	97	Independent Readers Science	Houghton Mifflin Harcourt
Down by the Swamp	F	RF	50	Little Celebrations	Pearson Learning Group
Down in the Sea	C	I	87	Bonnell, Kris	Reading Reading Books
Down in the Woods	I	F	155	Storyteller-Moon Rising	Wright Group/McGraw Hill
Down on the Farm	B	RF	59	Green Light Readers	Harcourt
Down on the Farm	E	F	244	Learn to Read	Creative Teaching Press
Down on the Ice	P	I	250+	Alchin, Rupert	Pacific Learning
Down Sand Mountain	X	HF	250+	Watkins, Steve	Candlewick Press
Down the Chimney with Googol and Googolplex	L	SF	250+	Orca Echoes	Orca Book Publishers
Down the Columbia	R	HF	1516	Leveled Readers	Houghton Mifflin Harcourt
Down the Columbia	R	HF	1516	Leveled Readers/CA	Houghton Mifflin Harcourt
Down the Columbia	R	HF	1516	Leveled Readers/TX	Houghton Mifflin Harcourt
Down the Hill	C	RF	32	KinderReaders	Rigby
Down the Hill	C	RF	94	New Way Red	Steck-Vaughn
Down the Laser Beam	P	SF	1752	Take Two Books	Wright Group/ McGraw Hill
Down the Nile	Q	I	250+	Windows on Literacy	National Geographic
Down the Path	B	F	43	Leveled Literacy Intervention/ Blue System	Heinemann
Down the Rabbit Hole	W	RF	250+	Abrahams, Peter	Harper Trophy
Down the River	C	RF	85	Leveled Literacy Intervention/ Blue System	Heinemann
Down the Side of the Sofa	B	RF	66	Lighthouse	Ginn & Co.
Down the Street	E	RF	66	Little Celebrations	Pearson Learning Group
Down the Well	E	F	200	Sun Sprouts	ETA Cuisenaire
Down to a Science	S	I	250+	Boldprint	Steck-Vaughn
Down to a Sunless Sea: The Strange World of Hydrothermal Vents	W	I	250+	Madin, Kate	Steck-Vaughn
Down to Town	A	F	26	Sunshine	Wright Group/McGraw Hill
Downhill BMX	M	I	250+	To the Extreme	Capstone Press
Downhill Fun: A Counting Book About Winter	J	I	123	Know Your Numbers	Picture Window Books
Downtown Lost & Found	E	F	55	New Reader Series	Bungalo Books
Dozen Dizzy Dogs, A	G	F	157	Bank Street	Bantam
Dozen Dogs, A	F	F	228	Ziefert, Harriet	Random House

TITLE	LEVEL	GENRE	WORD COUNT	AUTHOR / SERIES	PUBLISHER / DISTRIBUTOR
Dozen Eggs, A	LB	RF	14	Harry's Math Books	Outside the Box
Dr. Ben Carson: From Setbacks to Success	T	B	250+	Explore More	Wright Group/McGraw Hill
Dr. Charles Drew and the Blood Banks	S	B	1515	Independent Readers Science	Houghton Mifflin Harcourt
Dr. Faucet and the Case of the Missing Drops	L	F	650	Gear Up!	Wright Group/ McGraw Hill
Dr. Green	G	RF	141	Little Readers	Houghton Mifflin Harcourt
Dr. Jekyll, Orthodontist	N	RF	250+	The Zack Files	Grossett & Dunlap
Dr. MacTavish's Creature	N	RF	250+	PM Collection	Rigby
Dr. Quinn, Medicine Woman	T	B	250+	McKenna, Colleen O'Shaughnessy	Language for Learning Assoc.
Dr. Seuss	L	B	184	First Biographies	Red Brick Learning
Dr. Seuss and His Stories	N	B	250+	Sunshine	Wright Group/McGraw Hill
Dr. Sharma Is a Veterinarian	F	I	98	InfoTrek	ETA Cuisenaire
Dracula	Z+	F	250+	Stoker, Bram	Bantam Books
Dracula Doesn't Drink Lemonade	M	F	250+	Dadey, Debbie; Jones, Marcia Thornton	Scholastic
Dracula vs. Grampa at the Monster Truck Spectacular	Q	F	250+	Wiley & Grampa's Creature Features	Little, Brown & Co.
Drag Racers	W	I	6405	Motor Mania	Lerner Publications
Dragon	I	F	161	Pacific Literacy	Pacific Learning
Dragon Bones	O	F	250+	Hindman, Paul	Random House
Dragon Breath	L	F	250+	O'Connor, Jane	Grossett & Dunlap
Dragon Cauldron	W	F	250+	Yep, Laurence	HarperCollins
Dragon Chronicles, The: Dragon's Milk	V	F	250+	Fletcher, Susan	Aladdin
Dragon Family, The	J	F	250+	Scooters	ETA Cuisenaire
Dragon Feet	K	F	153	Books For Young Learners	Richard C. Owen
Dragon Fire	P	F	250+	Cowley, Joy	Pacific Learning
Dragon Flight	U	F	250+	George, Jessica Day	Bloomsbury Children's Books
Dragon for Sale	Q	F	250+	MacDonald, Marianne	Troll Associates
Dragon Gets By	I	F	250+	Pilkey, Dav	Orchard Books
*Dragon Hunt, The	F	F	53	New Way Red	Steck-Vaughn
Dragon in the Family, A	Q	F	250+	Koller, Jackie French	Pocket Books
Dragon in the Ghetto Caper, The	T	RF	250+	Konigsburg, E. L.	Aladdin
Dragon Inside, The	S	RF	250+	Power Up!	Steck-Vaughn
*Dragon King's Palace, The	T	TL	250+	Literacy 2000	Rigby
Dragon of Doom, The	P	F	250+	Coville, Bruce	Aladdin Paperbacks
Dragon of Krakow, The: A Polish Folktale	L	TL	366	Leveled Readers	Houghton Mifflin Harcourt
Dragon of Lonely Island, The	R	F	250+	Rupp, Rebecca	Scholastic
Dragon of the Lost Sea	W	F	250+	Yep, Laurence	HarperCollins
Dragon Parade: A Chinese New Year Story	O	I	250+	Chin, Steven A.	Steck-Vaughn
Dragon Prince, The: A Chinese Beauty and the Beast Tale	P	TL	250+	Yep, Laurence	HarperCollins
Dragon Quest	Q	F	250+	Koller, Jackie French	Pocket Books
Dragon Rider	V	F	250+	Funke, Cornelia	Scholastic
Dragon Slayer	P	F	250+	Cowley, Joy	Pacific Learning
Dragon Slippers	U	F	250+	George, Jessica Day	Bloomsbury Children's Books
Dragon Steel	W	F	250+	Yep, Laurence	HarperCollins
Dragon Trouble	Q	F	250+	Koller, Jackie French	Pocket Books
Dragon Trouble	N	F	250+	SupaDoopers	Sundance
Dragon War	W	F	250+	Yep, Laurence	HarperCollins
Dragon Who Came to Dinner, The	K	F	250+	The Wright Skills	Wright Group/McGraw Hill
Dragon Who Had the Measles, The	J	F	250+	Literacy 2000	Rigby

* Collection of short stories
# Graphic text

D

TITLE	LEVEL	GENRE	WORD COUNT	AUTHOR / SERIES	PUBLISHER / DISTRIBUTOR
Dragon with a Cold	J	F	250+	Sunshine	Wright Group/McGraw Hill
Dragon!	E	F	68	Wonder World	Wright Group/McGraw Hill
Dragon, The	I	F	250+	Story Box	Wright Group/McGraw Hill
Dragon, The	C	F	130	Sunshine	Wright Group/McGraw Hill
Dragon's Lullaby, A	M	F	670	Leveled Literacy Intervention/ Blue System	Heinemann
Dragonflies	G	I	53	Books for Young Learners	Richard C. Owen
Dragonflies	H	I	133	Bugs, Bugs, Bugs!	Capstone Press
Dragonflies	E	I	39	Insects	Capstone Press
Dragonflies	I	I	218	Sails	Rigby
Dragonflies	N	I	250+	World of Insects	Capstone Press
Dragonflies Are Super Bugs	G	I	101	Seedlings	Continental Press
Dragonfly and the Web of Dreams: The Fairy Chronicles	Q	F	13600	Sweet, J.H.	Sourcebooks
*Dragonfly Dreams and Other Stories	I	F	250+	Story Steps	Rigby
Dragonfly's Tale	N	TL	250+	Rodanas, Kristina	Clarion
Dragonling, The	Q	F	250+	Koller, Jackie French	Pocket Books
Dragons	X	I	5067	Monster Chronicles	Lerner Publications
Dragons and Kings	Q	F	250+	Koller, Jackie French	Pocket Books
Dragon's Birthday, The	K	F	250+	Literacy 2000	Rigby
Dragon's Blood	X	F	250+	Yolen, Jane	Harcourt Trade
Dragon's Coming After You, The	H	F	156	Voyages	SRA/McGraw Hill
Dragons Don't Cook Pizza	M	F	250+	Dadey, Debbie; Jones, Marcia Thornton	Scholastic
Dragons Don't Read Books	M	RF	250+	Bookshop	Mondo
Dragon's Dream	C	F	34	Learn to Read	Creative Teaching Press
Dragon's Fat Cat	I	F	250+	Pilkey, Dav	Orchard Books
Dragons Galore	N	F	250+	Wildcats	Wright Group/McGraw Hill
Dragon's Gate	W	HF	250+	Yep, Laurence	HarperCollins
Dragon's Halloween	I	F	250+	Pilkey, Dav	Orchard Books
Dragon's Lunch	F	F	85	Ready Readers	Pearson Learning Group
Dragon's Merry Christmas	I	F	250+	Pilkey, Dav	Orchard Books
Dragons of Blueland, The	L	F	250+	Gannett, Ruth	Random House
Dragons of Krad	Q	F	250+	Koller, Jackie French	Pocket Books
Dragon's Scales, The	J	F	250+	Albee, Sarah	Random House
Dragon's View, A	S	F	2317	Leveled Readers	Houghton Mifflin Harcourt
Dragon's View, A	S	F	2317	Leveled Readers/CA	Houghton Mifflin Harcourt
Dragon's View, A	S	F	2317	Leveled Readers/TX	Houghton Mifflin Harcourt
Dragonsong	V	F	250+	McCaffrey, Anne	Bantam
Dragonwings	W	HF	250+	Yep, Lawrence	HarperTrophy
Dragsters	M	I	250+	Horsepower	Capstone Press
Dragsters	L	I	113	On Deck	Rigby
Dragsters	T	I	250+	The World's Fastest	Red Brick Learning
Dragsters	Q	I	250+	Wild Rides!	Red Brick Learning
Drama Club	F	I	60	On Deck	Rigby
Drat That Cat!	I	F	250+	Cambridge Reading	Pearson Learning Group
Draw Me a Story	P	B	250+	Winter, Max	Scholastic
Drawbridge	E	I	29	Books for Young Learners	Richard C. Owen
Drawing	A	RF	40	Leveled Literacy Intervention/ Orange System	Heinemann
Drawing	B	I	48	Leveled Readers	Houghton Mifflin Harcourt
Drawing	B	I	48	Leveled Readers/CA	Houghton Mifflin Harcourt
Drawing	B	I	48	Leveled Readers/TX	Houghton Mifflin Harcourt

D

* Collection of short stories
# Graphic text

TITLE	LEVEL	GENRE	WORD COUNT	AUTHOR / SERIES	PUBLISHER / DISTRIBUTOR
Drawing, Sketching, and Cartooning: Techniques for Drawing People, Places, Pets, and Cartoon Characters	S	I	250+	Bookshop	Mondo
Dread Mountain	T	F	250+	Rodda, Emily	Scholastic
Dreadful Acts	U	F	250+	Ardagh, Philip	Scholastic
Dreadful Dinosaurs	N	F	250+	Springboard	Wright Group/McGraw Hill
Dreadful Future of Blossom Culp, The	U	SF	250+	Peck, Richard	Bantam
Dreadful Revenge of Ernest Gallen, The	U	F	250+	Collier, James Lincoln	Bloomsbury Children's Books
Dream Around the World	G	F	138	Instant Readers	Harcourt School Publishers
Dream Boat	M	RF	250+	Action Packs	Rigby
Dream Catcher	M	TL	159	Books for Young Learners	Richard C. Owen
Dream Catcher, The	H	RF	230	Adams, Lorraine; Bruvold, Lynn	Eagle Crest Books
Dream Catchers	M	RF	176	Storyteller-Night Crickets	Wright Group/McGraw Hill
Dream Come True, A	O	B	250+	Meet The Author	Richard C. Owen
Dream Comes True, A	N	B	250+	On Our Way to English	Rigby
Dream Eater, The	N	F	250+	Garrison, Christian	Aladdin
Dream Horse	C	F	47	Pair-It Books	Steck-Vaughn
Dream in the Wishing Well	H	F	250+	Van Allen, Roach	SRA/McGraw Hill
Dream of Flight, The	O	I	250+	Rigby Focus	Rigby
Dream Team, The	I	RF	250+	Lighthouse	Rigby
Dream Weaver	W	HF	3045	Leveled Readers	Houghton Mifflin Harcourt
Dream, The	F	RF	54	Oxford Reading Tree	Oxford University Press
Dreamer Behind the Dome, The: Judge Roy Hofheinz	O	I	250+	On Our Way to English	Rigby
Dreamers and Doers	S	B	250+	On Our Way to English	Rigby
Dreaming	B	RF	23	Smart Starts	Rigby
Dreaming in Black and White	Z	HF	250+	Jung, Reinhardt	Penguin Group
Dreaming Place, The	S	RF	250+	PM Plus Chapter Books	Rigby
Dreamquest: Tales of Slumberia	X	F	250+	Hartinger, Brent	Tom Doherty
Dreams	E	RF	93	Book Bank	Wright Group/McGraw Hill
Dreams	T	HF	250+	Reading Safari	Mondo
Dreams	G	RF	98	Sunshine	Wright Group/McGraw Hill
Dreams of Flying	O	I	250+	Rigby Literacy	Rigby
Dred Scott Decision, The	X	I	250+	Cornerstones of Freedom	Children's Press
Dress Up	D	RF	80	Carousel Readers	Pearson Learning Group
Dress Up	B	RF	49	Leveled Readers	Houghton Mifflin Harcourt
Dress Up	B	RF	49	Leveled Readers/CA	Houghton Mifflin Harcourt
Dress Up	B	RF	49	Leveled Readers/TX	Houghton Mifflin Harcourt
Dressed for School Success	P	I	731	Reading Street	Pearson
Dressed Up Dogs	A	F	25	Bonnell, Kris	Reading Reading Books
Dressed-Up Sammy	E	F	91	Urmston, Kathleen; Evans, Karen	Kaeden Books
Dressing Up	G	RF	104	Breakthrough	Longman
Dressing Up	B	I	50	InfoTrek	ETA Cuisenaire
Dressing Up	A	RF	12	Jellybeans	Rigby
Dressing Up	B	RF	66	Leveled Readers	Houghton Mifflin Harcourt
Dressing Up	B	RF	66	Leveled Readers/CA	Houghton Mifflin Harcourt
Dressing Up	C	RF	31	Literacy 2000	Rigby
Dressing Up	A	F	32	PM Starters	Rigby
Dressing Up	B	RF	25	Smart Starts	Rigby
Dressing Up	I	RF	222	Stepping Stones	Nelson/Michaels Assoc.
Dressing Up	LB	RF	12	Sunshine	Wright Group/McGraw Hill
Dressing-up Box, The	C	RF	61	Book Bank	Wright Group/McGraw Hill

* Collection of short stories
# Graphic text

D

TITLE	LEVEL	GENRE	WORD COUNT	AUTHOR / SERIES	PUBLISHER / DISTRIBUTOR
Dress-Up	E	RF	104	Real Kids Readers	Millbrook Press
Dress-Up Corner, The	H	RF	68	City Kids	Rigby
Drew and the Homeboy Question	U	RF	250+	Armstrong, Robb	HarperTrophy
Dribble, Dribble, Shoot	F	RF	198	Handprints D, Set 2	Educators Publishing Service
Drier than a Bone	S	RF	250+	Reading Safari	Mondo
Drift Cars	M	I	250+	Horsepower	Capstone Press
Drinking Gourd, The	M	HF	250+	Monjo, F. N.	HarperTrophy
Drinking Water	H	I	79	The Food Guide Pyramid	Capstone Press
Drip, The	D	RF	103	Leveled Literacy Intervention/ Blue System	Heinemann
Driscoll and the Singing Fish	Q	F	1005	Leveled Readers	Houghton Mifflin Harcourt
Drita My Homegirl	T	RF	250+	Lombard, Jenny	Scholastic
Drive Toward the Future	U	I	250+	In Step Readers	Rigby
Drive Toward the Future	U	I	250+	Literacy by Design	Rigby
Drive-By	W	RF	250+	Ewing, Lynne	HarperCollins
Driving Mom Crazy	H	RF	131	City Stories	Rigby
Driving on Mars	T	I	936	Leveled Readers	Houghton Mifflin Harcourt
Drooling and Dangerous: The Riot Brothers Return!	O	RF	250+	Amato, Mary	Holiday House
Drop in the Ocean, A: The Story of Water	Q	I	250+	Science Works	Picture Window Books
Drop of Water, A	S	I	250+	Wick, Walter	Scholastic
Drought and Wildfire	V	I	3297	Vocabulary Readers	Houghton Mifflin Harcourt
Drought and Wildfire	V	I	3297	Vocabulary Readers/CA	Houghton Mifflin Harcourt
Drought and Wildfire	V	I	3297	Vocabulary Readers/TX	Houghton Mifflin Harcourt
Drought Marker, The	M	F	250+	Literacy 2000	Rigby
Droughts	W	I	250+	Disasters Up Close	Lerner Publications
Droughts	Q	I	250+	Natural Disasters	Red Brick Learning
Droughts	S	I	250+	Theme Sets	National Geographic
Droughts	O	I	250+	Weather Update	Capstone Press
Drowned Maiden's Hair, A	W	HF	250+	Schlitz, Laura A.	Candlewick Press
Drum Beats On, The	O	I	250+	Cherrington, Janelle	Scholastic
Drum Dancers: An Inuit Story	Q	RF	873	Leveled Readers	Houghton Mifflin Harcourt
Drum, The	D	TL	117	Instant Readers	Harcourt School Publishers
Drummer Boy, The	S	I	1164	Leveled Readers	Houghton Mifflin Harcourt
Drummer Boy, The	Q	B	250+	WorldScapes	ETA Cuisenaire
Drummer Hoff	J	TL	173	Emberly, Barbara	Prentice-Hall
Drummers, The	H	RF	80	Gould, Carol	Kaeden Books
Dry and Snug and Warm	G	RF	64	Book Bank	Wright Group/McGraw Hill
Drylongso	V	RF	250+	Hamilton, Virginia	Harcourt Trade
Duck & Company	K	F	250+	Caple, Kathy	Holiday House
Duck and Hen	H	F	193	Sunshine	Wright Group/McGraw Hill
Duck and Pig	C	F	101	Sails	Rigby
Duck and Rooster	C	F	81	Sails	Rigby
Duck and Rooster Go Out	F	F	193	Sails	Rigby
Duck and Rooster Go to School	H	F	365	Sails	Rigby
Duck and Rooster in Trouble	G	F	192	Sails	Rigby
Duck Feet	L	RF	751	Rigby Flying Colors	Rigby
Duck Goes to the Farm	J	F	373	Leveled Readers	Houghton Mifflin Harcourt
Duck Hunting	S	I	250+	The Great Outdoors	Capstone Press
Duck in the Gun, The	M	F	250+	Literacy 2000	Rigby
Duck in the Truck	J	F	250+	Alborough, Jez	Kane/Miller
Duck Magic	N	I	250+	Literacy 2000 Satellites	Rigby
Duck Pond, The	G	RF	276	Leveled Readers	Houghton Mifflin Harcourt

* Collection of short stories
# Graphic text

TITLE	LEVEL	GENRE	WORD COUNT	AUTHOR / SERIES	PUBLISHER / DISTRIBUTOR
Duck with the Broken Wing, The	F	RF	189	PM Extensions-Blue	Rigby
Duck, Duck, Goose!	E	F	92	My First Reader	Grolier Press
Duck-Billed Dinosaurs	P	I	1159	Meet the Dinosaurs	Lerner Publications
Duckling Diary	O	RF	250+	Baglio, Ben M.	Scholastic
Ducks	F	I	98	Life Cycles	Lerner Publications
Ducks	D	F	94	Story Box	Wright Group/McGraw Hill
Ducks	D	I	54	Vocabulary Readers	Houghton Mifflin Harcourt
Ducks	D	I	54	Vocabulary Readers/CA	Houghton Mifflin Harcourt
Ducks	D	I	54	Vocabulary Readers/TX	Houghton Mifflin Harcourt
Ducks Crossing	M	RF	250+	Orbit Chapter Books	Pacific Learning
Ducks Have Ducklings	M	I	250+	Animals and Their Young	Compass Point Books
Ducks on the Farm	I	I	91	Pebble Books	Red Brick Learning
Ducks on the Run	I	RF	250+	PM Plus Story Books	Rigby
Ducks, The	H	RF	326	Rigby Flying Colors	Rigby
Duel! Burr and Hamilton's Deadly War of Words	S	I	250+	Fradin, Dennis Brindell	Walker & Company
Duke and Duchess	I	RF	250+	Reading Safari	Mondo
Duke Ellington	T	B	250+	Amazing Americans	Wright Group/McGraw Hill
Duke Ellington	Q	B	250+	Pinkey, Andrea Davis	Scholastic
Duke Ellington	R	B	250+	Venezia, Mike	Children's Press
Duke Ellington: A Life in Music	Q	B	905	Leveled Readers	Houghton Mifflin Harcourt
Duke Ellington: Man of Music	P	B	250+	Leveled Readers Language Support	Houghton Mifflin Harcourt
Duke Kahanamoku	U	B	250+	Amazing Americans	Wright Group/McGraw Hill
Duke the Mule	H	F	59	Easy Phonics Readers	Teacher Created Materials
Duma and the Lion	I	F	250+	Storyworlds	Heinemann Educational Books
Dumb Bunnies, The	J	F	250+	Pilkey, Dav	Scholastic
Dump Trucks	F	I	119	Mighty Machines	Capstone Press
Dump Trucks	L	I	356	Pull Ahead Books	Lerner Publications
Dumpsideary Jelly	H	RF	250+	Momentum Literacy Program	Troll Associates
Dunc and Amos and the Red Tattoos	R	RF	250+	Paulsen, Gary	Bantam
Dunc and Amos Go to the Dogs	R	RF	250+	Paulsen, Gary	Bantam
Dunc and Amos Hit the Big Top	R	RF	250+	Paulsen, Gary	Bantam
Dunc and Amos Meet the Slasher	R	RF	250+	Paulsen, Gary	Bantam
Dunc and the Flaming Ghost	R	F	250+	Paulsen, Gary	Bantam
Dunc and the Greased Sticks of Doom	R	RF	250+	Paulsen, Gary	Bantam
Dunc and the Haunted Castle	R	RF	250+	Paulsen, Gary	Bantam
Dunc and the Scam Artists	R	RF	250+	Paulsen, Gary	Bantam
Dunc Breaks the Record	R	RF	250+	Paulsen, Gary	Bantam
Dunc Gets Tweaked	R	RF	250+	Paulsen, Gary	Bantam
Duncan the Dancing Duck	J	F	250+	Hoff, Syd	Clarion Books
Dunc's Doll	R	RF	250+	Paulsen, Gary	Bantam
Dunc's Dump	R	RF	250+	Paulsen, Gary	Bantam
Dunc's Halloween	R	RF	250+	Paulsen, Gary	Bantam
Dunc's Undercover Christmas	R	RF	250+	Paulsen, Gary	Bantam
Dune Buggies	M	I	250+	Horsepower	Capstone Press
Dunkin' Dazza's Daring Dribble	O	RF	250+	SupaDoopers	Sundance
Dunkin' Dazza's Soaring Slammer	O	RF	250+	SupaDoopers	Sundance
During the Day	A	I	32	Springboard	Wright Group/McGraw Hill
DuSable - Chicago's First Citizen	T	B	1522	Leveled Readers Social Studies	Houghton Mifflin Harcourt
Dust Bowl Survivors	W	I	250+	Literacy by Design	Rigby
Dust Bowl, The	P	I	1204	Leveled Readers Social Studies	Houghton Mifflin Harcourt
Dust from Comets	U	I	1735	Leveled Readers	Houghton Mifflin Harcourt

* Collection of short stories
# Graphic text

TITLE	LEVEL	GENRE	WORD COUNT	AUTHOR / SERIES	PUBLISHER / DISTRIBUTOR
Dust from Comets	U	I	1735	Leveled Readers/CA	Houghton Mifflin Harcourt
Dust from Comets	U	I	1735	Leveled Readers/TX	Houghton Mifflin Harcourt
Dust from Old Bones	X	HF	250+	Forrester, Sandra	William Morrow
Dusted and Busted!	W	I	250+	24/7 Science Behind the Scenes	Scholastic
Dustland	V	F	250+	Hamilton, Virginia	Scholastic
Dusty's Big Day	H	RF	290	Handprints D	Educators Publishing Service
Dutch Colonies in the Americas	S	I	250+	On Deck	Rigby
Dwight D. Eisenhower	S	B	250+	Amazing Americans	Wright Group/McGraw Hill
Dwight D. Eisenhower	S	B	3605	History Maker Bios	Lerner Publications
Dwight D. Eisenhower	U	B	250+	Profiles of the Presidents	Compass Point Books
Dwight D. Eisenhower: Thirty-fourth President	R	B	250+	Getting to Know the U.S. Presidents	Children's Press
Dwyane Wade	Q	B	2059	Amazing Athletes	Lerner Publications
Dylan: The Clique Summer Collection	X	RF	250+	Harrison, Lisi	Little, Brown & Co.
Dynamic Dance	S	I	250+	InfoQuest	Rigby
Dynamic Duos	P	F	250+	Moore, David	Scholastic

D

* Collection of short stories
# Graphic text

TITLE	LEVEL	GENRE	WORD COUNT	AUTHOR / SERIES	PUBLISHER / DISTRIBUTOR
*E is for Elisa	N	RF	250+	Hurwitz, Johanna	Puffin/Penguin
E-(t)mail	R	F	250+	Bookshop	Mondo
EA-6B Prowler, The	U	I	250+	Cross-Sections	Capstone Press
Each Peach, Pear, Plum	G	TL	115	Ahlberg, Allan & Janet	Penguin Group
Eagle Feather	M	RF	250+	Bulla, Clyde Robert	Puffin/Penguin
Eagle Feathers	N	TL	250+	Story Vines	Wright Group/McGraw Hill
Eagle Flies High, An	G	I	142	Ready Readers	Pearson Learning Group
Eagle Has Landed, The	O	I	250+	Merchant, Peter	Scholastic
Eagle in the Sky	L	RF	250+	Little Celebrations	Pearson Learning Group
Eagle Song	S	RF	250+	Bruchac, Joseph	Puffin/Penguin
Eagle Watchers	N	RF	765	Leveled Readers	Houghton Mifflin Harcourt
Eagle, The	D	RF	72	Adams, Lorraine; Bruvold, Lynn	Eagle Crest Books
Eagles	L	I	425	Time for Kids	Teacher Created Materials
Eagles and Birds of Prey	V	I	250+	Eyewitness Books	DK Publishing
*Eagle's Reflection and Other Northwest Coast Stories	P	TL	250+	Challenger, James Robert	Heritage House
Eagles, Hawks, and Falcons	O	I	992	Take Two Books	Wright Group/McGraw Hill
Eagles: Birds of Prey	M	I	250+	The Wild World of Animals	Red Brick Learning
Ear Book	E	I	119	Perkins, Al	Random House
Ear, the Eye, and the Arm, The	Y	SF	250+	Farmer, Nancy	Puffin/Penguin
Earl and Eggster Float Away	M	F	918	Leveled Readers	Houghton Mifflin Harcourt
Earl and Eggster Float Away	M	F	918	Leveled Readers/CA	Houghton Mifflin Harcourt
Earl and Eggster Float Away	M	F	918	Leveled Readers/TX	Houghton Mifflin Harcourt
Earl and His Egg	L	F	1014	Leveled Readers	Houghton Mifflin Harcourt
Earl and His Egg	L	F	1014	Leveled Readers/CA	Houghton Mifflin Harcourt
Earl and His Egg	L	F	1014	Leveled Readers/TX	Houghton Mifflin Harcourt
Earliest American, The	S	I	250+	Kids Discover Reading	Wright Group/McGraw Hill
Early American Indian Tribes	T	I	250+	Primary Source Readers	Teacher Created Materials
Early American Industrial Revolution, 1793-1850, The	V	I	250+	Let Freedom Ring	Capstone Press
Early Bird's Alarm Clock, The	J	F	250+	Pair-It Books	Steck-Vaughn
Early Congresses	T	I	250+	Primary Source Readers	Teacher Created Materials
Early in the Morning	D	RF	55	Rise & Shine	Hampton-Brown
Early in the Morning	C	RF	56	Windows on Literacy	National Geographic
Early Inventions	M	I	250+	Rigby Focus	Rigby
Early Winter, An	T	RF	250+	Bauer, Marion Dane	Houghton Mifflin Harcourt
Earning Money	L	I	250+	Learning About Money	Capstone Press
Earning Money	O	I	250+	Let's See	Compass Point Books
Earning Money	E	I	104	Money	Lerner Publishing
Earning Money My Own Way	L	RF	625	Reading Street	Pearson
Ears	B	I	21	Animal Traits	Lerner Publications
Ears	E	I	74	Rigby Literacy	Rigby
Ears	C	I	37	Rise & Shine	Hampton-Brown
Ears	I	I	166	Sails	Rigby
Earth	Q	I	250+	A True Book	Children's Press
Earth	J	I	148	Exploring the Galaxy	Capstone Press
Earth	S	I	250+	Our Solar System	Compass Point Books
Earth	N	I	842	Our Universe	Lerner Publications
Earth	H	I	122	Space	Lerner Publications
Earth	Q	I	250+	The Galaxy	Capstone Press
Earth and Moon	G	I	250	Sunshine	Wright Group/McGraw Hill
Earth at Risk	V	I	250+	Sunshine	Wright Group/McGraw Hill
Earth Day	F	I	111	American Holidays	Lerner Publications
Earth Day	M	I	250+	Holiday Histories	Heinemann Library

* Collection of short stories
# Graphic text

TITLE	LEVEL	GENRE	WORD COUNT	AUTHOR / SERIES	PUBLISHER / DISTRIBUTOR
Earth Day	N	I	1559	On My Own Holidays	Lerner Publications
Earth Evidence	S	I	250+	Forensic Crime Solvers	Capstone Press
Earth in Space	N	I	250+	Reading Expeditions	National Geographic
Earth in Space, The	T	I	250+	Straightforward Science	Franklin Watts
Earth Is Mostly Ocean, The	M	I	250+	Rookie Read About Science	Children's Press
Earth Movement	R	I	1473	Reading Street	Pearson
Earth on Turtle's Back, The	L	TL	508	Early Connections	Benchmark Education
Earth Rocks!	N	I	402	Pair-It Turn and Learn	Steck-Vaughn
Earth to Matthew	U	RF	250+	Danziger, Paula	PaperStar
Earth, The	B	I	35	On Our Way to English	Rigby
Earth, The	H	I	112	Windows on Literacy	National Geographic
Earth: The Inside Story	V	I	2030	Reading Street	Pearson
Earthborn	Z	F	250+	Card, Orson Scott	Tor
Earthfall	Z	F	250+	Card, Orson Scott	Tor
Earth-Friendly Design	X	I	10486	Saving Our Living Earth	Lerner Publications
Earth-Friendly Energy	Y	I	10298	Saving Our Living Earth	Lerner Publications
Earth-Friendly Waste Management	Y	I	10669	Saving Our Living Earth	Lerner Publications
Earthlings in Space	U	SF	250+	Sunshine	Wright Group/McGraw Hill
Earthmovers	G	I	121	Mighty Machines	Capstone Press
Earthmovers	K	I	377	Pull Ahead Books	Lerner Publications
Earthquake	S	HF	250+	Duey, Kathleen; Bale, Karen A.	Simon & Schuster
Earthquake	M	RF	415	Jellybeans	Rigby
Earthquake	E	RF	40	Wonder World	Wright Group/McGraw Hill
Earthquake Alaska	U	HF	2192	Leveled Readers	Houghton Mifflin Harcourt
Earthquake in the Third Grade	N	RF	250+	Myers, Laurie	Clarion
Earthquake Scientists	T	I	1579	Vocabulary Readers	Houghton Mifflin Harcourt
Earthquake Scientists	T	I	1579	Vocabulary Readers/CA	Houghton Mifflin Harcourt
Earthquake Terror	X	RF	250+	Kehret, Peg	Puffin/Penguin
Earthquake!	N	RF	250+	Bookweb	Rigby
Earthquake!	S	HF	2376	Leveled Readers	Houghton Mifflin Harcourt
Earthquake!	S	I	2075	Leveled Readers Science	Houghton Mifflin Harcourt
Earthquake!	V	I	250+	WorldScapes	ETA Cuisenaire
Earthquake!: A Story of Old San Francisco	S	I	250+	Kudlinski, Kathleen V.	Penguin Group
Earthquake!: San Francisco, 1906	R	I	250+	Wilson, Kate	Steck-Vaughn
Earthquake!: The Disaster that Rocked San Francisco	R	HF	1753	Reading Street	Pearson
Earthquakes	O	I	250+	A True Book	Children's Press
Earthquakes	O	I	250+	Branley, Franklyn M.	HarperCollins
Earthquakes	W	I	250+	Disasters Up Close	Lerner Publications
Earthquakes	T	I	250+	Earth Science	Franklin Watts
Earthquakes	R	I	250+	Explorers	Wright Group/McGraw Hill
Earthquakes	S	I	250+	Natural Disasters	Capstone Press
Earthquakes	M	I	763	Pull Ahead Books	Lerner Publications
Earthquakes	T	I	250+	Simon, Seymour	Mulberry Books
Earthquakes	R	I	250+	The Wonders of Our World	Crabtree
Earthquakes	L	I	390	Time for Kids	Teacher Created Materials
Earthquakes and Tsunamis	O	I	250+	PM Plus Story Books	Rigby
Earthquakes and Volcanoes	Q	I	250+	Theme Sets	National Geographic
Earthquakes That Shook America	U	I	250+	Explore More	Wright Group/McGraw Hill
Earth's Changing Land	Q	I	250+	Reading Expeditions	National Geographic
Earth's Crust	R	I	1863	Early Bird Earth Systems	Lerner Publications
Earth's Land and Water	J	I	234	Yellow Umbrella Books	Capstone Press
Earth's Place in Space	V	I	2535	Reading Street	Pearson
Earth's Riches	M	I	386	Gear Up!	Wright Group/ McGraw Hill

E

* Collection of short stories
# Graphic text

TITLE	LEVEL	GENRE	WORD COUNT	AUTHOR / SERIES	PUBLISHER / DISTRIBUTOR
Earth's Riches	P	I	250+	WorldScapes	ETA Cuisenaire
Earth's Seasons & Cycles	S	I	250+	Time for Kids	Teacher Created Materials
Earth's Structure	T	I	2279	Science Support Readers	Houghton Mifflin Harcourt
Earthworm, The	H	I	157	Wonder World	Wright Group/McGraw Hill
Earthworms	O	I	250+	Holmes, Kevin J.	Red Brick Learning
Earthworms	J	I	185	Leveled Readers	Houghton Mifflin Harcourt
Earthworms	K	I	212	Rigby Focus	Rigby
Earthworms	I	I	156	Take Two Books	Wright Group/McGraw Hill
Earthworm's Life, An	L	I	250+	Himmelman, John	Scholastic
Earthworm's Life, An	L	I	250+	Nature Up Close	Children's Press
East Meets West: Japan and America	M	I	396	Reading Street	Pearson
East of the Sun & West of the Moon	P	TL	250+	Mayer, Mercer	Aladdin
East of the Sun and West of the Moon	R	TL	250+	Hague, Kathleen & Michael	Harcourt Trade
Easter	E	I	112	Fiesta Holiday Series	Pearson Learning Group
Easter	J	I	127	Holidays and Celebrations	Capstone Press
Easter	M	I	250+	Holidays and Celebrations	Picture Window Books
Easter Around the World	N	I	1494	On My Own Holidays	Lerner Publications
Easter Bunny that Ate My Sister, The	Q	F	250+	Marney, Dean	Scholastic
Easter Bunny's Lost Egg	G	F	174	First Start	Troll Associates
Easter Island Odyssey	T	RF	250+	Reading Safari	Mondo
Easter Island: Giant Stone Statues Tell of a Rich and Tragic Past	W	I	250+	Arnold, Caroline	Houghton Mifflin Harcourt
Easy Origami	R	I	250+	Origami	Capstone Press
Eat and Run!	L	I	289	Vocabulary Readers	Houghton Mifflin Harcourt
Eat It, Print It	B	I	70	Rigby Literacy	Rigby
Eat Right!: How You Can Make Good Food Choices	U	I	6703	Health Zone	Lerner Publications
Eat Right, Feel Good	K	I	250+	Rosen Real Readers	Rosen Publishing Group
Eat to Win	T	I	250+	The News	Richard C. Owen
Eat Up!	G	RF	95	Sunshine	Wright Group/McGraw Hill
Eat Up, Chick!	I	F	274	Sun Sprouts	ETA Cuisenaire
Eat Up, Gemma	I	RF	463	Hayes, Sarah	Sundance
Eat Your Broccoli	D	RF	72	Books for Young Learners	Richard C. Owen
Eat Your Peas, Louise	E	RF	83	Rookie Readers	Children's Press
Eat Your Peas, Please!	G	F	84	Pair-It Turn and Learn	Steck-Vaughn
Eat Your Vegetables	J	I	157	iOpeners	Pearson Learning Group
Eat Your Vegetables! Drink Your Milk!	P	I	250+	My Health	Franklin Watts
Eat Your Veggies	K	RF	704	Springboard	Wright Group/McGraw Hill
Eat!	M	RF	250+	Kroll, Steven	Hyperion
Eating	A	RF	29	Foundations	Wright Group/McGraw Hill
Eating Apples	LB	I	17	Apples	Capstone Press
Eating Breakfast	B	I	18	Rosen Real Readers	Rosen Publishing Group
Eating Fish	B	I	37	Sails	Rigby
Eating Food	I	I	392	Sails	Rigby
Eating Healthy Meals	P	I	1219	Vocabulary Readers	Houghton Mifflin Harcourt
Eating Healthy Meals	P	I	1219	Vocabulary Readers/CA	Houghton Mifflin Harcourt
Eating Lunch at School	I	RF	170	City Kids	Rigby
Eating Mud	D	I	35	Bonnell, Kris	Reading Reading Books
Eating Out	C	RF	31	Sunshine	Wright Group/McGraw Hill
Eating Right	H	I	151	The Food Guide Pyramid	Capstone Press
Eating Right	I	I	250	Time for Kids	Teacher Created Materials
Eating Well	M	I	457	Pull Ahead Books	Lerner Publications
Eating Well	H	I	214	Yellow Umbrella Books	Red Brick Learning
Eats	R	I	250+	Boldprint	Steck-Vaughn

* Collection of short stories
\# Graphic text

TITLE	LEVEL	GENRE	WORD COUNT	AUTHOR / SERIES	PUBLISHER / DISTRIBUTOR
Ebenezer and the Sneeze	D	RF	77	Story Box	Wright Group/McGraw Hill
Echohawk	X	HF	250+	Durrant, Lynda	Bantam
Echolocation: Animals Making Sound Waves	U	I	2125	Reading Street	Pearson
Eclipse	Z+	F	250+	Meyer, Stephanie	Little, Brown & Co.
Eclipses: Nature's Blackouts	T	I	250+	Aronson, Billy	Franklin Watts
Ecology: Earth's Balancing Act	T	I	250+	Kids Discover Reading	Wright Group/McGraw Hill
Ecosystems	T	I	250+	Pair-It Books	Steck-Vaughn
Ecosystems of the Rain Forests	T	I	1790	Reading Street	Pearson
Ecosystems: Changing and Conserving	R	I	250+	ConceptLinks	Millmark Education
Ecosystems: Energy Flow and Use	R	I	250+	ConceptLinks	Millmark Education
Ecosystems: Food Chains and Food Webs	R	I	250+	ConceptLinks	Millmark Education
Ecosystems: Populations and Communities	R	I	250+	ConceptLinks	Millmark Education
Ed and Me	L	RF	250+	McPhail, David	Harcourt Brace
Eddie and the Fire Engine	P	RF	250+	Haywood, Carolyn	Beech Tree Books
Eddie and the Jets	U	RF	26549	Attanas, John	Darby Creek Publishing
Eddy's Hair	G	RF	322	Sails	Rigby
Edgar Badger's Balloon Day	K	F	864	Kulling, Monica	Mondo
Edgar Badger's Butterfly Day	K	F	250+	Kulling, Monica	Mondo
Edgar Badger's Fishing Day	K	F	250+	Kulling, Monica	Mondo
Edgar Badger's Fix-it Day	K	F	250+	Kulling, Monica	Mondo
Edge of the Clearing, The	K	RF	760	Gear Up!	Wright Group/ McGraw Hill
Edge of the Sword, The	Y	HF	250+	Tingle, Rebecca	Scholastic
Edmond Went Splash	B	F	69	First Stories	Pacific Learning
Edna Bakes Cookies	D	F	37	Brand New Readers	Candlewick Press
Edna Dances	C	F	25	Brand New Readers	Candlewick Press
Edna's Flowers	D	F	41	Brand New Readers	Candlewick Press
Edna's New Coat	D	F	39	Brand New Readers	Candlewick Press
Educating Arthur	J	F	250+	Soar To Success	Houghton Mifflin Harcourt
Edward's Night Light	M	RF	622	Reading Corners	Pearson Learning Group
Edwin and Emily	K	RF	250+	Williams, Suzanne	Hyperion
Edwina Victorious	O	RF	250+	Bonners, Susan	Farrar, Straus and Giroux
Eeek! Look at This!	C	I	66	Rigby Star Quest	Rigby
Eek!	D	F	103	Lester the Lion Series	Pioneer Valley
Eek! Look at This!	C	I	66	Rigby Literacy	Rigby
Eels	I	I	200	Sails	Rigby
Eels	H	I	113	Under the Sea	Capstone Press
Eency Weency Spider	I	F	250+	Bank Street	Bantam
Eenie, Meanie, Murphy, NO!	S	RF	250+	McKenna, Colleen O'Shaughnessy	Scholastic
Eeny, Meeny, Miney Mole	M	F	250+	Yolen, Jane	Harcourt Brace
Effect of Gamma Rays on Man-in-the-Moon Marigolds, The	Z+	RF	250+	Zindel, Paul	Bantam Books
Effie	K	F	250+	Allison, Beverly	Scholastic
Egg	K	F	250+	Logan, Dick	Cypress
Egg Incubators	T	I	250+	Sails	Rigby
Egg Saga, The	N	RF	250+	Sails	Rigby
Egg to Chick	J	I	250+	Selsam, Millicent E.	HarperTrophy
Egg Watching	Q	RF	2840	Reading Street	Pearson
Egg, The	C	F	48	Joy Readers	Pearson Learning Group
Eggs	C	I	87	Leveled Literacy Intervention/ Green System	Heinemann
Eggs	L	I	250+	Rigby Literacy	Rigby
Eggs	B	I	56	Sails	Rigby
Eggs	U	RF	250+	Spinelli, Jerry	Little, Brown & Co.

E

* Collection of short stories
# Graphic text

TITLE	LEVEL	GENRE	WORD COUNT	AUTHOR / SERIES	PUBLISHER / DISTRIBUTOR
Eggs	C	I	30	Windows on Literacy	National Geographic
Eggs and Baby Birds	M	I	539	Sunshine	Wright Group/McGraw Hill
Eggs and Dandelions	F	F	182	PM Stars	Rigby
Eggs for Breakfast	D	I	126	PM Nonfiction-Red	Rigby
Eggs from the Chicken to You!	L	I	565	Rigby Flying Colors	Rigby
Eggs in the Sun	J	RF	384	Sails	Rigby
Eggs!	B	RF	28	Ready Readers	Pearson Learning Group
Eggs, Eggs, Eggs	H	I	248	Sails	Rigby
Eggs, Eggs, Eggs	J	I	188	Wonder World	Wright Group/McGraw Hill
Eggs, Larvae, and Flies	K	I	450	Sunshine	Wright Group/McGraw Hill
Eggshell Garden, The	LB	RF	14	Sunshine	Wright Group/McGraw Hill
Egypt	P	I	2018	Country Explorers	Lerner Publications
Egypt	Q	I	250+	First Reports: Countries	Compass Point Books
Egypt	W	I	250+	Primary Source Readers	Teacher Created Materials
Egypt (Ancient Civilizations)	V	I	250+	Theme Sets	National Geographic
Egypt (Cultures and Celebrations)	R	I	250+	Theme Sets	National Geographic
Egypt ABCs: A Book About the People and Places of Egypt	Q	I	250+	Country ABCs	Picture Window Books
Egypt Game, The	X	RF	250+	Snyder, Zilpha Keatley	Bantam
Egypt in Colors	N	I	250+	World of Colors	Capstone Press
Egypt in the Past and Present	S	I	250+	Reading Expeditions	National Geographic
Egypt: A Question and Answer Book	P	I	250+	Questions and Answers: Countries	Capstone Press
Egypt: Everyday Kids Now and Then	S	HF	250+	Reading Expeditions	National Geographic
Egypt: The Culture	U	I	250+	Kalman, Bobbie	Crabtree
Egypt: The Land	U	I	250+	Kalman, Bobbie	Crabtree
Egypt: The People	U	I	250+	Kalman, Bobbie	Crabtree
Egyptian News, The	W	I	250+	The History News	Candlewick Press
Egyptian Town	U	I	250+	Steedman, Scott	Franklin Watts
Egypt's Greatest Treasure	Q	HF	250+	Lighthouse	Ginn & Co.
Eight Friends in All	D	RF	64	Ready Readers	Pearson Learning Group
Eight Little Legs	H	RF	137	Gravelle, Karen	Kaeden Books
Eileen Collins: First Woman in Space	V	B	2488	Leveled Readers	Houghton Mifflin Harcourt
Einstein, Father of Physics	Z	B	250+	Independent Readers Science	Houghton Mifflin Harcourt
Einstein: Champion of the World	N	RF	250+	Trussell-Cullen, Alan	Pacific Learning
*El Bronx Remembered	Z	RF	250+	Mohr, Nicholas	HarperTrophy
El Camino Real	S	RF	2361	Leveled Readers	Houghton Mifflin Harcourt
El Camino Real	S	RF	2361	Leveled Readers/CA	Houghton Mifflin Harcourt
El Camino Real	S	RF	2361	Leveled Readers/TX	Houghton Mifflin Harcourt
El Chino	P	B	250+	Say, Allen	Houghton Mifflin Harcourt
El Greco	R	B	250+	Venezia, Mike	Children's Press
El Nino	I	RF	250+	Reading Safari	Mondo
El Sid and the Flea	V	RF	2632	Leveled Readers	Houghton Mifflin Harcourt
Elaine	J	B	250+	Stepping Stones	Nelson/Michaels Assoc.
Elaine and the Flying Frog	M	RF	250+	Chang, Heidi	Scholastic
Elbert's Bad Word	M	RF	250+	Wood, Audrey	Harcourt Trade
Eleanor	S	B	250+	Cooney, Barbara	Puffin/Penguin
Eleanor Everywhere: The Life of Eleanor Roosevelt	O	B	250+	Step into Reading	Random House
Eleanor Roosevelt	U	B	250+	Blevins, Wiley	Scholastic
Eleanor Roosevelt	P	B	250+	Early Biographies	Compass Point Books
Eleanor Roosevelt	S	B	3773	History Maker Bios	Lerner Publications
Eleanor Roosevelt	N	B	250+	Pebble Books	Capstone Press
Eleanor Roosevelt	P	B	250+	Photo-Illustrated Biographies	Red Brick Learning

* Collection of short stories
# Graphic text

TITLE	LEVEL	GENRE	WORD COUNT	AUTHOR / SERIES	PUBLISHER / DISTRIBUTOR
Eleanor Roosevelt	R	B	250+	Primary Source Readers	Teacher Created Materials
Eleanor Roosevelt: A Life of Discovery	W	B	250+	Freedman, Russell	Clarion
Eleanor Roosevelt: A Lifetime of Giving	Q	B	250+	Literacy by Design	Rigby
Eleanor Roosevelt: Fighter for Social Justice	O	B	250+	Childhood of Famous Americans	Aladdin
Eleanor Roosevelt: First Lady of the World	R	B	250+	Faber, Doris	Penguin Group
Eleanor Roosevelt: More Than a First Lady	P	B	250+	On Deck	Rigby
Election Connection	T	I	250+	Ring, Susan	Chronicle Books
Election Day	Q	I	250+	Holiday Histories	Heinemann Library
Election Day	H	RF	250+	McNamara, Margaret	Aladdin
Elections in the United States	W	I	250+	American Civics	Red Brick Learning
Electric Eels	O	I	2314	Early Bird Nature Books	Lerner Publications
Electric Mischief	W	I	250+	Bartholomew, Alan	Kids Can Press
*Electric Spark and Other Cases, The	O	RF	250+	Simon, Seymour	Avon
Electricity	Q	I	2246	Early Bird Energy	Lerner Publishing
Electricity	P	I	250+	Our Physical World	Capstone Press
Electricity	Y	I	250+	Reading Street	Pearson
Electricity	R	I	1437	Science Support Readers	Houghton Mifflin Harcourt
Electricity	O	I	250+	Sunshine	Wright Group/McGraw Hill
Electricity Adds Up	W	I	250+	Navigators Math Series	Benchmark Education
Electricity at Home	U	I	250+	Theme Sets	National Geographic
Electricity at Play	U	I	250+	Theme Sets	National Geographic
Electricity at School	U	I	250+	Theme Sets	National Geographic
Electricity at Work	U	I	250+	Theme Sets	National Geographic
Electricity Makes Things Work	N	I	250+	PM Plus Nonfiction	Rigby
Electricity Mystery, The	W	I	250+	Literacy by Design	Rigby
Electricity: Bulbs, Batteries, and Sparks	N	I	250+	Amazing Science	Picture Window Books
*Electrifying Cows and Other Cases, The	O	RF	250+	Simon, Seymour	Avon
Electrifying Personalities	S	B	250+	Navigators Biography Series	Benchmark Education
Elements in Nature	V	I	1001	Leveled Readers Science	Houghton Mifflin Harcourt
Elements in Our Universe	Z	I	2755	Reading Street	Pearson
Elements, The	V	I	841	Leveled Readers Science	Houghton Mifflin Harcourt
Elena in America	O	HF	575	Leveled Readers	Houghton Mifflin Harcourt
Elena Makes Tortillas	A	I	18	Pacific Literacy	Pacific Learning
Elena's Two Homes	M	HF	250+	Leveled Readers Language Support	Houghton Mifflin Harcourt
Elena's Wish	J	RF	708	Leveled Readers	Houghton Mifflin Harcourt
Elena's Wish	J	RF	708	Leveled Readers/CA	Houghton Mifflin Harcourt
Elena's Wish	J	RF	708	Leveled Readers/TX	Houghton Mifflin Harcourt
Elephant	V	I	250+	Eyewitness Books	DK Publishing
Elephant and Envelope	G	F	158	Start to Read	School Zone
Elephant and Mouse	B	F	50	Sails	Rigby
Elephant and the Bad Baby, The	J	F	250+	Hayes, Sarah	Sundance
Elephant and the Six Wise Men, The	L	TL	692	Rigby Flying Colors	Rigby
Elephant and Tiger	J	F	486	Leveled Literacy Intervention/ Blue System	Heinemann
Elephant Costume, The	A	RF	29	Leveled Readers	Houghton Mifflin Harcourt
Elephant Costume, The	A	RF	29	Leveled Readers/CA	Houghton Mifflin Harcourt
Elephant for the Holidays, An	I	F	118	Sunshine	Wright Group/McGraw Hill
Elephant in the House, An	J	F	546	Read Alongs	Rigby
Elephant in Trouble	H	F	98	First Start	Troll Associates
Elephant Play	E	F	35	Sun Sprouts	ETA Cuisenaire
Elephant Rescue	J	RF	250+	Leveled Readers Language Support	Houghton Mifflin Harcourt

E

TITLE	LEVEL	GENRE	WORD COUNT	AUTHOR / SERIES	PUBLISHER / DISTRIBUTOR
Elephant That Forgot, The	I	F	250+	Storyworlds	Heinemann Educational Books
Elephant Trick	B	F	30	Sails	Rigby
Elephant Tricks	F	F	147	Sun Sprouts	ETA Cuisenaire
Elephant Walk	C	RF	50	Rigby Literacy	Rigby
Elephant Walk	C	RF	51	Rigby Star	Rigby
Elephant Walk	L	I	250+	Storyteller Chapter Books	Wright Group/ McGraw Hill
Elephant Walk	C	F	44	Sunshine	Wright Group/McGraw Hill
Elephants	I	I	125	African Animals	Capstone Press
Elephants	I	I	224	Foundations	Wright Group/McGraw Hill
Elephants	N	I	250+	Meadows, Graham; Vial, Claire	Pearson Learning Group
Elephants	C	F	224	Phonics and Friends	Hampton-Brown
Elephants	K	I	250+	PM Animal Facts: Turquoise	Rigby
Elephants	U	I	250+	The Untamed World	Steck-Vaughn
Elephants Are Coming, The	E	F	138	Little Readers	Houghton Mifflin Harcourt
Elephants Can't Hop	C	F	75	Sails	Rigby
Elephant's Trunk, An	C	F	31	Little Celebrations	Pearson Learning Group
Elephant's Trunk, An	D	I	49	Windows on Literacy	National Geographic
Elephant's Trunk, The	E	I	60	Seedlings	Continental Press
Elevator	D	F	90	Story Box	Wright Group/McGraw Hill
Eleven Kids, One Summer	O	RF	250+	Martin, Ann M.	Scholastic
Eleven on a Team	H	RF	326	PM Math Readers	Rigby
Eli Whitney	R	B	250+	Amazing Americans	Wright Group/McGraw Hill
#Eli Whitney and the Cotton Gin	S	B	250+	Graphic Library	Capstone Press
Eli Whitney: American Inventor	U	B	250+	Let Freedom Ring	Capstone Press
Elie Wiesel: A Holocaust Survivor Cries Out for Peace	X	B	250+	High Five Reading	Red Brick Learning
Elijah McCoy	U	B	250+	Independent Readers Science	Houghton Mifflin Harcourt
*Elisa in the Middle	N	RF	250+	Hurwitz, Johanna	Penguin Group
Elisha Otis's Ups and Downs	U	I	1759	Leveled Readers	Houghton Mifflin Harcourt
Elissa and the Stone	R	RF	250+	PM Plus Chapter Books	Rigby
Eliza Pinckney	M	B	325	Independent Readers Social Studies	Houghton Mifflin Harcourt
Eliza the Hypnotizer	M	RF	250+	Granger, Michele	Scholastic
Elizabeth Blackwell	N	B	200	First Biographies	Capstone Press
Elizabeth Blackwell: First Woman Doctor	O	B	250+	Greene, Carol	Children's Press
Elizabeth Blackwell: First Woman Doctor	Q	B	250+	High-Fliers	Pacific Learning
Elizabeth Blackwell: Girl Doctor	O	B	250+	Henry, Joanne Landers	Simon & Schuster
Elizabeth Cady Stanton	P	B	250+	Photo-Illustrated Biographies	Red Brick Learning
Elizabeth Cady Stanton and Susan B. Anthony: Fighting Together for Women's Rights	P	B	250+	On Deck	Rigby
Elizabeth the First: Queen of England	O	B	250+	Greene, Carol	Children's Press
Elizabeth's Stormy Ride	N	HF	815	Leveled Readers	Houghton Mifflin Harcourt
Elizabeth's Stormy Ride	N	HF	815	Leveled Readers/CA	Houghton Mifflin Harcourt
Elizabeth's Stormy Ride	N	HF	815	Leveled Readers/TX	Houghton Mifflin Harcourt
Elizabeti's Doll	M	RF	250+	Bebop Books	Lee & Low Books Inc.
Elizabite: Adventures of a Carnivorous Plant	K	F	250+	Rey, H. A.	Houghton Mifflin Harcourt
Elk Hunters, The	N	TL	434	Reading Street	Pearson
Ella and the Toy Rabbit	D	RF	108	PM Stars	Rigby
Ella Enchanted	U	F	250+	Carson Levine, Gail	HarperTrophy
Ella Minnow Pea	Z	F	250+	Dunn, Mark	MacAdam/Cage Publishing
Ella the Superstar	I	F	239	Big Cat	Pacific Learning
Ella's Time Line	H	RF	101	Windows on Literacy	National Geographic
Ellen Ochoa	L	B	250+	Biography	Benchmark Education

* Collection of short stories
# Graphic text

TITLE	LEVEL	GENRE	WORD COUNT	AUTHOR / SERIES	PUBLISHER / DISTRIBUTOR
Ellen Ochoa	N	B	703	Leveled Readers Science	Houghton Mifflin Harcourt
Ellen Ochoa	G	B	250+	Welcome Books	Children's Press
Ellen Ochoa, Astronaut	M	B	726	Leveled Readers Science	Houghton Mifflin Harcourt
Ellen Ochoa: Reaching for the Stars	T	B	250+	Explore More	Wright Group/McGraw Hill
Ellen Tebbits	P	RF	250+	Cleary, Beverly	Dell
Ellie	Z	RF	250+	Borntrager, Mary Christner	Herald Press
Ellie and the Steel Drum	S	B	1344	Leveled Readers	Houghton Mifflin Harcourt
Ellie and the Steel Drum	S	B	1344	Leveled Readers/CA	Houghton Mifflin Harcourt
Ellie Brader Hates Mr. G.	R	RF	250+	Johnston, Janet	Pocket Books
#Ellie McDoodle: Have Pen, Will Travel	P	RF	250+	Barshaw, Ruth McNally	Bloomsbury Children's Books
#Ellie McDoodle: New Kid in School	P	RF	250+	Barshaw, Ruth McNally	Bloomsbury Children's Books
Ellis Island	S	I	250+	A True Book	Children's Press
Ellis Island	V	I	250+	Cornerstones of Freedom	Children's Press
Ellis Island	N	I	250+	Early Connections	Benchmark Education
Ellis Island	N	I	263	Independent Readers Social Studies	Houghton Mifflin Harcourt
Ellis Island	V	I	250+	Jango-Cohen, Judith	Scholastic
Ellis Island	U	I	250+	We the People	Compass Point Books
Ellis Island: Welcome to America	P	I	250+	Rosen Real Readers	Rosen Publishing Group
Elm River Airport	K	RF	603	Gear Up!	Wright Group/McGraw Hill
Elm Tree, The	K	RF	483	Gear Up!	Wright Group/McGraw Hill
Elmer and the Dragon	M	F	250+	Gannett, Ruth	Random House
Eloise Greenfield: Poetry to Grow On	P	B	886	Leveled Readers	Houghton Mifflin Harcourt
Eloise Greenfield: The Music of Poetry	O	B	250+	Leveled Readers Language Support	Houghton Mifflin Harcourt
Elsewhere	Y	F	250+	Zevin, Gabrielle	Farrar, Straus and Giroux
Elves and the Shoemaker, The	F	TL	214	Folk Tales	Pioneer Valley
Elves and the Shoemaker, The	J	TL	300	PM Tales and Plays-Turquoise	Rigby
Elves and the Shoemaker, The	I	TL	250+	Storyworlds	Heinemann Educational Books
Elves and the Shoemaker, The: A Tale by the Brothers Grimm	K	TL	250+	Rigby Literacy	Rigby
*Elves and the Shoemaker, The	K	TL	622	New Way Orange	Steck-Vaughn
Elves and the Shoemakers, The	J	TL	250+	Rigby Star	Rigby
Elves Don't Wear Hard Hats	M	F	250+	Dadey, Debbie; Jones, Marcia Thornton	Scholastic
Elvis and the Camping Trip	E	F	60	Rigby Star	Rigby
Elvis and the Scooter	C	F	83	Rigby Rocket	Rigby
Elvis and the Space Junk	I	F	250+	Rigby Star	Rigby
Elvis the Turnip and Me	N	F	250+	The Zack Files	Gosset & Dunlap
E-Mail Pals	M	RF	250+	InfoTrek	ETA Cuisenaire
E-Mails from the Teacher	N	RF	915	Leveled Readers	Houghton Mifflin Harcourt
E-Mails from the Teacher	N	RF	915	Leveled Readers/CA	Houghton Mifflin Harcourt
E-Mails from the Teacher	N	RF	915	Leveled Readers/TX	Houghton Mifflin Harcourt
Emancipation Proclamation, The	V	I	250+	Cornerstones of Freedom	Children's Press
Emancipation Proclamation, The: Hope of Freedom for the Slaves	V	I	250+	Let Freedom Ring	Capstone Press
Emerald Cathedral, The	V	I	1983	Leveled Readers	Houghton Mifflin Harcourt
Emerald Throne, The	T	F	250+	Baldry, Cherith	Mondo
Emergency Medical Technicians	J	I	223	On Deck	Rigby
Emergency Vehicles	K	I	250+	PM Plus	Rigby
Emergency Workers	L	I	250+	Rigby Focus	Rigby

TITLE	LEVEL	GENRE	WORD COUNT	AUTHOR / SERIES	PUBLISHER / DISTRIBUTOR
Emil	J	RF	250+	Stepping Stones	Nelson/Michaels Assoc.
Emil and Karl	Y	HF	250+	Glatshteyn, Yankev	Square Fish
Emilio and the River	J	RF	403	Sunshine	Wright Group/McGraw Hill
Emily and Alice	L	RF	250+	Champion, Joyce	Harcourt Trade
Emily Arrow Promises to Do Better This Year	M	RF	250+	Giff, Patricia Reilly	Bantam
Emily at School	L	RF	250+	Williams, Suzanne	Hyperion
Emily Can't Sleep	F	RF	124	Early Emergent, Set 2	Pioneer Valley
Emily Carr	X	B	250+	The Canadians	Fitzhenry & Whiteside
Emily Dickinson: American Poet	O	B	250+	Greene, Carol	Children's Press
Emily Eyefinger	M	F	250+	Ball, Duncan	Aladdin
Emily Geiger's Dangerous Mission	T	I	1273	Leveled Readers/CA	Houghton Mifflin Harcourt
Emily Geiger's Dangerous Mission	T	I	1273	Leveled Readers/TX	Houghton Mifflin Harcourt
Emily Loved Yellow	I	RF	99	Sunshine	Wright Group/McGraw Hill
Emily Murphy	X	B	250+	The Canadians	Fitzhenry & Whiteside
Emily Rodda's Raven Hill Mysteries: Dirty Tricks	T	RF	250+	Rodda, Emily & Rowe, Kate	Scholastic
Emily Windsnap and the Monster from the Deep	T	F	250+	Kessler, Liz	Candlewick Press
Emily's Babysitter	C	RF	67	Emergent	Pioneer Valley
Emily's Runaway Imagination	P	F	250+	Cleary, Beverly	Avon Camelot
Emma	L	RF	250+	Kesselman, Wendy	HarperTrophy
Emma Rides on the Erie Canal	T	HF	1904	Leveled Readers	Houghton Mifflin Harcourt
Emma, the Birthday Clown	M	RF	1887	Sunshine	Wright Group/McGraw Hill
Emma-Jean Lazarus Fell Out of a Tree	R	RF	250+	Tarshis, Lauren	Dial Books
Emma's Emu	N	F	250+	First Flight	Fitzhenry & Whiteside
Emma's Problem	H	RF	190	Literacy 2000	Rigby
Emperor and the Nightingale, The	L	TL	250+	Literacy 2000	Rigby
Emperor Penguins	L	I	420	Pull Ahead Books	Lerner Publications
Emperor Penguins	J	I	597	Vocabulary Readers	Houghton Mifflin Harcourt
Emperor Penguins	J	I	597	Vocabulary Readers/CA	Houghton Mifflin Harcourt
Emperor Penguins	J	I	597	Vocabulary Readers/TX	Houghton Mifflin Harcourt
Emperor's Egg, The	O	I	250+	Read and Wonder	Candlewick Press
Emperor's New Clothes, The	k	TL	250+	Literacy by Design	Rigby
Emperor's New Clothes, The	J	TL	250+	Rigby Literacy	Rigby
Emperor's New Clothes, The	J	TL	571	Tales from Hans Andersen	Wright Group/McGraw Hill
Empire Builders	T	I	250+	Rigby Focus	Rigby
Empty Envelope, The	N	RF	250+	A to Z Mysteries	Random House
Empty Lot, The	M	RF	606	Leveled Readers	Houghton Mifflin Harcourt
Empty Lunch Box, The	C	RF	73	Storyworlds	Heinemann Educational Publishers
Empty Pot, The	M	TL	250+	Demi	Henry Holt & Co.
EMTs	M	I	401	Pull Ahead Books	Lerner Publications
Emu Who Wanted to Be a Horse, The	J	F	250+	Voyages	SRA/McGraw Hill
Enchanted Horse, The	R	F	250+	Nabb, Magdalen	Hyperion
*Encyclopedia Brown Boy Detective	P	RF	250+	Sobol, Donald J.	Bantam
*Encyclopedia Brown Carries On	P	RF	250+	Sobol, Donald J.	Bantam
*Encyclopedia Brown Finds the Clues	P	RF	250+	Sobol, Donald J.	Bantam
*Encyclopedia Brown Gets His Man	P	RF	250+	Sobol, Donald J.	Bantam
*Encyclopedia Brown Keeps the Peace	P	RF	250+	Sobol, Donald J.	Bantam
*Encyclopedia Brown Lends a Hand	P	RF	250+	Sobol, Donald J.	Bantam
*Encyclopedia Brown Saves the Day	P	RF	250+	Sobol, Donald J.	Bantam
*Encyclopedia Brown Sets the Pace	P	RF	250+	Sobol, Donald J.	Bantam
*Encyclopedia Brown Shows the Way	P	RF	250+	Sobol, Donald J.	Bantam
*Encyclopedia Brown Solves Them All	P	RF	250+	Sobol, Donald J.	Bantam

E

* Collection of short stories
# Graphic text

TITLE	LEVEL	GENRE	WORD COUNT	AUTHOR / SERIES	PUBLISHER / DISTRIBUTOR
*Encyclopedia Brown Takes the Cake	P	RF	250+	Sobol, Donald J.	Bantam
*Encyclopedia Brown Tracks Them Down	P	RF	250+	Sobol, Donald J.	Bantam
*Encyclopedia Brown: Case of Pablo's Nose	P	RF	250+	Sobol, Donald J.	Scholastic
*Encyclopedia Brown: Case of the Dead Eagles	P	RF	250+	Sobol, Donald J.	Bantam
*Encyclopedia Brown: Case of the Disgusting Sneakers	P	RF	250+	Sobol, Donald J.	Bantam
*Encyclopedia Brown: Case of the Midnight Visitor	P	RF	250+	Sobol, Donald J.	Bantam
*Encyclopedia Brown: Case of the Mysterious Handprints	P	RF	250+	Sobol, Donald J.	Bantam
*Encyclopedia Brown: Case of the Secret Pitch	P	RF	250+	Sobol, Donald J.	Bantam
*Encyclopedia Brown: Case of the Sleeping Dog	P	RF	250+	Sobol, Donald J.	Scholastic
*Encyclopedia Brown: Case of the Slippery Salamander	P	RF	250+	Sobol, Donald J.	Scholastic
*Encyclopedia Brown: Case of the Treasure Hunt	P	RF	250+	Sobol, Donald J.	Bantam
*Encyclopedia Brown: Case of the Two Spies	P	RF	250+	Sobol, Donald J.	Bantam
Encyclopedia Brown's Book of Strange But True Crimes	P	RF	250+	Sobol, Donald J.; Sobol, Rose	Scholastic
Encyclopedia of a Rain Forest	N	I	250+	Rigby Literacy	Rigby
Encyclopedia of Animals, An	M	I	250+	Literacy by Design	Rigby
Encyclopedia of Animals, An	M	I	250+	On Our Way to English	Rigby
Encyclopedia of Birds, An	N	I	1021	In Step Readers	Rigby
Encyclopedia of Fantastic Fish	L	I	250+	Rigby Literacy	Rigby
Encyclopedia of Fantastic Fish	L	I	250+	Rigby Star Quest	Rigby
Encyclopedia of Fossils, An	O	I	250+	Literacy by Design	Rigby
Encyclopedia of Fossils, An	O	I	250+	On Our Way to English	Rigby
Encyclopedia of Life in the Smokies, An	P	I	250+	In Step Readers	Rigby
Encyclopedia of New Year's Celebrations Around the World	T	I	250+	Literacy by Design	Rigby
Encyclopedia of Rocks, An	P	I	250+	Literacy by Design	Rigby
Encyclopedia of Tiny Creatures	J	I	250+	Discovery World	Rigby
End of the Ice Age, The	U	I	2221	Independent Readers Science	Houghton Mifflin Harcourt
End of the Line, The	T	F	250+	Crew, Gary	Stone Arch Books
End, The	C	RF	106	Tiger Cub	Peguis
Endangered Animals	N	I	250+	A New True Book	Children's Press
Endangered Animals	K	I	148	Early Connections	Benchmark Education
Endangered Animals	T	I	1448	Reading Street	Pearson
Endangered Birds	O	I	250+	Wonder World	Wright Group/McGraw Hill
Endangered Desert Animals	R	I	250+	Taylor, Dave	Crabtree
Endangered Forest Animals	R	I	250+	Taylor, Dave	Crabtree
Endangered Grassland Animals	R	I	250+	Taylor, Dave	Crabtree
Endangered Island Animals	R	I	250+	Taylor, Dave	Crabtree
Endangered Mammals	P	I	250+	Rigby Focus	Rigby
Endangered Mountain Animals	R	I	250+	Taylor, Dave	Crabtree
Endangered Ocean Animals	R	I	250+	Taylor, Dave	Crabtree
Endangered or Extinct!	U	I	250+	The News	Richard C. Owen
Endangered Savannah Animals	R	I	250+	Taylor, Dave	Crabtree
Endangered Wetland Animals	R	I	250+	Taylor, Dave	Crabtree
Endless Puzzle, The	J	RF	416	Leveled Readers	Houghton Mifflin Harcourt
Endless Steppe, The	Y	B	250+	Hautzig, Esther	HarperTrophy
Ends of the Earth	S	I	250+	The News	Richard C. Owen
Endurance: Shackleton's Antarctic Expedition	S	I	250+	Orbit Chapter Books	Pacific Learning

E

* Collection of short stories
# Graphic text

TITLE	LEVEL	GENRE	WORD COUNT	AUTHOR / SERIES	PUBLISHER / DISTRIBUTOR
Endurance: Shipwreck and Survival on a Sea of Ice	T	I	250+	High Five Reading	Red Brick Learning
Enduro Racing	Q	I	250+	Dirt Bikes	Capstone Press
Energy	P	I	250+	Our Physical World	Capstone Press
Energy	P	I	250+	Sails	Rigby
Energy	Y	I	250+	The Heinle Reading Library	Thomson Learning
Energy and Me	U	I	250+	The News	Richard C. Owen
Energy and Weather	T	I	1828	Science Support Readers	Houghton Mifflin Harcourt
Energy at the Airport	W	I	250+	Theme Sets	National Geographic
Energy at the Sports Arena	W	I	250+	Theme Sets	National Geographic
Energy Chain	S	I	250+	Bookweb	Rigby
Energy Contest, The	K	RF	564	In Step Readers	Rigby
Energy for the Future	O	I	250+	Rigby Focus	Rigby
Energy in Ecosystems	Q	I	1106	Science Support Readers	Houghton Mifflin Harcourt
Energy in the Factory	W	I	250+	Theme Sets	National Geographic
Energy in the Home	W	I	250+	Theme Sets	National Geographic
Energy Resources	V	I	1964	Science Support Readers	Houghton Mifflin Harcourt
Energy Stars, The	U	RF	250+	Reading Expeditions	National Geographic
Energy: Heat, Light, and Fuel	M	I	250+	Amazing Science	Picture Window Books
Engelbert the Hero	H	F	113	Little Celebrations	Pearson Learning Group
Engelbert's Exercises	E	F	23	Little Celebrations	Pearson Learning Group
Engines	E	I	81	Sunshine	Wright Group/McGraw Hill
England	Q	I	250+	First Reports: Countries	Compass Point Books
England	P	I	250+	Many Cultures, One World	Capstone Press
England: A Question and Answer Book	P	I	250+	Questions and Answers: Countries	Capstone Press
English Channel, The	M	I	433	Reading Street	Pearson
English Colonies in the Armericas	S	I	250+	On Deck	Rigby
English Springer Spaniels	I	I	139	Dogs	Capstone Press
Enormous Crocodile, The	N	F	250+	Dahl, Roald	Penguin Group
Enormous Egg, The	R	F	250+	Butterworth, Oliver	Little, Brown & Co.
Enormous Egg, The	C	F	52	Learn to Read	Creative Teaching Press
Enormous Turnip, The	H	TL	431	Hunia, Fran	Ladybird Books
Enormous Turnip, The	H	TL	250+	Storyworlds	Heinemann Educational Books
Enormous Watermelon, The	H	TL	304	Traditional Tales & More	Rigby
Entertainment Then and Now	U	I	1627	Vocabulary Readers	Houghton Mifflin Harcourt
Entertainment Then and Now	U	I	1627	Vocabulary Readers/CA	Houghton Mifflin Harcourt
Environmental Disasters	W	I	8442	Disasters Up Close	Lerner Publications
Environmentally Friendly World	L	F	929	Early Connections	Benchmark Education
E-Pals	L	RF	347	Reading Street	Pearson
Equal Parts	I	I	233	Shutterbug Books	Steck-Vaughn
Equality in American Schools	X	I	1597	Reading Street	Pearson
Eragon	Y	F	250+	Paolini, Christopher	Alfred A. Knopf
Erana's Land: A Story from New Zealand	S	RF	250+	Reading Expeditions	National Geographic
Ereth's Birthday	S	F	250+	Avi	Harper Trophy
Eric's Birthday	H	RF	77	City Stories	Rigby
Eric's Greek Travel Diary	T	RF	250+	PM Extensions	Rigby
Eric's Thai Travel Diary	T	RF	250+	PM Extensions	Rigby
Erik and the Three Goats	H	F	257	Ready Readers	Pearson Learning Group
Erik's Story: From Sweden to Minnesota	T	HF	250+	Reading Expeditions	National Geographic
Erin Meets Tiffy	D	RF	104	PM Photo Stories	Rigby
Erin Rides Tiffy	F	RF	154	PM Photo Stories	Rigby
Er-Lang and the Suns: A Tale from China	M	TL	250+	Folk Tales	Mondo

* Collection of short stories
\# Graphic text

TITLE	LEVEL	GENRE	WORD COUNT	AUTHOR / SERIES	PUBLISHER / DISTRIBUTOR
Ernesto the Engine	C	F	50	Reading Safari	Mondo
Erosion	R	I	1896	Early Bird Earth Systems	Lerner Publications
Erosion	M	I	250+	Early Connections	Benchmark Education
Erosion	Q	I	250+	Exploring the Earth	Capstone Press
Erosion	L	I	300	Independent Readers Social Studies	Houghton Mifflin Harcourt
Erosion Shapes the Earth	N	I	882	Pair-It Turn and Learn	Steck-Vaughn
Erosion: The Changing Shape of the Land	M	I	250+	Explorations	Eleanor Curtain Publishing
Erosion: The Changing Shape of the Land	M	I	250+	Explorations	Okapi Educational Materials
Errol the Peril	Q	F	250+	Literacy 2000	Rigby
Ersatz Elevator, The	V	F	250+	Snicket, Lemony	Scholastic
Eruption	R	I	250+	Wildcats	Wright Group/McGraw Hill
Eruption of Mount St. Helens, The	V	HF	250+	Reading Expeditions	National Geographic
Escalator Escapade	N	RF	250+	Girlz Rock!	Mondo
Escalator, The	A	RF	23	Story Box	Wright Group/McGraw Hill
Escape	X	I	250+	InfoQuest	Rigby
Escape from Castle Cant	S	F	250+	Bath, K.P.	Little, Brown & Co.
Escape from Death Valley	M	I	419	Books for Young Learners	Richard C. Owen
Escape From Slavery: Five Journeys to Freedom	Q	B	250+	Rappaport, Doreen	HarperTrophy
Escape from the Comics	Q	RF	250+	Bookweb	Rigby
Escape from the Dark	W	F	250+	Dark Man	Ransom
Escape from the Deep	O	SF	1715	Take Two Books	Wright Group/ McGraw-Hill
Escape from the Nazis	Y	I	1620	Vocabulary Readers	Houghton Mifflin Harcourt
Escape from the Nazis	Y	I	1620	Vocabulary Readers/CA	Houghton Mifflin Harcourt
Escape from the Pop-Up Prison	T	F	250+	Dahl, Michael	Stone Arch Books
Escape from the Tower	W	HF	250+	WorldScapes	ETA Cuisenaire
Escape From the Zoo	E	F	108	Springboard	Wright Group/McGraw Hill
Escape from Vesuvius	U	HF	250+	PM Plus	Rigby
Escape of the Deadly Dinosaur, The	P	SF	250+	Secret Agent Jack Stalwart	Weinstein Books
Escape to Canada	P	I	513	Vocabulary Readers	Houghton Mifflin Harcourt
Escape to Freedom	V	HF	250+	Davis, Ossie	Puffin/Penguin
Escape!	N	SF	250+	Orbit Chapter Books	Pacific Learning
e-search	S	F	250+	Storyteller - Autumn Leaves	Wright Group/McGraw Hill
ESP	Z	I	8314	The Unexplained	Lerner Publications
ESP TV	R	SF	250+	Rodgers, Mary	HarperTrophy
Esperanza Rising	V	HF	250+	Ryan, Pam Munoz	Scholastic
Ethel the Emu	K	RF	1700	Wiley, Pamela	Kaeden Books
Ethiopia: A Question and Answer Book	P	I	250+	Questions & Answers: Countries	Capstone Press
Eugenie Clark Shark Lady	N	I	566	Leveled Literacy Intervention/ Blue System	Heinemann
Eureka!	Q	I	250+	Orbit Collections	Pacific Learning
Eureka! It's an Airplane	T	I	250+	Bendick, Jeanne	Scholastic
Eureka! It's Television!	T	I	250+	Bendick, Jeanne & Robert	Scholastic
Eureka! Stories of Everyday Inventions	P	I	250+	Literacy 2000	Rigby
Europe	N	I	250+	Continents	Capstone Press
Europe	N	I	330	Pull Ahead Books	Lerner Publications
Europe: Geography of Conquest	X	I	1830	Leveled Readers Social Studies	Houghton Mifflin Harcourt
Eva	Z	F	250+	Dickenson, Eva	Laurel-Leaf Books
Eva and Max	C	RF	27	Appleton-Smith, Laura	Flyleaf Publishing
Eva Perón: First Lady of the People	P	B	250+	Great Hispanics	Capstone Press
Eva the Beekeeper	J	I	250+	iOpeners	Pearson Learning Group
Evangeline Mudd's Great Mink Rescue	U	F	250+	Elliott, David	Candlewick Press
Eva's Lost and Found Report	K	F	250+	On Our Way to English	Rigby
Eve Shops	F	RF	146	Ready Readers	Pearson Learning Group

* Collection of short stories
# Graphic text

TITLE	LEVEL	GENRE	WORD COUNT	AUTHOR / SERIES	PUBLISHER / DISTRIBUTOR
Evelyn Cisneros: Prima Ballerina	P	B	250+	Great Hispanics	Capstone Press
Even Bread Has a Home	M	F	1888	Take Two Books	Wright Group/McGraw Hill
Even Steven and Odd Todd	K	F	250+	Cristaldi, Kathryn	Scholastic
Evening Meals Around the World	M	I	250+	Meals Around the World	Picture Window Books
Evening Song	L	RF	115	Books for Young Learners	Richard C. Owen
Everest	V	I	250+	PM Collection	Rigby
Everest Adventures	T	I	250+	WorldScapes	ETA Cuisenaire
Everest Challenge	Q	I	489	Vocabulary Readers	Houghton Mifflin Harcourt
Everglades	T	I	250+	George, Jean Craighead	HarperTrophy
Everglades, The	M	I	250+	Early Connections	Benchmark Education
Every Bird Has a Beak	E	I	49	Birds Series	Pearson Learning Group
Every Bird Has Feathers	E	I	50	Birds Series	Pearson Learning Group
Every Bird Has Two Feet	E	I	46	Birds Series	Pearson Learning Group
Every Body Tells a Story	R	I	250+	Explorers	Wright Group/McGraw Hill
Every Cat	F	RF	91	Instant Readers	Harcourt School Publishers
Every Cloud Has a Silver Lining	Q	RF	250+	Mazer, Anne	Scholastic
Every Day But Sunday	E	RF	83	Home Connection Collection	Rigby
Every Flower Is Beautiful	K	TL	250+	Turner, Teresa	Steck-Vaughn
Every Kind of Wish	K	RF	664	Leveled Readers	Houghton Mifflin Harcourt
Every Kind of Wish	K	RF	664	Leveled Readers/CA	Houghton Mifflin Harcourt
Every Kind of Wish	K	RF	664	Leveled Readers/TX	Houghton Mifflin Harcourt
*Every Living Thing	R	RF	250+	Rylant, Cynthia	Aladdin
Every Monday	C	F	52	Pair-It Books	Steck-Vaughn
Every Morning	A	I	30	Twig	Wright Group/McGraw Hill
Every Mother Bird Builds a Nest	E	I	62	Birds Series	Pearson Learning Group
Every Shape and Size	G	I	97	Wonder World	Wright Group/McGraw Hill
Every Soul a Star	U	RF	250+	Mass, Wendy	Little, Brown & Co.
Everybody Bakes Bread	M	RF	1828	Dooley, Norah	Carolrhoda Books
Everybody Brings Noodles	M	RF	1887	Dooley, Norah	Carolrhoda Books
Everybody Cooks Rice	M	RF	1041	Dooley, Norah	Scholastic
Everybody Dances	T	I	250+	Literacy 2000	Rigby
Everybody Eats Bread	J	I	241	Literacy 2000	Rigby
Everybody Makes Soup	M	RF	2416	Dooley, Norah	Carolrhoda Books
Everybody Says	G	RF	70	Rookie Readers	Children's Press
Everybody Wears Braids	B	RF	30	Bebop Books	Lee & Low Books Inc.
Everybody Wins! The Story of Special Olympics	S	I	1734	Reading Street	Pearson
Everybody Works	I	I	82	Shelley Rotner's Early Childhood	Millbrook Press
Everyday	D	I	45	Bonnell, Kris	Reading Reading Books
Everyday Forces	M	I	250+	Discovery World	Rigby
Everyday Hero	I	I	249	Vocabulary Readers	Houghton Mifflin Harcourt
Everyday Hero	I	I	249	Vocabulary Readers/CA	Houghton Mifflin Harcourt
Everyday Hero	I	I	249	Vocabulary Readers/TX	Houghton Mifflin Harcourt
Everyday Inventions	N	I	641	Vocabulary Readers	Houghton Mifflin Harcourt
Everyday Inventions	N	I	641	Vocabulary Readers/CA	Houghton Mifflin Harcourt
Everyday Inventions	N	I	641	Vocabulary Readers/TX	Houghton Mifflin Harcourt
Everyday Machines	J	I	188	Rigby Focus	Rigby
Everyday Math	D	I	102	Early Connections	Benchmark Education
Everyday Patterns	F	I	110	Early Connections	Benchmark Education
Everyone	J	F	553	Sun Sprouts	ETA Cuisenaire
Everyone Eats	C	I	44	Discovery Links	Newbridge
Everyone Eats Bread	G	I	139	Yellow Umbrella Books	Red Brick Learning
Everyone Else's Parents Said Yes	U	RF	250+	Danziger, Paula	PaperStar
Everyone Is a Scientist	I	I	197	Yellow Umbrella Books	Red Brick Learning
Everyone Is Coming	B	I	21	On Our Way to English	Rigby

* Collection of short stories
# Graphic text

TITLE	LEVEL	GENRE	WORD COUNT	AUTHOR / SERIES	PUBLISHER / DISTRIBUTOR
Everyone Is Reading	H	RF	225	Cambridge Reading	Pearson Learning Group
Everyone Knows About Cars	L	I	176	Bookshop	Mondo
Everyone Says Sh-h-h!	E	RF	93	Rigby Literacy	Rigby
Everyone Says Sh-h-h-h!	E	RF	93	Literacy By Design	Rigby
Everyone Uses Math	G	I	211	Yellow Umbrella Books	Red Brick Learning
Everyone Wears Wool	A	I	21	Pair-It Books	Steck-Vaughn
Everything Cat: What Kids Really Want to Know About Cats	R	I	250+	Crisp, Marty	NorthWord Press
Everything Changes	L	I	250+	Discovery World	Rigby
Everything Dog: What Kids Really Want to Know About Dogs	R	I	250+	Crisp, Marty	NorthWord Press
Everything Is Fine	Z+	RF	250+	Ellis, Ann Dee	Little, Brown & Co.
Everything Is Made of Matter	M	I	250+	Windows on Literacy	National Geographic
Everything Is Matter!	L	I	226	Yellow Umbrella Books	Capstone Press
Everything New Under the Sun	Q	RF	250+	Mazer, Anne	Scholastic
Everything on a Waffle	V	RF	250+	Horvath, Polly	Farrar, Straus and Giroux
Everywhere	R	RF	250+	Brooks, Bruce	Scholastic
Everywhere You Look	H	I	191	Sunshine	Wright Group/McGraw Hill
Evidence of Plate Tectonics	W	I	2446	Science Support Readers	Houghton Mifflin Harcourt
Evil Queen Tut and the Great Ant Pyramids	N	F	250+	The Zack Files	Grossett & Dunlap
Evvy's Civil War	X	HF	250+	Brenaman, Miriam	Putnam/Penguin
Exactly Right	I	RF	250+	Reading Safari	Mondo
Excavating a Castle	T	RF	250+	Reading Expeditions	National Geographic
Excuses, Excuses	E	RF	104	Tadpoles	Rigby
Exercise Time	O	F	250+	Sails	Rigby
Exercising	L	I	390	Pull Ahead Books	Lerner Publications
Exit Point	Z+	RF	250+	Orca Soundings	Orca Book Publishers
Exotic Cats	I	I	104	Cats	Capstone Press
Exotic Tropical Fish	L	I	250+	Marine Life for Young Readers	Pearson Learning Group
Expanding the Nation	U	I	250+	Primary Source Readers	Teacher Created Materials
Expect the Unexpected	Q	I	250+	Orbit Double Takes	Pacific Learning
Experiment with Movement	Q	I	250+	Murphy, Bryan	Scholastic
Experiment with Water	Q	I	250+	Murphy, Bryan	Scholastic
Experiments on Myself	R	I	250+	High-Fliers	Pacific Learning
Experiments with Electricity	S	I	250+	A True Book	Children's Press
Experiments with Sound	S	I	3457	Take Two Books	Wright Group/McGraw Hill
Exploration	V	I	250+	High-Fliers	Pacific Learning
Exploration and Conquest: The Americas After Columbus, 1500-1620	T	I	250+	Maestro, Betsy & Giulio	William Morrow
Exploration: Questing for Knowledge	R	I	250+	Explore More	Wright Group/McGraw Hill
Explore the Deciduous Forest	Q	I	250+	Explore the Biomes	Capstone Press
Explore the Desert	Q	I	250+	Explore the Biomes	Capstone Press
Explore the Galaxy	N	I	580	Reading Street	Pearson
Explore the Grasslands	Q	I	250+	Explore the Biomes	Capstone Press
Explore the Midwest	Q	I	250+	Reading Expeditions	National Geographic
Explore the Northeast	Q	I	250+	Reading Expeditions	National Geographic
Explore the Ocean	Q	I	250+	Explore the Biomes	Capstone Press
Explore the Southeast	Q	I	250+	Reading Expeditions	National Geographic
Explore the Southwest	Q	I	250+	Reading Expeditions	National Geographic
Explore the Tropical Rain Forest	Q	I	250+	Explore the Biomes	Capstone Press
Explore the Tundra	Q	I	250+	Explore the Biomes	Capstone Press
Explore the West	Q	I	250+	Reading Expeditions	National Geographic
Explore Your World	V	I	250+	iOpeners	Pearson Learning Group
Explorer	X	I	250+	Eyewitness Books	DK Publishing

E

* Collection of short stories
\# Graphic text

TITLE	LEVEL	GENRE	WORD COUNT	AUTHOR / SERIES	PUBLISHER / DISTRIBUTOR
Explorer of Glaciers	U	B	2110	Leveled Readers	Houghton Mifflin Harcourt
Explorer of Glaciers	U	B	2110	Leveled Readers/CA	Houghton Mifflin Harcourt
Explorer of the Gobi	X	B	3142	Leveled Readers	Houghton Mifflin Harcourt
Explorer of the Gobi	X	B	3142	Leveled Readers/CA	Houghton Mifflin Harcourt
Explorer, The	F	RF	73	City Stories	Rigby
Explorers News	W	I	250+	The History News	Candlewick Press
Explorers: Searching for Adventure	M	I	250+	Pair-It Books	Steck-Vaughn
*Explorers: Women in Profile	T	B	250+	Hacker, Carolotta	Crabtree
Exploring a Park	H	I	65	Vocabulary Readers	Houghton Mifflin Harcourt
Exploring an Ocean Tide Pool	W	I	250+	Bendick, Jeanne	Henry Holt & Co.
Exploring Antarctica	P	I	745	Leveled Readers	Houghton Mifflin Harcourt
Exploring Antarctica	P	I	745	Leveled Readers/CA	Houghton Mifflin Harcourt
Exploring Antarctica	P	I	745	Leveled Readers/TX	Houghton Mifflin Harcourt
Exploring Brazil	X	I	2434	Reading Street	Pearson
Exploring Caves	Q	I	250+	Explorer Books-Pathfinder	National Geographic
Exploring Caves	P	I	250+	Explorer Books-Pioneer	National Geographic
Exploring Earth's Oceans	Z	I	2880	Vocabulary Readers	Houghton Mifflin Harcourt
Exploring Earth's Oceans	Z	I	2880	Vocabulary Readers/CA	Houghton Mifflin Harcourt
Exploring Fossils	K	I	242	Windows on Literacy	National Geographic
Exploring Freshwater Habitats	P	I	250+	Snowball, Diane	Mondo
Exploring Land Habitats	P	I	250+	Phinney, Margaret Yatsevitch	Mondo
Exploring Mars	X	I	7261	Cool Science	Lerner Publications
Exploring Mars	W	I	2853	Reading Street	Pearson
Exploring Mars: The Red Planet	O	I	250+	In Step Readers	Rigby
Exploring Mars: The Red Planet	O	I	250+	Literacy by Design	Rigby
Exploring Medicine	V	I	250+	Kids Discover Reading	Wright Group/McGraw Hill
Exploring National Parks	L	I	250+	Rigby Literacy	Rigby
Exploring New Worlds	T	I	250+	News Extra	Richard C. Owen
Exploring Saltwater Habitats	P	I	250+	Smith, Sue	Mondo
Exploring Saturn	L	I	250+	Rosen Real Readers	Rosen Publishing Group
Exploring Space	R	I	250+	Explorers	Wright Group/McGraw Hill
Exploring Space	Y	I	250+	High-Fliers	Pacific Learning
Exploring Space	I	I	250+	Sunshine	Wright Group/McGraw Hill
Exploring the Frozen North	X	I	250+	Berton, Pierre	Fitzhenry & Whiteside
Exploring the Grand Canyon	Q	I	250+	Rosen Real Readers	Rosen Publishing Group
Exploring the Mysteries of Space	U	I	2893	Reading Street	Pearson
Exploring the New World	S	I	250+	Primary Source Readers	Teacher Created Materials
Exploring the New World: An Interactive History Adventure	U	HF	250+	You Choose Books	Capstone Press
Exploring the Titanic	Q	I	250+	Ballard, Robert D.	Scholastic
Exploring the World	O	I	250+	Literacy by Design	Rigby
Exploring the World	O	I	250+	On Our Way to English	Rigby
Exploring Tree Habitats	P	I	250+	Seifert, Patti	Mondo
Exploring with Lewis and Clark	O	I	250+	People, Spaces & Places	Rand McNally
Exploring with Science	T	I	1675	Reading Street	Pearson
Exposure	Z+	RF	250+	Orca Soundings	Orca Book Publishers
Expressway Jewels	M	RF	368	Evangeline Nicholas Collection	Wright Group/McGraw Hill
Extinct	S	I	2101	Leveled Readers Science	Houghton Mifflin Harcourt
Extinct and Endangered Animals	Q	I	2014	Take Two Books	Wright Group/ McGraw Hill
Extraordinary Adventures of Ordinary Basil, The	R	F	250+	Miller, Wiley	Blue Sky Press/Scholastic
*Extraordinary American Indians	W	B	250+	Avery, Susan; Skinner, Linda	Children's Press
Extraordinary Animals!	Q	I	250+	Tristars	Richard C. Owen

* Collection of short stories
# Graphic text

TITLE	LEVEL	GENRE	WORD COUNT	AUTHOR / SERIES	PUBLISHER / DISTRIBUTOR
*Extraordinary Black Americans: From Colonial to Contemporary Times	W	B	250+	Altman, Susan	Children's Press
Extraordinary House, The	L	F	762	Springboard	Wright Group/McGraw Hill
*Extraordinary Jewish Americans	W	B	250+	Brooks, Philip	Children's Press
Extraordinary Life of Thomas Peters, The	U	I	2250	Leveled Readers	Houghton Mifflin Harcourt
Extraordinary Life of Thomas Peters, The	U	I	2250	Leveled Readers/CA	Houghton Mifflin Harcourt
Extraordinary Life of Thomas Peters, The	U	I	2250	Leveled Readers/TX	Houghton Mifflin Harcourt
Extraordinary Life, An: The Story of a Monarch Butterfly	V	I	250+	Pringle, Laurence	Orchard Books
*Extraordinary People with Disabilities	W	B	250+	Kent, Deborah; Quinlan, Kathryn A.	Children's Press
Extraordinary Volcanoes	Q	I	250+	Gaff, Jackie & Polt, Gabrielle	Scholastic
*Extraordinary Women in Politics	W	B	250+	Gulatta, Charles	Children's Press
*Extraordinary Women Journalists	W	B	250+	Price-Groff, Claire	Children's Press
*Extraordinary Women of Medicine	W	B	250+	Stille, Darlene R.	Children's Press
*Extraordinary Women of the American West	W	B	250+	Alter, Judy	Children's Press
*Extraordinary Women Scientists	W	B	250+	Stille, Darlene R.	Children's Press
*Extraordinary Young People	W	B	250+	Brill, Marlene Targ	Children's Press
Extreme Animals: The Toughest Creatures on Earth	S	I	250+	Davies, Nicola	Candlewick Press
Extreme Environments	V	I	250+	Literacy by Design	Rigby
Extreme Environments - Challenges to Survival	U	I	250+	Connectors	Pacific Learning
Extreme Freestyle Motocross Moves	S	I	250+	Behind the Moves	Capstone Press
Extreme Lives	N	I	250+	Wildcats	Wright Group/McGraw Hill
Extreme Machines	U	I	250+	DK Readers	DK Publishing
Extreme Mountain Biking Moves	S	I	250+	Behind the Moves	Capstone Press
Extreme Racer	M	RF	696	Springboard	Wright Group/ McGraw Hill
Extreme Rock Climbing Moves	S	I	250+	Behind the Moves	Capstone Press
Extreme Scientists	T	I	250+	Connectors	Pacific Learning
Extreme Solutions	Q	I	1478	Leveled Readers	Houghton Mifflin Harcourt
Extreme Solutions	Q	I	1478	Leveled Readers/CA	Houghton Mifflin Harcourt
Extreme Sports	R	I	250+	Bookweb	Rigby
Extreme Sports	T	I	250+	High-Fliers	Pacific Learning
Extreme Sports	O	I	978	Leveled Readers	Houghton Mifflin Harcourt
Extreme Sports	O	I	978	Leveled Readers/CA	Houghton Mifflin Harcourt
Extreme Sports	R	I	250+	PM Nonfiction-Ruby	Rigby
Extreme Sports	P	I	250+	Wildcats	Wright Group/McGraw Hill
Extreme Surfing	M	I	250+	To the Extreme	Capstone Press
Extreme U.S.A.	R	I	250+	Literacy by Design	Rigby
Extreme Wakeboarding Moves	S	I	250+	Behind the Moves	Capstone Press
Extreme Weather	R	I	250+	Explore More	Wright Group/McGraw Hill
Exxon Valdez, The:The Oil Spill off the Alaskan Coast	R	I	250+	Disaster!	Capstone Press
Eye and Ear Pollution	V	I	250+	Connectors	Pacific Learning
Eye Doctor, The	D	I	50	Little Celebrations	Pearson Learning Group
Eye in the Graveyard, The	T	F	250+	Dahl, Michael	Stone Arch Books
Eye in the Sky	P	F	250+	Orbit Chapter Books	Pacific Learning
Eye of the Law, The	T	I	250+	Connectors	Pacific Learning
Eye on Invention	S	I	250+	WorldScapes	ETA Cuisenaire
Eye on the Ball	S	I	250+	InfoQuest	Rigby
Eye on the Wild: A Story about Ansel Adams	R	B	8848	Creative Minds Biographies	Carolrhoda Books
Eye Spy	P	I	250+	Wildcats	Wright Group/McGraw Hill
Eye Wonder	W	I	250+	Rigby Literacy	Rigby
Eyedropper	C	I	23	Simple Tools	Lerner Publishing

* Collection of short stories
# Graphic text

TITLE	LEVEL	GENRE	WORD COUNT	AUTHOR / SERIES	PUBLISHER / DISTRIBUTOR
Eyes	B	I	21	Animal Traits	Lerner Publications
Eyes	I	I	211	Explorations	Eleanor Curtain Publishing
Eyes	I	I	211	Explorations	Okapi Eductional Materials
Eyes	B	I	48	Sails	Rigby
Eyes	C	I	64	Wonder World	Wright Group/McGraw Hill
Eyes Are Everywhere	E	I	131	Ready Readers	Pearson Learning Group
Eyes in the Sky	R	I	250+	Literacy 2000	Rigby
Eyes of the Amaryllis, The	V	RF	250+	Babbitt, Natalie	Farrar, Straus and Giroux
Eyes of the Jungle	S	RF	4816	Take Two Books	Wright Group/McGraw Hill
Eyes of Wisdom: The Buffalo Woman Trilogy Book One	Z	HF	250+	Merrifield, Heyoka	Atria Books
Eyes on the Sky	T	I	250+	Kids Discover Reading	Wright Group/McGraw Hill
Eyewitness!	Q	RF	250+	Tristars	Richard C. Owen

E

* Collection of short stories
# Graphic text

TITLE	LEVEL	GENRE	WORD COUNT	AUTHOR / SERIES	PUBLISHER / DISTRIBUTOR
F is for Fabuloso	W	RF	250+	Lee, Marie G.	Avon
F/A-22 Raptor, The	U	I	250+	Cross-Sections	Capstone Press
Fab Four from Liverpool, The	U	B	1862	Leveled Readers	Houghton Mifflin Harcourt
*Fables	N	TL	250+	Lobel, Arnold	HarperCollins
Fables	D	I	40	Vocabulary Readers	Houghton Mifflin Harcourt
*Fables by Aesop	K	TL	250+	Reading Unlimited	Pearson Learning Group
Fabric Painting for Fun!	S	I	250+	For Fun! Crafts	Compass Point Books
Fabulous Animal Families	K	I	250+	Home Connection Collection	Rigby
Fabulous Creatures - Are They Real?	Q	I	1708	Big Cat	Pacific Learning
Fabulous Female Athletes	Q	B	1653	Reading Street	Pearson
Fabulous Fish	K	I	178	Rigby Focus	Rigby
Fabulous Freckles	K	RF	250+	Literacy 2000	Rigby
Fabulous Fruits	D	I	121	Fiesta Series	Pearson Learning Group
Fabulous Principal Pie, The	G	F	250+	Start to Read	School Zone
*Fabulous Spotted Egg, The	T	TL	250+	Literacy 2000	Rigby
Face in the Dark Mirror, The	W	F	250+	Dark Man	Ransom
Face in the Dark, The	D	RF	64	Storyteller-Setting Sun	Wright Group/McGraw Hill
Face on the Milk Carton, The	Y	RF	250+	Cooney, Caroline B.	Bantam Doubleday Dell
Face Painting	B	RF	24	Rigby Rocket	Rigby
Face Painting	G	RF	90	Wonder World	Wright Group/McGraw Hill
Face Sandwich, The	LB	RF	16	Sunshine	Wright Group/McGraw Hill
Face to Face	W	RF	250+	Bauer, Marion Dane	Bantam
Face to Face	P	RF	250+	Bookweb	Rigby
Face to the Sky	P	RF	250+	Greetings	Rigby
Face-Off	Q	RF	250+	Christopher, Matt	Little, Brown & Co.
Face-Off	P	RF	4301	Maddox, Jake	Stone Arch Books
Faceoff!	T	I	250+	Boldprint	Steck-Vaughn
Faces	D	I	250+	Little Celebrations	Pearson Learning Group
Faces	B	RF	27	Sunshine	Wright Group/McGraw Hill
Faces on Mount Rushmore	D	I	36	Leveled Readers Social Studies	Houghton Mifflin Harcourt
Facing My Music	Q	RF	250+	Pair-It Books	Steck-Vaughn
Facing the Flood	Q	RF	250+	Kleinhenz, Sydnie Meltzer	Steck-Vaughn
Facing West: A Story of the Oregon Trail	S	I	250+	Kudlinski, Kathleen V.	Penguin Group
Fact Finding	X	I	250+	Connectors	Pacific Learning
Fact or Fiction?	S	I	250+	Connectors	Pacific Learning
Factory Through the Ages	U	I	250+	Steele, Philip	Troll Associates
Facts About 50 States	Q	I	250+	Rigby Literacy	Rigby
Facts About Earthquakes	O	I	250+	Rosen Real Readers	Rosen Publishing Group
Facts About Forest Fires	J	I	250+	Rosen Real Readers	Rosen Publishing Group
Facts About Honeybees	K	I	575	Rigby Flying Colors	Rigby
Facts About Magnets	L	I	237	Leveled Readers Science	Houghton Mifflin Harcourt
Facts About Tornadoes	L	I	250+	Rosen Real Readers	Rosen Publishing Group
Facts and Fictions of Minna Pratt, The	U	RF	250+	MacLachlan, Patricia	HarperTrophy
Facts and Fun About the Presidents	S	I	250+	Sullivan, George	Scholastic
Facts on Film: How to Make a Documentary	U	I	250+	Bookshop	Mondo
Fading Forests: The Destruction of Our Rainforests	O	I	250+	On Deck	Rigby
Fahrenheit 451	Z+	SF	250+	Bradbury, Ray	Ballantine Books
Fair Day	J	RF	184	City Kids	Rigby
Fair Share	K	I	332	Yellow Umbrella Books	Red Brick Learning
Fair Swap, A	K	TL	250+	PM Story Books-Silver	Rigby
Fair Weather	T	HF	250+	Peck, Richard	Scholastic
Fair, Brown and Trembling	S	TL	250+	WorldScapes	ETA Cuisenaire
Fair, The	A	RF	40	First Stories	Pacific Learning

F

TITLE	LEVEL	GENRE	WORD COUNT	AUTHOR / SERIES	PUBLISHER / DISTRIBUTOR
Fairest	V	F	250+	Levine, Gail Carson	Harper Trophy
Fairies and Magical Creatures	V	I	250+	Reinhart, Matthew and Sabuda, Robert	Candlewick Press
Fairy World Crafts	P	I	3881	Ross, Kathy	Millbrook Press
Fairy's Guide to Understanding Humans, A	S	F	250+	Meacham, Margaret	Holiday House
Faith's Journey	S	HF	1263	Leveled Readers	Houghton Mifflin Harcourt
Falcon, The	N	RF	250+	PM Collection	Rigby
Falcon's Feathers, The	N	RF	250+	A to Z Mysteries	Random House
Falcons Nest on Skyscrapers	P	I	250+	Soar To Success	Houghton Mifflin Harcourt
Fall	B	I	12	Discovery Links	Newbridge
Fall	A	I	22	Little Books for Early Readers	University of Maine
Fall	E	I	54	Seasons	Lerner Publishing
Fall	E	I	73	Sunshine	Wright Group/McGraw Hill
Fall Changes	L	I	320	Leveled Readers	Houghton Mifflin Harcourt
Fall Changes	L	I	320	Leveled Readers/CA	Houghton Mifflin Harcourt
Fall Changes	L	I	320	Leveled Readers/TX	Houghton Mifflin Harcourt
Fall Colors	D	I	53	Bonnell, Kris	Reading Reading Books
Fall Colors	D	I	23	Windows on Literacy	National Geographic
Fall Fair Contest	J	RF	511	InfoTrek	ETA Cuisenaire
Fall Harvest	LB	I	16	Little Books for Early Readers	University of Maine
Fall Harvest	E	I	39	Preparing for Winter	Capstone Press
Fall Harvest	I	I	179	Vocabulary Readers/TX	Houghton Mifflin Harcourt
Fall Leaves	J	I	222	Leveled Readers	Houghton Mifflin Harcourt
Fall of Tenochtitlan	X	I	3489	Leveled Readers Social Studies	Houghton Mifflin Harcourt
Fallen Angels	Z+	HF	250+	Myers, Walter Dean	Scholastic
Falling From Grace	Z	RF	250+	Godwin, Jane	Holiday House
Falling Off a Log	Q	RF	1290	Leveled Readers	Houghton Mifflin Harcourt
Fallout	Z+	HF	250+	Krisher, Trudy	Holiday House
Fallout: Nuclear Disasters in Our World	R	I	250+	On Deck	Rigby
Families	H	I	160	Early Connections	Benchmark Education
Families	B	I	49	Interaction	Rigby
Families	D	I	60	Pebble Books	Capstone Press
Families	C	I	32	Rosen Real Readers	Rosen Publishing Group
Families	J	F	184	Storyteller-Night Crickets	Wright Group/McGraw Hill
Families	F	I	132	Twig	Wright Group/McGraw Hill
Families	C	I	94	Vocabulary Readers	Houghton Mifflin Harcourt
Families	C	I	94	Vocabulary Readers/CA	Houghton Mifflin Harcourt
Families	LB	I	8	Windows on Literacy	National Geographic
Families	F	I	159	Yellow Umbrella Books	Capstone Press
Families and Feasts	I	I	196	PM Plus Nonfiction	Rigby
Families Are Different	K	RF	250+	Pellegrini, Nina	Scholastic
Families in Many Cultures	I	I	114	Life Around the World	Capstone Press
Families in the City	D	I	134	Vocabulary Readers	Houghton Mifflin Harcourt
Families in the City	D	I	134	Vocabulary Readers/CA	Houghton Mifflin Harcourt
Families of 1608 Ash Street, The	L	RF	571	Leveled Readers	Houghton Mifflin Harcourt
Families of the Deep Blue Sea	P	I	250+	Mallory, Kenneth	Charlesbridge
Families Share	E	RF	72	Learn to Read	Creative Teaching Press
Family Bike Ride	C	RF	55	Handprints C, Set 1	Educators Publishing Service
Family Birthday, A	C	RF	55	Gear Up!	Wright Group/McGraw Hill
Family Counts	B	RF	19	Rise & Shine	Hampton-Brown
Family Dinner	Q	RF	250+	Cutler, Jane	Farrar, Straus and Giroux
Family Fun	A	RF	24	Handprints A	Educators Publishing Service

* Collection of short stories
\# Graphic text

TITLE	LEVEL	GENRE	WORD COUNT	AUTHOR / SERIES	PUBLISHER / DISTRIBUTOR
Family Fun	E	I	40	Shutterbug Books	Steck-Vaughn
Family Fun	A	I	20	Vocabulary Readers	Houghton Mifflin Harcourt
Family Fun	A	I	20	Vocabulary Readers/CA	Houghton Mifflin Harcourt
Family Life in the U.S.A., Then & Now	P	I	744	Time for Kids	Teacher Created Materials
Family Names	D	RF	36	Visions	Wright Group/McGraw Hill
Family of Beavers, A	J	RF	141	Books for Young Learners	Richard C. Owen
Family of Five, A	C	F	26	Pair-It Books	Steck-Vaughn
Family on Lake Street, The	F	RF	159	Teacher's Choice Series	Pearson Learning Group
Family Pets	F	I	61	Families	Capstone Press
Family Pets	C	I	37	Pebble Books	Capstone Press
Family Photo	L	RF	909	InfoTrek	ETA Cuisenaire
Family Photos	F	RF	106	Literacy 2000	Rigby
Family Picnic	B	RF	18	Bebop Books	Lee & Low Books Inc.
Family Picture, A	R	RF	1570	Leveled Readers	Houghton Mifflin Harcourt
Family Pictures	A	RF	32	Leveled Literacy Intervention/ Green System	Heinemann
Family Reunion	G	RF	243	Visions	Wright Group/McGraw Hill
Family Soccer	D	RF	55	Geddes, Diana	Kaeden Books
Family Table, The	J	RF	274	Leveled Readers Language Support	Houghton Mifflin Harcourt
Family Ties	Z	I	250+	Boldprint	Steck-Vaughn
Family Time	B	I	16	Pair-It Books	Steck-Vaughn
Family Traditions and Celebrations	N	I	1431	Reading Street	Pearson
Family Tree	S	RF	250+	Ayres, Katherine	Bantam
Family Tree, The	K	RF	250+	PM Plus Story Books	Rigby
Family Tree, The	G	F	213	Ready Readers	Pearson Learning Group
Family Under the Bridge, The	R	RF	250+	Savage Carlson, Natalie	Scholastic
Family Work and Fun	B	I	38	Little Red Readers	Sundance
Family, The	A	F	24	Sails	Rigby
Family, The	E	RF	55	Sunshine	Wright Group/McGraw Hill
*Famous Animals	Q	I	250+	Literacy Tree	Rigby
*Famous Children	O	I	250+	Literacy 2000	Rigby
Famous Faces	X	I	250+	InfoQuest	Rigby
Famous Feet	E	F	34	Instant Readers	Harcourt School Publishers
Famous Friendships	Z	I	2538	Independent Readers Social Studies	Houghton Mifflin Harcourt
Famous Immigrants	T	B	250+	Primary Source Readers	Teacher Created Materials
Famous Rocks	Q	I	578	Independent Readers Science	Houghton Mifflin Harcourt
Famous Trials	Z	I	250+	Boldprint	Steck-Vaughn
Famous Trios in World Literature	Z	I	3306	Vocabulary Readers	Houghton Mifflin Harcourt
Famous Trios in World Literature	Z	I	3306	Vocabulary Readers/CA	Houghton Mifflin Harcourt
Famous Women Athletes	S	B	2630	Reading Street	Pearson
Fancy Dance	H	RF	155	Bebop Books	Lee & Low Books, Inc.
Fancy Dress	B	RF	28	Rigby Star	Rigby
Fancy Dress Parade, The	H	RF	171	Stepping Stones	Nelson/Michaels Assoc.
Fancy Feet	L	RF	250+	Giff, Patricia Reilly	Bantam
Fancy Feet	M	I	250+	Yellow Umbrella Books	Red Brick Learning
Fanfare for Food	O	I	497	Vocabulary Readers	Houghton Mifflin Harcourt
Fangs	F	I	100	Sails	Rigby
Fangs and Me	N	RF	250+	Gilmore, Rachna	Fitzhenry & Whiteside
Fangs and Teeth	M	I	250+	Sails	Rigby
Fans and Umbrellas	E	TL	107	Joy Readers	Pearson Learning Group
Fantail, Fantail	D	F	67	Pacific Literacy	Pacific Learning
Fantastic Animal Features	Q	I	250+	Parker, Heather	Steck-Vaughn

TITLE	LEVEL	GENRE	WORD COUNT	AUTHOR / SERIES	PUBLISHER / DISTRIBUTOR
Fantastic Cake, The	E	RF	169	Story Box	Wright Group/McGraw Hill
Fantastic Field Trip, A	O	SF	1854	Reading Street	Pearson
Fantastic Fish	B	I	37	Gear Up!	Wright Group/McGraw Hill
Fantastic Flying Squirrel, The	G	I	127	Big Cat	Pacific Learning
Fantastic Forest, The	R	I	250+	Explorer Books-Pathfinder	National Geographic
Fantastic Forest, The	P	I	250+	Explorer Books-Pioneer	National Geographic
Fantastic Frogs	I	I	156	Sails	Rigby
Fantastic Frogs!	J	I	204	Robinson, Fay	Scholastic
Fantastic Fungi	K	I	234	Rigby Focus	Rigby
Fantastic Mr. Fox	P	F	250+	Dahl, Roald	Penguin Group
Fantastic Pumpkin, The	H	F	216	Rigby Literacy	Rigby
Fantastic Rocks	H	I	128	Shutterbug Books	Steck-Vaughn
Fantastic Washing Machine	J	F	250+	Sunshine	Wright Group/McGraw Hill
*Fantastic Water Pot and Other Cases, The	O	RF	250+	Simon, Seymour	Avon
Fantasy	V	I	250+	Boldprint	Steck-Vaughn
Far Away at Home	T	RF	5638	Reading Street	Pearson
Far Away Moon	G	I	80	Pacific Literacy	Pacific Learning
Far from Home	W	RF	2000	Leveled Readers/TX	Houghton Mifflin Harcourt
Far North	V	RF	250+	Hobbs, Will	Avon
Far Out!	Q	I	250+	Orbit Collections	Pacific Learning
Faraway Farm	H	RF	171	Whybrow, Ian	Carolrhoda Books
Farewell to Boyhood	O	I	250+	WorldScapes	ETA Cuisenaire
Farewell to Manzanar	Z	B	250+	Houston, Jeanne; Houston, James D.	Houghton Mifflin Harcourt
Farewell, My Lunchbag: A Chet Gecko Mystery	R	F	250+	Hale, Bruce	Harcourt, Inc.
Far-Flung Places	T	I	250+	Connectors	Pacific Learning
Farley Frog	B	F	33	Pair-It Books	Steck-Vaughn
Farm	W	I	250+	Eyewitness Books	DK Publishing
Farm Alarm	E	F	103	Early Connections	Benchmark Education
Farm Animals	A	I	28	Belle River Readers	Belle River Readers, Inc.
Farm Animals	A	I	28	Nonfiction Set 1	Literacy Footprints
Farm Animals	A	I	24	Vocabulary Readers	Houghton Mifflin Harcourt
Farm Chores	D	RF	35	Early Emergent, Set 4	Pioneer Valley
Farm Concert, The	C	F	74	Story Box	Wright Group/McGraw Hill
Farm Day	D	F	36	Little Celebrations	Pearson Learning Group
Farm Feet	B	I	40	Bonnell, Kris	Reading Reading Books
Farm for Wild Animals, A	K	I	161	Vocabulary Readers	Houghton Mifflin Harcourt
Farm Friends	K	I	197	Spyglass Books	Compass Point Books
Farm in Spring, The	C	I	69	PM Starters	Rigby
Farm Life Long Ago	L	I	436	Pair-It Books	Steck-Vaughn
Farm Patterns	J	I	308	Finding Patterns	Capstone Press
Farm Through the Ages	U	I	250+	Steele, Philip	Troll Associates
Farm Tractors	H	I	79	Mighty Machines	Capstone Press
Farm Tractors	L	I	416	Pull Ahead Books	Lerner Publications
Farm Work	D	F	80	Early Connections	Benchmark Education
Farm, The	A	F	46	InfoTrek	ETA Cuisenaire
Farm, The	B	I	79	Leveled Readers Emergent	Houghton Mifflin Harcourt
Farm, The	LB	I	14	Literacy 2000	Rigby
Farm, The	A	I	28	Little Books for Early Readers	University of Maine
Farm, The	A	I	42	Little Readers	Houghton Mifflin Harcourt
Farm, The	I	I	228	Pebble Books	Capstone Press
Farm, The	LB	I	14	Ready Readers	Pearson Learning Group
Farm, The	LB	F	12	Sails	Rigby
Farm, The	LB	I	14	Smart Starts	Rigby

F

TITLE	LEVEL	GENRE	WORD COUNT	AUTHOR / SERIES	PUBLISHER / DISTRIBUTOR
Farm, The	LB	I	21	Sunshine	Wright Group/McGraw Hill
Farmer and His Two Lazy Sons, The	I	TL	250+	Aesop's Fables	Pearson Learning Group
Farmer and the Skunk	E	F	139	Tiger Cub	Peguis
Farmer Boy	Q	HF	250+	Wilder, Laura Ingalls	HarperTrophy
Farmer Boy Birthday, A	J	HF	250+	Wilder, Laura Ingalls	HarperCollins
Farmer Boy Days	M	HF	250+	Wilder, Laura Ingalls	HarperTrophy
Farmer Brown and Dapple Gray	J	RF	166	Books for Young Learners	Richard C. Owen
Farmer Brown's Garden	C	F	48	Windmill Books	Rigby
Farmer Dan's Ducks	D	F	126	Leveled Literacy Intervention/ Green System	Heinemann
Farmer Didn't Wake Up, The	F	F	185	Learn to Read	Creative Teaching Press
Farmer Duck	K	F	250+	Waddell, Martin	Candlewick Press
Farmer Had a Pig, A	G	TL	149	Tiger Cub	Peguis
Farmer in the Dell	E	F	114	Parkinson, Kathy	Whitman
Farmer in the Dell, The	F	TL	159	PM Readalongs	Rigby
Farmer in the Dell, The	K	TL	250+	Traditional Songs	Picture Window Books
Farmer in the Soup, The	K	TL	250+	Littledale, Freya	Scholastic
Farmer Joe's Hot Day	J	F	406	Richards, Nancy W.	Scholastic
Farmer Mike	E	RF	52	Leveled Readers	Houghton Mifflin Harcourt
Farmer Upsy-Daisy	E	F	129	Start to Read	School Zone
Farmers	M	I	250+	Community Helpers	Red Brick Learning
Farmers	M	I	250+	Community Workers	Compass Point Books
Farmer's Journey, The	M	RF	250+	Little Celebrations	Pearson Learning Group
Farmers, The	A	RF	28	Leveled Literacy Intervention/ Green System	Heinemann
Farmers: Then and Now	P	I	250+	Primary Source Readers	Teacher Created Materials
Farming in the 1800s	U	I	2188	Reading Street	Pearson
Farms	F	I	153	Foundations	Wright Group/McGraw Hill
Farms	F	RF	102	Sunshine	Wright Group/McGraw Hill
Farms	N	I	606	Wonders	Hampton-Brown
Farmyard Fiasco, A	H	F	186	Book Bank	Wright Group/McGraw Hill
*Far-Out Frisbee and Other Cases, The	O	RF	250+	Simon, Seymour	Avon
Farthest Shore, The	Z	F	250+	Le Guin, Ursula	Bantam
Fascinating Faces	J	I	99	Literacy Tree	Rigby
Fascinating Families	O	I	717	Leveled Readers	Houghton Mifflin Harcourt
Fashion	V	I	250+	10 Things You Need to Know About	Capstone Press
Fashion Careers: Finding the Right Fit	V	I	250+	The World of Fashion	Capstone Press
Fashion Crafts: Create Your Own Style	Q	I	250+	Crafts	Capstone Press
Fashion Design School: Learning the Skills to Succeed	V	I	250+	The World of Fashion	Capstone Press
Fashion Design: The Art of Style	V	I	250+	The World of Fashion	Capstone Press
Fashion History: Looking Great Through the Ages	V	I	250+	The World of Fashion	Capstone Press
Fashion Modeling: Being Beautiful, Selling Clothes	V	I	250+	The World of Fashion	Capstone Press
Fashion Trends: How Popular Style Is Shaped	V	I	250+	The World of Fashion	Capstone Press
Fasi Sings and Fasi's Fish	I	RF	204	Pacific Literacy	Pacific Learning
Fast and Faster	B	I	24	Windows on Literacy	National Geographic
Fast and Faster!	D	I	77	Yellow Umbrella Books	Red Brick Learning
*Fast and Funny	J	RF	1499	Story Box	Wright Group/McGraw Hill
Fast and Furious	Q	I	250+	InfoQuest	Rigby
Fast and Slow	F	I	55	Pair-It Turn and Learn	Steck-Vaughn
Fast and Slow	B	F	48	Springboard	Wright Group/McGraw Hill

* Collection of short stories
# Graphic text

Storable Database at www.fountasandpinnellleveledbooks.com

TITLE	LEVEL	GENRE	WORD COUNT	AUTHOR / SERIES	PUBLISHER / DISTRIBUTOR
Fast and Slow: An Animal Opposites Book	K	I	250+	Animal Opposites	Capstone Press
Fast Athletes	C	I	104	Careers Series	Benchmark Education
Fast Food	E	RF	112	Foundations	Wright Group/McGraw Hill
Fast Food Felicity	L	F	250+	Bookweb	Rigby
Fast Food for Butterflies	I	I	170	Storyteller-Moon Rising	Wright Group/McGraw Hill
Fast Forward: Cities of the Future	U	I	250+	Explore More	Wright Group/McGraw Hill
Fast Fox, A	F	F	247	Leveled Literacy Intervention/Blue System	Heinemann
Fast Machines	D	RF	146	Foundations	Wright Group/McGraw Hill
Fast Sam, Cool Clyde, and Stuff	Y	RF	250+	Myers, Walter Dean	Puffin/Penguin
Fast Track	W	RF	250+	Redline Racing Series	Fitzhenry & Whiteside
Fast Track to Success	T	I	250+	WorldScapes	ETA Cuisenaire
Fast, Faster, Fastest	C	I	66	Twig	Wright Group/McGraw Hill
Fast, Not Last	H	F	233	Sunshine	Wright Group/McGraw Hill
Fastback Beach	W	RF	250+	Orca Soundings	Orca Book Publishers
Fast-Draw Freddie	D	F	50	Rookie Readers	Children's Press
Faster! Faster!	H	F	285	Leveled Readers	Houghton Mifflin Harcourt
Fastest Dinosaurs, The	P	I	1070	Meet the Dinosaurs	Lerner Publications
Fastest Gazelle, The	E	RF	146	Literacy 2000	Rigby
*Fastest Ketchup in the Cafeteria and Other Cases, The	O	RF	250+	Simon, Seymour	Avon
Fastest, Longest, Biggest, Lightest	O	I	1769	Reading Street	Pearson
Fat Cat	I	TL	250+	Kent, Jack	Scholastic
Fat Cat Sat on the Mat, The	G	F	250+	Karlin, Nurit	HarperTrophy
Fat Cat Tompkin	I	F	196	Voyages	SRA/McGraw Hill
Fat Cat's Chair	F	F	140	PM Stars	Rigby
Fat Ducks	G	F	253	Sails	Rigby
Fat Pig, The	I	TL	250+	Tiger Cub	Peguis
Fate of Achilles, The	W	TL	1891	Leveled Readers	Houghton Mifflin Harcourt
Fate of Achilles, The	W	TL	1891	Leveled Readers/CA	Houghton Mifflin Harcourt
Father Bear Comes Home	I	F	331	Minarik, Else H.	HarperCollins
Father Bear Goes Fishing	D	F	98	PM Story Books	Rigby
Father Bear's Surprise	H	RF	224	PM Extensions-Green	Rigby
Father Eusebio Francisco Kino: Changing the Colonial Southwest	W	I	2436	Independent Readers Science	Houghton Mifflin Harcourt
Father Fights Back: Franklin Delano Roosevelt and Polio	M	B	250+	Twig	Wright Group/McGraw Hill
Father of the Constitution: A Story about James Madison	S	B	8998	Creative Minds Biographies	Lerner Publications
Father Turk	X	B	250+	WorldScapes	ETA Cuisenaire
*Father Water, Mother Woods	V	RF	250+	Paulsen, Gary	Bantam
Father Who Walked on His Hands, The	K	RF	344	Literacy 2000	Rigby
Father Who Walked on His Hands, The	H	RF	250+	Mahy, Margaret	Scholastic
Fathers	F	I	46	Families	Capstone Press
Fathers	B	I	26	Pebble Books	Capstone Press
Father's Arcane Daughter	V	RF	250+	Konigsburg, E. L.	Aladdin
Father's Garden, A	P	RF	1000	Leveled Readers/TX	Houghton Mifflin Harcourt
Fatima	Q	RF	250+	Bookshop	Mondo
Fats, Oils, and Sweets	F	I	107	Food Groups	Lerner Publications
Fats, Oils, and Sweets	I	I	190	The Food Guide Pyramid	Capstone Press
Favorite Books	H	RF	251	PM Math Readers	Rigby
Favorite Fables	J	TL	667	Leveled Readers/TX	Houghton Mifflin Harcourt
Favorite Games Around the World	Q	I	250+	Sunshine	Wright Group/McGraw Hill
*Favorite Greek Myths	Y	TL	250+	Pope, Mary Osborne	Scholastic

* Collection of short stories
# Graphic text

TITLE	LEVEL	GENRE	WORD COUNT	AUTHOR / SERIES	PUBLISHER / DISTRIBUTOR
Favorite Medieval Tales	S	TL	250+	Pope, Mary Osborne	Scholastic
Favorite Places	C	I	75	Explorations	Eleanor Curtain Publishing
Favorite Places	C	I	75	Explorations	Okapi Educational Materials
Favorite Things	A	I	28	Vocabulary Readers	Houghton Mifflin Harcourt
Favorite Things	A	I	28	Vocabulary Readers/CA	Houghton Mifflin Harcourt
Favorite Things	A	I	28	Vocabulary Readers/TX	Houghton Mifflin Harcourt
Fawn in the Forest, The	H	RF	227	PM Plus Story Books	Rigby
Fawn, The	E	F	69	Reading Street	Pearson
Fawn, The	J	RF	701	The Fawn	Pioneer Valley
Fayim's Incredible Journey	T	RF	250+	High-Fliers	Pacific Learning
Fear in the Dark	W	F	250+	Dark Man	Ransom
Fear of White Water	S	RF	250+	Leveled Readers Language Support	Houghton Mifflin Harcourt
*Fearless Explorer and Other Cases, The	O	RF	250+	Simon, Seymour	Avon
Fearless Feats	U	I	250+	Connectors	Pacific Learning
Fearsome Four, The	M	RF	250+	Bookweb	Rigby
Feast For 10	E	RF	97	Falwell, Cathryn	Scholastic
Feast or Famine?	V	I	250+	WorldScapes	ETA Cuisenaire
Feast, The	E	F	58	Leveled Readers	Houghton Mifflin Harcourt
Featherbys	S	RF	250+	Steele, Mary	Peachtree
Feathered Dinosaurs	P	I	1180	Meet the Dinosaurs	Lerner Publications
Feathered Friends	F	RF	147	Sails	Rigby
Feathered Hunters of the Night	Q	I	959	Vocabulary Readers	Houghton Mifflin Harcourt
Feathered Hunters of the Night	Q	I	959	Vocabulary Readers/CA	Houghton Mifflin Harcourt
Feathered Hunters of the Night	Q	I	959	Vocabulary Readers/TX	Houghton Mifflin Harcourt
Feathers	C	I	39	Bonnell, Kris	Reading Reading Books
Feathers	C	I	104	Sails	Rigby
Feathers	K	RF	250+	Storyteller- Lightning Bolts	Wright Group/McGraw Hill
Feathers and Flight	Q	I	250+	Explorers	Wright Group/McGraw Hill
Feathers and Flight	I	I	790	Sunshine	Wright Group/McGraw Hill
*Feathery Fables	P	TL	250+	Action Packs	Rigby
Federal Bureau of Investigation, The: Hunting Criminals	S	I	250+	Line of Duty	Capstone Press
Feed Me! An Aesop Fable	I	TL	250+	Bank Street	Bantam
Feeding	A	I	40	Sun Sprouts	ETA Cuisenaire
Feeding Our Pets	A	I	25	Leveled Readers	Houghton Mifflin Harcourt
Feeding Our Pets	A	I	25	Leveled Readers/CA	Houghton Mifflin Harcourt
Feeding the Baby	C	I	51	Home Connection Collection	Rigby
Feeding the Lambs	H	RF	61	PM Plus Nonfiction	Rigby
Feeding the Otters	K	I	250+	On Our Way to English	Rigby
Feeding Time	C	RF	55	Carousel Readers	Pearson Learning Group
Feeding Time	A	RF	35	Rigby Rocket	Rigby
Feeding Time at the Zoo	L	I	250+	Scooters	ETA Cuisenaire
Feeding Time at the Zoo	D	RF	73	Windmill Books	Rigby
Feel the Power: Energy All Around	K	I	250+	Spyglass Books	Compass Point Books
Feel, Think, Move	U	I	2136	Reading Street	Pearson
Feeling	G	I	205	PM Science Readers	Rigby
Feeling Angry	F	I	70	Emotions	Red Brick Learning
Feeling Funny	J	F	250+	Sunshine	Wright Group/McGraw Hill
Feeling Great!	S	I	250+	Orbit Collections	Pacific Learning
Feeling Happy	F	I	57	Emotions	Red Brick Learning
Feeling Sad	F	I	62	Emotions	Red Brick Learning
Feeling Scared	F	I	62	Emotions	Red Brick Learning
Feelings	LB	I	12	Canizares, Susan	Scholastic

F

* Collection of short stories
# Graphic text

TITLE	LEVEL	GENRE	WORD COUNT	AUTHOR / SERIES	PUBLISHER / DISTRIBUTOR
Feelings	E	I	133	Rigby Rocket	Rigby
Feelings	D	RF	39	Rise & Shine	Hampton-Brown
Feelings	P	I	250+	Sunshine	Wright Group/McGraw Hill
Feelings	A	I	24	Windows on Literacy	National Geographic
Feet	B	I	21	Animal Traits	Lerner Publications
Feet	H	F	76	Book Bank	Wright Group/McGraw Hill
Feet	A	I	14	Foundations	Wright Group/McGraw Hill
Feet	D	RF	18	Story Box	Wright Group/McGraw Hill
Feet!	LB	I	28	Ray's Readers	Outside the Box
Feisty Old Woman Who Lived in the Cozy Cave	J	F	301	Foundations	Wright Group/McGraw Hill
Felicia the Critic	P	RF	250+	Conford, Ellen	Little, Brown & Co.
Felicity Learns a Lesson	Q	HF	250+	The American Girls Collection	Pleasant Company
Felicity Saves the Day	Q	HF	250+	The American Girls Collection	Pleasant Company
Felicity's Surprise	Q	HF	250+	The American Girls Collection	Pleasant Company
Felita	P	RF	250+	Mohr, Nicholas	Dell
Felix, the Very Hungry Fish	C	F	32	Little Books	Sadlier-Oxford
Fence, The	B	F	44	Bookshop	Mondo
Fence, The	A	RF	24	Handprints A	Educators Publishing Service
Ferdinand Magellan	S	B	3385	History Maker Bios	Lerner Publications
Ferdinand Saves the Day	N	RF	888	Leveled Readers	Houghton Mifflin Harcourt
Ferdinand Saves the Day	N	RF	888	Leveled Readers/CA	Houghton Mifflin Harcourt
Ferdinand Saves the Day	N	RF	888	Leveled Readers/TX	Houghton Mifflin Harcourt
Fergus and Bridey	K	F	250+	Little Celebrations	Pearson Learning Group
Fergus and the Princess	M	F	250+	Rigby Literacy	Rigby
Fern and Burt	H	F	250+	Ready Readers	Pearson Learning Group
Fern Goes Away	F	F	208	Sails	Rigby
Fernitickles	R	HF	250+	Literacy 2000	Rigby
Fern's Purple Birthday	I	F	250+	Phonics Readers Plus	Steck-Vaughn
Ferret Fun	O	RF	250+	Baglio, Ben M.	Scholastic
Ferret in The Bedroom, Lizards in the Fridge	T	RF	250+	Wallace, Bill	Language for learning Assoc.
Ferret Rescue	Q	RF	250+	Reading Expeditions	National Geographic
Ferry, The	C	RF	27	Sunshine	Wright Group/McGraw Hill
Festival Foods Around the World	M	I	250+	Stull, Becky	Steck-Vaughn
Festival Fun	N	I	250+	Wildcats	Wright Group/McGraw Hill
Festival in Valencia	L	RF	301	Leveled Readers	Houghton Mifflin Harcourt
Festival, The	D	I	146	Fiesta Series	Pearson Learning Group
Festival, the	B	I	37	Windows on Literacy	National Geographic
Festivals	F	I	40	Berger, Samantha; Chanko, Pamela	Scholastic
Festivals and Feasts	O	I	250+	InfoQuest	Rigby
Festus the Clownfish Finds a Home	Q	F	250+	Pair-It Books	Steck-Vaughn
Fever 1793	Z	HF	250+	Anderson, Laurie Halse	Simon & Schuster
Fibers from Plants	I	I	392	Sunshine	Wright Group/McGraw Hill
Fibers in Fashion	U	I	250+	PM Plus	Rigby
Fibers Made by People	M	I	442	Sunshine	Wright Group/McGraw Hill
Fibonacci's Cows	U	I	250+	Storyteller -Mountain Peaks	Wright Group/ McGraw Hill
*Fiddle and the Gun, The	M	F	250+	Literacy 2000	Rigby
Fiddle Maker, The	P	RF	4745	Take Two Books	Wright Group/ McGraw Hill
Field Day with Alex, A	D	F	96	Javernick, Ellen	Kaeden Books
Field Full of Horses, A	M	I	250+	Read and Wonder	Candlewick Press
Field Mouse and the Dinosaur Named Sue, The	L	F	250+	Wahl, Jan	Scholastic
Field of Gold	H	TL	172	Rigby Star	Rigby

F

TITLE	LEVEL	GENRE	WORD COUNT	AUTHOR / SERIES	PUBLISHER / DISTRIBUTOR
Field Trip, The	L	RF	853	Springboard	Wright Group/McGraw Hill
Fields of Hope	V	I	250+	WorldScapes	ETA Cuisenaire
Fiesta	D	RF	50	Javernick, Ellen	Kaeden Books
Fiesta Time	C	I	28	Little Celebrations	Pearson Learning Group
Fiesta!	M	I	250+	Festivals and Holidays	Children's Press
Fife and Drum Boys	S	HF	1584	Leveled Readers	Houghton Mifflin Harcourt
Fife and Drum Boys	S	HF	1584	Leveled Readers/CA	Houghton Mifflin Harcourt
Fife and Drum Boys	S	HF	1584	Leveled Readers/TX	Houghton Mifflin Harcourt
FiFi's Bath	K	RF	436	Leveled Readers	Houghton Mifflin Harcourt
FiFi's Bath	K	RF	436	Leveled Readers/CA	Houghton Mifflin Harcourt
FiFi's Bath	K	RF	436	Leveled Readers/TX	Houghton Mifflin Harcourt
Fifth Grade: Here Comes Trouble	S	RF	250+	McKenna, Colleen O'Shaughnessy	Scholastic
Fig Pudding	R	RF	250+	Fletcher, Ralph	Clarion
Figaro	K	F	250+	Voyages	SRA/McGraw Hill
Fight For Freedom: The American Revolutionary War	X	I	250+	Bobrick, Benson	Scholastic
Fight for Right, The	V	I	250+	Power Up!	Steck-Vaughn
Fight in the Schoolyard, The	K	RF	129	City Kids	Rigby
Fight on the Hill, The	I	F	336	Read Alongs	Rigby
Fighter Planes	G	I	115	Mighty Machines	Capstone Press
Fighter Planes	V	I	4968	Military Hardware in Action	Lerner Publications
Fighter Planes	N	I	470	Pull Ahead Books	Lerner Publications
Fighting Fire with Fire	W	I	2951	Leveled Readers	Houghton Mifflin Harcourt
Fighting Fire with Fire	W	I	2951	Leveled Readers/CA	Houghton Mifflin Harcourt
Fighting Fire With Fire	M	I	250+	Rigby Literacy	Rigby
Fighting Fires	G	I	198	Leveled Literacy Intervention/Blue System	Heinemann
Fighting Fires Then and Now	L	I	381	Leveled Readers	Houghton Mifflin Harcourt
Fighting Fish	O	I	250+	Life Cycles	Creative Teaching Press
Fighting for Equal Rights: A Story About Susan B. Anthony	R	B	8730	Creative Minds Biographies	Carolrhoda Books
Fighting for Freedom	Q	B	250+	WorldScapes	ETA Cuisenaire
Fighting for History	R	I	250+	Explorer Books-Pathfinder	National Geographic
Fighting for History	Q	I	250+	Explorer Books-Pioneer	National Geographic
Fighting Ground, The	V	HF	250+	Avi	HarperTrophy
Fighting Tackle	R	RF	250+	Christopher, Matt	Little, Brown & Co.
Figure in the Shadows, The	S	F	250+	Bellairs, John	Penguin Group
Fiji Facts and Figures	O	I	250+	WorldScapes	ETA Cuisenaire
Fiji Flood, The	M	F	250+	Woodland Mysteries	Wright Group/McGraw Hill
Filbert the Fly	C	F	28	Literacy 2000	Rigby
Film	Z	I	250+	Eyewitness Books	DK Publishing
Final Freedom, The	V	RF	250+	Wallace, Bill	Pocket Books
Fina's Story: From Mexico to Texas	U	HF	250+	Reading Expeditions	National Geographic
*Finch Family Summer	M	F	250+	Sunshine	Wright Group/McGraw Hill
Finches' Fabulous Furnace, The	O	F	250+	Drury, Roger	Scholastic
Find a Caterpillar	E	I	102	Book Bank	Wright Group/McGraw Hill
Find a Stranger, Say Goodbye	X	RF	250+	Lowry, Lois	Dell
Find It	C	RF	63	Carousel Earlybirds	Pearson Learning Group
Find It on the Map	G	I	61	Shutterbug Books	Steck-Vaughn
Find Out About It!	T	I	250+	iOpeners	Pearson Learning Group
Find the Bug	A	RF	29	Leveled Readers	Houghton Mifflin Harcourt
Find the Bug	A	RF	29	Leveled Readers/CA	Houghton Mifflin Harcourt

* Collection of short stories
# Graphic text

F

TITLE	LEVEL	GENRE	WORD COUNT	AUTHOR / SERIES	PUBLISHER / DISTRIBUTOR
Find the Prize	E	RF	39	Independent Readers Social Studies	Houghton Mifflin Harcourt
Find the Shapes	B	I	36	InfoTrek	ETA Cuisenaire
Find the Wild Animal	F	I	108	Foley, Cate	Scholastic
Find Yourself a Friend	F	RF	261	Visions	Wright Group/McGraw Hill
Finders Keepers?	T	I	250+	WorldScapes	ETA Cuisenaire
Finding a Dinosaur Named Sue	N	I	615	Reading Street	Pearson
Finding a Way: Six Historic U.S. Routes	W	I	250+	iOpeners	Pearson Learning Group
Finding a Wooly Mammoth	F	I	120	Independent Readers Science	Houghton Mifflin Harcourt
Finding Aunt Maria	N	RF	250+	Windows on Literacy	National Geographic
Finding Buck McHenry	S	RF	250+	Slote, Alfred	Scholastic
Finding Chance	S	RF	250+	Bookshop	Mondo
Finding Elmo	S	RF	250+	Orca Currents	Orca Book Publishers
Finding Gold	N	I	848	Leveled Readers Science	Houghton Mifflin Harcourt
Finding Home Again	U	RF	250+	Reading Expeditions	National Geographic
Finding My Hat	Z	RF	250+	Son, John	Scholastic
Finding Out About the Past	H	I	155	Windows on Literacy	National Geographic
Finding Providence: The Story of Roger Williams	P	B	250+	Avi	HarperTrophy
Finding Talent	L	RF	250+	Literacy by Design	Rigby
Finding Talent	L	RF	250+	On Our Way to English	Rigby
Finding the Party	J	RF	613	Leveled Readers	Houghton Mifflin Harcourt
Finding the Party	J	RF	613	Leveled Readers/CA	Houghton Mifflin Harcourt
Finding the Party	J	RF	613	Leveled Readers/TX	Houghton Mifflin Harcourt
Finding the Pharaohs	V	I	250+	WorldScapes	ETA Cuisenaire
Finding the Titanic	Q	I	250+	Ballard, Robert D.	Scholastic
Finding Your Way	R	I	250+	Orbit Chapter Books	Pacific Learning
Fine Lines	O	B	250+	Meet the Author	Richard C. Owen
Fine Print: A Story about Johann Gutenberg	S	B	7897	Creative Minds Biographies	Lerner Publications
Finger Puppet, The	B	RF	18	Sunshine	Wright Group/McGraw Hill
Finger Puppets, Finger Plays	I	I	268	Storyteller-Night Crickets	Wright Group/McGraw Hill
Fingernail Art: Dazzling Fingers and Terrific Toes	Q	I	250+	Crafts	Capstone Press
Fingerprint Family	C	I	24	Rigby Literacy	Rigby
Fingers and Thumbs	E	I	108	Sails	Rigby
Finicky Fish	L	RF	250+	Rigby Gigglers	Rigby
Finland: A Question and Answer Book	P	I	250+	Questions & Answers: Countries	Capstone Press
Finn MacCool and Big Head MacTavish	J	TL	250+	Lighthouse	Ginn & Co.
Fins, Wings, and Legs	J	I	250+	iOpeners	Pearson Learning Group
Fire	S	HF	250+	Duey, Kathleen; Bale, Karen A.	Aladdin
Fire	S	HF	250+	Duey, Kathleen; Bale, Karen A.	Simon & Schuster
Fire and Ash	P	I	250+	WorldScapes	ETA Cuisenaire
Fire and Ice: Warriors, Book 2	U	F	250+	Hunter, Erin	Avon Books
Fire and Snow: A Tale of the Alaskan Gold Rush	P	HF	250+	Gunderson, J	Stone Arch Books
Fire and Water	E	TL	127	Story Box	Wright Group/McGraw Hill
Fire and Wind	L	TL	250+	PM Story Books-Silver	Rigby
Fire at the Triangle Factory	P	HF	250+	Littlefield, Holly	Carolrhoda Books
Fire at the Zoo, A	I	F	229	Sunshine	Wright Group/McGraw Hill
Fire Boats	I	I	188	Community Vehicles	Capstone Press
Fire Bug Connection, The	S	RF	250+	George, Jean Craighead	HarperTrophy
Fire Cat, The	J	F	250+	Averill, Esther	HarperTrophy
Fire Engines	I	I	184	Community Vehicles	Capstone Press
Fire Fighter!	L	I	250+	DK Readers	DK Publishing
Fire Fighter, The	A	I	25	Leveled Readers	Houghton Mifflin Harcourt

* Collection of short stories
# Graphic text

F

TITLE	LEVEL	GENRE	WORD COUNT	AUTHOR / SERIES	PUBLISHER / DISTRIBUTOR
Fire Fighter, The	A	I	25	Leveled Readers/CA	Houghton Mifflin Harcourt
Fire Fighters	M	I	250+	Community Helpers	Red Brick Learning
Fire Fighters	L	I	250+	Community Workers	Compass Point Books
Fire in the Hills	Y	RF	250+	Myers, Anna	Puffin/Penguin
Fire in the Sky	R	I	1215	Leveled Readers	Houghton Mifflin Harcourt
Fire in the Sky	R	I	1215	Leveled Readers/CA	Houghton Mifflin Harcourt
Fire in the Sky	R	HF	250+	Ransom, Candice F.	Carolrhoda Books
Fire in the Wind	U	RF	250+	Levin, Betty	Beech Tree Books
Fire in Wild Wood	G	F	214	Storyworlds	Heinemann Educational Books
Fire on Toytown Hill, The	F	F	166	PM Plus Story Books	Rigby
Fire Safety Day	M	RF	749	Leveled Readers	Houghton Mifflin Harcourt
Fire Station, The	J	I	237	Pebble Books	Capstone Press
Fire Trucks	G	I	127	Mighty Machines	Capstone Press
Fire Trucks	K	I	327	Pull Ahead Books	Lerner Publications
Fire Trucks	M	I	250+	Transportation	Compass Point Books
Fire Zenith, The	R	F	250+	Sails	Rigby
Fire!	Q	I	250+	Bookweb	Rigby
Fire!	I	RF	224	Breakthrough	Longman
Fire!	M	RF	250+	Rigby Flying Colors	Rigby
Fire!	K	F	250+	Rigby Literacy	Rigby
Fire! Fire!	I	I	384	Big Cat	Pacific Learning
Fire! Fire!	P	I	250+	Orbit Chapter Books	Pacific Learning
Fire! Fire!	E	RF	164	PM Story Books	Rigby
Fire! Fire!	L	I	250+	Storyteller Chapter Books	Wright Group/ McGraw Hill
Fire! Fire!	O	I	250+	Wildcats	Wright Group/McGraw Hill
Fire! in Yellowstone: A True Adventure	O	I	250+	Soar To Success	Houghton Mifflin Harcourt
Fire! The Beginnings of the Labor Movement	R	HF	250+	Goldin, Barbara Diamond	Puffin/Penguin
Fire, Bed & Bone	X	HF	250+	Branford, Henrietta	Candlewick Press
Fire, The	D	RF	120	Sails	Rigby
*Fire-Bird, The	U	TL	250+	Literacy 2000	Rigby
Firedog!	G	RF	217	Leveled Readers	Houghton Mifflin Harcourt
Firedog!	G	RF	217	Leveled Readers/CA	Houghton Mifflin Harcourt
Firedog!	G	RF	217	Leveled Readers/TX	Houghton Mifflin Harcourt
Firefighter	C	I	23	Work People Do	Lerner Publishing
Firefighter Wears a Helmet, A	F	I	79	Windows on Literacy	National Geographic
Firefighters	E	RF	250+	Bookshop	Mondo
Firefighters	L	I	250+	Mitten, Christopher	Scholastic
Firefighters	J	I	167	Nonfiction Set 7	Literacy Footprints
Firefighters	K	I	470	Pull Ahead Books	Lerner Publications
Firefighters	L	I	623	Sun Sprouts	ETA Cuisenaire
Firefighters	T	I	250+	The News	Richard C. Owen
Firefighters in America	M	I	619	Leveled Readers	Houghton Mifflin Harcourt
Firefighters in America	M	I	619	Leveled Readers/CA	Houghton Mifflin Harcourt
Firefighters in America	M	I	619	Leveled Readers/TX	Houghton Mifflin Harcourt
Firefighters: Then and Now	M	I	250+	Primary Source Readers	Teacher Created Materials
Firefighting Then and Now	T	I	2226	Leveled Readers	Houghton Mifflin Harcourt
Firefighting Then and Now	T	I	2226	Leveled Readers/CA	Houghton Mifflin Harcourt
Fireflies	H	I	135	Bugs, Bugs, Bugs!	Capstone Press
Fireflies	Q	I	2704	Early Bird Nature Books	Lerner Publications
Fireflies	L	I	289	Leveled Readers	Houghton Mifflin Harcourt
Fireflies	L	I	289	Leveled Readers/CA	Houghton Mifflin Harcourt
Fireflies	L	I	289	Leveled Readers/TX	Houghton Mifflin Harcourt
Fireflies	F	I	85	Little Celebrations	Pearson Learning Group

F

* Collection of short stories
# Graphic text

TITLE	LEVEL	GENRE	WORD COUNT	AUTHOR / SERIES	PUBLISHER / DISTRIBUTOR
Fireflies	O	I	250+	Nature's Friends	Compass Point Books
Fireflies	E	I	49	Pebble Books	Capstone Press
Fireflies	E	I	57	Vocabulary Readers	Houghton Mifflin Harcourt
Fireflies in the Night	M	I	250+	Hawes, Judy	HarperTrophy
Fireflies!	L	I	250+	Twig	Wright Group/McGraw Hill
Firefly and the Quest of the Black Squirrel: The Fairy Chronicles	Q	F	12800	Sweet, J.H.	Sourcebooks
Firefly Named Torchy, A	L	F	250+	Waber, Bernard	Houghton Mifflin Harcourt
Firehouse	A	I	36	Vocabulary Readers	Houghton Mifflin Harcourt
Firehouse	A	I	36	Vocabulary Readers/CA	Houghton Mifflin Harcourt
Firehouse	A	I	36	Vocabulary Readers/TX	Houghton Mifflin Harcourt
Firehouse Sal	F	RF	52	Rookie Readers	Children's Press
Firelight Secrets	O	RF	250+	PM Collection	Rigby
Fires	W	I	250+	Disasters Up Close	Lerner Publications
Fires in the Wild	U	I	250+	Sails	Rigby
Firetalking	O	B	250+	Meet The Author	Richard C. Owen
Firewing	Y	F	250+	Oppel, Kenneth	Aladdin
Firework-Maker's Daughter, The	V	F	250+	Pullman, Philip	Scholastic
Fireworks	C	RF	29	Joy Readers	Pearson Learning Group
Fireworks!	P	I	889	Leveled Readers Science	Houghton Mifflin Harcourt
First Aid	F	I	44	Canizares, Susan; Chanko, Pamela	Scholastic
First Americans, The	O	I	250+	People, Spaces & Places	Rand McNally
First and Final Voyage, The: The Sinking of the Titanic	O	HF	250+	Peters, Stephanie	Stone Arch Books
First and Last	C	I	44	Teacher's Choice Series	Pearson Learning Group
First Apple	N	RF	250+	Russell, Ching Yueng	Penguin Group
First Art Class, The	G	RF	250+	Leveled Readers Language Support	Houghton Mifflin Harcourt
First Big Game, The	N	HF	821	Reading Street	Pearson
First Book About Africa: An Introduction for Young Readers	Q	I	250+	Ellis, Veronica Freeman	Just Us Books
First Builders, The	O	I	250+	Orbit Chapter Books	Pacific Learning
First Cowboys, The	Q	I	1180	Vocabulary Readers	Houghton Mifflin Harcourt
First Day	C	RF	64	InfoTrek	ETA Cuisenaire
First Day Back at School	H	RF	132	City Kids	Rigby
First Day for Carlos	P	RF	764	Leveled Readers	Houghton Mifflin Harcourt
First Day Jitters	L	RF	250+	Danneberg, Julie	Charlesbridge
First Day of School	D	RF	60	Carousel Readers	Pearson Learning Group
First Day of School	LB	RF	16	Visions	Wright Group/McGraw Hill
First Day of School, The	A	RF	28	Bookshop	Mondo
First Day of School, The	G	RF	262	Handprints D	Educators Publishing Service
First Day of Second Grade	H	RF	263	Leveled Readers	Houghton Mifflin Harcourt
First Day of Second Grade	H	RF	263	Leveled Readers/CA	Houghton Mifflin Harcourt
First Day of Second Grade	H	RF	263	Leveled Readers/TX	Houghton Mifflin Harcourt
First Day of Winter, The	I	RF	250+	Fleming, Denise	Scholastic
First Emperor, The	W	I	1617	Vocabulary Readers	Houghton Mifflin Harcourt
First Emperor, The	W	I	1617	Vocabulary Readers/CA	Houghton Mifflin Harcourt
First Family on Mars, The	P	SF	250+	Orbit Double Takes	Pacific Learning
First Family: The Roosevelts	U	B	2374	Independent Readers Social Studies	Houghton Mifflin Harcourt
First Fire Company, The	J	I	182	Leveled Readers	Houghton Mifflin Harcourt
First Fire, The	K	F	250+	Little Celebrations	Pearson Learning Group

* Collection of short stories
\# Graphic text

F

TITLE	LEVEL	GENRE	WORD COUNT	AUTHOR / SERIES	PUBLISHER / DISTRIBUTOR
First Fire: A Traditional Native American Tale	K	TL	250+	Rigby Literacy	Rigby
First Flight	Q	I	250+	Explorer Books-Pathfinder	National Geographic
First Flight	P	I	250+	Explorer Books-Pioneer	National Geographic
First Flight	J	RF	250+	PM Plus Story Books	Rigby
First Flight	K	B	250+	Shea, George	HarperTrophy
First Flight: The Story of the Wright Brothers	R	B	250+	DK Readers	DK Publishing
First Four Years, The	R	HF	250+	Wilder, Laura Ingalls	HarperTrophy
First French Kiss and Other Traumas	Z+	RF	250+	Bagdasarian, Adam	Farrar, Straus and Giroux
First Geologists, The	U	B	250+	Science Readers	Teacher Created Materials
First Grade Takes a Test	J	RF	250+	Cohen, Miriam	Bantam
First Hot-Air Balloons, The	M	I	250+	Take Two Books	Wright Group/McGraw Hill
First Humans, The	U	I	1814	Leveled Readers Social Studies	Houghton Mifflin Harcourt
First in Line	D	RF	77	Teacher's Choice Series	Pearson Learning Group
First in Space	R	I	250+	WorldScapes	ETA Cuisenaire
First Journeys	X	I	250+	iOpeners	Pearson Learning Group
First Ladies	U	B	250+	Cornerstones of Freedom	Children's Press
*First Ladies of the White House	U	B	250+	Skarmeas, Nancy	Ideals Publications Inc.
*First Ladies: Women Who Called the White House Home	U	B	250+	Gormley, Beatrice	Scholastic
First Lady of Track, The	O	I	885	Vocabulary Readers	Houghton Mifflin Harcourt
First Lady of Track, The	O	I	885	Vocabulary Readers/CA	Houghton Mifflin Harcourt
First Lady of Track, The	O	I	885	Vocabulary Readers/TX	Houghton Mifflin Harcourt
First Morning, The	N	TL	250+	Literacy 2000	Rigby
First Olympians, The	Y	I	2437	Vocabulary Readers	Houghton Mifflin Harcourt
First Olympians, The	Y	I	2437	Vocabulary Readers/CA	Houghton Mifflin Harcourt
First on the Moon	Y	I	250+	Hehner, Barbara	Hyperion
First Part Last, The	Z+	RF	250+	Johnson, Angela	Simon & Schuster
First Snow	WB	RF	N/A	McCully, Emily Arnold	Harper & Row
First Son and President: A Story about John Quincy Adams	S	B	8707	Creative Minds Biographies	Lerner Publications
First Thanksgiving, The	R	I	250+	The Library of the Pilgrims	Rosen Publishing Group
First Things	LB	RF	18	Home Connection Collection	Rigby
First Things	N	RF	250+	Stepping Stones	Nelson/Michaels Assoc.
First Woman Doctor, The	P	B	880	Leveled Readers	Houghton Mifflin Harcourt
First Woman Doctor, The	P	B	880	Leveled Readers/CA	Houghton Mifflin Harcourt
First Woman Doctor, The	P	B	880	Leveled Readers/TX	Houghton Mifflin Harcourt
First Woman Doctor, The	T	B	250+	Rachel Baker	Scholastic
First Year Letters	M	RF	250+	Danneberg, Julie	Charlesbridge
First Year, The	N	HF	922	Reading Street	Pearson
First, Second, Third	D	I	28	Shutterbug Books	Steck-Vaughn
First, Take the Flour	L	I	186	Rigby Literacy	Rigby
First-Aid Handbook	S	I	250+	iOpeners	Pearson Learning Group
Firsts in Forecasting	T	I	1439	Vocabulary Readers	Houghton Mifflin Harcourt
Firsts in Forecasting	T	I	1439	Vocabulary Readers/CA	Houghton Mifflin Harcourt
Fish	D	I	34	All About Pets	Red Brick Learning
Fish	M	I	250+	Exploring the Animal Kingdom	Capstone Press
Fish	W	I	250+	Eyewitness Books	DK Publishing
Fish	L	I	298	Marine Life For Young Readers	Pearson Learning Group
Fish	O	I	250+	Nature's Friends	Compass Point Books
Fish	D	I	58	Sun Sprouts	ETA Cuisenaire
Fish	D	I	58	Wonder World	Wright Group/McGraw Hill
Fish and the Cat, The	C	F	91	Sun Sprouts	ETA Cuisenaire
Fish Bowl, The	C	I	48	Sun Sprouts	ETA Cuisenaire
Fish Can Swim	E	I	102	Reading Street	Pearson

F

TITLE	LEVEL	GENRE	WORD COUNT	AUTHOR / SERIES	PUBLISHER / DISTRIBUTOR
Fish Colors	LB	I	6	Vocabulary Readers	Houghton Mifflin Harcourt
Fish Colours	C	I	37	Rigby Rocket	Rigby
Fish Face	M	RF	250+	Giff, Patricia Reilly	Bantam
Fish Facts	D	I	55	Rigby Rocket	Rigby
Fish Facts	C	I	27	Shutterbug Books	Steck-Vaughn
Fish for Dinner	C	RF	93	Sails	Rigby
Fish for Lunch, A	D	F	62	Rigby Star	Rigby
Fish for Sale	K	RF	250+	SupaDoopers	Sundance
Fish for You, A: Caring for Your Fish	M	I	250+	Pet Care	Picture Window Books
Fish from the Rainbow	I	F	239	Sunshine	Wright Group/McGraw Hill
Fish Gut Experiment, The	T	F	250+	Starke, R.	Stone Arch Books
Fish Guts	J	RF	439	Rigby Gigglers	Rigby
Fish Is Fish	L	F	250+	Lionni, Leo	Scholastic
Fish Named Goggles, A	H	RF	218	PM Photo Stories	Rigby
Fish on the Move	P	I	1061	Leveled Readers	Houghton Mifflin Harcourt
Fish on the Move	P	I	1061	Leveled Readers/CA	Houghton Mifflin Harcourt
Fish on the Move	P	I	1061	Leveled Readers/TX	Houghton Mifflin Harcourt
Fish Picture, A	B	RF	58	First Stories	Pacific Learning
Fish Print	B	I	25	Bebop Books	Lee & Low Books Inc.
Fish Stew for Supper	C	I	56	First Stories	Pacific Learning
Fish Story, A	C	I	51	Coulton, Mia	Maryruth Books
Fish Tank, The	C	I	91	Leveled Literacy Intervention/ Blue System	Heinemann
Fish that Hide	L	I	250+	Marine Life For Young Readers	Pearson Learning Group
Fish That Migrate	P	I	1039	Leveled Readers	Houghton Mifflin Harcourt
Fish That Migrate	P	I	1039	Leveled Readers/CA	Houghton Mifflin Harcourt
Fish That Migrate	P	I	1039	Leveled Readers/TX	Houghton Mifflin Harcourt
Fishers: Then and Now	N	I	250+	Primary Source Readers	Teacher Created Materials
Fishing	G	RF	180	Foundations	Wright Group/McGraw Hill
Fishing	C	RF	15	Instant Readers	Harcourt School Publishers
Fishing	C	I	35	KinderReaders	Rigby
Fishing	C	I	100	Leveled Literacy Intervention/ Blue System	Heinemann
Fishing	B	I	41	Little Books for Early Readers	University of Maine
Fishing	C	RF	63	PM Starters	Rigby
Fishing	B	F	40	Reed, Janet	Scholastic
Fishing	C	RF	35	Story Box	Wright Group/McGraw Hill
Fishing	E	RF	47	Wonder World	Wright Group/McGraw Hill
Fishing	D	RF	48	Yukish, Joe	Kaeden Books
Fishing Adventure, The	H	F	232	Arctic Stories	Pioneer Valley
Fishing Bears	K	I	321	Pull Ahead Books	Lerner Publications
Fishing Contest, The	E	RF	84	Literacy Tree	Rigby
Fishing Contest, The	H	RF	250+	Yukish, Joe	Kaeden Books
Fishing Family	L	I	281	Independent Readers Science	Houghton Mifflin Harcourt
Fishing Fun	I	RF	250+	Bebop Books	Lee & Low Books Inc.
Fishing Game, The	D	RF	69	Windows on Literacy	National Geographic
Fishing Is Fun	G	I	207	Rigby Flying Colors	Rigby
Fishing Off the Wharf	M	RF	274	Pacific Literacy	Pacific Learning
Fishing Trip, The	E	RF	121	Adams, Lorraine; Bruvold, Lynn	Eagle Crest Books
Fishing Trip, The	B	RF	74	Literacy by Design	Rigby
Fishing Trip, The	K	RF	250+	PM Plus Story Books	Rigby
Fishing Trip, The	D	RF	89	Springboard	Wright Group/McGraw Hill
Fishing with Sam	U	RF	2764	Leveled Readers	Houghton Mifflin Harcourt
Fishing with Sam	U	RF	2764	Leveled Readers/CA	Houghton Mifflin Harcourt

* Collection of short stories
\# Graphic text

TITLE	LEVEL	GENRE	WORD COUNT	AUTHOR / SERIES	PUBLISHER / DISTRIBUTOR
Fishing with the Birds	N	I	250+	WorldScapes	ETA Cuisenaire
Fishing!	C	RF	40	Sails	Rigby
Fishy Alphabet Story	F	F	126	Wylie, Joanne & David	Children's Press
Fishy Color Story	D	F	142	Wylie, Joanne & David	Children's Press
Fishy Mystery, The	N	RF	250+	Orbit Chapter Books	Pacific Learning
Fishy Scales	I	F	107	Mathtales	Mimosa
Fishy Story, A	L	F	174	Books for Young Learners	Richard C. Owen
Fishy Story, A	C	F	102	Pair-It Books	Steck-Vaughn
Fishy, Flashy Fourth, The	M	RF	250+	Woodland Mysteries	Wright Group/McGraw Hill
Fitness	C	F	60	Foundations	Wright Group/McGraw Hill
Fitness and Training	N	I	667	Vocabulary Readers	Houghton Mifflin Harcourt
Fitness and Training	N	I	667	Vocabulary Readers/CA	Houghton Mifflin Harcourt
Fitting In	T	I	250+	WorldScapes	ETA Cuisenaire
Five and Five are Ten	F	I	128	PM Math Readers	Rigby
Five Beans	H	I	197	Sun Sprouts	ETA Cuisenaire
Five Bears All in a Den	E	E	88	Reading Street	Pearson
Five Birds and Five Mice	D	RF	108	PM Math Readers	Rigby
Five Boxes	F	RF	203	In Step Readers	Rigby
*Five Brave Explorers	Q	B	250+	Hudson, Wade	Scholastic
*Five Brilliant Scientists	Q	B	250+	Jones, Lynda	Scholastic
Five Danny Dogs	F	F	122	Coulton, Mia	Maryruth Books
Five Days to Go!	K	RF	250+	Rigby Literacy	Rigby
Five Ducks	D	RF	89	Joy Readers	Pearson Learning Group
*Five Funny Frights	K	RF	250+	Bauer, Judith	Scholastic
Five Funny Uncles	I	RF	269	Story Box	Wright Group/McGraw Hill
Five Little Dinosaurs	E	F	113	Ready Readers	Pearson Learning Group
Five Little Dogs	D	F	123	Bella and Rosie Series	Literacy Footprints
Five Little Monkeys	F	F	81	Bookshop	Mondo
Five Little Monkeys	G	F	160	Cambridge Reading	Pearson Learning Group
Five Little Monkeys Going to the Zoo	E	F	201	Valerie Cutteridge's First Grade	Continental Press
Five Little Monkeys Jumping on the Bed	E	TL	200	Christelow, Eileen	Houghton Mifflin Harcourt
Five Little Monsters	D	F	146	Learn to Read	Creative Teaching Press
Five Little Monsters Went to School	E	F	65	Learn to Read	Creative Teaching Press
Five Little Speckled Frogs	G	RF	180	Tiger Cub	Peguis
*Five Notable Inventors	Q	B	250+	Hudson, Wade	Scholastic
Five Senses	G	I	122	Dominie Factivity Series	Pearson Learning Group
Five Senses	D	RF	101	Sun Sprouts	ETA Cuisenaire
Five Senses, The	C	I	53	Rigby Focus	Rigby
Five Senses, The	K	I	280	Story Box	Wright Group/McGraw Hill
Five Senses, The	S	I	250+	Time for Kids	Teacher Created Materials
Five Silly Fishermen	G	TL	250+	Edwards, Roberta	Random House
*Five True Dog Stories	M	I	250+	Davidson, Margaret	Scholastic
*Five True Horse Stories	M	I	250+	Davidson, Margaret	Scholastic
Five-Dog Night, The	P	RF	250+	Christelow, Eileen	Clarion
Fix It	C	I	35	InfoTrek	ETA Cuisenaire
Fix It	I	F	171	McPhail, David	Penguin Group
Fix It, Fox	E	F	62	Ready Readers	Pearson Learning Group
Fixing Things	L	I	250+	Explorations	Okapi Eductional Materials
Fixing Things	L	I	250+	Explorations	Eleanor Curtain Publishing
Fizz and Splutter	E	F	92	Story Box	Wright Group/McGraw Hill
Fizzkid the Inventor	J	F	250+	Rigby Literacy	Rigby
Flag	W	I	250+	Eyewitness Books	DK Publishing
Flag Book, The	N	I	792	InfoTrek	ETA Cuisenaire
Flag Day	Q	I	250+	Holiday Histories	Heinemann Library

TITLE	LEVEL	GENRE	WORD COUNT	AUTHOR / SERIES	PUBLISHER / DISTRIBUTOR
Flag Day	L	I	116	National Holidays	Red Brick Learning
Flag for All, A	I	RF	250+	Rookie Choices	Children's Press
Flag for Our Country, A	N	I	250+	Spencer, Eve	Steck-Vaughn
Flag Throwers, The	R	I	250+	WorldScapes	ETA Cuisenaire
Flag with Fifty-six Stars: A Gift from the Survivors of Mauthausen, The	Y	I	250+	Rubin, Susan Goldman	Holiday House
Flags	R	I	250+	Action Packs	Rigby
Flags	U	I	250+	iOpeners	Pearson Learning Group
Flags	D	RF	41	Windows on Literacy	National Geographic
Flags Everywhere!	B	I	25	Independent Readers Social Studies	Houghton Mifflin Harcourt
Flakes and Flurries: A Book About Snow	M	I	250+	Amazing Science	Picture Window Books
Flamenco, Ole!	U	I	1729	Vocabulary Readers	Houghton Mifflin Harcourt
Flamenco, Olé!	U	I	1729	Vocabulary Readers/CA	Houghton Mifflin Harcourt
Flaming Arrows	T	HF	250+	Steele, William O.	Harcourt Trade
Flamingo Chick Grows Up, A	L	I	447	Baby Animals	Lerner Publications
Flamingos	N	I	250+	Take Two Books	Wright Group/McGraw Hill
Flap and Sing: Birds	E	I	100+	Douglas, Ian	Scholastic
Flap, Flap, Fly	C	F	93	Leveled Literacy Intervention/Orange System	Heinemann
Flash Flood	N	RF	853	Reading Street	Pearson
Flash Flood!	O	I	1784	Independent Readers Science	Houghton Mifflin Harcourt
Flash Point	Y	RF	250+	Collard, Sneed B.	Peachtree
Flash: The Puppy Place	N	RF	250+	Miles, Ellen	Scholastic
Flashlights	J	I	250+	Sunshine	Wright Group/McGraw Hill
Flat Hat, The	C	I	24	KinderReaders	Rigby
Flat Stanley	M	F	250+	Brown, Jeff	HarperTrophy
Flatboat Mondays	U	I	2452	Independent Readers Social Studies	Houghton Mifflin Harcourt
Flavors and Fragrances	T	I	1987	Leveled Readers Science	Houghton Mifflin Harcourt
Flea and Big Bill	E	F	126	Sails	Rigby
Flea and Robber Cat	G	F	185	Sails	Rigby
Flea at the Football Game	I	F	248	Sails	Rigby
Flea Gets Wet	C	F	106	Sails	Rigby
Flea Goes Out!	E	F	151	Sails	Rigby
Flea Story, A	L	F	250+	Lionni, Leo	Scholastic
Flea Treat	L	F	250+	Rigby Rocket	Rigby
Fledgling, The	U	F	250+	Langton, Jane	Scholastic
Flicking the Switch	O	I	250+	Pacific Literacy	Pacific Learning
Flies	O	I	250+	A True Book	Children's Press
Flies	F	I	56	Pebble Books	Capstone Press
Flies for Dinner	C	I	37	Gear Up!	Wright Group/McGraw Hill
Flight #116 Is Down!	Z	RF	250+	Cooney, Caroline B.	Scholastic
Flight Deck	C	I	30	Wonder World	Wright Group/McGraw Hill
Flight of the Swallows	N	I	606	Vocabulary Readers	Houghton Mifflin Harcourt
Flight of the Swallows	N	I	606	Vocabulary Readers/CA	Houghton Mifflin Harcourt
Flight of the Swallows	N	I	606	Vocabulary Readers/TX	Houghton Mifflin Harcourt
Flight of the Union, The	L	B	250+	White, Tekla	Carolrhoda Books
Flight Path	P	I	250+	InfoQuest	Rigby
Flight: The Journey of Charles Lindbergh	R	I	250+	Burleigh, Robert	Putnam/Penguin
Flip Flop	G	RF	70	Books for Young Learners	Richard C. Owen
Flip, Flap, Flop	I	F	252	Sunshine	Wright Group/McGraw Hill
Flipped	U	RF	250+	Van Draanen, Wendelin	Random House
Flip's Trick	H	RF	134	Ready Readers	Pearson Learning Group

* Collection of short stories
\# Graphic text

F

TITLE	LEVEL	GENRE	WORD COUNT	AUTHOR / SERIES	PUBLISHER / DISTRIBUTOR
Flips, Twists, and Somersaults	T	RF	250+	Reading Safari	Mondo
Float and Sink	E	I	44	Forces and Motion	Lerner Publishing
Floating	C	I	29	Little Blue Readers	Sundance
Floating	K	RF	250+	Sunshine	Wright Group/McGraw Hill
Floating and Paddling	N	I	250+	Take Two Books	Wright Group/McGraw Hill
Floating and Sinking	J	I	221	Alphakids	Sundance
Floating and Sinking	J	I	168	Bookshop	Mondo
Floating and Sinking	P	I	250+	Our Physical World	Capstone Press
Floating and Sinking	H	I	168	Sunshine	Wright Group/McGraw Hill
Floating Circus, The	W	HF	250+	Zimmer, Tracie Vaughn	Bloomsbury Children's Books
Floating Island, The	X	F	250+	Haydon, Elizabeth	Tom Doherty
Floating Jellyfish	L	I	390	Pull Ahead Books	Lerner Publications
Floating Markets of Bangkok, The	L	I	250+	Sunshine	Wright Group/McGraw Hill
Floating on Air	Q	F	1332	Leveled Readers	Houghton Mifflin Harcourt
Floating on Airships	V	I	2715	Vocabulary Readers	Houghton Mifflin Harcourt
Floating on Airships	V	I	2715	Vocabulary Readers/CA	Houghton Mifflin Harcourt
Flood	S	HF	250+	Duey, Kathleen; Bale, Karen A.	Simon & Schuster
Flood	H	RF	170	Story Box	Wright Group/McGraw Hill
Flood!	K	RF	250+	Rigby Literacy	Rigby
Flood, The	H	RF	237	PM Story Books	Rigby
Flood, The	I	I	138	Wonder World	Wright Group/McGraw Hill
Floods	O	I	250+	A True Book	Children's Press
Floods	W	I	250+	Disasters Up Close	Lerner Publications
Floods	R	I	1142	Leveled Readers	Houghton Mifflin Harcourt
Floods	M	I	708	Pull Ahead Books	Lerner Publications
Floods	S	I	250+	Theme Sets	National Geographic
Floppy the Hero	F	F	74	Oxford Reading Tree	Oxford University Press
Floppy's Bath	E	F	55	Oxford Reading Tree	Oxford University Press
Flora the Fly Saves the Spiders	J	RF	353	Leveled Readers	Houghton Mifflin Harcourt
Flora the Fly Saves the Spiders	J	RF	353	Leveled Readers/CA	Houghton Mifflin Harcourt
Flora the Fly Saves the Spiders	J	RF	353	Leveled Readers/TX	Houghton Mifflin Harcourt
Flora to the Rescue	H	F	250+	Storyworlds	Heinemann Educational Books
Flora, a Friend for the Animals	J	RF	337	Sunshine	Wright Group/McGraw Hill
Florence Griffith-Joyner: Olympic Champion	K	B	184	Leveled Readers	Houghton Mifflin Harcourt
Florence Griffith-Joyner: Olympic Runner	J	B	184	Leveled Readers Language Support	Houghton Mifflin Harcourt
Florence Kelley	P	B	250+	Saller, Carol	Carolrhoda Books
Florence Nightingale	P	B	1996	On My Own Biography	Lerner Publications
Florence Nightingale	N	B	228	Pebble Books	Capstone Press
Florence Nightingale	P	B	250+	Photo-Illustrated Biographies	Red Brick Learning
#Florence Nightingale: Lady with the Lamp	R	B	250+	Graphic Library	Capstone Press
Florida	T	I	250+	Hello U.S.A.	Lerner Publications
Florida	S	I	250+	Land of Liberty	Red Brick Learning
Florida	Q	I	250+	One Nation	Capstone Press
Florida	R	I	250+	This Land Is Your Land	Compass Point Books
Florida Everglades, The	P	I	712	Gear Up	Wright Group/ McGraw Hill
Florida Everglades: Its Plants & Animals	O	I	670	Reading Street	Pearson
Florida Marlins, The	S	I	250+	Team Spirit	Norwood House Press
Flossie and the Fox	O	F	250+	McKissack, Patricia	Scholastic
Flossing Teeth	G	I	142	Healthy Teeth	Capstone Press
Flour	K	I	174	Wonder World	Wright Group/McGraw Hill
Flower Box, The	LB	I	14	Twig	Wright Group/McGraw Hill

* Collection of short stories
# Graphic text

F

TITLE	LEVEL	GENRE	WORD COUNT	AUTHOR / SERIES	PUBLISHER / DISTRIBUTOR
Flower Farms	L	I	445	Rigby Flying Colors	Rigby
Flower for a Bee, A	D	F	71	Bonnell, Kris	Reading Reading Books
Flower Garden	J	RF	146	Bunting, Eve	Scholastic
Flower Girl, The	C	RF	90	PM Extensions-Red	Rigby
Flower Girls # 1: Violet	L	RF	250+	Leverich, Kathleen	HarperTrophy
Flower Girls # 2: Daisy	L	RF	250+	Leverich, Kathleen	HarperTrophy
Flower Girls # 3: Heather	L	RF	250+	Leverich, Kathleen	HarperTrophy
Flower Girls # 4: Rose	L	RF	250+	Leverich, Kathleen	HarperTrophy
Flower of Sheba, The	L	TL	250+	Orgel, Doris; Schecter, Ellen	Bantam
Flower Power	S	RF	250+	Orca Currents	Orca Book Publishers
Flower Robber, The	G	RF	173	Sails	Rigby
Flower, The	A	I	32	Leveled Literacy Intervention/ Orange System	Heinemann
Flower, The	A	I	20	Vocabulary Readers	Houghton Mifflin Harcourt
Flower, The	A	I	20	Vocabulary Readers/CA	Houghton Mifflin Harcourt
Flowers	A	I	27	Bookshop	Mondo
Flowers	B	I	31	Explorations	Okapi Eductaional Materials
Flowers	B	I	31	Explorations	Eleanor Curtain Publishing
Flowers	A	I	27	Hoenecke, Karen	Kaeden Books
Flowers	E	I	29	Parts of Plants	Lerner Publishing
Flowers	L	I	270	Pebble Books	Capstone Press
Flowers	I	I	118	Plant Parts	Capstone Press
Flowers for Algernon	Z	RF	250+	Keyes, Daniel	Harcourt Trade
Flowers for Grandma	E	RF	131	PM Stars	Rigby
Flowers for Grandma	LB	RF	8	Windows on Literacy	National Geographic
Flowers for Mom	E	RF	88	Carousel Readers	Pearson Learning Group
Flowers for Mrs. Falepau	M	RF	857	Book Bank	Wright Group/McGraw Hill
Flowers Have Colors	B	I	29	Cherrington, Janelle	Scholastic
Flowers Like Worms	C	F	45	Bonnell, Kris	Reading Reading Books
Flows & Quakes and Spinning Winds	K	I	250+	Home Connection Collection	Rigby
Flu	K	I	250+	Health Matters	Capstone Press
Fluffy Chicks	E	RF	50	Book Bank	Wright Group/McGraw Hill
Fluffy: Scourge of the Sea	Q	F	250+	Bateman, Teresa	Charlesbridge
Fluffy's Accident	F	RF	136	Adams, Lorraine; Bruvold, Lynn	Eagle Crest Books
Fluffy's Trip	K	F	250+	Sunshine	Wright Group/McGraw Hill
Flunking of Joshua T. Bates, The	Q	RF	250+	Shreve, Susan	Alfred A. Knopf
Flutey Family Fruitcake, The	K	F	250+	Storyteller- Lightning Bolts	Wright Group/McGraw Hill
Fly Away	H	RF	195	Reading Street	Pearson
Fly Away Home	A	F	28	Big Cat	Pacific Learning
Fly Away Home	P	RF	250+	Bunting, Eve	Clarion Books
Fly Away Home	I	I	250+	Wonder World	Wright Group/McGraw Hill
Fly Away, Children	S	I	548	Vocabulary Readers	Houghton Mifflin Harcourt
Fly Facts	M	I	423	Big Cat	Pacific Learning
Fly Fishing	S	I	250+	The Great Outdoors	Capstone Press
Fly High	B	RF	24	Visions	Wright Group/McGraw Hill
Fly Homer Fly	N	F	250+	Peet, Bill	Houghton Mifflin Harcourt
Fly Like a Bird	R	I	1212	Reading Street	Pearson
Fly Like the Eagle	K	RF	603	Rigby Flying Colors	Rigby
Fly Spy	I	RF	350	InfoTrek	ETA Cuisenaire
Fly to the Rescue!	J	RF	384	Leveled Readers	Houghton Mifflin Harcourt
Fly to the Rescue!	J	RF	384	Leveled Readers/CA	Houghton Mifflin Harcourt
Fly to the Rescue!	J	RF	384	Leveled Readers/TX	Houghton Mifflin Harcourt
Fly Trap	L	F	250+	Anastasio, Dina	Grossett & Dunlap
Fly, Butterfly	F	I	49	Discovery Links	Newbridge

* Collection of short stories
# Graphic text

F

TITLE	LEVEL	GENRE	WORD COUNT	AUTHOR / SERIES	PUBLISHER / DISTRIBUTOR
Fly, The	D	F	78	Story Steps	Rigby
Fly-away Umbrella, The	M	F	250+	Voyages	SRA/McGraw Hill
Flyer Flew, The: The Invention of the Airplane	O	I	1815	On My Own Science	Lerner Publications
Flyers	I	RF	250+	Rigby Literacy	Rigby
Flyers	I	RF	250+	Rigby Star	Rigby
Flyers and Swimmers	B	I	39	Sails	Rigby
Fly-Fishing with Grandpa	O	RF	1029	Leveled Readers	Houghton Mifflin Harcourt
Flying	C	I	49	Crews, Donald	Mulberry Books
Flying	A	F	40	Leveled Literacy Intervention/ Green System	Heinemann
Flying	H	F	226	Leveled Readers	Houghton Mifflin Harcourt
Flying	H	F	226	Leveled Readers/CA	Houghton Mifflin Harcourt
Flying	H	F	226	Leveled Readers/TX	Houghton Mifflin Harcourt
Flying	C	F	26	Story Box	Wright Group/McGraw Hill
Flying Ace: The Story of Amelia Earhart	Q	B	250+	Eyewitness Readers	DK Publishing
Flying Across the Ocean: Yesterday and Today	T	I	1752	Reading Street	Pearson
Flying Against the Wind: A Story about Beryl Markham	R	B	8214	Creative Minds Biographies	Carolrhoda Books
Flying and Floating	B	I	64	Little Red Readers	Sundance
Flying Balloons	B	I	69	Literacy by Design	Rigby
Flying Brown Pelicans	K	I	421	Pull Ahead Books	Lerner Publications
Flying Car, The	J	RF	519	Pair-It Turn and Learn	Steck-Vaughn
Flying Doctor, The	H	F	246	Springboard	Wright Group/McGraw Hill
Flying Doctor, The	M	RF	250+	Windows on Literacy	National Geographic
Flying Fingers	K	RF	250+	Literacy 2000	Rigby
Flying Fish, The	H	RF	215	PM Extensions-Green	Rigby
Flying Flea, Callie, and Me, The	S	F	250+	Wallace, Carol & Bill	Pocket Books
Flying Football, The	I	RF	250+	Cambridge Reading	Pearson Learning Group
*Flying Free: America's First Black Aviators	T	B	250+	Hart, Philip S.	Lerner Publishing
Flying Free: Corey's Underground Railroad Diary	Q	HF	250+	Wyeth, Sharon Dennis	Scholastic
Flying Giants of Dinosaur Time	P	I	1090	Meet the Dinosaurs	Lerner Publications
Flying High	R	RF	250+	Orbit Double Takes	Pacific Learning
Flying High	F	RF	250+	Predictable Storybooks	SRA/McGraw Hill
Flying in an Airplane	H	F	272	Leveled Readers	Houghton Mifflin Harcourt
Flying in an Airplane	H	F	272	Leveled Readers/CA	Houghton Mifflin Harcourt
Flying in an Airplane	H	F	272	Leveled Readers/TX	Houghton Mifflin Harcourt
Flying into History	P	I	846	Leveled Readers/CA	Houghton Mifflin Harcourt
Flying into History	P	I	846	Leveled Readers/TX	Houghton Mifflin Harcourt
Flying into History	P	I	846	Leveled Readers	Houghton Mifflin Harcourt
Flying into the 21st Century	T	I	2565	Reading Street	Pearson
Flying Jewels	I	I	178	On Our Way to English	Rigby
Flying Lessons	W	HF	250+	Matthews, Kezi	Cricket Books
Flying Machines	J	I	270	Sails	Rigby
Flying Mosquitoes	L	I	383	Pull Ahead Books	Lerner Publications
Flying Saucer	I	RF	250+	Phonics Readers Plus	Steck-Vaughn
Flying Solo	S	RF	250+	Fletcher, Ralph	Bantam
Flying Spider	C	F	112	Sails	Rigby
Flying Squirrels	K	I	413	Pull Ahead Books	Lerner Publications
Flying Trunk,The	M	TL	644	Tales from Hans Andersen	Wright Group/McGraw Hill
*Flying With the Eagle, Racing the Great Bear: Stories from Native North America	U	TL	250+	Bruchac, Joseph	Troll Associates
*Flying-Saucer People and Other Cases, The	O	RF	250+	Simon, Seymour	Avon
Focus: Different Ways of Seeing	T	I	250+	Power Up!	Steck-Vaughn

* Collection of short stories
# Graphic text

TITLE	LEVEL	GENRE	WORD COUNT	AUTHOR / SERIES	PUBLISHER / DISTRIBUTOR
Folk Dancer	C	I	36	The Candid Collection	Pearson Learning Group
Folk Tales, Fables and Fairy Tales	L	I	204	Take Two Books	Wright Group/McGraw Hill
Folktales Around the World	N	I	757	Vocabulary Readers	Houghton Mifflin Harcourt
Folktales Around the World	N	I	757	Vocabulary Readers/CA	Houghton Mifflin Harcourt
*Folktales from Asia	O	TL	250+	Bookshop	Mondo
Folktales from China	N	TL	250+	Lawson, Barbara	Scholastic
Folktales from Ecosystems Around the World	Q	TL	250+	Pair-It Books	Steck-Vaughn
Folktales of the Midwest	R	TL	250+	Reading Expeditions	National Geographic
Folktales of the Northeast	R	TL	250+	Reading Expeditions	National Geographic
Folktales of the Southeast	R	TL	250+	Reading Expeditions	National Geographic
Folktales of the Southwest	R	TL	250+	Reading Expeditions	National Geographic
Folktales of the West	R	TL	250+	Reading Expeditions	National Geographic
Follow a River	L	I	198	iOpeners	Pearson Learning Group
Follow Me!	I	F	250+	Ziefert, Harriet	Puffin/Penguin
Follow Me!: How People Track Animals	P	I	1722	Reading Street	Pearson
Follow Me, Be a Bee	N	I	250+	Emerson, Dhanna	Houghton Mifflin Harcourt
Follow Me, Be a Bee	K	I	428	Independent Readers Science	Houghton Mifflin Harcourt
Follow My Leader	H	RF	96	Cambridge Reading	Pearson Learning Group
Follow That Car!	R	I	250+	Power Up!	Steck-Vaughn
Follow That Fin!: Studying Dolphin Behavior	T	I	250+	Samuels, Amy	Steck-Vaughn
Follow That Fish	K	F	250+	Bank Street	Bantam
Follow That Spy!	P	RF	250+	Action Packs	Rigby
Follow the Appalachian Trail	I	I	129	Leveled Readers Social Studies	Houghton Mifflin Harcourt
Follow the Leader	C	RF	62	First Stories	Pacific Learning
Follow the Leader	B	RF	32	Independent Readers Social Studies	Houghton Mifflin Harcourt
Follow the Leader	X	RF	2911	Leveled Readers	Houghton Mifflin Harcourt
Follow the Leader	X	RF	2911	Leveled Readers/CA	Houghton Mifflin Harcourt
Follow the Leader	D	RF	75	Teacher's Choice Series	Pearson Learning Group
Follow the Leader	B	RF	15	Windmill Books	Wright Group/McGraw Hill
Follow the Sun	D	RF	60	Leveled Readers Science	Houghton Mifflin Harcourt
Follower, The	P	F	494	Thompson, Richard	Fitzhenry & Whiteside
Following Rules	E	I	73	Citizenship	Lerner Publishing
Food	C	I	24	Basic Human Needs	Lerner Publishing
Food & Feasts Between the Two World Wars	T	I	250+	Steele, Philip	Dillon Press
Food & Feasts In Ancient Egypt	T	I	250+	Balkwill, Richard	Dillon Press
Food & Feasts In Ancient Greece	T	I	250+	Steele, Philip	Dillon Press
Food & Feasts In Ancient Rome	T	I	250+	Steele, Philip	Dillon Press
Food & Feasts In the Middle Ages	T	TL	250+	Dawson, Imogen	Dillon Press
Food & Feasts In Tudor Times	T	I	250+	Balkwill, Richard	Dillon Press
Food & Feasts With the Aztecs	T	I	250+	Dawson, Imogen	Dillon Press
Food & Feasts With the Vikings	T	I	250+	Martell, Hazel	Dillon Press
Food and Festivals: Israel	O	I	250+	Randall, Ronne	Steck-Vaughn
Food and Festivals: Italy	O	I	250+	Pirotta, Saviour	Steck-Vaughn
Food and Recipes of the Pilgrims	R	I	250+	Cooking Throughout American History	Rosen Publishing Group
Food and Recipes of the Thirteen Colonies	R	I	250+	Cooking Throughout American History	Rosen Publishing Group
Food and Recipes of the Westward Expansion	R	I	250+	Cooking Throughout American History	Rosen Publishing Group
Food Around the World	I	I	298	Early Connections	Benchmark Education
Food Chain	K	I	160	Pair-It Turn and Learn	Steck-Vaughn
Food Chains	O	I	677	Leveled Readers Science	Houghton Mifflin Harcourt
Food Chains	O	I	250+	Rigby Focus	Rigby

* Collection of short stories
# Graphic text

TITLE	LEVEL	GENRE	WORD COUNT	AUTHOR / SERIES	PUBLISHER / DISTRIBUTOR
Food Chains and Webs	P	I	974	Springboard	Wright Group/ McGraw Hill
Food Comes From Farms	F	I	75	Windows on Literacy	National Geographic
Food for a Mouse	C	I	94	Sails	Rigby
Food for Animals	H	I	223	Explorations	Eleanor Curtain Publishing
Food for Animals	H	I	223	Explorations	Okapi Eductional Materials
Food for Healthy Teeth	E	I	40	Dental Health	Capstone Press
Food for the World	W	I	250+	Rigby Literacy	Rigby
Food for Thought	U	I	250+	WorldScapes	ETA Cuisenaire
Food for Thought	I	I	250+	Yellow Umbrella Books	Red Brick Learning
Food for You	H	I	232	Leveled Readers	Houghton Mifflin Harcourt
Food for You	F	I	85	Leveled Readers Science	Houghton Mifflin Harcourt
Food for You	H	I	232	Leveled Readers/CA	Houghton Mifflin Harcourt
Food for You	H	I	232	Leveled Readers/TX	Houghton Mifflin Harcourt
Food Found All Around	L	I	220	Spyglass Books	Compass Point Books
Food From Another Country	H	I	91	Windows on Literacy	National Geographic
Food from Plants	D	RF	66	Rigby Literacy	Rigby
Food from the Farm	D	RF	78	Home Connection Collection	Rigby
Food From the Water	I	I	416	Sails	Rigby
Food Is Fun	H	RF	250+	PM Plus Poetry	Rigby
Food Journey, The	K	I	116	Home Connection Collection	Rigby
Food Patterns	J	I	263	Finding Patterns	Capstone Press
Food Pyramid, The	L	I	155	Spyglass Books	Compass Point Books
Food Science	Y	I	7194	Cool Science	Lerner Publications
Food Service Workers	M	I	250+	Community Helpers	Red Brick Learning
Food to Eat	B	I	29	Little Readers	Houghton Mifflin Harcourt
Food Trappers	I	I	165	Wonder World	Wright Group/McGraw Hill
Foods	C	I	18	We Are Alike and Different	Lerner Publishing
Foods of Mexico	S	I	1398	Vocabulary Readers	Houghton Mifflin Harcourt
Foods of Mexico	S	I	1398	Vocabulary Readers/CA	Houghton Mifflin Harcourt
Foolish Goose	F	F	141	Start To Read	School Zone
Foolish Gretel	O	TL	250+	Armstrong, Jennifer	Random House
Fool's Gold	T	RF	250+	Reading Safari	Mondo
Foot Book	E	F	108	Seuss, Dr.	Random House
Football	B	I	28	Visions	Wright Group/McGraw Hill
Football Book, The	I	RF	242	Breakthrough	Longman
Football Fever	H	RF	51	Pacific Literacy	Pacific Learning
Football for Fun	S	I	250+	Sports for Fun	Compass Point Books
Football Friends	L	RF	250+	Marzollo, Jean, Dan & Dave	Scholastic
Football Fugitive	Q	RF	250+	Christopher, Matt	Little, Brown & Co.
Footprints	H	RF	96	Book Bus	Creative Edge
Footprints	H	F	241	Leveled Literacy Intervention/ Blue System	Heinemann
Footprints	G	RF	96	Literacy Tree	Rigby
Footprints	C	I	69	Rigby Focus	Rigby
Footprints in the Garden	J	RF	250+	Literacy by Design	Rigby
Footprints in the Park	M	RF	748	Springboard	Wright Group/ McGraw Hill
Footprints in the Snow	D	RF	39	Benjamin, Cynthia	Scholastic
Footwork: The Story of Fred and Adele Astaire	P	B	250+	Orgill, Roxane	Candlewick Press
For a Better Life	T	B	250+	Power Up!	Steck-Vaughn
For Breakfast	LB	I	22	Visions	Wright Group/McGraw Hill
For My Birthday	B	RF	48	Lighthouse	Rigby
For the Birds!	R	I	250+	Boldprint	Steck-Vaughn
For the Feet	E	I	146	Sails	Rigby
For The Life of Laetitia	Y	RF	250+	Hodge, Merle	Farrar, Straus and Giroux

TITLE	LEVEL	GENRE	WORD COUNT	AUTHOR / SERIES	PUBLISHER / DISTRIBUTOR
For the Love of Pooch	N	RF	250+	Literacy 2000	Rigby
For the Love of Turtles	N	RF	250+	Greetings	Rigby
Forced Out	O	I	889	Independent Readers Science	Houghton Mifflin Harcourt
Forces and Movement	S	I	250+	Straightforward Science	Franklin Watts
Forecasting the Weather	K	I	235	Gear Up!	Wright Group/McGraw Hill
Forecasting the Weather	T	I	2435	Reading Street	Pearson
Forensic Science	X	I	7703	Cool Science	Lerner Publications
Forensic Science: Putting the Pieces Together	X	I	250+	Explore More	Wright Group/McGraw Hill
Forest	F	I	101	Habitats	Lerner Publications
Forest Animals	P	I	250+	Theme Sets	National Geographic
Forest Community, A	Q	I	250+	Massie, Elizabeth	Steck-Vaughn
Forest Fire	I	I	347	Rigby Flying Colors	Rigby
Forest Fire!	O	I	769	Leveled Readers Science	Houghton Mifflin Harcourt
Forest Fire!	J	I	250+	On Our Way to English	Rigby
Forest Fires	S	I	250+	Natural Disasters	Capstone Press
Forest Fires	M	I	648	Pull Ahead Books	Lerner Publications
Forest Fires: Run for Your Life!	T	I	250+	Bookshop	Mondo
Forest Giants	N	I	250+	InfoQuest	Rigby
Forest Mammals	R	I	250+	Kalman, Bobbie	Crabtree
Forest of Secrets: Warriors, Book 3	U	F	250+	Hunter, Erin	Avon Books
Forest Stew	H	F	239	Leveled Readers	Houghton Mifflin Harcourt
Forest Stew	H	F	239	Leveled Readers/CA	Houghton Mifflin Harcourt
Forest Stew	H	F	239	Leveled Readers/TX	Houghton Mifflin Harcourt
Forest, The	L	I	250+	Cambridge Reading	Pearson Learning Group
Forest, The	A	I	32	Literacy by Design	Rigby
Forest, The	A	I	34	On Our Way to English	Rigby
Forest, The	E	I	74	Reading Street	Pearson
Forests	N	I	250+	Habitats of the World	Pearson Learning Group
Forests	M	I	250+	PM Plus Nonfiction	Rigby
Forests	R	I	250+	The Wonders of Our World	Crabtree
Forest's Life, A: From Meadow to Mature Woodland	T	I	250+	A First Book	Franklin Watts
Forests, Grasslands, Deserts	M	I	250+	People, Spaces & Places	Rand McNally
Forever Amber Brown	O	RF	250+	Danziger, Paula	Scholastic
Forever Friends	X	RF	250+	Boyd, Candy Dawson	Puffin/Penguin
Forever Green	P	I	846	Vocabulary Readers	Houghton Mifflin Harcourt
Forever Green	P	I	846	Vocabulary Readers/CA	Houghton Mifflin Harcourt
Forever Green	P	I	846	Vocabulary Readers/TX	Houghton Mifflin Harcourt
Forged by Fire	Z	RF	250+	Draper, Sharon M.	Aladdin
Forget It!	L	RF	250+	Rigby Literacy	Rigby
Forgetful Bee, The	E	F	80	Reading Safari	Mondo
Forgetful Fran	J	RF	250+	Sunshine	Wright Group/McGraw Hill
Forgetful Fred	E	RF	78	Tadpoles	Rigby
Forgiveness	M	I	250+	Character Education	Red Brick Learning
Forgotten Door, The	T	SF	250+	Key, Alexander	Language for Learning Assoc.
Forgotten Heroes, The: The Story of the Buffalo Soldiers	X	I	250+	Cox, Clinton	Scholastic
Forgotten Hiding Place, The	M	RF	250+	Woodland Mysteries	Wright Group/McGraw Hill
Forgotten Princess, The	L	TL	250+	Literacy 2000	Rigby
Forklifts	L	I	371	Pull Ahead Books	Lerner Publications
Formation of the Continents	X	I	2046	Reading Street	Pearson
Forms of Energy	R	I	1168	Science Support Readers	Houghton Mifflin Harcourt
Formula One Cars	M	I	250+	Horsepower	Capstone Press

* Collection of short stories
\# Graphic text

F

TITLE	LEVEL	GENRE	WORD COUNT	AUTHOR / SERIES	PUBLISHER / DISTRIBUTOR
Formula One Cars	Q	I	250+	Wild Rides!	Capstone Press
Formula One Race Cars	W	I	6230	Motor Mania	Lerner Publications
Formula One Race Cars	N	I	498	Pull Ahead Books	Lerner Publications
Fort Life	T	I	250+	Historic Communities	Crabtree
Fort Sumter	V	I	250+	Cornerstones of Freedom	Children's Press
Fort Sumter: Where the Civil War Began	Q	I	250+	Rosen Real Readers	Rosen Publishing Group
Fortune Branches Out, A	R	RF	250+	Mahy, Margaret	Bantam
*Fortune's Friend: Tales of Rivalry and Riches	Q	TL	250+	Literacy 2000	Rigby
Fortune's Magic Farm	S	F	250+	Selfors, Suzanne	Little, Brown & Co.
Fortune-Tellers, The	O	TL	250+	Alexander, Lloyd	Puffin/Penguin
Forty Acres and Maybe a Mule	V	HF	250+	Robinet, Harriette Gillem	Scholastic
Forty-Three Cats	K	RF	232	Sunshine	Wright Group/McGraw Hill
Fossil Fuel Power	V	I	250+	Energy at Work	Capstone Press
Fossil Fuels	M	I	250+	Rigby Focus	Rigby
Fossil Fuels: A Resource Our World Depends On	V	I	250+	Managing Our Resources	Heinemann
Fossil Hunters	Q	I	1048	Vocabulary Readers	Houghton Mifflin Harcourt
Fossil Hunters	Q	I	1048	Vocabulary Readers/CA	Houghton Mifflin Harcourt
Fossil Hunters, The	J	I	207	Instant Readers	Harcourt School Publishers
Fossil Hunting	L	I	170	Rigby Focus	Rigby
Fossil Seekers	U	I	250+	iOpeners	Pearson Learning Group
Fossilized	T	I	3,782	Take Two Books	Wright Group/McGraw Hill
Fossils	R	I	1526	Early Bird Earth Systems	Lerner Publications
Fossils	L	I	250+	Early Connections	Benchmark Education
Fossils	Q	I	250+	Exploring the Earth	Capstone Press
Fossils	R	I	1272	Leveled Readers Science	Houghton Mifflin Harcourt
Fossils	Q	I	250+	On Deck	Rigby
Fossils	P	I	250+	Simply Science	Compass Point Books
Fossils	K	I	238	Windows on Literacy	National Geographic
Fossils Alive!	Q	I	250+	Pair-It Books	Steck-Vaughn
Fossils Tell of Long Ago	O	I	250+	Soar To Success	Houghton Mifflin Harcourt
Fossils: Pictures from the Past	Q	I	250+	Pair-It Books	Steck-Vaughn
Foster's Famous Farm	J	RF	353	Leveled Readers	Houghton Mifflin Harcourt
Foster's Famous Farm	J	RF	353	Leveled Readers/CA	Houghton Mifflin Harcourt
Foster's Famous Farm	J	RF	353	Leveled Readers/TX	Houghton Mifflin Harcourt
Foster's Farm	J	RF	323	Leveled Readers	Houghton Mifflin Harcourt
Foster's Farm	J	RF	323	Leveled Readers/CA	Houghton Mifflin Harcourt
Foster's Farm	J	RF	323	Leveled Readers/TX	Houghton Mifflin Harcourt
Foster's War	V	HF	250+	Reeder, Carolyn	Scholastic
Foul Play on the Sidelines	R	RF	250+	Costello, Emily	Dell
Foul Play: Jokes That Won't Strike Out	O	F	1775	Make Me Laugh!	Lerner Publications
Foundling and Other Tales of Prydain, The	T	F	250+	Alexander, Lloyd	Puffin Books
Fountains of Life: The Story of Deep-Sea Vents	S	I	250+	A First Book	Franklin Watts
Four A's, The	Q	RF	250+	Wildcats	Wright Group/McGraw Hill
Four Cars	C	I	96	PM Math Readers	Rigby
Four Cheerful Chipmunks	H	F	250+	Phonics and Friends	Hampton-Brown
Four Days in the Life of Zoe Coznaut	L	SF	250+	Foundations	Wright Group/McGraw Hill
Four Faces in Rock	M	I	300	Early Connections	Benchmark Education
*Four Friends and Other Stories, The	L	TL	250+	New Way Literature	Steck-Vaughn
Four Frogs	A	RF	25	Leveled Readers	Houghton Mifflin Harcourt
Four Frogs	A	RF	25	Leveled Readers/CA	Houghton Mifflin Harcourt
Four Getters and Arf, The	G	F	123	Little Celebrations	Pearson Learning Group
Four Good Friends	F	TL	274	Fairy Tales and Folklore	Norwood House Press
Four Great Cities	W	I	250+	iOpeners	Pearson Learning Group

F

* Collection of short stories
# Graphic text

TITLE	LEVEL	GENRE	WORD COUNT	AUTHOR / SERIES	PUBLISHER / DISTRIBUTOR
Four Great Inventions of Ancient China	W	I	2534	Independent Readers Social Studies	Houghton Mifflin Harcourt
Four Ice Creams	C	RF	61	PM Starters	Rigby
*Four on the Shore	J	F	250+	Marshall, Edward	Puffin/Penguin
Four Pictures By Emily Carr	X	B	250+	Debon, Nicolas	Groundwood Books
Four Seasons, The	E	I	154	Early Connections	Benchmark Education
Four Seasons, The	C	RF	20	Learn to Read	Creative Teaching Press
Four Seasons, The	S	I	1820	Leveled Readers Science	Houghton Mifflin Harcourt
Four Seasons, The	C	I	57	Windows on Literacy	National Geograhic
Four Stops on the Sante Fe Trail	S	I	1224	Vocabulary Readers	Houghton Mifflin Harcourt
Four Stops on the Sante Fe Trail	S	I	1224	Vocabulary Readers/CA	Houghton Mifflin Harcourt
Four Stops on the Sante Fe Trail	S	I	1224	Vocabulary Readers/TX	Houghton Mifflin Harcourt
Four Very Big Beans	E	RF	79	Instant Readers	Harcourt School Publishers
Four-Legged Friends	N	TL	250+	Literacy 2000	Rigby
Fourteen Marbles	J	RF	181	PM Math Readers	Rigby
Fourth Grade Celebrity	Q	RF	250+	Giff, Patricia Reilly	Bantam
Fourth Grade Is a Jinx	P	RF	250+	McKenna, Colleen	Scholastic
Fourth Grade Wizards, The	Q	RF	250+	DeClements, Barthe	Penguin Group
Fourth Little Pig, The	K	TL	250+	Ready Set Read	Steck-Vaughn
Fourth of July, The	G	I	120	Fiesta Holiday Series	Pearson Learning Group
Fourth of July, The	F	I	153	Ready Readers	Pearson Learning Group
Fourth of July, The	I	I	206	Rosen Real Readers	Rosen Publishing Group
Fourth of July, The	H	I	142	Shutterbug Books	Steck-Vaughn
Fourth of July, The	B	I	17	Windows on Literacy	National Geographic
Fourth-Graders Don't Believe in Witches	P	F	250+	Fields, Terri	Scholastic
Fowler's Family Tree	J	F	418	Storyteller	Wright Group/McGraw Hill
*Fox All Week	J	F	250+	Marshall, Edward	Puffin/Penguin
Fox and Crow	I	TL	333	Leveled Readers	Houghton Mifflin Harcourt
Fox and Crow	I	TL	333	Leveled Readers/CA	Houghton Mifflin Harcourt
Fox and Crow	I	TL	333	Leveled Readers/TX	Houghton Mifflin Harcourt
Fox and Crow, The	H	TL	201	Alphakids	Sundance
*Fox and His Friends	J	F	250+	Marshall, Edward	Puffin/Penguin
Fox and the Crow, The	I	TL	250+	Aesop's Fables	Pearson Learning Group
Fox and the Crow, The	J	F	240	Instant Readers	Harcourt School Publishers
Fox and the Crow, The	M	TL	614	Leveled Readers	Houghton Mifflin Harcourt
Fox and the Crow, The	J	TL	250+	PM Plus Story Books	Rigby
Fox and the Crow, The	K	TL	250+	Ready Readers	Pearson Learning Group
Fox and the Crow, The	H	TL	148	Sun Sprouts	ETA Cuisenaire
Fox and the Goat, The	J	TL	365	Aesop's Fables	Pearson Learning Group
Fox and the Grapes, The	G	TL	60	Jumbled Tumbled Tales & Rhymes	Rigby
Fox and the Gulls, The	M	TL	499	Leveled Literacy Intervention/Blue System	Heinemann
Fox and the Little Red Hen, The	L	TL	250+	Traditional Tales & More	Rigby
Fox and the Rabbit, The	C	TL	48	Storyworlds	Heinemann Educational Publishers
Fox and the Stork	H	F	149	New Way Blue	Steck-Vaughn
Fox and the Stork, The	H	TL	250+	Green Light Readers	Harcourt
Fox and the Stork, The	K	TL	399	Rigby Flying Colors	Rigby
Fox and the Stork, The	C	TL	51	Storyworlds	Heinemann Educational Publishers
*Fox at School	J	F	250+	Marshall, Edward	Puffin/Penguin
*Fox Be Nimble	J	F	250+	Marshall, James	Puffin/Penguin
Fox Fables	J	F	250+	Sunshine	Wright Group/McGraw Hill

* Collection of short stories
# Graphic text

TITLE	LEVEL	GENRE	WORD COUNT	AUTHOR / SERIES	PUBLISHER / DISTRIBUTOR
Fox Gets a Note	G	F	152	Gear Up!	Wright Group/McGraw Hill
*Fox in Love	J	F	250+	Marshall, Edward	Puffin/Penguin
Fox in the Frost	Q	RF	250+	Baglio, Ben M.	Scholastic
Fox Lives Here, A	I	I	160	Ready Readers	Pearson Learning Group
*Fox on Stage	J	F	250+	Marshall, James	Puffin/Penguin
Fox on the Box, The	C	RF	36	Little Readers	Houghton Mifflin Harcourt
Fox on the Box, The	C	RF	36	Start to Read	School Zone
Fox on the Job	J	F	250+	Marshall, James	Puffin/Penguin
*Fox on Wheels	J	F	250+	Marshall, Edward	Puffin/Penguin
*Fox Outfoxed	J	F	250+	Marshall, James	Puffin/Penguin
Fox Steals Home, The	Q	RF	250+	Christopher, Matt	Little, Brown & Co.
Fox Who Foxed, The	H	F	212	PM Story Books	Rigby
Fox, The	C	RF	24	Books for Young Learners	Richard C. Owen
Foxes	M	I	250+	PM Animal Facts: Gold	Rigby
Foxes	H	I	164	Sails	Rigby
Foxes and Their Dens	J	I	146	Animal Homes	Capstone Press
Foxes: Clever Hunters	M	I	250+	The Wild World of Animals	Red Brick Learning
Fox's Box	D	I	72	Dominie Phonics Reader	Pearson Learning Group
Fox's Hungry Day	H	RF	227	On Our Way to English	Rigby
Fractions: Making Fair Shares	M	I	250+	Exploring Math	Capstone Press
Fraidy Cats	J	F	250+	Krensky, Stephen	Scholastic
Frame by Frame	T	I	250+	Boldprint	Steck-Vaughn
Framed	V	RF	250+	Boyce, Frank Cottrell	Harper Collins
Fran That Time Forgot, The	N	SF	250+	Benton, Jim	Aladdin Paperbacks
France	U	I	250+	Countries and Cultures	Red Brick Learning
France	O	I	250+	Countries of the World	Red Brick Learning
France	P	I	2269	Country Explorers	Lerner Publications
France: A Question and Answer Book	P	I	250+	Questions and Answers: Countries	Capstone Press
Frances Hodgson Burnett: Beyond the Secret Garden	U	B	250+	Carpenter, Angelica Shirley; Shirley, Jean	Lerner Publishing
Frances the Fairy Dressmaker	L	F	736	Early Connections	Benchmark Education
Francie	W	RF	250+	English, Karen	Farrar, Straus and Giroux
Francis Frog Meets a Space Snake	H	F	250+	Reading Safari	Mondo
Francis Scott Key and "The Star-Spangled Banner"	M	I	250+	Bookshop	Mondo
Francis Scott Key: Patriotic Poet	U	B	250+	Let Freedom Ring	Capstone Press
Francisco Goya	R	B	250+	Venezia, Mike	Children's Press
Francisco's Collection	H	RF	250+	Pacific Literacy	Pacific Learning
Frank and Sam's Summer at Aramoana	M	RF	250+	Voyages	SRA/McGraw Hill
Frank Lloyd Wright	O	B	346	Independent Readers Social Studies	Houghton Mifflin Harcourt
Frank the Fish Gets His Wish	I	F	250+	Appleton-Smith, Laura	Flyleaf Publishing
Frankenstein	W	SF	250+	High-Fliers	Pacific Learning
Frankenstein	X	I	5158	Monster Chronicles	Lerner Publications
Frankenstein	Z+	SF	250+	Shelley, Mary	Penguin Group
Frankenstein Doesn't Plant Petunias	M	F	250+	Dadey, Debbie; Jones, Marcia Thornton	Scholastic
Frankenstein Doesn't Slam Hockey Pucks	M	F	250+	Dadey, Debbie; Jones, Marcia Thornton	Scholastic
Frankenstein Moved on to the 4th Floor	M	RF	250+	Levy, Elizabeth	Harper & Row
Frankie's Facts	K	RF	443	Leveled Readers	Houghton Mifflin Harcourt
Frankie's Facts	K	RF	443	Leveled Readers/CA	Houghton Mifflin Harcourt
Frankie's Facts	K	RF	443	Leveled Readers/TX	Houghton Mifflin Harcourt

* Collection of short stories
# Graphic text

TITLE	LEVEL	GENRE	WORD COUNT	AUTHOR / SERIES	PUBLISHER / DISTRIBUTOR
Franklin Chang-Diaz in Space	M	B	250	Vocabulary Readers	Houghton Mifflin Harcourt
Franklin D. Roosevelt	S	B	3374	History Maker Bios	Lerner Publications
Franklin D. Roosevelt	N	B	223	Pebble Books	Capstone Press
Franklin D. Roosevelt	P	B	250+	Photo-Illustrated Biographies	Red Brick Learning
Franklin D. Roosevelt	U	B	250+	Profiles of the Presidents	Compass Point Books
Franklin D. Roosevelt: Thirty-second President	R	B	250+	Getting to Know the U.S. Presidents	Children's Press
Franklin Delano Roosevelt	R	B	250+	Amazing Americans	Wright Group/McGraw Hill
Franklin Delano Roosevelt	W	B	250+	Freedman, Russell	Clarion
Franklin Goes to School	K	F	250+	Bourgeois, Paulette; Clark, Brenda	Scholastic
Franklin Pierce	U	B	250+	Profiles of the Presidents	Compass Point Books
Franklin Pierce: Fourteenth President	R	B	250+	Getting to Know the U.S. Presidents	Children's Press
Franklin Plays the Game	K	F	250+	Bourgeois, Paulette; Clark, Brenda	Scholastic
Frantastic Voyage	N	SF	250+	Benton, Jim	Aladdin Paperbacks
Freak the Mighty	W	RF	250+	Philbrick, Rodman	Scholastic
Freaky Flowers	S	I	250+	Plants and Fungi	Franklin Watts
Freaky Friday	R	F	250+	Rodgers, Mary	HarperTrophy
Freaky Frogs	P	I	250+	Explorer Books-Pioneer	National Geographic
Freaky Frogs	R	I	250+	Explorer Books-Pathfinder	National Geographic
Freckle Juice	M	RF	250+	Blume, Judy	Bantam
Fred and the Ball	G	RF	171	Rigby Flying Colors	Rigby
Fred and Zack in the Sandbox	F	RF	61	Appleton-Smith, Laura	Flyleaf Publishing
Fred Fixes a Faucet	I	F	250+	Popcorn	Sundance
Fred Goes Shopping	I	F	250+	Popcorn	Sundance
Fred Helps, Too	F	RF	218	Rigby Flying Colors	Rigby
Fred Joins the Band	I	F	250+	Popcorn	Sundance
Fred Plays a Trick	H	RF	237	Rigby Flying Colors	Rigby
Fred Said	D	RF	35	Sunshine	Wright Group/McGraw Hill
Freda's Signs	K	F	528	Reading Street	Pearson
Freddie the Frog	D	F	132	First Start	Troll Associates
Freddie the Frog	G	F	250+	Supersonics	Rigby
Freddie's Spaghetti	F	RF	250+	Doyle, Charlotte	Random House
Freddy Adu	P	B	1742	Amazing Athletes	Lerner Publications
Freddy Frog's Note	H	F	253	Ready Readers	Pearson Learning Group
Freddy's Train Ride	K	RF	573	Pair-It Books	Steck-Vaughn
Frederick Douglass	T	B	250+	Amazing Americans	Wright Group/McGraw Hill
Frederick Douglass	P	B	250+	Early Biographies	Compass Point Books
Frederick Douglass	N	B	257	First Biographies	Red Brick Learning
Frederick Douglass	S	B	3743	History Maker Bios	Lerner Publications
Frederick Douglass	P	B	250+	Photo-Illustrated Biographies	Red Brick Learning
Frederick Douglass: Fights for Freedom	M	B	250+	Davidson, Margaret	Language for Learning Assoc.
Frederick Douglass: His Story Made History	U	B	2008	Leveled Readers	Houghton Mifflin Harcourt
Frederick Douglass: The Last Days of Slavery	R	B	250+	Miller, William	Lee & Low Books Inc.
Fred's Big Lunch	I	F	250+	Popcorn	Sundance
Fred's Cold	I	F	250+	Popcorn	Sundance
Fred's Doghouse	H	RF	288	Rigby Flying Colors	Rigby
Fred's Little Snack	I	F	250+	Popcorn	Sundance
Fred's Polka-Dot Sock	I	F	250+	Popcorn	Sundance
Fred's Weekend	I	F	250+	Popcorn	Sundance
Fred's Wish for Fish	E	RF	128	Landman, Yael	Scholastic

F

* Collection of short stories
\# Graphic text

TITLE	LEVEL	GENRE	WORD COUNT	AUTHOR / SERIES	PUBLISHER / DISTRIBUTOR
Free at Last	S	B	250+	DK Readers	DK Publishing
Free Black Communities in the Time of Slavery	W	I	3120	Leveled Readers Social Studies	Houghton Mifflin Harcourt
Free Black Girl Before the Civil War, A	U	I	250+	Diaries and Memoirs	Capstone Press
Free Climb	Q	RF	250+	Maddox, Jake	Stone Arch Books
Free Fall	Q	I	250+	Basalaj, Kathy	Pacific Learning
Free Fall	WB	F	N/A	Wiesner, David	Lothrop, Lee & Shepard
Free Throw	P	RF	4509	Maddox, Jake	Stone Arch Books
Free to Fly	E	RF	96	Gibson, Kathleen	Continental Press
Freedom	M	RF	250+	Rigby Literacy	Rigby
Freedom Crossing	R	HF	250+	Clark, Margaret Goff	Scholastic
Freedom Debate	W	I	250+	WorldScapes	ETA Cuisenaire
Freedom Fighters: The Massachusetts 54th Regiment	V	I	2052	Leveled Readers Social Studies	Houghton Mifflin Harcourt
Freedom of Speech and Assembly in the United States	X	I	2852	Reading Street	Pearson
Freedom Quilt	M	HF	300	Books for Young Learners	Richard C. Owen
Freedom Readers	R	I	250+	Explorer Books-Pathfinder	National Geographic
Freedom Readers	Q	I	250+	Explorer Books-Pioneer	National Geographic
Freedom Seeker: A Story about William Penn	S	B	9841	Creative Minds Biographies	Lerner Publications
#Freedom Sings: A Tale of the Underground Railroad	R	HF	250+	Robbins, Trina	Stone Arch Books
Freedom Songs: A Tale of the Underground Railroad	T	HF	250+	Moore, Yvette	Language for Learning Assoc.
Freedom Train	T	B	250+	Sterling, Dorothy	Scholastic
Freedom Walkers: The Story of the Montgomery Bus Boycott	X	I	250+	Freedman, Russell	Holiday House
Freedom's Fire	U	HF	250+	Bookshop	Mondo
Freedom's Wings: Corey's Underground Railroad Diary	Q	HF	250+	Wyeth, Sharon Dennis	Scholastic
Freeman's Fax Machine, The	J	F	250+	Reading Safari	Mondo
Freewill	Z+	RF	250+	Lynch, Chris	Harper Tempest
Freeze Tag	G	RF	112	City Stories	Rigby
Freeze, Goldilocks!	M	F	250+	Pacific Literacy	Pacific Learning
Freezing and Melting	H	I	101	Water	Lerner Publications
Freight Trains	M	I	250+	Transportation	Compass Point Books
French Colonies in the Americas	S	I	250+	On Deck	Rigby
French Roots in North America	S	I	1612	Reading Street	Pearson
Frenzy of Sharks, A	U	I	250+	Jean-Michel Cousteau Presents	London Town Press
Fresh Air	O	RF	250+	Leveled Readers Language Support	Houghton Mifflin Harcourt
Fresh Fall Leaves	E	RF	50	Franco, Betsy	Scholastic
Fresh from the Farm!	M	I	727	Rigby Flying Colors	Rigby
Freshwater Fishing	S	I	250+	The Great Outdoors	Capstone Press
Freshwater Giants: Hippopatamus, River Dolphins, and Manatees	S	I	250+	Perry, Phyllis J.	Franklin Watts
Freshwater Habitats	N	I	250+	Habitats of the World	Pearson Learning Group
Freshwater Pond, A	T	I	250+	Small Worlds	Crabtree
Freshwater Seas: The Great Lakes	S	I	1905	Independent Readers Social Studies	Houghton Mifflin Harcourt
Friction	Z+	RF	250+	Frank, E.R.	Simon & Schuster
Friction	P	I	250+	Our Physical World	Capstone Press
Frida Kahlo	R	B	250+	Venezia, Mike	Children's Press
Frida Kahlo: Mexican Painter	R	B	250+	The Heinle Reading Library	Thomson Learning
Frida Kahlo: Painter of Strength	P	B	250+	Great Hispanics	Capstone Press

F

TITLE	LEVEL	GENRE	WORD COUNT	AUTHOR / SERIES	PUBLISHER / DISTRIBUTOR
Frida María: A Story of the Old Southwest	M	RF	250+	Lattimore, Deborah Nourse	Harcourt Trade
Friday Pizza	I	RF	334	Pair-It Turn and Learn	Steck-Vaughn
Friedrich	Z	HF	250+	Richter, Hans Peter	Puffin/Penguin
Friend for Ben, A	K	RF	250+	Literacy by Design	Rigby
Friend for Dear Dragon, A	E	F	279	Dear Dragon	Norwood House Press
Friend for Dragon, A	I	F	250+	Pilkey, Dav	Orchard Books
Friend for Jasper, A	J	F	584	Jasper the Cat	Pioneer Valley
Friend for Jellyfish, A	E	F	121	Bonnell, Kris	Reading Reading Books
Friend for Kate, A	I	RF	250+	Cambridge Reading	Pearson Learning Group
Friend for Little White Rabbit, A	E	F	113	PM Story Books	Rigby
Friend for Max, A	G	RF	228	PM Plus Story Books	Rigby
Friend for Me, A	A	I	48	First Stories	Pacific Learning
Friend for Peanut, A	E	RF	88	Emergent Set 4	Pioneer Valley
Friend in the Wild, A	T	RF	250+	Storyteller - Whispering Pines	Wright Group/McGraw Hill
Friend, A	G	RF	57	Literacy 2000	Rigby
Friendliness	L	I	250+	Character Education	Red Brick Learning
Friendliness	K	I	250+	Everyday Character Education	Capstone Press
Friendly Crocodile, The	I	F	218	Hiris, Monica	Kaeden Books
Friendly Field Trip, A	P	RF	1000	Leveled Readers/TX	Houghton Mifflin Harcourt
Friendly Snowman	F	F	134	First Start	Troll Associates
Friendly Snowman	F	F	144	Joyce, William	Scholastic
Friends	U	I	250+	Boldprint	Steck-Vaughn
Friends	F	RF	57	Bookshop	Mondo
Friends	I	I	313	Early Connections	Benchmark Education
Friends	D	I	134	Fiesta Series	Pearson Learning Group
Friends	D	F	98	Joy Starters	Pearson Learning Group
Friends	A	F	80	Leveled Literacy Intervention/ Green System	Heinemann
Friends	I	I	302	Leveled Readers	Houghton Mifflin Harcourt
Friends	A	I	21	Leveled Readers Emergent	Houghton Mifflin Harcourt
Friends	I	I	302	Leveled Readers/CA	Houghton Mifflin Harcourt
Friends	I	I	302	Leveled Readers/TX	Houghton Mifflin Harcourt
Friends	B	RF	36	Little Readers	Houghton Mifflin Harcourt
Friends	G	RF	195	Reading Unlimited	Pearson Learning Group
Friends	B	I	21	Rigby Literacy	Rigby
Friends	B	I	30	Rigby Star Quest	Rigby
Friends	D	I	60	Sun Sprouts	ETA Cuisenaire
Friends	A	I	20	Vocabulary Readers	Houghton Mifflin Harcourt
Friends	A	I	20	Vocabulary Readers/CA	Houghton Mifflin Harcourt
Friends	G	RF	250+	Well-Being Series	Pearson Learning Group
Friends Along the Way	W	I	1500	Leveled Readers/TX	Houghton Mifflin Harcourt
Friends and Competitors	X	B	2333	Leveled Readers	Houghton Mifflin Harcourt
Friends and Family	Q	I	250+	Orbit Collections	Pacific Learning
Friends Are Forever	K	F	585	Literacy 2000	Rigby
Friends Forever	K	F	250+	I Am Reading	Kingfisher
Friends Forever	K	RF	559	Leveled Readers	Houghton Mifflin Harcourt
Friends Forever	I	TL	250+	Ready Readers	Pearson Learning Group
Friends Go Together	D	RF	36	Pair-It Books	Steck-Vaughn
Friends of the Earth	J	RF	264	InfoTrek	ETA Cuisenaire
Friends on a Field Trip	O	RF	1000	Leveled Readers/TX	Houghton Mifflin Harcourt
Friends Online	I	RF	318	Leveled Readers	Houghton Mifflin Harcourt
Friends or Enemies?	R	I	250+	Leveled Readers Language Support	Houghton Mifflin Harcourt
Friends or Foes?	N	TL	250+	WorldScapes	ETA Cuisenaire

F

* Collection of short stories
\# Graphic text

TITLE	LEVEL	GENRE	WORD COUNT	AUTHOR / SERIES	PUBLISHER / DISTRIBUTOR
Friends Share	C	I	34	Vocabulary Readers	Houghton Mifflin Harcourt
Friends Who Share	C	I	118	Leveled Readers	Houghton Mifflin Harcourt
Friends Who Share	C	I	118	Leveled Readers/CA	Houghton Mifflin Harcourt
Friends Who Share	C	I	118	Leveled Readers/TX	Houghton Mifflin Harcourt
Friends with Wings	R	RF	1249	Leveled Readers	Houghton Mifflin Harcourt
Friends with Wings	R	RF	1249	Leveled Readers/CA	Houghton Mifflin Harcourt
Friends with Wings	R	RF	1249	Leveled Readers/TX	Houghton Mifflin Harcourt
Friends, The	Z	RF	250+	Guy, Rosa	Bantam
Friends, The	T	RF	250+	Yumoto, Kazumi	Yearling
Friendship and the Gold Cadillac, The	S	HF	250+	Taylor, Mildred	Bantam
Friendship Garden, The	S	RF	2232	Leveled Readers	Houghton Mifflin Harcourt
Friendship Garden, The	S	RF	2232	Leveled Readers/CA	Houghton Mifflin Harcourt
Friendship Garden, The	S	RF	2232	Leveled Readers/TX	Houghton Mifflin Harcourt
Friendship Garden, The	K	RF	250+	Little Celebrations	Pearson Learning Group
Friendship in Action	O	I	250+	Literacy Tree	Rigby
Friendship Pact, The	Q	RF	250+	Pfeffer, Susan Beth	Scholastic
Friendship Rules!	I	I	256	Vocabulary Readers	Houghton Mifflin Harcourt
Friendship Rules!	I	I	256	Vocabulary Readers/CA	Houghton Mifflin Harcourt
Friendship Rules!	I	I	256	Vocabulary Readers/TX	Houghton Mifflin Harcourt
Friendship Salad	D	RF	42	Instant Readers	Harcourt School Publishers
Friendship, The	S	HF	250+	Taylor, Mildred	Puffin/Penguin
Frightened	B	F	42	Story Box	Wright Group/McGraw Hill
Frightened Scarecrow, The	L	F	896	Springboard	Wright Group/McGraw Hill
Frightful's Mountain	U	RF	250+	George, Jean Craighead	Puffin/Penguin
Frindle	R	RF	250+	Clements, Andrew	Aladdin
Frisky and the Cat	D	F	117	Storyworlds	Heinemann Educational Publishers
Frisky and the Ducks	D	F	90	Storyworlds	Heinemann Educational Publishers
Frisky Plays a Trick	D	F	102	Storyworlds	Heinemann Educational Publishers
Frisky Wants to Sleep	C	F	66	Storyworlds	Heinemann Educational Publishers
Frito Jumps In	D	RF	34	Step-By-Step Series	Pearson Learning Group
Frog	B	RF	50	Sails	Rigby
Frog Alert	K	I	452	Explorations	Eleanor Curtain Publishing
Frog Alert	K	I	452	Explorations	Okapi Eductional Materials
Frog and the Fly, The	D	F	33	Cat on the Mat	Oxford University Press
*Frog and Toad All Year	K	F	250+	Little Readers	Houghton Mifflin Harcourt
*Frog and Toad Are Friends	K	F	250+	Lobel, Arnold	Harper & Row
Frog and Toad Together	K	F	250+	Little Readers	Houghton Mifflin Harcourt
Frog and Toad Together	K	F	1927	Lobel, Arnold	HarperCollins
Frog Bog	M	I	250+	Explorations	Eleanor Curtain Publishing
Frog Bog	M	I	250+	Explorations	Okapi Educational Materials
Frog Catchers of Fairfax, The	L	F	856	InfoTrek	ETA Cuisenaire
Frog Day	J	RF	442	Storyteller	Wright Group/McGraw Hill
Frog Food	A	F	38	Leveled Literacy Intervention/ Green System	Heinemann
Frog Friends	K	F	415	Reading Street	Pearson
Frog Fun	C	I	45	Bonnell, Kris	Reading Reading Books
Frog Goes to Dinner	WB	F	N/A	Mayer, Mercer	Dial/Penguin
Frog Has a Sticky Tongue, A	H	I	176	Windows on Literacy	National Geographic
Frog in a Bog	M	RF	250+	Himmelman, John	Charlesbridge
Frog in the Pond, The	H	RF	175	Rookie Readers	Children's Press

F

TITLE	LEVEL	GENRE	WORD COUNT	AUTHOR / SERIES	PUBLISHER / DISTRIBUTOR
Frog on His Own	WB	F	N/A	Mayer, Mercer	Dial/Penguin
Frog or Toad?	I	I	241	Ready Readers	Pearson Learning Group
Frog Prince, The	I	TL	250+	Jumbled Tumbled Tales & Rhymes	Rigby
Frog Prince, The	K	TL	250+	Literacy by Design	Rigby
Frog Prince, The	I	TL	250+	Storyworlds	Heinemann Educational Books
Frog Prince, The	K	TL	250+	Tarcov, Edith H.	Scholastic
Frog Prince, The	I	TL	572	Traditional Tales	Pearson Learning Group
Frog Princess, The	K	TL	206	Literacy 2000	Rigby
Frog Princess, The	N	TL	250+	WorldScapes	ETA Cuisenaire
Frog Report, The	K	I	184	Rigby Focus	Rigby
Frog Songs	J	F	377	Leveled Literacy Intervention/ Blue System	Heinemann
Frog Under the Tree, The	G	RF	194	PM Photo Stories	Rigby
Frog Who Thought He Was a Horse, The	L	F	250+	Literacy 2000	Rigby
Frog Who Would Be King, The	N	TL	250+	Walker, Kate	Mondo
Frog, The	D	RF	69	Adams, Lorraine; Bruvold, Lynn	Eagle Crest Books
Frog, The	M	I	250+	Crewe, Sabrina	Steck-Vaughn
Frogfish, The	J	I	130	Weird Animals	Capstone Press
Froggy Learns to Swim	J	F	250+	London, Jonathan	Scholastic
Froggy Tale, A	I	F	250+	Literacy 2000	Rigby
Frogs	N	I	250+	Bookshop	Mondo
Frogs	N	I	250+	Gibbons, Gail	Holiday House
Frogs	O	I	250+	Holmes, Kevin J.	Red Brick Learning
Frogs	C	F	36	Joy Readers	Pearson Learning Group
Frogs	F	I	94	Life Cycles	Lerner Publications
Frogs	N	I	250+	Nature's Friends	Compass Point Books
Frogs	C	I	34	Pair-It Books	Steck-Vaughn
Frogs	D	I	28	Pebble Books	Capstone Press
Frogs	G	I	192	Rigby Flying Colors	Rigby
Frogs	G	I	100	Storyteller-First Snow	Wright Group/McGraw Hill
Frogs	A	I	13	Twig	Wright Group/McGraw Hill
Frogs	K	I	170	Windows on Literacy	National Geographic
Frogs	K	I	311	Wonder World	Wright Group/McGraw Hill
Frogs and Tadpoles	L	I	913	Sun Sprouts	ETA Cuisenaire
Frogs and Toads	P	I	250+	Crabapples	Crabtree
Frogs and Toads	G	I	323	Sails	Rigby
Frogs and Toads	J	I	187	Shutterbug Books	Steck-Vaughn
Frogs and Turtles	A	I	58	InfoTrek	ETA Cuisenaire
Frogs Can Jump	C	I	41	Book Bank	Wright Group/McGraw Hill
Frog's Day	E	F	101	Instant Readers	Harcourt School Publishers
Frogs in the House	J	F	355	Sails	Rigby
Frogs in the Pond	D	I	122	PM Science Readers	Rigby
Frog's Life, A	L	I	246	Reading Street	Pearson
Frog's Life, A	G	I	100	Time for Kids	Teacher Created Materials
Frog's Lunch	E	F	89	Lillegard, Dee	Scholastic
Frogs of Betts, The	N	RF	250+	SupaDoopers	Sundance
Frogs on a Log	D	F	75	Teacher's Choice Series	Pearson Learning Group
From a Tree	K	I	351	Rigby Focus	Rigby
From Acorn to Oak Tree	I	I	199	Welcome Books	Children's Press
From Apples to Applesauce	M	I	250+	From Farm to Table	Capstone Press
From Axes to Zippers: Simple Machines	Q	I	250+	Navigators Social Studies Series	Benchmark Education

* Collection of short stories
# Graphic text

TITLE	LEVEL	GENRE	WORD COUNT	AUTHOR / SERIES	PUBLISHER / DISTRIBUTOR
From Barbados to Brooklyn: The Story of Shirley Chisholm	S	B	2374	Leveled Readers Social Studies	Houghton Mifflin Harcourt
From Bee to Honey	J	I	102	Take Two Books	Wright Group/McGraw Hill
From Big Bands to Rap	S	I	3915	Take Two Books	Wright Group/McGraw Hill
From Blossom to Fruit	E	I	44	Pebble Books	Capstone Press
From Bud to Blossom	D	I	40	Pebble Books	Capstone Press
From Camel Cart to Canoe	L	I	250+	Sunshine	Wright Group/McGraw Hill
From Cane to Crystals	R	I	250+	Orbit Chapter Books	Pacific Learning
From Cane to Sugar	L	I	250+	From Farm to Table	Capstone Press
From Cane to Sugar	M	I	350	Start to Finish	Lerner Publications
From Caves to Canvas	V	I	250+	Navigators Social Studies Series	Benchmark Education
From Cement to Bridge	L	I	400	Start to Finish	Lerner Publications
From Chili to Chocolate	S	I	250+	WorldScapes	ETA Cuisenaire
From Clay to Bricks	L	I	289	Start to Finish	Lerner Publications
From Cloth to American Flag	L	I	320	Start to Finish	Lerner Publications
From Cocoa Bean to Chocolate	L	I	301	Start to Finish	Lerner Publications
From Corn to Cereal	L	I	250+	From Farm to Table	Capstone Press
From Cotton Plant to Cotton Shirt	L	I	250+	Early Connections	Benchmark Education
From Cotton to Blue Jeans	Q	I	250+	Theme Sets	National Geographic
From Cotton to T-Shirt	K	I	311	Start to Finish	Lerner Publications
From Cow to Milk Carton	M	I	250+	Take Two Books	Wright Group/McGraw Hill
From Cows to Ice Cream	Q	I	250+	Theme Sets	National Geographic
From Cub to King	J	I	316	Leveled Readers	Houghton Mifflin Harcourt
From Cub to King	J	I	316	Leveled Readers/CA	Houghton Mifflin Harcourt
From Cuneiform to Computers	V	I	250+	High-Fliers	Pacific Learning
From Day to Night	B	I	23	On Our Way to English	Rigby
From Drummers to Satellites	R	I	250+	Take Two Books	Wright Group/McGraw Hill
From Earth to Art	U	I	250+	Rigby Literacy	Rigby
From Egg to Butterfly	J	I	262	Start to Finish	Lerner Publications
From Egg to Chicken	K	I	268	Start to Finish	Lerner Publications
From Egg to Robin	D	I	31	Canizares, Susan; Chessen, Betsey	Scholastic
From Farm to Store	J	I	181	Phonics Readers	Compass Point Books
From Field to Florist	I	I	142	Windows on Literacy	National Geographic
From Flower to Honey	J	I	274	Start to Finish	Lerner Publications
From Foal to Horse	M	I	337	Start to Finish	Lerner Publications
From Fruit to Jelly	L	I	302	Start to Finish	Lerner Publications
From Grain to Pita	M	I	1331	Take Two Books	Wright Group/McGraw Hill
From Grass to Milk	M	I	300	Start to Finish	Lerner Publications
From Here to There	M	I	250+	Sails	Rigby
From Here to There	G	I	179	Yellow Umbrella Books	Red Brick Learning
From Here to There: Transportation Timelines	P	I	250+	Discovery World	Rigby
From Hive to Home	J	I	200	Windows on Literacy	National Geographic
From Hubble to Hubble Astronomers and Outer Space	S	B	250+	Science Readers	Teacher Created Materials
From Idea to Book	K	I	407	Start to Finish	Lerner Publications
From Idea to Law: The Legislative Process	S	I	1625	Leveled Readers Social Studies	Houghton Mifflin Harcourt
From Iron to Car	L	I	339	Start to Finish	Lerner Publications
From Kernel to Corn	L	I	364	Start to Finish	Lerner Publications
From Maple Tree to Syrup	L	I	274	Start to Finish	Lerner Publications
From Maple Trees to Maple Syrup	M	I	250+	From Farm to Table	Capstone Press
From Metal to Airplane	K	I	278	Start to Finish	Lerner Publications
From Milk to Cheese	M	I	332	From Farm to Table	Capstone Press
From Milk to Cheese	M	I	318	Start to Finish	Lerner Publications

* Collection of short stories
# Graphic text

TITLE	LEVEL	GENRE	WORD COUNT	AUTHOR / SERIES	PUBLISHER / DISTRIBUTOR
From Milk to Ice Cream	M	I	250+	From Farm to Table	Capstone Press
From Milk to Ice Cream	L	I	365	Leveled Literacy Intervention/ Blue System	Heinemann
From Milk to Ice Cream	K	I	347	Start to Finish	Lerner Publications
From Oil to Gas	K	I	314	Start to Finish	Lerner Publications
From One to Eight	F	I	171	PM Math Readers	Rigby
From Oranges to Orange Juice	M	I	250+	From Farm to Table	Capstone Press
From Oscar Micheaux to the Oscars	X	I	2858	Reading Street	Pearson
From Paper Airplanes to Outer Space	O	B	250+	Meet The Author	Richard C. Owen
From Parking Lot to Garden	R	I	1236	Vocabulary Readers	Houghton Mifflin Harcourt
From Parking Lot to Garden	R	I	1236	Vocabulary Readers/CA	Houghton Mifflin Harcourt
From Parking Lot to Garden	R	I	1236	Vocabulary Readers/TX	Houghton Mifflin Harcourt
From Peanut to Peanut Butter	L	I	357	Start to Finish	Lerner Publications
From Peanuts to Peanut Butter	M	I	250+	From Farm to Table	Capstone Press
From Plan to House	K	I	252	Take Two Books	Wright Group/ McGraw Hill
From Pyramids to Skyscrapers: Building in the Americas	R	I	250+	Navigators Social Studies Series	Benchmark Education
From Raider to Peacemaker	U	I	1307	Leveled Readers	Houghton Mifflin Harcourt
From Raider to Peacemaker	U	I	1307	Leveled Readers/CA	Houghton Mifflin Harcourt
From Rock to Road	J	I	241	Start to Finish	Lerner Publications
From Rocks to Sand: The Story of a Beach	J	I	224	Wonder World	Wright Group/McGraw Hill
From Salt to Silk: Precious Goods	U	I	2867	Reading Street	Pearson
From Sand to Glass	K	I	352	Start to Finish	Lerner Publications
From Sea to Salt	M	I	322	Start to Finish	Lerner Publications
From Seed to Plant	M	I	250+	Gibbons, Gail	Holiday House
From Seed to Pumpkin	F	I	148	Kottke, Jan	Scholastic
From Seedling to Tree	E	I	78	Rigby Star Quest	Rigby
From Seeds to Plants	E	RF	80	Reading Street	Pearson
From Sheep to Sweater	J	I	266	Leveled Readers	Houghton Mifflin Harcourt
From Sheep to Sweater	J	I	266	Leveled Readers/CA	Houghton Mifflin Harcourt
From Sheep to Sweater	J	I	266	Leveled Readers/TX	Houghton Mifflin Harcourt
From Sheep to Sweater	L	I	308	Start to Finish	Lerner Publications
From Sheep to Sweater	B	I	28	Tarlow, Ellen	Scholastic
From Shoot to Apple	J	I	271	Start to Finish	Lerner Publications
From Sky to Sea	H	I	40	Pacific Literacy	Pacific Learning
From Spain to America	T	I	1096	Reading Street	Pearson
From Tadpole to Frog	L	I	327	Start to Finish	Lerner Publications
From Texas to California	L	RF	250+	On Our Way to English	Rigby
From the Air	E	I	107	Wonder World	Wright Group/McGraw Hill
From the Earth	J	I	186	Discovery Links	Newbridge
From the Farm to the Table	D	I	26	Rosen Real Readers	Rosen Publishing Group
From the Garden: A Counting Book About Growing Food	J	I	118	Know Your Numbers	Picture Window Books
From the Lake to Your Faucet	M	I	250+	On Our Way to English	Rigby
From the Mixed-up Files of Mrs. Basil E. Frankweiler	S	RF	250+	Konigsburg, E. L.	Bantam
From the Mountain to the Ocean	K	I	99	Independent Readers Social Studies	Houghton Mifflin Harcourt
From the Notebooks of Melanin Sun	Z	RF	250+	Woodson, Jacqueline	Scholastic
From the Sea	O	I	250+	Rigby Focus	Rigby
From the Skyscraper	E	I	82	Windows on Literacy	National Geographic
From Tomato to Ketchup	L	I	250+	From Farm to Table	Capstone Press
From Trails to Highways	Q	I	919	Leveled Readers	Houghton Mifflin Harcourt

F

* Collection of short stories
# Graphic text

TITLE	LEVEL	GENRE	WORD COUNT	AUTHOR / SERIES	PUBLISHER / DISTRIBUTOR
From Trails to Highways	Q	I	919	Leveled Readers/CA	Houghton Mifflin Harcourt
From Trails to Highways	Q	I	919	Leveled Readers/TX	Houghton Mifflin Harcourt
From Tree to House	J	I	319	Start to Finish	Lerner Publications
From Tree to Table	K	I	338	Start to Finish	Lerner Publications
From Tree to Table	E	I	89	Yellow Umbrella Books	Red Brick Learning
From Trees to Paper	Q	I	250+	Theme Sets	National Geographic
From Typewriters to Computers	K	I	312	Vocabulary Readers	Houghton Mifflin Harcourt
From Typewriters to Computers	K	I	312	Vocabulary Readers/CA	Houghton Mifflin Harcourt
From Typewriters to Computers	K	I	312	Vocabulary Readers/TX	Houghton Mifflin Harcourt
From Wax to Crayon	L	I	303	Start to Finish	Lerner Publications
From Wheat to Bread	M	I	250+	From Farm to Table	Capstone Press
From Wheat to Bread	K	I	305	Start to Finish	Lerner Publications
From Wheat to Bread	Q	I	250+	Theme Sets	National Geographic
From Wheels to Wings	J	I	149	Shutterbug Books	Steck-Vaughn
From Zeus to Aliens	V	I	250+	Power Up!	Steck-Vaughn
Frost in the Night, A: A Girlhood on the Eve of the Third Reich	X	B	250+	Baer, Edith	Sunburst
Frosty: The Adventures of a Morgan Horse	S	RF	250+	Feld, Ellen F.	Willow Bend Publishing
Frown, The	K	RF	228	Read Alongs	Rigby
Frozen Man	T	I	250+	Getz, David	Henry Holt & Co.
Frozen Music	L	TL	432	Books for Young Learners	Richard C. Owen
Frozen Wasteland, The	S	RF	250+	Reading Safari	Mondo
Fruit	A	I	28	Leveled Readers Emergent	Houghton Mifflin Harcourt
Fruit	K	I	551	Rigby Flying Colors	Rigby
Fruit	B	I	20	Rise & Shine	Hampton-Brown
Fruit Facts	E	I	198	Rosen Real Readers	Rosen Publishing Group
Fruit for Fly	E	F	103	Bonnell, Kris	Reading Reading Books
Fruit Group, The	H	I	96	The Food Guide Pyramid	Capstone Press
Fruit Pops	H	I	89	Windows on Literacy	National Geographic
Fruit Salad	B	I	24	Early Emergent	Pioneer Valley
Fruit Salad	D	I	18	Hoenecke, Karen	Kaeden Books
Fruit Salad	LB	I	15	Literacy 2000	Rigby
Fruit Salad	B	I	27	Rigby Rocket	Rigby
Fruit Salad	A	I	37	Sun Sprouts	ETA Cuisenaire
Fruit Salad	LB	I	7	Windows on Literacy	National Geographic
Fruit Salad	D	I	37	Wonder World	Wright Group/McGraw Hill
Fruit Trees	LB	I	24	Visions	Wright Group/McGraw Hill
Fruits	F	I	87	Food Groups	Lerner Publications
Fruits	H	I	114	Plant Parts	Capstone Press
Fudge	O	RF	250+	Graeber, Charlotte Towner	Simon & Schuster
Fudge-a-Mania	Q	RF	250+	Blume, Judy	Bantam
Full Court Dreams	P	RF	250+	Maddox, Jake	Stone Arch Books
Full Court Fever	Q	RF	250+	Bowen, Fred	Peachtree
Full House: Club Stephanie	Q	RF	250+	Herman, Gail	Pocket Books
Full House; Stephanie	Q	RF	250+	Herman, Gail	Pocket Books
Full of Air	E	I	97	Gear Up!	Wright Group/McGraw Hill
Full Throttle	W	RF	250+	Redline Racing Series	Fitzhenry & Whiteside
Fun	D	RF	45	Yannone, Deborah	Kaeden Books
Fun All Year	A	I	25	Leveled Readers	Houghton Mifflin Harcourt
Fun All Year	A	I	25	Leveled Readers/CA	Houghton Mifflin Harcourt
Fun and Food to Eat	D	F	68	Leveled Readers Language Support	Houghton Mifflin Harcourt
Fun and Games	O	I	250+	Orbit Chapter Books	Pacific Learning

F

* Collection of short stories
# Graphic text

TITLE	LEVEL	GENRE	WORD COUNT	AUTHOR / SERIES	PUBLISHER / DISTRIBUTOR
Fun and Games	O	I	250+	Rigby Focus	Rigby
Fun and Games, Then and Now	C	I	42	Independent Readers Social Studies	Houghton Mifflin Harcourt
Fun at Camp	H	RF	178	First Start	Troll Associates
Fun at Camp	A	F	35	Leveled Readers	Houghton Mifflin Harcourt
Fun at Camp	A	F	35	Leveled Readers/CA	Houghton Mifflin Harcourt
Fun at School	C	RF	50	Foundations	Wright Group/McGraw Hill
Fun at School	B	I	40	Leveled Literacy Intervention/ Orange System	Heinemann
Fun at the Amusement Park	G	RF	176	Frankford, Marilyn	Kaeden Books
Fun at the Beach	E	RF	88	Rigby Focus	Rigby
Fun Baseball Game, A	H	I	376	Leveled Readers	Houghton Mifflin Harcourt
Fun Baseball Game, A	H	I	376	Leveled Readers/CA	Houghton Mifflin Harcourt
Fun Baseball Game, A	H	I	376	Leveled Readers/TX	Houghton Mifflin Harcourt
Fun Club Goes to a Dairy Farm, The	H	I	233	Leveled Literacy Intervention/ Blue System	Heinemann
Fun Club Goes to the Aquarium, The	K	I	635	Leveled Literacy Intervention/ Blue System	Heinemann
Fun Club Goes to the Post Office, The	I	I	230	Leveled Literacy Intervention/ Blue System	Heinemann
Fun Club Goes to the Vet Clinic, The	I	I	258	Leveled Literacy Intervention/ Blue System	Heinemann
Fun Days	F	RF	250+	Let's Play	Norwood House Press
Fun Days!	D	RF	79	Literacy by Design	Rigby
Fun Days!	D	RF	79	On Our Way to English	Rigby
Fun Facts About Fossils	S	I	1129	Leveled Readers Science	Houghton Mifflin Harcourt
Fun Food	C	I	29	Home Connection Collection	Rigby
Fun for All Seasons	A	RF	24	Literacy by Design	Rigby
Fun for Everyone	K	RF	250+	On Our Way to English	Rigby
Fun For Families	D	I	28	Reading Street	Pearson
Fun for Hugs	I	RF	307	Leveled Literacy Intervention/ Green System	Heinemann
Fun for Pickles	J	F	608	Pickles the Dog Series	Pioneer Valley
Fun in Colonial Times	R	I	1431	Vocabulary Readers	Houghton Mifflin Harcourt
Fun in Colonial Times	R	I	1431	Vocabulary Readers/CA	Houghton Mifflin Harcourt
Fun in Colonial Times	R	I	1431	Vocabulary Readers/TX	Houghton Mifflin Harcourt
Fun in July	A	I	20	Vocabulary Readers	Houghton Mifflin Harcourt
Fun in July	A	I	20	Vocabulary Readers/CA	Houghton Mifflin Harcourt
Fun in the Mud	G	RF	182	Foundations	Wright Group/McGraw Hill
Fun in the Snow	C	F	56	Bella and Rosie Series	Pioneer Valley
Fun in the Snow	D	I	76	Leveled Readers	Houghton Mifflin Harcourt
Fun on the Sled	G	RF	269	Adams, Lorraine; Bruvold, Lynn	Eagle Crest Books
Fun on the Slide	C	RF	37	Early Emergent	Pioneer Valley
Fun Pets	H	I	190	Vocabulary Readers	Houghton Mifflin Harcourt
Fun Pets	H	I	190	Vocabulary Readers/CA	Houghton Mifflin Harcourt
Fun Pets	H	I	190	Vocabulary Readers/TX	Houghton Mifflin Harcourt
Fun Place to Eat, A	E	RF	90	Ready Readers	Pearson Learning Group
Fun Run, The	C	RF	27	Rigby Star	Rigby
Fun Things to Make and Do	I	I	250+	Discovery World	Rigby
Fun with Fingerprints	K	I	250+	How-To Series	Benchmark Education
Fun with Fingerprints	M	I	250+	Sunshine	Wright Group/McGraw Hill
Fun with Fizz and Frost	P	I	250+	Storyteller - Raging Rivers	Wright Group/ McGraw Hill
Fun with Fractions	P	I	250+	Rosen Real Readers	Rosen Publishing Group
Fun with Friends	A	RF	21	Bookshop	Mondo

* Collection of short stories
\# Graphic text

F

TITLE	LEVEL	GENRE	WORD COUNT	AUTHOR / SERIES	PUBLISHER / DISTRIBUTOR
Fun with Friends	A	I	28	Gear Up!	Wright Group/McGraw Hill
Fun with Friends	LB	RF	18	Rise & Shine	Hampton-Brown
Fun with Fruit	B	I	37	Storyteller	Wright Group/McGraw Hill
Fun with Hats	B	F	38	Bookshop	Mondo
Fun with Magnets	M	I	250+	Early Connections	Benchmark Education
Fun with Magnets	L	I	394	Rigby Focus	Rigby
Fun with Magnets	D	I	38	Rosen Real Readers	Rosen Publishing Group
Fun with Mo and Toots	C	F	41	Pacific Literacy	Pacific Learning
Fun with Paper	A	I	29	Gear Up!	Wright Group/McGraw Hill
Fun with Plaster	H	I	150	Rigby Focus	Rigby
Fun with Science	O	I	801	Reading Street	Pearson
Fun with Science	L	I	433	Vocabulary Readers/TX	Houghton Mifflin Harcourt
Fun with Shadows	M	I	250+	iOpeners	Pearson Learning Group
Fun with Simple Machines	C	RF	28	Tarlow, Ellen	Scholastic
Fun Zone	N	F	250+	Sails	Rigby
Fun, Fun, Fun	D	I	71	Leveled Readers	Houghton Mifflin Harcourt
Fungi	M	I	326	Take Two Books	Wright Group/McGraw Hill
Funky Flamingos	I	I	202	Sails	Rigby
Funny Baby, The	F	TL	217	Fairy Tales and Folklore	Norwood House Press
Funny Bananas: The Mystery in the Museum	N	RF	250+	McHargue, Georgess	Dell
Funny Bones	J	F	250+	Ahlberg, Allan & Janet	Viking/Penguin
Funny Cars	M	I	250+	Horsepower	Capstone Press
Funny Dog Facts	L	I	250+	Scooters	ETA Cuisenaire
Funny Ears	E	I	77	Rigby Star Quest	Rigby
Funny Face	A	RF	11	InfoTrek	ETA Cuisenaire
Funny Face	M	RF	250+	Rigby Gigglers	Rigby
Funny Faces	Q	I	250+	Rigby Literacy	Rigby
Funny Faces and Funny Places	D	I	45	Ready Readers	Pearson Learning Group
Funny Faces, Wacky Wings, and Other Silly Big Bird Things	J	I	387	Silly Millies	Millbrook Press
Funny Fish	E	F	130	Big Cat	Pacific Learning
Funny Fish	I	I	211	Sails	Rigby
Funny Fish	C	I	86	Springboard	Wright Group/McGraw Hill
Funny Fish Story	E	F	152	Rookie Readers	Children's Press
Funny Garden, A	I	RF	234	Reading Street	Pearson
Funny Insects	D	I	117	Sails	Rigby
Funny Man, A	E	F	244	Jensen, Patricia	Scholastic
Funny Old Man and the Funny Old Woman, The	M	F	250+	Bookshop	Mondo
Funny Ride, The	F	RF	250+	Let's Play	Norwood House Press
Funny Talk and More	I	F	250+	Bookshop	Mondo
Funny Things	A	I	40	Leveled Literacy Intervention/ Orange System	Heinemann
Funny, Funny Clown Face, The	M	F	250+	Sunshine	Wright Group/McGraw Hill
Fur	D	RF	32	Mark, Jan	Harper & Row
Fur	J	I	287	Springboard	Wright Group/McGraw Hill
Fur	U	I	250+	Theme Sets	National Geographic
Fur Traders of New France	X	I	2576	Independent Readers Social Studies	Houghton Mifflin Harcourt
Fur, Feathers, and Flippers: How Animals Live Where They Do	T	I	250+	Lauber, Patricia	Scholastic
Fur, Feathers, or Skin	I	I	354	Sails	Rigby
Fur, Feathers, Scales, Skin	H	I	173	Discovery Links	Newbridge
Furball to the Rescue	E	F	133	Rigby Rocket	Rigby

F

TITLE	LEVEL	GENRE	WORD COUNT	AUTHOR / SERIES	PUBLISHER / DISTRIBUTOR
Furry	B	I	19	Little Celebrations	Pearson Learning Group
Fussy Heron	F	TL	177	PM Stars	Rigby
Fussy Wolf	D	F	60	Sun Sprouts	ETA Cuisenaire
Future of NASA, The	U	I	1498	Leveled Readers	Houghton Mifflin Harcourt
Future of NASA, The	U	I	1498	Leveled Readers/CA	Houghton Mifflin Harcourt
*Future-Telling Lady and Other Stories, The	S	RF	250+	Berry, James	HarperTrophy
Fuzz and the Glass Eye	M	RF	250+	Literacy Tree	Rigby
Fuzz, Feathers, Fur	E	I	131	Twig	Wright Group/McGraw Hill

F

* Collection of short stories
# Graphic text

TITLE	LEVEL	GENRE	WORD COUNT	AUTHOR / SERIES	PUBLISHER / DISTRIBUTOR
G is for Googol	U	I	250+	Schwartz, David M.	Scholastic
Gabby and the Christmas Tree	G	F	113	Developing Books, Set 2	Pioneer Valley
Gabby Is Hungry	C	RF	78	Emergent	Pioneer Valley
Gabby Runs Away	G	RF	223	Developing Books, Set 1	Pioneer Valley
Gabby Visits Buster	C	RF	39	Early Emergent	Pioneer Valley
Gabrielle Lyon and the Fossil Hunt	P	I	250+	On Our Way to English	Rigby
Gabrielle's Team	G	RF	250+	Reading Safari	Mondo
Gadget War, The	N	RF	250+	Duffey, Betsy	Penguin Group
Gail & Me	L	RF	250+	Literacy 2000	Rigby
Gail Devers: A Runner's Dream	M	B	250+	Pair-It Books	Steck-Vaughn
Galapagos Giants	P	I	250+	Orbit Double Takes	Pacific Learning
Galapagos Islands, The	R	I	250+	Rosen Real Readers	Rosen Publishing Group
Galaxies	Q	I	250+	A True Book	Children's Press
Galaxies	T	I	250+	Simon, Seymour	Mulberry Books
Galaxies, Galaxies!	S	I	250+	Gibbons, Gail	Holiday House
Gale and Brian, Friends Forever	S	I	1984	Vocabulary Readers	Houghton Mifflin Harcourt
Gale and Brian, Friends Forever	S	I	1984	Vocabulary Readers/CA	Houghton Mifflin Harcourt
Galileo	W	I	2592	Leveled Readers	Houghton Mifflin Harcourt
Galileo	W	I	2592	Leveled Readers/CA	Houghton Mifflin Harcourt
Galileo Galilee, Astronomer	Q	B	455	Independent Readers Science	Houghton Mifflin Harcourt
Galileo, Messenger of Modern Science	Z	B	3428	Leveled Readers	Houghton Mifflin Harcourt
Galileo: Man of Science	R	B	250+	Rosen Real Readers	Rosen Publishing Group
Galileo's Journal 1609-1610	S	HF	250+	Pettenati, Jeanne K.	Charlesbridge
Galileo's Telescope	X	I	2796	Leveled Readers	Houghton Mifflin Harcourt
Galileo's Telescope	X	I	2796	Leveled Readers/CA	Houghton Mifflin Harcourt
Gallo and Zorro	J	F	369	Literacy 2000	Rigby
Game for Jamie, A	M	RF	572	Sunshine	Wright Group/McGraw Hill
Game for Scruffy, A	D	RF	109	PM Photo Stories	Rigby
Game of Bowling, A	G	RF	295	PM Math Stories	Rigby
Game Show, The	K	RF	610	InfoTrek	ETA Cuisenaire
Game with Shapes, A	D	I	74	PM Math Readers	Rigby
Game-Day Gigglers: Winning Jokes to Score Some Laughs	O	F	2287	Make Me Laugh!	Lerner Publications
Gamer	P	F	250+	Durant, Alan	Stone Arch Books
Gamer: Next Level	P	F	250+	Durant, Alan	Stone Arch Books
Games	C	RF	69	Berger, Samantha; Moreton, Daniel	Scholastic
Games	B	I	28	Berger, Samantha; Moreton, Daniel	Scholastic
Games	W	I	250+	Boldprint	Steck-Vaughn
Games	A	F	28	KinderReaders	Rigby
Games Around the World	D	I	110	Dominie Factivity Series	Pearson Learning Group
Games Around the World	N	I	873	Time for Kids	Teacher Created Materials Publishing
Games at School	D	I	121	Vocabulary Readers	Houghton Mifflin Harcourt
Games at School	D	I	121	Vocabulary Readers/CA	Houghton Mifflin Harcourt
Games from Long Ago	T	I	250+	Historic Communities	Crabtree
Games We Play	Q	I	1368	Leveled Readers	Houghton Mifflin Harcourt
Games We Play	Q	I	1368	Leveled Readers/CA	Houghton Mifflin Harcourt
Games We Play	Q	I	1368	Leveled Readers/TX	Houghton Mifflin Harcourt
Games We Play	J	I	250+	PM Plus Nonfiction	Rigby
Gampy's Lamps	P	RF	1296	Leveled Readers	Houghton Mifflin Harcourt
Gannets	L	I	250+	Sunshine	Wright Group/McGraw Hill
Garage Sale, The	D	RF	44	Harry's Math Books	Outside the Box

G

* Collection of short stories
# Graphic text

TITLE	LEVEL	GENRE	WORD COUNT	AUTHOR / SERIES	PUBLISHER / DISTRIBUTOR
Garbage	C	I	51	Wonder World	Wright Group/McGraw Hill
Garbage Collectors	M	I	250+	Community Helpers	Red Brick Learning
Garbage Trucks	I	I	131	Mighty Machines	Capstone Press
Garbage Trucks	K	I	444	Pull Ahead Books	Lerner Publications
Garbage, Waste, Dumps, and You; The Disgusting Story Behind What We Leave Behind	S	I	250+	Sanitation Investigation	Capstone Press
Garden Birthday	LB	F	15	Instant Readers	Harcourt School Publishers
Garden Colors	LB	F	15	Pair-It Books	Steck-Vaughn
Garden in a Bottle, A	K	I	370	Springboard	Wright Group/McGraw Hill
Garden in Your Bedroom, A	O	I	250+	Sunshine	Wright Group/McGraw Hill
Garden Is Fun, A	B	RF	36	Bonnell, Kris	Reading Reading Books
Garden of Eden Motel, The	W	RF	250+	Hamilton, Morse	William Morrow
Garden of Happiness, The	O	RF	1100	Tamar, Erika	Harcourt, Brace, and Company
Garden on Green Street, The	L	RF	250+	Goldish, Meish	Scholastic
Garden Tools	J	I	165	Spyglass Books	Compass Point Books
Garden, A	A	I	40	Foundations	Wright Group/McGraw Hill
Garden, A	LB	F	12	Sails	Rigby
Garden, The	G	RF	21	Hoenecke, Karen	Kaeden Books
Garden, The	LB	I	14	Instant Readers	Harcourt School Publishers
Garden, The	A	I	27	Leveled Readers	Houghton Mifflin Harcourt
Garden, The	B	RF	63	Leveled Readers Emergent	Houghton Mifflin Harcourt
Garden, The	A	I	27	Leveled Readers/CA	Houghton Mifflin Harcourt
Garden, The	G	RF	107	Reading Street	Pearson
Gardener, The	M	RF	250+	Stewart, Sarah	Farrar, Straus and Giroux
Gardening	D	RF	77	Foundations	Wright Group/McGraw Hill
Gardening with Grandpa	K	RF	310	Reading Street	Pearson
Gardens of the Sea	I	I	195	Sails	Rigby
Gardens on Green Street, The	I	RF	174	TOTTS	Tott Publications
Garfield and the Beast in the Basement	Q	F	250+	Davis, Jim	Troll Associates
Garfield and the Mysterious Mummy	Q	F	250+	Davis, Jim	Troll Associates
Gargoyles Don't Drive School Buses	M	F	250+	Dadey, Debbie; Jones, Marcia Thornton	Scholastic
Gargoyles on Guard	K	I	269	Books for Young Learners	Richard C. Owen
Garter Snakes	M	I	250+	Snakes	Capstone Press
Gary Soto	Y	B	2464	Leveled Readers	Houghton Mifflin Harcourt
Gases	J	I	93	What Earth Is Made Of	Lerner Publications
Gasp!	L	F	250+	Bookshop	Mondo
*Gaston the Giant and Other Stories	K	F	331	New Way Orange	Steck-Vaughn
Gathering Blue	X	F	250+	Lowry, Lois	Houghton Mifflin Harcourt
Gathering of Days, A: A New England Girl's Journal, 1830-32	U	HF	250+	Blos, Joan	Aladdin
*Gathering of Flowers, A	Z	RF	250+	Thomas, Joyce Carol	HarperTrophy
Gathering of Gargoyles, A	Y	F	250+	Pierce, Meredith Ann	Little, Brown & Co.
Gathering, The	V	F	250+	Hamilton, Virginia	Harcourt Brace
Gathering: A Northwoods Counting Book	Q	I	250+	Bowen, Betsy	Houghton Mifflin Harcourt
Gator Girls, The	L	F	250+	Calmenson, Stephanie & Cole	Beech Tree Books
Gator or Croc?	K	I	250+	Rookie Read About Science	Children's Press
Gecko That Came to School, The	H	RF	302	Leveled Literacy Intervention/Green System	Heinemann
Geckos	N	I	250+	World of Reptiles	Capstone Press
Gecko's Story	F	F	61	Books for Young Learners	Richard C. Owen
Geena's Project	H	I	212	Springboard	Wright Group/McGraw Hill

* Collection of short stories
# Graphic text

TITLE	LEVEL	GENRE	WORD COUNT	AUTHOR / SERIES	PUBLISHER / DISTRIBUTOR
Gee's Bend Quilts, The	X	I	2901	Leveled Readers	Houghton Mifflin Harcourt
Gee's Bend Quilts, The	X	I	2901	Leveled Readers/CA	Houghton Mifflin Harcourt
Geese on the Farm	I	I	69	On the Farm	Red Brick Learning
Gem of a Tale, A	P	I	1500	Reading Street	Pearson
Gems	Q	I	250+	On Deck	Rigby
General Butterfingers	O	RF	250+	Gardiner, John Reynolds	Puffin/Penguin
Genetic Engineering	Z	I	250+	Cool Science	Lerner Publications
Genghis Khan: A Dog Star Is Born	L	RF	250+	Sharmat, Marjorie Weinman	Random House
Genie of the Bike Lamp	P	F	250+	Storyteller - Mountain peaks	Wright Group/ McGraw Hill
Genie, The	O	F	250+	Hooper, M.	Stone Arch Books
Genies Don't Ride Bicycles	M	F	250+	Dadey, Debbie; Jones, Marcia Thornton	Scholastic
Gentle and Friendly Sea Lions	S	I	1000	Leveled Readers/TX	Houghton Mifflin Harcourt
Gentle Annie: The True Story of a Civil War Nurse	R	I	250+	Shura, Mary Frances	Scholastic
Gentle Giant Octopus	M	I	250+	Read and Wonder	Candlewick Press
Gentle Lions of the Sea	T	I	1000	Leveled Readers/TX	Houghton Mifflin Harcourt
Gentle Manatees	K	I	381	Pull Ahead Books	Lerner Publications
Gentle Redwood Giants	S	I	1776	Leveled Readers	Houghton Mifflin Harcourt
Gentle Redwood Giants	S	I	1776	Leveled Readers/CA	Houghton Mifflin Harcourt
Gentle Redwood Giants	S	I	1776	Leveled Readers/TX	Houghton Mifflin Harcourt
Gentlehands	Z	RF	250+	Kerr, M. E.	HarperTrophy
Gentleman Outlaw and Me - Eli, The: A Story of the Old West	T	HF	250+	Hahn, Mary Downing	Avon Camelot
Geoffrey the Dinosaur	D	F	36	Sunshine	Wright Group/McGraw Hill
Geographic Information Systems: Locating Ourselves	T	I	1493	Leveled Readers Social Studies	Houghton Mifflin Harcourt
Geography Bee, The	V	RF	3165	Leveled Readers	Houghton Mifflin Harcourt
Geography Bee, The	V	RF	3165	Leveled Readers/CA	Houghton Mifflin Harcourt
Geography Bee, The	V	RF	3165	Leveled Readers/TX	Houghton Mifflin Harcourt
Geography of an Empire: Ancient Rome	X	I	2392	Independent Readers Social Studies	Houghton Mifflin Harcourt
Geography of War, The: The Battle of Salamis	Y	I	2877	Independent Readers Social Studies	Houghton Mifflin Harcourt
Geography Shapes Our World	T	I	1701	Reading Street	Pearson
George and Martha	L	F	250+	Marshall, James	Houghton Mifflin Harcourt
George and Martha Back in Town	L	F	250+	Marshall, James	Houghton Mifflin Harcourt
George and Martha Encore	L	F	250+	Marshall, James	Houghton Mifflin Harcourt
George and Martha One Fine Day	L	F	250+	Marshall, James	Houghton Mifflin Harcourt
George and Martha Rise and Shine	L	F	250+	Marshall, James	Houghton Mifflin Harcourt
George and Martha Round and Round	L	F	250+	Marshall, James	Houghton Mifflin Harcourt
George and the Whopper	L	F	250+	Rigby Literacy	Rigby
George Armstrong Custer	P	B	250+	Early Biographies	Compass Point Books
George at the Zoo	H	F	250+	Voyages	SRA/McGraw Hill
George Bush: Forty-first President	R	B	250+	Getting to Know the U.S. Presidents	Children's Press
George C. Marshall	T	B	4008	History Maker Bios	Lerner Publications
George Catlin, Frontier Painter	Y	B	3371	Leveled Readers	Houghton Mifflin Harcourt
George Eastman	S	B	3213	History Maker Bios	Lerner Publications
#George Eastman and the Kodak Camera	R	B	250+	Graphic Library	Capstone Press
George Goes to Town	M	F	250+	Literacy by Design	Rigby
George H. W. Bush	T	B	3602	History Maker Bios	Lerner Publications
George H. W. Bush	U	B	250+	Profiles of the Presidents	Compass Point Books
George Handel	R	B	250+	Venezia, Mike	Children's Press

G

* Collection of short stories
# Graphic text

Storable Database at www.fountasandpinnellleveledbooks.com

TITLE	LEVEL	GENRE	WORD COUNT	AUTHOR / SERIES	PUBLISHER / DISTRIBUTOR
George Most Wanted	M	F	250+	Orca Echoes	Orca Book Publishers
George Rogers Clark and the American Revolution in the Midwest	V	B	2534	Leveled Readers Social Studies	Houghton Mifflin Harcourt
George S. Patton Jr.	T	B	3807	History Maker Bios	Lerner Publications
George Shrinks	H	F	114	Joyce, William	Scholastic
George the Drummer Boy	K	HF	250+	Benchley, Nathaniel	HarperTrophy
George W. Bush	U	B	250+	Profiles of the Presidents	Compass Point Books
George W. Bush: Forty-third President	R	B	250+	Getting to Know the U.S. Presidents	Children's Press
George Washington	U	B	250+	Amazing Americans	Wright Group/McGraw Hill
George Washington	P	B	250+	Early Biographies	Compass Point Books
George Washington	M	B	270	Famous Americans	Capstone Press
George Washington	N	B	196	First Biographies	Capstone Press
George Washington	S	B	250+	History Maker Bios	Lerner Publications
George Washington	E	B	69	Independent Readers Social Studies	Houghton Mifflin Harcourt
George Washington	U	B	250+	Let Freedom Ring	Red Brick Learning
George Washington	Q	I	250+	Photo-Illustrated Biographies	Red Brick Learning
George Washington	Q	B	250+	Primary Source Readers	Teacher Created Materials
George Washington	U	B	250+	Profiles of the Presidents	Compass Point Books
George Washington	P	B	799	Time for Kids	Teacher Created Materials
George Washington Carver	T	B	250+	Amazing Americans	Wright Group/McGraw Hill
George Washington Carver	M	B	250+	Biography	Benchmark Education
George Washington Carver	Q	B	250+	Early Biographies	Compass Point Books
George Washington Carver	O	B	967	Leveled Readers	Houghton Mifflin Harcourt
George Washington Carver	M	B	521	Leveled Readers	Houghton Mifflin Harcourt
George Washington Carver	O	B	967	Leveled Readers/CA	Houghton Mifflin Harcourt
George Washington Carver	O	B	967	Leveled Readers/TX	Houghton Mifflin Harcourt
George Washington Carver	N	B	1406	On My Own Biography	Lerner Publications
George Washington Carver	N	B	224	Pebble Books	Capstone Press
George Washington Carver	P	B	250+	Photo-Illustrated Biographies	Red Brick Learning
George Washington Carver: Agriculture Pioneer	R	B	250+	Science Readers	Teacher Created Materials
George Washington Carver: Scientist and Inventor	P	B	250+	Great African Americans	Capstone Press
George Washington Carver: Scientist and Teacher	O	B	250+	Greene, Carol	Children's Press
George Washington Carver: The Peanut Wizard	Q	B	250+	Driscoll, Laura	Grossett & Dunlap
George Washington Elected: How America's First President Was Chosen	S	I	250+	Headlines from History	Rosen Publishing Group
George Washington: A Life of Leadership	O	B	530	Pull Ahead Books	Lerner Publications
George Washington: A Picture Book Biography	R	B	250+	Giblin, James Cross	Scholastic
George Washington: Farmer, Soldier, President	M	B	250+	Biographies	Picture Window Books
George Washington: First President	R	B	250+	Getting to Know the U.S. Presidents	Children's Press
George Washington: First President of the U.S.	N	B	250+	Rookie Biographies	Children's Press
George Washington: Our First President	M	B	200	Rosen Real Readers	Rosen Publishing Group
George Washington: The Man Who Would Not Be King	U	B	250+	Krensky, Stephen	Scholastic
George Washington: Young Leader	O	B	250+	Childhood of Famous Americans	Aladdin
George Washington: Young Leader	R	B	250+	Santrey, Laurence	Troll Associates
George Washington's Breakfast	P	B	250+	Fritz, Jean	Putnam/Penguin
George Washington's Invisible Enemy	W	I	2874	Leveled Readers	Houghton Mifflin Harcourt
George Washington's Invisible Enemy	W	I	2874	Leveled Readers/CA	Houghton Mifflin Harcourt
George Washington's Invisible Enemy	W	I	2874	Leveled Readers/TX	Houghton Mifflin Harcourt

* Collection of short stories
# Graphic text

TITLE	LEVEL	GENRE	WORD COUNT	AUTHOR / SERIES	PUBLISHER / DISTRIBUTOR
George Washington's Mother	M	B	250+	Fritz, Jean	Scholastic
George Washington's Socks	T	F	250+	Woodruff, Elvira	Language for Learning Assoc.
George Washington's Socks	T	F	250+	Woodruff, Elvira	Scholastic
George's Marvelous Medicine	P	F	250+	Dahl, Roald	Penguin Group
George's Show and Tell	E	RF	133	Early Emergent	Pioneer Valley
George's Story	G	RF	133	Developing Books	Pioneer Valley
Georgia	T	I	250+	Hello U.S.A.	Lerner Publications
Georgia	T	I	250+	Hello U.S.A.	Lerner Publications
Georgia	S	I	250+	Land of Liberty	Red Brick Learning
Georgia	Q	I	250+	One Nation	Capstone Press
Georgia	T	I	250+	Sea to Shining Sea	Children's Press
Georgia	R	I	250+	This Land Is Your Land	Compass Point Books
Georgia Colony, The	R	I	250+	The American Colonies	Capstone Press
Georgia O'Keeffe	M	B	250+	Lowery, Linda	Carolrhoda Books
Georgia O'Keeffe	R	B	250+	Venezia, Mike	Children's Press
Georgie Giraffe, the Detective	E	F	96	Georgie Giraffe	Literacy Footprints
Georgina and the Dragon	K	F	250+	Rigby Rocket	Rigby
Geothermal Power	X	I	250+	Energy at Work	Capstone Press
Gerald R. Ford	T	B	3660	History Maker Bios	Lerner Publications
Gerald R. Ford	U	B	250+	Profiles of the Presidents	Compass Point Books
Gerald R. Ford: Thirty-eighth President	R	B	250+	Getting to Know the U.S. Presidents	Children's Press
Geraldine's Big Snow	I	RF	250+	Keller, Holly	Scholastic
Gerard Giraffe: Private Investigator	M	F	250+	Foundations	Wright Group/McGraw Hill
Gerbil Genius	O	RF	250+	Baglio, Ben M.	Scholastic
Gerbilitis	P	RF	250+	Soar To Success	Houghton Mifflin Harcourt
Gerbilitis	P	RF	250+	Spinner, Stephanie; Weiss, Ellen	HarperTrophy
Germ Warfare	T	I	250+	Bookweb	Rigby
German Immigrants in America: An Interactive History Adventure	U	HF	250+	You Choose Books	Capstone Press
German Shepherds	I	I	149	Dogs	Capstone Press
German Shepherds	R	I	250+	All About Dogs	Capstone Press
German Shepherds	R	I	250+	All About Dogs	Capstone Press
German-Jewish Immigration	V	I	250+	Theme Sets	National Geographic
Germany	O	I	250+	Countries of the World	Red Brick Learning
Germany	Q	I	250+	First Reports: Countries	Compass Point Books
Germany ABCs: A Book About the People and Places of Germany	Q	I	250+	Country ABCs	Picture Window Books
Germany: A Question and Answer Book	P	I	250+	Questions and Answers: Countries	Capstone Press
Germs	L	I	250+	Twig	Wright Group/McGraw Hill
Germs Make Me Sick!	O	I	250+	Berger, Melvin	Scholastic
Germs!	W	I	250+	WorldScapes	ETA Cuisenaire
Germs! Germs! Germs!	L	F	250+	Katz, Bobbi	Scholastic
Geronimo	R	B	3449	History Maker Bios	Lerner Publications
Geronimo	U	B	1903	Leveled Readers Social Studies	Houghton Mifflin Harcourt
Geronimo: A Novel	Y	HF	250+	Bruchac, Joseph	Scholastic
Gershwin's Rhapsoday in Blue	S	B	250+	Celenza, A. H.	Charlesbridge
Gertie's Green Thumb	O	F	250+	Dexter, Catherine	Dell
Gertrude McClatter Finds Some Friends	J	F	250+	Reading Safari	Mondo
Get A Grip, Pip!	P	RF	250+	Literacy 2000	Rigby
Get Down Danny	C	RF	32	Coulton, Mia	Maryruth Books
Get Lost Becka!	E	RF	102	Start to Read	School Zone

G

* Collection of short stories
# Graphic text

TITLE	LEVEL	GENRE	WORD COUNT	AUTHOR / SERIES	PUBLISHER / DISTRIBUTOR
Get Lost!	F	RF	219	Foundations	Wright Group/McGraw Hill
Get Me Out of Here!	M	F	250+	Rigby Rocket	Rigby
Get on Board: The Story of the Underground Railroad	V	I	250+	Haskins, Jim	Scholastic
Get On Out of Here, Philip Hall	Y	RF	250+	Greene, Bette	Puffin/Penguin
Get on the Train	C	F	42	Gear Up!	Wright Group/McGraw Hill
Get Ready for Second Grade, Amber Brown	K	RF	250+	Danziger, Paula	Puffin Books
Get Ready to Race	H	F	98	Instant Readers	Harcourt School Publishers
Get Ready!	B	I	22	On Our Way to English	Rigby
Get Set and Go	J	F	250+	Real Reading	Steck-Vaughn
Get Set for a Pet Hen	D	RF	31	Reading Street	Pearson
Get Set, Go!	E	RF	97	Reading Street	Pearson
Get Stronger	D	I	66	Little Celebrations	Pearson Learning Group
Get That Ghost to Go!	R	F	5931	MacPhail, C.	Stone Arch Books
Get That Pest!	F	F	179	Green Light Readers	Harcourt
Get the Ball, Slim	E	RF	94	Real Kids Readers	Millbrook Press
Get the Fruit!	WB	F	N/A	Big Cat	Pacific Learning
Get the Message	J	I	110	iOpeners	Pearson Learning Group
Get the Picture?	Q	I	250+	PM Plus Nonfiction	Rigby
Get Up!	D	RF	70	Reading Street	Pearson
Getting a Game	J	RF	250+	Reading Safari	Mondo
Getting Along - Contests, Conflicts, and Combats	V	I	250+	Connectors	Pacific Learning
Getting Around	F	I	182	Chessen, Betsey; Moreton, Daniel	Scholastic
Getting Around	H	I	211	Momentum Literacy Program	Troll Associates
Getting Around	Q	I	250+	Orbit Collections	Pacific Learning
Getting Away With Murder: The True Story of the Emmett Till Case	Z+	I	250+	Crowe, Chris	Ideals Children's Books
Getting Cold! Getting Hot!	K	RF	753	Sunshine	Wright Group/McGraw Hill
Getting Dressed	B	RF	40	Carousel Earlybirds	Pearson Learning Group
Getting Dressed	A	I	31	Leveled Literacy Intervention/ Green System	Heinemann
Getting Dressed	LB	RF	16	Sunshine	Wright Group/McGraw Hill
Getting Energy from Food	K	I	283	Vocabulary Readers	Houghton Mifflin Harcourt
Getting Energy from Food	K	I	283	Vocabulary Readers/CA	Houghton Mifflin Harcourt
Getting Fit	C	I	15	Wonder World	Wright Group/McGraw Hill
Getting Glasses	G	I	82	Wonder World	Wright Group/McGraw Hill
Getting Home	A	I	24	Windows on Literacy	National Geographic
Getting Lincoln's Goat	V	RF	250+	Goldman, E. M.	Bantam
Getting Near to Baby	V	RF	250+	Couloumbis, Audrey	Penguin Group
Getting Ready	A	I	42	Leveled Literacy Intervention/ Orange System	Heinemann
Getting Ready	B	I	29	Little Books for Early Readers	University of Maine
Getting Ready	WB	I	N/A	Windows on Literacy	National Geographic
Getting Ready for School	E	RF	109	Foundations	Wright Group/McGraw Hill
Getting Ready for School	C	I	109	Little Red Readers	Sundance
Getting Ready for School	B	I	72	Vocabulary Readers	Houghton Mifflin Harcourt
Getting Ready for School	B	I	72	Vocabulary Readers/CA	Houghton Mifflin Harcourt
Getting Ready for the Ball	C	F	27	Literacy 2000	Rigby
Getting Ready for Winter	C	F	43	Gear Up!	Wright Group/McGraw Hill
Getting Rest	L	I	350	Pull Ahead Books	Lerner Publications
Getting Rid of Katherine	Q	RF	250+	Wright, Betty Ren	Troll Associates
Getting the Lay of the Land	P	I	997	Reading Street	Pearson
Getting the Mail	G	RF	213	Voyages	SRA/McGraw Hill

* Collection of short stories
# Graphic text

TITLE	LEVEL	GENRE	WORD COUNT	AUTHOR / SERIES	PUBLISHER / DISTRIBUTOR
Getting the Message	Q	I	250+	Orbit Collections	Pacific Learning
Getting the Message Across	U	I	250+	Connectors	Pacific Learning
Getting There	B	I	71	Johns, Edwin	Scholastic
Getting There	P	I	250+	Literacy by Design	Rigby
Getting There	B	I	36	Wonder World	Wright Group/McGraw Hill
Getting to Know Sharks	K	I	379	Little Books	Sadlier-Oxford
Getting to Know Your Neighbors	M	RF	250+	On Our Way To English	Rigby
Getting to Know Your Toilet: The Disgusting Story Behind Your Home's Strangest Feature	S	I	250+	Sanitation Investigation	Capstone Press
Getting Together	R	I	250+	InfoQuest	Rigby
Getting Water	H	I	409	Sails	Rigby
Gettysburg Address in Translation, The: What It Really Means	V	I	250+	Kids' Translations	Capstone Press
Gettysburg Address, The	V	I	250+	Cornerstones of Freedom	Children's Press
Gettysburg Address, The	T	I	250+	Lincoln, Abraham	Houghton Mifflin Harcourt
Gettysburg: Bold Battle in the North	Y	I	250+	The Civil War	Carus Publishing
Get-Up Machine, The	I	F	115	Sunshine	Wright Group/McGraw Hill
Geysers	P	I	250+	A True Book	Children's Press
Geysers: When Earth Roars	U	I	250+	A First Book	Franklin Watts
Ghana	O	I	250+	Countries of the World	Red Brick Learning
Ghana: Ancient Empire	Y	I	2070	Leveled Readers Social Studies	Houghton Mifflin Harcourt
Ghost and the Sausage, The	I	F	250+	Story Box	Wright Group/McGraw Hill
Ghost Belonged to Me, The	V	F	250+	Peck, Richard	Penguin Group
Ghost Cadet	T	SF	250+	Alphin, Elaine Marie	Language for Learning Assoc.
Ghost Canoe	X	HF	250+	Hobbs, Will	Avon Books
Ghost Comes Calling, The	Q	F	250+	Wright, Betty	Scholastic
Ghost Dog	M	F	250+	Allen, Eleanor	Scholastic
Ghost Dog, The	N	F	250+	Warren, C	Stone Arch Books
Ghost Fox, The	P	F	250+	Yep, Laurence	Scholastic
Ghost in Tent 19, The	M	F	250+	O'Connor, Jim	Random House
Ghost in the Tokaido Inn, The	U	F	250+	Hoobler, Dorothy & Thomas	Penguin Group
Ghost Named Wanda, A	N	F	250+	The Zack Files	Grossett & Dunlap
Ghost of Popcorn Hill, The	N	F	250+	Wright, Betty Ren	Scholastic
Ghost on Saturday Night, The	Q	F	250+	Fleischman, Sid	Beech Tree Books
Ghost School	M	F	250+	Clifford, Eth	Scholastic
Ghost School	R	F	10091	Purkiss, S.	Stone Arch Books
Ghost Town at Sundown	M	F	250+	Osborne, Mary Pope	Random House
Ghost Town Treasure	M	RF	250+	Bulla, Clyde Robert	Penguin Group
Ghost Train	Q	HF	250+	Capeci, Anne	Peachtree
Ghost Tree, The	K	RF	250+	Voyages	SRA/McGraw Hill
Ghost Twins: Mystery at Kickingbird Lake	P	F	250+	Regan, Diane Curtis	Scholastic
Ghost Wolf	N	RF	250+	Orca Echoes	Orca Book Publishers
Ghost, The	A	RF	26	Story Box	Wright Group/McGraw Hill
Ghost, the White House, and Me, The	R	RF	250+	St. George, Judith	Holiday House
Ghostgirl	Z	F	250+	Hurley, Tonya	Little, Brown & Co.
Ghostmobile, The	S	F	250+	Tapp, Kathy Kennedy	Scholastic
Ghosts	X	I	250+	The Unexplained	Capstone Press
Ghosts Away	R	F	10285	Purkiss, S.	Stone Arch Books
Ghosts Beneath Our Feet	R	F	250+	Wright, Betty Ren	Scholastic
Ghosts Don't Eat Potato Chips	M	F	250+	Dadey, Debbie; Jones, Marcia Thornton	Scholastic
Ghosts of Cougar Island, The	N	RF	250+	Parish, Peggy	Yearling
Ghosts of Flight 401	Z	I	250+	Unsolved Mysteries	Steck-Vaughn

G

TITLE	LEVEL	GENRE	WORD COUNT	AUTHOR / SERIES	PUBLISHER / DISTRIBUTOR
Ghost's Revenge, The	T	F	9,889	Peschke, M.	Stone Arch Books
Ghosts' Secret, The	D	F	79	TOTTS	Tott Publications
*Ghosts!: Ghostly Tales from Folklore	J	TL	250+	Schwartz, Alvin	HarperTrophy
Ghouls Don't Scoop Ice Cream	M	F	250+	Dadey, Debbie; Jones, Marcia Thornton	Scholastic
Giant and the Boy, The	C	F	44	Sunshine	Wright Group/McGraw Hill
Giant and the Frippit, The	H	F	250+	Rigby Literacy	Rigby
Giant Anteaters	O	I	2097	Early Bird Nature Books	Lerner Publications
Giant Balloons	J	I	185	Rigby Focus	Rigby
Giant Bugs Were Real!	I	I	54	Seedlings	Continental Press
Giant Forest, The	H	F	269	Leveled Readers	Houghton Mifflin Harcourt
Giant Forest, The	H	F	269	Leveled Readers/CA	Houghton Mifflin Harcourt
Giant Forest, The	H	F	269	Leveled Readers/TX	Houghton Mifflin Harcourt
Giant Games	K	F	250+	Phonics and Friends	Hampton-Brown
Giant Gingerbread Man, The	G	TL	248	Alphakids	Sundance
Giant Grass	J	I	250+	Story Steps	Rigby
Giant Humanlike Beasts	Z	I	250+	Unsolved Mysteries	Steck-Vaughn
Giant in the Bed, The	H	F	253	New Way Green	Steck-Vaughn
Giant in the Forest, A	J	F	250+	Reading Unlimited	Pearson Learning Group
Giant Jack's Boots	M	F	420	Book Bank	Wright Group/McGraw Hill
Giant Jam Sandwich, The	K	F	250+	Vernon Lord, John	Houghton Mifflin Harcourt
Giant Jumperee	J	F	250+	Literacy by Design	Rigby
Giant Jumperee, The: A Play	J	F	250+	Rigby Literacy	Rigby
Giant Jumperee, The: A Play	J	F	250+	Rigby Star	Rigby
Giant Kangaroo	N	I	250+	Extinct Monsters	Capstone Press
Giant Meat-Eating Dinosaurs	P	I	940	Meet the Dinosaurs	Lerner Publications
Giant Octopuses	L	I	399	Pull Ahead Books	Lerner Publications
Giant Pandas	O	I	1904	Early Bird Nature Books	Lerner Publications
Giant Pandas	G	I	72	Pebble Books	Capstone Press
Giant Pandas	K	I	345	Pull Ahead Books	Lerner Publications
Giant Pandas	U	I	250+	The Untamed World	Steck-Vaughn
Giant Pandas	R	I	250+	Theme Sets	National Geographic
Giant Pandas: Gifts from China	I	I	250+	Rookie Read-About Science	Children's Press
Giant Plant-Eating Dinosaurs	P	I	1035	Meet the Dinosaurs	Lerner Publications
Giant Ripper Lizard	N	I	250+	Extinct Monsters	Capstone Press
Giant Rock of Yosemite, The: A Sierra Miwok Tale	Q	F	1028	Leveled Readers	Houghton Mifflin Harcourt
Giant Seeds, The	K	RF	507	PM Plus Story Books	Rigby
Giant -Sized Day, A	I	F	245	Ready Readers	Pearson Learning Group
Giant Snakes	O	I	1347	Take Two Books	Wright Group/McGraw Hill
*Giant Soup	J	F	419	Pacific Literacy	Pacific Learning
Giant, The	LB	F	20	Joy Readers	Pearson Learning Group
Giant, The	M	F	250+	Voyages	SRA/McGraw Hill
Giants	F	F	52	Blaxland, Wendy	Scholastic
Giant's Boy, The	H	F	89	Sunshine	Wright Group/McGraw Hill
Giant's Breakfast, The	B	F	42	Literacy 2000	Rigby
Giant's Cake	M	F	250+	Learning Media	Pacific Learning
Giant's Cake, The	H	F	162	Literacy 2000	Rigby
Giant's Cake, The	I	F	280	Sun Sprouts	ETA Cuisenaire
Giant's Day Out, The	B	F	26	Smart Starts	Rigby
Giants Don't Go Snowboarding	M	F	250+	Dadey, Debbie; Jones, Marcia Thornton	Scholastic
Giant's Fire, The	J	F	351	Springboard	Wright Group/McGraw Hill
Giant's Job, The	H	F	180	Stewart, Josie; Salem, Lynn	Continental Press

G

* Collection of short stories
# Graphic text

TITLE	LEVEL	GENRE	WORD COUNT	AUTHOR / SERIES	PUBLISHER / DISTRIBUTOR
Giant's Pizza, The	C	RF	28	Joy Readers	Pearson Learning Group
Giant's Rice, The	C	F	28	Joy Readers	Pearson Learning Group
Giant's Stew, The	I	F	259	Sunshine	Wright Group/McGraw Hill
Giants, Monsters & Mythical Beasts	O	I	250+	Literacy 2000	Rigby
Giant-Size Hamburger, A	C	F	38	Wonder World	Wright Group/McGraw Hill
Gib Got It	B	F	28	Reading Street	Pearson
Gib Rides Home	V	RF	250+	Snyder, Zilpha Keatley	Bantam
Gibbon Island	K	RF	444	PM Plus Story Books	Rigby
Gibbons, the Singing Apes	J	I	250+	Literacy by Design	Rigby
Giddy Up	C	RF	49	Cat on the Mat	Oxford University Press
Giddyoocha!	I	F	297	Story Box	Wright Group/McGraw Hill
Gift for Abuela, A	K	RF	670	Gear Up!	Wright Group/McGraw Hill
Gift for Grandpa, A	S	RF	1440	Leveled Readers	Houghton Mifflin Harcourt
Gift for Grandpa, A	S	RF	1440	Leveled Readers/CA	Houghton Mifflin Harcourt
Gift for Grandpa, A	S	RF	1440	Leveled Readers/TX	Houghton Mifflin Harcourt
Gift for Mama, A	N	RF	250+	Hautzig, Esther	Penguin Group
Gift for Yoshi, A	J	RF	282	Leveled Readers	Houghton Mifflin Harcourt
*Gift From Zeus, A: Sixteen Favorite Myths	X	TL	250+	Steig, Jeanne	HarperCollins
Gift of Crayons, A	G	RF	226	Leveled Readers Language Support	Houghton Mifflin Harcourt
Gift of Light, The: A Japanese Myth	Y	TL	2018	Leveled Readers	Houghton Mifflin Harcourt
Gift of Magic, A	W	F	250+	Duncan, Lois	Laurel-Leaf Books
Gift of the Girl Who Couldn't Hear, The	U	RF	250+	Shreve, Susan	Beech Tree Books
Gift of the Pirate Queen, The	S	RF	250+	Giff, Patricia Reilly	Yearling
Gift to Share, A	K	RF	544	Pair-It Books	Steck-Vaughn
Gift, The	WB	RF	N/A	Prater, J.	Wright Group/McGraw Hill
Gift, The	Q	RF	2340	Reading Street	Pearson
Gift, The	N	TL	250+	Story Vines	Wright Group/McGraw Hill
Gift-Giver, The	S	RF	250+	Hansen, Joyce	Houghton Mifflin Harcourt
Gifts for Dad	H	RF	178	Urmston, Kathleen; Evans, Karen	Kaeden Books
Gifts for Everyone	B	F	35	Rigby Literacy	Rigby
Gifts from Greece	Q	I	250+	InfoQuest	Rigby
Gifts of the Dineh	Q	RF	1301	Leveled Readers	Houghton Mifflin Harcourt
Gifts to Make	K	I	509	Pair-It Books	Steck-Vaughn
Gifts, The	B	RF	34	Story Box	Wright Group/McGraw Hill
*Gigantic Ants and Other Cases, The	O	RF	250+	Simon, Seymour	Avon
Gigantic Bell, The	K	TL	250+	PM Plus Story Books	Rigby
Gigantic George	H	F	224	Little Celebrations	Pearson Learning Group
Giggle Belly	G	RF	108	Rookie Readers	Children's Press
Giggle Box, The	E	F	176	Story Box	Wright Group/McGraw Hill
Gila Monsters	O	I	2003	Early Bird Nature Books	Lerner Publications
Gilbert Galaxy, Space Hero	L	SF	250+	Rigby Gigglers	Rigby
Gilbert Goes on a Picnic	F	F	152	Gilbert the Pig	Pioneer Valley
Gilbert in the Snow	I	F	706	Gilbert the Pig	Pioneer Valley
Gilbert the Pig Goes on a Diet	E	F	118	Gilbert the Pig	Pioneer Valley
Gilbert the Pig Has an Adventures	H	F	262	Gilbert the Pig	Pioneer Valley
Gilbert the Pig Wears a Dress	E	F	124	Gilbert the Pig	Pioneer Valley
Gilbert the Prize Winning Pig	B	RF	20	Gilbert the Pig	Pioneer Valley
Gilbert the Special Pig	H	F	238	Gilbert the Pig	Pioneer Valley
Gillian's Nines	C	RF	29	Harry's Math Books	Outside the Box
Gina's Puppy	L	RF	250+	Windows on Literacy	National Geographic
Ginger	I	RF	232	Little Readers	Houghton Mifflin Harcourt
Ginger	D	RF	43	Parker, Ant	Mondo

G

* Collection of short stories
# Graphic text

TITLE	LEVEL	GENRE	WORD COUNT	AUTHOR / SERIES	PUBLISHER / DISTRIBUTOR
Ginger Brown: The Nobody Boy	L	RF	250+	Wyeth, Sharon Dennis	Random House
Ginger Brown: Too Many Houses	L	RF	250+	Wyeth, Sharon Dennis	Random House
Ginger Pye	U	RF	250+	Estes, Eleanor	Scholastic
Gingerbread	Z+	RF	250+	Cohn, Rachel	Simon & Schuster
Gingerbread	I	I	134	Windows on Literacy	National Geographic
Gingerbread Boy	F	TL	137	New Way Red	Steck-Vaughn
Gingerbread Boy, The	C	TL	107	Folk Tales	Pioneer Valley
Gingerbread Boy, The	L	TL	1097	Galdone, Paul	Clarion
Gingerbread Boy, The	G	TL	250+	Ziefert, Harriet	Puffin/Penguin
Gingerbread Man	I	TL	250+	Hunia, Fran	Ladybird Books
Gingerbread Man, The	G	TL	139	Cambridge Reading	Pearson Learning Group
Gingerbread Man, The	G	TL	250+	Cherrington, Janelle	Scholastic
Gingerbread Man, The	E	F	79	Instant Readers	Harcourt School Publishers
Gingerbread Man, The	H	TL	447	Leveled Literacy Intervention/ Green System	Heinemann
Gingerbread Man, The	H	TL	250+	Literacy 2000	Rigby
Gingerbread Man, The	F	TL	180	Little Readers	Houghton Mifflin Harcourt
Gingerbread Man, The	I	TL	180	Rose, Rita	Scholastic
Gingerbread Man, The	I	TL	250+	Storyworlds	Heinemann Educational Books
Gingerbread Man, The	H	TL	197	Sunshine	Wright Group/McGraw Hill
Gingerbread Man, The	I	TL	250+	Tiger Cub	Peguis
Gingerbread Man, The	I	TL	544	Traditional Tales	Pearson Learning Group
Gingerbread Man, The	J	TL	535	Traditional Tales & More	Rigby
Gingerbread Men, The	D	I	37	Sunshine	Wright Group/McGraw Hill
Ginger's War	N	HF	250+	Sunshine	Wright Group/McGraw Hill
Giraffe and the Pelly and Me, The	P	F	250+	Dahl, Roald	Penguin Group
Giraffe Calf Grows Up, A	L	I	429	Baby Animals	Lerner Publications
Giraffe Goes Skating	E	F	101	Springboard	Wright Group/McGraw Hill
Giraffe Grows Up	D	I	72	Little Celebrations	Pearson Learning Group
Giraffe Made Her Laugh, The	E	F	70	Learn to Read	Creative Teaching Press
Giraffe, The	P	I	250+	Animal Close-Ups	Charlesbridge
Giraffes	I	I	137	African Animals	Capstone Press
Giraffes	P	I	250+	Crabapples	Crabtree
Giraffes	O	I	2038	Early Bird Nature Books	Lerner Publications
Giraffes	N	I	250+	Meadows, Graham; Vial, Claire	Pearson Learning Group
Giraffes	D	I	63	Nonfiction Set 3	Literacy Footprints
Giraffes	O	I	250+	Take Two Books	Wright Group/McGraw Hill
Giraffes Can't Dance	M	F	250+	Andreae, Giles	Scholastic
Giraffe's Neck	E	TL	109	Leveled Readers	Houghton Mifflin Harcourt
Giraffe's Neck	E	TL	109	Leveled Readers/CA	Houghton Mifflin Harcourt
Giraffe's Neck	E	TL	109	Leveled Readers/TX	Houghton Mifflin Harcourt
Giraffe's Sad Tale (With a Happy Ending)	H	F	250+	Alma Flor Ada	Hampton-Brown
Girl and the Wolf, The	N	RF	1038	Leveled Readers	Houghton Mifflin Harcourt
Girl and the Wolf, The	N	RF	1038	Leveled Readers/CA	Houghton Mifflin Harcourt
Girl and the Wolf, The	N	RF	1038	Leveled Readers/TX	Houghton Mifflin Harcourt
Girl Called Al, A	P	RF	250+	Greene, Constance C.	Puffin/Penguin
Girl Called Boy, A	U	F	250+	Hurmence, Belinda	Clarion
Girl From Yamhill, A	W	B	250+	Cleary, Beverly	Bantam
Girl in a Cage	X	HF	250+	Yolen, Jane; Harris, Robert J.	Scholastic
Girl in the Golden Bower, The	Q	TL	250+	Yolen, Jane	Little, Brown & Co.
Girl in the Window, The	U	RF	250+	Yeo, Wilma	Scholastic
Girl Named Amira, A	X	RF	2450	Leveled Readers	Houghton Mifflin Harcourt
Girl Named Amira, A	X	RF	2450	Leveled Readers/CA	Houghton Mifflin Harcourt

G

* Collection of short stories
\# Graphic text

TITLE	LEVEL	GENRE	WORD COUNT	AUTHOR / SERIES	PUBLISHER / DISTRIBUTOR
Girl Named Disaster, A	X	RF	250+	Farmer, Nancy	Penguin Group
Girl Named Helen Keller, A	K	B	250+	Lundell, Margo	Scholastic
Girl Overboard	Y	RF	250+	Headley, Justina Chen	Little, Brown & Co.
Girl Pirates	N	RF	250+	Girlz Rock!	Mondo
Girl Saves Giant	M	RF	250+	Wonder World	Wright Group/McGraw Hill
Girl Who Chased Away Sorrow, The: The Diary of Sarah Nita, a Navajo Girl	U	HF	250+	Dear America	Scholastic
Girl Who Climbed to the Moon, The	L	F	604	Sunshine	Wright Group/McGraw Hill
Girl Who Helped the Wolf, The	N	RF	999	Leveled Readers	Houghton Mifflin Harcourt
Girl Who Helped the Wolf, The	N	RF	999	Leveled Readers/CA	Houghton Mifflin Harcourt
Girl Who Helped the Wolf, The	N	RF	999	Leveled Readers/TX	Houghton Mifflin Harcourt
Girl Who Knew It All, The	Q	RF	250+	Giff, Patricia Reilly	Bantam
Girl Who Loved Meerkats, The	M	F	250+	World Quest Adventures	World Quest Learning
Girl Who Loved the Wind, The	Q	TL	250+	Yolen, Jane	HarperTrophy
Girl Who Loved Wild Horses, The	N	TL	250+	Goble, Paul	Scholastic
*Girl Who Married the Moon, The: Tales from Native North America	U	TL	250+	Bruchac, Joseph; Ross, Gayle	Troll Associates
Girl Who Owned a City, The	X	F	250+	Nelson, O. T.	Laurel-Leaf Books
Girl Who Struck Out Babe Ruth, The	N	HF	1715	On My Own History	Lerner Publications
Girl With the Silver Eyes, The	U	F	250+	Roberts, Willo Davis	Scholastic
Girl Wonder: A Baseball Story in Nine Innings	P	HF	250+	Hopkinson, Deborah	Aladddin Paperbacks
Girls' Basketball: Making Your Mark on the Court	R	I	250+	Girls Got Game	Capstone Press
Girls' Figure Skating: Ruling the Rink	R	I	250+	Girls Got Game	Capstone Press
Girls' Golf: Teeing Up	R	I	250+	Girls Got Game	Capstone Press
Girls' Ice Hockey: Dominating the Rink	R	I	250+	Girls Got Game	Capstone Press
Girls of Many Lands	W	HF	250+	Croutier, Alev Lytle	Pleasant Company
Girls' Skateboarding: Skating to Be the Best	R	I	250+	Girls Got Game	Capstone Press
Girls' Snowboarding:Showing Off Your Style	R	I	250+	Girls Got Game	Capstone Press
Girls' Soccer: Going for the Goal	R	I	250+	Girls Got Game	Capstone Press
Girls' Softball: Winning on the Diamond	R	I	250+	Girls Got Game	Capstone Press
Girls' Tennis: Conquering the Court	R	I	250+	Girls Got Game	Capstone Press
Girl's Think of Everything: Stories of Ingenious Inventions by Women	S	I	250+	Thimmesh, Catherine	Houghton Mifflin Harcourt
Girls to the Rescue, Book 3	Q	RF	250+	Lansky, Bruce	Meadowbrook Press
Girls to the Rescue, Book 4	Q	RF	250+	Lansky, Bruce	Meadowbrook Press
Girls to the Rescue, Book 6	Q	RF	250+	Lansky, Bruce	Meadowbrook Press
Girls' Volleyball: Setting Up Success	R	I	250+	Girls Got Game	Capstone Press
Girls, The	Y	RF	250+	Koss, Amy Goldman	Scholastic
Girl-Son, The	R	HF	250+	Neuberger, Anne E.	Carolrhoda Books
Give and Take	D	RF	122	Literacy by Design	Rigby
Give Me a Hug	B	RF	28	Sunshine	Wright Group/McGraw Hill
Give Me Liberty: The Story of the Declaration of Independence	V	I	250+	Freedman, Russell	Holiday House
Giver, The	Y	F	250+	Lowry, Lois	Bantam
Giving Thanks A Native American Good Morning Message	M	RF	305	Swamp, Chief Jake	Scholastic
Giving Thanks Around the World	K	I	350	Reading Street	Pearson
Gizmos' Party, The	J	F	250+	Rigby Literacy	Rigby
Gizmos' Party, The	J	F	250+	Rigby Star	Rigby
Gizmos' Trip, The	J	F	250+	Rigby Literacy	Rigby
Gizmos' Trip, The	J	F	250+	Rigby Star	Rigby
Glaciers	T	I	250+	Gallant, Roy A.	Franklin Watts
Glaciers	V	I	2117	Leveled Readers Social Studies	Houghton Mifflin Harcourt

G

* Collection of short stories
# Graphic text

TITLE	LEVEL	GENRE	WORD COUNT	AUTHOR / SERIES	PUBLISHER / DISTRIBUTOR
Gladiators	T	I	250+	Warriors of History	Capstone Press
Gladly, Here I Come	R	RF	250+	Cowley, Joy	Wright Group/McGraw Hill
Gladys and Max Love Bob	M	RF	459	Book Bank	Wright Group/McGraw Hill
Glass	M	I	250+	Materials	Capstone Press
Glass	G	I	112	Rigby Focus	Rigby
Glass Blowing	M	I	663	Reading Street	Pearson
Glass Café, The	Z	RF	250+	Paulsen, Gary	Random House
Glass Slipper for Rosie, A	N	RF	250+	Giff, Patricia Reilly	Penguin Group
Glass-Bottomed Boat, The	L	RF	854	Springboard	Wright Group/McGraw Hill
Glasses	D	RF	19	Visions	Wright Group/McGraw Hill
Glenda	P	F	250+	Udry, Janice May	HarperTrophy
Glenda Glinka: Witch-At-Large	P	F	250+	Udry, Janice May	HarperTrophy
Glenda the Lion	E	F	88	Ready Readers	Pearson Learning Group
Glessner House: An American Home and Family	T	I	250+	Rigby Literacy	Rigby
Glide, Wriggle, Zoom	M	I	250+	Pacific Literacy	Pacific Learning
Gliders and Sliders	H	I	198	Sails	Rigby
Gliding Garter Snakes	K	I	400	Pull Ahead Books	Lerner Publications
Glitter Trouble	C	RF	32	Learn to Read	Creative Teaching Press
Glitz Girls, The	R	RF	250+	Literacy by Design	Rigby
Global Alert	Q	I	250+	Navigators Social Studies Series	Benchmark Education
Global Energy	Y	I	2359	Independent Readers Science	Houghton Mifflin Harcourt
Global Warming	U	I	250+	Our Planet in Peril	Capstone Press
Globes	C	I	11	Geography	Lerner Publishing
Glorious Days, Dreadful Days: The Battle of Bunker Hill	R	I	250+	Kirby, Philippa	Steck-Vaughn
Glorious Flight, The: Across the Channel with Louis Blériot	O	B	250+	Provensen, Alice & Martin	Puffin/Penguin
Glory Field, The	X	HF	250+	Myers, Walter Dean	Scholastic
Glory Gate	U	SF	250+	Storyteller - Mountain Peaks	Wright Group/McGraw Hill
Glory Girl, The	S	RF	250+	Byars, Betsy	Penguin Group
Gloves	E	RF	103	Story Box	Wright Group/McGraw Hill
Glow from Lighthouse Cove, The	S	RF	2501	Leveled Readers	Houghton Mifflin Harcourt
Glow Stone, The	Z	RF	250+	Dreyer, Ellen	Peachtree
Gluepots	K	RF	205	Book Bank	Wright Group/McGraw Hill
Glumly	Q	F	250+	Literacy 2000	Rigby
Gnu Named Blue, A	K	F	250+	Phonics and Friends	Hampton-Brown
Go and Get It!	C	RF	68	Rigby Rocket	Rigby
Go and Hush the Baby	K	RF	250+	Byars, Betsy	Viking/Penguin
Go Annie, Go!	K	RF	250+	Pacific Literacy	Pacific Learning
Go Away Dog	I	RF	250+	Nodset, Joan	HarperCollins
Go Away!	B	I	36	Sails	Rigby
Go Away, Tooth Decay	T	I	250+	Leveled Readers Language Support	Houghton Mifflin Harcourt
Go Back to Bed!	L	RF	627	Guy, Ginger Foglesong	Carolrhoda Books
Go Back to Sleep	E	RF	74	Literacy 2000	Rigby
Go Dog Go	E	F	250+	Eastman, Philip D.	Random House
Go Fish	O	RF	250+	Stolz, Mary	Scholastic
Go Fly a Kite!	T	I	250+	WorldScapes	ETA Cuisenaire
Go Free or Die: A Story About Harriet Tubman	R	B	250+	Ferris, Jeri	Carolrhoda Books
Go Green	R	RF	1542	Leveled Readers	Houghton Mifflin Harcourt
Go Green	R	RF	1542	Leveled Readers/CA	Houghton Mifflin Harcourt
Go Home, Chick!	B	F	77	Literacy by Design	Rigby
Go Home, Daisy	F	RF	100+	Hill, Barbara	Scholastic

* Collection of short stories
\# Graphic text

G

TITLE	LEVEL	GENRE	WORD COUNT	AUTHOR / SERIES	PUBLISHER / DISTRIBUTOR
Go Sea It!	A	I	16	Little Celebrations	Pearson Learning Group
Go Teddy!	B	I	27	Windows on Literacy	National Geographic
Go to Bed!	D	RF	45	Joy Readers	Pearson Learning Group
Go To School	A	F	21	Reading Street	Pearson
Go to Sleep, Dear Dragon	E	F	313	Dear Dragon	Norwood House Press
Go Turtle! Go Hare!	D	TL	100	Leveled Readers	Houghton Mifflin Harcourt
Go Turtle! Go Hare!	D	TL	100	Leveled Readers/CA	Houghton Mifflin Harcourt
Go Turtle! Go Hare!	D	TL	100	Leveled Readers/TX	Houghton Mifflin Harcourt
Go West!	S	I	250+	Reading Expeditions	National Geographic
Go!	D	RF	44	Little Readers	Houghton Mifflin Harcourt
Go, Gina!	I	RF	519	Rigby Flying Colors	Rigby
Go, Go, Go	LB	RF	12	Handprints A	Educators Publishing Service
Go, Go, Go	A	I	23	Little Books for Early Readers	University of Maine
Go, Go, Go	A	RF	17	Story Box	Wright Group/McGraw Hill
Go, Go, Go!	A	I	24	On Our Way to English	Rigby
Go, Meg, Go!	D	RF	70	Pair-It Turn and Learn	Steck-Vaughn
Goal!	H	RF	232	Lighthouse	Rigby
Goalie from Nowhere, The	O	F	250+	High-Fliers	Pacific Learning
Goat Goes to Town, The	H	RF	131	Bebop Books	Lee & Low Books Inc.
Goat in the Chile Patch, The	H	TL	250+	Kratky, Lada Josefa	Hampton-Brown
Goat in the Garden	Q	RF	250+	Baglio, Ben M.	Scholastic
Goat in the Garden, The	G	TL	227	Leveled Literacy Intervention/ Green System	Heinemann
*Goat Monster and Other Stories, The	L	F	250+	New Way Literature	Steck-Vaughn
Goat Who Wouldn't Come Home, The	G	F	184	Seedlings	Continental Press
Goat, The	C	RF	17	KinderReaders	Rigby
Goat, The	B	F	40	Sails	Rigby
Goats	L	I	250+	PM Animal Facts: Purple	Rigby
Goat's Beard, The	H	F	325	Sails	Rigby
Goats in the Turnip Field, The	I	TL	250+	PM Plus Story Books	Rigby
Goats on the Farm	I	I	67	Pebble Books	Red Brick Learning
Goats, The	A	F	24	Sails	Rigby
Gobble Up the Moon	J	F	289	Gear Up!	Wright Group/McGraw Hill
Gobble! Gobble! Munch!	F	F	64	Rhythm 'N' Rhyme Readers	Pearson Learning Group
Gobble, Gobble, Gone	D	F	58	Little Celebrations	Pearson Learning Group
Goblins Don't Play Video Games	M	RF	250+	Dadey, Debbie; Jones, Marcia Thornton	Scholastic
Go-cart Day	K	RF	165	City Kids	Rigby
Go-cart Team, The	O	I	250+	PM Nonfiction-Emerald	Rigby
Go-cart, The	E	RF	47	Oxford Reading Tree	Oxford University Press
Go-carts, The	B	RF	46	PM Starters	Rigby
God of Mischief, The	U	F	250+	Bajoria, Paul	Little, Brown & Co.
Gods and Goddesses of Ancient Egypt	S	I	250+	Ancient Egypt	Capstone Press
Godzilla Ate My Homework	O	F	250+	Jones, Marcia	Scholastic
Goggly Gookers	H	F	100	Story Basket	Wright Group/McGraw Hill
Goha and His Donkey	I	F	114	Books for Young Learners	Richard C. Owen
Going Along With Lewis and Clark	T	I	250+	Fifer, Barbara	Montana Magazine
Going Back to Harlem	P	I	522	Vocabulary Readers	Houghton Mifflin Harcourt
Going Bowling	J	I	338	Springboard	Wright Group/McGraw Hill
Going Camping	F	RF	238	Leveled Literacy Intervention/ Blue System	Heinemann
Going Fast	N	I	449	Big Cat	Pacific Learning
Going Fast	D	I	116	Leveled Readers	Houghton Mifflin Harcourt

G

TITLE	LEVEL	GENRE	WORD COUNT	AUTHOR / SERIES	PUBLISHER / DISTRIBUTOR
Going Fast	D	I	116	Leveled Readers/CA	Houghton Mifflin Harcourt
Going Fast	H	I	197	Sails	Rigby
Going Fishing	E	F	99	Arctic Stories	Pioneer Valley
Going Fishing	G	RF	117	Cambridge Reading	Pearson Learning Group
Going Fishing	F	F	240	Leveled Readers	Houghton Mifflin Harcourt
Going Fishing	E	RF	26	Literacy 2000	Rigby
Going Fishing	I	RF	250+	Momentum Literacy Program	Troll Associates
Going Fishing	B	F	22	Ready Readers	Pearson Learning Group
Going Fishing	C	RF	30	Visions	Wright Group/McGraw Hill
Going Fishing	F	RF	26	Voyages	SRA/McGraw Hill
Going Fishing	I	I	161	Windows on Literacy	National Geographic
Going for a Hay Ride	A	I	26	Leveled Readers	Houghton Mifflin Harcourt
Going for a Hay Ride	A	I	26	Leveled Readers/CA	Houghton Mifflin Harcourt
Going for a Hike	A	I	20	Vocabulary Readers	Houghton Mifflin Harcourt
Going for a Hike	A	I	20	Vocabulary Readers/CA	Houghton Mifflin Harcourt
Going for a Ride	C	RF	52	Early Emergent	Pioneer Valley
Going for a Ride	B	I	67	Leveled Readers Emergent	Houghton Mifflin Harcourt
Going for a Ride	B	RF	40	Little Books for Early Readers	University of Maine
Going for a Walk	F	RF	82	DeRegniers, Beatrice Schenk	Harper & Row
Going for Gold	O	B	250+	WorldScapes	ETA Cuisenaire
Going for Gold!	P	B	250+	Eyewitness Readers	DK Publishing
Going Green	R	I	250+	High-Fliers	Pacific Learning
Going Here and There	D	RF	124	Early Connections	Benchmark Education
Going Home	T	RF	250+	Mohr, Nicholas	Penguin Group
Going in the Car	B	RF	24	Sunshine	Wright Group/McGraw Hill
Going Lobstering	O	I	250+	Pallotta, Jerry; Bolster, Rob	Charlesbridge
Going Nowhere Faster	Z	RF	250+	Beaudoin, Sean	Little, Brown & Co.
Going on an Airplane	C	I	83	Vocabulary Readers/CA	Houghton Mifflin Harcourt
Going on a Dinosaur Dig	K	I	342	Reading Street	Pearson
Going on a Field Trip	I	RF	288	Visions	Wright Group/McGraw Hill
Going on a Train Ride	C	RF	76	Leveled Literacy Intervention/ Orange System	Heinemann
Going on an Airplane	C	I	83	Vocabulary Readers	Houghton Mifflin Harcourt
Going on Safari	M	I	250+	Pacific Literacy	Pacific Learning
Going on Vacation	B	RF	51	Leveled Literacy Intervention/ Orange System	Heinemann
Going on Vacation	A	I	40	PM Plus Starters	Rigby
Going Out	D	RF	94	Foundations	Wright Group/McGraw Hill
Going Out	A	F	42	KinderReaders	Rigby
Going Out	B	RF	48	PM Plus Starters	Rigby
Going Outside	A	RF	35	Adams, Lorraine; Bruvold, Lynn	Eagle Crest Books
Going Outside	M	F	118	Voyages	SRA/McGraw Hill
Going Places	K	I	410	Early Connections	Benchmark Education
Going Places	B	F	49	First Stories	Pacific Learning
Going Places	R	I	250+	Orbit Collections	Pacific Learning
Going Places	C	I	32	Rosen Real Readers	Rosen Publishing Group
Going Places	E	I	101	Sails	Rigby
Going Shopping	F	I	112	Bookshop	Mondo
Going Shopping	D	RF	92	Carousel Readers	Pearson Learning Group
Going Shopping	F	RF	99	Leveled Readers Social Studies	Houghton Mifflin Harcourt
Going Shopping	B	RF	31	Rigby Literacy	Rigby
Going Shopping	B	F	24	Sails	Rigby
Going Sledding	A	I	31	Leveled Literacy Intervention/ Orange System	Heinemann

G

* Collection of short stories
\# Graphic text

TITLE	LEVEL	GENRE	WORD COUNT	AUTHOR / SERIES	PUBLISHER / DISTRIBUTOR
Going Solo	T	B	250+	Dahl, Roald	Puffin/Penguin
Going Solo	T	I	250+	iOpeners	Pearson Learning Group
Going Swimming	J	RF	210	City Kids	Rigby
Going Swimming	J	I	250+	Explorations	Eleanor Curtain Publishing
Going Swimming	J	I	250+	Explorations	Okapi Educational Materials
Going the Distance	T	RF	1626	Leveled Readers	Houghton Mifflin Harcourt
Going to a Football Game	I	RF	131	City Kids	Rigby
Going to America	K	HF	250+	Leveled Readers Language Support	Houghton Mifflin Harcourt
Going to America	N	RF	250+	Orbit Chapter Books	Pacific Learning
Going to Be a Butterfly	L	I	250+	Sunshine	Wright Group/McGraw Hill
Going to Bed	B	F	36	Sails	Rigby
Going to Grandma's	I	RF	136	Tarlton, John	Scholastic
Going to Grandma's Farm	C	RF	56	Rookie Readers	Children's Press
Going to Grandma's House	D	RF	122	Joy Starters	Pearson Learning Group
Going to Grandpa's House	C	RF	37	Frankford, Marilyn	Kaeden Books
Going to Lucy's House	E	RF	151	Sunshine	Wright Group/McGraw Hill
Going to School	I	F	476	Bella and Rosie Series	Literacy Footprints
Going to School	H	RF	250	Cambridge Reading	Pearson Learning Group
Going to School	F	I	171	Foundations	Wright Group/McGraw Hill
Going to School	C	I	45	Gear Up!	Wright Group/McGraw Hill
Going to School	O	I	21	iOpeners	Pearson Learning Group
Going to School	B	I	77	Leveled Literacy Intervention/ Blue System	Heinemann
Going to School	B	I	40	Leveled Readers	Houghton Mifflin Harcourt
Going to School	A	RF	28	Leveled Readers Emergent	Houghton Mifflin Harcourt
Going to School	B	I	40	Leveled Readers/CA	Houghton Mifflin Harcourt
Going to School	LB	RF	21	Smart Starts	Rigby
Going to School	C	I	43	Story Box	Wright Group/McGraw Hill
Going to School	C	I	50	Sunshine	Wright Group/McGraw Hill
Going to School	D	I	104	Vocabulary Readers	Houghton Mifflin Harcourt
Going to School	D	I	104	Vocabulary Readers/CA	Houghton Mifflin Harcourt
Going to School	D	I	104	Vocabulary Readers/TX	Houghton Mifflin Harcourt
Going to School	C	I	30	Windows on Literacy	National Geographic
Going to the Bank	J	I	317	Foundations	Wright Group/McGraw Hill
Going to the Beach	C	RF	75	Carousel Readers	Pearson Learning Group
Going to the Beach	E	I	30	Little Red Readers	Sundance
Going to the Beach	LB	RF	30	Pacific Literacy	Pacific Learning
Going to the Beach	C	I	60	Rigby Flying Colors	Rigby
Going to the Beach	E	RF	49	Rookie Readers	Children's Press
Going to the City	J	I	250+	People, Spaces & Places	Rand McNally
Going to the Dentist	F	I	122	Dental Health	Capstone Press
Going to the Doctor	F	RF	101	City Stories	Rigby
Going to the Hairdresser	J	I	227	Foundations	Wright Group/McGraw Hill
Going to the Hospital	H	RF	335	Foundations	Wright Group/McGraw Hill
Going to the Moon	C	F	75	Springboard	Wright Group/McGraw Hill
Going to the Movies	L	I	432	Rigby Flying Colors	Rigby
Going to the Park	C	RF	41	Home Connection Collection	Rigby
Going to the Park with Grandaddy	C	RF	30	Visions	Wright Group/McGraw Hill
Going to the Pool	D	RF	55	Pair-It Books	Steck-Vaughn
Going to the South Pole	O	I	843	Leveled Readers	Houghton Mifflin Harcourt
Going to the South Pole	O	I	843	Leveled Readers/CA	Houghton Mifflin Harcourt
Going to the South Pole	O	I	843	Leveled Readers/TX	Houghton Mifflin Harcourt
Going to the Symphony	G	I	132	Twig	Wright Group/McGraw Hill

* Collection of short stories
# Graphic text

TITLE	LEVEL	GENRE	WORD COUNT	AUTHOR / SERIES	PUBLISHER / DISTRIBUTOR
Going to the Vet	D	I	46	Sunshine	Wright Group/McGraw Hill
Going to Town	B	RF	63	Springboard	Wright Group/McGraw Hill
Going to Town	J	HF	250+	Wilder, Laura Ingalls	HarperCollins
Going to Town With Mom and Dad	D	RF	85	Early Connections	Benchmark Education
Going Up	P	I	250+	Scooters	ETA Cuisenaire
Going Up and Down	B	RF	51	Early Emergent	Pioneer Valley
Going Up the Mountain	K	I	251	Windows on Literacy	National Geographic
Going Up the Wall	N	I	250+	Pacific Literacy	Pacific Learning
Going Up?	B	F	26	Little Celebrations	Pearson Learning Group
Going West	O	HF	250+	Van Leeuwen, Jean	Penguin Group
Going West	N	I	428	Vocabulary Readers	Houghton Mifflin Harcourt
Going West	J	HF	250+	Wilder, Laura Ingalls	HarperCollins
Going West: Trials and Tradeoffs	S	I	2572	Independent Readers Social Studies	Houghton Mifflin Harcourt
Going Wild at the Zoo	R	I	1320	Leveled Readers	Houghton Mifflin Harcourt
Going Wild at the Zoo	R	I	1320	Leveled Readers/CA	Houghton Mifflin Harcourt
Going Wild at the Zoo	R	I	1320	Leveled Readers/TX	Houghton Mifflin Harcourt
Go-Kart Rush	Q	RF	4681	Maddox, Jake	Stone Arch Books
Go-Karts	Q	I	250+	Wild Rides!	Capstone Press
Gold and Earth's Treasures	U	I	250+	The News	Richard C. Owen
Gold Cadillac, The	S	HF	250+	Taylor, Mildred D.	Puffin/Penguin
Gold Dust Kids, The	N	HF	250+	Sunshine	Wright Group/McGraw Hill
Gold Dust Letters, The	S	RF	250+	Lisle, Janet Taylor	Avon Camelot
Gold Fever!	N	HF	250+	Step into Reading	Random House
Gold for Chan Li	T	HF	2647	Leveled Readers	Houghton Mifflin Harcourt
Gold for Chan Li	T	HF	2647	Leveled Readers/CA	Houghton Mifflin Harcourt
Gold for Chan Li	T	HF	2647	Leveled Readers/TX	Houghton Mifflin Harcourt
Gold Mountain	R	HF	250+	Pair-It Books	Steck-Vaughn
Gold Rush of 1849, The	S	I	1192	Reading Street	Pearson
Gold Rush!	T	I	250+	Navigators Social Studies Series	Benchmark Education Company
Gold Rush, The: California or Bust!	Q	I	250+	On Deck	Rigby
Gold! Gold! Gold!	C	F	37	Dominie Math Stories	Pearson Learning Group
Golden Age of Baghdad, The	W	I	2406	Reading Street	Pearson
Golden Age of Pirates, The: An Interactive History Adventure	S	HF	250+	You Choose Books	Capstone Press
Golden Age of Sail, The	P	I	1200	Vocabulary Readers/TX	Houghton Mifflin Harcourt
Golden Book of Death, The	T	F	250+	Dahl, Michael	Stone Arch Books
Golden Compass, The	Z	F	250+	Pullman, Philip	Ballantine Books
Golden Dragon	J	F	250+	Supersonics	Rigby
Golden Fish, The	N	TL	250+	WorldScapes	ETA Cuisenaire
Golden Fleece and the Heroes Who Lived Before Achilles, The	X	TL	250+	Colum, Padraic	Scholastic
Golden Fleece, The	Y	TL	250+	Colum, Padraic	Aladdin Paperbacks
Golden Games	Q	I	250+	Zemanski, Stella	Scholastic
Golden Glove, The	O	RF	250+	Bowen, Fred	Peachtree
Golden Goblet, The	V	RF	250+	McGraw, Eloise Jarvis	Scholastic
Golden Goose, The	M	TL	250+	Literacy 2000	Rigby
Golden Goose, The	L	TL	731	Sunshine	Wright Group/McGraw Hill
Golden Land, The	L	HF	505	Leveled Readers	Houghton Mifflin Harcourt
Golden Lasso, The	H	F	250+	Home Connection Collection	Rigby
Golden Locket, The	M	F	250+	Greene, Carol	Harcourt Brace
Golden Retrievers	R	I	250+	All About Dogs	Capstone Press
Golden Retrievers	I	I	104	Dogs	Capstone Press

G

* Collection of short stories
\# Graphic text

TITLE	LEVEL	GENRE	WORD COUNT	AUTHOR / SERIES	PUBLISHER / DISTRIBUTOR
Golden Rule, The	K	I	360	Vocabulary Readers	Houghton Mifflin Harcourt
Golden Rule, The	K	I	360	Vocabulary Readers/CA	Houghton Mifflin Harcourt
Golden Sword of Dragonwalk	Q	F	250+	Stine, R. L.	Scholastic
Golden Touch, The	K	TL	783	Gear Up!	Wright Group/ McGraw Hill
Golden Year, The	T	HF	3713	Reading Street	Pearson
Goldfish	J	I	250+	PM Animal Facts: Orange	Rigby
Goldfish Charlie and the Case of the Missing Planet	R	SF	250+	Mazer, Anne	Troll Associates
Goldie and the Fawn	J	RF	632	The Fawn	Pioneer Valley
Goldie and the Three Bears	G	TL	365	Leveled Literacy Intervention/ Green System	Heinemann
Goldie: The Puppy Place	N	RF	250+	Miles, Ellen	Scholastic
Goldilocks	I	TL	250+	Jumbled Tumbled Tales & Rhymes	Rigby
Goldilocks	G	TL	244	Sunshine	Wright Group/McGraw Hill
Goldilocks	C	TL	19	Tarlow, Ellen	Scholastic
Goldilocks and the Three Bears	WB	TL	N/A	Big Cat	Pacific Learning
Goldilocks and the Three Bears	E	TL	184	Hunia, Fran	Ladybird Books
Goldilocks and the Three Bears	G	TL	250+	Literacy Tree	Rigby
Goldilocks and the Three Bears	C	TL	54	Little Books	Sadlier-Oxford
Goldilocks and The Three Bears	M	TL	250+	Marshall, James	Scholastic
Goldilocks and the Three Bears	K	TL	250+	New Way Literature	Steck-Vaughn
Goldilocks and the Three Bears	K	TL	250+	Once Upon a Time	Wright Group/McGraw Hill
Goldilocks and The Three Bears	H	TL	250+	PM Tales and Plays-Turquoise	Rigby
Goldilocks and the Three Bears	M	TL	1102	Reading Street	Pearson
Goldilocks and the Three Bears	F	TL	200+	Shapiro, Sara	Scholastic
Goldilocks and the Three Bears	G	TL	265	Storyteller Nonfiction	Wright Group/McGraw Hill
Goldilocks and the Three Bears	H	TL	250+	Traditional Tales & More	Rigby
Goldilocks Comes Back	F	TL	134	Pair-It Books	Steck-Vaughn
Goldsworthy and Mort Blast Off	L	F	250+	Little Celebrations	Pearson Learning Group
Golf for Fun!	S	I	250+	Sports for Fun	Compass Point Books
Golf Legends	N	RF	250+	Boyz Rule!	Mondo
Goliath and the Burglar	L	RF	250+	Dicks, Terrance	Barron's Educational
Goliath and the Buried Treasure	L	RF	250+	Dicks, Terrance	Barron's Educational
Goliath and the Cub Scouts	L	RF	250+	Dicks, Terrance	Barron's Educational
Goliath at the Dog Show	L	RF	250+	Dicks, Terrance	Barron's Educational
Goliath at the Seaside	L	RF	250+	Dicks, Terrance	Barron's Educational
Goliath Goes to Summer School	L	RF	250+	Dicks, Terrance	Barron's Educational
Goliath on Vacation	L	RF	250+	Dicks, Terrance	Barron's Educational
Goliath's Birthday	L	RF	250+	Dicks, Terrance	Barron's Educational
Goliath's Christmas	L	RF	250+	Dicks, Terrance	Barron's Educational
Goliath's Easter Parade	L	RF	250+	Dicks, Terrance	Barron's Educational
Golly Sisters Go West, The	K	RF	250+	Byars, Betsy	HarperTrophy
Golly Sisters Ride Again, The	K	RF	250+	Byars, Betsy	HarperTrophy
Gollywhopper Eggs, The: A Play	K	F	250+	Windows on Literacy	National Geographic
Gone Fishing	N	RF	250+	Boyz Rule!	Mondo
*Gone Fishing	G	RF	180	Long, Erlene	Houghton Mifflin Harcourt
*Gone from Home	W	RF	250+	Johnson, Angela	Alfred A. Knopf
Gone-Away Lake	V	RF	250+	Enright, Elizabeth	Harcourt Trade
Gonna Bird, The	H	F	209	Storyteller-Night Crickets	Wright Group/McGraw Hill
Good As New	L	RF	250+	Douglass, Barbara	Scholastic
Good Bad Cat, The	D	RF	65	Little Readers	Houghton Mifflin Harcourt
Good Bad Cat, The	D	RF	65	Start to Read	School Zone
Good Bad Day, The	I	RF	451	Real Kids Readers	Millbrook Press

* Collection of short stories
# Graphic text

Organized Alphabetically by Title   **229**
Storable Database at www.fountasandpinnellleveledbooks.com

TITLE	LEVEL	GENRE	WORD COUNT	AUTHOR / SERIES	PUBLISHER / DISTRIBUTOR
Good Big Brother, A	F	RF	216	Reading Street	Pearson
Good Boy, Andrew!	E	RF	85	Literacy 2000	Rigby
*Good Catch!, A	E	RF	191	New Way Red	Steck-Vaughn
Good Choices for Cat and Dog	E	F	97	Learn to Read	Creative Teaching Press
Good Citizen	J	RF	372	Leveled Readers	Houghton Mifflin Harcourt
Good Citizen	J	RF	372	Leveled Readers/CA	Houghton Mifflin Harcourt
Good Citizen	J	RF	372	Leveled Readers/TX	Houghton Mifflin Harcourt
Good Dessert, A	J	F	250+	Leveled Readers Language Support	Houghton Mifflin Harcourt
Good Dog	C	RF	43	Sun Sprouts	ETA Cuisenaire
Good Dog!	P	I	1932	Vocabulary Readers	Houghton Mifflin Harcourt
Good Dog!	P	I	1932	Vocabulary Readers/CA	Houghton Mifflin Harcourt
Good Dog!	J	I	251	Yellow Umbrella Books	Red Brick Learning
Good Dog, Bonita	N	RF	250+	Giff, Patricia Reilly	Bantam
Good Dog, Carl	WB	F	N/A	Day, Alexandra	Green Tiger Press
Good Dog, The	S	F	250+	Avi	Simon & Schuster
Good Dog, The	D	F	125	Leveled Literacy Intervention/ Green System	Heinemann
Good Dogs, Guide Dogs	N	I	911	Leveled Readers	Houghton Mifflin Harcourt
Good Dogs, Guide Dogs	N	I	911	Leveled Readers/CA	Houghton Mifflin Harcourt
Good Dogs, Guide Dogs	O	I	911	Leveled Readers/TX	Houghton Mifflin Harcourt
Good Driving, Amelia Bedelia	L	F	250+	Parish, Peggy	Harper & Row
Good Earth, The	Z+	HF	250+	Buck, Pearl S.	Simon & Schuster
Good Fires, Bad Fires	L	I	885	Sun Sprouts	ETA Cuisenaire
Good Food	F	I	78	Leveled Readers Science	Houghton Mifflin Harcourt
Good for You	D	F	44	Sunshine	Wright Group/McGraw Hill
Good Fortune	U	B	250+	Wong, Li Keng	Peachtree
Good Friends	L	F	482	Leveled Literacy Intervention/ Blue System	Heinemann
Good Friends	A	I	21	Shutterbug Books	Steck-Vaughn
Good Friends	H	I	169	Vocabulary Readers	Houghton Mifflin Harcourt
Good Friends	H	I	169	Vocabulary Readers/CA	Houghton Mifflin Harcourt
Good Fun Farm	J	F	532	Big Cat	Pacfic Learning
Good Gauley!	O	I	250+	Literacy by Design	Rigby
Good Girl	B	F	18	Ready Readers	Pearson Learning Group
Good Grief . . . Third Grade	O	RF	250+	McKenna, Colleen	Scholastic
Good Hat for a Cat, A	E	F	104	Bonnell, Kris	Reading Reading Books
Good Home, A	C	F	77	Leveled Readers Language Support	Houghton Mifflin Harcourt
Good Idea, A	H	RF	250+	Leveled Readers Language Support	Houghton Mifflin Harcourt
Good Ideas for People	G	I	125	Sails	Rigby
Good Job, Little Bear	K	F	250+	Waddell, Martin	Candlewick Press
Good Job, Sam!	D	F	108	Leveled Readers	Houghton Mifflin Harcourt
Good Job, Sam!	D	F	108	Leveled Readers/CA	Houghton Mifflin Harcourt
Good Knee for a Cat, A	I	RF	205	Pacific Literacy	Pacific Learning
Good Luck Elephant	I	F	171	Sunshine	Wright Group/McGraw Hill
Good Manners	H	RF	222	Well-Being Series	Dominie Press
Good Master, The	S	RF	250+	Seredy, Kate	Scholastic
Good Masters! Sweet Ladies!: Voices From a Medieval Village	Z	I	250+	Schlitz, Laura Amy	Candlewick Press
Good Morning Isabel	G	RF	143	Literacy 2000	Rigby
Good Morning Mrs. Martin	K	F	156	Book Bank	Wright Group/McGraw Hill
Good Morning!	C	F	51	Science	Outside the Box

* Collection of short stories
\# Graphic text

TITLE	LEVEL	GENRE	WORD COUNT	AUTHOR / SERIES	PUBLISHER / DISTRIBUTOR
Good Morning, Monday	H	RF	77	Keenan, Sheila	Scholastic
Good Morning, Who's Snoring?	E	F	127	Story Steps	Rigby
Good Neighbors	E	RF	104	InfoTrek	ETA Cuisenaire
Good News	I	TL	250+	Brenner, Barbara	Bantam
Good Night	M	RF	753	Leveled Readers	Houghton Mifflin Harcourt
Good Night	E	RF	114	Start to Read	School Zone
Good Night Sky	D	RF	32	Seedlings	Continental Press
Good Night!	D	F	73	Leveled Readers Language Support	Houghton Mifflin Harcourt
Good Night, City Lights	F	RF	74	City Stories	Rigby
Good Night, Little Brother	F	RF	69	Literacy 2000	Rigby
Good Night, Little Bug	D	F	54	Ready Readers	Pearson Learning Group
Good Night, Little Kitten	D	F	78	My First Reader	Grolier Press
Good Night, Mr. Tom	Z	HF	250+	Magorian, Michelle	HarperTrophy
Good Night's Sleep, A	P	RF	1091	Leveled Readers	Houghton Mifflin Harcourt
Good Old Mom	C	RF	34	Oxford Reading Tree	Oxford University Press
Good Old Wood	L	I	293	Gear Up!	Wright Group/ McGraw Hill
Good Place for a City, A	N	I	194	Windows on Literacy	National Geographic
Good Place to Live, A	G	I	97	Windows on Literacy	National Geographic
Good Sport: Games, Sports, and Festivals	S	I	250+	Kids Discover Reading	Wright Group/McGraw Hill
Good Sports	H	I	206	Foundations	Wright Group/McGraw Hill
Good Sports	R	B	250+	InfoQuest	Rigby
Good Times Book, The	K	RF	851	Rigby Flying Colors	Rigby
Good to Eat	H	I	152	Rigby Focus	Rigby
Good to Eat	B	I	31	Twig	Wright Group/McGraw Hill
Good Vibrations: Experimenting with Sound	K	I	250+	Rigby Literacy	Rigby
Good Work, Amelia Bedelia	L	F	250+	Parish, Peggy	Avon Camelot
Good, the Bad, and Everything Else, The	R	RF	250+	Action Packs	Rigby
Good, the Bad, and the Goofy, The	P	SF	250+	Scieszka, Jon	Penguin Group
Goodbye Gabby	I	RF	400	Early Transitional, Set 1	Pioneer Valley
Goodbye Goose	L	F	264	Books for Young Learners	Richard C. Owen
Good-Bye Marianne	T	B	250+	Watts, Irene N.	Tundra Books
Good-Bye My Wishing Star	S	RF	250+	Grove, Vicki	Scholastic
Good-bye Perky	E	RF	54	Twig	Wright Group/McGraw Hill
Good-bye Summer, Hello Fall	H	I	169	Ready Readers	Pearson Learning Group
Goodbye to Angel Island	R	HF	1055	Leveled Readers	Houghton Mifflin Harcourt
Good-Bye, Billy Radish	V	HF	250+	Skurzynski, Gloria	Aladdin
Good-Bye, Chicken Little	Q	RF	250+	Byars, Betsy	HarperTrophy
Good-Bye, Fox	D	F	27	Instant Readers	Harcourt School Publishers
Good-Bye, Lucy	D	RF	60	Sunshine	Wright Group/McGraw Hill
Good-Bye, Vietnam	V	RF	250+	Whelan, Gloria	Alfred A. Knopf
Good-bye, Zoo	C	RF	48	Ready Readers	Pearson Learning Group
Good-Byes	J	I	184	Shelley Rotner's Early Childhood	Millbrook Press
Good-for-Nothing Dog, The	M	RF	250+	Woodland Mysteries	Wright Group/McGraw Hill
Goodness Gracious	I	I	190	Literacy 2000	Rigby
Goodness Me, Mr. Magee!	F	F	251	Sails	Rigby
Goodnight	F	F	131	Rigby Rocket	Rigby
Goodnight	D	RF	83	Voyages	SRA/McGraw Hill
Goodnight Bobbie	LB	RF	15	Rigby Literacy	Rigby
Goodnight Goodnight	H	F	185	Literacy Tree	Rigby
Goodnight Josie	LB	RF	15	Rigby Star	Rigby
Goodnight Moon	H	F	130	Brown, Margaret Wise	HarperCollins
Goodnight Peter	G	RF	107	Windmill Books	Wright Group/McGraw Hill
Goodnight!	D	RF	61	Joy Readers	Pearson Learning Group

* Collection of short stories
# Graphic text

TITLE	LEVEL	GENRE	WORD COUNT	AUTHOR / SERIES	PUBLISHER / DISTRIBUTOR
Goodnight, Gorilla	LB	F	25	Rothmann, Peggy	Putnam/Penguin
Goodnight, Owl!	I	F	181	Hutchins, Pat	Aladdin
Goodnight, Owl!	I	F	181	Hutchins, Pat	Macmillan
Goodnight-Loving Trail, The	U	I	2736	Leveled Readers	Houghton Mifflin Harcourt
Goodnight-Loving Trail, The	U	I	2736	Leveled Readers/CA	Houghton Mifflin Harcourt
Goodnight-Loving Trail, The	U	I	2736	Leveled Readers/TX	Houghton Mifflin Harcourt
Goods and Services	N	I	909	Reading Street	Pearson
Goods and Services	N	I	909	Reading Street	Pearson
Goody Hall	V	RF	250+	Babbitt, Natalie	Farrar, Straus and Giroux
Gooey Chewy Contest, The	L	F	1512	Goldsmith, Howard	Mondo
Gooney Bird Greene	N	RF	250+	Lowry, Lois	Dell Yearling
Goooaaalll!	P	RF	250+	Sails	Rigby
Goose Chase	D	F	43	Ready Readers	Pearson Learning Group
Goose on the Loose	Q	RF	250+	Baglio, Ben M.	Scholastic
Goose That Laid the Golden Egg, The	G	TL	73	Aesop	Wright Group/McGraw Hill
Goose Who Acted Like a Cow, The	J	F	250+	Phonics and Friends	Hampton-Brown
Gooseberry Park	P	F	250+	Rylant, Cynthia	Scholastic
Goosebumps: It Came From Beneath the Sink	T	F	250+	Stine, R. L.	Language for Learning Assoc.
Goose's Gold, The	N	RF	250+	A to Z Mysteries	Random House
Gordon Gets Even	M	RF	250+	Lighthouse	Ginn & Co.
Gorganzola Zombies in the Park	O	F	250+	Levy, Elizabeth	HarperTrophy
Gorgo Meets Her Match	K	HF	453	PM Story Books	Rigby
Gorilla Families	L	I	250+	Rosen Real Readers	Rosen Publishing Group
Gorilla Games	B	F	27	Phonics and Friends	Hampton-Brown
Gorilla Guardian	L	RF	250+	World Quest Adventures	World Quest Learning
Gorilla, Monkey, and Ape	V	I	250+	Eyewitness Books	DK Publishing
Gorillas	T	I	250+	Burgel, Paul H.; Hartwig, M.	Carolrhoda Books
Gorillas	J	I	250+	Pebble Books	Red Brick Learning
Gorillas	I	I	173	Sails	Rigby
Gorillas	H	I	185	Seedlings	Continental Press
Gorillas	U	I	250+	The Untamed World	Steck-Vaughn
Gorillas and Chimpanzees	S	I	4454	Take Two Books	Wright Group/McGraw Hill
Gorillas: Gentle Giants on the Forest	L	I	250+	Milton, Joyce	Random House
Gossamer	V	F	250+	Lowry, Lois	Yearling
Gotcha Box, The	A	RF	30	Story Box	Wright Group/McGraw Hill
Government in Action	T	I	250+	Reading Expeditions	National Geographic
Government Leaders: Then and Now	Q	I	250+	Primary Source Readers	Teacher Created Materials
Government Rules	U	I	250+	News Extra	Richard C. Owen
Go-With Words	F	I	133	Rookie Readers	Children's Press
Gowler's Horn	Z	RF	250+	Misfits Inc.	Peachtree
GPS Mystery, The	R	RF	250+	Take Two Books	Wright Group/McGraw Hill
Grab Bag, The	C	RF	85	PM Plus Story Books	Rigby
Grab Hands and Run	V	RF	250+	Temple, Frances	HarperTrophy
Grab It!	C	RF	45	Leveled Readers Language Support	Houghton Mifflin Harcourt
Grabbing Bird, The	L	F	250+	Cambridge Reading	Pearson Learning Group
Grace	U	HF	250+	Walsh, Jill Paton	Farrar, Straus and Giroux
Grace Hopper: Computer Pioneer	P	B	250+	On Deck	Rigby
Grace the Pirate	O	F	250+	High-Fliers	Pacific Learning
Grace the Pirate	O	F	250+	Lasky, Kathryn	Hyperion
Grace's Letter to Lincoln	P	HF	250+	Roop, Peter & Connie	Hyperion
Graciela Finds the Fair	Q	RF	250+	On Our Way to English	Rigby
Gracie's Cat	I	RF	250+	Cambridge Reading	Pearson Learning Group

* Collection of short stories
\# Graphic text

TITLE	LEVEL	GENRE	WORD COUNT	AUTHOR / SERIES	PUBLISHER / DISTRIBUTOR
Graduation of Jake Moon, The	U	RF	250+	Park, Barbara	Scholastic
Graffiti	L	RF	688	Rigby Flying Colors	Rigby
Graffiti	I	RF	168	Sunshine	Wright Group/McGraw Hill
Graham Hawkes: Underwater Pilot	U	B	1492	Leveled Readers	Houghton Mifflin Harcourt
Grain Group, The	H	I	108	The Food Guide Pyramid	Capstone Press
Grain of Rice, A	P	TL	250+	Pittman, Helena Clare	Bantam
Grains	F	I	88	Food Groups	Lerner Publications
Grampa's Zombie BBQ	Q	F	250+	Wiley & Grampa's Creature Features	Little, Brown & Co.
Gramp's Favorite Gift	S	RF	1481	Leveled Readers	Houghton Mifflin Harcourt
Gramp's Favorite Gift	S	RF	1481	Leveled Readers/CA	Houghton Mifflin Harcourt
Gramp's Favorite Gift	S	RF	1481	Leveled Readers/TX	Houghton Mifflin Harcourt
Gram's Hat	D	RF	76	Leveled Readers	Houghton Mifflin Harcourt
Grams, Her Boyfriend, My Family, and Me	U	RF	250+	Derby, Pat	Sunburst
Grand Canyon Adventure	N	I	250+	Windows on Literacy	National Geographic
Grand Canyon Doesn't Scare Me, The	R	RF	250+	Pair-It Books	Steck-Vaughn
Grand Canyon Journey, A: Tracing Time in Stone	W	I	250+	A First Book	Franklin Watts
Grand Canyon National Park	O	I	250+	A True Book	Children's Press
Grand Central Terminal: Gateway to New York City	U	I	250+	Bookshop	Mondo
Grand Coulee Dam, The	Q	I	793	Leveled Readers Social Studies	Houghton Mifflin Harcourt
Grand Duchess Anastasia Romanov	T	B	250+	Queens and Princesses	Capstone Press
Grand Escape, The	S	F	250+	Naylor, Phyllis Reynolds	Bantam
*Grand Mothers: Poems, Reminiscences, and Short Stories About Keepers of Our Traditions	Y	B	250+	Giovanni, Nikki	Henry Holt & Co.
Grand Trees of America: Our State and Champion Trees	T	I	250+	Jorgenson, Lisa	Roberts Rinehart
Grandad	L	RF	250+	Literacy 2000	Rigby
Grandad's Dinosaur	K	F	250+	Storyteller-Shooting Stars	Wright Group/McGraw Hill
Grandad's Mask	K	RF	250+	PM Collection	Rigby
Grandad's Wild Stories	O	F	250+	Tristars	Richard C. Owen
Granddad's Dinosaur	J	F	250+	I Am Reading	Kingfisher
Grandfather Horned Toad	K	F	250+	Little Celebrations	Pearson Learning Group
Grandfathers	F	I	49	Families	Capstone Press
Grandfathers	C	I	41	Pebble Books	Capstone Press
Grandfather's Ghost	M	F	250+	Sunshine	Wright Group/McGraw Hill
Grandfather's Mask	I	RF	245	Leveled Readers Language Support	Houghton Mifflin Harcourt
Grandma Alma's Special Room	H	RF	246	On Our Way to English	Rigby
Grandma and Me	D	I	68	Sun Sprouts	ETA Cuisenaire
Grandma and the Pirate	F	RF	105	Lloyd, David	Crown
Grandma Betty's Banjo	R	RF	3968	Reading Street	Pearson
Grandma Carol's Plant	I	RF	250+	Home Connection Collection	Rigby
Grandma Chicken Legs	O	TL	250+	McCaughrean, Geraldine	Carolrhoda Books
Grandma Comes to Stay	E	RF	118	Sails	Rigby
Grandma Comes to Stay Again	I	F	389	Sails	Rigby
Grandma Go	R	RF	250+	Reading Safari	Mondo
Grandma Helps Out!	G	RF	202	Sails	Rigby
Grandma J	I	RF	170	Instant Readers	Harcourt School Publishers
Grandma Mixup, The	K	RF	250+	Little Readers	Houghton Mifflin Harcourt
Grandma Mix-Up, The	K	RF	250+	McCully, Emily Arnold	HarperTrophy
Grandma Moses	N	B	250+	Biography	Benchmark Education
Grandma Moses: Painter of Rural America	T	B	250+	O'Neal, Zibby	Penguin Group

G

TITLE	LEVEL	GENRE	WORD COUNT	AUTHOR / SERIES	PUBLISHER / DISTRIBUTOR
Grandma Moves In	I	RF	250+	Greetings	Rigby
Grandma Pickleberry's Cold	I	RF	268	Springboard	Wright Group/McGraw Hill
Grandma's Glasses	F	RF	193	Leveled Literacy Intervention/ Green System	Heinemann
Grandmas at Bat	K	RF	250+	McCully, Emily Arnold	HarperTrophy
Grandmas at the Lake	K	RF	250+	McCully, Emily Arnold	HarperTrophy
Grandma's Bicycle	G	RF	74	Read Alongs	Rigby
Grandma's Bird	R	RF	250+	Sails	Rigby
Grandma's Birthday	G	RF	197	On Our Way to English	Rigby
Grandma's Cane	H	RF	250+	Story Box	Wright Group/McGraw Hill
Grandma's Cookie Cutters	K	RF	577	Leveled Readers	Houghton Mifflin Harcourt
Grandma's Flying Adventure	O	RF	250+	Tristars	Richard C. Owen
Grandma's Garden	K	I	340	Rigby Focus	Rigby
Grandma's Good Food	H	RF	200	InfoTrek	ETA Cuisenaire
Grandma's Hearing Aids	K	RF	361	Sails	Rigby
Grandma's Heart	K	I	90	Wonder World	Wright Group/McGraw Hill
Grandma's House	D	RF	113	Jasper the Cat	Pioneer Valley
Grandma's Letter	D	RF	67	Foundations	Wright Group/McGraw Hill
Grandma's Memories	F	RF	102	Literacy 2000	Rigby
Grandma's Other Life	X	RF	2480	Leveled Readers	Houghton Mifflin Harcourt
Grandma's Other Life	X	RF	2480	Leveled Readers/CA	Houghton Mifflin Harcourt
Grandma's Patchy Pocket	F	RF	55	Polette, Nancy	Kaeden Books
Grandma's Pictures of the Past	J	RF	250+	Home Connection Collection	Rigby
Grandma's Present	F	RF	191	Foundations	Wright Group/McGraw Hill
Grandma's Records	O	RF	250+	Velasquez, Eric	Scholastic
Grandma's Stick	H	RF	250+	Story Box	Wright Group/McGraw Hill
Grandma's Surprise	G	RF	220	Leveled Readers	Houghton Mifflin Harcourt
Grandma's Surprise	G	RF	220	Leveled Readers/CA	Houghton Mifflin Harcourt
Grandma's Surprise	G	RF	220	Leveled Readers/TX	Houghton Mifflin Harcourt
Grandma's Surprise	H	RF	216	Storyworlds	Heinemann Educational Books
Grandma's Table	K	RF	287	Leveled Readers	Houghton Mifflin Harcourt
Grandmother	E	RF	60	Joy Readers	Pearson Learning Group
Grandmother and I	C	RF	53	Home Connection Collection	Rigby
Grandmother Is Tired	C	RF	31	Joy Readers	Pearson Learning Group
Grandmothers	F	I	50	Families	Capstone Press
Grandmothers	C	I	50	Pebble Books	Capstone Press
Grandpa	C	RF	61	Literacy by Design	Rigby
Grandpa	S	RF	250+	Reading Safari	Mondo
Grandpa	C	RF	61	Rigby Literacy	Rigby
Grandpa	C	RF	69	Rigby Star	Rigby
Grandpa	E	RF	70	Sunshine	Wright Group/McGraw Hill
Grandpa	A	I	36	Vocabulary Readers	Houghton Mifflin Harcourt
Grandpa	A	I	36	Vocabulary Readers/CA	Houghton Mifflin Harcourt
Grandpa	A	I	36	Vocabulary Readers/TX	Houghton Mifflin Harcourt
Grandpa and I	C	RF	40	Home Connection Collection	Rigby
Grandpa and Me	E	RF	124	Gear Up!	Wright Group/McGraw Hill
Grandpa and Me	C	RF	86	Leveled Readers	Houghton Mifflin Harcourt
Grandpa and Me	C	RF	86	Leveled Readers/CA	Houghton Mifflin Harcourt
Grandpa and Me	C	RF	86	Leveled Readers/TX	Houghton Mifflin Harcourt
Grandpa and Me	D	I	36	Sun Sprouts	ETA Cuisenaire
*Grandpa at the Beach	J	F	250+	Lewis, Rob	Mondo
*Grandpa Comes to Stay	J	F	1083	Lewis, Rob	Mondo
Grandpa Knits Hats	E	RF	55	Wonder World	Wright Group/McGraw Hill

* Collection of short stories
\# Graphic text

G

TITLE	LEVEL	GENRE	WORD COUNT	AUTHOR / SERIES	PUBLISHER / DISTRIBUTOR
Grandpa Moves In	I	RF	158	InfoTrek	ETA Cuisenaire
Grandpa Snored	F	RF	51	Literacy 2000	Rigby
Grandpa, Grandma, and the Tractor	H	RF	220	Ready Readers	Pearson Learning Group
Grandpa, Grandpa	G	RF	122	Story Box	Wright Group/McGraw Hill
Grandparents Are Fun!	H	I	216	Leveled Readers Language Support	Houghton Mifflin Harcourt
Grandparents Are Great	I	I	257	Leveled Readers	Houghton Mifflin Harcourt
Grandpa's Baseball Card	P	RF	1022	Leveled Readers	Houghton Mifflin Harcourt
Grandpa's Birthday	J	RF	250+	Literacy 2000	Rigby
Grandpa's Boat	E	RF	108	Developing Books	Pioneer Valley
Grandpa's Bright Ideas	J	RF	250+	Lighthouse	Ginn & Co.
Grandpa's Candy Store	F	RF	65	Books for Young Learners	Richard C. Owen
Grandpa's Clues	F	RF	198	Rigby Literacy	Rigby
Grandpa's Cookies	F	F	193	Little Readers	Houghton Mifflin Harcourt
Grandpa's Face	Q	RF	250+	Greenfield, Eloise	Putnam/Penguin
Grandpa's Garden Shed	G	I	68	Windows on Literacy	National Geographic
Grandpa's Lemonade	G	RF	138	Storyteller Nonfiction	Wright Group/McGraw Hill
Grandpa's Mountain	T	RF	250+	Reeder, Carolyn	Avon Camelot
Grandpa's Rail Tales	T	F	1730	Leveled Readers	Houghton Mifflin Harcourt
Grandpa's Scrapbook	M	HF	660	Reading Street	Pearson
Grandpa's Sign	I	RF	304	Reading Street	Pearson
Grandpa's Special Present	I	RF	286	Foundations	Wright Group/McGraw Hill
Grandpa's Train	E	RF	69	Early Emergent, Set 3	Pioneer Valley
Grandpa's Tricky Puzzles	J	RF	537	InfoTrek	ETA Cuisenaire
Grandpa's Visit	H	RF	226	PM Stars	Rigby
Grandpa's Visit	C	RF	38	Vocabulary Readers	Houghton Mifflin Harcourt
Granny	A	RF	36	Leveled Readers	Houghton Mifflin Harcourt
Granny	A	RF	36	Leveled Readers/CA	Houghton Mifflin Harcourt
Granny	A	RF	36	Leveled Readers/TX	Houghton Mifflin Harcourt
Granny	G	RF	186	Sails	Rigby
Granny and the Desperadoes	J	RF	250+	Parish, Peggy	Simon & Schuster
Granny Bundle's Boring Walk	H	RF	250+	Stepping Stones	Nelson/Michaels Assoc.
Granny Gadget	J	F	250+	Rigby Rocket	Rigby
Granny Garcia's Gifts	J	RF	366	Storyteller	Wright Group/McGraw Hill
Granny Lina's Bedtime Story	M	RF	250+	Springboard	Wright Group/McGraw Hill
Granny Torrelli Makes Soup	S	RF	250+	Creech, Sharon	Scholastic
Granny's Teeth	H	RF	169	Cambridge Reading	Pearson Learning Group
Granny's Visit	E	RF	144	Leveled Readers Language Support	Houghton Mifflin Harcourt
Grant Wood	R	B	250+	Venezia, Mike	Children's Press
Granville T. Woods	P	I	1344	Vocabulary Readers	Houghton Mifflin Harcourt
Granville T. Woods	P	B	1344	Vocabulary Readers/CA	Houghton Mifflin Harcourt
Grapes of Math, The	N	I	250+	Tang, Greg	Scholastic
Graph It	K	I	250+	Yellow Umbrella Books	Capstone Press
Grass Circles Mystery, The	K	F	250+	Talking Points Series	Pearson Learning Group
Grass for Dinner	B	F	36	Sails	Rigby
Grass Is for Goats	D	RF	84	Joy Readers	Pearson Learning Group
Grasshopper and the Ants	K	TL	452	Sunshine	Wright Group/McGraw Hill
Grasshopper and the Flea, The	B	F	63	Springboard	Wright Group/McGraw Hill
Grasshopper Learns a Lesson: A Play	K	TL	250+	On Our Way to English	Rigby
Grasshopper on the Road	K	F	250+	Lobel, Arnold	HarperTrophy
Grasshopper Summer	T	HF	250+	Turner, Ann	Aladdin
Grasshoppers	H	I	84	Bugs, Bugs, Bugs!	Red Brick Learning
Grasshoppers	F	I	50	Insects	Capstone Press

G

TITLE	LEVEL	GENRE	WORD COUNT	AUTHOR / SERIES	PUBLISHER / DISTRIBUTOR
Grasshoppers	N	I	250+	Nature's Friends	Compass Point Books
Grassland Safari	Q	I	250+	InfoQuest	Rigby
Grasslands	O	I	250+	A True Book	Children's Press
Grasslands	Q	I	250+	Ecosystems	Red Brick Learning
Grasslands	Q	I	250+	First Reports	Compass Point Books
Gratefully Yours	T	HF	250+	Buchanan, Jane	Puffin/Penguin
*Graven Images: Three Stories by Paul Fleischman	U	F	250+	Fleischman, Paul	HarperTrophy
Gravity	O	I	250+	Early Connections	Benchmark Education
Gravity	I	I	77	Forces and Motion	Lerner Publications
Gravity	P	I	250+	Our Physical World	Capstone Press
Gravity	D	I	33	Wonder World	Wright Group/McGraw Hill
Gravity and the Solar System	O	I	250+	PM Plus Story Books	Rigby
Gravity: Simple Experiments for Young Scientists	T	I	250+	White, Larry	Millbrook Press
Gray Blanket, The: Rabbits in Australia	V	I	1878	Leveled Readers Social Studies	Houghton Mifflin Harcourt
Gray Heroes Elder Tales from Around the World	Z	TL	250+	Yolen, Jane	Penguin Group
Gray Whales	P	I	828	Reading Street	Pearson
Gray Wolves	O	I	2281	Early Bird Nature Books	Lerner Publications
*Great African Americans in Business	T	B	250+	Rediger, Pat	Crabtree
*Great African Americans in Civil Rights	T	B	250+	Rediger, Pat	Crabtree
*Great African Americans in Entertainment	T	B	250+	Rediger, Pat	Crabtree
*Great African Americans in Film	T	B	250+	Parker, Janice	Crabtree
*Great African Americans in Government	T	B	250+	Dudley, Karen	Crabtree
*Great African Americans in History	T	B	250+	Hacker, Carlotta	Crabtree
*Great African Americans in Jazz	T	B	250+	Hacker, Carlotta	Crabtree
*Great African Americans in Literature	T	B	250+	Rediger, Pat	Crabtree
*Great African Americans in Music	T	B	250+	Rediger, Pat	Crabtree
*Great African Americans in Sports	T	B	250+	Rediger, Pat	Crabtree
*Great African Americans in the Arts	T	B	250+	Hacker, Carlotta	Crabtree
*Great African Americans in the Olympics	T	B	250+	Hunter, Shaun	Crabtree
Great and Shining Road, The	R	I	250+	Orbit Chapter Books	Pacific Learning
Great Apes	T	I	2309	Reading Street	Pearson
Great Apes, The	S	I	250+	A First Book	Franklin Watts
Great Astronomers	Y	B	250+	High-Fliers	Pacific Learning
Great Attitude, A	F	B	196	Learn to Read	Creative Teaching Press
Great Basin Indians, The: Daily Life in the 1700s	O	I	250+	Native American Life	Capstone Press
Great Bay, The	M	RF	706	Leveled Readers	Houghton Mifflin Harcourt
Great Bay, The	M	RF	706	Leveled Readers/CA	Houghton Mifflin Harcourt
Great Bay, The	M	RF	706	Leveled Readers/TX	Houghton Mifflin Harcourt
Great Bean Race, The	K	RF	295	Pacific Literacy	Pacific Learning
Great Big Enormous Turnip, The	H	TL	355	Leveled Literacy Intervention/ Blue System	Heinemann
Great Big Enormous Turnip, The	H	TL	317	Reading Unlimited	Pearson Learning Group
Great Big Enormous Turnip, The	H	TL	250+	Tolstoi, Aleksei; Nikolaevich, Graf	Watts
Great Brain at the Academy, The	T	RF	250+	Fitzgerald, John D.	Yearling
Great Brain Does It Again, The	T	RF	250+	Fitzgerald, John D.	Yearling
Great Brain Reforms, The	T	RF	250+	Fitzgerald, John D.	Yearling
Great Brain, The	T	RF	250+	Fitzgerald, John D.	Language for Learning Assoc.
Great Bug Hunt, The	G	RF	96	Rookie Readers	Children's Press
Great Car Race, The	E	F	162	Carousel Readers	Pearson Learning Group

* Collection of short stories
# Graphic text

TITLE	LEVEL	GENRE	WORD COUNT	AUTHOR / SERIES	PUBLISHER / DISTRIBUTOR
Great Chicago Fire, 1871, The	Z	HF	250+	Massie, Elizabeth	Pocket Books
Great Danes	I	I	149	Dogs	Capstone Press
Great Day	G	RF	161	Alphakids	Sundance
Great Day for Snorkeling, A	K	RF	238	Leveled Readers	Houghton Mifflin Harcourt
Great Day for Up	J	F	180	Seuss, Dr.	Random House
Great Day, A	C	F	94	Literacy by Design	Rigby
Great Depression, The	X	I	250+	Cornerstones of Freedom	Children's Press
Great Dimpole Oak, The	S	RF	250+	Lisle, Janet Taylor	Puffin/Penguin
Great Dinosaur Hunt, The	M	F	250+	Woodland Mysteries	Wright Group/McGraw Hill
Great Dinosaur Race, The	L	F	250+	Popcorn	Sundance
Great Dog Wash, The	O	RF	250+	Rigby Focus	Rigby
Great Egg Problem, The	P	HF	250+	Bookweb	Rigby
Great Enormous Hamburger, The	B	F	36	Sunshine	Wright Group/McGraw Hill
Great Escape, The	P	RF	250+	In Step Readers	Rigby
Great Escape, The	L	RF	250+	Rigby Literacy	Rigby
Great Escapes & Amazing Tricks	V	I	250+	Boldprint	Steck-Vaughn
*Great Escapes of World War II	Z	I	250+	Sullivan, George	Scholastic
Great Expectations	S	HF	250+	Bullseye Step Into Classics	Random House
Great Explorations	T	HF	250+	Neufeld, David	Scholastic
Great Fire of London, The	P	I	250+	Rigby Star Quest	Rigby
Great Fire, The	W	I	250+	Murphy, Jim	Scholastic
Great Genghis Khan Look-Alike Contest, The	L	RF	250+	Sharmat, Marjorie Weinman	Random House
Great Ghosts	L	F	250+	Cohen, Daniel	Scholastic
Great Gilly Hopkins, The	S	RF	250+	Paterson, Katherine	Hearst
Great Gobs of Gum!	N	I	250+	Rigby Literacy	Rigby
Great Gracie Chase, Stop That Dog, The	K	RF	250+	Rylant, Cynthia	Scholastic
Great Great Grandfather's Railroad	J	HF	250+	Sunshine	Wright Group/McGraw Hill
Great Green Place, The	K	I	242	Story Box	Wright Group/McGraw Hill
Great Grumbler and the Wonder Tree, The	K	F	250+	Mahy, Margaret	Pacific Learning
Great Hearts: Heroes of Special Olympics	S	I	250+	High-Fliers	Pacific Learning
Great Houdini, The: World Famous Magician and Escape Artist	M	B	250+	Kulling, Monica	Random House
Great Ice Battle, The	M	F	250+	Abbott, Tony	Scholastic
Great Idea!	S	I	250+	Boldprint	Steck-Vaughn
Great Interactive Dream Machine, The	Y	SF	250+	Peck, Richard	Puffin/Penguin
Great Invention, The	H	RF	108	City Stories	Rigby
Great Inventions and Where They Came From	P	I	250+	Navigators Social Studies Series	Benchmark Education
Great Inventor, A: An Wang	J	B	207	Leveled Readers Social Studies	Houghton Mifflin Harcourt
Great Joy	O	RF	250+	DiCamillo, Kate	Candlewick Press
Great Kapok Tree, The	R	I	250+	Cherry, Lynne	Scholastic
Great Little Madison, The	X	B	250+	Fritz, Jean	G.P. Putnam's Sons
Great Migration, The	R	I	250+	Lawrence, Jacob	HarperCollins
Great Monsieur Vertelli, The	O	I	250+	Wonder World	Wright Group/McGraw Hill
Great Ocean, The	K	I	250+	Spyglass Books	Compass Point Books
Great Partnership, A	T	I	2132	Vocabulary Readers	Houghton Mifflin Harcourt
Great Partnership, A	T	I	2132	Vocabulary Readers/CA	Houghton Mifflin Harcourt
Great Piano Hoist, The	O	RF	250+	Orbit Chapter Books	Pacific Learning
Great Plague, The	T	HF	250+	Story Surfers	ETA Cuisenaire
Great Plains Indians, The: Daily Life in the 1700s	O	I	250+	Native American Life	Capstone Press
Great Plains, The	T	I	250+	Theme Sets	National Geographic
Great Pumpkin, The	I	F	239	Sunshine	Wright Group/McGraw Hill
Great Pyramid, The	T	I	250+	Lighthouse	Ginn & Co.
Great Pyramid, The	S	I	250+	Windows on Literacy	National Geographic

TITLE	LEVEL	GENRE	WORD COUNT	AUTHOR / SERIES	PUBLISHER / DISTRIBUTOR
Great Quarterback Switch, The	Q	RF	250+	Christopher, Matt	Little, Brown & Co.
Great Race, The	G	F	250+	McPhail, David	Scholastic
Great Riddle Mystery, The	M	RF	250+	MacClean, James R.	Pearson Learning Group
Great Rivers	R	I	250+	InfoQuest	Rigby
Great Sand Dunes National Monument	O	I	250+	A True Book	Children's Press
Great Scientist Detectives at Work	N	I	643	Reading Street	Pearson
Great Shakes: The Science of Earthquakes	X	I	250+	Headline Science	Compass Point Books
Great Smoky Mountains Encyclopedia	R	I	250+	Literacy by Design	Rigby
Great Snake Escape, The	J	F	250+	Coxe, Molly	HarperTrophy
Great Snake Swindle, The	O	RF	250+	Klooz	Stone Arch Books
Great Snakes!	I	I	161	Robinson, Fay	Scholastic
Great Sporting Events	R	I	250+	PM Nonfiction-Ruby	Rigby
Great Storyteller, The	O	RF	1095	Leveled Readers/TX	Houghton Mifflin Harcourt
Great Tomato Battle, The	S	RF	250+	Story Surfers	ETA Cuisenaire
Great Tree Mouse Adventure, The	J	F	250+	Rigby Rocket	Rigby
Great Wall of China, The	R	I	250+	Explorer Books-Pathfinder	National Geographic
Great Wall of China, The	P	I	250+	Explorer Books-Pioneer	National Geographic
Great Wall of China, The	Q	I	250+	Fisher, Leonard Everett	Aladdin
Great Wall of China, The	Q	I	250+	Rosen Real Readers	Rosen Publishing Group
Great Wall of China, The	N	I	141	Vocabulary Readers	Houghton Mifflin Harcourt
Great Whales: The Gentle Giants	W	I	250+	Lauber, Patricia	Henry Holt & Co.
Great Wheel, The	U	RF	250+	Lawson, Robert	Scholastic
Great White Shark	J	I	157	Sharks	Capstone Press
Great White Sharks	P	I	1633	Animal Predators	Lerner Publishing
Great White Sharks	O	I	1853	Early Bird Nature Books	Lerner Publications
Great White Sharks	F	I	98	Pair-It Books	Steck-Vaughn
Great White Sharks	U	I	250+	The Untamed World	Steck-Vaughn
Great, Big, Giant Turnip, The	J	TL	610	Early Connections	Benchmark Education
Greatest Baseball Records, The	S	I	250+	Sports Records	Capstone Press
Greatest Basketball Records, The	S	I	250+	Sports Records	Capstone Press
Greatest Binnie in the World, The	M	RF	709	Sunshine	Wright Group/McGraw Hill
Greatest Digger of All, The	M	F	250+	Pair-It Turn and Learn	Steck-Vaughn
Greatest Electrician in the World, The	W	B	1926	Leveled Readers	Houghton Mifflin Harcourt
Greatest Football Records, The	S	I	250+	Sports Records	Capstone Press
Greatest Hockey Records, The	S	I	250+	Sports Records	Capstone Press
Greatest of All, The: A Japanese Folktale	L	TL	250+	Kimmel, Eric A.	Holiday House
Greatest Player, The	V	B	250+	WorldScapes	ETA Cuisenaire
Greatest Wall of All, The	Q	I	250+	WorldScapes	ETA Cuisenaire
Greatest, The	R	I	250+	Literacy 2000	Rigby
Greatest, The: Muhammad Ali	Z	B	250+	Myers, Walter Dean	Scholastic
Great-Grandpa	G	RF	130	Voyages	SRA/McGraw Hill
Great-Grandpa's In The Litter Box	N	F	250+	The Zack Files	Grossett & Dunlap
Greebies	I	F	171	Gear Up!	Wright Group/McGraw Hill
Greece	W	I	250+	Countries and Cultures	Capstone Press
Greece	W	I	250+	Primary Source Readers	Teacher Created Materials
Greece	V	I	250+	Theme Sets	National Geographic
Greece in the Past and Present	T	I	250+	Reading Expeditions	National Geographic
Greece: A Question and Answer Book	P	I	250+	Question and Answer: Countries	Capstone Press
Greece: Everyday Kids Now and Then	S	HF	250+	Reading Expeditions	National Geographic
Greece: The Culture	U	I	250+	Kalman, Bobbie	Crabtree
Greece: The Land	U	I	250+	Kalman, Bobbie	Crabtree
Greece: The People	U	I	250+	Kalman, Bobbie	Crabtree
Greedy Cat	G	F	166	Pacific Literacy	Pacific Learning
Greedy Cat and the Birthday Cake	M	F	250+	Cowley, Joy	Pacific Learning

G

* Collection of short stories
\# Graphic text

TITLE	LEVEL	GENRE	WORD COUNT	AUTHOR / SERIES	PUBLISHER / DISTRIBUTOR
Greedy Cat Is Hungry	D	RF	103	Pacific Literacy	Pacific Learning
Greedy Cat's Breakfast	E	F	53	Story Basket	Wright Group/McGraw Hill
Greedy Crows, The	M	TL	250+	Story Vines	Wright Group/McGraw Hill
Greedy Dog, The	H	F	148	New Way Blue	Steck-Vaughn
Greedy Giant	LB	RF	14	Rigby Rocket	Rigby
Greedy Goat, The	L	TL	250+	Bookshop	Mondo
Greedy Gray Octopus, The	G	F	195	Tadpoles	Rigby
Greedy King, The	J	RF	250+	Lighthouse	Rigby
Greedy Mouse	G	F	187	Sails	Rigby
Greek and Roman Eras, The	R	I	250+	Journey Through History	Barron's Educational
Greek Myths	Y	TL	250+	Coolidge, Olivia	Houghton Mifflin Harcourt
Greek News, The	W	I	250+	The History News	Candlewick Press
Greeks, The	O	I	250+	Footsteps in Time	Children's Press
Green	B	I	26	Colors	Lerner Publications
Green and Blue, Yellow, Too!	B	I	38	Little Celebrations	Pearson Learning Group
Green and Growing	M	I	250+	Rigby Focus	Rigby
Green and Growing: A Book About Plants	M	I	250+	Growing Things	Picture Window Books
Green Angel	Z	RF	250+	Hoffman, Alice	Scholastic
Green Bananas	F	F	49	Tadpoles	Rigby
Green Bay Packers, The	S	I	250+	Team Spirit	Norwood House Press
Green Berets	T	I	250+	Warriors of History	Capstone Press
Green Book, The	V	F	250+	Walsh, Jill Paton	Farrar, Straus and Giroux
Green Bread, The	J	RF	338	Storyteller	Wright Group/McGraw Hill
Green Dragon, The	I	F	131	Sunshine	Wright Group/McGraw Hill
Green Dragons, The	J	RF	250+	PM Story Books	Rigby
Green Eggs and Ham	J	F	250+	Seuss, Dr.	Random House
Green Eyes	F	RF	111	Literacy 2000	Rigby
Green Footprints	E	RF	42	Literacy 2000	Rigby
Green Glass Sea, The	W	HF	250+	Klages, Ellen	Viking/Penguin
Green Grass	B	F	26	Story Box	Wright Group/McGraw Hill
Green Grass Grows All Around, The	H	TL	144	Instant Readers	Harcourt School Publishers
Green Grasshoppers	K	F	229	Sunshine	Wright Group/McGraw Hill
Green Green Green	E	F	218	Instant Readers	Harcourt School Publishers
Green Iguanas	N	I	250+	World of Reptiles	Capstone Press
Green Means Go	D	I	25	Yellow Umbrella Books	Red Brick Learning
Green Men of Gressingham, The	O	F	250+	Ardagh, Philip	Stone Arch Books
Green Plants	H	RF	213	Foundations	Wright Group/McGraw Hill
Green Scene, The	T	I	250+	InfoQuest	Rigby
Green Snake	N	I	250+	Life Cycles	Creative Teaching Press
Green Snake, The	D	I	131	Twig	Wright Group/McGraw Hill
Green Team, The	L	RF	957	Leveled Readers	Houghton Mifflin Harcourt
Green Team, The	L	RF	957	Leveled Readers/CA	Houghton Mifflin Harcourt
Green Team, The	L	RF	957	Leveled Readers/TX	Houghton Mifflin Harcourt
Green Technology	W	I	2470	Leveled Readers	Houghton Mifflin Harcourt
Green Technology	W	I	2470	Leveled Readers/CA	Houghton Mifflin Harcourt
Green Thumbs	Q	I	250+	Literacy 2000	Rigby
Green Thumbs, Everyone	N	RF	250+	Giff, Patricia Reilly	Bantam
Green Transportation	V	I	2575	Vocabulary Readers	Houghton Mifflin Harcourt
Green Transportation	V	I	2575	Vocabulary Readers/CA	Houghton Mifflin Harcourt
Green Transportation	V	I	2575	Vocabulary Readers/TX	Houghton Mifflin Harcourt
Green Turtle Rescue	J	RF	279	Gear Up!	Wright Group/McGraw Hill
Green with Red Spots Horrible	N	RF	250+	SupaDoopers	Sundance
Green, Green	D	RF	114	Little Readers	Houghton Mifflin Harcourt
Green: Seeing Green All Around Us	L	I	250+	Colors	Capstone Press

G

TITLE	LEVEL	GENRE	WORD COUNT	AUTHOR / SERIES	PUBLISHER / DISTRIBUTOR
Greenland's Ocean Region	Q	I	250+	Theme Sets	National Geographic
Greenwitch	X	F	250+	Cooper, Susan	Scholastic
Greeting Card Making: Sending Your Personal Message	Q	I	250+	Crafts	Capstone Press
Gregor and the Code of the Claw	V	F	250+	Collins, Suzanne	Scholastic
Gregor and the Curse of the Warmbloods	V	F	250+	Collins, Suzanne	Scholastic
Gregor and the Marks of Secret	V	F	250+	Collins, Suzanne	Scholastic
Gregor and the Prophecy of Bane	V	F	250+	Collins, Suzanne	Scholastic
Gregor Mendel: Genetics Pioneer	V	B	250+	Science Readers	Teacher Created Materials
Gregor the Grumblesome Giant	G	F	212	Literacy 2000	Rigby
Gregor the Overlander	V	F	250+	Collins, Suzanne	Scholastic
Gregory, the Mean Dragon	I	F	250+	Phonics and Friends	Hampton-Brown
Gregory, the Terrible Eater	L	F	250+	Sharmat, Marjorie Weinman	Scholastic
Gregory's Dog	C	RF	23	Cat on the Mat	Oxford University Press
Gregory's Garden	F	RF	70	Cat on the Mat	Oxford University Press
Greg's Microscope	K	I	250+	Selsam, Millicent E.	HarperTrophy
Gremlins Don't Chew Bubble Gum	M	F	250+	Dadey, Debbie; Jones, Marcia Thornton	Scholastic
Grey King, The	X	F	250+	Cooper, Susan	Simon & Schuster
Grey Lady and the Strawberry Snatcher, The	WB	F	N/A	Bang, Molly	Aladdin
Gribblegrot from Outer Space, The	N	F	250+	Literacy 2000 Satellites	Rigby
Griffin, the School Cat	I	RF	160	Sunshine	Wright Group/McGraw Hill
Grilled Cheese Sandwich	G	I	61	Windows on Literacy	National Geographic
Grilled Pizza Sandwich and Other Vegetarian Recipes	S	I	250+	Fun Food for Cool Cooks	Capstone Press
Grim Grotto, The	V	F	250+	Snicket, Lemony	HarperCollins
Grimms' Fairy Tales	X	B	2480	Leveled Readers	Houghton Mifflin Harcourt
Grimms' Fairy Tales	X	B	2402	Leveled Readers/CA	Houghton Mifflin Harcourt
Grin and Bear It: Zoo Jokes to Make You Roar	O	F	1762	Make Me Laugh!	Lerner Publications
Grind	U	RF	250+	Orca Soundings	Orca Book Publishers
Grist	Z+	RF	250+	Waldorf, Heather	Fitzhenry & Whiteside
Gristmill, The	T	I	250+	Historic Communities	Crabtree
Grizzled Bill Turns Over a New Leaf	U	HF	9080	Reading Street	Pearson
Grizzlies	M	I	250+	Phonics Plus	Educators Publishing Service
Grizzly and the Bumble-Bee	I	F	183	Sunshine	Wright Group/McGraw Hill
Grizzly Bear, The	R	I	250+	Wildlife of North America	Red Brick Learning
Grizzly Bears	R	I	250+	Predators in the Wild	Red Brick Learning
Grizzly Bears	N	I	250+	Woolley, M.; Pigdon, K.	Mondo
Grizzly Bears Return to Yellowstone	S	I	2009	Leveled Readers	Houghton Mifflin Harcourt
Grizzly Bears Return to Yellowstone	S	I	2009	Leveled Readers/CA	Houghton Mifflin Harcourt
Grizzly Bears Return to Yellowstone	S	I	2009	Leveled Readers/TX	Houghton Mifflin Harcourt
*Grizzly Mistake and Other Cases, The	O	RF	250+	Simon, Seymour	Avon
Grizzly Toothache, A	O	F	250+	Tristars	Richard C. Owen
Grizzwold	I	F	250+	Hoff, Syd	HarperTrophy
Grocers	M	I	610	Pull Ahead Books	Lerner Publications
Grocery Shopping	D	RF	34	Yannone, Deborah	Kaeden Books
Groovy Gran and the Karaoke Kid	R	RF	250+	Storyteller -Whispering Pines	Wright Group/McGraw Hill
Groundhog Day!	N	I	250+	Gibbons, Gail	Holiday House
Groundhog's New Home	N	TL	1070	Leveled Readers/TX	Houghton Mifflin Harcourt
Grouping Shells	H	RF	344	PM Math Readers	Rigby
Groups of Animals	N	I	250+	Windows on Literacy	National Geographic
Grover Cleveland	U	B	250+	Profiles of the Presidents	Compass Point Books

G

* Collection of short stories
\# Graphic text

TITLE	LEVEL	GENRE	WORD COUNT	AUTHOR / SERIES	PUBLISHER / DISTRIBUTOR
Grover Cleveland: Twenty-second and Twenty-fourth President	R	B	250+	Getting to Know the U.S. Presidents	Children's Press
Grow a Bean Plant!	I	I	220	Vocabulary Readers	Houghton Mifflin Harcourt
Grow a Bean Plant!	I	I	220	Vocabulary Readers/CA	Houghton Mifflin Harcourt
Grow a Bean Plant!	I	I	220	Vocabulary Readers/TX	Houghton Mifflin Harcourt
Grow a Plant Inch by Inch	H	I	142	Rosen Real Readers	Rosen Publishing Group
Grow a Tomato!	J	I	315	Reading Street	Pearson
Grow Up, Dad!	R	F	5022	Dhami, Narinder	Stone Arch Books
Grow, Seed, Grow	E	I	36	Discovery Links	Newbridge
Growin'	R	RF	250+	Grimes, Nikki	Puffin/Penguin
Growing	B	I	22	Little Celebrations	Pearson Learning Group
Growing	A	I	15	On Our Way to English	Rigby
Growing	C	I	42	Story Steps	Rigby
Growing	B	I	23	Windmill Books	Wright Group/McGraw Hill
Growing a Kitchen Garden	O	I	250+	Navigators How-To Series	Benchmark Education
Growing a Plant	G	I	115	Discovery World	Rigby
Growing a Plant	C	I	43	Early Connections	Benchmark Education
Growing a Salad	E	RF	59	Gear Up!	Wright Group/McGraw Hill
Growing and Changing	O	I	250+	InfoTrek	ETA Cuisenaire
Growing and Changing	N	I	869	Springboard	Wright Group/McGraw Hill
Growing Cotton	M	I	581	Rigby Flying Colors	Rigby
Growing Frogs	L	RF	250+	French, Vivian	Candlewick Press
Growing Ideas	O	B	250+	Meet The Author	Richard C. Owen
Growing in my Garden	I	I	208	Dominie Factivity Series	Pearson Learning Group
Growing Older	I	I	216	Early Connections	Benchmark Education
Growing Peas	I	I	346	Rigby Flying Colors	Rigby
Growing Radishes and Carrots	I	I	125	Bookshop	Mondo
Growing Sprouts and Eva's Sprout Diary	J	RF	250+	Voyages	SRA/McGraw Hill
Growing Tomatoes	G	I	87	Alphakids	Sundance
Growing Tomatoes	M	I	626	Leveled Readers Science	Houghton Mifflin Harcourt
Growing Up	D	I	47	Dominie Factivity Series	Pearson Learning Group
Growing Up	P	I	250+	It's Science	Children's Press
Growing Up Abenaki	N	B	250+	On Our Way to English	Rigby
Growing Up in a New Century	V	I	250+	Our America	Lerner Publications
Growing Up in a New World	T	I	8949	Our America	Lerner Publications
Growing Up in China	U	I	2537	Reading Street	Pearson
Growing Up in Coal Country	X	I	250+	Bartoletti, Susan Campbell	Houghton Mifflin Harcourt
Growing Up in Pioneer America	T	I	8785	Our America	Lerner Publications
Growing Up in Revolution and the New Nation	T	I	7946	Our America	Lerner Publications
Growing Up in the Civil War	V	I	250+	Our America	Lerner Publications
Growing Up in the Great Depression	W	I	250+	Our America	Lerner Publications
Growing Up in the Pond	N	I	799	Vocabulary Readers	Houghton Mifflin Harcourt
Growing Up in the Pond	N	I	799	Vocabulary Readers/CA	Houghton Mifflin Harcourt
Growing Up in World War II	V	I	7922	Our America	Lerner Publications
Growing Up Is Fun	C	I	87	The Candid Collection	Pearson Learning Group
*Growing Up Stories	T	RF	250+	Byars, Betsy	Kingfisher
Growing Up, Up, Up Book	F	RF	120	First Start	Troll Associates
Growing Vegetables	K	RF	423	Reading Street	Pearson
Grown-ups Make You Grumpy	J	RF	250+	Lighthouse	Ginn & Co.
Grown-ups Say the Silliest Things	J	F	250+	Lighthouse	Rigby
Gruff Brothers, The	I	TL	250+	Hooks, William H.	Bantam
Grumbles, Growls, and Roars	F	I	133	Twig	Wright Group/McGraw Hill
Grump, The	F	RF	73	Literacy 2000	Rigby
Grumputer, The	G	F	235	Story Basket	Wright Group/McGraw Hill

G

* Collection of short stories
# Graphic text

TITLE	LEVEL	GENRE	WORD COUNT	AUTHOR / SERIES	PUBLISHER / DISTRIBUTOR
Grumpy Bear	I	F	367	Gear Up!	Wright Group/McGraw Hill
Grumpy Elephant	E	F	100	Story Box	Wright Group/McGraw Hill
Grumpy Grizzly	C	RF	40	Learn to Read	Creative Teaching Press
Grumpy Millionaire, The	O	RF	250+	Bookweb	Rigby
Grumpy Rella	I	TL	251	Literacy by Design	Rigby
Guan Yu: Blood Brothers to the End	V	TL	3684	Graphic Myths and Legends	Lerner Publications
Guard Dog Diggory	L	RF	250+	Pacific Literacy	Pacific Learning
Guard the House, Sam!	G	RF	46	Rookie Readers	Children's Press
Guardian of the Dark	W	F	250+	Spencer, Bev	Scholastic
Guardian of the Everglades	R	I	1441	Leveled Readers	Houghton Mifflin Harcourt
Guardian of the Everglades	R	I	1441	Leveled Readers/CA	Houghton Mifflin Harcourt
Guardian of the Everglades	R	I	1441	Leveled Readers/TX	Houghton Mifflin Harcourt
Guardians of Ga'Hoole: The Journey	V	F	250+	Lasky, Kathryn	Scholastic
Guatemala	O	I	250+	Countries of the World	Red Brick Learning
Guatemala	Q	I	250+	Theme Sets	National Geographic
Guatemala in Colors	N	I	250+	World of Colors	Capstone Press
Guatemala: A Question and Answer Book	P	I	250+	Question and Answer Countries	Capstone Press
Guess How Many	N	I	250+	Rosen Real Readers	Rosen Publishing Group
Guess How Many I Have	A	I	24	Early Connections	Benchmark Education
Guess What Kind of Ball	E	RF	219	Urmston, Kathleen; Evans, Karen	Kaeden Books
Guess What the Moon Saw?	C	RF	38	Home Connection Collection	Rigby
Guess What the Sun Saw?	C	RF	36	Home Connection Collection	Rigby
Guess What Today Is?	I	F	250+	Popcorn	Sundance
Guess What!	E	RF	28	Literacy 2000	Rigby
Guess What?	E	RF	120	Foundations	Wright Group/McGraw Hill
Guess Who We Saw	F	RF	170	Windows on Literacy	National Geographic
Guess Who?	L	I	250+	Home Connection Collection	Rigby
Guess Who?	A	RF	40	Rigby Star	Rigby
Guess Who's Coming to Dinner?	F	RF	130	Literacy 2000	Rigby
Guessing Game, The	H	RF	183	InfoTrek	ETA Cuisenaire
Guessing Games	E	I	144	InfoTrek	ETA Cuisenaire
Guessing Jar, The	K	I	395	Early Connections	Benchmark Education
Guests	T	HF	250+	Dorris, Michael	Hyperion
Guide Dog School	J	I	348	Leveled Readers/TX	Houghton Mifflin Harcourt
Guide Dog, The	K	I	338	Foundations	Wright Group/McGraw Hill
Guide Dogs	H	I	107	Rosen Real Readers	Rosen Publishing Group
Guilty by a Hair!	W	I	250+	24/7 Science Behind the Scenes	Scholastic
Guilty!: The Complicated Life of Claudia Cristina Cortez	S	RF	250+	Gallagher, Diana G.	Stone Arch Books
Guinea Pig for You, A: Caring for Your Guinea Pig	M	I	250+	Pet Care	Picture Window Books
Guinea Pig Gang	O	RF	250+	Baglio, Ben M.	Scholastic
Guinea Pig Grass	I	RF	140	Literacy 2000	Rigby
Guinea Pig Scientists: Bold Self Experimenter in Science and Medicine	Y	B	250+	Dendy, Leslie and Boring, Mel	Henry Holt & Co.
Guinea Pigs	E	I	50	All About Pets	Capstone Press
Guinea Pigs	S	I	250+	Hansen, Elvig	Carolrhoda Books
Guinea Pigs	J	I	250+	PM Animal Facts: Orange	Rigby
Guinea Pigs	C	I	34	Sun Sprouts	ETA Cuisenaire
Gulf	X	F	250+	Westfall, Robert	Scholastic
Gulliver's Stories	Q	F	250+	Dolch, E. W.; Marguerite, P.	Scholastic
Gulliver's Travels	Z+	F	250+	Swift, Jonathan	Penguin Group
Gulp!	D	F	103	Story Box	Wright Group/McGraw Hill

G

* Collection of short stories
\# Graphic text

TITLE	LEVEL	GENRE	WORD COUNT	AUTHOR / SERIES	PUBLISHER / DISTRIBUTOR
Gum on the Drum, The	E	F	41	Start to Read	School Zone
Gumball, The	E	RF	67	Bonnell, Kris	Reading Reading Books
Gumby Shop, The	I	F	359	Read Alongs	Rigby
Gumshoe Goose Private Eye	K	F	250+	Kwitz, Mary DeBall	Puffin/Penguin
Gun, The	Y	RF	250+	Langan, Paul	Townsend Press
Gung Hay Fat Choy	N	I	250+	Behrens, June	Children's Press
Gunpowder and Tea	W	HF	3290	Leveled Readers	Houghton Mifflin Harcourt
Guns for General Washington	U	HF	250+	Reit, Seymour	Harcourt Achieve
Gurgles and Growls: Learning About Your Stomach	L	I	250+	Amazing Body	Picture Window Books
Gus and Grandpa	J	RF	250+	Mills, Claudia	Sunburst
Gus and His Bus	D	F	72	Reading Street	Pearson
Gusts and Gales: A Book About Wind	M	I	250+	Amazing Science	Picture Window Books
Guys Write for Guys Read	Z	B	250+	Scieszka, Jon	Scholastic
Gwen Torrence	P	B	250+	Stewart, Mark	Children's Press
Gwendolyn Brooks: A Life of Poetry	R	B	811	Leveled Readers	Houghton Mifflin Harcourt
Gym Teacher from the Black Lagoon, The	K	F	250+	Thaler, Mike	Scholastic
Gymnastics Competitions: On Your Way to Victory	S	I	250+	Gymnastics	Capstone Press
Gymnastics Essentials: Safety and Equipment	S	I	250+	Gymnastics	Capstone Press
Gymnastics Events: Floor, Vault, Bars, and Beam	S	I	250+	Gymnastics	Capstone Press
Gymnastics for Fun!	S	I	250+	Sports for Fun!	Compass Point Books
Gymnastics Skills: Beginning Tumbling	S	I	250+	Gymnastics	Capstone Press
Gymnastics Training and Fitness: Being Your Best	S	I	250+	Gymnastics	Capstone Press
Gypsy Game, The	U	RF	250+	Snyder, Zilpha Keatly	Yearling

G

TITLE	LEVEL	GENRE	WORD COUNT	AUTHOR / SERIES	PUBLISHER / DISTRIBUTOR
H for Horrible	Q	RF	250+	PM Extensions	Rigby
Habibi	V	B	250+	Nye, Naomi Shihab	Simon & Schuster
Habitat Is Where We Live, A	F	I	132	Twig	Wright Group/McGraw Hill
Habitat Rescue	O	I	250+	Navigators Social Studies Series	Benchmark Education
Habitats in Need of Help	T	I	2357	Reading Street	Pearson
Haddie's Caps	D	F	90	Ready Readers	Pearson Learning Group
Hades	W	I	250+	World Mythology	Capstone Press
Ha-Ha Party, The	J	RF	250	Sunshine	Wright Group/McGraw Hill
Hailstorm, The	J	RF	386	PM Collection	Rigby
Hair	A	RF	32	Carousel Earlybirds	Pearson Learning Group
Hair	B	I	37	Foundations	Wright Group/McGraw Hill
Hair	C	RF	35	Little Celebrations	Pearson Learning Group
Hair	A	I	28	Springboard	Wright Group/McGraw Hill
Hair	C	I	60	Sun Sprouts	ETA Cuisenaire
Hair Ball From Outer Space	Q	F	250+	Wiley & Grampa's Creature Features	Little, Brown & Co.
Hair Party, The	J	RF	250+	Literacy 2000	Rigby
Hair Scare	N	RF	250+	Girlz Rock!	Mondo
Haircut, The	D	RF	27	Hartley, Susan; Armstrong, Shane	Scholastic
Haircuts	G	RF	307	Yukish, Joe	Kaeden Books
Haircuts for Bella & Rosie	E	F	129	Bella and Rosie Series	Literacy Footprints
Hairdresser, The	G	I	164	PM Nonfiction-Blue	Rigby
Hairem Scarem	K	TL	250+	Rigby Rocket	Rigby
Hairs Pelitos	L	RF	159	Cisneros, Sandra	Alfred A. Knopf
Hairy Bear	G	F	109	Story Box	Wright Group/McGraw Hill
Hairy Caterpillars	I	I	164	Sails	Rigby
Hairy Harry	G	I	92	Windows on Literacy	National Geographic
Hairy Little Critters	O	I	250+	Literacy Tree	Rigby
Hairy Story, A	L	F	802	Springboard	Wright Group/McGraw Hill
Hairy, Scary, Ordinary: What Is an Adjective?	O	I	337	Words Are CATegorical	Millbrook Press
Haiti	U	I	250+	Countries and Cultures	Red Brick Learning
Haiti: A Question and Answer Book	P	I	250+	Questions & Answers: Countries	Capstone Press
Half and Half	I	F	389	InfoTrek	ETA Cuisenaire
Half for You, Half for Me	K	TL	399	Literacy 2000	Rigby
Half Magic	T	F	250+	Eager, Edward	Harcourt
Half Marathon, The	S	RF	250+	Reading Safari	Mondo
Half Moon Investigations	U	RF	250+	Colfer, Eoin	Hyperion
Halloween	Q	I	250+	Celebrate!	Capstone Press
Halloween	E	I	128	Fiesta Holiday Series	Pearson Learning Group
Halloween	C	RF	87	Handprints C, Set 1	Educators Publishing Service
Halloween	Q	I	250+	Holiday Histories	Heinemann Library
Halloween	M	I	250+	Holidays and Celebrations	Picture Window Books
Halloween	J	I	114	Holidays and Celebrations	Capstone Press
Halloween	O	I	250+	Holidays and Festivals	Compass Point Books
Halloween	P	I	250+	Let's See	Compass Point Books
Halloween	N	I	1209	On My Own Holidays	Lerner Publications
Halloween	B	RF	44	Story Box	Wright Group/McGraw Hill
Halloween	D	RF	32	Visions	Wright Group/McGraw Hill
Halloween Book of Facts & Fun, The	Q	I	250+	Old, Wendie	Albert Whitman & Co.
Halloween Caper, The	J	F	863	Spaceboy	Literacy Footprints
Halloween Danny	E	F	51	Coulton, Mia	Maryruth Books
Halloween Gotcha	N	RF	250+	Boyz Rule!	Mondo

* Collection of short stories
\# Graphic text

H

TITLE	LEVEL	GENRE	WORD COUNT	AUTHOR / SERIES	PUBLISHER / DISTRIBUTOR
*Halloween Horror and Other Cases, The	O	RF	250+	Simon, Seymour	Avon
Halloween Is…	M	I	250+	Gibbons, Gail	Holiday House
Halloween Mask for Monster	C	F	38	Mueller, Virginia	Whitman
Halloween Parade	F	RF	101	Ziefert, Harriet	Puffin/Penguin
Halloween: Why We Celebrate It the Way We Do	P	I	250+	Hintz, Martin & Kate	Red Brick Learning
Hamburger	H	RF	49	City Kids	Rigby
Hamburger Heaven	T	I	250+	The News	Richard C. Owen
Hamlet the Hamster	G	RF	189	Breakthrough	Longman/Bow
Hammerhead Shark	J	I	146	Sharks	Capstone Press
Hammurabi and the Glory of Mesopotamia	Y	B	2564	Independent Readers Social Studies	Houghton Mifflin Harcourt
Hammurabi: Babylonian Ruler	X	B	250+	Primary Source Readers	Teacher Created Materials
Hamper's Great Escape	M	RF	250+	High-Fliers	Pacific Learning
Hamster Hotel	O	RF	250+	Baglio, Ben M.	Scholastic
Hamster in a Handbasket	Q	RF	250+	Baglio, Ben M.	Scholastic
Hamster of the Baskervilles, The: A Chet Gecko Mystery	R	F	250+	Hale, Bruce	Harcourt Trade
Hamsters	D	I	39	All About Pets	Red Brick Learning
Hamster's Tale, A	M	RF	250+	Literacy by Design	Rigby
Hana's Suitcase	Y	I	250+	Levine, Karen	Albert Whitman & Co.
Hand Me Downs, The	G	RF	156	Little Readers	Houghton Mifflin Harcourt
Hand Tools	M	I	367	Wonder World	Wright Group/McGraw Hill
Hand, Hand, Fingers, Thumb	J	F	250+	Perkins, Al	Random House
Handbook for Boys	W	RF	250+	Myers, Walter Dean	Harper Trophy
Handful of Time, A	U	F	250+	Pearson, Kit	Puffin/Penguin
Handle with Care	S	I	250+	Orbit Collections	Pacific Learning
Hands	D	I	90	Big Cat	Pacific Learning
Hands	C	RF	39	Literacy 2000	Rigby
Hands	C	I	24	Rookie Readers	Children's Press
Hands	B	I	15	Twig	Wright Group/McGraw Hill
Hands at Work	C	I	50	Windows on Literacy	National Geographic
Hands Up, Wolf	L	F	250+	Pacific Literacy	Pacific Learning
Hands, Hands, Hands	F	I	85	Bookshop	Mondo
Hands, Hands, Hands	B	RF	17	Little Celebrations	Pearson Learning Group
Handwriting Evidence	S	I	250+	Forensic Crime Solvers	Capstone Press
Handy Dragon, A	H	F	159	Literacy 2000	Rigby
Handy Handbook for Harrowing Events	R	I	250+	Sails	Rigby
Hang a Left at Venus	N	F	250+	The Zack Files	Grossett & Dunlap
Hang in There, Oscar Martin!	N	RF	250+	Orbit Chapter Books	Pacific Learning
Hanged Man, The	Z	RF	250+	Block, Francesca Lia	HarperCollins
Hanging on to Max	Z+	RF	250+	Bechard, Margaret	Millbrook Press
Hank Aaron	O	B	877	Leveled Readers/CA	Houghton Mifflin Harcourt
Hank Aaron	O	B	877	Leveled Readers/TX	Houghton Mifflin Harcourt
Hannah	P	HF	250+	Book Blazers	ETA Cuisenaire
Hannah	I	RF	250+	Stepping Stones	Nelson/Michaels Assoc.
Hannah	N	RF	250+	Whelan, Gloria	Random House
Hannah and Her Dad	J	RF	250+	Voyages	SRA/McGraw Hill
Hannah and the Angels	Q	F	250+	Lowery, Linda	Random House
Hannah and the Golden Thread	Q	HF	250+	Book Blazers	ETA Cuisenaire
Hannah Brown, Union Army Spy	V	HF	2231	Leveled Readers	Houghton Mifflin Harcourt
Hannah of Fairfield	Q	HF	250+	Pioneer Daughters	Puffin/Penguin
Hannah's Fancy Notions: A Story of Industrial New England	R	HF	250+	Ross, Pat	Penguin Group
Hannah's Halloween	LB	I	14	Little Books for Early Readers	University of Maine

TITLE	LEVEL	GENRE	WORD COUNT	AUTHOR / SERIES	PUBLISHER / DISTRIBUTOR
Hannah's Helping Hands	Q	HF	250+	Van Leeuwen, Jean	Puffin/Penguin
Hannah's Hiccups	G	RF	196	Home Connection Collection	Rigby
Hannah's Voyage	Q	HF	250+	Book Blazers	ETA Cuisenaire
Hannah's Winter of Hope	Q	HF	250+	Van Leeuwen, Jean	Puffin/Penguin
Hanna's Butterfly	I	RF	158	Start to Read	School Zone
Hannibal	T	B	250+	Green, Robert	Franklin Watts
Hans Christian Andersen: Prince of Storytellers	N	B	250+	Rookie Biographies	Children's Press
Hansel and Gretel	K	TL	250+	Enrichment	Wright Group/McGraw Hill
Hansel and Gretel	G	TL	451	Hunia, Fran	Ladybird Books
Hansel and Gretel	O	TL	250+	Morpurgo, Michael	Candlewick Press
Hansel and Gretel	K	TL	250+	Storyworlds	Heinemann Educational Books
Hanukkah	N	I	250+	Festivals and Holidays	Children's Press
Hanukkah	K	I	206	Holidays and Celebrations	Capstone Press
Hanukkah	P	I	250+	Let's See	Compass Point Books
Hanukkah	O	I	1443	On My Own Holidays	Lerner Publications
Hanukkah at Valley Forge	T	HF	250+	Krensky, Stephen	Dutton Children's Books
Hanukkah Party, The	I	RF	250+	Early Transitional, Set 1	Pioneer Valley
Hap is Hot	B	F	30	Reading Street	Pearson
Happily Ever After	O	F	250+	Quindlen, Anna	Penguin Group
Happily Ever After!	K	TL	250+	Storyteller- Lightning Bolts	Wright Group/McGraw Hill
Happy	D	I	13	Feelings	Lerner Publishing
Happy 100th Day!	C	RF	35	Little Celebrations	Pearson Learning Group
Happy Accidents!	Q	I	250+	Action Packs	Rigby
Happy and Sad	I	F	232	Sunshine	Wright Group/McGraw Hill
Happy Birthday	G	RF	130	First Start	Troll Associates
Happy Birthday	C	F	26	Instant Readers	Harcourt School Publishers
Happy Birthday Book, The	P	I	250+	Sunshine	Wright Group/McGraw Hill
Happy Birthday Josie	LB	I	14	Rigby Rocket	Rigby
Happy Birthday to Me	D	I	60	Bonnell, Kris	Reading Reading Books
Happy Birthday!	C	RF	28	Literacy 2000	Rigby
Happy Birthday!	A	I	40	Vocabulary Readers	Houghton Mifflin Harcourt
Happy Birthday!	A	I	40	Vocabulary Readers/CA	Houghton Mifflin Harcourt
Happy Birthday!	A	I	40	Vocabulary Readers/TX	Houghton Mifflin Harcourt
Happy Birthday, Addy!	Q	HF	250+	The American Girls Collection	Pleasant Company
Happy Birthday, America!	L	I	388	Reading Street	Pearson
Happy Birthday, Anna, Sorpresa!	N	RF	250+	Giff, Patricia Reilly	Bantam
Happy Birthday, Brother!	A	I	24	Vocabulary Readers	Houghton Mifflin Harcourt
Happy Birthday, Danny and the Dinosaur	H	F	250+	Little Readers	Houghton Mifflin Harcourt
Happy Birthday, Danny and the Dinosaur!	H	F	250+	Hoff, Syd	HarperTrophy
Happy Birthday, Dear Dragon	E	F	290	Dear Dragon	Norwood House Press
Happy Birthday, Dear Duck	K	F	250+	Bunting, Eve	Clarion
Happy Birthday, Duckling	I	I	154	Literacy Tree	Rigby
Happy Birthday, Estela!	LB	RF	30	Pacific Literacy	Pacific Learning
Happy Birthday, Everyone	J	I	337	Leveled Readers	Houghton Mifflin Harcourt
Happy Birthday, Everyone	J	I	337	Leveled Readers/CA	Houghton Mifflin Harcourt
Happy Birthday, Everyone	J	I	337	Leveled Readers/TX	Houghton Mifflin Harcourt
Happy Birthday, Felicity!	Q	HF	250+	The American Girls Collection	Pleasant Company
Happy Birthday, Frog	C	F	87	Story Box	Wright Group/McGraw Hill
Happy Birthday, Josefina!	Q	HF	250+	The American Girls Collection	Pleasant Company
Happy Birthday, Kirsten!	Q	HF	250+	The American Girls Collection	Pleasant Company
Happy Birthday, Mallory!	O	RF	250+	Friedman, Laurie	Lerner Publications
Happy Birthday, Martin Luther King	L	B	250+	Marzollo, Jean	Scholastic
Happy Birthday, Molly!	Q	HF	250+	The American Girls Collection	Pleasant Company

* Collection of short stories
# Graphic text

H

TITLE	LEVEL	GENRE	WORD COUNT	AUTHOR / SERIES	PUBLISHER / DISTRIBUTOR
Happy Birthday, Moon	L	F	345	Asch, Frank	Simon & Schuster
Happy Birthday, Mrs. Boedecker	L	RF	250+	Little Celebrations	Pearson Learning Group
Happy Birthday, Sam	I	RF	213	Hutchins, Pat	Greenwillow
Happy Birthday, Sam!	I	RF	258	Leveled Readers	Houghton Mifflin Harcourt
Happy Birthday, Samantha!	Q	HF	250+	The American Girls Collection	Pleasant Company
Happy Birthday, Toad	E	F	144	Leveled Readers	Houghton Mifflin Harcourt
Happy Birthday, Toad	E	F	144	Leveled Readers/CA	Houghton Mifflin Harcourt
Happy Birthday, Toad	E	F	144	Leveled Readers/TX	Houghton Mifflin Harcourt
Happy Café, The	I	RF	238	Story Box	Wright Group/McGraw Hill
Happy Dogs	A	I	18	Bonnell, Kris	Reading Reading Books
Happy Easter, Dear Dragon	F	F	257	Dear Dragon	Norwood House Press
Happy Egg	E	F	210	Kraus, Robert	Scholastic
Happy Endings	I	F	213	Sunshine	Wright Group/McGraw Hill
Happy Face, Sad Face	C	I	77	Foundations	Wright Group/McGraw Hill
Happy Faces	H	RF	210	Reading Unlimited	Pearson Learning Group
Happy Hanukkah, Dear Dragon	F	F	250+	Dear Dragon	Norwood House Press
Happy Harriet	I	RF	326	Sails	Rigby
Happy Holidays	B	I	27	Teacher's Choice Series	Pearson Learning Group
Happy House, The	F	RF	224	Sails	Rigby
Happy Jack	F	F	99	First Start	Troll Associates
Happy Monkey in the Shed	C	F	30	Joy Readers	Pearson Learning Group
Happy Monkey's Peanuts	D	F	63	Joy Readers	Pearson Learning Group
Happy Moon, The	D	F	81	Bonnell, Kris	Reading Reading Books
Happy Mother's Day!	G	RF	101	Teacher's Choice Series	Pearson Learning Group
Happy New Year!	M	I	114	Independent Readers Social Studies	Houghton Mifflin Harcourt
Happy Pets, Healthy Pets	H	I	98	Spyglass Books	Compass Point Books
Happy Valentine's Day, Miss Hildy!	K	RF	250+	Grambling, Lois	Random House
Happy's Hat	C	F	69	Joy Starters	Pearson Learning Group
Harbor Seal Pup Grows Up, A	L	I	449	Baby Animals	Lerner Publications
Harbour, The	M	I	250+	Cambridge Reading	Pearson Learning Group
Hard at Work	B	RF	66	Early Emergent	Pioneer Valley
Hard Drive to Short	Q	RF	250+	Christopher, Matt	Little, Brown & Co.
Hard Workers	J	I	186	Phonics Readers	Compass Point Books
Hare and the Tortoise, The	J	TL	587	Aesop's Fables	Pearson Learning Group
Hare and the Tortoise, The	J	TL	531	Leveled Literacy Intervention/Blue System	Heinemann
Hare and the Tortoise, The	K	TL	250+	Literacy 2000	Rigby
Hare and the Tortoise, The	K	TL	250+	PM Tales and Plays-Purple	Rigby
Hare and the Tortoise, The	D	TL	93	Storyworlds	Heinemann Educational Publishers
Hare and Tortoise Go to School	D	F	66	Rigby Rocket	Rigby
Hare's Big Tug-of-War	I	TL	207	Instant Readers	Harcourt School Publishers
Harlem	Y	I	3083	Vocabulary Readers	Houghton Mifflin Harcourt
Harlem	Y	I	3083	Vocabulary Readers/CA	Houghton Mifflin Harcourt
Harlem Globetrotters, The: Clown Princes of Basketball	T	I	250+	High Five Reading	Red Brick Learning
Harlem Stomp! A Cultural History of the Harlem Renaissance	Z	I	250+	Hill, Laban Carrick	Little, Brown & Co.
Harlem Summer	X	HF	250+	Myers, Walter Dean	Scholastic
Harley-Davidson Motorcycles	M	I	250+	Horsepower	Capstone Press
Harold and the Purple Crayon	K	F	660	Johnson, Crockett	Harper & Row
Harold's Flyaway Kite	G	F	166	First Start	Troll Associates
Harp Seals	O	I	1669	Early Bird Nature Books	Lerner Publications

H

TITLE	LEVEL	GENRE	WORD COUNT	AUTHOR / SERIES	PUBLISHER / DISTRIBUTOR
Harriet and George's Christmas Treat	L	F	400	Carlson, Nancy	Carolrhoda Books
Harriet and the Garden	K	F	363	Carlson, Nancy	Carolrhoda Books
Harriet and the Roller Coaster	K	F	283	Carlson, Nancy	Carolrhoda Books
Harriet and Walt	K	F	376	Carlson, Nancy	Carolrhoda Books
Harriet Beecher Stowe	T	B	250+	Amazing Americans	Wright Group/McGraw Hill
Harriet Beecher Stowe and the Beecher Preachers	X	B	250+	Fritz, Jean	Penguin Group
Harriet Higby	J	F	250+	Howard-Hess, Susan	Kaeden Books
Harriet the Spy	T	RF	250+	Fitzhugh, Louise	HarperCollins
Harriet Tubman	P	B	250+	Early Biographies	Compass Point Books
Harriet Tubman	S	B	3390	History Maker Bios	Lerner Publications
Harriet Tubman	U	B	250+	Let Freedom Ring	Red Brick Learning
Harriet Tubman	N	B	239	Pebble Books	Capstone Press
Harriet Tubman	P	B	250+	Photo-Illustrated Biographies	Red Brick Learning
Harriet Tubman	Q	B	250+	Primary Source Readers	Teacher Created Materials
Harriet Tubman and the Underground Railroad	U	I	250+	Graphic Library	Capstone Press
#Harriet Tubman and the Underground Railroad	X	B	2159	Leveled Readers	Houghton Mifflin Harcourt
Harriet Tubman, Secret Agent: How Daring Slaves and Free Blacks Spied for the Union During the Civil War	W	B	250+	Allen, Thomas B.	National Geographic
Harriet Tubman: A Lesson in Bravery	M	B	250+	Rosen Real Readers	Rosen Publishing Group
Harriet Tubman: A Woman of Courage	K	B	170	Independent Readers Social Studies	Houghton Mifflin Harcourt
Harriet's Halloween Candy	K	F	285	Carlson, Nancy	Carolrhoda Books
Harriet's Hare	O	F	250+	King-Smith, Dick	Alfred A. Knopf
Harriet's Recital	K	F	196	Carlson, Nancy	Carolrhoda Books
Harris and Me	V	RF	250+	Paulsen, Gary	Bantam
Harry	P	RF	1868	Take Two Books	Wright Group/ McGraw Hill
Harry and Chicken	S	F	250+	Sheldon, Dyan	Candlewick Press
Harry and the Lady Next Door	J	F	250+	Zion, Gene	HarperTrophy
Harry and the Terrible Whatzit	K	F	250+	Gackenbach, Dick	Clarion Books
Harry and Willy and Carrothead	K	RF	250+	Caseley, Judith	Scholastic
Harry Cat's Pet Puppy	R	F	250+	Selden, George	Bantam
Harry Gets Ready for School	G	F	170	Ziefert, Harriet	Puffin/Penguin
Harry Goes to Day Camp	F	F	250+	Ziefert, James	Puffin/Penguin
Harry Goes to Fun Land	F	F	166	Ziefert, Harriet	Puffin/Penguin
Harry Hates Shopping!	K	F	250+	Armitage, Ronda & David	Scholastic
Harry Houdini: Master of Magic	R	B	250+	Kraske, Robert	Scholastic
Harry Houdini: The Man and His Magic	P	B	863	Reading Street	Pearson
Harry Houdini: Wonderdog!	N	RF	250+	Orbit Chapter Books	Pacific Learning
Harry Houdini: Young Magician	O	B	250+	Childhood of Famous Americans	Aladdin
Harry on Vacation	S	SF	250+	Sheldon, Dyan	Candlewick Press
Harry Potter and the Chamber of Secrets	V	F	250+	Rowling, J. K.	Scholastic
Harry Potter and the Deathly Hallows	Z	F	250+	Rowling, J. K.	Scholastic
Harry Potter and the Goblet of Fire	W	F	250+	Rowling, J. K.	Scholastic
Harry Potter and the Half-Blood Prince	W	F	250+	Rowling, J. K.	Scholastic
Harry Potter and the Order of the Phoenix	W	F	250+	Rowling, J. K.	Scholastic
Harry Potter and the Prisoner of Azkaban	V	F	250+	Rowling, J. K.	Scholastic
Harry Potter and the Sorcerer's Stone	V	F	250+	Rowling, J. K.	Scholastic
Harry S. Truman	U	B	250+	Profiles of the Presidents	Compass Point Books
Harry S. Truman: Thirty-third President	R	B	250+	Getting to Know the U.S. Presidents	Children's Press
Harry Takes a Bath	G	F	132	Ziefert, Harriet	Puffin/Penguin

* Collection of short stories
# Graphic text

H

TITLE	LEVEL	GENRE	WORD COUNT	AUTHOR / SERIES	PUBLISHER / DISTRIBUTOR
Harry the Explorer	S	F	250+	Sheldon, Dyan	Candlewick Press
Harry's Caterpillars	I	RF	381	Gear Up!	Wright Group/McGraw Hill
Harry's Elephant	H	F	250+	Storyworlds	Heinemann Educational Books
Harry's Garden	H	I	138	Big Cat	Pacific Learning
Harry's Great Big Burp	J	RF	361	Springboard	Wright Group/McGraw Hill
Harry's Hat	B	RF	45	Little Books	Sadlier-Oxford
Harry's Hats	D	F	49	Teacher's Choice Series	Pearson Learning Group
Harry's Hiccups	J	F	439	Rigby Gigglers	Rigby
Harry's House	F	RF	83	Medearis, Angela; Keeter, Susan	Scholastic
Harry's Mad	P	F	250+	King-Smith, Dick	Alfred A. Knopf
Harry's Monkey	H	F	250+	Storyworlds	Heinemann Educational Books
Harry's New Hat	F	RF	171	PM Stars	Rigby
Harry's Seal	H	F	250+	Storyworlds	Heinemann Educational Books
Harry's Snake	H	F	250+	Storyworlds	Heinemann Educational Books
Harvest Festivals	O	I	250+	Windows on Literacy	National Geographic
Harvest Holidays	J	RF	399	Reading Street	Pearson
Harvest Time	J	I	228	Spyglass Books	Compass Point Books
Harvest Time	H	I	184	Yellow Umbrella Books	Red Brick Learning
Harvesting Medicine on the Hill	U	HF	2388	Reading Street	Pearson
Hat Came Back, The	K	RF	250+	Literacy 2000	Rigby
Hat Chat	H	I	124	Storyteller	Wright Group/McGraw Hill
Hat for Cat, A	C	F	85	Leveled Readers	Houghton Mifflin Harcourt
Hat for Cat, A	C	F	85	Leveled Readers/CA	Houghton Mifflin Harcourt
Hat for Hippo, A	C	F	137	Sails	Rigby
Hat for Monster, A	LB	F	14	Handprints A	Educators Publishing Service
Hat Trick	C	RF	38	Literacy 2000	Rigby
Hat, The	B	TL	43	Leveled Literacy Intervention/ Orange System	Heinemann
Hat, The	M	RF	250+	Literacy by Design	Rigby
Hat, The	LB	F	12	Ready Readers	Pearson Learning Group
Hat, The	B	RF	35	Sails	Rigby
Hatchet	R	RF	250+	Paulsen, Gary	Aladdin
Hatching Chickens at School	H	RF	94	City Kids	Rigby
Hatching Chicks	H	I	132	Nonfiction Set 6	Literacy Footprints
Hatchling, The	J	F	516	Sun Sprouts	ETA Cuisenaire
Hats	C	RF	35	Joy Readers	Pearson Learning Group
Hats	C	RF	43	Little Readers	Houghton Mifflin Harcourt
Hats	B	F	30	Sails	Rigby
Hats	F	I	88	Talk About Books	Pearson Learning Group
Hats	C	I	27	Twig	Wright Group/McGraw Hill
Hats	LB	I	46	Williams, Deborah	Kaeden Books
Hats	F	I	114	Wonder World	Wright Group/McGraw Hill
Hats Around the World	B	I	59	Charlesworth, Liza	Scholastic
Hats for the Carnival	H	RF	231	Lighthouse	Rigby
Hats!	E	RF	59	Early Readers	Compass Point Books
Hats!	C	F	28	Learn to Read	Creative Teaching Press
Hats, Hats, Hats	LB	I	14	Shutterbug Books	Steck-Vaughn
Hatshepsut and Nerfertiti: Egyptian Queens	X	B	2135	Leveled Readers Social Studies	Houghton Mifflin Harcourt
Hatshepsut Egypt's Woman King	Y	I	250+	iOpeners	Pearson Learning Group

H

* Collection of short stories
# Graphic text

TITLE	LEVEL	GENRE	WORD COUNT	AUTHOR / SERIES	PUBLISHER / DISTRIBUTOR
Hatshepsut: First Female Pharaoh	X	B	250+	Primary Source Readers	Teacher Created Materials
Hattie and the Fox	I	TL	321	Fox, Mem	Bradbury/Trumpet
Hattie Big Sky	W	HF	250+	Larson, Kirby	Delacorte Press
Hatty and Tatty and the Bumping Boats	G	F	235	Gear Up!	Wright Group/McGraw Hill
Hatty and Tatty and the Deep Blue Sea	H	F	199	Gear Up!	Wright Group/McGraw Hill
Hatty and Tatty and the Greedy Gull	F	F	165	Gear Up!	Wright Group/McGraw Hill
Hatty and Tatty and the Polar Bear	I	F	291	Gear Up!	Wright Group/McGraw Hill
Hatupatu and the Birdwoman	J	F	250+	Story Box	Wright Group/McGraw Hill
Hau Kola Hello Friend	O	B	250+	Meet The Author	Richard C. Owen
Haunted	Q	F	250+	Ragged Island Mysteries	Wright Group/McGraw Hill
Haunted	J	F	383	Take Two Books	Wright Group/McGraw Hill
Haunted Bike, The	L	F	250+	Herman, Gail	Grossett & Dunlap
Haunted Halloween, The	M	F	250+	Woodland Mysteries	Wright Group/McGraw Hill
Haunted Hotel, The	N	RF	250+	A to Z Mysteries	Random House
Haunted House, The	N	RF	250+	Parish, Peggy	Yearling
Haunted House, The	M	RF	937	Springboard	Wright Group/McGraw Hill
Haunted House, The	E	F	77	Story Box	Wright Group/McGraw Hill
Haunted Playground, The	S	F	250+	Tan, Shaun	Stone Arch Books
Haunting of Grade Three, The	O	RF	250+	Maccarone, Grace	Scholastic
Have a Ball!	K	I	456	Gear Up!	Wright Group/McGraw Hill
Have a Cookout	A	RF	21	Little Books for Early Readers	University of Maine
Have Numbers, Will Travel	WB	I	N/A	Gosset, Rachel	Scholastic
Have Wheels, Will Travel	Q	RF	250+	Mazer, Anne	Scholastic
Have You Ever Found a Beetle?	F	I	94	Voyages	SRA/McGraw Hill
Have You Ever Seen a Shell Walking?	M	I	460	Springboard	Wright Group/McGraw Hill
Have You Ever?	E	F	33	Big Cat	Pacific Learning
Have You Got Everything, Colin?	E	RF	72	Rigby Literacy	Rigby
Have You Got Everything, Colin?	E	RF	76	Rigby Star	Rigby
Have You Seen a Javelina?	K	F	250+	Literacy 2000	Rigby
Have You Seen Birds?	K	I	250+	Oppenheim, Joanne; Reid, Barbara	Scholastic
Have You Seen Hyacinth Macaw?	R	RF	250+	Giff, Patricia Reilly	Dell
Have You Seen Joe?	D	RF	57	Home Connection Collection	Rigby
Have You Seen My Cat?	B	F	93	Carle, Eric	Putnam/Penguin
Have You Seen My Duckling?	WB	F	N/A	Tafuri, Nancy	Greenwillow
Have You Seen the Crocodile?	F	F	150	West, Colin	Harper & Row
Have You Seen the Tooth Fairy?	E	RF	187	Visions	Wright Group/McGraw Hill
Have You Seen?	C	RF	38	Literacy 2000	Rigby
Haven't Got a Clue	W	I	250+	Boldprint	Steck-Vaughn
Having a Ball	U	I	250+	Rigby Literacy	Rigby
Having a Haircut	J	RF	298	City Kids	Rigby
Having Fun	B	RF	35	Early Emergent	Pioneer Valley
Having Fun	D	I	78	Windows on Literacy	National Geographic
Having Fun Then and Now	R	I	250+	PM Extensions	Rigby
Having Healthful Habits	Q	I	250+	Navigators How-to Series	Benchmark Education
Having My Hair Washed	I	RF	171	City Kids	Rigby
Hawaii	T	I	250+	Hello U.S.A.	Lerner Publications
Hawaii	S	I	250+	Land of Liberty	Red Brick Learning
Hawaii	T	I	250+	Sea to Shining Sea	Children's Press
Hawaii	R	I	250+	This Land Is Your Land	Compass Point Books
Hawaii	L	I	240	Windows on Literacy	National Geographic
Hawaii: The Aloha State	Q	I	250+	Rosen Real Readers	Rosen Publishing Group
Hawaiin Magic	R	I	250+	Orbit Chapter Books	Pacific Learning
Hawaiin Sea Life	R	I	1386	Vocabulary Readers/CA	Houghton Mifflin Harcourt

* Collection of short stories
\# Graphic text

H

TITLE	LEVEL	GENRE	WORD COUNT	AUTHOR / SERIES	PUBLISHER / DISTRIBUTOR
Hawaiin Sea Life	R	I	1386	Vocabulary Readers	Houghton Mifflin Harcourt
Hawk Drum, The	D	RF	81	Adams, Lorraine; Bruvold, Lynn	Eagle Crest Books
Hawkers' Amazing Machines, The: A Play	K	F	250+	Phonics and Friends	Hampton-Brown
Hawks	R	I	250+	Predators in the Wild	Red Brick Learning
Hawks	F	RF	87	Seedlings	Continental Press
Hay for Ambrosia	G	I	86	Pacific Literacy	Pacific Learning
Hay Making	F	I	62	Wonder World	Wright Group/McGraw Hill
Hay Ride, The	A	I	16	Leveled Readers	Houghton Mifflin Harcourt
Hay Ride, The	A	I	16	Leveled Readers/CA	Houghton Mifflin Harcourt
Haymeadow, The	T	RF	250+	Paulsen, Gary	Dell
Haystack, The	L	RF	250+	Cambridge Reading	Pearson Learning Group
He Bear, She Bear	J	F	250+	Berenstain, Stan & Jan	Random House
He Who Listens	K	RF	250+	Literacy 2000	Rigby
Head For the Hills!	O	I	250+	Walker, Paul Robert	Random House
Head Full of Notions, A: A Story about Robert Fulton	S	B	250+	Russell Bowen, Andy	Carolrhoda Books
Head Lice	K	I	250+	Health Matters	Capstone Press
Head to Toe: The Human Body	S	I	250+	Boldprint	Steck-Vaughn
Headache, The	B	RF	20	Oxford Reading Tree	Oxford University Press
Headfirst into the Oatmeal	L	F	250+	Rigby Literacy	Rigby
Headfirst into the Porridge	L	F	250+	Rigby Star Plus	Rigby
Headgear	I	I	362	Sails	Rigby
Headless Horseman, The	L	TL	250+	Standiford, Natalie	Random House
Headline News	J	F	357	Sails	Rigby
Headlines	Y	I	250+	Boldprint	Steck-Vaughn
Headlines from Space	Q	I	250+	Rigby Focus	Rigby
Heads and Tails	LB	I	29	Windmill Books	Rigby
Heads or Tails	O	RF	250+	On Our Way to English	Rigby
Healthy and Happy	J	I	251	Gear Up!	Wright Group/McGraw Hill
Healthy Food	I	I	162	PM Plus Nonfiction	Rigby
Healthy Visit, A	E	I	44	New Way Red	Steck-Vaughn
Hear Our Stories	Y	I	250+	iOpeners	Pearson Learning Group
Hearing	J	I	107	Pebble Books	Capstone Press
Hearing	G	I	212	PM Science Readers	Rigby
Hearing	E	I	86	Senses	Lerner Publishing
Hearing	M	I	250+	The Senses	Capstone Press
Heart and Lungs, The	Q	I	697	Time for Kids	Teacher Created Materials
Heart of a Champion	Z	RF	250+	Deuker, Carl	Little, Brown & Co.
Heart of a Chief, The	U	RF	250+	Bruchac, Joseph	Puffin/Penguin
Heart to Heart with Mallory	O	RF	250+	Friedman, Laurie	Carolrhoda Books
Heartbeat	W	RF	250+	Creech, Sharon	HarperCollins
Heartbreak and Roses: Real Life Stories of Troubled Love	Z+	RF	250+	Bode, Janet & Mack, Stan	Grolier Press
Heart's Blood	X	F	250+	Yolen, Jane	Harcourt Trade
Heat	Q	I	2290	Early Bird Energy	Lerner Publishing
Heat	I	I	203	Early Connections	Benchmark Education
Heat	V	RF	250+	Lupica, Mike	Puffin Books
Heat	J	I	146	Take Two Books	Wright Group/ McGraw Hill
Heat All Around	E	I	120	Leveled Readers Science	Houghton Mifflin Harcourt
Heat and Eat!	C	I	79	Independent Readers Science	Houghton Mifflin Harcourt
Heat Changes Things	G	I	101	Instant Readers	Harcourt School Publishers
Heat Changes Things	E	I	46	Windows on Literacy	National Geographic
Heat Is On, The	U	I	250+	Tanaka, Shelley	Firefly Books
Heather and the Pink Poodles	Q	RF	250+	Engle, Marion	Magic Attic

TITLE	LEVEL	GENRE	WORD COUNT	AUTHOR / SERIES	PUBLISHER / DISTRIBUTOR
Heather at the Barre	Q	RF	250+	Sinykin, Sheri Cooper	Magic Attic
Heather Goes to Hollywood	Q	RF	250+	Sinykin, Sheri Cooper	Magic Attic
Heather Takes the Reins	Q	RF	250+	Sinykin, Sheri Cooper	Magic Attic
Heather, Belle of the Ball	Q	RF	250+	Sinykin, Sheri Cooper	Magic Attic
Heather's Book	K	RF	250+	Ready Readers	Pearson Learning Group
Heather's Story	R	I	250+	Orbit Double Takes	Pacific Learning
Heating Earth	T	I	2023	Science Support Readers	Houghton Mifflin Harcourt
Heaven	U	RF	250+	Johnson, Angela	Scholastic
Heaven Looks a Lot Like the Mall	Z+	RF	250+	Mass, Wendy	Little, Brown & Co.
Heaviest Pumpkin Contest, The	J	RF	689	InfoTrek	ETA Cuisenaire
Heavy and Light: An Animal Opposites Book	J	I	250+	Animal Opposites	Capstone Press
Heavy Bombers: The B-52 Stratofortresses	V	I	250+	War Planes	Capstone Press
Heavy Hippo, The	H	RF	211	Windows on Literacy	National Geographic
Heavy Weight and Other Cases, The	O	RF	250+	Simon, Seymour	Avon
Heavyweights	O	I	250+	Take Two Books	Wright Group/McGraw Hill
Hector and the Cello	J	F	440	Big Cat	Pacfic Learning
Hedgehog Bakes a Cake	J	F	250+	Bank Street	Bantam
Hedgehog Day	I	I	121	Seedlings	Continental Press
Hedgehog in the Hall	Q	RF	250+	Daniels, Lucy	Barron's Educational
Hedgehog Is Hungry	C	RF	48	PM Story Books	Rigby
Hedgehog Mountain	K	F	489	Rigby Gigglers	Rigby
Hedgehogs	I	I	286	Sails	Rigby
Helen Keller	K	B	250+	Adler, David A.	Holiday House
Helen Keller	N	B	250+	Davidson, Margaret	Scholastic
Helen Keller	N	B	1884	On My Own Biography	Lerner Publications
Helen Keller	P	B	250+	Photo-Illustrated Biographies	Red Brick Learning
Helen Keller: A Life of Adventure	O	B	250+	Orbit Chapter Books	Pacific Learning
Helen Keller: A Light for the Blind	R	B	250+	Kudlinski, Kathleen V.	Penguin Group
Helen Keller: Courage in Darkness	Y	B	250+	Sterling Biographies	Sterling Publishing
Helen Keller: Courage in the Dark	N	B	250+	Hurwitz, Johanna	Random House
Helen Keller: Crusader for the Blind and Deaf	P	B	250+	Graff, Stewart & Polly Anne	Bantam
Helen Keller: From Tragedy to Triumph	O	B	250+	Childhood of Famous Americans	Aladdin
Helen Keller's Lifelong Friend	S	I	1377	Leveled Readers	Houghton Mifflin Harcourt
Helen Keller's Lifelong Friend	S	I	1377	Leveled Readers/CA	Houghton Mifflin Harcourt
Helen Keller's Lifelong Friend	S	I	1377	Leveled Readers/TX	Houghton Mifflin Harcourt
Helen Keller's Special Friend	S	I	1472	Leveled Readers	Houghton Mifflin Harcourt
Helen Keller's Special Friend	S	I	1472	Leveled Readers/CA	Houghton Mifflin Harcourt
Helen Keller's Special Friend	S	I	1472	Leveled Readers/TX	Houghton Mifflin Harcourt
Helen Keller's Teacher	N	B	250+	Davidson, Margaret	Scholastic
Helen's Job	A	RF	24	Phonics and Friends	Hampton-Brown
Helga and the Ogre	J	F	495	Sun Sprouts	ETA Cuisenaire
Helga's Secret	J	RF	250+	Rigby Literacy	Rigby
Helicopter Over Hawaii	LB	I	21	Twig	Wright Group/McGraw Hill
Helicopters	O	I	250+	A True Book	Children's Press
Helicopters	M	I	250+	Horsepower	Capstone Press
Helicopters	V	I	4384	Military Hardware in Action	Lerner Publications
Helicopters	L	I	294	Pull Ahead Books	Lerner Publications
Helicopters	T	I	250+	The World's Fastest	Red Brick Learning
Hello	C	F	63	Story Box	Wright Group/McGraw Hill
Hello Chick!	D	I	54	Leveled Readers Language Support	Houghton Mifflin Harcourt
Hello Creatures!	K	I	250+	Literacy 2000	Rigby
Hello Doctor	C	RF	43	Rookie Readers	Children's Press
Hello Flower	B	RF	20	Bebop Books	Lee & Low Books Inc.

H

* Collection of short stories
# Graphic text

TITLE	LEVEL	GENRE	WORD COUNT	AUTHOR / SERIES	PUBLISHER / DISTRIBUTOR
Hello Goodbye	B	F	29	Literacy 2000	Rigby
Hello Hello	J	F	164	Takeshita, Fumiko	Kane/Miller Book Publishers
Hello Ocean	N	RF	302	Ryan, Pam Munoz	Charlesbridge
Hello Puppet	C	I	26	Voyages	SRA/McGraw Hill
Hello!	F	I	17	Chessen, Betsey; Bergen, Samantha	Scholastic
Hello, Bingo!	C	RF	42	PM Stars	Rigby
Hello, Cat: You Need a Hat	I	F	250+	Gelman, Rita	Scholastic
Hello, Dad!	D	RF	16	Pacific Literacy	Pacific Learning
Hello, First Grade	I	RF	250+	Ryder, Joanne	Troll Associates
Hello, Friend	C	F	39	Instant Readers	Harcourt School Publishers
Hello, Goodbye, I Love You: The Story of Aloha, A Guide Dog for the Blind	S	RF	250+	Mueller, Pamela Bauer	Pinata Publishing
Hello, Hello, Hello	E	RF	56	Sunshine	Wright Group/McGraw Hill
Hello, I'm Joe	J	RF	652	Rigby Flying Colors	Rigby
Hello, Little Chick!	D	I	56	Leveled Readers	Houghton Mifflin Harcourt
*Hello, Mrs. Piggle-Wiggle	O	F	250+	MacDonald, Betty	HarperTrophy
Hello, My Name Is Scrambled Eggs	R	RF	250+	Gilson, Jamie	Pocket Books
Hello, Peter-Bonjour, Remy	L	F	250+	Little Celebrations	Pearson Learning Group
Help for Dear Dragon	E	F	304	Dear Dragon	Norwood House Press
Help for Eyes	H	I	156	Sails	Rigby
Help for Loc: A Play	H	RF	202	Literacy by Design	Rigby
Help for Loc: A Play	H	RF	202	On Our Way to English	Rigby
Help for Rhino!	E	F	131	Sails	Rigby
Help for Rosie	H	F	165	Bella and Rosie Series	Pioneer Valley
Help for Santa	F	F	147	Little Elf	Literacy Footprints
Help Is on the Way	Q	I	372	Vocabulary Readers	Houghton Mifflin Harcourt
Help Me	D	RF	107	Emergent	Pioneer Valley
Help Me	H	TL	196	Story Box	Wright Group/McGraw Hill
Help Me!	C	F	55	New Way Red	Steck-Vaughn
Help the Forest	G	I	122	Reading Street	Pearson
Help with the Herd	T	RF	1830	Leveled Readers	Houghton Mifflin Harcourt
Help Yourself to Health	L	I	538	Springboard	Wright Group/ McGraw Hill
Help!	H	RF	82	Giant Step Readers	Educational Insights
Help!	C	I	57	Reading Corners	Pearson Learning Group
Help!	C	RF	57	Rigby Literacy	Rigby
Help! A Vampire's Coming!	L	RF	250+	Klein, Abby	Scholastic
Help! Help!	LB	RF	14	Joy Readers	Pearson Learning Group
Help! I'm a Prisoner in the Library	Q	RF	250+	Clifford, Eth	Scholastic
Help! I'm Stuck!	J	F	250+	Little Celebrations	Pearson Learning Group
Help! I'm Trapped in an Alien's Body	Q	F	250+	Strasser, Todd	Scholastic
Help! I'm Trapped in My Lunch Lady's Body	Q	F	250+	Strasser, Todd	Scholastic
Help! I'm Trapped in My Teacher's Body	Q	F	250+	Strasser, Todd	Scholastic
Help! I'm Trapped in Obedience School	Q	F	250+	Strasser, Todd	Scholastic
Help! I'm Trapped in Obedience School Again	Q	F	250+	Strasser, Todd	Scholastic
Help! I'm Trapped in Santa's Body	Q	F	250+	Strasser, Todd	Scholastic
Help! I'm Trapped in the First Day of School	Q	F	250+	Strasser, Todd	Scholastic
Help! I'm Trapped in the First Day of Summer Camp	Q	F	250+	Strasser, Todd	Scholastic
Help! I'm Trapped in the President's Body	Q	F	250+	Strasser, Todd	Scholastic
Help! Said Jed	C	TL	35	Instant Readers	Harcourt School Publishers
Help! Somebody Get Me Out of Fourth Grade!	R	RF	250+	Winkler, Henry and Oliver, Lin	Grosset & Dunlap
Helper Monkeys	L	I	499	Leveled Readers	Houghton Mifflin Harcourt

* Collection of short stories
# Graphic text

H

TITLE	LEVEL	GENRE	WORD COUNT	AUTHOR / SERIES	PUBLISHER / DISTRIBUTOR
Helper Monkeys	L	I	499	Leveled Readers/CA	Houghton Mifflin Harcourt
Helper Monkeys	L	I	499	Leveled Readers/TX	Houghton Mifflin Harcourt
Helper, The	A	I	31	InfoTrek	ETA Cuisenaire
Helpers	D	RF	57	Joy Starters	Pearson Learning Group
Helpers	C	RF	31	Storyworlds	Heinemann Educational Publishers
Helpful Becky	J	RF	250+	Phonics Readers Plus	Steck-Vaughn
Helpful Change, A	L	RF	250+	Behr, Alexandra	Hampton-Brown
*Helpful Harry and Other Stories	L	RF	250+	New Way Literature	Steck-Vaughn
Helpful Hints for Boring Moments	R	I	250+	Sails	Rigby
Helpful or Harmful?	O	I	250+	Orbit Double Takes	Pacific Learning
Helping	F	RF	79	Bookshop	Mondo
Helping	A	RF	22	Johns, Linda	Scholastic
Helping	D	RF	79	Joy Readers	Pearson Learning Group
Helping	C	RF	74	Leveled Literacy Intervention/ Orange System	Heinemann
Helping	A	I	36	Leveled Readers	Houghton Mifflin Harcourt
Helping	A	I	36	Leveled Readers/CA	Houghton Mifflin Harcourt
Helping	A	I	36	Leveled Readers/TX	Houghton Mifflin Harcourt
Helping	F	RF	103	Well-Being Series	Pearson Learning Group
Helping at Home	C	I	86	Vocabulary Readers	Houghton Mifflin Harcourt
Helping at Home	E	I	157	Vocabulary Readers	Houghton Mifflin Harcourt
Helping at Home	B	I	86	Vocabulary Readers/CA	Houghton Mifflin Harcourt
Helping at Home	E	I	157	Vocabulary Readers/CA	Houghton Mifflin Harcourt
Helping at Home	E	I	157	Vocabulary Readers/TX	Houghton Mifflin Harcourt
Helping Dad	B	RF	31	Storyteller	Wright Group/McGraw Hill
Helping Dad	C	RF	34	Sunshine	Wright Group/McGraw Hill
Helping Each Other	C	RF	80	Literacy by Design	Rigby
Helping Each Other	C	RF	80	On Our Way to English	Rigby
Helping Grandma	G	RF	164	Adams, Lorraine; Bruvold, Lynn	Eagle Crest Books
Helping Hand, A	P	I	250+	Rigby Focus	Rigby
Helping Hands	K	I	372	Gear Up!	Wright Group/ McGraw Hill
Helping Hands	I	RF	350	Rigby Flying Colors	Rigby
Helping Hands	J	I	387	Vocabulary Readers	Houghton Mifflin Harcourt
Helping Hands	J	I	387	Vocabulary Readers/CA	Houghton Mifflin Harcourt
Helping Hands	P	I	250+	WorldScapes	ETA Cuisenaire
Helping Hands	J	I	250+	Yellow Umbrella Books	Red Brick Learning
Helping Mom	E	RF	165	Leveled Literacy Intervention/ Green System	Heinemann
Helping Mom and Dad	E	RF	121	Learn to Read	Creative Teaching Press
Helping Mr. Horse	D	F	82	Leveled Readers	Houghton Mifflin Harcourt
Helping Mr. Horse	D	F	82	Leveled Readers/CA	Houghton Mifflin Harcourt
Helping My Dad	D	RF	90	Teacher's Choice Series	Pearson Learning Group
Helping Out	L	RF	317	Independent Readers Social Studies	Houghton Mifflin Harcourt
Helping Out	F	I	121	Sails	Rigby
Helping Paws: Dogs That Serve	O	I	250+	Luke, Melinda	Scholastic
Helping the Everglades	J	I	369	In Step Readers	Rigby
Helping the Hoiho	S	I	250+	Literacy 2000	Rigby
Helping Toby's Team	E	RF	98	Windows on Literacy	National Geographic
Helping Wild Animals	T	I	2126	Leveled Readers	Houghton Mifflin Harcourt
Helping Wild Animals	T	I	2126	Leveled Readers/CA	Houghton Mifflin Harcourt
Helping Wild Animals	T	I	2126	Leveled Readers/TX	Houghton Mifflin Harcourt
Helping Wild Animals	R	I	582	Vocabulary Readers	Houghton Mifflin Harcourt

H

* Collection of short stories
# Graphic text

TITLE	LEVEL	GENRE	WORD COUNT	AUTHOR / SERIES	PUBLISHER / DISTRIBUTOR
Helping With Baby	E	RF	115	Adams, Lorraine; Bruvold, Lynn	Eagle Crest Books
Helping You	D	I	53	Interaction	Rigby
Helping You Heal: A Book About Nurses	H	I	145	Community Workers	Picture Window Books
Helping You Learn: A Book About Teachers	H	I	147	Community Workers	Picture Window Books
Helter-Skelter	J	F	250+	Rigby Rocket	Rigby
Hemingway Tradition, The	Z	RF	250+	Orca Soundings	Orca Book Publishers
Hen Can, A	E	F	159	Tiger Cub	Peguis
Hen, the Rooster, and the Bean, The	I	TL	250+	Kratky, Lada Josefa	Hampton-Brown
Henny Penny	I	TL	582	Galdone, Paul	Clarion
Henny Penny	H	TL	292	New Way Green	Steck-Vaughn
Henny Penny	I	TL	250+	Zimmerman, H. Werner	Scholastic
Henri de Toulouse-Lautrec	R	B	250+	Venezia, Mike	Children's Press
Henri Matisse	R	B	250+	Venezia, Mike	Children's Press
Henri Rousseau	T	B	250+	Rabott, Ernest	HarperTrophy
Henrietta There's No One Better	Q	F	250+	Murray, Martine	Scholastic
Henry	T	RF	250+	Bawden, Nina	Bantam
Henry	E	RF	77	Books for Young Learners	Richard C. Owen
Henry	F	F	141	Instant Readers	Harcourt School Publishers
Henry and Beezus	O	RF	250+	Cleary, Beverly	Avon
Henry and Mudge and Annie's Good Move	J	RF	250+	Rylant, Cynthia	Aladdin
Henry and Mudge and Annie's Perfect Pet	J	RF	250+	Rylant, Cynthia	Aladddin Paperbacks
Henry and Mudge and the Bedtime Thumps	J	RF	250+	Rylant, Cynthia	Aladdin
Henry and Mudge and the Best Day of All	J	RF	250+	Rylant, Cynthia	Aladdin
Henry and Mudge and the Careful Cousin	J	RF	250+	Rylant, Cynthia	Aladdin
Henry and Mudge and the Forever Sea	J	RF	250+	Rylant, Cynthia	Aladdin
Henry and Mudge and the Funny Lunch	I	RF	250+	Rylant, Cynthia	Scholastic
Henry and Mudge and the Happy Cat	J	RF	250+	Rylant, Cynthia	Aladdin
Henry and Mudge and the Long Weekend	J	RF	250+	Rylant, Cynthia	Aladdin
Henry and Mudge and the Sneaky Crackers	J	RF	250+	Rylant, Cynthia	Aladdin
Henry and Mudge and the Snowman Plan	J	RF	250+	Rylant, Cynthia	Aladdin
Henry and Mudge and the Starry Night	J	RF	250+	Rylant, Cynthia	Aladdin
Henry and Mudge and the Wild Goose Chase	J	RF	250+	Rylant, Cynthia	Aladddin Paperbacks
Henry and Mudge and the Wild Wind	J	RF	250+	Rylant, Cynthia	Aladdin
Henry and Mudge Get the Cold Shivers	J	RF	250+	Rylant, Cynthia	Aladdin
Henry and Mudge in Puddle Trouble	J	RF	250+	Rylant, Cynthia	Aladdin
Henry and Mudge in the Family Trees	J	RF	250+	Rylant, Cynthia	Aladdin
Henry and Mudge in the Green Time	J	RF	250+	Rylant, Cynthia	Aladdin
Henry and Mudge in the Sparkle Days	J	RF	250+	Rylant, Cynthia	Aladdin
Henry and Mudge Take the Big Test	J	RF	250+	Rylant, Cynthia	Aladdin
Henry and Mudge Under the Yellow Moon	J	RF	250+	Rylant, Cynthia	Aladdin
Henry and Mudge: The First Book	J	RF	250+	Rylant, Cynthia	Aladdin
Henry and Ribsy	O	RF	250+	Cleary, Beverly	Hearst
Henry and the Clubhouse	O	RF	250+	Cleary, Beverly	Avon
Henry and the Fox	K	RF	388	Leveled Readers	Houghton Mifflin Harcourt
Henry and the Helicopter	D	RF	58	Literacy 2000	Rigby
Henry and the Paper Route	O	RF	250+	Cleary, Beverly	Hearst
Henry Ford	T	B	250+	Amazing Americans	Wright Group/McGraw Hill
Henry Ford	L	B	216	Famous People in Transportation	Red Brick Learning
Henry Ford	P	B	250+	Photo-Illustrated Biographies	Red Brick Learning
Henry Ford and the Automobile Industry	R	B	250+	On Deck	Rigby
Henry Ford: Young Man with Ideas	O	B	250+	Childhood of Famous Americans	Aladdin
Henry Gonzales, U.S. Representative	N	B	491	Leveled Readers Social Studies	Houghton Mifflin Harcourt
Henry Huggins	O	RF	250+	Cleary, Beverly	Avon
Henry Morgan, the Pirate	Q	B	947	Springboard	Wright Group/ McGraw Hill

* Collection of short stories
# Graphic text

TITLE	LEVEL	GENRE	WORD COUNT	AUTHOR / SERIES	PUBLISHER / DISTRIBUTOR
Henry Reed, Inc.	X	F	250+	Robertson, Keith	Puffin/Penguin
Henry Runs Away	F	RF	150	Books for Young Learners	Richard C. Owen
Henry's Busy Day	E	F	112	Campbell, Rod	Penguin Group
Henry's Choice	M	RF	527	Reading Unlimited	Pearson Learning Group
Henry's New Friend	I	RF	250+	Leveled Readers Language Support	Houghton Mifflin Harcourt
Henry's Tricks	H	RF	162	Books for Young Learners	Richard C. Owen
Her Name Is Amira	U	RF	2510	Leveled Readers/CA	Houghton Mifflin Harcourt
Her Name Is Amira	U	RF	2510	Leveled Readers	Houghton Mifflin Harcourt
Her Piano Sang: A Story About Clara Schumann	R	B	250+	Allman, Barbara	Carolrhoda Books
Her Seven Brothers	O	TL	250+	Goble, Paul	Aladdin
Herbert Fieldmouse, Secret Agent	R	F	250+	Bookshop	Mondo
Herbert Hoover	U	B	250+	Profiles of the Presidents	Compass Point Books
Herbert Hoover: Thirty-first President	R	B	250+	Getting to Know the U.S. Presidents	Children's Press
Herbie Jones	N	RF	250+	Kline, Suzy	Penguin Group
Herbie Jones and Hamburger Head	N	RF	250+	Kline, Suzy	Penguin Group
Herbie Jones and the Birthday Showdown	N	RF	250+	Kline, Suzy	Penguin Group
Herbie Jones and the Class Gift	N	RF	250+	Kline, Suzy	Penguin Group
Herbie Jones and the Dark Attic	N	RF	250+	Kline, Suzy	Puffin/Penguin
Herbie Jones and the Monster Ball	N	RF	250+	Kline, Suzy	Penguin Group
Hercules	W	I	250+	World Mythology	Capstone Press
Hercules and Other Greek Legends	T	TL	250+	Wildcats	Wright Group/McGraw Hill
Hercules Doesn't Pull Teeth	M	F	250+	Dadey, Debbie; Jones, Marcia Thornton	Scholastic
Hercules: Superhero	Q	TL	1809	Big Cat	Pacific Learning
Here Are My Hands	H	I	127	Bobber Book	SRA/McGraw Hill
Here Come the Bison!	L	I	212	Sunshine	Wright Group/McGraw Hill
Here Come the Shapes	E	F	118	PM Plus Story Books	Rigby
Here Comes a Bus	F	F	171	Ziefert, Harriet	Penguin Group
Here Comes a Storm	O	I	1021	Reading Street	Pearson
Here Comes a Storm	O	I	1021	Reading Street	Pearson
Here Comes Annette!	E	RF	143	Voyages	SRA/McGraw Hill
Here Comes Everyone	F	RF	78	Cambridge Reading	Pearson Learning Group
Here Comes Kate!	J	RF	250+	Real Reading	Steck-Vaughn
Here Comes Little Chimp	D	F	69	PM Plus Story Books	Rigby
*Here Comes McBroom	O	F	250+	Fleischman, Sid	Beech Tree Books
Here Comes the Bus	B	RF	21	Bebop Books	Lee & Low Books Inc.
Here Comes the Bus	D	RF	143	Rigby Flying Colors	Rigby
Here Comes the Cat	LB	RF	24	Asch, Frank	Scholastic
Here Comes the Parade!	B	RF	32	Pair-It Books	Steck-Vaughn
Here Comes the Rain!	C	I	47	Little Books	Sadlier-Oxford
Here Comes the Strikeout	K	RF	250+	Kessler, Leonard	HarperTrophy
Here Comes the Strikeout	I	RF	250+	Little Readers	Houghton Mifflin Harcourt
Here Comes Trouble	N	RF	250+	High-Fliers	Pacific Learning
Here Comes Winter	G	RF	134	First Start	Troll Associates
Here I Am!	B	RF	36	First Stories	Pacific Learning
Here Is . . .	B	I	49	Carousel Earlybirds	Pearson Learning Group
Here Is a Bird	A	RF	24	Sails	Rigby
Here Is a Box	B	I	91	Rigby Literacy	Rigby
Here Is a Carrot	C	I	96	Foundations	Wright Group/McGraw Hill
Here Is a Seed	C	RF	23	Science	Outside the Box

H

* Collection of short stories
\# Graphic text

TITLE	LEVEL	GENRE	WORD COUNT	AUTHOR / SERIES	PUBLISHER / DISTRIBUTOR
Here Is Hen	A	F	21	Leveled Readers Language Support	Houghton Mifflin Harcourt
Here is Rosa!	B	RF	20	Brand New Readers	Candlewick Press
Here Is the Butter	D	I	48	Rigby Flying Colors	Rigby
Here It Is!	B	RF	64	Literacy by Design	Rigby
Here It Is!	B	RF	64	On Our Way to English	Rigby
Here Lies the Librarian	V	RF	250+	Peck, Richard	Puffin Books
*Here There Be Dragons	Y	F	250+	Yolen, Jane	Harcourt Trade
*Here There Be Witches	Y	F	250+	Yolen, Jane	Harcourt Trade
Here We All Are	N	B	250+	DePaola, Tomie	Penguin Group
Here We Go Round the Mulberry Bush	D	RF	187	Little Readers	Houghton Mifflin Harcourt
Here We Go Round the Mulberry Bush	F	TL	208	PM Readalongs	Rigby
Here We Go Round the Mulberry Bush	L	TL	250+	Trapani, Iza	Charlesbridge
Here's a House	C	I	45	Windmill Books	Wright Group/McGraw Hill
Here's Bobby's World! How a TV Cartoon Is	L	I	250+	Little Celebrations	Pearson Learning Group
Here's Looking at Me: How Artists See Themselves	S	I	2768	Raczka, Bob	Millbrook Press
Here's My Home Page	N	RF	250+	InfoTrek	ETA Cuisenaire
Here's Skipper	B	RF	28	Salem, Lynn; Stewart, Josie	Continental Press
Here's to Hats	L	I	250+	Sunshine	Wright Group/McGraw Hill
Here's to You, Rachel Robinson	T	RF	250+	Blume, Judy	Bantam
Here's What I Made	C	RF	38	Literacy 2000	Rigby
Herman Henry's Dog	I	F	250+	Little Readers	Houghton Mifflin Harcourt
Herman the Helper	J	F	94	Kraus, Robert	Simon & Schuster
Herman the Helper Lends a Hand	F	F	198	Kraus, Robert	Windmill
Herman's Tooth	H	F	210	Foundations	Wright Group/McGraw Hill
Hermie the Crab	J	RF	250+	PM Plus Story Books	Rigby
Hermit Crab	E	I	111	PM Story Books	Rigby
Hermit Crab, The	G	RF	119	Sunshine	Wright Group/McGraw Hill
Hero	Z+	F	250+	Moore, Perry	Hyperion
Hero Ain't Nothin' but a Sandwich, A	Z+	RF	250+	Childress, Alice	Puffin Books
Hero and the Crown, The	Z	F	250+	McKinley, Robin	Puffin/Penguin
Hero in the Mirror, The	M	RF	250+	Rigby Literacy	Rigby
Hero of Lesser Causes	W	RF	250+	Johnston, Julie	Tundra Books
Hero of the Poor	W	I	2410	Leveled Readers	Houghton Mifflin Harcourt
Hero of the Poor	W	I	2410	Leveled Readers/CA	Houghton Mifflin Harcourt
Hero of Ticonderoga, The	V	HF	250+	Gauthier, Gail	Scholastic
Hero Twins, The: Against the Lords of Death	U	TL	2460	Graphic Myths and Legends	Lerner Publications
Hero Weighs In, A	S	SF	1488	Leveled Readers	Houghton Mifflin Harcourt
Hero Weighs In, A	S	SF	1488	Leveled Readers/CA	Houghton Mifflin Harcourt
Hero Weighs In, A	S	SF	1488	Leveled Readers/TX	Houghton Mifflin Harcourt
Hero, The	T	RF	250+	Woods, Ron	Dell Yearling
Heroes	N	I	250+	Wildcats	Wright Group/McGraw Hill
Heroes & Idealists	U	B	250+	Real Lives	Troll Associates
Heroes for Civil Rights	S	B	250+	Adler, David A.	Holiday House
Heroes in the Sky	k	I	204	Literacy by Design	Rigby
Heroes of the American Revolution	P	B	626	Reading Street	Pearson
Heroes of the Antarctic	V	I	1994	Leveled Readers	Houghton Mifflin Harcourt
Heroes of the Antarctic	V	I	1994	Leveled Readers/CA	Houghton Mifflin Harcourt
Heroes of the Antarctic	V	I	1994	Leveled Readers/TX	Houghton Mifflin Harcourt
Heroes of the Holocaust: True Stories of Rescues by Teens	Y	I	250+	Zullo, Allan & Bovsun, Mara	Scholastic
Heroes of the Revolution	S	B	250+	Adler, David A.	Holiday House
Heroic Animals	U	I	2926	Reading Street	Pearson

H

TITLE	LEVEL	GENRE	WORD COUNT	AUTHOR / SERIES	PUBLISHER / DISTRIBUTOR
Herons	H	I	106	Wetland Animals	Capstone Press
Heros and Heroines	S	I	250+	Literacy 2000	Rigby
Hey Coach!	C	RF	37	TOTTS	Tott Publications
Hey Diddle Diddle	D	F	53	Seedlings	Continental Press
Hey Kid, Want to Buy a Bridge?	P	F	250+	Scieszka, Jon	Penguin Group
Hey There, Bear!	C	F	39	Little Celebrations	Pearson Learning Group
*Hey World, Here I Am!	S	RF	250+	Little, Jean	HarperTrophy
Hey! You're Eating My Homework	H	RF	250+	Bebop Books	Lee & Low Books Inc.
Hey, Al	N	F	250+	Yorinks, Arthur	Farrar, Straus and Giroux
Hey, Diddle, Diddle!	D	TL	30	Sunshine	Wright Group/McGraw Hill
Hey, Four-Eyes!	K	RF	469	Rigby Flying Colors	Rigby
Hey, New Kid!	N	RF	250+	Duffey, Betsy	Penguin Group
Hi Dog	D	RF	137	Ready Readers	Pearson Learning Group
Hi! Fly Guy	I	F	250+	Arnold, Tedd	Scholastic
Hi, Clouds	D	RF	56	Rookie Readers	Children's Press
Hiawatha, American Leader	M	B	535	Leveled Readers Social Studies	Houghton Mifflin Harcourt
Hibernation	I	I	170	Patterns in Nature	Capstone Press
Hiccups	I	F	250+	Bookshop	Mondo
Hiccups for Elephant	I	F	250+	Preller, James	Scholastic
Hiccups for Hippo	I	F	100	Sunshine	Wright Group/McGraw Hill
Hiccups for Rachel	I	RF	250+	Scooters	ETA Cuisenaire
Hiccups Would Not Stop, The	H	F	177	Ready Readers	Pearson Learning Group
Hickory Dickory Dock	D	F	20	Instant Readers	Harcourt School Publishers
Hickory, Dickory Pizza Clock	C	F	92	Little Celebrations	Pearson Learning Group
Hidden Animals	C	I	32	Gear Up!	Wright Group/McGraw Hill
Hidden Cave, The	P	RF	1739	Gear Up!	Wright Group/ McGraw Hill
Hidden Flower	T	B	250+	WorldScapes	ETA Cuisenaire
Hidden Hand, The	M	RF	250+	Woodland Mysteries	Wright Group/McGraw Hill
Hidden Heritage	T	I	250+	WorldScapes	ETA Cuisenaire
Hidden Insects	I	I	244	Sails	Rigby
Hidden on the Mountain: Stories of Children Sheltered from the Nazis in Le Chambon	Z	I	250+	DeSaix, Deborah and Ruelle, Karen Gray	Holiday House
Hidden Spiders	I	I	239	Sails	Rigby
Hidden Stairs and the Magic Carpet, The	O	F	250+	Abbott, Tony	Scholastic
Hidden World	R	I	250+	Explorers	Wright Group/McGraw Hill
Hidden World of Mold, The	U	I	1541	Vocabulary Readers	Houghton Mifflin Harcourt
Hidden World of Mold, The	U	I	1541	Vocabulary Readers/CA	Houghton Mifflin Harcourt
Hide & Seek	H	I	138	Wonder World	Wright Group/McGraw Hill
Hide and Seek	K	I	250+	World Quest Adventures	World Quest Learning
Hide and Seek	D	F	63	Brown, Roberta; Carey, Sue	Scholastic
Hide and Seek	H	RF	215	Foundations	Wright Group/McGraw Hill
Hide and Seek	E	F	60	Instant Readers	Harcourt School Publishers
Hide and Seek	J	F	398	Leveled Literacy Intervention/ Blue System	Heinemann
Hide and Seek	B	RF	38	Literacy 2000	Rigby
Hide and Seek	D	RF	49	New Way Red	Steck-Vaughn
Hide and Seek	I	I	250+	Phonics and Friends	Hampton-Brown
Hide and Seek	D	RF	108	PM Extensions-Red	Rigby
Hide and Seek	C	F	78	Reed, Janet	Scholastic
Hide and Seek	LB	F	24	Rigby Star	Rigby
Hide and Seek	A	F	38	Smart Starts	Rigby
Hide and Seek	D	RF	49	Start to Read	School Zone
Hide and Seek	H	F	171	Storyworlds	Heinemann Educational Books

* Collection of short stories
# Graphic text

TITLE	LEVEL	GENRE	WORD COUNT	AUTHOR / SERIES	PUBLISHER / DISTRIBUTOR
Hide and Seek	E	F	228	Sun Sprouts	ETA Cuisenaire
Hide and Seek With Allie Alligator	G	F	174	Springboard	Wright Group/McGraw Hill
Hide to Survive	L	I	250+	Home Connection Collection	Rigby
Hide!	C	F	81	Sun Sprouts	ETA Cuisenaire
Hide, Spider!	G	F	179	Momentum Literacy Program	Troll Associates
Hide-and-Go-Seek	C	F	66	First Stories	Pacific Learning
Hide-and-Seek	H	F	546	Leveled Readers	Houghton Mifflin Harcourt
Hide-and-Seek	H	F	250+	Momentum Literacy Program	Troll Associates
Hide-and-Seek All Week	I	RF	250+	DePaola, Tomie	Grossett & Dunlap
*Hide-and-Seek with Grandpa	J	F	250+	Lewis, Rob	Mondo
Hi-De-Hi	E	F	110	Little Celebrations	Pearson Learning Group
Hiders, The	M	I	250+	Sails	Rigby
Hiding	E	I	97	Foundations	Wright Group/McGraw Hill
Hiding	A	F	28	KinderReaders	Rigby
Hiding	B	F	57	Leveled Literacy Intervention/ Orange System	Heinemann
Hiding	B	I	56	Sails	Rigby
Hiding from Bella	D	RF	114	PM Photo Stories	Rigby
Hiding in Plain Sight	I	I	173	Instant Readers	Harcourt School Publishers
Hiding Places	J	I	250+	Storyteller-Night Crickets	Wright Group/McGraw Hill
Hiding Toads	K	I	438	Pull Ahead Books	Lerner Publications
Hieroglyphs	S	I	250+	Ancient Egypt	Capstone Press
High- Altitude Spy Planes: The U-2s	V	I	250+	War Planes	Capstone Press
High and Low: An Animal Opposites Book	J	I	355	Animal Opposites	Capstone Press
High Flying	R	I	250+	Explorers	Wright Group/McGraw Hill
High King, The: The Chronicles of Prydain-Book 5	X	F	250+	Alexander, Lloyd	Henry Holt & Co.
High Life, The	T	I	250+	WorldScapes	ETA Cuisenaire
High Noon	P	F	250+	Storyteller Chapter Books	Wright Group/ McGraw Hill
High Tide	X	I	2084	Independent Readers Science	Houghton Mifflin Harcourt
High Wire	N	RF	250+	Orbit Double Takes	Pacific Learning
Higher Power of Lucky, The	W	RF	250+	Patron, Susan	Atheneum
Highest Tide, The	Z+	RF	250+	Lynch, Jim	Bloomsbury
High-Flying Contest, The: An African American	N	F	639	Leveled Readers	Houghton Mifflin Harcourt
Highland Cattle, The	J	RF	250+	Storyworlds	Heinemann Educational Books
Highland Games, The	J	RF	250+	Storyworlds	Heinemann Educational Books
High-Water Heroes	T	RF	2242	Leveled Readers	Houghton Mifflin Harcourt
Highway Turtles, The	K	RF	250+	PM Plus Story Books	Rigby
Hike at Day Camp, The	C	RF	32	Visions	Wright Group/McGraw Hill
Hiking	S	I	250+	The Great Outdoors	Capstone Press
Hiking for Fun!	S	I	250+	Sports for Fun!	Compass Point Books
Hiking in the Wilds	P	I	1894	Take Two Books	Wright Group/ McGraw Hill
Hiking the Appalachian Trail	R	I	250+	Explore More	Wright Group/McGraw Hill
Hiking Together	K	RF	250+	On Our Way to English	Rigby
Hiking with Dad	H	RF	189	Wonder World	Wright Group/McGraw Hill
Hilary and the Lions	M	F	250+	Desaix, Frank	Farrar, Straus and Giroux
Hill of Fire	L	RF	1099	Lewis, Thomas P.	HarperCollins
Hillary Rodham Clinton: A New Kind of First Lady	S	B	250+	Guernsey, JoAnn Bren	Lerner Publishing
Hindu Holiday	P	I	494	Independent Readers Social Studies	Houghton Mifflin Harcourt
Hip Hop	LB	F	19	Rigby Star	Rigby

H

* Collection of short stories
# Graphic text

TITLE	LEVEL	GENRE	WORD COUNT	AUTHOR / SERIES	PUBLISHER / DISTRIBUTOR
Hip Hop Dancing	S	I	250+	Dance	Capstone Press
Hippo from Another Planet	M	F	250+	Little Celebrations	Pearson Learning Group
Hippo in June's Tub, A	H	F	85	Little Books	Sadlier-Oxford
Hippo Lesson	T	RF	8031	Reading Street	Pearson
Hippo Pot and Hippo Tot	G	F	88	Supersonics	Rigby
Hippocrates: Making the Way for Medicine	T	B	250+	Science Readers	Teacher Created Materials
Hippopotamus Ate the Teacher, A	J	F	250+	Thaler, Mike	Avon
Hippos	O	I	1595	Early Bird Nature Books	Lerner Publications
Hippos	U	I	5579	Nature Watch Books	Lerner Publications
Hippos	K	I	250+	PM Animal Facts: Turquoise	Rigby
Hippos	H	I	394	Sails	Rigby
Hippos	H	I	117	Story Steps	Rigby
Hippo's Hiccups	G	F	208	Literacy 2000	Rigby
Hiram Fong, Hawaii's First Senator	S	B	1726	Leveled Readers Social Studies	Houghton Mifflin Harcourt
Hiroshima	S	HF	250+	Yep, Laurence	Scholastic
His Majesty the King	J	F	250+	Little Celebrations	Pearson Learning Group
Hispaniola: Island of Two Nations	T	I	1871	Independent Readers Social Studies	Houghton Mifflin Harcourt
Historic Santa Fe Trail, The	V	I	2546	Vocabulary Readers	Houghton Mifflin Harcourt
Historic Santa Fe Trail, The	V	I	2546	Vocabulary Readers/CA	Houghton Mifflin Harcourt
Historic Santa Fe Trail, The	V	I	2546	Vocabulary Readers/TX	Houghton Mifflin Harcourt
History Behind the Holidays	N	I	250+	Early Connections	Benchmark Education
History Nook, The	O	SF	250+	Phonics and Friends	Hampton-Brown
History of Baseball	S	I	1203	Time for Kids	Teacher Created Materials
History of Bread, The	P	I	951	Springboard	Wright Group/ McGraw Hill
History of Electricity, A	S	I	794	Leveled Readers Science	Houghton Mifflin Harcourt
History of Firefighting, The	T	I	2304	Leveled Readers	Houghton Mifflin Harcourt
History of Firefighting, The	T	I	2304	Leveled Readers/CA	Houghton Mifflin Harcourt
History of Guitars, The	S	I	250+	Literacy by Design	Rigby
History of Guitars, The	S	I	250+	On Our Way to English	Rigby
History of Hip-Hop, A: The Roots of Rap	R	I	250+	High Five Reading	Red Brick Learning
History of Machines, The	O	I	250+	Home Connection Collection	Rigby
History of Money	S	I	250+	Time for Kids	Teacher Created Materials
History of Money, The	N	I	515	Gear Up!	Wright Group/McGraw Hill
History of Pirates, The: From Privateers to Outlaws	T	I	250+	The Real World of Pirates	Capstone Press
History of School	R	I	1249	Time for Kids	Teacher Created Materials
History of the Blues, The	S	I	250+	Rosen Real Readers	Rosen Publishing Group
History of the Flu, A	R	I	250+	High-Fliers	Pacific Learning
History of the Fur Trade	V	I	2295	Leveled Readers	Houghton Mifflin Harcourt
History of the Fur Trade	V	I	2295	Leveled Readers/CA	Houghton Mifflin Harcourt
History of the Fur Trade	V	I	2200	Leveled Readers/TX	Houghton Mifflin Harcourt
History Walk	M	RF	250+	Pacific Literacy	Pacific Learning
Hit and Run	Z	RF	250+	Misfits Inc.	Peachtree
Hit By a Blade	K	RF	250+	Foundations	Wright Group/McGraw Hill
Hit Squad	Z+	RF	250+	Orca Soundings	Orca Book Publishers
Hit the Beach	N	RF	250+	Boyz Rule!	Mondo
Hit-Away Kid, The	M	RF	250+	Christopher, Matt	Little, Brown & Co.
Hitler's Daughter	W	RF	250+	French, Jackie	Scholastic
Hitmen Triumph	V	RF	250+	Orca Sports	Orca Book Publishers
Hitty: Her First Hundred Years	U	F	250+	Field, Rachel	Aladdin
Hiyomi and the Moon Men	S	HF	250+	Orbit Chapter Books	Pacific Learning
HMMWV Humvee, The	U	I	250+	Cross-Sections	Capstone Press

H

* Collection of short stories
# Graphic text

TITLE	LEVEL	GENRE	WORD COUNT	AUTHOR / SERIES	PUBLISHER / DISTRIBUTOR
*Ho Yi the Archer and Other Classic Chinese Tales	X	TL	250+	Fu, Shelley	Linnet Books
Ho, Ho, Benjamin, Feliz Navidad	N	RF	250+	Giff, Patricia Reilly	Bantam
Hoang Anh: A Vietnamese-American Boy	T	B	250+	Hoyt-Goldsmith, Diane	Scholastic
Hoaxes	Z	I	6559	The Unexplained	Lerner Publications
Hobbit, The	Z	F	250+	Tolkien, J.R.R.	Ballantine Books
Hobby: The Young Merlin Trilogy	V	F	250+	Yolen, Jane	Scholastic
Hobnob the Troll	H	F	165	Supersonics	Rigby
Hobson Family Vacation, The	H	RF	250+	Momentum Literacy Program	Troll Associates
Hockey for Fun!	S	I	250+	Sports for Fun	Compass Point Books
Hockey Machine, The	S	RF	250+	Christopher, Matt	Norwood House Press
Hockey Practice	G	RF	134	Geddes, Diana	Kaeden Books
Hocus Pocus	M	I	250+	Wildcats	Wright Group/McGraw Hill
Hocus-Pocus Hound	M	F	250+	I Am Reading	Kingfisher
Hofus the Stonecutter	N	TL	250+	Literacy by Design	Rigby
Hogboggit, The	D	RF	65	Pacific Literacy	Pacific Learning
Hoiho's Chicks	D	I	38	Pacific Literacy	Pacific Learning
Hoketichee and the Manatee	I	RF	113	Books for Young Learners	Richard C. Owen
Hold on Tight!	B	I	60	Sails	Rigby
Hole in Harry's Pocket, The	I	RF	250+	Little Readers	Houghton Mifflin Harcourt
Hole in the Garden, The	G	RF	277	Sails	Rigby
Hole in the Hedge, The	F	F	188	Sunshine	Wright Group/McGraw Hill
Hole in the Hill, The	N	RF	250+	Action Packs	Rigby
Hole in the Tub, The	F	F	174	The Story Basket	Wright Group/McGraw Hill
Hole Is a Great Home, A	F	RF	236	Phonics and Friends	Hampton-Brown
Hole, The	A	F	24	Sails	Rigby
Holes	V	RF	250+	Sachar, Louis	Random House
Holiday Howlers: Jokes for Punny Parties!	O	F	1701	Make Me Laugh!	Lerner Publications
Holiday!: Celebration Days Around the World	L	I	250+	DK Readers	DK Publishing
Holidays	I	I	195	Time for Kids	Teacher Created Materials
Holidays	C	I	23	We Are Alike and Different	Lerner Publishing
Holidays	J	I	191	Windows on Literacy	National Geographic
Holidays at Our Home	I	RF	88	Leveled Readers Social Studies	Houghton Mifflin Harcourt
Hollow Log, The	J	RF	361	Leveled Readers	Houghton Mifflin Harcourt
Hollow Log, The	J	RF	361	Leveled Readers/CA	Houghton Mifflin Harcourt
Holly & Mac	N	RF	250+	SupaDoopers	Sundance
Holly's Surprise	C	RF	50	Adams, Lorraine; Bruvold, Lynn	Eagle Crest Books
Hollywood Special Effects	V	I	2667	Reading Street	Pearson
Holocaust Rescuers	Y	I	1941	Reading Street	Pearson
Holy Enchilada!	R	RF	250+	Winkler, Henry and Oliver, Lin	Grosset & Dunlap
Home	M	RF	250+	Voyages	SRA/McGraw Hill
Home at Last	D	F	94	Sun Sprouts	ETA Cuisenaire
Home at Mount Vernon, A	W	I	2941	Leveled Readers	Houghton Mifflin Harcourt
Home at Mount Vernon, A	W	I	2941	Leveled Readers/CA	Houghton Mifflin Harcourt
Home at Mount Vernon, A	W	I	2941	Leveled Readers/TX	Houghton Mifflin Harcourt
Home Crafts	T	I	250+	Historic Communities	Crabtree
Home for a Dog, A	G	RF	146	Book Bus	Creative Edge
Home for a Puppy	G	RF	194	First Start	Troll Associates
Home for Curly, A	A	F	30	Rigby Star	Rigby
Home for Diggory, A	K	RF	250+	Pacific Literacy	Pacific Learning
Home for Flap the Cat, A	E	RF	100	Reading Street	Pearson
Home for Humans in Outer Space, A: Is It Possible?	U	I	1989	Reading Street	Pearson
Home for Little Teddy, A	D	F	153	PM Extensions-Red	Rigby

H

TITLE	LEVEL	GENRE	WORD COUNT	AUTHOR / SERIES	PUBLISHER / DISTRIBUTOR
Home for Mindy, A	H	I	250+	Rigby Literacy	Rigby
Home for Star and Patches, A	J	RF	250+	PM Plus Story Books	Rigby
Home for the Howl-idays	S	F	250+	Regan, Diane Curtis	Scholastic
Home Green Home	U	I	250+	Literacy by Design	Rigby
Home in the Sky	K	RF	250+	Baker, Jeannie	Scholastic
Home in the Wilderness, A	O	HF	948	Reading Street	Pearson
Home Invasion	Z+	RF	250+	Orca Soundings	Orca Book Publishers
Home of the Brave	W	RF	250+	Applegate, Katherine	Feiwel and Friends
Home of the Brave	R	I	958	Reading Street	Pearson
Home of the Braves	Z+	RF	250+	Klass, David	HarperCollins
Home on the Range	P	I	851	Reading Street	Pearson
Home Run!	B	RF	42	Peters, Catherine	Scholastic
Home Run, The	E	RF	92	Teacher's Choice Series	Pearson Learning Group
Home Sweet Home	G	F	299	Leveled Literacy Intervention/ Green System	Heinemann
Home Sweet Home	N	I	250+	Literacy 2000	Rigby
Home Sweet Home	T	RF	250+	Reading Expeditions	National Geographic
Home Sweet Home	I	F	250+	Rigby Rocket	Rigby
Home Sweet Home	E	I	172	Roffey, Maureen	Bodley
Home Sweet Home, Goodbye	R	RF	250+	Stowe, Cynthia	Scholastic
Home Technology	O	I	250+	Bookweb	Rigby
Home Then and Now	I	I	110	Then and Now	Lerner Publications
Home, A	D	I	40	Instant Readers	Harcourt School Publishers
Home, A	LB	F	12	Sails	Rigby
Home: A Journey Through America	R	I	250+	Locker, Thomas	Voyager Books
Home-Alone Kids	S	I	250+	Rigby Literacy	Rigby
Homecoming	X	RF	250+	Voigt, Cynthia	Ballantine Books
Homegirl on the Range (Sister Sister)	S	RF	250+	Quin-Harkin, Janet	Pocket Books
Homeless Bird	X	RF	250+	Whelan, Gloria	HarperCollins
*Homer Price	Q	RF	250+	McCloskey, Robert	Puffin/Penguin
Home-Run King, The	O	B	856	Leveled Readers	Houghton Mifflin Harcourt
Home-Run King, The	O	B	856	Leveled Readers/CA	Houghton Mifflin Harcourt
Home-Run King, The	O	B	856	Leveled Readers/TX	Houghton Mifflin Harcourt
Homes	C	I	34	Basic Human Needs	Lerner Publishing
Homes	B	I	63	Bookshop	Mondo
Homes	A	I	35	Handprints A	Educators Publishing Service
Homes	C	I	90	Leveled Literacy Intervention/ Green System	Heinemann
Homes	D	I	42	Rise & Shine	Hampton-Brown
Homes	C	I	69	Storyteller Nonfiction	Wright Group/McGraw Hill
Homes	I	I	244	Yellow Umbrella Books	Red Brick Learning
Homes Are for Living	M	I	417	Cumpiano, Ina	Hampton-Brown
Homes Around the World	C	I	73	Early Connections	Benchmark Education
Homes Around the World	D	I	41	iOpeners	Pearson Learning Group
Homes Around the World	I	I	192	Rigby Focus	Rigby
Homes Around the World	J	I	294	Time for Kids	Teacher Created Materials
Homes for People	B	I	40	Early Connections	Benchmark Education
Homes in Many Cultures	I	I	98	Life Around the World	Capstone Press
Homes on Wheels	M	I	788	Rigby Flying Colors	Rigby
Homes Through Time	N	I	755	Rigby Flying Colors	Rigby
Homesick, My Own Story	X	B	250+	Fritz, Jean	Penguin Group
Homesteaders in Nebraska	T	HF	4356	Reading Street	Pearson
Hometown Turtles	P	RF	1175	Leveled Readers	Houghton Mifflin Harcourt

* Collection of short stories
# Graphic text

TITLE	LEVEL	GENRE	WORD COUNT	AUTHOR / SERIES	PUBLISHER / DISTRIBUTOR
Homework	F	RF	57	City Stories	Rigby
Homework	E	RF	154	Emergent Set 4	Pioneer Valley
Homework Machine, The	R	RF	250+	Gutman, Dan	Aladddin Paperbacks
Honest-to-Goodness Truth, The	O	RF	250+	McKissack, Fredrick & Patricia	Aladddin Paperbacks
Honesty	L	I	250+	Character Education	Red Brick Learning
Honesty	L	I	250+	Everyday Character Education	Capstone Press
Honey Bees	D	I	61	Honeybees	Capstone Press
Honey Bees	M	I	250+	Kahkonen, Sharon	Steck-Vaughn
Honey Bees and Flowers	G	I	67	Honeybees	Capstone Press
Honey Bees and Hives	E	I	58	Honeybees	Capstone Press
Honey Bees and Honey	F	I	57	Honeybees	Capstone Press
Honey for Baby Bear	F	F	200	PM Story Books	Rigby
Honey for Wolf	I	F	246	Sun Sprouts	ETA Cuisenaire
Honey Hunt	E	RF	63	Sunshine	Wright Group/McGraw Hill
Honey Tree, The	L	F	250+	Literacy 2000	Rigby
Honey, Honey	E	F	53	Sails	Rigby
Honey, My Rabbit	E	RF	56	Voyages	SRA/McGraw Hill
Honeybees	L	I	379	Leveled Readers	Houghton Mifflin Harcourt
Honeybees	L	I	379	Leveled Readers/CA	Houghton Mifflin Harcourt
Honeybees	L	I	379	Leveled Readers/TX	Houghton Mifflin Harcourt
Honk!	B	F	36	Bookshop	Mondo
Honolulu, Hawaii	Q	I	250+	Theme Sets	National Geographic
Honorable Prison, The	W	HF	250+	Becerra de Jenkins, Lyll	Penguin Group
Honus & Me	T	F	250+	Gutman, Dan	Harper Trophy
Hoofprints	D	RF	62	Teacher's Choice Series	Pearson Learning Group
Hoop Dancers	L	I	250+	Phonics and Friends	Hampton-Brown
Hoops	X	RF	250+	Myers, Walter Dean	Bantam
Hoops and Me	K	RF	929	Books for Young Learners	Richard C. Owen
Hoops!	L	RF	250+	On Our Way to English	Rigby
Hoopstars: Go to the Hoop!	M	RF	250+	Hughes, Dean	Random House
Hooray for Hollywood	U	I	1725	Vocabulary Readers	Houghton Mifflin Harcourt
Hooray for Hollywood	U	I	1725	Vocabulary Readers/CA	Houghton Mifflin Harcourt
Hooray for Midsommar!	J	RF	250+	Greetings	Rigby
Hooray for Snail	F	F	102	Stadler, John	HarperCollins
Hooray for Snow	D	RF	15	Voyages	SRA/McGraw Hill
Hooray for the Golly Sisters!	K	RF	250+	Byars, Betsy	HarperTrophy
Hoot	W	RF	250+	Hiaasen, Carl	Alfred A. Knopf
Hoover Dam	N	I	934	Pair-It Turn and Learn	Steck-Vaughn
Hop and Stop	C	RF	35	Books for Young Learners	Richard C. Owen
Hop In!	D	F	23	Small-Gamby, Julie	Scholastic
Hop on Pop	J	F	250+	Seuss, Dr.	Random House
Hop on Top!	C	F	42	Reading Street	Pearson
Hop to it, Minty!	O	RF	250+	PM Collection	Rigby
Hop! Spring! Leap! Animals That Jump	H	I	150+	Bayrock, Fiona	Scholastic
Hop, Hop, Hop	B	F	51	Leveled Literacy Intervention/ Orange System	Heinemann
Hop, Skip, and Jump	A	RF	22	Cherrington, Janelle	Scholastic
Hop, Skip, Run	E	RF	109	Real Kids Readers	Millbrook Press
Hope Not	D	RF	83	Salem, Lynn; Stewart, Josie	Continental Press
Hope Was Here	W	RF	250+	Bauer, Joan	G.P. Putnam's Sons
Hopes and Dreams: A Story from Northern Thailand	S	RF	250+	Reading Expeditions	National Geographic
Hopeville Book of Records, The	L	RF	250+	Rigby Gigglers	Rigby
Hopi, The	P	I	250+	Native Peoples	Red Brick Learning

TITLE	LEVEL	GENRE	WORD COUNT	AUTHOR / SERIES	PUBLISHER / DISTRIBUTOR
Hopi, The	S	I	250+	The Heinle Reading Library	Thomson Learning
Hopping Henry	O	F	1216	Leveled Readers	Houghton Mifflin Harcourt
Hopping Henry	O	F	1216	Leveled Readers/CA	Houghton Mifflin Harcourt
Hopping Henry	O	F	1216	Leveled Readers/TX	Houghton Mifflin Harcourt
Hopscotch	P	I	250+	Games Around the World	Compass Point Books
Hopscotch	D	F	61	Reading Street	Pearson
Horace	D	F	56	Story Box	Wright Group/McGraw Hill
Horace's Home Helpers	K	RF	250+	Windows on Literacy	National Geographic
Horacio's Hiccups	G	RF	205	In Step Readers	Rigby
Horatio Whale	J	F	165	Book Bus	Creative Edge
Horned Dinosaurs	P	I	967	Meet the Dinosaurs	Lerner Publications
Hornets: Incredible Insect Architects	T	I	3366	Insect World	Lerner Publications
Horns	C	I	102	Sails	Rigby
Horns, Scales, Claws, and Tales	I	I	208	Story Steps	Rigby
*Horrakapotchkin	M	F	250+	Pacific Literacy	Pacific Learning
Horrible Big Black Bug, The	D	RF	50	Tadpoles	Rigby
Horrible Harry and the Ant Invasion	L	RF	250+	Kline, Suzy	Scholastic
Horrible Harry and the Christmas Surprise	L	RF	250+	Kline, Suzy	Scholastic
Horrible Harry and the Drop of Doom	L	RF	250+	Kline, Suzy	Puffin/Penguin
Horrible Harry and the Dungeon	L	RF	250+	Kline, Suzy	Penguin Group
Horrible Harry and the Green Slime	L	RF	250+	Kline, Suzy	Penguin Group
Horrible Harry and the Kickball Wedding	L	RF	250+	Kline, Suzy	Penguin Group
Horrible Harry and the Purple People	L	F	250+	Kline, Suzy	Puffin/Penguin
Horrible Harry in Room 2B	L	RF	250+	Kline, Suzy	Penguin Group
Horrible Harry Moves Up to Third Grade	L	RF	250+	Kline, Suzy	Puffin/Penguin
Horrible Harry's Secret	L	RF	250+	Kline, Suzy	Penguin Group
Horrible Thing with Hairy Feet	H	TL	208	Read Alongs	Rigby
Horrible Urktar of Or, The	G	F	143	Sunshine	Wright Group/McGraw Hill
Horrie the Hoarder	K	RF	250+	Voyages	SRA/McGraw Hill
Horrors of the Haunted Museum	Q	RF	250+	Stine, R. L.	Scholastic
Horse	W	I	250+	Eyewitness Books	DK Publishing
Horse	M	I	250+	Life Cycles	Creative Teaching Press
Horse and His Boy, The	T	F	250+	Lewis, C. S.	Collier Books
Horse and the Bell, The	J	TL	250+	PM Plus Story Books	Rigby
*Horse and the Donkey, The	I	F	382	New Way Green	Steck-Vaughn
Horse Called Sky, A	M	RF	250+	Leveled Readers Language Support	Houghton Mifflin Harcourt
Horse Feathers	D	I	41	Pair-It Books	Steck-Vaughn
Horse Heroes: True Stories of Amazing Horses	S	I	250+	DK Readers	DK Publishing
Horse in Harry's Room, The	J	F	425	Hoff, Syd	HarperCollins
Horse in the House, A	Q	I	250+	Ablow, Gail	Candlewick Press
Horse Power	S	RF	250+	Orca Currents	Orca Book Publishers
Horse Power	O	I	250+	Pacific Literacy	Pacific Learning
Horse Rescue!	K	I	344	Reading Street	Pearson
Horse, of Course, The	Q	I	250+	Action Packs	Rigby
Horseback Riding for Fun!	S	I	250+	Activities for Fun	Compass Point Books
Horsepower	Q	I	250+	InfoQuest	Rigby
Horses	N	I	250+	A New True Book	Children's Press
Horses	D	I	43	All About Pets	Red Brick Learning
Horses	R	I	250+	Boldprint	Steck-Vaughn
Horses	P	I	250+	Crabapples	Crabtree
Horses	O	I	2279	Early Bird Nature Books	Lerner Publications
Horses	E	I	104	Nonfiction Set 4	Literacy Footprints
Horses	E	I	131	Pebble Books	Capstone Press

H

TITLE	LEVEL	GENRE	WORD COUNT	AUTHOR / SERIES	PUBLISHER / DISTRIBUTOR
Horses	L	I	250+	PM Animal Facts: Purple	Rigby
Horses	K	I	417	Springboard	Wright Group/ McGraw Hill
Horses	L	I	438	Time for Kids	Teacher Created Materials
Horses	F	I	131	Twig	Wright Group/McGraw Hill
Horses Have Foals	M	I	250+	Animals and Their Young	Compass Point Books
Horse's Hiccups	F	F	83	Storyteller-Moon Rising	Wright Group/McGraw Hill
Horses' Holiday	J	F	302	Big Cat	Pacfic Learning
Horses in North America	R	I	1007	Vocabulary Readers	Houghton Mifflin Harcourt
Horses in North America	R	I	1007	Vocabulary Readers/CA	Houghton Mifflin Harcourt
Horses in North America	R	I	1007	Vocabulary Readers/TX	Houghton Mifflin Harcourt
Horses of the Air	N	I	250+	Little Celebrations	Pearson Learning Group
Horses of the Sea	P	I	250+	Lighthouse	Ginn & Co.
Horses of the Sea	P	I	250+	Rigby Literacy	Rigby
Horses on the Farm	I	I	120	Pebble Books	Red Brick Learning
Horsing Around	N	RF	250+	Girlz Rock!	Mondo
Horsing Around	S	I	250+	WorldScapes	ETA Cuisenaire
Horsing Around: Jokes to Make Ewe Smile	O	F	1667	Make Me Laugh!	Lerner Publications
Hospital Party, The	H	RF	237	PM Plus Story Books	Rigby
Hospitals	L	I	177	Bookshop	Mondo
Hostile Hospital, The	V	F	250+	Snicket, Lemony	Scholastic
Hosting Grandpa Joseph	O	RF	1424	Reading Street	Pearson
Hot Air Balloons	L	I	479	Pair-It Books	Steck-Vaughn
Hot and Cold	F	I	219	Sails	Rigby
Hot and Cold	C	I	47	Windows on Literacy	National Geographic
Hot and Cold Summer	O	RF	250+	Hurwitz, Johanna	Scholastic
Hot and Cold Weather	K	I	922	Sunshine	Wright Group/McGraw Hill
Hot Chocolate for Sale	H	F	242	Gear Up!	Wright Group/McGraw Hill
Hot Competition	R	RF	250+	Story Surfers	ETA Cuisenaire
Hot Day at the Farm	H	F	321	Springboard	Wright Group/McGraw Hill
Hot Day, A	C	RF	86	Handprints B	Educators Publishing Service
Hot Day, A	E	I	61	Pebble Books	Capstone Press
Hot Day, The	N	RF	647	Leveled Literacy Intervention/ Blue System	Heinemann
Hot Dogs	I	RF	196	City Kids	Rigby
Hot Dogs (Sausages)	C	RF	84	PM Story Books	Rigby
Hot Fudge Hero	L	RF	250+	Brisson, Pat	Henry Holt & Co.
Hot Iron: The Adventure of a Civil War Powder Boy	T	HF	250+	Burgan, Michael	Stone Arch Books
Hot Moose Stew	H	RF	251	Adams, Lorraine; Bruvold, Lynn	Eagle Crest Books
Hot or Cold?	F	I	106	Yellow Umbrella Books	Red Brick Learning
Hot Potato and Cold Potato	C	I	77	Foundations	Wright Group/McGraw Hill
Hot Rod Harry	E	RF	66	Rookie Readers	Children's Press
Hot Rods	M	I	250+	Horsepower	Capstone Press
Hot Rods	W	I	6714	Motor Mania	Lerner Publications
Hot Sidewalks	C	RF	28	Visions	Wright Group/McGraw Hill
Hot Stuff to Help Kids Cheer Up: The Depression and Self-Esteem Workbook	X	I	13200	Wilde, Ph.D., Jerry	Sourcebooks
Hot Sunny Days	F	I	122	PM Plus Nonfiction	Rigby
Hot Surprise, A	H	RF	162	Rigby Literacy	Rigby
Hot-Air Balloon Day	F	I	115	Springboard	Wright Group/McGraw Hill
Hottest Week in Sun City, The	I	F	250+	Reading Safari	Mondo
Houdini's Last Trick	O	B	250+	Hass, Elizabeth	Random House
Hound of Rowan, The: The Tapestry Book I	X	F	250+	Neff, Henry H.	Random House

H

TITLE	LEVEL	GENRE	WORD COUNT	AUTHOR / SERIES	PUBLISHER / DISTRIBUTOR
Hound of the Baskervilles, The	T	HF	250+	Doyle, Sir Arthur Conan	Stone Arch Books
Houndsley and Catina	K	F	250+	Howe, James	Candlewick Press
Houndsley and Catina and the Birthday Surprise	K	F	250+	Howe, James	Candlewick Press
Houndsley and Catina and the Quiet Time	K	F	250+	Howe, James	Candlewick Press
Hour of the Olympics	M	F	250+	Osborne, Mary Pope	Random House
House	WB	I	N/A	Felix, Monique	Stewart, Tabori & Chang
House	C	I	47	Little Celebrations	Pearson Learning Group
House Book, The	LB	I	17	Windows on Literacy	National Geographic
House Called Awful End, A	U	F	250+	Ardagh, Philip	Scholastic
House Cleaning	LB	RF	19	Book Bank	Wright Group/McGraw Hill
House for a Mouse, A	E	F	182	On Our Way to English	Rigby
House for a Mouse, A	LB	RF	21	Pacific Literacy	Pacific Learning
House for a Mouse, A	E	F	124	Sails	Rigby
House for Hickory, A	H	F	174	Bookshop	Mondo
House for Little Red	F	RF	78	Just Beginning	Pearson Learning Group
House for Little Red, A	E	RF	283	Easy Stories	Norwood House Press
House for Me, A	C	I	71	Twig	Wright Group/McGraw Hill
House for My Fish, A	D	RF	34	Reading Street	Pearson
House for Sergin, A	M	RF	250+	Greetings	Rigby
House for Squirrel, A	C	F	55	Bonnell, Kris	Reading Reading Books
House for the Alien, A	C	F	158	Sails	Rigby
House Gobbaleen, The	P	F	250+	Alexander, Lloyd	Penguin Group
House Hunting	G	RF	223	PM Story Books	Rigby
House in the Snow, The	S	RF	250+	Engh, M. J.	Scholastic
House in the Tree, The	F	RF	202	PM Story Books	Rigby
House of Dies Drear	V	HF	250+	Hamilton, Virginia	Aladdin
House of History	N	I	470	Pair-It Turn and Learn	Steck-Vaughn
House of Mirrors, The	M	F	250+	Take Two Books	Wright Group/McGraw Hill
House of Power, The	U	F	250+	Carman, Patrick	Little, Brown & Co.
House of Stairs	Z	F	250+	Sleator, William	Puffin/Penguin
House of the Horrible Ghosts	M	F	250+	Hayes, Geoffrey	Random House
House of the Scorpion, The	Y	SF	250+	Farmer, Nancy	Simon Pulse
House of the Scorpion, The	Z+	SF	250+	Farmer, Nancy	Simon & Schuster
House of Wings, The	R	RF	250+	Byars, Betsy	Penguin Group
House on Mango Street, The	W	RF	250+	Cisneros, Sandra	Alfred A. Knopf
House on the Hill, The	F	F	189	PM Plus Story Books	Rigby
House on Walenska Street, The	N	RF	250+	Herman, Charlotte	Penguin Group
House Party	Z+	RF	250+	Orca Soundings	Orca Book Publishers
House Sitters, The	G	RF	211	Sails	Rigby
House Spider's Life, A	K	I	230	Himmelman, John	Scholastic
House that Jack Built, The	I	TL	201	Cat on the Mat	Oxford University Press
House that Jack Built, The	J	TL	250+	Peppe, Rodney	Delacorte Press
House that Jack's Friends Built, The	J	RF	254	Pair-It Books	Steck-Vaughn
House that Stood on Booker Hill, The	J	RF	250+	Ready Readers	Pearson Learning Group
House Through the Ages	U	I	250+	Steele, Philip	Troll Associates
House with a Clock in its Walls, The	S	F	250+	Bellairs, John	Penguin Group
House with No Name, The	Q	F	4864	Goodhart, P.	Stone Arch Books
House, A	A	I	32	PM Starters	Rigby
House, A	A	F	30	Sails	Rigby
Houses	G	I	51	Learn to Read	Creative Teaching Press
Houses	C	I	35	Little Celebrations	Pearson Learning Group
Houses	B	I	64	Rigby Literacy	Rigby
Houses	C	I	64	Story Box	Wright Group/McGraw Hill

H

* Collection of short stories
# Graphic text

TITLE	LEVEL	GENRE	WORD COUNT	AUTHOR / SERIES	PUBLISHER / DISTRIBUTOR
Houses	C	RF	38	Windmill Books	Wright Group/McGraw Hill
Houses	I	I	103	Windows on Literacy	National Geographic
Houses	M	I	279	Wonder World	Wright Group/McGraw Hill
Houses and Homes	G	RF	250+	PM Plus Poetry	Rigby
Houses That Move	K	I	250+	Voyages	SRA/McGraw Hill
Houses, Then and Now	L	I	407	Take Two Books	Wright Group/ McGraw Hill
Houses: Past and Present	Q	I	1751	Reading Street	Pearson
Houston Astros, The	S	I	250+	Team Spirit	Norwood House Press
Houston Texans, The	S	I	250+	Team Spirit	Norwood House Press
Hovercrafts	M	I	250+	Horsepower	Capstone Press
Hovering Hummingbirds	K	I	407	Pull Ahead Books	Lerner Publications
How 100 Dandelions Grew	E	I	173	Instant Readers	Harcourt School Publishers
How a Book Gets Published	S	I	1765	Vocabulary Readers	Houghton Mifflin Harcourt
How a Book Gets Published	S	I	1765	Vocabulary Readers/CA	Houghton Mifflin Harcourt
How a Book Is Made	N	I	250+	Aliki	Harper & Row
How a Butterfly Farm Works	J	I	392	Sun Sprouts	ETA Cuisenaire
How a Frog Grows	I	I	136	Phonics Readers	Compass Point Books
How a House Is Built	M	I	250+	Gibbons, Gail	Scholastic
How a Plant Grows	O	I	250+	Kalman, Bobbie	Crabtree
How a Seed Grows	J	I	250+	Let's Read and Find Out About	HarperCollins
How a Volcano Is Formed	M	I	135	Wonder World	Wright Group/McGraw Hill
How Advertising Works: The Amazing Adventures of the GOB Mob and the Gang From OWW!	U	I	250+	Bookshop	Mondo
*How Angel Peterson Got His Name: And Other Outrageous Tales About Extreme Sports	U	RF	250+	Paulsen, Gary	Random House
How Animals Change: The Interaction of Animals and Scientists	U	I	250+	Reading Street	Pearson
How Animals Hide	F	I	98	Wonder World	Wright Group/McGraw Hill
How Animals Move	L	I	250+	Animal Behavior	Capstone Press
How Animals Move	G	I	132	Discovery Links	Newbridge
How Animals Move	L	I	132	Discovery World	Rigby
How Animals Move	J	I	401	Leveled Readers	Houghton Mifflin Harcourt
How Animals Move	J	I	401	Leveled Readers/CA	Houghton Mifflin Harcourt
How Animals Move	J	I	401	Leveled Readers/TX	Houghton Mifflin Harcourt
How Animals Move	M	I	700	Springboard	Wright Group/McGraw Hill
How Animals Move Around	L	I	593	PM Plus Nonfiction	Rigby
How Ants Live	I	I	159	Sunshine	Wright Group/McGraw Hill
How Are Magnets Used?	I	I	166	Windows on Literacy	National Geographic
How Are We the Same?	D	I	100	Teacher's Choice Series	Pearson Learning Group
How Barbed Wire Changed the West	V	I	3269	Leveled Readers	Houghton Mifflin Harcourt
How Barbed Wire Changed the West	V	I	3269	Leveled Readers/CA	Houghton Mifflin Harcourt
How Barbed Wire Changed the West	V	I	3269	Leveled Readers/TX	Houghton Mifflin Harcourt
How Bat Learned to Fly	H	TL	168	Storyteller-Night Crickets	Wright Group/McGraw Hill
How Bear Lost His Tail	K	TL	492	Leveled Literacy Intervention/ Blue System	Heinemann
How Ben Franklin Stole the Lightning	R	B	250+	Schanzer, Rosalyn	HarperCollins
How Beth Feels	I	RF	272	Reading Street	Pearson
How Big Is a Foot?	K	F	250+	Myller, Rolf	Bantam
How Big Is Big?	F	I	158	Ziefert, Harriet	Puffin/Penguin
How Big Is It?	J	RF	250+	Lighthouse	Rigby
How Big? How Much?	H	I	134	Hutchins, Jeannie	Scholastic
How Birds Live	I	I	1090	Sunshine	Wright Group/McGraw Hill
How Bizarre	R	I	250+	Orbit Collections	Pacific Learning

H

TITLE	LEVEL	GENRE	WORD COUNT	AUTHOR / SERIES	PUBLISHER / DISTRIBUTOR
How Bullfrog Found His Sound	M	F	250+	Michaels, Eric	Pearson Learning Group
How Can I Help?	E	RF	73	Learn to Read	Creative Teaching Press
How Can I Help?	D	I	65	Questions & Answers	Pearson Learning Group
How Can We See in the Dark?	H	I	157	Sunshine	Wright Group/McGraw Hill
How Can You Fix It?	B	I	56	Rigby Literacy	Rigby
How Chocolate Is Made	L	I	250+	Lighthouse	Rigby
How Could You?	Q	I	250+	Kids Talk	Picture Window Books
How Coyote Stole Fire	K	TL	544	Leveled Readers	Houghton Mifflin Harcourt
How Coyote Stole Fire	K	TL	544	Leveled Readers/CA	Houghton Mifflin Harcourt
How Coyote Stole Fire	K	TL	544	Leveled Readers/TX	Houghton Mifflin Harcourt
How Coyote Stole the Summer	N	TL	1653	On My Own Folklore	Millbrook Press
How Did Ancient Greece Get So Great?	Y	I	2402	Reading Street	Pearson
How Did the Lights Go Out? The Story of the New York City Blackout	R	I	1175	Independent Readers Science	Houghton Mifflin Harcourt
How Did They Do That?	Q	I	250+	On Our Way to English	Rigby
How Did This City Grow?	M	I	250+	Early Connections	Benchmark Education
How Do Airplanes Fly?	Q	I	250+	Rosen Real Readers	Rosen Publishing Group
How Do Animals Stay Alive?	I	I	193	Early Connections	Benchmark Education
How Do Dinosaurs Go to School?	J	F	191	Yolen, Jane	The Blue Sky Press
How Do Fish Live?	I	I	1242	Sunshine	Wright Group/McGraw Hill
How Do Flies Walk Upside Down?	R	I	250+	Berger, Melvin & Gilda	Scholastic
How Do Frogs Grow?	G	I	42	Discovery Links	Newbridge
How Do Frogs Swallow with Their Eyes?	R	I	250+	Berger, Melvin	Scholastic
How Do I Become a Firefighter?	P	I	250+	The Heinle Reading Library	Thomson Learning
How Do I Feel?	D	I	64	Questions & Answers	Pearson Learning Group
How Do I Put It On?	H	I	168	Watanabe, Shiego	Penguin Group
How Do Plants Get Food?	L	I	250+	Goldish, Meish	Steck-Vaughn
How Do Plants Grow Here?	K	I	250+	Explorations	Eleanor Curtain Publishing
How Do Plants Grow Here?	K	I	250+	Explorations	Okapi Eductaional Materials
How Do Plants Grow?	L	I	250+	Rosen Real Readers	Rosen Publishing Group
How Do Seeds Travel?	J	I	179	Windows on Literacy	National Geographic
How Do Trees Grow?	L	I	250+	Rosen Real Readers	Rosen Publishing Group
How Do We Use Water?	O	I	250+	Reading Expeditions	National Geographic
How Do You Feel Today?	C	I	71	Gear Up!	Wright Group/McGraw Hill
How Do You Feel Today?	L	I	250+	Rosen Real Readers	Rosen Publishing Group
How Do You Make a Bubble?	G	RF	250+	Hooks, William H.	Bantam
How Do You Measure a Dinosaur?	M	F	257	Pacific Literacy	Pacific Learning
How Do You Move?	J	I	250+	Yellow Umbrella Books	Red Brick Learning
How Do You Say Hello to a Ghost?	F	F	149	Tiger Cub	Peguis
How Do You Sleep?	H	I	188	On Our Way to English	Rigby
How Do Your Lungs Work?	P	I	250+	Rookie Read-About Health	Children's Press
How Does a Plant Grow?	I	I	115	Instant Readers	Harcourt School Publishers
How Does a Tree Help?	B	I	69	Literacy by Design	Rigby
How Does It Breathe?	K	I	250+	Home Connection Collection	Rigby
How Does It Change?	F	I	127	InfoTrek	ETA Cuisenaire
How Does It Feel?	B	I	28	Properties of Matter	Lerner Publications
How Does It Feel?	LB	I	11	Windows on Literacy	National Geographic
How Does It Grow?	L	I	250+	Home Connection Collection	Rigby
How Does It Work?	O	I	694	Big Cat	Pacific Learning
How Does My Bike Work?	J	I	127	Windows on Literacy	National Geographic
How Does My Garden Grow?	H	I	73	Windows on Literacy	National Geographic
How Does Sound Travel?	J	I	148	Instant Readers	Harcourt School Publishers
How Does the Mail Work?	H	I	169	Reading Street	Pearson
How Does This Sound?	L	I	260	Independent Readers Science	Houghton Mifflin Harcourt

* Collection of short stories
\# Graphic text

TITLE	LEVEL	GENRE	WORD COUNT	AUTHOR / SERIES	PUBLISHER / DISTRIBUTOR
How Does Water Change?	J	I	176	Rigby Star Quest	Rigby
How Does Your Garden Grow?	Q	I	250+	PM Extensions	Rigby
How Does Your Salad Grow?	H	I	136	Alexander, Francie	Scholastic
How Dog Lost His Bone	E	TL	100	Leveled Readers Language Support	Houghton Mifflin Harcourt
How Far Is It?	L	I	250+	Rosen Real Readers	Rosen Publishing Group
How Far Will I Fly?	F	RF	94	Oyama, Sachi	Scholastic
How Far Would You Have Gotten If I Hadn't Called You Back?	Z+	RF	250+	Hobbs, Valerie	Scholastic
How Fire Came to Earth	K	TL	250+	Literacy 2000	Rigby
How Flamingos Came to Have Red Legs: A South American Folk Tale	M	TL	250+	Take Two Books	Wright Group/McGraw Hill
How Flexible Are You?	M	I	250+	Take Two Books	Wright Group/McGraw Hill
How Flies Live	I	I	448	Sunshine	Wright Group/McGraw Hill
How Flowers Grow	E	I	68	Rosen Real Readers	Rosen Publishing Group
How Fly Saved the River	J	TL	426	Rigby Flying Colors	Rigby
How Fox Became Red	I	TL	163	Books for Young Learners	Richard C. Owen
How Frogs Grow	G	I	116	Leveled Literacy Intervention/ Green System	Heinemann
*How Glooskap Found Summer and Other Curious Tales	Q	TL	250+	Literacy by Design	Rigby
How Goods Are Moved	K	I	250+	People, Spaces & Places	Rand McNally
How Grandmother Spider Got the Sun	J	TL	115	Little Readers	Houghton Mifflin Harcourt
How Has It Changed?	D	I	103	Rigby Literacy	Rigby
How Have I Grown	G	RF	235	Reid, Mary	Scholastic
How I Came to Be a Writer	W	B	250+	Naylor, Phyllis Reynolds	Scholastic
How I Fixed the Year 1000 Problem	N	F	250+	The Zack Files	Grossett & Dunlap
How I Go	F	I	138	Early Connections	Benchmark Education
How I Met Archie	M	RF	250+	Kenna, Anna	Pacific Learning
How I Met Einstein: A Character Comes to Life	S	I	250+	Orbit Chapter Books	Pacific Learning
How I Move	A	RF	21	Leveled Readers Science	Houghton Mifflin Harcourt
How I Went from Bad to Verse	N	F	250+	The Zack Files	Grossett & Dunlap
How Is a Crayon Made?	P	I	250+	Oz, Charles	Scholastic
How Is a Moose Like a Goose?	I	I	408	Silly Millies	Millbrook Press
How Kittens Grow	L	I	250+	Selsam, Millicent E.	Scholastic
How Leaves Change Color	M	I	250+	Rosen Real Readers	Rosen Publishing Group
How Living Things Help Each Other	I	I	221	Literacy by Design	Rigby
How Lizard Lost His Colors	J	TL	197	Literacy Tree	Rigby
How Lizard Lost His Colors	F	TL	139	Shapiro, Sara	Scholastic
How Long Do Animals Live?	D	I	65	Pacific Literacy	Pacific Learning
How Long Is a Dog's Tail?	H	RF	209	InfoTrek	ETA Cuisenaire
How Long Is a Foot?	M	I	250+	Twig	Wright Group/McGraw Hill
How Long Is a Piece of String?	L	RF	250+	Voyages	SRA/McGraw Hill
How Machines Help	D	I	143	Sunshine	Wright Group/McGraw Hill
How Magic Tricks Work	P	I	250+	PM Extensions	Rigby
How Many Animals?	LB	I	27	Big Cat	Pacific Learning
How Many Animals?	A	I	25	Vocabulary Readers	Houghton Mifflin Harcourt
How Many Ants?	E	RF	35	Rookie Readers	Children's Press
How Many Are Left?	I	I	225	Early Connections	Benchmark Education
How Many Bugs in a Box?	LB	F	126	Carter, David	Simon & Schuster
How Many Can Play?	D	I	46	Canizares, Susan; Chessen, Betsey	Scholastic
How Many Climates Does One Island Need?	R	RF	250+	Pair-It Books	Steck-Vaughn

* Collection of short stories
# Graphic text

TITLE	LEVEL	GENRE	WORD COUNT	AUTHOR / SERIES	PUBLISHER / DISTRIBUTOR
How Many Days to America?: A Thanksgiving Story	S	I	250+	Bunting, Eve	Houghton Mifflin Harcourt
How Many Ducks?	F	F	88	Chapman, Cindy	Scholastic
How Many Ducks?	A	I	22	Vocabulary Readers	Houghton Mifflin Harcourt
How Many Ducks?	A	I	22	Vocabulary Readers/CA	Houghton Mifflin Harcourt
How Many Fish in the Sea?	N	I	250+	Why In the World?	Capstone Press
How Many Fish?	B	F	30	Gosset, Rachel; Ballinger, Margaret	Scholastic
How Many Fish?	F	I	114	Yellow Umbrella Books	Red Brick Learning
How Many Frogs?	C	I	44	Leveled Readers Language Support	Houghton Mifflin Harcourt
How Many Hats?	C	I	57	On Our Way to English	Rigby
How Many Hot Dogs?	E	I	115	Story Box	Wright Group/McGraw Hill
How Many Jelly Beans	B	RF	61	Phonics and Friends	Hampton-Brown
How Many Kisses Do You Want Tonight?	J	F	250+	Bajaj, Varsha	Little, Brown & Co.
How Many Kittens?	C	I	37	Twig	Wright Group/McGraw Hill
How Many Legs?	D	I	74	Bookshop	Mondo
How Many Legs?	E	I	104	Early Connections	Benchmark Education
How Many Legs?	D	I	103	Sails	Rigby
How Many Legs?	C	F	47	Science	Outside the Box
How Many Legs?	B	I	19	Windmill Books	Wright Group/McGraw Hill
How Many Monkeys?	B	F	16	Pair-It Books	Steck-Vaughn
How Many Pennies?	H	I	180	Shutterbug Books	Steck-Vaughn
How Many Pets?	D	RF	37	Bookshop	Mondo
How Many Sandwiches?	K	RF	463	In Step Readers	Rigby
How Many Seeds?	E	I	42	Pair-It Books	Steck-Vaughn
How Many Toes?	B	I	48	Sails	Rigby
How Many?	E	I	147	Early Connections	Benchmark Education
How Many?	C	I	45	Gear Up!	Wright Group/McGraw Hill
How Many?	C	I	45	Learn to Read	Creative Teaching Press
How Many?	B	I	49	Nonfiction Set 2	Literacy Footprints
How Many?	WB	I	N/A	Reading Street	Pearson
How Many?	C	I	39	Windows on Literacy	National Geographic
How Moon Tricked Sun	H	TL	241	Rigby Rocket	Rigby
How Much Can a Bare Bear Bear?: What Are Homonyms and Homophones?	O	I	421	Words Are CATegorical	Millbrook Press
How Much Does It Weigh?	I	I	253	On Our Way to English	Rigby
How Much Does This Hold?	K	RF	179	Coulton, Mia	Kaeden Books
How Much Is a Million?	M	I	250+	Schwartz, David M.	Scholastic
How Much Is That Guinea Pig in the Window?	L	RF	250+	Rocklin, Joanne	Scholastic
How Much Money?	L	I	360	Yellow Umbrella Books	Red Brick Learning
How Music Came to Earth	P	TL	250+	WorldScapes	ETA Cuisenaire
How Music Is Made	K	I	250+	Rigby Star Quest	Rigby
How My Family Lives in America	O	I	250+	Kuklin, Susan	Aladdin
How My Pet Grew	I	RF	235	Leveled Readers Science	Houghton Mifflin Harcourt
How News Travels	M	I	250+	PM Plus Nonfiction	Rigby
How Not to Catch the Moon	N	TL	250+	Storyteller Summer Skies	Wright Group/McGraw Hill
How Owl Changed His Hoot	I	TL	227	Sunshine	Wright Group/McGraw Hill
How People Got Fire	K	TL	580	Leveled Readers	Houghton Mifflin Harcourt
How People Got Fire	K	TL	580	Leveled Readers/CA	Houghton Mifflin Harcourt
How People Got Fire	K	TL	580	Leveled Readers/TX	Houghton Mifflin Harcourt
How People Got Wisdom: An Ashanti Tale	N	TL	891	Leveled Readers	Houghton Mifflin Harcourt
How People Move Around	L	I	541	PM Plus Nonfiction	Rigby
How Plants Grow	F	I	69	Time for Kids	Teacher Created Materials

* Collection of short stories
\# Graphic text

TITLE	LEVEL	GENRE	WORD COUNT	AUTHOR / SERIES	PUBLISHER / DISTRIBUTOR
How Plants Survive	P	I	250+	Science Links	Chelsea Clubhouse
How Smart Are Animals?	U	I	2123	Vocabulary Readers	Houghton Mifflin Harcourt
How Smart Are Animals?	U	I	2123	Vocabulary Readers/CA	Houghton Mifflin Harcourt
How Spider Tricked Snake	K	TL	250+	Real Reading	Steck-Vaughn
How Spiders Catch Their Food	K	I	250+	Explorations	Eleanor Curtain Publishing
How Spiders Catch Their Food	K	I	250+	Explorations	Okapi Eductional Materials
How Spiders Got Eight Legs	L	F	884	Pair-It Books	Steck-Vaughn
How Spiders Live	F	I	145	Sunshine	Wright Group/McGraw Hill
How the Animals Got Their Tails	L	TL	250+	Cambridge Reading	Pearson Learning Group
How the Camel Got His Hump and Other Stories	K	TL	250+	Storyteller- Shooting Stars	Wright Group/McGraw Hill
How the Chick Tricked the Fox	G	F	167	Ready Readers	Pearson Learning Group
How the Dinosaurs Disappeared	L	I	250+	Rosen Real Readers	Rosen Publishing Group
How the Elephant Got His Trunk	J	TL	250+	Rigby Rocket	Rigby
How the Giraffe Became a Giraffe	M	TL	648	Sunshine	Wright Group/McGraw Hill
How the Government Works	S	I	1142	Vocabulary Readers	Houghton Mifflin Harcourt
How the Government Works	S	I	1142	Vocabulary Readers/CA	Houghton Mifflin Harcourt
How the Guinea Fowl Got Her Spots	L	TL	635	Knutson, Barbara	Carolrhoda Books
How the Leaves Got Their Colors	K	F	474	Leveled Readers/TX	Houghton Mifflin Harcourt
How the Mouse Got Brown Teeth	I	F	250+	Bookshop	Mondo
How the Rattlesnake Got Its Rattle	L	TL	1006	Pair-It Books	Steck-Vaughn
How the Sky Got Its Stars	G	TL	208	Instant Readers	Harcourt School Publishers
How the Three Great Mountains Came to Be	N	TL	710	Gear Up!	Wright Group/ McGraw Hill
*How the Tortoise Got His Shell and Other Stories	K	TL	250+	New Way Literature	Steck-Vaughn
How the Walrus Got to the Arctic	Q	TL	250+	Reading Safari	Mondo
How the Water Got to the Plains	L	TL	250+	Home Connection Collection	Rigby
How Things Move	H	I	214	Yellow Umbrella Books	Red Brick Learning
How Things Work	R	I	250+	Explorers	Wright Group/McGraw Hill
How Tia Lola Came to Stay	R	RF	250+	Alvarez, Julia	Yearling
How to Be a Detective	N	RF	4197	Damian Drooth Supersleuth	Stone Arch Books
How to Be a Pirate in 10 Easy Stages	N	F	1077	Big Cat	Pacific Learning
How to Be Cool in the Third Grade	N	RF	250+	Duffey, Betsy	Penguin Group
How to Be Healthy	K	I	250+	Rosen Real Readers	Rosen Publishing Group
How to Be Nice…And Other Lessons I Didn't Learn	Q	RF	250+	Bookshop	Mondo
How to Build a Dinosaur	L	I	457	Pair-It Turn and Learn	Steck-Vaughn
How to Build a Robot	T	I	1660	Leveled Readers	Houghton Mifflin Harcourt
How to Build a Robot	T	I	1660	Leveled Readers/CA	Houghton Mifflin Harcourt
How to Cheat a Dragons's Curse: The Heroic Misadventures of Hiccup the Viking	T	F	250+	Cowell, Cressida	Little, Brown & Co.
How to Choose a Pet	L	I	250+	Discovery World	Rigby
How to Clean a Dinosaur	G	F	208	Windmill Books	Rigby
How to Cook Scones	J	I	250+	Bookshop	Mondo
How to Draw Amazing Motorcycles	Q	I	250+	Drawing Cool Stuff	Capstone Press
How to Draw Cartoons	N	I	944	Big Cat	Pacific Learning
How to Draw Comic Heroes	Q	I	250+	Drawing Cool Stuff	Capstone Press
How to Draw Crazy Fighter Planes	Q	I	250+	Drawing Cool Stuff	Capstone Press
How to Draw Disgusting Aliens	Q	I	250+	Drawing Cool Stuff	Capstone Press
How to Draw Ferocious Animals	Q	I	250+	Drawing Cool Stuff	Capstone Press
How to Draw Ferocious Dinosaurs	Q	I	250+	Drawing Cool Stuff	Capstone Press
How to Draw Grotesque Monsters	Q	I	250+	Drawing Cool Stuff	Capstone Press
How to Draw Incredible Cars	Q	I	250+	Drawing Cool Stuff	Capstone Press
How to Draw Indestructible Tanks	Q	I	250+	Drawing Cool Stuff	Capstone Press

H

* Collection of short stories
# Graphic text

TITLE	LEVEL	GENRE	WORD COUNT	AUTHOR / SERIES	PUBLISHER / DISTRIBUTOR
How to Draw Manga Warriors	Q	I	250+	Drawing Cool Stuff	Capstone Press
How to Draw Monster Trucks	Q	I	250+	Drawing Cool Stuff	Capstone Press
How to Draw Terrifying Robots	Q	I	250+	Drawing Cool Stuff	Capstone Press
How to Draw Unreal Spaceships	Q	I	250+	Drawing Cool Stuff	Capstone Press
How to Eat Fried Worms	R	RF	250+	Rockwell, Thomas	Bantam
How to Grow a Plant	E	I	172	Visions	Wright Group/McGraw Hill
How to Grow Crystals	P	I	250+	Bookshop	Mondo
How to Have a Party	F	I	85	Big Cat	Pacific Learning
How to Help Your Community	P	I	1190	Vocabulary Readers	Houghton Mifflin Harcourt
How to Help Your Community	P	I	1190	Vocabulary Readers/CA	Houghton Mifflin Harcourt
How to Make a Bird Feeder	D	I	80	Rigby Literacy	Rigby
How to Make a Bird Feeder	E	I	84	Rigby Star Quest	Rigby
How to Make a Card	G	I	69	Urmston, Kathleen; Evans, Karen	Kaeden Books
How to Make a Clown Costume	G	I	90	Rigby Rocket	Rigby
How to Make a Crocodile	H	F	62	Little Books	Sadlier-Oxford
How to Make a Family Tree	N	I	929	Leveled Readers	Houghton Mifflin Harcourt
How to Make a Family Tree	N	I	929	Leveled Readers/CA	Houghton Mifflin Harcourt
How to Make a Family Tree	N	I	929	Leveled Readers/TX	Houghton Mifflin Harcourt
How to Make a Hen House	B	I	25	Ready Readers	Pearson Learning Group
How to Make a Hot Dog	C	I	48	Story Box	Wright Group/McGraw Hill
How to Make a Kite	M	I	250+	Take Two Books	Wright Group/McGraw Hill
How to Make a Lion Mask	G	I	133	Instant Readers	Harcourt School Publishers
How to Make a Mud Pie	H	RF	127	Little Readers	Houghton Mifflin Harcourt
How to Make a Mudpie	A	I	32	Learn to Read	Creative Teaching Press
How to Make a Paper Frog	I	I	140	Windows on Literacy	National Geographic
How to Make a Salad	A	I	12	Vocabulary Readers	Houghton Mifflin Harcourt
How to Make a Sandwich	C	I	27	Visions	Wright Group/McGraw Hill
How to Make a Scarecrow	WB	I	N/A	Big Cat	Pacific Learning
How to Make a Sun Hat	E	I	87	Home Connection Collection	Rigby
How to Make a Wind Sock	B	F	20	Tarlow, Ellen	Scholastic
How to Make Can Stilts	C	I	28	Story Box	Wright Group/McGraw Hill
How to Make Cheese Muffins	K	I	220	Voyages	SRA/McGraw Hill
How to Make Paper	L	I	250+	On Our Way to English	Rigby
How to Make Pop-up Cards	I	I	434	Big Cat	Pacific Learning
How to Make Salsa	J	I	192	Bookshop	Mondo
How to Make Smoothies!	E	I	75	Literacy by Design	Rigby
How to Make Snack Mix	C	I	47	Oppenlander, Meredith	Kaeden Books
How to Make Sock Puppets	H	I	229	Bookshop	Mondo
How to Ride a Giraffe	I	F	191	Little Readers	Houghton Mifflin Harcourt
How to Speak Dolphin in Three Easy Lessons	N	F	250+	The Zack Files	Grossett & Dunlap
How to Speak Dragonese: The Heroic Misadventures of Hiccup the Viking	T	F	250+	Cowell, Cressida	Little, Brown & Co.
How to Start Your Own Business	U	I	250+	Bookshop	Mondo
How to Stay Safe at Home and On-Line	M	I	250+	Rosen Real Readers	Rosen Publishing Group
How to Survive a Totally Boring Summer	N	RF	250+	Delacroix, Alice	Holiday House
How to Survive in Antarctica	U	I	250+	Bledsoe, Lucy Jane	Holiday House
How to Talk to Your Cat	Q	I	250+	George, Jean Craighead	Harper Collins
How to Talk to Your Dog	Q	I	250+	George, Jean Craighead	Harper Collins
How to Train Your Dragon by Hiccup Horrendous Haddock III	T	F	250+	Cowell, Cressida	Little, Brown & Co.
How to Twist a Dragon's Tale: The Heroic Misadventures of Hiccup Horrendous Haddock III	T	F	250+	Cowell, Cressida	Little, Brown & Co.

H

* Collection of short stories
# Graphic text

TITLE	LEVEL	GENRE	WORD COUNT	AUTHOR / SERIES	PUBLISHER / DISTRIBUTOR
How to Weigh an Elephant	K	F	390	Pacific Literacy	Pacific Learning
How Turtle Got His Tail	H	F	248	Rigby Literacy	Rigby
How Turtle Raced Beaver	J	TL	182	Literacy 2000	Rigby
How We Get Food	G	I	291	Leveled Readers	Houghton Mifflin Harcourt
How We Get Food	G	I	291	Leveled Readers/CA	Houghton Mifflin Harcourt
How We Get Food	G	I	291	Leveled Readers/TX	Houghton Mifflin Harcourt
How We Make Music	H	I	104	Rosen Real Readers	Rosen Publishing Group
How We Use Wool	M	I	654	Leveled Readers	Houghton Mifflin Harcourt
How We Use Wool	M	I	654	Leveled Readers/CA	Houghton Mifflin Harcourt
How We Use Wool	M	I	654	Leveled Readers/TX	Houghton Mifflin Harcourt
How We Vote	L	I	314	Independent Readers Social Studies	Houghton Mifflin Harcourt
How Will I Get to Grandma's House?	D	F	103	Blevins, Wiley	Scholastic
How Wisdom Came to the World: An Ashanti Tale	M	TL	250+	Khan, Benjamin	Houghton Mifflin Harcourt
How Women Got the Vote	U	I	1760	Vocabulary Readers	Houghton Mifflin Harcourt
How Women Got the Vote	U	I	1760	Vocabulary Readers/CA	Houghton Mifflin Harcourt
Howard Carter: Searching for King Tut	W	B	250+	Ford, Barbara	W. H. Freeman & Co.
Howie Has a Stomachache	E	F	100	Moore, Johnny R.	Continental Press
Howie Merton and the Magic Dust	M	F	250+	Reeves, Faye Couch	Random House
Howliday Inn	P	F	250+	Howe, James	Atheneum
Howling at the Hauntly's	M	RF	250+	Dadey, Debbie; Jones, Marcia Thornton	Scholastic
*Howling Dog and Other Cases, The	O	RF	250+	Simon, Seymour	Avon
How's the Weather	B	I	29	Learn to Read	Creative Teaching Press
How's the Weather?	N	I	250+	Berger, Melvin & Gilda	Ideals Children's Books
How's the Weather?	R	I	250+	On Our Way to English	Rigby
Hubble Space Telescope, The	Q	I	250+	A True Book	Children's Press
Hubert and Frankie	K	F	572	Reading Street	Pearson
Hubert the Sad Giant	J	F	602	InfoTrek	ETA Cuisenaire
Huberta the Hiking Hippo	L	RF	250+	Literacy 2000	Rigby
Hudson: Henry Hudson Searches for a Passage to Asia	U	B	250+	Exploring the World	Compass Point Books
Hue Boy	M	RF	250+	Mitchell, Rita Phillips	Penguin Group
Hug Bug	F	F	65	Start to Read	School Zone
Hug Is Warm, A	C	F	60	Sunshine	Wright Group/McGraw Hill
Hug, The	E	F	162	Leveled Literacy Intervention/Blue System	Heinemann
Huge Carrot, The	D	F	50	Leveled Readers	Houghton Mifflin Harcourt
Huge Paintings of Thomas Hart Benton, The	Q	B	1182	Reading Street	Pearson
Huggles Breakfast	LB	F	14	Sunshine	Wright Group/McGraw Hill
Huggles Can Juggle	LB	F	15	Sunshine	Wright Group/McGraw Hill
Huggles Goes Away	LB	F	14	Sunshine	Wright Group/McGraw Hill
Huggly, Snuggly Pets	F	RF	142	Giant Step Readers	Educational Insights
Hugo and Splot	O	F	250+	Bookweb	Rigby
Hugo Hogget: Story Based on an Ecuadoran Legend	K	TL	528	Cumpiano, Ina	Hampton-Brown
Hullabaloo at the Zoo	G	F	172	Lighthouse	Rigby
Human Barriers - The Walls of the World	T	I	250+	Connectors	Pacific Learning
Human Body	U	I	250+	Navigators Science Series	Benchmark Education Company
Human Body Math	T	I	250+	Navigators Math Series	Benchmark Education
Human Body Systems	R	I	1831	Science Support Readers	Houghton Mifflin Harcourt
Human Body, The	Q	I	250+	Explorers	Wright Group/McGraw Hill

H

TITLE	LEVEL	GENRE	WORD COUNT	AUTHOR / SERIES	PUBLISHER / DISTRIBUTOR
Human Emotions	Q	I	250+	Navigators Science Series	Benchmark Education
Human Growth	T	I	250+	Sun Sprouts	ETA Cuisenaire
Human Life Cycle, The	S	I	1193	Time for Kids	Teacher Created Materials
Hummingbird	N	I	250+	Life Cycles	Creative Teaching Press
Hummingbird Garden	K	RF	252	Story Box	Wright Group/McGraw Hill
Hummingbird, The	I	I	189	Sails	Rigby
Humongous Cat, The	I	F	250+	Sunshine	Wright Group/McGraw Hill
Humpback Teddy, The	E	RF	144	Take Two Books	Wright Group/McGraw Hill
Humpback Whale, The	S	I	250+	Frahm, Randy	Red Brick Learning
Humpback Whales	E	I	48	Pair-It Books	Steck-Vaughn
Humpback Whales	F	I	72	Ready Readers	Pearson Learning Group
Humphrey	M	RF	250+	Literacy Tree	Rigby
Humpity-Bump!	C	F	36	Little Celebrations	Pearson Learning Group
Humpty Dumpty	D	F	28	Instant Readers	Harcourt School Publishers
Humpty Dumpty	D	TL	26	Jumbled Tumbled Tales & Rhymes	Rigby
Humpty Dumpty	D	TL	27	Peppe, Rodney	Penguin Group
Humpty Dumpty	C	F	42	Seedlings	Continental Press
Humpty Dumpty Jr: Hardboiled Detective, in he Case of the Fiendish Flapjack Flop	Q	F	11470	Evans, Nate and Hindman, Paul	Sourcebooks
Humpty Dumpty Jr: Hardboiled Detective, in the Mystery of Merlin and the Gruesome Ghost	Q	F	14000	Evans, Nate and Hindman, Paul	Sourcebooks
Humvees	J	I	87	Mighty Machines	Capstone Press
Humvees	N	I	432	Pull Ahead Books	Lerner Publications
Hundred Dresses, The	P	RF	250+	Estes, Eleanor	Scholastic
Hundred Hugs, A	I	F	229	Sunshine	Wright Group/McGraw Hill
Hundred Penny Box, The	P	RF	250+	Mathis, Sharon Bell	Puffin/Penguin
Hunger for Learning: A Story About Booker T. Washington, A	R	B	8474	Creative Minds Biographies	Carolrhoda Books
Hungry Animals	G	I	127	Little Readers	Houghton Mifflin Harcourt
Hungry Bear	C	F	22	Smart Starts	Rigby
Hungry Chickens, The	G	F	107	Literacy Tree	Rigby
Hungry Dragon, The	B	F	26	Rigby Rocket	Rigby
Hungry Farmer, The	E	RF	149	Learn to Read	Creative Teaching Press
Hungry Fox, The	E	F	158	Early Connections	Benchmark Education
Hungry Fox, The	LB	RF	12	Rigby Literacy	Rigby
Hungry Giant, The	F	F	183	Story Box	Wright Group/McGraw Hill
Hungry Giant's Birthday Cake, The	G	F	241	Story Basket	Wright Group/McGraw Hill
Hungry Giant's Lunch, The	F	F	140	Story Box	Wright Group/McGraw Hill
Hungry Giant's Soup, The	G	F	42	Story Basket	Wright Group/McGraw Hill
Hungry Goat, The	D	F	30	Ray's Readers	Outside the Box
Hungry Goat, The	C	RF	33	Rise & Shine	Hampton-Brown
Hungry Happy Monkey	E	F	77	Joy Readers	Pearson Learning Group
Hungry Hedgehog	C	F	79	Story Steps	Rigby
Hungry Holidays for Bella and Rosie	I	F	586	Bella and Rosie Series	Literacy Footprints
Hungry Hoppers: Grasshoppers in Your Backyard	M	I	250+	Backyard Bugs	Picture Window Books
Hungry Horse	E	RF	35	Literacy 2000	Rigby
Hungry Kitten	C	F	50	Teacher's Choice Series	Pearson Learning Group
Hungry Kitten, The	D	F	95	PM Story Books	Rigby
Hungry Ladybugs	L	I	388	Pull Ahead Books	Lerner Publications
Hungry Monster	H	F	241	Story Box	Wright Group/McGraw Hill
Hungry Puppy, A	D	F	103	Bella and Rosie Series	Literacy Footprints
Hungry Red Fox	F	F	125	Adams, Lorraine; Bruvold, Lynn	Eagle Crest Books

H

* Collection of short stories
\# Graphic text

TITLE	LEVEL	GENRE	WORD COUNT	AUTHOR / SERIES	PUBLISHER / DISTRIBUTOR
Hungry Red Hawk, A	K	I	2312	Independent Readers Science	Houghton Mifflin Harcourt
Hungry Sea Star, The	I	I	69	Books for Young Learners	Richard C. Owen
Hungry Spiders	G	I	97	Gear Up!	Wright Group/McGraw Hill
Hungry Squirrel, The	C	RF	77	PM Stars	Rigby
Hungry Thing, The	M	F	250+	Slepian, Jan & Seidler, Ann	Scholastic
Hungry Turtle	F	I	173	Handprints D, Set 1	Educators Publishing Service
Hungry, Hungry Jack	I	RF	173	Lighthouse	Rigby
Hungry, Hungry Sharks	L	I	250+	Cole, Joanna	Random House
Hunt for Clues, A	G	RF	157	Ready Readers	Pearson Learning Group
Hunt for Pirate Gold, The	M	F	250+	Woodland Mysteries	Wright Group/McGraw Hill
Hunted, The	O	I	250+	Rigby Focus	Rigby
Hunter and the Animals, The	WB	RF	N/A	DePaola, Tomie	Holiday House
Hunterman and the Crocodile, The	P	TL	250+	Diakite, Baba Wague	Scholastic
Hunter's Moon	R	RF	5887	Townsend, John	Stone Arch Books
Hunting for Mummies	T	RF	250+	Reading Expeditions	National Geographic
Hunting Sharks	M	I	250+	Pull Ahead Books	Lerner Publications
Hunting the Horned Lizard	R	I	250+	Orbit Chapter Books	Pacific Learning
Hunting with My Camera	S	I	250+	Literacy 2000	Rigby
Hup Pups	F	F	89	Supersonics	Rigby
Hurdles and Jumps	M	I	250+	Take Two Books	Wright Group/McGraw Hill
*Hurray For Ali Baba Bernstein	O	RF	250+	Hurwitz, Johanna	Scholastic
Hurricane	S	HF	250+	Duey, Kathleen; Bale, Karen A.	Simon & Schuster
Hurricane	D	RF	36	Joy Readers	Pearson Learning Group
Hurricane at the Zoo!	N	I	250+	Literacy by Design	Rigby
Hurricane Diary	T	RF	3392	Leveled Readers Science	Houghton Mifflin Harcourt
Hurricane Hunters	R	I	250+	Explorer Books-Pathfinder	National Geographic
Hurricane Hunters	P	I	250+	Explorer Books-Pioneer	National Geographic
Hurricane Katrina Dogs	K	I	250+	All About Dogs	Literacy Footprints
*Hurricane Machine and Other Cases, The	O	RF	250+	Simon, Seymour	Avon
Hurricane Music	Y	RF	2564	Leveled Readers	Houghton Mifflin Harcourt
Hurricane on Its Way!	N	I	250+	Greetings	Rigby
Hurricane Opal: Into the Storm	U	RF	1931	Leveled Readers	Houghton Mifflin Harcourt
Hurricane Power	X	RF	250+	Orca Sports	Orca Book Publishers
Hurricanes	W	I	250+	Disasters Up Close	Lerner Publications
Hurricanes	T	I	250+	iOpeners	Pearson Learning Group
Hurricanes	S	I	250+	Natural Disasters	Capstone Press
Hurricanes	M	I	564	Pull Ahead Books	Lerner Publications
Hurricanes	S	I	250+	Theme Sets	National Geographic
Hurricanes	N	I	250+	Weather Update	Capstone Press
Hurricanes & Tornadoes	R	I	250+	The Wonders of Our World	Crabtree
Hurricanes and Storms	M	I	250+	Rosen Real Readers	Rosen Publishing Group
Hurricanes!	N	I	250+	Hopping, Jean	Scholastic
Hurricanes: Earth's Mightiest Storms	T	I	250+	Lauber, Patricia	Scholastic
Hurry Squirrel!	E	RF	72	Start to Read	School Zone
Hurry Up	D	RF	49	Voyages	SRA/McGraw Hill
Hurry Up!	D	RF	81	Explorations	Eleanor Curtain Publishing
Hurry Up!	D	I	81	Explorations	Okapi Educational Materials
Hurry Up!	J	RF	250+	Literacy by Design	Rigby
Hurry Up!	G	RF	131	Rookie Readers	Children's Press
Hurry Up, Hippo!	B	F	54	Literacy by Design	Rigby
Hurry Up, Lucy!	I	RF	340	Sun Sprouts	ETA Cuisenaire
Hurt Go Happy	W	RF	250+	Rorby, Ginny	Tom Doherty
Hush	U	RF	250+	Woodson, Jacqueline	Scholastic

H

* Collection of short stories
# Graphic text

TITLE	LEVEL	GENRE	WORD COUNT	AUTHOR / SERIES	PUBLISHER / DISTRIBUTOR
Hush Harbor: Praying in Secret	T	HF	1945	Evans, Freddi Williams	Carolrhoda Books
Hush Up!	L	F	250+	Little Celebrations	Pearson Learning Group
Hushtown: A Peaceful Community	Q	RF	250+	Massie, Elizabeth	Steck-Vaughn
Husky in a Hut	Q	RF	250+	Baglio, Ben M.	Scholastic
Hut in the Old Tree, The	I	RF	250+	PM Plus Story Books	Rigby
Huzzard Buzzard	F	F	112	Reese, Bob	Children's Press
Hydroelectric Power	V	I	250+	Energy at Work	Capstone Press
Hydroplanes	M	I	250+	Horsepower	Capstone Press
Hyena Tricks Vulture	N	F	1472	Take Two Books	Wright Group/McGraw Hill
Hyenas	P	I	1999	Animal Scavengers	Lerner Publishing
Hyenas	O	I	250+	Holmes, Kevin J.	Red Brick Learning
Hypnotized	Z	RF	250+	Orca Currents	Orca Book Publishers
*Hypnotized Frog and Other Cases, The	O	RF	250+	Simon, Seymour	Avon
Hyrax of Top-Knot Island, The	S	I	1762	Leveled Readers	Houghton Mifflin Harcourt
Hyrax, The: An Interesting Puzzle	R	I	250+	Leveled Readers Language Support	Houghton Mifflin Harcourt

H

* Collection of short stories
# Graphic text

TITLE	LEVEL	GENRE	WORD COUNT	AUTHOR / SERIES	PUBLISHER / DISTRIBUTOR
I Almost Love You, Eddie Clegg	W	RF	250+	Supplee, Audra	Peachtree
I Am	A	RF	21	Klein, Adria	Scholastic
I Am	B	RF	32	Little Readers	Houghton Mifflin Harcourt
I Am	D	RF	27	Rookie Readers	Children's Press
I Am	B	RF	32	Seedlings	Continental Press
I Am . . .	A	RF	20	Sunshine	Wright Group/McGraw Hill
I Am a Bee	A	F	24	Sails	Rigby
I Am a Book	M	F	730	Silly Millies	Millbrook Press
I Am a Bookworm	C	F	32	Sunshine	Wright Group/McGraw Hill
I Am a Dentist	C	I	20	Read-More Books	Pearson Learning Group
I Am a Drummer	E	I	32	iOpeners	Pearson Learning Group
I Am a Fireman	D	I	45	Read-More Books	Pearson Learning Group
I Am a Gypsy Pot	K	F	220	Evangeline Nicholas Collection	Wright Group/McGraw Hill
I Am a Leader	I	I	120	Character Values	Capstone Press
I Am a Painter	A	F	24	Sails	Rigby
I Am a Pencil	M	F	778	Silly Millies	Millbrook Press
I Am a Photographer	E	I	32	Read-More Books	Pearson Learning Group
I Am a Rock	J	I	250+	Marzollo, Jean	Scholastic
I Am a Star	B	RF	32	Little Readers	Houghton Mifflin Harcourt
I Am a Star	I	I	195	Marzollo, Jean	Scholastic
I Am a Star: Child of the Holocaust	W	I	250+	Auerbacher, Inge	Penguin Group
I Am a Tiger!	B	I	35	Rigby Flying Colors	Rigby
I Am a Train Driver	D	I	32	Read-More Books	Pearson Learning Group
I Am Alive!	D	I	109	Literacy by Design	Rigby
I Am an American: A True Story of Japanese Internment	Z	I	250+	Stanley, Jerry	Scholastic
I Am an Artist	C	I	30	Rosen Real Readers	Rosen Publishing Group
I Am an Explorer	D	RF	32	Rookie Readers	Children's Press
I Am Apache	Y	HF	250+	Landman, Tanya	Candlewick Press
I Am Blind	G	I	160	PM Science Readers	Rigby
I Am Busy	C	RF	43	Windows on Literacy	National Geographic
I Am Cold	E	RF	136	Foundations	Wright Group/McGraw Hill
I Am Courageous	I	I	110	Character Values	Capstone Press
I Am Danny	A	RF	23	Coulton, Mia	Maryruth Books
I Am Deaf	H	I	227	PM Science Readers	Rigby
I Am Fire	G	I	162	Marzollo, Jean	Scholastic
I Am Friendly	G	I	103	Character Values	Capstone Press
I Am Frightened	B	RF	41	Story Box	Wright Group/McGraw Hill
I Am Generous	G	I	89	Pebble Books	Capstone Press
I Am Going	B	RF	31	Sun Sprouts	ETA Cuisenaire
I Am Here	B	F	36	Sails	Rigby
I Am Hot	E	RF	123	Foundations	Wright Group/McGraw Hill
I Am Jumping	A	RF	18	Sails	Rigby
I Am Jumping	A	RF	24	Sun Sprouts	ETA Cuisenaire
I Am King!	E	F	57	My First Reader	Grolier Press
I Am Mad!	E	RF	112	Real Kids Readers	Millbrook Press
I Am Not Afraid	K	RF	250+	Mann, Kenny	Bantam
I Am Not Esther	Z+	RF	250+	Beale, Fleur	Hyperion
I Am Patriotic	H	I	76	Pebble Books	Red Brick Learning
I Am Planet Earth	G	I	124	Marzollo, Jean	Scholastic
I Am Polite	G	I	76	Pebble Books	Capstone Press
I Am Regina	U	HF	250+	Keehn, Sally	Bantam
I Am Rosa Parks	O	B	250+	Parks, Rosa	Dial/Penguin
I Am Running	A	I	24	PM Plus Starters	Rigby

* Collection of short stories
# Graphic text

TITLE	LEVEL	GENRE	WORD COUNT	AUTHOR / SERIES	PUBLISHER / DISTRIBUTOR
I Am Special	C	RF	38	Learn to Read	Creative Teaching Press
I Am Thankful	A	RF	42	Carousel Earlybirds	Pearson Learning Group
I Am the Cheese	Z	RF	250+	Cormier, Robert	Laurel-Leaf Books
I Am the Ice Worm	S	F	250+	Easley, Mary Ann	Yearling
I Am the Walrus	R	I	250+	Storyteller -Autumn Leaves	Wright Group/McGraw Hill
I Am Tolerant	H	I	132	Pebble Books	Red Brick Learning
I Am Too Absolutely Small for School	M	RF	250+	Child, Lauren	Candlewick Press
I Am Water	A	I	25	Independent Readers Science	Houghton Mifflin Harcourt
I Am Water	A	I	25	Science Support Readers	Houghton Mifflin Harcourt
I Am Working	A	F	18	Sails	Rigby
I and You and Don't Forget Who: What Is a Pronoun?	O	I	382	Words Are CATegorical	Millbrook Press
I Bought My Lunch Today	I	I	90	City Kids	Rigby
I Can	A	RF	21	Carousel Earlybirds	Pearson Learning Group
I Can	B	I	40	InfoTrek	ETA Cuisenaire
I Can	B	RF	54	Little Readers	Houghton Mifflin Harcourt
I Can	B	RF	21	New Way	Steck-Vaughn
I Can	B	RF	40	Ready Readers	Pearson Learning Group
I Can	A	F	18	Sails	Rigby
I Can	C	RF	27	Visions	Wright Group/McGraw Hill
I Can Be Anything	E	RF	242	Pair-It Books	Steck-Vaughn
I Can Breathe Underwater	G	RF	44	Windows on Literacy	National Geographic
I Can Build a House	D	I	52	Watanabe, Shiego	Viking/Penguin
I Can Change Things!	A	RF	29	Leveled Readers Science	Houghton Mifflin Harcourt
I Can Dig	C	I	45	Can You Do This?	SRA/McGraw Hill
I Can Do Anything!	C	RF	21	Sunshine	Wright Group/McGraw Hill
I Can Do It	I	RF	200	Bookshop	Mondo
I Can Do It Myself	C	RF	37	Literacy 2000	Rigby
I Can Do It Myself	E	RF	150	Visions	Wright Group/McGraw Hill
I Can Do It!	D	RF	74	Early Learning Modules	Steck-Vaughn
I Can Do It!	A	RF	30	Gear Up!	Wright Group/McGraw Hill
I Can Do It!	Q	I	250+	Kids Talk	Picture Window Books
I Can Do It, I Really Can	G	RF	195	Teacher's Choice Series	Pearson Learning Group
I Can Do Lots of Stuff!	E	RF	72	Reading Street	Pearson
I Can Do Many Things	C	RF	43	Carousel Readers	Pearson Learning Group
I Can Draw	C	RF	75	Carousel Earlybirds	Pearson Learning Group
I Can Draw	C	RF	57	Gear Up!	Wright Group/McGraw Hill
I Can Draw	C	RF	37	Learn to Read	Creative Teaching Press
I Can Draw	A	I	35	Pacific Literacy	Pacific Learning
I Can Draw	A	I	33	Sun Sprouts	ETA Cuisenaire
I Can Eat	C	I	51	Can You Do This?	SRA/McGraw Hill
I Can Find	E	I	131	Teacher's Choice Series	Pearson Learning Group
I Can Fly	F	F	107	Carousel Readers	Pearson Learning Group
I Can Fly	B	RF	86	InfoTrek	ETA Cuisenaire
I Can Fly	C	F	68	Lighthouse	Rigby
I Can Fly	B	F	21	Sunshine	Wright Group/McGraw Hill
I Can Hear	A	RF	32	TOTTS	Tott Publications
I Can Help	A	F	30	Sails	Rigby
I Can Help	D	RF	65	Teacher's Choice Series	Pearson Learning Group
I Can Hop. Can You?	B	I	41	Independent Readers Science	Houghton Mifflin Harcourt
I Can Jump	C	F	40	Sunshine	Wright Group/McGraw Hill
I Can Laugh	A	RF	18	Sails	Rigby
I Can Make a Flower	A	I	32	InfoTrek	ETA Cuisenaire
I Can Make Music	B	I	41	Little Red Readers	Sundance

* Collection of short stories
# Graphic text

TITLE	LEVEL	GENRE	WORD COUNT	AUTHOR / SERIES	PUBLISHER / DISTRIBUTOR
I Can Make You Red	B	F	43	The Book Project	Sundance
I Can Measure an Elephant	R	I	521	Independent Readers Science	Houghton Mifflin Harcourt
I Can Move!	B	I	39	Leveled Readers Science	Houghton Mifflin Harcourt
I Can Move!	A	I	18	Vocabulary Readers	Houghton Mifflin Harcourt
I Can Paint	A	RF	35	Book Bank	Wright Group/McGraw Hill
I Can Paint a Picture	C	I	26	Rosen Real Readers	Rosen Publishing Group
I Can Play	C	I	45	Can You Do This?	SRA/McGraw Hill
I Can Play	B	RF	32	Handprints B	Educators Publishing Service
I Can Play Soccer	F	I	120	Welcome Books	Children's Press
I Can Play Tangram	E	I	99	Pacific Literacy	Pacific Learning
I Can Push	A	RF	29	Bookshop	Mondo
I Can Read	A	I	35	Learn to Read	Creative Teaching Press
I Can Read	A	I	47	Leveled Literacy Intervention/ Orange System	Heinemann
I Can Read	A	RF	35	Pacific Literacy	Pacific Learning
I Can Read	C	RF	38	Teacher's Choice Series	Pearson Learning Group
I Can Read Anything	C	F	42	Sunshine	Wright Group/McGraw Hill
I Can Read with My Eyes Shut	J	F	250+	Seuss, Dr.	Random House
I Can Read! I Can Read!	L	RF	250+	Little Celebrations	Pearson Learning Group
I Can Ride	C	I	66	Can You Do This?	SRA/McGraw Hill
I Can Ride	A	I	66	Sun Sprouts	ETA Cuisenaire
I Can Ride My Bike	E	RF	224	Rigby Flying Colors	Rigby
I Can See	A	F	40	Carousel Earlybirds	Pearson Learning Group
I Can See	E	RF	38	Cervantes, Jesus	Scholastic
I Can See	A	I	35	Independent Readers Science	Houghton Mifflin Harcourt
I Can See	B	RF	36	Rigby Focus	Rigby
I Can See	C	I	35	Science Support Readers	Houghton Mifflin Harcourt
I Can See My Shadow	F	I	55	Windows on Literacy	National Geographic
I Can See the Leaves	K	RF	368	Pacific Literacy	Pacific Learning
I Can See You	D	RF	66	Sun Sprouts	ETA Cuisenaire
I Can Spell Dinosaur	F	RF	82	Predictable Storybooks	SRA/McGraw Hill
I Can Squeak	E	RF	154	Windmill Books	Wright Group/McGraw Hill
I Can Swim	D	RF	61	Ready Readers	Pearson Learning Group
I Can Swim	A	F	18	Sails	Rigby
I Can Take Care of the Earth	C	I	72	Independent Readers Science	Houghton Mifflin Harcourt
I Can Talk with My Hands	G	RF	146	Learn to Read	Creative Teaching Press
I Can Taste	C	I	31	Teacher's Choice Series	Pearson Learning Group
I Can Use a Computer	D	RF	52	Teacher's Choice Series	Pearson Learning Group
I Can Wash	C	RF	66	Carousel Earlybirds	Pearson Learning Group
I Can Write	A	RF	40	Learn to Read	Pacific Learning
I Can Write, Can You?	B	RF	30	Stewart, Josie; Salem, Lynn	Continental Press
I Can!	B	I	26	Time for Kids	Teacher Created Materials
I Can!	F	I	131	Twig	Wright Group/McGraw Hill
I Can!	A	I	15	Vocabulary Readers	Houghton Mifflin Harcourt
I Can!	A	I	15	Vocabulary Readers/CA	Houghton Mifflin Harcourt
I Can, Can You	B	RF	35	Springboard	Wright Group/McGraw Hill
I Can, I Can!	A	I	21	Little Readers	Houghton Mifflin Harcourt
I Can't Find It!	WB	RF	N/A	Rigby Literacy	Rigby
I Can't Open It!	E	F	76	Rigby Literacy	Rigby
I Can't Said the Ant	M	F	250+	Cameron, Polly	Scholastic
I Can't See	C	RF	36	Little Celebrations	Pearson Learning Group
I Can't Sleep	D	F	71	Learn to Read	Creative Teaching Press
I Can't Wait to Read	H	RF	185	Adventures in Reading	Pearson Learning Group

I

TITLE	LEVEL	GENRE	WORD COUNT	AUTHOR / SERIES	PUBLISHER / DISTRIBUTOR
I Care: American Reformers	S	I	914	Independent Readers Social Studies	Houghton Mifflin Harcourt
I Climb	C	I	57	This Is the Way I Go	SRA/McGraw Hill
I Could Be	D	RF	71	Sun Sprouts	ETA Cuisenaire
I Could Be	B	RF	40	Visions	Wright Group/McGraw Hill
I Crawl	C	I	56	This Is the Way I Go	SRA/McGraw Hill
I Did It!	E	RF	213	Handprints D, Set 1	Educators Publishing Service
I Did That!	I	RF	250+	Momentum Literacy Program	Troll Associates
I Do Not Like Peas	D	RF	32	Visions	Wright Group/McGraw Hill
I Don't Believe It!	L	RF	250+	Home Connection Collection	Rigby
I Don't Care	H	F	250+	Reading Friends	Pearson Learning Group
I Don't Care!	H	RF	250	TOTTS	Tott Publications
I Don't Like Peas	F	RF	89	Start to Read	School Zone
I Don't Think It's Fair	G	RF	147	Teacher's Choice Series	Pearson Learning Group
I Don't Want To	E	RF	144	Rigby Rocket	Rigby
I Double Dare You	S	RF	1910	Leveled Readers	Houghton Mifflin Harcourt
I Dream	K	RF	583	Sunshine	Wright Group/McGraw Hill
I Dress Up Like Mama	C	RF	35	Visions	Wright Group/McGraw Hill
I Eat Leaves	C	I	47	Bookshop	Mondo
I Feel Cold	C	RF	57	Home Connection Collection	Rigby
I Feel Hot	C	RF	58	Home Connection Collection	Rigby
I Feel Sick	A	RF	15	Science	Outside the Box
I Fixed Breakfast	H	RF	176	Teacher's Choice Series	Pearson Learning Group
I Fly	C	I	57	This Is the Way I Go	SRA/McGraw Hill
I Found a Can	C	I	33	Twig	Wright Group/McGraw Hill
I Get Ready for School	C	RF	37	Visions	Wright Group/McGraw Hill
I Get the Creeps	K	RF	250+	Reading Corners	Pearson Learning Group
I Get Tired	B	RF	37	Carousel Earlybirds	Pearson Learning Group
I Go to Gymnastics	D	I	58	Sun Sprouts	ETA Cuisenaire
I Go with Grandpa	E	RF	100+	Landman, Yael	Scholastic
I Go, Go, Go	B	F	21	Sunshine	Wright Group/McGraw Hill
I Got a "D" in Salami	R	RF	250+	Winkler, Henry and Oliver, Lin	Grosset & Dunlap
I Got a Goldfish	E	F	92	Ready Readers	Pearson Learning Group
I Grow Too!	C	I	30	Start to Read	School Zone
I Hadn't Meant to Tell You This	Z	RF	250+	Woodson, Jacqueline	Bantam
I Hate Camping	M	RF	250+	Petersen, P. J.	Penguin Group
I Hate English	L	RF	250+	Levine, Ellen	Scholastic
I Hate My Best Friend	L	RF	250+	Rosner, Ruth	Hyperion
I Have 10	A	RF	29	InfoTrek	ETA Cuisenaire
I Have a Dream	Q	B	250+	Davidson, Margaret	Scholastic
I Have a Home	E	RF	79	Sunshine	Wright Group/McGraw Hill
I Have a New Baby Brother	F	F	163	Learn to Read	Creative Teaching Press
I Have a Paper Route	I	I	90	City Kids	Rigby
I Have a Pet	B	RF	35	Reading Corners	Pearson Learning Group
I Have a Question, Grandma	G	RF	124	Literacy 2000	Rigby
I Have a Watch!	C	RF	60	Williams, Deborah	Kaeden Books
I Have Another Language	F	RF	92	Instant Readers	Harcourt School Publishers
I Have Feelings!	J	F	250+	Bookshop	Mondo
I Have Five Senses	D	I	89	Literacy by Design	Rigby
I Have Five Senses	D	I	89	On Our Way to English	Rigby
I Have Heard of a Land	Q	HF	250+	Thomas, Joyce Carol	Harper Trophy
I Have Lived a Thousand Years	Y	B	250+	Bitton-Jackson, Livia	Simon & Schuster

280   Organized Alphabetically by Title
Storable Database at www.fountasandpinnellleveledbooks.com

* Collection of short stories
\# Graphic text

TITLE	LEVEL	GENRE	WORD COUNT	AUTHOR / SERIES	PUBLISHER / DISTRIBUTOR
I Have Not Yet Begun to Fight: A Story About John Paul Jones	R	B	8692	Creative Minds Biographies	Carolrhoda Books
I Have Self-Respect	I	I	112	Character Values	Capstone Press
I Have Shoes	C	RF	24	Visions	Wright Group/McGraw Hill
I Hear!	A	I	33	Early Connections	Benchmark Education
I Heard the Owl Call My Name	Z	RF	250+	Craven, Margaret	Random House
I Help My Dad	A	I	24	Windows on Literacy	National Geographic
I Hope It Floats!	R	I	250+	Literacy by Design	Rigby
I Jump	C	I	56	This Is the Way I Go	SRA/McGraw Hill
I Just Forgot	G	F	250+	Mayer, Mercer	Scholastic
I Know a Lady	L	RF	221	Zolotow, Charlotte	Penguin Group
I Know an Old Lady	H	F	82	Readalong Rhythms	Wright Group/McGraw Hill
I Know an Old Lady	K	TL	250+	Traditional Songs	Picture Window Books
I Know It Is Living	E	I	26	Living or Nonliving	Lerner Publishing
I Know It Is Nonliving	E	I	34	Living or Nonliving	Lerner Publishing
I Know Karate	E	RF	62	Packard, Mary	Scholastic
I Know That Tune!	F	RF	201	Foundations	Wright Group/McGraw Hill
I Know That!	I	I	99	Sunshine	Wright Group/McGraw Hill
I Know Why the Caged Bird Sings	Z+	B	250+	Angelou, Maya	Bantam Books
I Know, I Know!	U	RF	1820	Leveled Readers	Houghton Mifflin Harcourt
I Like	B	RF	53	Early Connections	Benchmark Education
I Like	C	RF	24	Literacy 2000	Rigby
I Like	A	RF	24	Sunshine	Wright Group/McGraw Hill
I Like Apples	A	RF	12	Windows on Literacy	National Geographic
I Like Balloons	A	RF	27	Reading Corners	Pearson Learning Group
I Like Being Outdoors	WB	I	N/A	Windows on Literacy	National Geographic
I Like Bikes	A	I	24	Sun Sprouts	ETA Cuisenaire
I Like Books	D	F	168	Browne, Anthony	Random House
I Like Boxes	B	F	30	Sails	Rigby
I Like Cars	B	RF	36	Rigby Rocket	Rigby
I Like Cheese	G	I	105	Welcome Books	Children's Press
I Like Dogs	C	RF	35	Rigby Literacy	Rigby
I Like Elephants	A	F	18	Sails	Rigby
I Like Fruit	LB	RF	18	Visions	Wright Group/McGraw Hill
I Like Green	C	RF	47	Literacy 2000	Rigby
I Like Green	B	F	28	The Book Project	Sundance
I Like Hats	A	RF	18	Sails	Rigby
I Like It When . . .	E	RF	82	Ready Set Read	Steck-Vaughn
I Like Jam	B	F	30	Sails	Rigby
I Like Me	A	RF	31	Visions	Wright Group/McGraw Hill
I Like Mess	E	RF	74	Real Kids Readers	Millbrook Press
I Like My Picture!	D	RF	160	Teacher's Choice Series	Pearson Learning Group
I Like Painting	C	RF	42	Little Red Readers	Sundance
I Like Playing	B	RF	38	Rigby Flying Colors	Rigby
I Like Red	A	RF	18	Sails	Rigby
I Like Rice	B	I	36	First Stories	Pacific Learning
I Like Riding	A	F	18	Sails	Rigby
I Like Salad	A	I	24	InfoTrek	ETA Cuisenaire
I Like School	C	I	107	Vocabulary Readers	Houghton Mifflin Harcourt
I Like School	C	I	107	Vocabulary Readers/CA	Houghton Mifflin Harcourt
I Like Shapes	LB	RF	21	Armstrong, Shane	Scholastic
I Like Shopping	J	RF	287	Sunshine	Wright Group/McGraw Hill
I Like That Horse	B	RF	68	First Stories	Pacific Learning
I Like Things	F	RF	250+	Let's Play	Norwood House Press

* Collection of short stories
\# Graphic text

TITLE	LEVEL	GENRE	WORD COUNT	AUTHOR / SERIES	PUBLISHER / DISTRIBUTOR
I Like to Count	C	RF	40	Ready Readers	Pearson Learning Group
I Like to Eat	A	RF	41	Reading Corners	Pearson Learning Group
I Like to Eat...	C	RF	56	Sunshine	Wright Group/McGraw Hill
I Like to Find Things	C	I	40	Sunshine	Wright Group/McGraw Hill
I Like to Help	E	I	137	In Step Readers	Rigby
I Like to Help	B	RF	46	Little Books for Early Readers	University of Maine
I Like to Jump	C	F	50	Rigby Literacy	Rigby
I Like to Jump	C	F	50	Rigby Star	Rigby
I Like to Paint	A	RF	29	Reading Corners	Pearson Learning Group
I Like to Play	C	RF	50	Carousel Readers	Pearson Learning Group
I Like to Read	A	RF	44	Early Emergent	Pioneer Valley
I Like to Read	B	RF	49	Little Books for Early Readers	University of Maine
I Like to Ride	C	RF	72	Little Readers	Houghton Mifflin Harcourt
I Like to Win!	E	RF	96	Real Kids Readers	Millbrook Press
I Like to Write	C	RF	62	Carousel Readers	Pearson Learning Group
I Like Worms!	D	F	213	Sunshine	Wright Group/McGraw Hill
I Listen	F	RF	84	Windows on Literacy	National Geographic
I Live in a House	D	I	51	Read-More Books	Pearson Learning Group
I Live in an Apartment	D	I	41	Read-More Books	Pearson Learning Group
I Live in an Apartment Building	I	I	111	City Kids	Rigby
I Live in the Rockies	L	I	259	Windows on Literacy	National Geographic
I Live on a Farm	C	I	42	Read-More Books	Pearson Learning Group
I Lost My Tooth in Africa	N	RF	250+	Diakite, Penda	Scholastic
I Love a Parade	C	I	38	Yellow Umbrella Books	Red Brick Learning
I Love Bugs	C	RF	40	Bookshop	Mondo
I Love Camping	E	RF	83	Carousel Readers	Pearson Learning Group
I Love Camping	B	RF	34	Early Emergent	Pioneer Valley
I Love Cats	I	RF	104	Bookshop	Mondo
I Love Cats	E	RF	116	Rookie Readers	Children's Press
I Love Chickens	D	F	67	Story Box	Wright Group/McGraw Hill
I Love Fishing	D	RF	37	Rookie Readers	Children's Press
I Love Guinea Pigs	O	I	250+	King-Smith, Dick	Candlewick Press
I Love Guinea Pigs	M	I	250+	Read and Wonder	Candlewick Press
I Love Ladybugs	C	RF	68	Van Allen, Roach	Wright Group/McGraw Hill
I Love Mud and Mud Loves Me	D	RF	121	Stephens, Vicki	Scholastic
I Love Music	C	RF	41	Carousel Readers	Pearson Learning Group
I Love My Family	B	RF	34	Foundations	Wright Group/McGraw Hill
I Love My Family	B	RF	31	Sunshine	Wright Group/McGraw Hill
I Love My Grandma	D	RF	36	Rise & Shine	Hampton-Brown
I Love Rocks	G	RF	150	Rigby Rocket	Rigby
I Love Rocks	F	RF	95	Rookie Readers	Children's Press
I Love the Beach	M	I	250+	Literacy 2000	Rigby
I Love the Beach!	E	RF	57	Windows on Literacy	National Geographic
I Love to Sneeze	J	F	250+	Bank Street	Bantam
I Love to Write!	F	RF	131	Mader, Jan	Kaeden Books
I Love You	E	F	121	Teacher's Choice Series	Pearson Learning Group
I Love You, Dear Dragon	E	F	278	Dear Dragon	Norwood House Press
I Made a Picture	B	I	39	Storyteller	Wright Group/McGraw Hill
I Made a Trail	I	RF	191	InfoTrek	ETA Cuisenaire
I Make Clay Pots	C	I	29	Bebop Books	Lee & Low Books Inc.
I Meowed	D	RF	58	Books for Young Learners	Richard C. Owen
I Miss Grandpa	E	RF	65	InfoTrek	ETA Cuisenaire
I Need . . .	C	RF	23	Ray's Readers	Outside the Box
I Need a Book	F	RF	113	Sunshine	Wright Group/McGraw Hill

* Collection of short stories
# Graphic text

TITLE	LEVEL	GENRE	WORD COUNT	AUTHOR / SERIES	PUBLISHER / DISTRIBUTOR
I Need a Lunch Box	H	RF	216	Caines, Jeannette	Scholastic
I Need a Rest	F	RF	119	Home Connection Collection	Rigby
I Need Glasses: My Visit to the Optometrist	M	RF	250+	Bookshop	Mondo
I Need Something Round	H	RF	239	On Our Way to English	Rigby
I Need to Clean My Room	F	RF	157	Learn to Read	Creative Teaching Press
I Need You	F	RF	121	Rookie Readers	Children's Press
I Never Promised You a Rose Garden	Z+	RF	250+	Greenberg, Joanne	Penguin Group
I Paint	A	RF	22	Bookshop	Mondo
I Paint	A	I	22	Literacy 2000	Rigby
I Picked a Flower	C	RF	33	Science	Outside the Box
I Play Soccer	C	RF	31	Bebop Books	Lee & Low Books Inc.
I Play Soccer	J	RF	97	City Kids	Rigby
I Pledge Allegiance	Q	I	250+	Martin Jr., Bill & Sampson, Michael	Candlewick Press
I Pledge Allegiance	O	I	1421	On My Own History	Lerner Publications
I Push, I Pull	B	I	40	On Our Way to English	Rigby
I Read	A	RF	38	Reading Corners	Pearson Learning Group
I Read Signs	LB	I	12	Hoban, Tana	Greenwillow
I Read Symbols	LB	I	14	Hoban, Tana	Greenwillow
I Remember	C	RF	26	Literacy 2000	Rigby
I Ride the Waves	I	RF	61	Books for Young Learners	Richard C. Owen
I Rode a Horse of Milk White Jade	V	HF	250+	Wilson, Diane Lee	HarperTrophy
I Run	B	RF	22	Carousel Earlybirds	Pearson Learning Group
I Run	C	I	56	This Is the Way I Go	SRA/McGraw Hill
I Said to Sam	M	F	250+	Molnar, Gwen	Scholastic
I Saw a Dinosaur	E	F	98	Book Bus	Creative Edge
I Saw a Dinosaur	G	F	55	Literacy 2000	Rigby
I Saw a Sign	F	RF	100	Literacy Tree	Rigby
I Saw the Boston Tea Party	J	HF	273	Independent Readers Social Studies	Houghton Mifflin Harcourt
I Saw You in the Bathtub	J	TL	250+	Schwartz, Alvin	HarperTrophy
I Say, You Say	Q	I	250+	Orbit Collections	Pacific Learning
I See	B	F	29	Bookshop	Mondo
I See	A	I	32	Early Connections	Benchmark Education
I See	A	I	32	Sun Sprouts	ETA Cuisenaire
I See	C	RF	29	Teacher's Choice Series	Pearson Learning Group
I See Animals Hiding	M	I	250+	Arnosky, Jim	Scholastic
I See Bugs	A	I	30	Blevins, Wiley	Scholastic
I See Colors	B	I	23	Learn to Read	Creative Teaching Press
I See Colors	B	RF	50	Little Readers	Houghton Mifflin Harcourt
I See Dad	A	RF	24	Literacy by Design	Rigby
I See Fish	B	I	45	Curry, Don L.	Scholastic
I See Flags	C	I	31	Blevins, Wiley	Scholastic
I See Monkeys	C	RF	39	Williams, Deborah	Kaeden Books
I See Patterns	A	I	42	Learn to Read	Creative Teaching Press
I See Patterns	C	I	43	Yellow Umbrella Books	Red Brick Learning
I See Shapes	B	I	37	Learn to Read	Creative Teaching Press
I See Spring!	A	I	18	Vocabulary Readers	Houghton Mifflin Harcourt
I See Tails!	B	I	42	Rise & Shine	Hampton-Brown
I See You	C	I	56	Twig	Wright Group/McGraw Hill
I Shop with My Daddy	G	RF	131	Maccarone, Grace	Scholastic
I Smell Smoke!	E	RF	49	Sunshine	Wright Group/McGraw Hill
I Speak English and Chinese	F	RF	159	On Our Way to English	Rigby
I Spy	A	RF	31	Lighthouse	Rigby

* Collection of short stories
\# Graphic text

TITLE	LEVEL	GENRE	WORD COUNT	AUTHOR / SERIES	PUBLISHER / DISTRIBUTOR
I Spy	I	RF	302	Literacy 2000	Rigby
I Spy	C	RF	29	Literacy Tree	Rigby
I Spy	B	RF	30	Story Steps	Rigby
I Spy a Fly	I	I	132	Wonder World	Wright Group/McGraw Hill
I Swim	C	I	57	This Is the Way I Go	SRA/McGraw Hill
I Take Care of My Dog	WB	RF	N/A	Rigby Literacy	Rigby
I Take Care of My Dog	D	I	121	Rigby Star Quest	Rigby
I Thought I Couldn't	C	RF	40	Visions	Wright Group/McGraw Hill
I Try to Be a Good Person	H	RF	192	Learn to Read	Creative Teaching Press
I Use My Senses	B	I	28	On Our Way to English	Rigby
I Walk and Read	LB	I	16	Hoban, Tana	Greenwillow
I Want a Dog	F	RF	192	Sun Sprouts	ETA Cuisenaire
I Want a Pet	C	RF	46	Little Readers	Houghton Mifflin Harcourt
I Want a Pet	C	RF	46	Start to Read	School Zone
I Want a Pet!	H	F	167	Big Cat	Pacific Learning
I Want a Red Ball	B	F	29	The Book Project	Sundance
I Want Ice Cream	C	RF	18	Story Box	Wright Group/McGraw Hill
I Want My Own Room!	LB	RF	25	Visions	Wright Group/McGraw Hill
I Want Some Honey	E	F	152	Take Two Books	Wright Group/McGraw Hill
I Want to be a Ballerina	D	RF	66	Teacher's Choice Series	Pearson Learning Group
I Want to Be a Clown	F	RF	82	Start to Read	School Zone
I Want to Be an Astronaut	I	RF	79	Barton, Byron	HarperCollins
I Want to Be Me	I	F	214	Sun Sprouts	ETA Cuisenaire
I Want to Be…	B	F	46	The Book Project	Sundance
I Want to Go Camping	I	RF	407	Leveled Readers	Houghton Mifflin Harcourt
I Want To Live: The Diary of a Young Girl in Stalin's Russia	Z	B	250+	Lugovskaya, Nina	Houghton Mifflin Harcourt
I Was a Sixth Grade Alien	S	F	250+	Coville, Bruce	Pocket Books
I Was a Third Grade Science Project	N	RF	250+	Auch, Mary Jane	Yearling
I Was at the Zoo	J	I	250+	Literacy Tree	Rigby
I Was Just About to Go to Bed	E	RF	107	Instant Readers	Harcourt School Publishers
I Was So Mad	J	RF	232	Mayer, Mercer	Donovan
I Was Walking Down the Road	H	F	299	Barchas, Sarah	Scholastic
I Wash	B	RF	33	First Stories	Pacific Learning
I Went to the Beach	C	RF	25	Books for Young Learners	Richard C. Owen
I Went to the Dentist	K	RF	152	City Kids	Rigby
I Went to the Movies	J	RF	120	City Kids	Rigby
I Went to Visit a Friend One Day	F	F	111	Voyages	SRA/McGraw Hill
I Went Walking	C	RF	105	Williams, Sue	Harcourt Trade
I Will Never Not Ever Eat a Tomato	M	RF	250+	Child, Lauren	Candlewick Press
I Will Not Eat That!	R	RF	1344	Leveled Readers	Houghton Mifflin Harcourt
I Will Not Eat That!	R	RF	1344	Leveled Readers/CA	Houghton Mifflin Harcourt
I Will Not Eat That!	R	RF	1344	Leveled Readers/TX	Houghton Mifflin Harcourt
I Will Plant You a Lilac Tree: A Memoir of a Schindler's List Survivor	Z	B	250+	Hillman, Laura	Atheneum
I Wish I Had a Dinosaur	D	F	46	Little Celebrations	Pearson Learning Group
I Wish I Was a Bat	C	F	31	Rigby Rocket	Rigby
I Wish I Was Sick Too	G	RF	94	Brandenburg, Franz	Morrow
I Wish, I Wish	O	F	250+	High-Fliers	Pacific Learning
I Wonder	H	I	151	Green Light Readers	Harcourt
I Wonder	C	RF	49	Little Celebrations	Pearson Learning Group
I Wonder	F	RF	67	Sunshine	Wright Group/McGraw Hill
I Wonder Why	E	RF	73	Foundations	Wright Group/McGraw Hill

* Collection of short stories
\# Graphic text

TITLE	LEVEL	GENRE	WORD COUNT	AUTHOR / SERIES	PUBLISHER / DISTRIBUTOR
I Wonder Why Snakes Shed Their Skins and Other Questions About Reptiles	O	I	250+	O'Neill, Amanda	Scholastic
I Wonder Why the Sky Is Blue	O	I	250+	Rosen Real Readers	Rosen Publishing Group
I Wonder Why?	F	I	95	Wonder World	Wright Group/McGraw Hill
I Work at Night	D	RF	49	Windows on Literacy	National Geographic
I Write	B	RF	40	Little Books for Early Readers	University of Maine
I Write	C	RF	19	Sunshine	Wright Group/McGraw Hill
I Write for the Newspaper	I	I	145	Rosen Real Readers	Rosen Publishing Group
I, Amber Brown	O	RF	250+	Danziger, Paula	Scholastic
I, Dred Scott	U	HF	250+	Moses, Sheila P.	Margaret K. McElderry Books
I. M. Pei	M	B	250+	Biography	Benchmark Education
I.D.	Z+	RF	250+	Orca Soundings	Orca Book Publishers
I.M. Pei	S	B	250+	Amazing Americans	Wright Group/McGraw Hill
I.M. Pei	T	B	250+	On Our Way to English	Rigby
Iain's Eagle Eye	M	RF	250+	Lighthouse	Ginn & Co.
Ibis: A True Whale Story	K	I	250+	Himmelman, John	Scholastic
Ice	B	I	34	Gear Up!	Wright Group/McGraw Hill
Ice	Q	I	250+	Theme Sets	National Geographic
Ice	I	I	92	Windows on Literacy	National Geographic
Ice - A Cold Blanket	S	I	250+	Connectors	Pacific Learning
Ice Age Safari	P	I	250+	Rigby Focus	Rigby
Ice and Snow	D	I	71	Explorations	Eleanor Curtain Publishing
Ice and Snow	D	I	71	Explorations	Okapi Educational Materials
Ice Climbing	M	I	250+	To the Extreme	Capstone Press
Ice Cream	O	I	1078	Big Cat	Pacific Learning
Ice Cream	N	I	250+	Gibbons, Gail	Holiday House
Ice Cream	B	F	36	Sails	Rigby
Ice Cream	L	I	450	Springboard	Wright Group/ McGraw Hill
Ice Cream	C	RF	49	Sunshine	Wright Group/McGraw Hill
Ice Cream Dream	I	F	250+	Rigby Rocket	Rigby
Ice Cream for You	J	I	214	Windows on Literacy	National Geographic
*Ice Dove and Other Stories, The	M	RF	250+	deAnda, Diane	Arte Publico
Ice Fishing	H	I	140	Ready Readers	Pearson Learning Group
Ice Fishing	S	I	250+	The Great Outdoors	Red Brick Learning
Ice Hockey	K	I	250+	On Deck	Rigby
Ice Is . . . Whee!	D	RF	59	Rookie Readers	Children's Press
Ice Magic	Q	RF	250+	Christopher, Matt	Little, Brown & Co.
Ice Man, The: A Traditional Native American Tale	L	TL	250+	Rigby Literacy	Rigby
Ice Mummies: Frozen in Time	V	I	250+	Mummies	Capstone Press
Ice Mummy: The Discovery of a 5,000-Year-Old Man	P	I	250+	Dubowski, Mark & Cathy East	Random House
Ice on the Move	K	I	362	Rigby Focus	Rigby
Ice Storms	Q	I	250+	Natural Disasters	Red Brick Learning
Iceberg Ahead!	R	I	1240	Vocabulary Readers	Houghton Mifflin Harcourt
Iceberg Ahead!	R	I	1240	Vocabulary Readers/CA	Houghton Mifflin Harcourt
Iceberg Hermit, The	X	RF	250+	Roth, Arthur	Scholastic
Iceberg Rescue	N	I	464	Leveled Readers	Houghton Mifflin Harcourt
Icebergs	L	I	250+	Sunshine	Wright Group/McGraw Hill
Ice-Cream Factory, The	J	I	250+	Rigby Literacy	Rigby
Ice-Cream Factory, The	J	I	250+	Rigby Star Quest	Rigby
Ice-Cream Stick	B	RF	35	Story Box	Wright Group/McGraw Hill
Iceman	Z	RF	250+	Lynch, Chris	HarperCollins

* Collection of short stories
# Graphic text

TITLE	LEVEL	GENRE	WORD COUNT	AUTHOR / SERIES	PUBLISHER / DISTRIBUTOR
Ice-Skating	G	RF	219	Rigby Flying Colors	Rigby
Ichiro Suzuki	P	B	1546	Amazing Athletes	Lerner Publications
Ichthyosaurus	N	I	250+	Discovering Dinosaurs	Red Brick Learning
Icky Bug Alphabet Book, The	N	I	250+	Pallotta, Jerry	Charlesbridge
Icy Adventure, An	R	I	1176	Leveled Readers	Houghton Mifflin Harcourt
Icy Adventure, An	R	I	1176	Leveled Readers/CA	Houghton Mifflin Harcourt
Icy Adventure, An	R	I	1176	Leveled Readers/TX	Houghton Mifflin Harcourt
*Icy Question and Other Cases, The	O	RF	250+	Simon, Seymour	Avon
Ida B. Wells	T	B	250+	Amazing Americans	Wright Group/McGraw Hill
Ida Lewis and the Lighthouse	S	I	973	Leveled Readers	Houghton Mifflin Harcourt
Idaho	T	I	250+	Hello U.S.A.	Lerner Publications
Idaho	S	I	250+	Land of Liberty	Red Brick Learning
Idaho	R	I	250+	This Land Is Your Land	Compass Point Books
Idea Seed, An - Inventions That Change Our Lives	S	I	250+	Connectors	Pacific Learning
Ideas to Inventions	O	I	1009	Reading Street	Pearson
Iditarod, The: Story of the Last Great Race	S	I	250+	High Five Reading	Red Brick Learning
Iditarod: Dogsled Race Across Alaska	Q	I	250+	Sunshine	Wright Group/McGraw Hill
If	H	F	83	Sunshine	Wright Group/McGraw Hill
If a Tree Could Talk	G	F	62	Learn to Read	Creative Teaching Press
If Animals Came to School	F	F	125	Learn to Read	Creative Teaching Press
If Anything Ever Goes Wrong at the Zoo	L	F	250+	Hendrick, Mary Jean	Harcourt Trade
If Dogs Ruled the World	J	F	250+	McNulty, Faith	Scholastic
If Germs Were Purple	D	F	53	Carousel Readers	Pearson Learning Group
If Horses Could Talk!	E	RF	32	Teacher's Choice Series	Pearson Learning Group
If I Forget, You Remember	V	RF	250+	Williams, Carol Lynch	Bantam
If I Had an Alligator	H	F	214	Mayer, Mercer	Dial/Penguin
If I Had an Elephant	F	F	90	Teacher's Choice Series	Pearson Learning Group
If I Were a Penguin	H	RF	159	Goeneil, Heidi	Little, Brown & Co.
If I Were an Ant	I	F	51	Rookie Readers	Children's Press
If I Were You	E	RF	77	Wildsmith, Brian	Oxford University Press
If I Were You...	S	F	250+	Power Up!	Steck-Vaughn
If We Could Do What the Animals Do	G	F	188	Learn to Read	Creative Teaching Press
If You Come Softly	Y	RF	250+	Woodson, Jacqueline	G.P. Putnam's Sons
If You Could Be Anything	Q	I	250+	Power Up!	Steck-Vaughn
If You Give A Moose a Muffin	K	F	250+	Numeroff, Laura Joffe	HarperCollins
If You Give A Mouse a Cookie	K	F	291	Numeroff, Laura Joffe	HarperCollins
If You Give a T-Rex a Bone	N	I	842	Myers, Tim	Dawn Publications
If You Give an Author a Pencil	O	B	250+	Meet the Author	Richard C. Owen
If You Grew Up with Abraham Lincoln	Q	I	250+	McGovern, Ann	Scholastic
If You Grew Up with George Washington	Q	I	250+	Gross, Ruth Belov	Scholastic
If You Like Strawberries, Don't Read this Book	H	RF	101	Literacy 2000	Rigby
If You Lived 100 Years Ago	Q	I	250+	McGovern, Ann	Scholastic
If You Lived at the Time of Martin Luther King	Q	I	250+	Levine, Ellen	Scholastic
If You Lived at the Time of the American Revolution	Q	I	250+	Moore, Kay	Scholastic
If You Lived at the Time of the Civil War	Q	I	250+	Moore, Kay	Scholastic
If You Lived at the Time of the Great San Francisco Earthquake	Q	I	250+	Levine, Ellen	Scholastic
If You Lived in Colonial Times	Q	I	250+	McGovern, Ann	Scholastic
If You Lived in the Alaska Territory	Q	I	250+	Levinson, Nancy Smiler	Scholastic
If You Lived with the Cherokee	Q	I	250+	Roop, Peter & Connie	Scholastic
If You Lived with the Hopi	Q	I	250+	Kamma, Anne	Scholastic

* Collection of short stories
# Graphic text

TITLE	LEVEL	GENRE	WORD COUNT	AUTHOR / SERIES	PUBLISHER / DISTRIBUTOR
. . . If You Lived with the Indians of the Northwest Coast	Q	I	250+	Kamma, Anne	Scholastic
If You Lived with the Iroquois	Q	I	250+	Levine, Ellen	Scholastic
If You Lived with the Sioux Indians	Q	I	250+	McGovern, Ann	Scholastic
If You Meet a Dragon	C	F	31	Story Box	Wright Group/McGraw Hill
If You Miss Your Bus	F	F	160	Leveled Readers	Houghton Mifflin Harcourt
If You Sailed on the Mayflower in 1620	Q	I	250+	McGovern, Ann	Scholastic
If You Traveled on the Underground Railroad	Q	I	250+	Levine, Ellen	Scholastic
If You Traveled West in a Covered Wagon	Q	I	250+	Levine, Ellen	Scholastic
If You Were a Bat	K	I	227	Gear Up!	Wright Group/McGraw Hill
If You Were a Bat	F	F	78	Instant Readers	Harcourt School Publishers
If You Were My Baby	L	F	338	Hodgkins, Fran	Dawn Publications
If You Were There in 1492: Everyday Life in the Time of Columbus	U	I	250+	Brenner, Barbara	Aladdin
If You Were There When They Signed the Constitution	Q	I	250+	Levy, Elizabeth	Scholastic
If You Won 100 Dollars	P	I	250+	Literacy by Design	Rigby
If Your Name was Changed at Ellis Island	Q	I	250+	Levine, Ellen	Scholastic
If You're Reading This, It's Too Late	U	F	250+	Bosch, Pseudonymous	Little, Brown & Co.
Iggie's House	R	RF	250+	Blume, Judy	Bantam
Iggy Iguana's Trip	B	F	43	Phonics and Friends	Hampton-Brown
Ignatius MacFarland: Frequenaut!	W	F	250+	Feig Paul	Little, Brown & Co.
Igneous Rocks	Q	I	250+	On Deck	Rigby
Iguanodon	N	I	250+	Discovering Dinosaurs	Capstone Press
Ike in the Spotlight	M	RF	992	Leveled Readers	Houghton Mifflin Harcourt
Ike in the Spotlight	M	RF	992	Leveled Readers/CA	Houghton Mifflin Harcourt
Ike in the Spotlight	M	RF	992	Leveled Readers/TX	Houghton Mifflin Harcourt
Iliad, The	Z+	TL	250+	Homer	Penguin Group
I'll Be a Pirate	E	F	53	Eifrig, Kate	Kaeden Books
I'll Be Good	K	RF	862	Rigby Gigglers	Rigby
I'll Do It Later	I	RF	574	Real Kids Readers	Millbrook Press
I'll Make You a Card	G	RF	180	Early Readers	Compass Point Books
I'll Run Away	D	RF	53	Home Connection Collection	Rigby
Illinois	T	I	250+	Hello U.S.A.	Lerner Publications
Illinois	S	I	250+	Land of Liberty	Red Brick Learning
Illinois	Q	I	250+	One Nation	Capstone Press
I'm a Caterpillar	G	I	169	Marzollo, Jean	Scholastic
I'm a Chef	M	I	250+	Literacy 2000	Rigby
I'm a Good Reader	H	RF	188	Carousel Readers	Pearson Learning Group
I'm a Little Seed	D	F	30	Pair-It Books	Steck-Vaughn
I'm a Little Teapot	L	TL	250+	Trapani, Iza	Charlesbridge
I'm a Pill Bug	M	I	640	Tokuda, Yukihisa	Kane/Miller Book Publishers
I'm a Seed	G	F	181	Marzollo, Jean	Scholastic
I'm a Wimp!	R	RF	250+	Sails	Rigby
I'm an Artist	N	I	250+	Literacy 2000	Rigby
I'm an Astronaut	H	F	162	Voyages	SRA/McGraw Hill
I'm an Entrepreneur	N	B	501	Independent Readers Social Studies	Houghton Mifflin Harcourt
I'm Bigger Than You!	C	F	48	Sunshine	Wright Group/McGraw Hill
I'm Brave	D	RF	51	Sunshine	Wright Group/McGraw Hill
I'm Glad I'm Me	F	RF	147	Windmill Books	Rigby
I'm Glad to Say	H	RF	165	Sunshine	Wright Group/McGraw Hill
I'm Heading to the Rodeo	I	RF	160	Bebop Books	Lee & Low Books Inc.

TITLE	LEVEL	GENRE	WORD COUNT	AUTHOR / SERIES	PUBLISHER / DISTRIBUTOR
I'm Hungry	B	I	25	Fitros, Pamela	Kaeden Books
I'm Hungry	D	RF	84	Tuer, Judy	Scholastic
I'm Hungry	C	RF	37	Visions	Wright Group/McGraw Hill
I'm in the Fish Tank	M	I	865	Springboard	Wright Group/McGraw Hill
I'm King of the Castle	F	F	184	Watanabe, Shigeo	Philomel/Penguin
I'm King of the Mountain	G	F	285	Pacific Literacy	Pacific Learning
I'm Looking for My Hat	F	RF	89	Book Bank	Wright Group/McGraw Hill
I'm No One Else But Me	M	RF	1010	Book Bank	Wright Group/McGraw Hill
I'm Not Jess	I	RF	174	Gear Up!	Wright Group/McGraw Hill
I'm Not Scared	J	F	408	Rigby Gigglers	Rigby
I'm Not, I'm Not	C	RF	19	Windmill Books	Wright Group/McGraw Hill
I'm Out of My Body . . . Please Leave a Message	N	F	250+	The Zack Files	Grossett & Dunlap
I'm Red	B	F	25	The Book Project	Sundance
I'm Sick Today	H	RF	150	Carousel Readers	Pearson Learning Group
I'm So Hungry and Other Plays	M	F	250+	Orbit Chapter Books	Pacific Learning
I'm Telling	E	RF	71	Teacher's Choice Series	Pearson Learning Group
Images of Nikki Grimes, The	Y	B	1974	Leveled Readers	Houghton Mifflin Harcourt
Imagination	O	B	250+	Meet The Author	Richard C. Owen
Imagine That	J	F	250+	Story Box	Wright Group/McGraw Hill
Imagine This, James Robert	P	F	250+	Action Packs	Rigby
Immigrant Children in New York City	V	I	1614	Reading Street	Pearson
Immigrants	T	I	250+	Sandler, Martin W.	HarperTrophy
Immigrants at Work: A Look at Migrant Labor	V	I	2264	Reading Street	Pearson
Immigrants: Coming to America	R	I	250+	Thompson, Gare	Children's Press
Immigration	U	I	250+	Primary Source Readers	Teacher Created Materials
Immortal	S	HF	250+	Tristars	Richard C. Owen
Imogene's Antlers	L	F	191	Small, David	Scholastic
*Impossible Bend and Other Cases, The	O	RF	250+	Simon, Seymour	Avon
Impossible Bridge, The	N	I	250+	Pacific Literacy	Pacific Learning
Impossible Victory: The Battle of Stalingrad	X	I	250+	Bloodiest Battles	Capstone Press
Impressionism	Z	I	250+	Eyewitness Books	DK Publishing
Imran and the Watch	J	RF	415	Cambridge Reading	Pearson Learning Group
In a Cave	LB	I	11	Animal Homes	Lerner Publications
*In a Dark, Dark Room	J	TL	250+	Schwartz, Alvin	HarperTrophy
In a Dark, Dark Wood	E	TL	168	Carter, David	Simon & Schuster Trade
In a Dark, Dark Wood	E	F	81	Story Box	Wright Group/McGraw Hill
In a Faraway Forest	K	F	347	Kratky, Lada Josefa	Hampton-Brown
In a Muddle	G	RF	93	Voyages	SRA/McGraw Hill
In a New Land	L	HF	378	Sunshine	Wright Group/McGraw Hill
In a Painting	E	I	52	Canizares, Susan; Moreton, Daniel	Scholastic
In a Pickle	M	RF	250+	SupaDoopers	Sundance
In a Town	E	RF	47	Little Celebrations	Pearson Learning Group
In a Tree	LB	I	12	Animal Homes	Lerner Publications
In a Tree	M	I	250+	Look Once Look Again	Creative Teaching Press
In and Out	C	I	41	Location	Lerner Publishing
In and Out	I	I	254	Where Words	Capstone Press
In Aunt Lucy's Kitchen	M	RF	250+	Rylant, Cynthia	Aladdin
In Business with Mallory	O	RF	250+	Friedman, Laurie	Lerner Publications
In City Gardens	L	I	250+	Little Celebrations	Pearson Learning Group
In Danger	M	I	250+	Home Connection Collection	Rigby
In Defense of Liberty: The Story of America's Bill of Rights	Z	I	250+	Freedman, Russell	Holiday House
In Flight	U	I	250+	The News	Richard C. Owen

* Collection of short stories
# Graphic text

TITLE	LEVEL	GENRE	WORD COUNT	AUTHOR / SERIES	PUBLISHER / DISTRIBUTOR
In Front of the Ant: Walking with Beetles and Other Insects	K	I	166	Kuwahara, Ryuichi	Kane/Miller Book Publishers
In Grandma Rita's Garden	K	RF	191	Books for Young Learners	Richard C. Owen
In Grandma's Garden	H	RF	244	Sunshine	Wright Group/McGraw Hill
In Her Stride	T	B	250+	WorldScapes	ETA Cuisenaire
In Hiding, Animals Under Cover	L	I	250+	Burke, Melissa Blackwell	Steck-Vaughn
In My Backyard	LB	RF	18	Visions	Wright Group/McGraw Hill
In My Bag	H	RF	237	Windows on Literacy	National Geographic
In My Bed	C	RF	57	Literacy 2000	Rigby
In My Bucket	F	RF	94	Carousel Readers	Pearson Learning Group
In My Country	G	I	119	My World	Capstone Press
In My Desert	D	I	24	Little Celebrations	Pearson Learning Group
In My Family	B	I	35	Explorations	Okapi Eductional Materials
In My Family	B	I	35	Explorations	Eleanor Curtain Publishing
In My Family	D	RF	61	Windows on Literacy	National Geographic
In My Garden	B	RF	35	Bookshop	Mondo
In My Garden	C	RF	36	Carousel Readers	Pearson Learning Group
In My Garden	I	I	250+	Momentum Literacy Program	Troll Associates
In My Head	G	RF	74	Voyages	SRA/McGraw Hill
In My Home	E	I	126	My World	Capstone Press
In My Neighborhood	E	I	110	My World	Capstone Press
In My Pocket	E	RF	195	Carousel Readers	Pearson Learning Group
In My Pocket	B	RF	34	Instant Readers	Harcourt School Publishers
In My Pocket	A	I	28	Sun Sprouts	ETA Cuisenaire
In My Room	C	I	74	Leveled Literacy Intervention/ Blue System	Heinemann
In My Room	C	F	44	Literacy 2000	Rigby
In My Room	D	RF	58	Seedlings	Continental Press
In My School	A	I	27	Little Books for Early Readers	University of Maine
In My State	G	I	137	My World	Capstone Press
In My Toolbox	B	I	36	Foundations	Wright Group/McGraw Hill
In My Town	F	I	111	My World	Capstone Press
In My World	H	I	120	My World	Capstone Press
In My Yard	A	I	28	Leveled Readers	Houghton Mifflin Harcourt
In My Yard	A	I	28	Leveled Readers/CA	Houghton Mifflin Harcourt
In Nonna's Kitchen	C	I	32	Home Connection Collection	Rigby
In One Tidepool	P	I	937	Sharing Nature with Children	Dawn Publications
In Our Classroom	A	I	33	PM Plus Starters	Rigby
In Our Classroom	F	I	89	Windows on Literacy	National Geographic
In Our Country	F	I	63	Canizares, Susan; Moreton, Daniel	Scholastic
In Our Own Words: Teen Art and Writing	W	RF	250+	Power Up!	Steck-Vaughn
In Our Yard	G	RF	150+	Reed, Janet	Scholastic
In Ravi's Fort	C	RF	78	Lighthouse	Rigby
In School	A	I	21	On Our Way to English	Rigby
In Search of Food	M	SF	923	Springboard	Wright Group/McGraw Hill
In Search of Something Delicious	G	F	202	Seedlings	Continental Press
In Search of the Giant Pandas	P	RF	250+	Reading Safari	Mondo
In Search of the Grand Canyon	W	I	250+	Fraser, Mary Ann	Henry Holt & Co.
In Search of the Great Bears	S	I	250+	Literacy 2000	Rigby
In Search of Treasure	L	TL	250+	PM Story Books	Rigby
*In Short: A Collection of Brief Creative Nonfiction	Z	I	250+	Kitchen, J.; Jones, M. P.	W. W. Norton
In Spring	B	I	15	Discovery Links	Newbridge

* Collection of short stories
# Graphic text

TITLE	LEVEL	GENRE	WORD COUNT	AUTHOR / SERIES	PUBLISHER / DISTRIBUTOR
In Spring	B	I	34	Science	Outside the Box
In Summer	D	I	36	Discovery Links	Newbridge
In the Afternoon	H	I	156	PM Nonfiction-Green	Rigby
In the Air	D	I	38	Berger, Samantha & Chessen, Betsey	Scholastic
In the Air	B	I	54	Sails	Rigby
In the Air	B	I	20	Sunshine	Wright Group/McGraw Hill
In the Arctic	C	I	43	Science	Outside the Box
In the Backyard	H	F	197	Little Celebrations	Pearson Learning Group
In the Bank	H	I	140	Independent Readers Social Studies	Houghton Mifflin Harcourt
In the Barn	D	I	38	Vocabulary Readers	Houghton Mifflin Harcourt
In the Barrio	J	RF	130	Ada, Alma Flor	Scholastic
In the Bathroom	B	RF	24	Smart Starts	Rigby
In the Boat	LB	F	30	Big Cat	Pacific Learning
In the Box	C	RF	64	Leveled Readers Emergent	Houghton Mifflin Harcourt
In the Box	C	RF	33	Phonics and Friends	Hampton-Brown
In the Box	D	I	36	Sun Sprouts	ETA Cuisenaire
In the Box	B	F	64	The Book Project	Sundance
In the Car	B	RF	32	First Stories	Pacific Learning
In the Chicken Coop	D	I	56	Twig	Wright Group/McGraw Hill
In the City	LB	RF	22	Home Connection Collection	Rigby
In the City	A	I	20	Leveled Readers	Houghton Mifflin Harcourt
In the City	A	I	20	Leveled Readers/CA	Houghton Mifflin Harcourt
In the City	C	RF	45	Pasternac, Susana	Scholastic
In the City	C	RF	50	Rise & Shine	Hampton-Brown
In the City of Rome	J	TL	250+	Literacy 2000	Rigby
In the Clouds	M	RF	250+	Literacy 2000	Rigby
In the Clouds	H	RF	192	Literacy by Design	Rigby
In the Country	D	RF	21	Home Connection Collection	Rigby
In the Country	D	I	54	Vocabulary Readers	Houghton Mifflin Harcourt
In the Country, In the City	B	I	71	Rigby Literacy	Rigby
In the Dark	B	RF	36	Big Cat	Pacific Learning
In the Dark Forest	C	I	24	Pacific Literacy	Pacific Learning
In the Days of Missions and Ranchos	T	I	1029	Vocabulary Readers	Houghton Mifflin Harcourt
In the Days of Missions and Ranchos	T	I	1029	Vocabulary Readers/CA	Houghton Mifflin Harcourt
In the Days of Missions and Ranchos	T	I	1029	Vocabulary Readers/TX	Houghton Mifflin Harcourt
In the Days of the Dinosaur	V	I	3182	Leveled Readers Science	Houghton Mifflin Harcourt
In the Days of the Dinosaurs: Arky, the Dinosaur With Feathers	K	HF	250+	PM Plus Story Books	Rigby
In the Desert	D	I	109	Leveled Readers	Houghton Mifflin Harcourt
In the Desert	D	I	109	Leveled Readers/CA	Houghton Mifflin Harcourt
In the Desert	M	I	250+	Look Once Look Again	Creative Teaching Press
In the Desert	D	I	51	Pacific Literacy	Pacific Learning
In the Desert	H	I	138	Shutterbug Books	Steck-Vaughn
In the Desert	D	I	62	Sunshine	Wright Group/McGraw Hill
In the Desert	N	I	558	Time for Kids	Teacher Created Materials
In the Dinosaur's Paw	M	RF	250+	Giff, Patricia Reilly	Bantam
In the Doghouse	K	RF	250+	Kimmelman, Leslie	Holiday House
In the Fall	H	I	286	Leveled Readers	Houghton Mifflin Harcourt
In the Fall	H	I	286	Leveled Readers/CA	Houghton Mifflin Harcourt
In the Fall	H	I	286	Leveled Readers/TX	Houghton Mifflin Harcourt
In the Fast Lane	R	I	250+	Literacy 2000	Rigby
In the Forest	B	I	48	Adams, Lorraine; Bruvold, Lynn	Eagle Crest Books

* Collection of short stories
\# Graphic text

TITLE	LEVEL	GENRE	WORD COUNT	AUTHOR / SERIES	PUBLISHER / DISTRIBUTOR
In the Forest	L	I	581	Leveled Readers	Houghton Mifflin Harcourt
In the Forest	N	I	250+	Look Once Look Again	Creative Teaching Press
In the Forest	C	F	71	Schiller, Melissa	Scholastic
In the Forest	B	I	38	Science	Outside the Box
In the Forest	M	I	556	Time for Kids	Teacher Created Materials
In the Forest	C	RF	42	Twig	Wright Group/McGraw Hill
In the Forest	G	RF	95	Voyages	SRA/McGraw Hill
In the Garage	Z+	RF	250+	Fullerton, Alma	Fitzhenry & Whiteside
In the Garden	LB	RF	18	Big Cat	Pacific Learning
In the Garden	A	I	20	Leveled Readers	Houghton Mifflin Harcourt
In the Garden	A	I	20	Leveled Readers/CA	Houghton Mifflin Harcourt
In the Garden	D	I	90	Literacy 2000	Rigby
In the Garden	M	I	250+	Look Once Look Again	Creative Teaching Press
In the Garden	A	I	32	PM Plus Starters	Rigby
In the Garden	A	F	24	Sails	Rigby
In The Garden	E	I	N/A	Sun Sprouts	ETA Cuisenaire
In the Garden	WB	I	N/A	Windows on Literacy	National Geographic
In the Green Room	Q	RF	250+	Reading Safari	Mondo
In the Hen House	G	RF	82	Oppenlander, Meredith	Kaeden Books
In the Jungle	F	F	247	Dominie Math Stories	Pearson Learning Group
In the Jungle River	I	I	214	Sails	Rigby
In the Kitchen	N	I	250+	Bookweb	Rigby
In the Kitchen	C	I	16	Canizares, Susan; Chessen, Betsey	Scholastic
In the Land of the Polar Bear	J	RF	250+	Robinson, F. R.	Steck-Vaughn
*In the Line of Fire: Eight Women War Spies	U	B	250+	Sullivan, George	Scholastic
In the Meadow	M	I	250+	Look Once Look Again	Creative Teaching Press
In the Middle of the Night	I	RF	250+	Sunshine	Wright Group/McGraw Hill
In the Mirror	B	RF	26	Story Box	Wright Group/McGraw Hill
In the Morning	H	I	218	PM Nonfiction-Green	Rigby
In the Mountains	U	I	250+	iOpeners	Pearson Learning Group
In the Mountains	LB	I	14	Twig	Wright Group/McGraw Hill
In the Mud	B	F	30	Sails	Rigby
In the News	Q	I	250+	Wildcats	Wright Group/McGraw Hill
In the News	O	I	250+	Wonder World	Wright Group/McGraw Hill
In the Park	D	RF	65	Foundations	Wright Group/McGraw Hill
In the Park	B	I	37	Gear Up!	Wright Group/McGraw Hill
In the Park	F	I	96	Literacy 2000	Rigby
In the Park	M	I	250+	Look Once Look Again	Creative Teaching Press
In the Park	A	I	35	On Our Way to English	Rigby
In the Path of Lewis & Clark: Traveling the Missouri	V	I	250+	Lourie, Peter	Silver Burdett Press
In the Pond	B	RF	32	Gear Up!	Wright Group/McGraw Hill
In the Pool	E	RF	158	Joy Starters	Pearson Learning Group
In the Rain	E	RF	121	On Our Way to English	Rigby
In the Rain	B	F	19	Ready Readers	Pearson Learning Group
In the Rain Forest	B	I	65	Leveled Readers	Houghton Mifflin Harcourt
In the Rain Forest	B	I	65	Leveled Readers/CA	Houghton Mifflin Harcourt
In the Rain Forest	E	I	57	Twig	Wright Group/McGraw Hill
In the Rain Forest	Q	I	250+	Wildcats	Wright Group/McGraw Hill
In the Rainforest	M	I	567	Time for Kids	Teacher Created Materials
In the Sea	D	I	87	Leveled Readers	Houghton Mifflin Harcourt
In the Sea	D	I	87	Leveled Readers/CA	Houghton Mifflin Harcourt
In the Sea	D	I	87	Leveled Readers/TX	Houghton Mifflin Harcourt

* Collection of short stories
# Graphic text

TITLE	LEVEL	GENRE	WORD COUNT	AUTHOR / SERIES	PUBLISHER / DISTRIBUTOR
In the Sea	B	I	41	Little Red Readers	Sundance
In the Sea	C	I	41	Sunshine	Wright Group/McGraw Hill
In the Shade of the Nispero Tree	S	HF	250+	Bernier-Grand, Carmen T.	Orchard Books
In the Shopping Cart	A	I	24	PM Starters	Rigby
In the Sky	B	I	42	Little Red Readers	Sundance
In the Sky	B	I	96	Vocabulary Readers/CA	Houghton Mifflin Harcourt
In the Sky	A	I	20	Vocabulary Readers/CA	Houghton Mifflin Harcourt
In the Sky	B	I	96	Vocabulary Readers/TX	Houghton Mifflin Harcourt
#In the Small	Z	F	250+	Hague, Michael	Little, Brown & Co.
In the Small, Small Pond	K	RF	65	Fleming, Denise	Scholastic
In the Summer	A	I	36	Gear Up!	Wright Group/McGraw Hill
In the Sun	C	F	95	Phonics and Friends	Hampton-Brown
In the Supermarket	A	RF	24	Smart Starts	Rigby
In the Teacup	A	F	35	KinderReaders	Rigby
In the Toy Shop	C	F	29	The Book Project	Sundance
In the Tree	C	I	110	Leveled Readers	Houghton Mifflin Harcourt
In the Tree	B	RF	48	Leveled Readers Emergent	Houghton Mifflin Harcourt
In the Tree	C	I	110	Leveled Readers/CA	Houghton Mifflin Harcourt
In the Tree	B	I	36	Windows on Literacy	National Geographic
In the Treetops	J	I	250+	Explorations	Eleanor Curtain Publishing
In the Treetops	J	I	250+	Explorations	Okapi Educational Materials
In the Treetops	M	I	250+	Woolley, M.; Pigdon, K.	Mondo
In the Van	C	RF	55	Leveled Readers	Houghton Mifflin Harcourt
In the Water	LB	I	12	Animal Homes	Lerner Publications
In the Woods	B	I	48	Bookshop	Mondo
In the Woods	WB	I	N/A	Christini, Ermanno; Puricelli, Luigi	Scholastic
In the Woods	B	F	25	Gibson, Akimi	Scholastic
In the Woods	B	I	60	Literacy by Design	Rigby
In the Woods	B	I	60	On Our Way to English	Rigby
In the Woods	G	I	304	Reading Corners	Pearson Learning Group
In the Yard	F	RF	40	Early Readers	Compass Point Books
In the Yard	D	RF	88	Rigby Literacy	Rigby
In the Year of the Boar and Jackie Robinson	S	HF	250+	Lord, Bette Bao	HarperTrophy
In the Zoo	H	F	252	Lane, Jerry	Ginn & Co.
In Times Long Ago	G	I	196	Learn to Read	Creative Teaching Press
In Went Goldilocks	C	TL	30	Literacy 2000	Rigby
In Winter	H	RF	263	Leveled Literacy Intervention/ Green System	Heinemann
In-Between Days, The	P	RF	250+	Bunting, Eve	HarperTrophy
Incantation	Y	HF	250+	Hoffman, Alice	Little, Brown & Co.
Inch by Inch	K	F	183	Lionni, Leo	Scholastic
Incident at Hawk's Hill	V	F	250+	Eckert, Allen W.	Little, Brown & Co.
Inclined Plane, The	K	I	237	Reading Street	Pearson
Inclined Planes and Wedges	Q	I	1869	Early Bird Energy Physics Books	Lerner Publishing
Inclined Planes to the Rescue	O	I	250+	Simple Machine to the Rescue	Capstone Press
Incognito	S	RF	2619	Leveled Readers	Houghton Mifflin Harcourt
Incognito	S	RF	2619	Leveled Readers/CA	Houghton Mifflin Harcourt
Incognito	S	RF	2619	Leveled Readers/TX	Houghton Mifflin Harcourt
*Incredible Animal Adventures	N	I	250+	George, Jean Craighead	HarperCollins
Incredible Creatures	P	I	250+	Explorers	Wright Group/McGraw Hill
Incredible Insects	M	I	250+	Sunshine	Wright Group/McGraw Hill
Incredible Journey of Thor Heyerdahl and the Kon-Tiki Raft, The	T	I	2415	Reading Street	Pearson

* Collection of short stories
# Graphic text

TITLE	LEVEL	GENRE	WORD COUNT	AUTHOR / SERIES	PUBLISHER / DISTRIBUTOR
Incredible Journey, The	V	F	250+	Burnford, Sheila	Bantam
Incredible Places	P	I	250+	Wildcats	Wright Group/McGraw Hill
Incredible Rescue of Apollo 13, The	O	I	521	Springboard	Wright Group/ McGraw Hill
Incredible Sea Journey, The	R	HF	2921	Reading Street	Pearson
Incredible Shrinking Kid, The	P	F	250+	Abbott, Tony	Scholastic
*Incredible Shrinking Machine and Other Cases, The	O	RF	250+	Simon, Seymour	Avon
Incredible, Edible Plants	L	I	250+	Early Connections	Benchmark Education
Independence Day	J	I	131	American Holidays	Lerner Publications
Independence Day	Q	I	250+	Holiday Histories	Heinemann Library
Independence Day	L	I	182	Pebble Books	Red Brick Learning
Independence Hall	I	I	77	Leveled Readers	Houghton Mifflin Harcourt
India	W	I	250+	Countries and Cultures	Capstone Press
India	O	I	250+	Countries of the World	Red Brick Learning
India	P	I	2187	Country Explorers	Lerner Publications
India	S	I	250+	First Reports: Countries	Compass Point Books
India	W	I	250+	Primary Source Readers	Teacher Created Materials
India in the Past and Present	T	I	250+	Reading Expeditions	National Geographic
Indian Captive, The Story of Mary Jemison	V	HF	250+	Lenski, Lois	Harper Trophy
Indian Chiefs	Y	B	250+	Freedman, Russell	Scholastic
Indian in the Cupboard, The	R	F	250+	Banks, Lynne Reid	Avon
Indian Ocean, The	N	I	250+	Oceans	Capstone Press
Indian School, The	P	RF	250+	Whelan, Gloria	HarperTrophy
Indian Wars, The	Q	I	250+	On Deck	Rigby
Indian Winter, An	X	I	250+	Freedman, Russell	Holiday House
Indiana	T	I	250+	Hello U.S.A.	Lerner Publications
Indiana	S	I	250+	Land of Liberty	Red Brick Learning
Indiana	R	I	250+	This Land Is Your Land	Compass Point Books
Indiana Pacers, The	S	I	250+	Team Spirit	Norwood House Press
Indianapolis Colts, The	S	I	5063	Team Spirit	Norwood House Press
*Indian-Head Pennies and Other Cases, The	O	RF	250+	Simon, Seymour	Avon
India's Amazing Geography	Y	I	1953	Leveled Readers	Houghton Mifflin Harcourt
India's Amazing Geography	Y	I	1953	Leveled Readers/CA	Houghton Mifflin Harcourt
India's Monsoons	X	I	1124	Leveled Readers	Houghton Mifflin Harcourt
India's Monsoons	X	I	1124	Leveled Readers/CA	Houghton Mifflin Harcourt
Indigo Jackal, The	N	TL	250+	WorldScapes	ETA Cuisenaire
Indigo's Star	W	RF	250+	McKay, Hilary	Aladdin
Indonesia	O	I	1546	A Ticket to …	Carolrhoda Books
Indonesia	O	I	250+	Countries of the World	Red Brick Learning
Indonesia	T	I	250+	First Reports: Countries	Compass Point Books
Indonesia: A Question and Answer Book	P	I	250+	Questions & Answers: Countries	Capstone Press
Indonesia's Rain Forests	Q	I	250+	Theme Sets	National Geographic
Industrial Giants	U	B	250+	Primary Source Readers	Teacher Created Materials
Industrial Revolution	U	I	250+	Primary Source Readers	Teacher Created Materials
Industry Changes America	S	I	250+	Reading Expeditions	National Geographic
Indy Cars	M	I	250+	Horsepower	Capstone Press
Indy Cars	T	I	250+	The World's Fastest	Red Brick Learning
Infinite Imagination, The	S	I	250+	Kids Discover Reading	Wright Group/McGraw Hill
Inkheart	W	F	250+	Funke, Cornelia	Scholastic
In-Line Skates, The	F	RF	137	Foundations	Wright Group/McGraw Hill
Inn Keeper's Apprentice	Z	B	250+	Say, Allen	Penguin Group
Innocent Prisoners!: Life in a Japanese American Internment Camp	T	HF	1621	Reading Street	Pearson
Innocent's Story, The	Z	F	250+	Singer, Nicky	Holiday House

* Collection of short stories
# Graphic text

TITLE	LEVEL	GENRE	WORD COUNT	AUTHOR / SERIES	PUBLISHER / DISTRIBUTOR
Innovations from Ancient China	Y	I	2264	Leveled Readers	Houghton Mifflin Harcourt
Innovations from Ancient China	Y	I	2264	Leveled Readers/CA	Houghton Mifflin Harcourt
Insect	W	I	250+	Eyewitness Books	DK Publishing
Insect and Spider	C	F	50	Science	Outside the Box
Insect Army, The	O	I	250+	InfoQuest	Rigby
Insect Evidence	S	I	250+	Forensic Crime Solvers	Capstone Press
Insect Luck	G	RF	131	Appleton-Smith, Laura	Flyleaf Publishing
Insect or Arachnid?	K	I	284	Reading Street	Pearson
Insect-Eaters	J	I	213	Rigby Focus	Rigby
Insectigations	V	I	250+	Blobaum, Cindy	Chicago Review Press
Insects	N	I	250+	A New True Book	Children's Press
Insects	U	I	250+	Bird, Bettina; Short, Joan	Mondo
Insects	M	I	250+	Exploring the Animal Kingdom	Capstone Press
Insects	R	I	250+	Eyewitness Explorers	DK Publishing
Insects	J	I	171	MacLulich, Carolyn	Scholastic
Insects	A	I	28	Nonfiction Set 1	Literacy Footprints
Insects	G	I	107	Rigby Focus	Rigby
Insects & Spiders	U	I	250+	World Book Looks at Science	World Book
Insects & Spiders	R	I	250+	Worldwise	Franklin Watts
Insects All Around	K	I	229	Early Connections	Benchmark Education
Insects and Spiders	H	I	150	Time for Kids	Teacher Created Materials
Insects Change	J	I	202	Shutterbug Books	Steck-Vaughn
Insects That Bother Us	G	I	87	Foundations	Wright Group/McGraw Hill
Insects That Use Color	I	I	310	Sails	Rigby
Insects Up Close	D	I	85	Shutterbug Books	Steck-Vaughn
Insects, Insects, Insects	G	I	167	Appleton-Smith, Laura	Flyleaf Publishing
Inside a Cave	J	I	331	In Step Readers	Rigby
Inside a Cell	S	I	1651	Leveled Readers Science	Houghton Mifflin Harcourt
Inside a Rain Forest	M	I	353	Pair-It Books	Steck-Vaughn
Inside All	K	I	110	Sharing Nature with Children	Dawn Publications
Inside an Ant Colony	K	I	250+	Rookie Read-About Science	Children's Press
Inside Caves	L	I	306	Sails	Rigby
Inside Caves	P	I	250+	Scooters	ETA Cuisenaire
Inside Ecosystems and Biomes	T	I	250+	Science Readers	Teacher Created Materials
Inside Insects	G	I	89	Sails	Rigby
Inside Look at Zoos, An	S	I	1864	Leveled Readers	Houghton Mifflin Harcourt
Inside Look at Zoos, An	S	I	1864	Leveled Readers/CA	Houghton Mifflin Harcourt
Inside Look at Zoos, An	S	I	1864	Leveled Readers/TX	Houghton Mifflin Harcourt
Inside Nests	D	I	115	Sails	Rigby
Inside or Outside?	E	RF	57	Literacy 2000	Rigby
Inside School	A	I	35	Little Books for Early Readers	University of Maine
Inside Story, The	E	RF	43	Teacher's Choice Series	Pearson Learning Group
Inside the Game - Rex Jones	P	SF	1649	Zucker, Jonny	Stone Arch Books
Inside the Sun	O	I	250+	Rosen Real Readers	Rosen Publishing Group
Inside the Volcano	T	F	2272	Leveled Readers	Houghton Mifflin Harcourt
Inside the Volcano	T	F	2272	Leveled Readers/CA	Houghton Mifflin Harcourt
Inside the Water Cycle	U	I	250+	Science Readers	Teacher Created Materials
Inside the World of Matter	Y	I	250+	Science Readers	Teacher Created Materials
Inside the Zoo	R	I	1322	Leveled Readers	Houghton Mifflin Harcourt
Inside the Zoo	R	I	1322	Leveled Readers/CA	Houghton Mifflin Harcourt
Inside the Zoo	R	I	1322	Leveled Readers/TX	Houghton Mifflin Harcourt
Inside, Outside, Upside Down	E	F	118	Berenstain, Stan & Jan	Random House
Inside-Outside Book of London, The	WB	I	N/A	Monro, Roxie	Dutton/Penguin
Inside-Outside Book of Washington, DC	WB	I	N/A	Monro, Roxie	Dutton/Penguin

* Collection of short stories
# Graphic text

TITLE	LEVEL	GENRE	WORD COUNT	AUTHOR / SERIES	PUBLISHER / DISTRIBUTOR
Inspector Grub and the Fizzer-X Spy	S	RF	250+	Bookweb	Rigby
Inspector Grub and the Gourmet Mystery	Q	RF	250+	Bookweb	Rigby
Inspector Grub and the Jelly Bean Robber	L	RF	250+	Bookweb	Rigby
Inspiration of Art, The	V	I	2437	Reading Street	Pearson
Inspirational Artists	T	I	250+	Take Two Books	Wright Group/McGraw Hill
Instead of a Car	H	RF	250+	Reading Safari	Mondo
*Instead of Three Wishes: Magical Short Stories	Y	F	250+	Turner, Megan Whalen	Penguin Group
Instrument Families	O	I	250+	Bookweb	Rigby
Interactions of Living Things	Q	I	1588	Science Support Readers	Houghton Mifflin Harcourt
International Children's Day	U	I	250+	WorldScapes	ETA Cuisenaire
International Day	D	I	47	Home Connection Collection	Rigby
International Food Fair, An	K	RF	381	Reading Street	Pearson
International Space Station, The	M	I	560	Rigby Flying Colors	Rigby
International Space Station, The	V	I	2708	Vocabulary Readers	Houghton Mifflin Harcourt
International Space Station, The	V	I	2708	Vocabulary Readers/CA	Houghton Mifflin Harcourt
International Space Station, The	V	I	2708	Vocabulary Readers/TX	Houghton Mifflin Harcourt
Internet	S	I	250+	Theme Sets	National Geographic
Interrupted Journey: Saving Endangered Sea Turtles	U	I	250+	Lasky, Kathryn	Candlewick Press
Interrupting the Big Sleep	P	RF	250+	Orbit Chapter Books	Pacific Learning
Interruptions	F	F	81	Bookshop	Mondo
Interview with Alan Ant, An	L	I	441	Springboard	Wright Group/McGraw Hill
Interview with Cindy Centipede	N	I	864	Springboard	Wright Group/McGraw Hill
Into Space	J	I	250+	Momentum Literacy Program	Troll Associates
Into the Eye of a Hurricane	T	I	2712	Leveled Readers Science	Houghton Mifflin Harcourt
Into the Jungle: Searching for the Rare Mountain Gorilla	L	I	250+	World Quest Adventures	World Quest Learning
Into the Sea	L	I	208	Leveled Literacy Intervention/ Blue System	Heinemann
Into the Unknown	V	I	250+	WorldScapes	ETA Cuisenaire
Into the Wild: Warriors, Book 1	U	F	250+	Hunter, Erin	Avon Books
Into the Woods	W	F	250+	Gardner, Lyn	David Fickling Books
Introducing the Euro	W	I	1930	Leveled Readers Social Studies	Houghton Mifflin Harcourt
Inuit of Arctic Canada, The	X	I	2714	Vocabulary Readers	Houghton Mifflin Harcourt
Inuit of Arctic Canada, The	X	I	2714	Vocabulary Readers/CA	Houghton Mifflin Harcourt
Invaders!	Y	I	3289	Leveled Readers	Houghton Mifflin Harcourt
Invasion of the Boy Snatchers	X	RF	250+	Harrison, Lisi	Little, Brown & Co.
Invasive Species	T	I	250+	Connectors	Pacific Learning
Inventing Oatmeal	P	F	784	Reading Street	Pearson
Inventing the Telephone	L	I	250+	iOpeners	Pearson Learning Group
Invention of Hugo Cabret, The	W	RF	250+	Selznick, Brian	Scholastic
Inventions from Space Travel	T	I	2639	Reading Street	Pearson
Inventions in Communication	O	I	789	Pair-It Turn and Learn	Steck-Vaughn
Inventions in Communications	R	I	1045	Time for Kids	Teacher Created Materials
Inventions in the Clothing Industry	R	I	1049	Time for Kids	Teacher Created Materials
Inventions in the Food Industry	R	I	1039	Time for Kids	Teacher Created Materials
Inventions of Alexander Graham Bell, The	Q	B	250+	On Deck	Rigby
Inventions of Amanda Jones, The	Q	B	250+	On Deck	Rigby
Inventions of Eli Whitney, The	Q	B	250+	On Deck	Rigby
Inventions of Granville Woods, The	Q	B	250+	On Deck	Rigby
Inventions of Martha Coston, The	Q	B	250+	On Deck	Rigby
Inventions of Thomas Alva Edison, The	Q	B	250+	On Deck	Rigby
Inventions of Thomas Edison, The	O	I	250+	Rigby Star Quest	Rigby
Inventions That Changed the World	P	I	250+	Reading Expeditions	National Geographic

I

* Collection of short stories
# Graphic text

TITLE	LEVEL	GENRE	WORD COUNT	AUTHOR / SERIES	PUBLISHER / DISTRIBUTOR
Inventions: Great Ideas and Where They Came From	U	I	250+	High Five Reading	Red Brick Learning
Inventions: Stonger, Faster, Better	U	I	250+	Kids Discover Reading	Wright Group/McGraw Hill
Inventive Mind of Jules Verne, The	X	B	1828	Leveled Readers	Houghton Mifflin Harcourt
Inventor of the Telephone	M	B	448	Leveled Readers	Houghton Mifflin Harcourt
Inventor of the Telephone	M	B	448	Leveled Readers/CA	Houghton Mifflin Harcourt
Inventor of the Telephone	M	B	448	Leveled Readers/TX	Houghton Mifflin Harcourt
Inventors	T	I	250+	Sandler, Martin W.	HarperTrophy
Inventors at Work	U	I	2596	Reading Street	Pearson
Inventor's Diary, The	M	RF	271	Pacific Literacy	Pacific Learning
Inventor's Vision, An	V	B	250+	WorldScapes	ETA Cuisenaire
Inventors: Making Things Better	M	I	250+	Pair-It Books	Steck-Vaughn
Invertebrates	Q	I	943	Time for Kids	Teacher Created Materials
Investigating Electromagnetism	Y	I	250+	Science Readers	Teacher Created Materials
Investigating Forces and Motion	W	I	250+	Science Readers	Teacher Created Materials
Investigating Inverterbrates	N	I	964	Rigby Flying Colors	Rigby
Investigating Landforms	T	I	250+	Science Readers	Teacher Created Materials
Investigating Plate Tectonics	W	I	250+	Science Readers	Teacher Created Materials
Investigating Simple Organisms	Y	I	250+	Science Readers	Teacher Created Materials
Investigating Storms	S	I	250+	Science Readers	Teacher Created Materials
Investigating the Chemistry of Atoms	Y	I	250+	Science Readers	Teacher Created Materials
Investigating the Human Body	U	I	250+	Science Readers	Teacher Created Materials
Invincible Louisa	Z	B	250+	Meigs, Cornelia	Scholastic
Invisible	I	F	111	Read Alongs	Rigby
Invisible Clues	W	I	250+	Sails	Rigby
Invisible Dog, The	M	F	250+	King-Smith, Dick	Alfred A. Knopf
Invisible Fran, The	N	SF	250+	Benton, Jim	Aladdin Paperbacks
Invisible in the Third Grade	M	RF	250+	Cuyler, Margery	Scholastic
Invisible Spy, The	J	F	227	Foundations	Wright Group/McGraw Hill
Invisible Stanley	N	F	250+	Brown, Jeff	HarperTrophy
Iowa	T	I	250+	Hello U.S.A.	Lerner Publications
Iowa	S	I	250+	Land of Liberty	Red Brick Learning
Iowa	T	I	250+	Sea to Shining Sea	Children's Press
Iowa	R	I	250+	This Land Is Your Land	Compass Point Books
Iqbal	X	RF	250+	D'Adamo, Francesco	Atheneum
Iran	T	I	250+	First Reports: Countries	Compass Point Books
Iraq: A Question and Answer Book	P	I	250+	Questions and Answers: Countries	Capstone Press
Ireland	W	I	250+	Countries and Cultures	Capstone Press
Ireland: A Question and Answer Book	P	I	250+	Question and Answer Countries	Capstone Press
Iris Rose Maple	O	RF	1913	Take Two Books	Wright Group/ McGraw-Hill
Irish Experience, The	U	I	250+	Literacy by Design	Rigby
Irish Immigrants in America: An Interactive History Adventure	T	HF	250+	You Choose Books	Capstone Press
Irish Immigration	V	I	250+	Theme Sets	National Geographic
Irish Step Dancing	S	I	250+	Dance	Capstone Press
Irma Imogen: Inventor	R	RF	250+	Take Two Books	Wright Group/McGraw Hill
Irniq and the Eagles	M	TL	250+	Orbit Chapter Books	Pacific Learning
Iron Giant, The	O	SF	250+	Hughes, Ted	Alfred A. Knopf
Iron Hans: A Grimms' Fairy Tale	S	TL	250+	Mitchell, Stephen	Candlewick Press
Iron Horse, The	A	F	21	Smart Starts	Rigby
Iron Mikkos the Magnet Man	T	F	250+	Reading Safari	Mondo
Iron Ring, The	W	F	250+	Alexander, Lloyd	Puffin/Penguin
Ironman	Z	RF	250+	Crutcher, Chris	Laurel-Leaf Books

* Collection of short stories
\# Graphic text

TITLE	LEVEL	GENRE	WORD COUNT	AUTHOR / SERIES	PUBLISHER / DISTRIBUTOR
Iroquois Indians, The	P	I	250+	Native Peoples	Red Brick Learning
Iroquois League, The	Q	I	250+	Rosen Real Readers	Rosen Publishing Group
Iroquois, The	R	I	250+	First Reports	Compass Point Books
Iroquois, The	T	I	4385	Native American Stories	Lerner Publications
Iroquois, The: Longhouse Builders	R	I	250+	America's First Peoples	Capstone Press
Iroquois, The: People of the Longhouse	S	I	250+	Explore More	Wright Group/McGraw Hill
Iroquois, The: People of the Northeast	S	I	250+	Theme Sets	National Geographic
Irrational Season, The	Z	B	250+	L'Engle, Madeleine	HarperCollins
Irritating Irma	N	F	250+	Literacy 2000	Rigby
Is a Dollar Enough?	D	RF	75	Visions	Wright Group/McGraw Hill
Is Anyone Home?	F	RF	65	Maris, Ron	Greenwillow
Is It a Fish?	K	I	606	Sunshine	Wright Group/McGraw Hill
Is It a Fruit?	G	I	101	Rigby Literacy	Rigby
Is It Alive?	C	RF	26	Learn to Read	Creative Teaching Press
Is It almost Ready?	C	RF	53	Book Bus	Creative Edge
Is It Almost Time?	H	RF	252	InfoTrek	ETA Cuisenaire
Is It an Insect?	C	I	85	First Stories	Pacific Learning
Is It Better to be Judged by a Jury of Your Peers Than by a Judge?	W	I	250+	Bookshop	Mondo
Is It Big Or Little?	B	I	31	Properties of Matter	Lerner Publications
Is It Floating?	E	I	146	Sunshine	Wright Group/McGraw Hill
Is It Heavy Or Light?	B	I	25	Properties of Matter	Lerner Publications
Is It Hot? Is It Not?	C	I	30	Phonics Readers	Compass Point Books
Is It Living or Nonliving?	E	I	30	Living or Nonliving	Lerner Publishing
Is It Metal?	C	I	19	Rigby Focus	Rigby
Is It Odd or Even?	K	I	344	Yellow Umbrella Books	Red Brick Learning
Is It Red? Is It Yellow? Is It Blue?	WB	F	N/A	Hoban, Tana	Greenwillow
Is It Rough? Is It Smooth?	D	I	45	Rosen Real Readers	Rosen Publishing Group
Is It Time Yet?	G	RF	162	Foundations	Wright Group/McGraw Hill
Is It Time?	C	RF	52	Campbell, J. G.	Scholastic
Is Jim In?	F	RF	106	Supersonics	Rigby
Is That a Bear?	H	RF	225	Sunshine	Wright Group/McGraw Hill
Is That Fair?	W	I	250+	WorldScapes	ETA Cuisenaire
Is the Spaghetti Ready?	E	F	80	New Reader Series	Bungalo Books
Is the Wise Owl Wise?	I	F	250+	Literacy by Design	Rigby
Is the Wise Owl Wise?	I	F	250+	Rigby Literacy	Rigby
Is the Wise Owl Wise?	I	F	250+	Rigby Star	Rigby
Is There Anyone Out There?	O	I	1625	Big Cat	Pacific Learning
Is There Life in Outer Space	O	I	250+	Branley, Franklyn M.	HarperCollins
Is This a Collection?	F	I	88	Gear Up!	Wright Group/McGraw Hill
Is This a Monster?	C	F	93	Bookshop	Mondo
Is This a Moose?	G	I	150+	Armstrong, Jenny	Scholastic
Is This My Dinner?	I	F	162	Black/Fry	Whitman
Is This You?	F	RF	250+	Krauss, Ruth	Scholastic
Is Tomorrow My Birthday?	E	RF	87	Blaxland, Wendy	Scholastic
Is Your Mama a Llama?	L	F	250+	Guarino, Deborah	Scholastic
Is Your Pail Full?	F	RF	162	Mishica, Clare	Continental Press
Isaac Asimov	W	I	1575	Vocabulary Readers	Houghton Mifflin Harcourt
Isaac Asimov	W	B	1575	Vocabulary Readers/CA	Houghton Mifflin Harcourt
Isaac Newton	Y	B	250+	Krull, Kathleen	Scholastic
#Isaac Newton and the Laws of Motion	V	B	250+	Graphic Library	Capstone Press
Isaac Newton and the Laws of the Universe	X	B	250+	Science Readers	Teacher Created Materials
Isabel Allende	X	B	3430	Leveled Readers	Houghton Mifflin Harcourt
Isabel Allende	X	B	3430	Leveled Readers/CA	Houghton Mifflin Harcourt

* Collection of short stories
# Graphic text

TITLE	LEVEL	GENRE	WORD COUNT	AUTHOR / SERIES	PUBLISHER / DISTRIBUTOR
Isabel Allende	X	B	3430	Leveled Readers/TX	Houghton Mifflin Harcourt
Isabella: A Wish for Miguel	Q	HF	250+	Childhood Journeys	Aladdin
Isabel's Day	C	I	88	Literacy by Design	Rigby
Isabel's Day	C	I	88	On Our Way to English	Rigby
Isabel's Story: From Guatemala to Georgia	V	HF	250+	Reading Expeditions	National Geographic
Isadora Duncan	O	B	915	Leveled Readers	Houghton Mifflin Harcourt
Isadora Duncan	O	B	915	Leveled Readers/CA	Houghton Mifflin Harcourt
Isadora Duncan	O	B	915	Leveled Readers/TX	Houghton Mifflin Harcourt
Ish	L	RF	250+	Reynolds, Peter H.	Candlewick Press
Ishi's Tale of Lizard	P	TL	250+	Hinton, Leanne; Roth, Susan L.	Farrar, Straus and Giroux
Island Baby	M	RF	250+	Keller, Holly	Scholastic
Island Far From Home, An	W	HF	250+	Donahue, John	Carolrhoda Books
Island Keeper	T	RF	250+	Mazer, Harry	Language for Learning Assoc.
Island Life	R	I	250+	iOpeners	Pearson Learning Group
*Island Like You, An: Stories of the Barrio	Z	RF	250+	Cofer, Judith Ortiz	Penguin Group
Island of the Blue Dolphins	V	HF	250+	O'Dell, Scott	Bantam
Island of the Skog, The	M	F	250+	Kellogg, Steven	Dial/Penguin
Island of Wingo, The	N	F	250+	Sails	Rigby
Island on Bird Street, The	X	HF	250+	Orlev, Uri	Houghton Mifflin Harcourt
Island Picnic, The	H	RF	236	PM Story Books	Rigby
Island to Island	K	RF	250+	Ready to Read	Pacific Learning
Island, The	R	RF	250+	Paulsen, Gary	Bantam
Island, The	D	RF	24	Wildsmith, Brian	Oxford University Press
Islander, The	T	F	250+	Rylant, Cynthia	Random House
Islands	J	I	294	Landforms	Lerner Publications
Isn't It Cool?	R	I	250+	Action Packs	Rigby
Isn't It Strange?	H	I	128	Polette, Nancy	Kaeden Books
Israel	O	I	2096	A Ticket to …	Carolrhoda Books
Israel	O	I	250+	Countries of the World	Red Brick Learning
Israel	P	I	2361	Country Explorers	Lerner Publications
Israel	Q	I	250+	First Reports: Countries	Compass Point Books
Israel ABCs: A Book About the People and Places of Israel	Q	I	250+	Country ABCs	Picture Window Books
It All Adds Up	J	I	329	Pair-It Turn and Learn	Steck-Vaughn
It Came From Ohio!: My Life as a Writer	R	B	250+	Stine, R. L.	Scholastic
It Came Through the Wall	O	F	1182	Healey, Tim	Mondo
It Can Fly	LB	I	8	Windows on Literacy	National Geographic
It Could Be Worse	E	F	108	Home Connection Collection	Rigby
It Didn't Frighten Me	D	F	250+	Bookshop	Mondo
It Happened to Nancy	Z+	B	250+	Sparks, Beatrice (Ed.)	Avon
It Is Halloween!	J	RF	404	Appleton-Smith, Laura	Flyleaf Publishing
It Is My Birthday, Too!	E	RF	50	Pair-It Turn and Learn	Steck-Vaughn
It Is Raining	F	I	56	PM Plus Nonfiction	Rigby
It Looked Like Spilt Milk	E	RF	172	Shaw, Charles	Harper & Row
It Must Be Clay	H	I	173	Independent Readers Science	Houghton Mifflin Harcourt
It Only Looks Easy	T	RF	250+	Swallow, Pamela Curtis	Scholastic
It Smells Like Friday	L	F	250+	Popcorn	Sundance
It Sounds Like Music	D	I	56	Pair-It Books	Steck-Vaughn
It Started as a Seed	F	I	126	Learn to Read	Creative Teaching Press
It Started as an Egg	G	I	179	Learn to Read	Creative Teaching Press
It Starts as a Seed	E	I	36	Rosen Real Readers	Rosen Publishing Group
It Takes a Village	L	RF	250+	Cowen-Fletcher, J.	Scholastic
It Takes All Kinds	N	I	250+	Voyages	SRA/McGraw Hill

Organized Alphabetically by Title
Storable Database at www.fountasandpinnellleveledbooks.com

* Collection of short stories
\# Graphic text

TITLE	LEVEL	GENRE	WORD COUNT	AUTHOR / SERIES	PUBLISHER / DISTRIBUTOR
It Takes Balance	M	I	250+	Rigby Literacy	Rigby
It Takes Three	K	F	501	Silly Millies	Millbrook Press
It Takes Time to Grow	H	RF	57	Sunshine	Wright Group/McGraw Hill
*It Was on Fire When I Lay Down on It	Z	I	250+	Fulghum, Robert	Ballantine Books
It Wasn't My Fault	L	RF	250+	Lester, Helen	Houghton Mifflin Harcourt
It Would Be Fun!	F	F	203	Start to Read	School Zone
Italy	H	I	34	Canizares, Susan; Chessen, Betsey	Scholastic
Italy	O	I	250+	Countries of the World	Red Brick Learning
Italy	Q	I	250+	First Reports: Countries	Compass Point Books
Italy	R	I	250+	Theme Sets	National Geographic
Itch! Itch!	C	RF	76	Bookshop	Mondo
Itchy Mitch	U	RF	250+	Bookshop	Mondo
Itchy, Itchy Chicken Pox	F	RF	131	Maccarone, Grace	Scholastic
Ithaka	Z+	TL	250+	Geras, Adele	Harcourt
It'll Be All Right on the Night!	Q	I	250+	Orbit Chapter Books	Pacific Learning
It's a Beautiful Day!	H	F	229	Silly Millies	Millbrook Press
It's a Big Country	Q	I	250+	WorldScapes	ETA Cuisenaire
It's a Bit Tricky	G	RF	250+	Home Connection Collection	Rigby
It's a Blizzard!	L	I	250+	Rosen Real Readers	Rosen Publishing Group
It's a Butterfly's Life	O	I	250+	Kelly, Irene	Holiday House
It's a Dog's Life	R	I	250+	Explore More	Wright Group/McGraw Hill
It's a Fair Swap	P	I	393	Reading Street	Pearson
It's a Fiesta, Benjamin	N	RF	250+	Giff, Patricia Reilly	Bantam
It's a Frog's Life	Q	I	250+	Literacy 2000 Satellites	Rigby
It's a Gift	H	I	156	Lighthouse	Rigby
It's a Goal!	V	I	250+	WorldScapes	ETA Cuisenaire
It's a Good Thing That There Are Insects	H	I	250+	Fowler, Allan	Scholastic
It's a Mammal!	Q	I	250+	iOpeners	Pearson Learning Group
It's a Party	D	I	24	Berger, Samantha; Moreton, Daniel	Scholastic
It's a Party!	A	F	15	Leveled Readers	Houghton Mifflin Harcourt
It's a Party!	A	F	15	Leveled Readers/CA	Houghton Mifflin Harcourt
It's a Rule	E	I	128	Yellow Umbrella Books	Red Brick Learning
It's a World of Time Zones	R	I	2055	Reading Street	Pearson
It's a Zoo!	H	RF	100	City Stories	Rigby
It's About Time	Q	I	250+	Orbit Collections	Pacific Learning
It's About Time	M	I	481	Storyteller Nonfiction	Wright Group/McGraw Hill
It's About Time	B	I	39	Twig	Wright Group/McGraw Hill
It's About Time	K	I	250+	Yellow Umbrella Books	Capstone Press
It's About Time!	I	I	224	In Step Readers	Rigby
It's About Time!	X	I	2675	Reading Street	Pearson
It's Alive!	L	I	432	Reading Street	Pearson
It's Alive: Earth's Plants and Animals	T	I	250+	Kids Discover Reading	Wright Group/McGraw Hill
It's All Greek to Me	P	F	250+	Scieszka, Jon	Penguin Group
It's All in the Soil	Q	I	250+	iOpeners	Pearson Learning Group
It's All in Your Mind, James Robert	P	F	250+	Literacy 2000	Rigby
It's Alright to Cry	F	RF	138	Teacher's Choice Series	Pearson Learning Group
*It's Back to School We Go: First Day Stories From Around the World	Q	I	3508	Jackson, Ellen	Millbrook Press
It's Broken	E	RF	88	Dominie Phonics Reader	Pearson Learning Group
It's Circus Time, Dear Dragon	F	F	322	Dear Dragon	Norwood House Press
It's Cold Where I Live	H	RF	98	Windows on Literacy	National Geographic
It's Dinner Time	WB	I	N/A	Windows on Literacy	National Geographic

TITLE	LEVEL	GENRE	WORD COUNT	AUTHOR / SERIES	PUBLISHER / DISTRIBUTOR
It's Easy!	O	RF	250+	Leveled Readers Language Support	Houghton Mifflin Harcourt
It's Electric!	T	I	250+	Rosen Real Readers	Rosen Publishing Group
It's Fall!	K	RF	875	Glaser, Linda	Millbrook Press
It's Football Time	C	RF	24	Geddes, Diana	Kaeden Books
It's Fun to Exercise	J	I	250+	Rosen Real Readers	Rosen Publishing Group
It's Game Day	D	RF	65	Salem, Lynn; Stewart, Josie	Continental Press
It's George!	H	RF	250+	Cohen, Miriam	Bantam
It's Halloween!	K	RF	250+	Prelutsky, Jack	Scholastic
It's Halloween, Dear Dragon	F	F	309	Dear Dragon	Norwood House Press
It's Hot	D	RF	54	Ready Readers	Pearson Learning Group
It's in the Air	Z	I	2025	Independent Readers Science	Houghton Mifflin Harcourt
It's Just a Trick	O	RF	250+	Literacy 2000	Rigby
It's Justin Time, Amber Brown	K	RF	250+	Danziger, Paula	Puffin Books
It's Magic	H	F	204	Start to Read	School Zone
It's Melting	C	RF	16	Learn to Read	Creative Teaching Press
It's Mine!	P	F	250+	Lionni, Leo	Scholastic
It's My Bread	B	F	43	Pacific Literacy	Pacific Learning
It's New, It's Improved, It's Terrible!	Q	RF	250+	Manes, Stephen	Bantam
It's Noisy at Night	E	RF	80	Wonder World	Wright Group/McGraw Hill
It's Not All Ancient History	Y	I	250+	iOpeners	Pearson Learning Group
It's Not Easy Being a Bunny	I	F	250+	Sadler, Marilyn	Random House
It's Not Easy Being George	S	RF	250+	Smith, Janice Lee	HarperTrophy
It's Not Fair	F	RF	51	Tadpoles	Rigby
It's Not Going to Rain	J	F	363	Gear Up!	Wright Group/McGraw Hill
It's Not the End of the World	T	RF	250+	Blume, Judy	Dell
It's Not the Same	I	RF	250+	Sunshine	Wright Group/McGraw Hill
It's Our Right	V	I	2676	Reading Street	Pearson
It's Our World	Q	I	250+	Orbit Collections	Pacific Learning
It's Our World, Too!	T	I	250+	Hoose, Phillip	Sunburst
It's Pumpkin Time!	J	RF	234	Hall, Zoe	Scholastic
It's Raining	E	I	86	Teacher's Choice Series	Pearson Learning Group
It's Raining!	C	I	32	Pair-It Books	Steck-Vaughn
It's Shearing Time, Max!	H	F	225	Sun Sprouts	ETA Cuisenaire
It's Show Time	S	I	250+	InfoQuest	Rigby
It's Snowing!	J	I	193	Find Out Readers	Continental Press
It's Spring	A	I	24	Vocabulary Readers	Houghton Mifflin Harcourt
It's Spring!	H	F	124	Berger, Samantha; Chanko, Pamela	Scholastic
It's Spring!	K	RF	941	Glaser, Linda	Millbrook Press
It's St. Patrick's Day, Dear Dragon	F	F	250+	Dear Dragon	Norwood House Press
It's Summer!	K	RF	972	Glaser, Linda	Millbrook Press
It's Super Mouse!	C	F	40	Brand New Readers	Candlewick Press
It's Taco Time	F	I	56	Teacher's Choice Series	Pearson Learning Group
It's Test Day, Tiger Turcotte	M	RF	4628	Flood, Pansie Hart	Carolrhoda Books
It's the Fashion	S	I	250+	Literacy 2000	Rigby
It's Time for Bed	E	RF	126	Visions	Wright Group/McGraw Hill
It's Time to Eat!	C	I	49	Davidson, Avelyn	Scholastic
It's Time to Get Up	E	RF	143	Visions	Wright Group/McGraw Hill
It's Time!	A	I	24	Early Connections	Benchmark Education
It's Time!	H	I	175	Yellow Umbrella Books	Red Brick Learning
It's Too Loud	C	I	53	Independent Readers Science	Houghton Mifflin Harcourt
It's Up to Me	T	I	250+	InfoTrek	ETA Cuisenaire
Itsy Bitsy Spider, The	K	TL	225	Trapani, Iza	Charlesbridge

* Collection of short stories
\# Graphic text

TITLE	LEVEL	GENRE	WORD COUNT	AUTHOR / SERIES	PUBLISHER / DISTRIBUTOR
I've Been Working on the Railroad	J	TL	250+	Traditional Songs	Picture Window Books
I've Got Mail	N	RF	250+	InfoTrek	ETA Cuisenaire
I've Got New Sneakers	H	RF	111	City Kids	Rigby
I've Lost My Boot	C	RF	18	Windmill Books	Wright Group/McGraw Hill
Ivy & Bean	M	RF	250+	Barrows, Annie	Chronicle Books
Ivy & Bean and the Ghost That Had to Go	M	RF	250+	Barrows, Annie	Scholastic
Ivy's Journal: A Trip to the Yucatán	R	RF	250+	Bookshop	Mondo
Izzy, Willy-Nilly	X	RF	250+	Voigt, Cynthia	Aladdin
Izzy's Move	D	F	129	Leveled Readers	Houghton Mifflin Harcourt
Izzy's Move	D	F	129	Leveled Readers/CA	Houghton Mifflin Harcourt
Izzy's Move	D	F	129	Leveled Readers/TX	Houghton Mifflin Harcourt

I

* Collection of short stories
# Graphic text

TITLE	LEVEL	GENRE	WORD COUNT	AUTHOR / SERIES	PUBLISHER / DISTRIBUTOR
J. Pierpont Morgan and Wall Street	R	I	250+	On Deck	Rigby
J. T.	Q	RF	250+	Wagner, Jane	Bantam
*J.J. Rabbit and the Monster	M	F	250+	I Am Reading	Kingfisher
J: My Name Is Jess	C	RF	61	Little Books	Sadlier-Oxford
Jace, Mace, and the Big Race	F	RF	124	Start to Read	School Zone
Jack	D	TL	11	Jumbled Tumbled Tales & Rhymes	Rigby
Jack and Billy	C	RF	50	PM Plus Story Books	Rigby
Jack and Billy and Rose	G	RF	179	PM Plus Story Books	Rigby
Jack and Chug	I	F	337	PM Story Books-Orange	Rigby
Jack and Jill	D	TL	25	Jumbled Tumbled Tales & Rhymes	Rigby
Jack and Jill	D	F	40	Seedlings	Continental Press
Jack and Jill	E	TL	51	Sunshine	Wright Group/McGraw Hill
Jack and the Bean Stalk	D	TL	109	Folk Tales	Pioneer Valley
Jack and the Beanstalk	K	TL	901	Hunia, Fran	Ladybird Books
Jack and the Beanstalk	L	TL	664	Leveled Literacy Intervention/ Blue System	Heinemann
Jack and the Beanstalk	I	TL	250+	Literacy 2000	Rigby
Jack and the Beanstalk	K	TL	250+	Storyworlds	Heinemann Educational Books
Jack and the Beanstalk	H	TL	170	Sunshine	Wright Group/McGraw Hill
Jack and the Beanstalk	K	TL	250+	Weisner, David	Scholastic
Jack and the Magic Harp	K	TL	250+	PM Tales and Plays-Gold	Rigby
Jack DePert at the Supermarket	G	RF	188	Wonder World	Wright Group/McGraw Hill
Jack in the Box	I	F	250+	Story Box	Wright Group/McGraw Hill
Jack Plays the Violin	H	RF	250+	Schultz, Jessica	Scholastic
Jack Prelutsky	M	B	690	Leveled Readers	Houghton Mifflin Harcourt
Jack Prelutsky	M	B	690	Leveled Readers/CA	Houghton Mifflin Harcourt
Jack Prelutsky	M	B	690	Leveled Readers/TX	Houghton Mifflin Harcourt
Jack Russell Dog Detective: Dog Den Mystery	N	F	250+	Odgers, Darrel & Sally	Kane/Miller Book Publishers
Jack Russell Dog Detective: The Awful Pawful	N	F	250+	Odgers, Darrel & Sally	Kane/Miller Book Publishers
Jack Russell Dog Detective: The Lying Postman	N	F	250+	Odgers, Darrel & Sally	Kane/Miller Book Publishers
Jack Russell Dog Detective: The Mugged Pug	N	F	250+	Odgers, Darrel & Sally	Kane/Miller Book Publishers
Jack Russell Dog Detective: The Phantom Mudder	N	F	250+	Odgers, Darrel & Sally	Kane/Miller Book Publishers
Jack Russell Dog Detective: The Sausage Situation	N	F	250+	Odgers, Darrel & Sally	Kane/Miller Book Publishers
Jack Russell Terriers	I	I	161	Dogs	Capstone Press
Jackals	P	I	1812	Animal Scavengers	Lerner Publishing
Jackaroo	Y	RF	250+	Voigt, Cynthia	Scholastic
Jacket, The	R	RF	250+	Clements, Andrew	Aladddin Paperbacks
Jackets	C	RF	42	Joy Readers	Pearson Learning Group
Jackie & Me	T	F	250+	Gutman, Dan	Harper Trophy
Jackie Robinson	T	B	250+	Amazing Americans	Wright Group/McGraw Hill
Jackie Robinson	P	B	250+	Early Biographies	Compass Point Books
Jackie Robinson	N	B	235	First Biographies	Capstone Press
Jackie Robinson	O	B	1991	On My Own Biography	Lerner Publications
Jackie Robinson	P	B	250+	Photo-Illustrated Biographies	Red Brick Learning
Jackie Robinson	R	B	1789	Reading Street	Pearson

* Collection of short stories
# Graphic text

J

TITLE	LEVEL	GENRE	WORD COUNT	AUTHOR / SERIES	PUBLISHER / DISTRIBUTOR
Jackie Robinson	N	B	250+	Soar To Success	Houghton Mifflin Harcourt
Jackie Robinson and the Breaking of the Color Barrier	S	B	250+	Shorto, Russell	Millbrook Press
Jackie Robinson and the Story of All-Black Baseball	N	I	250+	O'Connor, Jim	Random House
Jackie Robinson Breaks the Color Line	V	B	250+	Cornerstones of Freedom	Children's Press
Jackie Robinson Breaks Through	Q	I	1350	Vocabulary Readers	Houghton Mifflin Harcourt
Jackie Robinson Breaks Through	Q	B	1350	Vocabulary Readers/CA	Houghton Mifflin Harcourt
Jackie Robinson, Breaking Barriers	X	I	2907	Vocabulary Readers	Houghton Mifflin Harcourt
Jackie Robinson, Breaking Barriers	X	B	2907	Vocabulary Readers/CA	Houghton Mifflin Harcourt
Jackie Robinson: Baseball's First Black Major Leaguer	O	B	250+	Greene, Carol	Children's Press
Jackie's New Friend	F	I	168	O'Connor, C. M.	Continental Press
Jack-in-the-Box	B	RF	34	Literacy 2000	Rigby
Jacko of Baker Street	I	RF	369	Sails	Rigby
Jacko, the Dreamer	I	F	306	Sails	Rigby
Jack-O-Lantern	B	I	37	Twig	Wright Group/McGraw Hill
Jack-O-Lanterns	D	I	47	Pebble Books	Capstone Press
Jacks	P	I	250+	Games Around the World	Compass Point Books
Jacks and More Jacks	F	F	79	Little Celebrations	Pearson Learning Group
Jack's Balloon	D	RF	69	Reading Safari	Mondo
Jack's Birthday	C	RF	89	PM Plus Story Books	Rigby
Jack's Boat	I	I	172	Windows on Literacy	National Geographic
*Jack's New Power: Stories From a Caribbean Year	W	RF	250+	Gantos, Jack	Sunburst
Jack's New Skates	E	RF	148	Developing Books	Pioneer Valley
Jack's Pack	C	I	22	KinderReaders	Rigby
Jack's Road	C	RF	59	PM Stars	Rigby
Jackson Pollock in Action	S	B	1263	Leveled Readers	Houghton Mifflin Harcourt
Jackson Pollock in Action	S	B	1263	Leveled Readers/CA	Houghton Mifflin Harcourt
Jackson Pollock in Action	S	B	1263	Leveled Readers/TX	Houghton Mifflin Harcourt
Jackson's Bear	K	F	678	Springboard	Wright Group/ McGraw Hill
Jackson's Monster	I	F	250+	Little Readers	Houghton Mifflin Harcourt
Jacksonville Jaguars, The	S	I	250+	Team Spirit	Norwood House Press
Jacob Have I Loved	X	RF	250+	Paterson, Katherine	HarperTrophy
Jacob Two-Two and the Dinosaur	P	F	250+	Richler, Mordecai	Tundra Books
Jacob Two-Two Meets the Hooded Fang	P	F	250+	Richler, Mordecai	Seal Books
Jacob's Day	F	RF	51	Windows on Literacy	National Geographic
Jacob's Rescue: A Holocaust Story	Y	HF	250+	Drucker, M.; Halperin, M.	Bantam
Jacques Cousteau	L	B	250+	Biography	Benchmark Education
Jacques Cousteau: In Love with the Sea	R	B	250+	Explore More	Wright Group/McGraw Hill
Jade Dragon, The	P	RF	250+	Marsden, Carolyn & Shin-Mui Loh, Virginia"	Candlewick Press
Jade Emperor and the Four Dragons, The	K	TL	250+	Lighthouse	Rigby
Jade Green	Z	F	250+	Naylor, Phyllis Reynolds	Simon & Schuster
Jaguar Attack!	P	RF	250+	Bookweb	Rigby
Jaguars	O	I	250+	First Reports	Compass Point Books
Jaguars	U	I	250+	High Performance	Red Brick Learning
Jaguars	U	I	6508	Nature Watch Books	Lerner Publications
Jaguars	J	I	78	Pebble Books	Red Brick Learning
Jaguar's Jewel, The	N	RF	250+	A to Z Mysteries	Random House
Jaime Escalante	T	B	250+	Literacy by Design	Rigby
Jaime Escalante, A Great Teacher	M	B	273	Independent Readers Social Studies	Houghton Mifflin Harcourt

J

* Collection of short stories
# Graphic text

TITLE	LEVEL	GENRE	WORD COUNT	AUTHOR / SERIES	PUBLISHER / DISTRIBUTOR
Jake	A	I	35	Little Books for Early Readers	University of Maine
Jake and the Big Fish	E	RF	130	PM Photo Stories	Rigby
Jake and the Copycats	J	RF	250+	Rocklin, Joanne	Bantam
Jake Can Play	B	RF	42	Little Books for Early Readers	University of Maine
Jake Drake Bully Buster	O	RF	250+	Clements, Andrew	Aladddin Paperbacks
Jake Drake Class Clown	O	RF	250+	Clements, Andrew	Aladddin Paperbacks
Jake Drake Know-It-All	O	RF	250+	Clements, Andrew	Aladdin
Jake Drake Teacher's Pet	O	RF	250+	Clements, Andrew	Aladddin Paperbacks
Jake Greenthumb	J	F	250+	Bookshop	Mondo
Jake Kicks a Goal	D	RF	87	PM Photo Stories	Rigby
Jake Makes a Map	D	RF	55	Leveled Readers	Houghton Mifflin Harcourt
Jake the Snake	K	F	250+	Supersonics	Rigby
Jake Was a Pirate	M	F	250+	Voyages	SRA/McGraw Hill
Jake, the Juggler	J	RF	403	Sails	Rigby
Jake's Bird Feeder	J	RF	514	Kanninen, Barbara	Kaeden Books
Jake's Car	D	RF	80	PM Photo Stories	Rigby
Jake's Dream	N	RF	846	Reading Street	Pearson
Jake's First Word	H	RF	204	Books for Young Learners	Richard C. Owen
Jake's Lemonade Stand	H	RF	294	Kanninen, Barbara	Kaeden Books
Jake's Map	C	RF	63	Leveled Readers Language Support	Houghton Mifflin Harcourt
Jake's Plane	E	RF	137	PM Photo Stories	Rigby
Jake's Toad House	I	RF	382	Kanninen, Barbara	Kaeden Books
Jamaica	O	I	1895	A Ticket to …	Carolrhoda Books
Jamaica	G	I	97	Nonfiction Set 4	Literacy Footprints
Jamaica	Q	I	250+	Theme Sets	National Geographic
Jamaica and Brianna	K	RF	250+	Little Readers	Houghton Mifflin Harcourt
Jamaica's Find	K	RF	250+	Havill, Juanita	Scholastic
Jamall's City Garden	I	I	250+	Rigby Literacy	Rigby
Jamberry	J	F	111	Degen, Bruce	Harper & Row
James A. Garfield	U	B	250+	Profiles of the Presidents	Compass Point Books
James A. Garfield: Twentieth President	R	B	250+	Getting to Know the U.S. Presidents	Children's Press
James and the Alien Experiment	P	SF	9643	Prue, S	Stone Arch Books
James and the Giant Peach	Q	F	250+	Dahl, Roald	Penguin Group
James Buchanan	U	B	250+	Profiles of the Presidents	Compass Point Books
James Buchanan: Fifteenth President	R	B	250+	Getting to Know the U.S. Presidents	Children's Press
James Earl Carter, Jr.	U	B	250+	Profiles of the Presidents	Compass Point Books
James Is Hiding	A	RF	24	Windmill Books	Wright Group/McGraw Hill
James K. Polk	U	B	250+	Profiles of the Presidents	Compass Point Books
James K. Polk: Eleventh President	R	B	250+	Getting to Know the U.S. Presidents	Children's Press
James Madison	U	B	250+	Amazing Americans	Wright Group/McGraw Hill
James Madison	S	B	250+	Primary Source Readers	Teacher Created Materials
James Madison	U	B	250+	Profiles of the Presidents	Compass Point Books
James Madison: Founding Father	Q	B	250+	Rosen Real Readers	Rosen Publishing Group
James Madison: Fourth President	R	B	250+	Getting to Know the U.S. Presidents	Children's Press
James Monroe	U	B	250+	Profiles of the Presidents	Compass Point Books
James Monroe: Fifth President	R	B	250+	Getting to Know the U.S. Presidents	Children's Press
James Stuart: Motocross Great	Q	B	250+	Dirt Bikes	Capstone Press
Jamestown Colony, The	V	I	250+	Cornerstones of Freedom	Children's Press

J

* Collection of short stories
\# Graphic text

TITLE	LEVEL	GENRE	WORD COUNT	AUTHOR / SERIES	PUBLISHER / DISTRIBUTOR
Jamestown Colony, The	V	I	250+	Let Freedom Ring	Capstone Press
Jamestown Colony, The	T	I	250+	We The People	Compass Point Books
Jamestown, 1607	W	I	250+	Cooper, Michael L.	Holiday House
Jamestown: New World Adventure	T	I	250+	Adventures in Colonial America	Troll Associates
*Jamie and Angus Stories, The	N	RF	250+	Fine, Anne	Candlewick Press
*Jamie and Angus Together	N	RF	250+	Fine, Anne	Candlewick Press
Jamila Joins the Team	K	RF	509	Springboard	Wright Group/McGraw Hill
Jan and the Jacket	E	RF	74	Oxford Reading Tree	Oxford University Press
Jan Can Juggle	B	RF	25	Ready Readers	Pearson Learning Group
Jan Matzeliger, Inventor	T	B	1916	Leveled Readers Science	Houghton Mifflin Harcourt
Jane Addams	U	B	250+	Amazing Americans	Wright Group/ McGraw Hill
Jane Addams	P	B	250+	Community Builders	Children's Press
Jane Addams	Q	B	250+	Early Biographies	Compass Point Books
Jane Addams	O	B	586	Leveled Readers Social Studies	Houghton Mifflin Harcourt
Jane Addams: A Life of Cooperation	P	B	592	Pull Ahead Books	Lerner Publications
Jane and the Beanstalk	Q	TL	1534	Leveled Readers	Houghton Mifflin Harcourt
Jane Eyre	Z	RF	250+	Bronte, Charlotte	Scholastic
Jane Eyre	Z	RF	250+	High-Fliers	Pacific Learning
Jane Goodall	N	B	250+	Biography	Benchmark Education
Jane Goodall	M	B	250+	First Biographies	Capstone Press
Jane Goodall	O	B	250+	Leveled Readers	Houghton Mifflin Harcourt
Jane Goodall	E	B	183	Leveled Readers Science	Houghton Mifflin Harcourt
Jane Goodall	R	B	1298	Time for Kids	Teacher Created Materials
Jane Goodall and the Chimps	L	B	250+	Twig	Wright Group/McGraw Hill
Jane Goodall and the Wild Chimpanzees	L	B	250+	Birnbaum, Bette	Steck-Vaughn
Jane Goodall: A Chimp's Best Friend	K	I	247	Shutterbug Books	Steck-Vaughn
Jane Goodall: A Good and True Heart	S	B	250+	Pair-It Books	Steck-Vaughn
Jane Goodall: A Life of Loyalty	N	B	522	Pull Ahead- Biographies	Lerner Publications
Jane Goodall: Animal Scientist and Friend	R	B	250+	Science Readers	Teacher Created Materials
Jane Goodall: Finding Hope in the Wilds of Africa	R	B	250+	High Five Reading	Red Brick Learning
Jane Goodall: Living With Chimpanzees	E	B	162	Leveled Readers Science	Houghton Mifflin Harcourt
Jane Goodall: Living With the Chimpanzees	M	B	250+	Rigby Literacy	Rigby
Jane Goodall: Living With the Chimpanzees	M	B	250+	Rigby Star Quest	Rigby
Jane Mt. Pleasant	H	B	134	Leveled Readers Science	Houghton Mifflin Harcourt
Jane's Car	F	RF	121	PM Story Books	Rigby
Jane's Mansion	N	I	250+	Literacy 2000	Rigby
Janitor's Boy, The	S	RF	250+	Clements, Andrew	Aladddin Paperbacks
Jan's New Fan	C	RF	34	KinderReaders	Rigby
January to March	N	RF	2082	Take Two Books	Wright Group/McGraw Hill
Japan	P	I	250+	A True Book	Children's Press
Japan	O	I	250+	Countries of the World	Red Brick Learning
Japan	P	I	2162	Country Explorers	Lerner Publications
Japan	Q	I	250+	First Reports: Countries	Compass Point Books
Japan	P	I	250+	Many Cultures, One World	Capstone Press
Japan	M	I	488	Pair-It Books	Steck-Vaughn
Japan	R	I	250+	Theme Sets	National Geographic
Japan ABCs: A Book About the People and Places of Japan	Q	I	250+	Country ABCs	Picture Window Books
Japan: A Question and Answer Book	P	I	250+	Questions and Answers: Countries	Capstone Press
Japan: Land of Contrasts	R	I	250+	Orbit Chapter Books	Pacific Learning
Japanese American Internment, The: An Interactive History Adventure	W	HF	250+	You Choose Books	Capstone Press

J

* Collection of short stories
# Graphic text

TITLE	LEVEL	GENRE	WORD COUNT	AUTHOR / SERIES	PUBLISHER / DISTRIBUTOR
Japanese Garden, The	K	RF	250+	PM Plus Story Books	Rigby
Japanese Giant Hornet, The	M	I	250+	Literacy by Design	Rigby
Japanese Language, The	R	I	1945	Reading Street	Pearson
Jar of Dreams, A	R	HF	250+	Uchida, Yoshiko	Aladdin
Jasmine's Duck	H	RF	207	Lighthouse	Rigby
Jason and the Aliens Down the Street	O	F	250+	Greer, Greg; Ruddick, Bob	HarperTrophy
Jason and the Blind Puppy	I	RF	605	Rigby Flying Colors	Rigby
Jason and the Space Creature	K	F	643	Leveled Readers	Houghton Mifflin Harcourt
Jason and the Space Creature	K	F	643	Leveled Readers/CA	Houghton Mifflin Harcourt
Jason and the Space Creature	K	F	643	Leveled Readers/TX	Houghton Mifflin Harcourt
Jason Kidd Story, The	P	RF	250+	Moore, David	Scholastic
Jason's Bus Ride	G	F	117	Ziefert, Harriet	Penguin Group
Jason's Gold	T	HF	250+	Hobbs, Will	William Morrow
Jason's Journey	N	RF	250+	InfoTrek	ETA Cuisenaire
Jasper	F	RF	107	Books for Young Learners	Richard C. Owen
Jasper and the Bully	K	F	250+	Jasper the Cat	Pioneer Valley
Jasper and the Kitten	I	F	647	Jasper the Cat	Pioneer Valley
Jasper the Fat Cat	C	RF	68	Jasper the Cat	Pioneer Valley
Javed's Pet	K	RF	250+	Reading Safari	Mondo
Javelinas	P	I	2056	Early Bird Nature Books	Lerner Publications
Jaws of Life, The	T	I	4144	A Great Idea	Norwood House Press
Jazmin's Notebook	Z	RF	250+	Grimes, Nikki	Penguin Group
Jazz Age Poet: A Story About Langston Hughes	R	B	8795	Creative Minds Biographies	Carolrhoda Books
Jazz Baby	J	RF	125	Bebop Books	Lee & Low Books Inc.
Jazz Dance	S	I	250+	Dance	Capstone Press
Jazz Great	U	RF	3296	Leveled Readers	Houghton Mifflin Harcourt
Jazz Kid, The	Y	RF	250+	Lincoln Collier, James	Penguin Group
Jazz Man, The	T	RF	250+	Weik, Mary Hays	Simon & Schuster
Jazz, Jazz, Jazz	V	I	1696	Reading Street	Pearson
Jazz, Pizzazz, and the Silver Threads	P	RF	250+	Quattlebaum, Mary	Bantam
Jean Baptiste Pointe du Sable: Father of Chicago	T	B	250+	Literacy by Design	Rigby
Jean Batten: Pioneer of the Sky	P	B	250+	Wonder World	Wright Group/McGraw Hill
Jean Craighead George	S	B	250+	Cary, Alice	Learning Works, The
Jean Fritz Comes Home	X	B	2268	Leveled Readers	Houghton Mifflin Harcourt
Jeans From Mines to Malls	P	I	250+	Explorer Books-Pioneer	National Geographic
Jeans: From Mines to Malls	Q	I	250+	Explorer Books-Pathfinder	National Geographic
Jeb's Barn	G	RF	86	Little Celebrations	Pearson Learning Group
Jeepers	L	RF	250+	Books for Young Learners	Richard C. Owen
Jeff Gordon	P	B	1580	Amazing Athletes	Lerner Publications
Jeff Gordon	R	B	250+	Sports Heroes	Red Brick Learning
Jefferson Davis	U	B	250+	Let Freedom Ring	Red Brick Learning
Jefferson Davis and the Confederacy	Y	B	250+	The Civil War	Carus Publishing
Jeff's Hero	U	RF	7218	Reading Street	Pearson
Jeff's Magnets	I	I	168	Instant Readers	Harcourt School Publishers
Jelly Beans	M	I	250+	Early Connections	Benchmark Education
Jellybean Jar, The	F	RF	107	InfoTrek	ETA Cuisenaire
Jellybean Tree, The	H	F	231	Sunshine	Wright Group/McGraw Hill
Jellyfish	O	I	1188	Early Bird Nature Books	Lerner Publications
Jellyfish	I	I	58	Pebble Books	Red Brick Learning
Jellyfish	F	I	125	Sails	Rigby
Jellyfish	J	I	95	Under the Sea	Capstone Press
Jemma's Big Leap	K	RF	542	Rigby Gigglers	Rigby
Jeni's Lettuce	G	RF	194	Rigby Flying Colors	Rigby

J

* Collection of short stories
\# Graphic text

TITLE	LEVEL	GENRE	WORD COUNT	AUTHOR / SERIES	PUBLISHER / DISTRIBUTOR
Jenius: The Amazing Guinea Pig	N	F	250+	King-Smith, Dick	Hyperion
Jenna's Pet	E	RF	179	Windows on Literacy	National Geographic
Jennifer Pockets	I	RF	205	Book Bank	Wright Group/McGraw Hill
Jennifer, Hecate, Macbeth, William McKinley, and Me, Elizabeth	R	RF	250+	Konigsburg, E. L.	Yearling
Jennifer, Too	L	RF	250+	Havill, Juanita	Hyperion
Jenny and the Cornstalk	L	TL	890	Pair-It Books	Steck-Vaughn
Jenny Archer to the Rescue	M	RF	250+	Conford, Ellen	Little, Brown & Co.
Jenny Archer, Author	M	RF	250+	Conford, Ellen	Little, Brown & Co.
Jenny in Bed	D	RF	76	Lighthouse	Rigby
Jenny Lives on Hunter Street	H	RF	141	Book Bank	Wright Group/McGraw Hill
Jenny's Garden	E	RF	45	Leveled Readers Science	Houghton Mifflin Harcourt
Jenny's Socks	G	RF	94	Rookie Readers	Children's Press
Jen's Best Gift Ever	I	RF	310	Appleton-Smith, Laura	Flyleaf Publishing
Jeremy and the Enchanted Theater	M	F	250+	Orca Echoes	Orca Book Publishers
Jeremy Fink and the Meaning of Life	U	RF	250+	Mass, Wendy	Little, Brown & Co.
Jeremy Thatcher, Dragon Hatcher	R	F	250+	Coville, Bruce	Aladdin
Jeremy's Cake	F	RF	97	Storyteller-Moon Rising	Wright Group/McGraw Hill
Jericho	T	RF	250+	Hickman, Janet	Hearst
Jericho Walls	V	HF	250+	Collier, Kristi	Henry Holt & Co.
Jericho's Journey	U	RF	250+	Wisler, G. Clifton	Penguin Group
Jerry on the Line	R	RF	250+	Seabrooke, Brenda	Puffin/Penguin
Jerry Yang, Chief Yahoo	T	B	250+	Bookshop	Mondo
Jess in the Snow	E	RF	109	Handprints C, Set 2	Educators Publishing Service
Jesse	A	RF	38	Leveled Literacy Intervention/ Green System	Heinemann
Jesse	Y	RF	250+	Soto, Gary	Scholastic
Jesse Jackson	P	B	250+	Simon, Charnan	Children's Press
Jesse Owens	N	B	200	First Biographies	Capstone Press
Jesse Owens	P	B	1746	On My Own Biography	Lerner Publications
Jesse Owens An American Hero	R	B	1336	Vocabulary Readers/CA	Houghton Mifflin Harcourt
Jesse Owens An American Hero	R	I	1336	Vocabulary Readers	Houghton Mifflin Harcourt
Jesse Owens: Olympic Hero	P	B	250+	Sabin, Francene	Troll Associates
Jessica in the Dark	I	RF	362	PM Story Books-Orange	Rigby
Jessica's Dress-Ups	F	RF	130	Voyages	SRA/McGraw Hill
Jessie's Flower	G	F	132	Read Alongs	Rigby
Jet Fighter Planes	Q	I	250+	Wild Rides!	Capstone Press
Jets	M	I	250+	Horsepower	Capstone Press
Jets	H	I	88	Mighty Machines	Capstone Press
Jets	L	I	337	Pull Ahead Books	Lerner Publications
Jets and the Rockets, The	J	RF	250+	PM Plus Story Books	Rigby
Jetty's Journey to Freedom	S	HF	250+	Pair-It Books	Steck-Vaughn
Jewel of the Desert	V	HF	2994	Leveled Readers	Houghton Mifflin Harcourt
Jewelers to the Palace	O	HF	250+	Windows on Literacy	National Geographic
Jewels of the Sea	M	I	250+	Rigby Flying Colors	Rigby
J-Files, The	L	RF	250+	Bookweb	Rigby
Jigaree, The	E	F	128	Story Box	Wright Group/McGraw Hill
Jigaree's Breakfast, The	I	F	203	The Story Basket	Wright Group/McGraw Hill
Jill Jumps	C	F	35	Ray's Readers	Outside the Box
Jillian Jiggs	J	RF	250+	Gilman, Phoebe	Scholastic
Jilly the Kid	M	RF	250+	Krailing, Tessa	Barron's Educational
Jim Abbott: Making the Most of It	X	B	2451	Leveled Readers	Houghton Mifflin Harcourt
Jim Henson, the Puppet Man	E	I	93	Leveled Readers	Houghton Mifflin Harcourt

J

* Collection of short stories
# Graphic text

TITLE	LEVEL	GENRE	WORD COUNT	AUTHOR / SERIES	PUBLISHER / DISTRIBUTOR
Jim Henson, the Puppet Man	E	I	93	Leveled Readers/CA	Houghton Mifflin Harcourt
Jim Henson, the Puppet Man	E	I	93	Leveled Readers/TX	Houghton Mifflin Harcourt
Jim Meets the Thing	I	F	250+	Cohen, Miriam	Bantam
Jim Morrison	Z	B	250+	Rock Music Library	Capstone Press
Jim Thorpe	N	I	528	Vocabulary Readers	Houghton Mifflin Harcourt
Jim Thorpe	N	I	528	Vocabulary Readers/CA	Houghton Mifflin Harcourt
Jim Thorpe	N	I	528	Vocabulary Readers/TX	Houghton Mifflin Harcourt
#Jim Thorpe: Greatest Athlete in the World	R	B	250+	Graphic Library	Capstone Press
Jim Thorpe: The Greatest Athlete in the World	S	B	2443	Reading Street	Pearson
Jim Ugly	Q	RF	250+	Fleischman, Sid	Bantam
Jimmy	D	RF	83	Foundations	Wright Group/McGraw Hill
Jimmy Carter	R	B	4103	History Maker Bios	Lerner Publications
Jimmy Carter: A Life of Friendship	N	B	532	Pull Ahead- Biographies	Lerner Publications
Jimmy Carter: Thirty-ninth President	R	B	250+	Getting to Know the U.S. Presidents	Children's Press
Jimmy Lee Did It	J	RF	250+	Cummings, Pat	Lothrop
Jimmy Parker's New Job	J	RF	250+	Voyages	SRA/McGraw Hill
Jimmy the Gymnast	K	RF	250+	Foundations	Wright Group/McGraw Hill
Jimmy Zangwow's Out-of-This-World Moon Pie Adventure	N	F	250+	DiTerlizzi, Tony	Aladddin Paperbacks
Jimmy's Birthday Balloon	F	RF	95	Foundations	Wright Group/McGraw Hill
Jimmy's Goal	E	RF	159	Foundations	Wright Group/McGraw Hill
Jim's Dog Muffins	K	RF	250+	Cohen, Miriam	Bantam
Jim's Trumpet	H	RF	304	Sunshine	Wright Group/McGraw Hill
Jim's Visit to Kim	G	RF	149	Ready Readers	Pearson Learning Group
Jingo Django	V	RF	250+	Fleischman, Sid	Bantam
Jinx	Z	RF	250+	Wild, Margaret	Walker & Company
Jip the Pirate	F	F	142	New Way Blue	Steck-Vaughn
Jip: His Story	V	HF	250+	Paterson, Katherine	Penguin Group
*JJ Rabbit and the Monster	K	F	250+	Storyteller-Shooting Stars	Wright Group/McGraw Hill
Jo and the Spider	D	RF	78	Sun Sprouts	ETA Cuisenaire
Jo Jo Winnie Again	O	RF	250+	Sachs, Marilyn	Dutton/Penguin
Jo Jo's Flying Side Kick	M	RF	250+	Soar To Success	Houghton Mifflin Harcourt
Jo the Model Maker	K	I	250+	Lighthouse	Rigby
Joan of Arc	Y	B	250+	DK Readers	DK Publishing
Joan of Arc: Heavenly Warrior	Y	B	250+	Sterling Biographies	Sterling Publishing
Joanie's House Becomes a Home	M	RF	860	Reading Street	Pearson
Joan's Garden	B	F	34	Sun Sprouts	ETA Cuisenaire
Joan's Hat	F	F	174	Sun Sprouts	ETA Cuisenaire
Job at the Zoo, A	K	RF	525	Rigby Gigglers	Rigby
Job for a Day, A	K	RF	250+	On Our Way to English	Rigby
Job for Giant Jim, A	I	RF	298	Sunshine	Wright Group/McGraw Hill
Job for Jenny Archer, A	M	RF	250+	Conford, Ellen	Random House
Job for Jojo, A	J	F	326	Leveled Readers	Houghton Mifflin Harcourt
Job for Jojo, A	J	F	326	Leveled Readers/CA	Houghton Mifflin Harcourt
Job for Jojo, A	J	F	326	Leveled Readers/TX	Houghton Mifflin Harcourt
Job for Little Elf, A	F	F	197	Little Elf	Literacy Footprints
Job for Pup, A	F	F	89	Pair-It Turn and Learn	Steck-Vaughn
Job for You, A	D	I	56	Independent Readers Social Studies	Houghton Mifflin Harcourt
Job Sense	P	I	1472	Vocabulary Readers	Houghton Mifflin Harcourt
Job Sense	P	I	1472	Vocabulary Readers/CA	Houghton Mifflin Harcourt
Job Sense	P	I	1472	Vocabulary Readers/TX	Houghton Mifflin Harcourt
Job to Do, A	T	I	250+	Connectors	Pacific Learning

* Collection of short stories
# Graphic text

J

TITLE	LEVEL	GENRE	WORD COUNT	AUTHOR / SERIES	PUBLISHER / DISTRIBUTOR
Job Well Done, A	Q	I	250+	Orbit Collections	Pacific Learning
Jobs	C	I	30	Basic Human Needs	Lerner Publishing
Jobs	E	F	112	Benger, Wendy	Kaeden Books
Jobs	B	I	29	Bookshop	Mondo
Jobs	I	I	112	Canizares, Susan; Chessen, Betsey	Scholastic
Jobs	D	I	71	Leveled Readers	Houghton Mifflin Harcourt
Jobs Around Town	A	I	31	Leveled Readers Social Studies	Houghton Mifflin Harcourt
Jobs at Home	C	I	35	Leveled Readers Language Support	Houghton Mifflin Harcourt
Jobs for Dogs	H	I	188	Rigby Focus	Rigby
Jobs for Everyone	E	I	51	Pair-It Turn and Learn	Steck-Vaughn
Jobs for Some People	E	I	146	Sails	Rigby
Jobs on the Farm	D	I	107	Leveled Readers	Houghton Mifflin Harcourt
Jobs on the Farm	D	I	107	Leveled Readers/CA	Houghton Mifflin Harcourt
Jobs to Do	J	I	368	Vocabulary Readers	Houghton Mifflin Harcourt
Jobs to Do	J	I	368	Vocabulary Readers/CA	Houghton Mifflin Harcourt
Jobs Up High	C	I	62	Early Connections	Benchmark Education
Jobs: Making and Helping	E	I	63	Windows on Literacy	National Geographic
Jock Jerome	E	F	99	Voyages	SRA/McGraw Hill
Jody's Beans	K	RF	250+	Doyle, Malachy	Candlewick Press
Joe and Betsy the Dinosaur	K	F	250+	Hoban, Lillian	HarperTrophy
Joe and the BMX Bike	E	RF	91	Oxford Reading Tree	Oxford University Press
Joe and the Mouse	F	RF	138	Oxford Reading Tree	Oxford University Press
Joe Cocker Spaniel	N	RF	250+	SupaDoopers	Sundance
Joe Joe	LB	RF	22	Montezinos, Nina	McElderry
Joe Lion's Big Boots	L	F	250+	I Am Reading	Kingfisher
Joe Makes a House	G	RF	174	PM Plus Story Books	Rigby
Joe Mauer	P	B	250+	Amazing Athletes	Lerner Publications
Joe on the Go	I	F	250+	Anderson, Peggy Perry	Houghton Mifflin Harcourt
Joe's Blue Shoes	G	RF	130	Books for Young Learners	Richard C. Owen
Joe's Father	E	RF	138	Book Bank	Wright Group/McGraw Hill
Joe's Letter	G	RF	219	Springboard	Wright Group/McGraw Hill
Joe's Pizza Parlor	I	RF	113	City Stories	Rigby
Joey	G	RF	243	PM Extensions-Green	Rigby
Joey Pigza Loses Control	T	RF	250+	Gantos, Jack	Farrar, Straus and Giroux
Joey Pigza Swallowed the Key	T	RF	250+	Gantos, Jack	HarperTrophy
Joey's Head	L	F	250+	Cretan, G.	Simon & Schuster
Joey's Rowboat	H	RF	83	Little Books	Sadlier-Oxford
Jog, Frog, Jog	F	F	72	Start to Read	School Zone
Johann Sebastian Bach: Great Man of Music	O	B	250+	Greene, Carol	Children's Press
John & Abigail Adams: An American Love Story	W	B	250+	St. George, Judith	Scholastic
John A. Macdonald	X	B	250+	The Canadians	Fitzhenry & Whiteside
John Adams	S	B	3770	History Maker Bios	Lerner Publications
John Adams	S	B	250+	Photo-Illustrated Biographies	Red Brick Learning
John Adams	U	B	250+	Profiles of the Presidents	Compass Point Books
John Adams and the Boston Massacre	Y	I	2307	Leveled Readers	Houghton Mifflin Harcourt
John Adams: Second President	R	B	250+	Getting to Know the U.S. Presidents	Children's Press
John Brown	P	B	1609	On My Own Biography	Lerner Publications
John Chapman: The Man Who Was Johnny	N	B	250+	Rookie Biographies	Children's Press
John Charles and Jessie Fremont: Pathfinders of the West	V	B	2453	Leveled Readers Social Studies	Houghton Mifflin Harcourt
John D. Rockefeller and the Oil Industry	R	I	250+	On Deck	Rigby

J

TITLE	LEVEL	GENRE	WORD COUNT	AUTHOR / SERIES	PUBLISHER / DISTRIBUTOR
John F. Kennedy	S	B	250+	Amazing Americans	Wright Group/McGraw Hill
John F. Kennedy	P	B	250+	Early Biographies	Compass Point Books
John F. Kennedy	N	B	250+	First Biographies	Red Brick Learning
John F. Kennedy	S	B	3373	History Maker Bios	Lerner Publications
John F. Kennedy	N	B	250+	Pebble Books	Capstone Press
John F. Kennedy	Q	B	250+	Photo-Illustrated Biographies	Red Brick Learning
John F. Kennedy	U	B	250+	Profiles of the Presidents	Compass Point Books
John F. Kennedy	V	B	250+	World Leaders: Past and Present	Chelsea House
#John F. Kennedy: American Visionary	R	B	250+	Graphic Library	Capstone Press
John F. Kennedy: America's Youngest President	O	B	250+	Childhood of Famous Americans	Aladdin
John F. Kennedy: Thirty-fifth President	R	B	250+	Getting to Know the U.S. Presidents	Children's Press
John Glenn	N	B	250+	Explore Space!	Capstone Press
John H. Johnson, Business Leader	K	B	130	Independent Readers Social Studies	Houghton Mifflin Harcourt
John Hancock	S	B	3514	History Maker Bios	Lerner Publications
John Henry	N	TL	1865	On My Own Folklore	Lerner Publications
John Henry	N	TL	250+	Tall Tales	Compass Point Books
John Henry and the Steam Drill	Q	F	1203	Leveled Readers	Houghton Mifflin Harcourt
John Jacob Astor and the Fur Trade	R	B	250+	On Deck	Rigby
John James Audubon	M	B	250+	Biography	Benchmark Education
John James Audubon, American Painter	M	B	538	Leveled Readers Social Studies	Houghton Mifflin Harcourt
John James Audubon: Wildlife Artist	V	B	250+	A First Book	Franklin Watts
John Jay	Q	B	250+	Primary Source Readers	Teacher Created Materials
John Lennon	Z	B	250+	Rock Music Library	Capstone Press
John Lewis	W	I	3390	Vocabulary Readers	Houghton Mifflin Harcourt
John Lewis	W	B	3390	Vocabulary Readers/CA	Houghton Mifflin Harcourt
John Muir: A Man of the Wilderness	T	B	2317	Reading Street	Pearson
John Muir: Man of the Wild Places	N	B	250+	Rookie Biographies	Children's Press
John Paul Jones	X	I	2828	Vocabulary Readers	Houghton Mifflin Harcourt
John Paul Jones	X	B	2828	Vocabulary Readers/CA	Houghton Mifflin Harcourt
John Paul Jones	X	B	2828	Vocabulary Readers/TX	Houghton Mifflin Harcourt
John Paul Jones and the Battle at Sea	W	B	2095	Independent Readers Social Studies	Houghton Mifflin Harcourt
John Peter Zenger and Freedom of the Press	V	B	2213	Leveled Readers Social Studies	Houghton Mifflin Harcourt
John Philip Duck	O	HF	250+	Polacco, Patricia	Scholastic
John Philip Sousa: The March King	N	B	250+	Rookie Biographies	Children's Press
John Quincy Adams	U	B	250+	Profiles of the Presidents	Compass Point Books
John Quincy Adams in Paris	W	I	3091	Vocabulary Readers	Houghton Mifflin Harcourt
John Quincy Adams in Paris	W	I	3091	Vocabulary Readers/CA	Houghton Mifflin Harcourt
John Quincy Adams in Paris	W	I	3091	Vocabulary Readers/TX	Houghton Mifflin Harcourt
John Quincy Adams: Sixth President	R	B	250+	Getting to Know the U.S. Presidents	Children's Press
John Tyler	U	B	250+	Profiles of the Presidents	Compass Point Books
John Tyler: Tenth President	R	B	250+	Getting to Know the U.S. Presidents	Children's Press
John Wesley Powell	O	B	888	Leveled Readers	Houghton Mifflin Harcourt
John Wesley Powell	O	B	888	Leveled Readers/CA	Houghton Mifflin Harcourt
John Wesley Powell	O	B	888	Leveled Readers/TX	Houghton Mifflin Harcourt
John Williams: Musical Storyteller	S	I	250+	Explore More	Wright Group/McGraw Hill
John Winthrop: Governor of the Massachusetts Bay Colony	U	B	250+	Let Freedom Ring	Red Brick Learning
Johnny Appleseed	M	B	250+	First Biographies	Red Brick Learning
Johnny Appleseed	Q	TL	250+	Kellogg, Steven	Scholastic

* Collection of short stories
# Graphic text

J

TITLE	LEVEL	GENRE	WORD COUNT	AUTHOR / SERIES	PUBLISHER / DISTRIBUTOR
Johnny Appleseed	O	B	622	Leveled Readers	Houghton Mifflin Harcourt
Johnny Appleseed	K	TL	250+	Moore, Eva	Scholastic
Johnny Appleseed	N	B	1453	On My Own Biography	Lerner Publications
Johnny Appleseed	N	TL	250+	Tall Tales	Compass Point Books
Johnny Kelley's Tale	X	HF	2162	Leveled Readers	Houghton Mifflin Harcourt
Johnny Lion's Book	J	F	250+	Hurd, Edith Thacher	HarperCollins
Johnny Lion's Rubber Boots	F	F	80	Hurd, Edith Thacher	HarperCollins
Johnny Long Legs	R	RF	250+	Christopher, Matt	Little, Brown & Co.
Johnny Tremain	Z	HF	250+	Forbes, Esther	Bantam Doubleday Dell
Johnston Flood, The	V	HF	250+	Reading Expeditions	National Geographic
Join Us	D	RF	54	InfoTrek	ETA Cuisenaire
Jojo and the Robot	J	F	250+	Sunshine	Wright Group/McGraw Hill
Joke Book, The	H	I	143	Vocabulary Readers	Houghton Mifflin Harcourt
Joke, The	H	F	186	Little Readers	Houghton Mifflin Harcourt
Jokers	H	F	190	Breakthrough	Longman/Bow
Jokes and Riddles	O	I	250+	Literacy 2000	Rigby
Jolly Jumping Jelly Beans	E	F	121	Sunshine	Wright Group/McGraw Hill
Jolly Roger and the Spyglass	G	F	200	PM Stars	Rigby
Jolly Roger and the Treasure	E	F	129	PM Plus Story Books	Rigby
Jolly Roger, the Pirate	D	F	138	PM Extensions-Yellow	Rigby
Jon Scieszka Gets Kids Reading	Q	B	1155	Leveled Readers	Houghton Mifflin Harcourt
Jon Sleeps On	G	RF	147	Little Red Readers	Sundance
Jonathan and His Mommy	L	RF	250+	Smalls, Irene	Scholastic
Jonathan Buys a Present	J	RF	353	PM Story Books-Turquoise	Rigby
Jono's Rescue	O	RF	250+	PM Plus	Rigby
Jordan and the Northside Reps	K	RF	250+	PM Story Books-Silver	Rigby
Jordan at the Big Game	I	RF	250+	PM Plus Story Books	Rigby
Jordan Is Hiding	A	RF	24	Little Books for Early Readers	University of Maine
Jordan's Catch	J	RF	250+	PM Story Books	Rigby
Jordan's Lucky Day	K	RF	466	PM Story Books-Turquoise	Rigby
Jordan's Soccer Ball	G	RF	210	PM Plus Story Books	Rigby
Jordan's Zoo	G	RF	90	City Stories	Rigby
Jo's Troubled Heart	Q	HF	250+	The Little Women Journals	Avon
Josefina Learns a Lesson	Q	HF	250+	The American Girls Collection	Pleasant Company
Josefina Saves the Day	Q	HF	250+	The American Girls Collection	Pleasant Company
Josefina Story Quilt	L	F	250+	Coerr, Eleanor	HarperTrophy
Josefina's Surprise	Q	HF	250+	The American Girls Collection	Pleasant Company
Joseph Brant: Iroquois Leader in the Revolution	Y	B	1743	Leveled Readers	Houghton Mifflin Harcourt
Joseph Warren, An American Hero	U	I	2577	Leveled Readers/CA	Houghton Mifflin Harcourt
Joseph Warren, An American Hero	U	I	2577	Leveled Readers/TX	Houghton Mifflin Harcourt
Joseph Warren, An American Hero	U	I	2577	Leveled Readers	Houghton Mifflin Harcourt
Joseph, the Greedy Octopus	H	F	290	Springboard	Wright Group/McGraw Hill
Joseph: 1861 - A Rumble of War	V	HF	250+	Pryor, Bonnie	Avon
Josephine's Imagination	L	RF	250+	Dobrin, Arnold	Scholastic
Josh	I	RF	582	Rigby Flying Colors	Rigby
Josh and Scruffy	C	RF	48	PM Photo Stories	Rigby
Josh and the Bad Hair Day	K	RF	837	Rigby Flying Colors	Rigby
Josh and the Big Boys	C	RF	82	PM Photo Stories	Rigby
Josh and the Kite	C	RF	58	PM Photo Stories	Rigby
Josh Rides a Skateboard	D	RF	107	PM Photo Stories	Rigby
Joshua James Likes Trucks	C	RF	50	Rookie Readers	Children's Press
Joshua Poole and Sunrise	L	RF	250+	Rigby Literacy	Rigby
Joshua T. Bates	Q	RF	250+	Shreve, Susan	Alfred A. Knopf
Joshua T. Bates in Trouble Again	Q	RF	250+	Shreve, Susan	Alfred A. Knopf

* Collection of short stories
# Graphic text

J

TITLE	LEVEL	GENRE	WORD COUNT	AUTHOR / SERIES	PUBLISHER / DISTRIBUTOR
Joshua T. Bates Takes Charge	Q	RF	250+	Shreve, Susan	Alfred A. Knopf
Josie and the Baby	C	RF	62	Rigby Star	Rigby
Josie and the Bully	E	RF	149	Rigby Rocket	Rigby
Josie and the Cake Sale	D	RF	91	Rigby Rocket	Rigby
Josie and the Juke Box	B	RF	28	Rigby Star	Rigby
Josie and the Parade	B	RF	49	Rigby Star	Rigby
Josie and the Play	F	RF	185	Rigby Star	Rigby
Josie and the Puppy	G	RF	206	Rigby Star	Rigby
Josie Cleans Up	I	RF	213	Little Readers	Houghton Mifflin Harcourt
Josie Goes on Holiday	F	RF	240	Rigby Star	Rigby
Josie Helps Out	E	RF	71	Rigby Star	Rigby
Josie's New Coat	F	RF	189	Rigby Star	Rigby
Journal of Douglas Allen Deeds, The: The Donner Party Expedition, 1846	W	HF	250+	My Name Is America	Scholastic
Journal of James Edmond Pease, The	V	HF	250+	Dear America	Scholastic
Journal of Patrick Seamus Flaherty, The	Z	HF	250+	White, Ellen Emerson	Scholastic
Journal of Sean Sullivan, The	W	HF	250+	Dear America	Scholastic
Journal, The: Dear Future II	Q	SF	250+	Literacy 2000	Rigby
Journals of the West	R	I	1300	Vocabulary Readers/TX	Houghton Mifflin Harcourt
Journery into an Estuary, A	T	I	2444	Biomes of North America	Lerner Publications
Journey	S	RF	250+	MacLachlan, Patricia	Yearling
Journey Home	V	RF	250+	Uchida, Yoshika	Aladdin
Journey Home, The	S	RF	250+	Holland, Isabelle	Scholastic
Journey into a Lake, A	T	I	2317	Biomes of North America	Lerner Publications
Journey into a River, A	T	I	2598	Biomes of North America	Lerner Publications
Journey into a Wetland, A	T	I	2256	Biomes of North America	Lerner Publications
Journey into Terror	U	RF	250+	Wallace, Bill	Simon & Schuster
Journey into the Earth	I	F	250+	Storyworlds	Heinemann Educational Books
Journey of a Butterfly, The	P	I	250+	Scrace, Carolyn	Scholastic
Journey of the Kon-Tiki	O	I	1036	Leveled Readers	Houghton Mifflin Harcourt
Journey of the Kon-Tiki	O	I	1036	Leveled Readers/CA	Houghton Mifflin Harcourt
Journey of the Kon-Tiki	O	I	1036	Leveled Readers/TX	Houghton Mifflin Harcourt
Journey on a Patriotic Path	R	I	250+	In Step Readers	Rigby
Journey Outside	V	F	250+	Steele, Mary Q.	Penguin Group
Journey Through the Earth	T	SF	4548	Reading Street	Pearson
Journey to a Free Town	S	HF	1747	Leveled Readers	Houghton Mifflin Harcourt
Journey to a New Land	M	HF	250+	Rigby Literacy	Rigby
Journey to a New Land: An Oral History	R	B	250+	Bookshop	Mondo
Journey to America	U	HF	250+	Levitin, Sonia	Simon & Schuster
Journey to an 800 Number	V	RF	250+	Konigsburg, E. L.	Aladdin
Journey to Antarctica	V	I	250+	PM Collection	Rigby
Journey to Ellis Island: How My Father Came to America	T	B	250+	Bierman, Carol	Scholastic
Journey to Jo'burg	S	HF	250+	Naidoo, Beverly	HarperTrophy
Journey to Kansas	R	HF	250+	Leveled Readers Language Support	Houghton Mifflin Harcourt
Journey to Mars	T	I	644	Vocabulary Readers	Houghton Mifflin Harcourt
Journey to Nowhere	T	HF	250+	Auch, Mary Jane	Bantam
Journey to Statehood	T	I	2596	Reading Street	Pearson
Journey to the Center of the Earth, A	X	SF	250+	Verne, Jules	HarperCollins
Journey to the New World	S	HF	250+	Action Packs	Rigby
Journey to the New World	V	HF	250+	My America	Scholastic
Journey to the Undersea Gardens	Q	I	250+	iOpeners	Pearson Learning Group

J

* Collection of short stories
\# Graphic text

TITLE	LEVEL	GENRE	WORD COUNT	AUTHOR / SERIES	PUBLISHER / DISTRIBUTOR
Journey to Topaz	U	HF	250+	Uchida, Yoshiko	Creative Arts Book Co.
Journey West, The	N	I	250+	Rigby Literacy	Rigby
Journeys of Courage on the Underground Railroad	T	I	250+	Pair-It Books	Steck-Vaughn
Journeys of Sojourner Truth, The	R	B	1217	Leveled Readers Social Studies	Houghton Mifflin Harcourt
Joy Crowley Writes	K	B	250+	Sunshine	Wright Group/McGraw Hill
Joy Luck Club, The	Z+	HF	250+	Tan, Amy	Random House
Joy of Making Music, The	N	I	280	Vocabulary Readers	Houghton Mifflin Harcourt
Joy's Great Idea	M	RF	250+	Ellis, Veronica Freeman	Houghton Mifflin Harcourt
Joy's Planet Patrol Plan	M	RF	889	Leveled Readers	Houghton Mifflin Harcourt
Joy's Planet Patrol Plan	M	RF	889	Leveled Readers/CA	Houghton Mifflin Harcourt
Joy's Planet Patrol Plan	M	RF	889	Leveled Readers/TX	Houghton Mifflin Harcourt
Juan	H	RF	77	City Kids	Rigby
Juan Bobo	E	TL	55	Leveled Readers	Houghton Mifflin Harcourt
Juan Ponce De Leon	Q	B	250+	Biographies-Great Explorers	Capstone Press
Juan Ponce de Leon	S	B	3232	History Maker Bios	Lerner Publications
Juan's Journey	T	RF	1980	Reading Street	Pearson
Juan's Three Wishes	V	F	1842	Leveled Readers	Houghton Mifflin Harcourt
Judge Rabbit Helps the Fish	N	TL	250+	Story Vines	Wright Group/McGraw Hill
Judo	P	I	1644	Take Two Books	Wright Group/ McGraw Hill
Judy Moody	M	RF	250+	McDonald, Megan	Candlewick Press
Judy Moody & Stink: The Holly Joliday	M	RF	250+	McDonald, Megan	Candlewick Press
Judy Moody Around the World in 8 1/2 Days	M	RF	250+	McDonald, Megan	Candlewick Press
Judy Moody Declares Independence	M	RF	250+	McDonald, Megan	Candlewick Press
Judy Moody Gets Famous!	M	RF	250+	McDonald, Megan	Candlewick Press
Judy Moody Goes to College	M	RF	250+	McDonald, Megan	Candlewick Press
Judy Moody Predicts the Future	M	RF	250+	McDonald, Megan	Candlewick Press
Judy Moody Saves the World	M	RF	250+	McDonald, Megan	Candlewick Press
Judy Moody was in a Mood. Not a Good Mood. A Bad Mood.	M	RF	250+	McDonald, Megan	Candlewick Press
Judy Moody, M.D. The Doctor Is In!	M	RF	250+	McDonald, Megan	Candlewick Press
Juggling	P	I	250+	Games Around the World	Compass Point Books
Juggling	LB	RF	15	Rigby Literacy	Rigby
Juggling	LB	RF	15	Rigby Star	Rigby
Juice	B	RF	38	Bonnell, Kris	Reading Reading Books
Juice	T	RF	250+	Orca Soundings	Orca Book Publishers
Juicy Peach	C	RF	18	Bebop Books	Lee & Low Books Inc.
Julia Alvarez, Storyteller	L	B	515	In Step Readers	Rigby
Julia Alvarez: One Author, Two Cultures	Q	B	1029	Leveled Readers	Houghton Mifflin Harcourt
Julia Gillian (and the Art of Knowing)	R	RF	250+	McGhee, Alison	Scholastic
Julian Rodriguez: Trash Crisis on Earth	R	SF	250+	Stadler, Alexander	Scholastic
Julian, Dream Doctor	N	RF	250+	Cameron, Ann	Random House
Julian, Secret Agent	N	RF	250+	Cameron, Ann	Random House
Julian's Glorious Summer	N	RF	250+	Cameron, Ann	Random House
Julia's Lists	D	RF	47	Little Celebrations	Pearson Learning Group
Julia's New Home	R	RF	1950	Reading Street	Pearson
Julie	U	RF	250+	George, Jean Craighead	HarperTrophy
Julie Gets Lost	T	RF	3624	Reading Street	Pearson
Julie Krone	Y	B	250+	The Achievers	Lerner Publishing
Julie of the Wolves	U	RF	250+	George, Jean Craighead	HarperCollins
Julie of the Wolves	U	RF	250+	inZone Books	Hampton-Brown
Julie Rescues Big Mack	M	RF	250+	Voyages	SRA/McGraw Hill
Julie Taymor: Art on Stage and Screen	W	B	250+	Explore More	Wright Group/McGraw Hill
Julie's Mornings	K	F	250+	Ready Readers	Pearson Learning Group

TITLE	LEVEL	GENRE	WORD COUNT	AUTHOR / SERIES	PUBLISHER / DISTRIBUTOR
Julie's Wolf Pack	U	RF	250+	George, Jean Craighead	HarperTrophy
Juliette: The Modern Art Monkey	Q	F	250+	Bookweb	Rigby
Julius Caesar: Roman General and Statesman	Y	B	250+	Signature Lives	Compass Point Books
Julius Caesar: Roman Leader	W	B	250+	Primary Source Readers	Teacher Created Materials
Julius: The Baby of the World	N	F	250+	Henkes, Kevin	Scholastic
July 4th	C	RF	20	Instant Readers	Harcourt School Publishers
July Fourth!	F	I	137	In Step Readers	Rigby
Jumbaroo, The	H	F	173	Story Basket	Wright Group/McGraw Hill
Jumble Power	L	F	250+	Cambridge Reading	Pearson Learning Group
Jumble Sale, The	E	RF	81	Oxford Reading Tree	Oxford University Press
Jumbo	E	RF	133	PM Plus Story Books	Rigby
Jump	A	F	30	Leveled Literacy Intervention/ Green System	Heinemann
Jump and Swim	H	RF	293	Leveled Readers	Houghton Mifflin Harcourt
Jump and Thump!	C	RF	18	Home Connection Collection	Rigby
Jump Ball!: You Can Play Basketball	M	I	250+	Game Day	Picture Window Books
Jump in the Pool, A	H	RF	243	Leveled Readers Language Support	Houghton Mifflin Harcourt
Jump Jets: The AV-88 Harriers	U	I	250+	War Planes	Capstone Press
Jump Right In	D	RF	50	Ready Readers	Pearson Learning Group
Jump Rope	B	RF	18	Bebop Books	Lee & Low Books Inc.
Jump Rope, The	H	RF	241	PM Plus Story Books	Rigby
Jump Serve	P	RF	250+	Maddox, Jake	Stone Arch Books
Jump Ship to Freedom	U	HF	250+	Collier, James & Christopher	Bantam
Jump the Broom	L	RF	119	Books For Young Learners	Richard C. Owen
*Jump!: The Adventures of Brer Rabbit	T	TL	250+	Harris, Joel Chandler	Harcourt Brace
Jump, Frog	C	F	33	Stewart, Josie; Salem, Lynn	Continental Press
Jump, Jump, Jump	I	F	236	Sunshine	Wright Group/McGraw Hill
Jump, Jump, Kangaroo	B	F	31	Story Box	Wright Group/McGraw Hill
Jump, Trundle, Climb, Slither, Flap, Snap!	N	I	565	Springboard	Wright Group/ McGraw Hill
Jumper	E	RF	125	Literacy Tree	Rigby
Jumper	T	RF	250+	Orca Sports	Orca Book Publishers
Jumper for James, A	C	RF	34	Rigby Rocket	Rigby
Jumpers	B	F	21	Sunshine	Wright Group/McGraw Hill
Jumping Fish, The	D	F	114	Rigby Flying Colors	Rigby
Jumping into Nothing	M	RF	250+	Willner-Pardo, Gina	Houghton Mifflin Harcourt
Jumping into the Flames	P	I	675	Vocabulary Readers	Houghton Mifflin Harcourt
Jumping Jack	J	F	250+	Rigby Literacy	Rigby
Jumping Jack	J	F	250+	Rigby Star	Rigby
Jumping Jesters, The	H	F	217	Rigby Rocket	Rigby
Jumping Kangaroos	K	I	377	Pull Ahead Books	Lerner Publications
Jumping Shoes	C	RF	34	Joy Readers	Pearson Learning Group
Jumping Spider	O	I	250+	Life Cycles	Creative Teaching Press
Jumping Spiders	I	I	404	Sails	Rigby
Jumping Tree, The	Y	RF	250+	Saldana, Jr., Rene	Scholastic
Jumprope	D	RF	31	Visions	Wright Group/McGraw Hill
Jun and Pepper Grow Up	J	RF	362	Reading Street	Pearson
June Bacon-Bercey: A Meteorologist Talks About the Weather	K	I	192	Leveled Readers Science	Houghton Mifflin Harcourt
June Vacation	C	I	86	Leveled Readers	Houghton Mifflin Harcourt
June Vacation	C	I	86	Leveled Readers/CA	Houghton Mifflin Harcourt
Junebug	S	RF	250+	Mead, Alice	Bantam
Junebug and the Reverend	S	RF	250+	Mead, Alice	Dell Yearling
Junebug in Trouble	T	RF	250+	Mead, Alice	Dell Yearling

* Collection of short stories
# Graphic text

TITLE	LEVEL	GENRE	WORD COUNT	AUTHOR / SERIES	PUBLISHER / DISTRIBUTOR
Juneteenth	Q	I	250+	Holiday Histories	Heinemann Library
Juneteenth	O	I	1632	On My Own Holidays	Lerner Publications
Juneteenth: Celebrating the End of Slavery	Q	I	250+	Rosen Real Readers	Rosen Publishing Group
Jungle	V	I	250+	Eyewitness Books	DK Publishing
Jungle Book, The	U	F	250+	Kipling, Rudyard	Scholastic
Jungle Friends	I	RF	250+	Reading Safari	Mondo
Jungle Frogs	G	F	195	PM Plus Story Books	Rigby
Jungle Jenny	M	F	250+	Literacy by Design	Rigby
Jungle Law	S	RF	250+	Sails	Rigby
Jungle Life	K	I	268	Spyglass Books	Compass Point Books
Jungle Parade: A Singing Game	D	F	105	Little Celebrations	Pearson Learning Group
Jungle Scout: A Vietnam War Story	W	HF	250+	Hoppey, Tim	Stone Arch Books
Jungle Spots	B	F	28	Little Celebrations	Pearson Learning Group
Jungle Sun, The	M	F	250+	Sails	Rigby
Jungle Tiger Cat	G	F	120	Frankford, Marilyn	Kaeden Books
Jungle Trek	S	RF	250+	PM Extensions	Rigby
Jungle Walk	WB	RF	N/A	Tafuri, Nancy	Greenwillow
Jungle, The	LB	F	12	Sails	Rigby
Junie B. Jones and a Little Monkey Business	M	RF	250+	Park, Barbara	Random House
Junie B. Jones and Her Big Fat Mouth	M	RF	250+	Park, Barbara	Random House
Junie B. Jones and Some Sneaky Peeky Spying	M	RF	250+	Park, Barbara	Random House
Junie B. Jones and that Meanie Jim's Birthday	M	RF	250+	Park, Barbara	Random House
Junie B. Jones and the Mushy Gushy Valentine	M	RF	250+	Park, Barbara	Random House
Junie B. Jones and the Stupid Smelly Bus	M	RF	250+	Park, Barbara	Random House
Junie B. Jones and the Yucky Blucky Fruitcake	M	RF	250+	Park, Barbara	Random House
Junie B. Jones Has a Monster Under Her Bed	M	RF	250+	Park, Barbara	Random House
Junie B. Jones Has a Peep in Her Pocket	M	RF	250+	Park, Barbara	Random House
Junie B. Jones Is (almost) a Flower Girl	M	RF	250+	Park, Barbara	Random House
Junie B. Jones Is a Beauty Shop Guy	M	RF	250+	Park, Barbara	Random House
Junie B. Jones Is a Party Animal	M	RF	250+	Park, Barbara	Random House
Junie B. Jones Is Not a Crook	M	RF	250+	Park, Barbara	Random House
Junie B. Jones Loves Handsome Warren	M	RF	250+	Park, Barbara	Random House
Junie B. Jones Smells Something Fishy	M	RF	250+	Park, Barbara	Random House
Junie B., First Grader (at last!)	M	RF	250+	Park, Barbara	Random House
Junior Concert, The	J	RF	266	PM Math Readers	Rigby
Junior Gymnasts: Katie's Big Move	M	RF	250+	Slater, Teddy	Scholastic
Junk Box, The	C	RF	54	Windmill Books	Rigby
Junk into Art	K	RF	587	Leveled Readers	Houghton Mifflin Harcourt
Junk Sculpture	O	I	250+	PM Extensions	Rigby
Junk-Food Files, The	S	F	250+	Power Up!	Steck-Vaughn
Junkpile Robot, The	L	F	250+	Ready Readers	Pearson Learning Group
Junkyard Dog, The	N	RF	250+	PM Collection	Rigby
Juno Loves Barney	I	RF	249	Voyages	SRA/McGraw Hill
Jupiter	Q	I	250+	A True Book	Children's Press
Jupiter	J	I	131	Exploring the Galaxy	Capstone Press
Jupiter	S	I	250+	Our Solar System	Compass Point Books
Jupiter	N	I	785	Our Universe	Lerner Publications
Jupiter	Q	I	250+	The Galaxy	Capstone Press
Jupiter	R	I	250+	Theme Sets	National Geographic
Jupiter Spiders and Other Scary Creatures	K	SF	250+	Popcorn	Sundance
Jupiter: The Moon King	Q	I	250+	Explorer Books-Pathfinder	National Geographic
Jupiter: The Moon King	P	I	250+	Explorer Books-Pioneer	National Geographic
Jurassic Grampa	Q	F	250+	Wiley & Grampa's Creature Features	Little, Brown & Co.

J

TITLE	LEVEL	GENRE	WORD COUNT	AUTHOR / SERIES	PUBLISHER / DISTRIBUTOR
Jurassic Park	Z+	SF	250+	Crichton, Michael	Ballantine Books
Just a Box	J	RF	424	Appleton-Smith, Laura	Flyleaf Publishing
Just a Few Words, Mr. Lincoln	N	I	250+	Fritz, Jean	Putnam/Penguin
Just a Mess	I	F	206	Mayer, Mercer	Donovan
Just a Seed	E	I	74	Blaxland, Wendy	Scholastic
Just Add Water	C	I	41	Discovery World	Rigby
Just As Long As We're Together	T	RF	250+	Blume, Judy	Bantam
Just Call Me Stupid	R	RF	250+	Birdseye, Tom	Puffin/Penguin
Just Clowning Around: Two Stories	E	F	62	Green Light Readers	Harcourt
Just Ella	Y	F	250+	Haddix, Margaret Peterson	Simon & Schuster
Just Enough	G	RF	107	Salem, Lynn; Stewart, Josie	Continental Press
Just for Fun	J	F	250+	Literacy 2000	Rigby
Just for Fun	Q	I	250+	Orbit Collections	Pacific Learning
Just for the Fun of It	W	RF	2792	Leveled Readers	Houghton Mifflin Harcourt
Just for the Fun of It	W	RF	2792	Leveled Readers/CA	Houghton Mifflin Harcourt
Just for You	G	F	160	Mayer, Mercer	Donovan
Just Grandma and Me	I	F	186	Mayer, Mercer	Donovan
Just Graph It!	G	I	156	Learn to Read	Creative Teaching Press
Just Hanging Around	J	I	223	Storyteller-Night Crickets	Wright Group/McGraw Hill
Just in Passing	WB	RF	N/A	Bonners, Susan	Lothrop, Lee & Shepard
Just Juice	Q	RF	250+	Hesse, Karen	Scholastic
Just Like Dad	D	RF	44	Hiris, Monica	Kaeden Books
Just Like Daddy	F	F	93	Asch, Frank	Simon & Schuster
Just Like Everyone Else	I	RF	225	Kuskin, Karla	HarperCollins
Just Like Grandpa	E	RF	81	Literacy 2000	Rigby
Just Like Grandpa	C	RF	49	Little Celebrations	Pearson Learning Group
Just Like Me	F	RF	86	First Start	Troll Associates
*Just Like Me	G	RF	108	Learn to Read	Creative Teaching Press
Just Like Me	F	RF	115	Reading Street	Pearson
Just Like Me	E	RF	138	Rookie Readers	Children's Press
Just Like Me	J	F	2154	Story Box	Wright Group/McGraw Hill
Just Like Me!	D	RF	62	Sunshine	Wright Group/McGraw Hill
Just Like Mom	D	RF	56	Hiris, Monica	Kaeden Books
Just Like Mom and Dad	O	I	1099	Leveled Readers Science	Houghton Mifflin Harcourt
Just Like My Grandpa	D	RF	48	Rise & Shine	Hampton-Brown
Just Like Us	E	RF	55	Ready Readers	Pearson Learning Group
Just Like You	D	F	160	Dominie Readers	Pearson Learning Group
Just Like You!	C	F	28	Instant Readers	Harcourt School Publishers
Just Look at You	B	RF	16	Sunshine	Wright Group/McGraw Hill
*Just Mabel	K	RF	250+	I Am Reading	Kingfisher
Just Me	C	RF	51	Literacy 2000	Rigby
Just Me and My Babysitter	H	F	182	Mayer, Mercer	Donovan
Just Me and My Dad	H	F	161	Mayer, Mercer	Donovan
Just Me and My Puppy	H	F	190	Mayer, Mercer	Donovan
Just My Luck	G	RF	136	Literacy 2000	Rigby
Just One Fish Would Do	I	RF	250+	Home Connection Collection	Rigby
Just One Guinea Pig	I	RF	339	PM Story Books-Orange	Rigby
Just One More, Mom	I	F	423	Grady, Kit S.	Kaeden Books
Just Plain Cat	O	RF	250+	Robinson, Nancy K.	Scholastic
Just Right	C	F	35	Brand New Readers	Candlewick Press
Just Right for the Night	E	RF	69	Voyages	SRA/McGraw Hill
Just Right!	C	F	75	Leveled Readers	Houghton Mifflin Harcourt
Just Right!	G	RF	105	Sunshine	Wright Group/McGraw Hill
Just Tell Me When We're Dead!	O	RF	250+	Clifford, Eth	Scholastic

J

* Collection of short stories
\# Graphic text

TITLE	LEVEL	GENRE	WORD COUNT	AUTHOR / SERIES	PUBLISHER / DISTRIBUTOR
Just the Bee's Knees	K	I	250+	Story Steps	Rigby
Just This Once	H	F	252	Sunshine	Wright Group/McGraw Hill
Just Us Women	J	RF	250+	Caines, Jeannette	Scholastic
Just Wait and See	F	F	185	Leveled Literacy Intervention / Green System	Heinemann
Justin and the Best Biscuits in the World	P	RF	250+	Pitts, Walter & Mildred	Alfred A. Knopf
Justin Morgan Had a Horse	R	HF	250+	Henry, Marguerite	Scholastic
Justin's Big Fish	I	RF	509	Pair-It Turn and Learn	Steck-Vaughn
Justin's New Bike	G	RF	150+	Hill, Barbara	Scholastic
Just-Right House, The	F	F	201	Leveled Readers	Houghton Mifflin Harcourt

J

* Collection of short stories
# Graphic text

TITLE	LEVEL	GENRE	WORD COUNT	AUTHOR / SERIES	PUBLISHER / DISTRIBUTOR
K. C. at the Bat	U	F	1939	Leveled Readers	Houghton Mifflin Harcourt
K-9 Team on Patrol	G	I	138	Literacy by Design	Rigby
Kabuki Kid, The	P	RF	773	Leveled Readers	Houghton Mifflin Harcourt
Kabuki Kid, The	P	RF	773	Leveled Readers/CA	Houghton Mifflin Harcourt
Kabuki Kid, The	P	RF	773	Leveled Readers/TX	Houghton Mifflin Harcourt
Kali and the Rat Snake	O	RF	250+	Whitaker, Zai	Kane/ Miller Book Publishers
Kalpana Chawla, Astronaut	T	B	250+	Independent Readers Science	Houghton Mifflin Harcourt
Kalulu's Pumpkins	K	F	250+	Rigby Literacy	Rigby
Kamala's Art	G	I	150	Vocabulary Readers	Houghton Mifflin Harcourt
Kamala's Art	G	I	150	Vocabulary Readers/CA	Houghton Mifflin Harcourt
Kamala's Art	G	I	150	Vocabulary Readers/TX	Houghton Mifflin Harcourt
Kama's Lei	H	RF	134	Bebop Books	Lee & Low Books Inc.
Kandake, The: Queens of Kush	X	I	2040	Independent Readers Social Studies	Houghton Mifflin Harcourt
Kangaroo from Wooloomooloo	H	F	254	Jellybeans	Rigby
Kangaroo in the Kitchen	D	F	72	Ready Readers	Pearson Learning Group
Kangaroo Joey Grows Up, A	L	I	397	Baby Animals	Lerner Publications
Kangaroo, The	M	I	250+	Crewe, Sabrina	Steck-Vaughn
Kangaroos	N	I	250+	A New True Book	Children's Press
Kangaroos	K	I	250+	PM Animal Facts: Turquoise	Rigby
Kangaroos	F	I	111	Springboard	Wright Group/McGraw Hill
Kangaroos Have Joeys	M	I	250+	Animals and Their Young	Compass Point Books
Kangaroos in the Land Down Under	M	I	250+	Rosen Real Readers	Rosen Publishing Group
Kangaroo's Pouch	C	F	36	Sails	Rigby
Kansas	T	I	250+	Hello U.S.A.	Lerner Publications
Kansas	S	I	250+	Land of Liberty	Red Brick Learning
Kansas	R	I	250+	This Land Is Your Land	Compass Point Books
Kansas City Chiefs, The	S	I	250+	Team Spirit	Norwood House Press
Kansas City Royals, The	S	I	250+	Team Spirit	Norwood House Press
Kantjil and Tiger	M	TL	250+	Story Vines	Wright Group/McGraw Hill
Kapuapua's Magic Shell	O	TL	1374	Reading Street	Pearson
Karina	D	RF	40	Step-By-Step Series	Pearson Learning Group
Kart Crash	Q	RF	250+	Maddox, Jake	Stone Arch Books
Kat the Curious	R	RF	1723	Leveled Readers	Houghton Mifflin Harcourt
Katarina	X	HF	250+	Winter, Kathryn	Scholastic
Kate Shelley and the Midnight Express	M	B	250+	Wetterer, Margaret	Carolrhoda Books
Kate's Truck	C	RF	92	Leveled Literacy Intervention/ Green System	Heinemann
Kate's Surprise	F	RF	143	Rookie Readers	Children's Press
Katharine Graham: American Publisher	P	B	250+	On Deck	Rigby
Katherine Dunham, Black Dancer	N	B	250+	Rookie Biographies	Children's Press
Katherine Paterson	S	B	250+	Cary, Alice	Learning Works, The
Katie Couldn't	F	RF	176	Rookie Readers	Children's Press
Katie Did It	G	RF	105	Rookie Readers	Children's Press
Katie Kazoo Switcheroo: No Messin' with My Lesson	M	F	250+	Krulik, Nancy	Scholastic
Katie's Butterfly	H	RF	222	PM Plus Story Books	Rigby
Katie's Caterpillar	E	RF	149	PM Plus Story Books	Rigby
Katy and the Big Snow	L	F	250+	Burton, Virginia L.	Scholastic
Katydids	E	I	20	Books for Young Learners	Richard C. Owen
Katydid's Life, A	M	I	250+	Twig	Wright Group/McGraw Hill
Katy's Inventions	N	F	804	Leveled Readers	Houghton Mifflin Harcourt
Katy's Inventions	N	F	804	Leveled Readers/CA	Houghton Mifflin Harcourt

K

* Collection of short stories
\# Graphic text

TITLE	LEVEL	GENRE	WORD COUNT	AUTHOR / SERIES	PUBLISHER / DISTRIBUTOR
Katy's Inventions	N	F	804	Leveled Readers/TX	Houghton Mifflin Harcourt
Katy's Last-Minute Book Report	M	RF	831	Reading Street	Pearson
Kawi, Pawi, Po	K	RF	472	Take Two Books	Wright Group/McGraw Hill
Kayaking	Q	I	250+	Extreme Sports	Red Brick Learning
Kayaking at Blue Lake	J	RF	250+	PM Plus Story Books	Rigby
Kayla Chronicles, The	Z+	RF	250+	Winston, Sherri	Little, Brown & Co.
Kay's Birthday	C	RF	26	KinderReaders	Rigby
Kazam All Wet	D	RF	40	Brand New Readers	Candlewick Press
Kazam's Birds	D	F	38	Brand New Readers	Candlewick Press
Kazam's Cards	D	F	34	Brand New Readers	Candlewick Press
Kazam's Coins	D	F	35	Brand New Readers	Candlewick Press
Kazam's Rabbit	D	RF	40	Brand New Readers	Candlewick Press
Kazam's Scarf	D	RF	41	Brand New Readers	Candlewick Press
Kazam's Wand	D	F	29	Brand New Readers	Candlewick Press
Keelboat Annie	N	TL	250+	Johnson, Janet P.	Troll Associates
Keep Calm!	Q	RF	250+	Bookweb	Rigby
Keep Ms. Sugarman in the Fourth Grade	M	RF	250+	Levy, Elizabeth	HarperTrophy
Keep Out!	B	RF	19	Ready Readers	Pearson Learning Group
Keep Out: Our Dog Buries What It Can't Eat	P	RF	250+	Beale, Fleur	Pacific Learning
Keep Rivers Clean	M	I	405	Sun Sprouts	ETA Cuisenaire
Keep Smiling Through	V	RF	250+	Rinaldi, Ann	Harcourt Trade
Keep the Beat	D	RF	48	Little Celebrations	Pearson Learning Group
Keep the Lights Burning Abbie	K	HF	250+	Roop, Peter & Connie	Scholastic
Keep Your Cool!: What You Should Know about Stress	V	I	7034	Health Zone	Lerner Publications
Keep Your Eye on Amanda!	R	F	250+	Avi	Avon
Keeper of Soles	Q	F	250+	Bateman, Teresa	Holiday House
Keeper of the Night	Z+	RF	250+	Holt, Kimberly Willis	Henry Holt & Co.
Keeping Baby Animals Safe	C	I	56	Little Books	Sadlier-Oxford
Keeping Clean	I	I	220	Sails	Rigby
Keeping Clean	WB	I	N/A	Windows on Literacy	National Geographic
Keeping Cool	D	I	18	Foundations	Wright Group/McGraw Hill
Keeping Cool	C	I	18	Pacific Literacy	Pacific Learning
Keeping Count	Q	I	250+	WorldScapes	ETA Cuisenaire
Keeping Days, The	Z	HF	250+	Johnston, Norma	Puffin/Penguin
Keeping Fit with Sports	I	I	250	Time for Kids	Teacher Created Materials
Keeping Fit!	E	F	36	Little Celebrations	Pearson Learning Group
Keeping Ice Cold	L	I	567	Sun Sprouts	ETA Cuisenaire
Keeping in Touch	S	I	250+	Connectors	Pacific Learning
Keeping in Touch	K	I	328	Gear Up!	Wright Group/ McGraw Hill
Keeping Israel Safe: Serving in the Israel Defense Forces	X	I	7210	Sofer, Barbara	Kar-Ben Publishing
Keeping Records	V	I	250+	WorldScapes	ETA Cuisenaire
Keeping Room, The	V	HF	250+	Myers, Anna	Puffin/Penguin
Keeping Safe in an Earthquake	O	I	949	Vocabulary Readers	Houghton Mifflin Harcourt
Keeping Safe in an Earthquake	O	I	949	Vocabulary Readers/CA	Houghton Mifflin Harcourt
Keeping Safe in an Earthquake	O	I	949	Vocabulary Readers/TX	Houghton Mifflin Harcourt
Keeping Score	J	I	240	Early Connections	Benchmark Education
Keeping Tadpoles	N	I	250+	Discovery World	Rigby
Keeping the Balance	P	I	250+	WorldScapes	ETA Cuisenaire
Keeping the Promise: A Torah's Journey	R	I	1277	Lehman-Wilzig, Tami	Kar-Ben Publishing
Keeping Time	J	I	231	Early Connections	Benchmark Education
Keeping Time	S	I	250+	InfoQuest	Rigby
Keeping Up with Claire	O	RF	250+	On Our Way to English	Rigby

* Collection of short stories
# Graphic text

K

TITLE	LEVEL	GENRE	WORD COUNT	AUTHOR / SERIES	PUBLISHER / DISTRIBUTOR
Keeping Warm	E	I	105	Yellow Umbrella Books	Red Brick Learning
Keeping Warm in Winter	P	I	516	Vocabulary Readers	Houghton Mifflin Harcourt
Keeping Warm! Keeping Cool!	K	I	946	Sunshine	Wright Group/McGraw Hill
Keeping Watch	J	F	520	Bella and Rosie Series	Literacy Footprints
Keeping Water Clean	I	I	117	Pebble Books	Red Brick Learning
Keeping You a Secret	Z+	RF	250+	Peters, Julie Anne	Little, Brown & Co.
Keeping You Healthy: A Book About Doctors	I	I	185	Community Workers	Picture Window Books
Keeping You Safe: A Book About Police Officers	I	I	112	Community Workers	Picture Window Books
Keisha Discovers Harlem	Q	RF	250+	Lewis, Zoe	Magic Attic
Keisha Leads the Way: Magic Attic Club	Q	RF	250+	Reed, Teresa	Magic Attic
Keisha the Fairy Snow Queen: Magic Attic Club	Q	RF	250+	Reed, Teresa	Magic Attic
Keisha to the Rescue: Magic Attic Club	Q	RF	250+	Reed, Teresa	Magic Attic
Keisha's Maze Mystery: Magic Attic Club	Q	RF	250+	Benson, Lauren	Magic Attic
Kelly the Rescue Dog	S	HF	250+	High-Fliers	Pacific Learning
Kelly's Trip	L	RF	250	Sunshine	Wright Group/McGraw Hill
Ken Griffey, Jr. & Ken Griffey, Sr.	T	B	250+	Star Families	Crestwood House
Kendria's Watch	S	SF	2316	Leveled Readers	Houghton Mifflin Harcourt
Kendria's Watch	S	SF	2316	Leveled Readers/CA	Houghton Mifflin Harcourt
Kendria's Watch	S	SF	2316	Leveled Readers/TX	Houghton Mifflin Harcourt
Kenji's Haircut	D	RF	105	Lighthouse	Rigby
Kenny and the Little Kickers	J	F	250+	Marzollo, Claudio	Scholastic
Kenny's Big Present	H	RF	181	Leveled Readers	Houghton Mifflin Harcourt
Kensuke's Kingdom	V	RF	250+	Morpurgo, Michael	Scholastic
Kent State Shootings, The	X	I	250+	We the People	Compass Point Books
Kentucky	T	I	250+	Hello U.S.A.	Lerner Publications
Kentucky	S	I	250+	Land of Liberty	Red Brick Learning
Kentucky	R	I	250+	This Land Is Your Land	Compass Point Books
Kenya	O	I	2440	A Ticket to …	Carolrhoda Books
Kenya	O	I	250+	Countries of the World	Red Brick Learning
Kenya	P	I	1993	Country Explorers	Lerner Publications
Kenya	Q	I	250+	First Reports: Countries	Compass Point Books
Kenya ABCs: A Book About the People and Places of Kenya	Q	I	250+	Country ABCs	Picture Window Books
Kenya in Colors	N	I	250+	World of Colors	Capstone Press
Kenya: A Question and Answer Book	P	I	250+	Questions & Answers: Countries	Capstone Press
Kenya's Word	L	RF	250+	Trice, Linda	Charlesbridge
Kermit and Robin's Scary Story	J	F	250+	Muntean, Michaela	Puffin/Penguin
Kerplunk!	J	I	250	Spyglass Books	Compass Point Books
Kerri Strug: Heart of Gold	L	B	250+	Strug, K.; Brown, G.	Scholastic
Kerry	K	RF	250+	PM Story Books-Silver	Rigby
Kerry's Double	K	RF	250+	PM Story Books-Silver	Rigby
Ketchup Deal, The	P	F	250+	Orbit Chapter Books	Pacific Learning
Kevin and Lucy	E	RF	130	Leveled Readers	Houghton Mifflin Harcourt
Kevin and Lucy	E	RF	130	Leveled Readers/CA	Houghton Mifflin Harcourt
Kevin Counts	D	RF	83	Seedlings	Continental Press
Kevin Garnett	P	B	1501	Amazing Athletes	Lerner Publications
Kevin Garnett	R	B	250+	Sports Heroes	Red Brick Learning
Key to Maps, The	K	I	222	Windows on Literacy	National Geographic
Key to the Playhouse, The	O	RF	250+	York, Carol	Scholastic
Key to the Treasure	N	RF	250+	Parish, Peggy	Bantam
Key, The	L	F	250+	On Our Way to English	Rigby
Keys	B	I	31	Ready Readers	Pearson Learning Group
Khyber Pass, The	W	I	1993	Leveled Readers Social Studies	Houghton Mifflin Harcourt

* Collection of short stories
# Graphic text

K

TITLE	LEVEL	GENRE	WORD COUNT	AUTHOR / SERIES	PUBLISHER / DISTRIBUTOR
Kiboko and the Water Snake	I	F	250+	Storyworlds	Heinemann Educational Books
Kick, Pass, and Run	J	RF	250+	Kessler, Leonard	HarperTrophy
Kick-a-Lot Shoes, The	H	F	433	Story Box	Wright Group/McGraw Hill
Kickball	F	RF	148	Handprints D, Set 1	Educators Publishing Service
Kickboxing	M	I	250+	To the Extreme	Capstone Press
Kickboxing	S	I	250+	X-Sports	Capstone Press
Kicked Out	Z	RF	250+	Orca Soundings	Orca Book Publishers
Kicker	T	RF	250+	Orca Sports	Orca Book Publishers
Kickin' It	Y	I	250+	Boldprint	Steck-Vaughn
Kid Heroes of the Environment	Q	I	250+	Dee, Catherine	Scholastic
Kid in the Red Jacket, The	O	RF	250+	Park, Barbara	Random House
Kid Next Door, The	N	RF	250+	Smith, Janice Lee	HarperTrophy
Kid Power	P	RF	250+	Pfeffer, Susan Beth	Scholastic
Kid Who Only Hit Homers, The	P	RF	250+	Christopher, Matt	Little, Brown & Co.
Kid Who Ran for President, The	T	RF	250+	Gutman, Dan	Language for Learning Assoc.
Kidnapped King, The	N	RF	250+	A to Z Mysteries	Random House
Kids Against Hunger	Q	RF	250+	We Are Heroes	Stone Arch Books
Kids Around the World	K	I	294	Time for Kids	Teacher Created Materials
Kids at Our School	I	RF	107	City Kids	Rigby
Kids at Work: Lewis Hine and the Crusade Against Child Labor	T	B	250+	Freedman, Russell	Clarion
Kids Can Be Safe!	D	I	65	On Our Way to English	Rigby
Kids Can Cook	M	I	250+	Literacy 2000	Rigby
Kids Can Read	C	RF	158	Sails	Rigby
Kids Care Club, The	I	RF	414	Reading Street	Pearson
Kids from Quiller's Bend	P	RF	250+	Action Packs	Rigby
Kids' Guide to Family Reunions, A	O	I	351	Vocabulary Readers	Houghton Mifflin Harcourt
Kid's Guide to Social Action	V	I	250+	Lewis, Barbara A.	Free Spirit Publishing
Kids in Ms. Colman's Class: Author Day	M	RF	250+	Martin, Ann M.	Scholastic
Kids in Pioneer Times	Q	I	250+	Kids Throughout History	Rosen Publishing Group
Kids in the Circus	L	I	250+	Sunshine	Wright Group/McGraw Hill
Kids in the Kitchen	C	RF	127	Sails	Rigby
Kids' Invention Book, The	T	I	250+	Erlbach, Arlene	Lerner Publishing
Kids Rule!	O	I	250+	Bookshop	Mondo
Kids Say	N	F	250+	Sails	Rigby
Kids to the Rescue	W	I	2421	Vocabulary Readers	Houghton Mifflin Harcourt
Kids to the Rescue	W	I	2421	Vocabulary Readers/CA	Houghton Mifflin Harcourt
Kids to the Rescue	W	I	2421	Vocabulary Readers/TX	Houghton Mifflin Harcourt
Kids You Ought to Know	U	B	250+	Bookshop	Mondo
Kiki Strike: Empress's Tomb, The	W	F	250+	Miller Kirsten	Bloomsbury Children's Books
Kiki Strike: Inside the Shadow City	W	F	250+	Miller Kirsten	Bloomsbury Children's Books
Killer Bees	S	I	250+	Blau, Melinda	Steck-Vaughn
Killer Lipstick	W	I	250+	24/7 Science Behind the Scenes	Scholastic
Killer Plants	K	I	469	Explorations	Okapi Eductional Materials
Killer Plants	K	I	469	Explorations	Eleanor Curtain Publishing
Killer Sharks	Q	SF	250+	Cullimore, Stan	Stone Arch Books
Killer Whales	P	I	1678	Animal Predators	Lerner Publishing
Killer Whales	R	I	250+	Predators in the Wild	Red Brick Learning
Killer Whales	K	I	250+	Simon, Seymour	Chronicle Books

K

TITLE	LEVEL	GENRE	WORD COUNT	AUTHOR / SERIES	PUBLISHER / DISTRIBUTOR
Killing Germs	K	I	677	Pull Ahead Books	Lerner Publications
Kilmer's Pet Monster	L	RF	250+	Dadey, Debbie; Jones, Marcia Thornton	Scholastic
Kim and the Computer Giant	J	F	250+	Storyworlds	Heinemann Educational Books
Kim and the Computer Mouse	J	F	250+	Storyworlds	Heinemann Educational Books
Kim and the Missing Paint Pot	J	F	250+	Storyworlds	Heinemann Educational Books
Kim and the Shape Dragon	J	F	250+	Storyworlds	Heinemann Educational Books
Kim Carries the Flag	H	RF	130	Pair-It Turn and Learn	Steck-Vaughn
Kim Does It	P	RF	250+	Reading Safari	Mondo
Kim's New Shoes	G	RF	234	Leveled Literacy Intervention/ Blue System	Heinemann
Kimiko Quest	O	F	250+	Literacy by Design	Rigby
Kind Child, The	I	RF	250+	Hechinger, Nancy	Scholastic
Kind Emma	I	F	224	Big Cat	Pacific Learning
Kind of Thief, A	U	RF	250+	Alcock, Vivien	Bantam
*Kind Prince and Rupert, The	L	F	250+	New Way Literature	Steck-Vaughn
Kindergarten	D	RF	118	Carousel Readers	Pearson Learning Group
Kindest Family, The	K	TL	536	PM Plus Story Books	Rigby
Kindling, The (Fire-Us Trilogy: Book 1)	Y	SF	250+	Armstrong, Jennifer; Butcher, Nancy	HarperCollins
Kinds of Environments	I	I	382	Science Support Readers	Houghton Mifflin Harcourt
King Arthur	M	F	250+	Brown, Marc	Little, Brown & Co.
King Beast's Birthday	L	F	250+	Literacy 2000	Rigby
King Bidgood's in the Bathtub	L	F	250+	Wood, Audrey	Scholastic
King Crab Is Coming!	J	F	250+	Rigby Rocket	Rigby
King Emmett the Second	R	RF	250+	Stolz, Mary	Bantam
King Glitter and the Stars	J	F	318	Talking Point Series	Pearson Learning Group
King Max	Q	F	250+	King-Smith, Dick	Troll Associates
King Midas and the Golden Touch	K	TL	721	PM Collection	Rigby
King Midas and the Golden Touch	J	TL	250+	Traditional Tales	Pearson Learning Group
King of Egypt, The	R	HF	250+	Rigby Literacy	Rigby
King of Shadows	Z	F	250+	Cooper, Susan	McElderry
King of the Birds, The	J	F	250+	Rigby Literacy	Rigby
King of the Birds, The	J	F	250+	Rigby Star	Rigby
King of the Mild Frontier: An Ill-Advised Autobiography	Z+	RF	250+	Crutcher, Chris	HarperCollins
King of the Pygmies	Z+	RF	250+	Fuqua, Jonathon Scott	Candlewick Press
King of the Sky	J	RF	250+	Foundations	Wright Group/McGraw Hill
King of the Wind	R	HF	250+	Henry, Marguerite	Aladdin
King Philip	V	B	250+	Amazing Americans	Wright Group/ McGraw Hill
King Tut	R	I	250+	Explorer Books-Pathfinder	National Geographic
King Tut	Q	I	250+	Explorer Books-Pioneer	National Geographic
King Tut: Tales from the Tomb	W	I	250+	High Five Reading	Red Brick Learning
King Tut's Tomb	S	I	250+	Ancient Egypt	Capstone Press
King Who Could Knit, The	J	F	250+	The Wright Skills	Wright Group/McGraw Hill
King Who Had Dirty Feet, The: A Play	M	TL	250+	Rigby Literacy	Rigby
King Who Loved to Dance, The	F	F	82	Instant Readers	Harcourt School Publishers
King, the Mice, and the Cheese, The	K	F	250+	Gurney, Nancy	Random House
Kingdom of Kush, The	Z	I	3395	Leveled Readers	Houghton Mifflin Harcourt
Kingdom of the Golden Dragon	X	F	250+	Allende, Isabel	Harper Trophy

* Collection of short stories
# Graphic text

K

TITLE	LEVEL	GENRE	WORD COUNT	AUTHOR / SERIES	PUBLISHER / DISTRIBUTOR
Kingfisher's Gift, The	W	F	250+	Beckhorn, Susan Williams	Penguin Group
Kingfisher's Tale, The	Z	RF	250+	Misfits Inc.	Peachtree
King's Big Foot, The	I	F	249	On Our Way to English	Rigby
King's Birthday, The	B	F	35	Ray's Readers	Outside the Box
King's Crossing	G	RF	258	Handprints D	Educators Publishing Service
*King's Dream and Sammy's New Yellow Sweater, The	L	TL	250+	New Way Literature	Steck-Vaughn
King's Equal, The	O	TL	250+	Paterson, Katherine	HarperTrophy
King's Job	F	F	155	Handprints C	Educators Publishing Service
King's New Castle, The	L	F	1222	InfoTrek	ETA Cuisenaire
Kings of Persia, The	X	I	2093	Leveled Readers	Houghton Mifflin Harcourt
Kings of Persia, The	X	I	2093	Leveled Readers/CA	Houghton Mifflin Harcourt
King's Pudding, The	I	F	214	Literacy Tree	Rigby
*King's Race and Other Stories, The	L	F	250+	New Way Literature	Steck-Vaughn
King's Ring, The	C	F	38	KinderReaders	Rigby
King's Slippers, The	E	F	107	Sun Sprouts	ETA Cuisenaire
King's Surprise, The	D	F	54	Stewart, Josie; Salem, Lynn	Continental Press
Kink the Mink	C	F	18	KinderReaders	Rigby
Kip and Tip	C	I	24	KinderReaders	Rigby
Kipper's Birthday	E	RF	64	Oxford Reading Tree	Oxford University Press
Kira-Kira	T	RF	250+	Kadohata, Cynthia	Aladddin Paperbacks
Kirsten Learns a Lesson	Q	HF	250+	The American Girls Collection	Pleasant Company
Kirsten Saves the Day	Q	HF	250+	The American Girls Collection	Pleasant Company
Kirsten's Surprise	Q	HF	250+	The American Girls Collection	Pleasant Company
Kiss for Little Bear, A	H	F	250+	Minarik, Else H.	HarperTrophy
Kiss Me, I'm Perfect	L	F	250+	Munsch, Robert	Scholastic
Kiss the Cow!	L	F	250+	Root, Phyllis	Candlewick Press
Kiss the Dust	W	RF	250+	Laird, Elizabeth	Penguin Group
Kit Carson: Mountain Man	V	B	250+	Let Freedom Ring	Capstone Press
Kit Finds a Mitt	H	RF	198	Leveled Readers	Houghton Mifflin Harcourt
Kitchen Garden	F	I	174	Explorations	Eleanor Curtain Publishing
Kitchen Garden	F	I	174	Explorations	Okapi Educational Materials
Kitchen Knight, The	T	TL	250+	Hodges, Margaret	Holiday House
Kitchen Rules	J	I	153	Windows on Literacy	National Geographic
Kitchen Science	P	I	958	Independent Readers Science	Houghton Mifflin Harcourt
Kitchen Science	M	I	552	Vocabulary Readers	Houghton Mifflin Harcourt
Kitchen Science	M	I	552	Vocabulary Readers/CA	Houghton Mifflin Harcourt
Kitchen Science	M	I	552	Vocabulary Readers/TX	Houghton Mifflin Harcourt
Kitchen Science	M	I	250+	Windows on Literacy	National Geographic
Kitchen Scientist	M	I	792	Sun Sprouts	ETA Cuisenaire
Kitchen Table Science	M	I	250+	Literacy by Design	Rigby
Kitchen Tools	E	I	104	Foundations	Wright Group/McGraw Hill
Kitchen, The	T	I	250+	Historic Communities	Crabtree
Kite and the Butterflies, The	I	F	364	Book Bank	Wright Group/McGraw Hill
Kite Contest, The	I	RF	346	Leveled Readers	Houghton Mifflin Harcourt
Kite Contest, The	I	RF	346	Leveled Readers/CA	Houghton Mifflin Harcourt
Kite Contest, The	I	RF	346	Leveled Readers/TX	Houghton Mifflin Harcourt
Kite Dance	E	RF	65	Danforth, Audrey	Continental Press
Kite Day	E	RF	120	Springboard	Wright Group/McGraw Hill
Kite Flying	E	I	190	Vocabulary Readers	Houghton Mifflin Harcourt
Kite Flying	E	I	190	Vocabulary Readers/CA	Houghton Mifflin Harcourt
Kite Flying	E	I	190	Vocabulary Readers/TX	Houghton Mifflin Harcourt

* Collection of short stories
# Graphic text

Storable Database at www.fountasandpinnellleveledbooks.com

K

TITLE	LEVEL	GENRE	WORD COUNT	AUTHOR / SERIES	PUBLISHER / DISTRIBUTOR
Kite Shapes	C	I	31	Little Celebrations	Pearson Learning Group
Kite That Flew Away, The	H	RF	279	Ready Readers	Pearson Learning Group
Kite That Got Away, The	I	RF	250+	PM Plus Story Books	Rigby
Kite, The	D	RF	59	My First Reader	Grolier Press
Kite, The	J	RF	468	Springboard	Wright Group/McGraw Hill
Kites	I	I	166	Explorations	Eleanor Curtain Publishing
Kites	I	I	166	Explorations	Okapi Eductional Materials
Kites	C	RF	41	Joy Readers	Pearson Learning Group
Kites	C	RF	42	Ling, Bettina	Scholastic
Kites	N	I	250+	Literacy 2000	Rigby
Kites	B	F	41	Phonics and Friends	Hampton-Brown
Kites	O	I	250+	PM Nonfiction-Emerald	Rigby
Kites, The	B	RF	36	Sails	Rigby
Kitesurfing	O	I	250+	Sails	Rigby
Kit's Castle	L	RF	250+	Storyteller-Shooting Stars	Wright Group/McGraw Hill
Kit's Wilderness	Y	RF	250+	Almond, David	Random House
Kitten Chased a Fly	C	RF	57	Windmill Books	Wright Group/McGraw Hill
Kitten Crowd	O	RF	250+	Baglio, Ben M.	Scholastic
Kitten for Kate, A	E	RF	137	On Our Way to English	Rigby
Kitten in the Cold	Q	RF	250+	Baglio, Ben M.	Scholastic
Kitten Is a Baby Cat, A	D	I	64	Blevins, Wiley	Scholastic
Kitten That Won First Prize, The	Q	RF	250+	Baglio, Ben M.	Scholastic
Kitten, The	A	RF	40	Sun Sprouts	ETA Cuisenaire
Kittens	B	RF	33	Curry, Don L.	Scholastic
Kittens	G	I	107	Discovery Links	Newbridge
Kittens	C	I	87	Leveled Literacy Intervention/ Blue System	Heinemann
Kittens	C	RF	22	Literacy 2000	Rigby
Kittens	E	I	32	Pair-It Turn and Learn	Steck-Vaughn
Kittens in the Kitchen	Q	RF	250+	Daniels, Lucy	Barron's Educational
Kitty and the Birds	C	F	64	PM Story Books	Rigby
Kitty Cat	C	RF	57	PM Plus Story Books	Rigby
Kitty Cat and Fat Cat	D	F	98	PM Plus Story Books	Rigby
Kitty Cat and the Bird	C	RF	78	PM Stars	Rigby
Kitty Cat and the Fish	D	F	73	PM Plus Story Books	Rigby
Kitty Cat and the Paint Can	F	F	165	PM Plus Story Books	Rigby
Kitty Cat Plays Inside	E	F	134	PM Plus Story Books	Rigby
Kitty Cat Runs up a Tree	E	F	134	PM Stars	Rigby
Kitty Goes on Vacation	I	RF	354	Rigby Flying Colors	Rigby
Kitty Goes Splash	E	RF	112	Books for Young Learners	Richard C. Owen
Kitzikuba	G	F	198	Story Basket	Wright Group/McGraw Hill
Klondike Gold Rush, The	S	I	250+	A First Book	Franklin Watts
Klutzy Cat, The	M	F	250+	Storyteller Summer Skies	Wright Group/McGraw Hill
Knee Knock Rise	S	F	250+	Babbitt, Natalie	Farrar, Straus and Giroux
Knife, The	N	RF	250+	Orbit Chapter Books	Pacific Learning
Knight	X	I	250+	Eyewitness Books	DK Publishing
Knight at Dawn, The	M	F	250+	Osborne, Mary Pope	Random House
Knight in Armor, A	U	I	1224	Vocabulary Readers	Houghton Mifflin Harcourt
Knight in Armor, A	U	I	1224	Vocabulary Readers/CA	Houghton Mifflin Harcourt
Knight in Armor, A	U	I	1224	Vocabulary Readers/TX	Houghton Mifflin Harcourt
Knightly News	P	RF	250+	Kenna, Anna	Pacific Learning
Knights	T	I	250+	Warriors of History	Capstone Press
Knights	T	I	250+	Warriors of History	Capstone Press
Knights & Armor	Q	I	250+	Worldwise	Franklin Watts

K

* Collection of short stories
\# Graphic text

TITLE	LEVEL	GENRE	WORD COUNT	AUTHOR / SERIES	PUBLISHER / DISTRIBUTOR
Knight's Castle	T	F	250+	Eager, Edward	Harcourt
Knights Don't Teach Piano	M	F	250+	Dadey, Debbie; Jones, Marcia Thornton	Scholastic
Knights in Shining Armor	O	I	250+	Gibbons, Gail	Little, Brown & Co.
Knights of the Kitchen Table	P	F	250+	Scieszka, Jon	Penguin Group
Knit, Knit, Knit, Knit	J	F	250+	Literacy 2000	Rigby
Knitting for Fun!	S	I	250+	For Fun! Crafts	Compass Point Books
Knitting for Penguins	J	I	179	Storyteller	Wright Group/ McGraw Hill
Knitwits	Q	RF	250+	Taylor, William	Scholastic
Knobby Knuckles, Knobby Knees	I	F	236	Sunshine	Wright Group/McGraw Hill
Knock! Knock!	K	RF	250+	Carter, Jackie	Scholastic
Knock, Knock	E	RF	96	Leveled Readers	Houghton Mifflin Harcourt
Knock, Knock	C	F	56	Little Celebrations	Pearson Learning Group
*Knot in the Grain (and Other Stories)	X	F	250+	McKinley, Robin	HarperTrophy
Knots in My Yo-yo String: The Autobiography of a Kid	U	B	250+	Spinelli, Jerry	Alfred A. Knopf
Knots on a Counting Rope	P	RF	250+	Martin, Jr., B.; Archambault, J.	Henry Holt & Co.
Know Where to Go	M	I	250+	Pacific Literacy	Pacific Learning
Know Your Birthday Manners	D	F	38	Instant Readers	Harcourt School Publishers
Know Your Noodles	K	I	115	Gear Up!	Wright Group/McGraw Hill
Know-Nothing Birthday, A	K	RF	250+	Spirn, Michele Sobel	HarperTrophy
Know-Nothings, The	K	RF	250+	Spirn, Michele Sobel	HarperTrophy
Knuffle Bunny	K	RF	212	Willems, Mo	Scholastic
Koala Bears	D	I	37	Rosen Real Readers	Rosen Publishing Group
Koala Is Not a Bear, A	P	I	250+	Crabapples	Crabtree
Koala Joey Grows Up, A	J	I	728	Baby Animals	Carolrhoda Books
Koalas	N	I	250+	A New True Book	Children's Press
Koalas	O	I	2111	Early Bird Nature Books	Lerner Publications
Koalas	R	I	250+	Explorer Books-Pathfinder	National Geographic
Koalas	P	I	250+	Explorer Books-Pioneer	National Geographic
Koalas	E	I	36	Literacy 2000	Rigby
Koalas	F	I	45	Pebble Books	Capstone Press
Kobe Bryant	P	B	1474	Amazing Athletes	Lerner Publications
Kobe Bryant	T	B	250+	Sports Heroes	Red Brick Learning
Koi's Python	P	RF	250+	Moore, Miriam	Hyperion
Koko Communicates	O	I	822	Leveled Readers	Houghton Mifflin Harcourt
Koko Communicates	O	I	822	Leveled Readers/CA	Houghton Mifflin Harcourt
Koko Communicates	O	I	822	Leveled Readers/TX	Houghton Mifflin Harcourt
Komodo Dragons	R	I	250+	Predators in the Wild	Red Brick Learning
Komodo Dragons	I	I	238	Sails	Rigby
Komodo Dragons	R	I	250+	Theme Sets	National Geographic
Kon-Tiki	Z+	I	250+	Heyerdahl, Thor	Simon & Schuster
Kon-Tiki, The	O	I	1201	Leveled Readers	Houghton Mifflin Harcourt
Kon-Tiki, The	O	I	1201	Leveled Readers/CA	Houghton Mifflin Harcourt
Kon-Tiki, The	O	I	1201	Leveled Readers/TX	Houghton Mifflin Harcourt
Korka the Mighty Elf	H	F	250+	Rigby Literacy	Rigby
Korka the Mighty Elf	H	F	250+	Rigby Star	Rigby
Korky Paul: Biography of an Illustrator	M	B	250+	Discovery World	Rigby
Koya DeLaney and the Good Girl Blues	P	RF	250+	Greenfield, Eloise	Scholastic
Krakus and the Dragon: A Polish Folktale	J	TL	250+	Leveled Readers Language Support	Houghton Mifflin Harcourt
Kristen: The Clique Summer Collection	X	RF	250+	Harrison, Lisi	Little, Brown & Co.
Kristy and the Walking Disaster	O	RF	250+	Martin, Ann M.	Scholastic
Kudzu Invasion, The	T	I	1438	Reading Street	Pearson

TITLE	LEVEL	GENRE	WORD COUNT	AUTHOR / SERIES	PUBLISHER / DISTRIBUTOR
Kurt Cobain	Z	B	250+	Rock Music Library	Capstone Press
Kwanza	J	I	143	Holidays and Celebrations	Capstone Press
Kwanzaa	Q	I	250+	Celebrate!	Capstone Press
Kwanzaa	O	I	250+	Chocolate, Deborah M. Newton	Children's Press
Kwanzaa	O	I	1518	On My Own Holidays	Lerner Publications
Kwanzaa	K	I	225	Visions	Wright Group/McGraw Hill
Kwasi: A Storysong	J	RF	250+	Greetings	Rigby
Kyle's First Kwanzaa	L	RF	250+	Little Celebrations	Pearson Learning Group

K

* Collection of short stories
\# Graphic text

TITLE	LEVEL	GENRE	WORD COUNT	AUTHOR / SERIES	PUBLISHER / DISTRIBUTOR
La Causa: The Migrant Farmworkers' Story	U	I	250+	deRuiz, Dana Catharine	Steck-Vaughn
La Mariposa	P	RF	250+	Jimenez, Franciso	Scholastic
La Salle: La Salle and the Mississippi River	U	B	250+	Exploring the World	Compass Point Books
Labor Day	Q	I	250+	Holiday Histories	Heinemann Library
Labor Day	L	I	125	National Holidays	Red Brick Learning
Labradoodles	R	I	250+	All About Dogs	Capstone Press
Labrador Retrievers	R	I	250+	All About Dogs	Capstone Press
Labradors	I	I	157	Dogs	Capstone Press
Lacey's Loud Voice	L	RF	589	Leveled Readers	Houghton Mifflin Harcourt
Lacrosse Firestorm	Q	RF	250+	Christopher, Matt	Little, Brown & Co.
Lacrosse for Fun!	S	I	250+	Sports for Fun!	Compass Point Books
Lad Who Went to the North Wind, The	J	F	250+	Bookshop	Mondo
Ladders	G	I	162	Sails	Rigby
Ladies and Gentlemen	G	RF	120	Early Readers	Compass Point Books
Ladies First	U	B	250+	Rappaport, Ken	Peachtree
Lady Bird Johnson	Q	B	250+	Simon, Charnan	Children's Press
Lady Liberty	J	I	229	Twig	Wright Group/McGraw Hill
Lady Liberty: A Biography	T	B	250+	Rappaport, Doreen	Candlewick Press
Lady Lollipop	P	F	250+	King-Smith, Dick	Candlewick Press
Lady Red Rose and the Woods	S	RF	2621	Reading Street	Pearson
Lady with the Alligator Purse	F	F	218	Wescott, Nadine Bernard	Little, Brown & Co.
Lady with the Hat, The	Z	HF	250+	Orlev, Uri	Penguin Group
Ladybug	N	I	250+	Life Cycles	Creative Teaching Press
Ladybug and the Cricket, The	J	F	388	Leveled Literacy Intervention/Blue System	Heinemann
Ladybug and the Legislature, The	O	I	484	Independent Readers Social Studies	Houghton Mifflin Harcourt
Ladybug, Ladybug	D	I	118	Rigby Flying Colors	Rigby
Ladybug, The	O	I	250+	Crewe, Sabrina	Steck-Vaughn
Ladybug, The	O	I	250+	Exploring History & Geography	Rigby
Ladybugs	G	I	98	Bugs, Bugs, Bugs	Red Brick Learning
Ladybugs	D	I	42	Insects	Capstone Press
Ladybugs	F	I	163	Leveled Readers	Houghton Mifflin Harcourt
Ladybugs	F	I	163	Leveled Readers/CA	Houghton Mifflin Harcourt
Ladybugs	F	I	163	Leveled Readers/TX	Houghton Mifflin Harcourt
Ladybugs	N	I	250+	Minibeasts	Franklin Watts
Ladybugs	N	I	250+	Nature's Friends	Compass Point Books
Ladybugs: Red, Fiery, and Bright	M	I	735	Posada, Mia	Carolrhoda Books
Lady's Big Surprise: Lucky Foot Stable Series	R	RF	36261	Dawson, JoAnn S.	Sourcebooks
Laggan Lard Butts	V	RF	250+	Orca Currents	Orca Book Publishers
Lake Critter Journal	O	RF	250+	Little Celebrations	Pearson Learning Group
Lake Life	Q	I	250+	Orbit Chapter Books	Pacific Learning
Lake of Secrets	V	RF	250+	Little, Lael	Henry Holt & Co.
Lake of Stars, The	F	F	248	Storyworlds	Heinemann Educational Publishers
Lake, The	G	I	53	Windows on Literacy	National Geographic
Lakes	H	I	240	Rigby Flying Colors	Rigby
Lamb in the Laundry	Q	RF	250+	Baglio, Ben M.	Scholastic
Lamb Lessons	O	RF	250+	Baglio, Ben M.	Scholastic
Lamb Who Came for Dinner, The	M	F	250+	Smallman, Steve	Scholastic
Lamborghinis	U	I	250+	High Performance	Red Brick Learning
Lamby's Breakfast	D	RF	105	PM Photo Stories	Rigby
Lamp from the Warlock's Tomb, The	S	F	250+	Bellairs, John	Puffin/Penguin
Lampfish of Twill, The	U	F	250+	Lisle, Janet Taylor	Scholastic

* Collection of short stories
# Graphic text

L

TITLE	LEVEL	GENRE	WORD COUNT	AUTHOR / SERIES	PUBLISHER / DISTRIBUTOR
Lan Xang, Kingdom of the Million Elephants	Y	I	2056	Leveled Readers Social Studies	Houghton Mifflin Harcourt
Lana and Miguel's Park	J	RF	381	Leveled Readers	Houghton Mifflin Harcourt
Lana and Miguel's Park	J	RF	381	Leveled Readers/CA	Houghton Mifflin Harcourt
Lana and Miguel's Park	J	RF	381	Leveled Readers/TX	Houghton Mifflin Harcourt
Lance Armstrong	P	B	2052	Amazing Athletes	Lerner Publications
Lance Armstrong	L	I	444	Leveled Readers	Houghton Mifflin Harcourt
Lance Armstrong	L	I	444	Leveled Readers/CA	Houghton Mifflin Harcourt
Lance Armstrong	L	I	444	Leveled Readers/TX	Houghton Mifflin Harcourt
Lance Armstrong: Champion for Life!	S	B	250+	High Five Reading	Red Brick Learning
Land	C	I	12	Geography	Lerner Publishing
Land	D	I	50	Time for Kids	Teacher Created Materials
Land and Water	K	I	106	Independent Readers Social Studies	Houghton Mifflin Harcourt
Land and Water of the United States, The: A Dictionary,	k	I	219	Literacy by Design	Rigby
Land Around Us, The	J	I	249	Explorations	Okapi Educational Materials
Land Around Us, The	J	I	249	Explorations	Eleanor Curtain Publishing
Land I Lost, The	P	I	250+	Nhuong, Huynh Quang	HarperTrophy
Land of Opportunity, The	T	I	2550	Reading Street	Pearson
Land of the Dragons	P	I	250+	Orbit Chapter Books	Pacific Learning
Land of the Great Big "No!"	L	RF	250+	Trussell-Cullen, Alan	Pearson Learning Group
Land Predators of North America	T	I	250+	Animals in Order	Franklin Watts
Land, The	Z	HF	250+	Taylor, Mildred D.	Penguin Group
Landforms	T	I	250+	Pair-It Books	Steck-Vaughn
Landry News, The	R	RF	250+	Clements, Andrew	Simon & Schuster
Lands of Ice and Snow	Q	I	250+	InfoQuest	Rigby
Lands of Mystery	Z	I	6907	The Unexplained	Lerner Publications
Lands of Rock	Q	I	250+	InfoQuest	Rigby
Lands of the Rainforest	T	I	1698	Leveled Readers Social Studies	Houghton Mifflin Harcourt
Landslides	R	I	1127	Leveled Readers	Houghton Mifflin Harcourt
Landslides	Q	I	250+	Natural Disasters	Red Brick Learning
Landslides	M	I	609	Pull Ahead Books	Lerner Publications
Landslides, Slumps & Creep	U	I	250+	A First Book	Franklin Watts
Langston Hughes	L	B	168	Vocabulary Readers	Houghton Mifflin Harcourt
Langston Hughes: An Illustrated Edition	X	B	250+	Meltzer, Milton	Millbrook Press
Langston Hughes: Young Black Poet	O	B	250+	Childhood of Famous Americans	Aladdin
Lara Ladybug	C	F	68	Rookie Readers	Children's Press
Lara Saves the Concert	J	RF	250+	Rigby Flying Colors	Rigby
Lara's Team	H	RF	287	Take Two Books	Wright Group/McGraw Hill
Lark Sings in Many Colors, The	T	TL	2159	Leveled Readers	Houghton Mifflin Harcourt
Lark Sings in Many Colors, The	T	TL	2159	Leveled Readers/CA	Houghton Mifflin Harcourt
Lark Sings in Many Colors, The	T	TL	2159	Leveled Readers/TX	Houghton Mifflin Harcourt
Larklight: A Rousing Tale of Dauntless Pluck in the Farthest Reaches of Space	Y	F	250+	Reeve, Philip	Bloomsbury Children's Books
Larry and Rita Dance	C	F	24	Brand New Readers	Candlewick Press
Larry and the Cookie	E	RF	56	Rookie Readers	Children's Press
Larry and the Crab	C	F	38	Brand New Readers	Candlewick Press
Larry the Singing Chicken	J	F	333	Leveled Readers	Houghton Mifflin Harcourt
Larry the Singing Chicken	J	F	333	Leveled Readers/CA	Houghton Mifflin Harcourt
Larry the Singing Chicken	J	F	333	Leveled Readers/TX	Houghton Mifflin Harcourt
Laser Shows	M	I	250+	Rigby Literacy	Rigby
Lasers	V	I	250+	Sunshine	Wright Group/McGraw Hill
Last Book in the Universe, The	W	SF	250+	Philbrick, Rodman	Scholastic
Last Chance for Magic	P	F	250+	Chew, Ruth	Scholastic

L

* Collection of short stories
# Graphic text

TITLE	LEVEL	GENRE	WORD COUNT	AUTHOR / SERIES	PUBLISHER / DISTRIBUTOR
Last Day Blues	M	RF	250+	Danneberg, Julie	Charlesbridge
Last Game, The	G	RF	89	Start to Read	School Zone
Last Holiday Concert, The	R	RF	250+	Clements, Andrew	Aladdin Paperbacks
Last Inca Emperor, The	V	I	1642	Leveled Readers/CA	Houghton Mifflin Harcourt
Last Inca Emperer, The	V	I	1642	Leveled Readers	Houghton Mifflin Harcourt
Last Laugh, The	WB	F	0	Aruego, Jose & Dewey, Ariane	Dial Books
Last Look	P	RF	250+	Bulla, Clyde Robert	Puffin/Penguin
Last One in Is a Rotten Egg	J	RF	250+	Kessler, Leonard	HarperTrophy
Last Princess, The: The Story of Princess Ka'iulani of Hawaii	T	B	250+	Stanley, Fay	Aladddin Paperbacks
Last Puppy, The	K	F	244	Asch, Frank	Simon & Schuster
Last Rider, The: The Final Days of the Pony Express	T	HF	3,357	Gunderson, J.	Stone Arch Books
Last Summer with Maizon	Q	RF	250+	Woodson, Jacqueline	G.P. Putnam's Sons
Last Treasure, The	W	F	250+	Anderson, Janet S.	Puffin Books
Last-Minute Rescue	M	RF	250+	Rigby Rocket	Rigby
Late for Soccer (Football)	G	RF	185	PM Story Books	Rigby
Late for the Party	H	RF	235	PM Photo Stories	Rigby
Late One Night	D	RF	97	Mader, Jan	Kaeden Books
Later	D	RF	106	Teacher's Choice Series	Pearson Learning Group
Later, Gator	R	RF	250+	Yep, Laurence	Hyperion
Later, Rover	G	RF	200	Ziefert, Harriet	Puffin/Penguin
Latino Legends: Hispanics in Major League Baseball	S	B	250+	High Five Reading	Red Brick Learning
Laugh Stand, The: Adventures in Humor	U	I	1597	Cleary, Brian P.	Millbrook Press
Laughing Cake, The	G	RF	89	Reading Corners	Pearson Learning Group
Laughing Hyena	I	F	250+	Lighthouse	Rigby
Laughing Place, The	K	F	250+	Story Steps	Rigby
Laughter Is the Best Medicine	P	I	250+	Literacy Tree	Rigby
Laundromat, The	D	RF	25	Sunshine	Wright Group/McGraw Hill
Laundromat, The	B	RF	25	Visions	Wright Group/McGraw Hill
Laundry Day	C	RF	28	Bebop Books	Lee & Low Books Inc.
Laura and Mr. Edwards	M	HF	250+	Wilder, Laura Ingalls	HarperTrophy
Laura and Nellie	M	HF	250+	Wilder, Laura Ingalls	HarperTrophy
Laura Ingalls Wilder	O	B	250+	Allen, Thomas B.	Putnam/Penguin
Laura Ingalls Wilder	L	B	250+	Biography	Benchmark Education
Laura Ingalls Wilder	P	B	250+	Blair, Gwenda; Allen, Thomas	Lerner Publishing
Laura Ingalls Wilder	R	B	1477	Leveled Readers	Houghton Mifflin Harcourt
Laura Ingalls Wilder	R	B	1477	Leveled Readers/CA	Houghton Mifflin Harcourt
Laura Ingalls Wilder	R	B	1477	Leveled Readers/TX	Houghton Mifflin Harcourt
Laura Ingalls Wilder	M	B	1439	On My Own Biography	Lerner Publications
Laura Ingalls Wilder	R	B	250+	Primary Source Readers	Teacher Created Materials
Laura Ingalls Wilder: A Biography	R	B	250+	Anderson, William	HarperTrophy
Laura Ingalls Wilder: An Author's Story	N	B	250+	Pair-It Books	Steck-Vaughn
Laura Ingalls Wilder: Author of the Little House Books	O	B	250+	Greene, Carol	Children's Press
Laura Ingalls Wilder: Growing Up in the Little House	P	B	250+	Giff, Patricia Reilly	Puffin/Penguin
Laura's Ma	M	HF	250+	Wilder, Laura Ingalls	HarperTrophy
Laura's Pa	M	HF	250+	Wilder, Laura Ingalls	HarperTrophy
Lauren Helps Sammy	M	F	817	Leveled Readers	Houghton Mifflin Harcourt
Lauren Helps Sammy	M	F	817	Leveled Readers/CA	Houghton Mifflin Harcourt
Lauren Helps Sammy	M	F	817	Leveled Readers/TX	Houghton Mifflin Harcourt
Lauren Otter	N	F	772	Leveled Readers	Houghton Mifflin Harcourt

L

TITLE	LEVEL	GENRE	WORD COUNT	AUTHOR / SERIES	PUBLISHER / DISTRIBUTOR
Lauren Otter	N	F	772	Leveled Readers/CA	Houghton Mifflin Harcourt
Lauren Otter	O	I	785	Leveled Readers/TX	Houghton Mifflin Harcourt
Lavender	O	RF	250+	Hesse, Karen	Henry Holt & Co.
Lavender the Library Cat	K	RF	418	Jellybeans	Rigby
Law and Order	K	I	250+	Spyglass Books	Compass Point Books
Lazily, Crazily, Just a Bit Nasally: More about Adverbs	O	I	342	Words Are CATegorical	Millbrook Press
Lazy Bones Jones	P	F	250+	Orbit Chapter Books	Pacific Learning
Lazy Fox	I	F	268	Leveled Readers	Houghton Mifflin Harcourt
Lazy Jackal, The	M	F	561	Sunshine	Wright Group/McGraw Hill
Lazy Lions, Lucky Lambs	M	RF	250+	Giff, Patricia Reilly	Bantam
Lazy Mary	D	RF	191	Story Box	Wright Group/McGraw Hill
Lazy Moon, The	I	F	242	Take Two Books	Wright Group/McGraw Hill
Lazy Pig, The	C	F	78	PM Story Books	Rigby
Lazy Sailor Sam	G	F	227	Sails	Rigby
Lazy Sloth	I	F	418	Sails	Rigby
LCAC Military Hovercraft, The	U	I	250+	Cross-Sections	Capstone Press
LCAC Military Hovercraft, The	U	I	250+	Cross-Sections	Capstone Press
Leader for All, A	U	B	1500	Leveled Readers/CA	Houghton Mifflin Harcourt
Leader for All, A	U	B	1500	Leveled Readers	Houghton Mifflin Harcourt
Leader for All, A	U	B	1500	Leveled Readers/TX	Houghton Mifflin Harcourt
Leader of the Pack	U	RF	2770	Leveled Readers	Houghton Mifflin Harcourt
Leader of the Pack	U	RF	2770	Leveled Readers/CA	Houghton Mifflin Harcourt
Leaders of the Middle East	U	B	250+	Primary Source Readers	Teacher Created Materials
Leaders of the People	U	B	250+	Real Lives	Troll Associates
Leaders: People Who Make a Difference	R	B	250+	You Are There	Children's Press
Leading the Way	P	B	250+	InfoQuest	Rigby
Leaf Boats, The	E	RF	132	PM Plus Story Books	Rigby
Leaf Jumpers	J	RF	207	Gerber, Carole	Charlesbridge
Leaf Rain	F	RF	82	Book Bank	Wright Group/McGraw Hill
Leaf Raker, The	M	RF	250+	Voyages	SRA/McGraw Hill
Leafcutter Ant, The	H	I	77	Vocabulary Readers	Houghton Mifflin Harcourt
Leafcutter Ants	J	I	425	Sails	Rigby
Leaf-Cutter Ants	M	I	462	Springboard	Wright Group/McGraw Hill
Leafy Sea Dragons	F	I	183	Sun Sprouts	ETA Cuisenaire
Leap Frog	WB	RF	N/A	Ready to Read	Pacific Learning
Leaping Grasshoppers	K	I	389	Pull Ahead Books	Lerner Publications
Leaping Lena	L	F	250+	Rigby Literacy	Rigby
Leaping Lizards	M	I	250+	Early Connections	Benchmark Education
Leaps and Bounds	R	I	250+	WorldScapes	ETA Cuisenaire
Learning About Art	K	I	401	Rigby Flying Colors	Rigby
Learning About Clouds	D	I	18	Rosen Real Readers	Rosen Publishing Group
Learning About Leaves	D	I	37	Rosen Real Readers	Rosen Publishing Group
Learning About Rain	E	I	26	Rosen Real Readers	Rosen Publishing Group
Learning About Sand	E	I	42	Rosen Real Readers	Rosen Publishing Group
Learning About Snow	F	I	42	Rosen Real Readers	Rosen Publishing Group
Learning About the Library	I	I	164	Rosen Real Readers	Rosen Publishing Group
Learning from Fossils	P	I	870	Leveled Readers	Houghton Mifflin Harcourt
Learning from Fossils	Q	I	3234	Leveled Readers Science	Houghton Mifflin Harcourt
Learning from Fossils	P	I	870	Leveled Readers/CA	Houghton Mifflin Harcourt
Learning from Fossils	P	I	870	Leveled Readers/TX	Houghton Mifflin Harcourt
Learning from Ms. Liang	T	RF	2968	Reading Street	Pearson
Learning New Things	H	RF	156	Foundations	Wright Group/McGraw Hill
Learning to Play the Game	R	RF	2614	Reading Street	Pearson

* Collection of short stories
# Graphic text

L

TITLE	LEVEL	GENRE	WORD COUNT	AUTHOR / SERIES	PUBLISHER / DISTRIBUTOR
Learning to Swim	I	RF	234	My World	Steck-Vaughn
Leather Boat, The	V	B	250+	WorldScapes	ETA Cuisenaire
Leave It to Beavers	F	RF	102	Leveled Readers Science	Houghton Mifflin Harcourt
Leaves	C	I	34	Explorations	Okapi Educational Materials
Leaves	C	I	34	Explorations	Eleanor Curtain Publishing
Leaves	C	I	29	Hoenecke, Karen	Kaeden Books
Leaves	I	I	250+	Momentum Literacy Program	Troll Associates
Leaves	E	I	29	Parts of Plants	Lerner Publishing
Leaves	K	I	236	Pebble Books	Capstone Press
Leaves	I	I	130	Plant Parts	Capstone Press
Leaves in Fall	F	I	86	All About Fall	Capstone Press
Leaves, Fruits, Seeds, and Roots	C	I	26	Pacific Literacy	Pacific Learning
Leaving a Mark - Dinosaur Discoveries	U	I	250+	Connectors	Pacific Learning
Leaving Home	N	F	727	Gear Up!	Wright Group/ McGraw Hill
Leaving Home	R	I	250+	InfoQuest	Rigby
*Leaving Home	Z	RF	250+	Keillor, Garrison	Penguin Group
Leaving Home	K	RF	509	Pair-It Turn and Learn	Steck-Vaughn
*Leaving Home: 15 Distinguished Authors Explore Personal Journeys	Z	RF	250+	Rochman, Hazel; McCampbell, Darlene	HarperTrophy
Lebanon: A Question and Answer Book	P	I	250+	Questions & Answers: Countries	Capstone Press
LeBron James	Q	B	1791	Amazing Athletes	Lerner Publications
LeBron James: King of the Court	V	B	250+	High Five Reading	Capstone Press
Leeches	P	I	1861	Early Bird Nature Books	Lerner Publishing
Left and Right	C	I	43	Location	Lerner Publishing
Left Behind	L	RF	250+	Carrick, Carol	Clarion
Left for Dead!: Lincoln Hall's Story of Survival	S	I	250+	True Tales of Survival	Capstone Press
Left for Dead!: Lincoln Hall's Story of Survival	S	I	250+	True Tales of Survival	Capstone Press
Left Hand of Darkness, The	Z+	SF	250+	Le Guin, Ursula K.	Ace Books
Left, Right	G	RF	182	Sunshine	Wright Group/McGraw Hill
Leftovers, The: Catch Flies!	N	RF	250+	Howard, Tristan	Scholastic
Leftovers, The: Fast Break	N	RF	250+	Howard, Tristan	Scholastic
Leftovers, The: Get Jammed	N	RF	250+	Howard, Tristan	Scholastic
Leftovers, The: Reach Their Goal	N	RF	250+	Howard, Tristan	Scholastic
Leftovers, The: Strike Out!	N	RF	250+	Howard, Tristan	Scholastic
Leftovers, The: Use Their Heads!	N	RF	250+	Howard, Tristan	Scholastic
Legend of Dirty Bert the Bandit, The	M	TL	250+	Lighthouse	Ginn & Co.
Legend of Scarface, The	Q	I	900	Books for Young Learners	Richard C. Owen
Legend of the Bluebonnet, The	O	TL	250+	DePaola, Tomie	Scholastic
Legend of the Bluebonnet, The	N	TL	250+	On Our Way to English	Rigby
Legend of the Hummingbird, The	K	TL	250+	Folk Tales	Mondo
Legend of the Indian Paintbrush, The	O	TL	250+	DePaola, Tomie	Scholastic
Legend of the Lonesome Bear, The	M	TL	2047	Take Two Books	Wright Group/McGraw Hill
Legend of the Red Bird, The	K	TL	389	Sunshine	Wright Group/McGraw Hill
Legend of the Underwater Cave, The	Q	RF	250+	Reading Safari	Mondo
Legendary Heroes	P	B	1448	Take Two Books	Wright Group/ McGraw Hill
Legendary Places	N	I	250+	Wildcats	Wright Group/McGraw Hill
*Legends	S	TL	250+	Goodman, R.; Pierce, R.; Wagner, Betty Jane	Houghton Mifflin Harcourt
Legends of the Blues	T	B	2196	Reading Street	Pearson
Legends of the Past	S	TL	4820	Take Two Books	Wright Group/McGraw Hill
Legends of the Wild West	R	B	250+	Storyteller -Autum Leaves	Wright Group/McGraw Hill
LEGO Toys	T	I	4953	A Great Idea	Norwood House Press
Legs	B	F	15	Gosset, Rachel; Ballinger, Margaret	Scholastic

L

TITLE	LEVEL	GENRE	WORD COUNT	AUTHOR / SERIES	PUBLISHER / DISTRIBUTOR
Legs	D	I	21	Literacy 2000	Rigby
Legs	B	I	36	Sails	Rigby
Legs	LB	I	21	Twig	Wright Group/McGraw Hill
Legs	B	I	36	Windows on Literacy	National Geographic
Legs, Legs, Legs	C	I	36	Wonder World	Wright Group/McGraw Hill
Legs, No Legs	H	I	167	Sails	Rigby
Leif Eriksson	Q	B	250+	Biographies-Great Explorers	Capstone Press
Leif Eriksson	P	B	1419	On My Own Biography	Lerner Publications
Lemon Tree, The	D	RF	28	Harry's Math Books	Outside the Box
Lemonade	C	I	27	Bonnell, Kris	Reading Reading Books
Lemonade	F	F	140	Learn to Read	Creative Teaching Press
Lemonade for Gilbert	H	F	144	Gilbert the Pig	Pioneer Valley
Lemonade for Sale	D	F	36	Brand New Readers	Candlewick Press
Lemonade for Sale	K	RF	1343	Real Kids Readers	Millbrook Press
Lemonade Mouth	Z	RF	250+	Hughes, Mark Peter	Delacorte Press
Lemonade on the Double	H	RF	204	On Our Way to English	Rigby
Lemonade Stand, The	G	RF	148	City Stories	Rigby
Lemonade Stand, The	J	I	166	Early Connections	Benchmark Education
Lemonade Stand, The	L	RF	385	Leveled Readers	Houghton Mifflin Harcourt
Lemonade Stand, The	L	RF	385	Leveled Readers/CA	Houghton Mifflin Harcourt
Lemonade Stand, The	L	RF	385	Leveled Readers/TX	Houghton Mifflin Harcourt
Lemonade Trick, The	Q	RF	250+	Corbett, Scott	Scholastic
Lemony Snicket: The Unauthorized Autobiography	W	F	250+	Snicket, Lemony	Harper Collins
Lemurs	M	I	250+	The Wild World of Animals	Capstone Press
Lena's Garden	J	F	302	Leveled Readers	Houghton Mifflin Harcourt
Lena's Garden	J	F	302	Leveled Readers/CA	Houghton Mifflin Harcourt
Lena's Garden	J	F	302	Leveled Readers/TX	Houghton Mifflin Harcourt
Lend a Hand	E	I	26	iOpeners	Pearson Learning Group
Lend a Hand	K	F	250+	Kratky, Lada	Hampton-Brown
Lenny and Tweek	K	F	250+	Bookshop	Mondo
Len's Tomato Plant	L	RF	294	Leveled Readers	Houghton Mifflin Harcourt
Len's Tomato Plant	L	RF	294	Leveled Readers/CA	Houghton Mifflin Harcourt
Len's Tomato Plant	L	RF	294	Leveled Readers/TX	Houghton Mifflin Harcourt
Len's Tomatoes	L	RF	289	Leveled Readers	Houghton Mifflin Harcourt
Len's Tomatoes	L	RF	289	Leveled Readers/CA	Houghton Mifflin Harcourt
Len's Tomatoes	L	RF	289	Leveled Readers/TX	Houghton Mifflin Harcourt
Lenses and Light	V	I	250+	Literacy By Design	Rigby
Lentil	M	RF	250+	McCloskey, Robert	Scholastic
Leo and Lester	L	F	250+	Bookshop	Mondo
Leo and the Butterflies	K	I	250+	Bebop Books	Lee & Low Books Inc.
Leo and the School of Fish	K	F	393	Reading Street	Pearson
Leo the Late Bloomer	I	F	164	Kraus, Robert	Simon & Schuster
Leo, You Are a Star	I	RF	401	Rigby Flying Colors	Rigby
Leon and Bob	K	RF	250+	James, Simon	Candlewick Press
Leona Goes Home	N	F	952	Leveled Readers	Houghton Mifflin Harcourt
Leona Goes Home	N	F	952	Leveled Readers/CA	Houghton Mifflin Harcourt
Leona Goes Home	N	F	952	Leveled Readers/TX	Houghton Mifflin Harcourt
Leonard Bernstein	R	B	250+	Venezia, Mike	Children's Press
Leonardo and His Times	Y	I	250+	Eyewitness Books	DK Publishing
Leonardo Da Vinci	Z	B	250+	Krull, Kathleen	Scholastic
Leonardo da Vinci	U	I	1623	Leveled Readers	Houghton Mifflin Harcourt
Leonardo da Vinci	T	B	1776	Leveled Readers Science	Houghton Mifflin Harcourt
Leonardo da Vinci	U	I	1623	Leveled Readers/CA	Houghton Mifflin Harcourt

Organized Alphabetically by Title
Storable Database at www.fountasandpinnellleveledbooks.com

L

* Collection of short stories
# Graphic text

TITLE	LEVEL	GENRE	WORD COUNT	AUTHOR / SERIES	PUBLISHER / DISTRIBUTOR
Leonardo da Vinci	S	B	250+	Masterpieces: Artists and Their Works	Capstone Press
Leona's Sneakers	M	RF	1691	In Step Readers	Rigby
Leon's Story	T	B	250+	Tillage, Leon Walter	Farrar, Straus and Giroux
Leontyne Price: Opera Superstar	N	B	250+	Williams, Sylvia B.	Children's Press
Leopards	I	I	119	African Animals	Capstone Press
Leopards	K	I	343	Vocabulary Readers	Houghton Mifflin Harcourt
Leopards	K	I	343	Vocabulary Readers/CA	Houghton Mifflin Harcourt
Leo's Italian Lesson	R	RF	1041	Leveled Readers	Houghton Mifflin Harcourt
Leo's Italian Lesson	R	RF	1041	Leveled Readers/CA	Houghton Mifflin Harcourt
Leo's Tree	H	F	135	Pearson, Debora	Annick Press
Leprechauns Don't Play Basketball	M	F	250+	Dadey, Debbie; Jones, Marcia Thornton	Scholastic
LeRoy and the Old Man	Z+	RF	250+	Butterworth, W.E.	Scholastic
Les Paul: Master of the Electric Guitar	S	B	250+	Literacy By Design	Rigby
Leslie Ludel's Apple Strudel	M	RF	250+	Literacy by Design	Rigby
Lesson Before Dying, A	Z+	HF	250+	Gaines, Ernest J.	Vintage Books
Lesson of Icarus, The	Q	TL	325	Reading Street	Pearson
Lesson, The	H	RF	133	Cummings, Pat	Scholastic
Lessons About Lightning	N	I	850	Leveled Readers	Houghton Mifflin Harcourt
Lessons About Lightning	N	I	850	Leveled Readers/CA	Houghton Mifflin Harcourt
Lessons About Lightning	N	I	850	Leveled Readers/TX	Houghton Mifflin Harcourt
Lessons from Lester	J	F	250+	Rigby Rocket	Rigby
Lester's Bedtime	B	F	39	Lester the Lion Series	Pioneer Valley
Lester's Haircut	I	F	250+	Lester the Lion Series	Pioneer Valley
Lester's Song	F	F	155	Lester the Lion Series	Pioneer Valley
Let Art Do the Talking	T	I	250+	Rigby Literacy	Rigby
Let It Begin Here!	S	HF	250+	Fradin, Dennis Brindell	Scholastic
Let It Rain!	I	I	257	Vocabulary Readers	Houghton Mifflin Harcourt
Let It Rain!	I	I	257	Vocabulary Readers/CA	Houghton Mifflin Harcourt
Let It Rain!	I	I	257	Vocabulary Readers/TX	Houghton Mifflin Harcourt
Let Me Help!	I	RF	451	Real Kids Readers	Millbrook Press
*Let Me In	I	TL	1814	Story Box	Wright Group/McGraw Hill
Let the Circle Be Unbroken	X	HF	250+	Taylor, Mildred D.	Penguin Group
Let the Fun Begin: Wacky What-Do-You-Get-Jokes, Playful Puns, and More	O	F	1793	Make Me Laugh!	Lerner Publications
Let the Games Begin	T	I	250+	The News	Richard C. Owen
Let the Games Begin: History of the Olympics	S	I	979	Reading Street	Pearson
Let the River Run Silver Again!	V	I	250+	Burk, Sandy	The McDonald & Woodward Publishing Co.
Let's All Dance!	G	I	148	Vocabulary Readers	Houghton Mifflin Harcourt
Let's Bake	G	I	195	Discovery Links	Newbridge
Let's Be Enemies	J	RF	250+	Sendak, Maurice	Harper & Row
Let's Be Friends	D	I	23	Pair-It Books	Steck-Vaughn
Let's Be Safe and Healthy	I	I	291	InfoTrek	ETA Cuisenaire
Let's Brush Our Teeth	F	I	78	Rosen Real Readers	Rosen Publishing Group
Let's Build a Playground	O	I	250+	Myers, Edward	Pearson Learning Group
Let's Build a Tower	LB	RF	15	Literacy 2000	Rigby
Let's Camp at Crescent Lake	J	RF	262	Reading Street	Pearson
Let's Celebrate	T	I	250+	News Extra	Richard C. Owen
Let's Celebrate	T	I	250+	News Extra	Richard C. Owen
Let's Celebrate	C	I	33	Rise & Shine	Hampton-Brown
Let's Clean Up	K	I	326	Gear Up!	Wright Group/McGraw Hill
Let's Clean Up!	H	F	181	Anderson, Peggy Perry	Houghton Mifflin Harcourt

* Collection of short stories
# Graphic text

L

TITLE	LEVEL	GENRE	WORD COUNT	AUTHOR / SERIES	PUBLISHER / DISTRIBUTOR
Let's Climb!	A	I	19	Leveled Readers	Houghton Mifflin Harcourt
Let's Climb!	A	I	19	Leveled Readers/CA	Houghton Mifflin Harcourt
Let's Compare	K	I	567	In Step Readers	Rigby
Let's Dance	J	I	131	Gear Up!	Wright Group/McGraw Hill
Let's Do Karate!	I	I	119	Sports and Activities	Capstone Press
Let's Downhill Ski!	H	I	131	Sports and Activities	Capstone Press
Let's Draw!	F	I	21	Rosen Real Readers	Rosen Publishing Group
Let's Eat	D	I	110	Sails	Rigby
Let's Eat	E	RF	63	Teacher's Choice Series	Pearson Learning Group
Let's Eat: Foods of Our World	K	I	250+	Spyglass Books	Compass Point Books
Let's Explore Antarctica!	T	I	2356	Reading Street	Pearson
Let's Find Out about Money	O	I	250+	Barabas, Kathy	Scholastic
Let's Find Shapes	A	I	30	Gear Up!	Wright Group/McGraw Hill
Let's Get a Pet	F	RF	22	Jellybeans	Rigby
Let's Get a Pup! Said Kate	L	RF	250+	Graham, Bob	Candlewick Press
Let's Get Dressed: What People Wear	K	I	250+	Spyglass Books	Compass Point Books
Let's Get Moving	M	I	250+	Literacy 2000	Rigby
Let's Get Those Stingers Out of Here!	L	RF	901	Springboard	Wright Group/McGraw Hill
Let's Get to Know the Incas	S	I	1264	Reading Street	Pearson
Let's Go	B	I	81	Early Connections	Benchmark Education
Let's Go	A	RF	32	Reading Corners	Pearson Learning Group
Let's Go	C	RF	30	Windmill Books	Wright Group/McGraw Hill
Let's Go Camping	E	I	44	Vocabulary Readers	Houghton Mifflin Harcourt
*Let's Go Camping and Other Stories	H	F	250+	New Way Literature	Steck-Vaughn
Let's Go Camping!	L	I	692	Rigby Flying Colors	Rigby
Let's Go Camping!	H	I	114	Sports and Activities	Capstone Press
Let's Go Downtown	F	RF	85	City Stories	Rigby
Let's Go Fishing	M	RF	250+	Voyages	SRA/McGraw Hill
Let's Go Have Fun!	P	I	1516	Reading Street	Pearson
Let's Go Marching	E	RF	94	Ready Readers	Pearson Learning Group
Let's Go Rock Climbing!	I	I	128	Vocabulary Readers	Houghton Mifflin Harcourt
Let's Go Rock Collecting	N	I	250+	Soar To Success	Houghton Mifflin Harcourt
Let's Go Shopping	C	I	34	Rise & Shine	Hampton-Brown
Let's Go Shopping!	G	I	120	Pair-It Turn and Learn	Steck-Vaughn
Let's Go Shopping!	N	I	250+	Rigby Focus	Rigby
Let's Go to a Fair	F	I	139	Welcome Books	Children's Press
Let's Go to a Museum	E	RF	181	Blevins, Wiley	Scholastic
Let's Go to Mars	N	I	782	Big Cat	Pacific Learning
Let's Go to the Bank	I	I	233	Rosen Real Readers	Rosen Publishing Group
Let's Go to the Supermarket	I	I	198	Rosen Real Readers	Rosen Publishing Group
Let's Go to the Theater!	N	I	320	Vocabulary Readers	Houghton Mifflin Harcourt
Let's Go!	B	I	28	On Our Way to English	Rigby
Let's Go!	A	I	30	Vocabulary Readers	Houghton Mifflin Harcourt
Let's Go, Dear Dragon	E	F	293	Dear Dragon	Norwood House Press
Let's Go, Philadelphia!	M	RF	250+	Giff, Patricia Reilly	Bantam
Let's Grab It!	D	RF	60	Leveled Readers	Houghton Mifflin Harcourt
Let's Graph	M	I	239	Yellow Umbrella Books	Capstone Press
Let's Graph It!	S	I	250+	Rosen Real Readers	Rosen Publishing Group
Let's Have a Play	F	RF	250+	Let's Play	Norwood House Press
Let's Have a Swim	C	F	74	Sunshine	Wright Group/McGraw Hill
Let's Have Fun!	A	I	20	Vocabulary Readers	Houghton Mifflin Harcourt
Let's Have Fun!	A	I	20	Vocabulary Readers/CA	Houghton Mifflin Harcourt
Let's Look After Our World	L	I	250+	Sunshine	Wright Group/McGraw Hill
Let's Look at Animal Bottoms	H	I	131	Looking at Animal Parts	Capstone Press

L

Organized Alphabetically by Title
Storable Database at www.fountasandpinnellleveledbooks.com

* Collection of short stories
\# Graphic text

TITLE	LEVEL	GENRE	WORD COUNT	AUTHOR / SERIES	PUBLISHER / DISTRIBUTOR
Let's Look at Animal Ears	H	I	132	Looking at Animal Parts	Capstone Press
Let's Look at Animal Eyes	H	I	137	Looking at Animal Parts	Capstone Press
Let's Look at Animal Feathers	H	I	136	Looking at Animal Parts	Capstone Press
Let's Look at Animal Feet	H	I	113	Looking at Animal Parts	Capstone Press
Let's Look at Animal Legs	H	I	124	Looking at Animal Parts	Capstone Press
Let's Look at Animal Noses	H	I	134	Looking at Animal Parts	Capstone Press
Let's Look at Animal Tails	I	I	129	Looking at Animal Parts	Capstone Press
Let's Look at Animal Teeth	H	I	133	Looking at Animal Parts	Capstone Press
Let's Look at Animal Wings	H	I	137	Looking at Animal Parts	Capstone Press
Let's Look at Fall	H	I	106	Investigate the Seasons	Capstone Press
Let's Look at Leopards	H	I	155	Rosen Real Readers	Rosen Publishing Group
Let's Look at Rocks	I	I	186	Yellow Umbrella Books	Red Brick Learning
Let's Look at Spring	H	I	104	Investigate the Seasons	Capstone Press
Let's Look at Summer	H	I	110	Investigate the Seasons	Capstone Press
Let's Look at Venus	L	I	250+	Rosen Real Readers	Rosen Publishing Group
Let's Look at Winter	H	I	113	Investigate the Seasons	Capstone Press
Let's Look Outside	B	I	38	Early Connections	Benchmark Education
Let's Make a Club Hut	G	RF	119	Reading Street	Pearson
Let's Make a Kite	J	I	250+	Bookshop	Mondo
Let's Make a Trade!	L	I	450	Reading Street	Pearson
Let's Make Butter	I	I	224	Yellow Umbrella Books	Red Brick Learning
Let's Make Music	J	I	220	iOpeners	Pearson Learning Group
Let's Make Music!	I	I	185	Leveled Readers	Houghton Mifflin Harcourt
Let's Make Music!	I	I	185	Leveled Readers/CA	Houghton Mifflin Harcourt
Let's Make Music!	I	I	185	Leveled Readers/TX	Houghton Mifflin Harcourt
Let's Make Something New	G	I	116	Discovery Links	Newbridge
Let's Measure It!	D	F	100	Learn to Read	Creative Teaching Press
Let's Measure It!	G	I	252	Shutterbug Books	Steck-Vaughn
Let's Move!	B	RF	29	Ready Readers	Pearson Learning Group
Let's Move!	B	I	55	Vocabulary Readers	Houghton Mifflin Harcourt
Let's Move!	B	I	55	Vocabulary Readers/CA	Houghton Mifflin Harcourt
Let's Paint	C	RF	51	Rise & Shine	Hampton-Brown
Let's Party	L	I	476	Explorations	Eleanor Curtain Publishing
Let's Party	L	I	476	Explorations	Okapi Eductional Materials
Let's Play	B	RF	40	Little Books for Early Readers	University of Maine
Let's Play	B	RF	37	Peters, Catherine	Scholastic
Let's Play Ball	C	F	68	New Way Red	Steck-Vaughn
Let's Play Baseball!	H	RF	157	Reading Street	Pearson
Let's Play Basketball	E	RF	46	Geddes, Diana	Kaeden Books
Let's Play Football!	H	I	117	Sports and Activities	Capstone Press
Let's Play Games Around the World	O	I	250+	iOpeners	Pearson Learning Group
Let's Play in the Forest	E	F	209	Rueda, Claudia	Scholastic
Let's Play Soccer	E	I	100+	Douglas, Ian	Scholastic
Let's Play Today	D	RF	68	Leveled Readers Language Support	Houghton Mifflin Harcourt
Let's Pretend	B	RF	40	Home Connection Collection	Rigby
Let's Pretend	C	RF	82	PM Plus Story Books	Rigby
Let's Race	E	F	77	Reading Street	Pearson
Let's Recycle!	I	I	154	Caring for the Earth	Capstone Press
Let's Reduce Garbage!	I	I	141	Caring for the Earth	Capstone Press
Let's Reuse!	I	I	120	Caring for the Earth	Capstone Press
Let's Ride	G	RF	90	Reading Street	Pearson
Let's Save Energy	I	I	136	Caring for the Earth	Capstone Press
Let's Save Money	N	RF	583	Reading Street	Pearson

L

* Collection of short stories
# Graphic text

TITLE	LEVEL	GENRE	WORD COUNT	AUTHOR / SERIES	PUBLISHER / DISTRIBUTOR
Let's Save Water	I	I	121	Caring For The Earth	Capstone Press
Let's Sell Things!	A	I	28	Leveled Readers	Houghton Mifflin Harcourt
Let's Sell Things!	A	I	28	Leveled Readers/CA	Houghton Mifflin Harcourt
Let's Skip-Count	I	I	197	Shutterbug Books	Steck-Vaughn
Let's Sleep	D	I	73	Sails	Rigby
Let's Sort	F	I	100	Yellow Umbrella Books	Red Brick Learning
Let's Swim	A	I	19	Leveled Readers	Houghton Mifflin Harcourt
Let's Swim	A	I	19	Leveled Readers/CA	Houghton Mifflin Harcourt
Let's Take a Trip	H	F	178	Leveled Readers	Houghton Mifflin Harcourt
Let's Take Care of the Earth	E	I	121	Learn to Read	Creative Teaching Press
Let's Take the Bus	H	RF	250+	Real Reading	Steck-Vaughn
Let's Talk: How We Communicate	K	I	250+	Spyglass Books	Compass Point Books
Let's Visit the Moon	E	F	130	Instant Readers	Harcourt School Publishers
Let's Wash Up	F	I	69	Rosen Real Readers	Rosen Publishing Group
Letter Carriers	L	I	250+	Community Workers	Compass Point Books
Letter from Fish Bay, A	N	B	250+	Cowley, Joy	Pacific Learning
Letter From Phoenix Farm, A	O	B	250+	Meet The Author	Richard C. Owen
Letter to a Friend	L	I	250+	Early Connections	Benchmark Education
Letter to Amy, A	K	RF	250+	Keats, Ezra Jack	Harper & Row
Letter to Mrs. Roosevelt, A	R	HF	250+	DeYoung, C. Coco	Delacorte Press
Letter, The	E	I	76	Little Celebrations	Pearson Learning Group
Letter, The	LB	RF	15	Twig	Wright Group/McGraw Hill
Letter, the Witch, and the Ring, The	S	F	250+	Bellairs, John	Penguin Group
Letters for Mr. James	H	RF	203	Sunshine	Wright Group/McGraw Hill
Letters From a Mill Town	T	HF	1662	Leveled Readers Social Studies	Houghton Mifflin Harcourt
Letters From a Slave Girl: The Story of Harriet Jacobs	X	HF	250+	Lyons, Mary E.	Simon & Schuster
Letters From Camp: A Mystery	V	RF	250+	Klise, Kate	HarperTrophy
Letters from Rifka	S	HF	250+	Hesse, Karen	Puffin/Penguin
Letters from the Front	W	HF	2118	Leveled Readers	Houghton Mifflin Harcourt
Letters from the Front	W	HF	2118	Leveled Readers/CA	Houghton Mifflin Harcourt
Letters from the Sea	S	I	250+	Voyages in Time	Wright Group/McGraw Hill
Letters from the War	V	HF	1998	Leveled Readers	Houghton Mifflin Harcourt
Letters from the War	V	HF	1998	Leveled Readers/CA	Houghton Mifflin Harcourt
Letters to Cupid	Z	RF	250+	Lantz, Francess	Pleasant Company
Letters to Julia	W	RF	250+	Holmes, Barbara Ware	HarperTrophy
Letters to Leah	U	RF	250+	Book Blazers	ETA Cuisenaire
Lettie's North Star	T	HF	250+	Bookshop	Mondo
Letting Swift River Go	M	HF	250+	Yolen, Jane	Little, Brown & Co.
Levers	Q	I	1736	Early Bird Energy Physics Books	Lerner Publishing
Levers to the Rescue	O	I	250+	Simple Machine to the Rescue	Capstone Press
Levi Sings	C	RF	29	Teacher's Choice Series	Pearson Learning Group
Levi Strauss	R	B	250+	Amazing Americans	Wright Group/McGraw Hill
Levi Strauss	P	B	250+	Early Biographies	Compass Point Books
Lewis & Clark	S	I	250+	Primary Source Readers	Teacher Created Materials
Lewis & Clark: Explorers of the American West	S	I	250+	Kroll, Steven	Holiday House
Lewis and Clark	Q	B	250+	Biographies-Great Explorers	Capstone Press
Lewis and Clark	V	B	250+	Cornerstones of Freedom	Children's Press
Lewis and Clark	S	B	250+	History Maker Bios	Lerner Publications
Lewis and Clark	R	I	250+	Navigators Social Studies Series	Benchmark Education
Lewis and Clark	S	B	1476	Reading Street	Pearson
Lewis and Clark	N	B	250+	Rookie Biographies	Children's Press
Lewis and Clark	T	B	250+	Santella, Andrew	Franklin Watts
Lewis and Clark	T	HF	250+	Sullivan, George	Scholastic

* Collection of short stories
\# Graphic text

L

TITLE	LEVEL	GENRE	WORD COUNT	AUTHOR / SERIES	PUBLISHER / DISTRIBUTOR
Lewis and Clark Expedition, The	V	I	250+	Let Freedom Ring	Red Brick Learning
Lewis and Clark Expedition, The	T	I	250+	We The People	Compass Point Books
Lewis and Clark's Packing List	Q	I	936	Vocabulary Readers	Houghton Mifflin Harcourt
Lewis and Clark's Packing List	Q	I	936	Vocabulary Readers/CA	Houghton Mifflin Harcourt
Lewis and Clark's Packing List	Q	I	936	Vocabulary Readers/TX	Houghton Mifflin Harcourt
Lewis and Clark's Voyage of Discovery	S	I	250+	The Library of the Westward Expansion	Rosen Publishing Group
Lexington and Concord	V	I	250+	Cornerstones of Freedom	Children's Press
Liang and the Magic Paintbrush	M	TL	250+	Demi	Henry Holt & Co.
Liar, Liar Pants on Fire	I	RF	250+	Cohen, Miriam	Bantam
Liar, Liar, Pants on Fire	O	RF	250+	Korman, Gordon	Scholastic
Libby's New Friend	L	F	403	Leveled Literacy Intervention/ Blue System	Heinemann
Liberty Bell, The	N	I	250+	American Symbols	Capstone Press
Liberty Bell, The	V	I	250+	Cornerstones of Freedom	Children's Press
Liberty Bell, The	P	I	669	Pull Ahead Books	Lerner Publications
Liberty or Death: A Story about Patrick Henry	S	B	8519	Creative Minds Biographies	Lerner Publications
Librarian Who Measured the Earth, The	S	B	250+	Lasky, Kathryn	Scholastic
Librarians	M	I	250+	Community Helpers	Red Brick Learning
Librarians	L	I	250+	Community Workers	Compass Point Books
Librarians	L	I	363	Pull Ahead Books	Lerner Publications
Librarians: Then and Now	O	I	250+	Primary Source Readers	Teacher Created Materials
Library Card, The	R	RF	250+	Spinelli, Jerry	Scholastic
Library Comes to Town, A	I	HF	136	Reading Street	Pearson
Library Day	J	F	250+	Sunshine	Wright Group/McGraw Hill
Library of Congress, The	V	I	250+	Cornerstones of Freedom	Children's Press
Library, The	C	RF	33	Carousel Readers	Pearson Learning Group
Library, The	D	RF	96	Emergent	Pioneer Valley
License Plates	J	RF	411	PM Collection	Rigby
Licken Chicken	I	TL	250+	Tiger Cub	Peguis
Lid, The	G	RF	111	Books for Young Learners	Richard C. Owen
Liddy's Sayings	N	RF	880	Leveled Readers	Houghton Mifflin Harcourt
Liddy's Sayings	N	RF	880	Leveled Readers/CA	Houghton Mifflin Harcourt
Liddy's Sayings	N	RF	880	Leveled Readers/TX	Houghton Mifflin Harcourt
Life Among the Redwoods	S	I	1410	Leveled Readers	Houghton Mifflin Harcourt
Life Among the Redwoods	S	I	1410	Leveled Readers/CA	Houghton Mifflin Harcourt
Life Among the Redwoods	S	I	1410	Leveled Readers/TX	Houghton Mifflin Harcourt
Life and Death of Crazy Horse, The	X	B	250+	Freedman, Russell	Holiday House
Life and Death of Martin Luther King, Jr.,The	Y	B	250+	Haskins, James	Beech Tree Books
Life and Death of Stars, The	Y	I	250+	Spangenburg, Ray and Moser, Kit	Franklin Watts
Life and Times of Frederick Douglass, The	Z+	B	250+	Douglass, Frederick	Dover Publications
Life and Times of the Peanut, The	Q	I	250+	Micucci, Charles	Houghton Mifflin Harcourt
Life and Words of Martin Luther King, Jr., The	W	B	250+	Peck, Ira	Scholastic
Life as We Knew It	Z	SF	250+	Pfeffer, Susan Beth	Harcourt
Life at Plimoth	L	I	210	Leveled Readers Social Studies	Houghton Mifflin Harcourt
Life at the Bottom of the Sea	U	I	250+	Leveled Readers Language Support	Houghton Mifflin Harcourt
Life Birds	N	RF	250+	Sails	Rigby
Life Cycle of a Bean, The	I	I	117	Plant Life Cycles	Capstone Press
Life Cycle of a Butterfly, The	J	I	94	Life Cycles	Capstone Press
Life Cycle of a Carrot, The	I	I	115	Plant Life Cycles	Capstone Press
Life Cycle of a Cat, The	J	I	108	Life Cycles	Capstone Press
Life Cycle of a Chicken, The	J	I	103	Life Cycles	Capstone Press

L

* Collection of short stories
# Graphic text

TITLE	LEVEL	GENRE	WORD COUNT	AUTHOR / SERIES	PUBLISHER / DISTRIBUTOR
Life Cycle of a Cow, The	J	I	108	Life Cycles	Capstone Press
Life Cycle of a Dog, The	J	I	110	Life Cycles	Capstone Press
Life Cycle of a Frog, The	J	I	115	Life Cycles	Capstone Press
Life Cycle of a Kangaroo, The	J	I	155	Life Cycles	Capstone Press
Life Cycle of a Pine Tree, The	I	I	111	Plant Life Cycles	Capstone Press
Life Cycle of a Salmon, The	K	I	121	Life Cycles	Capstone Press
Life Cycle of a Sunflower, The	I	I	90	Plant Life Cycles	Capstone Press
Life Cycle of a Swan	J	I	250+	Rigby Rocket	Rigby
Life Cycle of a Whale, The	J	I	135	Life Cycles	Capstone Press
Life Cycle of an Apple Tree, The	I	I	128	Plant Life Cycles	Capstone Press
Life Cycle of an Oak Tree, The	I	I	109	Plant Life Cycles	Capstone Press
Life Cycles	J	I	226	Explorations	Eleanor Curtain Publishing
Life Cycles	J	I	226	Explorations	Okapi Educational Materials
Life Cycles of a Wolf, The	P	I	250+	Kalman, Bobbie and Bishop, Amanda	Crabtree
Life in a Cave	U	I	250+	The Heinle Reading Library	Thomson Learning
Life in a Coral Reef	L	I	250+	Rosen Real Readers	Rosen Publishing Group
Life in a Desert	I	I	123	Living in a Biome	Capstone Press
Life in a Forest	I	I	124	Living in a Biome	Capstone Press
Life in a Polar Region	H	I	133	Living in a Biome	Capstone Press
Life in a Pond	I	I	147	Living in a Biome	Capstone Press
Life in a Rain Forest	I	I	146	Living in a Biome	Capstone Press
Life in a Shell	K	I	206	Gear Up!	Wright Group/McGraw Hill
Life in a Stream	H	I	109	Living in a Biome	Capstone Press
Life in a Wetland	I	I	140	Living in a Biome	Capstone Press
Life in an Ocean	H	I	109	Living in a Biome	Capstone Press
Life in Ancient Egypt	U	I	1473	Vocabulary Readers	Houghton Mifflin Harcourt
Life in Ancient Egypt	U	I	1473	Vocabulary Readers/CA	Houghton Mifflin Harcourt
Life in Colonial America	L	I	405	Leveled Readers Social Studies	Houghton Mifflin Harcourt
Life in the 1950s	U	I	1576	Vocabulary Readers/CA	Houghton Mifflin Harcourt
Life in the 1950's	U	I	1576	Vocabulary Readers	Houghton Mifflin Harcourt
Life in the Arctic	K	I	293	Leveled Readers Science	Houghton Mifflin Harcourt
Life in the Arctic	T	I	250+	Reading Street	Pearson
Life in the Arctic	M	I	250+	Rosen Real Readers	Rosen Publishing Group
Life in the Arctic	U	I	1518	Vocabulary Readers	Houghton Mifflin Harcourt
Life in the Arctic	U	I	1518	Vocabulary Readers/CA	Houghton Mifflin Harcourt
Life in the City	J	I	307	Early Connections	Benchmark Education
Life in the City	E	RF	184	Handprints D, Set 1	Educators Publishing Service
Life in the Colonies	T	I	250+	Primary Source Readers	Teacher Created Materials
Life in the Colonies: A Diary	O	RF	826	Gear Up!	Wright Group/ McGraw Hill
Life in the Coral Reefs	G	I	198	Leveled Readers	Houghton Mifflin Harcourt
Life in the Coral Reefs	G	I	198	Leveled Readers/CA	Houghton Mifflin Harcourt
Life in the Coral Reefs	G	I	198	Leveled Readers/TX	Houghton Mifflin Harcourt
Life in the Desert	K	I	326	Gear Up!	Wright Group/ McGraw Hill
Life in the Desert	M	I	250+	Pair-It Books	Steck-Vaughn
Life in the Desert	L	I	250+	Sails	Rigby
Life in the Mangroves	I	I	172	Home Connection Collection	Rigby
Life in the Ocean	M	I	250+	Windows on Literacy	National Geographic
Life in the Ocean Depths	T	I	2165	Leveled Readers Science	Houghton Mifflin Harcourt
Life in the Oceans: Animals, People, Plants	T	I	250+	Baker, Lucy	Scholastic
Life in the Rain Forest	L	I	250+	Rosen Real Readers	Rosen Publishing Group
Life in the Rain Forests: Animals, People, Plants	T	I	250+	Baker, Lucy	Scholastic
Life in the Sahara	U	I	1804	Leveled Readers Social Studies	Houghton Mifflin Harcourt

* Collection of short stories
# Graphic text

L

TITLE	LEVEL	GENRE	WORD COUNT	AUTHOR / SERIES	PUBLISHER / DISTRIBUTOR
Life in the Sea	T	I	2027	Reading Street	Pearson
Life in the Trees	I	I	340	Rigby Flying Colors	Rigby
Life in the Trees	F	I	147	Springboard	Wright Group/McGraw Hill
Life in Their Hands, A	T	RF	250+	Power Up!	Steck-Vaughn
Life in Tide Pools	K	I	383	Leveled Readers	Houghton Mifflin Harcourt
Life in Tide Pools	K	I	383	Leveled Readers/CA	Houghton Mifflin Harcourt
Life in Tide Pools	K	I	383	Leveled Readers/TX	Houghton Mifflin Harcourt
Life Inside the Arctic Circle	T	I	2632	Reading Street	Pearson
Life Long Ago	K	I	250+	Spyglass Books	Compass Point Books
Life of a Bean, The	J	I	201	Independent Readers Science	Houghton Mifflin Harcourt
Life of a Butterfly, The	E	I	46	Vocabulary Readers	Houghton Mifflin Harcourt
Life of a Continental Soldier, The	W	I	3160	Vocabulary Readers	Houghton Mifflin Harcourt
Life of a Continental Soldier, The	W	I	3160	Vocabulary Readers/CA	Houghton Mifflin Harcourt
Life of a Continental Soldier, The	W	I	3160	Vocabulary Readers/TX	Houghton Mifflin Harcourt
Life of a Dollar Bill, The	N	I	301	Leveled Readers Social Studies	Houghton Mifflin Harcourt
Life of a Lion, The	E	I	28	Rosen Real Readers	Rosen Publishing Group
Life of a Miner	T	I	250+	Life in the Old West	Crabtree
Life of Abraham Lincoln, The	M	B	250+	Rosen Real Readers	Rosen Publishing Group
Life of B. B. King, The	U	B	2522	Leveled Readers/CA	Houghton Mifflin Harcourt
Life of B. B. King, The	U	B	2522	Leveled Readers/TX	Houghton Mifflin Harcourt
Life of B.B. King, The	U	B	2522	Leveled Readers	Houghton Mifflin Harcourt
Life of Cesar Chavez	U	B	2568	Reading Street	Pearson
Life of Emily Pauline Johnson, The	Y	B	2363	Leveled Readers	Houghton Mifflin Harcourt
Life of Emily Pauline Johnson, The	Y	B	2363	Leveled Readers/CA	Houghton Mifflin Harcourt
Life of George Washington Carver, The	O	B	991	Leveled Readers	Houghton Mifflin Harcourt
Life of George Washington Carver, The	O	B	991	Leveled Readers/CA	Houghton Mifflin Harcourt
Life of George Washington Carver, The	O	B	991	Leveled Readers/TX	Houghton Mifflin Harcourt
Life of Jack London, The	T	B	1643	Leveled Readers	Houghton Mifflin Harcourt
Life of Jack London, The	T	B	1643	Leveled Readers/CA	Houghton Mifflin Harcourt
Life of Jack Prelutsky, The	M	B	631	Leveled Readers	Houghton Mifflin Harcourt
Life of Jack Prelutsky, The	M	B	631	Leveled Readers/CA	Houghton Mifflin Harcourt
Life of Jack Prelutsky, The	M	B	631	Leveled Readers/TX	Houghton Mifflin Harcourt
Life of Jackson Pollock, The	S	B	1155	Leveled Readers	Houghton Mifflin Harcourt
Life of Jackson Pollock, The	S	B	1155	Leveled Readers/CA	Houghton Mifflin Harcourt
Life of Jackson Pollock, The	S	B	1155	Leveled Readers/TX	Houghton Mifflin Harcourt
Life of Langston Hughes, The	P	B	1003	Leveled Readers	Houghton Mifflin Harcourt
Life of Langston Hughes, the	P	B	1003	Leveled Readers/CA	Houghton Mifflin Harcourt
Life of Langston Hughes, The	P	B	1003	Leveled Readers/TX	Houghton Mifflin Harcourt
Life of Phillis Wheatley, The	T	I	2202	Leveled Readers	Houghton Mifflin Harcourt
Life of Phillis Wheatley, The	T	I	2202	Leveled Readers/CA	Houghton Mifflin Harcourt
Life of Phillis Wheatley, The	T	B	2202	Leveled Readers/TX	Houghton Mifflin Harcourt
Life on a Farm	A	I	24	Early Connections	Benchmark Education
Life on a Plantation	T	I	250+	Historic Communities	Crabtree
Life on a Ranch	P	I	1202	Vocabulary Readers	Houghton Mifflin Harcourt
Life on a Ranch	P	I	1202	Vocabulary Readers/CA	Houghton Mifflin Harcourt
Life on a Space Station	U	I	2670	Leveled Readers	Houghton Mifflin Harcourt
Life on a Space Station	U	I	2670	Leveled Readers/CA	Houghton Mifflin Harcourt
Life on a Wagon Train	Q	I	250+	Rosen Real Readers	Rosen Publishing Group
Life on Land, Water, and Air	N	I	781	Pair-It Turn and Learn	Steck-Vaughn
Life on Mars: The Real Story	R	RF	1834	Reading Street	Pearson
Life on the Edge	Y	I	6699	Cool Science	Lerner Publications
Life on the Mississippi	Z+	HF	250+	Twain, Mark	Bantam Books
Life on the Oregon Trail	W	I	2967	Vocabulary Readers	Houghton Mifflin Harcourt
Life on the Oregon Trail	W	I	2967	Vocabulary Readers/CA	Houghton Mifflin Harcourt

L

* Collection of short stories
# Graphic text

TITLE	LEVEL	GENRE	WORD COUNT	AUTHOR / SERIES	PUBLISHER / DISTRIBUTOR
Life on the Oregon Trail	W	I	2967	Vocabulary Readers/TX	Houghton Mifflin Harcourt
Life on the Ranch	M	RF	1733	Reading Street	Pearson
Life on the Ranch	M	RF	1733	Reading Street	Pearson
Life on the Serengeti	V	I	1811	Independent Readers Science	Houghton Mifflin Harcourt
Life Savers	H	I	198	Sails	Rigby
Life Savers at Point Reyes	W	I	2992	Vocabulary Readers	Houghton Mifflin Harcourt
Life Savers at Point Reyes	W	I	2992	Vocabulary Readers/CA	Houghton Mifflin Harcourt
Life Savers at Point Reyes	W	I	2992	Vocabulary Readers/TX	Houghton Mifflin Harcourt
Life Stinks	L	F	250+	Rigby Gigglers	Rigby
Lifeboat in Space	Z	I	3358	Leveled Readers	Houghton Mifflin Harcourt
Lifeguards	M	I	250+	Community Helpers	Red Brick Learning
Lifesavers: Discoveries in Medicine	Y	I	250+	High-Fliers	Pacific Learning
Lift Off!	G	I	121	Pair-It Books	Steck-Vaughn
Lift Off!: The Story of Space Flight	O	I	669	Rigby Flying Colors	Rigby
Lift the Sky Up	H	RF	133	Little Celebrations	Pearson Learning Group
Lift the Sky Up	H	RF	133	Little Readers	Houghton Mifflin Harcourt
Lift-Off!	I	SF	141	Pacific Literacy	Pacific Learning
Light	Q	I	1781	Early Bird Energy	Lerner Publishing
Light	J	I	150	Early Connections	Benchmark Education
Light	Z	I	250+	Eyewitness Books	DK Publishing
Light	J	I	250+	Momentum Literacy Program	Troll Associates
Light	P	I	250+	Our Physical World	Capstone Press
Light	Q	I	1063	Science Support Readers	Houghton Mifflin Harcourt
Light	T	I	250+	The News	Richard C. Owen
Light	T	I	250+	The News	Richard C. Owen
Light	C	I	30	Twig	Wright Group/McGraw Hill
Light and Color	T	I	250+	Straightforward Science	Franklin Watts
Light and Shade	X	I	250+	iOpeners	Pearson Learning Group
Light and Shadow	G	I	138	Discovery Links	Newbridge
Light and Shadow	F	I	82	Yellow Umbrella Books	Red Brick Learning
Light at Tern Rock, The	N	RF	250+	Sauer, Julia L.	Scholastic
Light Bulb, The	P	I	250+	Great Inventions	Red Brick Learning
Light in the Forest, The	Y	HF	250+	Richter, Conrad	Random House
Light in the Storm, A	T	HF	250+	Hesse, Karen	Scholastic
Light: Shadows, Mirrors, and Rainbows	M	I	250+	Amazing Science	Picture Window Books
Lighter Than Air	S	I	1494	Vocabulary Readers	Houghton Mifflin Harcourt
Lighter Than Air	S	I	1494	Vocabulary Readers/CA	Houghton Mifflin Harcourt
Lighthouse Children, The	I	F	250+	Hoff, Syd	HarperTrophy
Lighthouse Mermaid, The	M	F	250+	Karr, Kathleen	Hyperion
Lighthouse People, The	N	RF	250+	Orbit Chapter Books	Pacific Learning
Lightning	T	I	250+	Kramer, Stephen	Carolrhoda Books
Lightning	S	I	1110	Leveled Readers	Houghton Mifflin Harcourt
Lightning	T	I	250+	Simon, Seymour	Scholastic
Lightning	L	I	279	Weather	Capstone Press
Lightning Bugs	E	RF	45	Ketch, Ann	Kaeden Books
Lightning Liz	F	F	41	Rookie Readers	Children's Press
Lightning Strikes	R	I	250+	Explorer Books-Pathfinder	National Geographic
Lightning Strikes	P	I	250+	Explorer Books-Pioneer	National Geographic
Lightning Thief, The	W	F	250+	Riordan, Rick	Scholastic
Lights	E	I	65	Big Cat	Pacific Learning
Lights at Night	LB	I	33	Pacific Literacy	Pacific Learning
Lights Go On	C	I	45	Windows on Literacy	National Geographic
Lights in the Night	J	RF	368	Leveled Readers	Houghton Mifflin Harcourt
Lights in the Night	J	RF	368	Leveled Readers/CA	Houghton Mifflin Harcourt

* Collection of short stories
\# Graphic text

L

TITLE	LEVEL	GENRE	WORD COUNT	AUTHOR / SERIES	PUBLISHER / DISTRIBUTOR
Lights On!	S	I	1450	Independent Readers Science	Houghton Mifflin Harcourt
Lights! Camera! Magic!: Making Movies	S	I	250+	Explore More	Wright Group/McGraw Hill
Lights, Camera, Amalee	W	RF	250+	Williams, Dar	Scholastic
*Lightweight Rocket and Other Cases, The	O	RF	250+	Simon, Seymour	Avon
Like Jake and Me	O	RF	250+	Jukes, Mavis	Alfred A. Knopf
Like Me	D	RF	20	Book Bank	Wright Group/McGraw Hill
Like My Daddy	E	RF	129	Visions	Wright Group/McGraw Hill
Like Sisters on the Homefront	Z+	RF	250+	Williams-Garcia, Rita	Penguin Group
Lila the Fair	L	RF	250+	Social Studies Connects	The Kane Press
Lilacs, Lotuses, and Ladybugs	L	RF	402	Evangeline Nicholas Collection	Wright Group/McGraw Hill
Lili the Brave	N	RF	250+	Armstrong, Jennifer	Random House
Lili's Breakfast	F	RF	156	Storyteller-Setting Sun	Wright Group/McGraw Hill
Lillian the Librarian	I	RF	315	Seedlings	Continental Press
Lillian's Fish	P	F	250+	Menk, James	Peachtree
Lilly-Lolly-Little-Legs	H	RF	129	Literacy 2000	Rigby
Lilly's Purple Plastic Purse	N	F	250+	Henkes, Kevin	Scholastic
Lily and Miss Liberty	N	HF	250+	Stephens, Carla	Scholastic
Lily and the Leaf Boats	C	RF	55	PM Photo Stories	Rigby
Lily B. on the Brink of Love	U	RF	250+	Kimmel, Elizabeth Cody	HarperTrophy
Lily Dale: Awakening	Z	F	250+	Staub, Wendy Corsi	Walker & Company
Lily Dale: Believing	Z	F	250+	Staub, Wendy Corsi	Walker & Company
Lily's Crossing	S	HF	250+	Giff, Patricia Reilly	Delacorte Press
Lily's New Home	J	RF	557	Rigby Flying Colors	Rigby
Lily's Playhouse	D	RF	69	PM Photo Stories	Rigby
Lily's Special Garden	E	RF	156	Reading Safari	Mondo
Lime, a Mime, a Pool of Slime, A: More About Nouns	O	I	252	Words Are CATegorical	Millbrook Press
Limestone Cave	N	I	250+	Habitats	Children's Press
Limestone Caves	N	I	250+	A First Book	Franklin Watts
Lincoln Memorial, The	V	I	250+	Cornerstones of Freedom	Children's Press
Lincoln Memorial, The	Q	I	250+	National Landmarks	Red Brick Learning
Lincoln Memorial, The	P	I	661	Pull Ahead Books	Lerner Publications
Lincoln: A Photobiography	V	B	250+	Freedman, Russell	Clarion
Lincoln-Douglas Debates, The	W	I	250+	Cornerstones of Freedom	Children's Press
Ling and the Turtle	D	F	65	Rigby Star	Rigby
Lingospeak	S	I	250+	Rigby Literacy	Rigby
Ling's Monster	I	RF	274	Sun Sprouts	ETA Cuisenaire
Ling's New Friend	F	RF	164	Sun Sprouts	ETA Cuisenaire
Links in the Food Chain	L	I	284	Reading Street	Pearson
Lin-Lin and The Gulls	J	RF	478	Appleton-Smith, Laura	Flyleaf Publishing
Linney Twins Get Cooking, The	M	SF	968	Leveled Readers	Houghton Mifflin Harcourt
Linney Twins Get Cooking, The	M	SF	968	Leveled Readers/CA	Houghton Mifflin Harcourt
Linney Twins Get Cooking, The	M	SF	968	Leveled Readers/TX	Houghton Mifflin Harcourt
Lin's Backpack	C	RF	49	Little Celebrations	Pearson Learning Group
Lion and the Hare, The	N	TL	1655	On My Own Folklore	Millbrook Press
Lion and the Mouse	E	TL	87	Herman, Gail	Random House
Lion and the Mouse, The	I	TL	499	Aesop's Fables	Pearson Learning Group
Lion and the Mouse, The	E	SF	91	Cambridge Reading	Pearson Learning Group
Lion and the Mouse, The	J	TL	427	Leveled Literacy Intervention/ Green System	Heinemann
Lion and The Mouse, The	G	TL	250	Literacy 2000	Rigby
Lion and the Mouse, The	J	TL	325	Little Books	Sadlier-Oxford
*Lion and the Mouse, The	F	TL	115	New Way Literature	Steck-Vaughn
Lion and the Mouse, The	K	TL	557	Pair-It Books	Steck-Vaughn

* Collection of short stories
\# Graphic text

L

TITLE	LEVEL	GENRE	WORD COUNT	AUTHOR / SERIES	PUBLISHER / DISTRIBUTOR
Lion and the Mouse, The	G	TL	125	PM Story Books	Rigby
Lion and the Mouse, The	I	TL	250+	Storyworlds	Heinemann Educational Books
Lion and the Mouse, The	J	TL	285	Sunshine	Wright Group/McGraw Hill
Lion and the Mouse, The	G	TL	250	Traditional Tales & More	Rigby
Lion and the Rabbit, The	F	TL	99	PM Story Books	Rigby
Lion Dancer: Ernie Wan's Chinese New Year	N	B	250+	Waters, Kate; Slovenz-Low, Madeline	Scholastic
Lion in the Night, The	J	F	250+	Momentum Literacy Program	Troll Associates
Lion Roars, The	I	RF	270	Ready Readers	Pearson Learning Group
Lion Talk	I	I	216	Storyteller-Night Crickets	Wright Group/McGraw Hill
*Lion Tamer's Daughter And Other Stories, The	Z	F	250+	Dickinson, Peter	Laurel-Leaf Books
Lion to Guard Us, A	P	HF	250+	Bulla, Clyde Robert	HarperTrophy
Lion, The	A	I	20	Vocabulary Readers	Houghton Mifflin Harcourt
Lion, The	A	I	20	Vocabulary Readers/CA	Houghton Mifflin Harcourt
Lion, the Witch, and the Wardrobe, The	T	F	250+	Lewis, C. S.	HarperTrophy
Lionel and Amelia	L	F	250+	Bookshop	Mondo
*Lionel and His Friends	K	RF	250+	Krensky, Stephen	Puffin/Penguin
*Lionel and Louise	K	RF	250+	Krensky, Stephen	Puffin/Penguin
*Lionel at Large	K	RF	250+	Krensky, Stephen	Puffin/Penguin
*Lionel In The Fall	K	RF	250+	Krensky, Stephen	Puffin/Penguin
*Lionel In The Spring	K	RF	250+	Krensky, Stephen	Puffin/Penguin
*Lionel In The Summer	K	RF	250+	Krensky, Stephen	Puffin/Penguin
*Lionel In The Winter	K	RF	250+	Krensky, Stephen	Puffin/Penguin
Lions	I	I	111	African Animals	Capstone Press
Lions	P	I	1662	Animal Predators	Lerner Publishing
Lions	O	I	250+	Holmes, Kevin J.	Red Brick Learning
Lions	N	I	250+	Meadows, Graham; Vial, Claire	Pearson Learning Group
Lions	L	I	644	Pair-It Books	Steck-Vaughn
Lions & Tigers	K	I	250+	PM Animals in the Wild-Yellow	Rigby
Lions and the Water Buffaloes, The	I	RF	250+	PM Plus Story Books	Rigby
Lions at Lunchtime	M	F	250+	Osborne, Mary Pope	Random House
Lion's Dinner, The	E	F	111	Rigby Literacy	Rigby
Lions Dinner, The: A Play	E	F	110	Rigby Star	Rigby
Lion's Dinner, The: A Play	E	F	111	Literacy By Design	Rigby
Lion's Lunch	F	F	201	Lighthouse	Rigby
Lion's Tail, The	F	F	147	Reading Unlimited	Pearson Learning Group
Liquids	K	I	240	Gear Up!	Wright Group/McGraw Hill
Lisa, Bright and Dark	Z+	RF	250+	Neufeld, John	Penguin Group
Lisa's Diary	L	RF	250+	Home Connection Collection	Rigby
Lisa's Ices	G	RF	106	City Stories	Rigby
Lise Meitner	Y	B	3362	Leveled Readers Science	Houghton Mifflin Harcourt
Listen	D	RF	35	Visions	Wright Group/McGraw Hill
*Listen Children: An Anthology of Black Literature	U	RF	250+	Strickland, Dorothy S.	Bantam
Listen to Me	E	RF	113	Rookie Readers	Children's Press
Listen to Me	I	F	327	Springboard	Wright Group/McGraw Hill
Listening in Bed	M	RF	116	Book Bank	Wright Group/McGraw Hill
Listening to Crickets: A Story About Rachel Carson	R	B	7387	Creative Minds Biographies	Carolrhoda Books
Little Adventure, A	J	RF	250+	PM Story Books-Silver	Rigby
Little and Big	B	I	77	InfoTrek	ETA Cuisenaire
Little and Big	C	I	57	Little Red Readers	Sundance
Little Animals	A	F	22	Reed, Janet	Scholastic

L

* Collection of short stories
\# Graphic text

TITLE	LEVEL	GENRE	WORD COUNT	AUTHOR / SERIES	PUBLISHER / DISTRIBUTOR
Little Ant, The: A Folktale From New Mexico	J	TL	250+	Costigan, Shirleyann	Hampton-Brown
Little Ballerina, The	L	RF	250+	DK Readers	DK Publishing
Little Bat	E	F	196	Leveled Literacy Intervention/ Blue System	Heinemann
Little Bear	J	F	1664	Minarik, Else H.	HarperCollins
Little Bear	D	F	77	My First Reader	Grolier Press
Little Bear and the Bee	E	F	184	Rigby Flying Colors	Rigby
Little Bears	A	I	37	Bookshop	Mondo
Little Bear's Friend	J	F	250+	Minarik, Else H.	HarperTrophy
Little Bear's Visit	J	F	250+	Minarik, Else H.	HarperTrophy
Little Bike, The	C	F	29	Joy Readers	Pearson Learning Group
Little Bill	L	RF	250+	Cosby, Bill	Scholastic
Little Bird	E	TL	42	Sunshine	Wright Group/McGraw Hill
Little Bit Hotter Can't Hurt, A	L	RF	466	Leveled Readers	Houghton Mifflin Harcourt
Little Black: A Pony	J	RF	250+	Farley, Walter	Random House
Little Blue and Little Yellow	J	F	250+	Lionni, Leo	Scholastic
Little Blue Fish	C	RF	58	Evans, Lynette	Scholastic
Little Blue Horse, The	I	RF	250+	PM Plus Story Books	Rigby
Little Blue, Big Blue	K	RF	250+	Rigby Literacy	Rigby
Little Blue, Big Blue	K	RF	250+	Rigby Star	Rigby
Little Boat, The	D	F	77	Bonnell, Kris	Reading Reading Books
Little Book of Street Rods, The	H	I	79	Books for Young Learners	Richard C. Owen
Little Bo-Peep	C	F	48	Seedlings	Continental Press
Little Box, The	L	F	250+	Rigby Gigglers	Rigby
Little Boy and the Balloon Man	E	F	16	Tiger Cub	Peguis
Little Boy Blue	D	TL	32	Sunshine	Wright Group/McGraw Hill
*Little Boy with Three Names and Other Short Stories	S	TL	250+	Clark, Ann Nolan	Kiva Publishing
Little Brother	C	RF	31	Story Box	Wright Group/McGraw Hill
Little Brother	A	RF	14	Sunshine	Wright Group/McGraw Hill
Little Brother's Haircut	J	RF	250+	Story Box	Wright Group/McGraw Hill
Little Brown House	H	RF	266	Jellybeans	Rigby
Little Brown Jay, The: A Tale from India	K	TL	366	Claire, Elizabeth	Mondo
Little Bulldozer	E	F	170	PM Story Books	Rigby
Little Bulldozer Helps Again	F	F	197	PM Extensions-Blue	Rigby
Little Car	F	F	181	Sunshine	Wright Group/McGraw Hill
Little Caribou	N	I	250+	Fox-Davies, Sarah	Candlewick Press
Little Cat Big Cat	L	I	472	Leveled Literacy Intervention/ Blue System	Heinemann
Little Cats	P	I	250+	Crabapples	Crabtree
Little Chick's Friend Duckling	I	F	572	Kwitz, Mary Deball	HarperTrophy
Little Chicks Sing, The	E	F	52	Instant Readers	Harcourt School Publishers
Little Chief	K	F	250+	Hoff, Syd	HarperCollins
Little Chimp	C	F	50	PM Plus Story Books	Rigby
Little Chimp and Baby Chimp	E	F	184	PM Plus Story Books	Rigby
Little Chimp and Big Chimp	C	RF	66	PM Plus Story Books	Rigby
Little Chimp and the Bees	F	F	160	PM Plus Story Books	Rigby
Little Chimp and the Buffalo	G	F	195	PM Stars	Rigby
Little Chimp and the Termites	H	F	192	PM Plus Story Books	Rigby
Little Chimp Finds Some Fruit	G	F	192	PM Stars	Rigby
Little Chimp Is Brave	D	F	92	PM Stars	Rigby
Little Chimp Runs Away	D	F	104	PM Plus Story Books	Rigby
Little Clearing in the Woods	Q	HF	250+	Wilkes, Maria D.	HarperTrophy
Little Cookie, The	E	TL	310	Fairy Tales and Folklore	Norwood House Press

L

TITLE	LEVEL	GENRE	WORD COUNT	AUTHOR / SERIES	PUBLISHER / DISTRIBUTOR
Little Cousins' Visit, The	C	RF	123	Emergent	Pioneer Valley
Little Critter Sleeps Over	H	F	267	Mayer, Mercer	Random House
Little Critters	I	RF	127	Books for Young Learners	Richard C. Owen
Little Cub	A	F	24	Leveled Literacy Intervention/ Orange System	Heinemann
*Little Dancer and Other Short Stories, The	K	F	250+	New Way Literature	Steck-Vaughn
Little Danny Dinosaur	G	F	195	First Start	Troll Associates
Little Dinosaur	D	F	55	The Vocabulary Development Collection	Pearson Learning Group
Little Dinosaur	K	F	250+	Voyages	SRA/McGraw Hill
Little Dinosaur Escapes	J	HF	389	PM Collection	Rigby
Little Dinosaur Runs Away	J	F	847	Little Dinosaur	Literacy Footprints
Little Dinosaur, the Hero	E	F	159	Little Dinosaur	Literacy Footprints
Little Dinosaur's Skateboard	H	F	186	Little Dinosaur	Literacy Footprints
Little Dog Moon	Q	RF	250+	Trottier, Maxine	Stoddart Kids
Little Dragon Boats	I	RF	250+	Literacy by Design	Rigby
Little Dragon Boats	I	RF	250+	On Our Way to English	Rigby
Little Duchess, The	T	B	250+	WorldScapes	ETA Cuisenaire
Little Duck for Lily, A	C	RF	42	PM Photo Stories	Rigby
Little Duckling Is Lost	C	F	66	Nelson, May	Scholastic
Little Ducklings	B	RF	56	First Stories	Pacific Learning
Little Dutch Boy, The	J	TL	250+	Jumbled Tumbled Tales & Rhymes	Rigby
Little Egg, The	F	F	78	Big Cat	Pacific Learning
Little Elephant	G	F	192	New Way Blue	Steck-Vaughn
Little Farm in the Ozarks	R	HF	250+	MacBride, Roger Lea	HarperTrophy
Little Firefighter, The	M	RF	867	Sunshine	Wright Group/McGraw Hill
Little Fireman	J	RF	250+	Brown, Margaret Wise	HarperCollins
Little Fish	C	F	106	Sails	Rigby
Little Fish	C	F	192	Tiger Cub	Peguis
Little Fish that Got Away	I	F	250+	Cook, Bernadine	Scholastic
Little Frog, Big Pond	J	F	250+	The Wright Skills	Wright Group/McGraw Hill
Little Frog's Monster Story	E	F	144	Ready Readers	Pearson Learning Group
Little Frogs of Puerto Rico, The	J	RF	143	Books for Young Learners	Richard C. Owen
Little Ghost Goes to School	G	F	210	TOTTS	Tott Publications
Little Ghost's Baby Brother	G	F	221	TOTTS	Tott Publications
Little Ghost's Vacation	G	F	118	TOTTS	Tott Publications
Little Giraffe, The	C	RF	70	PM Stars	Rigby
Little Girl and Her Beetle, The	I	TL	250+	Literacy 2000	Rigby
Little Girl and the Bear, The	K	TL	250+	Storyworlds	Heinemann Educational Books
Little Gorilla	J	F	167	Bornstein, Ruth	Clarion
Little Green Car, The	G	RF	252	Rigby Flying Colors	Rigby
Little Green Dandelion, A	H	RF	191	Books for Young Learners	Richard C. Owen
Little Green Frog	F	F	121	Learn to Read	Creative Teaching Press
Little Green Man Visits a Farm, The	E	F	183	Learn to Read	Creative Teaching Press
Little Green Witch, The	K	F	250+	McGrath, Barbara Barbieri	Charlesbridge
Little Half Chick	K	F	250+	Literacy Tree	Rigby
Little Hare and the Thundering Earth	S	HF	1426	Leveled Readers	Houghton Mifflin Harcourt
Little Hare and the Thundering Earth	S	HF	1426	Leveled Readers/CA	Houghton Mifflin Harcourt
Little Hare and the Thundering Earth	S	HF	1426	Leveled Readers/TX	Houghton Mifflin Harcourt
Little Hawk's New Name	M	HF	250+	Bolognese, Don	Scholastic
Little Hearts	C	RF	44	Story Box	Wright Group/McGraw Hill
Little Help, A	M	F	250+	Pair-It Turn and Learn	Steck-Vaughn

* Collection of short stories
# Graphic text

L

TITLE	LEVEL	GENRE	WORD COUNT	AUTHOR / SERIES	PUBLISHER / DISTRIBUTOR
Little Helpers	I	I	203	Sails	Rigby
Little Hen, The	D	F	107	Ready Readers	Pearson Learning Group
Little Horse and Big Horse	D	F	162	Rigby Flying Colors	Rigby
Little House	LB	F	14	Ready Readers	Pearson Learning Group
Little House Birthday, A	J	HF	250+	Wilder, Laura Ingalls	HarperCollins
Little House by Boston Bay	Q	HF	250+	Wiley, Melissa	HarperTrophy
Little House Farm Days	M	HF	250+	Wilder, Laura Ingalls	HarperTrophy
Little House Friends	M	HF	250+	Wilder, Laura Ingalls	HarperTrophy
Little House in Brookfield	Q	HF	250+	Wilkes, Maria D.	HarperTrophy
Little House in the Big Woods	Q	HF	250+	Wilder, Laura Ingalls	HarperTrophy
Little House in the Highlands	Q	HF	250+	Wiley, Melissa	HarperTrophy
Little House on Rocky Ridge	R	HF	250+	MacBride, Roger Lea	HarperTrophy
Little House on the Prairie	Q	HF	250+	Wilder, Laura Ingalls	HarperTrophy
Little House, The	I	TL	391	Pacific Literacy	Pacific Learning
Little Icicle	O	RF	250+	Szymanski, Lois	Avon Camelot
Little Iguana	C	RF	28	Reading Street	Pearson
Little Jack Horner	D	TL	29	Jumbled Tumbled Tales & Rhymes	Rigby
Little Kid	H	F	169	Literacy 2000	Rigby
Little Kittens	B	F	27	Ready Readers	Pearson Learning Group
Little Klein	T	HF	250+	Ylvisaker, Anne	Candlewick Press
Little Knight, The	K	F	250+	Reading Unlimited	Pearson Learning Group
Little Lady, The	C	RF	37	Ray's Readers	Outside the Box
Little Leaf- Leaper, The	O	RF	250+	WorldScapes	ETA Cuisenaire
*Little Leaf's Journey and the Lost Tooth, The	K	F	564	New Way Orange	Steck-Vaughn
Little Lefty	P	RF	250+	Christopher, Matt	Little, Brown & Co.
Little Lion, The	A	I	29	Phonics and Friends	Hampton-Brown
Little Match Girl, The	M	TL	250+	Lighthouse	Ginn & Co.
Little Meanie's Lunch	D	F	90	Story Box	Wright Group/McGraw Hill
Little Mermaid, The	S	TL	250+	Bookshop	Mondo
Little Mermaid, The	M	TL	735	Springboard	Wright Group/McGraw Hill
Little Miss Muffet	D	TL	26	Jumbled Tumbled Tales & Rhymes	Rigby
Little Miss Muffet	F	TL	146	Literacy 2000	Rigby
Little Miss Muffet	D	RF	59	Seedlings	Continental Press
Little Miss Stoneybrook and Dawn	O	RF	250+	Martin, Ann M.	Scholastic
Little Monkey	I	F	250+	Alphakids	Sundance
Little Monkey Is Stuck	E	F	251	Foundations	Wright Group/McGraw Hill
Little Monkeys	A	I	21	Windows on Literacy	National Geographic
Little Mouse	C	F	59	Handprints B	Educators Publishing Service
Little Mouse	E	RF	74	Hoenecke, Karen	Kaeden Books
Little Mouse's Trail Tale	I	F	250+	Bookshop	Mondo
Little Number Stories: Addition	G	I	154	Learn to Read	Creative Teaching Press
Little Number Stories: Subtraction	G	I	133	Learn to Read	Creative Teaching Press
Little Old Lady Who Danced on the Moon, The	M	RF	711	Sunshine	Wright Group/McGraw Hill
Little One Inch	K	TL	384	Gibson, Akimi	Scholastic
Little Overcoat, The	F	TL	237	Bookshop	Mondo
Little Painter of Sabana Grande, The	M	RF	250+	Soar to Success	Houghton Mifflin Harcourt
Little Panda	G	F	143	Books for Young Learners	Richard C. Owen
Little Panda, The	D	I	40	Windows on Literacy	National Geographic
*Little Pear	O	HF	250+	Lattimore, Eleanor F.	Harcourt Trade
*Little Pear and His Friends	O	HF	250+	Lattimore, Eleanor F.	Harcourt Trade
Little Penguin Is Lost	D	F	56	Reading Safari	Mondo

* Collection of short stories
# Graphic text

L

TITLE	LEVEL	GENRE	WORD COUNT	AUTHOR / SERIES	PUBLISHER / DISTRIBUTOR
Little Penguin's Tale	L	F	250+	Wood, Audrey	Scholastic
Little Pickle	WB	F	N/A	Collington, Peter	Dutton/Penguin
Little Pig	C	F	63	Story Box	Wright Group/McGraw Hill
Little Polar Bear and the Brave Little Hare	K	F	250+	de Beer, Hans	North-South Books
Little Porro	N	F	250+	Sun Sprouts	ETA Cuisenaire
Little Prairie House, A	J	HF	250+	Wilder, Laura Ingalls	HarperCollins
Little Prince, The	X	F	250+	De Saint-Exupery, Antoine	Harcourt Trade
Little Princess	E	F	99	Seedlings	Continental Press
Little Princess, A	L	RF	250+	All Aboard Reading	Grossett & Dunlap
Little Puffer Fish	H	F	133	Books for Young Learners	Richard C. Owen
Little Puppy Rap	I	F	211	Sunshine	Wright Group/McGraw Hill
Little Quack's New Friend	J	F	250+	Thompson, Lauren	Scholastic
Little Rabbit	E	TL	202	Storyworlds	Heinemann Educational Publishers
Little Rabbit Is Sad	D	F	97	Williams, Deborah	Kaeden Books
Little Rabbit Who Wanted Red Wings, The	H	F	364	Seedlings	Continental Press
Little Rat Makes Music	L	F	250+	Bang-Campbell, Monika	Harcourt
Little Rat Rides	L	F	250+	Bang-Campbell, Monika	Harcourt
Little Rat Sets Sail	L	F	250+	Bang-Campbell, Monika	Harcourt
Little Red and the Wolf	I	TL	316	Pair-It Books	Steck-Vaughn
Little Red Bus, The	H	RF	222	PM Story Books	Rigby
Little Red Hen	I	TL	250+	Hunia, Fran	Ladybird Books
Little Red Hen	H	TL	255	New Way Green	Steck-Vaughn
Little Red Hen, The	G	TL	250+	Cambridge Reading	Pearson Learning Group
Little Red Hen, The	D	TL	200+	Cherrington, Janelle	Scholastic
Little Red Hen, The	B	TL	96	Folk Tales	Pioneer Valley
Little Red Hen, The	C	TL	93	Leveled Literacy Intervention/ Blue System	Heinemann
Little Red Hen, The	I	TL	250+	Literacy 2000	Rigby
Little Red Hen, The	G	TL	206	Literacy by Design	Rigby
Little Red Hen, The	I	TL	250+	PM Traditional Tales Orange	Rigby
Little Red Hen, The	G	TL	256	Storyteller-Moon Rising	Wright Group/McGraw Hill
Little Red Hen, The	H	TL	250+	Storyworlds	Heinemann Educational Books
Little Red Hen, The	I	TL	226	Sunshine	Wright Group/McGraw Hill
Little Red Hen, The	H	TL	375	Traditional Tales	Pearson Learning Group
Little Red Hen, The	B	TL	87	Windmill Books	Wright Group/McGraw Hill
Little Red Hen, The	G	TL	250+	Ziefert, Harriet	Puffin/Penguin
Little Red Pig, The	G	F	214	Ready Readers	Pearson Learning Group
Little Red Riding Hood	E	TL	140	Bookshop	Mondo
Little Red Riding Hood	K	TL	250+	Enrichment	Wright Group/McGraw Hill
Little Red Riding Hood	E	TL	355	Fairy Tales and Folklore	Norwood House Press
Little Red Riding Hood	G	TL	140	Folk Tales	Pioneer Valley
Little Red Riding Hood	WB	TL	N/A	Goodall, John	McElderry
Little Red Riding Hood	H	TL	250+	Hunia, Fran	Ladybird Books
Little Red Riding Hood	I	TL	250+	Jumbled Tumbled Tales & Rhymes	Rigby
Little Red Riding Hood	J	TL	250+	PM Tales and Plays-Turquoise	Rigby
Little Red Riding Hood	H	TL	250+	Shapiro, Sara	Scholastic
Little Red Riding Hood	K	TL	250+	Story Steps	Rigby
Little Red Riding Hood	I	TL	250+	Storyworlds	Heinemann Educational Books
Little Red Riding Hood	G	TL	140	Sun Sprouts	ETA Cuisenaire
Little Red Sports Car	G	F	231	The Story Basket	Wright Group/McGraw Hill

L

* Collection of short stories
\# Graphic text

TITLE	LEVEL	GENRE	WORD COUNT	AUTHOR / SERIES	PUBLISHER / DISTRIBUTOR
Little Round Husband, The	M	F	250+	Sunshine	Wright Group/McGraw Hill
Little Runner of the Longhouse	K	HF	250+	Baker, Betty	HarperTrophy
Little Sea Pony, The	N	F	250+	Cresswell, Helen	HarperTrophy
Little Seed, A	B	I	18	Smart Starts	Rigby
Little Seeds	C	I	75	First Stories	Pacific Learning
Little Shapes and Big Shapes	A	I	40	InfoTrek	ETA Cuisenaire
Little Shopping, A	M	RF	250+	Rylant, Cynthia	Aladdin
Little Sima and the Giant Bowl	N	TL	1645	On My Own Folklore	Millbrook Press
Little Sister	C	RF	40	Mitchell, Robin	Scholastic
Little Snowman, The	C	RF	59	PM Extensions-Red	Rigby
Little Soup's Birthday	K	HF	250+	Peck, Robert Newton	Bantam
Little Sparrow, The: A Cinderella Story From Italy	O	TL	795	Leveled Readers	Houghton Mifflin Harcourt
Little Spider, The	K	F	250+	Literacy 2000	Rigby
Little Sprout, The	E	F	105	Bonnell, Kris	Reading Reading Books
Little Swan	M	RF	250+	Geras, Adele	Random House
Little Teddy and the Monkey	C	F	50	PM Stars	Rigby
Little Things	A	I	40	Leveled Literacy Intervention/ Orange System	Heinemann
Little Things	A	I	33	PM Starters	Rigby
Little Tin Soldier,The	M	TL	766	Tales from Hans Andersen	Wright Group/McGraw Hill
Little Tommy Tucker	E	TL	30	Jumbled Tumbled Tales & Rhymes	Rigby
Little Town at the Crossroads	Q	HF	250+	Wilkes, Maria D.	HarperTrophy
Little Town in the Ozarks	R	HF	250+	MacBride, Roger Lea	HarperTrophy
Little Town on the Prairie	Q	HF	250+	Wilder, Laura Ingalls	HarperTrophy
Little Tree, The	D	I	114	Vocabulary Readers	Houghton Mifflin Harcourt
Little Tree, The	D	I	114	Vocabulary Readers/CA	Houghton Mifflin Harcourt
Little Tuppen	I	TL	250+	Galdone, Paul	Houghton Mifflin Harcourt
Little Turtle	WB	RF	N/A	Books for Young Learners	Richard C. Owen
Little Turtle, The	D	F	57	Lindsay, Vachel	Scholastic
Little Vampire and the Midnight Bear	L	F	250+	Kwitz, Mary DeBall	Puffin/Penguin
Little Walrus Rising	K	F	250+	Young, Carol	Scholastic
Little Whale, The	M	F	1057	Sunshine	Wright Group/McGraw Hill
Little White Hen, The	E	F	159	PM Plus Story Books	Rigby
Little Witch Goes to School	K	F	250+	Hautzig, Deborah	Random House
Little Witch's Big Night	K	F	250+	Hautzig, Deborah	Random House
Little Wolf's New Home	F	F	253	Leveled Literacy Intervention/ Blue System	Heinemann
Little Women	Z	HF	250+	Alcott, Louisa May	Aladdin
Little Women	M	HF	250+	Bullseye	Random House
Little Work Plane, The	I	F	250+	PM Plus Story Books	Rigby
Little Yellow Chicken, The	I	F	322	Sunshine	Wright Group/McGraw Hill
Little Yellow Chicken's House, The	F	F	287	Story Basket	Wright Group/McGraw Hill
Little Zoot	E	F	33	Little Celebrations	Pearson Learning Group
Little, Little Man, The	M	F	741	Book Bank	Wright Group/McGraw Hill
Littles and the Great Halloween Scare, The	M	F	250+	Peterson, John	Scholastic
Littles and the Lost Children, The	M	F	250+	Peterson, John	Scholastic
Littles and the Terrible Tiny Kid, The	M	F	250+	Peterson, John	Scholastic
Littles and the Trash Tinies, The	M	F	250+	Peterson, John	Scholastic
Littles Give a Party, The	M	F	250+	Peterson, John	Scholastic
Littles Go Exploring, The	M	F	250+	Peterson, John	Scholastic
Littles Go to School, The	M	F	250+	Peterson, John	Scholastic
Littles Have a Wedding, The	M	F	250+	Peterson, John	Scholastic

* Collection of short stories
# Graphic text

L

TITLE	LEVEL	GENRE	WORD COUNT	AUTHOR / SERIES	PUBLISHER / DISTRIBUTOR
Littles Take a Trip, The	M	F	250+	Peterson, John	Scholastic
Littles to the Rescue, The	M	F	250+	Peterson, John	Scholastic
Littles, The	M	F	250+	Peterson, John	Scholastic
Littlest Glowworm, The	N	F	1517	Take Two Books	Wright Group/McGraw Hill
Lives of Ants, The	O	I	1054	Leveled Readers	Houghton Mifflin Harcourt
Lives of Ants, The	O	I	1054	Leveled Readers/CA	Houghton Mifflin Harcourt
Lives of Ants, The	O	I	1054	Leveled Readers/TX	Houghton Mifflin Harcourt
Lives of Social Insects, The	P	I	886	Leveled Readers	Houghton Mifflin Harcourt
Lives of Social Insects, The	p	I	886	Leveled Readers/CA	Houghton Mifflin Harcourt
Lives of Social Insects, The	P	I	886	Leveled Readers/TX	Houghton Mifflin Harcourt
Living Abroad	S	I	1619	Reading Street	Pearson
Living and Growing	J	I	250+	PM Plus Nonfiction	Rigby
Living and Nonliving	I	I	132	Nature Basics	Capstone Press
Living and Working in Space	J	I	383	Leveled Readers	Houghton Mifflin Harcourt
Living and Working in Space	J	I	383	Leveled Readers/CA	Houghton Mifflin Harcourt
Living and Working in Space	J	I	383	Leveled Readers/TX	Houghton Mifflin Harcourt
Living Desert, The	J	I	230	On Our Way to English	Rigby
Living Desert, The	I	I	123	Pair-It Turn and Learn	Steck-Vaughn
Living Dinosaurs	O	I	641	Big Cat	Pacific Learning
Living History	V	I	250+	iOpeners	Pearson Learning Group
Living in a City	F	I	133	Communities	Capstone Press
Living in a Rural Area	G	I	129	Communities	Capstone Press
Living in a Small Town	F	I	117	Communities	Capstone Press
Living in a Suburb	G	I	114	Communities	Capstone Press
Living in Alaska	C	I	101	In Step Readers	Rigby
Living in Alaska	C	I	101	Literacy by Design	Rigby
Living in an Igloo	H	RF	181	Bebop Books	Lee & Low Books Inc.
Living in Groups	O	I	250+	Rigby Flying Colors	Rigby
Living in Hard Times	S	I	594	Vocabulary Readers	Houghton Mifflin Harcourt
Living in Harsh Lands	X	I	250+	iOpeners	Pearson Learning Group
Living in Rural Communities	I	I	243	Communities	Lerner Publications
Living in Space	V	I	2329	Leveled Readers	Houghton Mifflin Harcourt
Living in Space	U	I	250+	Leveled Readers Language Support	Houghton Mifflin Harcourt
Living in Space	V	I	2329	Leveled Readers/CA	Houghton Mifflin Harcourt
Living in Space	O	I	250+	Nayer, Judy	Pearson Learning Group
Living in Space	M	I	250+	Rigby Star Quest	Rigby
Living in Space	O	I	250+	Scooters	ETA Cuisenaire
Living in Space	R	I	1121	Time for Kids	Teacher Created Materials
Living in Suburban Communities	I	I	279	Communities	Lerner Publications
Living in the Extreme	O	I	250+	Literacy by Design	Rigby
Living in the Rain Forest	N	I	818	Rigby Flying Colors	Rigby
Living in the Sky	K	RF	328	Sunshine	Wright Group/McGraw Hill
Living in Trees	Q	I	1328	Leveled Readers	Houghton Mifflin Harcourt
Living in Trees	Q	I	1328	Leveled Readers/CA	Houghton Mifflin Harcourt
Living in Trees	Q	I	1328	Leveled Readers/TX	Houghton Mifflin Harcourt
Living in Trees	B	I	36	Sails	Rigby
Living in Two Worlds	N	I	250+	InfoQuest	Rigby
Living in Urban Communities	I	I	212	Communities	Lerner Publications
Living It Up in Space	R	I	250+	Explorer Books-Pathfinder	National Geographic
Living It Up in Space	P	I	250+	Explorer Books-Pioneer	National Geographic
Living Lights: Fireflies in Your Backyard	M	I	250+	Backyard Bugs	Picture Window Books
Living Ocean, The	U	I	250+	Pair-It Books	Steck-Vaughn
Living on the Edge	R	I	250+	High-Fliers	Pacific Learning

Organized Alphabetically by Title
Storable Database at www.fountasandpinnellleveledbooks.com

L

* Collection of short stories
\# Graphic text

TITLE	LEVEL	GENRE	WORD COUNT	AUTHOR / SERIES	PUBLISHER / DISTRIBUTOR
Living on the Farm	D	I	155	Early Connections	Benchmark Education
Living or Nonliving	B	I	27	Instant Readers	Harcourt School Publishers
Living Rain Forest, The	S	I	250+	Orbit Chapter Books	Pacific Learning
Living Things	E	I	75	Avery, Dorothy	Scholastic
Living Things	C	I	57	Independent Readers Science	Houghton Mifflin Harcourt
Living Things	C	I	43	Leveled Readers Science	Houghton Mifflin Harcourt
Living Things	G	I	151	Rosen Real Readers	Rosen Publishing Group
Living Things	I	I	383	Science Support Readers	Houghton Mifflin Harcourt
Living Things Need Food	H	I	66	Windows on Literacy	National Geographic
Living Things Need Water	C	I	26	Windows on Literacy	National Geographic
Living Through a Natural Disaster	W	I	250+	iOpeners	Pearson Learning Group
Living to Tell the Tale - Survival Stories	T	I	250+	Connectors	Pacific Learning
Living Together	L	I	284	Gear Up!	Wright Group/ McGraw Hill
Living Together	F	I	176	Sails	Rigby
Living Up the Street	Y	RF	250+	Soto, Gary	Bantam
Living with Llamas	R	I	250+	WorldScapes	ETA Cuisenaire
Living with Others	J	I	250+	PM Plus Nonfiction	Rigby
Living with Salties	P	I	250+	Orbit Double Takes	Pacific Learning
Living with Vampires	S	F	3653	Strong, Jeremy	Stone Arch Books
Lizard	E	RF	80	Foundations	Wright Group/McGraw Hill
Lizard Loses His Tail	D	RF	54	PM Story Books	Rigby
Lizard Music	T	F	250+	Pinkwater, D. Manus	Bantam
Lizard on a Stick	C	RF	38	Wonder World	Wright Group/McGraw Hill
Lizard on the Loose	K	RF	667	In Step Readers	Rigby
Lizard Tongue	Q	RF	250+	PM Extensions	Rigby
Lizards	H	I	106	Desert Animals	Capstone Press
Lizards	G	I	228	Sails	Rigby
Lizards	L	I	356	Wonder World	Wright Group/McGraw Hill
Lizards and Salamanders	M	I	250+	Reading Unlimited	Pearson Learning Group
Lizards and Snakes	O	I	250+	Rigby Literacy	Rigby
Lizard's Grandmother	J	F	336	Sunshine	Wright Group/McGraw Hill
Lizard's Song	M	TL	250+	Voyages	SRA/McGraw Hill
Lizzie's Lizard	L	I	289	Storyteller Nonfiction	Wright Group/McGraw Hill
Lizzie's Lunch	I	F	118	Literacy Tree	Rigby
Lizzy	E	RF	155	Leveled Literacy Intervention/ Green System	Heinemann
Llama in the Family, A	O	RF	250+	Hurwitz, Johanna	Scholastic
Llama Pajamas	N	RF	250+	Clymer, Susan	Scholastic
Llamas	O	I	1297	Early Bird Nature Books	Lerner Publishing
Loading the Airplane	G	RF	140	Windows on Literacy	National Geographic
Loans for the Poor	W	I	2313	Leveled Readers	Houghton Mifflin Harcourt
Loans for the Poor	W	I	2313	Leveled Readers/CA	Houghton Mifflin Harcourt
Lobster	I	I	132	Under the Sea	Capstone Press
Lobster Fishing at Dawn	I	I	194	Ready Readers	Pearson Learning Group
Lobstering	LB	I	14	Little Books for Early Readers	University of Maine
Lobster's Tale, A	W	I	2114	Leveled Readers	Houghton Mifflin Harcourt
*Local News	W	RF	250+	Soto, Gary	Scholastic
Loch Ness Monster Mystery, The	S	I	250+	Literacy 2000	Rigby
Loch Ness Monster, The	U	I	250+	The Unexplained	Capstone Press
Loch Ness Monster, The	L	I	359	Vocabulary Readers	Houghton Mifflin Harcourt
Loch Ness Monster, The	L	I	359	Vocabulary Readers/CA	Houghton Mifflin Harcourt
Loch Ness Monster, The	I	I	359	Vocabulary Readers/TX	Houghton Mifflin Harcourt
Lock the Gate!	D	RF	41	Leveled Readers	Houghton Mifflin Harcourt
Locked In	H	RF	228	PM Plus Story Books	Rigby

* Collection of short stories
# Graphic text

L

| --- | --- | --- | --- | --- | --- |
Locked in the Library!	M	F	250+	Brown, Marc	Little, Brown & Co.
Locked Out	G	RF	15	PM Story Books	Rigby
Locked Out!	B	RF	15	Twig	Wright Group/McGraw Hill
Lockgate Mystery, The	P	RF	250+	Storyteller - Raging Rivers	Wright Group/ McGraw Hill
Locomotion	V	RF	250+	Woodson, Jacqueline	Penguin Group
Locusts: Insects on the Move	T	I	2877	Insect World	Lerner Publications
Log Cabin in the Woods	R	HF	250+	Henry, Joanne Landers	Scholastic
Log Cabin Wedding, The	O	HF	250+	Howard, Ellen	Holiday House
Log Garfish	M	TL	114	Books for Young Learners	Richard C. Owen
Log Hotel	J	RF	261	Schreiber, Anne	Scholastic
Log Hotel, The	A	F	22	Little Celebrations	Pearson Learning Group
Log, The	C	RF	29	New Way Red	Steck-Vaughn
Log, The	E	RF	179	Sails	Rigby
Logan West, Printer's Devil	T	HF	250+	Bookshop	Mondo
Lois Lowry	T	B	250+	Markham, Lois	Learning Works, The
Lola and Miss Kitty	H	RF	250+	Little Readers	Houghton Mifflin Harcourt
Lola at the Library	I	RF	288	McQuinn, Anna & Beardshaw, Rosalind	Charlesbridge
Lola, the Muddy Dog	D	RF	107	Leveled Readers	Houghton Mifflin Harcourt
Lola, the Muddy Dog	D	RF	107	Leveled Readers/CA	Houghton Mifflin Harcourt
Lollipop	G	F	59	Watson, Wendy	Crowell
Lollipop Please, A	H	RF	73	Literacy 2000	Rigby
Lon Po Po: A Red-Riding Hood Story from China	S	TL	250+	Young, Ed	Scholastic
Lone Wolf	Y	RF	2697	Leveled Readers	Houghton Mifflin Harcourt
Lonely Bull, The	E	F	116	Pacific Literacy	Pacific Learning
Lonely Dragon, The	J	F	250+	Momentum Literacy Program	Troll Associates
Lonely Giant, The	K	F	449	Literacy 2000	Rigby
Lonely Man, The	P	TL	767	Leveled Readers	Houghton Mifflin Harcourt
Lonely Man, The	P	TL	767	Leveled Readers/CA	Houghton Mifflin Harcourt
Lonely Man, The	P	TL	767	Leveled Readers/TX	Houghton Mifflin Harcourt
Long Ago	D	I	105	Early Connections	Benchmark Education
Long Ago and Far Away	T	I	250+	Wildcats	Wright Group/McGraw Hill
Long Ago and Today	D	I	72	Learn to Read	Creative Teaching Press
Long Ago and Today	E	I	64	Shutterbug Books	Steck-Vaughn
Long and Short	D	RF	108	PM Math Readers	Rigby
Long and Short	I	F	228	Sunshine	Wright Group/McGraw Hill
Long and Short: An Animal Opposites Book	K	I	250+	Animal Opposites	Capstone Press
Long Arrow and the Elk Dogs	Q	TL	250+	Leveled Readers Language Support	Houghton Mifflin Harcourt
Long Bike Ride, The	G	RF	183	PM Photo Stories	Rigby
Long Cattle Drive, The	T	HF	2463	Leveled Readers	Houghton Mifflin Harcourt
Long Cattle Drive, The	T	HF	2463	Leveled Readers/CA	Houghton Mifflin Harcourt
Long Cattle Drive, The	T	HF	2463	Leveled Readers/TX	Houghton Mifflin Harcourt
Long Grass of Tumbledown Road	M	F	283	Read Alongs	Rigby
Long Hair	B	I	30	Sails	Rigby
Long Limousines	L	I	160	On Deck	Rigby
Long Road to Freedom: Journey of the Hmong	V	I	250+	High Five Reading	Red Brick Learning
Long Shot for Paul	Q	RF	250+	Christopher, Matt	Little, Brown & Co.
Long Texas Trail, The	R	HF	250+	Literacy by Design	Rigby
Long Time Ago, A	H	I	112	Sails	Rigby
Long Trail Home, The	S	HF	250+	On Our Way to English	Rigby
Long Trip West, The	R	I	633	Reading Street	Pearson
Long Walk Home, The	P	RF	250+	Action Packs	Rigby

L

* Collection of short stories
\# Graphic text

TITLE	LEVEL	GENRE	WORD COUNT	AUTHOR / SERIES	PUBLISHER / DISTRIBUTOR
Long Walk, A	E	I	131	Twig	Wright Group/McGraw Hill
Long Way from Chicago, A	V	HF	250+	Peck, Richard	Puffin/Penguin
Long Way Home, The	G	RF	94	Rookie Readers	Children's Press
Long Way to a New Land, A	L	HF	250+	Sandin, Joan	HarperTrophy
Long Way to Go, A	R	I	250+	O'Neal, Zibby	Penguin Group
Long Way Westward, The	L	HF	250+	Sandin, Joan	HarperTrophy
Long Winter, The	Q	HF	250+	Wilder, Laura Ingalls	HarperTrophy
Long, Long Ago	M	I	250+	Literacy 2000	Rigby
Long, Long Ago	M	TL	250+	Literacy by Design	Rigby
Long, Long Tail, The	B	F	33	Sunshine	Wright Group/McGraw Hill
Long-Arm Quarterback	S	RF	250+	Christopher, Matt	Norwood House Press
Longest Necklace, The	B	RF	64	InfoTrek	ETA Cuisenaire
Longest Noodle in the World, The	D	F	66	Joy Readers	Pearson Learning Group
Longest Shortcut, The	O	RF	250+	Literacy by Design	Rigby
Long-Lost Friends, The	M	RF	250+	Woodland Mysteries	Wright Group/McGraw Hill
Long-Neck: The Adventure of Apatosaurus	N	I	250+	Dinosaur World	Picture Window Books
Long-Range Bombers: The B-1B Lancers	V	I	250+	War Planes	Capstone Press
Loni's Town	J	RF	353	Reading Street	Pearson
Look	A	F	20	Sunshine	Wright Group/McGraw Hill
Look Again	C	I	47	Bookshop	Mondo
Look and See	G	I	208	Learn to Read	Creative Teaching Press
Look Around!	LB	I	7	Reading Street	Pearson
Look at All the Money!	F	I	110	InfoTrek	ETA Cuisenaire
Look at Australia, A	M	I	185	Pebble Books	Red Brick Learning
Look at Bix	B	I	25	Reading Street	Pearson
Look at Both Sides	K	I	236	Yellow Umbrella Books	Capstone Press
Look at Canada, A	M	I	180	Pebble Books	Red Brick Learning
Look at China, A	M	I	178	Our World	Capstone Press
Look at Conor	A	RF	27	Little Books for Early Readers	University of Maine
Look at Cuba, A	M	I	149	Our World	Capstone Press
Look at Danny	C	RF	39	Coulton, Mia	Maryruth Books
Look at Dogs, A	M	I	551	Pair-It Books	Steck-Vaughn
Look at Egypt, A	M	I	179	Our World	Capstone Press
Look at France, A	M	I	152	Pebble Books	Red Brick Learning
Look at Germany, A	M	I	162	Our World	Capstone Press
Look at Japan, A	M	I	185	Pebble Books	Red Brick Learning
Look at Kenya, A	M	I	161	Our World	Capstone Press
Look at Kyle	B	I	46	Little Books for Early Readers	University of Maine
Look at Lady Liberty, A	M	B	250+	Rosen Real Readers	Rosen Publishing Group
Look at Me	D	RF	67	Carousel Readers	Pearson Learning Group
Look at Me	C	RF	62	Early Connections	Benchmark Education
Look at Me	B	I	24	InfoTrek	ETA Cuisenaire
Look at Me	F	RF	104	Literacy 2000	Rigby
Look at Me	LB	I	17	Little Books for Early Readers	University of Maine
Look at Me	B	RF	48	PM Starters	Rigby
Look at Me	LB	I	13	Windows on Literacy	National Geographic
Look at Me!	B	F	59	In Step Readers	Rigby
Look at Me!	A	F	27	KinderReaders	Rigby
Look at Me!	A	RF	27	Leveled Readers Emergent	Houghton Mifflin Harcourt
Look at Me!	B	RF	35	Lighthouse	Rigby
Look at Me!	D	F	94	Rigby Rocket	Rigby
Look at Me!	B	F	62	Sails	Rigby
Look at Me!	A	I	19	Vocabulary Readers	Houghton Mifflin Harcourt
Look at Me!	A	I	19	Vocabulary Readers/CA	Houghton Mifflin Harcourt

L

TITLE	LEVEL	GENRE	WORD COUNT	AUTHOR / SERIES	PUBLISHER / DISTRIBUTOR
Look at Mexico, A	M	I	159	Our World	Capstone Press
Look at Minerals, A: From Galena to Gold	S	I	250+	A First Book	Franklin Watts
Look at Monkey	C	F	95	Sails	Rigby
Look at My Eggs!	C	F	39	Sails	Rigby
Look at My Friends	A	RF	32	In Step Readers	Rigby
Look at My Weaving	C	I	69	First Stories	Pacific Learning
Look at Pets, A	J	I	250+	Rigby Rocket	Rigby
Look at Pickles	B	RF	90	Pickles the Dog Series	Pioneer Valley
Look at Rocks, A: From Coal to Kimerlite	S	I	250+	A First Book	Franklin Watts
Look at Russia, A	M	I	161	Our World	Capstone Press
Look at Snakes, A	M	I	250+	Pair-It Books	Steck-Vaughn
Look at Spiders, A	M	I	785	Pair-It Books	Steck-Vaughn
Look at That Cat!	I	RF	407	Reading Street	Pearson
Look at the Animals	B	I	64	Early Connections	Benchmark Education
Look at the Animals	B	RF	49	Little Readers	Houghton Mifflin Harcourt
Look at the Animals	B	RF	24	Sails	Rigby
Look at the Ball	B	I	58	Storyteller	Wright Group/McGraw Hill
Look at the Bears	A	F	28	Leveled Readers	Houghton Mifflin Harcourt
Look at the Bears	A	F	28	Leveled Readers/CA	Houghton Mifflin Harcourt
Look at the Calendar, A	H	I	139	Rosen Real Readers	Rosen Publishing Group
Look at the Clock, Max!	C	F	28	Reading Street	Pearson
Look at the Garden	A	I	43	Windmill Books	Rigby
Look at the House	B	F	53	PM Plus Starters	Rigby
Look at the Leaves	I	I	350	Rigby Flying Colors	Rigby
Look at the Lizard	A	I	33	Bookshop	Mondo
Look at the Moon	N	I	250+	Bookshop	Mondo
Look at the Ocean, A	B	I	50	Little Books for Early Readers	University of Maine
Look at the Robot	A	F	24	Sails	Rigby
Look at the Stars	H	I	144	Rigby Focus	Rigby
Look at the Tree	B	I	22	Windows on Literacy	National Geographic
Look at This	B	I	57	Carousel Earlybirds	Pearson Learning Group
Look at This Mess!	C	RF	50	First Stories	Pacific Learning
Look at This!	B	I	71	Literacy by Design	Rigby
Look at Us	B	RF	42	Johns, Linda	Scholastic
Look at Vietnam, A	M	I	163	Our World	Capstone Press
Look Before You Leap	Q	RF	250+	Mazer, Anne	Scholastic
Look Closer	A	I	21	Ready Readers	Pearson Learning Group
Look Down Low	F	I	66	Early Readers	Compass Point Books
Look Down!	B	I	51	Early Connections	Benchmark Education
Look for Bugs	A	RF	35	Leveled Readers	Houghton Mifflin Harcourt
Look for Bugs	A	RF	35	Leveled Readers/CA	Houghton Mifflin Harcourt
Look for Me	D	RF	71	Story Box	Wright Group/McGraw Hill
Look for Me!	F	I	208	Little Readers	Houghton Mifflin Harcourt
Look Here!	E	RF	67	Wonder World	Wright Group/McGraw Hill
Look How Tall I Am!	E	RF	108	Windows on Literacy	National Geographic
Look in Mom's Purse	D	RF	60	Carousel Readers	Pearson Learning Group
Look in the Garden	G	RF	208	PM Plus Story Books	Rigby
Look in the Garden	D	I	115	Rigby Flying Colors	Rigby
Look in the Tree	D	I	97	Springboard	Wright Group/McGraw Hill
Look in the Woods	C	RF	71	Leveled Readers	Houghton Mifflin Harcourt
Look in the Woods	C	RF	71	Leveled Readers/CA	Houghton Mifflin Harcourt
Look Inside	E	I	77	Sails	Rigby
Look Inside	J	I	168	Storyteller Nonfiction	Wright Group/McGraw Hill
Look into Space, A	D	I	71	Discovery World	Rigby

L

Organized Alphabetically by Title
Storable Database at www.fountasandpinnellleveledbooks.com

* Collection of short stories
\# Graphic text

TITLE	LEVEL	GENRE	WORD COUNT	AUTHOR / SERIES	PUBLISHER / DISTRIBUTOR
Look Out - Minibeasts About!	N	I	250+	Rigby Rocket	Rigby
Look Out for Bingo	E	RF	138	PM Plus Story Books	Rigby
Look Out for Space Monster	C	F	54	Spaceboy	Literacy Footprints
Look Out for Your Tail	J	F	250+	Literacy 2000	Rigby
Look Out the Window	C	RF	67	Story Steps	Rigby
Look Out!	B	F	15	Literacy 2000	Rigby
Look Out!	I	RF	250+	PM Plus Story Books	Rigby
Look Out!	B	F	29	Rigby Rocket	Rigby
Look Out!	D	F	53	Sunshine	Wright Group/McGraw Hill
Look Out, Butterfly!	WB	I	N/A	Big Cat	Pacific Learning
Look Out, Dan!	B	F	34	Story Box	Wright Group/McGraw Hill
Look Out, Fish!	C	F	65	Lighthouse	Rigby
Look Out, Fox!	B	F	32	Sails	Rigby
Look Out, Washington D.C.!	O	RF	250+	Giff, Patricia Reilly	Bantam
Look Up	C	RF	25	Bonnell, Kris	Reading Reading Books
Look Up	R	I	250+	iOpeners	Pearson Learning Group
Look Up	E	I	44	Little Celebrations	Pearson Learning Group
Look Up!	A	I	25	Leveled Readers	Houghton Mifflin Harcourt
Look Up!	A	I	25	Leveled Readers/CA	Houghton Mifflin Harcourt
Look Up, Look Down	D	I	165	PM Nonfiction-Red	Rigby
Look What Came from China	O	I	250+	Harvey, Miles	Franklin Watts
Look What Came from Egypt	O	I	250+	Harvey, Miles	Franklin Watts
Look What Came from France	O	I	250+	Harvey, Miles	Franklin Watts
Look What Came from Italy	O	I	250+	Harvey, Miles	Franklin Watts
Look What Came from Mexico	O	I	250+	Harvey, Miles	Franklin Watts
Look What Came from Russia	O	I	250+	Harvey, Miles	Franklin Watts
Look What Came from the United States	O	I	250+	Davis, Kevin	Franklin Watts
Look What Feet Can Do	P	I	1546	Look What Animals Can Do	Lerner Publications
Look What I Can Do	WB	F	N/A	Aruego, Jose	Macmillan
Look What I Can Read!	E	RF	49	Instant Readers	Harcourt School Publishers
Look What I Found!	B	RF	29	Lighthouse	Rigby
Look What I Found!	B	RF	29	Science	Outside the Box
Look What I Made!	D	I	40	Gear Up!	Wright Group/McGraw Hill
Look What I Made!	M	I	250+	Literacy 2000	Rigby
Look What Mouths Can Do	P	I	2123	Look What Animals Can Do	Lerner Publications
Look What Tails Can Do	P	I	1963	Look What Animals Can Do	Lerner Publications
Look What Whiskers Can Do	P	I	1970	Look What Animals Can Do	Lerner Publications
Look What You Can Make!	G	I	203	Story Steps	Rigby
Look Who Is at the Zoo	C	I	59	Bonnell, Kris	Reading Reading Books
Look Who Is Eating	C	I	41	Bonnell, Kris	Reading Reading Books
Look Who's Playing First Base	P	RF	250+	Christopher, Matt	Little, Brown & Co.
Look Who's Talking!	L	I	250+	Rigby Literacy	Rigby
Look!	A	F	31	Leveled Literacy Intervention/ Green System	Heinemann
Look!	C	RF	43	Little Celebrations	Pearson Learning Group
Look! Bugs!	C	I	32	Seedlings	Continental Press
Look! I Can Read!	F	RF	124	Hood, Susan	Grossett & Dunlap
Look! Now Look!	B	I	9	Rigby Literacy	Rigby
Look! Snow!	LB	RF	14	Montezinos, Nina	McElderry
Look, Bear	D	F	51	Sun Sprouts	ETA Cuisenaire
Look, Listen, and Learn	E	I	49	Canizares, Susan; Chanko, Pamela	Scholastic
Look, Listen, Taste, Touch, and Smell: Learning About Your Five Senses	M	I	250+	Amazing Body	Picture Window Books

L

* Collection of short stories
# Graphic text

TITLE	LEVEL	GENRE	WORD COUNT	AUTHOR / SERIES	PUBLISHER / DISTRIBUTOR
Look, We Can Fly Too	I	F	250+	Phonics Readers Plus	Steck-Vaughn
Look-Alike Animals	H	I	130	Bernard, Robin	Scholastic
Look-and-Find Shapes	B	I	42	Blevins, Wiley	Scholastic
Looking After a Dog	C	I	58	Sun Sprouts	ETA Cuisenaire
Looking After Baby	E	I	143	Storyteller Nonfiction	Wright Group/McGraw Hill
Looking After Eggs	M	I	250+	Explorations	Eleanor Curtain Publishing
Looking After Eggs	M	I	250+	Explorations	Okapi Educational Materials
Looking After Grandpa	D	RF	91	Foundations	Wright Group/McGraw Hill
Looking After Our World	S	I	250+	Connectors	Pacific Learning
Looking After Suzie	G	RF	209	Well-Being Series	Dominie Press
Looking at Animals in Cold Places	O	I	250+	Butterfield, Moira	Steck-Vaughn
Looking at Animals in Hot Places	N	I	250+	Butterfield, Moira	Steck-Vaughn
Looking at Animals in the Ocean	O	I	250+	Butterfield, Moira	Steck-Vaughn
Looking at Ants	I	I	250+	Yellow Umbrella Books	Red Brick Learning
Looking at Baby Animals	E	I	54	Teacher's Choice Series	Pearson Learning Group
Looking at Cities	E	I	30	iOpeners	Pearson Learning Group
Looking at Fish	A	I	35	Bonnell, Kris	Reading Reading Books
Looking at Fish	D	I	148	Sails	Rigby
Looking at Insects	L	I	250+	Discovery World	Rigby
Looking at Insects	E	I	110	Rigby Flying Colors	Rigby
Looking at Light	T	I	250+	Orbit Chapter Books	Pacific Learning
Looking at Low Tide	M	RF	642	Leveled Readers	Houghton Mifflin Harcourt
Looking at Maps and Globes	K	I	250+	Brederson, Carmen	Scholastic
Looking at Materials	F	I	137	Rigby Rocket	Rigby
Looking at Our World	I	I	188	Early Connections	Benchmark Education
Looking at Pets	C	I	99	Vocabulary Readers	Houghton Mifflin Harcourt
Looking at Pets	C	I	99	Vocabulary Readers/CA	Houghton Mifflin Harcourt
Looking at Plants	C	I	44	Leveled Readers Science	Houghton Mifflin Harcourt
Looking at Shapes	G	I	235	Yellow Umbrella Books	Red Brick Learning
Looking at Snails	D	I	90	Rigby Flying Colors	Rigby
Looking at the Moon	I	I	228	PM Science Readers	Rigby
Looking at Worms	D	I	94	Rigby Flying Colors	Rigby
Looking Back: A Book of Memories	X	B	250+	Lowry, Lois	Delacorte Press
Looking Down	E	I	130	Early Connections	Benchmark Education
Looking Down	B	RF	64	First Stories	Pacific Learning
Looking Down	C	RF	70	PM Starters	Rigby
Looking for a Letter	F	RF	223	New Way Green	Steck-Vaughn
Looking for a New House	I	RF	250+	Windows on Literacy	National Geographic
Looking for Amelia	S	RF	250+	PM Plus Chapter Books	Rigby
Looking for Angus	H	F	99	Ready Readers	Pearson Learning Group
Looking for Bears	H	RF	80	Books for Young Learners	Richard C. Owen
Looking for Birds	D	I	74	Leveled Readers	Houghton Mifflin Harcourt
Looking for Buddy	N	RF	250+	Leveled Readers Language Support	Houghton Mifflin Harcourt
Looking for Dad	M	RF	250+	SupaDoopers	Sundance
Looking for Eggs	C	RF	47	Windmill Books	Rigby
Looking for Frogs	D	I	50	Leveled Readers	Houghton Mifflin Harcourt
Looking for Halloween	LB	RF	49	Urmston, Kathleen; Evans, Karen	Kaeden Books
Looking for Home	B	I	63	In Step Readers	Rigby
Looking for Leo	G	RF	253	Rigby Flying Colors	Rigby
Looking for Lions	L	I	250+	World Quest Adventures	World Quest Learning
Looking for Luke	I	RF	250+	Sunshine	Wright Group/McGraw Hill
Looking for Numbers	D	I	91	Early Connections	Benchmark Education

L

* Collection of short stories
\# Graphic text

TITLE	LEVEL	GENRE	WORD COUNT	AUTHOR / SERIES	PUBLISHER / DISTRIBUTOR
Looking for Patterns	J	I	160	Early Connections	Benchmark Education
Looking for Shapes	K	I	289	Early Connections	Benchmark Education
Looking for Symmetry	I	I	224	Windows on Literacy	National Geographic
Looking for Taco	C	F	94	Leveled Literacy Intervention/ Green System	Heinemann
Looking for the Queen	O	I	250+	Frederick, Shirley	Hampton-Brown
Looking Great	V	I	250+	10 Things You Need to Know About	Capstone Press
Looking in Mirrors	L	I	316	Explorations	Eleanor Curtain Publishing
Looking in Mirrors	L	I	316	Explorations	Okapi Eductional Materials
Looking Inside Cells	Y	I	250+	Science Readers	Teacher Created Materials
Looking into Space	L	I	345	Early Connections	Benchmark Education
Looking the Part	X	I	2322	Leveled Readers	Houghton Mifflin Harcourt
Looking Through a Telescope	K	I	250+	Rookie Read-About Science	Children's Press
Looks Like Rain!	C	RF	24	Science	Outside the Box
Loose Bolts	O	SF	250+	Sunshine	Wright Group/McGraw Hill
Loose Laces	J	RF	209	Reading Unlimited	Pearson Learning Group
Loose Tooth	B	RF	51	Bebop Books	Lee & Low Books Inc.
Loose Tooth	G	I	147	Healthy Teeth	Capstone Press
Loose Tooth	F	RF	123	Schaefer, Lola M.	Scholastic
Loose Tooth, The	H	RF	168	Breakthrough	Longman/Bow
Loose Tooth, The	E	F	134	Galaxy Girl	Literacy Footprints
Loose-Tooth Luke	K	RF	1304	Real Kids Readers	Millbrook Press
Lord Mount Dragon, The	M	TL	250+	Cambridge Reading	Pearson Learning Group
Lord of the Nutcracker Men	Z	HF	250+	Lawrence, Iain	Random House
Lord of the Rings, The	Z	F	250+	Tolkien, J.R.R.	Houghton Mifflin Harcourt
Lorenzo's Secret Mission	W	HF	250+	Guzman Lila and Rick	Pinata Books
Los Angeles Angels of Anaheim, The	S	I	250+	Team Spirit	Norwood House Press
Los Angeles Dodgers, The	S	I	250+	Team Spirit	Norwood House Press
Los Angeles Lakers, The	S	I	250+	Team Spirit	Norwood House Press
Loser	U	RF	250+	Spinelli, Jerry	HarperCollins
Losing Joe's Place	Y	RF	250+	Korman, Gordon	Scholastic
Lost	E	RF	82	Literacy Tree	Rigby
Lost	C	RF	38	Story Box	Wright Group/McGraw Hill
Lost	E	RF	29	Sun Sprouts	ETA Cuisenaire
Lost	P	RF	2082	Take Two Books	Wright Group/ McGraw Hill
Lost	A	RF	29	TOTTS	Tott Publications
Lost and Found	G	RF	203	Adams, Lorraine; Bruvold, Lynn	Eagle Crest Books
Lost and Found	D	RF	64	Carousel Readers	Pearson Learning Group
*Lost and Found	G	F	55	Instant Readers	Harcourt School Publishers
Lost and Found	D	RF	55	New Way Red	Steck-Vaughn
Lost and Found	I	RF	534	Real Kids Readers	Millbrook Press
Lost and Found	Z	RF	250+	Schraff, Anne	Townsend Press
Lost and Found Game, The	M	RF	250+	Nayer, Judy	Pearson Learning Group
Lost At Sea!: Tami Oldham Ashcraft's Story of Survival	S	I	250+	True Tales of Survival	Capstone Press
Lost at the Fun Park	F	RF	192	PM Extensions-Blue	Rigby
Lost at the White House: A 1909 Easter Story	L	HF	250+	Griest, Lisa	Carolrhoda Books
Lost Cat!	E	RF	156	Bookshop	Mondo
Lost Children, The	M	TL	250+	Goble, Paul	Aladdin
Lost Cities	T	I	250+	Navigators Social Studies Series	Benchmark Education Company
Lost Cities	Q	I	1581	Take Two Books	Wright Group/ McGraw Hill

TITLE	LEVEL	GENRE	WORD COUNT	AUTHOR / SERIES	PUBLISHER / DISTRIBUTOR
Lost Coat, The	D	RF	98	Storyworlds	Heinemann Educational Publishers
Lost Colony of Roanoke, The	T	I	1081	Leveled Readers Social Studies	Houghton Mifflin Harcourt
Lost Comic Book, The	S	RF	2655	Leveled Readers/CA	Houghton Mifflin Harcourt
Lost Comic Book, The	S	RF	2655	Leveled Readers/TX	Houghton Mifflin Harcourt
*Lost Continent and Other Cases, The	O	RF	250+	Simon, Seymour	Avon
Lost Costume, The	I	RF	250+	Storyworlds	Heinemann Educational Books
Lost Dog, The	N	RF	908	Reading Street	Pearson
Lost Flower Children, The	Q	RF	250+	Lisle, Janet Taylor	Philomel/Penguin
Lost Garden, The	W	B	250+	Yep, Laurence	Beech Tree Books
Lost Glasses	G	RF	270	Rigby Flying Colors	Rigby
Lost Glove, The	D	RF	105	Foundations	Wright Group/McGraw Hill
Lost Goat Lane	W	RF	250+	Jordan, Rosa	Peachtree
*Lost Hikers and Other Cases, The	O	RF	250+	Simon, Seymour	Avon
Lost in a Cave	P	RF	250+	On Our Way to English	Rigby
Lost in Cyberspace	Y	SF	250+	Peck, Richard	Puffin/Penguin
Lost in English	N	RF	999	Springboard	Wright Group/McGraw Hill
Lost in Space	M	SF	250+	Pacific Literacy	Pacific Learning
Lost in Space	P	SF	960	Springboard	Wright Group/ McGraw Hill
Lost in the Dark	Q	I	250+	Orbit Double Takes	Pacific Learning
Lost in the Fog	D	F	59	Ready Readers	Pearson Learning Group
Lost in the Forest	I	HF	298	PM Story Books-Orange	Rigby
Lost in the Forest	K	RF	250+	Sunshine	Wright Group/McGraw Hill
Lost in the Jungle	E	F	131	Little Dinosaur	Literacy Footprints
Lost in the Mist	J	RF	250+	Storyworlds	Heinemann Educational Books
Lost in the Museum	I	RF	250+	Cohen, Miriam	Bantam
Lost in the Wilderness!	Q	I	660	Vocabulary Readers	Houghton Mifflin Harcourt
Lost in the Woods	D	F	120	Bella and Rosie Series	Pioneer Valley
Lost in Time	V	B	250+	WorldScapes	ETA Cuisenaire
Lost Keys, The	G	RF	223	PM Plus Story Books	Rigby
Lost Lake, The	M	RF	250+	Soar To Success	Houghton Mifflin Harcourt
Lost Money, The	E	F	100	Georgie Giraffe	Literacy Footprints
Lost Mother, The	E	RF	112	Alphakids	Sundance
Lost Necklace, The	E	RF	132	Adams, Lorraine; Bruvold, Lynn	Eagle Crest Books
Lost Comic Book, The	S	RF	2655	Leveled Readers	Houghton Mifflin Harcourt
Lost on a Mountain in Maine	R	RF	250+	Fendler, Donn	Peter Smith Publications
Lost Sandals, The	N	RF	250+	Bennett, Jean	Pacific Learning
Lost Scroll, The	K	RF	253	Pair-It Turn and Learn	Steck-Vaughn
Lost Sheep, The	I	F	219	Little Readers	Houghton Mifflin Harcourt
Lost Socks	F	RF	159	PM Plus Story Books	Rigby
Lost Star: The Story of Amelia Earhart	T	B	250+	Lauber, Patricia	Language for Learning Assoc.
Lost Storybook, The	F	RF	172	Storyworlds	Heinemann Educational Publishers
Lost Toy, The	G	F	184	Storyworlds	Heinemann Educational Books
Lost Treasure of the Emerald Eye	O	F	250+	Stilton, Geronimo	Scholastic
Lost Underground	T	RF	250+	Reading Safari	Mondo
Lost Valentines, The	G	RF	159	Developing Set 4	Pioneer Valley
Lost World of the Olmec	V	I	2149	Independent Readers Social Studies	Houghton Mifflin Harcourt
Lost!	J	RF	452	Gear Up!	Wright Group/McGraw Hill

L

* Collection of short stories
# Graphic text

TITLE	LEVEL	GENRE	WORD COUNT	AUTHOR / SERIES	PUBLISHER / DISTRIBUTOR
Lost!	F	F	82	Green Light Readers	Harcourt
Lost!	D	RF	57	Harry's Math Books	Outside the Box
Lost!	L	F	57	Home Connection Collection	Rigby
Lost!	B	RF	18	Smart Starts	Rigby
Lost: One Cat!	N	RF	250+	Tristars	Richard C. Owen
Lot Happened Today, A	I	RF	193	Ready Readers	Pearson Learning Group
Lots and Lots of Stairs	B	RF	33	Little Books for Early Readers	University of Maine
Lots of Balloons	F	RF	72	Early Readers	Compass Point Books
Lots of Birds	A	I	25	Vocabulary Readers	Houghton Mifflin Harcourt
Lots of Birds	A	I	25	Vocabulary Readers/CA	Houghton Mifflin Harcourt
Lots of Boats	K	I	468	Vocabulary Readers	Houghton Mifflin Harcourt
Lots of Boats	K	I	468	Vocabulary Readers/CA	Houghton Mifflin Harcourt
Lots of Caps	G	F	205	New Way Blue	Steck-Vaughn
Lots of Clocks	G	I	88	Gear Up!	Wright Group/McGraw Hill
Lots of Dogs	C	I	68	Teacher's Choice Series	Pearson Learning Group
Lots of Dolls!	C	I	61	The Candid Collection	Pearson Learning Group
Lots of Feelings	J	I	72	Shelley Rotner's Early Childhood	Millbrook Press
Lots of Flowers	A	I	28	Leveled Readers	Houghton Mifflin Harcourt
Lots of Flowers	A	I	28	Leveled Readers/CA	Houghton Mifflin Harcourt
Lots of Grandparents	J	I	156	Shelley Rotner's Early Childhood	Millbrook Press
Lots of Helpers	C	I	92	Leveled Readers	Houghton Mifflin Harcourt
Lots of Helpers	C	I	92	Leveled Readers/CA	Houghton Mifflin Harcourt
Lots of Socks	B	I	30	Gear Up!	Wright Group/McGraw Hill
Lots of Things	B	RF	23	Reading Corners	Pearson Learning Group
Lots of Toys	B	I	47	Carousel Earlybirds	Pearson Learning Group
Lottie Goat & Donny Goat	H	F	145	Ready Readers	Pearson Learning Group
Lotus Seed, The	P	HF	250+	Garland, Sherry	Harcourt Trade
Lou Gehrig: A Life of Dedication	N	B	614	Pull Ahead- Biographies	Lerner Publications
Lou Gehrig: One of Baseball's Greatest	O	B	250+	Childhood of Famous Americans	Aladdin
Lou Gehrig: The Luckiest Man	O	B	2200	Adler, David A.	Harcourt Inc.
Louanne Pig in Making the Team	K	F	325	Carlson, Nancy	Carolrhoda Books
Louanne Pig in the Mysterious Valentine	K	F	490	Carlson, Nancy	Carolrhoda Books
Louanne Pig in the Perfect Family	L	F	588	Carlson, Nancy	Carolrhoda Books
Louanne Pig in the Talent Show	K	F	302	Carlson, Nancy	Carolrhoda Books
Louanne Pig in Witch Lady	L	F	489	Carlson, Nancy	Carolrhoda Books
Loud and Quiet: An Animal Opposites Book	K	I	250+	Animal Opposites	Capstone Press
Loud Sounds, Quiet Sounds	B	I	26	Rosen Real Readers	Rosen Publishing Group
Loudmouth George and the Big Race	L	F	531	Carlson, Nancy	Carolrhoda Books
Loudmouth George and the Cornet	L	F	460	Carlson, Nancy	Carolrhoda Books
Loudmouth George and the Sixth-Grade Bully	L	F	544	Carlson, Nancy	Carolrhoda Books
Louie's Hat	C	RF	53	Adams, Lorraine; Bruvold, Lynn	Eagle Crest Books
Louis Agassiz Fuertes, Painter of the Bird	L	B	250+	Independent Readers Science	Houghton Mifflin Harcourt
Louis Armstrong	Z	B	250+	Brown, Sandford	Franklin Watts
Louis Armstrong	S	B	3775	History Maker Bios	Lerner Publications
Louis Armstrong: Jazz Legend	P	B	250+	Great African Americans	Capstone Press
Louis Braille	G	B	132	Independent Readers Science	Houghton Mifflin Harcourt
Louis Braille: Boy Who Invented Books for the Blind	N	B	250+	Davidson, Margaret	Scholastic
Louis Is Hungry	C	RF	31	Bonnell, Kris	Reading Reading Books
Louis Pasteur	N	B	250+	Biography	Benchmark Education
Louis Pasteur	P	B	250+	Photo-Illustrated Biographies	Red Brick Learning
#Louis Pasteur and Pasteurization	V	B	250+	Graphic Library	Capstone Press
Louis Pasteur and the Fight Against Germs	S	B	250+	Science Readers	Teacher Created Materials
Louis Riel	X	B	250+	The Canadians	Fitzhenry & Whiteside

* Collection of short stories
# Graphic text

L

TITLE	LEVEL	GENRE	WORD COUNT	AUTHOR / SERIES	PUBLISHER / DISTRIBUTOR
Louisa May Alcott: Young Novelist	O	B	250+	Childhood of Famous Americans	Aladdin
Louise Arner Boyd and Glaciers	V	B	2384	Leveled Readers	Houghton Mifflin Harcourt
Louise Arner Boyd and Glaciers	V	B	2384	Leveled Readers/CA	Houghton Mifflin Harcourt
Louisiana	T	I	250+	Hello U.S.A.	Lerner Publications
Louisiana	S	I	250+	Land of Liberty	Red Brick Learning
Louisiana	R	I	250+	This Land Is Your Land	Compass Point Books
Louisiana Purchase, The	V	I	250+	Cornerstones of Freedom	Children's Press
Louisiana Purchase, The	V	I	250+	Let Freedom Ring	Red Brick Learning
Love	B	RF	24	Handprints A	Educators Publishing Service
Love from Your Friend, Hannah	Y	HF	250+	Skolsky, Mindy Warshaw	HarperTrophy
Love Is	LB	RF	11	Visions	Wright Group/McGraw Hill
Love Me, Love My Broccoli	S	RF	250+	Peters, Julie Anne	Avon Camelot
Love That Dog	T	RF	250+	Creech, Sharon	HarperCollins
Love Those Bugs!	T	I	1798	Leveled Readers	Houghton Mifflin Harcourt
Love Those Bugs!	T	I	1798	Leveled Readers/CA	Houghton Mifflin Harcourt
Love Those Bugs!	T	I	1798	Leveled Readers/TX	Houghton Mifflin Harcourt
Love You, Soldier	R	HF	250+	Hest, Amy	Puffin/Penguin
Love, Football, and Other Contact Sports	X	RF	250+	Carter, Alden R.	Holiday House
Love, from the Fifth-Grade Celebrity	Q	RF	250+	Giff, Patricia Reilly	Bantam
Love, Ruby Lavender	U	RF	250+	Wiles, Deborah	Harcourt Achieve
Low Riders	L	I	110	On Deck	Rigby
Lowriders	M	I	250+	Horsepower	Capstone Press
Lowriders	W	I	4919	Motor Mania*	Lerner Publications
Lowriders	Q	I	250+	Wild Rides!	Capstone Press
Lucas the Lizard	K	F	474	Rigby Gigglers	Rigby
Luciano Pavarotti	W	B	1706	Leveled Readers	Houghton Mifflin Harcourt
Luciano Pavarotti	W	B	1706	Leveled Readers/CA	Houghton Mifflin Harcourt
Luciano Pavarotti	W	B	1706	Leveled Readers/TX	Houghton Mifflin Harcourt
Lucky Baseball Bat, The	M	RF	250+	Christopher, Matt	Little, Brown & Co.
Lucky Buster	M	F	250+	Rigby Gigglers	Rigby
Lucky Candlesticks, The	N	RF	764	Leveled Readers	Houghton Mifflin Harcourt
Lucky Chuck's Least Favorite Cousin	V	HF	5761	Reading Street	Pearson
Lucky Day for Little Dinosaur, A	F	HF	135	PM Extensions-Yellow	Rigby
Lucky Duck, The	E	F	73	Ready Readers	Pearson Learning Group
Lucky Feather, The	L	F	250+	Literacy 2000	Rigby
Lucky Goes to Dog School	E	RF	127	PM Story Books	Rigby
Lucky Last Luke	M	RF	250+	Clark, Margaret	Sundance
Lucky Me!	K	RF	1573	Real Kids Readers	Millbrook Press
Lucky Penny, The	G	RF	259	Leveled Literacy Intervention/Green System	Heinemann
Lucky Pony, A	D	F	76	Coulton, Mia	Maryruth Books
Lucky Socks	K	RF	250+	Literacy by Design	Rigby
Lucky Socks	K	RF	250+	On Our Way to English	Rigby
Lucky Stars	L	RF	250+	Adler, David A.	Random House
Lucky Stone, The	Q	RF	250+	Clifton, Lucille	Bantam
Lucky We Have a Station Wagon	F	RF	259	Foundations	Wright Group/McGraw Hill
Lucky Whale, The	J	RF	351	Springboard	Wright Group/McGraw Hill
Lucy and Billy	L	RF	317	Leveled Readers/TX	Houghton Mifflin Harcourt
Lucy Loses Red Ted	E	RF	187	Storyworlds	Heinemann Educational Publishers
Lucy Maud Montgomery	Q	B	250+	Wallner, Alexandra	Holiday House
Lucy Meets a Dragon	L	F	250+	Literacy 2000	Rigby
Lucy Rose: Big on Plans	O	RF	250+	Kelly, Katy	Yearling

* Collection of short stories
\# Graphic text

L

TITLE	LEVEL	GENRE	WORD COUNT	AUTHOR / SERIES	PUBLISHER / DISTRIBUTOR
Lucy Rose: Busy Like You Can't Believe	O	RF	250+	Kelly, Katy	Yearling
Lucy Rose: Here's the Thing About Me	O	RF	250+	Kelly, Katy	Yearling
Lucy Rose: Working Myself to Pieces and Bits	O	RF	250+	Kelly, Katy	Delacorte Press
Lucy Takes a Holiday	M	F	250+	Bookshop	Mondo
Lucy's Boot	F	F	210	Dominie Readers	Pearson Learning Group
Lucy's Box	E	F	108	Cambridge Reading	Pearson Learning Group
Lucy's Garden	I	RF	303	PM Math Readers	Rigby
Lucy's Loose Tooth	D	RF	88	Springboard	Wright Group/McGraw Hill
Lucy's Quiet Book	I	RF	237	Green Light Readers	Harcourt
Lucy's Sore Knee	F	RF	93	Windmill Books	Wright Group/McGraw Hill
Ludwig van Beethoven: Musical Pioneer	N	B	250+	Rookie Biographies	Children's Press
Luis Alvarez	S	B	871	Leveled Readers Science	Houghton Mifflin Harcourt
Luis Munoz Marin: Father of Modern Puerto Rico	P	B	250+	Community Builders	Children's Press
Luis Rodriguez	S	B	250+	Schwartz, Michael	Steck-Vaughn
Luis W. Alvarez	R	B	250+	Hispanic Stories	Steck-Vaughn
Luka Plays Baseball	H	RF	328	Rigby Flying Colors	Rigby
Luka's Campout	I	RF	384	Rigby Flying Colors	Rigby
Luka's New Kite	C	RF	104	Rigby Flying Colors	Rigby
Luka's Tortoise	F	RF	178	Rigby Flying Colors	Rigby
Luke Lively and the Castle of Sleep	P	F	250+	High-Fliers	Pacific Learning
Luke's Adventures	H	F	98	City Stories	Rigby
Luke's Bully	N	RF	250+	Winthrop, Elizabeth	Puffin/Penguin
Luke's Go-cart	L	RF	656	PM Collection	Rigby
Lullabob, The	N	I	250+	Sails	Rigby
Lulu Goes to Witch School	K	F	250+	O'Connor, Jane	HarperTrophy
Lulu's Lost Shoes	LB	F	43	We Both Read	Treasure Bay
Lumberjacks	P	I	1110	Reading Street	Pearson
Lumberjacks	M	I	255	Vocabulary Readers	Houghton Mifflin Harcourt
Lump in My Bed, A	D	RF	48	Book Bank	Wright Group/McGraw Hill
Lumpy Rug	D	RF	86	Dominie Phonics Reader	Pearson Learning Group
Luna	L	F	371	Leveled Readers	Houghton Mifflin Harcourt
Luna and the Well of Secrets: The Fairy Chronicles	Q	F	11900	Sweet, J.H.	Sourcebooks
Luna Moths: Masters of Change	T	I	2731	Insect World	Lerner Publications
Lunch	C	RF	42	Harry's Math Books	Outside the Box
Lunch	F	RF	156	Urmston, Kathleen; Evans, Karen	Kaeden Books
Lunch at the Joy House Café	K	RF	250+	Blackaby, Susan	Hampton-Brown
Lunch at the Park	E	I	132	Rigby Flying Colors	Rigby
Lunch at the Pond	E	F	146	Foundations	Wright Group/McGraw Hill
Lunch at the Zoo	B	RF	64	Blaxland, Wendy; Brimage, C.	Scholastic
Lunch at the Zoo	A	RF	32	Bookshop	Mondo
Lunch Bunch, The	I	RF	594	Real Kids Readers	Millbrook Press
Lunch Bunch, The	I	I	169	Storyteller-Moon Rising	Wright Group/McGraw Hill
Lunch in Space	G	RF	156	Instant Readers	Harcourt School Publishers
Lunch in the Park	D	F	108	Springboard	Wright Group/McGraw Hill
Lunch Money	R	RF	250+	Clements, Andrew	Aladddin Paperbacks
Lunch Orders	C	RF	18	Tadpoles	Rigby
Lunch Room, The	M	F	259	Leveled Readers	Houghton Mifflin Harcourt
Lunch Time	C	RF	69	Carousel Readers	Pearson Learning Group
Lunch Walks Among Us	N	SF	250+	Benton, Jim	Aladdin Paperbacks
Lunch with Cat and Dog	F	F	122	Learn to Read	Creative Teaching Press
Lunchbox Mystery, The	N	RF	250+	Lohans, Alison	Scholastic

* Collection of short stories
# Graphic text

TITLE	LEVEL	GENRE	WORD COUNT	AUTHOR / SERIES	PUBLISHER / DISTRIBUTOR
Lunchbox, The	H	RF	90	Pacific Literacy	Pacific Learning
Lunchroom, The	F	RF	80	City Stories	Rigby
Lunchtime	D	RF	82	Rigby Literacy	Rigby
Lunchtime at the Zoo	B	RF	53	First Stories	Pacific Learning
Luther Burbank	O	B	250+	Faber, Doris	Garrard Publishing Co.
Luz and the Garden	J	RF	446	Leveled Readers	Houghton Mifflin Harcourt
Luz and the Garden	J	RF	446	Leveled Readers/CA	Houghton Mifflin Harcourt
Luz and the Garden	J	RF	446	Leveled Readers/TX	Houghton Mifflin Harcourt
Lyddie	V	HF	250+	Paterson, Katherine	Penguin Group
Lydia and Her Cat	G	RF	77	Oxford Reading Tree	Oxford University Press
Lydia and Her Garden	G	RF	88	Oxford Reading Tree	Oxford University Press
Lydia and Her Kitten	G	RF	77	Oxford Reading Tree	Oxford University Press
Lydia and the Ducks	G	RF	87	Oxford Reading Tree	Oxford University Press
Lydia and the Letters	F	RF	84	Oxford Reading Tree	Oxford University Press
Lydia and the Present	F	RF	77	Oxford Reading Tree	Oxford University Press
Lydia at the Shops	G	RF	72	Oxford Reading Tree	Oxford University Press
Lying as Still as I Can	L	RF	250+	Greetings	Rigby
Lying Down Mountain: The Buffalo Woman Trilogy, Book Three	Z	HF	250+	Merrifield, Heyoka	Atria Books
Lyla and the New Piano	D	F	85	Lester the Lion Series	Pioneer Valley
Lyndon B. Johnson: Thirty-sixth President	R	B	250+	Getting to Know the U.S. Presidents	Children's Press
Lyndon Baines Johnson	U	B	250+	Profiles of the Presidents	Compass Point Books
Lynxes	O	I	2051	Early Bird Nature Books	Lerner Publications

L

* Collection of short stories
# Graphic text

TITLE	LEVEL	GENRE	WORD COUNT	AUTHOR / SERIES	PUBLISHER / DISTRIBUTOR
M & M and the Bad News Babies	K	RF	250+	Ross, Pat	Penguin Group
M & M and the Big Bag	K	RF	250+	Ross, Pat	Penguin Group
M & M and the Halloween Monster	K	RF	250+	Ross, Pat	Penguin Group
M & M and the Haunted House Game	K	RF	250+	Ross, Pat	Penguin Group
M & M and the Mummy Mess	K	RF	250+	Ross, Pat	Penguin Group
M & M and the Santa Secrets	K	RF	250+	Ross, Pat	Penguin Group
M & M and the Super Child Afternoon	K	RF	250+	Ross, Pat	Penguin Group
M. C. Higgins the Great	X	RF	250+	Hamilton, Virginia	Macmillan
M1 Abrams Main Battle Tank, The	U	I	250+	Cross-Sections	Capstone Press
M109A6 Paladin, The	U	I	250+	Cross-Sections	Capstone Press
M2 Bradley Infantry Fighting Vehicle, The	U	I	250+	Cross-Sections	Capstone Press
M270 Multiple Rocket Launcher, The	U	I	250+	Cross-Sections	Capstone Press
Ma and Pa Dracula	O	F	250+	Martin, Ann M.	Scholastic
Maasai Dreamer: A Story from Kenya	R	RF	250+	Reading Expeditions	National Geographic
MacGregors and the MacDougalls, The	N	RF	250+	Bookweb	Rigby
Machines	C	I	36	Little Celebrations	Pearson Learning Group
Machines	J	I	44	Sunshine	Wright Group/McGraw Hill
Machines	E	I	44	Twig	Wright Group/McGraw Hill
Machines at Work	H	I	101	Little Red Readers	Sundance
Machines in Construction	U	I	250+	Theme Sets	National Geographic
Machines in Health	U	I	250+	Theme Sets	National Geographic
Machines in Sports	U	I	250+	Theme Sets	National Geographic
Machines in the Home	N	I	250+	Home Connection Collection	Rigby
Machines in the Home	U	I	250+	Theme Sets	National Geographic
Machines Make Fun Rides	I	I	182	Windows on Literacy	National Geographic
Machines That Fly	I	I	111	Windows on Literacy	National Geographic
Machines That Work	D	I	93	Shutterbug Books	Steck-Vaughn
Mack Forgot!	B	RF	56	Literacy by Design	Rigby
Mack the Cat	C	RF	59	Reading Street	Pearson
Mack's Big Day	L	RF	464	PM Plus Story Books	Rigby
Mad Scientist, The	M	F	250+	Woodland Mysteries	Wright Group/McGraw Hill
Mad Scientist's Secret, The	P	SF	250+	Miller, Marvin	Scholastic
Madagascar	O	I	1550	A Ticket to ...	Carolrohoda Books
Madam C.J. Walker	S	B	250+	Amazing Americans	Wright Group/McGraw Hill
Madam C.J. Walker: Pioneer Buisnesswoman	P	B	250+	Great African Americans	Capstone Press
Madame C. J. Walker	Q	B	494	Independent Readers Social Studies	Houghton Mifflin Harcourt
Made in America	U	I	250+	WorldScapes	ETA Cuisenaire
Made of Wood	J	I	264	Rigby Flying Colors	Rigby
Made with Glass	F	I	106	Cherrington, Janelle	Scholastic
Madeline	K	F	250+	Bemelmans, Ludwig	Scholastic
Madeline's Rescue	K	F	250+	Bemelmans, Ludwig	Scholastic
Made's Birthday	L	RF	250+	Little Celebrations	Pearson Learning Group
Mae Jemison	R	B	250+	Bookshop	Mondo
Mae Jemison	N	B	250+	Explore Space!	Capstone Press
Mae Jemison	N	B	240	First Biographies	Capstone Press
Mae Jemison: Making Dreams Come True	N	B	540	Leveled Readers	Houghton Mifflin Harcourt
Mae Jemison: Space Pioneer	P	B	250+	Great African Americans	Capstone Press
Mae-Nerd	C	F	44	Teacher's Choice Series	Pearson Learning Group
Magellan: Ferdinand Magellan and the First Trip Around the World	U	B	250+	Exploring the World	Compass Point Books
Maggie McGee and Me at the Mint	O	RF	1579	Reading Street	Pearson
Maggie Moves Away	H	RF	327	Adventures in Reading	Pearson Learning Group
Maggie's Pets	I	RF	250+	Early Transitional	Pioneer Valley

* Collection of short stories
# Graphic text

TITLE	LEVEL	GENRE	WORD COUNT	AUTHOR / SERIES	PUBLISHER / DISTRIBUTOR
Magic All Around	L	F	250+	Literacy 2000	Rigby
Magic Beans, The	E	TL	239	Fairy Tales and Folklore	Norwood House Press
Magic Boots, The	I	F	250+	Storyworlds	Heinemann Educational Books
Magic Box, The	K	F	250+	Brenner, Barbara	Bantam
Magic by Heart	U	F	250+	Gordon, Amy	Holiday House
Magic by the Lake	T	F	250+	Eager, Edward	Harcourt
Magic Carpet, The	J	F	250+	Storyworlds	Heinemann Educational Books
Magic Coat, The	J	F	250+	Storyworlds	Heinemann Educational Books
Magic Finger, The	N	F	250+	Dahl, Roald	Penguin Group
Magic Fish, The	L	TL	870	Littledale, Freya	Scholastic
Magic Fish, The	J	TL	250+	Rylant, Cynthia	Scholastic
Magic Food	C	F	26	Smart Starts	Rigby
Magic Glasses Day	K	RF	718	Rigby Flying Colors	Rigby
Magic Hat, The	I	F	250+	Storyworlds	Heinemann Educational Books
Magic Horse, The	L	TL	839	Springboard	Wright Group/McGraw Hill
Magic Jigsaw, The	K	F	250+	Rigby Star Quest	Rigby
Magic Machine, The	C	F	163	Sunshine	Wright Group/McGraw Hill
Magic Money	L	RF	250+	Adler, David A.	Random House
Magic Money Box, The	E	I	71	Learn to Read	Creative Teaching Press
Magic Moscow, The	P	RF	250+	Pinkwater, Daniel	Aladdin
Magic Noodle Show, The	N	RF	250+	Orbit Chapter Books	Pacific Learning
Magic of Coyote, The	O	RF	2265	Reading Street	Pearson
Magic of Movies, The	T	I	1303	Leveled Readers	Houghton Mifflin Harcourt
Magic of Movies, The	T	I	1303	Leveled Readers/CA	Houghton Mifflin Harcourt
Magic of Movies, The	T	I	1303	Leveled Readers/TX	Houghton Mifflin Harcourt
Magic of Teamwork, The	M	F	873	Leveled Readers	Houghton Mifflin Harcourt
Magic of Teamwork, The	M	F	873	Leveled Readers/CA	Houghton Mifflin Harcourt
Magic of Teamwork, The	M	F	873	Leveled Readers/TX	Houghton Mifflin Harcourt
Magic Passport, The	N	F	250+	Navigators Fiction Series	Benchmark Education
Magic Pear Tree, The	I	TL	207	Little Celebrations	Pearson Learning Group
Magic Porridge Pot, The	I	TL	321	New Way Orange	Steck-Vaughn
Magic Porridge Pot, The	L	TL	497	Sunshine	Wright Group/McGraw Hill
Magic Pot, The	E	F	100+	Smith, Laura	Scholastic
Magic Ride, The	M	F	170	Book Bank	Wright Group/McGraw Hill
Magic School Bus	P	F	250+	Cole, Joanna; Degen, Bruce	Scholastic
Magic School Bus and the Electric Field Trip, The	P	F	250+	Cole, Joanna; Degen, Bruce	Scholastic
Magic School Bus and the Science Fair Expedition, The	P	F	250+	Cole, Joanna & Degen, Bruce	Scholastic
Magic School Bus Answers Questions, The	P	F	250+	Cole, Joanna; Degen, Bruce	Scholastic
Magic School Bus at the Waterworks, The	P	F	250+	Cole, Joanna; Degen, Bruce	Scholastic
Magic School Bus Blows Its Top, The	P	F	250+	Cole, Joanna; Degen, Bruce	Scholastic
Magic School Bus Briefcase, The	P	F	250+	Cole, Joanna; Degen, Bruce	Scholastic
Magic School Bus Butterfly and the Bog Beast, The	P	F	250+	Cole, Joanna; Degen, Bruce	Scholastic
Magic School Bus Explores the Senses, The	P	F	250+	Cole, Joanna; Degen, Bruce	Scholastic
Magic School Bus Explores the World of Animals, The	P	F	250+	Cole, Joanna; Degen, Bruce	Scholastic
Magic School Bus Food Chain Frenzy, The	Q	F	250+	Capeci, Anne	Scholastic
Magic School Bus Gets a Bright Idea, The	P	F	250+	Cole, Joanna; Degen, Bruce	Scholastic

* Collection of short stories
\# Graphic text

TITLE	LEVEL	GENRE	WORD COUNT	AUTHOR / SERIES	PUBLISHER / DISTRIBUTOR
Magic School Bus Gets All Dried Up, The	P	F	250+	Cole, Joanna; Degen, Bruce	Scholastic
Magic School Bus Gets Ants in Its Pants, The	P	F	250+	Cole, Joanna; Degen, Bruce	Scholastic
Magic School Bus Gets Baked in a Cake, The	P	F	250+	Cole, Joanna; Degen, Bruce	Scholastic
Magic School Bus Gets Cold Feet, The	P	F	250+	Cole, Joanna; Degen, Bruce	Scholastic
Magic School Bus Gets Eaten, The	P	F	250+	Cole, Joanna; Degen, Bruce	Scholastic
Magic School Bus Gets Programmed, The	P	F	250+	Cole, Joanna; Degen, Bruce	Scholastic
Magic School Bus Goes Upstream, The	P	F	250+	Cole, Joanna; Degen, Bruce	Scholastic
Magic School Bus Going Batty, The	P	F	250+	Cole, Joanna; Degen, Bruce	Scholastic
Magic School Bus Hops Home, The	P	F	250+	Cole, Joanna; Degen, Bruce	Scholastic
Magic School Bus in a Pickle, The	P	F	250+	Cole, Joanna; Degen, Bruce	Scholastic
Magic School Bus in the Arctic, The	P	F	250+	Cole, Joanna; Degen, Bruce	Scholastic
Magic School Bus in the Haunted Museum, The	P	F	250+	Cole, Joanna; Degen, Bruce	Scholastic
Magic School Bus in the Rain Forest, The	P	F	250+	Cole, Joanna; Degen, Bruce	Scholastic
Magic School Bus in the Time of the Dinosaurs, The	P	F	250+	Cole, Joanna; Degen, Bruce	Scholastic
Magic School Bus Inside a Beehive, The	P	F	250+	Cole, Joanna; Degen, Bruce	Scholastic
Magic School Bus Inside a Hurricane, The	P	F	250+	Cole, Joanna; Degen, Bruce	Scholastic
Magic School Bus Inside Ralphie, The	P	F	250+	Cole, Joanna; Degen, Bruce	Scholastic
Magic School Bus Inside the Earth, The	P	F	250+	Cole, Joanna; Degen, Bruce	Scholastic
Magic School Bus Inside the Human Body, The	P	F	250+	Cole, Joanna; Degen, Bruce	Scholastic
Magic School Bus Kicks Up a Storm, The	P	F	250+	Cole, Joanna; Degen, Bruce	Scholastic
Magic School Bus Liz Sorts It Out, The	P	F	250+	Cole, Joanna; Degen, Bruce	Scholastic
Magic School Bus Lost in the Solar System, The	P	F	250+	Cole, Joanna; Degen, Bruce	Scholastic
Magic School Bus Makes a Rainbow, The	P	F	250+	Cole, Joanna; Degen, Bruce	Scholastic
Magic School Bus Meets the Rot Squad, The	P	F	250+	Cole, Joanna; Degen, Bruce	Scholastic
Magic School Bus on the Ocean Floor, The	P	F	250+	Cole, Joanna; Degen, Bruce	Scholastic
Magic School Bus Out of This World, The	P	F	250+	Cole, Joanna; Degen, Bruce	Scholastic
Magic School Bus Plants Seeds, The	P	F	250+	Cole, Joanna; Degen, Bruce	Scholastic
Magic School Bus Plays Ball, The	P	F	250+	Cole, Joanna; Degen, Bruce	Scholastic
Magic School Bus Science Explorations, The	P	F	250+	Cole, Joanna; Degen, Bruce	Scholastic
Magic School Bus Search for the Missing Bones, The	P	F	250+	Cole, Joanna; Degen, Bruce	Scholastic
Magic School Bus Sees Stars, The	P	F	250+	Cole, Joanna; Degen, Bruce	Scholastic
Magic School Bus Shows and Tells, The	P	F	250+	Cole, Joanna; Degen, Bruce	Scholastic
Magic School Bus Space Explorers, The	P	F	250+	Cole, Joanna; Degen, Bruce	Scholastic
Magic School Bus Spins a Web, The	P	F	250+	Cole, Joanna; Degen, Bruce	Scholastic
Magic School Bus Takes a Dive, The	P	F	250+	Cole, Joanna; Degen, Bruce	Scholastic
Magic School Bus Taking Flight, The	P	F	250+	Cole, Joanna; Degen, Bruce	Scholastic
Magic School Bus the Truth About Bats, The	P	F	250+	Cole, Joanna; Degen, Bruce	Scholastic
Magic School Bus the Wild Whale Watch, The	P	F	250+	Cole, Joanna; Degen, Bruce	Scholastic
Magic School Bus Twister Trouble, The	P	F	250+	Cole, Joanna; Degen, Bruce	Scholastic
Magic School Bus Ups and Downs, The	P	F	250+	Cole, Joanna; Degen, Bruce	Scholastic
Magic School Bus Visits the Planets, The	P	F	250+	Cole, Joanna; Degen, Bruce	Scholastic
Magic School Bus Wet All Over, The	P	F	250+	Cole, Joanna; Degen, Bruce	Scholastic
Magic Shoes, The	M	RF	250+	Storyteller Summer Skies	Wright Group/McGraw Hill
Magic Shoes, The	I	F	250+	Storyworlds	Heinemann Educational Books
Magic Show, The	B	RF	29	Sails	Rigby
Magic Squad and the Dog of Great Potential, The	P	RF	250+	Quattlebaum, Mary	Bantam
Magic Squares and More	Q	I	250+	WorldScapes	ETA Cuisenaire
Magic Store, The	I	RF	203	Sunshine	Wright Group/McGraw Hill
Magic Sword, The	L	F	250+	Cambridge Reading	Pearson Learning Group

* Collection of short stories
# Graphic text

TITLE	LEVEL	GENRE	WORD COUNT	AUTHOR / SERIES	PUBLISHER / DISTRIBUTOR
Magic Tricks	P	I	250+	Games Around the World	Compass Point Books
Magic Trident, The	H	F	250+	Storyworlds	Heinemann Educational Books
Magic Wand, The	E	F	100	Start to Read	School Zone
Magic Wheel, The	P	I	250+	Voyages	SRA/McGraw Hill
Magic!	LB	RF	23	Twig	Wright Group/McGraw Hill
Magical Adventures of Pretty Pearl, The	W	F	250+	Hamilton, Virginia	HarperTrophy
Magical Mischief: Jokes that Shock and Amaze	O	F	1795	Make Me Laugh!	Lerner Publications
Magician's House, A	I	F	214	Sunshine	Wright Group/McGraw Hill
Magician's Lunch	I	F	272	Jellybeans	Rigby
Magician's Nephew, The	T	F	250+	Lewis, C. S.	HarperTrophy
Magnet Book, The	T	I	250+	Levine, Shar; Johnstone, Leslie	Sterling
Magnet Fishing Game	A	I	28	How-To Series	Benchmark Education
Magnet Time	I	I	212	Independent Readers Science	Houghton Mifflin Harcourt
Magnet, The	D	I	115	Sun Sprouts	ETA Cuisenaire
Magnetism	Q	I	1722	Early Bird Energy	Lerner Publishing
Magnetism and Electromagnets	R	I	1261	Science Support Readers	Houghton Mifflin Harcourt
Magnets	E	I	52	Discovery Links	Newbridge
Magnets	C	I	55	Early Connections	Benchmark Education
Magnets	K	I	352	Explorations	Eleanor Curtain Publishing
Magnets	K	I	352	Explorations	Okapi Eductional Materials
Magnets	F	I	77	Forces and Motion	Lerner Publications
Magnets	P	I	250+	Our Physical World	Capstone Press
Magnets	G	I	71	Phonics Readers	Compass Point Books
Magnets	K	I	250+	Rigby Star Quest	Rigby
Magnets	M	I	458	Science Support Readers	Houghton Mifflin Harcourt
Magnets	B	I	28	Seedlings	Continental Press
Magnets	F	I	79	Sunshine	Wright Group/McGraw Hill
Magnets	J	I	259	Windows on Literacy	National Geographic
Magnets in Medicine	Y	I	2083	Leveled Readers Science	Houghton Mifflin Harcourt
Magnets Quiz	N	I	549	Springboard	Wright Group/ McGraw Hill
Magnets: Pulling Together, Pushing Apart	M	I	250+	Amazing Science	Picture Window Books
Magnificent Masks	S	I	250+	Bookweb	Rigby
Magnifying Glass	C	I	32	Simple Tools	Lerner Publishing
Magnifying Glass, A	N	I	475	Sun Sprouts	ETA Cuisenaire
Magnifying Glass, The	C	I	45	Foundations	Wright Group/McGraw Hill
Magpie's Baking Day	F	F	132	PM Story Books	Rigby
Magpie's Tail, The	L	F	543	Pacific Literacy	Pacific Learning
Mahatma Gandhi	Z	I	3171	Leveled Readers	Houghton Mifflin Harcourt
Mahatma Gandhi	Z	I	3171	Leveled Readers/CA	Houghton Mifflin Harcourt
Mai Li's Surprise	F	RF	63	Books for Young Learners	Richard C. Owen
Mail Came Today, The	C	RF	35	Carousel Readers	Pearson Learning Group
Mail Carriers	M	I	250+	Community Helpers	Red Brick Learning
Mail Harry to the Moon!	J	F	250+	Harris, Robie & Emberley, Michael	Little, Brown & Co.
Mail It...From Here to There	Q	I	915	Reading Street	Pearson
Mail Myself to You	E	RF	60	Little Celebrations	Pearson Learning Group
Mailman Mario & His Boris-Busters	L	RF	250+	Parker, John	Pearson Learning Group
Main Street	F	I	87	Leveled Readers Social Studies	Houghton Mifflin Harcourt
Main Street	Q	RF	250+	Martin, Ann M.	Scholastic
Main Street Mystery, The	H	RF	196	Literacy by Design	Rigby
Maine	T	I	250+	Hello U.S.A.	Lerner Publications
Maine	S	I	250+	Land of Liberty	Red Brick Learning
Maine	R	I	250+	This Land Is Your Land	Compass Point Books

* Collection of short stories
# Graphic text

TITLE	LEVEL	GENRE	WORD COUNT	AUTHOR / SERIES	PUBLISHER / DISTRIBUTOR
Maine Coon Cats	I	I	112	Cats	Capstone Press
Mai's Big Surprise	J	RF	250+	The Wright Skills	Wright Group/McGraw Hill
Maisie's Race	L	RF	250+	Take Two Books	Wright Group/McGraw Hill
Major Jump	B	F	21	Sunshine	Wright Group/McGraw Hill
Makah, The: Whaling Tribe of the Northwest	S	I	250+	Explore More	Wright Group/McGraw Hill
Make A Bird Feeder	D	I	62	How-To Series	Benchmark Education
Make a Boat That Floats	I	I	126	Book Bank	Wright Group/McGraw Hill
Make a Bottle Garden	L	I	250+	Lighthouse	Rigby
Make a Bottle Orchestra	J	I	250	Sunshine	Wright Group/McGraw Hill
Make a Cloud, Measure the Wind	M	I	250+	Take Two Books	Wright Group/McGraw Hill
Make a Dinosaur	H	I	208	Sun Sprouts	ETA Cuisenaire
Make a Drum	C	I	29	Early Connections	Benchmark Education
Make a Fruit Salad	D	I	102	Springboard	Wright Group/McGraw Hill
Make a Funny Face	C	I	41	InfoTrek	ETA Cuisenaire
Make a Glider	G	I	57	Storyteller-Setting Sun	Wright Group/McGraw Hill
Make a Guitar	J	I	540	Sunshine	Wright Group/McGraw Hill
Make a House	F	I	41	iOpeners	Pearson Learning Group
Make a Kite	F	I	49	Story Steps	Rigby
Make a Kite	A	I	20	Vocabulary Readers	Houghton Mifflin Harcourt
Make a Kite	A	I	20	Vocabulary Readers/CA	Houghton Mifflin Harcourt
Make a Lei	F	I	39	Pacific Literacy	Pacific Learning
Make a Marionette	K	I	349	How-To Series	Benchmark Education
Make a Monster	E	I	31	Windows on Literacy	National Geographic
Make a Music Shaker	E	RF	113	InfoTrek	ETA Cuisenaire
Make a Necklace	E	I	106	How-To Series	Benchmark Education
Make a Paper Airplane	J	I	158	How-To Series	Benchmark Education
Make a Pinata	C	I	16	Little Celebrations	Pearson Learning Group
Make a Pinata	I	I	152	Windows on Literacy	National Geographic
Make a Plan of Your Classroom	E	I	94	How-To Series	Benchmark Education
Make a Raft	F	I	186	Take Two Books	Wright Group/McGraw Hill
Make a Rainbow Fish	G	I	139	Sun Sprouts	ETA Cuisenaire
Make a Safety Puppet	E	I	107	How-To Series	Benchmark Education
Make a Salad Face	F	I	82	Voyages	SRA/McGraw Hill
Make a Shake and a Bakeless Cake	L	I	250+	Take Two Books	Wright Group/McGraw Hill
Make a Sundial	K	I	250+	How-To Series	Benchmark Education
Make a "Talking" Card	H	I	165	Sunshine	Wright Group/McGraw Hill
Make a Tune	J	I	246	Kratky, Lada	Hampton-Brown
Make a Turkey	C	I	14	Bebop Books	Lee & Low Books Inc.
Make a Valentine	D	RF	33	Bookshop	Mondo
Make a wish, Molly	O	RF	250+	Cohen, Barbara	Bantam
Make a Worm Farm	E	I	98	Sun Sprouts	ETA Cuisenaire
Make an Animal Mobile	H	I	116	How-to Series	Benchmark Education
Make an Island	J	I	199	How-To Series	Benchmark Education
Make Dinosaur Eggs	I	I	188	Sunshine	Wright Group/McGraw Hill
Make It Go	S	I	250+	PM Extensions	Rigby
Make It Move!	E	I	29	Canizares, Susan; Chessen, Betsey	Scholastic
Make It Move!	N	I	215	Yellow Umbrella Books	Capstone Press
Make It Spin	D	I	18	Pacific Literacy	Pacific Learning
Make It!	A	RF	21	Phonics and Friends	Hampton-Brown
Make It! Ship It!	K	I	250+	Spyglass Books	Compass Point Books
Make It, Wear It	P	I	250+	iOpeners	Pearson Learning Group
Make Lemonade	Z	RF	250+	Wolff, Virginia Euwer	Scholastic
Make Like a Tree and Leave	U	RF	250+	Danziger, Paula	PaperStar

TITLE	LEVEL	GENRE	WORD COUNT	AUTHOR / SERIES	PUBLISHER / DISTRIBUTOR
Make Masks for a Play	J	I	540	Sunshine	Wright Group/McGraw Hill
Make Mini Movies	I	I	309	Sunshine	Wright Group/McGraw Hill
Make My Name	E	F	63	Reading Safari	Mondo
Make Prints and Patterns	K	I	454	Sunshine	Wright Group/McGraw Hill
*Make Room For Elisa	N	RF	250+	Hurwitz, Johanna	Penguin Group
Make Sense!	F	RF	115	Silly Millies	Millbrook Press
Make Things That Move	O	I	250+	Sunshine	Wright Group/McGraw Hill
Make Way for Ducklings	L	RF	250+	McCloskey, Robert	Puffin/Penguin
Make Way for Sam Houston	X	B	250+	Fritz, Jean	Putnam/Penguin
Make Way for Tooth Decay	K	F	250+	Katz, Bobbi	Scholastic
Make Your Own Crystals	N	I	395	In Step Readers	Rigby
Make Your Own Monster	I	I	239	Rigby Star Quest	Rigby
Make Your Own Party	I	I	314	Sunshine	Wright Group/McGraw Hill
Make Your Own Terrarium	P	I	1380	Leveled Readers Science	Houghton Mifflin Harcourt
Maker of Machines: A Story about Eli Whitney	S	B	8690	Creative Minds Biographies	Lerner Publications
Maker of Things	O	B	250+	Meet The Author	Richard C. Owen
Making a Bird	B	I	32	PM Plus Nonfiction	Rigby
Making a Book	L	I	401	Rigby Flying Colors	Rigby
Making a Bug Habitat	K	I	250+	How-To Series	Benchmark Education
Making a Butterfly	C	I	71	PM Math Readers	Rigby
Making a Cake	G	I	125	Little Red Readers	Sundance
Making a Castle	H	I	184	PM Math Readers	Rigby
Making a Cat and a Mouse	D	I	121	PM Plus Nonfiction	Rigby
Making a Caterpillar	E	I	115	PM Plus Nonfiction	Rigby
Making a Clock Cake	J	RF	389	PM Math Readers	Rigby
Making a Difference	N	RF	1648	Gear Up!	Wright Group/McGraw Hill
Making a Difference	V	B	250+	Literacy By Design	Rigby
Making a Difference in the World	O	B	250+	Meet the Author	Richard C. Owen
Making a Dinosaur	B	I	32	PM Plus Nonfiction	Rigby
Making a Friend	B	F	30	Bonnell, Kris	Reading Reading Books
Making a Garden	A	RF	28	Foundations	Wright Group/McGraw Hill
Making a Hat	C	I	24	Windows on Literacy	National Geographic
Making a Home	D	I	102	Leveled Readers	Houghton Mifflin Harcourt
Making a Home	D	I	102	Leveled Readers/CA	Houghton Mifflin Harcourt
Making a Home	D	I	102	Leveled Readers/TX	Houghton Mifflin Harcourt
Making a House	C	I	89	Early Connections	Benchmark Education
Making a Magazine	O	I	496	Vocabulary Readers	Houghton Mifflin Harcourt
Making a Magnet	I	I	185	Sun Sprouts	ETA Cuisenaire
Making a Map	L	I	293	Rigby Focus	Rigby
Making a Memory	D	I	53	Ballinger, Margaret	Scholastic
Making a Mud Pie	C	RF	105	Leveled Readers	Houghton Mifflin Harcourt
Making a Mud Pie	C	RF	105	Leveled Readers/CA	Houghton Mifflin Harcourt
Making a Mural	H	I	128	Vocabulary Readers	Houghton Mifflin Harcourt
Making a Newspaper	M	I	317	Leveled Readers	Houghton Mifflin Harcourt
Making a Newspaper	M	I	317	Leveled Readers/CA	Houghton Mifflin Harcourt
Making a Newspaper	M	I	317	Leveled Readers/TX	Houghton Mifflin Harcourt
Making a Park	F	I	168	On Our Way to English	Rigby
Making a Pizza	A	I	32	Leveled Literacy Intervention/ Orange System	Heinemann
Making a Plate	H	I	183	Ready Readers	Pearson Learning Group
Making a Rabbit	B	I	32	PM Plus Nonfiction	Rigby
Making a Snowman	A	I	32	Leveled Literacy Intervention/ Orange System	Heinemann
Making a Terrarium	L	I	250+	How-To Series	Benchmark Education

* Collection of short stories
# Graphic text

TITLE	LEVEL	GENRE	WORD COUNT	AUTHOR / SERIES	PUBLISHER / DISTRIBUTOR
Making a Toy House	G	I	132	PM Plus Nonfiction	Rigby
Making a Tree House	A	F	27	Leveled Readers	Houghton Mifflin Harcourt
Making a Tree House	A	F	27	Leveled Readers/CA	Houghton Mifflin Harcourt
Making a TV Documentary	P	I	250+	Wonder World	Wright Group/McGraw Hill
Making a Weather Station	M	I	250+	How-To Series	Benchmark Education
Making Art	J	I	250+	Rosen Real Readers	Rosen Publishing Group
Making Books for Fun!	S	I	250+	For Fun! Crafts	Compass Point Books
Making Breakfast	E	I	129	Rigby Flying Colors	Rigby
Making Breakfast	F	I	59	Windows on Literacy	National Geographic
Making Butter	H	I	187	Literacy by Design	Rigby
Making Caterpillars and Butterflies	I	I	162	Literacy 2000	Rigby
Making Clay	O	I	792	Leveled Readers Science	Houghton Mifflin Harcourt
Making Collages	J	I	250+	Bookshop	Mondo
Making Concrete	I	I	136	Alphakids	Sundance
Making Crafts From Around the World	O	I	250+	Navigators How-To Series	Benchmark Education
Making Flavors and Fragrances	S	I	2032	Leveled Readers Science	Houghton Mifflin Harcourt
Making Friends	J	RF	214	Foundations	Wright Group/McGraw Hill
Making Friends in Mali	T	RF	5116	Reading Street	Pearson
Making Friends on Beacon Street	M	RF	250+	Literacy 2000	Rigby
Making Gingerbread Men	M	I	806	Springboard	Wright Group/McGraw Hill
Making Granny Grasshead	K	I	362	Sun Sprouts	ETA Cuisenaire
Making Great Greeting Cards & Gifts	Q	I	250+	Navigators How-To Series	Benchmark Education Company
Making Holes	E	I	134	Sails	Rigby
Making Ice Cream	J	I	176	How-To Series	Benchmark Education
Making Ice Cream	H	I	162	Sun Sprouts	ETA Cuisenaire
Making It Go: The Life and Work of Robert Fulton	T	B	250+	Science Readers	Teacher Created Materials
Making It Go?	F	I	106	Independent Readers Science	Houghton Mifflin Harcourt
Making Lily Laugh!	M	RF	250+	Dreyer, Ellen	Pearson Learning Group
Making Lunch	D	I	70	Rigby Flying Colors	Rigby
Making Maple Syrup	F	I	91	Nonfiction Set 5	Literacy Footprints
Making Maps	T	I	250+	Navigators Science Series	Benchmark Education Company
Making Money	H	I	129	Rosen Real Readers	Rosen Publishing Group
Making Money	I	I	234	Yellow Umbrella Books	Red Brick Learning
Making Mount Rushmore	M	I	250+	Twig	Wright Group/McGraw Hill
Making Mountains	B	I	35	Gosset, Rachel; Ballinger, Margaret	Scholastic
Making Movies	T	I	1297	Leveled Readers	Houghton Mifflin Harcourt
Making Movies	T	I	1297	Leveled Readers/CA	Houghton Mifflin Harcourt
Making Movies	T	I	1297	Leveled Readers/TX	Houghton Mifflin Harcourt
Making Movies	LB	I	43	Sunshine	Wright Group/McGraw Hill
Making Moving Models	T	I	250+	High-Fliers	Pacific Learning
Making Murals	K	I	423	Leveled Readers	Houghton Mifflin Harcourt
Making Murals	K	I	423	Leveled Readers/CA	Houghton Mifflin Harcourt
Making Murals	K	I	423	Leveled Readers/TX	Houghton Mifflin Harcourt
Making Music	H	RF	71	Early Readers	Compass Point Books
Making Music	L	I	356	Rigby Flying Colors	Rigby
Making Music	K	I	174	Windows on Literacy	National Geographic
Making Music	C	I	35	Wonder World	Wright Group/McGraw Hill
Making Myths	T	I	250+	The News	Richard C. Owen
Making Oatmeal	E	I	38	Interaction	Rigby
Making Pancakes	D	RF	39	Carousel Readers	Pearson Learning Group

TITLE	LEVEL	GENRE	WORD COUNT	AUTHOR / SERIES	PUBLISHER / DISTRIBUTOR
Making Paper	H	I	128	Rigby Focus	Rigby
Making Party Food	I	I	221	PM Plus Nonfiction	Rigby
Making Party Hats	F	I	168	PM Math Readers	Rigby
Making Patterns	L	I	250+	Early Connections	Benchmark Education
Making Patterns	C	I	30	Twig	Wright Group/McGraw Hill
Making Pictures	B	RF	48	Foundations	Wright Group/McGraw Hill
Making Pictures	C	I	48	Gear Up!	Wright Group/McGraw Hill
Making Pictures	G	I	132	Vocabulary Readers	Houghton Mifflin Harcourt
Making Pizza	C	I	60	Nonfiction	Literacy Footprints
Making Pizza with Math	J	I	250+	On Our Way to English	Rigby
Making Pop-ups	N	I	250+	Bookshop	Mondo
Making Pop-ups	O	I	250+	Brian, Janeen	Mondo
Making Puppets	C	I	86	Vocabulary Readers	Houghton Mifflin Harcourt
Making Puppets	C	I	86	Vocabulary Readers/CA	Houghton Mifflin Harcourt
Making Raisins	E	I	35	Windows on Literacy	National Geographic
Making Roads	I	I	176	Sails	Rigby
Making Sense of Dollars and Cents	M	I	393	Reading Street	Pearson
Making Sense of Your Senses	P	I	250+	Navigators Science Series	Benchmark Education
Making Shapes	H	I	206	Early Connections	Benchmark Education
Making Shapes	S	I	250+	PM Plus Nonfiction	Rigby
Making Shapes	K	I	250+	Yellow Umbrella Books	Capstone Press
Making Snack Mix	G	I	188	In Step Readers	Rigby
Making Sound	N	I	422	Science Support Readers	Houghton Mifflin Harcourt
Making Soup	B	I	53	Leveled Literacy Intervention/ Orange System	Heinemann
Making Soup	C	RF	77	Leveled Readers Emergent	Houghton Mifflin Harcourt
Making the World a Better Place	K	I	544	Reading Street	Pearson
Making the World a Better Place: The Stories of Social Reformers	T	B	250+	Rigby Literacy	Rigby
Making Things	D	RF	64	Foundations	Wright Group/McGraw Hill
Making Tortillas	H	I	104	Windows on Literacy	National Geographic
Making Work Easy	M	I	250+	Explorations	Okapi Educational Materials
Making Work Easy	M	I	250+	Explorations	Eleanor Curtain Publishing
Making Yogurt	N	I	250+	Pacific Literacy	Pacific Learning
Mako Shark	J	I	123	Sharks	Capstone Press
Malawi: Keeper of the Trees	D	I	250+	Little Celebrations	Pearson Learning Group
Malcolm Magpie	F	I	126	Storyteller-Setting Sun	Wright Group/McGraw Hill
Malcolm X: By Any Means Necessary	Z	B	250+	Myers, Walter Dean	Scholastic
Malcolm X: Force for Change	S	B	250+	Great African Americans	Capstone Press
Malinali: The Slave Who Traded Words for Freedom	T	B	250+	Bookshop	Mondo
Malka	Z	HF	250+	Pressler, Mirjam	Philomel/Penguin
Mall Mystery, The	M	F	250+	Woodland Mysteries	Wright Group/McGraw Hill
Mallard Ducks	K	I	346	Pull Ahead Books	Lerner Publications
Mallards	H	I	105	Wetland Animals	Capstone Press
Mallory on the Move	O	RF	250+	Friedman, Laurie	Lerner Publications
Mallory vs. Max	O	RF	250+	Friedman, Laurie	Lerner Publications
Malted Falcon, The: A Chet Gecko Mystery	R	F	250+	Hale, Bruce	Harcourt, Inc.
Maltese Falcon, The	Z+	RF	250+	Hammett, Dashiell	Random House
Mama and Kit Go Away	D	F	84	Leveled Readers	Houghton Mifflin Harcourt
Mama Cut My Hair	H	RF	134	Books for Young Learners	Richard C. Owen
Mama Goes to School	D	RF	47	Visions	Wright Group/McGraw Hill
Mama Hen, Come Quick	C	F	35	Ready Readers	Pearson Learning Group
Mama Zooms	I	F	174	Cowen-Fletcher, J.	Scholastic

* Collection of short stories
\# Graphic text

TITLE	LEVEL	GENRE	WORD COUNT	AUTHOR / SERIES	PUBLISHER / DISTRIBUTOR
Mama, Let's Dance	W	RF	250+	Hermes, Patricia	Scholastic
Mama's Llamas	J	F	159	Books for Young Learners	Richard C. Owen
Mamba and the Crocodile Bird	I	F	250+	Storyworlds	Heinemann Educational Books
Mammal	W	I	250+	Eyewitness Books	DK Publishing
Mammals	M	I	134	Exploring the Animal Kingdom	Capstone Press
Mammals	N	I	250+	Simply Science	Compass Point Books
Mammals	P	I	950	Time for Kids	Teacher Created Materials
Mammals	H	I	134	Yellow Umbrella Books	Red Brick Learning
Mammals Around the World	N	I	979	Rigby Flying Colors	Rigby
Mammals of the Sea	Q	I	250+	Explorers	Wright Group/McGraw Hill
Mammoth	T	I	250+	Sails	Rigby
Mammoth Hunters, The	Q	F	250+	Bookweb	Rigby
Mammoth Mammals	Q	I	250+	Explorer Books-Pathfinder	National Geographic
Mammoth Mammals	P	I	250+	Explorer Books-Pioneer	National Geographic
Mammoth Mistake, A	K	RF	250+	Rigby Literacy	Rigby
Mammoth Mistake, A	K	RF	250+	Rigby Star Plus	Rigby
Mammoths: Ice-Age Giants	Z	I	250+	Agenbroad, Dr. Larry D.; Nelson, Lisa	Lerner Publishing
Man from Mars, The	K	SF	250+	Popcorn	Sundance
Man from the Sky	S	RF	250+	Avi	Beech Tree Books
Man in the Iron Mask, The	V	HF	250+	WorldScapes	ETA Cuisenaire
Man in the Moon and Other Moon Tales, The	N	RF	322	Independent Readers Science	Houghton Mifflin Harcourt
Man in the Moon, The	H	I	173	Pair-It Books	Steck-Vaughn
Man in the Moon, The	L	F	928	Pair-It Turn and Learn	Steck-Vaughn
Man in the Moon, The	I	F	248	Storyteller	Wright Group/McGraw Hill
Man Out at First	M	RF	250+	Christopher, Matt	Little, Brown & Co.
Man Who Digs Dinosaurs, The	Q	I	1278	Leveled Readers	Houghton Mifflin Harcourt
Man Who Digs Dinosaurs, The	Q	I	1278	Leveled Readers/CA	Houghton Mifflin Harcourt
Man Who Digs Dinosaurs, The	Q	I	1278	Leveled Readers/TX	Houghton Mifflin Harcourt
Man Who Enjoyed Grumbling, The	L	F	250+	Sunshine	Wright Group/McGraw Hill
Man Who Kept His Heart in a Bucket, The	S	TL	250+	Levitin, Sonia	Penguin Group
Man Who Made Puppets, The	E	I	106	Leveled Readers	Houghton Mifflin Harcourt
Man Who Made Puppets, The	E	I	106	Leveled Readers/CA	Houghton Mifflin Harcourt
Man Who Made Puppets, The	E	I	106	Leveled Readers/TX	Houghton Mifflin Harcourt
Man Who Measured the World, The	V	HF	250+	PM Extensions	Rigby
Man Who Paints Nature, The	O	B	250+	Meet The Author	Richard C. Owen
Man Who Rode the Tiger, The	L	TL	250+	PM Story Books	Rigby
Man Who Tricked a Ghost, The	N	TL	250+	Yep, Laurence	Troll Associates
Man Who Was Poe, The	Y	HF	250+	Avi	Avon
Man, the Boy, and the Donkey, The	I	TL	234	Story Box	Wright Group/McGraw Hill
Manatee Mom	F	F	172	Silly Millies	Millbrook Press
Manatee Winter	K	RF	250+	Zoehfeld, Kathleen Weidnetz	Scholastic
Manatee, The	V	I	250+	Silverstein, A.; Nunn, L.	Millbrook Press
Manatees	O	I	1589	Early Bird Nature Books	Lerner Publications
Manatees	G	I	73	Pebble Books	Red Brick Learning
Manatees	H	I	124	Under the Sea	Capstone Press
Manatees	N	I	250+	World of Mammals	Capstone Press
Manatees and Dugongs	M	I	250+	Take Two Books	Wright Group/McGraw Hill
Manet	Z	B	250+	Eyewitness Books	DK Publishing
Manga Touch	V	RF	250+	Orca Currents	Orca Book Publishers
Mango Tree, The	H	RF	272	Storyworlds	Heinemann Educational Books
Mango Tree, The	E	F	163	Sun Sprouts	ETA Cuisenaire

* Collection of short stories
# Graphic text

TITLE	LEVEL	GENRE	WORD COUNT	AUTHOR / SERIES	PUBLISHER / DISTRIBUTOR
Mango's Revenge	R	F	250+	Bookshop	Mondo
Mangrove Swamp	R	I	1136	Vocabulary Readers	Houghton Mifflin Harcourt
Mangrove Swamp	R	I	1136	Vocabulary Readers/CA	Houghton Mifflin Harcourt
Mangrove Swamp	R	I	1136	Vocabulary Readers/TX	Houghton Mifflin Harcourt
Manhattan Project, The: The Race to the Atomic Bomb	Y	I	2925	Leveled Readers Science	Houghton Mifflin Harcourt
Maniac Magee	W	RF	250+	Spinelli, Jerry	Scholastic
Manly Ferry Pigeon, The	K	RF	250+	Sunshine	Wright Group/McGraw Hill
Manners at a Friend's Home	L	I	250+	Manners	Capstone Press
Manners at a Restaurant	L	I	250+	Manners	Capstone Press
Manners at the Library	L	I	250+	Manners	Capstone Press
Manners in the Classroom	L	I	250+	Manners	Capstone Press
Manners of a Pig, The	I	F	250+	Bookshop	Mondo
Manners on the Playground	L	I	250+	Manners	Capstone Press
Manners on the Telephone	L	I	250+	Manners	Capstone Press
Manners Please	C	RF	27	Pair-It Books	Steck-Vaughn
Mannings, The: Football's Famous Family	R	B	250+	High Five Reading	Capstone Press
Manny's Story	L	RF	869	Leveled Readers	Houghton Mifflin Harcourt
Manny's Story	L	RF	869	Leveled Readers/CA	Houghton Mifflin Harcourt
Manny's Story	L	RF	869	Leveled Readers/TX	Houghton Mifflin Harcourt
Mansa Musa: Leader of Mali	X	B	250+	Primary Source Readers	Teacher Created Materials
Mansion in the Mist, The	S	F	250+	Bellairs, John	Puffin/Penguin
Mantu the Elephant	K	F	250+	Rigby Literacy	Rigby
Manual of House Monsters, A	O	F	250+	Marijanovic, Stanislav	Mondo
Manx Cats	I	I	133	Cats	Capstone Press
Many Friends, Many Languages	D	I	98	Fiesta Series	Pearson Learning Group
Many Happy Returns: A Review of Recycling	R	I	250+	Literacy 2000	Rigby
Many Homes	B	I	48	Literacy by Design	Rigby
Many Kinds of Bats	J	I	292	Leveled Readers	Houghton Mifflin Harcourt
Many Kinds of Bats	J	I	292	Leveled Readers/CA	Houghton Mifflin Harcourt
Many Kinds of Bats	J	I	292	Leveled Readers/TX	Houghton Mifflin Harcourt
Many Kinds of Birds	I	I	290	Leveled Readers	Houghton Mifflin Harcourt
Many Plants, Many Places	P	I	1077	Reading Street	Pearson
Many Thousand Gone: African Americans From Slavery to Freedom	X	TL	250+	Hamilton, Virginia	Alfred A. Knopf
Many Waters	V	F	250+	L'Engle, Madeleine	Bantam
Many Ways to 100	I	I	250+	Yellow Umbrella Books	Red Brick Learning
Many Ways to be a Soldier	O	HF	1486	On My Own History	Millbrook Press
Many Ways to Work	J	I	250+	Literacy by Design	Rigby
Many Ways: How Families Practice Their Beliefs and Religions	N	I	156	Shelley Rotner's Early Childhood	Millbrook Press
Maori of New Zealand, The	U	I	1168	Vocabulary Readers	Houghton Mifflin Harcourt
Maori of New Zealand, The	U	I	1168	Vocabulary Readers/CA	Houghton Mifflin Harcourt
Mao's Last Dancer	Y	B	250+	Cunxin, Li	Walker & Co.
Map and the Treasure, The	L	F	292	Leveled Readers	Houghton Mifflin Harcourt
Map and the Treasure, The	L	F	292	Leveled Readers/CA	Houghton Mifflin Harcourt
Map and the Treasure, The	L	F	292	Leveled Readers/TX	Houghton Mifflin Harcourt
Map Book, The	F	I	144	Sunshine	Wright Group/McGraw Hill
Map Mania	S	I	250+	DiSpezio, Michael A.	Sterling Publishing
Map Mysteries	M	I	250+	Home Connection Collection	Rigby
Map of Our School, A	E	I	142	Dominie Factivity Series	Pearson Learning Group
Map Search	F	I	164	Shutterbug Books	Steck-Vaughn
Map to Fun, A	G	RF	182	InfoTrek	ETA Cuisenaire
Maple Thanksgiving, The	L	F	250+	Little Celebrations	Pearson Learning Group

* Collection of short stories
\# Graphic text

TITLE	LEVEL	GENRE	WORD COUNT	AUTHOR / SERIES	PUBLISHER / DISTRIBUTOR
Maple Tree	O	I	250+	Life Cycles	Creative Teaching Press
Maple Tree, The	R	I	1573	Reading Street	Pearson
Maple Trees	F	I	118	Pebble Books	Capstone Press
Mapping North America	M	I	148	Windows on Literacy	National Geographic
Mapping Our World	K	I	250+	Spyglass Books	Compass Point Books
Mapping the World	Q	I	250+	InfoQuest	Rigby
Mapping the World	O	I	250+	Orbit Chapter Books	Pacific Learning
Maps	G	I	142	Early Connections	Benchmark Education
Maps	C	I	11	Geography	Lerner Publishing
Maps	R	I	250+	Haslam, Andrew	World Book
Maps	G	I	99	Learn to Read	Creative Teaching Press
Maps	K	I	150	Phonics Readers	Compass Point Books
Maps	Q	I	250+	Rigby Focus	Rigby
Maps	K	I	237	Take Two Books	Wright Group/McGraw Hill
Maps & Globes	O	I	250+	Knowlton, Jack	Harper Collins
Maps and Codes	P	I	250+	Wildcats	Wright Group/McGraw Hill
Maps and Mapping	P	I	250+	Science Kids	Kingfisher
Maps and Mapping	R	I	250+	Young Discoverers	Kingfisher
Maps and Our World	Q	I	250+	Explorers	Wright Group/McGraw Hill
Maps Are Cool: How to Read Them, Plan Them, and Create Them	U	I	250+	Bookshop	Mondo
Maps Show Us the Way	H	I	94	Rosen Real Readers	Rosen Publishing Group
Maps, Maps, Maps	E	I	47	Rosen Real Readers	Rosen Publishing Group
Maps: Getting From Here to There	V	I	250+	Weiss, Harvey	Houghton Mifflin Harcourt
Mara's Clouds	J	F	414	Springboard	Wright Group/McGraw Hill
Marathon	M	I	551	Big Cat	Pacific Learning
Marathon, The	P	RF	250+	Literacy by Design	Rigby
Marble Game, The	F	RF	250+	Reading Safari	Mondo
Marble Patch, The	J	RF	250+	PM Story Books	Rigby
Marbles	P	I	250+	Games Around the World	Compass Point Books
Marcella	L	RF	250+	Literacy 2000	Rigby
March Along with Me	D	F	56	Literacy 2000	Rigby
March for Freedom	J	I	132	Twig	Wright Group/McGraw Hill
March on Washington, The	P	I	304	Vocabulary Readers	Houghton Mifflin Harcourt
March to the Park	K	F	444	Leveled Literacy Intervention/ Blue System	Heinemann
March, March, Marching	D	RF	60	Teacher's Choice Series	Pearson Learning Group
Marching Band	LB	RF	35	Urmston, Kathleen; Evans, Karen	Kaeden Books
Marching Bands	L	I	166	Vocabulary Readers	Houghton Mifflin Harcourt
Marching Bands	L	I	166	Vocabulary Readers/CA	Houghton Mifflin Harcourt
Marching to Freedom: The Story of Martin Luther King, Jr.	P	B	250+	Milton, Joyce	Bantam
Marcie's Birthday Dig	Q	RF	250+	Leveled Readers Language Support	Houghton Mifflin Harcourt
Marco Polo: Marco Polo and the Silk Road to China	U	B	250+	Exploring the World	Compass Point Books
Marco Saves Grandpa	I	RF	232	Foundations	Wright Group/McGraw Hill
Marco's Run	G	RF	199	Green Light Readers	Harcourt
Mardi Gras	H	I	84	Vocabulary Readers	Houghton Mifflin Harcourt
Mare for Young Wolf, A	L	HF	250+	Shefelman, Janice	Random House
Margaret Bourke-White	O	B	250+	Welch, Catherine	Carolrhoda Books
Margaret Bourke-White: A Photographer's Life	P	B	250+	Keller, Emily	Lerner Publishing
Margaret Bourke-White: Life Through the Lens	X	B	3041	Leveled Readers	Houghton Mifflin Harcourt

* Collection of short stories
# Graphic text

TITLE	LEVEL	GENRE	WORD COUNT	AUTHOR / SERIES	PUBLISHER / DISTRIBUTOR
Margaret E. Mooney: Essentially M	R	B	250+	Author at Work	Richard C. Owen
Margaret Mahy	L	B	250+	Sunshine	Wright Group/McGraw Hill
Margaret Wise Brown	O	B	250+	Greene, Carol	Children's Press
Margarito's Carvings	L	I	250+	Little Celebrations	Pearson Learning Group
Margret and Hans Rey	J	I	237	Leveled Readers	Houghton Mifflin Harcourt
Margret and Hans Rey	J	I	237	Leveled Readers/CA	Houghton Mifflin Harcourt
Margret and Hans Rey	J	I	237	Leveled Readers/TX	Houghton Mifflin Harcourt
Maria	I	RF	72	City Kids	Rigby
Maria Goes to School	E	RF	174	Foundations	Wright Group/McGraw Hill
Maria Mitchell	O	B	291	Independent Readers Science	Houghton Mifflin Harcourt
Maria Sanz de Sautuola	S	B	250+	Bookshop	Mondo
Maria Sharapova	P	B	250+	Amazing Athletes	Lerner Publications
Maria Tallchief	E	B	48	Independent Readers Social Studies	Houghton Mifflin Harcourt
Maria Tallchief	R	B	250+	Native American Stories	Steck-Vaughn
Maria Tallchief, American Ballerina	P	B	1355	Leveled Readers/CA	Houghton Mifflin Harcourt
Maria Tallchief, American Ballerina	P	B	1355	Leveled Readers/TX	Houghton Mifflin Harcourt
Maria Tallchief, American Ballerina	P	B	1355	Leveled Readers	Houghton Mifflin Harcourt
Maria: A Christmas Story	R	RF	250+	Taylor, Theodore	Avon Camelot
Mariachi Band, The	A	I	32	In Step Readers	Rigby
Mariachi Kid, The	O	B	250+	WorldScapes	ETA Cuisenaire
Marian Anderson	N	B	246	First Biographies	Capstone Press
Marian Anderson	R	B	4112	History Maker Bios	Lerner Publications
Marian Anderson, American Hero	M	B	645	Leveled Readers Social Studies	Houghton Mifflin Harcourt
Marian Anderson: Singer	V	B	250+	American Women of Achievement	Chelsea House
Marian Wright Edelman: For Every Child	S	B	2406	Leveled Readers	Houghton Mifflin Harcourt
Maria's Diary	R	RF	250+	Wonder World	Wright Group/McGraw Hill
Maria's Dream	U	SF	250+	Reading Safari	Mondo
Maria's House	F	RF	138	Seedlings	Continental Press
Maria's Nonna	I	RF	467	Rigby Flying Colors	Rigby
Marie Antoinette Queen of France	T	B	250+	Queens and Princesses	Capstone Press
Marie Curie	P	B	250+	Early Biographies	Compass Point Books
Marie Curie	R	B	250+	Getting to Know the World's Greatest Inventors and Scientists	Children's Press
Marie Curie	R	B	3486	History Maker Bios	Lerner Publications
Marie Curie	S	B	1924	Independent Readers Science	Houghton Mifflin Harcourt
Marie Curie	N	B	182	Pebble Books	Capstone Press
Marie Curie: Mother of Modern Physics	Y	B	250+	Sterling Biographies	Sterling Publishing
Marie Curie: Pioneering Physicist	V	B	250+	Science Readers	Teacher Created Materials
Marie Mitchell	O	B	250+	Independent Readers Science	Houghton Mifflin Harcourt
Marie: Summer in the Country	Q	HF	250+	Girlhood Journeys	Aladdin
Mariel of Redwall	Z	F	250+	Jacques, Brian	Avon
Mariela's Camping Adventure	I	RF	338	In Step Readers	Rigby
Marie-Maud Becomes a Citizen	L	RF	563	Leveled Readers Social Studies	Houghton Mifflin Harcourt
Marigold and Grandma on the Town	J	F	250+	Calmenson, Stephanie	HarperTrophy
Marigold and the Feather of Hope, the Journey Begins: The Fairy Chronicles	Q	F	13340	Sweet, J.H.	Sourcebooks
Marigolds for Dona Remedios	M	RF	250+	Story Vines	Wright Group/McGraw Hill
Marina Silva: Conserving the Rain Forest	N	B	812	Leveled Readers Science	Houghton Mifflin Harcourt
Marine Life	S	I	2605	Reading Street	Pearson
Mario Mixwell	M	B	250+	Take Two Books	Wright Group/McGraw Hill
Mario Molina: Above the Clouds	X	B	2464	Leveled Readers Science	Houghton Mifflin Harcourt
Marion Jones: Quest for Gold	R	B	1337	Leveled Readers	Houghton Mifflin Harcourt

* Collection of short stories
\# Graphic text

TITLE	LEVEL	GENRE	WORD COUNT	AUTHOR / SERIES	PUBLISHER / DISTRIBUTOR
Mario's Mayan Journey	P	F	250+	Bookshop	Mondo
Marisol's Mystery	H	RF	245	Literacy by Design	Rigby
Marjorie Harris Carr	O	B	546	Leveled Readers Science	Houghton Mifflin Harcourt
Marjory Stoneman Douglas	N	B	294	Independent Readers Social Studies	Houghton Mifflin Harcourt
Mark McGuire, Home Run King	P	B	250+	Leveled Readers Language Support	Houghton Mifflin Harcourt
Mark McGwire	R	B	250+	Sports Heroes	Red Brick Learning
Mark McGwire: Home Run Hero	Q	B	960	Leveled Readers	Houghton Mifflin Harcourt
Mark Twain	W	B	250+	Cox, Clinton	Scholastic
Mark T-W-A-I-N: A Story About Samuel Clemens	R	B	8718	Creative Minds Biographies	Carolrhoda Books
Mark Twain: Young Writer	O	B	250+	Childhood of Famous Americans	Aladdin
Market Day for Mrs. Wordy	J	RF	177	Sunshine	Wright Group/McGraw Hill
Market, The	D	RF	48	Joy Readers	Pearson Learning Group
Market, The	A	I	15	Leveled Readers	Houghton Mifflin Harcourt
Market, The	A	I	15	Leveled Readers/CA	Houghton Mifflin Harcourt
Market, The	B	F	30	Sails	Rigby
Marketplace, The	E	RF	58	Visions	Wright Group/McGraw Hill
Markets	D	I	44	Chanko, Pamela; Berger, Samantha	Scholastic
Markets Around the World	O	I	871	Time for Kids	Teacher Created Materials Publishing
Markie the Moonman	T	SF	2759	Reading Street	Pearson
Marks in the Sand	F	I	121	Windows on Literacy	National Geographic
Mark's Monster	I	F	250+	Reading Unlimited	Pearson Learning Group
Marla's Idea	J	RF	443	Reading Street	Pearson
Marlfox: A Novel of Redwall	Z	F	250+	Jacques, Brian	Ace Books
Marmalade's Nap	F	F	57	Wheeler, Cindy	Alfred A. Knopf
Marmalade's Snowy Day	F	F	61	Wheeler, Cindy	Alfred A. Knopf
Marrying Malcolm Murgatroyd	T	RF	250+	Farrell, Mame	Sunburst
Mars	J	I	139	Exploring the Galaxy	Capstone Press
Mars	S	I	250+	Our Solar System	Compass Point Books
Mars	N	I	829	Our Universe	Lerner Publications
Mars	L	I	220	Rigby Focus	Rigby
Mars	Q	I	250+	The Galaxy	Capstone Press
Mars	R	I	250+	Theme Sets	National Geographic
Mars	W	I	250+	World Mythology	Capstone Press
Mars on Earth	W	I	2610	Leveled Readers	Houghton Mifflin Harcourt
Mars on Earth	W	I	2610	Leveled Readers/CA	Houghton Mifflin Harcourt
Mars on Earth	W	I	2610	Leveled Readers/TX	Houghton Mifflin Harcourt
Mars, Our Closest Neighbor	S	I	1366	Leveled Readers Science	Houghton Mifflin Harcourt
Mars: Mysteries of the Red Planet	X	I	3297	Leveled Readers	Houghton Mifflin Harcourt
Mars: The Red Planet	L	I	250+	Rosen Real Readers	Rosen Publishing Group
Marshfield Dreams: When I Was a Kid	S	B	250+	Fletcher, Ralph	Henry Holt & Co.
Martha Graham, Modern Dancer	P	B	982	Leveled Readers	Houghton Mifflin Harcourt
Martha in the Middle	L	F	250+	Fearnley, Jan	Candlewick Press
Martha Washington	N	B	1793	On My Own Biography	Lerner Publications
Martha Washington: America's First First Lady	O	B	250+	Childhood of Famous Americans	Aladdin
Martial Arts	U	I	250+	Boldprint	Steck-Vaughn
Martial Arts	U	I	250+	Boldprint	Steck-Vaughn
Martial Arts	R	I	250+	Orbit Chapter Books	Pacific Learning
Martial Arts for Fun!	S	I	250+	Activities for Fun	Compass Point Books
Martian Goo	E	F	65	Salem, Lynn; Stewart, Josie	Continental Press

TITLE	LEVEL	GENRE	WORD COUNT	AUTHOR / SERIES	PUBLISHER / DISTRIBUTOR
Martians Are People, Too	N	F	250+	Navigators Fiction Series	Benchmark Education
Martians Don't Take Temperatures	M	F	250+	Dadey, Debbie; Jones, Marcia Thornton	Scholastic
Martin and the Teacher's Pets	K	RF	250+	Chardiet, Bernice; Maccarone, Grace	Scholastic
Martin and the Tooth Fairy	K	RF	250+	Chardiet, Bernice; Maccarone, Grace	Scholastic
Martin Luther King	T	B	250+	Bray, Rosemary L.	William Morrow
Martin Luther King Jr. Day	L	I	250+	Lowery, Linda	Scholastic
Martin Luther King Jr.	S	B	250+	Amazing Americans	Wright Group/McGraw Hill
Martin Luther King Jr.	Q	B	250+	Early Biographies	Compass Point Books
Martin Luther King Jr.	S	B	3426	History Maker Bios	Lerner Publications
Martin Luther King Jr.	S	B	250+	Primary Source Readers	Teacher Created Materials
Martin Luther King Jr. Day	I	I	125	American Holidays	Lerner Publications
Martin Luther King Jr. Day	Q	I	250+	Holiday Histories	Heinemann Library
Martin Luther King Jr. Day	O	I	1693	On My Own Holidays	Lerner Publications
Martin Luther King Jr.: A Life of Determination	O	B	486	Pull Ahead Books	Lerner Publications
Martin Luther King, Jr.	M	B	290	Famous Americans	Capstone Press
Martin Luther King, Jr.	P	B	250+	Photo-Illustrated Biographies	Red Brick Learning
Martin Luther King, Jr.	O	B	250+	Rookie Biographies	Children's Press
Martin Luther King, Jr.	B	I	110	Shutterbug Books	Steck-Vaughn
Martin Luther King, Jr.	Q	B	798	Time for Kids	Teacher Created Materials
Martin Luther King, Jr. and the March Toward Freedom	R	B	250+	Hakim, Rita	Millbrook Press
Martin Luther King, Jr. Day	L	I	138	National Holidays	Capstone Press
Martin Luther King, Jr., A Man Who Changed Things	O	B	250+	Greene, Carol	Children's Press
Martin Luther King, Jr.: Preacher, Freedom Fighter, Peacemaker	M	B	250+	Biographies	Picture Window Books
Martin Luther King, Jr.: Young Man with a Dream	O	B	250+	Childhood of Famous Americans	Aladdin
Martin Van Buren	U	B	250+	Profiles of the Presidents	Compass Point Books
Martin Van Buren: Eighth President	R	B	250+	Getting to Know the U.S. Presidents	Children's Press
Martina the Beautiful Cockroach	P	TL	1037	Deedy, Carmen Agra	Peachtree
Martin's Mice	P	F	250+	King-Smith, Dick	Alfred A. Knopf
Martin's Mighty Hit	M	RF	390	Windmill Books	Rigby
Marty Solves a Mystery	M	RF	1391	In Step Readers	Rigby
Marty's Job	M	RF	1258	Reading Street	Pearson
Marvella and the Moon	F	F	250+	Bookshop	Mondo
Marvelous Mammals	F	I	99	Independent Readers Science	Houghton Mifflin Harcourt
Marvelous Marine Animals	S	I	1000	Leveled Readers/TX	Houghton Mifflin Harcourt
Marvelous Me	F	F	29	Literacy 2000	Rigby
Marvelous Me Inside and Out	K	RF	250+	All About Me	Picture Window Books
Marvelous Menus	N	F	250+	Sails	Rigby
Marvelous Metals	U	I	1616	Independent Readers Science	Houghton Mifflin Harcourt
Marvelous Migration	Q	I	1398	Reading Street	Pearson
Marvelous Treasure, The	M	RF	481	Sunshine	Wright Group/McGraw Hill
Marvin and the Mean Words	M	RF	250+	Kline, Suzy	PaperStar
Marvin One Too Many	J	RF	250+	Paterson, Katherine	HarperCollins
Marvin Redpost (Class President)	M	RF	250+	Sachar, Louis	Random House
Marvin Redpost, Super Fast, Out of Control!	M	RF	250+	Sachar, Louis	Random House
Marvin Redpost: A Flying Birthday Cake?	M	RF	250+	Sachar, Louis	Random House
Marvin Redpost: Alone in His Teacher's House	M	RF	250+	Sachar, Louis	Random House

Organized Alphabetically by Title
Storable Database at www.fountasandpinnellleveledbooks.com

* Collection of short stories
\# Graphic text

TITLE	LEVEL	GENRE	WORD COUNT	AUTHOR / SERIES	PUBLISHER / DISTRIBUTOR
Marvin Redpost: Is He a Girl?	M	RF	250+	Sachar, Louis	Random House
Marvin Redpost: Kidnapped at Birth?	M	RF	250+	Sachar, Louis	Random House
Marvin Redpost: Why Pick on Me?	M	RF	250+	Sachar, Louis	Random House
Marvin, the Christmas Cat	N	F	250+	Tristars	Richard C. Owen
Marvin's Birthday	K	RF	250+	Pacific Literacy	Pacific Learning
Marvin's Egg	H	F	501	Sails	Rigby
Marvin's Manners	E	RF	32	Pair-It Books	Steck-Vaughn
Marvin's Trip to Mars	I	F	571	Appleton-Smith, Laura	Flyleaf Publishing
Marvin's Woolly Mammoth	I	F	264	Sails	Rigby
Marwe: Into the Land of the Dead	R	TL	1780	Graphic Myths and Legends	Lerner Publications
Mary and Jody in the Movies: Lucky Foot Stable Series	R	RF	41500	Dawson, JoAnn S.	Sourcebooks
Mary Anning, Fossil Hunter	R	B	1307	Independent Readers Science	Houghton Mifflin Harcourt
Mary Anning: Fossil Hunter	O	B	1576	On My Own Biography	Lerner Publications
Mary by Myself	Q	F	250+	Smith, Jane Denitz	HarperTrophy
Mary Cassatt	S	B	250+	Masterpieces: Artists and Their Works	Capstone Press
Mary Celeste Mystery, The	S	I	250+	Storyteller - Mountain Peaks	Wright Group/ McGraw Hill
Mary Had a Little Lamb	K	TL	250+	Trapani, Iza	Charlesbridge
Mary Leakey	W	B	2174	Leveled Readers Social Studies	Houghton Mifflin Harcourt
Mary Marony and the Chocolate Surprise	M	RF	250+	Kline, Suzy	Bantam
Mary Marony and the Snake	M	RF	250+	Kline, Suzy	Bantam
Mary Marony Hides Out	M	RF	250+	Kline, Suzy	Bantam
Mary Marony, Mummy Girl	M	RF	250+	Kline, Suzy	Bantam
Mary McLeod Bethune	U	B	250+	Amazing Americans	Wright Group/ McGraw Hill
Mary McLeod Bethune	U	B	250+	Cornerstones of Freedom	Children's Press
Mary McLeod Bethune	O	B	250+	Greenfield, Eloise	HarperTrophy
Mary McLeod Bethune	P	B	250+	Photo-Illustrated Biographies	Red Brick Learning
Mary McLeod Bethune - Voice of Black Hope	S	B	250+	Meltzer, Milton	Puffin/Penguin
Mary McLeod Bethune: A Life of Resourcefulness	O	B	552	Pull Ahead- Biographies	Lerner Publications
Mary McLeod Bethune: Empowering Educator	P	B	250+	Great African Americans	Capstone Press
*Mary on Horseback	Q	RF	250+	Wells, Rosemary	Puffin/Penguin
Mary Todd Lincoln: Girl of the Bluegrass	O	B	250+	Childhood of Famous Americans	Aladdin
Mary Wore Her Red Dress	D	F	170	Peek, Merle	Clarion
Mary, Mary	D	TL	21	Jumbled Tumbled Tales & Rhymes	Rigby
Maryland	T	I	250+	Hello U.S.A.	Lerner Publications
Maryland	S	I	250+	Land of Liberty	Red Brick Learning
Maryland	R	I	250+	This Land Is Your Land	Compass Point Books
Maryland Colony, The	R	I	250+	The American Colonies	Capstone Press
Mascot, The	K	RF	558	In Step Readers	Rigby
Mask Book, The	L	I	217	Twig	Wright Group/McGraw Hill
Mask Makers, The	K	RF	242	Leveled Readers	Houghton Mifflin Harcourt
Mask, The	E	I	45	Pair-It Books	Steck-Vaughn
Masks	J	I	136	Gear Up!	Wright Group/McGraw Hill
Masks	M	I	250+	Literacy 2000	Rigby
Masks	C	I	41	Pebble Books	Capstone Press
Masks	D	I	109	Sails	Rigby
Masks	E	I	62	Wonder World	Wright Group/McGraw Hill
Mass Production and the Model T: Building the Car for Everyone	R	I	250+	Literacy by Design	Rigby
Massachusetts	T	I	250+	Hello U.S.A.	Lerner Publications
Massachusetts	S	I	250+	Land of Liberty	Red Brick Learning

* Collection of short stories
# Graphic text

TITLE	LEVEL	GENRE	WORD COUNT	AUTHOR / SERIES	PUBLISHER / DISTRIBUTOR
Massachusetts	T	I	250+	Theme Sets	National Geographic
Massachusetts	R	I	250+	This Land Is Your Land	Compass Point Books
Massachusetts 54th, The: African American Soldiers of the Union	V	I	250+	Let Freedom Ring	Capstone Press
Massachusetts Bay Colony, The	R	I	250+	The American Colonies	Capstone Press
Massie: The Clique Summer Collection	X	RF	250+	Harrison, Lisi	Little, Brown & Co.
Master of the Weather	O	F	250+	The Adventures of Sam X	Stone Arch Books
Master Puppeteer, The	X	HF	250+	Paterson, Katherine	HarperCollins
Masterpiece, The	K	F	250+	Storyteller-Lightning Bolts	Wright Group/McGraw Hill
Matchbox Collection, A	K	I	250+	Stepping Stones	Nelson/Michaels Assoc.
Matchbox, The	S	HF	250+	Literacy 2000	Rigby
Matchlock Gun, The	P	HF	250+	Edmonds, Walter D.	Putnam/Penguin
Material Resources	R	I	1932	Science Support Readers	Houghton Mifflin Harcourt
Materializer, The	S	SF	250+	Sails	Rigby
Materials	L	I	250+	Discovery World	Rigby
Materials Science	Z	I	7192	Cool Science	Lerner Publications
Math Around the Globe	T	I	250+	Navigators Math Series	Benchmark Education Company
Math at the Olympics	T	I	250+	Navigators Math Series	Benchmark Education
Math at the Store	G	I	127	Amato, William	Scholastic
Math Bee, The	P	B	795	Leveled Readers	Houghton Mifflin Harcourt
Math Chat: A Glossary of Terms	M	I	250+	Twig	Wright Group/McGraw Hill
Math Counts	L	I	250+	Pluckrose, Henry	Scholastic
Math in a Democracy	T	I	250+	Navigators Math Series	Benchmark Education
Math in the Garden	R	I	250+	Navigators Math Series	Benchmark Education
Math Is Everywhere	F	I	95	Sunshine	Wright Group/McGraw Hill
Math Master, The	N	RF	250+	Literacy by Design	Rigby
Math on the Moon	O	I	250+	Navigators Math Series	Benchmark Education
Math to Build On	U	I	250+	Navigators Math Series	Benchmark Education Company
Math to Munch On	T	I	250+	Navigators Math Series	Benchmark Education
Math Today and Tomorrow	T	SF	2035	Leveled Readers	Houghton Mifflin Harcourt
Math Today and Tomorrow	T	SF	2035	Leveled Readers/CA	Houghton Mifflin Harcourt
Math Today and Tomorrow	T	SF	2035	Leveled Readers/TX	Houghton Mifflin Harcourt
Math- Who Needs It?	J	I	366	In Step Readers	Rigby
Math Wiz, The	N	RF	250+	Duffey, Betsy	Penguin Group
Mathematical Thinkers	T	I	250+	Navigators Math Series	Benchmark Education Company
Mathew Brady: Civil War Photographer	T	B	250+	A First Book	Franklin Watts
Matilda	S	F	250+	Dahl, Roald	Penguin Group
Matilda Bone	X	HF	250+	Cushman, Karen	Clarion
Matilda's Plans	O	F	250+	Sails	Rigby
Matisse	S	B	250+	Masterpieces: Artists and Their Works	Capstone Press
Matsumura's Ice Sculpture	I	I	94	iOpeners	Pearson Learning Group
Matt Drives the Car	D	RF	136	Early Emergent, Set 3	Pioneer Valley
Matter	Q	I	2389	Early Bird Energy	Lerner Publishing
Matter	P	I	250+	Our Physical World	Capstone Press
Matter in Ecosystems	R	I	1861	Science Support Readers	Houghton Mifflin Harcourt
Matter of Balance, A	L	B	250+	Voyages	SRA/McGraw Hill
Matter of Conscience, A: The Trial of Anne Hutchinson	U	I	250+	Nichols, Joan Kane	Steck-Vaughn
Matter of Trust, A	Z	RF	250+	Schraff, Anne	Townsend Press
Matter Splatter!	T	I	250+	InfoQuest	Rigby

* Collection of short stories
\# Graphic text

TITLE	LEVEL	GENRE	WORD COUNT	AUTHOR / SERIES	PUBLISHER / DISTRIBUTOR
Matter: See It, Touch It, Taste It, Smell It	N	I	250+	Amazing Science	Picture Window Books
Matthew and Emma	C	RF	49	PM Stars	Rigby
Matthew and Tilly	L	RF	250+	Jones, Rebecca C.	Penguin Group
Matthew Henson	L	B	250+	Biography	Benchmark Education
Matthew Henson	N	B	207	First Biographies	Capstone Press
Matthew Henson	S	B	3437	History Maker Bios	Lerner Publications
Matthew Henson: Arctic Explorer	O	B	250+	Sunshine	Wright Group/McGraw Hill
Matthew Likes to Read	J	RF	144	Pacific Literacy	Pacific Learning
Matthew the Magician	E	RF	116	Learn to Read	Creative Teaching Press
Matthew's Meadow	V	RF	250+	Bliss, Corinne Demas	Harcourt Brace
Matthew's Story: From England to Plimouth Colony	T	HF	250+	Reading Expeditions	National Geographic
Matthew's Tantrum	J	RF	250+	Literacy 2000	Rigby
Mattimeo: A Tale from Redwall	Z	F	250+	Jacques, Brian	Avon
Matt's Cairo Caper	U	RF	250+	WorldScapes	ETA Cuisenaire
Matt's Good Idea	G	RF	226	PM Stars	Rigby
Maud and Anne	W	B	2073	Leveled Readers	Houghton Mifflin Harcourt
Maud and Anne	W	B	2073	Leveled Readers/CA	Houghton Mifflin Harcourt
Maui and the Sun	M	TL	359	Pacific Literacy	Pacific Learning
Maui and the Sun	I	TL	267	Story Box	Wright Group/McGraw Hill
Maui and the Wind	N	TL	799	Springboard	Wright Group/McGraw Hill
Maura's Angel	X	F	250+	Banks, Lynne Reid	Avon
Maurice Sendak	L	B	201	First Biographies	Red Brick Learning
Max	M	F	250+	Graham, Bob	Candlewick Press
Max	J	RF	234	Isadora, Rachel	Macmillan
Max and Jake	G	RF	212	PM Plus Story Books	Rigby
Max and Me and the Time Machine	T	SF	250+	Greer, Gery; Ruddick, Bob	HarperTrophy
Max and Mintie	K	F	250+	Home Connection Collection	Rigby
Max and the Alpaca	L	F	828	Sun Sprouts	ETA Cuisenaire
Max and the Apples	E	F	189	Storyworlds	Heinemann Educational Publishers
Max and the Birdhouse	G	RF	190	PM Plus Story Books	Rigby
Max and the Cat	E	F	154	Storyworlds	Heinemann Educational Publishers
Max and the Clouds	E	F	211	Sun Sprouts	ETA Cuisenaire
Max and the Drum	E	F	171	Storyworlds	Heinemann Educational Publishers
Max and the Little Plant	E	RF	134	PM Plus Story Books	Rigby
Max and the Storm	I	F	475	Sun Sprouts	ETA Cuisenaire
Max at the Fair	H	F	245	Sun Sprouts	ETA Cuisenaire
Max Comes Home	A	RF	24	First Stories	Pacific Learning
Max Gets Ready	C	RF	48	Rigby Literacy	Rigby
Max Gets Ready	C	RF	48	Rigby Star	Rigby
Max Goes Fishing	E	RF	147	PM Plus Story Books	Rigby
Max in a Tree	D	F	86	Sun Sprouts	ETA Cuisenaire
Max Is a Star!	F	RF	160	Leveled Readers Language Support	Houghton Mifflin Harcourt
Max Jumps	B	F	37	Sun Sprouts	ETA Cuisenaire
Max Malone and the Great Cereal Rip-off	N	RF	250+	Herman, Charlotte	Henry Holt & Co.
Max Malone Makes a Million	N	RF	250+	Herman, Charlotte	Henry Holt & Co.
Max Malone the Magnificent	N	RF	250+	Herman, Charlotte	Scholastic
Max Malone, Superstar	N	RF	250+	Herman, Charlotte	Scholastic
Max on a Hill	E	F	80	Sun Sprouts	ETA Cuisenaire
Max on Ice	E	F	219	Sun Sprouts	ETA Cuisenaire

TITLE	LEVEL	GENRE	WORD COUNT	AUTHOR / SERIES	PUBLISHER / DISTRIBUTOR
Max Planck: Uncovering the World of Matter	W	B	250+	Science Readers	Teacher Created Materials
Max Rides His Bike	E	RF	143	PM Plus Story Books	Rigby
Max Saves a Frog	G	RF	208	PM Stars	Rigby
Max the Man Mountain	Q	RF	250+	McFarlane, Peter	HarperCollins
Max the Mighty	W	RF	250+	Philbrick, Rodman	Scholastic
Max the Mouse and the Moon	Q	F	250+	Reading Safari	Mondo
Max the Pet Show Star	G	RF	175	Leveled Readers	Houghton Mifflin Harcourt
Max Visits London	K	RF	250+	Leveled Readers Language Support	Houghton Mifflin Harcourt
Max Wants to Fly	E	F	159	Storyworlds	Heinemann Educational Publishers
Max, Honey and Hay	J	F	496	Sun Sprouts	ETA Cuisenaire
Maxie, Rosie, and Earl - Partners in Grime	O	RF	250+	Park, Barbara	Random House
Maximum Ride: Saving the World and Other Extreme Sports	X	SF	250+	Patterson, James	Little, Brown & Co.
Maximum Ride: School's Out-Forever	X	SF	250+	Patterson, James	Little, Brown & Co.
Maximum Ride: The Angel Experiment	X	SF	250+	Patterson, James	Little, Brown & Co.
Maximum Ride: The Final Warning	X	SF	250+	Patterson, James	Little, Brown & Co.
Max's Box	B	RF	43	Little Celebrations	Pearson Learning Group
Max's Glasses	L	RF	250+	Navigators Fiction Series	Benchmark Education
Max's New Friend	K	F	250+	Rigby Rocket	Rigby
May Chinn: The Best Medicine	U	B	250+	Butts, Ellen; Schwartz, Joyce	W. H. Freeman & Co.
May I Stay Home Today?	E	RF	73	Tadpoles	Rigby
Maya Angelou	W	B	250+	Spain, Valerie	Random House
Maya Angelou: Greeting the Morning	W	B	250+	King, Sarah E.	Millbrook Press
Maya Angelou: Journey of the Heart	W	B	250+	Pettit, Jayne	Puffin/Penguin
Maya in the Past and Present, The	T	I	250+	Reading Expeditions	National Geographic
Maya the Adventureless	P	F	250+	Scooters	ETA Cuisenaire
Maya, The	P	I	250+	A New True Book	Children's Press
Maya, The	R	I	250+	First Reports	Compass Point Books
Maya, The	S	I	250+	Journey Into Civilization	Chelsea House
Mayan Writing in Mesoamerica	U	I	250+	On Deck	Rigby
Mayas Incas and Aztecs	X	I	250+	Primary Source Readers	Teacher Created Materials
Maya's Storm	P	RF	250+	In Step Readers	Rigby
Maybe I'll Be	D	F	49	Carousel Readers	Pearson Learning Group
Maybe Yes, Maybe No, Maybe Maybe	M	RF	250+	Patron, Susan	Bantam
Mayflower, The	R	I	250+	The Library of the Pilgrims	Rosen Publishing Group
Mayor Mom	K	RF	315	Reading Street	Pearson
Mayors	L	I	250+	Community Workers	Compass Point Books
Mayors	M	I	630	Pull Ahead Books	Lerner Publications
Maze Craze, The	N	I	250+	Pacific Literacy	Pacific Learning
Maze Race, The	J	F	442	Springboard	Wright Group/McGraw Hill
Maze, The	V	RF	250+	Hobbs, Will	Morrow Junior Books
Mazes Are Amazing!	K	I	220	Vocabulary Readers	Houghton Mifflin Harcourt
*McBroom's Wonderful One-Acre Farm	O	F	250+	Fleischman, Sid	Beech Tree Books
McBungle's African Safari	I	F	336	Traditional Tales & More	Rigby
McGinty's Friend	L	F	250+	Sails	Rigby
McMurdo Station	P	I	860	Leveled Readers	Houghton Mifflin Harcourt
McMurdo Station	P	I	860	Leveled Readers/CA	Houghton Mifflin Harcourt
McMurdo Station	P	I	860	Leveled Readers/TX	Houghton Mifflin Harcourt
Me	LB	RF	15	Handprints A	Educators Publishing Service
Me	A	I	24	PM Starters	Rigby
Me	C	RF	41	Reading Corners	Pearson Learning Group

* Collection of short stories
# Graphic text

TITLE	LEVEL	GENRE	WORD COUNT	AUTHOR / SERIES	PUBLISHER / DISTRIBUTOR
Me (boy)	C	I	34	Tonon, Terry	Kaeden Books
Me (girl)	C	I	34	Tonon, Terry	Kaeden Books
Me and My Brother	C	RF	36	Ohi, Ruth	Annick Press
Me and My Dog	B	RF	55	Lighthouse	Ginn & Co.
Me and My Dog	F	RF	115	Sunshine	Wright Group/McGraw Hill
Me and My Little Brain	T	RF	250+	Fitzgerald, John D.	Dell
Me and My Newt	N	F	250+	High-Fliers	Pacific Learning
Me and My Pup	C	RF	34	Leveled Readers Language Support	Houghton Mifflin Harcourt
Me and My Shadow	H	F	247	Momentum Literacy Program	Troll Associates
Me and My Sister	C	RF	33	Ohi, Ruth	Annick Press
Me and Rupert Goody	Q	RF	250+	O'Connor, Barbara	Scholastic
Me Oh Maya	P	F	250+	Scieszka, Jon	Penguin Group
Me on the Map	I	I	250+	Sweeney, Joan	Dragonfly Books
Me Too	K	RF	136	Mayer, Mercer	Donovan
Me Too!	G	F	200	Bookshop	Mondo
Me Too!	D	F	70	Sunshine	Wright Group/McGraw Hill
Me!	B	RF	19	Reading Street	Pearson
Me!: Healthy Body, Healthy Mind	Y	I	250+	Boldprint	Steck-Vaughn
Me, Mop, and the Moondance Kid	S	RF	250+	Myers, Walter Dean	Bantam
Mealworms	P	I	250+	Life Cycles	Capstone Press
Mean Dream Wonder Machine, The	O	F	250+	High-Fliers	Pacific Learning
Mean Giant, The	C	F	69	Sun Sprouts	ETA Cuisenaire
Meanest Thing to Say, The	K	RF	250+	Cosby, Bill	Scholastic
Meanies	F	F	158	Story Box	Wright Group/McGraw Hill
Meanies Came to School, The	E	F	135	Story Basket	Wright Group/McGraw Hill
Meanie's Party, A	I	F	250+	The Story Basket	Wright Group/McGraw Hill
Meanies' Trick, The	E	F	93	Story Box	Wright Group/McGraw Hill
Measure	L	I	229	Spyglass Books	Compass Point Books
Measure and Cook	I	I	408	Shutterbug Books	Steck-Vaughn
Measure for Measure	U	I	250+	PM Plus	Rigby
Measure It	C	I	56	Twig	Wright Group/McGraw Hill
Measure Me	E	I	112	InfoTrek	ETA Cuisenaire
Measure the Motion	H	I	146	Leveled Readers Science	Houghton Mifflin Harcourt
Measure Up!	K	I	303	Early Connections	Benchmark Education
Measurement Action	M	I	250+	Yellow Umbrella Books	Red Brick Learning
Measurement Mysteries	G	I	124	Learn to Read	Creative Teaching Press
Measurement Tools	I	I	131	Windows on Literacy	National Geographic
Measuring Cup	C	I	29	Simple Tools	Lerner Publishing
Measuring Day	J	RF	607	InfoTrek	ETA Cuisenaire
Measuring Motion	H	I	113	Leveled Readers Science	Houghton Mifflin Harcourt
Measuring the Weather	R	I	250+	Gaynor, Bill	Pacific Learning
Measuring the Weather	L	I	401	Reading Street	Pearson
Measuring Time	E	I	217	Early Connections	Benchmark Education
Measuring Tools	M	I	250+	Early Connections	Benchmark Education
Measuring Up	R	I	250+	Orbit Chapter Books	Pacific Learning
Measuring Weather	E	I	99	Independent Readers Science	Houghton Mifflin Harcourt
Meat and Protein Group, The	H	I	117	The Food Guide Pyramid	Capstone Press
Meat Eaters, Plant Eaters	K	I	156	Planet Earth	Rigby
Meat Pies	D	I	21	Bebop Books	Lee & Low Books Inc.
Meat-Eating Plants Next Door, The	Q	RF	250+	Pair-It Books	Steck-Vaughn
Meats and Proteins	F	I	103	Food Groups	Lerner Publications
Medal for Molly, A	N	RF	250+	PM Collection	Rigby
Medal for Nickie, A	K	RF	262	Sunshine	Wright Group/McGraw Hill

* Collection of short stories
\# Graphic text

TITLE	LEVEL	GENRE	WORD COUNT	AUTHOR / SERIES	PUBLISHER / DISTRIBUTOR
Medical Pioneers	P	B	250+	Navigators Biography Series	Benchmark Education
Medieval Days	S	I	250+	InfoQuest	Rigby
Medieval Feast, A	Q	I	250+	Aliki	HarperCollins
Medieval Life	X	I	250+	Eyewitness Books	DK Publishing
Medieval Times	T	I	250+	Boldprint	Steck-Vaughn
Medieval Town	Q	I	250+	Worldwise	Franklin Watts
Medieval Warfare	Z	I	250+	Boldprint	Steck-Vaughn
Medusa	W	I	250+	World Mythology	Capstone Press
Meerkat Chat	L	I	250+	Story Steps	Rigby
Meerkats	I	I	125	African Animals	Capstone Press
Meerkats	O	I	250+	Weaver, Robyn	Red Brick Learning
Meet a Community Helper	D	RF	41	Independent Readers Social Studies	Houghton Mifflin Harcourt
Meet Abraham Lincoln	O	B	250+	Cary, Barbara	Step-Up Books
Meet Addy	Q	HF	250+	The American Girls Collection	Pleasant Company
Meet an Author: Laura Kvasnosky	E	B	54	Sunshine	Wright Group/McGraw Hill
Meet Benjamin Franklin	O	B	250+	Scarf, Maggi	Step-Up Books
Meet Calliope Day	R	F	250+	Haddad, Charles	Random House
Meet Dino Sue!	L	I	394	Vocabulary Readers	Houghton Mifflin Harcourt
Meet Dino Sue!	L	I	394	Vocabulary Readers/CA	Houghton Mifflin Harcourt
Meet Dino Sue!	L	I	394	Vocabulary Readers/TX	Houghton Mifflin Harcourt
Meet Erdene	P	I	250+	iOpeners	Pearson Learning Group
Meet Felicity	Q	HF	250+	The American Girls Collection	Pleasant Company
Meet Firefighter Jen	I	I	250+	Rosen Real Readers	Rosen Publishing Group
Meet George Washington	O	B	250+	Heilbroner, Joan	Random House
Meet Hillary Rodham Clinton	Q	B	250+	Spain, Valerie	Random House
Meet Jane Mt. Pleasant	H	B	183	Leveled Readers Science	Houghton Mifflin Harcourt
Meet John F. Kennedy	Q	B	250+	White, Nancy Bean	Random House
Meet Johnny Appleseed	D	B	32	Independent Readers Social Studies	Houghton Mifflin Harcourt
Meet Josefina	Q	HF	250+	The American Girls Collection	Pleasant Company
Meet Kirsten	Q	HF	250+	The American Girls Collection	Pleasant Company
Meet M & M	K	RF	250+	Ross, Pat	Penguin Group
Meet Martin Luther King, Jr.	R	B	250+	DeKay, James T.	Random House
Meet Me at the Water Hole	H	I	144	Storyteller-Night Crickets	Wright Group/McGraw Hill
Meet Messy Fred	I	F	250+	Popcorn	Sundance
Meet Molly	Q	HF	250+	The American Girls Collection	Pleasant Company
Meet Mr. Cricket	E	F	86	Carousel Readers	Pearson Learning Group
Meet Mr. Hydeous	Q	F	250+	Extreme Monsters	Penny Candy Press
Meet My Family	C	RF	71	Early Connections	Benchmark Education
Meet My Mouse	H	RF	135	Little Celebrations	Pearson Learning Group
Meet Officer Jerry	H	I	173	Rosen Real Readers	Rosen Publishing Group
Meet Our Families	D	RF	108	InfoTrek	ETA Cuisenaire
Meet Samantha	Q	HF	250+	The American Girls Collection	Pleasant Company
Meet Samuel Adams	P	B	447	Vocabulary Readers	Houghton Mifflin Harcourt
Meet Some Tricksters!	J	I	301	Vocabulary Readers	Houghton Mifflin Harcourt
Meet the Austins	W	RF	250+	L'Engle, Madeleine	Laurel-Leaf Books
Meet the Bugs!	L	I	250+	Scooters	ETA Cuisenaire
Meet the Feet	J	I	189	Leveled Readers	Houghton Mifflin Harcourt
Meet the Johnson Family	G	RF	52	Windows on Literacy	National Geographic
Meet the Lincoln Lions Band	L	RF	250+	Giff, Patricia Reilly	Bantam
Meet the Manatee	M	I	841	Vocabulary Readers	Houghton Mifflin Harcourt
Meet the Manatee	M	I	841	Vocabulary Readers/CA	Houghton Mifflin Harcourt
Meet the Maya	V	I	1783	Reading Street	Pearson

* Collection of short stories
\# Graphic text

TITLE	LEVEL	GENRE	WORD COUNT	AUTHOR / SERIES	PUBLISHER / DISTRIBUTOR
Meet the Meerkats	L	I	250+	World Quest Adventures	World Quest Learning
*Meet the Molesons	L	F	250+	Bos, Burny	North-South Books
Meet the Octopus	K	I	250+	Bookshop	Mondo
Meet the Ojibwa	R	I	1383	Vocabulary Readers	Houghton Mifflin Harcourt
Meet the Ojibwa	R	I	1383	Vocabulary Readers/CA	Houghton Mifflin Harcourt
Meet the Ojibwa	R	I	1383	Vocabulary Readers/TX	Houghton Mifflin Harcourt
Meet the United States Government	S	I	1173	Reading Street	Pearson
Meet the Villarreals	M	B	387	Kratky, Lada Josefa	Hampton-Brown
Meet Thomas Jefferson	O	B	250+	Barrett, Marvin	Step-Up Books
Meet Tom Paxton	I	B	229	Little Celebrations	Pearson Learning Group
Meet William Joyce	I	B	207	Little Celebrations	Pearson Learning Group
Meet Yo-Yo Ma	R	B	1406	Leveled Readers	Houghton Mifflin Harcourt
Meeting Amelia Earhart	O	HF	969	Reading Street	Pearson
Meeting Sqauwky	N	I	250+	Books for Young Learners	Richard C. Owen
Meg and Jim's Sled Trip	I	RF	264	Appleton-Smith, Laura	Flyleaf Publishing
Meg and Mog	J	F	236	Nicoll, Helen	Viking/Penguin
Meg and the Lost Pencil Case	F	RF	226	Parasmo, Greg	Scholastic
Meg Goes to Bed	B	RF	48	PM Photo Stories	Rigby
Meg Mackintosh and the Case of the Curious Whale Watch	O	RF	250+	Landon, Lucinda	Secret Passage Press
Meg Mackintosh and the Case of the Missing Babe Ruth Baseball	O	RF	250+	Landon, Lucinda	Secret Passage Press
Meg Mackintosh and the Mystery at Camp Creepy	O	RF	250+	Landon, Lucinda	Secret Passage Press
Meg Mackintosh and the Mystery at the Medieval Castle	O	RF	250+	Landon, Lucinda	Secret Passage Press
Meg Mackintosh and the Mystery at the Soccer Match	O	RF	250+	Landon, Lucinda	Secret Passage Press
Meg Mackintosh and the Mystery in the Locked Library	O	RF	250+	Landon, Lucinda	Secret Passage Press
Megacites	S	I	250+	Connectors	Pacific Learning
Megamouths and Hammerheads	I	I	403	Sails	Rigby
Megan in Ancient Greece	Q	HF	250+	Korman, Susan	Magic Attic
Megan's Balancing Act	Q	RF	250+	Korman, Susan	Magic Attic
Megan's Island	R	RF	250+	Roberts, Willo Davis	Aladdin
Meg's Cat	F	RF	117	Lighthouse	Rigby
Meg's Dearest Wish	Q	HF	250+	The Little Women Journals	Avon
Meg's Eggs	C	F	38	New Way Red	Steck-Vaughn
Meg's Mad Magnet	H	F	145	Supersonics	Rigby
Meg's Messy Room	C	RF	52	PM Photo Stories	Rigby
Meg's Tiny Red Teddy	C	RF	64	PM Photo Stories	Rigby
Meg's Warm Clothes	B	RF	34	Gear Up!	Wright Group/McGraw Hill
Mei Fuh: Memories From China	P	B	250+	Schaeffer, Edith	Houghton Mifflin Harcourt
Mel Spells	M	RF	822	Leveled Readers	Houghton Mifflin Harcourt
Mel Spells	M	RF	822	Leveled Readers/CA	Houghton Mifflin Harcourt
Meli at School	G	I	207	Leveled Literacy Intervention/ Blue System	Heinemann
Meli at the Pet Shop	E	I	148	Leveled Literacy Intervention/ Blue System	Heinemann
Meli at the Vet	E	I	141	Leveled Literacy Intervention/ Blue System	Heinemann
Meli on the Stairs	C	I	91	Leveled Literacy Intervention/ Green System	Heinemann
Melleron's Magic	Q	F	250+	High-Fliers	Pacific Learning

* Collection of short stories
# Graphic text

TITLE	LEVEL	GENRE	WORD COUNT	AUTHOR / SERIES	PUBLISHER / DISTRIBUTOR
Melleron's Monsters	Q	F	250+	High-Fliers	Pacific Learning
Melt It, Shape It: Glass	F	I	250+	Nelson, May	Scholastic
Melting	F	I	69	Bookshop	Mondo
Melting Away	R	I	250+	Explorer Books-Pathfinder	National Geographic
Melting Away	P	I	250+	Explorer Books-Pioneer	National Geographic
Melting Ice Cubes	C	I	50	Rigby Flying Colors	Rigby
*Melting Snow Sculptures and Other Cases, The	O	RF	250+	Simon, Seymour	Avon
Memorial Day	I	I	96	American Holidays	Lerner Publications
Memorial Day	Q	I	250+	Holiday Histories	Heinemann Library
Memorial Day	L	I	250+	National Holidays	Red Brick Learning
Memories	Q	RF	250+	Reading Safari	Mondo
Memories for Mom	P	RF	1517	Leveled Readers	Houghton Mifflin Harcourt
Memories of Anne Frank	X	B	250+	Gold, Alison Leslie	Scholastic
Memories of Vietnam: War in the First Person	Z	HF	250+	Weiss, Ellen	Scholastic
Memory Boy	Z	F	250+	Weaver, Will	HarperCollins
Men in Baseball	N	I	611	Reading Street	Pearson
Meow, What Now?	G	F	186	Seedlings	Continental Press
Merchant of Venice, The	Z+	HF	250+	Hinds, Gareth	Candlewick Press
Mercury	Q	I	250+	A True Book	Children's Press
Mercury	J	I	126	Exploring the Galaxy	Capstone Press
Mercury	S	I	250+	Our Solar System	Compass Point Books
Mercury	N	I	705	Our Universe	Lerner Publications
Mercury	Q	I	250	The Galaxy	Capstone Press
Mercury	R	I	250+	Theme Sets	National Geographic
Mercy Otis Warren: A Woman of the Revolution	X	B	2210	Leveled Readers	Houghton Mifflin Harcourt
Mercy Watson Fights Crime	K	F	250+	DiCamillo, Kate	Candlewick Press
Mercy Watson Goes for a Ride	K	F	250+	DiCamillo, Kate	Candlewick Press
Mercy Watson Thinks Like a Pig	K	F	250+	Di Camillo, Kate	Candlewick Press
Mercy Watson to the Rescue	K	F	250+	DiCamillo, Kate	Candlewick Press
Merlin and the Dragons	U	F	250+	Yolen, Jane	Penguin Group
Merlin: The Young Merlin Trilogy	V	TL	250+	Yolen, Jane	Scholastic
Mermaid and the Octopus	F	F	139	Big Cat	Pacific Learning
Mermaid in the Bathtub	O	F	11700	Peetom, Laura	Fitzhenry & Whiteside
Mermaid Island	L	F	250+	Frith, Margaret	Grossett & Dunlap
Mermaids Don't Run Track	M	F	250+	Dadey, Debbie; Jones, Marcia Thornton	Scholastic
Merry Christmas, Amelia Bedelia	L	F	250+	Parish, Peggy	William Morrow
Merry Christmas, Dear Dragon	F	F	312	Dear Dragon	Norwood House Press
Merry-Go-Round	C	RF	66	Teacher's Choice Series	Pearson Learning Group
Merry-Go-Round, The	C	RF	84	PM Story Books	Rigby
Merry-Go-Round, The	C	RF	45	Ready Readers	Pearson Learning Group
Merry-Go-Round, The	C	RF	62	Sunshine	Wright Group/McGraw Hill
Mesopotamia	X	I	250+	Primary Source Readers	Teacher Created Materials
Mess Monster	G	F	179	Literacy 2000	Rigby
Mess, A	D	F	34	Ready Readers	Pearson Learning Group
Mess, The	D	RF	55	My First Reader	Grolier Press
Mess, The	B	RF	40	Sun Sprouts	ETA Cuisenaire
Message from Danny Bell, A	I	RF	587	Rigby Flying Colors	Rigby
Message to the World, A	S	I	813	Vocabulary Readers	Houghton Mifflin Harcourt
Message, The	R	F	250+	Applegate, K. A.	Scholastic
Messages Without Words	Q	I	250+	Sunshine	Wright Group/McGraw Hill
Messenger	Y	F	250+	Lowry, Lois	Houghton Mifflin Harcourt
Messy Bessey	I	RF	63	Rookie Readers	Children's Press

* Collection of short stories
# Graphic text

TITLE	LEVEL	GENRE	WORD COUNT	AUTHOR / SERIES	PUBLISHER / DISTRIBUTOR
Messy Bessey's Closet	K	RF	92	Rookie Readers	Children's Press
Messy Bessey's Family Reunion	J	RF	190	McKissack, Patricia & Fredrick	Scholastic
Messy Bessey's Garden	I	RF	60	Rookie Readers	Children's Press
Messy Bessey's School Desk	J	RF	104	Rookie Readers	Children's Press
Messy Mark	F	RF	180	First Start	Troll Associates
Messy Meals	J	F	87	Franco, Betsy	Scholastic
Messy Monsters, The	G	F	167	Carousel Readers	Pearson Learning Group
Messy Moose	C	F	45	Little Books	Sadlier-Oxford
Messy Rooms, The	F	F	103	Lester the Lion Series	Pioneer Valley
Metal	G	I	129	Materials	Lerner Publications
Metal Detector Detective	K	RF	377	Reading Street	Pearson
Metamorphic Rocks	Q	I	250+	On Deck	Rigby
#Metamorphosis, The	Z+	F	250+	Kafka, Franz	Hampton-Brown
Meteorite!: The Last Days of the Dinosaurs	W	I	250+	Norris, Richard	Steck-Vaughn
Meteorologists	M	I	250+	Community Helpers	Red Brick Learning
Meteors and Meteorites	Q	I	250+	The Galaxy	Red Brick Learning
Meteors, Comets, and Asteroids	X	I	3166	Leveled Readers	Houghton Mifflin Harcourt
Meteors, Comets, and Asteroids	X	I	3166	Leveled Readers/CA	Houghton Mifflin Harcourt
Meteors: The Truth Behind Shooting Stars	T	I	250+	Aronson, Billy	Franklin Watts
Metric Math	T	I	250+	Navigators Math Series	Benchmark Education
Metropolitan Cow	N	F	250+	Egan, Tim	Houghton Mifflin Harcourt
Mexican Community, A	J	I	606	Vocabulary Readers	Houghton Mifflin Harcourt
Mexican Community, A	J	I	606	Vocabulary Readers/CA	Houghton Mifflin Harcourt
Mexican Feast, A: The Foods and Recipes of Mexico	P	I	250+	Rosen Real Readers	Rosen Publishing Group
Mexican Festival, A	J	RF	267	Leveled Readers	Houghton Mifflin Harcourt
Mexican Festival, A	J	RF	267	Leveled Readers/CA	Houghton Mifflin Harcourt
Mexican Festival, A	J	RF	267	Leveled Readers/TX	Houghton Mifflin Harcourt
Mexican Holiday, A	C	I	24	The Candid Collection	Pearson Learning Group
Mexican Immigrants in America: An Interactive History Adventure	V	HF	250+	You Choose Books	Capstone Press
Mexican Immigration	V	I	250+	Theme Sets	National Geographic
Mexican War, 1846-1848, The	V	I	250+	Let Freedom Ring	Capstone Press
Mexican-American War, The	R	I	250+	On Deck	Rigby
Mexico	LB	I	22	Canizares, Susan; Chanko, Pamela	Scholastic
Mexico	O	I	250+	Countries of the World	Red Brick Learning
Mexico	Q	I	250+	First Reports: Countries	Compass Point Books
Mexico	P	I	250+	Many Cultures, One World	Capstone Press
Mexico	R	I	250+	Theme Sets	National Geographic
Mexico	M	I	340	Time for Kids	Teacher Created Materials
Mexico ABCs: A Book About the People and Places of Mexico	Q	I	250+	Country ABCs	Picture Window Books
Mexico City Is Muy Grande	M	I	250+	Twig	Wright Group/McGraw Hill
Mexico in Colors	N	I	250+	World of Colors	Capstone Press
Mexico: A Question and Answer Book	P	I	250+	Questions and Answers: Countries	Capstone Press
Mexico: Everyday Kids Now and Then	S	HF	250+	Reading Expeditions	National Geographic
Mexico's Smoking Mountains	W	I	1955	Leveled Readers	Houghton Mifflin Harcourt
Mia and Nomar	K	I	464	Vocabulary Readers	Houghton Mifflin Harcourt
Mia and Nomar	K	I	464	Vocabulary Readers/CA	Houghton Mifflin Harcourt
Mia and Nomar	K	I	464	Vocabulary Readers/TX	Houghton Mifflin Harcourt
Mia Hamm	R	B	250+	Sports Heroes	Red Brick Learning
Mia Hamm, Journey of a Soccer Champion	S	B	1730	Leveled Readers	Houghton Mifflin Harcourt

TITLE	LEVEL	GENRE	WORD COUNT	AUTHOR / SERIES	PUBLISHER / DISTRIBUTOR
Mia Hamm, Soccer Star	J	I	390	Vocabulary Readers	Houghton Mifflin Harcourt
Mia Hamm, Soccer Star	J	B	390	Vocabulary Readers/CA	Houghton Mifflin Harcourt
Mia Hamm: Soccer Star	Q	B	250+	Leveled Readers Language Support	Houghton Mifflin Harcourt
Miami Dolphins, The	S	I	250+	Team Spirit	Norwood House Press
Miami Gets It Straight	M	RF	250+	McKissack, Fredrick & Patricia	Random House
Miami Heat, The	S	I	4014	Team Spirit	Norwood House Press
Mia's Sun Hat	E	RF	32	Start to Read	School Zone
Mice	O	I	250+	Holmes, Kevin J.	Red Brick Learning
Mice	H	I	143	Literacy 2000	Rigby
Mice	J	I	250+	PM Animal Facts: Orange	Rigby
Mice and Beans	N	F	250+	Ryan, Pam Munoz	Scholastic
Mice and Max	G	F	169	Carousel Readers	Pearson Learning Group
Mice at Bat	I	F	250+	Oechsli, Kelly	HarperTrophy
Mice Have a Meeting, The	I	TL	250+	PM Plus Story Books	Rigby
Mice on Ice	H	F	51	Easy Phonics Readers	Teacher Created Materials
Mice on Ice	C	F	34	KinderReaders	Rigby
Mice on Ice	I	F	211	Sunshine	Wright Group/McGraw Hill
Mice, The	B	F	30	Sails	Rigby
Michael and the Chicks	G	RF	210	Developing	Pioneer Valley
Michael and the Eggs	G	RF	154	Oxford Reading Tree	Oxford University Press
Michael in the Hospital	E	RF	91	Oxford Reading Tree	Oxford University Press
Michael Jordan	R	B	250+	Christopher, Matt	Little, Brown & Co.
Michael Jordan	M	B	250+	Edwards, Nick	Scholastic
Michael Jordan	Q	B	250+	Lovitt, Chip	Scholastic
Michael Jordan: The Best Ever	T	B	250+	High Five Reading	Red Brick Learning
Michael Phelps	P	B	1848	Amazing Athletes	Lerner Publications
Michael Vick	P	B	250+	Amazing Athletes	Lerner Publications
Michael's Picture	C	RF	33	Little Celebrations	Pearson Learning Group
Michelangelo	S	B	250+	Masterpieces: Artists and Their Works	Red Brick Learning
Michelangelo and the Italian Renaissance	U	B	2119	Reading Street	Pearson
Michelangelo: His Life and Art	R	B	250+	Rosen Real Readers	Rosen Publishing Group
Michelle Kwan	N	B	250+	Biography	Benchmark Education
Michelle Kwan	R	B	250+	Sports Heroes	Red Brick Learning
Michelle Kwan, Champion	M	B	499	Leveled Readers	Houghton Mifflin Harcourt
Michelle Kwan, Champion	M	B	499	Leveled Readers/CA	Houghton Mifflin Harcourt
Michelle Kwan, Champion	M	B	499	Leveled Readers/TX	Houghton Mifflin Harcourt
Michelle Wie	F	B	153	Leveled Readers	Houghton Mifflin Harcourt
Michelle Wie	F	B	153	Leveled Readers/CA	Houghton Mifflin Harcourt
Michelle Wie	F	B	153	Leveled Readers/TX	Houghton Mifflin Harcourt
Michelle Wie: She's Got the Power!	Q	B	250+	High Five Reading	Red Brick Learning
Michigan	T	I	250+	Hello U.S.A.	Lerner Publications
Michigan	S	I	250+	Land of Liberty	Red Brick Learning
Michigan	Q	I	250+	One Nation	Capstone Press
Michigan	R	I	250+	This Land Is Your Land	Compass Point Books
Michigan Outdoor Photos	A	I	28	Larkin, Bruce	Books for a Cause, Inc.
Mick and Max	G	RF	169	Carousel Readers	Pearson Learning Group
Mickey & Me	T	F	250+	Gutman, Dan	Harper Trophy
Mickey Maloney	I	RF	371	Sails	Rigby
Mickey Maloney - Spy	N	RF	250+	Sails	Rigby
Mickey Maloney's Mail	M	RF	250+	Sails	Rigby
Mickey Maloney's Missing Bag	G	RF	230	Sails	Rigby
Mickey's Secret	K	RF	250+	Rigby Literacy	Rigby

Organized Alphabetically by Title
Storable Database at www.fountasandpinnellleveledbooks.com

* Collection of short stories
\# Graphic text

TITLE	LEVEL	GENRE	WORD COUNT	AUTHOR / SERIES	PUBLISHER / DISTRIBUTOR
Micro Monsters	U	I	250+	DK Readers	DK Publishing
Microscope	C	I	46	Story Box	Wright Group/McGraw Hill
Midday Meals Around the World	M	I	250+	Meals Around the World	Picture Window Books
Middle Ages, The	R	I	250+	Journey Through History	Barron's Educational
Middle Moffat, The	T	RF	250+	Estes, Eleanor	Language for Learning Assoc.
Middle of Nowhere, The	K	RF	250+	Rigby Literacy	Rigby
Midge in the Hospital	E	RF	91	Oxford Reading Tree	Oxford University Press
Midnight Bakery	R	I	250+	Bookweb	Rigby
Midnight Circus, The	WB	F	N/A	Collington, Peter	Alfred A. Knopf
Midnight for Charlie Bone	U	F	250+	Nimmo, Jenny	Orchard Books
Midnight Fox, The	R	RF	250+	Byars, Betsy	Scholastic
Midnight Horse, The	V	F	250+	Fleischman, Sid	Bantam
Midnight Journeys: Travels in the Mysterious World of Sleep	R	S	250+	Literacy by Design	Rigby
Midnight Journeys: Travels in the Mysterious World of Sleep	S	I	250+	Rigby Literacy	Rigby
Midnight Library, The	S	F	250+	Graves, Damien	Scholastic
Midnight Lightning	P	RF	250+	Bookweb	Rigby
Midnight Magic	U	F	250+	Avi	Scholastic
Midnight Menace, The	Q	RF	250+	Reading Expeditions	National Geographic
Midnight on the Moon	M	F	250+	Osborne, Mary Pope	Random House
Midnight Pig, The	M	F	250+	Action Packs	Rigby
Midnight Rescue	N	RF	250+	Literacy Tree	Rigby
Midnight Ride of Sybil Ludington, The	P	B	250+	Literacy by Design	Rigby
Midnight Ride of Sybil Ludington, The	P	B	250+	On Our Way to English	Rigby
Midwife's Apprentice, The	X	HF	250+	Cushman, Karen	HarperTrophy
Midwinter Nightingale	X	F	250+	Aiken, Joan	Yearling
Mieko and the Fifth Treasure	O	HF	250+	Coerr, Eleanor	Bantam
Mighty 12, The: Superheroes of Greek Myth	U	TL	250+	Smith, Charles R.	Little, Brown & Co.
Mighty Bison	K	I	297	Pull Ahead Books	Lerner Publications
Mighty Forces	S	I	250+	Orbit Collections	Pacific Learning
Mighty Hippopotamus, The	T	I	250+	Bookshop	Mondo
Mighty Hurricane, The	L	I	250+	Gear Up!	Wright Group/ McGraw Hill
Mighty Ironclads and Other Amazements	U	I	2454	Independent Readers Social Studies	Houghton Mifflin Harcourt
Mighty Lever, The	P	I	250+	InfoTrek	ETA/Cuisenaire
Mighty Machines	I	I	127	Windows on Literacy	National Geographic
Mighty Mammals	Q	I	250+	Explorers	Wright Group/McGraw Hill
Mighty Maya, The	U	I	250+	Leveled Readers Language Support	Houghton Mifflin Harcourt
Mighty Mekong, The	T	I	250+	WorldScapes	ETA Cuisenaire
Mighty Minibeasts	N	I	250+	Sun Sprouts	ETA Cuisenaire
Mighty Mountains	K	I	246	Explorations	Eleanor Curtain Publishing
Mighty Mountains	K	I	246	Explorations	Okapi Eductional Materials
Mighty Movers, Mighty Diggers	K	I	250+	Scooters	ETA Cuisenaire
Mighty Mississippi, The	K	I	250+	On Our Way to English	Rigby
Mighty Rome!	S	I	250+	InfoQuest	Rigby
Mighty, Mighty Daffodils, The	Q	RF	1373	Leveled Readers/TX	Houghton Mifflin Harcourt
Mighty, Mighty Daffodils, The	Q	RF	1373	Leveled Readers	Houghton Mifflin Harcourt
Mighty, Mighty Daffodils, The	Q	RF	1373	Leveled Readers/CA	Houghton Mifflin Harcourt
Mighty, The	V	RF	250+	Philbrick, Rodman	Scholastic
Migrant Music, A	W	I	2170	Reading Street	Pearson
Migration, The	D	I	45	Wonder World	Wright Group/McGraw Hill

TITLE	LEVEL	GENRE	WORD COUNT	AUTHOR / SERIES	PUBLISHER / DISTRIBUTOR
Miguel Hidalgo, Father of Mexican Independence	Q	B	1145	Leveled Readers Social Studies	Houghton Mifflin Harcourt
Mike and Tony: Best Friends	G	RF	171	Ziefert, Harriet	Penguin Group
Mike Fink	N	TL	2003	On My Own Folklore	Lerner Publications
Mike Ghost's Delicious Rainbow	F	F	157	TOTTS	Tott Publications
Mike Swan, Sink or Swim	J	RF	250+	Heiligman, Deborah	Bantam
Mike's Bike	E	RF	82	Dominie Phonics Readers	Pearson Learning Group
Mike's Bike	J	RF	250+	Supersonics	Rigby
Mike's First Haircut	G	RF	136	First Start	Troll Associates
Mike's New Bike	F	RF	183	First Start	Troll Associates
Mile High, A	K	F	331	Book Bank	Wright Group/McGraw Hill
Mile-a-Minute Vine, The	K	F	511	Reading Street	Pearson
Miles on the Mississippi	M	I	337	Independent Readers Social Studies	Houghton Mifflin Harcourt
Miles Standish: Colonial Leader	U	B	250+	Let Freedom Ring	Red Brick Learning
Military Helicopters	H	I	106	Mighty Machines	Capstone Press
Milk From a Cow	G	I	129	Rigby Flying Colors	Rigby
Milking	F	RF	67	Wonder World	Wright Group/McGraw Hill
Milkshake Man, The	L	F	250+	Take Two Books	Wright Group/McGraw Hill
Milkweed	Y	HF	250+	Spinelli, Jerry	Random House
Mill Girls	S	I	884	Vocabulary Readers	Houghton Mifflin Harcourt
Mill Girls	S	I	884	Vocabulary Readers/CA	Houghton Mifflin Harcourt
Mill Girls	S	I	884	Vocabulary Readers/TX	Houghton Mifflin Harcourt
Mill on the Hill, The	I	F	187	Supersonics	Rigby
Millard Fillmore	U	B	250+	Profiles of the Presidents	Compass Point Books
Millard Fillmore: Thirteenth President	R	B	250+	Getting to Know the U.S. Presidents	Children's Press
Millennium Prophecies	Z	I	250+	Unsolved Mysteries	Steck-Vaughn
Miller Who Tried to Please Everyone, The	K	TL	250+	Aesop's Fables	Pearson Learning Group
Millicent Min, Girl Genius	X	RF	250+	Yee, Lisa	Scholastic
Millie Monster	I	F	315	Springboard	Wright Group/McGraw Hill
Millie's Adventure	J	RF	250+	Scooters	ETA Cuisenaire
Million Dollar Putt, The	S	RF	250+	Gutman, Dan	Hyperion
Million Dollar Shot, The	S	RF	250+	Gutman, Dan	Hyperion
Million Dollar Strike, The	S	RF	250+	Gutman, Dan	Hyperion
Milo and the Fire Engine Parade	J	RF	250+	Bookshop	Mondo
Milo and the Greatest Trick Ever!	J	RF	250+	Bookshop	Mondo
Milo's Great Invention	M	RF	250+	Pair-It Books	Steck-Vaughn
Milton Hershey	R	B	3529	History Maker Bios	Lerner Publications
Milton Hershey: Chocolate King Town Builder	P	B	250+	Simon, Charnan	Children's Press
Milton the Early Riser	J	F	148	Kraus, Robert	Aladdin
Milwaukee Brewers, The	S	I	250+	Team Spirit	Norwood House Press
Milwaukee Bucks, The	S	I	250+	Team Spirit	Norwood House Press
Milwaukee Cows	E	F	79	Story Box	Wright Group/McGraw Hill
Mimosa and the River of Wisdom: The Fairy Chronicles	Q	F	11700	Sweet, J.H.	Sourcebooks
Mina's Day	J	I	292	Reading Street	Pearson
Mina's Spring of Colors	S	RF	250+	Gilmore, Rachna	Fitzhenry & Whiteside
Minerals	R	I	1713	Early Bird Earth Systems	Lerner Publications
Minerals	Q	I	250+	Exploring the Earth	Capstone Press
Minerals	Q	I	250+	On Deck	Rigby
Minerals: A Resource Our World Depends On	V	I	250+	Managing Our Resources	Heinemann
Minerva's Dream	M	F	250+	Pair-It Books	Steck-Vaughn
Mine's the Best	G	RF	104	Bonsall, Crosby	HarperCollins

* Collection of short stories
\# Graphic text

TITLE	LEVEL	GENRE	WORD COUNT	AUTHOR / SERIES	PUBLISHER / DISTRIBUTOR
Ming Lo Moves the Mountain	J	F	250+	Lobel, Arnold	Scholastic
Ming on Mars	O	F	250+	In Step Readers	Rigby
Ming the Messenger	F	RF	91	Reading Street	Pearson
Minh's New Life	L	RF	250+	PM Plus Story Books	Rigby
Mini Mammals	R	I	250+	Explorers	Wright Group/McGraw Hill
Mini Markets or Mega Stores?	R	I	250+	WorldScapes	ETA Cuisenaire
Minibeasts	LB	I	12	Big Cat	Pacific Learning
Minibeasts	LB	I	15	Rigby Rocket	Rigby
Minibeasts	Q	I	250+	The News	Richard C. Owen
Minister's Daughter, The	Z+	F	250+	Hearn, Julie	Simon Pulse
Mink, a Fink, a Skating Rink, A: What Is a Noun?	O	I	335	Words Are CATegorical	Millbrook Press
Minnesota	T	I	250+	Hello U.S.A.	Lerner Publications
Minnesota	R	I	250+	This Land Is Your Land	Compass Point Books
Minnesota Twins, The	S	I	250+	Team Spirit	Norwood House Press
Minnesota Vikings, The	S	I	250+	Team Spirit	Norwood House Press
Minnie and Moo Go to Paris	J	F	250+	Cazet, Denys	DK Publishing
Minnie and Moo: The Attack of the Easter Bunnies	J	F	250+	Cazet, Denys	HarperCollins
Minnie and Moo: Will You Be My Valentine?	J	F	250+	Cazet, Denys	HarperCollins
Minpins, The	P	F	250+	Dahl, Roald	Penguin Group
Min's Plane Ride	B	RF	49	Bookshop	Mondo
Min-Yo and the Moon Dragon	N	TL	250+	Hillman, Elizabeth	Harcourt Brace
Miracle at the Plate	P	RF	250+	Christopher, Matt	Little, Brown & Co.
Miracle Material, A	V	I	250+	Navigators Science Series	Benchmark Education
Miracle Worker, The	Z	B	250+	Gibson, William	Bantam
Miracle's Boys	Z	RF	250+	Woodson, Jacqueline	Penguin Group
Miracles on Maple Hill	R	RF	250+	Sorensen, Virginia	Scholastic
Miraculous Journey of Edward Tulane, The	U	F	250+	DiCamillo, Kate	Candlewick Press
Miranda and the Movies	U	HF	250+	Kendall, Jane	Harcourt Brace
Mirandy and Brother Wind	R	F	250+	McKissack, Patricia	Alfred A. Knopf
Miriam Dives Into a Good Book	N	F	653	Leveled Readers	Houghton Mifflin Harcourt
Mirounga's Pup	L	RF	250+	Books for Young Learners	Richard C. Owen
Mirror Image	W	RF	250+	Orca Currents	Orca Book Publishers
Mirror Image, A	G	I	198	Shutterbug Books	Steck-Vaughn
Mirror Magic	C	RF	20	Harry's Math Books	Outside the Box
Mirror, The	D	RF	112	Story Box	Wright Group/McGraw Hill
Misa Learns to Ride	I	RF	342	Rigby Flying Colors	Rigby
Mischief	M	RF	250+	Pacific Literacy	Pacific Learning
Mischief and Mayhem	P	F	250+	Storyteller Chapter Books	Wright Group/ McGraw Hill
Miserable Mill, The	V	F	250+	Snicket, Lemony	Scholastic
Misfits, The	W	RF	250+	Howe, James	Aladdin
Misfortune Cookie, The	N	F	250+	The Zack Files	Grossett & Dunlap
Misha Disappears	K	RF	250+	Literacy 2000	Rigby
Mishi-Na	I	F	217	Sunshine	Wright Group/McGraw Hill
Mishmash	N	RF	250+	Cone, Molly	Pocket Books
Miss Flutter Remembers	K	F	2100	Sims, Henrietta Barbara	Kaeden Books
Miss Fuzzy	H	F	219	Handprints D	Educators Publishing Service
Miss Geeta's Hair	D	F	44	Joy Readers	Pearson Learning Group
Miss Geneva's Lantern	P	RF	250+	Bookshop	Mondo
Miss Grimble	I	RF	265	Sails	Rigby
Miss Hen's Feast	I	F	434	Leveled Readers	Houghton Mifflin Harcourt
Miss McKenzie Had a Farm	J	F	515	Pair-It Books	Steck-Vaughn

* Collection of short stories
\# Graphic text

TITLE	LEVEL	GENRE	WORD COUNT	AUTHOR / SERIES	PUBLISHER / DISTRIBUTOR
Miss Messier's Mess	J	RF	596	InfoTrek	ETA Cuisenaire
Miss Mouse Gets Married	K	TL	250+	Folk Tales	Wright Group/McGraw Hill
Miss Muffett and the Spider	I	F	270	Ready Readers	Pearson Learning Group
Miss Nelson Has a Field Day	L	RF	250+	Allard, Harry	Scholastic
Miss Nelson Is Missing	L	RF	598	Allard, Harry	Houghton Mifflin Harcourt
Miss Piggy's Night Out	J	F	250+	Hunter, Sandra H.	Puffin/Penguin
Miss Popple's Pets	A	RF	28	Literacy 2000	Rigby
Miss Rumphius	M	RF	250+	Cooney, Barbara	Penguin Group
Miss Smith's Incredible Storybook	M	F	250+	Garland, Michael	Scholastic
Miss Wire's Christmas Surprise	K	F	250+	I Am Reading	Kingfisher
Missiles and Rockets	V	I	4341	Military Hardware in Action	Lerner Publications
Missing	Q	RF	250+	Spirn, M. Sobel	Stone Arch Books
Missing Cat, The	I	RF	414	Leveled Literacy Intervention/ Green System	Heinemann
Missing Earrings, The	D	F	98	Georgie Giraffe	Literacy Footprints
Missing Fossil Mystery, The	L	RF	250+	Herman, Emily	Hyperion
Missing 'Gator of Gumbo Limbo, The	S	RF	250+	George, Jean Craighead	HarperTrophy
Missing Glasses, The	D	RF	99	Emergent	Pioneer Valley
Missing Glove, The	F	RF	212	Leveled Readers	Houghton Mifflin Harcourt
Missing Glove, The	F	RF	212	Leveled Readers/CA	Houghton Mifflin Harcourt
Missing Glove, The	F	RF	212	Leveled Readers/TX	Houghton Mifflin Harcourt
Missing Keys, The	K	RF	819	Rigby Flying Colors	Rigby
Missing Lighthouse, The	Q	RF	250+	Reading Expeditions	National Geographic
Missing May	W	RF	250+	Rylant, Cynthia	Bantam
Missing Necklace, The	H	F	231	Reading Unlimited	Pearson Learning Group
Missing Osprey Nest, The	Q	RF	250+	Ragged Island Mysteries	Wright Group/McGraw Hill
Missing Parrot, The	J	RF	491	Early Connections	Benchmark Education
Missing Pet Mystery, The	H	RF	174	Instant Readers	Harcourt School Publishers
Missing Pet, The	K	RF	618	Pair-It Books	Steck-Vaughn
Missing Pieces	Q	RF	250+	Power Up!	Steck-Vaughn
Missing Puppy Spots, The	F	RF	168	In Step Readers	Rigby
Missing Puppy, The	C	F	67	Bella and Rosie Series	Literacy Footprints
Missing Suit, The	H	F	250+	Phonics and Friends	Hampton-Brown
Missing Tooth, The	J	RF	250+	Cole, Joanna	Random House
Missing Will, The	M	RF	250+	Woodland Mysteries	Wright Group/McGraw Hill
Missing!	Q	HF	250+	Capeci, Anne	Peachtree
Missing!	L	RF	699	Rigby Flying Colors	Rigby
Mission Control	N	I	250+	Explore Space!	Red Brick Learning
Mission: Steel	P	I	250+	Rigby Focus	Rigby
Mississippi	R	I	250+	This Land Is Your Land	Compass Point Books
Mississippi Bridge	S	HF	250+	Taylor, Mildred	Bantam
Mississippi Marvis Barnes	P	TL	1000	Leveled Readers/TX	Houghton Mifflin Harcourt
Mississippi River, The	M	I	250+	Rookie Read-About Geography	Children's Press
Mississippi Trial, 1955	Z+	HF	250+	Crowe, Chris	Penguin Group
Missoula, Montana	Q	I	250+	Theme Sets	National Geographic
Missouri	T	I	250+	Hello U.S.A.	Lerner Publications
Missouri	R	I	250+	This Land Is Your Land	Compass Point Books
Mistakes That Worked	T	I	250+	Jones, Charlotte Foltz	Bantam Doubleday Dell
Mister Mole's Stove	J	F	604	Appleton-Smith, Laura	Flyleaf Publishing
Mister Wolf's Plan	E	F	84	Rigby Rocket	Rigby
Misty of Chincoteague	R	RF	250+	Henry, Marguerite	Aladdin
Misty Sleeps	E	RF	56	Books for Young Learners	Richard C. Owen
Misty's Mischief	H	F	61	Campbell, Rod	Viking/Penguin
Misty's Twilight	R	RF	250+	Henry, Marguerite	Aladdin

* Collection of short stories
# Graphic text

TITLE	LEVEL	GENRE	WORD COUNT	AUTHOR / SERIES	PUBLISHER / DISTRIBUTOR
Mitch and Amy	O	RF	250+	Cleary, Beverly	HarperCollins
Mitch to the Rescue	I	RF	302	PM Story Books-Orange	Rigby
Mitchell Is Moving	J	F	250+	Sharmat, Marjorie Weinman	Simon & Schuster
Mitchell's Readathon	J	RF	665	InfoTrek	ETA Cuisenaire
Mitt for Me, A	B	RF	34	First Stories	Pacific Learning
Mitten, The	M	TL	250+	Brett, Jan	Scholastic
Mitten, The	D	TL	212	Leveled Literacy Intervention/ Blue System	Heinemann
Mix It Up	C	I	35	Twig	Wright Group/McGraw Hill
Mix It Up!	C	I	44	Leveled Readers Science	Houghton Mifflin Harcourt
Mix It Up!	D	I	52	Rigby Focus	Rigby
Mix, Make, and Munch	J	I	245	Home Connection Collection	Rigby
Mixed-up Max	Q	F	250+	King-Smith, Dick	Troll Associates
Mixed-Up Mystery, A	T	I	1541	Independent Readers Science	Houghton Mifflin Harcourt
Mixed-Up Vegetables	U	I	1591	Reading Street	Pearson
Mixed-Up Wigs, The	I	F	199	Leveled Readers	Houghton Mifflin Harcourt
Mixed-Up Wishing Well, The	N	F	250+	Rigby Rocket	Rigby
Mixing Colors	B	I	15	Rigby Literacy	Rigby
Mixing Things	C	I	51	Leveled Readers Science	Houghton Mifflin Harcourt
Mixing, Kneading, and Baking: The Baker's Art	P	I	2248	Reading Street	Pearson
Miyu and the Cranes for Peace	Q	RF	949	Leveled Readers	Houghton Mifflin Harcourt
MM Mouse at the Movies	J	RF	318	Sails	Rigby
Mmm . . . Very Nice	E	F	91	Home Connection Collection	Rigby
Mmm Apples	E	F	92	Bonnell, Kris	Reading Reading Books
Mmm Milk	D	I	46	Little Celebrations	Pearson Learning Group
Moana Makana	R	RF	250+	WorldScapes	ETA Cuisenaire
Moana's Island	J	RF	450	Sunshine	Wright Group/McGraw Hill
Mobile Days	U	I	250+	PM Extensions	Rigby
Moccasin Trail	W	RF	250+	McGraw, Eloise	Scholastic
Moccasins	LB	I	20	Twig	Wright Group/McGraw Hill
Model, The	B	I	18	Smart Starts	Rigby
Models	G	I	231	Yellow Umbrella Books	Red Brick Learning
Modern Dance	S	I	250+	Dance	Capstone Press
Modern Middle East	V	I	250+	Primary Source Readers	Teacher Created Materials
Modern Times	R	I	250+	Journey Through History	Barron's Educational
Mog at the Zoo	L	F	250+	Nicoll, Helen	Penguin Group
Moggy the Mouser	J	F	250+	Voyages	SRA/McGraw Hill
Mog's Mumps	L	F	250+	Nicoll, Helen	Penguin Group
Mohandas Gandhi	U	B	1298	Time for Kids	Teacher Created Materials
Mohandas Gandhi: A Life of Integrity	P	B	584	Pull Ahead Books	Lerner Publications
Mojo and Weeza and the Funny Thing	G	F	147	Big Cat	Pacific Learning
Mojo and Weeza and the New Hat	F	F	146	Big Cat	Pacific Learning
Moki	Q	HF	250+	Penny, Grace Jackson	Penguin Group
Moldy Mystery, A	M	RF	250+	Science Solves It!	Kane Press
Mole Sisters and the Blue Egg, The	G	F	84	Schwartz, Roslyn	Annick Press
Mole Sisters and the Busy Bees, The	I	F	115	Schwartz, Roslyn	Annick Press
Mole Sisters and the Cool Breeze, The	I	F	121	Schwartz, Roslyn	Annick Press
Mole Sisters and the Fairy Ring, The	H	F	83	Schwartz, Roslyn	Annick Press
Mole Sisters and the Moonlit Night, The	I	F	111	Schwartz, Roslyn	Annick Press
Mole Sisters and the Piece of Moss, The	I	F	111	Schwartz, Roslyn	Annick Press
Mole Sisters and the Question, The	I	F	105	Schwartz, Roslyn	Annick Press
Mole Sisters and the Rainy Day, The	G	F	91	Schwartz, Roslyn	Annick Press
Mole Sisters and the Wavy Wheat, The	I	F	110	Schwartz, Roslyn	Annick Press
Mole Sisters and the Way Home, The	H	F	85	Schwartz, Roslyn	Annick Press

* Collection of short stories
# Graphic text

TITLE	LEVEL	GENRE	WORD COUNT	AUTHOR / SERIES	PUBLISHER / DISTRIBUTOR
*Mollie Whuppie	K	TL	250+	New Way Orange	Steck-Vaughn
Molly and Harry	H	F	328	Sails	Rigby
Molly in the Middle	K	RF	1413	Real Kids Readers	Millbrook Press
Molly Learns a Lesson	Q	HF	250+	The American Girls Collection	Pleasant Company
Molly Makes a Graph	G	RF	110	Seedlings	Continental Press
Molly Monster's Party	C	F	86	Springboard	Wright Group/McGraw Hill
Molly Pitcher	N	B	208	First Biographies	Capstone Press
Molly Pitcher: Young Patriot	O	B	250+	Childhood of Famous Americans	Aladdin
Molly Saves the Day	Q	HF	250+	The American Girls Collection	Pleasant Company
Molly the Brave and Me	K	RF	250+	O'Connor, Jane	Random House
Molly's Bracelet	I	RF	250+	Voyages	SRA/McGraw Hill
Molly's Broccoli	I	RF	233	Ready Readers	Pearson Learning Group
Molly's Hard Bargain	I	RF	180	Instant Readers	Harcourt School Publishers
Molly's Mailbox	F	RF	122	Teacher's Choice Series	Pearson Learning Group
Molly's New Team	F	RF	161	Leveled Readers	Houghton Mifflin Harcourt
Molly's New Team	F	RF	161	Leveled Readers/CA	Houghton Mifflin Harcourt
Molly's New Team	F	RF	161	Leveled Readers/TX	Houghton Mifflin Harcourt
Molly's Pilgrim	M	RF	250+	Cohen, Barbara	Bantam
Molly's Surprise	Q	HF	250+	The American Girls Collection	Pleasant Company
Molly's Trampoline	J	F	407	Sails	Rigby
Mom	B	I	32	InfoTrek	ETA Cuisenaire
Mom	A	RF	25	Leveled Literacy Intervention/Orange System	Heinemann
Mom	A	I	24	PM Starters	Rigby
Mom and Kayla	B	RF	69	Leveled Literacy Intervention/Green System	Heinemann
Mom at the Football Game	J	F	381	Sails	Rigby
Mom at the Market	J	RF	301	Sails	Rigby
Mom at Work	B	I	56	Rigby Flying Colors	Rigby
Mom Can Fix Anything	D	RF	74	Learn to Read	Creative Teaching Press
Mom Dresses Up	A	RF	46	Mom and Dad Series	Pioneer Valley
Mom Goes Shopping	A	RF	34	Mom and Dad Series	Pioneer Valley
Mom Is a Painter	B	I	34	Bebop Books	Lee & Low Books Inc.
Mom Is Busy	B	RF	33	Handprints A	Educators Publishing Service
Mom Likes Hats	A	RF	40	Mom and Dad Series	Pioneer Valley
Mom Named Dad, A	L	RF	250+	Rigby Literacy	Rigby
Mom Paints the House	H	RF	220	Foundations	Wright Group/McGraw Hill
Mom, You're Fired!	O	RF	250+	Robinson, Nancy K.	Scholastic
Momentous Decision, A	X	I	3354	Leveled Readers	Houghton Mifflin Harcourt
Momentous Decision, A	X	I	3354	Leveled Readers/CA	Houghton Mifflin Harcourt
Mommy, Where Are You?	B	RF	64	Ziefert, Harriet	Puffin/Penguin
Momotaro	M	F	631	Sunshine	Wright Group/McGraw Hill
Moms	B	RF	34	Handprints B	Educators Publishing Service
Moms and Dads	A	I	36	PM Starters	Rigby
Mom's Bag	I	RF	404	Sails	Rigby
Mom's Birthday	I	RF	229	Sunshine	Wright Group/McGraw Hill
Mom's Diet	I	RF	228	Sunshine	Wright Group/McGraw Hill
Mom's Getting Married	K	RF	376	Sunshine	Wright Group/McGraw Hill
Mom's Haircut	H	RF	99	Literacy 2000	Rigby
Mom's Hat	C	RF	39	Joy Readers	Pearson Learning Group
Mom's Hat	C	RF	114	Sails	Rigby
Mom's New Car	D	RF	116	Foundations	Wright Group/McGraw Hill

* Collection of short stories
# Graphic text

TITLE	LEVEL	GENRE	WORD COUNT	AUTHOR / SERIES	PUBLISHER / DISTRIBUTOR
Mom's New Car	D	RF	119	Springboard	Wright Group/McGraw Hill
Mom's Salsa Garden	F	RF	196	On Our Way to English	Rigby
Mom's Secret	H	RF	143	Costain, Meredith	Scholastic
Mom's Shoes	E	RF	133	Handprints C	Educators Publishing Service
Mom's Shoes	J	RF	298	Sails	Rigby
Mom's Stories	D	RF	32	Vocabulary Readers	Houghton Mifflin Harcourt
Mon Hung and Mon Lung	I	RF	250+	On Our Way to English	Rigby
Monarch Butterflies	G	I	56	Pebble Books	Capstone Press
Monarch Butterflies	K	I	414	Pull Ahead Books	Lerner Publications
Monarch Butterflies	R	I	250+	Theme Sets	National Geographic
Monarch Butterfly	I	I	28	Book Bank	Wright Group/McGraw Hill
Monarch Butterfly	N	I	250+	Gibbons, Gail	Holiday House
Monarch Butterfly	N	I	250+	Life Cycles	Creative Teaching Press
Monarch Butterfly, The	I	I	152	Foundations	Wright Group/McGraw Hill
Monarch Mystery	E	I	117	Literacy by Design	Rigby
Monarchs on the Move	N	I	629	Leveled Readers	Houghton Mifflin Harcourt
Monarchs on the Move	N	I	629	Leveled Readers/CA	Houghton Mifflin Harcourt
Monarchs on the Move	N	I	629	Leveled Readers/TX	Houghton Mifflin Harcourt
Monday Came	K	RF	250+	Voyages	SRA/McGraw Hill
Mondo and Gordo Weather the Storm	L	F	759	Early Connections	Benchmark Education
Monet	X	B	250+	Eyewitness Books	DK Publishing
Monet	S	B	250+	Masterpieces: Artists and Their Works	Red Brick Learning
Monet	R	B	250+	Venezia, Mike	Children's Press
Money	M	I	250+	Early Connections	Benchmark Education
Money	U	I	250+	News Extra	Richard C. Owen
Money	M	I	250+	Spyglass Books	Compass Point Books
Money	J	I	250+	Twig	Wright Group/McGraw Hill
Money and You	O	I	250+	Reading Expeditions	National Geographic
Money Boot, The	N	RF	250+	Russell, Ginny	Fitzhenry & Whiteside
Money Hungry	V	RF	250+	Flake, Sharon G.	Scholastic
Money in My Pocket	G	I	133	Twig	Wright Group/McGraw Hill
Money Math	H	I	247	Yellow Umbrella Books	Red Brick Learning
Money Riddles That Count	K	I	250+	Pair-It Books	Steck-Vaughn
Money Saving and Spending	I	I	174	Rosen Real Readers	Rosen Publishing Group
Money, Money, Money	R	I	1242	Vocabulary Readers	Houghton Mifflin Harcourt
Money, Money, Money	R	I	1242	Vocabulary Readers/CA	Houghton Mifflin Harcourt
Money, Money, Money!	O	I	250+	Bookweb	Rigby
Mongol Warriors	T	I	250+	Warriors of History	Capstone Press
Mongols, The	S	I	250+	Journey Into Civilization	Chelsea House
Monica and the Summer Party	M	RF	250+	Sunflower	Intercultural Center for Research in Education
Monica Goes to the Zoo	M	RF	250+	Sunflower	Intercultural Center for Research in Education
Monique's Moon Log	M	I	644	In Step Readers	Rigby
Monkey	A	I	32	Leveled Literacy Intervention/ Green System	Heinemann
Monkey and Fire	J	F	372	Literacy 2000	Rigby
Monkey and Gorilla	E	F	150	Sails	Rigby
Monkey Baby Grows Up, A	L	I	363	Baby Animals	Lerner Publications
Monkey Bridge, The	D	F	66	Sunshine	Wright Group/McGraw Hill
Monkey Business	L	I	250+	Storyteller- Shooting Stars	Wright Group/ McGraw Hill
Monkey Hop, The	C	F	26	Joy Readers	Pearson Learning Group

TITLE	LEVEL	GENRE	WORD COUNT	AUTHOR / SERIES	PUBLISHER / DISTRIBUTOR
Monkey Island	V	RF	250+	Fox, Paula	Orchard Books
Monkey Moves	B	I	16	Pair-It Books	Steck-Vaughn
Monkey on the Roof	D	RF	92	PM Plus Story Books	Rigby
Monkey Paint	F	F	157	Gear Up!	Wright Group/McGraw Hill
Monkey Pudding and Other Dessert Recipes	S	I	250+	Fun Food for Cool Cooks	Capstone Press
Monkey See, Monkey Do	E	F	89	Gave, Marc	Scholastic
Monkey Tricks	E	F	81	Joy Readers	Pearson Learning Group
Monkey Tricks	H	RF	328	PM Collection	Rigby
Monkey Trouble	O	RF	250+	WorldScapes	ETA Cuisenaire
Monkey Watch	I	F	262	Sails	Rigby
Monkey, The	A	I	32	On Our Way to English	Rigby
Monkeys	B	I	27	Canizares, Susan; Chanko, Pamela	Scholastic
Monkeys	G	I	27	Reading Unlimited	Pearson Learning Group
Monkeys	A	F	18	Sails	Rigby
Monkeys & Apes	K	I	250+	PM Animal Facts: Turquoise	Rigby
Monkey's Friends	C	F	36	Literacy 2000	Rigby
Monkey's Ride	I	F	350	Sails	Rigby
Monkey's Tail	B	F	76	Sails	Rigby
Monkeys, Diverse Animals	U	I	250+	Sails	Rigby
Monsoon Civilizations	V	I	2591	Independent Readers Social Studies	Houghton Mifflin Harcourt
Monsoon Makers, The	U	RF	250+	WorldScapes	ETA Cuisenaire
Monsoons of India	W	I	2070	Leveled Readers	Houghton Mifflin Harcourt
Monsoons of India	W	I	2070	Leveled Readers/CA	Houghton Mifflin Harcourt
Monster	Z	RF	250+	inZone Books	Hampton-Brown
Monster	Z	RF	250+	Myers, Walter Dean	HarperCollins
Monster	I	F	201	Read Alongs	Rigby
Monster and the Baby	D	F	48	Mueller, Virginia	Puffin/Penguin
Monster at the Beach, The	E	RF	82	Storyteller-Moon Rising	Wright Group/McGraw Hill
Monster Bones, The Story of a Dinosaur Fossil	Q	I	250+	Science Works	Picture Window Books
Monster Bus	F	F	103	The Monster Bus Series	Pearson Learning Group
Monster Bus Goes on a Hot Air Balloon Trip	I	F	254	The Monster Bus Series	Pearson Learning Group
Monster Bus Goes to the Races	H	F	158	The Monster Bus Series	Pearson Learning Group
Monster Bus Goes to Yellowstone Park	I	F	259	The Monster Bus Series	Pearson Learning Group
Monster Can't Sleep	D	F	52	Mueller, Virginia	Puffin/Penguin
Monster Fish Frenzy	Q	F	250+	Wiley & Grampa's Creature Features	Little, Brown & Co.
Monster for Hire	M	F	250+	Wilson, Trevor	Mondo
Monster for Miss Owen, A	H	RF	185	Storyworlds	Heinemann Educational Books
Monster from Mercury, The	L	F	250+	Popcorn	Sundance
Monster from the Sea, The	K	TL	250+	Bank Street	Bantam
Monster House, A	LB	F	12	Sails	Rigby
Monster in the Attic, The	F	RF	151	Literacy by Design	Rigby
Monster in the Backpack, The	K	F	250+	Moser, Lisa	Candlewick Press
Monster in the Cave, The	J	F	250+	Lighthouse	Ginn & Co.
Monster in the Wardrobe, The	O	F	250+	High-Fliers	Pacific Learning
Monster Is Coming!, The	K	F	250+	Rigby Star	Rigby
Monster Is Coming, The	K	F	250+	Rigby Literacy	Rigby
Monster Machines	V	I	250+	Boldprint	Steck-Vaughn
Monster Machines	M	I	250+	Explorations	Okapi Educational Materials
Monster Machines	M	I	250+	Explorations	Eleanor Curtain Publishing
Monster Manners	J	F	250+	Cole, Joanna	Scholastic

* Collection of short stories
# Graphic text

TITLE	LEVEL	GENRE	WORD COUNT	AUTHOR / SERIES	PUBLISHER / DISTRIBUTOR
Monster Math Picnic	G	F	98	Maccarone, Grace	Scholastic
Monster Math School Time	G	F	120	Maccarone, Grace	Scholastic
Monster Mayhem: Jokes to Scare You Silly!	O	F	1641	Make Me Laugh!	Lerner Publications
Monster Meal	C	F	47	Rigby Star	Rigby
Monster Meals	C	F	33	Literacy 2000	Rigby
Monster Mess	A	F	18	Big Cat	Pacific Learning
Monster Money	H	F	130	Maccarone, Grace	Scholastic
Monster Mop	LB	F	8	Ready Readers	Pearson Learning Group
Monster Movie	K	F	250+	Cole, Joanna	Scholastic
Monster of Mirror Mountain, The	K	F	250+	Literacy 2000	Rigby
Monster of the Year	S	F	250+	Coville, Bruce	Pocket Books
Monster Party	A	F	29	Bookshop	Mondo
Monster Party	A	F	20	Literacy 2000	Rigby
Monster Party	A	F	20	Smart Starts	Rigby
Monster Planet	Q	SF	250+	Orme, David	Stone Arch Books
Monster Rabbit Runs Amuck!	M	RF	250+	Giff, Patricia Reilly	Bantam
Monster Sandwich, A	C	F	36	Story Box	Wright Group/McGraw Hill
Monster Songs	I	RF	527	Real Kids Readers	Millbrook Press
Monster Soup	LB	F	33	Rigby Literacy	Rigby
Monster Stew	F	F	117	Learn to Read	Creative Teaching Press
Monster Town, The	A	F	24	Sails	Rigby
Monster Trucks	M	I	250+	Horsepower	Capstone Press
Monster Trucks	H	I	133	Mighty Machines	Capstone Press
Monster Trucks	L	I	137	On Deck	Rigby
Monster Trucks	L	I	354	Pull Ahead Books	Lerner Publications
Monster Trucks	Q	I	250+	Wild Rides!	Red Brick Learning
Monster Under the Bed, The	K	F	250+	Ready Readers	Pearson Learning Group
Monster, Monster	C	F	38	Reading Corners	Pearson Learning Group
Monster, The	D	RF	29	Harry's Math Books	Outside the Box
Monster, The	C	RF	83	Sun Sprouts	ETA Cuisenaire
Monsterology: The Complete Book of Monstrous Beasts	X	I	250+	Steer, Dugald	Candlewick Press
Monsters	Z	I	7201	The Unexplained	Lerner Publications
Monsters	C	F	30	TOTTS	Tott Publications
Monster's Clothes, The	LB	F	12	Sails	Rigby
Monsters Don't Scuba Dive	M	F	250+	Dadey, Debbie; Jones, Marcia Thornton	Scholastic
Monster's New Friend, The	K	F	250+	Rigby Literacy	Rigby
Monsters Next Door, The	L	RF	250+	Dadey, Debbie; Jones, Marcia Thornton	Scholastic
Monsters of the Deep	L	I	250+	Marine Life For Young Readers	Pearson Learning Group
Monsters of the Myth	T	I	522	Vocabulary Readers	Houghton Mifflin Harcourt
Monster's Party, The	C	F	92	Story Box	Wright Group/McGraw Hill
Monster's Ring, The	R	F	250+	Coville, Bruce	Pocket Books
Monsters' Tea Party, The	E	F	129	Learn to Read	Creative Teaching Press
Monsters!	D	F	45	My First Reader	Grolier Press
Montana	T	I	250+	Hello U.S.A.	Lerner Publications
Montana	R	I	250+	This Land Is Your Land	Compass Point Books
Montezuma and the Aztecs	X	I	2755	Leveled Readers	Houghton Mifflin Harcourt
Montezuma and the Aztecs	X	I	2755	Leveled Readers/CA	Houghton Mifflin Harcourt
Montezuma: Aztec Ruler	X	B	250+	Primary Source Readers	Teacher Created Materials
Montgomery Bus Boycott, The	T	I	1432	Leveled Readers	Houghton Mifflin Harcourt
Montgomery Bus Boycott, The	T	I	1432	Leveled Readers/CA	Houghton Mifflin Harcourt
Months	F	I	93	Calendars	Lerner Publications

* Collection of short stories
# Graphic text

TITLE	LEVEL	GENRE	WORD COUNT	AUTHOR / SERIES	PUBLISHER / DISTRIBUTOR
Months	H	I	135	The Calendar	Capstone Press
Monticello	V	I	250+	Cornerstones of Freedom	Children's Press
Monticello	T	I	250+	We The People	Compass Point Books
Monty and the Ghost Train	C	F	48	Storyworlds	Heinemann Educational Publishers
Monty at McBurgers	D	F	40	Storyworlds	Heinemann Educational Publishers
Monty at the Party	C	F	46	Storyworlds	Heinemann Educational Publishers
Monty at the Seaside	C	F	38	Storyworlds	Heinemann Educational Publishers
Monty, the Missing Cat	E	RF	100	Developing Books	Pioneer Valley
Monuments and Mummies	T	I	250+	InfoQuest	Rigby
Moog-Moog, Space Barber	N	F	250+	Teague, Mark	Scholastic
Moon	F	RF	38	Books for Young Learners	Richard C. Owen
Moon	S	I	250+	Our Solar System	Compass Point Books
Moon	H	I	108	Space	Lerner Publications
Moon and Beyond, The	U	I	250+	Power Up!	Steck-Vaughn
Moon and the Mirror, The	M	TL	250+	Literacy 2000	Rigby
Moon Boy	J	F	250+	Bank Street	Bantam
Moon Bridge, The	W	HF	250+	Savin, Marcia	Scholastic
Moon Cake, The	E	RF	127	Joy Readers	Pearson Learning Group
Moon Car Race, The	D	F	107	Springboard	Wright Group/McGraw Hill
Moon Festival, The	G	RF	202	Reading Street	Pearson
Moon Journal	L	RF	250+	Rigby Literacy	Rigby
Moon Kids	T	SF	5379	Reading Street	Pearson
Moon Lady and Her Festival, The	M	F	635	Reading Street	Pearson
Moon Landing	V	I	250+	Platt, Richard	Candlewick Press
Moon Landing, The	G	RF	189	Springboard	Wright Group/McGraw Hill
Moon Over Tennessee: A Boy's Civil War Journal	W	B	250+	Crist-Evans, Craig	Houghton Mifflin Harcourt
Moon Rope: Un Lazo a la Luna	K	TL	250+	Ehlert, Lois	Harcourt
Moon Shadow	W	RF	250+	Platt, Chris	Peachtree
Moon Stories	J	F	250+	Ready Readers	Pearson Learning Group
Moon Story	E	RF	157	Sunshine	Wright Group/McGraw Hill
Moon, The	U	I	250+	A First Book	Franklin Watts
Moon, The	I	I	165	Exploring the Galaxy	Capstone Press
Moon, The	Q	I	250+	Eye on the Universe	Crabtree
Moon, The	L	I	295	Gear Up!	Wright Group/McGraw Hill
Moon, The	D	F	139	Joy Readers	Pearson Learning Group
Moon, The	N	I	250+	Literacy 2000	Rigby
Moon, The	N	I	754	Our Universe	Lerner Publications
Moon, The	K	I	126	Out In Space	Red Brick Learning
Moon, The	S	I	1601	Reading Street	Pearson
Moon, The	D	I	51	Rigby Focus	Rigby
Moon, The	A	F	30	Sails	Rigby
Moon, The	L	I	139	Twig	Wright Group/McGraw Hill
Moonbeam Cow	K	TL	228	Books for Young Learners	Richard C. Owen
Moonhorse	M	F	250+	Osborne, Mary Pope	Alfred A. Knopf
Moonlight	D	RF	48	Literacy 2000	Rigby
Moonlight Man, The	U	F	250+	Wright, Betty Ren	Scholastic
Moonlight on the River	R	RF	250+	Kovacs, Deborah	Penguin Group
Moonlit Owl, The	I	RF	225	Cambridge Reading	Pearson Learning Group
Moonwalk: The First Trip to the Moon	O	I	250+	Donnelly, Judy	Random House

* Collection of short stories
\# Graphic text

TITLE	LEVEL	GENRE	WORD COUNT	AUTHOR / SERIES	PUBLISHER / DISTRIBUTOR
Moorchild, The	W	F	250+	McGraw, Eloise	Scholastic
Moose	O	I	1633	Early Bird Nature Books	Lerner Publications
Moose	E	I	100	Vocabulary Readers	Houghton Mifflin Harcourt
Moose	E	I	100	Vocabulary Readers/CA	Houghton Mifflin Harcourt
Moose and Mouse	J	F	250+	I Am Reading	Kingfisher
Moose Is Loose, A	F	F	120	Little Readers	Houghton Mifflin Harcourt
Moose Tales	J	F	250+	Van Laan, Nancy	Houghton Mifflin Harcourt
Moose, The	R	I	250+	Wildlife of North America	Red Brick Learning
Moose's Loose Tooth	G	F	142	Spinelle, Nancy Louise	Kaeden Books
Moosling in Winter	K	F	429	Leveled Literacy Intervention/ Blue System	Heinemann
Moosling the Baby Sitter	G	F	230	Leveled Literacy Intervention/ Blue System	Heinemann
Moosling the Hero	L	F	374	Leveled Literacy Intervention/ Blue System	Heinemann
Mop	C	RF	74	Leveled Literacy Intervention/ Orange System	Heinemann
Moppet on the Run	J	RF	250+	PM Story Books	Rigby
More Adventures of the Great Brain	T	RF	250+	Fitzgerald, John D.	Yearling
More and More Clowns	D	F	249	Van Allen, Roach	SRA/McGraw Hill
More Food for the Big Cat	E	RF	82	Bonnell, Kris	Reading Reading Books
More Monsters in School	N	RF	250+	Godfrey, M.	Fitzhenry & Whiteside
More or Less Fish Story	E	F	68	Wylie, Joanne & David	Children's Press
More or Less: A Rain Forest Counting Book	I	I	139	Counting Books	Capstone Press
More Perfect than the Moon	R	HF	250+	MacLachlan, Patricia	HarperCollins
More Perfect Union, A: The Story of Our Constitution	S	I	250+	Maestro, Betsy & Giulio	William Morrow
More Places to Visit	L	I	238	Windows on Literacy	National Geographic
More Spaghetti I Say	G	F	340	Gelman, Rita	Scholastic
More Spaghetti!	I	RF	250+	PM Plus Story Books	Rigby
*More Stories from Grandma's Attic	O	RF	250+	Richardson, Arleta	Chariot Victor Publishing
*More Stories Huey Tells	N	RF	250+	Cameron, Ann	Alfred A. Knopf
*More Stories Julian Tells	N	RF	250+	Cameron, Ann	Random House
*More Tales of Amanda Pig	L	F	1939	Van Leeuwen, Jean	Penguin Group
*More Tales of Oliver Pig	L	F	250+	Van Leeuwen, Jean	Puffin/Penguin
More Than Anything Else	R	HF	250+	Bradby, Marie	Scholastic
More Than One	I	F	238	Sunshine	Wright Group/McGraw Hill
More Trouble	H	F	264	Bella and Rosie Series	Literacy Footprints
More Water, Please! Animals in Dry Places	M	I	250+	Literacy by Design	Rigby
*More! More! More!	M	TL	250+	Story Box	Wright Group/McGraw Hill
More, the Merrier, The	Q	RF	250+	Mazer, Anne	Scholastic
Morgan's Zoo	Q	F	250+	Howe, James	Aladdin
Mormon Pioneer Trail, The	Q	I	250+	On Deck	Rigby
Morning and Night	C	I	112	Vocabulary Readers	Houghton Mifflin Harcourt
Morning and Night	C	I	112	Vocabulary Readers/CA	Houghton Mifflin Harcourt
Morning Bath	J	F	250+	Sunshine	Wright Group/McGraw Hill
Morning Dance, The	K	RF	268	Jellybeans	Rigby
Morning Girl	S	HF	250+	Dorris, Michael	Hyperion
Morning Meals Around the World	M	I	250+	Meals Around the World	Picture Window Books
Morning Queen, The	J	F	250+	Sunshine	Wright Group/McGraw Hill
Morning Star	J	F	250+	Literacy 2000	Rigby
Morphing Monster, The	T	F	250+	Reading Safari	Mondo
Morris and Boris at the Circus	J	F	250+	Wiseman, Bernard	HarperTrophy
Morris Goes to School	J	F	250+	Wiseman, Bernard	HarperTrophy

* Collection of short stories
# Graphic text

TITLE	LEVEL	GENRE	WORD COUNT	AUTHOR / SERIES	PUBLISHER / DISTRIBUTOR
Morris Plays Hide and Seek	I	F	304	Big Cat	Pacific Learning
Morris the Moose	H	F	250+	Wiseman, Bernard	HarperTrophy
Morse and the Telegraph	N	B	524	Leveled Readers Science	Houghton Mifflin Harcourt
Morte D' Arthur, Le	Z+	TL	250+	Malory, Sir Thomas	Hyperion
Moses	V	B	250+	Weatherford, Carole Boston	Hyperion
Mosquito	C	I	46	Book Bank	Wright Group/McGraw Hill
Mosquito Buzzed, A	E	F	133	Little Readers	Houghton Mifflin Harcourt
Mosquito King, The	T	F	250+	Welvaert, Scott R.	Stone Arch Books
Mosquitoes	P	I	2297	Early Bird Nature Books	Lerner Publications
Mosquitoes	E	I	39	Pebble Books	Grolier Press
Mosquitoes	I	I	193	Sails	Rigby
Mosquitoes: Tiny Insect Troublemakers	T	I	3101	Insect World	Lerner Publications
Mossflower	Z	F	250+	Jacques, Brian	Ace Books
Most Beautiful Child, The	M	TL	250+	Cambridge Reading	Pearson Learning Group
Most Beautiful Place in the World, The	O	RF	250+	Cameron, Ann	Alfred A. Knopf
Most Excellent Community Service Project, The	R	RF	250+	Reading Street	Pearson
Most Scary Ghost	H	F	355	Jellybeans	Rigby
Most Terrible Creature in the World, The	M	F	340	Pacific Literacy	Pacific Learning
Most Unusual Pet, The	J	RF	250+	Scooters	ETA Cuisenaire
Most Wonderful Doll in the World, The	O	RF	250+	McGinley, Phyllis	Scholastic
Mostly Michael	Q	RF	250+	Smith, Robert Kimmel	Bantam
Mother and Me	B	RF	48	Spinelle, Nancy Louise	Kaeden Books
Mother Animals	B	I	45	Bonnell, Kris	Reading Reading Books
Mother Bear's Scarf	E	F	152	PM Stars	Rigby
Mother Bird	C	RF	75	PM Plus Story Books	Rigby
Mother Dog and Her Puppies, A	L	I	250+	All About Dogs	Literacy Footprints
Mother Giant's Book Review	N	F	250+	Springboard	Wright Group/ McGraw Hill
Mother Goose Caper, The	K	F	799	Georgie Giraffe	Literacy Footprints
Mother Hen	G	F	205	Book Bank	Wright Group/McGraw Hill
Mother Hippopotamus	LB	F	7	Foundations	Wright Group/McGraw Hill
Mother Hippopotamus Gets Wet	J	F	421	Foundations	Wright Group/McGraw Hill
Mother Hippopotamus Goes Canoeing	L	F	250+	Foundations	Wright Group/McGraw Hill
Mother Hippopotamus Goes Shopping	C	F	79	Foundations	Wright Group/McGraw Hill
Mother Hippopotamus's Dry Skin	I	F	201	Foundations	Wright Group/McGraw Hill
Mother Hippopotamus's Hiccups	I	F	162	Foundations	Wright Group/McGraw Hill
Mother Nature Goes Nuts! Amazing Natural Disasters	W	I	250+	Klutz	Scholastic
Mother Octopus	J	RF	119	Books for Young Learners	Richard C. Owen
Mother Sea Turtle	K	I	240	Foundations	Wright Group/McGraw Hill
Mother Sea Turtle	F	I	155	Leveled Literacy Intervention/ Blue System	Heinemann
Mother Sun's Rest Day	H	F	250+	Momentum Literacy Program	Troll Associates
Mother Teresa	M	B	250+	First Biographies	Red Brick Learning
Mother Teresa	O	B	1672	On My Own Biography	Lerner Publications
Mother Teresa of Calcutta	Q	B	250+	WorldScapes	ETA Cuisenaire
Mother Teresa: A Life of Caring	O	B	454	Pull Ahead Books	Lerner Publications
Mother Tiger and Her Cubs	G	F	212	PM Plus Story Books	Rigby
Mothers	F	I	49	Families	Capstone Press
Mothers	B	I	26	Pebble Books	Capstone Press
Mothers and Babies	F	I	163	PM Science Readers	Rigby
Mother's Day	F	I	128	Fiesta Holiday Series	Pearson Learning Group

* Collection of short stories
\# Graphic text

TITLE	LEVEL	GENRE	WORD COUNT	AUTHOR / SERIES	PUBLISHER / DISTRIBUTOR
Mother's Day	E	RF	118	PM Plus Story Books	Rigby
Mother's Helpers	K	RF	250+	Ready Readers	Pearson Learning Group
Mother's Journey, A	O	RF	1660	Markle, Sandra	Charlesbridge
Moths	I	I	102	Bugs, Bugs, Bugs	Capstone Press
Moths	I	I	65	Pebble Books	Red Brick Learning
Motion	I	I	155	Instant Readers	Harcourt School Publishers
Motion	P	I	250+	Our Physical World	Capstone Press
Motion	Q	I	250+	Simply Science	Compass Point Books
Motion: Push and Pull, Fast and Slow	N	I	250+	Amazing Science	Picture Window Books
Motocross Cycles	Q	I	250+	Wild Rides!	Capstone Press
Motocross Freestyle	M	I	250+	To the Extreme	Capstone Press
Motorbike Race, The	C	RF	48	Joy Readers	Pearson Learning Group
Motorbike Racer	O	B	250+	Wonder World	Wright Group/McGraw Hill
Motorbikes	Y	I	250+	Boldprint	Steck-Vaughn
Motorcycle Photo, The	J	RF	250+	PM Plus Story Books	Rigby
Motorcycle Police	S	I	250+	Law Enforcement	Capstone Press
Motorcycles	H	I	112	Mighty Machines	Capstone Press
Motorcycles	N	I	367	Pull Ahead Books	Lerner Publications
Motorcycles of the Past	M	I	250+	On Deck	Rigby
Mound Builders, The	P	I	426	Independent Readers Social Studies	Houghton Mifflin Harcourt
Mound of the Dead: The City of Mohenjo-Daro	X	I	2018	Independent Readers Social Studies	Houghton Mifflin Harcourt
Mount Rushmore	Q	I	250+	Let's See	Compass Point Books
Mount Rushmore	P	I	653	Pull Ahead Books	Lerner Publications
Mount St. Helens	O	I	250+	Early Connections	Benchmark Education
Mount St. Helen's	P	I	782	Reading Street	Pearson
Mount St. Helen's: A Mountain Explodes	O	I	250+	Literacy by Design	Rigby
Mount Vernon	V	I	250+	Cornerstones of Freedom	Children's Press
Mountain Adventure	R	RF	250+	Reading Expeditions	National Geographic
Mountain Bike Challenge, The	Q	I	250+	Orbit Chapter Books	Pacific Learning
Mountain Bike Mania	O	RF	250+	Action Packs	Rigby
Mountain Bikes	Q	I	250+	Wild Rides!	Capstone Press
Mountain Biking	M	I	250+	To the Extreme	Capstone Press
Mountain Gorillas	O	I	2986	Early Bird Nature Books	Lerner Publishing
Mountain Gorillas	O	I	250+	Wonder World	Wright Group/McGraw Hill
Mountain Gorillas in Danger	N	I	250+	Soar To Success	Houghton Mifflin Harcourt
Mountain Hike, The	F	RF	176	Developing Books	Pioneer Valley
Mountain Lion, The	O	I	250+	Crewe, Sabrina	Steck-Vaughn
Mountain Man and the President, The	Q	B	250+	First Reports	Compass Point Books
Mountain Manor Mystery	S	RF	250+	Bookshop	Mondo
Mountain Men of the West	S	I	250+	The Library of the Westward Expansion	Rosen Publishing Group
Mountain Mona	L	F	820	Big Cat	Pacific Learning
Mountain Rescue	I	I	209	Sails	Rigby
Mountain, The	J	F	348	Leveled Readers	Houghton Mifflin Harcourt
Mountain, The	J	F	348	Leveled Readers/CA	Houghton Mifflin Harcourt
Mountain, The	J	F	348	Leveled Readers/TX	Houghton Mifflin Harcourt
Mountains	L	I	250+	Early Connections	Benchmark Education
Mountains	Q	I	250+	First Reports	Compass Point Books
Mountains	J	I	293	Landforms	Lerner Publications

TITLE	LEVEL	GENRE	WORD COUNT	AUTHOR / SERIES	PUBLISHER / DISTRIBUTOR
Mountains	R	I	250+	The Wonders of Our World	Crabtree
Mountains	S	I	250+	Weitzman, David	Steck-Vaughn
Mountains of Fire	M	I	153	Windows on Literacy	National Geographic
Mountains of Quilt, The	N	F	250+	Willard, Nancy	Harcourt Brace
Mountains, Earthquakes and Volcanoes	U	I	2583	Science Support Readers	Houghton Mifflin Harcourt
Mountains, Hills, and Cliffs	M	I	250+	PM Plus Nonfiction	Rigby
Mounted Police	S	I	250+	Law Enforcement	Capstone Press
Mounted Police	I	I	200	On Deck	Rigby
Mouse	C	F	78	Leveled Literacy Intervention/ Orange System	Heinemann
Mouse	C	F	40	Story Box	Wright Group/McGraw Hill
Mouse and Bear	A	F	26	Leveled Readers	Houghton Mifflin Harcourt
Mouse and Bear	A	F	26	Leveled Readers/CA	Houghton Mifflin Harcourt
Mouse and Bear Are Friends	A	F	35	Leveled Readers	Houghton Mifflin Harcourt
Mouse and Bear Are Friends	A	F	35	Leveled Readers/CA	Houghton Mifflin Harcourt
Mouse and Crocodile	L	TL	573	Leveled Readers	Houghton Mifflin Harcourt
Mouse and Crocodile	L	TL	573	Leveled Readers/CA	Houghton Mifflin Harcourt
Mouse and Crocodile	L	TL	573	Leveled Readers/TX	Houghton Mifflin Harcourt
Mouse and Moose	LB	I	7	Reading Street	Pearson
Mouse and Owl	I	RF	250+	Start to Read	School Zone
Mouse and the Elephant, The	J	TL	250+	Little Readers	Houghton Mifflin Harcourt
Mouse and the Motorcycle, The	O	F	250+	Cleary, Beverly	Avon Camelot
Mouse Around	WB	F	N/A	Collington, Peter	Alfred A. Knopf
Mouse Called Wolf, A	O	F	250+	King-Smith, Dick	Alfred A. Knopf
Mouse Deer and the Crocodiles, The	J	TL	250+	PM Plus Story Books	Rigby
Mouse Deer Escapes, The	J	TL	250+	PM Plus Story Books	Rigby
Mouse Finds a House	D	F	72	Start to Read	School Zone
Mouse Hunt	C	RF	40	Brand New Readers	Candlewick Press
Mouse in the Forest, The	I	I	211	Leveled Readers	Houghton Mifflin Harcourt
Mouse in the House, A	G	RF	228	Jasper the Cat	Pioneer Valley
Mouse Magic	O	RF	250+	Baglio, Ben M.	Scholastic
Mouse Manual	M	F	250+	Sails	Rigby
Mouse Mapper, The	I	F	273	Take Two Books	Wright Group/McGraw Hill
Mouse Monster	J	F	302	Jellybeans	Rigby
Mouse of Amherst, The	Q	F	250+	Spires, Elizabeth	Farrar, Straus and Giroux
Mouse Party!	M	F	250+	Little Celebrations	Pearson Learning Group
Mouse Rap, The	W	RF	250+	Myers, Walter Dean	HarperTrophy
*Mouse Soup	J	F	1350	Lobel, Arnold	HarperCollins
Mouse Stone, The	K	F	250+	Lighthouse	Ginn & Co.
*Mouse Tales	J	F	1519	Lobel, Arnold	HarperCollins
Mouse Train	B	F	48	Story Box	Wright Group/McGraw Hill
Mouse Views	LB	RF	12	McMillan, Bruce	Holiday House
Mouse Who Wanted to Marry, The	J	F	250+	Bank Street	Bantam
Mouse, The	C	F	26	Pacific Literacy	Pacific Learning
Mousehunter, The	T	F	250+	Milway, Alex	Little, Brown & Co.
Mouse's Baby Blanket	D	F	68	Brown, Beverly Swerdlow	Continental Press
Mouse's House	D	F	70	New Way Red	Steck-Vaughn
Mouse's Meadow	C	I	62	Independent Readers Science	Houghton Mifflin Harcourt
Mousetrap	G	RF	49	Snowball, Diane	Scholastic
Mountaineering Adventures	S	I	250+	Dangerous Adventures	Red Brick Learning
Mouths	B	I	33	Animal Traits	Lerner Publications
Move it	E	I	58	Wonder World	Wright Group/McGraw Hill
Move It!	R	I	250+	Orbit Chapter Books	Pacific Learning
Move It!	L	I	268	Spyglass Books	Compass Point Books

* Collection of short stories
# Graphic text

TITLE	LEVEL	GENRE	WORD COUNT	AUTHOR / SERIES	PUBLISHER / DISTRIBUTOR
Move It!: The Story of Animation	P	I	250+	Rigby Literacy	Rigby
Move Like Us!	H	RF	250+	Home Connection Collection	Rigby
Move Over!	E	F	118	Story Basket	Wright Group/McGraw Hill
Moves Make the Man, The	Z	RF	250+	Brooks, Bruce	HarperTrophy
Movie FX	U	I	250+	Boldprint	Steck-Vaughn
Movie Magic	T	I	250+	Sunshine	Wright Group/McGraw Hill
Moving	B	I	56	Little Red Readers	Sundance
Moving	R	RF	2569	Reading Street	Pearson
Moving	G	I	156	Vocabulary Readers	Houghton Mifflin Harcourt
Moving	G	I	156	Vocabulary Readers/CA	Houghton Mifflin Harcourt
Moving	G	I	156	Vocabulary Readers/TX	Houghton Mifflin Harcourt
Moving and Shaking	Q	I	250+	Bookweb	Rigby
Moving Away	F	RF	140	InfoTrek	ETA Cuisenaire
Moving Day	D	RF	90	Foundations	Wright Group/McGraw Hill
Moving Day	G	RF	215	Momentum Literacy Program	Troll Associates
Moving Day	K	F	379	Reading Street	Pearson
Moving Day	H	RF	315	Rigby Flying Colors	Rigby
Moving Day	LB	RF	28	Rigby Literacy	Rigby
Moving Day	C	RF	35	Rigby Star	Rigby
Moving Day	D	RF	64	Rookie Readers	Children's Press
Moving Day	F	RF	55	Shuter, Jane and Reynoldson, Fiona	Rigby
Moving Day	E	RF	110	Sunshine	Wright Group/McGraw Hill
Moving Day Surprise	H	RF	209	Bebop Books	Lee & Low Books Inc.
Moving From Place to Place	E	I	86	Shutterbug Books	Steck-Vaughn
Moving Home	M	I	250+	Explorations	Okapi Educational Materials
Moving Home	M	I	250+	Explorations	Eleanor Curtain Publishing
Moving In	E	RF	82	Foundations	Wright Group/McGraw Hill
Moving Mama to Town	X	RF	250+	Young, Ronder Thomas	Bantam
Moving on Sand and Snow	E	I	156	Sails	Rigby
Moving Things	M	I	250+	Sunshine	Wright Group/McGraw Hill
Moving to America	E	RF	81	Carousel Readers	Pearson Learning Group
Moving to America: My Travel Scrapbook	K	I	308	Dominie Factivity Series	Pearson Learning Group
Moving World, A	W	I	250+	PM Extensions	Rigby
Mozart Question, The	W	RF	250+	Morpurgo, Michael	Candlewick Press
Mozart Season, The	X	RF	250+	Wolff, Virginia Euwer	Henry Holt & Co.
Mr. and Mrs. Murphy and Bernard	K	F	250+	Little Celebrations	Pearson Learning Group
Mr. Ape	O	F	250+	King-Smith, Dick	Alfred A. Knopf
Mr. Beekman's Deli	H	F	96	Story Basket	Wright Group/McGraw Hill
Mr. Beep	M	F	250+	Read Alongs	Rigby
Mr. Big Goes on Holiday	G	F	177	Storyworlds	Heinemann Educational Books
Mr. Big Goes to the Park	F	F	186	Storyworlds	Heinemann Educational Publishers
Mr. Big Has a Party	G	F	177	Storyworlds	Heinemann Educational Books
Mr. Big Is a Big Help	G	F	212	Storyworlds	Heinemann Educational Books
Mr. Bitter's Butter	H	F	231	Story Basket	Wright Group/McGraw Hill
Mr. Brown	C	RF	20	KinderReaders	Rigby
Mr. Bumbleticker	B	F	28	Foundations	Wright Group/McGraw Hill
Mr. Bumbleticker Goes Shopping	J	F	391	Foundations	Wright Group/McGraw Hill
Mr. Bumbleticker Goes to the Zoo	L	RF	250+	Foundations	Wright Group/McGraw Hill
Mr. Bumbleticker Likes to Cook	I	F	196	Foundations	Wright Group/McGraw Hill

* Collection of short stories
# Graphic text

TITLE	LEVEL	GENRE	WORD COUNT	AUTHOR / SERIES	PUBLISHER / DISTRIBUTOR
Mr. Bumbleticker Likes to Fix Machines	I	F	142	Foundations	Wright Group/McGraw Hill
Mr. Bumbleticker's Apples	I	F	338	Foundations	Wright Group/McGraw Hill
Mr. Bumbleticker's Birthday	E	F	110	Foundations	Wright Group/McGraw Hill
Mr. Burger Is a Farmer	H	I	106	InfoTrek	ETA Cuisenaire
Mr. Clutterbus	H	F	250+	Voyages	SRA/McGraw Hill
Mr. Cool	K	F	250+	I Am Reading	Kingfisher
Mr. Crawford	E	RF	119	Foundations	Wright Group/McGraw Hill
Mr. Cricket Finds a Friend	G	F	134	Carousel Readers	Pearson Learning Group
Mr. Cricket Takes a Vacation	E	F	165	Carousel Readers	Pearson Learning Group
Mr. Cricket's New Home	F	F	121	Carousel Readers	Pearson Learning Group
Mr. Davis Is a Security Officer	F	I	101	InfoTrek	ETA Cuisenaire
Mr. Dugas Is a Carpenter	F	I	84	InfoTrek	ETA Cuisenaire
Mr. Egg	E	F	22	Pair-It Books	Steck-Vaughn
Mr. Fahrenheit and Mr. Celsius	T	I	1330	Leveled Readers Science	Houghton Mifflin Harcourt
Mr. Fin's Trip	E	F	130	Ready Readers	Pearson Learning Group
Mr. Fixit	H	RF	196	Sunshine	Wright Group/McGraw Hill
Mr. Fizzle, the Man Who Went "Boo!"	I	F	250+	Home Connection Collection	Rigby
Mr. Florentine's Violin	M	RF	250+	Bookweb	Rigby
Mr. Fluff at Laura's House	F	RF	134	Developing Books Set 4	Pioneer Valley
Mr. Greg's Garden	E	RF	118	Windows on Literacy	National Geographic
Mr. Grim and the Goose That Laid Golden Eggs	O	TL	1723	Reading Street	Pearson
Mr. Grump	D	F	73	Sunshine	Wright Group/McGraw Hill
Mr. Gumpy's Motor Car	L	RF	250+	Burningham, John	HarperCollins
Mr. Gumpy's Outing	L	RF	283	Burningham, John	Henry Holt & Co.
Mr. Hoot's Room	J	F	250+	The Wright Skills	Wright Group/McGraw Hill
Mr. Kean's Garden	M	RF	250+	Literacy by Design	Rigby
Mr. Lincoln's Drummer	W	HF	250+	Wisler, G. Clifton	Penguin Group
Mr. Magee's Goats	I	F	354	Sails	Rigby
Mr. Mancini's Rats	K	F	250+	Popcorn	Sundance
Mr. Marvel and the Cake	D	F	119	Storyworlds	Heinemann Educational Publishers
Mr. Marvel and the Car	D	F	118	Storyworlds	Heinemann Educational Publishers
Mr. Marvel and the Lemonade	D	F	100	Storyworlds	Heinemann Educational Publishers
Mr. Marvel and the Washing	D	F	100	Storyworlds	Heinemann Educational Publishers
Mr. McCready's Cleaning Day	H	F	119	Shilling, Tracy	Scholastic
Mr. McGillicuddy's Clocks	M	RF	250+	Voyages	SRA/McGraw Hill
Mr. McGrah's New Car	H	F	119	Book Bank	Wright Group/McGraw Hill
Mr. Merton's Vacation	K	RF	250+	Sails	Rigby
Mr. Miller's Old Car	F	RF	108	Seedlings	Continental Press
Mr. Mulch's Magic Mixtures	L	F	250+	Cambridge Reading	Pearson Learning Group
Mr. Mysterious & Company	R	F	250+	Fleischman, Sid	Beech Tree Books
Mr. Noisy	D	F	90	Learn to Read	Creative Teaching Press
Mr. Noisy Builds a House	D	F	35	Learn to Read	Creative Teaching Press
Mr. Noisy Paints His House	E	F	159	Learn to Read	Creative Teaching Press
Mr. Noisy's Book of Patterns	G	F	47	Learn to Read	Creative Teaching Press
Mr. Noisy's Helpers	F	F	81	Learn to Read	Creative Teaching Press
Mr. Pappas Is a Waiter	F	I	106	InfoTrek	ETA Cuisenaire
Mr. Pepperpot's Pet	K	F	250+	Literacy 2000	Rigby
Mr. Popper's Penguins	Q	F	250+	Atwater, Richard & Florence	Little, Brown & Co.
Mr. Post's Class	O	RF	1606	Reading Street	Pearson
Mr. Potter's Pet	N	F	250+	King-Smith, Dick	Hyperion

* Collection of short stories
\# Graphic text

TITLE	LEVEL	GENRE	WORD COUNT	AUTHOR / SERIES	PUBLISHER / DISTRIBUTOR
*Mr. President: A Book of U.S. Presidents	S	B	250+	Sullivan, George	Scholastic
Mr. Putter & Tabby Row the Boat	J	RF	250+	Rylant, Cynthia	Harcourt Trade
Mr. Putter & Tabby See the Stars	J	RF	250+	Rylant, Cynthia	Harcourt
Mr. Putter & Tabby Take the Train	J	RF	250+	Rylant, Cynthia	Harcourt Trade
Mr. Putter & Tabby Toot the Horn	J	RF	250+	Rylant, Cynthia	Harcourt Trade
Mr. Putter and Tabby Bake the Cake	J	RF	250+	Rylant, Cynthia	Harcourt Trade
Mr. Putter and Tabby Fly the Plane	J	RF	250+	Rylant, Cynthia	Harcourt Trade
Mr. Putter and Tabby Pick the Pears	J	RF	250+	Rylant, Cynthia	Harcourt Trade
Mr. Putter and Tabby Pour the Tea	J	RF	250+	Rylant, Cynthia	Harcourt Trade
Mr. Putter and Tabby Walk the Dog	J	RF	250+	Rylant, Cynthia	Harcourt Trade
Mr. Rabbit and the Moon	F	F	137	New Way Red	Steck-Vaughn
Mr. Revere and I	U	F	250+	Lawson, Robert	Little, Brown & Co.
Mr. Rice Is a Salesperson	F	I	93	InfoTrek	ETA Cuisenaire
Mr. Rover Takes Over	G	F	203	Maccarone, Grace	Scholastic
Mr. Sanchez and the Kick Ball Champ	I	RF	529	Appleton-Smith, Laura	Flyleaf Publishing
Mr. Sharp's Shapes	J	F	374	InfoTrek	ETA Cuisenaire
Mr. Smarty Loves to Party	F	F	101	Storyteller-Moon Rising	Wright Group/McGraw Hill
Mr. Strike Out	P	RF	4361	Maddox, Jake	Stone Arch Books
Mr. Sun and Mr. Sea	I	F	202	Little Celebrations	Pearson Learning Group
Mr. Sun and Mr. Sea	L	F	506	Sunshine	Wright Group/McGraw Hill
Mr. Tucket	U	HF	250+	Paulsen, Gary	Bantam
Mr. Turner Is an Actor	F	I	99	InfoTrek	ETA Cuisenaire
Mr. Verdi's New Path	I	F	250+	Home Connection Collection	Rigby
Mr. Whisper	H	F	325	Sunshine	Wright Group/McGraw Hill
Mr. Wind	F	F	37	Literacy 2000	Rigby
Mr. Wink	E	F	86	Ready Readers	Pearson Learning Group
Mr. Wolf	D	F	48	Joy Readers	Pearson Learning Group
Mr. Wolf Leaves Town	H	TL	208	Alphakids	Sundance
Mr. Wolf Tries Again	H	TL	218	Alphakids	Sundance
Mr. Wumple's Travels	I	F	259	Read Alongs	Rigby
Mr. Wu's Shop of Curiosities	R	F	250+	Literacy by Design	Rigby
Mrs. Always Goes Shopping	M	RF	423	Sunshine	Wright Group/McGraw Hill
Mrs. Barnett's Birthday	I	RF	135	Sunshine	Wright Group/McGraw Hill
Mrs. Bean	I	RF	250+	Rigby Rocket	Rigby
Mrs. Bold	F	RF	94	Literacy 2000	Rigby
Mrs. Brice's Mice	I	F	250+	Hoff, Syd	HarperTrophy
Mrs. Bubble's Baby	M	F	250+	Pacific Literacy	Pacific Learning
Mrs. Cheng's Surprise	G	RF	186	Leveled Readers	Houghton Mifflin Harcourt
Mrs. Cole Is a Bus Driver	F	I	105	InfoTrek	ETA Cuisenaire
Mrs. Cook's Hats	LB	RF	31	Mader, Jan	Kaeden Books
Mrs. Frisby and the Rats of NIMH	V	F	250+	O'Brien, Robert C.	Aladdin
Mrs. Grindy's Shoes	I	F	211	Sunshine	Wright Group/McGraw Hill
Mrs. Hippo's Pizza Parlor	J	F	250+	I Am Reading	Kingfisher
Mrs. Honey's List	J	RF	250+	Voyages	SRA/McGraw Hill
Mrs. Huggins and Her Hen Hannah	K	F	250+	Dabcovich, Lydia	Dutton/Penguin
Mrs. Jeepers' Batty Vacation	L	RF	250+	Dadey, Debbie; Jones, Marcia Thornton	Scholastic
Mrs. Jeepers in Outer Space	M	RF	250+	Dadey, Debbie; Jones, Marcia Thornton	Scholastic
Mrs. Keen	G	RF	88	City Stories	Rigby
Mrs. Lunch	LB	F	17	Joy Readers	Pearson Learning Group
Mrs. Marigold's Menagerie	Q	RF	250+	Sails	Rigby
Mrs. McNosh Hangs Up Her Wash	H	F	166	Little Celebrations	Pearson Learning Group
Mrs. Mog's Cats	F	F	124	Rigby Literacy	Rigby

TITLE	LEVEL	GENRE	WORD COUNT	AUTHOR / SERIES	PUBLISHER / DISTRIBUTOR
Mrs. Mog's Cats	F	F	126	Rigby Star	Rigby
Mrs. Muddle's Mud-Puddle	I	F	181	Sunshine	Wright Group/McGraw Hill
Mrs. Murphy's Bears	I	RF	188	Little Readers	Houghton Mifflin Harcourt
Mrs. Murphy's Crows	H	RF	120	Books for Young Learners	Richard C. Owen
Mrs. Patches and Her Fudge	J	F	250+	The Wright Skills	Wright Group/McGraw Hill
*Mrs. Piggle-Wiggle	O	F	250+	MacDonald, Betty	Scholastic
*Mrs. Piggle-Wiggle's Farm	O	F	250+	MacDonald, Betty	Scholastic
*Mrs. Piggle-Wiggle's Magic	O	F	250+	MacDonald, Betty	Scholastic
Mrs. Pomelili's Wet Week	G	F	215	Book Bank	Wright Group/McGraw Hill
Mrs. Popinpop's Ghost	G	RF	186	Springboard	Wright Group/McGraw Hill
Mrs. Popinpop's New Novel	N	RF	250+	Springboard	Wright Group/ McGraw Hill
"Mrs. Riley Bought Five Itchy Aardvarks" and Other Painless Tricks for Memorizing Science Facts	T	I	3465	Cleary, Brian P.	Millbrook Press
Mrs. Sato's Hens	D	F	51	Little Celebrations	Pearson Learning Group
Mrs. Sato's Hens	D	F	51	Little Readers	Houghton Mifflin Harcourt
Mrs. Sheep's Garden	K	F	953	Kratky, Lada	Hampton-Brown
Mrs. Spider's Beautiful Web	H	F	250+	PM Story Books	Rigby
Mrs. Tuck's Little Tune	F	RF	195	Ready Readers	Pearson Learning Group
Mrs. West Is a Daycare Worker	F	I	102	InfoTrek	ETA Cuisenaire
Mrs. Wishy-Washy	E	F	102	Story Box	Wright Group/McGraw Hill
Mrs. Wishy-Washy's Tub	B	F	38	Story Box	Wright Group/McGraw Hill
Mrs. Yee Is a Teacher	H	I	102	InfoTrek	ETA Cuisenaire
Ms. F Goes Back to School	O	RF	1114	Leveled Readers	Houghton Mifflin Harcourt
Ms. F Goes Back to School	O	RF	1114	Leveled Readers/CA	Houghton Mifflin Harcourt
Ms. F Goes Back to School	O	RF	1114	Leveled Readers/TX	Houghton Mifflin Harcourt
Ms. Hakeem Is a Food Bank Volunteer	H	I	90	InfoTrek	ETA Cuisenaire
Ms. Hawkins and the Bake Sale	K	RF	643	Leveled Readers	Houghton Mifflin Harcourt
Ms. Hawkins and the Bake Sale	K	RF	643	Leveled Readers/CA	Houghton Mifflin Harcourt
Ms. Hawkins and the Bake Sale	K	RF	643	Leveled Readers/TX	Houghton Mifflin Harcourt
Ms. Hill Is a Nurse	F	I	97	InfoTrek	ETA Cuisenaire
Ms. Kim Is a Web Designer	H	I	107	InfoTrek	ETA Cuisenaire
Ms. Pinkerville, You're Our Star!	M	RF	717	Leveled Readers	Houghton Mifflin Harcourt
Ms. Pinkerville, You're Our Star!	M	RF	717	Leveled Readers/CA	Houghton Mifflin Harcourt
Ms. Pinkerville, You're Our Star!	M	RF	717	Leveled Readers/TX	Houghton Mifflin Harcourt
Mt. St. Helens	S	I	1492	Independent Readers Science	Houghton Mifflin Harcourt
Much Ado About Aldo	O	RF	250+	Hurwitz, Johanna	Penguin Group
Mud	D	RF	68	Lewison, Wendy Cheyette	Random House
Mud	B	RF	30	Science	Outside the Box
Mud Girl	Z+	RF	250+	Acheson, Alison	Fitzhenry & Whiteside
Mud Pie	C	RF	14	Literacy 2000	Rigby
Mud Pies	E	RF	143	Start to Read	School Zone
Mud Pies	C	RF	56	TOTTS	Tott Publications
Mud Pony, The	M	TL	250+	Reading Rainbow	Scholastic
Mud Pony, The	L	TL	764	Sunshine	Wright Group/McGraw Hill
Mud Puddles	C	RF	24	TOTTS	Tott Publications
Mud Tortillas	I	RF	250+	Bebop Books	Lee & Low Books Inc.
Mud Walk	E	F	183	Story Box	Wright Group/McGraw Hill
Mud!	D	RF	68	Lewison, Wendy Cheyette	Scholastic
Mud!	E	RF	94	Real Kids Readers	Millbrook Press
Mud, Mud, Mud	G	I	83	Windows on Literacy	National Geographic
Muddle Farm	C	F	44	Rigby Star	Rigby
Muddledy Fuddledy Mixed-Up Day, The	M	F	250+	Redhead, Janet Slater	Steck-Vaughn

* Collection of short stories
\# Graphic text

TITLE	LEVEL	GENRE	WORD COUNT	AUTHOR / SERIES	PUBLISHER / DISTRIBUTOR
Muddy Mess, The	F	RF	147	Leveled Literacy Intervention/ Blue System	Heinemann
Mudflows and Landslides	W	I	250+	Disasters Up Close	Lerner Publications
Mudskipper	G	I	132	Twig	Wright Group/McGraw Hill
Mudskipper and the Water	D	F	57	Bonnell, Kris	Reading Reading Books
Mudskipper, The	A	F	30	Bonnell, Kris	Reading Reading Books
Mufaro's Beautiful Daughters: An African Tale	N	TL	250+	Steptoe, John	Scholastic
Muffin Is Trapped	J	RF	250+	PM Story Books	Rigby
Muffy and Fluffy	F	RF	155	First Start	Troll Associates
Muffy's Secret Admirer	M	RF	250+	Brown, Marc	Little, Brown & Co.
Muggie Maggie	O	RF	250+	Cleary, Beverly	Avon Camelot
Muhammad Ali	T	B	250+	Amazing Americans	Wright Group/McGraw Hill
#Muhammad Ali: American Champion	S	B	250	Graphic Library	Capstone Press
Muhammed Ali: The Greatest	P	B	250+	Great African Americans	Capstone Press
Mule's Hat, The	G	F	204	Dominie Readers	Pearson Learning Group
Multi-Tasker, The	V	RF	3226	Leveled Readers	Houghton Mifflin Harcourt
Mumbo Jumbo's Shoes	I	F	130	Book Bus	Creative Edge
Mummies	M	I	250+	All Aboard Reading	Grossett & Dunlap
Mummies	S	I	250+	Ancient Egypt	Capstone Press
Mummies and Their Mysteries	X	I	250+	Wilcox, Charlotte	Carolrhoda Books
Mummies Don't Coach Softball	M	F	250+	Dadey, Debbie; Jones, Marcia Thornton	Scholastic
Mummies in the Morning	M	F	250+	Osborne, Mary Pope	Random House
Mummies Made in Egypt	R	I	250+	Aliki	HarperCollins
Mummies, Pyramids, and Pharaohs: A Book About Ancient Egypt	Q	I	250+	Gibbons, Gail	Scholastic
Mummies, Tombs, and the Afterlife	T	I	250+	High-Fliers	Pacific Learning
Mummy	Y	I	250+	Eyewitness Books	DK Publishing
Mummy and Other Adventures of Sam & Alice, The	J	F	250+	Gutierrez, Akemi	Houghton Mifflin Harcourt
Mummy Mania	N	RF	250+	Girlz Rock!	Mondo
Mummy, The	X	I	4728	Monster Chronicles	Lerner Publications
Mummy's Curse, The	O	F	250+	SupaDoopers	Sundance
Mummy's Gold, The	L	F	250+	McMullan, Kate	Grossett & Dunlap
Mumps	D	RF	108	Carousel Readers	Pearson Learning Group
Mumps	D	RF	112	PM Story Books	Rigby
Munch Together	B	F	33	Reading Street	Pearson
Munch! Munch!	D	RF	109	Rigby Flying Colors	Rigby
Munching Mark	G	RF	88	Tadpoles	Rigby
Munching Monster	I	F	261	Storyteller-Moon Rising	Wright Group/McGraw Hill
Munching, Crunching, Sniffing, and Snooping	L	I	250+	DK Readers	DK Publishing
Munga, the Lonely Monster	K	F	566	Springboard	Wright Group/McGraw Hill
Mural, The	O	RF	801	Leveled Readers	Houghton Mifflin Harcourt
Mural, The	F	I	262	Visions	Wright Group/McGraw Hill
Murals for Joy	N	RF	745	Leveled Readers	Houghton Mifflin Harcourt
Muscle Cars	W	I	6462	Motor Mania	Lerner Publications
Muscles	T	I	250+	Theme Sets	National Geographic
Muscles: Our Muscular System	T	I	250+	Simon, Seymour	HarperTrophy
Muscular System, The	P	I	1929	Early Bird Body Systems	Lerner Publishing
Muscular System, The	K	I	131	Human Body Systems	Red Brick Learning
Museum Book, The: A Guide to Strange and Wonderful Collections	T	I	250+	Mark, Jan	Candlewick Press
Museum, The	D	RF	41	Sunshine	Wright Group/McGraw Hill
Mush, Mush!	O	I	250+	WorldScapes	ETA Cuisenaire

* Collection of short stories
# Graphic text

TITLE	LEVEL	GENRE	WORD COUNT	AUTHOR / SERIES	PUBLISHER / DISTRIBUTOR
Mushrooms and Other Fungi	P	I	250+	Sunshine	Wright Group/McGraw Hill
Mushrooms and Toadstools	K	I	250+	Explorations	Eleanor Curtain Publishing
Mushrooms and Toadstools	K	I	250+	Explorations	Okapi Educational Materials
Mushrooms for Dinner	G	F	177	PM Story Books	Rigby
Music	Z	I	250+	Eyewitness Books	DK Publishing
Music	A	I	45	Vocabulary Readers	Houghton Mifflin Harcourt
Music	A	I	45	Vocabulary Readers/CA	Houghton Mifflin Harcourt
Music	A	I	45	Vocabulary Readers/TX	Houghton Mifflin Harcourt
Music - Magic and Imagination	U	I	250+	Connectors	Pacific Learning
Music Counts	P	I	250+	Navigators Math Series	Benchmark Education
Music Gets the Blues	V	I	2463	Reading Street	Pearson
Music Machine, The	G	F	231	Sunshine	Wright Group/McGraw Hill
Music Madness: Questioning Music and Music Videos	U	I	250+	Media Literacy	Capstone Press
Music Makers	V	I	250+	High-Fliers	Pacific Learning
Music of Dolphins, The	V	RF	250+	Hesse, Karen	Scholastic
Music of Tito Puente, The	J	B	127	Vocabulary Readers	Houghton Mifflin Harcourt
Music Students	E	RF	83	Dominie Phonics Reader	Pearson Learning Group
Music, Music, Music!	T	I	250+	InfoQuest	Rigby
Musical Adventure, A	D	RF	78	Reading Street	Pearson
Musical Genius, A Story About Wolfgang Amadeus Mozart	T	B	8784	Creative Minds Biographies	Carolrhoda Books
Musicians and Their Music	S	B	250+	Pair-It Books	Steck-Vaughn
Muskrats	H	I	114	Wetland Animals	Capstone Press
Mustangs	U	I	250+	Gillespie, Lorraine	Red Brick Learning
Mutt and the Lifeguards	M	RF	754	Sunshine	Wright Group/McGraw Hill
Mutts	I	I	131	Dogs	Capstone Press
My Accident	C	RF	46	PM Starters	Rigby
My Airplane Trip	K	RF	684	Rigby Flying Colors	Rigby
My Alien	LB	F	12	Sails	Rigby
My Apartment	LB	RF	20	Visions	Wright Group/McGraw Hill
My Apple Tree	D	I	48	Yellow Umbrella Books	Red Brick Learning
My Baby	D	F	64	Storyteller-First Snow	Wright Group/McGraw Hill
My Baby Sister	A	RF	32	Leveled Literacy Intervention/Orange System	Heinemann
My Backpack	B	I	72	First Stories	Pacific Learning
My Backpack	A	F	21	Leveled Readers	Houghton Mifflin Harcourt
My Backpack	A	F	21	Leveled Readers/CA	Houghton Mifflin Harcourt
My Backyard	LB	I	14	Little Books for Early Readers	University of Maine
My Balloon Man	C	I	56	First Stories	Pacific Learning
My Bath	A	RF	32	Leveled Literacy Intervention/Green System	Heinemann
My Bean Plant	H	I	146	Windows on Literacy	National Geographic
My Bear	A	RF	48	Leveled Literacy Intervention/Orange System	Heinemann
My Bed	E	RF	65	Book Bus	Creative Edge
My Bed Is Soft	B	I	42	Windows on Literacy	National Geographic
My Best Friend	C	RF	63	Carousel Readers	Pearson Learning Group
My Best Friend	I	RF	147	Hutchins, Pat	Greenwillow
My Best Friend	C	RF	28	Little Celebrations	Pearson Learning Group
My Best Sandwich	D	RF	25	Hartley, Susan; Armstrong, Shane	Scholastic
My Big Bear	B	I	75	Leveled Literacy Intervention/Orange System	Heinemann

* Collection of short stories
\# Graphic text

TITLE	LEVEL	GENRE	WORD COUNT	AUTHOR / SERIES	PUBLISHER / DISTRIBUTOR
My Big Box	D	RF	94	Voyages	SRA/McGraw Hill
My Big Brother	B	RF	64	Leveled Literacy Intervention/ Orange System	Heinemann
My Big Brother	C	RF	49	On Our Way to English	Rigby
My Big Brother	E	I	103	PM Nonfiction-Yellow	Rigby
My Big Brother Ned	B	RF	38	Leveled Readers	Houghton Mifflin Harcourt
My Big Brother Ned	B	RF	38	Leveled Readers/CA	Houghton Mifflin Harcourt
My Big Car	C	RF	62	Handprints B	Educators Publishing Service
My Big Family	B	I	34	Time for Kids	Teacher Created Materials
My Big Pig	A	RF	32	Literacy by Design	Rigby
My Big Rock	B	RF	42	Bebop Books	Lee & Low Books Inc.
My Big Surprise	H	F	139	Instant Readers	Harcourt School Publishers
My Big Tree	D	I	120	PM Science Readers	Rigby
My Big Wheel	C	RF	38	Visions	Wright Group/McGraw Hill
My Bike	F	I	108	Pacific Literacy	Pacific Learning
My Bike	D	I	38	Storyteller-First Snow	Wright Group/McGraw Hill
My Bike	A	I	19	Vocabulary Readers	Houghton Mifflin Harcourt
My Bike	A	I	19	Vocabulary Readers/CA	Houghton Mifflin Harcourt
My Bike Ride	C	RF	30	Big Cat	Pacific Learning
My Birthday	F	RF	131	Rigby Flying Colors	Rigby
My Birthday Party	LB	RF	16	Little Readers	Houghton Mifflin Harcourt
My Birthday Party	C	RF	38	Visions	Wright Group/McGraw Hill
My Birthday Surprise	G	RF	153	Foundations	Wright Group/McGraw Hill
My Black Cat	C	RF	52	Early Emergent	Pioneer Valley
My Boat	G	RF	133	Sunshine	Wright Group/McGraw Hill
My Body	C	I	47	Discovery World	Rigby
My Body	M	I	250+	Early Connections	Benchmark Education
My Body	B	I	28	On Our Way to English	Rigby
My Body	D	I	250+	Sun Sprouts	ETA Cuisenaire
My Body Head to Toe	K	RF	250+	All About Me	Picture Window Books
My Body Works	E	I	131	Twig	Wright Group/McGraw Hill
My Bones	I	I	148	My Body	Capstone Press
My Book	A	RF	17	Maris, Ron	Viking/Penguin
My Book	C	RF	63	PM Plus Story Books	Rigby
My Book	C	RF	32	Sunshine	Wright Group/McGraw Hill
My Book of the Seasons	H	I	271	PM Science Readers	Rigby
My Box	D	RF	94	Books for Young Learners	Richard C. Owen
My Box	WB	RF	N/A	Instant Readers	Harcourt School Publishers
My Box	A	RF	94	Smart Starts	Rigby
My Brain	J	I	152	My Body	Capstone Press
My Breakfast	D	RF	54	Lighthouse	Rigby
My Breakfast	G	RF	167	Rigby Flying Colors	Rigby
My Brother	B	RF	48	Leveled Readers	Houghton Mifflin Harcourt
My Brother	B	RF	48	Leveled Readers/CA	Houghton Mifflin Harcourt
My Brother	D	RF	51	Rise & Shine	Hampton-Brown
My Brother Is a Superhero	S	RF	250+	Sheldon, Dyan	Candlewick Press
My Brother Is a Visitor from Another Planet	S	RF	250+	Sheldon, Dyan	Candlewick Press
*My Brother Louis Measures Worms and Other Louis Stories	T	RF	250+	Robinson, Barbara	HarperTrophy
My Brother Sam Is Dead	Y	HF	250+	Collier, James & Christopher	Scholastic
My Brother Wants to Be Like Me	D	RF	62	Mader, Jan	Kaeden Books
My Brother, Ant	J	RF	250+	Byars, Betsy	Viking/Penguin
My Brother, My Sister, and I	V	HF	250+	Watkins, Yoko Kawashima	Aladdin

* Collection of short stories
# Graphic text

TITLE	LEVEL	GENRE	WORD COUNT	AUTHOR / SERIES	PUBLISHER / DISTRIBUTOR
My Brother, Owen	I	RF	150	Book Bank	Wright Group/McGraw Hill
My Brother, the Brat	E	RF	62	Hall, Kirsten	Scholastic
My Brother, the Bridesmaid	M	RF	250+	Lighthouse	Ginn & Co.
My Brother, the Knight	M	RF	250+	Social Studies Connects	The Kane Press
My Brother, the Pest	I	RF	459	Real Kids Readers	Millbrook Press
My Brother, the Spy	N	RF	250+	SupaDoopers	Sundance
My Brother's Hero	W	RF	250+	Fogelin, Adrian	Peachtree
My Brother's Motorcycle	D	RF	45	Visions	Wright Group/McGraw Hill
My Brown Bear Barney	H	RF	82	Butler, Dorothy	Morrow
My Brown Cow	D	I	62	Story Box	Wright Group/McGraw Hill
My Buddy	B	RF	80	Adams, Lorraine; Bruvold, Lynn	Eagle Crest Books
My Buddy	B	RF	32	First Stories	Pacific Learning
My Buddy, My Friend	D	RF	33	Visions	Wright Group/McGraw Hill
My Bug Box	E	RF	99	Books for Young Learners	Richard C. Owen
My Busy Day	B	RF	41	Early Emergent	Pioneer Valley
My Busy Week	H	RF	122	InfoTrek	ETA Cuisenaire
My Calculator Book	E	RF	50	Gosset, Rachel; Ballinger, Margaret	Scholastic
My Camera	D	RF	67	Gear Up!	Wright Group/McGraw Hill
My Camera	C	RF	41	Rigby Literacy	Rigby
My Camera	C	RF	41	Rigby Star	Rigby
My Camp-Out	E	RF	81	Real Kids Readers	Millbrook Press
My Car	A	RF	40	On Our Way to English	Rigby
My Cat	A	I	37	Early Connections	Benchmark Education
My Cat	A	RF	47	First Stories	Pacific Learning
My Cat	A	RF	25	Leveled Readers	Houghton Mifflin Harcourt
My Cat	A	RF	28	Leveled Readers Science	Houghton Mifflin Harcourt
My Cat	A	RF	25	Leveled Readers/CA	Houghton Mifflin Harcourt
My Cat	B	RF	47	Lighthouse	Rigby
My Cat	F	RF	42	My World	Steck-Vaughn
My Cat	D	RF	40	Ready Readers	Pearson Learning Group
My Cat	D	I	42	Sunshine	Wright Group/McGraw Hill
My Cat	H	I	79	Taylor, Judy	Macmillan
My Cat Muffin	C	RF	35	Gardner, Marjory	Scholastic
My Cat Sam	H	F	147	Supersonics	Rigby
My Caterpillar Report	E	I	94	Rigby Flying Colors	Rigby
My Cats	B	RF	42	Gear Up!	Wright Group/McGraw Hill
My Cats	A	RF	41	Robinson, Eileen	Scholastic
*My Cat's Surprise	D	RF	71	New Way Blue	Steck-Vaughn
My Chair	B	RF	24	Pacific Literacy	Pacific Learning
My Cheese	B	F	35	Sails	Rigby
My Chinese New Year	D	I	56	Rigby Star Quest	Rigby
My Circus Family	C	F	42	Bookshop	Mondo
My Circus Friend	C	F	42	Lake, Mary Dixon	Mondo
My City	C	I	99	Rigby Literacy	Rigby
My Class	LB	I	14	Stewart, Josie; Salem, Lynn	Continental Press
My Classroom	A	I	31	At School Series	Pioneer Valley
My Clock is Sick	D	F	45	Ready Readers	Pearson Learning Group
My Clothes	LB	RF	16	Carousel Earlybirds	Pearson Learning Group
My Clothes	C	RF	86	Foundations	Wright Group/McGraw Hill
My Clothes	A	I	35	On Our Way to English	Rigby
My Clothes	B	RF	36	PM Plus Starters	Rigby
My Clothes	LB	F	12	Sails	Rigby
My Clothes	LB	I	12	Vocabulary Readers	Houghton Mifflin Harcourt

* Collection of short stories
# Graphic text

TITLE	LEVEL	GENRE	WORD COUNT	AUTHOR / SERIES	PUBLISHER / DISTRIBUTOR
My Color	B	I	22	Mann, Rachel	Scholastic
My Computer	F	I	76	Wonder World	Wright Group/McGraw Hill
My Continent	I	I	117	My World	Capstone Press
My Cousin Jake	H	RF	123	City Stories	Rigby
My Cousin, the Alien	T	SF	19335	Service, Pamela F.	Carolrhoda Books
My Cushion!	B	RF	20	Rigby Rocket	Rigby
My Dad	E	I	114	PM Nonfiction-Yellow	Rigby
My Dad	F	I	79	Talk About Books	Pearson Learning Group
My Dad and I	B	RF	52	Handprints B	Educators Publishing Service
My Dad Cooks	C	RF	29	Carousel Readers	Pearson Learning Group
My Dad Has Asthma	I	I	138	Wonder World	Wright Group/McGraw Hill
My Dad is a Chef	H	I	169	Dominie Factivity Series	Pearson Learning Group
My Dad Lost His Job	E	RF	76	Carousel Readers	Pearson Learning Group
My Dad the Dragon	Q	F	8874	French, Jackie	Stone Arch Books
My Dad's Truck	E	I	57	Costain, Merideth	Scholastic
My Daniel	T	HF	250+	Conrad, Pam	HarperTrophy
My Darling Kitten	WB	RF	N/A	Collington, Peter	Alfred A. Knopf
My Darling, My Hamburger	Z+	RF	250+	Zindel, Paul	Bantam Books
My Day	C	RF	51	Barney, Mike	Kaeden Books
My Day	D	RF	80	InfoTrek	ETA Cuisenaire
My Day	C	RF	44	Rise & Shine	Hampton-Brown
My Day	B	RF	24	Sunshine	Wright Group/McGraw Hill
My Day	LB	RF	29	We Both Read	Treasure Bay
My Day: Morning, Noon, and Night	J	RF	250+	All About Me	Picture Window Books
My Desperate Love Diary	Z+	RF	250+	Rettig, Liz	Holiday House
My Dog	C	RF	79	Early Emergent	Pioneer Valley
My Dog	A	RF	72	Instant Readers	Harcourt School Publishers
My Dog	A	RF	22	Leveled Readers	Houghton Mifflin Harcourt
My Dog	A	RF	22	Leveled Readers/CA	Houghton Mifflin Harcourt
My Dog	G	RF	79	My World	Steck-Vaughn
My Dog	A	I	32	Rigby Flying Colors	Rigby
My Dog	D	I	51	Sunshine	Wright Group/McGraw Hill
My Dog	G	I	72	Taylor, Judy	Macmillan
My Dog	D	RF	38	Visions	Wright Group/McGraw Hill
My Dog	C	I	46	Vocabulary Readers	Houghton Mifflin Harcourt
My Dog and I	B	RF	55	Lighthouse	Rigby
*My Dog and Other Stories	I	RF	250+	Story Steps	Rigby
My Dog Ben	C	RF	19	Voyages	SRA/McGraw Hill
My Dog Fluffy	A	I	27	Cherrington, Janelle	Scholastic
My Dog Fuzzy	B	RF	27	Books for Young Learners	Richard C. Owen
My Dog Kam	E	RF	73	InfoTrek	ETA Cuisenaire
My Dog Rusty	G	RF	75	City Stories	Rigby
My Dog Talks	E	RF	250+	Herman, Gail	Scholastic
My Dog the Dinosaur	Q	F	8918	French, Jackie	Stone Arch Books
My Dog Willy	C	RF	71	Little Readers	Houghton Mifflin Harcourt
My Dog, Miffy	D	RF	38	Visions	Wright Group/McGraw Hill
My Dog's a Scaredy Cat: A Halloween Tail	R	RF	250+	Winkler, Henry and Oliver, Lin	Grosset & Dunlap
My Dog's the Best	F	RF	175	Calmenson, Stephanie	Scholastic
My Doll	A	F	32	Sun Sprouts	ETA Cuisenaire
My Doll	E	RF	86	Yukish, Joe	Kaeden Books
My Dream	C	RF	34	Wildsmith, Brian	Oxford University Press
My Dream of Martin Luther King	R	I	250+	Ringgold, Faith	Crown
My Elephant, My Friend	O	I	250+	WorldScapes	ETA Cuisenaire

* Collection of short stories
# Graphic text

TITLE	LEVEL	GENRE	WORD COUNT	AUTHOR / SERIES	PUBLISHER / DISTRIBUTOR
My Face to the Wind	W	HF	250+	Dear America	Scholastic
My Faces	E	RF	62	Rhythm 'N' Rhyme Readers	Pearson Learning Group
My Family	B	RF	55	Adams, Lorraine; Bruvold, Lynn	Eagle Crest Books
My Family	B	RF	31	Bebop Books	Lee & Low Books Inc.
My Family	B	RF	87	Carousel Earlybirds	Pearson Learning Group
My Family	B	RF	46	First Stories	Pacific Learning
My Family	N	I	250+	Kinkade, Sheila	Charlesbridge
My Family	B	F	69	Leveled Literacy Intervention/ Orange System	Heinemann
My Family	D	I	88	Leveled Readers	Houghton Mifflin Harcourt
My Family	A	I	25	Leveled Readers	Houghton Mifflin Harcourt
My Family	A	RF	28	Leveled Readers Social Studies	Houghton Mifflin Harcourt
My Family	A	I	25	Leveled Readers/CA	Houghton Mifflin Harcourt
My Family	LB	F	12	Sails	Rigby
My Family	A	RF	28	Sunshine	Wright Group/McGraw Hill
My Family	LB	I	12	Vocabulary Readers	Houghton Mifflin Harcourt
My Family & the Wasps	N	F	250+	Parker, John	Pearson Learning Group
My Family Band	C	RF	50	Instant Readers	Harcourt School Publishers
My Family Has Fun	A	RF	28	Leveled Readers Emergent	Houghton Mifflin Harcourt
My Family Keeps Fit	G	RF	98	Windows on Literacy	National Geographic
My Family Love and Care, Give and Share	K	RF	250+	All About Me	Picture Window Books
My Family Pictures	B	I	20	Leveled Readers	Houghton Mifflin Harcourt
My Family Pictures	A	I	20	Leveled Readers/CA	Houghton Mifflin Harcourt
My Family Split Up	H	RF	85	City Kids	Rigby
My Family Tree	D	I	107	Story Steps	Rigby
My Family Tree	I	I	229	Windows on Literacy	National Geographic
My Farm	N	RF	250+	Lester, Alison	Houghton Mifflin Harcourt
My Father	J	RF	194	Mayer, Laura	Scholastic
My Father the Mad Professor	P	F	250+	Action Packs	Rigby
My Father, the Angel of Death	U	RF	250+	Villareal, Ray	Pinata Books
My Father, the Clown	Y	RF	3497	Leveled Readers	Houghton Mifflin Harcourt
My Father, the Clown	Y	RF	3497	Leveled Readers/CA	Houghton Mifflin Harcourt
My Father's Dragon	N	F	250+	Gannett, Ruth Stiles	Random House
My Favorite Bear	J	I	146	Books for Young Learners	Richard C. Owen
My Favorite Bear	F	F	70	Gabriel, Andrea	Charlesbridge
My Favorite Days	J	I	250+	Rigby Literacy	Rigby
My Favorite Foods	I	RF	100	Early Readers	Compass Point Books
My Favorite Foods	D	I	107	Vocabulary Readers	Houghton Mifflin Harcourt
My Favorite Foods	D	I	107	Vocabulary Readers/CA	Houghton Mifflin Harcourt
My Favorite Foods	D	I	107	Vocabulary Readers/TX	Houghton Mifflin Harcourt
My Favorite Fruit	B	I	35	Bonnell, Kris	Reading Reading Books
My Favorite Place	J	RF	464	Books for Young Learners	Richard C. Owen
My Favorite School Helper	E	I	61	Little Celebrations	Pearson Learning Group
My Feet	B	RF	35	Reed, Janet	Scholastic
My Feet	B	I	25	Twig	Wright Group/McGraw Hill
My Feet Are Just Right	I	I	220	Sunshine	Wright Group/McGraw Hill
My First Book About the Internet	M	I	250+	Cromwell, Sharon	Troll Associates
*My First Book of Biographies: Great Men and Women Every Child Should Know	P	B	250+	Marzollo, Jean	Scholastic
My First Business: Lemonade Stand	K	RF	548	Leveled Readers Social Studies	Houghton Mifflin Harcourt
My First Hike	F	RF	70	Woolf, Catherine Maria	Dawn Publications
My First Snow	F	I	127	Independent Readers Science	Houghton Mifflin Harcourt
My Fish	A	RF	24	Phonics and Friends	Hampton-Brown
My Fish Are Fine with Me	G	RF	78	City Stories	Rigby

* Collection of short stories
\# Graphic text

TITLE	LEVEL	GENRE	WORD COUNT	AUTHOR / SERIES	PUBLISHER / DISTRIBUTOR
My Fish Bowl	B	I	29	Foundations	Wright Group/McGraw Hill
My Fish Does Not Chirp	E	I	77	Ready Readers	Pearson Learning Group
My Fish Tank	J	I	238	Windows on Literacy	National Geographic
My Five Senses	F	I	142	Early Connections	Benchmark Education
My Five Senses	C	I	36	Independent Readers Science	Houghton Mifflin Harcourt
My Five Senses	D	I	127	Leveled Literacy Intervention/ Green System	Heinemann
My Five Senses	F	I	42	Rosen Real Readers	Rosen Publishing Group
My Five Senses	LB	I	5	Windows on Literacy	National Geographic
My Flower Garden	A	I	19	Leveled Readers	Houghton Mifflin Harcourt
My Flower Garden	A	I	19	Leveled Readers/CA	Houghton Mifflin Harcourt
My Fort	LB	I	17	Little Books for Early Readers	University of Maine
My Friend	E	RF	95	Foundations	Wright Group/McGraw Hill
My Friend	B	I	64	Leveled Literacy Intervention/ Green System	Heinemann
My Friend	B	RF	41	Sunshine	Wright Group/McGraw Hill
My Friend Alan	D	RF	65	Carousel Readers	Pearson Learning Group
My Friend and I	C	RF	78	Windows on Literacy	National Geographic
My Friend at School	C	RF	30	Visions	Wright Group/McGraw Hill
My Friend Goes Left	F	RF	72	Start to Read	School Zone
My Friend Gorilla	G	RF	125	Morozumi, Atsuko	Farrar, Straus, and Giroux
My Friend Jess	H	RF	124	Wonder World	Wright Group/McGraw Hill
My Friend Meg	U	RF	250+	Book Blazers	ETA Cuisenaire
My Friend the Monster	N	F	250+	Bulla, Clyde Robert	Harper & Row
My Friend Trent	H	RF	186	Foundations	Wright Group/McGraw Hill
My Friend, Mandela	R	B	250+	High-Fliers	Pacific Learning
My Friends	G	F	152	Gomi, Taro	Scholastic
My Friends	D	RF	58	Little Celebrations	Pearson Learning Group
My Friends at School	G	I	248	Dominie Factivity Series	Pearson Learning Group
My Friends at School	C	I	84	Vocabulary Readers	Houghton Mifflin Harcourt
My Friends at School	C	I	84	Vocabulary Readers/CA	Houghton Mifflin Harcourt
My Frisbee	B	RF	31	Rigby Literacy	Rigby
My Frog Log	N	RF	250+	On Our Way to English	Rigby
My Garden	B	I	37	Ostrow, Jesse S.	Scholastic
My Garden	C	I	33	Rosen Real Readers	Rosen Publishing Group
My Garden	B	F	40	Sails	Rigby
My Global Address	G	I	84	Learn to Read	Creative Teaching Press
My Go-Cart	K	I	467	Sun Sprouts	ETA Cuisenaire
My Goldfish	G	I	239	Walker, Pamela	Scholastic
My Goose Betsy	L	F	250+	Braun, Trudi	Candlewick Press
My Grandfather's Face	B	RF	27	Literacy 2000	Rigby
My Grandma	A	RF	24	Adams, Lorraine; Bruvold, Lynn	Eagle Crest Books
My Grandma	E	RF	67	Early Connections	Benchmark Education
My Grandma and Grandpa	E	I	130	PM Nonfiction	Rigby
My Grandma, the Rock Star	L	RF	250+	Rigby Literacy	Rigby
My Grandpa	B	RF	58	Adams, Lorraine; Bruvold, Lynn	Eagle Crest Books
My Grandpa	F	I	75	Bookshop	Mondo
My Great Big Brother	F	RF	65	Book Bank	Wright Group/McGraw Hill
My Great-Aunt Arizona	N	RF	250+	Houston, Gloria	HarperCollins
My Green Thumb	K	F	351	Leveled Readers	Houghton Mifflin Harcourt
My Gymnastics Class	F	I	33	iOpeners	Pearson Learning Group
My Hair	F	RF	124	Bookshop	Mondo
My Half Day	N	F	347	Fisher, Doris and Sneed, Dani	Sylvan Dell Publishing
My Hamburger	E	RF	108	Rigby Flying Colors	Rigby

* Collection of short stories
# Graphic text

TITLE	LEVEL	GENRE	WORD COUNT	AUTHOR / SERIES	PUBLISHER / DISTRIBUTOR
My Hamster, Van	E	RF	73	Ready Readers	Pearson Learning Group
My Hard-Boiled Egg	F	I	94	Windmill Books	Rigby
My Hat	A	RF	30	Sails	Rigby
My Heart	J	I	125	My Body	Capstone Press
My Heart Is on the Ground	W	HF	250+	Dear America	Scholastic
My Heartbeat	Z+	RF	250+	Freymann-Weyr, Garret	Houghton Mifflin Harcourt
My Helicopter Ride	C	F	42	Foundations	Wright Group/McGraw Hill
My Hero	J	I	250+	Literacy by Design	Rigby
My Hero!	B	I	37	Shutterbug Books	Steck-Vaughn
My Hiroshima	T	HF	250+	Morimoto, Junko	Penguin Group
My Hobby	H	I	155	Rigby Focus	Rigby
My Holiday Diary	F	RF	95	Stepping Stones	Nelson/Michaels Assoc.
My Home	B	I	67	On Our Way to English	Rigby
My Home	K	F	250+	Rhyme and Analogy	Oxford University Press
My Home	B	I	49	Science	Outside the Box
My Home	A	F	56	Smart Starts	Rigby
My Home	C	F	46	Story Box	Wright Group/McGraw Hill
My Home	C	RF	56	Sunshine	Wright Group/McGraw Hill
My Home Is High	B	F	23	Literacy 2000	Rigby
My Home Is Just Right for Me	G	F	250+	Momentum Literacy Program	Troll Associates
My Home: Walls, Floors, Ceilings, and Doors	L	RF	250+	All About Me	Picture Window Books
My Horse	B	I	22	Bebop Books	Lee & Low Books Inc.
My House	G	RF	43	Book Bunny Series	Creative Edge
My House	A	RF	40	Carousel Earlybirds	Pearson Learning Group
My House	F	RF	52	Cat on the Mat	Oxford University Press
My House	B	I	74	Leveled Readers	Houghton Mifflin Harcourt
My House	B	I	74	Leveled Readers/CA	Houghton Mifflin Harcourt
My House	F	RF	126	Literacy 2000	Rigby
My House	E	F	79	My First Reader	Grolier Press
My House	A	I	27	Peters, Catherine	Scholastic
My House	B	I	25	Voyages	SRA/McGraw Hill
My Island Reef	T	RF	250+	Reading Safari	Mondo
My Jobs	C	RF	58	InfoTrek	ETA Cuisenaire
My Kitchen	F	I	80	Rockwell, Harlow	Morrow
My Kite	C	RF	37	Williams, Deborah	Kaeden Books
My Left Hand	K	RF	828	Rigby Flying Colors	Rigby
My Letter	C	RF	51	Wonder World	Wright Group/McGraw Hill
My Life	K	RF	250+	Pistone, Paul	Scholastic
My Life as a Fifth-Grade Comedian	T	RF	250+	Levy, Elizabeth	HarperTrophy
My Life in a Town	C	I	24	Rosen Real Readers	Rosen Publishing Group
My Life in Dog Years	S	B	250+	Paulsen, Gary	Bantam
My Life in the Mountains	D	I	59	Rosen Real Readers	Rosen Publishing Group
My Life on an Island	C	I	43	Rosen Real Readers	Rosen Publishing Group
My Little Brother	C	RF	38	Gear Up!	Wright Group/McGraw Hill
My Little Brother	C	RF	59	Windmill Books	Rigby
My Little Brother Ben	D	RF	35	Books for Young Learners	Richard C. Owen
My Little Cat	B	RF	57	PM Plus Starters	Rigby
My Little Dog	C	F	90	PM Starters	Rigby
My Little Fish	B	RF	49	Rigby Flying Colors	Rigby
My Little House	D	RF	67	InfoTrek	ETA Cuisenaire
My Little Mouse	C	I	32	Book Bank	Wright Group/McGraw Hill
My Little Sister	C	RF	36	First Stories	Pacific Learning
My Little Sister	D	RF	44	Joy Readers	Pearson Learning Group
My Little Sister	E	I	120	PM Nonfiction-Yellow	Rigby

* Collection of short stories
\# Graphic text

TITLE	LEVEL	GENRE	WORD COUNT	AUTHOR / SERIES	PUBLISHER / DISTRIBUTOR
My Little Sister	G	RF	143	Story Box	Wright Group/McGraw Hill
My Lizard	G	RF	246	Handprints D	Educators Publishing Service
My Lost Top	E	RF	70	Ready Readers	Pearson Learning Group
My Louisiana Sky	T	RF	250+	Holt, Kimberly Willis	Random House
My Lucky Hat	J	F	250+	Bookshop	Mondo
My Lunch	C	RF	70	Early Emergent	Pioneer Valley
My Lunch	A	I	32	Leveled Literacy Intervention/ Orange System	Heinemann
My Lunch	A	I	35	On Our Way to English	Rigby
My Lunch	A	I	32	Rigby Flying Colors	Rigby
My Lungs	I	I	130	My Body	Capstone Press
My Magic Bike	G	F	121	Worthington, Lisa & Moon, Susan	Kaeden Books
My Mama	C	RF	25	Visions	Wright Group/McGraw Hill
My Mama Had a Dancing Heart	O	RF	250+	Gray, Libba Moore	Scholastic
My Messy Room	D	RF	82	Packard, Mary	Scholastic
My Models	E	RF	143	Early Connections	Benchmark Education
My Mom	B	I	40	Little Books for Early Readers	University of Maine
My Mom	F	I	91	Talk About Books	Pearson Learning Group
My Mom and Dad	D	RF	86	Story Box	Wright Group/McGraw Hill
My Mom and Dad Take Care of Me	B	I	44	Windows on Literacy	National Geographic
My Mom and I	A	RF	42	Little Books for Early Readers	University of Maine
My Mom the Mayor	N	RF	250+	Windows on Literacy	National Geographic
My Mom the Pirate	Q	F	9067	French, Jackie	Stone Arch Books
My Mom's Apron	I	RF	216	Books for Young Learners	Richard C. Owen
My Monster and Me	B	F	37	Ready Readers	Pearson Learning Group
My Monster Friends	F	F	94	Literacy 2000	Rigby
My Mother Got Married (and Other Disasters)	P	RF	250+	Park, Barbara	Random House
My Muscles	I	I	101	My Body	Capstone Press
My Mysterious World	O	B	250+	Meet The Author	Richard C. Owen
My Name Is America	Z	HF	250+	White, Ellen Emerson	Scholastic
My Name Is Erica Montoya de la Cruz	K	RF	804	Books for Young Learners	Richard C. Owen
My Name Is Maria Isabel	N	RF	250+	Ada, Alma Flor	Aladdin
My Name Is Not Angelica	V	HF	250+	O'Dell, Scott	Bantam
My Name Is Yun Jim	N	RF	250+	Sunshine	Wright Group/McGraw Hill
My Native American School	F	RF	86	Gould, Carol	Kaeden Books
My Neighborhood	K	I	250+	Early Connections	Benchmark Education
My Neighborhood	J	RF	391	Leveled Readers	Houghton Mifflin Harcourt
My Neighborhood	E	RF	71	Reading Street	Pearson
My Neighborhood Places and Faces	K	RF	250+	All About Me	Picture Window Books
My Nest	C	I	42	Little Celebrations	Pearson Learning Group
My Nest Is Best	D	RF	92	Foundations	Wright Group/McGraw Hill
My New Boy	F	F	102	Step into Reading	Random House
My New House	C	RF	26	Reading Corners	Pearson Learning Group
My New Mom	K	RF	282	Sunshine	Wright Group/McGraw Hill
My New Pet	A	RF	32	Literacy by Design	Rigby
My New Pet	F	RF	105	Little Readers	Houghton Mifflin Harcourt
My New Pet	E	I	151	Sun Sprouts	ETA Cuisenaire
My New Quilt	H	I	170	Rigby Focus	Rigby
My New Rocket	D	F	128	Bookshop	Mondo
My New Room	D	I	108	PM Science Readers	Rigby
My New School	A	I	40	Leveled Literacy Intervention/ Green System	Heinemann

* Collection of short stories
# Graphic text

TITLE	LEVEL	GENRE	WORD COUNT	AUTHOR / SERIES	PUBLISHER / DISTRIBUTOR
My New School	A	I	32	On Our Way to English	Rigby
My New Truck	C	I	71	First Stories	Pacific Learning
My Noodle Necklace	C	I	75	Rigby Flying Colors	Rigby
My Old Cat	E	RF	110	Foundations	Wright Group/McGraw Hill
My Old Cat and the Computer	F	RF	81	Foundations	Wright Group/McGraw Hill
My Old Gold Boat	G	F	51	Easy Phonics Readers	Teacher Created Materials
My Own Place	J	RF	250+	Voyages	SRA/McGraw Hill
My Own Two Feet	W	B	250+	Cleary, Beverly	Avon
My Painting	B	RF	31	First Stories	Pacific Learning
My Pal Al	E	RF	81	Real Kids Readers	Millbrook Press
My Party	WB	I	N/A	Big Cat	Pacific Learning
My Party	C	I	35	The Candid Collection	Pearson Learning Group
My Pen Pal	K	RF	250+	Twig	Wright Group/McGraw Hill
My Pen Pal, Pat	K	RF	1298	Real Kids Readers	Millbrook Press
My Pet	C	I	18	KinderReaders	Rigby
My Pet	A	I	25	Leveled Readers	Houghton Mifflin Harcourt
My Pet	A	I	25	Leveled Readers/CA	Houghton Mifflin Harcourt
My Pet	D	RF	65	Salem, Lynn; Stewart, Josie	Continental Press
My Pet Bobby	E	F	150	Little Readers	Houghton Mifflin Harcourt
My Pet Cat	A	RF	32	Leveled Readers	Houghton Mifflin Harcourt
My Pet Cat	A	RF	32	Leveled Readers/CA	Houghton Mifflin Harcourt
My Pet Ferrets	P	I	5911	All About Pets	Lerner Publications
My Pet Fish	P	I	7027	All About Pets	Lerner Publications
My Pet Lizards	P	I	5591	All About Pets	Lerner Publications
My Pet Rabbit	P	I	6188	All About Pets	Lerner Publications
My Pet Rat	P	I	5934	All About Pets	Lerner Publications
My Photo Journal	I	I	242	Shutterbug Books	Steck-Vaughn
My Picture	C	RF	37	Carousel Readers	Pearson Learning Group
My Picture	A	RF	23	Story Box	Wright Group/McGraw Hill
My Pigs	F	I	123	Miller, Heather	Scholastic
My Place	A	RF	28	Foundations	Wright Group/McGraw Hill
My Place	Q	I	250+	Orbit Collections	Pacific Learning
My Place	A	RF	34	Story Steps	Rigby
My Planet	A	I	28	Smart Starts	Rigby
My Plant	D	I	96	Rigby Literacy	Rigby
My Play House	B	RF	71	Leveled Readers	Houghton Mifflin Harcourt
My Play House	B	RF	71	Leveled Readers/CA	Houghton Mifflin Harcourt
My Pony	C	RF	49	Rise & Shine	Hampton-Brown
My Pony Minnie	E	RF	59	Sunshine	Wright Group/McGraw Hill
My Prairie Summer	M	RF	250+	Pair-It Books	Steck-Vaughn
My Pumpkin	C	I	52	Teacher's Choice Series	Pearson Learning Group
My Pup	D	RF	65	Leveled Readers	Houghton Mifflin Harcourt
My Puppy	B	RF	29	Gear Up!	Wright Group/McGraw Hill
My Puppy	A	RF	39	Leveled Literacy Intervention/ Green System	Heinemann
My Puppy	B	I	72	Literacy by Design	Rigby
My Puppy	C	RF	33	Little Celebrations	Pearson Learning Group
My Puppy	B	RF	14	Sunshine	Wright Group/McGraw Hill
My Red Rowboat	E	RF	89	Early Readers	Compass Point Books
My Red Scarf	F	I	120	Rigby Focus	Rigby
My Ride	C	RF	56	Foundations	Wright Group/McGraw Hill
My River	F	F	53	Halpern, Shari	Scholastic
My Rocket	A	F	28	KinderReaders	Rigby
My Rocks	C	RF	43	Early Connections	Benchmark Education

* Collection of short stories
\# Graphic text

TITLE	LEVEL	GENRE	WORD COUNT	AUTHOR / SERIES	PUBLISHER / DISTRIBUTOR
My Room	A	RF	28	Carousel Earlybirds	Pearson Learning Group
My Room	A	I	32	Leveled Literacy Intervention/ Orange System	Heinemann
My Room	A	RF	15	Leveled Readers Emergent	Houghton Mifflin Harcourt
My Room	LB	RF	14	Ready Readers	Pearson Learning Group
My Room	A	RF	15	Twig	Wright Group/McGraw Hill
My Sand Castle	C	RF	44	PM Plus Starters	Rigby
My Sand Pie	B	I	33	Rigby Flying Colors	Rigby
My School	A	I	34	At School Series	Pioneer Valley
My School	A	RF	32	Handprints A	Educators Publishing Service
My School	B	I	34	Little Readers	Houghton Mifflin Harcourt
My School	C	RF	40	TOTTS	Tott Publications
My School	A	I	20	Vocabulary Readers	Houghton Mifflin Harcourt
My School	A	I	20	Vocabulary Readers/CA	Houghton Mifflin Harcourt
My School Day	LB	I	6	Windows on Literacy	National Geographic
My School Lunch	C	I	54	Bonnell, Kris	Reading Reading Books
My School, Your School	F	I	72	Take Two Books	Wright Group/McGraw Hill
My Science Project	M	RF	250+	On Our Way To English	Rigby
My Scrapbook	K	I	312	Storyteller Nonfiction	Wright Group/McGraw Hill
My Search for Fossils	S	I	250+	Literacy by Design	Rigby
My Search for My Father	X	RF	2402	Leveled Readers	Houghton Mifflin Harcourt
My Search for My Father	X	RF	2402	Leveled Readers/CA	Houghton Mifflin Harcourt
My Secret Hiding Place	G	RF	155	First Start	Troll Associates
My Secret Life as a Ping-Pong Wizard	R	RF	250+	Winkler, Henry and Oliver, Lin	Grosset & Dunlap
My Secret Place	G	RF	121	Wonder World	Wright Group/McGraw Hill
My Secret War Diary	Z	HF	250+	Albright, Flossie	Candlewick Press
My Shadow	A	RF	29	Book Bank	Wright Group/McGraw Hill
My Shadow	C	RF	42	Foundations	Wright Group/McGraw Hill
My Shadow	E	I	46	Pacific Literacy	Pacific Learning
My Shadow	F	RF	116	Ready Readers	Pearson Learning Group
My Shadow	C	RF	35	Sunshine	Wright Group/McGraw Hill
My Shadow Clock	H	I	180	Sun Sprouts	ETA Cuisenaire
My Shoes	B	RF	25	Rise & Shine	Hampton-Brown
My Side of the Mountain	U	RF	250+	George, Jean Craighead	Penguin Group
My Sister Annie	S	RF	250+	Dodds, Bill	Boyds Mills Press
My Sister Is My Friend	B	RF	32	Instant Readers	Harcourt School Publishers
My Sister Jess	I	RF	120	Supersonics	Rigby
My Sister June	H	RF	182	Ready Readers	Pearson Learning Group
My Sister the Witch	R	RF	250+	Conford, Ellen	Troll Associates
My Sister's Getting Married	K	RF	300	Foundations	Wright Group/McGraw Hill
My Sister's Surprise	T	RF	2298	Leveled Readers	Houghton Mifflin Harcourt
My Sister's Surprise	T	RF	2298	Leveled Readers/CA	Houghton Mifflin Harcourt
My Sister's Surprise	T	RF	2298	Leveled Readers/TX	Houghton Mifflin Harcourt
My Skateboard	LB	I	11	Big Cat	Pacific Learning
My Skateboard	D	RF	89	Carousel Readers	Pearson Learning Group
My Skateboard	I	RF	81	City Kids	Rigby
My Skateboard	G	I	81	Sun Sprouts	ETA Cuisenaire
My Skin	D	I	64	Wonder World	Wright Group/McGraw Hill
My Skin Looks After Me	G	I	82	Pacific Literacy	Pacific Learning
My Sloppy Tiger	I	F	211	Sunshine	Wright Group/McGraw Hill
My Sloppy Tiger Goes to School	J	F	217	Sunshine	Wright Group/McGraw Hill
My Snowman	B	I	66	First Stories	Pacific Learning
My Snowman	D	I	113	PM Science Readers	Rigby

* Collection of short stories
# Graphic text

TITLE	LEVEL	GENRE	WORD COUNT	AUTHOR / SERIES	PUBLISHER / DISTRIBUTOR
My Son, the Time Traveler	N	F	250+	The Zack Files	Grossett & Dunlap
My Special Book	B	I	45	Storyteller	Wright Group/McGraw Hill
My Special Job	E	RF	110	Pacific Literacy	Pacific Learning
My Special Place	E	RF	33	Home Connection Collection	Rigby
My Special Place	E	RF	116	Teacher's Choice Series	Pearson Learning Group
My Stepmother	I	RF	121	City Stories	Rigby
My Steps	K	RF	250+	Bebop Books	Lee & Low Books Inc.
My Stomach	J	I	144	My Body	Capstone Press
My Story	A	RF	17	Wonder World	Wright Group/McGraw Hill
My Stuffed Animals	C	RF	50	Handprints B	Educators Publishing Service
My Suitcase	LB	RF	16	Handprints A	Educators Publishing Service
My Summer Without Baseball and Other Disasters	N	RF	3491	In Step Readers	Rigby
My Summertime Camping Trip	J	RF	585	Appleton-Smith, Laura	Flyleaf Publishing
My Take-Away Day	E	RF	115	InfoTrek	ETA Cuisenaire
My Teacher	A	I	32	At School Series	Pioneer Valley
My Teacher Flunked the Planet	S	F	250+	Coville, Bruce	Pocket Books
My Teacher Fried My Brains	S	F	250+	Coville, Bruce	Pocket Books
My Teacher Glows in the Dark	S	F	250+	Coville, Bruce	Pocket Books
My Teacher Helps Me	C	RF	37	Visions	Wright Group/McGraw Hill
My Teacher Is an Alien	S	F	250+	Coville, Bruce	Pocket Books
My Teacher Turns into a Tyrannosaurus	O	F	250+	SupaDoopers	Sundance
My Teacher, My Dad	J	RF	296	Leveled Readers	Houghton Mifflin Harcourt
My Teacher, My Dad	J	RF	296	Leveled Readers/CA	Houghton Mifflin Harcourt
My Teacher, My Dad	J	RF	296	Leveled Readers/TX	Houghton Mifflin Harcourt
My Teacher's Leaving	I	RF	154	City Kids	Rigby
My Things	LB	F	12	Sails	Rigby
My Three-Wheeler	C	RF	38	Visions	Wright Group/McGraw Hill
My Tiger Cat	E	F	76	Frankford, Marilyn	Kaeden Books
My Time as Caz Hazard	Z+	RF	250+	Orca Soundings	Orca Book Publishers
My Time Box	I	RF	225	Early Connections	Benchmark Education
My Tooth Is About to Fall Out	I	RF	173	Maccarone, Grace	Scholastic
My Tooth is Loose!	H	RF	250+	Silverman, Martin	Puffin/Penguin
My Tower	C	RF	61	PM Plus Story Books	Rigby
My Tower	A	RF	15	Windmill Books	Wright Group/McGraw Hill
My Town	A	I	33	Early Connections	Benchmark Education
My Town at Work	M	I	250+	Windows on Literacy	National Geographic
My Town Used to Be Small	G	I	79	Windows on Literacy	National Geographic
My Toy Box Is Heavy	D	RF	99	Windows on Literacy	National Geographic
My Toys	A	I	25	Explorations	Okapi Educational Materials
My Toys	A	I	25	Explorations	Eleanor Curtain Publishing
My Toys	A	RF	28	Little Books for Early Readers	University of Maine
My Treasure Garden	J	RF	134	Book Bank	Wright Group/McGraw Hill
My Trip	A	F	30	Sails	Rigby
My Turn Your Turn	D	RF	78	Book Bus	Creative Edge
My Twin!	C	RF	40	Ready Readers	Pearson Learning Group
My Two Families	K	RF	250+	PM Story Books-Silver	Rigby
My Two Grandmas	I	RF	235	Sun Sprouts	ETA Cuisenaire
My Two Homes	E	RF	69	Carousel Readers	Pearson Learning Group
My Uncle the Werewolf	Q	F	9674	French, Jackie	Stone Arch Books
My Uncle's Truck	C	RF	24	Visions	Wright Group/McGraw Hill
My Undersea World	Q	I	250+	Literacy by Design	Rigby

Organized Alphabetically by Title
Storable Database at www.fountasandpinnellleveledbooks.com

* Collection of short stories
\# Graphic text

TITLE	LEVEL	GENRE	WORD COUNT	AUTHOR / SERIES	PUBLISHER / DISTRIBUTOR
My Vacation	D	RF	60	Rigby Literacy	Rigby
My Very Hungry Pet	F	RF	334	Reading Corners	Pearson Learning Group
My Vivid Town	I	RF	332	Appleton-Smith, Laura	Flyleaf Publishing
My Walk	WB	I	N/A	Windows on Literacy	National Geographic
My Walk Home	F	RF	71	Windows on Literacy	National Geographic
My Wartime Summers	V	HF	250+	Cutler, Jane	HarperCollins
My Weather Station	G	I	313	Leveled Readers Science	Houghton Mifflin Harcourt
My Week	D	RF	137	Early Connections	Benchmark Education
My Weekly Chores	C	RF	44	Visions	Wright Group/McGraw Hill
My Weird Mother	M	RF	250+	SupaDoopers	Sundance
My Wild Woolly	F	F	87	Instant Readers	Harcourt Trade
My Wild Woolly	E	F	91	Rigby Rocket	Rigby
My Wonderful Aunt, Story Five	M	F	493	Sunshine	Wright Group/McGraw Hill
My Wonderful Aunt, Story Four	M	F	436	Sunshine	Wright Group/McGraw Hill
My Wonderful Aunt, Story One	M	F	193	Sunshine	Wright Group/McGraw Hill
My Wonderful Aunt, Story Six	M	F	432	Sunshine	Wright Group/McGraw Hill
My Wonderful Aunt, Story Three	M	F	392	Sunshine	Wright Group/McGraw Hill
My Wonderful Aunt, Story Two	M	F	199	Sunshine	Wright Group/McGraw Hill
My Wonderful Chair	F	F	109	Windmill Books	Wright Group/McGraw Hill
My Writing Day	O	B	250+	Meet The Author	Richard C. Owen
My Yard	A	I	19	Leveled Readers	Houghton Mifflin Harcourt
My Yard	A	I	19	Leveled Readers/CA	Houghton Mifflin Harcourt
My Zoo Album	F	I	168	PM Science Readers	Rigby
Mysteries from Long Ago	P	I	936	Leveled Readers	Houghton Mifflin Harcourt
Mysteries from Long Ago	P	I	936	Leveled Readers/CA	Houghton Mifflin Harcourt
Mysteries from Long Ago	P	I	936	Leveled Readers/TX	Houghton Mifflin Harcourt
Mysteries of Chaco Canyon, The	V	I	250+	Explore More	Wright Group/McGraw Hill
Mysteries of Pompeii	X	I	3180	Vocabulary Readers	Houghton Mifflin Harcourt
Mysteries of Pompeii	X	I	3180	Vocabulary Readers/CA	Houghton Mifflin Harcourt
Mysteries of the Ancients	Z	I	250+	Unsolved Mysteries	Steck-Vaughn
Mysteries of the Bermuda Triangle	Z	I	2348	Leveled Readers	Houghton Mifflin Harcourt
Mysteries of the Deep	R	I	531	Vocabulary Readers	Houghton Mifflin Harcourt
Mysteries of the Phoenicians	Z	I	2041	Leveled Readers	Houghton Mifflin Harcourt
Mysteries of the Phoenicians	Z	I	2041	Leveled Readers/CA	Houghton Mifflin Harcourt
Mysteries of UFOs, The	Z	I	250+	Unsolved Mysteries	Steck-Vaughn
Mysterious Animal Tracks, The	K	RF	250+	Literacy by Design	Rigby
Mysterious Bali	P	RF	250+	Reading Safari	Mondo
Mysterious Benedict Society and the Perilous Journey, The	V	SF	250+	Stewart, Trenton Lee	Little, Brown & Co.
Mysterious Benedict Society, The	V	SF	250+	Stewart, Trenton Lee	Little, Brown & Co.
Mysterious Bone, The	L	B	320	Leveled Readers	Houghton Mifflin Harcourt
Mysterious Bone, The	L	B	320	Leveled Readers/CA	Houghton Mifflin Harcourt
Mysterious Bone, The	L	B	320	Leveled Readers/TX	Houghton Mifflin Harcourt
Mysterious Edge of the Heroic World, The	Z	RF	250+	Konigsburg, E. L.	Atheneum
Mysterious Giant Squid, The	Z	I	2415	Leveled Readers	Houghton Mifflin Harcourt
*Mysterious Green Swimmer and Other Cases, The	O	RF	250+	Simon, Seymour	Avon
Mysterious Healing	Z	I	250+	Unsolved Mysteries	Steck-Vaughn
Mysterious I.O.U., The	M	RF	250+	Woodland Mysteries	Wright Group/McGraw Hill
Mysterious Mask, The	O	RF	250+	Klooz	Stone Arch Books
Mysterious Ms. Martin, The	N	RF	250+	On Our Way To English	Rigby
Mysterious Neighbor, The	L	RF	1014	In Step Readers	Rigby
Mysterious Neighbor, The	L	RF	250+	Literacy By Design	Rigby

TITLE	LEVEL	GENRE	WORD COUNT	AUTHOR / SERIES	PUBLISHER / DISTRIBUTOR
Mysterious Ocean Highway: Benjamin Franklin and the Gulf Stream	T	B	250+	Heiligman, Deborah	Steck-Vaughn
Mysterious Spinners	Q	TL	250+	Bookshop	Mondo
Mysterious Superhero, The	L	F	1104	Leveled Readers	Houghton Mifflin Harcourt
Mysterious Superhero, The	L	F	1104	Leveled Readers/CA	Houghton Mifflin Harcourt
Mysterious Superhero, The	L	F	1104	Leveled Readers/TX	Houghton Mifflin Harcourt
*Mysterious Tracks and Other Cases, The	O	RF	250+	Simon, Seymour	Avon
Mystery Ancestor	Q	I	250+	Rigby Focus	Rigby
Mystery at Summer Camp	Q	RF	250+	Reading Expeditions	National Geographic
Mystery at the White House	R	F	250+	Pair-It Books	Steck-Vaughn
Mystery at the Zoo	T	F	1733	Leveled Readers	Houghton Mifflin Harcourt
Mystery Bay	P	RF	250+	Action Packs	Rigby
Mystery Box, The	I	RF	326	New Way Orange	Steck-Vaughn
Mystery Coin	J	RF	379	Independent Readers Social Studies	Houghton Mifflin Harcourt
Mystery Fish: Secrets of the Coelacanth	O	I	1678	On My Own Science	Lerner Publications
Mystery Food	E	RF	62	Leveled Readers Science	Houghton Mifflin Harcourt
Mystery for Mickey Maloney, A	J	RF	383	Sails	Rigby
Mystery Fruit	K	I	364	Vocabulary Readers	Houghton Mifflin Harcourt
Mystery Fruit	K	I	364	Vocabulary Readers/CA	Houghton Mifflin Harcourt
Mystery in the Arctic	V	I	250+	PM Collection	Rigby
Mystery in the Attic, The	L	RF	250+	Leveled Readers Language Support	Houghton Mifflin Harcourt
Mystery in the Night Woods	M	F	250+	Peterson, John	Scholastic
Mystery Man, The	K	RF	250+	Rigby Literacy	Rigby
Mystery Mask, The	N	RF	250+	Literacy by Design	Rigby
Mystery of Campion Cave, The	P	RF	1950	Take Two Books	Wright Group/ McGraw Hill
Mystery of Hermit Dan, The	N	RF	250+	Parish, Peggy	Yearling
Mystery of Lighthouse Cave, The	P	RF	250+	Leveled Readers Language Support	Houghton Mifflin Harcourt
Mystery of Magnets, The	P	I	250+	iOpeners	Pearson Learning Group
Mystery of Mazes, The	O	I	250+	Wonder World	Wright Group/McGraw Hill
Mystery of Moody Manor, The	Q	F	250+	Ragged Island Mysteries	Wright Group/McGraw Hill
Mystery of Mr. Nice, The: A Chet Gecko Mystery	R	F	250+	Hale, Bruce	Harcourt, Inc.
Mystery of Mrs. Kim, The	M	RF	250+	Rigby Literacy	Rigby
Mystery of Mrs. Kim, The	M	RF	250+	Rigby Star Plus	Rigby
Mystery of Pony Hollow, The	N	F	250+	Hall, Lynn	Random House
Mystery of the Bay Monster	J	RF	250+	Literacy by Design	Rigby
Mystery of the Blue Box, The	N	I	841	Independent Readers Science	Houghton Mifflin Harcourt
Mystery of the Blue Ring, The	L	RF	250+	Giff, Patricia Reilly	Bantam
Mystery of the Clever Cat, The	J	RF	250+	Literacy by Design	Rigby
Mystery of the Clever Cat, The	J	RF	250+	On Our Way to English	Rigby
Mystery of the Clock Tower, The	Q	RF	250+	Reading Safari	Mondo
Mystery of the Cocos Gold	Q	HF	250+	High-Fliers	Pacific Learning
Mystery of the Cupboard	R	F	250+	Banks, Lynne Reid	Avon Camelot
Mystery of the Dark Old House, The	M	F	250+	Woodland Mysteries	Wright Group/McGraw Hill
Mystery of the Fire in the Sky	Q	RF	250+	Mystery Solvers	Troll Associates
Mystery of the Flattened Flowers, The	J	RF	454	Springboard	Wright Group/McGraw Hill
Mystery of the Fool & the Vanisher, The	W	F	250+	Ellwand, David & Ruth	Candlewick Press
Mystery of the Jubilee Emerald, The	R	RF	250+	Bookshop	Mondo
Mystery of the Missing Berries, The	J	RF	250+	Literacy by Design	Rigby
Mystery of the Missing Dog, The	J	F	250+	Levy, Elizabeth	Scholastic
Mystery of the Missing Dog, The	M	RF	250+	Woodland Mysteries	Wright Group/McGraw Hill
Mystery of the Missing Garden Gnome, The	R	RF	250+	Book Blazers	ETA Cuisenaire

* Collection of short stories
# Graphic text

TITLE	LEVEL	GENRE	WORD COUNT	AUTHOR / SERIES	PUBLISHER / DISTRIBUTOR
Mystery of the Missing Leopard, The	Q	F	250+	Leonhardt, Alice	Steck-Vaughn
Mystery of the Missing Malamute, The	M	RF	250+	Sunshine	Wright Group/McGraw Hill
Mystery of the Missing Mystery, The	M	RF	250+	Rigby Rocket	Rigby
Mystery of the Missing Red Mitten, The	H	RF	246	Little Readers	Houghton Mifflin Harcourt
Mystery of the Mona Lisa, The	P	SF	250+	Secret Agent Jack Stalwart	Weinstein Books
Mystery of the Noises in the Attic, The	N	F	606	Leveled Readers	Houghton Mifflin Harcourt
Mystery of the Phantom Pony, The	N	RF	250+	Hall, Lynn	Random House
Mystery of the Pirate Ghost, The	L	F	250+	Hayes, Geoffrey	Random House
Mystery of the Sea Jellies, The	N	RF	1350	Gear Up!	Wright Group/McGraw Hill
Mystery of the Silver Spoons, The	Q	RF	250+	Book Blazers	ETA Cuisenaire
Mystery of the Stolen Bike, The	M	F	250+	Brown, Marc	Little, Brown & Co.
Mystery of the Talking Tail, The	M	F	250+	SupaDoopers	Sundance
Mystery of the Three Keys, The	M	RF	250+	Woodland Mysteries	Wright Group/McGraw Hill
Mystery of the Tooth Gremlin	L	RF	250+	Graves, Bonnie	Hyperion
Mystery of the Trembling Earth, The	T	F	250+	Reading Safari	Mondo
Mystery on Maple Street, The	Q	RF	1153	Leveled Readers	Houghton Mifflin Harcourt
Mystery on Maple Street, The	Q	RF	1153	Leveled Readers/CA	Houghton Mifflin Harcourt
Mystery on Maple Street, The	Q	RF	1153	Leveled Readers/TX	Houghton Mifflin Harcourt
Mystery on October Road	O	RF	250+	Herzig, A. C.; Mali, Jane	Scholastic
Mystery on Penn Street	G	RF	214	On Our Way to English	Rigby
Mystery Seeds	L	RF	250+	Reading Unlimited	Pearson Learning Group
*Mystery Stories	R	RF	250+	Higgins, James	Houghton Mifflin Harcourt
Mystery to Me, A	Q	I	250+	Orbit Collections	Pacific Learning
Mystery Trip, The	L	RF	525	Rigby Flying Colors	Rigby
Mystery Valley	P	SF	250+	Bookweb	Rigby
Myth or Mystery?	Q	F	250+	Literacy Tree	Rigby
Mythical Beasts	T	F	250+	Wildcats	Wright Group/McGraw Hill
Mythical Horse, The	T	I	250+	Sunshine	Wright Group/McGraw Hill
Mythmakers	S	I	250+	Wildcats	Wright Group/McGraw Hill
Mythology	Y	I	250+	Eyewitness Books	DK Publishing
*Myths	S	TL	250+	Goodman, Ronald; Pierce, Robert; Wagner, Betty Jane	Houghton Mifflin Harcourt
Myths and Legends	T	I	250+	Kids Discover Reading	Wright Group/McGraw Hill
Myths of a Different Feather	U	TL	250+	Literacy By Design	Rigby

TITLE	LEVEL	GENRE	WORD COUNT	AUTHOR / SERIES	PUBLISHER / DISTRIBUTOR
Nadia Comaneci	M	B	250+	Take Two Books	Wright Group/McGraw Hill
Nailed	Z+	RF	250+	Jones, Patrick	Walker & Company
Naked Mole-Rat Letters, The	T	RF	250+	Amato, Mary	Holiday House
Naked Mole-Rat, The	J	I	134	Weird Animals	Capstone Press
Name for a Dog, A	I	RF	258	Windmill Books	Rigby
Name for Rabbit, A	H	F	94	Pacific Literacy	Pacific Learning
Name Garden, A	F	I	125	Sunshine	Wright Group/McGraw Hill
Name Is the Same, The	G	RF	115	Ready Readers	Pearson Learning Group
Name Jar, The	N	RF	250+	Choi, Yangsook	Dell Dragonfly Books
Name of Honor, A	T	HF	250+	Bookshop	Mondo
Name Of The Game Was Murder, The	Y	RF	250	Nixon, Joan Lowery	Laurel-Leaf Books
Name of This Book Is Secret, The	U	F	250+	Bosch, Pseudonymous	Little, Brown & Co.
Name That Plant	I	I	383	Shutterbug Books	Steck-Vaughn
Name That Style: All About Isms in Art	Y	I	3863	Raczka, Bob	Millbrook Press
Name, The	H	RF	159	Voyages	SRA/McGraw Hill
Named, The	Z	F	250+	Curly, Marianne	Bloomsbury Children's Books
Names and Games	H	I	115	Literacy Tree	Rigby
Naming the Cat	L	RF	250+	Soar To Success	Houghton Mifflin Harcourt
Nan the Red Hen!	C	RF	43	Reading Street	Pearson
Nana Rescue, The	J	RF	250+	Voyages	SRA/McGraw Hill
Nana's House	D	RF	133	Leveled Readers	Houghton Mifflin Harcourt
Nana's House	D	RF	133	Leveled Readers/CA	Houghton Mifflin Harcourt
Nana's House	D	RF	133	Leveled Readers/TX	Houghton Mifflin Harcourt
Nana's in the Plum Tree	M	RF	250+	Pacific Literacy	Pacific Learning
Nana's Kitchen	J	RF	250+	Walton, Darwin McBeth	Steck-Vaughn
Nana's Orchard	F	RF	92	Gould, Carol	Kaeden Books
Nana's Place	I	RF	211	Gibson, Akimi; Meyer, K.	Scholastic
Nana's Sweet Potato Pie	E	RF	233	Visions	Wright Group/McGraw Hill
Nana's Tomatoes	M	RF	587	Leveled Readers Science	Houghton Mifflin Harcourt
Nannies for Hire	M	RF	250+	Hest, Amy	William Morrow
Nanny Goat's Nap	C	F	96	Ready Readers	Pearson Learning Group
Nanotechnology	Z	I	6581	Cool Science	Lerner Publications
Nanotechnology	Z	I	2839	Leveled Readers	Houghton Mifflin Harcourt
Nanotechnology	Z	I	2839	Leveled Readers/CA	Houghton Mifflin Harcourt
Nap Time	C	RF	24	KinderReaders	Rigby
Nap Time for Gilbert	D	F	83	Gilbert the Pig	Pioneer Valley
Nap Time for Lily	D	RF	79	Emergent	Pioneer Valley
Napping House, The	I	F	268	Wood, Don & Audrey	Harcourt Trade
NASCAR at the Track	U	I	4409	The Science of NASCAR	Lerner Publications
NASCAR Behind the Scenes	U	I	4568	The Science of NASCAR	Lerner Publications
NASCAR Designed to Win	U	I	4465	The Science of NASCAR	Lerner Publications
NASCAR in the Driver's Seat	U	I	4425	The Science of NASCAR	Lerner Publications
NASCAR in the Pits	U	I	4973	The Science of NASCAR	Lerner Publications
NASCAR Safety on the Track	U	I	4635	The Science of NASCAR	Lerner Publications
NASCAR's Greatest Moments	S	I	250+	NASCAR Racing	Capstone Press
Nasty, Stinky Sneakers	R	RF	250+	Bunting, Eve	HarperTrophy
Nat and Harry Meet a Dinosaur	I	RF	416	Rigby Flying Colors	Rigby
Nat and Harry Play Soccer	G	RF	201	Rigby Flying Colors	Rigby
Nat Love	S	B	3919	History Maker Bios	Lerner Publications
Nat Turner: Rebellious Slave	U	B	250+	Let Freedom Ring	Capstone Press
Nat, Nan, and Pam	C	RF	30	Leveled Readers	Houghton Mifflin Harcourt
Natalia and Her Grandma	N	RF	250+	Sunflower	Intercultural Center for Research in Education

* Collection of short stories
\# Graphic text

TITLE	LEVEL	GENRE	WORD COUNT	AUTHOR / SERIES	PUBLISHER / DISTRIBUTOR
Natalie Du Toit	O	B	250+	Lighthouse	Ginn & Co.
Natchez Under the Hill	T	HF	250+	Applegate, Stan	Peachtree
Nate the Great	K	RF	250+	Sharmat, Marjorie Weinman	Bantam
Nate the Great and Me	K	RF	250+	Sharmat, Marjorie Weinman	Random House
Nate the Great and the Boring Beach Bag	K	RF	250+	Sharmat, Marjorie Weinman	Bantam
Nate the Great and the Crunchy Christmas	K	RF	250+	Sharmat, Marjorie Weinman	Bantam
Nate the Great and the Fishy Prize	K	RF	250+	Sharmat, Marjorie Weinman	Bantam
Nate the Great and the Halloween Hunt	K	RF	250+	Sharmat, Marjorie Weinman	Bantam
Nate the Great and the Lost List	K	RF	250+	Sharmat, Marjorie Weinman	Bantam
Nate the Great and the Missing Key	K	RF	250+	Sharmat, Marjorie Weinman	Bantam
Nate the Great and the Mushy Valentine	K	RF	250+	Sharmat, Marjorie Weinman	Bantam
Nate the Great and the Musical Note	K	RF	250+	Sharmat, Marjorie Weinman	Bantam
Nate the Great and the Phony Clue	K	RF	250+	Sharmat, Marjorie Weinman	Bantam
Nate the Great and the Pillowcase	K	RF	250+	Sharmat, Marjorie Weinman	Bantam
Nate the Great and the Snowy Trail	K	RF	250+	Sharmat, Marjorie Weinman	Bantam
Nate the Great and the Sticky Case	K	RF	250+	Sharmat, Marjorie Weinman	Bantam
Nate the Great and the Stolen Base	K	RF	250+	Sharmat, Marjorie Weinman	Bantam
Nate the Great and the Tardy Tortoise	K	RF	250+	Sharmat, Marjorie Weinman	Bantam
Nate the Great Goes Down in the Dumps	K	RF	250+	Sharmat, Marjorie Weinman	Bantam
Nate the Great Goes Undercover	K	RF	250+	Sharmat, Marjorie Weinman	Bantam
Nate the Great Saves the King of Sweden	K	RF	250+	Sharmat, Marjorie Weinman	Bantam
Nate the Great Stalks Stupidweed	K	RF	250+	Sharmat, Marjorie Weinman	Bantam
Nathan and Nicholas Alexander	K	F	250+	Delacre, Lulu	Scholastic
Nathan Hale Patriot Spy	P	B	1923	On My Own Biography	Lerner Publications
Nathaniel Comes to Town	S	RF	4072	Reading Street	Pearson
Nation at War: Soldiers, Saints, and Spies	Y	I	250+	The Civil War	Carus Publishing
Nation of Many Colors, A	T	I	2498	Reading Street	Pearson
Nation of Nations, A	S	HF	1931	Leveled Readers Social Studies	Houghton Mifflin Harcourt
Nation of Parks, A	O	I	250+	Literacy By Design	Rigby
National Anthem, The	S	I	250+	A True Book	Children's Press
National Guard, The: Modern Minutemen	T	I	1809	Reading Street	Pearson
National Parks	S	I	250+	iOpeners	Pearson Learning Group
National Parks	M	I	250+	Yellow Umbrella Books	Red Brick Learning
National Parks America's Best Idea	U	I	250+	Rigby Literacy	Rigby
National Security Agency, The: Cracking Secret Codes	S	I	250+	Line of Duty	Capstone Press
National Velvet	X	RF	250+	Bagnold, Enid	Avon Books
Native American Art	O	I	250+	Motil, Rebecca	Scholastic
Native American Art from the Pueblos	P	I	250+	Rosen Real Readers	Rosen Publishing Group
Native American Baskets	L	I	195	Phonics Readers	Compass Point Books
Native American Book of Change, The	W	I	250+	Native People Native Ways	Beyond Words
Native American Book of Knowledge, The	W	I	250+	Native People Native Ways	Beyond Words
Native American Book of Life, The	W	I	250+	Native People Native Ways	Beyond Words
Native American Book of Wisdom, The	W	I	250+	Native People Native Ways	Beyond Words
Native American Folktales	J	I	288	Vocabulary Readers	Houghton Mifflin Harcourt
Native American Folktales	J	I	288	Vocabulary Readers/CA	Houghton Mifflin Harcourt
Native American Folktales	J	I	288	Vocabulary Readers/TX	Houghton Mifflin Harcourt
Native American Foods and Recipes	O	I	250+	Rosen Real Readers	Rosen Publishing Group
Native American Homes	M	I	250+	Pair-It Turn and Learn	Steck-Vaughn
*Native American Stories	Q	TL	250+	Bruchac, Joseph	Fulcrum Publishing
Native Americans	P	I	250+	Explorers	Wright Group/McGraw Hill
Native Americans	O	I	250+	Navigators Social Studies Series	Benchmark Education
Native Peoples	R	I	250+	Navigators Social Studies Series	Benchmark Education
Nat's New Soccer Ball	G	RF	214	Rigby Flying Colors	Rigby

* Collection of short stories
# Graphic text

Organized Alphabetically by Title   **419**
Storable Database at www.fountasandpinnellleveledbooks.com

TITLE	LEVEL	GENRE	WORD COUNT	AUTHOR / SERIES	PUBLISHER / DISTRIBUTOR
Natural and Human-Made	I	I	107	Nature Basics	Capstone Press
Natural History Museum, The	K	I	250+	Stepping Stones	Nelson/Michaels Assoc.
Natural Writer: A Story About Marjorie Kinnan Rawlings	R	B	7847	Creative Minds Biographies	Carolrhoda Books
Nature Club, The	O	RF	755	Leveled Readers	Houghton Mifflin Harcourt
Nature Hike	C	HF	32	Twig	Wright Group/McGraw Hill
Nature in Focus	T	I	250+	Navigators Science Series	Benchmark Education Company
Nature of Cats and Dogs, The	X	I	3193	Vocabulary Readers	Houghton Mifflin Harcourt
Nature of Cats and Dogs, The	X	I	3193	Vocabulary Readers/CA	Houghton Mifflin Harcourt
Nature Reserves	N	I	720	Leveled Readers	Houghton Mifflin Harcourt
Nature Reserves	N	I	720	Leveled Readers/CA	Houghton Mifflin Harcourt
Nature Scales: Weighing Environmental Issues	U	I	250+	Rigby Literacy	Rigby
Nature Trail	B	RF	39	Rigby Star	Rigby
Nature Walk, The	A	RF	40	Handprints A	Educators Publishing Service
Nature! Wild and Wonderful	O	B	250+	Meet The Author	Richard C. Owen
Nature's Celebration	M	I	250+	Literacy 2000	Rigby
Nature's Extremes - Wild Weather	U	I	250+	Connectors	Pacific Learning
Nature's Fireworks: A Book About Lightning	M	I	250+	Amazing Science	Picture Window Books
Nature's Green Umbrella: Tropical Rain Forests	Q	I	250+	Gibbons, Gail	Harper Collins
Nature's Power	Q	I	250+	Pair-It Books	Steck-Vaughn
Nature's Sculptures	M	I	250+	Literacy by Design	Rigby
Nature's Wonders	V	I	250+	News Extra	Richard C. Owen
Nature's Wonders	V	I	250+	News Extra	Richard C. Owen
Naughty Ann, The	G	F	159	PM Story Books	Rigby
Naughty Hamster, The	G	RF	195	Storyworlds	Heinemann Educational Books
Naughty Happy Monkey	C	F	33	Joy Readers	Pearson Learning Group
Naughty Joe	C	RF	34	Storyworlds	Heinemann Educational Publishers
Naughty Kitten!	LB	RF	18	Smart Starts	Rigby
Naughty Monkey	B	F	30	Sails	Rigby
Naughty Nancy Goes to School	WB	F	N/A	Goodall, John S.	Andre Deutsch
Naughty Patch	D	RF	74	Foundations	Wright Group/McGraw Hill
Navajo Code Talkers, The	U	I	2549	Independent Readers Social Studies	Houghton Mifflin Harcourt
Navajo Longwalk	S	HF	250+	Armstrong, Nancy M.	Scholastic
Navajo, The	U	I	250+	The Heinle Reading Library	Thomson Learning
Navajo, The	P	I	830	Vocabulary Readers	Houghton Mifflin Harcourt
Navajo, The	P	I	830	Vocabulary Readers/CA	Houghton Mifflin Harcourt
Navajos, The	T	I	3668	Native American Stories	Lerner Publications
Near and Far	C	I	29	Location	Lerner Publishing
Near and Far	I	I	238	Where Words	Capstone Press
Near Death Experiences	X	I	250+	The Unexplained	Capstone Press
Near One Cattail	P	I	946	Sharing Nature with Children	Dawn Publications
Nebraska	T	I	250+	Hello U.S.A.	Lerner Publications
Nebraska	R	I	250+	This Land Is Your Land	Compass Point Books
*Necklace of Raindrops and Other Stories, A	S	TL	250+	Aiken, Joan	Random House
Necklace, The	D	RF	82	Dominie Math Stories	Pearson Learning Group
Necklaces	B	RF	34	Phonics and Friends	Hampton-Brown
Necks Out for Adventure	O	F	250+	Ering, Timothy Basil	Candlewick Press
Ned	C	RF	30	Leveled Readers Language Support	Houghton Mifflin Harcourt

* Collection of short stories
# Graphic text

TITLE	LEVEL	GENRE	WORD COUNT	AUTHOR / SERIES	PUBLISHER / DISTRIBUTOR
Ned Rides for the Pony Express	T	HF	2910	Leveled Readers	Houghton Mifflin Harcourt
Ned Rides for the Pony Express	T	HF	2910	Leveled Readers/CA	Houghton Mifflin Harcourt
Ned Rides for the Pony Express	T	HF	2910	Leveled Readers/TX	Houghton Mifflin Harcourt
Ned's Noise Machine	C	F	36	Rigby Literacy	Rigby
Ned's Noise Machine	C	F	32	Rigby Star	Rigby
Need for Speed, The	T	I	250+	Story Surfers	ETA Cuisenaire
Needs and Wants	C	I	43	Early Connections	Benchmark Education
Needs and Wants	H	I	154	Pebble Books	Capstone Press
Needs and Wants	D	I	107	Yellow Umbrella Books	Red Brick Learning
Neeny Coming, Neeny Going	Q	RF	250+	English, Karen	Bridge Water Paperback
Negro Leagues of Baseball, The	V	I	3319	Leveled Readers Social Studies	Houghton Mifflin Harcourt
Neighbor From Outer Space, The	N	F	250+	George, Maureen	Scholastic
Neighborhood Clubhouse, The	J	RF	474	Visions	Wright Group/McGraw Hill
Neighborhood Event, The	I	RF	309	Leveled Readers	Houghton Mifflin Harcourt
Neighborhood Nonsense	S	RF	250+	Sails	Rigby
Neighborhood Party, The	P	RF	250+	Leveled Readers Language Support	Houghton Mifflin Harcourt
Neighborhood Party, The	C	RF	60	Pair-It Books	Steck-Vaughn
Neighborhood Picnic, The	G	I	157	Visions	Wright Group/McGraw Hill
Neighborhoods	F	I	91	Reading Street	Pearson
Neighborhoods of Los Angeles	Y	I	2583	Vocabulary Readers	Houghton Mifflin Harcourt
Neighborhoods of Los Angeles	Y	I	2583	Vocabulary Readers/CA	Houghton Mifflin Harcourt
Neighbors	I	I	244	Leveled Readers	Houghton Mifflin Harcourt
Neighbors	I	I	244	Leveled Readers/CA	Houghton Mifflin Harcourt
Neighbors	I	I	244	Leveled Readers/TX	Houghton Mifflin Harcourt
Neil Armstrong	R	B	250+	Amazing Americans	Wright Group/McGraw Hill
Neil Armstrong	N	B	250+	Explore Space!	Capstone Press
Neil Armstrong	S	B	3498	History Maker Bios	Lerner Publications
Neil Armstrong: Young Flyer	O	B	250+	Childhood of Famous Americans	Aladdin
Nellie Bly	R	B	3270	History Maker Bios	Lerner Publications
Nellie Bly	J	B	270	Leveled Readers Social Studies	Houghton Mifflin Harcourt
Nellie McClung	X	B	250+	The Canadians	Fitzhenry & Whiteside
Nelson Gets a Fright	K	RF	387	PM Story Books	Rigby
Nelson Is Kidnapped	M	RF	250+	PM Story Books-Silver	Rigby
Nelson Mandela	Q	B	250+	First Biographies	Steck-Vaughn
Nelson Mandela	O	B	250+	Rookie Biographies	Children's Press
Nelson Mandela: A Life of Persistence	P	B	516	Pull Ahead Books	Lerner Publications
Nelson Mandela: Freedom for South Africa	T	B	250+	Dell, Pamela	Children's Press
Nelson Mandela: "No Easy Walk to Freedom"	X	B	250+	Denenberg, Barry	Scholastic
Nelson Mandela: South Africa's Silent Voice of Protest	X	B	250+	Hargrove, Jim	Children's Press
Nelson Mandela: The Fight for Freedom	T	B	250+	Orbit Chapter Books	Pacific Learning
Nelson the Baby Elephant	J	RF	350	PM Collection	Rigby
Nemo and the Ship of Gold	O	I	250+	Leveled Readers Language Support	Houghton Mifflin Harcourt
Neptune	Q	I	250+	A True Book	Children's Press
Neptune	J	I	125	Exploring the Galaxy	Capstone Press
Neptune	S	I	250+	Our Solar System	Compass Point Books
Neptune	N	I	713	Our Universe	Lerner Publications
Neptune	Q	I	250+	The Galaxy	Capstone Press
Neptune's Children	Z+	F	250+	Dobkin, Bonnie	Walker & Company
Nero Hawley's Fight for Freedom	Q	B	545	Vocabulary Readers	Houghton Mifflin Harcourt
Nervous	R	F	250+	Norman, Tony	Stone Arch Books
Nervous System, The	S	I	250+	A True Book	Children's Press

TITLE	LEVEL	GENRE	WORD COUNT	AUTHOR / SERIES	PUBLISHER / DISTRIBUTOR
Nervous System, The	P	I	1917	Early Bird Body Systems	Lerner Publishing
Nervous System, The	M	I	213	Human Body Systems	Red Brick Learning
Nest Full of Eggs, A	B	I	25	Pair-It Books	Steck-Vaughn
Nest of Grass, A	H	I	359	Sails	Rigby
Nest on the Beach, The	H	RF	243	PM Plus Story Books	Rigby
Nest, The	C	F	32	Story Box	Wright Group/McGraw Hill
Nest, The	B	I	21	Storyteller	Wright Group/McGraw Hill
Nest, The	C	F	34	Sunshine	Wright Group/McGraw Hill
Nesting Place, The	K	HF	356	PM Collection	Rigby
Nesting Places	B	I	36	Sails	Rigby
Nestor	K	F	250+	Bookshop	Mondo
Nests	D	I	58	Literacy 2000	Rigby
Nests	L	I	656	Rigby Flying Colors	Rigby
Nests	B	I	54	Sails	Rigby
Nests	M	I	222	Vocabulary Readers	Houghton Mifflin Harcourt
Nests	C	I	35	Wonder World	Wright Group/McGraw Hill
Nests, Nests, Nests	C	I	42	Canizares, Susan; Reid, Mary	Scholastic
Netherlands	Q	I	250+	First Reports: Countries	Compass Point Books
Netherlands, The	O	I	250+	Countries of the World	Red Brick Learning
Nettie's Journey	T	HF	250+	From Many Peoples	Fitzhenry & Whiteside
Nettie's Trip South	T	HF	250+	Turner, Ann	Scholastic
Nevada	T	I	250+	Hello U.S.A.	Lerner Publications
Nevada	R	I	250+	This Land Is Your Land	Compass Point Books
Never Be	D	RF	73	Salem, Lynn; Stewart, Josie	Continental Press
Never Bored on Boards	O	I	250+	Literacy 2000	Rigby
Never Cry Wolf	Z	B	250+	Mowat, Farley	Bantam
Never Hit a Ghost with a Baseball Bat	O	RF	250+	Clifford, Eth	Scholastic
Never Hitch a Ride With a Martian!	N	SF	250+	Orbit Chapter Books	Pacific Learning
Never Say Never	G	F	225	Ready Readers	Pearson Learning Group
Never Say Quit	T	RF	250+	Wallace, Bill	Pocket Books
Never Snap at a Bubble	G	F	89	Giant Step Reader	Educational Insights
Never So Green	Z+	RF	250+	Johnston, Tim	Farrar, Straus and Giroux
Never Trust a Cat Who Wears Earrings	N	F	250+	The Zack Files	Grossett & Dunlap
Never Turn Back: Father Serra's Mission	S	B	250+	Rawls, Jim	Steck-Vaughn
Never Wash Your Hair!	O	F	250+	High-Fliers	Pacific Learning
Never-Told Story, The	H	RF	138	Literacy Tree	Rigby
New Americans, The: Colonial Times 1620-1689	S	I	250+	Maestro, Betsy	Harper Collins
New and Old	B	I	46	Windows on Literacy	National Geographic
New at the Zoo	E	F	84	New Reader Series	Bungalo Books
New Baby	WB	RF	N/A	McCullu, Emily Arnold	Harper & Row
New Baby Calf, The	H	RF	240	Chase, Edith; Reid, Barbara	Scholastic
New Baby, The	E	RF	133	PM Story Books	Rigby
New Babysitter, The	E	RF	156	Rigby Rocket	Rigby
New Balloon, A	E	RF	36	Pacific Literacy	Pacific Learning
New Bear at School, The	L	F	250+	Weston, Carrie	Scholastic
New Beds	F	RF	173	Rigby Flying Colors	Rigby
New Beginnings	J	RF	277	Books for Young Learners	Richard C. Owen
New Bike, The	F	RF	96	Start to Read	School Zone
New Bike, The	J	RF	526	Sunshine	Wright Group/McGraw Hill
New Boots	E	RF	127	PM Plus Story Books	Rigby
New Boy, The	I	RF	250+	Storyworlds	Heinemann Educational Books
New Building, The	H	RF	78	Sunshine	Wright Group/McGraw Hill
New Butterfly, The	D	I	55	Sun Sprouts	ETA Cuisenaire

* Collection of short stories
# Graphic text

TITLE	LEVEL	GENRE	WORD COUNT	AUTHOR / SERIES	PUBLISHER / DISTRIBUTOR
New Car, The	K	RF	250+	Sunshine	Wright Group/McGraw Hill
New Cat, The	LB	F	29	Pacific Literacy	Pacific Learning
New Children, The	H	RF	161	Storyworlds	Heinemann Educational Books
New Citizens	L	I	250+	Twig	Wright Group/McGraw Hill
New Class Pet, The	J	RF	250+	On Our Way to English	Rigby
New Clothes	F	RF	107	Windows on Literacy	National Geographic
New Club, The	I	RF	267	Leveled Readers	Houghton Mifflin Harcourt
New Clubhouse, The	K	RF	553	Springboard	Wright Group/McGraw Hill
New Coach Blues	Q	RF	250+	Power Up!	Steck-Vaughn
New Coat for Anna, A	M	HF	250+	Ziefert, Harriet	Scholastic
New Cougars, The	V	I	2790	Vocabulary Readers	Houghton Mifflin Harcourt
New Cougars, The	V	I	2790	Vocabulary Readers/CA	Houghton Mifflin Harcourt
New Cougars, The	V	I	2790	Vocabulary Readers/TX	Houghton Mifflin Harcourt
New Dog in Town	L	RF	250+	Social Studies Connects	The Kane Press
New Dog, A	D	RF	52	Oxford Reading Tree	Oxford University Press
New England Patriots, The	S	I	5023	Team Spirit	Norwood House Press
New England's Whales	Q	I	856	Independent Readers Social Studies	Houghton Mifflin Harcourt
New Field, The	M	RF	945	Leveled Readers	Houghton Mifflin Harcourt
New Field, The	M	RF	945	Leveled Readers/CA	Houghton Mifflin Harcourt
New Field, The	M	RF	945	Leveled Readers/TX	Houghton Mifflin Harcourt
New Forest, The	J	RF	250+	Talking Points Series	Pearson Learning Group
New Found Land	Z+	HF	250+	Wolf, Allan	Candlewick Press
New France	S	I	250+	Orbit Chapter books	Pacific Learning
New Friend at the Beach, A	G	F	372	Bella and Rosie Series	Literacy Footprints
New Friend, A	G	RF	224	Literacy by Design	Rigby
New Friends	E	RF	159	InfoTrek	ETA Cuisenaire
New Friends	E	RF	89	Leveled Readers Language Support	Houghton Mifflin Harcourt
New Friends in a New Land: A Thanksgiving Story	N	I	250+	Stamper, Judith Bauer	Steck-Vaughn
New Girl in Class, A	S	RF	1942	Reading Street	Pearson
New Girl, The	I	RF	234	On Our Way to English	Rigby
New Girl, The	K	RF	250+	Pacific Literacy	Pacific Learning
New Glasses for Max	H	RF	239	PM Plus Story Books	Rigby
New Gym Shoes	F	RF	175	Yukish, Joe	Kaeden Books
New Hampshire	T	I	250+	Hello U.S.A.	Lerner Publications
New Hampshire	R	I	250+	This Land Is Your Land	Compass Point Books
New Hampshire Colony, The	R	I	250+	The American Colonies	Capstone Press
New Hat, The	C	RF	37	Rigby Literacy	Rigby
New Hat, The	C	RF	57	Rigby Star	Rigby
New Highway, The	C	I	67	Foundations	Wright Group/McGraw Hill
New Home, A	D	F	45	Green Light Readers	Harcourt
New Horizons	S	I	250+	Orbit Collections	Pacific Learning
New House for Mole and Mouse, A	G	F	223	Ziefert, Harriet	Penguin Group
New House, The	D	F	112	Bookshop	Mondo
New House, The	I	F	451	Pickles the Dog Series	Pioneer Valley
New House, The	B	F	31	Sails	Rigby
New House, The	LB	F	15	Sunshine	Wright Group/McGraw Hill
New House, The	I	RF	371	Take Two Books	Wright Group/McGraw Hill
New Ice-Cream Machine, A	G	RF	350	Sails	Rigby
New Jersey	T	I	250+	Hello U.S.A.	Lerner Publications
New Jersey	Q	I	250+	One Nation	Red Brick Learning

* Collection of short stories
# Graphic text

TITLE	LEVEL	GENRE	WORD COUNT	AUTHOR / SERIES	PUBLISHER / DISTRIBUTOR
New Jersey	R	I	250+	This Land Is Your Land	Compass Point Books
New Jersey Colony, The	R	I	250+	The American Colonies	Capstone Press
New Kid at School, The	T	I	2615	Reading Street	Pearson
New Kid in Town	N	RF	250+	Kroll, Stephen	Avon Camelot
New Kid on the Court	N	RF	776	Leveled Readers	Houghton Mifflin Harcourt
New Kid on the Court	N	RF	776	Leveled Readers/CA	Houghton Mifflin Harcourt
New Kid on the Court	N	RF	776	Leveled Readers/TX	Houghton Mifflin Harcourt
New Kid, The	J	RF	278	Reading Street	Pearson
New Kid, The	F	RF	124	Real Kids Readers	Millbrook Press
*New Kids In Town	Y	B	250+	Bode, Janet	Scholastic
New Kind of Art, A	T	I	527	Vocabulary Readers	Houghton Mifflin Harcourt
New Kind of Magic, The	P	F	250+	Szymanski, Lois	Avon Camelot
New Kite, The	E	RF	78	Big Cat	Pacific Learning
New Land, The: A First Year on the Prairie	M	I	250+	Reynolds, Marilynn	Orca Book Publishers
New Language, New Friends	Q	I	250+	iOpeners	Pearson Learning Group
New Life in the Big City, A	T	HF	2761	Reading Street	Pearson
New Light for the Lodge, A	L	F	250+	Take Two Books	Wright Group/McGraw Hill
New Mexico	T	I	250+	Hello U.S.A.	Lerner Publications
New Mexico	R	I	250+	This Land Is Your Land	Compass Point Books
New Mexico	S	I	250+	Thompson, Kathleen	Steck-Vaughn
New Moon	Z+	F	250+	Meyer, Stephanie	Little, Brown & Co.
New Name for Lois, A	R	HF	1382	Leveled Readers	Houghton Mifflin Harcourt
New Name for Lois, A	R	HF	1382	Leveled Readers/CA	Houghton Mifflin Harcourt
New Name for Lois, A	R	HF	1382	Leveled Readers/TX	Houghton Mifflin Harcourt
New Nest, A	LB	I	14	Pair-It Books	Steck-Vaughn
New Nest, The	F	RF	207	Foundations	Wright Group/McGraw Hill
New Orleans Saints, The	S	I	250+	Team Spirit	Norwood House Press
New Pants	B	F	20	Story Box	Wright Group/McGraw Hill
New Paper, Everyone!	G	I	53	Pacific Literacy	Pacific Learning
New Park, The	H	RF	256	Reading Street	Pearson
New Pen, The	L	F	250+	On Our Way to English	Rigby
New Pet, The	LB	RF	14	Rigby Star	Rigby
New Place to Live, A	E	F	144	Springboard	Wright Group/McGraw Hill
New Place, The	I	I	280	Sails	Rigby
New Places, New Faces	R	I	250+	WorldScapes	ETA Cuisenaire
New Playground, The	D	RF	80	Gear Up!	Wright Group/McGraw Hill
New Puppy, A	G	I	250+	Momentum Literacy Program	Troll Associates
New Puppy, The	A	I	40	Leveled Literacy Intervention/ Green System	Heinemann
New Red Bed, The	G	F	92	We Both Read	Treasure Bay
New Road, The	D	I	49	Joy Readers	Pearson Learning Group
New Roof, The	G	RF	237	Leveled Literacy Intervention/ Blue System	Heinemann
New School for Megan, A	J	RF	250+	PM Story Books	Rigby
New School, A	B	RF	24	Vocabulary Readers	Houghton Mifflin Harcourt
New School, A	G	RF	137	Windows on Literacy	National Geographic
New School, The	J	RF	210	City Kids	Rigby
New Schoolmates	J	RF	464	Springboard	Wright Group/McGraw Hill
New Scooter, The	G	RF	175	Gear Up!	Wright Group/McGraw Hill
New Shoes	C	RF	29	Wonder World	Wright Group/McGraw Hill
New Skin, A	D	I	71	Sails	Rigby
New Sled, The	E	RF	85	Leveled Readers	Houghton Mifflin Harcourt
New Slippers	E	RF	132	Adams, Lorraine; Bruvold, Lynn	Eagle Crest Books
New Sneakers	F	RF	34	Oxford Reading Tree	Oxford University Press

* Collection of short stories
# Graphic text

TITLE	LEVEL	GENRE	WORD COUNT	AUTHOR / SERIES	PUBLISHER / DISTRIBUTOR
New Soccer Nets	G	RF	123	Early Connections	Benchmark Education
New Tricks	I	RF	250+	Voyages	SRA/McGraw Hill
New Way, A	T	RF	250+	Reading Safari	Mondo
New Wheels, The	I	RF	266	Sails	Rigby
New Year Called Tet, A	K	I	250+	On Our Way to English	Rigby
New Year's Around the World	O	I	250+	Trumbore, Cindy	Pearson Learning Group
New Year's Day	Q	I	250+	Holiday Histories	Heinemann Library
New Year's Day	J	I	109	Holidays and Celebrations	Capstone Press
New York	T	I	250+	Hello U.S.A.	Lerner Publications
New York	S	I	250+	Land of Liberty	Red Brick Learning
New York	Q	I	250+	One Nation	Capstone Press
New York	R	I	250+	This Land Is Your Land	Compass Point Books
New York	S	I	250+	Thompson, Kathleen	Steck-Vaughn
New York City	T	I	250+	Kent, Deborah	Children's Press
New York City Buildings	F	I	59	Books for Young Learners	Richard C. Owen
New York Colony, The	R	I	250+	The American Colonies	Capstone Press
New York Giants, The	S	I	250+	Team Spirit	Norwood House Press
New York Knicks, The	S	I	250+	Team Spirit	Norwood House Press
New York Mets, The	S	I	250+	Team Spirit	Norwood House Press
New York Yankees, The	S	I	250+	Team Spirit	Norwood House Press
New Zealand ABCs: A Book About the People and Places of New Zealand	Q	I	250+	Country ABCs	Picture Window Books
*Newbery Christmas, A: Fourteen Stories of Christmas by Newbery Award-Winning Authors	W	RF	250+	Greenberg, Martin H.; Waugh, Charles G.	Delacorte Press
*Newbery Halloween, A: A Dozen Scary Stories by Newbery Award-Winning Authors	W	F	250+	Greenberg, Martin H.; Waugh, Charles G.	Delacorte Press
Newborn Animals	J	I	250+	Momentum Literacy Program	Troll Associates
Newf	N	TL	250+	Killilea, Marie	Putnam/Penguin
News Flash!	R	I	250+	Hill, Sharon	Pacific Learning
News on Shoes	J	I	153	Storyteller	Wright Group/McGraw Hill
News Rules	W	I	3219	Vocabulary Readers	Houghton Mifflin Harcourt
News Rules	W	I	3219	Vocabulary Readers/CA	Houghton Mifflin Harcourt
Newspaper Carriers	M	I	250+	Community Helpers	Red Brick Learning
Newspaper for Dad, A	G	RF	192	New Way Green	Steck-Vaughn
Newspaper Kids, The	Q	RF	250+	Phillips, Juanita	HarperCollins
Newspaper Scoop	N	RF	250+	Girlz Rock!	Mondo
Newspaper, The	G	RF	132	Twig	Wright Group/McGraw Hill
Newt	J	F	250+	Novak, Matt	HarperTrophy
Newton and Gravity	W	I	2603	Vocabulary Readers	Houghton Mifflin Harcourt
Newton and Gravity	W	I	2603	Vocabulary Readers/CA	Houghton Mifflin Harcourt
Newton and Gravity	W	I	2603	Vocabulary Readers/TX	Houghton Mifflin Harcourt
Newton's Laws	Z	I	2853	Leveled Readers Science	Houghton Mifflin Harcourt
Next Door	A	F	31	Rigby Literacy	Rigby
Next Door Neighbour, The	I	RF	250+	Storyworlds	Heinemann Educational Books
Next Door Pets	B	F	31	Rigby Star	Rigby
Next Spring an Oriole	N	HF	250+	Whelan, Gloria	Random House
Next Stop!	I	RF	250+	Ellis, Sarah	Fitzhenry & Whiteside
Next Stop, New York City!	O	RF	250+	Giff, Patricia Reilly	Bantam
Next Time I Will	K	RF	250+	Bank Street	Bantam
Nez Perce Tribe, The	P	I	250+	Native Peoples	Red Brick Learning
Nez Perce, The	R	I	250+	First Reports	Compass Point Books
Nez Perce, The: People of the Northwest	S	I	250+	Theme Sets	National Geographic
Niagara Falls or Does It?	R	RF	250+	Winkler, Henry and Oliver, Lin	Grosset & Dunlap

TITLE	LEVEL	GENRE	WORD COUNT	AUTHOR / SERIES	PUBLISHER / DISTRIBUTOR
Niagra Falls	L	I	184	Rosen Real Readers	Rosen Publishing Group
Niagra Falls, The Power of Water	T	I	1840	Independent Readers Science	Houghton Mifflin Harcourt
Nibble, Nibble, Jenny Archer	M	RF	250+	Conford, Ellen	Little, Brown & Co.
Nibbles	J	RF	250+	Cambridge Reading	Pearson Learning Group
Nibbly Mouse	E	F	116	Voyages	SRA/McGraw Hill
Nicaragua	O	I	250+	Countries of the World	Red Brick Learning
Nice Hit!: You Can Play Baseball	M	I	250+	Game Day	Picture Window Books
Nice New Neighbors	K	RF	250+	Brandenberg, Franz	Scholastic
Nicest Day, The	L	RF	400	Leveled Readers	Houghton Mifflin Harcourt
Nick Goes Fishing	I	RF	123	Yukish, Joe	Kaeden Books
Nick the Fix-It Man	D	RF	40	Reading Street	Pearson
Nick Wants a Puppy	J	F	250+	Scooters	ETA Cuisenaire
Nickels and Pennies	E	I	53	Williams, Deborah	Kaeden Books
Nicketty-Nacketty Noo-Noo-Noo	K	F	250+	Cowley, Joy	Mondo
Nickey's Meadow	N	RF	1745	Reading Street	Pearson
Nick's Glasses	D	RF	51	Pacific Literacy	Pacific Learning
Nick's Pet	E	F	119	Teacher's Choice Series	Pearson Learning Group
Nicky Upstairs and Downstairs	G	F	179	Ziefert, Harriet	Penguin Group
Nicolaus Copernicus: The Earth Is a Planet	S	B	250+	Bookshop	Mondo
Nicole Digs a Hole	G	RF	138	Start to Read	School Zone
Nicole Helps Grandma	B	I	35	Little Books for Early Readers	University of Maine
Nigeria	O	I	250+	Countries of the World	Red Brick Learning
Night	Z	B	250+	Wiesel, Elie	Bantam Books
Night and Day	E	I	112	Ready Readers	Pearson Learning Group
Night Animals	D	RF	56	Ready Readers	Pearson Learning Group
Night Animals	F	I	168	Rigby Rocket	Rigby
Night at the Beach, A	S	I	250+	Literacy By Design	Rigby
Night at the Beach, A	S	I	250+	Rigby Literacy	Rigby
Night Attack Gunships: The AC-130H Spectres	V	I	250+	War Planes	Capstone Press
Night Bird, The	Q	TL	1172	Leveled Readers/TX	Houghton Mifflin Harcourt
Night Birds on Nantucket	V	HF	250+	Aiken, Joan	Houghton Mifflin Harcourt
Night Cat	L	I	250+	World Quest Adventures	World Quest Learning
Night Crossing, The	O	HF	250+	Ackerman, Karen	Alfred A. Knopf
Night Crossing, The	P	SF	250+	Bookweb	Rigby
Night Diving	H	I	101	Twig	Wright Group/McGraw Hill
Night Dragon, The	J	F	494	Sun Sprouts	ETA Cuisenaire
Night Fishing	S	RF	250+	PM Plus Chapter Books	Rigby
Night Fliers: Moths in Your Backyard	M	I	250+	Backyard Bugs	Picture Window Books
Night Flyers, The	W	RF	250+	Jones, Elizabeth McDavid	Pleasant Company
Night I Disappeared, The	Z+	RF	250+	Deaver, Julie Reece	Simon & Schuster
Night I Flunked My Field Trip, The	R	RF	250+	Winkler, Henry and Oliver, Lin	Grosset & Dunlap
Night in the Desert	D	I	69	Carousel Readers	Pearson Learning Group
Night in the Kingdom, A	X	RF	3375	Leveled Readers	Houghton Mifflin Harcourt
Night in the Kingdom, A	X	RF	3375	Leveled Readers/CA	Houghton Mifflin Harcourt
Night in the Kingdom, A	X	RF	3375	Leveled Readers/TX	Houghton Mifflin Harcourt
Night Journey, The	T	HF	250+	Lasky, Kathryn	Puffin/Penguin
Night Journeys	U	HF	250+	Avi	Avon
Night Light, The	K	RF	554	Leveled Readers	Houghton Mifflin Harcourt
Night Lights	I	I	130	Gear Up!	Wright Group/McGraw Hill
Night Lights	H	I	172	Independent Readers Science	Houghton Mifflin Harcourt
Night Lights, A Cruise Around the Solar System	R	I	250+	Hill, David	Pacific Learning
Night Music	P	HF	250+	Voyages in Time	Wright Group/McGraw Hill
Night Noises	G	RF	97	Storyteller-Moon Rising	Wright Group/McGraw Hill
Night Noises	G	RF	104	Sunshine	Wright Group/McGraw Hill

* Collection of short stories
# Graphic text

TITLE	LEVEL	GENRE	WORD COUNT	AUTHOR / SERIES	PUBLISHER / DISTRIBUTOR
Night of the Blue Heads, The	O	RF	250+	Klooz	Stone Arch Books
Night of the Chupacabras	Y	RF	250+	Lee, Marie G.	Avon Camelot
Night of the Killer Waves	V	HF	3001	Leveled Readers	Houghton Mifflin Harcourt
Night of the Killer Waves	V	HF	3001	Leveled Readers/CA	Houghton Mifflin Harcourt
Night of the Killer Waves	V	HF	3001	Leveled Readers/TX	Houghton Mifflin Harcourt
Night of the Living Eggnog	Q	F	250+	Wiley & Grampa's Creature Features	Little, Brown & Co.
Night of the Ninjas	M	F	250+	Osborne, Mary Pope	Random House
Night of the Pumpkins, The	K	RF	250+	On Our Way to English	Rigby
Night of the Ticklers, The	N	SF	250+	High-Fliers	Pacific Learning
Night of the Twisters	U	RF	250+	Ruckman, Ivy	HarperTrophy
Night Out, The	M	RF	250+	Sails	Rigby
Night Owls, The	M	I	368	Wonder World	Wright Group/McGraw Hill
Night Queen's Blue Velvet Dress, The	Q	F	250+	Pair-It Books	Steck-Vaughn
Night Shift	Q	I	250+	Explorer Books-Pathfinder	National Geographic
Night Shift	P	I	250+	Explorer Books-Pioneer	National Geographic
Night Shift	B	I	47	Ryan, Josh	Scholastic
Night Sky	LB	I	15	Twig	Wright Group/McGraw Hill
Night Sky, The	G	RF	226	Ready Readers	Pearson Learning Group
Night Sky, The	G	I	120	Windows on Literacy	National Geographic
Night Swimmers, The	S	RF	250+	Byars, Betsy	Dell
*Night Terrors, Stories of Shadow and Substance	Z	F	250+	Duncan, Lois	Aladdin
Night the Heads Came, The	Y	SF	250+	Sleator, William	Puffin/Penguin
Night the Lights Went Out, The	H	RF	155	Little Readers	Houghton Mifflin Harcourt
Night the White Deer Died, The	Z	HF	250+	Paulsen, Gary	Dell
Night to Remember, A	U	HF	2377	Leveled Readers	Houghton Mifflin Harcourt
Night to Remember, A	U	HF	2377	Leveled Readers/CA	Houghton Mifflin Harcourt
Night to Remember, A	U	HF	2377	Leveled Readers/TX	Houghton Mifflin Harcourt
Night to Remember, A	Z+	HF	250+	Lord, Walter	Bantam Books
Night Train, The	E	F	65	Story Box	Wright Group/McGraw Hill
Night Walk	F	RF	51	Books for Young Learners	Richard C. Owen
Night Walk	E	RF	47	Prokopchak, Ann	Kaeden Books
Night Walk, The	G	RF	91	Instant Readers	Harcourt School Publishers
Night Walk, The	K	RF	667	PM Story Books-Gold	Rigby
Night Walker, The	P	RF	1189	Thompson, Richard	Fitzhenry & Whiteside
Night Without Stars, A	S	RF	250+	Howe, James	Aladdin
Night Work	I	I	193	Sails	Rigby
Night Workers	D	I	120	Leveled Literacy Intervention/ Blue System	Heinemann
Nightingale, The	J	TL	563	Tales from Hans Andersen	Wright Group/McGraw Hill
Nightjohn	Z	HF	250+	Paulsen, Gary	Bantam
Nightmare	M	RF	250+	Action Packs	Rigby
Nightmare Hill	F	RF	129	Developing Books, Set 1	Pioneer Valley
*Nightmare Hour: Time for Terror	W	F	250+	Stine, R. L.	HarperCollins
Nightmare Mountain	X	RF	250+	Kehret, Peg	Puffin/Penguin
Nighttime	C	RF	25	Science	Outside the Box
Nighttime	C	RF	44	Story Box	Wright Group/McGraw Hill
Nighttime: Too Dark to See	O	F	250+	Strasser, Todd	Scholastic
Nighty-Nightmare	R	F	250+	Howe, James	Avon Camelot
Niki's Walk	WB	RF	N/A	Tanner, Jane	Curriculum Press
Nikki Giovanni	T	B	1729	Leveled Readers	Houghton Mifflin Harcourt
Nikki Giovanni: A Special Poet	O	B	605	Leveled Readers	Houghton Mifflin Harcourt
Niles Likes to Smile	F	RF	80	Little Books	Sadlier-Oxford

* Collection of short stories
# Graphic text

TITLE	LEVEL	GENRE	WORD COUNT	AUTHOR / SERIES	PUBLISHER / DISTRIBUTOR
Nina Wows KWOW	N	RF	1200	Leveled Readers/TX	Houghton Mifflin Harcourt
Nina, the Pinta, and the Vanishing Treasure, The	P	RF	250+	Santopolo, Jill	Orchard Books
Nina's Shells	E	RF	111	Gear Up!	Wright Group/McGraw Hill
Nine Children at the Pool	F	I	157	PM Math Readers	Rigby
Nine Days of Camping, The	E	RF	254	Twig	Wright Group/McGraw Hill
Nine Lives of Adventure Cat, The	L	F	250+	Clymer, Susan	Scholastic
Nine Man Tree	Z	RF	250+	Peck, Robert Newton	Random House
Nine Men Chase a Hen	G	F	74	Start to Read	School Zone
*Nine True Dolphin Stories	M	I	250+	Davidson, Margaret	Scholastic
Ninja	T	I	250+	Warriors of History	Capstone Press
Ninjas Don't Bake Pumpkin Pies	M	RF	250+	Dadey, Debbie; Jones, Marcia Thornton	Scholastic
Ninjas, Piranhas, and Galileo	V	RF	250+	Smith, Greg Leitich	Little, Brown & Co.
Nishal's Box	I	F	250+	Cambridge Reading	Pearson Learning Group
Nissa's Place	Y	RF	250+	LaFaye, A.	Simon & Schuster
No Arm in Left Field	Q	RF	250+	Christopher, Matt	Little, Brown & Co.
No Ball Games	I	F	250+	Rigby Literacy	Rigby
No Ball Games Here	H	RF	128	Ziefert, Harriet	Penguin Group
No Biting Puma!	J	F	401	Be Nice at School	Carolrhoda Books
No Buzz for the Bees	G	F	245	Sails	Rigby
No Cookies Before Dinner	D	RF	138	Developing Books, Set 1	Pioneer Valley
No Copycats Allowed!	L	RF	250+	Graves, Bonnie	Hyperion
No Dinner for Black Cat!	I	F	253	Sails	Rigby
No Dinner for Sally	J	RF	340	Literacy 2000	Rigby
No Dogs Allowed	F	RF	73	Books for Young Learners	Richard C. Owen
*No Dogs Allowed	O	RF	250+	Cutler, Jane	Farrar, Straus and Giroux
No Extras	F	RF	90	Literacy 2000	Rigby
No Fair!	Q	I	250+	Kids Talk	Picture Window Books
No Fair!	P	RF	250+	On Our Way to English	Rigby
No Fighting, No Biting!	K	RF	250+	Minarik, Else Holmelund	HarperTrophy
No Flying in the House	P	F	250+	Brock, Betty	HarperCollins
No Good in Art	I	RF	250+	Cohen, Miriam	Bantam
No Jumping on the Bed!	L	F	250+	Arnold, Tedd	Scholastic
No Jumping!	C	RF	102	Sails	Rigby
No Laughing Matter	R	RF	250+	Power Up!	Steck-Vaughn
No Laughing Matter	Q	RF	250+	Ragged Island Mysteries	Wright Group/McGraw Hill
No Luck	F	RF	120	Stewart, Josie; Salem, Lynn	Continental Press
No Mail for Mitchell	H	F	250+	Siracusa, Catherine	Random House
No Matter How You Play It	J	I	129	Instant Readers	Harcourt School Publishers
No Money? No Problem!	L	RF	250+	Social Studies Connects	The Kane Press
No More Bread!	K	RF	876	Rigby Gigglers	Rigby
No More Cotton Blues	X	HF	3559	Leveled Readers	Houghton Mifflin Harcourt
No More Cotton Blues	X	HF	3559	Leveled Readers/CA	Houghton Mifflin Harcourt
No More Lost and Found	J	I	137	Vocabulary Readers	Houghton Mifflin Harcourt
No More Magic	R	SF	250+	Avi	Alfred A. Knopf
No More Monsters for Me!	J	F	250+	Parish, Peggy	HarperTrophy
No More Pranks	Z+	RF	250+	Orca Soundings	Orca Book Publishers
No Need for Words	S	I	250+	InfoQuest	Rigby
No New Pants!	E	RF	110	Real Kids Readers	Millbrook Press
No One Else Like Me	D	I	129	Early Connections	Benchmark Education
No One Is Going to Nashville	O	RF	250+	Jukes, Mavis	Alfred A. Knopf
No One Likes Me	D	F	71	Sun Sprouts	ETA Cuisenaire

TITLE	LEVEL	GENRE	WORD COUNT	AUTHOR / SERIES	PUBLISHER / DISTRIBUTOR
No One Saw: Ordinary Things Through the Eyes of an Artist	P	I	129	Raczka, Bob	Lerner Publications
No Pay? No Way!	T	RF	250+	Power Up!	Steck-Vaughn
No Peas, Please!	I	RF	247	Athey, Victoria	Kaeden Books
No Place Like Home	N	F	879	Leveled Readers	Houghton Mifflin Harcourt
No Place Like Home	N	F	879	Leveled Readers/CA	Houghton Mifflin Harcourt
No Place Like Home	N	F	879	Leveled Readers/TX	Houghton Mifflin Harcourt
No Place to Turn	Z	I	2820	Vocabulary Readers	Houghton Mifflin Harcourt
No Place to Turn	Z	I	2820	Vocabulary Readers/CA	Houghton Mifflin Harcourt
No Pretty Pictures: A Child of War	Z	B	250+	Lobel, Anita	Greenwillow
No Problem	Z+	RF	250+	Orca Soundings	Orca Book Publishers
No Problem!	M	RF	250+	Rigby Gigglers	Rigby
No Promises in the Wind	Z	HF	250+	Hunt, Irene	Berkley Books
No Room for a Dog	N	RF	250+	Nichols, Joan Kane	Hearst
No Rules for Rex!	L	RF	250+	Social Studies Connects	The Kane Press
No Running!	H	RF	183	Lighthouse	Rigby
No Safe Place	P	SF	250+	Orbit Double Takes	Pacific Learning
No Singing Today	H	RF	250+	Bookshop	Mondo
No Snacks, Jack!	E	RF	248	Reed, Janet	Scholastic
No Snow!	D	F	94	Leveled Readers	Houghton Mifflin Harcourt
No Snow!	D	F	94	Leveled Readers/CA	Houghton Mifflin Harcourt
No Space to Waste	K	RF	250+	Storyteller-Lightning Bolts	Wright Group/McGraw Hill
No Space to Waste	Q	I	250+	WorldScapes	ETA Cuisenaire
No Sword Fighting in the House	K	RF	250+	Hill, Susanna Leonard	Holiday House
No Talking	R	RF	250+	Clements, Andrew	Scholastic
No Time to Lose	S	HF	250+	Power Up!	Steck-Vaughn
No Tooth, No Quarter!	K	F	250+	Buller, Jon	Random House
No Trouble at All	J	RF	559	InfoTrek	ETA Cuisenaire
No Trouble at All!	M	RF	250+	Literacy Tree	Rigby
No TV	I	RF	299	Sails	Rigby
No Way Back	T	F	250+	Story Surfers	ETA Cuisenaire
No Way, Tooth Decay!	T	F	1186	Leveled Readers	Houghton Mifflin Harcourt
No Way, Winky Blue!	N	F	4053	Jane, Pamela	Mondo
No, Bo!	D	RF	109	Handprints C, Set 1	Educators Publishing Service
No, I Won't	E	F	174	Seedlings	Continental Press
No, No	D	F	91	Story Box	Wright Group/McGraw Hill
No, You Can't	D	RF	52	Sunshine	Wright Group/McGraw Hill
Noah's Ark	T	I	250+	Cambridge Reading	Pearson Learning Group
Noah's Ark	WB	F	N/A	Spier, Peter	Doubleday Books
*Nobel Prize Winners	T	B	250+	Hacker, Carlotta	Crabtree
Noble Boy and the Brick Maker, The	U	HF	3380	Reading Street	Pearson
Noble French Patriot, A	X	I	2958	Leveled Readers	Houghton Mifflin Harcourt
Noble French Patriot, A	X	I	2958	Leveled Readers/CA	Houghton Mifflin Harcourt
Noble French Patriot, A	X	I	2958	Leveled Readers/TX	Houghton Mifflin Harcourt
Nobody Gonna Turn Me 'Round: Stories and Songs of the Civil Rights Movement	V	I	250+	Rappaport, Doreen	Candlewick Press
Nobody Knew My Name	I	RF	276	Foundations	Wright Group/McGraw Hill
Nobody Listens to Andrew	I	F	250+	Little Readers	Houghton Mifflin Harcourt
Nobody Owns the Sky: The Story of "Brave Bessie" Coleman	M	B	250+	Lindbergh, Reeve	Candlewick Press
Nobody's Family Is Going to Change	U	RF	250+	Fitzhugh, Louise	Farrar, Straus and Giroux
Nocturnal Animals	N	I	725	Springboard	Wright Group/McGraw Hill
Noggin and Bobbin by the Sea	I	F	204	Little Celebrations	Pearson Learning Group

* Collection of short stories
# Graphic text

TITLE	LEVEL	GENRE	WORD COUNT	AUTHOR / SERIES	PUBLISHER / DISTRIBUTOR
Noggin and Bobbin in the Garden	E	F	57	Little Celebrations	Pearson Learning Group
Noise	G	RF	138	Sunshine	Wright Group/McGraw Hill
Noise Festival, The	J	RF	250+	Sunshine	Wright Group/McGraw Hill
Noise in the Night	I	F	250+	Start to Read	School Zone
Noises	E	I	49	Literacy 2000	Rigby
Noises in the Night	K	RF	250+	Literacy by Design	Rigby
Noises in the Night	K	RF	250+	On Our Way to English	Rigby
Noises!!!	C	RF	98	Teacher's Choice Series	Pearson Learning Group
Noisy and Quiet	A	I	26	Vocabulary Readers	Houghton Mifflin Harcourt
Noisy Breakfast	D	F	32	Blonder, Ellen	Scholastic
Noisy Neighbors	M	F	250+	I Am Reading	Kingfisher
Noisy Nora	I	F	204	Wells, Rosemary	Scholastic
Noisy Toys	E	RF	77	Home Connection Collection	Rigby
Nomads - A Wandering People	S	I	250+	Connectors	Pacific Learning
Noodle Race, The	G	RF	199	PM Photo Stories	Rigby
Noodle Up Your Nose, A	L	RF	250+	Orca Echoes	Orca Book Publishers
Nooks, Crannies, and Hiding Places	Q	RF	5282	Take Two Books	Wright Group/ McGraw Hill
Noonday Friends, The	R	RF	250+	Stolz, Mary	Scholastic
Nora Plays All Day	B	RF	42	Little Books	Sadlier-Oxford
Nora's Money	H	RF	254	On Our Way to English	Rigby
Norma Jean, Jumping Bean	J	F	250+	Cole, Joanna	Random House
Norman Newman and the Werewolf of Walnut Street	Q	F	250+	Conford, Ellen	Troll Associates
Norman Rockwell	T	B	250+	Cohen, Joel H.	Grolier Publishing
North America	N	I	250+	Continents	Capstone Press
North America	Q	I	250+	Petersen, David	Grolier Publishing
North America	L	I	494	Pull Ahead Books	Lerner Publications
North American Indian	V	I	250+	Eyewitness Books	DK Publishing
North Carolina	T	I	250+	Fradin, Dennis Brindell	Children's Press
North Carolina	T	I	250+	Hello U.S.A.	Lerner Publications
North Carolina	S	I	250+	Portrait of America	Steck-Vaughn
North Carolina	R	I	250+	This Land Is Your Land	Compass Point Books
North Carolina Colony, The	R	I	250+	The American Colonies	Capstone Press
North Dakota	T	I	250+	Hello U.S.A.	Lerner Publications
North Dakota	R	I	250+	This Land Is Your Land	Compass Point Books
North Pole Walk	R	I	250+	Orbit Double Takes	Pacific Learning
North Star to Freedom	U	I	250+	Gorrell, Gena K.	Random House
Northeast Indians, The: Daily Life in the 1500s	O	I	250+	Native American Life	Capstone Press
Northern Lights	M	I	578	Pull Ahead Books	Lerner Publications
Northwest Indians, The: Daily Life in the 1700s	O	I	250+	Native American Life	Capstone Press
Norway	O	I	1459	A Ticket to ...	Carolrhoda Books
Nory Ryan's Song	T	HF	250+	Giff, Patricia Reilly	Delacorte Press
Nose Book	E	I	111	Perkins, Al	Random House
Nose for Trouble, A	P	RF	250+	Wilson, Nancy Hope	Avon
Nose Horns, The	M	I	371	Sails	Rigby
Noses	B	I	33	Animal Traits	Lerner Publications
Noses	E	I	56	Literacy 2000	Rigby
Noses	C	RF	46	Science	Outside the Box
Nostradamus	X	B	250+	The Unexplained	Capstone Press
Nosy Spider, The	G	F	199	Springboard	Wright Group/McGraw Hill
Not Enough Cupcakes	I	F	292	Talking Point Series	Pearson Learning Group
Not Enough Water	D	RF	84	Armstrong, Shane; Hartley, Susan	Scholastic
*Not Guilty	X	B	250+	Sullivan, George	Scholastic

Organized Alphabetically by Title
Storable Database at www.fountasandpinnellleveledbooks.com

* Collection of short stories
# Graphic text

TITLE	LEVEL	GENRE	WORD COUNT	AUTHOR / SERIES	PUBLISHER / DISTRIBUTOR
Not I, Not I	E	TL	254	Fairy Tales and Folklore	Norwood House Press
Not in a Thousand Years	R	RF	250+	PM Chapter Books	Rigby
Not It!	E	RF	177	Handprints C	Educators Publishing Service
Not Just Any Boy	H	F	221	Reading Street	Pearson
Not Just Second Place	Q	RF	1200	Leveled Readers/TX	Houghton Mifflin Harcourt
Not Me, Said the Monkey	G	F	118	West, Colin	Harper & Row
Not Much Room on the Mushroom	J	F	310	Take Two Books	Wright Group/McGraw Hill
Not Now! Said the Cow	J	F	250+	Bank Street	Bantam
Not Now, Sam	F	RF	159	Early Connections	Benchmark Education
Not That I Care	V	RF	250+	Vail, Rachel	Scholastic
Not Too Many	G	RF	193	Sun Sprouts	ETA Cuisenaire
Not Too Small at All	I	F	251	Seedlings	Continental Press
*Not Too Young and Other Stories	L	RF	250+	New Way Literature	Steck-Vaughn
Not Very Messy, Unless . . .	F	F	94	Seedlings	Continental Press
Not What It Seems	P	RF	250+	Wildcats	Wright Group/McGraw Hill
Not With Our Blood	Y	HF	250+	Massie, Elizabeth	Tom Doherty
Not Worms!	K	RF	888	Rigby Gigglers	Rigby
Not Yet!	D	RF	64	Reading Links	Steck-Vaughn
Not Yet, Nathan	G	RF	127	Cambridge Reading	Pearson Learning Group
Not Your Usual Goat	K	F	656	Leveled Readers	Houghton Mifflin Harcourt
Notes From a Liar and Her Dog	T	RF	250+	Choldenko, Gennifer	Puffin Books
Notes from Mom	F	RF	99	Salem, Lynn; Stewart, Josie	Continental Press
Notes to Dad	F	RF	114	Stewart, Josie; Salem, Lynn	Continental Press
Nothing but Air	Q	RF	250+	Story Surfers	ETA Cuisenaire
Nothing But The Truth	U	RF	250+	Avi	Hearst
Nothing But Trouble, Trouble, Trouble	Q	RF	250+	Hermes, Patricia	Scholastic
Nothing Ever Happens	F	F	49	City Stories	Rigby
Nothing Ever Happens on 90th Street	Q	RF	250+	Schotter, Roni	Scholastic
Nothing in the Mailbox	F	RF	73	Books for Young Learners	Richard C. Owen
Nothing Stays the Same	E	RF	86	Reading Street	Pearson
Nothing to Be Scared About	K	RF	343	Sunshine	Wright Group/McGraw Hill
Nothing's Fair in Fifth Grade	R	RF	250+	DeClements, Barthe	Scholastic
Not-Just-Anybody Family, The	P	RF	250+	Byars, Betsy	Dell
Not-Quite-So-Easy Origami	R	I	250+	Origami	Capstone Press
*Not-So-Dead Fish and Other Cases, The	O	RF	250+	Simon, Seymour	Avon
Not-So-Jolly Roger, The	P	F	250+	Scieszka, Jon	Penguin Group
Not-So-Perfect Rosie	N	RF	250+	Giff, Patricia Reilly	Penguin Group
Not-So-Scary-Scarecrow, The	I	RF	166	Ready Readers	Pearson Learning Group
Not-So-Weird Emma	O	RF	250+	Warner, Sally	Puffin Books
Nouns and Verbs Have a Field Day	O	F	250+	Pulver, Robin	Holiday House
Noura Comes to Cleveland	L	RF	717	Leveled Readers Social Studies	Houghton Mifflin Harcourt
Novio Boy	X	TL	250+	Soto, Gary	Harcourt Trade
Now and Long Ago	L	I	189	Phonics Readers	Compass Point Books
Now and Then	Q	I	250+	Literacy by Design	Rigby
Now and Then	D	I	78	Windows on Literacy	National Geographic
Now I Am Eight	K	I	250+	Explorations	Eleanor Curtain Publishing
Now I Am Eight	K	I	250+	Explorations	Okapi Eductional Materials
Now I Am Five	I	RF	582	Sunshine	Wright Group/McGraw Hill
Now I Know: Animals at Night	I	I	207	Berger, Melvin & Gilda	Scholastic
Now I Know: Bears	I	I	218	Berger, Melvin & Gilda	Scholastic
Now I Know: Butterflies	I	I	159	Berger, Melvin & Gilda	Scholastic
Now I Know: Dolphins and Porpoises	I	I	201	Berger, Melvin & Gilda	Scholastic
Now I Ride	D	I	63	Carousel Readers	Pearson Learning Group

* Collection of short stories
# Graphic text

TITLE	LEVEL	GENRE	WORD COUNT	AUTHOR / SERIES	PUBLISHER / DISTRIBUTOR
Now Is Your Time! The African-American Struggle	Y	I	250+	Myers, Walter Dean	HarperCollins
Now It's Hot	C	I	49	Rigby Focus	Rigby
Now Listen, Stanley	K	F	250+	Literacy 2000	Rigby
Now Showing in Your Living Room	P	I	885	Leveled Readers	Houghton Mifflin Harcourt
Now Showing in Your Living Room	P	I	885	Leveled Readers/CA	Houghton Mifflin Harcourt
Now Showing in Your Living Room	P	I	885	Leveled Readers/TX	Houghton Mifflin Harcourt
Now We Can Go	C	RF	25	Jonas, Ann	Greenwillow
Now You See It, Now You Don't	M	I	204	Independent Readers Science	Houghton Mifflin Harcourt
Now You See Me . . . Now You Don't	N	F	250+	The Zack Files	Grossett & Dunlap
Nowhere and Nothing	I	RF	143	Sunshine	Wright Group/McGraw Hill
Nuclear Power	X	I	250+	Energy at Work	Capstone Press
Number Cruncher, The	L	F	250+	Sunshine	Wright Group/McGraw Hill
Number Games Around the World	S	I	250+	Navigators Math Series	Benchmark Education Company
Number One	J	F	170	Pacific Literacy	Pacific Learning
Number the Stars	U	HF	250+	Lowry, Lois	Bantam
Numbering All the Bones	Y	HF	250+	Rinaldi, Ann	Hyperion
Numbers	B	I	86	Canizares, Susan; Moreton, Daniel	Scholastic
Numbers All Around	LB	I	12	Canizares, Susan; Chessen, Betsey	Scholastic
Numbers All Around	B	I	40	Yellow Umbrella Books	Red Brick Learning
Numbers All around Me	G	F	140	Learn to Read	Creative Teaching Press
Numbers and You	O	I	250+	Windows on Literacy	National Geographic
Numbers Are Everywhere	E	I	125	Early Connections	Benchmark Education
Numbers Are Everywhere	E	I	131	Twig	Wright Group/McGraw Hill
Numbers We Know	J	I	139	Spyglass Books	Compass Point Books
Numbers: Counting It Up	L	I	250+	Exploring Math	Capstone Press
Nurses	M	I	250+	Community Helpers	Red Brick Learning
Nurses	M	I	250+	Community Workers	Compass Point Books
Nurses	M	I	509	Pull Ahead Books	Lerner Publications
Nurses: Then and Now	O	I	250+	Primary Source Readers	Teacher Created Materials
Nut Pie for Jud, A	D	I	46	Ready Readers	Pearson Learning Group
Nutcracker, The	J	F	250+	Rigby Rocket	Rigby

* Collection of short stories
# Graphic text

TITLE	LEVEL	GENRE	WORD COUNT	AUTHOR / SERIES	PUBLISHER / DISTRIBUTOR
Oak Tree, An	I	I	141	Book Bus	Creative Edge
Oak Street Party, The	C	RF	57	Peters, Catherine	Scholastic
Oak Tree and Fir Tree	G	F	102	New Way Red	Steck-Vaughn
Oak Tree Controversy	N	RF	250+	Bookweb	Rigby
Oak Tree, The	C	I	34	Big Cat	Pacific Learning
Oak Trees	F	I	91	Life Cycles	Lerner Publications
Oak Trees	F	I	132	Pebble Books	Capstone Press
Oak Trees	J	I	375	Reading Street	Pearson
Oakland A's, The	S	I	250+	Team Spirit	Norwood House Press
Oakland Fire, The	V	HF	250+	Reading Expeditions	National Geographic
Oatmeal	F	I	96	Wonder World	Wright Group/McGraw Hill
Obadiah	G	TL	105	Story Box	Wright Group/McGraw Hill
Obadiah the Bold	N	RF	250+	Turkle, Brinton	Penguin Group
Obee & Mungedeech	T	RF	250+	Martin, Trude	Aladdin
Objects in Motion	N	I	450	Science Support Readers	Houghton Mifflin Harcourt
Observations of Emma Boyle, The	U	RF	2623	Leveled Readers	Houghton Mifflin Harcourt
Obstacle Course, The	H	RF	211	Foundations	Wright Group/McGraw Hill
Obstacle Course, The	K	RF	531	Springboard	Wright Group/McGraw Hill
Obstacles in Our Way	L	RF	250+	Home Connection Collection	Rigby
Ocean	F	I	119	Habitats	Lerner Publications
Ocean Alphabet Book, The	M	I	250+	Pallotta, Jerry	Charlesbridge
Ocean Animals	J	I	204	Early Connections	Benchmark Education
Ocean Animals	P	I	250+	Theme Sets	National Geographic
Ocean by the Lake, The	N	I	250+	Little Celebrations	Pearson Learning Group
Ocean Detectives: Solving Mysteries of the Sea	W	I	250+	Cerullo, Mary	Steck-Vaughn
Ocean Exploration	P	I	250+	Reading Expeditions	National Geographic
Ocean Explorers	Q	I	250+	InfoQuest	Rigby
Ocean Facts	D	I	40	Rosen Real Readers	Rosen Publishing Group
Ocean Flight Adventure	O	RF	250+	Tristars	Richard C. Owen
Ocean Life	Q	I	250+	Explorers	Wright Group/McGraw Hill
Ocean Life Encyclopedia	V	I	250+	Bookshop	Mondo
Ocean Life: Tide Pool Creatures	Q	I	250+	Leonhardt, Alice	Steck-Vaughn
*Ocean of Story, The: Fairy Tales From India	U	TL	250+	Ness, Caroline	Lothrop, Lee & Shepard
Ocean Plants	N	I	250+	Life in the World's Biomes	Capstone Press
Ocean Tide Pool	N	I	250+	Habitats	Children's Press
Ocean Tides	M	I	250+	Rosen Real Readers	Rosen Publishing Group
Ocean Waves	B	I	21	Twig	Wright Group/McGraw Hill
Ocean, The	H	F	362	Bella and Rosie Series	Literacy Footprints
Ocean, The	H	I	139	Yellow Umbrella Books	Red Brick Learning
Oceanography	Q	I	2127	Independent Readers Social Studies	Houghton Mifflin Harcourt
Oceans	Q	I	250+	Ecosystems	Red Brick Learning
Oceans	Q	I	250+	First Reports	Compass Point Books
Oceans	R	I	250+	The Wonders of Our World	Crabtree
Oceans of Grass: The Prairie	O	I	707	Leveled Readers Social Studies	Houghton Mifflin Harcourt
Oceans of Resources	U	I	1962	Reading Street	Pearson
Oceans of the World	R	I	250+	InfoQuest	Rigby
Oceans, Seas, and Coasts	M	I	250+	PM Plus Nonfiction	Rigby
October Days	A	I	24	Leveled Readers	Houghton Mifflin Harcourt
October Days	A	I	24	Leveled Readers/CA	Houghton Mifflin Harcourt
Octopus for Dinner!	F	F	147	Sails	Rigby
Octopus Goes to School	C	F	42	Bordelon, Carolyn	Continental Press
Octopus, The	E	I	119	Sails	Rigby
Octopuses	O	I	1350	Early Bird Nature Books	Lerner Publications

TITLE	LEVEL	GENRE	WORD COUNT	AUTHOR / SERIES	PUBLISHER / DISTRIBUTOR
Octopuses	G	I	47	Ocean Life	Capstone Press
Octopuses	J	I	94	Under the Sea	Capstone Press
Octopuses and Squids	O	I	328	Wonder World	Wright Group/McGraw Hill
Octopuses, Squid & Cuttlefish	L	I	231	Marine Life For Young Readers	Pearson Learning Group
Odd and Even Numbers	I	I	250+	Yellow Umbrella Books	Red Brick Learning
Odd Jobs	U	I	250+	Boldprint	Steck-Vaughn
Odd or Not? - Transportation with a Difference	U	I	250+	Connectors	Pacific Learning
Odd Socks	G	RF	83	Literacy 2000	Rigby
*Oddballs	X	B	250+	Sleator, William	Puffin/Penguin
*Odder Than Ever	Z	F	250+	Coville, Bruce	Harcourt Trade
*Oddly Enough	Z	F	250+	Coville, Bruce	Pocket Books
Odds on Oliver	P	RF	250+	Greene, Carol	Puffin/Penguin
Odin's Wisdom	Z	TL	2644	Leveled Readers	Houghton Mifflin Harcourt
Odyssey, The: A Greek Play for Students	W	TL	250+	Bookshop	Mondo
Of Colors and Things	WB	I	N/A	Hoban, Tana	Scholastic
Of Heroes and Villians	Z	RF	250+	Misfits Inc.	Peachtree
Of Mice and Men	Z	RF	250+	Steinbeck, John	Penguin Group
Of Nightingales That Weep	U	HF	250+	Paterson, Katherine	HarperCollins
Off and Running	S	RF	250+	Soto, Gary	Dell
Off the Map: The Journals of Lewis and Clark	U	I	250+	Roop, Peter & Connie	Walker & Company
Off the Rim	Q	RF	250+	Bowen, Fred	Peachtree
Off to Africa	S	B	250+	WorldScapes	ETA Cuisenaire
Off to Grandma's House	D	RF	80	Little Celebrations	Pearson Learning Group
Off to School	C	RF	45	Story Steps	Rigby
Off to Sea: An Inside Look at a Research Cruise	T	I	250+	Kovacs, Deborah	Steck-Vaughn
Off to Squintum's/The Four Musicians	N	TL	1268	Bookshop	Mondo
Off to the City	B	F	43	Davidson, Avelyn	Scholastic
Off to the Library	C	RF	46	Seedlings	Continental Press
Off to the Shop	H	F	323	Storyteller-Night Crickets	Wright Group/McGraw Hill
Off to Work	B	RF	41	Literacy 2000	Rigby
Off We Go!	LB	RF	16	Pacific Literacy	Pacific Learning
Officer Buckle and Gloria	L	F	250+	Rathman, Peggy	Scholastic
Officer Gonzalez and Cindy	G	I	128	Dominie Factivity Series	Pearson Learning Group
Officially Interesting	Q	RF	1460	Leveled Readers	Houghton Mifflin Harcourt
Off-Road Truck Racing	S	I	250+	Motor Sports	Red Brick Learning
Ogden Nash: Playing with Words	U	B	1770	Leveled Readers	Houghton Mifflin Harcourt
Oggie Cooder	Q	RF	250+	Weeks, Sarah	Scholastic
Ogs Discover Fire and Other Stuff, The	N	F	250+	Navigators Drama Series	Benchmark Education
Oh a Hunting We Will Go	E	TL	346	Langstaff, John	Macmillan
Oh Boy, Boston!	O	RF	250+	Giff, Patricia Reilly	Bantam
Oh Dear	F	F	109	Campbell, Rod	Macmillan
Oh My! It Must Be the Sky!	K	F	1097	Appleton-Smith, Laura	Flyleaf Publishing
Oh No Otis!	E	F	45	Rookie Readers	Children's Press
Oh No!	E	RF	118	Bookshop	Mondo
Oh No!	E	F	118	Sun Sprouts	ETA Cuisenaire
Oh No!	F	RF	122	Traditional Tales & More	Rigby
Oh Say, I Can't See	P	F	250+	Scieszka, Jon	Penguin Group
Oh, Baby!	G	I	121	Literacy by Design	Rigby
Oh, Brother	P	RF	250+	Wilson, Johnniece M.	Scholastic
Oh, Cats!	E	RF	93	Buck, Nola	HarperTrophy
Oh, Columbus!	K	F	250+	Literacy 2000	Rigby
Oh, Jump in a Sack	E	F	130	Story Box	Wright Group/McGraw Hill
Oh, No!	C	F	53	Joy Readers	Pearson Learning Group

* Collection of short stories
# Graphic text

TITLE	LEVEL	GENRE	WORD COUNT	AUTHOR / SERIES	PUBLISHER / DISTRIBUTOR
Oh, No!	A	F	46	Leveled Literacy Intervention/ Green System	Heinemann
Oh, No!	G	RF	128	Little Celebrations	Pearson Learning Group
Oh, No, Sherman	E	RF	66	Erickson, Betty	Continental Press
Oh, the Places He Went: A Story About Dr. Seuss	R	B	8621	Creative Minds Biographies	Carolrhoda Books
Oh, What a Daughter!	L	F	250+	Literacy 2000	Rigby
Ohio	T	I	250+	Hello U.S.A.	Lerner Publications
Ohio	S	I	250+	Land of Liberty	Red Brick Learning
Ohio	Q	I	250+	One Nation	Capstone Press
Ohio	T	I	250+	Theme Sets	National Geographic
Ohio	R	I	250+	This Land Is Your Land	Compass Point Books
Ohio	S	I	250+	Thompson, Kathleen	Steck-Vaughn
Oil on Water	P	I	250+	Sails	Rigby
Oil Spill!	L	I	250+	Soar To Success	Houghton Mifflin Harcourt
Oil Spills	P	I	250+	Rigby Focus	Rigby
Oil!	P	I	450	Independent Readers Social Studies	Houghton Mifflin Harcourt
Oink Oink	LB	F	15	Geisert, Arthur	Houghton Mifflin Harcourt
Ojibwa Animal Stories	U	I	3204	Vocabulary Readers	Houghton Mifflin Harcourt
Ojibwa Animal Stories	U	I	3204	Vocabulary Readers/CA	Houghton Mifflin Harcourt
Ojibwa Animal Stories	U	I	3204	Vocabulary Readers/TX	Houghton Mifflin Harcourt
Ojibwa Indians, The	P	I	250+	Native Peoples	Red Brick Learning
Ojibwa, The: Wild Rice Gatherers	R	I	250+	America's First Peoples	Capstone Press
Ojibwe, The	T	I	4405	Native American Stories	Lerner Publications
Oklahoma	T	I	250+	Hello U.S.A.	Lerner Publications
Oklahoma	R	I	250+	This Land Is Your Land	Compass Point Books
Ola Shakes It Up	T	RF	250+	Hyppolite, Joanne	Random House
Ola's Wake	R	RF	250+	Stone, B. J.	Henry Holt & Co.
Old and New	B	I	54	Early Connections	Benchmark Education
Old and New	C	I	50	Interaction	Rigby
Old and New	G	I	54	Sun Sprouts	ETA Cuisenaire
Old Bark's Cure	X	HF	3382	Leveled Readers	Houghton Mifflin Harcourt
Old Bark's Cure	X	HF	3382	Leveled Readers/CA	Houghton Mifflin Harcourt
Old Bark's Cure	X	HF	3382	Leveled Readers/TX	Houghton Mifflin Harcourt
Old Bones	M	RF	848	Sunshine	Wright Group/McGraw Hill
Old Bumpy Alligator	E	F	69	Books for Young Learners	Richard C. Owen
Old Cans and Cars	I	I	224	Explorations	Okapi Eductional Materials
Old Cans and Cars	I	I	224	Explorations	Eleanor Curtain Publishing
Old Car, The	F	RF	135	Voyages	SRA/McGraw Hill
Old Cat, New Cat	G	RF	169	Wonder World	Wright Group/McGraw Hill
Old Cat, The	I	RF	302	Sails	Rigby
Old Devil Wind	J	F	250+	Martin, Jr., Bill	Harcourt Trade
Old Enough for Magic	L	F	250+	Pickett, A.	HarperTrophy
Old Friend, An	J	RF	250+	Sunshine	Wright Group/McGraw Hill
Old Friends	M	RF	345	Literacy 2000	Rigby
Old Friends, Near Friends	J	I	250+	Rigby Literacy	Rigby
Old Gold: Gold in the Ancient World	X	I	1197	Reading Street	Pearson
Old Grizzly	H	F	185	Sunshine	Wright Group/McGraw Hill
Old Hat, New Hat	H	F	115	Berenstain, Stan & Jan	Random House
Old House, The	J	RF	375	Story Box	Wright Group/McGraw Hill
Old Jacket, New Jacket	I	RF	375	Leveled Literacy Intervention/ Blue System	Heinemann
*Old Key, The	T	TL	250+	Literacy 2000	Rigby

* Collection of short stories
# Graphic text

TITLE	LEVEL	GENRE	WORD COUNT	AUTHOR / SERIES	PUBLISHER / DISTRIBUTOR
Old King Cole	E	TL	33	Jumbled Tumbled Tales & Rhymes	Rigby
Old King Cole	C	F	29	Seedlings	Continental Press
Old MacDonald Had a Farm	D	TL	103	Jones, Carol	Houghton Mifflin Harcourt
Old MacDonald Had a Farm	F	TL	250+	PM Readalongs	Rigby
Old MacDonald Had a Farm	D	TL	118	Rounds, Glen	Holiday House
Old MacDonald Had a Farm	J	TL	250+	Traditional Songs	Picture Window Books
Old MacDonald's Fun Time Farm	B	F	34	Instant Readers	Harcourt School Publishers
Old Magic	Z+	SF	250+	Curley, Marianne	Simon & Schuster
Old Malolo Had a Farm	H	F	250+	Sunshine	Wright Group/McGraw Hill
Old Man and the Bear, The	M	RF	250+	Hanel, Wolfram	North-South Books
Old Man and the Sea, The	Z+	RF	250+	Hemingway, Ernest	Scribner
Old Man's Mitten, The	I	TL	378	Bookshop	Mondo
Old Meadow, The	S	F	250+	Selden, George	Farrar, Straus and Giroux
Old Mother Hubbard	H	F	117	Literacy 2000	Rigby
Old New York City	S	I	250+	Leveled Readers	Houghton Mifflin Harcourt
Old Oak Tree, The	F	F	108	Little Celebrations	Pearson Learning Group
Old Recipe Book, The	L	F	250+	Take Two Books	Wright Group/McGraw Hill
Old Red Rocking Chair, The	M	RF	250+	Root, Phyllis	Scholastic
Old Spanish Trail, The	Q	I	250+	On Deck	Rigby
Old Steam Train, The	F	RF	43	Literacy 2000	Rigby
Old Store, New Store	C	I	56	Leveled Readers Social Studies	Houghton Mifflin Harcourt
Old Teddy	I	F	302	Sun Sprouts	ETA Cuisenaire
Old Teeth, New Teeth	F	I	53	Wonder World	Wright Group/McGraw Hill
Old Toad, The	E	F	189	Phonics and Friends	Hampton-Brown
Old Tom and the Rogue	M	HF	250+	Wilson, Trevor	Pearson Learning Group
Old Train, The	F	RF	68	Books for Young Learners	Richard C. Owen
Old Tree, The	T	RF	2667	Leveled Readers	Houghton Mifflin Harcourt
Old Tree, The	T	RF	2667	Leveled Readers/CA	Houghton Mifflin Harcourt
Old Tree, The	T	RF	2667	Leveled Readers/TX	Houghton Mifflin Harcourt
Old Tuatara	C	F	33	Pacific Literacy	Pacific Learning
Old Woman and Her Pig, The: An Old English Tale	K	TL	250+	Litzinger, Rosanne	Harcourt Brace
Old Woman and the Hen, The	C	TL	48	Storyworlds	Heinemann Educational Publishers
Old Woman and the Pig, The	D	RF	68	Tiger Cub	Peguis
Old Woman in a Shoe, The	E	TL	38	Jumbled Tumbled Tales & Rhymes	Rigby
Old Woman Who Lived in a Shoe, The	D	F	56	Seedlings	Continental Press
Old Woman Who Lived in a Vinegar Bottle	M	TL	1161	Douglas, Ann	Mondo
Old Woman Who Lived in a Vinegar Bottle	I	TL	250+	Storyworlds	Heinemann Educational Books
Old Woman, The	H	F	69	Sunshine	Wright Group/McGraw Hill
Old Woman's Nose, The	K	F	250+	Sunshine	Wright Group/McGraw Hill
Old Yeller	V	RF	250+	Gipson, Fred	Scholastic
Old-Timers	T	RF	2884	Reading Street	Pearson
Olga's New Mobile	D	RF	100	In Step Readers	Rigby
Olga's New Mobile	D	RF	100	Literacy by Design	Rigby
*Oliver and Amanda's Halloween	L	F	250+	Van Leeuwen, Jean	Puffin/Penguin
*Oliver Pig at School	L	F	250+	Van Leeuwen, Jean	Puffin/Penguin
Oliver Trades Places	L	F	250+	Scooters	ETA Cuisenaire
*Oliver, Amanda, and Grandmother Pig	L	F	250+	Van Leeuwen, Jean	Puffin/Penguin
Olive's Ocean	V	RF	250+	Henkes, Kevin	HarperCollins
Olivia Agnew's Wild Imagination	M	F	250+	Wonder World	Wright Group/McGraw Hill

* Collection of short stories
\# Graphic text

TITLE	LEVEL	GENRE	WORD COUNT	AUTHOR / SERIES	PUBLISHER / DISTRIBUTOR
Olivia Kidney Stops for No One	T	F	250+	Potter, Ellen	Puffin Books
Olly the Octopus	H	F	250+	Storyworlds	Heinemann Educational Books
Olympic Champions	N	RF	250+	Boyz Rule!	Mondo
Olympic Champions	S	I	250+	iOpeners	Pearson Learning Group
Olympic Dreams	O	RF	250+	Navigators Fiction Series	Benchmark Education
Olympic Softball Stars	R	I	577	Vocabulary Readers	Houghton Mifflin Harcourt
Olympics and the Mini Olympics, The	N	I	250+	Take Two Books	Wright Group/McGraw Hill
Olympics, The	R	I	250+	Christopher, Matt	Little, Brown & Co.
Olympics, The	Q	I	250+	Gear Up!	Wright Group/ McGraw Hill
Olympics, The	O	I	250+	Windows on Literacy	National Geographic
Omar's Surprise	E	RF	144	On Our Way to English	Rigby
Omen and the Ghost, The	T	F	250+	Townsend, John	Stone Arch Books
On a Boat	B	RF	20	Novek, Minda	Scholastic
On a Chair	C	F	30	Story Box	Wright Group/McGraw Hill
On a Cold, Cold Day	C	F	33	Tadpoles	Rigby
On a Dark and Scary Night	F	F	50	Shared Reading	Rigby
On a Hill	D	RF	53	Start to Read	School Zone
On a Log	A	I	42	On Our Way to English	Rigby
On a Map	D	I	60	Windows on Literacy	National Geographic
On a Ranch	Q	I	1676	Reading Street	Pearson
On a Reef	B	I	75	In Step Readers	Rigby
On a Tropical Island	T	I	250+	WorldScapes	ETA Cuisenaire
On a Walk	A	RF	5	Ready Readers	Pearson Learning Group
On All Kinds of Days	C	I	50	Yellow Umbrella Books	Red Brick Learning
On and Off	B	I	60	PM Plus Nonfiction	Rigby
On and Off the Road	M	I	250+	Wildcats	Wright Group/McGraw Hill
On Board the Santa Maria	T	I	2391	Independent Readers Social Studies	Houghton Mifflin Harcourt
On Board The Titanic	T	I	250+	Tanaka, Shelley	Hyperion/Madison Press
On Board with Captain Cook	Q	B	250+	WorldScapes	ETA Cuisenaire
On Christmas Eve	WB	RF	N/A	Collington, Peter	Alfred A. Knopf
On Course	S	RF	2360	Leveled Readers	Houghton Mifflin Harcourt
On Course	S	RF	2360	Leveled Readers/CA	Houghton Mifflin Harcourt
On Earth	B	I	35	Leveled Readers Social Studies	Houghton Mifflin Harcourt
On Fortune's Wheel	Z	F	250+	Voigt, Cynthia	Aladdin
On Friday the Giant	K	F	240	The Giant	Wright Group/McGraw Hill
On Guard	R	RF	250+	Napoli, Donna Jo	Puffin/Penguin
On Monday the Giant	K	F	250+	The Giant	Wright Group/McGraw Hill
On My Honor	S	RF	250+	Bauer, Marion Dane	Bantam
On My Street	H	I	292	Visions	Wright Group/McGraw Hill
On My Way	N	B	250+	DePaola, Tomie	Penguin Group
On My Way to Buy Eggs	K	RF	250+	Chen, Chih-Yuan	Scholastic
On One Flower Butterflies, Ticks and a Few More Icks	O	RF	990	Sharing Nature with Children	Dawn Publications
On Our Farm	A	I	14	Bebop Books	Lee & Low Books Inc.
On Our Street	C	RF	52	Little Red Readers	Sundance
On Safari	J	I	250+	Rigby Rocket	Rigby
On Safari	A	I	28	Smart Starts	Rigby
On Safari	N	I	250+	Windows on Literacy	National Geographic
On Saturday	C	RF	44	Handprints B	Educators Publishing Service
On Saturday	C	I	28	Little Red Readers	Sundance
On Site	S	I	250+	Pollock, John	Mondo

TITLE	LEVEL	GENRE	WORD COUNT	AUTHOR / SERIES	PUBLISHER / DISTRIBUTOR
On Stage	E	I	94	Early Connections	Benchmark Education
On Sunday the Giant	K	F	250+	The Giant	Wright Group/McGraw Hill
On the Air	L	I	250+	Rigby Literacy	Rigby
On the Air	S	I	250+	Wonder World	Wright Group/McGraw Hill
On the Ball	N	I	250+	Pacific Literacy	Pacific Learning
On the Banks of Plum Creek	Q	HF	250+	Wilder, Laura Ingalls	HarperCollins
On the Banks of the Bayou	Q	HF	250+	MacBride, Roger Lea	HarperCollins
On the Beach	J	I	258	Leveled Readers	Houghton Mifflin Harcourt
On the Beach	B	RF	28	Smart Starts	Rigby
On the Beams	N	I	328	Independent Readers Social Studies	Houghton Mifflin Harcourt
On the Bridge at Avignon	F	TL	250+	PM Readalongs	Rigby
On the Computer	D	I	67	Twig	Wright Group/McGraw Hill
On the Devil's Court	Z	RF	250+	Deuker, Carl	Little, Brown & Co.
On the Edge	S	I	250+	Action Packs	Rigby
On the Edge	S	I	250+	Orbit Collections	Pacific Learning
On the Far Side of the Mountain	V	RF	250+	George, Jean Craighead	Puffin/Penguin
On the Farm	N	RF	250+	Boyz Rule!	Mondo
On the Farm	N	I	250+	iOpeners	Pearson Learning Group
On the Farm	C	I	18	Literacy 2000	Rigby
On the Farm	I	RF	250+	Literacy by Design	Rigby
On the Farm	A	I	35	On Our Way to English	Rigby
On the Farm	D	RF	18	Sun Sprouts	ETA Cuisenaire
On the Farm	A	I	24	Vocabulary Readers	Houghton Mifflin Harcourt
On the Farm	A	I	21	Vocabulary Readers	Houghton Mifflin Harcourt
On the Farm	A	I	21	Vocabulary Readers/CA	Houghton Mifflin Harcourt
On the Field with...Peyton and Eli Manning	R	B	250+	Christopher, Matt	Little, Brown & Co.
On the Go	C	RF	43	Learn to Read	Creative Teaching Press
On the Go	C	I	39	Time for Kids	Teacher Created Materials
On the Go	G	I	250+	Yellow Umbrella Books	Red Brick Learning
On the Ground	LB	I	11	Animal Homes	Lerner Publications
On the Ground	C	I	40	Sunshine	Wright Group/McGraw Hill
On the Job	F	RF	79	City Stories	Rigby
On the Job	Q	I	250+	Orbit Collections	Pacific Learning
On the Launch Pad: A Counting Book About Rockets	J	I	71	Know Your Numbers	Picture Window Books
On the Limit	W	RF	250+	Redline Racing Series	Fitzhenry & Whiteside
On the Line	P	RF	4726	Maddox, Jake	Stone Arch Books
On the Line	B	RF	35	Teacher's Choice Series	Pearson Learning Group
On the List	N	F	250+	Sails	Rigby
On the Long Drive	T	HF	2505	Leveled Readers	Houghton Mifflin Harcourt
On the Long Drive	T	HF	2505	Leveled Readers/CA	Houghton Mifflin Harcourt
On the Long Drive	T	HF	2505	Leveled Readers/TX	Houghton Mifflin Harcourt
On the Map	J	I	280	Pair-It Turn and Learn	Steck-Vaughn
On the Menu	R	I	250+	Explorer Books-Pathfinder	National Geographic
On the Menu	P	I	250+	Explorer Books-Pioneer	National Geographic
On the Menu	N	F	250+	Sails	Rigby
On the Moon	H	I	77	Windows on Literacy	National Geographic
On the Move	S	I	250+	Sunshine	Wright Group/McGraw Hill
On the Move	U	I	250+	The News	Richard C. Owen
On the Move	B	I	28	Windows on Literacy	National Geographic
On the Move	D	I	26	Wonder World	Wright Group/McGraw Hill
On the Open Plains	J	I	250+	Momentum Literacy Program	Troll Associates
On the Playground	B	I	47	Early Connections	Benchmark Education

* Collection of short stories
\# Graphic text

TITLE	LEVEL	GENRE	WORD COUNT	AUTHOR / SERIES	PUBLISHER / DISTRIBUTOR
On the Playground	E	I	127	Explorations	Eleanor Curtain Publishing
On the Playground	E	I	127	Explorations	Okapi Educational Materials
On the Right Track	N	I	250+	Home Connection Collection	Rigby
On the Road	C	I	47	Teacher's Choice Series	Pearson Learning Group
On the Rocks	A	I	42	Windows on Literacy	National Geographic
On the Run	P	RF	3897	Townson, H	Stone Arch Books
On the Scale, a Weighty Tale	O	I	353	Cleary, Brian P.	Millbrook Press
On the School Bus	F	RF	62	Little Readers	Houghton Mifflin Harcourt
On the Seashore	A	I	24	Sails	Rigby
On the Silk Road: Ancient Baghdad	L	I	250+	Leveled Readers Language Support	Houghton Mifflin Harcourt
On the Way Home	S	HF	250+	Wilder, Laura Ingalls	HarperCollins
On the Way to School	D	I	143	Dominie Factivity Series	Pearson Learning Group
On the Way to School	A	I	32	Leveled Literacy Intervention/ Orange System	Heinemann
On the Way to the Moon	O	F	250+	Gold, Becky	Pearson Learning Group
On the Weekend	H	I	349	Explorations	Eleanor Curtain Publishing
On the Weekend	H	I	349	Explorations	Okapi Eductional Materials
On the Weekend	WB	I	N/A	Windows on Literacy	National Geographic
On the Wild Side	Q	B	250+	InfoQuest	Rigby
On Thin Ice	O	I	250+	WorldScapes	ETA Cuisenaire
On This Earth	D	I	71	Rise & Shine	Hampton-Brown
On Thursday the Giant	K	F	250+	The Giant	Wright Group/McGraw Hill
On Top of Concord Hill	Q	HF	250+	Wilkes, Maria D.	HarperCollins
On Top of Spaghetti	G	F	105	Little Celebrations	Pearson Learning Group
On Top of the World	Q	I	588	Vocabulary Readers	Houghton Mifflin Harcourt
On Top of the World	T	B	250+	WorldScapes	ETA Cuisenaire
On Tuesday the Giant	K	F	250+	The Giant	Wright Group/McGraw Hill
On Uncle John's Farm	P	RF	536	Fitz-Gibbon, Sally	Fitzhenry & Whiteside
On Vacation	D	I	88	Little Red Readers	Sundance
On Wednesday the Giant	K	F	250+	The Giant	Wright Group/McGraw Hill
On Wings of a Dragon	Y	F	250+	Taylor, Cora	Fitzhenry & Whiteside
On With the Show!	M	I	250+	Pair-It Books	Steck-Vaughn
On With the Show!	K	RF	1438	Real Kids Readers	Millbrook Press
Once and Future King, The	Z+	TL	250+	White, T.H.	Ace Books
Once I Was a Plum Tree	Q	RF	250+	Hurwitz, Johanna	Beech Tree Books
Once on this Island	S	HF	250+	Whelan, Gloria	HarperTrophy
Once Upon a Marigold	W	F	250+	Ferris, Jean	Harcourt Trade
Once Upon a Rhyme	M	F	250+	Pacific Literacy	Pacific Learning
Once Upon a Story	M	I	227	Vocabulary Readers	Houghton Mifflin Harcourt
Once Upon a Time	T	I	250+	Literacy 2000	Rigby
Once Upon a Time	O	B	250+	Meet The Author	Richard C. Owen
Once Upon a Time	H	F	243	Ready Readers	Pearson Learning Group
Once Upon a Time in Junior High	U	RF	250+	Norment, Lisa	Scholastic
Once When I Was Shipwrecked	L	F	250+	Literacy 2000	Rigby
One Blue Hen	F	F	108	Cambridge Reading	Pearson Learning Group
One and Only Special Me, The	E	RF	73	Learn to Read	Creative Teaching Press
One and Only You, The	W	I	250+	Rigby Literacy	Rigby
One Bad Thing About Father, The	M	RF	250+	Monjo, F. N.	HarperTrophy
One Bear All Alone	H	F	107	Bucknall, Caroline	Dial/Penguin
One Bee Got on the Bus	C	F	43	Ready Readers	Pearson Learning Group
One Big Building: A Counting Book About Construction	J	I	88	Know Your Numbers	Picture Window Books
One Bird	Y	RF	250+	Mori, Kyoko	Ballantine Books

TITLE	LEVEL	GENRE	WORD COUNT	AUTHOR / SERIES	PUBLISHER / DISTRIBUTOR
One Bird Sat on the Fence	C	I	40	Wonder World	Wright Group/McGraw Hill
One Birthday, Two Traditions	D	RF	56	Independent Readers Social Studies	Houghton Mifflin Harcourt
One Checkered Flag: A Counting Book About Racing	J	I	69	Know Your Numbers	Picture Window Books
One Chick, One Egg	D	F	64	Step-By-Step Series	Pearson Learning Group
One Chili Pepper	L	RF	722	Reading Street	Pearson
One Clean House	H	RF	250+	Literacy by Design	Rigby
One Cold, Wet Night	D	F	134	Story Box	Wright Group/McGraw Hill
One Day	C	RF	48	Teacher's Choice Series	Pearson Learning Group
One Day in May	N	F	710	Leveled Readers	Houghton Mifflin Harcourt
One Day in the Alpine Tundra	P	I	250+	George, Jean Craighead	HarperCollins
One Day in the Desert	P	I	250+	George, Jean Craighead	HarperCollins
One Day in the Tropical Rain Forest	S	I	250+	George, Jean Craighead	HarperTrophy
One Day in the Woods	P	I	250+	George, Jean Craighead	HarperTrophy
One Day, Two Stars	N	RF	250+	Leveled Readers Language Support	Houghton Mifflin Harcourt
One Drop of Water and a Million More	K	I	156	Book Bank	Wright Group/McGraw Hill
One Duck Stuck	L	F	250+	Root, Phyllis	Candlewick Press
One- Eyed Jake	M	F	547	Hutchins, Pat	Morrow
One Fat Frog	C	I	65	Vocabulary Readers	Houghton Mifflin Harcourt
One Fat Frog	C	I	65	Vocabulary Readers/CA	Houghton Mifflin Harcourt
One Fat Summer	Y	RF	250+	Lipsyte, Robert	HarperCollins
One for You and One for Me	C	RF	27	Blaxland, Wendy	Scholastic
One for You and One for Me	I	I	354	Early Connections	Benchmark Education
One Frog, One Fly	C	F	26	Blaxland, Wendy	Scholastic
One Giant Leap	S	I	250+	Fraser, Mary Ann	Henry Holt & Co.
One Giant Splash A Counting Book About The Ocean	L	I	105	Know Your Numbers	Picture Window Books
One Giant Step	T	I	2570	Reading Street	Pearson
One Green Frog	H	I	215	Yellow Umbrella Books	Red Brick Learning
One Happy Classroom	D	RF	49	Rookie Readers	Children's Press
One Hot Summer Night	I	RF	126	Bookshop	Mondo
One Hundred Books	I	I	217	Story Box	Wright Group/McGraw Hill
One Hundred Hungry Ants	K	F	250+	Pinczes, Elinor	Houghton Mifflin Harcourt
One Hundredth Thing about Caroline, The	R	RF	250+	Lowry, Lois	Bantam
One Hunter	LB	F	15	Hutchins, Pat	Greenwillow
One in the Middle Is the Green Kangaroo, The	M	RF	250+	Blume, Judy	Bantam
One Is a Snail, Ten Is a Crab	I	I	134	Sayre, April Pulley & Sayre, Jeff	Candlewick Press
One Little Elephant	H	F	174	Sunshine	Wright Group/McGraw Hill
One Little Slip	C	F	33	Instant Readers	Harcourt School Publishers
One Lucky Summer	O	RF	250+	Kvasnosky, Laura McGee	Penguin Group
One Man Show	O	B	250+	Meet The Author	Richard C. Owen
One Million Lost: The Battle of the Somme	X	I	250+	Bloodiest Battles	Capstone Press
One Monday Morning	G	F	180	Shulevitz, Uri	Scribner
One More Child	D	RF	28	Harry's Math Books	Outside the Box
One More Frog	F	RF	266	PM Math Readers	Rigby
One More River	V	HF	250+	Banks, Lynne Reid	Avon Camelot
*One More River to Cross	X	B	250+	Haskins, Jim	Scholastic
One More Step	Z	RF	250+	Orca Soundings	Orca Book Publishers
One More Time	C	RF	45	Instant Readers	Harcourt School Publishers
One Night	I	RF	92	Carter, Jackie	Scholastic
One Night	Z+	RF	250+	Qualey, Marsha	Penguin Group
One Night in the Coral Sea	R	I	250+	Collard III, Sneed B.	Charlesbridge

* Collection of short stories
\# Graphic text

TITLE	LEVEL	GENRE	WORD COUNT	AUTHOR / SERIES	PUBLISHER / DISTRIBUTOR
One O'Clock Is Time for One Nap	D	RF	56	Harry's Math Books	Outside the Box
One Picture	B	I	58	PM Math Readers	Rigby
One Piece at a Time	T	RF	250+	Power Up!	Steck-Vaughn
One Piece Missing	K	SF	250+	Rigby Literacy	Rigby
*One Potato, Tu	T	RF	250+	Pearson, Gayle	Scholastic
One Quiet Afternoon	I	F	155	Instant Readers	Harcourt School Publishers
One Racer	F	I	106	Leveled Readers Science	Houghton Mifflin Harcourt
One Room Schools	I	I	250	Vocabulary Readers/TX	Houghton Mifflin Harcourt
One Smart Chick	G	F	250	Rigby Literacy	Rigby
One Smart Goose	L	F	250+	Church, Caroline Jayne	Scholastic
One Soccer Game	C	RF	29	Harry's Math Books	Outside the Box
One Sock, Two Socks	H	RF	179	Reading Corners	Pearson Learning Group
One Special Dog	Q	RF	250+	Pair-It Books	Steck-Vaughn
One Step, Two Steps	D	I	98	Explorations	Eleanor Curtain Publishing
One Step, Two Steps	D	I	98	Explorations	Okapi Educational Materials
One Stormy Night	F	RF	165	Story Basket	Wright Group/McGraw Hill
One Sun in the Sky	E	RF	120	Windmill Books	Wright Group/McGraw Hill
One Thing I'm Good At	R	RF	250+	Williams, Karen Lynn	William Morrow
One Thousand Currant Buns	H	F	213	Sunshine	Wright Group/McGraw Hill
One Tiny Turtle	N	RF	250+	Read and Wonder	Candlewick Press
One Who Came Back, The	X	RF	250+	Mazzio, Joann	Houghton Mifflin Harcourt
One, One Is the Sun	B	RF	42	Story Box	Wright Group/McGraw Hill
One, Two, Buckle My Shoe	D	TL	27	Instant Readers	Harcourt School Publishers
One, Two, Three, Four	LB	F	21	KinderReaders	Rigby
One, Two, Three, Four	D	F	89	Rise & Shine	Hampton-Brown
One, Two, Three, Four, Five!	D	RF	44	Reading Street	Pearson
One-Eyed Cat	S	RF	250+	Fox, Paula	Bantam
Oneidas, The	S	I	1428	Leveled Readers	Houghton Mifflin Harcourt
Oneidas, The	S	I	1428	Leveled Readers/CA	Houghton Mifflin Harcourt
Oneidas, The	S	I	1428	Leveled Readers/TX	Houghton Mifflin Harcourt
One-Man Band	H	RF	144	Leveled Readers Science	Houghton Mifflin Harcourt
One-Minute Muffin	H	RF	250+	Reading Safari	Mondo
Oni Wa Soto	M	TL	250+	Story Vines	Wright Group/McGraw Hill
Onion John	U	HF	250+	Krumgold, Joseph	Harper & Row
Onion Sundaes	L	RF	250+	Adler, David A.	Random House
Onion Tears	Q	RF	250+	Kidd, Diana	William Morrow
*On-Line Spaceman and Other Cases, The	O	RF	250+	Simon, Seymour	Avon
Only an Octopus	H	RF	236	Literacy 2000	Rigby
Only Earth and Sky Last Forever	Y	HF	250+	Benchley, Nathaniel	HarperCollins
Only in Australia	P	I	250+	WorldScapes	ETA Cuisenaire
Ontario	T	I	250+	Hello Canada	Fitzhenry & Whiteside
Oodle Doodles Tuna Noodle and Other Salad Recipes	S	I	250+	Fun Food for Cool Cooks	Capstone Press
Oogly Gum Chasing Game, The	K	F	250+	Literacy 2000	Rigby
Ooh La La, Lottie	K	F	250+	I Am Reading	Kingfisher
Oops!	D	F	62	Mayer, Mercer	Penguin Group
Oops! Why Did I Do That?	K	RF	416	Early Connections	Benchmark Education
Open Door Club, The	L	RF	570	Leveled Readers	Houghton Mifflin Harcourt
Open It!	D	I	27	Pacific Literacy	Pacific Learning
Open Wide	G	I	189	Home Connection Collection	Rigby
Open Wide	C	F	56	Mitchell, Robin	Scholastic
Open Wide!	O	I	250+	Tristars	Richard C. Owen
Open Your Eyes, Sidney Miffet	H	RF	107	Seedlings	Continental Press
Open Your Mouth	F	F	201	Sunshine	Wright Group/McGraw Hill

O

* Collection of short stories
# Graphic text

Organized Alphabetically by Title **441**
Storable Database at www.fountasandpinnellleveledbooks.com

TITLE	LEVEL	GENRE	WORD COUNT	AUTHOR / SERIES	PUBLISHER / DISTRIBUTOR
Opening Night	X	I	2265	Leveled Readers	Houghton Mifflin Harcourt
Opening Night	M	RF	250+	Navigators Fiction Series	Benchmark Education
Operation Communication	V	I	250+	WorldScapes	ETA Cuisenaire
Operation Elephant Foot	G	RF	149	Springboard	Wright Group/McGraw Hill
Operation Migration	S	B	250+	WorldScapes	ETA Cuisenaire
Opossums	O	I	1853	Early Bird Nature Books	Lerner Publications
Opposite of Pig, The	K	F	250+	Little Celebrations	Pearson Learning Group
Oprah Winfrey, A Voice for the People	U	B	250+	Brooks, Philip	Grolier Publishing
Optometrist	O	I	250+	Bookweb	Rigby
Optometrist, The	G	I	191	PM Nonfiction-Blue	Rigby
Orange	B	I	26	Colors	Lerner Publications
Orange Floats, An	K	I	331	Reading Street	Pearson
Orange: Seeing Orange All Around Us	K	I	250+	Colors	Capstone Press
Oranges for Orange Juice	F	I	25	Learn to Read	Creative Teaching Press
Orangutans	I	I	208	Sails	Rigby
Orbiting the Sun	W	I	2326	Reading Street	Pearson
Orca Song	K	RF	250+	Armour	Scholastic
Orca Whales	F	I	85	Seedlings	Continental Press
*Orca's Family and More Northwest Coast Stories	P	TL	250+	Challenger, James Robert	Heritage House
Orchestra, The	C	F	33	Foundations	Wright Group/McGraw Hill
Ordinary Genius, The Story of Albert Einstein	U	B	250+	McPherson, Stephanie S.	The Lerner Group
Ordinary Miracles	Y	RF	250+	Tolan, Stephanie S.	Morrow
Oregon	T	I	250+	Hello U.S.A.	Lerner Publications
Oregon	T	I	250+	Theme Sets	National Geographic
Oregon	R	I	250+	This Land Is Your Land	Compass Point Books
Oregon Trail, The	S	I	250+	A True Book	Children's Press
Oregon Trail, The	V	I	250+	Cornerstones of Freedom	Children's Press
Oregon Trail, The	V	I	250+	Let Freedom Ring	Red Brick Learning
Oregon Trail, The	Q	I	250+	On Deck	Rigby
Oregon Trail, The	T	I	250+	The Heinle Reading Library	Thomson Learning
Oregon Trail, The	S	I	250+	The Library of the Westward Expansion	Rosen Publishing Group
Oregon Trail, The	S	I	1424	Vocabulary Readers	Houghton Mifflin Harcourt
Oregon Trail, The	S	I	1424	Vocabulary Readers/CA	Houghton Mifflin Harcourt
Oregon Trail, The	T	I	250+	We The People	Compass Point Books
Organisms of Long Ago	R	I	1012	Science Support Readers	Houghton Mifflin Harcourt
Oriental Cats	I	I	107	Cats	Capstone Press
Origami	L	I	250+	How-To Series	Benchmark Education
Origami for Fun!	S	I	250+	For Fun! Crafts	Compass Point Books
Origami: The Fun and Funky Art of Paper Folding	Q	I	250+	Crafts	Capstone Press
Original Adventures of Hank the Cowdog, The	Q	F	250+	Erickson, John R.	Gulf
Orphan of Ellis Island, The	S	HF	250+	Woodruff, Elvira	Scholastic
Orphan Train	K	RF	250+	The Wright Skills	Wright Group/McGraw Hill
Orphan Train Adventures: Caught in the Act	W	HF	250+	Nixon, Joan Lowery	Bantam
Orphan Train Adventures: Circle of Love	W	HF	250+	Nixon, Joan Lowery	Bantam
Orphan Train Adventures: A Dangerous Promise	W	HF	250+	Nixon, Joan Lowery	Dell
Orphan Train Adventures: A Family Apart	W	HF	250+	Nixon, Joan Lowery	Dell
Orphan Train Adventures: In the Face of Danger	W	HF	250+	Nixon, Joan Lowery	Dell
Orphan Train Adventures: Keeping Secrets	W	HF	250+	Nixon, Joan Lowery	Dell
Orphan Train Adventures: A Place to Belong	W	HF	250+	Nixon, Joan Lowery	Dell

* Collection of short stories
# Graphic text

TITLE	LEVEL	GENRE	WORD COUNT	AUTHOR / SERIES	PUBLISHER / DISTRIBUTOR
Orphan Train Children: Aggie's Home	Q	HF	250+	Nixon, Joan Lowery	Yearling
Orphan Train Journey	S	HF	1247	Leveled Readers	Houghton Mifflin Harcourt
Orphan Train Rider: One Boy's True Story	V	I	250+	Warren, Andrea	Scholastic
Orson Welles and the War of the Worlds	V	I	1917	Leveled Readers	Houghton Mifflin Harcourt
Orson's Tummy Ache	B	F	51	Leveled Literacy Intervention/ Green System	Heinemann
Oscar & Tatiana	N	RF	250+	Literacy 2000	Rigby
Oscar De La Hoya: The Golden Boy	P	B	250+	Great Hispanics	Capstone Press
Oscar Otter	J	F	250+	Benchley, Nathaniel	HarperTrophy
Oscar's Day	J	I	154	iOpeners	Pearson Learning Group
Osceola: Patriot and Warrior	T	B	250+	Jumper, Moses; Sonder, Ben	Steck-Vaughn
Osprey	M	I	250+	Cambridge Reading	Pearson Learning Group
Ostriches	O	I	1323	Early Bird Nature Books	Lerner Publications
Ostriches	M	I	250+	Sails	Rigby
Other Side of Dark, The	Z+	RF	250+	Nixon, Joan Lowery	Random House
Other Side of the Lake, The	L	F	250+	Little Celebrations	Pearson Learning Group
Other Side, The	G	F	182	Sun Sprouts	ETA Cuisenaire
Other Victims, The: First-Person Stories of Non-Jews Persecuted by the Nazis	Z+	I	250+	Friedman, Ina R.	Houghton Mifflin Harcourt
Others See Us	Z	F	250+	Sleator, William	Puffin/Penguin
Otherwise Known as Sheila the Great	R	RF	250+	Blume, Judy	Bantam
Otis Spofford	O	RF	250+	Cleary, Beverly	Avon
Otter Rescue	L	I	641	Gear Up!	Wright Group/McGraw Hill
Otter, Otter	C	I	39	Phonics and Friends	Hampton-Brown
Otters	H	I	437	Sails	Rigby
Otto the Cat	I	F	250+	Herman, Gail	Grossett & Dunlap
Otto's Lunchbox	I	F	250+	Rigby Rocket	Rigby
Ouch!	LB	RF	40	Literacy 2000	Rigby
Ouch!	L	RF	250+	Noonan, Diana	Pearson Learning Group
Ouch!	B	I	40	Science	Outside the Box
Ouch!: What Happens When a Bone Breaks or a Muscle Tears	P	I	250+	On Our Way to English	Rigby
Our Adobe House	L	I	250+	Greetings	Rigby
Our America	S	I	250+	Literacy By Design	Rigby
Our American Flag	O	I	250+	Sunshine	Wright Group/McGraw Hill
Our Baby	G	RF	164	Breakthrough	Longman
Our Baby	J	RF	128	Foundations	Wright Group/McGraw Hill
Our Baby	B	RF	14	Literacy 2000	Rigby
Our Baby	E	I	90	PM Nonfiction-Yellow	Rigby
Our Baby	D	RF	70	Voyages	SRA/McGraw Hill
Our Bakery	H	RF	230	Leveled Readers	Houghton Mifflin Harcourt
Our Bakery	H	RF	230	Leveled Readers/CA	Houghton Mifflin Harcourt
Our Bakery	H	RF	230	Leveled Readers/TX	Houghton Mifflin Harcourt
Our Bodies	J	I	250+	PM Plus Nonfiction	Rigby
Our Book of Maps	N	I	250+	Discovery World	Rigby
Our Busy Bodies	K	I	144	Home Connection Collection	Rigby
Our Butterflies	D	I	99	Rigby Flying Colors	Rigby
Our Camping Trip	E	RF	120	Lighthouse	Rigby
Our Car	G	I	94	Bookshop	Mondo
Our Car	C	RF	32	Sunshine	Wright Group/McGraw Hill
Our Cat	E	RF	99	Foundations	Wright Group/McGraw Hill
Our Changing Earth	R	I	250+	Belcher, Angie	Pacific Learning
Our Changing Earth: An Encyclopedia of Landforms	O	I	250+	Literacy by Design	Rigby

* Collection of short stories
\# Graphic text

TITLE	LEVEL	GENRE	WORD COUNT	AUTHOR / SERIES	PUBLISHER / DISTRIBUTOR
Our Changing Earth: An Encyclopedia of Landforms	O	I	250+	On Our Way to English	Rigby
Our Changing Planet	P	I	250+	InfoQuest	Rigby
Our Chore Chart	D	I	65	Storyteller-First Snow	Wright Group/McGraw Hill
Our Class	E	I	200	Leveled Readers	Houghton Mifflin Harcourt
Our Class	E	I	200	Leveled Readers/CA	Houghton Mifflin Harcourt
Our Class	E	I	200	Leveled Readers/TX	Houghton Mifflin Harcourt
Our Class and the Very Big Rabbit!	K	F	927	Big Cat	Pacific Learning
Our Class Band	A	RF	30	Leveled Readers	Houghton Mifflin Harcourt
Our Class Band	A	RF	30	Leveled Readers/CA	Houghton Mifflin Harcourt
Our Class Survey	F	I	128	Early Connections	Benchmark Education
Our Classroom	E	RF	53	Leveled Readers Social Studies	Houghton Mifflin Harcourt
Our Classroom	A	I	20	Vocabulary Readers	Houghton Mifflin Harcourt
Our Classroom	A	I	20	Vocabulary Readers/CA	Houghton Mifflin Harcourt
Our Clothes	J	I	250+	PM Plus Nonfiction	Rigby
Our Clubhouse	WB	I	N/A	Windows on Literacy	National Geographic
Our Crazy Class Election	N	RF	250+	Roland, Timothy	Scholastic
Our "Current" World	T	I	250+	Navigators Social Studies Series	Benchmark Education
Our Dad	C	RF	41	Little Books for Early Readers	University of Maine
Our Dairy Farm	L	I	562	Rigby Flying Colors	Rigby
Our Day	B	F	30	Sails	Rigby
Our Day at Nana's House	D	RF	137	Leveled Readers	Houghton Mifflin Harcourt
Our Day at Nana's House	D	RF	137	Leveled Readers/CA	Houghton Mifflin Harcourt
Our Day at Nana's House	D	RF	137	Leveled Readers/TX	Houghton Mifflin Harcourt
Our Day at the Bakery	H	RF	274	Leveled Readers	Houghton Mifflin Harcourt
Our Day at the Bakery	H	RF	274	Leveled Readers/CA	Houghton Mifflin Harcourt
Our Day at the Bakery	H	RF	274	Leveled Readers/TX	Houghton Mifflin Harcourt
Our Disappearing Rain Forest	Q	I	1467	Reading Street	Pearson
Our Dog	D	I	113	PM Science Readers	Rigby
Our Dog Sam	B	RF	56	Literacy 2000	Rigby
Our Earth	D	I	33	Discovery Links	Newbridge
Our Earth	F	I	53	Rosen Real Readers	Rosen Publishing Group
Our Earth	M	I	604	Time for Kids	Teacher Created Materials
Our Endangered Planet (Oceans)	W	I	250+	Hoff, Mary; Rodgers, Mary	Lerner Publishing
Our Eyes	I	I	869	Sunshine	Wright Group/McGraw Hill
Our Families	B	I	52	Leveled Readers Social Studies	Houghton Mifflin Harcourt
Our Families	B	I	26	Rigby Literacy	Rigby
Our Family Vacation	A	F	29	Leveled Readers	Houghton Mifflin Harcourt
Our Family Vacation	A	F	29	Leveled Readers/CA	Houghton Mifflin Harcourt
Our Farm	C	I	37	Rosen Real Readers	Rosen Publishing Group
Our Favorite Food	D	I	121	Explorations	Eleanor Curtain Publishing
Our Favorite Food	D	I	121	Explorations	Okapi Educational Materials
Our Favorite Things to Do	F	I	241	Yellow Umbrella Books	Capstone Press
Our Favorites	G	I	217	Learn to Read	Creative Teaching Press
Our Feelings	L	I	250+	Rigby Star Quest	Rigby
Our Fish	F	I	161	PM Science Readers	Rigby
Our Five Senses	G	I	100	Gear Up!	Wright Group/McGraw Hill
Our Five Senses	B	I	23	Rigby Star Quest	Rigby
Our Five Senses	E	I	99	Yellow Umbrella Books	Red Brick Learning
Our Flag	C	I	21	Leveled Readers Social Studies	Houghton Mifflin Harcourt
Our Flag	D	I	62	On Our Way to English	Rigby
Our Flag	I	I	93	Phonics Readers	Compass Point Books
Our Flag	M	HF	250+	Rothman, Cynthia	Scholastic
Our Four Walls	L	RF	422	Leveled Readers	Houghton Mifflin Harcourt

Organized Alphabetically by Title
Storable Database at www.fountasandpinnellleveledbooks.com

* Collection of short stories
\# Graphic text

TITLE	LEVEL	GENRE	WORD COUNT	AUTHOR / SERIES	PUBLISHER / DISTRIBUTOR
Our Garage	F	RF	80	Urmston, Kathleen; Evans, Karen	Kaeden Books
Our Garden	B	RF	54	Leveled Literacy Intervention/ Green System	Heinemann
Our Garden	B	I	16	Literacy 2000	Rigby
Our Garden	M	I	250+	On Our Way to English	Rigby
Our Garden	L	RF	1032	Reading Street	Pearson
Our Gift to the Beach	D	I	83	In Step Readers	Rigby
Our Gift to the Beach	D	I	83	Literacy by Design	Rigby
Our Goat	D	RF	27	Costain, Meredith	Scholastic
Our Government	M	I	250+	People, Spaces & Places	Rand McNally
Our Grandad	C	RF	30	Sunshine	Wright Group/McGraw Hill
Our Granny	C	RF	41	Sunshine	Wright Group/McGraw Hill
Our Heritage	S	I	250+	WorldScapes	ETA Cuisenaire
Our Home Is the Pond	E	I	52	Independent Readers Science	Houghton Mifflin Harcourt
Our Homes	C	I	50	Dominie Factivity Series	Pearson Learning Group
Our Homes	G	RF	277	InfoTrek	ETA Cuisenaire
Our House Had a Mouse	E	F	102	Worthington, Denise	Continental Press
Our House Is a Safe House	G	I	163	PM Plus Nonfiction	Rigby
Our Inside Story	W	I	250+	InfoQuest	Rigby
Our Jobs	A	I	15	Vocabulary Readers	Houghton Mifflin Harcourt
Our Jobs	A	I	15	Vocabulary Readers/CA	Houghton Mifflin Harcourt
Our Journey	P	I	250+	On Our Way to English	Rigby
Our Liberty Bell	T	I	250+	Magaziner, Henry Jonas	Holiday House
Our Library	I	RF	320	Leveled Readers	Houghton Mifflin Harcourt
Our Library	I	RF	320	Leveled Readers/CA	Houghton Mifflin Harcourt
Our Library	I	RF	320	Leveled Readers/TX	Houghton Mifflin Harcourt
Our Lunch Boxes	E	I	142	Rigby Flying Colors	Rigby
Our Magazine Article	P	I	250+	Rigby Focus	Rigby
Our Market	F	I	147	Explorations	Eleanor Curtain Publishing
Our Market	F	I	147	Explorations	Okapi Eductional Materials
Our Mom	E	I	107	PM Nonfiction-Yellow	Rigby
Our Money	J	I	255	Early Connections	Benchmark Education
Our Money	E	I	74	Leveled Readers Social Studies	Houghton Mifflin Harcourt
Our Moon	H	I	161	Early Connections	Benchmark Education
Our Moon	N	I	832	Pair-It Turn and Learn	Steck-Vaughn
Our Moon	N	I	250+	Yellow Umbrella Books	Red Brick Learning
Our Mysterious Universe	Y	I	250+	iOpeners	Pearson Learning Group
Our National Holidays	Q	I	250+	Let's See	Compass Point Books
Our National Park System	M	I	642	Gear Up!	Wright Group/ McGraw Hill
Our National Parks	Q	I	250+	Let's See	Compass Point Books
Our National Treasures	O	I	250+	Bookshop	Mondo
Our Natural Resources	M	I	1234	Leveled Readers Social Studies	Houghton Mifflin Harcourt
Our New Baby	F	RF	59	City Stories	Rigby
Our New House	G	RF	68	PM Plus Nonfiction	Rigby
Our New House	G	RF	167	Windows on Literacy	National Geographic
Our New Principal	K	RF	149	City Kids	Rigby
Our New Puppy	C	RF	29	Windows on Literacy	National Geographic
Our Old Friend, Bear	J	RF	250+	PM Story Books-Silver	Rigby
Our Only May Amelia	R	HF	250+	Holm, Jennifer	HarperCollins
Our Painted Village	P	I	250+	WorldScapes	ETA Cuisenaire
Our Parents	G	I	142	PM Nonfiction-Blue	Rigby
Our Party	B	RF	40	Leveled Readers Social Studies	Houghton Mifflin Harcourt
Our Pet Rabbit	B	I	35	Gear Up!	Wright Group/McGraw Hill

* Collection of short stories
# Graphic text

TITLE	LEVEL	GENRE	WORD COUNT	AUTHOR / SERIES	PUBLISHER / DISTRIBUTOR
Our Pets	C	I	109	Leveled Literacy Intervention/ Orange System	Heinemann
Our Pets	F	I	163	PM Science Readers	Rigby
Our Place, Their Place	Q	I	250+	WorldScapes	ETA Cuisenaire
Our Planet	R	I	250+	Worldwise	Franklin Watts
Our Playhouse	D	RF	46	Voyages	SRA/McGraw Hill
Our Polliwogs	I	RF	91	Books for Young Learners	Richard C. Owen
Our Pumpkin	B	I	29	Learn to Read	Creative Teaching Press
Our Puppy	M	I	873	Rigby Flying Colors	Rigby
Our Rocket	B	I	28	Pacific Literacy	Pacific Learning
Our Room	A	RF	22	Leveled Readers	Houghton Mifflin Harcourt
Our Room	A	RF	22	Leveled Readers/CA	Houghton Mifflin Harcourt
Our Sand Castle	H	RF	229	Rigby Flying Colors	Rigby
Our School	H	RF	98	City Kids	Rigby
Our School	A	F	22	Leveled Readers	Houghton Mifflin Harcourt
Our School	F	RF	182	Leveled Readers	Houghton Mifflin Harcourt
Our School	F	RF	182	Leveled Readers/CA	Houghton Mifflin Harcourt
Our School	A	F	22	Leveled Readers/CA	Houghton Mifflin Harcourt
Our School	F	RF	182	Leveled Readers/TX	Houghton Mifflin Harcourt
Our School	C	I	46	Twig	Wright Group/McGraw Hill
Our School	H	RF	46	Well-Being Series	Dominie Press
Our Senses	F	I	182	Discovery Links	Newbridge
Our Senses	F	I	77	Nonfiction	Literacy Footprints
Our Senses	D	I	39	Rise & Shine	Hampton-Brown
Our Senses	K	I	179	Spyglass Books	Compass Point Books
Our Skeleton	I	I	105	Sunshine	Wright Group/McGraw Hill
Our Soccer Team	G	RF	139	Literacy Tree	Rigby
Our Solar System	T	I	250+	Navigators Science Series	Benchmark Education Company
Our Solar System	Q	I	250+	Reading Expeditions	National Geographic
Our Solar System	O	I	1502	Science Support Readers	Houghton Mifflin Harcourt
Our Star, the Sun	N	I	599	Leveled Readers Science	Houghton Mifflin Harcourt
Our Stories, Our Songs: African Children Talk About AIDS	Y	I	28897	Ellis, Deborah	Fitzhenry & Whiteside
Our Street	C	RF	40	Sunshine	Wright Group/McGraw Hill
Our Sun	J	I	166	Early Connections	Benchmark Education
Our Sun	K	I	229	Pair-It Turn and Learn	Steck-Vaughn
Our Sun	I	I	189	Rosen Real Readers	Rosen Publishing Group
Our Teacher	G	RF	168	Windows on Literacy	National Geographic
Our Teacher, Miss Pool	D	F	62	Pacific Literacy	Pacific Learning
Our Town	C	I	103	Leveled Readers	Houghton Mifflin Harcourt
Our Town	C	I	103	Leveled Readers/CA	Houghton Mifflin Harcourt
Our Town	C	I	103	Leveled Readers/TX	Houghton Mifflin Harcourt
Our Town	I	I	189	Literacy by Design	Rigby
Our Town	B	RF	37	Little Red Readers	Sundance
Our Town	N	I	250+	Rigby Focus	Rigby
Our Town	G	RF	129	Well-Being Series	Pearson Learning Group
Our Town	H	I	129	Windows on Literacy	National Geographic
Our Town Mural	M	RF	660	Leveled Readers	Houghton Mifflin Harcourt
Our Tree	E	RF	53	Joy Starters	Pearson Learning Group
Our Tree House	E	RF	144	Twig	Wright Group/McGraw Hill
Our Vegetable Garden	I	I	344	Rigby Flying Colors	Rigby
Our Week	C	RF	37	Storyteller-First Snow	Wright Group/McGraw Hill

* Collection of short stories
# Graphic text

TITLE	LEVEL	GENRE	WORD COUNT	AUTHOR / SERIES	PUBLISHER / DISTRIBUTOR
Our White House: Looking in, Looking Out	Y	I	250+	National Children's Book and Literacy Alliance	Candlewick Press
*Our World of Mysteries: Fascinating Facts About the Planet Earth	X	I	250+	Lord, Suzanne	Scholastic
Our World of Wonders	Q	I	250+	Canetti, Yanitzia	Steck-Vaughn
Our Yard	E	I	120	PM Science Readers	Rigby
Out After Dark	H	RF	114	Book Bank	Wright Group/McGraw Hill
Out and About	Q	I	250+	Explorers	Wright Group/McGraw Hill
Out and About at the Apple Orchard	M	I	250+	Field Trips	Picture Window Books
Out and About at the Aquarium	M	I	250+	Field Trips	Picture Window Books
Out and About at the Bakery	M	I	250+	Field Trips	Picture Window Books
Out and About at the Dairy Farm	M	I	250+	Field Trips	Picture Window Books
Out and About at the Fire Station	M	I	250+	Field Trips	Picture Window Books
Out and About at the Orchestra	M	I	250+	Field Trips	Picture Window Books
Out and About at the Planetarium	M	I	250+	Field Trips	Picture Window Books
Out and About at the Post Office	M	I	250+	Field Trips	Picture Window Books
Out and About at the Science Center	M	I	250+	Field Trips	Picture Window Books
Out and About at the Supermarket	M	I	250+	Field Trips	Picture Window Books
Out and About at the Vet Clinic	M	I	250+	Field Trips	Picture Window Books
Out and About at the Zoo	M	I	250+	Field Trips	Picture Window Books
Out for Lunch	F	RF	235	Leveled Literacy Intervention/ Green System	Heinemann
Out in Space	L	I	224	Spyglass Books	Compass Point Books
Out in the Big Wild World	K	F	430	Jellybeans	Rigby
Out in the Weather	B	I	56	PM Starters	Rigby
Out of an Egg	I	I	103	Gear Up!	Wright Group/McGraw Hill
Out of Bounds	Z	HF	250+	Naidoo, Beverly	HarperCollins
Out of Control	T	I	250+	Orbit Collections	Pacific Learning
Out of Darkness: The Story of Louis Braille	S	B	250+	Freedman, Russell	Houghton Mifflin Harcourt
Out of His League	Z+	RF	250+	Flynn, Pat	Walker & Company
Out of Reach	G	RF	86	Literacy Tree	Rigby
Out of Sight	C	I	52	Rigby Literacy	Rigby
Out of Sight, Out of Mind	Q	RF	250+	Mazer, Anne	Scholastic
Out of the Dust	X	HF	250+	Hesse, Karen	Scholastic
Out of the Egg	E	I	118	Sails	Rigby
Out of the Ocean	M	RF	432	Frasier, Debra	Harcourt
Out of This World	U	I	250+	Story Surfers	ETA Cuisenaire
Out the Door	E	RF	150	Rookie Readers	Children's Press
Out the Window	D	I	79	Vocabulary Readers	Houghton Mifflin Harcourt
Out the Window	D	I	79	Vocabulary Readers/CA	Houghton Mifflin Harcourt
Out to Play	C	F	69	Leveled Literacy Intervention/ Orange System	Heinemann
Outback Adventure	R	RF	250+	Reading Expeditions	National Geographic
Outback Adventure, The	O	RF	250+	WorldScapes	ETA Cuisenaire
Outback School	G	RF	131	Take Two Books	Wright Group/McGraw Hill
Outcast of Redwall, The	Z	F	250+	Jacques, Brian	Ace Books
Outcasts of 19 Schuyler Place, The	W	RF	250+	Konigsburg, E. L.	Aladdin
Outdoor Adventures	W	I	250+	iOpeners	Pearson Learning Group
Outer Banks, The	R	I	1353	Leveled Readers	Houghton Mifflin Harcourt
Outer Banks, The	R	I	1353	Leveled Readers/CA	Houghton Mifflin Harcourt
Outer Space	O	I	622	Time for Kids	Teacher Created Materials
Outing, An	E	RF	68	Sunshine	Wright Group/McGraw Hill
Outrageously Alice	U	RF	250+	Naylor, Phyllis Reynolds	Aladdin
Outside and Inside	C	I	43	Twig	Wright Group/McGraw Hill

O

TITLE	LEVEL	GENRE	WORD COUNT	AUTHOR / SERIES	PUBLISHER / DISTRIBUTOR
Outside and Inside Bats	Q	I	250+	Markle, Sandra	Simon & Schuster
Outside and Inside Kangaroos	Q	I	250+	Markle, Sandra	Atheneum
Outside and Inside Sharks	Q	I	250+	Markle, Sandra	Simon & Schuster
Outside and Inside Snakes	Q	I	250+	Markle, Sandra	Simon & Schuster
Outside and Inside Spiders	Q	I	250+	Markle, Sandra	Simon & Schuster
Outside Dog, The	K	RF	250+	Pomerantz, Charlotte	HarperTrophy
Outside Games	H	I	230	Springboard	Wright Group/McGraw Hill
Outside the Window	B	I	31	Vocabulary Readers	Houghton Mifflin Harcourt
Outside, Inside	D	RF	97	Teacher's Choice Series	Pearson Learning Group
Outsiders, The	Z	RF	250+	Hinton, S. E.	Penguin Group
Outwitting the Tiger	L	TL	250+	Voyages	SRA/McGraw Hill
Ovals Around Town	J	I	275	Shapes Around Town	Capstone Press
Ovals: Seeing Ovals All Around Us	K	I	214	Shapes	Capstone Press
Over and Over	D	RF	39	Ray's Readers	Outside the Box
Over and Under	C	I	41	Location	Lerner Publishing
Over in the Arctic	M	F	462	Sharing Nature with Children	Dawn Publications
Over in the Jungle, A Rainforest Rhyme	M	F	427	Sharing Nature with Children	Dawn Publications
Over in the Meadow	F	F	228	Cambridge Reading	Pearson Learning Group
Over in the Meadow	G	F	242	Little Readers	Houghton Mifflin Harcourt
Over in the Meadow	F	TL	250+	PM Readalongs	Rigby
Over in the Ocean, in a Coral Reef	M	F	431	Sharing Nature with Children	Dawn Publications
Over Sea, Under Stone	X	F	250+	Cooper, Susan	Simon & Schuster
Over the Bridge	B	I	50	Little Red Readers	Sundance
Over the Marble Mountain	E	RF	92	Voyages	SRA/McGraw Hill
Over the Oregon Trail	D	I	131	Twig	Wright Group/McGraw Hill
Over the Rainbow	T	B	250+	High-Fliers	Pacific Learning
Over the River	B	F	72	Leveled Literacy Intervention/ Orange System	Heinemann
Over the Wall	Y	RF	250+	Ritter, John H.	Puffin Books
Over Under in the Garden	WB	I	N/A	Schories, Pat	Farrar, Straus and Giroux
Over, Under, in, and Ouch!	I	F	287	Silly Millies	Millbrook Press
Overcoming Challenges: The Life of Charles F. Bolden, Jr.	Q	B	250+	Walton, Darwin McBeth	Steck-Vaughn
Overdrive	X	RF	250+	Orca Soundings	Orca Book Publishers
Overground, Underground	S	I	250+	WorldScapes	ETA Cuisenaire
Overland Trail, The	Q	I	250+	On Deck	Rigby
Overnight	Y	RF	250+	Griffin, Adele	Speak
Over-Under	E	RF	29	Rookie Readers	Children's Press
Owen & Mzee: The True Story of a Remarkable Friendship	R	I	250+	Hatkoff, Isabella & Craig & Kahumbu, Dr. Paula	Scholastic
Owl and Mouse in the House	J	F	383	Sails	Rigby
Owl and the Pussy Cat	L	TL	215	Lear, Edward	Scholastic
*Owl at Home	J	F	1488	Lobel, Arnold	HarperCollins
Owl Babies	K	F	250+	Waddell, Martin	Candlewick Press
Owl in the Office	Q	RF	250+	Baglio, Ben M.	Scholastic
Owl Moon	O	B	250+	Yolen, Jane	Scholastic
Owl Rescue	G	RF	157	Gear Up!	Wright Group/McGraw Hill
Owl, That's Who!, An	E	I	31	Rosen Real Readers	Rosen Publishing Group
Owlbert	K	RF	250+	Soar To Success	Houghton Mifflin Harcourt
Owliver	H	F	106	Kraus, Robert	Simon & Schuster
Owls	P	I	1749	Animal Predators	Lerner Publishing
Owls	N	I	250+	Gibbons, Gail	Holiday House
Owls	O	I	250+	Holmes, Kevin J.	Red Brick Learning
Owls	R	I	250+	Kalman, Bobbie	Crabtree

* Collection of short stories
\# Graphic text

TITLE	LEVEL	GENRE	WORD COUNT	AUTHOR / SERIES	PUBLISHER / DISTRIBUTOR
Owls	I	I	250+	Pebble Books	Red Brick Learning
Owls	M	I	250+	PM Animal Facts: Gold	Rigby
Owls in the Family	P	F	250+	Mowat, Farley	Bantam
Owls in the Garden	L	RF	670	PM Collection	Rigby
Owls in the Snow	J	I	422	Sails	Rigby
Owls: The Silent Hunters	T	I	250+	Animals in Order	Franklin Watts
Ox-Bow Incident, The	Z+	HF	250+	Clark, Walter Van Tilburg	Random House
Oxcart Day	N	RF	250+	WorldScapes	ETA Cuisenaire
Ox-Cart Man	K	HF	250+	Hall, Donald	Scholastic
Ozlo's Beard	J	F	250+	Lighthouse	Ginn & Co.

O

* Collection of short stories
# Graphic text

TITLE	LEVEL	GENRE	WORD COUNT	AUTHOR / SERIES	PUBLISHER / DISTRIBUTOR
P. J. Funnybunny Camps Out	I	F	250+	Sadler, Marilyn	Random House
P. W. Cracker Sees the World	Q	F	250+	Yoshizawa, Linda	Steck-Vaughn
P.S. Longer Letter Later	U	RF	250+	Danziger, Paula; Martin, Ann M.	Scholastic
Pablo Picasso	P	B	250+	Lowery, Linda	Lerner Publishing
Pablo's Fiesta	E	RF	91	On Our Way to English	Rigby
Pacal: A Maya King	R	B	250+	High-Fliers	Pacific Learning
Pacific Island Scrapbook	N	I	591	Big Cat	Pacific Learning
Pacific Ocean, The	N	I	250+	Oceans	Capstone Press
Pacific Passage	T	RF	250+	Reading Safari	Mondo
Pack 109	J	F	164	Thaler, Mike	Scholastic
Pack a Picnic	E	F	140	Learn to Read	Creative Teaching Press
Package, The	E	RF	35	Bauer, Roger	Kaeden Books
Packed with Poison! Deadly Animal Defenses	O	I	1793	On My Own Science	Lerner Publications
Packing	B	RF	37	Foundations	Wright Group/McGraw Hill
Packing My Bag	A	I	32	Leveled Literacy Intervention/ Orange System	Heinemann
Packing My Bag	B	RF	52	PM Starters	Rigby
Paco's Garden	G	RF	118	Books for Young Learners	Richard C. Owen
Paco's Snowman	L	RF	330	Leveled Readers	Houghton Mifflin Harcourt
Paco's Snowman	L	RF	330	Leveled Readers/CA	Houghton Mifflin Harcourt
Paco's Snowman	L	RF	330	Leveled Readers/TX	Houghton Mifflin Harcourt
Pagan's Crusade	Y	HF	250+	Jinks, Catherine	Candlewick Press
Pagan's Vows	Z+	HF	250+	Jinks, Catherine	Candlewick Press
Pagemaster, The	P	F	250+	Horowitz, Jordan	Scholastic
Paint Brush Kid, The	M	RF	250+	Bulla, Clyde Robert	Random House
Paint the Sky	LB	F	14	Sunshine	Wright Group/McGraw Hill
Paintball	Q	I	250+	X-Sports	Capstone Press
Paintball Blast	Q	RF	4301	Maddox, Jake	Stone Arch Books
Paintball Invasion	Q	RF	250+	Maddox, Jake	Stone Arch Books
Painted Earth Temple: The Buffalo Woman Trilogy, Book Two	Z	HF	250+	Merrifield, Heyoka	Atria Books
Painter, The	A	F	39	Leveled Literacy Intervention/ Green System	Heinemann
Painter, The	C	RF	31	Ray's Readers	Outside the Box
Painters	A	I	23	Twig	Wright Group/McGraw Hill
Painting	A	RF	40	Leveled Literacy Intervention/ Orange System	Heinemann
Painting	E	RF	135	Scott, Janine	Scholastic
Painting	C	RF	24	Story Box	Wright Group/McGraw Hill
Painting Day, The	H	RF	250+	Voyages	SRA/McGraw Hill
Painting from Caves to Computers	O	I	578	Vocabulary Readers	Houghton Mifflin Harcourt
Painting from Caves to Computers	O	I	578	Vocabulary Readers/CA	Houghton Mifflin Harcourt
Painting from Caves to Computers	O	I	578	Vocabulary Readers/TX	Houghton Mifflin Harcourt
Painting History	J	RF	242	On Our Way to English	Rigby
Painting Lesson, The	K	F	250+	Pacific Literacy	Pacific Learning
Painting Patterns	A	RF	31	InfoTrek	ETA Cuisenaire
Painting Shapes	F	I	148	Early Connections	Benchmark Education
Painting the Ocean	M	RF	885	Leveled Readers	Houghton Mifflin Harcourt
Painting the Ocean	M	RF	885	Leveled Readers/CA	Houghton Mifflin Harcourt
Painting the Ocean	M	RF	885	Leveled Readers/TX	Houghton Mifflin Harcourt
Pair of Babies, A	D	I	70	Early Connections	Benchmark Education
Pajama Party	M	RF	250+	Hest, Amy	William Morrow
Pajama Party, The	D	F	46	Sunshine	Wright Group/McGraw Hill
Pakistan	W	I	250+	Countries and Cultures	Capstone Press

* Collection of short stories
\# Graphic text

TITLE	LEVEL	GENRE	WORD COUNT	AUTHOR / SERIES	PUBLISHER / DISTRIBUTOR
Pal the Pony	G	RF	224	Herman, R. A.	Grossett & Dunlap
Palapalooza	L	RF	250+	Social Studies Connects	The Kane Press
Paleontology: Digging for Dinosaurs and More	U	I	1597	Reading Street	Pearson
Palm Trees	H	I	123	Pebble Books	Capstone Press
Paloma's Party	L	I	250+	Little Celebrations	Pearson Learning Group
Pam	D	F	41	Reading Street	Pearson
Pam & Sam at the Park	C	F	108	Carousel Earlybirds	Pearson Learning Group
Pam & Sam at the Zoo	C	F	84	Carousel Earlybirds	Pearson Learning Group
Pam & Sam Fly Over the City	C	F	80	Carousel Earlybirds	Pearson Learning Group
Pam & Sam on the Beach	C	F	94	Carousel Earlybirds	Pearson Learning Group
Pam, Pam	F	F	231	Springboard	Wright Group/McGraw Hill
Pamphleteers of the Revolution	V	I	2717	Leveled Readers	Houghton Mifflin Harcourt
Pamphleteers of the Revolution	V	I	2717	Leveled Readers/CA	Houghton Mifflin Harcourt
Pamphleteers of the Revolution	V	I	2717	Leveled Readers/TX	Houghton Mifflin Harcourt
Pan Woman	P	RF	1145	Leveled Readers	Houghton Mifflin Harcourt
Panama Canal, The	W	I	250+	Cornerstones of Freedom	Children's Press
Pancake, The	K	TL	250+	Lobel, Anita	Bantam
Pancakes	G	RF	181	Foundations	Wright Group/McGraw Hill
Pancakes	W	SF	3080	Leveled Readers	Houghton Mifflin Harcourt
Pancakes	W	SF	3080	Leveled Readers/CA	Houghton Mifflin Harcourt
Pancakes	W	SF	3080	Leveled Readers/TX	Houghton Mifflin Harcourt
Pancakes	WB	RF	N/A	Rigby Literacy	Rigby
Pancakes	G	RF	294	Sails	Rigby
Pancakes	L	I	700	Springboard	Wright Group/McGraw Hill
Pancakes for Breakfast	H	F	99	Books for Young Learners	Richard C. Owen
Pancakes for Breakfast	WB	F	N/A	DePaola, Tomie	Doubleday Books
Pancakes for Breakfast	C	RF	108	Emergent	Pioneer Valley
Pancakes for Supper	H	RF	96	Literacy 2000	Rigby
Pancakes!	F	F	106	Ready Readers	Pearson Learning Group
Pancakes, Crackers, and Pizza	C	RF	63	Rookie Readers	Children's Press
Panda Babies	C	I	31	Little Celebrations	Pearson Learning Group
Panda Bear, The	D	I	28	Rosen Real Readers	Rosen Publishing Group
Panda Puzzle, The	N	RF	250+	A to Z Mysteries	Random House
Panda, The	L	I	250+	Sunshine	Wright Group/McGraw Hill
Pandas	K	I	243	Nonfiction	Literacy Footprints
Pandas	E	I	75	Time for Kids	Teacher Created Materials
Panda's Birthday Surprise	F	F	141	Seedlings	Continental Press
Pandas Have Cubs	M	I	250+	Animals and Their Young	Compass Point Books
Pandas in the Mountains	M	F	735	PM Collection	Rigby
Pandas Nap	B	F	28	Reading Street	Pearson
Panda's Surprise	H	F	242	Little Readers	Houghton Mifflin Harcourt
Pandora Gets Jealous	U	F	250+	Hennesy, Carolyn	Bloomsbury Children's Books
Pandora's Box	Q	RF	250+	Literacy 2000	Rigby
Pandora's Box: A Greek Myth	L	TL	250+	Storyteller Chapter Books	Wright Group/ McGraw Hill
Pangaea	X	I	3186	Leveled Readers Science	Houghton Mifflin Harcourt
Panning for Gold	O	RF	825	Leveled Readers Science	Houghton Mifflin Harcourt
Pansies for Mom	G	I	56	Windows on Literacy	National Geographic
Papa Penguin's Surprise	F	RF	136	Seedlings	Continental Press
Papa's Birthday	G	RF	249	Leveled Literacy Intervention/ Green System	Heinemann
Papagayo the Mischief Maker	N	TL	250+	McDermott, Gerald	Harcourt Trade
Papa's Spaghetti	G	F	248	Literacy 2000	Rigby
Paper Art	C	I	29	Little Celebrations	Pearson Learning Group

* Collection of short stories
# Graphic text

TITLE	LEVEL	GENRE	WORD COUNT	AUTHOR / SERIES	PUBLISHER / DISTRIBUTOR
Paper Bag Trail	E	RF	67	Schreiber, Anne; Doughty, A.	Scholastic
Paper Bag, The	D	RF	82	Books for Young Learners	Richard C. Owen
Paper Birds, The	K	RF	363	Foundations	Wright Group/McGraw Hill
Paper Capers	Q	I	250+	Storyteller - Raging Rivers	Wright Group/ McGraw Hill
Paper Chains to Ten	E	RF	139	InfoTrek	ETA Cuisenaire
Paper Crane, The	M	F	250+	Soar To Success	Houghton Mifflin Harcourt
Paper Crunch	K	I	250+	Rigby Literacy	Rigby
Paper Lanterns	N	F	250+	Czernecki, Stefan	Charlesbridge
Paper Patchwork	F	I	54	Pacific Literacy	Pacific Learning
Paper Pictures	H	I	196	Sun Sprouts	ETA Cuisenaire
Paper Route, The	K	RF	314	New Way Green	Steck-Vaughn
Paper Shapes	N	I	250+	Voyages	SRA/McGraw Hill
Paper Theater	Q	I	1275	Vocabulary Readers	Houghton Mifflin Harcourt
Paper Theater	Q	I	1275	Vocabulary Readers/CA	Houghton Mifflin Harcourt
Paper Trail, The	I	RF	253	Windmill Books	Rigby
Paper Wagon, The	M	TL	250+	Orca Echoes	Orca Book Publishers
Paperboy, The	N	RF	373	Pilkey, Dav	Orchard Books
Parachute Adventure	O	F	1868	Take Two Books	Wright Group/ McGraw Hill
Parachutes	J	RF	145	Storyteller-Moon Rising	Wright Group/McGraw Hill
Parade in Valencia	K	RF	214	Leveled Readers Language Support	Houghton Mifflin Harcourt
Parade, The	A	RF	32	Leveled Literacy Intervention/ Orange System	Heinemann
Parade, The	B	I	56	Leveled Readers Emergent	Houghton Mifflin Harcourt
Parade, The	B	RF	67	PM Plus Starters	Rigby
Parades!	C	I	24	Pair-It Books	Steck-Vaughn
Parakeet Girl, The	J	F	250+	Sadler, Marilyn	Random House
Parakeets	J	I	250+	PM Animal Facts: Orange	Rigby
Parallel Universe of Liars, The	Z+	RF	250+	Johnson, Kathleen Jeffrie	Millbrook Press
Paramedics to the Rescue: When Every Second Counts	U	I	250+	High Five Reading	Red Brick Learning
Parasites: Nature's Stowaways	S	I	250+	Orbit Chapter Books	Pacific Learning
Pardon? Said the Giraffe	F	F	123	West, Colin	Harper & Row
Parents	C	I	60	Pebble Books	Capstone Press
Parents' Night Fright	K	RF	250+	Levy, Elizabeth	Scholastic
Park for Everyone, A	L	I	668	Gear Up!	Wright Group/ McGraw Hill
Park Rangers	M	I	250+	Community Helpers	Red Brick Learning
Park Ranger's Day, A	H	I	195	Rosen Real Readers	Rosen Publishing Group
Park Soccer	N	RF	250+	Boyz Rule!	Mondo
Park Train, The	D	RF	88	Springboard	Wright Group/McGraw Hill
Park, The	A	RF	40	Leveled Literacy Intervention/ Orange System	Heinemann
Park, The	A	I	32	Rigby Flying Colors	Rigby
Park, The	G	RF	155	Windows on Literacy	National Geographic
Parker's Problem	P	RF	850	Leveled Readers	Houghton Mifflin Harcourt
Parker's Problem	P	RF	850	Leveled Readers/CA	Houghton Mifflin Harcourt
Parker's Problem	P	RF	850	Leveled Readers/TX	Houghton Mifflin Harcourt
Park's Quest	U	RF	250+	Paterson, Katherine	Puffin/Penguin
Parrot in the Bat's Cave	E	F	152	Sails	Rigby
Parrot Talk	K	RF	250+	Cambridge Reading	Pearson Learning Group
Parrotfish	G	I	51	Ocean Life	Capstone Press
Parrots	J	I	94	Pebble Books	Red Brick Learning
Parrots	I	I	181	Sails	Rigby
Parrots: Colorful Birds	M	I	250+	The Wild World of Animals	Capstone Press

* Collection of short stories
\# Graphic text

TITLE	LEVEL	GENRE	WORD COUNT	AUTHOR / SERIES	PUBLISHER / DISTRIBUTOR
Part of the Sky, A	Z	HF	250+	Peck, Robert Newton	Random House
Part of the Team	I	RF	288	InfoTrek	ETA Cuisenaire
Partners	L	I	159	Home Connection Collection	Rigby
Parts Make Up a Whole	J	I	219	Early Connections	Benchmark Education
Parts of a Plant	K	I	164	Phonics Readers	Compass Point Books
Parts of a Whole	G	I	161	Early Connections	Benchmark Education
Parts of a Whole	M	I	250+	Yellow Umbrella Books	Capstone Press
Parts of Ecosystems	R	I	1504	Science Support Readers	Houghton Mifflin Harcourt
Party Clothes	E	RF	132	Jasper the Cat	Pioneer Valley
Party Clown, The	F	RF	182	PM Photo Stories	Rigby
Party Food	A	I	25	Rigby Focus	Rigby
Party for a Rabbit, A	C	F	70	Early Connections	Benchmark Education
Party for Bear, A	B	F	27	Gear Up!	Wright Group/McGraw Hill
Party for Brown Mouse, A	E	F	149	PM Plus Story Books	Rigby
Party for Panda, A	G	I	162	Leveled Literacy Intervention/ Blue System	Heinemann
Party for Pedro, A	F	RF	87	Reading Street	Pearson
Party Game, The	G	RF	115	Home Connection Collection	Rigby
Party Games	J	RF	399	Foundations	Wright Group/McGraw Hill
Party Girl	Z+	RF	250+	Ewing, Lynne	Random House
Party Hats	B	RF	72	PM Plus Starters	Rigby
Party Is Here, The	A	RF	32	Literacy by Design	Rigby
Party Time	J	I	250+	Rigby Literacy	Rigby
Party Time at the Milky Way	I	F	160	Sunshine	Wright Group/McGraw Hill
Party, A	A	RF	28	Leveled Readers Emergent	Houghton Mifflin Harcourt
Party, A	LB	RF	14	Story Box	Wright Group/McGraw Hill
Party, The	F	RF	56	Book Bus	Creative Edge
Party, The	B	RF	93	First Stories	Pacific Learning
Party, The	D	RF	26	Ready Readers	Pearson Learning Group
Party, The	A	F	24	Sails	Rigby
Paru Has a Bath	J	RF	242	Pacific Literacy	Pacific Learning
Parvana's Journey	W	RF	250+	Ellis, Deborah	Douglas & McIntyre
Pasquale's Gift	J	RF	250+	Voyages	SRA/McGraw Hill
Pass the Pasta, Please	D	I	63	Storyteller-Setting Sun	Wright Group/McGraw Hill
Pass the Pasta, Please!	C	I	45	Johns, Linda	Scholastic
Pass the Present	C	F	86	Storyteller-First Snow	Wright Group/McGraw Hill
Passage to Freedom: The Sugihara Story	U	B	250+	Mochizuki, Ken	Lee & Low Books Inc.
Passage, The	Z	HF	250+	Killgore, James	Peachtree
Passager: The Young Merlin Trilogy	V	F	250+	Yolen, Jane	Scholastic
Passing Poetry	R	RF	785	Leveled Readers	Houghton Mifflin Harcourt
Passover	K	I	152	Holidays and Celebrations	Capstone Press
Passover	O	I	250+	Holidays and Festivals	Compass Point Books
Passover	O	I	1579	On My Own Holidays	Lerner Publications
Passport to Earth	P	I	250+	Sails	Rigby
Pasta	N	I	250+	Little Celebrations	Pearson Learning Group
Pasta	I	I	125	Rigby Rocket	Rigby
Pat and Nat	A	RF	21	Rigby Star	Rigby
Pat and Pea Soup	J	RF	187	Books for Young Learners	Richard C. Owen
Pat and Pig	B	F	34	Leveled Readers	Houghton Mifflin Harcourt
Pat Mora, the Storyteller	L	B	278	Vocabulary Readers	Houghton Mifflin Harcourt
Pat Mora: Two Languages, One Poet	P	B	769	Leveled Readers	Houghton Mifflin Harcourt
Pat the Penguin	C	F	23	Reading Street	Pearson
Pat, Pat, Pat	B	RF	37	Book Bank	Wright Group/McGraw Hill
Patches	M	RF	250+	Szymanski, Lois	Avon Camelot

P

TITLE	LEVEL	GENRE	WORD COUNT	AUTHOR / SERIES	PUBLISHER / DISTRIBUTOR
Patching Up the Past	W	I	250+	WorldScapes	ETA Cuisenaire
Patchwork Path, The	R	HF	250+	Stroud, Bettye	Candlewick Press
Patchwork Patterns	G	RF	64	Little Celebrations	Pearson Learning Group
Patchwork Quilt, The	O	RF	250+	Flournoy, Valerie	Scholastic
Patent Process, The	U	I	2067	Reading Street	Pearson
Path to Frog's New Home, The	E	RF	118	Reading Street	Pearson
Pathfinder: Mission to Mars	P	I	250+	Rigby Literacy	Rigby
Paths to Freedom	S	I	250+	Reading Expeditions	National Geographic
Patience	M	I	250+	Everyday Character Education	Capstone Press
Patrick and the Leprechaun	L	F	677	PM Collection	Rigby
Patrick Doyle Is Full of Blarney	O	HF	250+	Armstrong, Jennifer	Random House
Patrick Henry	S	B	250+	Amazing Americans	Wright Group/McGraw Hill
Patrick Henry	S	B	3990	History Maker Bios	Lerner Publications
Patron Saint of Butterflies, The	Z	RF	250+	Galante, Cecilia	Bloomsbury Children's Books
Pat's New Puppy	E	RF	88	Reading Unlimited	Pearson Learning Group
Pat's Perfect Pizza	C	RF	37	Ready Readers	Pearson Learning Group
Pat's Picture	G	RF	243	Take Two Books	Wright Group/McGraw Hill
Pat's Train	D	RF	22	KinderReaders	Rigby
Patsy Mink	W	I	2489	Leveled Readers	Houghton Mifflin Harcourt
Patsy Mink	W	I	2489	Leveled Readers/CA	Houghton Mifflin Harcourt
Patsy Mink	W	I	2489	Leveled Readers/TX	Houghton Mifflin Harcourt
Patsy Mink and Title IX	W	I	2170	Leveled Readers	Houghton Mifflin Harcourt
Patsy Mink and Title IX	W	I	2170	Leveled Readers/CA	Houghton Mifflin Harcourt
Patsy Mink and Title IX	W	I	2170	Leveled Readers/TX	Houghton Mifflin Harcourt
Pattern Parade, The	F	RF	96	InfoTrek	ETA Cuisenaire
Pattern Performers, The	J	RF	624	InfoTrek	ETA Cuisenaire
Pattern Walk, A	C	I	79	InfoTrek	ETA Cuisenaire
Patterns	C	I	32	Berger, Samantha; Moreton, Daniel	Scholastic
Patterns	C	I	35	Discovery Links	Newbridge
Patterns	A	I	24	In Step Readers	Rigby
Patterns	E	I	57	Literacy 2000	Rigby
Patterns	J	I	122	Spyglass Books	Compass Point Books
Patterns	C	I	57	Story Steps	Rigby
Patterns	K	I	307	Yellow Umbrella Books	Red Brick Learning
Patterns All Around	B	I	55	Early Connections	Benchmark Education
Patterns All Around	E	I	36	Shutterbug Books	Steck-Vaughn
Patterns All Around Me	E	I	181	Learn to Read	Creative Teaching Press
Patterns Are Fun!	C	I	35	Story Steps	Rigby
Patterns: What Comes Next?	L	I	250+	Exploring Math	Capstone Press
Patty and Pop's Picnic	C	RF	57	Little Books	Sadlier-Oxford
Paul	F	I	54	Pacific Literacy	Pacific Learning
Paul and Lucy	J	RF	250+	Stepping Stones	Nelson/Michaels Assoc.
Paul Bunyan	J	TL	250+	Jumbled Tumbled Tales & Rhymes	Rigby
Paul Bunyan	N	TL	1831	On My Own Folklore	Lerner Publications
Paul Bunyan	N	TL	250+	Tall Tales	Compass Point Books
Paul Cezanne	R	B	250+	Venezia, Mike	Children's Press
Paul Gauguin	R	B	250+	Venezia, Mike	Children's Press
Paul Harvey's the Rest of the Story	Z	I	250+	Harvey, Jr., Paul	Bantam
Paul Klee	R	B	250+	Venezia, Mike	Children's Press
Paul Laurence Dunbar, Poet	S	B	542	Vocabulary Readers	Houghton Mifflin Harcourt
Paul Revere	V	B	250+	Cornerstones of Freedom	Children's Press

* Collection of short stories
# Graphic text

TITLE	LEVEL	GENRE	WORD COUNT	AUTHOR / SERIES	PUBLISHER / DISTRIBUTOR
Paul Revere	N	B	237	First Biographies	Capstone Press
Paul Revere	S	B	3318	History Maker Bios	Lerner Publications
Paul Revere and the American Revolution	T	B	2218	Reading Street	Pearson
Paul Revere, Hero on Horseback	T	B	1292	Vocabulary Readers/CA	Houghton Mifflin Harcourt
Paul Revere, Hero on Horseback	T	B	1292	Vocabulary Readers/TX	Houghton Mifflin Harcourt
Paul Revere, Rider of the Revolution	T	B	1292	Vocabulary Readers	Houghton Mifflin Harcourt
Paul Revere's Midnight Ride	S	I	1177	Reading Street	Pearson
Paul Revere's Ride	S	HF	250+	Literacy 2000	Rigby
Paul Revere's Ride	T	I	250+	We The People	Compass Point Books
Paul Robeson	U	B	250+	Amazing Americans	Wright Group/McGraw Hill
Paul the Artist	P	RF	1356	Leveled Readers	Houghton Mifflin Harcourt
Paul the Pitcher	D	RF	86	Rookie Readers	Children's Press
Paula's Pickle Picnic	K	RF	688	Underwood, Barbara J.	Kaeden Books
Paulo the Pilot	C	RF	62	Reading Safari	Mondo
Paulo the Pilot	F	F	131	Windmill Books	Rigby
Paul's Day at School	B	I	38	Little Books for Early Readers	University of Maine
Pawnee Nation, The	P	I	250+	Native Peoples	Red Brick Learning
Pawpaw Patch	F	TL	174	PM Readalongs	Rigby
Paws and Claws and Other Stories	D	F	120	Story Steps	Rigby
Paws and Claws: Learn About Animal Tracks	L	I	465	Reading Street	Pearson
Pay Attention!	K	RF	458	Leveled Readers	Houghton Mifflin Harcourt
Pay Attention!	K	RF	458	Leveled Readers/CA	Houghton Mifflin Harcourt
Pay Attention!	K	RF	458	Leveled Readers/TX	Houghton Mifflin Harcourt
Pea or the Flea?, The	F	RF	66	Start to Read	School Zone
Peace Makers	V	B	250+	InfoQuest	Rigby
Peace Ring, The	L	F	250+	Cambridge Reading	Pearson Learning Group
Peaceful Protest	U	I	1710	Vocabulary Readers	Houghton Mifflin Harcourt
Peaceful Protest	U	I	1710	Vocabulary Readers/CA	Houghton Mifflin Harcourt
Peacefulness	L	I	250+	Character Education	Red Brick Learning
Peacefulness	N	I	250+	Everyday Character Education	Capstone Press
Peaches	Z+	RF	250+	Anderson, Jodi Lynn	HarperTrophy
Peaches All the Time	J	I	149	Early Connections	Benchmark Education
Peaches the Pig	E	F	120	Little Readers	Houghton Mifflin Harcourt
Peacocks	O	I	1681	Early Bird Nature Books	Lerner Publications
Peacock's Tail	L	TL	344	Leveled Readers	Houghton Mifflin Harcourt
Peacock's Tail	L	TL	344	Leveled Readers/CA	Houghton Mifflin Harcourt
Peacock's Tail	L	TL	344	Leveled Readers/TX	Houghton Mifflin Harcourt
Peanut	Q	I	250+	Selsam, Millicent	William Morrow
Peanut Butter	E	RF	60	Little Celebrations	Pearson Learning Group
Peanut Butter and Jelly	E	RF	164	Little Readers	Houghton Mifflin Harcourt
Peanut Butter and Jelly	H	I	136	Shutterbug Books	Steck-Vaughn
Peanut Butter and Jelly	G	F	156	Wescott, Nadine B.	Penguin Group
Peanut Butter Gang, The	K	F	250+	Siracusa, Catherine	Hyperion
Peanuts	K	I	250+	Rigby Literacy	Rigby
Peanuts	K	I	250+	Rigby Star Quest	Rigby
Peanuts	J	F	250+	Sunshine	Wright Group/McGraw Hill
Peanuts	J	I	149	Windows on Literacy	National Geographic
Pearl Learns a Lesson	L	F	1291	Appleton-Smith, Laura	Flyleaf Publishing
Pearl of the Soul of the World, The	Y	F	250+	Pierce, Meredith Ann	Little, Brown & Co.
Pearl, The	Z	RF	250+	Steinbeck, John	Penguin Group
Peas and Potatoes: 1, 2, 3	B	RF	44	Pair-It Books	Steck-Vaughn
Peas in a Pod	F	F	173	Cambridge Reading	Pearson Learning Group
Pebble First Guide to Horses, The	N	I	250+	Pebble First Guides	Capstone Press
Pebble First Guide to Lizards, The	N	I	250+	Pebble First Guides	Capstone Press

* Collection of short stories
# Graphic text

TITLE	LEVEL	GENRE	WORD COUNT	AUTHOR / SERIES	PUBLISHER / DISTRIBUTOR
Pebble First Guide to Rocks and Minerals, The	N	I	250+	Pebble First Guides	Capstone Press
Pebble First Guide to Spiders, The	N	I	250+	Pebble First Guides	Capstone Press
Pebble First Guide to Whales, The	N	I	250+	Pebble First Guides	Capstone Press
Pebble First Guide to Wildcats, The	N	I	250+	Pebble First Guides	Capstone Press
Pebbles	C	RF	30	Science	Outside the Box
Pecos Bill	N	TL	1965	On My Own Folklore	Lerner Publications
Pecos Bill	N	TL	250+	Tall Tales	Compass Point Books
Pedal Power	C	I	22	Pacific Literacy	Pacific Learning
Pedal Power	J	I	226	Rigby Literacy	Rigby
Pedal Power	J	I	226	Rigby Star Quest	Rigby
Peddler's Caps, The	J	TL	250+	PM Story Books-Purple	Rigby
Pedro's Gift	T	RF	250+	Reading Street	Pearson
Pedro's Journal	Q	HF	250+	Conrad, Pam	Scholastic
Pee Wee Scouts	L	RF	250+	Delton, Judy	Yearling
Pee Wee Scouts on First	L	RF	250+	Delton, Judy	Bantam
Pee Wee Scouts on Parade	L	RF	250+	Delton, Judy	Bantam
Pee Wee Scouts on Skis	L	RF	250+	Delton, Judy	Bantam
Pee Wee Scouts: A Big Box of Memories	L	RF	250+	Delton, Judy	Bantam
Pee Wee Scouts: A Pee Wee Christmas	L	RF	250+	Delton, Judy	Bantam
Pee Wee Scouts: Bad, Bad Bunnies	L	RF	250+	Delton, Judy	Bantam
Pee Wee Scouts: Blue Skies, French Fries	L	RF	250+	Delton, Judy	Bantam
Pee Wee Scouts: Bookworm Buddies	L	RF	250+	Delton, Judy	Bantam
Pee Wee Scouts: Camp Ghost Away	L	RF	250+	Delton, Judy	Bantam
Pee Wee Scouts: Computer Clues	L	RF	250+	Delton, Judy	Bantam
Pee Wee Scouts: Cookies and Crutches	L	RF	250+	Delton, Judy	Bantam
Pee Wee Scouts: Eggs with Legs	L	RF	250+	Delton, Judy	Bantam
Pee Wee Scouts: Fishy Wishes	L	RF	250+	Delton, Judy	Bantam
Pee Wee Scouts: Greedy Groundhogs	L	RF	250+	Delton, Judy	Bantam
Pee Wee Scouts: Grumpy Pumpkins	L	RF	250+	Delton, Judy	Bantam
Pee Wee Scouts: Halloween Helpers	L	RF	250+	Delton, Judy	Bantam
Pee Wee Scouts: Lights, Action, Land-Ho!	L	RF	250+	Delton, Judy	Bantam
Pee Wee Scouts: Lucky Dog Days	L	RF	250+	Delton, Judy	Bantam
Pee Wee Scouts: Moans and Groans and Dinosaur Bones	L	RF	250+	Delton, Judy	Bantam
Pee Wee Scouts: Molly for Mayor	L	RF	250+	Delton, Judy	Bantam
Pee Wee Scouts: Peanut-Butter Pilgrims	L	RF	250+	Delton, Judy	Bantam
Pee Wee Scouts: Pedal Power	L	RF	250+	Delton, Judy	Bantam
Pee Wee Scouts: Pee Wee Pool Party	L	RF	250+	Delton, Judy	Bantam
Pee Wee Scouts: Piles of Pets	L	RF	250+	Delton, Judy	Bantam
Pee Wee Scouts: Planet Pee Wee	L	RF	250+	Delton, Judy	Bantam
Pee Wee Scouts: Rosy Noses, Freezing Toes	L	RF	250+	Delton, Judy	Bantam
Pee Wee Scouts: Send in the Clowns	L	RF	250+	Delton, Judy	Bantam
Pee Wee Scouts: Sky Babies	L	RF	250+	Delton, Judy	Bantam
Pee Wee Scouts: Sonny's Secret	L	RF	250+	Delton, Judy	Bantam
Pee Wee Scouts: Spring Sprouts	L	RF	250+	Delton, Judy	Bantam
Pee Wee Scouts: Stage Frightened	L	RF	250+	Delton, Judy	Bantam
Pee Wee Scouts: Super Duper Pee Wee!	L	RF	250+	Delton, Judy	Bantam
Pee Wee Scouts: Teeny Weeny Zucchinis	L	RF	250+	Delton, Judy	Bantam
Pee Wee Scouts: That Mushy Stuff	L	RF	250+	Delton, Judy	Bantam
Pee Wee Scouts: The Pee Wee Jubilee	L	RF	250+	Delton, Judy	Bantam
Pee Wee Scouts: The Pooped Troop	L	RF	250+	Delton, Judy	Bantam
Pee Wee Scouts: Trash Bash	L	RF	250+	Delton, Judy	Bantam
Pee Wee Scouts: Tricks and Treats	L	RF	250+	Delton, Judy	Bantam
Pee Wee Scouts: Wild, Wild West	L	RF	250+	Delton, Judy	Bantam

P

* Collection of short stories
# Graphic text

TITLE	LEVEL	GENRE	WORD COUNT	AUTHOR / SERIES	PUBLISHER / DISTRIBUTOR
Peek-a-boo	F	F	131	Storyworlds	Heinemann Educational Publishers
Peek-a-boo at the Zoo	E	F	49	New Reader Series	Bungalo Books
Peeking Prairie Dogs	K	I	372	Pull Ahead Books	Lerner Publications
Pele	H	B	36	Canizares, Susan; Berger, Samantha	Scholastic
Pelicans, Cormorants, and Their Kin	T	I	250+	Animals in Order	Franklin Watts
Pemba's Song: A Ghost Story	Y	F	250+	Nelson, Marilyn & Hegamin, Tonya C.	Scholastic
Pen and a Painting, A	S	TL	1444	Leveled Readers	Houghton Mifflin Harcourt
Pen and a Painting, A	S	TL	1444	Leveled Readers/CA	Houghton Mifflin Harcourt
Pen and a Painting, A	S	TL	1444	Leveled Readers/TX	Houghton Mifflin Harcourt
Pen Is Mightier Than the Sword, The	Q	RF	250+	Mazer, Anne	Scholastic
Pen Pals	D	RF	92	Bookshop	Mondo
Pen Pals	K	RF	589	Leveled Literacy Intervention/Blue System	Heinemann
Pen Pals	J	RF	250+	On Our Way to English	Rigby
Penalty, The	Z+	F	250+	Peet, Mal	Candlewick Press
Pencil, The	B	I	97	PM Starters	Rigby
Penderwicks, The: A Summer Tale of Four Sisters, Two Rabbits, and a Very Interesting Boy	T	RF	250+	Birdsall, Jane	Yearling
Penguin and the Pea, The	M	TL	250+	Perlman, Janet	Scholastic
Penguin Chick Grows Up, A	J	I	744	Baby Animals	Carolrhoda Books
Penguin Chick, The	I	I	105	Windows on Literacy	National Geographic
Penguin Family, The	J	I	301	Leveled Readers	Houghton Mifflin Harcourt
Penguin Parents	Q	I	250+	Explorer Books-Pathfinder	National Geographic
Penguin Parents	P	I	250+	Explorer Books-Pioneer	National Geographic
Penguin Pete	L	F	250+	Pfister, Marcus	North-South Books
Penguin Rescue	L	RF	250+	PM Story Books	Rigby
Penguin, The	O	I	250+	Crewe, Sabrina	Steck-Vaughn
Penguins	O	I	1696	Early Bird Nature Books	Lerner Publishing
Penguins	O	I	250+	First Reports	Compass Point Books
Penguins	O	I	250+	Holmes, Kevin J.	Red Brick Learning
Penguins	J	I	311	Leveled Readers	Houghton Mifflin Harcourt
Penguins	J	I	311	Leveled Readers/CA	Houghton Mifflin Harcourt
Penguins	J	I	311	Leveled Readers/TX	Houghton Mifflin Harcourt
Penguins	H	I	106	Polar Animals	Capstone Press
Penguins	L	I	250+	Reed, Janet	Scholastic
Penguins	D	I	250+	Rosen Real Readers	Rosen Publishing Group
Penguins	K	I	265	Take Two Books	Wright Group/McGraw Hill
Penguins	H	I	109	Under the Sea	Capstone Press
Penguins	O	I	250+	Woolley, M.; Pigdon, K.	Mondo
Penguins Are Waterbirds	K	I	250+	Bookshop	Mondo
Penguin's Chicks	D	I	38	Pacific Literacy	Pacific Learning
Penguins of the Galápagos	P	I	250+	Young Readers' Series	Barron's Educational
Penguins on Parade	O	F	250+	Little Celebrations	Pearson Learning Group
Penguins On Parade	P	I	1593	Reading Street	Pearson
Penguins on the Go	D	I	24	Shutterbug Books	Steck-Vaughn
Penguins!	N	I	250+	Gibbons, Gail	Holiday House
Peninsulas	N	I	250+	Earthforms	Capstone Press
Pennsylvania	T	I	250+	Hello U.S.A.	Lerner Publications
Pennsylvania	Q	I	250+	One Nation	Capstone Press
Pennsylvania	T	I	250+	Theme Sets	National Geographic
Pennsylvania	R	I	250+	This Land Is Your Land	Compass Point Books

* Collection of short stories
# Graphic text

TITLE	LEVEL	GENRE	WORD COUNT	AUTHOR / SERIES	PUBLISHER / DISTRIBUTOR
Pennsylvania Colony, The	R	I	250+	The American Colonies	Capstone Press
Penny Candy	K	I	250+	Early Connections	Benchmark Education
Penny Changes the Day, A	J	RF	250+	Pair-It Books	Steck-Vaughn
Penny Pulls the Plug	J	F	407	Rigby Gigglers	Rigby
Penny's Plane	B	RF	30	Gear Up!	Wright Group/McGraw Hill
People and Places	R	I	250+	Rigby Focus	Rigby
People and Places	H	I	240	Yellow Umbrella Books	Red Brick Learning
People and the Environment	I	I	214	Ecology	Lerner Publications
People Are Living Things	K	I	250+	Home Connection Collection	Rigby
People Are Working	E	I	71	Pacific Literacy	Pacific Learning
People at Work	J	I	250+	Momentum Literacy Program	Troll Associates
People Build Dams	F	I	46	Windows on Literacy	National Geographic
People Can Build	E	I	46	Sunshine	Wright Group/McGraw Hill
People Change the Land	H	I	222	Yellow Umbrella Books	Red Brick Learning
*People Could Fly, American Black Folktales	X	TL	250+	Hamilton, Virginia	Alfred A. Knopf
People Dance	E	I	46	Wonder World	Wright Group/McGraw Hill
People Do Silly Things	F	RF	119	Worthington, Lisa & Moon, Susan	Kaeden Books
People from the Past	R	I	250+	Explorers	Wright Group/McGraw Hill
People Go Up	A	I	18	Windows on Literacy	National Geographic
People in Fall	F	I	86	All About Fall	Capstone Press
People in My Town	A	I	36	Rosen Real Readers	Rosen Publishing Group
People in Stories	G	RF	114	Breakthrough	Longman Group UK
People in the Rain Forest	O	I	250+	Pirotta, Saviour	Steck-Vaughn
People in the Town	D	I	91	Vocabulary Readers	Houghton Mifflin Harcourt
People in the Town	D	I	91	Vocabulary Readers/CA	Houghton Mifflin Harcourt
People in the Town	D	I	91	Vocabulary Readers/TX	Houghton Mifflin Harcourt
People in Winter	H	I	96	All About Winter	Capstone Press
People Live Here	F	I	42	Windows on Literacy	National Geographic
People Live in the Desert	J	I	163	Windows on Literacy	National Geographic
People of Action	Q	I	250+	Literacy by Design	Rigby
People of the Amazon Rain Forest	V	I	2381	Reading Street	Pearson
People of the Amazon Rain Forest, The	W	I	250+	Explore More	Wright Group/McGraw Hill
People of the Breaking Day	T	I	250+	Sewall, Marcia	Aladddin Paperbacks
People of the Ice Age	K	I	286	Rigby Focus	Rigby
People of the Pacific Rim	S	I	250+	InfoQuest	Rigby
People of the Past	Q	I	250+	Explorer Books-Pathfinder	National Geographic
People of the Past	P	I	250+	Explorer Books-Pioneer	National Geographic
People of the Past	W	I	250+	InfoQuest	Rigby
People on the Beach	F	RF	87	Carousel Readers	Pearson Learning Group
People on the Move	Q	I	250+	iOpeners	Pearson Learning Group
People Parts	B	I	42	Independent Readers Science	Houghton Mifflin Harcourt
People Patterns	K	I	348	Finding Patterns	Capstone Press
People Planet, The	V	I	250+	Orbit Chapter Books	Pacific Learning
People Power: Buying and Selling in the United States	U	I	250+	In Step Readers	Rigby
People Power: Buying and Selling in the United States	U	I	250+	Literacy By Design	Rigby
People Say Hello	C	I	37	Learn to Read	Creative Teaching Press
People Use Tools	A	I	24	Early Connections	Benchmark Education
People Who Help Us	D	I	62	Foundations	Wright Group/McGraw Hill
People Who Keep You Safe	C	I	84	Careers Series	Benchmark Education
People Who Lead Us	I	I	155	Windows on Literacy	National Geographic
People Who Save Animals	E	I	143	Careers Series	Benchmark Education

* Collection of short stories
\# Graphic text

TITLE	LEVEL	GENRE	WORD COUNT	AUTHOR / SERIES	PUBLISHER / DISTRIBUTOR
People Who Traveled with Lewis and Clark, The	N	B	555	Leveled Readers Social Studies	Houghton Mifflin Harcourt
People Who Use Magnets at Work	H	I	148	Early Connections	Benchmark Education
People Work	G	I	232	Yellow Umbrella Books	Red Brick Learning
People Work at the Supermarket	E	I	77	Windows on Literacy	National Geographic
People, Plants, and Animals	H	I	154	InfoTrek	ETA Cuisenaire
People's President, The	R	B	1372	Leveled Readers	Houghton Mifflin Harcourt
People's President, The	R	B	1372	Leveled Readers/CA	Houghton Mifflin Harcourt
People's President, The	R	B	1372	Leveled Readers/TX	Houghton Mifflin Harcourt
Pepper Goes to School	H	RF	125	Foundations	Wright Group/McGraw Hill
Pepper Sees Me	A	I	28	Little Books for Early Readers	University of Maine
Pepperland	Z	RF	250+	Delaney, Mark	Peachtree
Peppers	D	I	32	Rise & Shine	Hampton-Brown
Pepper's Adventure	H	RF	250+	PM Story Books	Rigby
Percival	I	RF	303	Literacy 2000	Rigby
Perfect Cat-Sitter, The	N	RF	250+	Nagda, Ann Whitehead	Holiday House
Perfect Dog, A	J	F	594	Pickles the Dog Series	Pioneer Valley
Perfect Instrument, The	O	RF	786	Leveled Readers	Houghton Mifflin Harcourt
Perfect Kite Weather	C	I	56	Vocabulary Readers	Houghton Mifflin Harcourt
Perfect Monster, The	L	F	250+	I Am Reading	Kingfisher
Perfect Paper	K	I	250+	Rigby Literacy	Rigby
Perfect Paper Planes	K	RF	250+	PM Plus Story Books	Rigby
Perfect Patterns	P	I	250+	WorldScapes	ETA Cuisenaire
Perfect Person, The	Q	SF	250+	Bookweb	Rigby
Perfect Pet, The	Q	F	250+	Bookweb	Rigby
Perfect Pet, The	C	RF	30	Instant Readers	Harcourt School Publishers
Perfect Pet, The	C	RF	29	Rigby Rocket	Rigby
Perfect Picnic, The	G	F	271	Leveled Literacy Intervention/ Blue System	Heinemann
Perfect Pizza, The	I	RF	250+	Rigby Star	Rigby
Perfect Pizza, The	G	RF	167	Windows on Literacy	National Geographic
Perfect Place to Paint, The	K	I	383	Leveled Readers	Houghton Mifflin Harcourt
Perfect Place to Paint, The	K	I	383	Leveled Readers/CA	Houghton Mifflin Harcourt
Perfect Place, The	H	RF	157	Pair-It Turn and Learn	Steck-Vaughn
Perfect Pony, A	O	RF	250+	Szymanski, Lois	Avon Camelot
Perfect Present, The	L	RF	250+	Lighthouse	Ginn & Co.
Perfect Pretzels	L	I	232	Twig	Wright Group/McGraw Hill
Perfect the Pig	L	F	250+	Jeschke, Susan	Scholastic
Peril in the Bessledorf Parachute Factory	U	RF	250+	Naylor, Phyllis Reynolds	Atheneum
Perilous Passage	S	HF	1273	Leveled Readers	Houghton Mifflin Harcourt
Perilous Passage	S	HF	1273	Leveled Readers/CA	Houghton Mifflin Harcourt
Perilous Passage	S	HF	1273	Leveled Readers/TX	Houghton Mifflin Harcourt
Perilous Road, The	U	HF	250+	Steele, William	Scholastic
Period Pieces: Stories for Girls	Z+	RF	250+	Deak, Erzsi & Litchman, Kristin Embry	HarperCollins
Periwinkle and the Cave of Courage: The Fairy Chronicles	Q	F	12100	Sweet, J.H.	Sourcebooks
Perks of Being a Wallflower, The	Z+	RF	250+	Chbosky, Jan	Simon & Schuster
Perla's Family	H	RF	207	Reading Safari	Mondo
Perlitas	I	RF	98	Books for Young Learners	Richard C. Owen
Perri Plays Possum	M	F	1276	Leveled Readers	Houghton Mifflin Harcourt
Perri Plays Possum	M	F	1276	Leveled Readers/CA	Houghton Mifflin Harcourt
Perri Plays Possum	M	F	1276	Leveled Readers/TX	Houghton Mifflin Harcourt
Perseus and Medusa	V	TL	250+	Leveled Readers Language Support	Houghton Mifflin Harcourt

P

* Collection of short stories
# Graphic text

TITLE	LEVEL	GENRE	WORD COUNT	AUTHOR / SERIES	PUBLISHER / DISTRIBUTOR
Perseus: The Hunt for Medusa's Head	W	TL	3133	Graphic Myths and Legends	Lerner Publications
Persian Cats	I	I	122	Cats	Capstone Press
Person from Planet X, The	H	F	250+	Sunshine	Wright Group/McGraw Hill
Personality Potion, The	O	F	250+	High-Fliers	Pacific Learning
Perspective: Discover the Theory and Techniques of Perspective, From the Renaissance to Pop Art	Z	I	250+	Eyewitness Books	DK Publishing
Peru	O	I	250+	Countries of the World	Red Brick Learning
Peru's Mountains	Q	I	250+	Theme Sets	National Geographic
Pesky Fly, The	A	F	35	Springboard	Wright Group/McGraw Hill
Pesky Paua, The	H	F	267	Book Bank	Wright Group/McGraw Hill
Pests and Plagues	U	I	250+	Story Surfers	ETA Cuisenaire
Pet Care	E	I	35	Chessen, Betsey	Scholastic
Pet Day	F	RF	92	Home Connection Collection	Rigby
Pet Day	G	RF	175	Instant Readers	Harcourt School Publishers
Pet Day	E	F	70	Sun Sprouts	ETA Cuisenaire
Pet Day at School	I	RF	198	City Kids	Rigby
Pet Day at School	E	I	103	Story Steps	Rigby
Pet Dogs and Working Dogs	E	I	99	Springboard	Wright Group/McGraw Hill
Pet Dreams	K	F	410	Leveled Readers	Houghton Mifflin Harcourt
Pet Fish	F	I	98	Classroom Pets	Lerner Publications
Pet for Me, A	E	RF	152	Alphakids	Sundance
Pet for Me, A	C	RF	73	Early Emergent	Pioneer Valley
Pet for Pat, A	D	RF	45	Rookie Readers	Children's Press
Pet for Sol, A	N	F	619	Leveled Readers	Houghton Mifflin Harcourt
Pet for You, A	K	I	531	Pair-It Books	Steck-Vaughn
Pet Frog	F	I	99	Classroom Pets	Lerner Publications
Pet Guinea Pig	F	I	96	Classroom Pets	Lerner Publications
Pet Hamster	F	I	93	Classroom Pets	Lerner Publications
Pet Hermit Crab	F	I	112	Classroom Pets	Lerner Publications
Pet Parade	O	RF	250+	Giff, Patricia Reilly	Bantam
Pet Parade	C	F	33	Literacy 2000	Rigby
Pet Peeves	M	RF	250+	Social Studies Connects	The Kane Press
Pet Perspectives	U	I	250+	Sails	Rigby
Pet Pictures	J	I	181	Vocabulary Readers	Houghton Mifflin Harcourt
Pet Rabbits	I	I	365	Vocabulary Readers/TX	Houghton Mifflin Harcourt
Pet Riddles and Jokes	I	F	154	Instant Readers	Harcourt School Publishers
Pet Shop	D	F	167	Story Box	Wright Group/McGraw Hill
Pet Shop, The	C	RF	32	Oxford Reading Tree	Oxford University Press
Pet Show, The	A	I	25	Leveled Readers	Houghton Mifflin Harcourt
Pet Show, The	A	I	25	Leveled Readers/CA	Houghton Mifflin Harcourt
Pet Sitters Plus Five	L	RF	250+	Springstubb, Tricia	Scholastic
Pet Store, The	A	I	49	Bookshop	Mondo
Pet Store, The	A	I	32	Leveled Literacy Intervention/Orange System	Heinemann
Pet Store, The	A	RF	32	On Our Way to English	Rigby
Pet Tarantula, The	I	I	208	Storyteller Nonfiction	Wright Group/McGraw Hill
Pet That Fits, A	M	RF	404	Leveled Readers/TX	Houghton Mifflin Harcourt
Pet That I Want, The	E	F	57	Packard, Mary	Scholastic
Pet Tricks	G	RF	208	In Step Readers	Rigby
Pet Vet	N	I	250+	Pacific Literacy	Pacific Learning
Pet Vet, The	E	RF	101	Real Kids Readers	Millbrook Press
Pet Your Pet	H	F	93	Early Readers	Compass Point Books
Pete Discovers Gravity	M	RF	947	Early Connections	Benchmark Education

* Collection of short stories
\# Graphic text

TITLE	LEVEL	GENRE	WORD COUNT	AUTHOR / SERIES	PUBLISHER / DISTRIBUTOR
Pete for President	M	RF	250+	Social Studies Connects	The Kane Press
Pete Little	G	F	222	PM Story Books	Rigby
Pete Paints a Picture	C	RF	87	Story Steps	Rigby
Pete the Parakeet	F	F	133	First Start	Troll Associates
Peter and the North Wind	L	TL	250+	Littledale, Freya	Scholastic
Peter and the Pennytree	G	F	119	First Start	Troll Associates
Peter and the Starcatchers	X	F	250+	Barry, Dave & Pearson, Ridley	Hyperion
Peter and the Wolf	J	TL	871	Big Cat	Pacfic Learning
Peter and the Wolf	J	TL	250+	PM Plus Story Books	Rigby
Peter Pan	X	F	250+	Barrie, J. M.	Aladdin
Peter Piper	E	TL	32	Jumbled Tumbled Tales & Rhymes	Rigby
Peter Salem: Hero of the Revolution	T	B	1096	Independent Readers Social Studies	Houghton Mifflin Harcourt
Peter Stuyvesant: New Amsterdam and the Origins of New York	W	B	250+	The Library of American Lives and Times	Rosen Publishing Group
Peter Tchaikovsky	R	B	250+	Venezia, Mike	Children's Press
Peter the Pumpkin-Eater	M	RF	250+	Action Packs	Rigby
Peter's Chair	J	RF	250+	Keats, Ezra Jack	HarperTrophy
Peter's Dream	I	F	186	Start to Read	School Zone
Peter's Harvest	Q	RF	1085	Leveled Readers	Houghton Mifflin Harcourt
Peter's Move	H	RF	224	Little Readers	Houghton Mifflin Harcourt
Peter's Painting	F	F	147	Bookshop	Mondo
Peter's Treasure Hunt	I	RF	280	Springboard	Wright Group/McGraw Hill
Pete's Bad Day	G	RF	164	Ready Readers	Pearson Learning Group
Pete's New Shoes	G	RF	91	Literacy 2000	Rigby
Pete's Peacock	F	RF	89	Dominie Phonics Reader	Pearson Learning Group
Pete's Secret Plan	J	F	342	Take Two Books	Wright Group/McGraw Hill
Pete's Story	L	F	250+	Literacy 2000	Rigby
Pete's Tickets	D	RF	65	Seedlings	Continental Press
Petey	O	SF	250+	High-Fliers	Pacific Learning
Pets	P	I	250+	Animals Are Amazing	Carus Publishing Company
Pets	D	I	64	Explorations	Okapi Educational Materials
Pets	D	I	64	Explorations	Eleanor Curtain Publishing
Pets	C	RF	88	Leveled Literacy Intervention/Green System	Heinemann
Pets	F	RF	56	Literacy 2000	Rigby
Pets	B	I	66	Little Readers	Houghton Mifflin Harcourt
Pets	J	I	196	Nonfiction	Literacy Footprints
Pets	J	F	90	Pacific Literacy	Pacific Learning
Pets	A	I	33	PM Starters	Rigby
Pets	B	I	31	Vocabulary Readers	Houghton Mifflin Harcourt
Pets at School	A	I	33	Leveled Readers	Houghton Mifflin Harcourt
Pets at School	A	I	33	Leveled Readers/CA	Houghton Mifflin Harcourt
Pets for the Twins	E	RF	101	Leveled Readers	Houghton Mifflin Harcourt
Pets for Us	D	I	69	Bonnell, Kris	Reading Reading Books
Pets from the Rain Forest	S	I	250+	Explore More	Wright Group/McGraw Hill
Pets in a Jar: Collecting and Caring for Small Wild Animals	W	I	250+	Simon, Seymour	Penguin Group
Pets Lost-and-Found	L	I	250+	Rigby Literacy	Rigby
Pets Need People	M	I	250+	Literacy 2000	Rigby
Pets, The	C	RF	28	Learn to Read	Creative Teaching Press
Pets, The	A	RF	24	Sails	Rigby
Petting Farm, The	E	I	67	Bonnell, Kris	Reading Reading Books

* Collection of short stories
# Graphic text

TITLE	LEVEL	GENRE	WORD COUNT	AUTHOR / SERIES	PUBLISHER / DISTRIBUTOR
Petting Gilbert	H	F	218	Gilbert the Pig	Pioneer Valley
Peyton Manning	P	B	1570	Amazing Athletes	Lerner Publications
Phan's Diary	N	RF	250+	PM Collection	Rigby
Phantom of the Water Park	Q	F	250+	Wiley & Grampa's Creature Features	Little, Brown & Co.
Phantom Robber Mystery, The	M	RF	792	Springboard	Wright Group/McGraw Hill
Phantom Striker, The	O	F	250+	Zucker, Jonny	Stone Arch Books
Phantom Tollbooth, The	W	F	250+	Juster, Norton	Bantam
Phantoms Don't Drive Sports Cars	M	F	250+	Dadey, Debbie; Jones, Marcia Thornton	Scholastic
Phases of the Moon	J	I	164	Patterns in Nature	Capstone Press
Pheasant and Kingfisher	L	TL	250+	Bookshop	Mondo
Pheasant Hunting	S	I	250+	The Great Outdoors	Red Brick Learning
Phenomena: Secrets of the Senses	Z	I	250+	Jackson, Donna M.	Little, Brown & Co.
Phenomena: Secrets of the Senses	Z	I	250+	Jackson, Donna M.	Little, Brown & Co.
Philadelphia 76ers, The	S	I	250+	Team Spirit	Norwood House Press
Philadelphia Phillies, The	S	I	250+	Team Spirit	Norwood House Press
Philadelphia, 1756	M	I	273	Vocabulary Readers	Houghton Mifflin Harcourt
Philadelphia, 1756	M	I	273	Vocabulary Readers/CA	Houghton Mifflin Harcourt
Philadelphia, 1756	M	I	273	Vocabulary Readers/TX	Houghton Mifflin Harcourt
Philadephia Eagles, The	S	I	5055	Team Spirit	Norwood House Press
Philip Hall Likes Me. I Reckon Maybe.	Y	RF	250+	Greene, Bette	Puffin/Penguin
Philippa and the Dragon	G	F	137	Literacy 2000	Rigby
Philippa Fisher's Fairy Godsister	S	F	250+	Kessler, Liz	Candlewick Press
Philippines	O	I	1482	A Ticket to …	Carolrohoda Books
Philippines, The	O	I	250+	Countries of the World	Red Brick Learning
Phillis Wheatley	S	B	250+	Amazing Americans	Wright Group/McGraw Hill
Phillis Wheatley	U	B	250+	Let Freedom Ring	Red Brick Learning
Phillis Wheatley	T	B	2200	Leveled Readers	Houghton Mifflin Harcourt
Phillis Wheatley	T	B	2200	Leveled Readers/CA	Houghton Mifflin Harcourt
Phillis Wheatley	T	B	2200	Leveled Readers/TX	Houghton Mifflin Harcourt
Phillis Wheatley	Q	B	250+	Primary Source Readers	Teacher Created Materials
Phoebe the Spy	R	HF	250+	Griffin, Judith Berry	Scholastic
Phoenix Rising	W	RF	250+	Hesse, Karen	Penguin Group
Phoenix Suns, The	S	I	4872	Team Spirit	Norwood House Press
Photo	Y	I	250+	Boldprint	Steck-Vaughn
Photo Album, The	J	RF	249	In Step Readers	Rigby
Photo Book, The	C	RF	50	PM Story Books	Rigby
Photo Contest, The	O	RF	250+	Leveled Readers Language Support	Houghton Mifflin Harcourt
Photo Time	C	RF	59	PM Plus Story Books	Rigby
Photograph, The	I	F	250+	Popcorn	Sundance
Photographic Memory	O	RF	250+	PM Collection	Rigby
Photograpy	R	I	250+	Tristars	Richard C. Owen
Photos Can Fool You!	W	I	250+	Rigby Literacy	Rigby
Photos, Photos	N	I	250+	Wildcats	Wright Group/McGraw Hill
Photosynthesis	W	I	250+	The Heinle Reading Library	Thomson Learning
Phyllis Wheatley: First African-American Poet	N	B	250+	Rookie Biographies	Children's Press
Piano Recital, The	K	RF	250+	Rigby Literacy	Rigby
Picasso	S	B	250+	Masterpieces: Artists and Their Works	Red Brick Learning
Picasso	R	B	250+	Venezia, Mike	Children's Press
Pick a Pet	C	RF	40	Little Celebrations	Pearson Learning Group

* Collection of short stories
# Graphic text

TITLE	LEVEL	GENRE	WORD COUNT	AUTHOR / SERIES	PUBLISHER / DISTRIBUTOR
Pick a Pumpkin	I	F	250+	Leveled Readers Language Support	Houghton Mifflin Harcourt
Pick Me	J	F	518	Sun Sprouts	ETA Cuisenaire
Pick Up Nick!	H	RF	219	Ready Readers	Pearson Learning Group
Picked for the Team	L	RF	709	PM Collection	Rigby
Picking a Pet	I	I	224	Sunshine	Wright Group/McGraw Hill
Picking a Pumpkin	D	I	49	Bonnell, Kris	Reading Reading Books
Picking Apples	E	RF	128	Developing Books	Pioneer Valley
Picking Apples	F	I	53	Pebble Books	Capstone Press
Picking Apples and Pumpkins	L	I	250+	Hutchings, Amy & Richard	Scholastic
Picking Blackberries	G	RF	171	Adams, Lorraine; Bruvold, Lynn	Eagle Crest Books
Picking Flowers	A	I	35	Adams, Lorraine; Bruvold, Lynn	Eagle Crest Books
Picking Up Papers	K	RF	161	City Kids	Rigby
Pickle Puss	L	RF	250+	Giff, Patricia Reilly	Bantam
Pickles and the Hole	I	F	517	Pickles the Dog Series	Pioneer Valley
Pickles Are Great	B	RF	25	Bonnell, Kris	Reading Reading Books
Pickles Gets Lost	G	RF	154	Pickles the Dog Series	Pioneer Valley
Pickles Goes to School	E	RF	90	Pickles the Dog Series	Pioneer Valley
Pickles Helps Out	F	RF	160	Pickles the Dog Series	Pioneer Valley
Pickles in My Soup	F	F	88	Rookie Reader	Children's Press
Pickup Trucks	L	I	392	Pull Ahead Books	Lerner Publications
Picky Eater, The	R	RF	1238	Leveled Readers	Houghton Mifflin Harcourt
Picky Eater, The	R	RF	1238	Leveled Readers/CA	Houghton Mifflin Harcourt
Picky Eater, The	R	RF	1238	Leveled Readers/TX	Houghton Mifflin Harcourt
Picky Prince, The	J	F	250+	Rigby Literacy	Rigby
Picnic	C	F	28	Brand New Readers	Candlewick Press
Picnic	WB	RF	N/A	McCully, Emily Arnold	Harper & Row
Picnic Boat, The	G	RF	210	PM Plus Story Books	Rigby
Picnic for Two, A	C	I	71	PM Math Readers	Rigby
Picnic in the Rain, A	D	F	158	Leveled Literacy Intervention/Blue System	Heinemann
Picnic in the Sand, A	LB	RF	14	Ready Readers	Pearson Learning Group
Picnic in the Sky, The	D	F	80	Foundations	Wright Group/McGraw Hill
Picnic Lunch, A	F	F	120	Little Dinosaur	Literacy Footprints
Picnic on the Sidewalk	F	RF	108	Seedlings	Continental Press
Picnic Plans	E	RF	144	InfoTrek	ETA Cuisenaire
Picnic Tea	I	RF	224	Stepping Stones	Nelson/Michaels Assoc.
Picnic Tree, The	H	RF	201	PM Photo Stories	Rigby
Picnic Weather	J	RF	282	Gear Up!	Wright Group/McGraw Hill
Picnic, The	E	RF	89	Adams, Lorraine; Bruvold, Lynn	Eagle Crest Books
Picnic, The	LB	RF	18	Book Bank	Wright Group/McGraw Hill
Picnic, The	LB	RF	48	First Stories	Pacific Learning
Picnic, The	B	F	38	Gear Up!	Wright Group/McGraw Hill
Picnic, The	D	RF	96	Handprints C	Educators Publishing Service
Picnic, The	G	RF	151	Home Connection Collection	Rigby
Picnic, The	A	F	32	Leveled Literacy Intervention/Green System	Heinemann
Picnic, The	C	RF	48	Teacher's Choice Series	Pearson Learning Group
Picnic, The	F	RF	122	Wonder World	Wright Group/McGraw Hill
Pictographs	K	I	250+	Making Graphs	Capstone Press
Picture Book of Abraham Lincoln, A	M	B	250+	Adler, David A.	Holiday House
Picture Book of Amelia Earhart, A	M	B	250+	Adler, David A.	Holiday House
Picture Book of Anne Frank, A	R	B	250+	Adler, David A.	Holiday House

TITLE	LEVEL	GENRE	WORD COUNT	AUTHOR / SERIES	PUBLISHER / DISTRIBUTOR
Picture Book of Benjamin Franklin, A	M	B	250+	Adler, David A.	Holiday House
Picture Book of Christopher Columbus, A	M	B	250+	Adler, David A.	Holiday House
Picture Book of Davy Crockett, A	M	B	250+	Adler, David A.	Holiday House
Picture Book of Eleanor Roosevelt, A	N	B	250+	Adler, David A.	Holiday House
Picture Book of Florence Nightingale, A	M	B	250+	Adler, David A.	Holiday House
Picture Book of Frederick Douglass, A	N	B	250+	Adler, David A.	Holiday House
Picture Book of George Washington, A	N	B	250+	Adler, David A.	Holiday House
Picture Book of George Washington Carver, A	O	B	250+	Adler, David A.	Holiday House
Picture Book of Harriet Tubman, A	P	B	250+	Adler, David A.	Holiday House
Picture Book of Helen Keller, A	M	B	250+	Adler, David A.	Holiday House
Picture Book of Jackie Robinson, A	M	B	250+	Adler, David A.	Holiday House
Picture Book of Jesse Owens, A	N	B	250+	Adler, David A.	Holiday House
Picture Book of John F. Kennedy, A	N	B	250+	Adler, David A.	Holiday House
Picture Book of John Hancock, A	Q	B	250+	Adler, David A. & Adler, Michael S.	Holiday House
Picture Book of Louis Braille, A	M	B	250+	Adler, David A.	Holiday House
Picture Book of Martin Luther King, Jr., A	M	B	250+	Adler, David A.	Holiday House
Picture Book of Patrick Henry, A	N	B	250+	Adler, David A.	Holiday House
Picture Book of Paul Revere, A	M	B	250+	Adler, David A.	Holiday House
Picture Book of Robert E. Lee, A	N	B	250+	Adler, David A.	Holiday House
Picture Book of Rosa Parks, A	P	B	250+	Adler, David A.	Holiday House
Picture Book of Sacagawea, A	P	B	250+	Adler, David A.	Holiday House
Picture Book of Samuel Adams, A	Q	B	250+	Adler, David A. & Adler, Michael S.	Holiday House
Picture Book of Simon Bolivar, A	Q	B	250+	Adler, David A.	Bantam
Picture Book of Sitting Bull, A	M	B	250+	Adler, David A.	Holiday House
Picture Book of Sojourner Truth, A	N	B	250+	Adler, David A.	Holiday House
Picture Book of Thomas Alva Edison, A	M	B	250+	Adler, David A.	Holiday House
Picture Book of Thomas Jefferson, A	N	B	250+	Adler, David A.	Holiday House
Picture Book of Thurgood Marshall, A	N	B	250+	Adler, David A.	Holiday House
Picture for Harold's Room, A	H	F	550	Johnson, Crockett	HarperCollins
Picture Numbers	V	I	250+	WorldScapes	ETA Cuisenaire
Picture of Freedom, A	T	HF	250+	McKissack, Patricia C.	Scholastic
Picture Perfect	Z	RF	250+	Alphin, Elaine Marie	Carolrhoda Books
Picture This!	U	I	250+	Bookweb	Rigby
Picture Tricks	I	I	250+	Phonics Readers Plus	Steck-Vaughn
Picture, A	C	I	58	Storyteller-First Snow	Wright Group/McGraw Hill
Picture-Perfect Pattern, A	L	RF	830	InfoTrek	ETA Cuisenaire
Pictures	E	RF	76	Teacher's Choice Series	Pearson Learning Group
Pictures in the Sky	P	I	648	Reading Street	Pearson
Pictures of Hollis Woods	V	RF	250+	Giff, Patricia Reilly	Scholastic
Pictures of Hugs	F	RF	230	Leveled Literacy Intervention/ Green System	Heinemann
Pictures of My Family	D	I	49	Gear Up!	Wright Group/McGraw Hill
Pictures to Words: The Origins of Writing	V	I	2032	Independent Readers Social Studies	Houghton Mifflin Harcourt
Pie Day	H	F	250+	Phonics and Friends	Hampton-Brown
Pie Graphs	K	I	411	Making Graphs	Capstone Press
Pie Magic	N	F	250+	Cornell, Laura	Beech Tree Books
Pie Thief, A: A Play	J	F	250+	Story Box	Wright Group/McGraw Hill
Pie, The	F	RF	117	Developing Books, Set 1	Pioneer Valley
Piece of Cake	I	I	250+	Home Connection Collection	Rigby
Pied Piper	L	TL	250+	Hunia, Fran	Ladybird Books
Pied Piper of Hamelin, The	K	TL	250+	Hautzig, Deborah	Random House

* Collection of short stories
\# Graphic text

TITLE	LEVEL	GENRE	WORD COUNT	AUTHOR / SERIES	PUBLISHER / DISTRIBUTOR
Pied Piper, The	I	TL	250+	Storyworlds	Heinemann Educational Books
Pied Piper, The	M	TL	585	Sunshine	Wright Group/McGraw Hill
Pierre	K	RF	490	Sendak, Maurice	Scholastic
Pierre August Renoir	R	B	250+	Venezia, Mike	Children's Press
Pig on the Swing	G	F	242	Reading Safari	Mondo
Pig Scrolls, The	X	F	250+	Shipton, Paul	Candlewick Press
Pig That Learned to Jig, The	I	F	140	Wonder World	Wright Group/McGraw Hill
Pig Who Saved the World, The	X	F	250+	Shipton, Paul	Candlewick Press
Pig William's Midnight Walk	H	F	354	Book Bank	Wright Group/McGraw Hill
Pig's New House	E	F	222	Leveled Literacy Intervention/ Blue System	Heinemann
Pigboy	T	RF	250+	Orca Currents	Orca Book Publishers
Pigeon Feathers	M	TL	250+	Books for Young Learners	Richard C. Owen
Pigeon Princess, The	P	F	250+	Storyteller - Autumn Leaves	Wright Group/ McGraw Hill
Piggle	K	F	250+	Bonsall, Crosby	HarperCollins
Piggy's Bath	B	F	29	Brand New Readers	Candlewick Press
Piggy's Bedtime	C	F	32	Brand New Readers	Candlewick Press
Piggy's Pictures	B	F	30	Brand New Readers	Candlewick Press
Piggy's Sandwich	C	F	36	Brand New Readers	Candlewick Press
Piglet in a Playpen	Q	RF	250+	Baglio, Ben M.	Scholastic
Piglet in a Playpen	P	RF	250+	Daniels, Lucy	Barron's Educational
Pigling: A Cinderella Story	R	TL	2527	Graphic Myths and Legends	Lerner Publications
Pigman & Me, The	Z	B	250+	Zindel, Paul	Dell
Pigman's Legacy, The	Z	RF	250+	Zindel, Paul	Harper & Row
Pignocchio	L	F	250+	Pair-It Books	Steck-Vaughn
Pigpen Party, The	I	F	186	Literacy Tree	Rigby
Pigs	C	F	29	Learn to Read	Creative Teaching Press
Pigs	L	I	250+	PM Animal Facts: Purple	Rigby
Pigs	D	I	54	Vocabulary Readers	Houghton Mifflin Harcourt
Pigs and Piglets	B	I	33	Animal Families	Lerner Publications
Pigs at Odds	L	F	250+	Axelrod, Amy	Aladdin
Pigs Have Piglets	M	I	250+	Animals and Their Young	Compass Point Books
Pig's Life, A	D	I	98	Reading Street	Pearson
Pigs Might Fly	R	F	250+	King-Smith, Dick	Scholastic
Pigs on the Farm	G	I	72	Pebble Books	Capstone Press
Pigs Peek	C	F	28	Books for Young Learners	Richard C. Owen
Pig's Tall Hat	E	F	81	Leveled Readers Language Support	Houghton Mifflin Harcourt
Pigs, The	B	TL	83	Leveled Readers	Houghton Mifflin Harcourt
Pigs, The	B	TL	83	Leveled Readers/CA	Houghton Mifflin Harcourt
Pigs, The	B	TL	83	Leveled Readers/TX	Houghton Mifflin Harcourt
Pike River Phantom, The	R	F	250+	Wright, Betty	Scholastic
Pilar Speaks Up	T	RF	1354	Leveled Readers	Houghton Mifflin Harcourt
Pile in Pete's Room, The	K	RF	745	Sunshine	Wright Group/McGraw Hill
Pilgrim Children Had Many Chores	F	I	47	Learn to Read	Creative Teaching Press
Pilgrim Voices: Our First Year in the New World	T	HF	250+	Roop, Connie & Peter	Walker & Company
Pilgrims' First Year, The	O	I	919	Reading Street	Pearson
Pilgrims of Plimouth, The	T	I	250+	Sewall, Marcia	Simon & Schuster
Pilgrims, The	V	I	250+	Cornerstones of Freedom	Children's Press
Pilgrims, The	R	I	250+	The Heinle Reading Library	Thomson Learning
Pillow Sale, The	B	F	26	KinderReaders	Rigby
Pilots	M	I	250+	Community Workers	Compass Point Books

TITLE	LEVEL	GENRE	WORD COUNT	AUTHOR / SERIES	PUBLISHER / DISTRIBUTOR
Pilots	J	I	219	On Deck	Rigby
Pin It! Fix It!	E	F	76	Phonics and Friends	Hampton-Brown
Pinata Party	C	RF	31	Bebop Books	Lee & Low Books Inc.
Pinata Time	D	RF	71	Teacher's Choice Series	Pearson Learning Group
Pinballs, The	S	RF	250+	Byars, Betsy	HarperTrophy
Pincher Martin	Z+	RF	250+	Golding, William	Harcourt Trade
Pinduli	O	F	250+	Cannon, Janell	Scholastic
Pine Hollow: Changing Leads	W	RF	250+	Bryant, Bonnie	Bantam
Pine Hollow: Conformation Faults	W	RF	250+	Bryant, Bonnie	Bantam
Pine Hollow: Reining In	W	RF	250+	Bryant, Bonnie	Bantam
Pine Hollow: The Long Ride	W	RF	250+	Bryant, Bonnie	Bantam
Pine Hollow: The Trail Home	W	RF	250+	Bryant, Bonnie	Bantam
Pine Trees	H	I	138	Pebble Books	Capstone Press
Ping-Pong	D	I	78	Nonfiction	Literacy Footprints
Ping-Pong	D	RF	89	Rigby Star	Rigby
Pink Pig	B	RF	23	Ready Readers	Pearson Learning Group
Pink: Seeing Pink All Around Us	L	I	250+	Colors	Capstone Press
Pinkeye	K	I	250+	Health Matters	Capstone Press
Pinky and Rex	L	RF	250+	Howe, James	Simon & Schuster
Pinky and Rex and the Bully	L	RF	250+	Howe, James	Simon & Schuster
Pinky and Rex and the Double-Dad Weekend	L	RF	250+	Howe, James	Simon & Schuster
Pinky and Rex and the Mean Old Witch	L	RF	250+	Howe, James	Simon & Schuster
Pinky and Rex and the New Baby	L	RF	250+	Howe, James	Simon & Schuster
Pinky and Rex and the New Neighbors	L	RF	250+	Howe, James	Simon & Schuster
Pinky and Rex and the Perfect Pumpkin	L	RF	250+	Howe, James	Simon & Schuster
Pinky and Rex and the School Play	L	RF	250+	Howe, James	Simon & Schuster
Pinky and Rex and the Spelling Bee	L	RF	250+	Howe, James	Simon & Schuster
Pinky and Rex Get Married	L	RF	250+	Howe, James	Simon & Schuster
Pinky and Rex Go to Camp	L	RF	250+	Howe, James	Aladdin
Pinky Dinky Doo Shrinky Pinky!	K	F	250+	Step into Reading	Random House
Pinky the Pig	C	RF	77	Leveled Literacy Intervention/ Blue System	Heinemann
Pinocchio	F	TL	357	Fairy Tales and Folklore	Norwood House Press
Pinocchio	J	TL	250+	Jumbled Tumbled Tales & Rhymes	Rigby
Pins in the Map	L	RF	566	Reading Street	Pearson
Pioneer Bear	L	F	250+	Sandin, Joan	Random House
Pioneer Cat	N	HF	250+	Hooks, William H.	Random House
Pioneer Families	L	I	250+	Rosen Real Readers	Rosen Publishing Group
Pioneer Girl, The Story of Laura Ingalls Wilder	R	B	250+	Anderson, William	HarperCollins
Pioneer Trails	V	I	250+	Primary Source Readers	Teacher Created Materials
Pioneer Way, The	Q	I	250+	Kummer, Patricia K.	Steck-Vaughn
Pioneering Ecologists	R	B	250+	Science Readers	Teacher Created Materials
Pioneers	T	I	250+	Sandler, Martin W.	HarperTrophy
Pioneers in Cell Biology	V	B	250+	Science Readers	Teacher Created Materials
Pioneers in Medicine	U	B	250+	Navigators Biography Series	Benchmark Education Company
Pioneers of Earth Science	T	B	250+	Science Readers	Teacher Created Materials
Pioneers of Light and Sound	W	B	250+	Science Readers	Teacher Created Materials
Pioneers: Life as a Homesteader	Q	I	250+	On Deck	Rigby
Pip and the Little Monkey	F	RF	112	Oxford Reading Tree	Oxford University Press
Pip at the Zoo	F	RF	70	Oxford Reading Tree	Oxford University Press
Pippa's Pet Pest	D	RF	35	Home Connection Collection	Rigby
Pippi Goes on Board	O	F	250+	Lindgren, Astrid	Puffin/Penguin

P

* Collection of short stories
\# Graphic text

TITLE	LEVEL	GENRE	WORD COUNT	AUTHOR / SERIES	PUBLISHER / DISTRIBUTOR
Pippi in the South Seas	O	F	250+	Lindgren, Astrid	Puffin/Penguin
Pippi Longstocking	O	F	250+	Lindgren, Astrid	Penguin Group
Piranhas	I	I	213	Sails	Rigby
Pirate	X	I	250+	Eyewitness Books	DK Publishing
Pirate Attack	N	RF	250+	Boyz Rule!	Mondo
Pirate Code, The: Life of a Pirate	T	I	250+	The Real World of Pirates	Capstone Press
Pirate Feast, The	H	F	172	Story Basket	Wright Group/McGraw Hill
Pirate Gear: Cannons, Swords, and the Jolly Roger	T	I	250+	The Real World of Pirates	Capstone Press
Pirate Hideouts: Secret Spots and Shelters	T	I	250+	The Real World of Pirates	Capstone Press
Pirate Island Adventure	N	RF	250+	Parish, Peggy	Yearling
Pirate Party	L	F	884	Big Cat	Pacific Learning
Pirate Pete and the Monster	E	F	144	Storyworlds	Heinemann Educational Publishers
Pirate Pete and the Treasure Island	E	F	145	Storyworlds	Heinemann Educational Publishers
Pirate Pete Keeps Fit	E	F	139	Storyworlds	Heinemann Educational Publishers
Pirate Pete Loses His Hat	E	F	139	Storyworlds	Heinemann Educational Publishers
Pirate Pie	M	F	250+	Orbit Chapter Books	Pacific Learning
Pirate Ships: Sailing the High Seas	T	I	250+	The Real World of Pirates	Capstone Press
Pirate Traps	K	F	370	Story Box	Wright Group/McGraw Hill
Pirate Treasure	H	F	168	Gear Up!	Wright Group/McGraw Hill
Pirate Treasure: Stolen Riches	T	I	250+	The Real World of Pirates	Capstone Press
Pirate, Big Fist, and Me, The	S	RF	10615	Gosson, M.J.	Stone Arch Books
Pirateology Handbook, The	X	HF	250+	Lubber, Captain William	Candlewick Press
Pirates	B	F	43	Big Cat	Pacific Learning
Pirates	R	I	250+	Take Two Books	Wright Group/McGraw Hill
Pirates Don't Wear Pink Sunglasses	M	F	250+	Dadey, Debbie; Jones, Marcia Thornton	Scholastic
Pirates Past Noon	M	F	250+	Osborne, Mary Pope	Scholastic
Pirate's Promise	N	RF	250+	Bulla, Clyde Robert	HarperTrophy
Pirate's Treasure, The	E	F	63	Joy Readers	Pearson Learning Group
Pirates, The	L	RF	621	Leveled Literacy Intervention/ Blue System	Heinemann
Pirates: Raiders of the High Seas	V	HF	250+	DK Readers	DK Publishing
Pita's Birthday	H	F	250+	Ready to Read	Pacific Learning
Pitch and Throw, Grasp and Know: What Is a Synonym?	O	I	246	Words Are CATegorical	Millbrook Press
Pitching Trouble	N	RF	250+	Kroll, Stephen	Avon Camelot
Pitt Street Pirates	O	F	5117	Dreary, Terry	Stone Arch Books
Pittsburgh Pirates, The	S	I	250+	Team Spirit	Norwood House Press
Pittsburgh Steelers, The	S	I	250+	Team Spirit	Norwood House Press
Pitty Pitty Pat	C	F	45	Little Celebrations	Pearson Learning Group
Pizza	C	F	24	Brand New Readers	Candlewick Press
Pizza Day	G	I	156	Springboard	Wright Group/McGraw Hill
Pizza for Carl	D	RF	66	Bonnell, Kris	Reading Reading Books
Pizza for Dinner	H	RF	164	Literacy 2000	Rigby
Pizza for Everyone	K	I	251	Pair-It Books	Steck-Vaughn
Pizza for Me	G	RF	225	In Step Readers	Rigby
Pizza Maker, The	D	RF	57	Harry's Math Books	Outside the Box
Pizza Parts	O	I	250+	Early Connections	Benchmark Education
Pizza Party!	F	RF	79	Maccarone, Grace	Scholastic

TITLE	LEVEL	GENRE	WORD COUNT	AUTHOR / SERIES	PUBLISHER / DISTRIBUTOR
Pizza Pokey	I	F	280	Pair-It Books	Steck-Vaughn
Pizza with a Twist	N	F	1684	Reading Street	Pearson
Pizza, The	D	RF	100	Foundations	Wright Group/McGraw Hill
Place Called Heartbreak, A: A Story of Vietnam	U	I	250+	Myers, Walter Dean	Steck-Vaughn
Place for a Bed, A	E	I	130	Sails	Rigby
Place for Nicholas, A	E	RF	82	Instant Readers	Harcourt Trade
Place in My Town, A	H	I	184	Vocabulary Readers	Houghton Mifflin Harcourt
Place in My Town, A	H	I	184	Vocabulary Readers/CA	Houghton Mifflin Harcourt
Place in the Sun, A	U	HF	250+	Rubalcaba, Jill	Puffin/Penguin
Place to Call Home, A	Y	RF	250+	Koller, Jackie French	Aladdin
*Place to Hide, A	Y	B	250+	Petit, Jayne	Scholastic
Place to Live, A	O	I	250+	Orbit Chapter Books	Pacific Learning
Place to Paint, A	K	I	335	Leveled Readers	Houghton Mifflin Harcourt
Place to Paint, A	K	I	335	Leveled Readers/CA	Houghton Mifflin Harcourt
Place to Sleep, A	B	F	25	Sails	Rigby
Place Value	N	I	324	Yellow Umbrella Books	Red Brick Learning
Places	C	I	88	Little Red Readers	Sundance
Places Around the World	K	I	287	Time for Kids	Teacher Created Materials
Places I Like	B	I	49	Little Red Readers	Sundance
Places in Our Town, The	D	I	108	Leveled Readers	Houghton Mifflin Harcourt
Places in Our Town, The	D	I	108	Leveled Readers/CA	Houghton Mifflin Harcourt
Places in Our Town, The	D	I	108	Leveled Readers/TX	Houghton Mifflin Harcourt
Places in the United States	J	I	200	Leveled Readers	Houghton Mifflin Harcourt
Places to Go	B	I	42	Time for Kids	Teacher Created Materials
Places to Visit	L	I	202	Windows on Literacy	National Geographic
Places We Live	L	I	383	Yellow Umbrella Books	Red Brick Learning
Places Where People Live	H	I	189	Springboard	Wright Group/McGraw Hill
Plague, The	T	F	250+	Harlen, Jonathan	Stone Arch Books
Plain and Fancy	WB	I	N/A	Vocabulary Readers	Houghton Mifflin Harcourt
Plain Girl	Q	RF	250+	Sorensen, Virginia	Harcourt Trade
Plains	J	I	262	Landforms	Lerner Publications
Plan a Party	E	I	47	Vocabulary Readers	Houghton Mifflin Harcourt
Plane Ride, The	F	I	68	Little Red Readers	Sundance
Plane Rides	G	I	160	Walker, Pamela	Scholastic
Planes and How They Work	Q	I	892	Time for Kids	Teacher Created Materials
Planes of the Past	M	I	238	On Deck	Rigby
Planes, Rockets, and Other Flying Machines	W	I	250+	Graham, Ian	Franklin Watts
Planes, Trains, and More	E	I	43	iOpeners	Pearson Learning Group
Planet Boring	P	F	250+	Cook, Nathan	Pacific Learning
Planet Earth	L	I	197	Rigby Focus	Rigby
Planet Earth Fact File	P	I	250+	Rigby Focus	Rigby
Planet of Junior Brown, The	Z	RF	250+	Hamilton, Virginia	Aladdin
Planet Patrol	V	I	250+	News Extra	Richard C. Owen
Planet Patrol: A Kid's Action Guide to Earth Care	R	I	250+	Lorbiecki, Marybeth	Two-Can Publishing
Planet Race, The	G	F	160	Take Two Books	Wright Group/McGraw Hill
Planet Watch	P	I	250+	Literacy by Design	Rigby
Planet X	L	SF	250+	Popcorn	Sundance
Planet Zogo	L	F	663	Leveled Readers	Houghton Mifflin Harcourt
Planet Zogo	L	F	663	Leveled Readers/CA	Houghton Mifflin Harcourt
Planet Zogo	L	F	663	Leveled Readers/TX	Houghton Mifflin Harcourt
Planets Around the Sun	L	I	250+	Simon, Seymour	Chronicle Books
Planets in Our Solar System	N	I	250+	Windows on Literacy	National Geographic
Planets of Our Solar System	M	I	250+	Rigby Focus	Rigby

* Collection of short stories
\# Graphic text

TITLE	LEVEL	GENRE	WORD COUNT	AUTHOR / SERIES	PUBLISHER / DISTRIBUTOR
Planets, The	Q	I	101	Explorers	Wright Group/McGraw Hill
Planets, The	M	I	250+	Gibbons, Gail	Holiday House
Planets, The	K	I	142	Out In Space	Red Brick Learning
Planets, The	L	I	95	Take Two Books	Wright Group/McGraw Hill
Planets, The	J	I	101	Wonder World	Wright Group/McGraw Hill
Planning a Birthday Party	N	I	250+	Bookshop	Mondo
Planning Dinner	H	RF	250+	Urmston, Kathleen; Evans, Karen	Kaeden Books
Plant	W	I	250+	Eyewitness Books	DK Publishing
Plant and Animal Partners	M	I	587	Early Connections	Benchmark Education
Plant Atlas	T	I	250+	Navigators Science Series	Benchmark Education Company
Plant Blossoms	M	I	250+	Look Once Look Again	Creative Teaching Press
Plant Discoveries	P	I	250+	Literacy by Design	Rigby
Plant Fruits and Seeds	M	I	250+	Look Once Look Again	Creative Teaching Press
Plant Genetics	U	I	250+	Navigators Science Series	Benchmark Education
Plant Kingdom, The	Q	I	250+	Explorers	Wright Group/McGraw Hill
Plant Leaves	N	I	250+	Look Once Look Again	Creative Teaching Press
Plant Life Cycles	L	I	670	Science Support Readers	Houghton Mifflin Harcourt
Plant Packages: A Book About Seeds	M	I	250+	Growing Things	Picture Window Books
Plant Patterns	K	I	286	Finding Patterns	Capstone Press
Plant Plumbing: A Book About Roots and Stems	M	I	250+	Growing Things	Picture Window Books
Plant Products	S	I	250+	The Life of Plants	Heinemann Educational Publishers
Plant Stems and Roots	N	I	250+	Look Once Look Again	Creative Teaching Press
Plant Systems	U	I	1177	Science Support Readers	Houghton Mifflin Harcourt
Plant That Ate Dirty Socks Goes Up in Space, The	S	F	250+	McArthur, Nancy	Avon Camelot
Plant, The	A	I	32	Sun Sprouts	ETA Cuisenaire
Planting a Garden	D	I	48	Leveled Readers Language Support	Houghton Mifflin Harcourt
Planting a Garden	E	I	62	Ready Readers	Pearson Learning Group
Planting and Growing	E	I	100	On Our Way to English	Rigby
Planting Beans and Beets	E	I	53	Leveled Readers	Houghton Mifflin Harcourt
Plants	J	I	162	Early Connections	Benchmark Education
Plants	B	I	51	Leveled Readers Science	Houghton Mifflin Harcourt
Plants	I	I	250+	Momentum Literacy Program	Troll Associates
Plants	O	I	250+	Rigby Focus	Rigby
Plants	I	I	325	Science Support Readers	Houghton Mifflin Harcourt
Plants	P	I	250+	Simply Science	Compass Point Books
Plants and Animals in Antarctica	R	I	1161	Reading Street	Pearson
Plants and Animals Live Here	F	I	54	Windows on Literacy	National Geographic
Plants and Flowers	M	I	250+	It's Science!	Children's Press
Plants and Seeds	I	I	148	Sunshine	Wright Group/McGraw Hill
Plants and Soil - A Great Partnership	P	I	250+	InfoTrek	ETA Cuisenaire
Plants and the Environment	I	I	239	Ecology	Lerner Publications
Plants Eat Meat, Too	I	I	215	Sails	Rigby
Plants Grow From Seeds	I	I	109	Phonics Readers	Compass Point Books
Plants in the Park	B	I	35	Windows on Literacy	National Geographic
Plants of My Aunt	J	F	429	Jellybeans	Rigby
Plants of the Coral Reef	W	I	1832	Leveled Readers Science	Houghton Mifflin Harcourt
Plants of the Redwood Forest	O	I	913	Leveled Readers	Houghton Mifflin Harcourt
Plants of the Redwood Forest	O	I	913	Leveled Readers/CA	Houghton Mifflin Harcourt
Plants of the Redwood Forest	O	I	913	Leveled Readers/TX	Houghton Mifflin Harcourt
Plants on My Plate	G	I	101	Windows on Literacy	National Geographic

P

* Collection of short stories
# Graphic text

TITLE	LEVEL	GENRE	WORD COUNT	AUTHOR / SERIES	PUBLISHER / DISTRIBUTOR
Plants that Eat Animals	L	I	250+	Read-About Science	Children's Press
Plants That Eat Bugs	H	I	150	Leveled Literacy Intervention/ Blue System	Heinemann
Plants We Use	R	I	250+	Navigators Science Series	Benchmark Education
Plants We Use	K	I	250+	On Our Way to English	Rigby
Plastic	G	I	93	Materials	Lerner Publications
Plateaus	J	I	267	Landforms	Lerner Publications
Platypus	P	I	1098	Short, Joan.; Green, J.; Bird, Bettina	Mondo
Platypus	P	I	1984	Take Two Books	Wright Group/ McGraw Hill
Play and Ride	C	RF	88	Leveled Literacy Intervention/ Orange System	Heinemann
Play Ball	LB	I	7	Bookshop	Mondo
Play Ball	F	RF	250+	Let's Play	Norwood House Press
*Play Ball Like the Hall of Famers: The Inside Scoop from 19 Baseball Greats	R	I	250+	Krasner, Steven	Peachtree
*Play Ball Like the Pros: Tips for Kids from 20 Big League Stars	R	I	250+	Krasner, Steven	Peachtree
Play Ball!	R	I	250+	Boldprint	Steck-Vaughn
Play Ball!	D	RF	30	Books for Young Learners	Richard C. Owen
Play Ball!	B	F	26	Brand New Readers	Candlewick Press
Play Ball!	R	I	250+	Explorer Books-Pathfinder	National Geographic
Play Ball!	P	I	250+	Explorer Books-Pioneer	National Geographic
Play Ball!	R	I	250+	Explorers	Wright Group/McGraw Hill
Play Ball!	F	RF	49	Instant Readers	Harcourt School Publishers
Play Ball!	C	I	80	Leveled Literacy Intervention/ Green System	Heinemann
Play Ball!	C	I	97	Literacy by Design	Rigby
Play Ball!	LB	I	14	Twig	Wright Group/McGraw Hill
Play Ball, Amelia Bedelia	L	F	250+	Parish, Peggy	Harper & Row
Play Ball, Kate	D	RF	39	Giant First Step	Troll Associates
Play Ball, Sherman	F	RF	88	Erickson, Betty	Continental Press
Play Date, The	G	RF	258	Leveled Literacy Intervention/ Blue System	Heinemann
Play Dough	C	RF	63	Foundations	Wright Group/McGraw Hill
Play It Again Sam	I	RF	139	Literacy 2000	Rigby
Play It Safe!	G	I	92	Phonics Readers	Compass Point Books
Play of the Day	S	RF	1485	Leveled Readers	Houghton Mifflin Harcourt
Play of the Day	S	RF	1485	Leveled Readers/CA	Houghton Mifflin Harcourt
Play the Game	R	I	250+	Orbit Collections	Pacific Learning
Play Together	B	F	25	Reading Street	Pearson
Play with Me	E	F	118	Bella and Rosie Series	Literacy Footprints
Play, Bear	G	F	219	Sun Sprouts	ETA Cuisenaire
Play, The	B	RF	33	First Stories	Pacific Learning
Play, The	A	I	32	Leveled Literacy Intervention/ Orange System	Heinemann
Play, The	L	RF	588	Leveled Readers	Houghton Mifflin Harcourt
Play, The	B	RF	52	PM Plus Starters	Rigby
Play, The	D	RF	61	Reading Street	Pearson
Play, The	C	RF	23	Rigby Literacy	Rigby
Play, The	C	RF	22	Rigby Star	Rigby
Playful Platypus, The	C	F	35	Learn to Read	Creative Teaching Press
Playground Fun	D	I	127	Early Connections	Benchmark Education
Playground in the Yard, The	G	RF	261	Springboard	Wright Group/McGraw Hill

* Collection of short stories
# Graphic text

TITLE	LEVEL	GENRE	WORD COUNT	AUTHOR / SERIES	PUBLISHER / DISTRIBUTOR
Playground Opposites	B	I	21	Pair-It Books	Steck-Vaughn
Playground Play	B	RF	39	Handprints B	Educators Publishing Service
Playground Problem Solvers	G	F	199	Learn to Read	Creative Teaching Press
Playground Science	R	I	250+	iOpeners	Pearson Learning Group
Playground, The	C	RF	108	Early Emergent	Pioneer Valley
Playground, The	A	I	16	Twig	Wright Group/McGraw Hill
Playhouse for Monster	C	F	34	Mueller, Virginia	Whitman
Playhouse, The	K	RF	197	Pacific Literacy	Pacific Learning
Playhouse, The	C	RF	34	Rigby Literacy	Rigby
Playhouse, The	F	RF	158	Springboard	Wright Group/McGraw Hill
Playing	A	RF	24	Davidson, Avelyn	Scholastic
Playing	B	RF	55	First Stories	Pacific Learning
Playing	A	I	39	PM Starters	Rigby
Playing at Home	B	RF	72	Rigby Flying Colors	Rigby
Playing at Lily's House	H	I	212	On Our Way to English	Rigby
Playing Ball	E	RF	170	Handprints C	Educators Publishing Service
Playing Dress Up	A	RF	40	Leveled Literacy Intervention/ Orange System	Heinemann
Playing Favorites	N	RF	250+	Kroll, Steven	Avon Camelot
Playing Games	F	RF	89	Phonics Readers	Pearson Learning Group
Playing in the Snow	C	RF	61	Early Emergent	Pioneer Valley
Playing It Safe	F	I	135	Early Connections	Benchmark Education
Playing Outside	A	I	36	Explorations	Okapi Educational Materials
Playing Outside	A	I	36	Explorations	Eleanor Curtain Publishing
Playing Outside	C	RF	56	PM Plus Starters	Rigby
Playing Safely	L	I	579	Pull Ahead Books	Lerner Publications
Playing Soccer	I	RF	123	Foundations	Wright Group/McGraw Hill
Playing Sports	B	I	24	Early Connections	Benchmark Education
Playing to Win: The Story of Althea Gibson	Q	B	250+	Deans, Karen	Holiday House
Playing Together	B	I	56	Leveled Literacy Intervention/ Orange System	Heinemann
Playing Together	D	I	110	Vocabulary Readers	Houghton Mifflin Harcourt
Playing Together	D	I	110	Vocabulary Readers/CA	Houghton Mifflin Harcourt
Playing with Blocks	C	RF	82	Leveled Literacy Intervention/ Orange System	Heinemann
Playing with Dad	F	RF	146	Foundations	Wright Group/McGraw Hill
Playing with Dough	D	I	94	PM Plus Nonfiction	Rigby
Playing with Milly	F	RF	151	PM Stars	Rigby
Playing with My Cat	C	RF	83	Early Emergent	Pioneer Valley
Playing with Shapes	C	I	57	InfoTrek	ETA Cuisenaire
Playing with Words	S	I	250+	Action Packs	Rigby
Playing with Words	O	B	250+	Meet The Author	Richard C. Owen
Play's the Thing: A Story About William Shakespeare, The	T	B	6778	Creative Minds Biographies	Carolrhoda Books
Playtime	C	I	49	Bonnell, Kris	Reading Reading Books
Playtime	C	F	66	Voyages	SRA/McGraw Hill
Please Don't Be Mine, Julie Valentine!	R	RF	250+	Strasser, Todd	Scholastic
Please Don't Sneeze!	I	TL	404	Storyteller	Wright Group/McGraw Hill
Please Read to Me	E	RF	98	Developing	Pioneer Valley
Please Write in This Book	Q	RF	250+	Amato, Mary	Holiday House
Please, Do Not Drop Your Jelly Beans	I	RF	180	Storyteller-Night Crickets	Wright Group/McGraw Hill
Please, Miss	H	RF	90	Cambridge Reading	Pearson Learning Group

* Collection of short stories
\# Graphic text

TITLE	LEVEL	GENRE	WORD COUNT	AUTHOR / SERIES	PUBLISHER / DISTRIBUTOR
Please, Mom!	D	RF	92	Lighthouse	Rigby
Pleased to Eat You	G	F	144	Silly Millies	Millbrook Press
Pleasing the Ghost	V	F	250+	Creech, Sharon	HarperCollins
Pledge of Allegiance in Translation, The: What It Really Means	V	I	250+	Kids' Translations	Capstone Press
Pledge of Allegiance, The	N	I	250+	American Symbols	Capstone Press
Plenty of Pets	F	RF	173	Instant Readers	Harcourt School Publishers
Plenty of Plants	E	I	89	Gear Up!	Wright Group/McGraw Hill
Plop and the Frog Tower	H	F	247	Rigby Flying Colors	Rigby
Plop!	G	F	176	Rigby Flying Colors	Rigby
Plop!	C	F	30	Story Box	Wright Group/McGraw Hill
Plop, the Water Monster	H	F	365	Rigby Flying Colors	Rigby
Plumbers	M	I	250+	Community Helpers	Red Brick Learning
Pluto	Q	I	250+	A First Book	Franklin Watts
Pluto	Q	I	250+	A True Book	Children's Press
Pluto	S	I	250+	Our Solar System	Compass Point Books
Pluto	N	I	760	Our Universe	Lerner Publications
Pluto	Q	I	250+	The Galaxy	Capstone Press
Pluto: A Dwarf Planet	J	I	157	Exploring the Galaxy	Capstone Press
Plymouth Colony, The	U	I	250+	Let Freedom Ring	Red Brick Learning
Plymouth Colony, The	T	I	250+	We The People	Compass Point Books
Plymouth Partnership, A: Pilgrims and Native Americans	R	I	250+	The Library of the Pilgrims	Rosen Publishing Group
Plymouth: Surviving the First Winter	R	I	250+	The Library of the Pilgrims	Rosen Publishing Group
Pocahontas	R	B	250+	Amazing Americans	Wright Group/McGraw Hill
Pocahontas	Q	B	250+	Early Biographies	Compass Point Books
Pocahontas	M	B	250+	First Biographies	Red Brick Learning
Pocahontas	Q	B	838	Independent Readers Social Studies	Houghton Mifflin Harcourt
Pocahontas	O	B	2137	On My Own Biography	Lerner Publications
Pocahontas	Q	B	250+	Primary Source Readers	Teacher Created Materials
Pocahontas and the Strangers	R	HF	250+	Bulla, Clyde Robert	Scholastic
Pocahontas: 1595-1617	S	B	250+	American Indian Biographies	Capstone Press
Pocahontas: Daughter of a Chief	N	B	250+	Rookie Biographies	Children's Press
Pocahontas: Peacemaker and Friend to the Colonists	M	B	250+	Biographies	Picture Window Books
Pocahontas: The Life of an Indian Princess	M	B	250+	Rosen Real Readers	Rosen Publishing Group
Pocket for Corduroy, A	K	F	250+	Freeman, Don	Scholastic
Pocket Full of Acorns, A	L	RF	250+	Beames, Michael	Pearson Learning Group
Pocket Full of Seeds, A	V	HF	250+	Sachs, Marilyn	Scholastic
Pocket Money	K	RF	835	Rigby Flying Colors	Rigby
Pocketful of Goobers, A: Story of George Washington Carver	Q	B	250+	Mitchell, Barbara	Carolrhoda Books
Pockets	D	RF	32	Visions	Wright Group/McGraw Hill
Pod of Killer Whales, A	U	I	250+	Jean-Michel Cousteau Presents	London Town Press
Poem for Grandma, A	M	RF	250+	Leveled Readers Language Support	Houghton Mifflin Harcourt
Poet from the Plains, A	N	B	353	Vocabulary Readers	Houghton Mifflin Harcourt
Poetry of Basketball, The	P	RF	250+	Leveled Readers Language Support	Houghton Mifflin Harcourt
Poggy Frog	F	F	151	Gear Up!	Wright Group/McGraw Hill
Poggy Frog and the Cows	I	F	229	Gear Up!	Wright Group/McGraw Hill
Poggy Frog and the Flies	G	F	204	Gear Up!	Wright Group/McGraw Hill
Poggy Frog's Contest	I	F	314	Gear Up!	Wright Group/McGraw Hill

* Collection of short stories
\# Graphic text

TITLE	LEVEL	GENRE	WORD COUNT	AUTHOR / SERIES	PUBLISHER / DISTRIBUTOR
Poggy Frog's Song	H	F	201	Gear Up!	Wright Group/McGraw Hill
Point Blank	Z	RF	250+	Horowitz, Anthony	Scholastic
Poison Dart Frogs	R	I	250+	Theme Sets	National Geographic
Poison Evidence	Z	I	250+	Forensic Crime Solvers	Capstone Press
Poison Pages	T	F	711	Dahl, Michael	Stone Arch Books
Poison Pen	R	RF	250+	Sunshine	Wright Group/ McGraw Hill
Poison Plate	U	RF	250+	Spirn, M. Sobel	Stone Arch Books
Poisoned Planet: Pollution in Our World	O	I	250+	On Deck	Rigby
Poisonous Animals	F	I	147	Sails	Rigby
Poland	O	I	1959	A Ticket to …	Carolrohoda Books
Polar Babies	F	I	115	Susan Ring	Random House
Polar Bear Pete	H	F	273	Leveled Readers	Houghton Mifflin Harcourt
Polar Bear Pete	H	F	273	Leveled Readers/CA	Houghton Mifflin Harcourt
Polar Bear Pete	H	F	273	Leveled Readers/TX	Houghton Mifflin Harcourt
Polar Bear, The	R	I	250+	Wildlife of North America	Red Brick Learning
Polar Bears	P	I	1807	Animal Predators	Lerner Publishing
Polar Bears	O	I	1683	Early Bird Nature Books	Lerner Publications
Polar Bears	F	I	50	Gear Up!	Wright Group/McGraw Hill
Polar Bears	F	I	77	Pebble Books	Capstone Press
Polar Bears	N	I	250+	PM Animal Facts: Silver	Rigby
Polar Bears	H	I	106	Polar Animals	Capstone Press
Polar Bears	K	I	412	Pull Ahead Books	Lerner Publications
Polar Bears	F	I	77	Story Steps	Rigby
Polar Bears	E	I	78	Vocabulary Readers	Houghton Mifflin Harcourt
Polar Bears	G	I	67	Windows on Literacy	National Geographic
Polar Bears	K	I	276	Wonder World	Wright Group/McGraw Hill
Polar Bears	N	I	250+	World of Mammals	Capstone Press
Polar Bears Past Bedtime	M	F	250+	Osborne, Mary Pope	Random House
Polar Bears: In Living Color	L	I	250+	Rigby Literacy	Rigby
Polar Climate	R	I	250+	Theme Sets	National Geographic
Polar Exploration Adventures	S	I	250+	Dangerous Adventures	Red Brick Learning
Polar Plants	N	I	250+	Life in the World's Biomes	Capstone Press
Polar Regions	N	I	250+	Habitats of the World	Pearson Learning Group
Poles Apart	J	F	250+	Rigby Literacy	Rigby
Poles Apart	J	F	250+	Rigby Star	Rigby
Poles Apart	Q	I	978	Vocabulary Readers	Houghton Mifflin Harcourt
Poles Apart	Q	I	978	Vocabulary Readers/CA	Houghton Mifflin Harcourt
Poles, The	M	I	675	Vocabulary Readers/CA	Houghton Mifflin Harcourt
Police Car	B	I	72	Leveled Literacy Intervention/ Blue System	Heinemann
Police Cars	I	I	177	Community Vehicles	Capstone Press
Police Cars	G	I	125	Mighty Machines	Capstone Press
Police Cars	L	I	466	Pull Ahead Books	Lerner Publications
Police Cars	M	I	250+	Transportation	Compass Point Books
Police Files	N	RF	250+	Sails	Rigby
Police in the Community	I	I	225	Vocabulary Readers	Houghton Mifflin Harcourt
Police in the Community	I	I	225	Vocabulary Readers/CA	Houghton Mifflin Harcourt
Police in the Community	I	I	225	Vocabulary Readers/TX	Houghton Mifflin Harcourt
Police Officer	C	I	24	Work People Do	Lerner Publishing
Police Officer Mom	E	RF	125	Joy Starters	Pearson Learning Group
Police Officers	M	I	250+	Community Helpers	Red Brick Learning
Police Officers	L	I	250+	Community Workers	Compass Point Books
Police Officers	K	I	399	Pull Ahead Books	Lerner Publications
Police Work	O	I	250+	Sails	Rigby

P

TITLE	LEVEL	GENRE	WORD COUNT	AUTHOR / SERIES	PUBLISHER / DISTRIBUTOR
Police: Then and Now	P	I	250+	Primary Source Readers	Teacher Created Materials
Politeness	M	I	250+	Character Education	Red Brick Learning
Polka Dots!	F	I	102	Little Celebrations	Pearson Learning Group
Pollution	F	I	46	Wonder World	Wright Group/McGraw Hill
Pollution Solution?	S	I	250+	WorldScapes	ETA Cuisenaire
Polly	A	RF	32	Leveled Literacy Intervention/ Orange System	Heinemann
Polly Perkins's Pictures	I	RF	377	Springboard	Wright Group/McGraw Hill
Polly's Pet Polar Bear	G	F	279	Leveled Readers	Houghton Mifflin Harcourt
Polly's Pet Polar Bear	G	F	279	Leveled Readers/CA	Houghton Mifflin Harcourt
Polly's Pet Polar Bear	G	F	279	Leveled Readers/TX	Houghton Mifflin Harcourt
Polly's Shop	E	RF	130	Ready Readers	Pearson Learning Group
Polonium's Treasure	S	RF	250+	Tristars	Richard C. Owen
Pompeii . . . Buried Alive!	N	I	250+	Kunhardt, Edith	Random House
Pompeii, The Lost City	V	I	2090	Reading Street	Pearson
Ponce de Leon: Juan Ponce de Leon Searches for the Fountain of Youth	U	B	250+	Exploring the World	Compass Point Books
Pond for Tim, A	D	RF	62	Counters & Seekers	Steck-Vaughn
Pond Hockey Challenge, The	K	RF	250+	Yevchak, Kathryn	Kaeden Books
Pond Party	D	F	33	Little Celebrations	Pearson Learning Group
Pond Where Harriet Lives, The	H	TL	151	Storyteller	Wright Group/McGraw Hill
Pond, A	LB	I	14	Discovery Links	Newbridge
Pond, The	B	I	34	Big Cat	Pacific Learning
Pond, The	C	I	25	Books for Young Learners	Richard C. Owen
Pond, The	C	F	54	Joy Readers	Pearson Learning Group
Pong Song, The	E	F	46	Rigby Star	Rigby
Ponies at the Point	Q	RF	250+	Baglio, Ben M.	Scholastic
Pony Club, The	H	RF	228	PM Photo Stories	Rigby
Pony Express Dreams	S	HF	250+	In Step Readers	Rigby
Pony Express, The	V	I	250+	Cornerstones of Freedom	Children's Press
Pony Express, The	I	I	128	Independent Readers Social Studies	Houghton Mifflin Harcourt
Pony Express, The	U	I	250+	We The People	Compass Point Books
Pony for Jeremiah, A	R	HF	250+	Miller, Robert H.	Silver Burdett Press
Pony Named Shawney, A	P	RF	3075	Small, Mary	Mondo
Pony on the Porch	Q	RF	250+	Baglio, Ben M.	Scholastic
Pony Pals: A Pony for Keeps	O	RF	250+	Betancourt, Jeanne	Scholastic
Pony Pals: A Pony in Trouble	O	RF	250+	Betancourt, Jeanne	Scholastic
Pony Pals: Detective Pony	O	RF	250+	Betancourt, Jeanne	Scholastic
Pony Pals: Don't Hurt My Pony	O	RF	250+	Betancourt, Jeanne	Scholastic
Pony Pals: Give Me Back My Pony	O	RF	250+	Betancourt, Jeanne	Scholastic
Pony Pals: Good-bye Pony	O	RF	250+	Betancourt, Jeanne	Scholastic
Pony Pals: I Want a Pony	O	RF	250+	Betancourt, Jeanne	Scholastic
Pony Pals: Keep Out, Pony!	O	RF	250+	Betancourt, Jeanne	Scholastic
Pony Pals: Pony to the Rescue	O	RF	250+	Betancourt, Jeanne	Scholastic
Pony Pals: Pony-Sitters	O	RF	250+	Betancourt, Jeanne	Scholastic
Pony Pals: Runaway Pony	O	RF	250+	Betancourt, Jeanne	Scholastic
Pony Pals: The Blind Pony	O	RF	250+	Betancourt, Jeanne	Scholastic
Pony Pals: The Ghost Pony	O	RF	250+	Betancourt, Jeanne	Scholastic
Pony Pals: The Girl Who Hated Ponies	O	RF	250+	Betancourt, Jeanne	Scholastic
Pony Pals: The Lonely Pony	O	RF	250+	Betancourt, Jeanne	Scholastic
Pony Pals: The Wild Pony	O	RF	250+	Betancourt, Jeanne	Scholastic
Pony Pals: Too Many Ponies	O	RF	250+	Betancourt, Jeanne	Scholastic
Pony Parade	O	RF	250+	Baglio, Ben M.	Scholastic

* Collection of short stories
# Graphic text

TITLE	LEVEL	GENRE	WORD COUNT	AUTHOR / SERIES	PUBLISHER / DISTRIBUTOR
Pony Tails: Jasmine and the Jumping Pony	P	RF	250+	Bryant, Bonnie	Bantam
Pony Tails: Jasmine's Christmas Ride	P	RF	250+	Bryant, Bonnie	Bantam
Pony Tails: May Takes the Lead	P	RF	250+	Bryant, Bonnie	Bantam
Pony Trouble	L	RF	250+	Gasque, Dale Blackwell	Hyperion
Poochie the Poodle	F	RF	155	Gear Up!	Wright Group/McGraw Hill
Poodles	I	I	115	Dogs	Capstone Press
Pookie and Joe	K	F	250+	Literacy 2000	Rigby
Pool Boy	Y	RF	250+	Simmons, Michael	Roaring Book Press
Pool of Fire, The	V	F	250+	Christopher, John	Aladdin
Pool Pals	N	RF	250+	Girlz Rock!	Mondo
Pool, The	D	RF	129	Handprints C	Educators Publishing Service
Pool, The	D	F	141	Leveled Literacy Intervention/ Green System	Heinemann
Poopsie Pomerantz Pick Up Your Feet	P	RF	250+	Giff, Patricia Reilly	Dell
Poor Girl, Rich Girl	T	RF	250+	Wilson, Johniece Marshall	Language for Learning Assoc.
Poor Little Kittens	P	RF	1173	Leveled Readers	Houghton Mifflin Harcourt
Poor Miss Dee!	I	RF	247	Story Box	Wright Group/McGraw Hill
Poor Old Polly	F	F	111	Story Box	Wright Group/McGraw Hill
Poor Panda	WB	F	N/A	Rigby Literacy	Rigby
Poor Polly Pig	F	F	57	Start to Read	School Zone
Poor Puppy!	B	RF	52	First Stories	Pacific Learning
Poor Sore Paw, The	I	F	244	Sunshine	Wright Group/McGraw Hill
Pop . . . Pop . . . Popcorn	C	I	40	Home Connection Collection	Rigby
Pop and Robby	I	F	328	Sails	Rigby
Pop Pop and Grandpa	G	RF	194	Bebop Books	Lee & Low Books Inc.
Pop Pop Popcorn!	F	RF	207	Leveled Literacy Intervention/ Blue System	Heinemann
POP Pops the Popcorn	E	RF	60	Ready Readers	Pearson Learning Group
Pop! A Play	D	F	105	Rigby Star	Rigby
Pop! Pop! Pop!	D	RF	84	Reading Street	Pearson
Popcorn	D	F	75	Green Light Readers	Harcourt
Popcorn	LB	RF	16	Handprints A	Educators Publishing Service
Popcorn and Candy	I	I	161	Windows on Literacy	National Geographic
Popcorn Book, The	N	I	250+	DePaola, Tomie	Holiday House
Popcorn Book, The	K	I	208	Reading Unlimited	Pearson Learning Group
Popcorn Days & Buttermilk Nights	U	RF	250+	Paulsen, Gary	Penguin Group
Popcorn Fun	H	RF	217	PM Plus Story Books	Rigby
Popcorn Plants	Q	I	1852	Early Bird Nature Books	Lerner Publications
Popcorn Shop, The	J	RF	250+	Low, Alice	Scholastic
*Poppleton	J	F	250+	Rylant, Cynthia	Scholastic
*Poppleton and Friends	J	F	250+	Rylant, Cynthia	Blue Sky Press
*Poppleton Everyday	J	F	250+	Rylant, Cynthia	Scholastic
*Poppleton Forever	J	F	250+	Rylant, Cynthia	Scholastic
*Poppleton Has Fun	J	F	250+	Rylant, Cynthia	Scholastic
*Poppleton in Fall	J	F	250+	Rylant, Cynthia	Scholastic
*Poppleton in Spring	J	F	250+	Rylant, Cynthia	Scholastic
Poppy	S	F	250+	Avi	Avon
Poppy and Rye	S	F	250+	Avi	Avon
Poppy, Josh, and the Hurricane	H	RF	225	Gear Up!	Wright Group/McGraw Hill
Poppy, The	K	I	152	Pacific Literacy	Pacific Learning
Poppy's Return	S	F	250+	Avi	Harper Trophy

* Collection of short stories
# Graphic text

Organized Alphabetically by Title   **475**
Storable Database at www.fountasandpinnellleveledbooks.com

TITLE	LEVEL	GENRE	WORD COUNT	AUTHOR / SERIES	PUBLISHER / DISTRIBUTOR
Poppy's Timeline	U	RF	1759	Leveled Readers	Houghton Mifflin Harcourt
Pop's Truck	K	RF	250+	Voyages	SRA/McGraw Hill
Populations	Y	I	2006	Science Support Readers	Houghton Mifflin Harcourt
Porcupine, A	D	I	49	Wonder World	Wright Group/McGraw Hill
Porcupine's Pajama Party	J	F	250+	Harshman, Terry Webb	HarperTrophy
Porridge That Was Too Hot, The	F	TL	286	Rigby Flying Colors	Rigby
Port, The	L	I	250+	Explorations	Eleanor Curtain Publishing
Port, The	L	I	250+	Explorations	Okapi Eductional Materials
Portia and the Math Problems	N	B	250+	Leveled Readers Language Support	Houghton Mifflin Harcourt
Portland Trail Blazers, The	S	I	250+	Team Spirit	Norwood House Press
Portraits in Greatness	U	B	250+	Navigators Biography Series	Benchmark Education
Portraits of African-American Heroes	V	B	250+	Bolden, Tonya	Scholastic
Portuguese Colonies in the Americas	S	I	250+	On Deck	Rigby
Possum Babies, The	H	F	252	Sails	Rigby
Possum's Bare Tail	N	TL	770	Leveled Readers	Houghton Mifflin Harcourt
Possum's Three Fine Friends	K	F	250+	Bannister, Barbara	Kaeden Books
Postal Carrier	C	I	29	Work People Do	Lerner Publishing
Postal Workers	M	I	720	Pull Ahead Books	Lerner Publications
Postal Workers: Then and Now	P	I	250+	Primary Source Readers	Teacher Created Materials
Postcard Pest, The	M	RF	250+	Giff, Patricia Reilly	Bantam
Postcard, The	X	RF	250+	Abbott, Tony	Little, Brown & Co.
Postcards From France	N	I	250+	Arnold, Helen	Steck-Vaughn
Postcards From Kenya	N	I	250+	Arnold, Helen	Steck-Vaughn
Postcards from Pluto: A Tour of the Solar System	N	F	250+	Leedy, Loren	Scholastic
Postcards from Pop	H	RF	122	Literacy Tree	Rigby
Postcards From South Africa	N	I	250+	Dawson, Zoe	Steck-Vaughn
Postcards From Vietnam	N	I	250+	Allard, Denise	Steck-Vaughn
Postcards to Paul	G	RF	147	Windows on Literacy	National Geographic
Postman Pete	J	RF	250+	Bookshop	Mondo
*Pot of Gold, A/Clever Farmer, The	L	TL	250+	Pacific Literacy	Pacific Learning
Pot of Gold, The	J	TL	655	Big Cat	Pacfic Learning
Pot of Gold, The	I	TL	266	Reading Unlimited	Pearson Learning Group
Pot of Stone Soup, A	L	TL	250+	Ready Readers	Pearson Learning Group
Potato	N	RF	250+	Peirce, Robin	Wright Group/McGraw Hill
Potato Chips	I	RF	101	City Kids	Rigby
Potato Harvest Time	A	I	33	Little Books for Early Readers	University of Maine
Potato Pride	P	RF	1000	Leveled Readers	Houghton Mifflin Harcourt
Potato Printing	G	I	174	Sun Sprouts	ETA Cuisenaire
Potato: A Tale From the Great Depression	L	HF	250+	Soar To Success	Houghton Mifflin Harcourt
Potatoes	F	I	92	Life Cycles	Lerner Publications
Potatoes	I	I	78	Windows on Literacy	National Geographic
Potatoes on Tuesday	C	F	28	Little Celebrations	Pearson Learning Group
Potatoes, Potatoes	H	I	91	Wonder World	Wright Group/McGraw Hill
Potter in Fiji, A	N	I	453	Wonder World	Wright Group/McGraw Hill
Pouncing Bobcats	K	I	411	Pull Ahead Books	Lerner Publications
Pourquoi Tales	N	TL	523	Vocabulary Readers	Houghton Mifflin Harcourt
Powder Monkey, The	Q	HF	250+	High-Fliers	Pacific Learning
Powder Puff Puzzle, The	L	RF	250+	Giff, Patricia Reilly	Bantam
Power Machines	N	I	250+	Robbins, Ken	Henry Holt & Co.
Power of Corn, The	P	I	1092	Leveled Readers/TX	Houghton Mifflin Harcourt
Power of Gandhi, The	U	B	250+	Power Up!	Steck-Vaughn

* Collection of short stories
\# Graphic text

TITLE	LEVEL	GENRE	WORD COUNT	AUTHOR / SERIES	PUBLISHER / DISTRIBUTOR
*Power of Light, The	V	TL	250+	Singer, Isaac Bashevis	Farrar, Straus and Giroux
Power of Nature, The	K	I	274	Early Connections	Benchmark Education
Power of Our People, The	U	I	1529	Reading Street	Pearson
Power of the Wind, The	L	I	250+	Literacy by Design	Rigby
Power of Un, The	T	SF	250+	Etchemendy, Nancy	Scholastic
Power of Water, The	L	I	250+	Home Connection Collection	Rigby
Power of Wind, The	V	I	1653	Leveled Readers	Houghton Mifflin Harcourt
Power of Wind, The	T	I	1983	Leveled Readers Science	Houghton Mifflin Harcourt
Power of Wind, The	V	I	1653	Leveled Readers/CA	Houghton Mifflin Harcourt
Power Partners	T	I	250+	Literacy by Design	Rigby
Powerboats	L	I	110	On Deck	Rigby
Powerboats	N	I	464	Pull Ahead Books	Lerner Publications
Powerful People	L	I	211	Pair-It Turn and Learn	Steck-Vaughn
Powerhouse, Inside a Nuclear Power Plant	Z	I	250+	Wilcox, Charlotte	Carolrhoda Books
Power-Packed Plants	O	I	250+	InfoQuest	Rigby
Powers of Congress, The	W	I	250+	Cornerstones of Freedom	Children's Press
Powers of the Mind	Z	I	250+	Unsolved Mysteries	Steck-Vaughn
Powhatan, The: A Confederacy of Native American Tribes	S	I	250+	American Indian Nations	Capstone Press
Powwow	F	I	29	Books for Young Learners	Richard C. Owen
Powwow	Q	I	250+	WorldScapes	ETA Cuisenaire
Powwow Summer: A Family Celebrates the Circle of Life	S	I	250+	Rendon, Marcie R.	Carolrhoda Books
Powwow, The	I	RF	328	Adams, Lorraine; Bruvold, Lynn	Eagle Crest Books
Practice Makes Perfect	K	RF	250+	On Our Way to English	Rigby
Practice Makes Perfect	D	RF	111	Teacher's Choice Series	Pearson Learning Group
Prairie Danger	T	HF	1722	Leveled Readers	Houghton Mifflin Harcourt
Prairie Dogs	L	I	212	Twig	Wright Group/McGraw Hill
Prairie Dogs - Social Animals	S	I	250+	Sails	Rigby
Prairie Dogs and Their Burrows	J	I	130	Animal Homes	Capstone Press
Prairie Plants	N	I	250+	Life in the World's Biomes	Capstone Press
Prairie School	Q	I	505	Vocabulary Readers	Houghton Mifflin Harcourt
Prairie Songs	Q	HF	250+	Conrad, Pam	HarperTrophy
Prairie Town	F	I	62	Seedlings	Continental Press
Praying Mantis, The	D	I	46	Pacific Literacy	Pacific Learning
Praying Mantises	H	I	96	Bugs, Bugs, Bugs!	Red Brick Learning
Praying Mantises: Hungry Insect Heroes	U	I	250+	Insect World	Lerner Publications
Praying Mantises	I	I	78	Insects	Red Brick Learning
Preacher's Boy	T	RF	250+	Paterson, Katherine	Houghton Mifflin Harcourt
Precious Stones	T	I	1331	Leveled Readers Science	Houghton Mifflin Harcourt
Precise Patterns	U	I	250+	WorldScapes	ETA Cuisenaire
Predators	N	I	803	Springboard	Wright Group/McGraw Hill
Predators in the Rain Forest	O	I	250+	Pirotta, Saviour	Steck-Vaughn
Predators!	U	I	250+	Boldprint	Steck-Vaughn
Predicting the Weather	P	I	857	Vocabulary Readers	Houghton Mifflin Harcourt
Predicting the Weather	P	I	857	Vocabulary Readers/CA	Houghton Mifflin Harcourt
Predictions	T	RF	250+	Halliday, John	Margaret K. McElderry Books
Prehistoric Record Breakers	N	I	250+	Discovery World	Rigby
Prehistory to Egypt	R	I	250+	Journey Through History	Barron's Educational
Preparing for Lift-Off	Q	I	453	Vocabulary Readers	Houghton Mifflin Harcourt
Present for Karl, A	C	RF	81	PM Photo Stories	Rigby
Present for LaNita, A	L	RF	835	Leveled Readers Social Studies	Houghton Mifflin Harcourt

P

TITLE	LEVEL	GENRE	WORD COUNT	AUTHOR / SERIES	PUBLISHER / DISTRIBUTOR
Present for Our Teacher, A	H	I	189	Explorations	Okapi Eductional Materials
Present for Our Teacher, A	H	I	189	Explorations	Eleanor Curtain Publishing
Present From Aunt Skidoo, The	M	RF	250+	Literacy 2000	Rigby
Present, The	B	I	36	First Stories	Pacific Learning
Present, The	E	F	30	Literacy 2000	Rigby
Presentation, The	S	RF	2568	Leveled Readers	Houghton Mifflin Harcourt
Presentation, The	S	RF	2568	Leveled Readers/CA	Houghton Mifflin Harcourt
Presentation, The	S	RF	2568	Leveled Readers/TX	Houghton Mifflin Harcourt
Presents	D	F	43	Storyteller-First Snow	Wright Group/McGraw Hill
Presents	H	RF	211	Storyworlds	Heinemann Educational Books
Presents for Jack and Billy	D	RF	105	PM Stars	Rigby
Presents for Mom	A	RF	18	Bonnell, Kris	Reading Reading Books
Presents, The	B	F	30	Sails	Rigby
Presidency of the United States, The	V	I	250+	American Civics	Red Brick Learning
Presidency, The	S	I	250+	A True Book	Children's Press
Presidency, The	Q	I	250+	Let's See	Compass Point Books
President for the People, A	R	B	1317	Leveled Readers	Houghton Mifflin Harcourt
President for the People, A	R	B	1317	Leveled Readers/CA	Houghton Mifflin Harcourt
President for the People, A	R	B	1317	Leveled Readers/TX	Houghton Mifflin Harcourt
President of the Underground Railroad: A Story about Levi Coffin	S	B	7965	Creative Minds Biographies	Lerner Publications
President of the United States, The	T	I	250+	Pair-It Books	Steck-Vaughn
Presidential Elections	W	I	250+	Cornerstones of Freedom	Children's Press
Presidents' Day	J	I	103	American Holidays	Lerner Publications
Presidents' Day	Q	I	250+	Holiday Histories	Heinemann Library
Presidents' Day	L	I	250+	National Holidays	Red Brick Learning
Presidents' Day	N	I	250+	Rookie Read-About Holidays	Children's Press
Press a Button	E	I	43	Windows on Literacy	National Geographic
Presto's New Pet	K	F	250+	Rigby Rocket	Rigby
Pretty Cool, For a Cat	Q	RF	1707	Leveled Readers	Houghton Mifflin Harcourt
Pretty Good Magic	J	RF	250+	Dubowski, Cathy East & Mark	Random House
Pretty in Print: Questioning Magazines	S	I	250+	Media Literacy	Capstone Press
Price of a Pipeline, The	U	I	2608	Reading Street	Pearson
Prickles the Porcupine	K	RF	430	PM Plus Story Books	Rigby
Prickly Porcupines	K	I	339	Pull Ahead Books	Lerner Publications
Pride of Puerto Rico: The Life of Roberto Clemente	W	B	250+	Walker, Paul Robert	Harcourt Trade
Pride of the Rockets	N	RF	250+	Kroll, Stephen	Avon Camelot
Primavera	X	HF	250+	Beaufrand, Mary Jane	Little, Brown & Co.
Prince Among Donkeys, A	K	RF	250+	Rigby Literacy	Rigby
Prince Amos	R	RF	250+	Paulsen, Gary	Bantam
Prince William	Q	B	250+	Rand, Gloria	Henry Holt & Co.
Prince's Carpet, The	L	TL	669	In Step Readers	Rigby
Princess Academy	V	F	250+	Hale, Shannon	Bloomsbury Children's Books
Princess and the Castle, The	J	F	250+	Leonhardt, Alice	Steck-Vaughn
Princess and the Dragon, The	C	F	20	Rigby Rocket	Rigby
Princess and the Manatee, The	O	F	1000	Leveled Readers/TX	Houghton Mifflin Harcourt
Princess and the Pea, The	J	TL	250+	Literacy by Design	Rigby
Princess and the Pea, The	I	TL	250+	Storyworlds	Heinemann Educational Books
Princess and the Pea, The	I	TL	304	Traditional Tales	Pearson Learning Group

* Collection of short stories
\# Graphic text

TITLE	LEVEL	GENRE	WORD COUNT	AUTHOR / SERIES	PUBLISHER / DISTRIBUTOR
Princess and the Peas, The	K	TL	250+	Enrichment	Wright Group/McGraw Hill
Princess and the Wise Woman, The	K	TL	250+	Ready Readers	Pearson Learning Group
Princess Bride, The	Z+	TL	250+	Goldman, William	Ballantine Books
Princess Diaries, The	Z	RF	250+	Cabot, Meg	HarperTrophy
Princess Euphorbia	N	RF	250+	SupaDoopers	Sundance
Princess for a Week	Q	F	250+	Wright, Betty Ren	Holiday House
Princess Grace of Monaco	S	B	250+	Queens and Princesses	Capstone Press
Princess in Love	Z	RF	250+	Cabot, Meg	HarperTrophy
Princess Josie's Pets	L	RF	250+	Macdonald, Maryann	Hyperion
Princess Kiko of Japan	S	B	250+	Queens and Princesses	Capstone Press
Princess Rosa's Winter	L	F	250+	I Am Reading	Kingfisher
Princess Rosa's Winter	L	F	250+	Storyteller-Shooting Stars	Wright Group/McGraw Hill
Princess Who Couldn't Cry, The	G	TL	300	Ready Readers	Pearson Learning Group
Princess Who Loved to Cook, The	M	F	250+	Cartwright, Pauline	Pearson Learning Group
Princess Who Wanted the Moon, The	M	F	250+	Lane, Sheila; Kemp, Marion	Wood Lock Educational
Princess, the Mud Pies, and the Dragon, The	I	TL	250+	Little Readers	Houghton Mifflin Harcourt
Princesses Don't Wear Jeans	M	RF	250+	Bookshop	Mondo
Principal from the Black Lagoon, The	K	F	250+	Thaler, Mike	Scholastic
Principals	J	I	546	Pull Ahead Books	Lerner Publications
Print It!	R	I	1209	Vocabulary Readers	Houghton Mifflin Harcourt
Print It!	R	I	1209	Vocabulary Readers/CA	Houghton Mifflin Harcourt
Print It!	R	I	1209	Vocabulary Readers/TX	Houghton Mifflin Harcourt
Printed Words of the Revolution	V	I	2645	Leveled Readers	Houghton Mifflin Harcourt
Printed Words of the Revolution	V	I	2645	Leveled Readers/CA	Houghton Mifflin Harcourt
Printed Words of the Revolution	V	I	2645	Leveled Readers/TX	Houghton Mifflin Harcourt
Printing Machine, The	G	F	102	Literacy 2000	Rigby
Printing Press, The: An Information Revolution	R	I	250+	On Deck	Rigby
Priscilla and the Dinosaurs	K	RF	340	Sunshine	Wright Group/McGraw Hill
Prisoner for Liberty	O	B	1465	On My Own History	Millbrook Press
Private Captain: A Story of Gettysburg	W	HF	250+	Crisp, Marty	Philomel/Penguin
Private Joel and the Sewell Mountain Seder	R	HF	2537	Fireside, Bryna J.	Kar-Ben Publishing
Private Notebook of Katie Roberts, Age 11, The	P	RF	250+	Hest, Amy	Candlewick Press
Prize for Purry, A	K	RF	250+	Literacy 2000	Rigby
Prize Goat	J	F	533	Sun Sprouts	ETA Cuisenaire
Pro Sports: How Did They Begin?	S	I	250+	Wulffson, Don L.	Mondo
Pro Stock Car Racing	S	I	250+	Motor Sports	Red Brick Learning
Pro Stock Cars	Q	I	250+	Wild Rides!	Red Brick Learning
Pro Stock Trucks	T	I	250+	The World's Fastest	Red Brick Learning
Probability	P	I	250+	Early Connections	Benchmark Education
Problem with Meli, The	J	I	333	Leveled Literacy Intervention/Blue System	Heinemann
Problems with My Pudding	N	I	950	Leveled Readers Science	Houghton Mifflin Harcourt
Proboscis Monkey, the	J	I	147	Weird Animals	Capstone Press
Processed Food	F	I	54	Wonder World	Wright Group/McGraw Hill
Professor Gylden Lox's Hair School	S	F	4800	Take Two Books	Wright Group/McGraw Hill
Professor Science and the Salamander Stumper	Q	RF	2579	Reading Street	Pearson
Profiles in Sports Courage	U	B	250+	Rappaport, Ken	Peachtree
Prohibition	X	I	2560	Independent Readers Social Studies	Houghton Mifflin Harcourt
Project Apollo	Q	I	250+	A True Book	Children's Press
Project Bug	V	RF	3641	Leveled Readers	Houghton Mifflin Harcourt
Project Bug	V	RF	3641	Leveled Readers/CA	Houghton Mifflin Harcourt
Project Bug	V	RF	3641	Leveled Readers/TX	Houghton Mifflin Harcourt

P

* Collection of short stories
# Graphic text

TITLE	LEVEL	GENRE	WORD COUNT	AUTHOR / SERIES	PUBLISHER / DISTRIBUTOR
Project Gemini	Q	I	250+	A True Book	Children's Press
Project Mercury	Q	I	250+	A True Book	Children's Press
Promise Me the Moon	V	RF	250+	Barnes, Joyce Annette	Penguin Group
Proof of Magic	Q	F	250+	Ragged Island Mysteries	Wright Group/McGraw Hill
Properties of Matter	S	I	1748	Science Support Readers	Houghton Mifflin Harcourt
Prophecy of the Stones, The	Z	F	250+	Bujor, Flavia	Hyperion
Protecting Earth's Air Quality	X	I	11018	Saving Our Living Earth	Lerner Publications
Protecting Earth's Land	X	I	10697	Saving Our Living Earth	Lerner Publications
Protecting Earth's Rain Forests	X	I	11411	Saving Our Living Earth	Lerner Publications
Protecting Earth's Water Supply	X	I	10317	Saving Our Living Earth	Lerner Publications
Protecting Endangered Animals	T	I	1928	Vocabulary Readers	Houghton Mifflin Harcourt
Protecting Endangered Animals	T	I	1928	Vocabulary Readers/CA	Houghton Mifflin Harcourt
Protecting Sea Turtles	R	I	250+	Leveled Readers Language Support	Houghton Mifflin Harcourt
Protecting Sea Turtles	M	I	250+	Windows on Literacy	National Geographic
Protecting the Past	W	I	250+	WorldScapes	ETA Cuisenaire
Protecting Your Home: A Book About Firefighters	H	I	89	Community Workers	Picture Window Books
Protectors, The	Y	RF	3223	Leveled Readers	Houghton Mifflin Harcourt
Protester's Song, The (Misfits Inc. #5)	Z	RF	250+	Delaney, Mark	Peachtree
Proud Achilles	V	TL	2386	Leveled Readers	Houghton Mifflin Harcourt
Proud Achilles	V	TL	2386	Leveled Readers/CA	Houghton Mifflin Harcourt
Proud Taste for Scarlet and Miniver	W	F	250+	Konigsburg, E. L.	Dell
Prudence	N	I	250+	Character Education	Red Brick Learning
PS, I Love You Gramps	O	RF	250+	Literacy Tree	Rigby
Psyche & Eros: The Lady and the Monster	W	TL	2679	Graphic Myths and Legends	Lerner Publications
Psychics	X	I	250+	The Unexplained	Capstone Press
PT Boats	T	I	250+	Land and Sea	Capstone Press
Pterodactyl at the Airport	K	F	185	Wesley & the Dinosaurs	Wright Group/McGraw Hill
Pterosaur's Long Flight	I	HF	301	PM Story Books-Orange	Rigby
PT's Terrible Problem	P	F	1240	Leveled Readers	Houghton Mifflin Harcourt
PT's Terrible Problem	P	F	1240	Leveled Readers/CA	Houghton Mifflin Harcourt
PT's Terrible Problem	P	F	1240	Leveled Readers/TX	Houghton Mifflin Harcourt
Public Library, The	K	I	250+	Stepping Stones	Nelson/Michaels Assoc.
Pudding Problems	N	RF	921	Leveled Readers Science	Houghton Mifflin Harcourt
Puddle Play	K	F	460	Leveled Literacy Intervention/ Blue System	Heinemann
Puddle, The	I	F	325	McPhail, David	Farrar, Straus, and Giroux
Puddles	D	I	114	PM Science Readers	Rigby
Pueblo	K	I	114	Leveled Readers Social Studies	Houghton Mifflin Harcourt
Pueblo Indians, The	P	I	250+	Native Peoples	Red Brick Learning
Pueblo Ruins	Q	I	250+	Rigby Literacy	Rigby
Pueblo, The	R	I	250+	First Reports	Compass Point Books
Pueblo, The: Southwestern Potters	R	I	250+	America's First Peoples	Capstone Press
Pueblos, The: People of the Southwest	S	I	250+	Theme Sets	National Geographic
Puerto Rico	O	I	1906	A Ticket to …	Carolrhoda Books
Puerto Rico	T	I	250+	Hello U.S.A.	Lerner Publications
Puerto Rico	K	I	175	Nonfiction	Literacy Footprints
Puerto Rico	R	I	250+	This Land Is Your Land	Compass Point Books
Puffer Fish	I	I	121	Under the Sea	Capstone Press
Puffins	H	I	121	Polar Animals	Capstone Press
Puffins	H	I	104	Seedlings	Continental Press
Pug and Chug	I	F	250+	Supersonics	Rigby

P

* Collection of short stories
\# Graphic text

TITLE	LEVEL	GENRE	WORD COUNT	AUTHOR / SERIES	PUBLISHER / DISTRIBUTOR
Pugs	R	I	250+	All About Dogs	Capstone Press
Pugs	I	I	128	Dogs	Capstone Press
Pug's Walk	E	RF	84	Joy Starters	Pearson Learning Group
Pukeko Morning	G	I	148	Pacific Literacy	Pacific Learning
Pulleys	Q	I	1643	Early Bird Energy Physics Books	Lerner Publishing
Pulleys to the Rescue	O	I	250+	Simple Machine to the Rescue	Capstone Press
Pulling Down the Walls: The Struggle of African American Performers	U	I	2697	Reading Street	Pearson
Pullman Strike, The	V	I	1541	Leveled Readers Social Studies	Houghton Mifflin Harcourt
Pumpkin Grows, A	E	I	176	Bookshop	Mondo
Pumpkin Grows, The	B	I	24	On Our Way to English	Rigby
Pumpkin Harvest	F	I	92	All About Fall	Capstone Press
Pumpkin House, The	J	F	250+	Literacy 2000	Rigby
Pumpkin Seeds, The	I	I	217	Storyteller	Wright Group/McGraw Hill
Pumpkin That Kim Carved, The	H	RF	149	Little Readers	Houghton Mifflin Harcourt
Pumpkin, The	E	I	56	Story Box	Wright Group/McGraw Hill
Pumpkins	M	I	250+	Ray, Mary Lyn	Harcourt Trade
Pumpkins and Apples	I	F	311	Reading Street	Pearson
Pumpkins in Fall	D	I	41	Shutterbug Books	Steck-Vaughn
Punched Paper	I	I	250+	Bebop Books	Lee & Low Books Inc.
Punchinello	F	TL	250+	PM Readalongs	Rigby
Punished!	Q	F	9988	Lubar, David	Darby Creek Publishing
Punny Places: Jokes to Make You Mappy!	O	F	1703	Make Me Laugh!	Lerner Publications
Punxsutawney Phyllis	K	F	250+	Hill, Susanna Leonard	Holiday House
Pup Camps Out	G	F	115	Reading Street	Pearson
Puppet Pals	C	I	35	Little Celebrations	Pearson Learning Group
Puppet Play, A	C	I	54	Storyteller-First Snow	Wright Group/McGraw Hill
Puppet Show	F	RF	105	First Start	Troll Associates
Puppet Show, The	A	RF	67	InfoTrek	ETA Cuisenaire
Puppet Show, The	A	RF	35	Leveled Literacy Intervention/ Orange System	Heinemann
Puppet Show, The	E	I	25	Literacy 2000	Rigby
Puppet Show, The	B	RF	25	Phonics and Friends	Hampton-Brown
Puppet, The	A	I	24	On Our Way to English	Rigby
Puppeteer's Apprentice, The	Z	HF	250+	Love, D. Anne	Simon & Schuster
Puppets	G	I	47	Canizares, Susan; Berger, Samantha	Scholastic
Puppets	P	I	250	Literacy Tree	Rigby
Puppets	J	I	250+	Little Celebrations	Pearson Learning Group
Puppets	K	I	380	Rigby Flying Colors	Rigby
Puppets for a Play	D	I	45	Home Connection Collection	Rigby
Puppets, Puppets, Puppets	K	I	537	Vocabulary Readers	Houghton Mifflin Harcourt
Puppets, Puppets, Puppets	K	I	537	Vocabulary Readers/CA	Houghton Mifflin Harcourt
Puppets, Puppets, Puppets	K	I	537	Vocabulary Readers/TX	Houghton Mifflin Harcourt
Puppets, The	C	F	91	Leveled Literacy Intervention/ Green System	Heinemann
Puppies Can Play	C	I	42	Bonnell, Kris	Reading Reading Books
Puppies in the Pantry	Q	RF	250+	Baglio, Ben M.	Scholastic
Puppies! Puppies! Puppies!	J	RF	250+	Meyers, Susan	Scholastic
Puppies, Dogs, and Blue Northers	S	I	250+	Paulsen, Gary	Delacorte Press
Puppy at the Door	J	RF	250+	PM Plus Story Books	Rigby
Puppy Chase, The	I	RF	250+	Cambridge Reading	Pearson Learning Group
Puppy Danny	E	RF	136	Coulton, Mia	Maryruth Books

TITLE	LEVEL	GENRE	WORD COUNT	AUTHOR / SERIES	PUBLISHER / DISTRIBUTOR
Puppy Love	N	RF	250+	Duffey, Betsy	Puffin/Penguin
Puppy Play	D	RF	67	Emergent Books	Pioneer Valley
Puppy Puzzle	O	RF	250+	Baglio, Ben M.	Scholastic
Puppy Raiser, A	J	F	437	Reading Street	Pearson
Puppy Trouble	G	F	168	Bella and Rosie Series	Literacy Footprints
Puppy Who Wanted a Boy, The	L	F	250+	Thayer, Jane	Scholastic
Puppy, The	B	RF	37	First Stories	Pacific Learning
Puppy, The	A	I	15	Vocabulary Readers	Houghton Mifflin Harcourt
Puppy, The	A	I	15	Vocabulary Readers/CA	Houghton Mifflin Harcourt
Pure Dead Wicked	W	F	250+	Gliori, Debi	Random House
Purple	B	I	26	Colors	Lerner Publications
Purple Climbing Days	M	RF	250+	Giff, Patricia Reilly	Bantam
Purple Is Part of a Rainbow	E	RF	131	Rookie Readers	Children's Press
Purple Pussycat, The	F	F	281	Easy Stories	Norwood House Press
Purple Snerd, The	H	F	216	Green Light Readers	Harcourt
Purple Walrus and Other Perfect Pets	O	RF	250+	Wildcats	Wright Group/McGraw Hill
Purple: Seeing Purple All Around Us	K	I	250+	Colors	Capstone Press
Pursuit of the Ivory Poachers, The	P	SF	250+	Secret Agent Jack Stalwart	Weinstein Books
Push and Pull	G	I	49	iOpeners	Pearson Learning Group
Push and Pull	E	I	36	The Way Things Move	Capstone Press
Push and Pull	H	I	184	Yellow Umbrella Books	Red Brick Learning
Push It or Pull It?	F	RF	162	Instant Readers	Harcourt School Publishers
Push or Pull	L	I	316	Independent Readers Science	Houghton Mifflin Harcourt
Push or Pull?	LB	I	7	Discovery Links	Newbridge
Push or Pull?	J	I	154	Phonics Readers	Compass Point Books
Push or Pull?	C	I	73	Windows on Literacy	National Geographic
Push!	D	RF	21	Oxford Reading Tree	Oxford University Press
Pushcart War, The	Y	F	250+	Merrill, Jean	Bantam
Pushing and Pulling	A	I	18	Big Cat	Pacific Learning
Pushing and Pulling	J	I	250+	Explorations	Okapi Educational Materials
Pushing and Pulling	J	I	250+	Explorations	Eleanor Curtain Publishing
Pushing the Limits	T	I	250+	Connectors	Pacific Learning
Puss-in-Boots	K	TL	250+	PM Tales and Plays-Purple	Rigby
Pussy Cat	F	TL	143	Literacy 2000	Rigby
Pussy Cat, Pussy Cat	D	F	44	Seedlings	Continental Press
Put Me in the Zoo	H	B	250+	Lopshire, Robert	Random House
Putting Frosting on the Cake	D	F	120	Leveled Readers	Houghton Mifflin Harcourt
Putting Frosting on the Cake	D	F	120	Leveled Readers/CA	Houghton Mifflin Harcourt
Putting Frosting on the Cake	D	F	120	Leveled Readers/TX	Houghton Mifflin Harcourt
Putting on a Concert and the Television News	L	RF	250+	Voyages	SRA/McGraw Hill
Putting on a Play	Q	I	424	Vocabulary Readers	Houghton Mifflin Harcourt
Putting Up the Tent	F	RF	119	Reading Street	Pearson
Puzzle of the Missing Panda, The	P	SF	250+	Secret Agent Jack Stalwart	Weinstein Books
Puzzle Power Drain, The	O	RF	250+	Klooz	Stone Arch Books
Puzzle, The	B	RF	32	Smart Starts	Rigby
Puzzle, The	A	I	32	Sun Sprouts	ETA Cuisenaire
Puzzle, The	B	I	28	Storyteller Nonfiction	Wright Group/McGraw Hill
Pyjama Party, The	K	RF	250+	Cambridge Reading	Pearson Learning Group
Pyramid	X	I	250+	Eyewitness Books	DK Publishing
Pyramid	X	I	250+	Macaulay, David	Scholastic
Pyramids	K	I	239	3-D Shapes	Capstone Press
Pyramids	S	I	250+	Ancient Egypt	Capstone Press
Pyramids & Mummies	R	I	250+	Simon, Seymour	Chronicle Books

Organized Alphabetically by Title
Storable Database at www.fountasandpinnellleveledbooks.com

* Collection of short stories
\# Graphic text

TITLE	LEVEL	GENRE	WORD COUNT	AUTHOR / SERIES	PUBLISHER / DISTRIBUTOR
Pyramids in the Bush: A Book about Mallee Fowl	T	I	250+	Sunshine	Wright Group/McGraw Hill
Pyramids of Ancient Egypt, The	V	I	250+	Leveled Readers Language Support	Houghton Mifflin Harcourt
Pyramids of Egypt, The	S	I	250+	Rosen Real Readers	Rosen Publishing Group
Pyramids of Giza, The	W	I	1718	Leveled Readers	Houghton Mifflin Harcourt
Python Caught the Eagle, The	C	F	60	Voyages	SRA/McGraw Hill
Pythons	I	I	139	African Animals	Capstone Press

P

* Collection of short stories
# Graphic text

TITLE	LEVEL	GENRE	WORD COUNT	AUTHOR / SERIES	PUBLISHER / DISTRIBUTOR
Qillak	M	RF	250+	Take Two Books	Wright Group/McGraw Hill
Quack!	E	F	48	Ready Readers	Pearson Learning Group
Quack, Quack, Quack	D	F	97	Carousel Readers	Pearson Learning Group
Quack, Quack, Quack!	I	F	219	Sunshine	Wright Group/McGraw Hill
Quack, Said the Billy Goat	H	F	88	Causley, Charles	Harper & Row
Quackers, the Troublesome Duck	M	F	250+	Ellen, Leslie	Pearson Learning Group
Quail Club, The	P	RF	250+	Marsden, Carolyn	Candlewick Press
Quake!	T	RF	250+	Cottonwood, Joe	Language for Learning Assoc.
Quake!: Disaster in San Francisco, 1906	T	HF	250+	Karwoski, Gail Langer	Peachtree
Quanah Parker	S	B	3563	History Maker Bios	Lerner Publications
Quarter Story, The	E	I	99	Williams, Deborah	Kaeden Books
Quarterback Sneak	P	RF	250+	Maddox, Jake	Stone Arch Books
Quarters for Everyone	S	RF	1798	Leveled Readers	Houghton Mifflin Harcourt
Quarters Toss, The	P	RF	250+	Leveled Readers Language Support	Houghton Mifflin Harcourt
Queen and the Dragon, The	I	F	243	New Way Green	Steck-Vaughn
Queen Bee Needs to be Free	K	F	738	Appleton-Smith, Laura	Flyleaf Publishing
Queen Eleanor: Independent Spirit in the Medieval World	X	B	250+	Brooks, Polly Schoyer	Houghton Mifflin Harcourt
Queen Isabella's Feast	K	F	900	InfoTrek	ETA Cuisenaire
Queen Jelly Bean	J	F	250+	The Wright Skills	Wright Group/McGraw Hill
Queen Made a Quilt	D	RF	46	Ray's Readers	Outside the Box
Queen of Egypt	V	B	250+	WorldScapes	ETA Cuisenaire
Queen of Everything, The	Z+	RF	250+	Caletti, Deb	Simon & Schuster
Queen of Hearts, The	E	TL	26	Jumbled Tumbled Tales & Rhymes	Rigby
Queen of the Bean	N	RF	250+	Action Packs	Rigby
Queen of the Pool	N	RF	250+	PM Collection	Rigby
Queen of the Toilet Bowl	S	RF	250+	Orca Currents	Orca Book Publishers
Queen on a Quilt	C	F	26	Ready Readers	Pearson Learning Group
Queen Rania of Jordan	S	B	250+	Queens and Princesses	Capstone Press
Queen's New Seat, The	H	F	230	Springboard	Wright Group/McGraw Hill
Queens of Ancient Egypt	Y	I	3160	Vocabulary Readers/CA	Houghton Mifflin Harcourt
Queens of Ancient Egypt	Y	I	3160	Vocabulary Readers	Houghton Mifflin Harcourt
Queen's Parrot, The: A Play	J	TL	365	Literacy 2000	Rigby
Quest for California's Gold, The	S	I	250+	The Library of the Westward Expansion	Rosen Publishing Group
Quest For Medusa's Head, The	W	TL	1385	Leveled Readers	Houghton Mifflin Harcourt
Quest for the Golden Seesaw, The	O	F	250+	High-Fliers	Pacific Learning
Quest for the Moon	X	I	3419	Vocabulary Readers	Houghton Mifflin Harcourt
Quest for the Moon	X	I	3419	Vocabulary Readers/CA	Houghton Mifflin Harcourt
Questions and Answers About Forest Animals	P	I	250+	Chinery, Michael	Kingfisher
Questions and Answers About Freshwater Animals	P	I	250+	Chinery, Michael	Kingfisher
Questions, Questions, Questions	F	RF	190	Visions	Wright Group/McGraw Hill
Quests for Gold	X	I	2050	Reading Street	Pearson
Quick and Quiet	B	F	38	Phonics and Friends	Hampton-Brown
Quick Chick	J	F	250+	Hoban, Julia	Puffin/Penguin
Quick Duck, The	H	F	165	Phonics Readers	Scholastic
Quick Thinking	L	RF	549	In Step Readers	Rigby
Quick, Go Peek!	E	F	83	Little Celebrations	Pearson Learning Group
Quiet in the Library	E	RF	102	Rigby Rocket	Rigby
Quiet in the Library!	H	F	113	Sunshine	Wright Group/McGraw Hill

* Collection of short stories
# Graphic text

TITLE	LEVEL	GENRE	WORD COUNT	AUTHOR / SERIES	PUBLISHER / DISTRIBUTOR
Quiet Morning for Mom, A	H	RF	169	Lighthouse	Rigby
Quiet Owls	K	I	385	Pull Ahead Books	Lerner Publications
Quiet TV Lunch, A	L	F	250+	Popcorn	Sundance
Quiet World, The	K	RF	250+	Voyages	SRA/McGraw Hill
Quilt for Kiri, A	K	RF	367	Pacific Literacy	Pacific Learning
Quilt for Kristy, A	J	RF	250+	The Wright Skills	Wright Group/McGraw Hill
Quilt Story, The	L	HF	250+	Johnston, Tony; DePaola, Tomie	Scholastic
Quilt with a Difference, A	N	I	250+	Pacific Literacy	Pacific Learning
Quilt, The	I	RF	165	Jonas, Ann	Morrow
Quilting for Fun!	S	I	250+	For Fun! Crafts	Compass Point Books
Quilting in America	I	I	152	Vocabulary Readers	Houghton Mifflin Harcourt
Quilting Memories	L	I	471	Reading Street	Pearson
Quilts	C	RF	35	Foundations	Wright Group/McGraw Hill
Quilts	E	I	131	Twig	Wright Group/McGraw Hill
Quirky Times at Quagmire Castle	R	F	9190	Wallace, Karen	Stone Arch Books
Quiz Show	N	RF	250+	On Our Way To English	Rigby
Quork Attack	L	F	250+	Rigby Literacy	Rigby
Quork Attack	L	F	250+	Rigby Star Plus	Rigby

Q

TITLE	LEVEL	GENRE	WORD COUNT	AUTHOR / SERIES	PUBLISHER / DISTRIBUTOR
R Is for Radish!	J	F	250+	Coxe, Molly	Random House
R.S.P.C.A.	O	I	250+	Tristars	Richard C. Owen
Rabbit and Coyote	J	TL	522	Rigby Flying Colors	Rigby
Rabbit and Fox	D	F	87	Sails	Rigby
Rabbit and the Coyote, The	Q	F	979	Leveled Readers	Houghton Mifflin Harcourt
Rabbit and Turtle Go to School	E	F	84	Green Light Readers	Harcourt
Rabbit and Turtle Go to School	E	F	67	Instant Readers	Harcourt Trade
Rabbit Catches the Sun	M	F	621	Sunshine	Wright Group/McGraw Hill
Rabbit Dance, The	L	TL	563	Gear Up!	Wright Group/ McGraw Hill
Rabbit for You, A: Caring for Your Rabbit	M	I	250+	Pet Care	Picture Window Books
Rabbit Makes Toast	K	F	250+	Popcorn	Sundance
Rabbit Race	O	RF	250+	Baglio, Ben M.	Scholastic
Rabbit Rescue	L	RF	427	Gear Up!	Wright Group/ McGraw Hill
Rabbit Stew	L	F	250+	Literacy 2000	Rigby
Rabbit, The	H	RF	59	Burningham, John	Crowell
Rabbits	D	I	37	All About Pets	Red Brick Learning
Rabbits	F	I	96	Life Cycles	Lerner Publications
Rabbits	N	I	250+	Literacy 2000	Rigby
Rabbits and Their Burrows	J	I	136	Animal Homes	Capstone Press
Rabbit's Birthday Kite	J	F	250+	Bank Street	Bantam
Rabbits' Ears	F	RF	179	PM Plus Story Books	Rigby
Rabbit's Feelings	C	F	53	Gear Up!	Wright Group/McGraw Hill
Rabbit's Garden	B	F	42	Gear Up!	Wright Group/McGraw Hill
Rabbit's Garden	L	F	661	Leveled Readers	Houghton Mifflin Harcourt
Rabbit's Garden	L	F	661	Leveled Readers/CA	Houghton Mifflin Harcourt
Rabbit's Garden	L	F	661	Leveled Readers/TX	Houghton Mifflin Harcourt
Rabbit's Garden Troubles	L	F	652	Leveled Readers	Houghton Mifflin Harcourt
Rabbit's Garden Troubles	L	F	652	Leveled Readers/CA	Houghton Mifflin Harcourt
Rabbit's Garden Troubles	L	F	652	Leveled Readers/TX	Houghton Mifflin Harcourt
Rabbits Have Bunnies	M	I	250+	Animals and Their Young	Compass Point Books
Rabbits in Space	J	F	216	Talking Point Series	Pearson Learning Group
Rabbits on the Farm	I	I	103	Pebble Books	Red Brick Learning
Rabbit's Party	G	F	351	Bunting, Eve; Sloan-Childers, E.	Scholastic
Rabbit's Pumpkin	B	F	29	Gear Up!	Wright Group/McGraw Hill
Rabbit's Real Birthday	J	F	250+	Rigby Literacy	Rigby
Rabbit's Robber	L	F	250+	Popcorn	Sundance
Rabbit's Skating Party	D	F	89	Handprints B	Educators Publishing Service
Rabbit's Surprise Birthday	J	F	250+	Rigby Star	Rigby
Rabbit's Tail	K	TL	250+	Cambridge Reading	Pearson Learning Group
Rabbit's Tricks	I	F	250+	Story Box	Wright Group/McGraw Hill
Rabble Starkey	T	RF	250+	Lowry, Lois	Bantam
Raccoon Cookies	H	F	136	Gear Up!	Wright Group/McGraw Hill
Raccoon on the Moon	I	RF	250+	Start to Read	School Zone
Raccoon Wakes Up	C	RF	66	PM Stars	Rigby
Raccoons	O	I	2107	Early Bird Nature Books	Lerner Publications
Raccoons	M	I	250+	PM Animal Facts: Gold	Rigby
Race Against Time	Q	I	250+	Bookweb	Rigby
Race Against Time	U	I	250+	High-Fliers	Pacific Learning
Race Car Dreamers	N	RF	250+	Boyz Rule!	Mondo
Race Car, The	B	F	30	Sails	Rigby
Race Cars	I	I	417	Sails	Rigby
Race Cars	M	I	250+	Transportation	Compass Point Books
Race Day	D	F	58	Reading Street	Pearson

* Collection of short stories
\# Graphic text

TITLE	LEVEL	GENRE	WORD COUNT	AUTHOR / SERIES	PUBLISHER / DISTRIBUTOR
Race Day	O	I	250+	Windows on Literacy	National Geographic
Race Is On, The	D	F	45	New Way Red	Steck-Vaughn
Race of a Lifetime, The	N	RF	1837	Norman, Tony	Stone Arch Books
Race of the River Runner	P	HF	540	Leveled Readers	Houghton Mifflin Harcourt
Race to Green End, The	J	F	506	PM Collection	Rigby
Race to the Mountain, The	H	TL	174	Leveled Readers Language Support	Houghton Mifflin Harcourt
Race to the North Pole	Q	B	250+	WorldScapes	ETA Cuisenaire
Race to the Pole	R	I	250+	Windows on Literacy	National Geographic
Race to the South Pole	S	I	1367	Vocabulary Readers	Houghton Mifflin Harcourt
Race to the South Pole	S	I	1367	Vocabulary Readers/CA	Houghton Mifflin Harcourt
Race to the South Pole, The	W	I	2859	Reading Street	Pearson
Race, The	B	RF	78	Leveled Readers Emergent	Houghton Mifflin Harcourt
Race, The	E	F	30	Little Celebrations	Pearson Learning Group
Race, The	F	RF	145	Little Readers	Houghton Mifflin Harcourt
Race, The	I	F	451	New Way Green	Steck-Vaughn
Race, The	C	RF	25	Sunshine	Wright Group/McGraw Hill
Race, The	B	RF	34	Windmill Books	Wright Group/McGraw Hill
Racecar Bob in Panama	Q	RF	1021	Leveled Readers	Houghton Mifflin Harcourt
Racecar Bob in Panama	Q	RF	1021	Leveled Readers/CA	Houghton Mifflin Harcourt
Racecar Bob in Panama	Q	RF	1021	Leveled Readers/TX	Houghton Mifflin Harcourt
Rachel Carson	J	B	279	Leveled Readers	Houghton Mifflin Harcourt
Rachel Carson, Scientist and Writer	N	B	370	Independent Readers Social Studies	Houghton Mifflin Harcourt
Rachel Carson: Friend of Nature	N	B	250+	Rookie Biographies	Children's Press
Rachel Carson: Nature's Guardian	S	B	250+	Science Readers	Teacher Created Materials
Rachel to the Rescue	O	RF	250+	SupaDoopers	Sundance
Racing Cars, The	C	RF	68	Rigby Flying Colors	Rigby
Racing Danger	Q	I	737	Leveled Readers	Houghton Mifflin Harcourt
Racing with the Sun	Q	I	250+	Orbit Double Takes	Pacific Learning
Radar Jammers: The EA-6B Prowlers	U	I	250+	War Planes	Capstone Press
Radio	O	I	250+	Let's See	Compass Point Books
Radio	S	I	250+	Theme Sets	National Geographic
Radio Scare	T	I	250+	Leveled Readers Language Support	Houghton Mifflin Harcourt
Radio, The	Q	I	250+	Great Inventions	Red Brick Learning
Radio, The: The World Tunes In	R	I	250+	On Deck	Rigby
Raewyn's Got the Writing Bug Again	N	B	250+	Voyages	SRA/McGraw Hill
Ragbag	G	F	41	Supersonics	Rigby
Ragdoll Cats	I	I	118	Cats	Capstone Press
Raggin': A Story about Scott Joplin	S	B	6409	Creative Minds Biographies	Lerner Publications
Raging Dragon, The (Will to Conquer Series: Book 2)	Z	F	250+	Lamensdorf, Len	SeaScape Press
Ragweed	U	F	250+	Avi	Avon
Railroad Revolution	R	I	618	Vocabulary Readers	Houghton Mifflin Harcourt
Railroad Toad	K	F	178	Schade, Susan	Random House
Railroad, The	R	I	250+	Theme Sets	National Geographic
Rain	LB	I	56	Kalan, Robert	Greenwillow
Rain	C	RF	34	Learn to Read	Creative Teaching Press
Rain	B	I	87	Leveled Literacy Intervention/ Orange System	Heinemann
Rain	G	RF	68	Literacy 2000	Rigby
Rain	D	I	44	Little Celebrations	Pearson Learning Group
Rain	B	RF	52	Reading Corners	Pearson Learning Group

TITLE	LEVEL	GENRE	WORD COUNT	AUTHOR / SERIES	PUBLISHER / DISTRIBUTOR
Rain	D	RF	45	Step-By-Step Series	Pearson Learning Group
Rain	J	I	250+	Voyages	SRA/McGraw Hill
Rain	K	I	263	Weather	Capstone Press
Rain and the Sun, The	E	I	45	Wonder World	Wright Group/McGraw Hill
Rain Came Down, The	J	RF	250+	Shannon, David	Scholastic
Rain Forest	N	F	250+	Cowcher, Helen	Scholastic
Rain Forest	R	I	250+	Worldwise	Franklin Watts
Rain Forest Adventure	L	F	482	Pair-It Books	Steck-Vaughn
Rain Forest Adventure	S	RF	250+	Reading Expeditions	National Geographic
Rain Forest Alert!	T	I	250+	Literacy by Design	Rigby
Rain Forest Animals	J	I	151	Phonics Readers	Compass Point Books
Rain Forest Animals	P	I	250+	Theme Sets	National Geographic
Rain Forest Encyclopedia	N	I	250+	Literacy by Design	Rigby
Rain Forest Plants	I	I	151	Alphakids	Sundance
Rain Forest Plants	N	I	250+	Life in the World's Biomes	Capstone Press
Rain Forest Plants	M	I	580	Lundberg, Linda	Harcourt School Publishers
Rain Forest Secrets	P	I	250+	Dorros, Arthur	Scholastic
Rain Forest Tree, A	Q	I	250+	Kite, Lorien	Crabtree
Rain Forest Vacation	P	I	250+	Literacy by Design	Rigby
Rain Forest, A	LB	I	18	Rigby Focus	Rigby
Rain Forest, The	Q	I	191	Action Packs	Rigby
Rain Forest, The	N	I	191	Windows on Literacy	National Geographic
Rain Forests	Q	I	250+	Ecosystems	Red Brick Learning
Rain Forests	Q	I	250+	First Reports	Compass Point Books
Rain Forests	S	I	250+	The Heinle Reading Library	Thomson Learning
Rain Forests: Facts vs. Fiction	T	I	250+	Explore More	Wright Group/McGraw Hill
Rain Ghost, The	X	F	250+	Kilworth, Garry	Scholastic
Rain in the Hills	D	RF	41	Book Bank	Wright Group/McGraw Hill
Rain Is Not My Indian Name	Z	RF	250+	Smith, Cynthia Leitich	HarperCollins
Rain Is Water	E	I	82	PM Plus Nonfiction	Rigby
Rain or Shine	Q	I	250+	Explorers	Wright Group/McGraw Hill
Rain or Shine?	C	I	21	Twig	Wright Group/McGraw Hill
Rain Puddle	J	RF	250+	Holl, Adelaide	Morrow
Rain Today	A	I	25	Leveled Readers	Houghton Mifflin Harcourt
Rain Today	A	I	25	Leveled Readers/CA	Houghton Mifflin Harcourt
Rain! Rain!	D	RF	29	Rookie Readers	Children's Press
Rain, Rain	E	RF	58	Pacific Literacy	Pacific Learning
Rain, Rain, and More Rain	H	RF	250+	Momentum Literacy Program	Troll Associates
Rain, Rain, Rain	C	F	36	Sails	Rigby
Rain, Rivers, and Rain Again	M	I	250+	Sunshine	Wright Group/McGraw Hill
Rain, Snow, and Hail	J	I	250+	Discovery World	Rigby
Rain, The	G	RF	171	Foundations	Wright Group/McGraw Hill
Rain, The	C	RF	76	Leveled Readers Emergent	Houghton Mifflin Harcourt
Rainbow Bird, A	LB	I	18	Pair-It Books	Steck-Vaughn
Rainbow Clown, The	C	RF	55	Reading Safari	Mondo
Rainbow Clubhouse, The	I	RF	483	Rigby Flying Colors	Rigby
Rainbow Glider, The	O	RF	250+	Reading Safari	Mondo
Rainbow of My Own	C	F	52	Freeman, Don	Penguin Group
Rainbow of Parrots, A	B	I	60	Springboard	Wright Group/McGraw Hill
Rainbow Parrot	I	TL	174	Literacy Tree	Rigby
*Rainbow People, The	V	F	250+	Yep, Lawrence	HarperTrophy
Rainbow Solution, The	N	RF	250+	Literacy 2000	Rigby
Rainbow Somewhere, A	G	RF	201	Ready Readers	Pearson Learning Group
Rainbow Town	B	RF	30	Sails	Rigby

Organized Alphabetically by Title
Storable Database at www.fountasandpinnellleveledbooks.com

* Collection of short stories
\# Graphic text

TITLE	LEVEL	GENRE	WORD COUNT	AUTHOR / SERIES	PUBLISHER / DISTRIBUTOR
Rainbow Wings	M	F	250+	Sunshine	Wright Group/McGraw Hill
Rainbow, A	B	I	29	Rigby Focus	Rigby
Rainbow, The	C	I	59	Rigby Flying Colors	Rigby
Rainbows	L	I	250+	Rigby Literacy	Rigby
Rainbows All Around	M	RF	250+	Hardin, Suzanne	Pacific Learning
Rainbows and Moonbeams	I	RF	238	Sunshine	Wright Group/McGraw Hill
Rainbows of the Sea	L	I	250+	Thomas, Meredith	Mondo
Raindrop, A	C	RF	41	Teacher's Choice Series	Pearson Learning Group
Raindrops	B	I	34	Bookshop	Mondo
Raindrops	C	RF	66	Gay, Sandy	Scholastic
Raindrops	I	I	70	Rookie Readers	Children's Press
Rainforest Math	O	I	250+	WorldScapes	ETA Cuisenaire
Rainy	T	RF	250+	Deans, Sis	Henry Holt & Co.
Rainy	B	I	23	Weather	Lerner Publications
Rainy Day	A	I	20	Leveled Readers	Houghton Mifflin Harcourt
Rainy Day	A	I	20	Leveled Readers/CA	Houghton Mifflin Harcourt
Rainy Day Alphabet Book	E	RF	82	Posner, Jackie; Wiener, Sara	Scholastic
Rainy Day Counting	B	I	30	Twig	Wright Group/McGraw Hill
Rainy Day Dream	WB	F	N/A	Chesworth, Michael	Farrar, Straus and Giroux
Rainy Day for Sammy, A	H	RF	249	Urmston, Kathleen; Urmston, Graig	Kaeden Books
Rainy Day Grump, The	H	RF	394	Real Kids Readers	Millbrook Press
Rainy Day Solution, A	K	I	161	Vocabulary Readers	Houghton Mifflin Harcourt
Rainy Day Story	K	RF	749	InfoTrek	ETA Cuisenaire
Rainy Day, A	D	RF	72	Evans, Lynette	Scholastic
Rainy Day, A	B	RF	61	Leveled Literacy Intervention/Green System	Heinemann
Rainy Day, A	A	RF	32	Literacy by Design	Rigby
Rainy Day, A	D	RF	105	New Way Blue	Steck-Vaughn
Rainy Day, A	E	I	52	Pebble Books	Capstone Press
Rainy Day, A	C	RF	27	Reading Street	Pearson
Rainy Day, A	E	I	90	Weather	Lerner Publishing
Rainy Day, Sunny Day	E	F	135	Early Connections	Benchmark Education
Rainy Days at School	H	RF	118	City Kids	Rigby
Rairarubia	S	F	250+	Adams, W. Royce	Lost Coast Press
Raising Funds	J	I	250	Vocabulary Readers	Houghton Mifflin Harcourt
Raising Funds	J	I	250	Vocabulary Readers/CA	Houghton Mifflin Harcourt
Raising Funds	J	I	250	Vocabulary Readers/TX	Houghton Mifflin Harcourt
Raising the Flag: The Battle of Iwo Jima	X	I	250+	Bloodiest Battles	Capstone Press
Rally Car Race	J	RF	250+	PM Plus Story Books	Rigby
Rally Cars	M	I	250+	Horsepower	Capstone Press
Ralph Fletcher: Reflections	S	B	250+	Author at Work	Richard C. Owen
Ralph S. Mouse	O	F	250+	Cleary, Beverly	HarperTrophy
Ramadan	O	I	1632	On My Own Holidays	Lerner Publications
Ramona and Her Father	O	RF	250+	Cleary, Beverly	Avon
Ramona and Her Mother	O	RF	250+	Cleary, Beverly	Avon
Ramona Forever	O	RF	250+	Cleary, Beverly	Hearst
Ramona Quimby, Age 8	O	RF	250+	Cleary, Beverly	Hearst
Ramona the Brave	O	RF	250+	Cleary, Beverly	Hearst
Ramona the Pest	O	RF	250+	Cleary, Beverly	Avon
Ranch Life	J	HF	395	Reading Street	Pearson
Rand and the Fox, The	H	TL	93	Cambridge Reading	Pearson Learning Group
Randy Moss	Y	B	250+	Sports Heroes	Red Brick Learning
Randy's Room	C	RF	32	Harry's Math Books	Outside the Box

* Collection of short stories
# Graphic text

R

TITLE	LEVEL	GENRE	WORD COUNT	AUTHOR / SERIES	PUBLISHER / DISTRIBUTOR
Ranger's Apprentice: The Ruins of Gorlan	U	F	250+	Flanagan, John	Scholastic
Rani Comes to Stay	E	RF	156	PM Photo Stories	Rigby
Ransom	Z	RF	250+	Duncan, Lois	Laurel-Leaf Books
Rap a Tap Tap Here's Bojangles- Think of That!	J	B	199	Dillon, Leo & Diane	Scholastic
Rap Party, The	H	RF	300	Foundations	Wright Group/McGraw Hill
Rapid Changes on Earth	Q	I	1135	Science Support Readers	Houghton Mifflin Harcourt
Rapid Robert Roadrunner	H	F	125	Reese, Bob	Children's Press
Raptors: Hunters in the Sky	R	I	250+	Sunshine.	Wright Group/McGraw Hill
Rapunzel	L	TL	250+	Literacy 2000	Rigby
#Rapunzel's Revenge	U	TL	250+	Hale, Shanon and Dean	Bloomsbury Children's Books
Rascal	V	HF	250+	North, Sterling	Scholastic
Rascal	G	RF	108	Rigby Literacy	Rigby
Rascal: The Puppy Place	N	RF	250+	Miles, Ellen	Scholastic
Rashee and the Seven Elephants	M	RF	250+	Little Celebrations	Pearson Learning Group
Rat	Z+	RF	250+	Cheripko, Jan	Boyds Mills Press
Rat Princess, The	M	TL	250+	Rigby Rocket	Rigby
Rat Squad	P	SF	250+	High-Fliers	Pacific Learning
Rat-a-tat-tat	E	F	98	Big Cat	Pacific Learning
Rat-a-tat-tat	E	F	107	Literacy 2000	Rigby
Rats	O	I	1406	Early Bird Nature Books	Lerner Publications
Rats	I	I	193	Sails	Rigby
Rat's Funny Story	C	F	39	Story Box	Wright Group/McGraw Hill
*Rats on the Range and Other Stories	O	F	250+	Marshall, James	Penguin Group
*Rats on the Roof and Other Stories	O	F	250+	Marshall, James	Penguin Group
Rat's Tale, A	T	F	250+	Seidler, Tor	HarperTrophy
*Rats!	O	RF	250+	Cutler, Jane	Farrar, Straus and Giroux
Rats, Bats, and Black Puddings	K	F	714	Pacific Literacy	Pacific Learning
Rattlesnake Looks for Food, The	E	RF	105	Foundations	Wright Group/McGraw Hill
Rattlesnakes	H	I	96	Desert Animals	Capstone Press
Rattlesnakes	M	I	250+	Snakes	Capstone Press
Rattletrap Car	L	F	250+	Root, Phyllis	Candlewick Press
Ratty Tatty	H	F	181	Sunshine	Wright Group/McGraw Hill
Raven Necklace, The	E	RF	83	Adams, Lorraine; Bruvold, Lynn	Eagle Crest Books
Raven, The	C	I	129	Adams, Lorraine; Bruvold, Lynn	Eagle Crest Books
Ravenmaster's Secret, The	U	HF	250+	Woodruff, Elvira	Scholastic
*Raven's Call and More Northwest Coast Stories	P	TL	250+	Challenger, James Robert	Heritage House
Raven's Gift	L	F	160	Books For Young Learners	Richard C. Owen
Raving about Rainforests	V	I	250+	News Extra	Richard C. Owen
Ray Charles	P	B	250+	Mathis, Sharon Bell	Lee & Low Books Inc.
Ray Ran	C	RF	34	Ray's Readers	Outside the Box
Rays	I	I	48	Pebble Books	Red Brick Learning
Rays	I	I	117	Under the Sea	Capstone Press
Reach for the Stars	Y	I	250+	High-Fliers	Pacific Learning
Reach for the Stars	Q	RF	250+	Mazer, Anne	Scholastic
Reach for Your Dreams	F	RF	115	Reading Street	Pearson
Reach Out	V	I	250+	WorldScapes	ETA Cuisenaire
Reaching for the Sky	T	I	250+	In Step Readers	Rigby
Reaching for the Sky	T	I	250+	Literacy by Design	Rigby
Reaching New Heights	T	I	250+	WorldScapes	ETA Cuisenaire
Reaching the Sky	C	RF	46	Sunshine	Wright Group/McGraw Hill
Reaction We Need, The	U	I	2708	Leveled Readers Science	Houghton Mifflin Harcourt
Reactor, The	R	SF	1854	Powell, J.	Stone Arch Books
Read a Zillion Books	O	B	250+	Meet The Author	Richard C. Owen

* Collection of short stories
# Graphic text

TITLE	LEVEL	GENRE	WORD COUNT	AUTHOR / SERIES	PUBLISHER / DISTRIBUTOR
Read All About It!	T	RF	1609	Leveled Readers	Houghton Mifflin Harcourt
Read All About It!	T	RF	1609	Leveled Readers/CA	Houghton Mifflin Harcourt
Read All About It!	S	HF	250+	On Our Way to English	Rigby
Read the Signs	I	F	250+	Literacy by Design	Rigby
Read to Your Bunny	F	F	38	Wells, Rosemary	Scholastic
Reading	B	I	60	Vocabulary Readers	Houghton Mifflin Harcourt
Reading	B	I	60	Vocabulary Readers/CA	Houghton Mifflin Harcourt
Reading	B	I	60	Vocabulary Readers/TX	Houghton Mifflin Harcourt
Reading a Graph	F	I	251	Early Connections	Benchmark Education
Reading a Map	M	I	250+	Rosen Real Readers	Rosen Publishing Group
Reading Buddies	B	F	34	Galaxy Girl	Literacy Footprints
Reading Is Everywhere	D	RF	53	Sunshine	Wright Group/McGraw Hill
Reading Lesson, The	F	RF	78	Teacher's Choice Series	Pearson Learning Group
Reading Partners	A	I	48	At School Series	Pioneer Valley
Reading Robot, The	H	F	224	Sunshine	Wright Group/McGraw Hill
Reading Room, The	G	RF	231	In Step Readers	Rigby
Reading Signs	D	I	37	Shutterbug Books	Steck-Vaughn
Reading Together	A	I	46	Vocabulary Readers	Houghton Mifflin Harcourt
Reading Together	A	I	46	Vocabulary Readers/CA	Houghton Mifflin Harcourt
Reading Together	A	I	46	Vocabulary Readers/TX	Houghton Mifflin Harcourt
Reading Under the Covers	D	RF	25	Visions	Wright Group/McGraw Hill
Reading with Eva and Pogo	I	RF	328	Gear Up!	Wright Group/McGraw Hill
Ready for Liftoff	L	I	294	Vocabulary Readers	Houghton Mifflin Harcourt
Ready for Liftoff	L	I	294	Vocabulary Readers/CA	Houghton Mifflin Harcourt
Ready for Liftoff	L	I	294	Vocabulary Readers/TX	Houghton Mifflin Harcourt
Ready for School	C	RF	41	Teacher's Choice Series	Pearson Learning Group
Ready for School	E	RF	77	Windmill Books	Rigby
Ready for Second Grade	L	RF	295	Leveled Readers	Houghton Mifflin Harcourt
Ready for Second Grade	L	RF	295	Leveled Readers/CA	Houghton Mifflin Harcourt
Ready for Second Grade	L	RF	295	Leveled Readers/TX	Houghton Mifflin Harcourt
Ready for Take-Off!	O	I	250+	Bookweb	Rigby
Ready Steady Jump	D	I	25	Pacific Literacy	Pacific Learning
Ready, Get Set, Go!	G	RF	137	First Start	Troll Associates
Ready, Set, Go	H	F	250+	Stadler, John	HarperTrophy
Ready, Set, Go!	D	I	26	Canizares, Susan; Chanko, Pamela	Scholastic
Ready, Set, Go!	K	RF	250+	Pacific Literacy	Pacific Learning
Ready, Set, Jump!	M	I	250+	Rigby Literacy	Rigby
Ready, Set, Pedal!	F	RF	165	On Our Way to English	Rigby
Ready, Steady, Rhyme!	J	RF	250+	Rigby Literacy	Rigby
Ready to Ride	F	RF	103	City Stories	Rigby
Real Band, A	G	RF	183	Leveled Readers	Houghton Mifflin Harcourt
Real Band, A	G	RF	183	Leveled Readers/CA	Houghton Mifflin Harcourt
Real Band, A	G	RF	183	Leveled Readers/TX	Houghton Mifflin Harcourt
Real Classy: Silly School Jokes	O	F	1880	Make Me Laugh!	Lerner Publications
Real Facts About Rivers	I	I	159	Rosen Real Readers	Rosen Publishing Group
Real McCoy, The: The Life of an African-American Inventor	T	B	250+	Towle, Wendy	Scholastic
Real or Not?- Art Fakes and Fakers	U	I	250+	Connectors	Pacific Learning
Real Princess, The	I	TL	193	Jumbled Tumbled Tales & Rhymes	Rigby
Real Question, The	Z+	RF	250+	Fogelin, Adrian	Fitzhenry & Whiteside
Real Team Soccer	R	RF	1207	Leveled Readers	Houghton Mifflin Harcourt
Real Thief, The	U	F	250+	Steig, William	Farrar, Straus and Giroux

* Collection of short stories
# Graphic text

TITLE	LEVEL	GENRE	WORD COUNT	AUTHOR / SERIES	PUBLISHER / DISTRIBUTOR
Really Rabbits	K	F	533	Kroll, Virginia	Charlesbridge
Really, Really Cold!	O	I	781	Vocabulary Readers	Houghton Mifflin Harcourt
Really, Really Cold!	O	I	781	Vocabulary Readers/CA	Houghton Mifflin Harcourt
Really, Really Cold!	O	I	781	Vocabulary Readers/TX	Houghton Mifflin Harcourt
Really?	K	RF	1506	Real Kids Readers	Millbrook Press
Real-Skin Rubber Monster Mask, The	H	F	104	Cohen, Miriam	Bantam
Reaper, The	R	I	250+	Theme Sets	National Geographic
Reason for a Flower, The	N	I	250+	Heller, Ruth	Scholastic
Reason to Run, A	Q	RF	250+	Leveled Readers Language Support	Houghton Mifflin Harcourt
Reasons for Seasons, The	M	I	250+	Gibbons, Gail	Holiday House
Rebecca and the Concert	I	RF	374	PM Story Books	Rigby
Rebecca at the Fun Fair	E	RF	87	Big Cat	Pacific Learning
Rebel Glory	U	RF	250+	Orca Sports	Orca Book Publishers
Rebels and Revolutions	X	I	250+	InfoQuest	Rigby
Rebel's Tag	V	RF	250+	Orca Currents	Orca Book Publishers
Rebuilding a Nation: Picking Up the Pieces	Y	I	250+	The Civil War	Carus Publishing
Rebus Bears, The	I	F	250+	Reit, Seymour	Bantam
Recess	A	I	27	At School Series	Pioneer Valley
Recess	B	RF	26	Teacher's Choice Series	Pearson Learning Group
Recipe for Learning	M	RF	879	Leveled Readers	Houghton Mifflin Harcourt
Recipe for Learning	M	RF	879	Leveled Readers/CA	Houghton Mifflin Harcourt
Recipe for Learning	M	RF	879	Leveled Readers/TX	Houghton Mifflin Harcourt
Reconstruction: Rebuilding after the Civil War	V	I	250+	Let Freedom Ring	Capstone Press
Rectangle	B	I	32	Shapes	Lerner Publications
Rectangles Around Town	J	I	309	Shapes Around Town	Capstone Press
Rectangles: Seeing Rectangles All Around Us	K	I	199	Shapes	Capstone Press
Recycle	C	I	16	Conservation	Lerner Publishing
Recycle It!	G	I	118	Discovery Links	Newbridge
Recycle Michael	F	RF	134	Storyteller	Wright Group/McGraw Hill
Recycle!	B	I	33	Leveled Readers Science	Houghton Mifflin Harcourt
Recycle, Reuse, and Reduce!	K	I	445	Vocabulary Readers	Houghton Mifflin Harcourt
Recycle, Reuse, and Reduce!	K	I	445	Vocabulary Readers/CA	Houghton Mifflin Harcourt
Recycle, Reuse, and Reduce!	K	I	445	Vocabulary Readers/TX	Houghton Mifflin Harcourt
Recycling a Can	M	I	250+	Rosen Real Readers	Rosen Publishing Group
Recycling Contest, The	K	RF	604	Leveled Readers	Houghton Mifflin Harcourt
Recycling Contest, The	K	RF	604	Leveled Readers/CA	Houghton Mifflin Harcourt
Recycling Contest, The	K	RF	604	Leveled Readers/TX	Houghton Mifflin Harcourt
Recycling Dump	D	I	48	Little Celebrations	Pearson Learning Group
Recycling Plastic	V	I	250+	Sauklis, Anthony	Houghton Mifflin Harcourt
Red	B	I	26	Colors	Lerner Publications
Red	E	F	71	Instant Readers	Harcourt School Publishers
Red Adair: The Story of an Oil Well Fighter	U	B	250+	High-Fliers	Pacific Learning
Red and Blue and Yellow	D	I	100	PM Nonfiction-Red	Rigby
Red and Blue Mittens	M	RF	250+	Reading Unlimited	Pearson Learning Group
Red and I Visit the Vet	F	RF	196	Ready Readers	Pearson Learning Group
Red and the Big Bad Wolf	W	F	1357	Leveled Readers	Houghton Mifflin Harcourt
Red Apples for Me	D	RF	69	Bonnell, Kris	Reading Reading Books
Red Balloon, The	C	RF	34	Joy Readers	Pearson Learning Group
Red Balloons, The	B	RF	55	Literacy by Design	Rigby
Red Balloons, The	B	RF	55	On Our Way to English	Rigby
Red Bird, The	D	RF	64	Reading Street	Pearson
Red Bird's Nest	E	F	149	Sails	Rigby
Red Block, Blue Block	D	I	108	PM Math Readers	Rigby

* Collection of short stories
\# Graphic text

TITLE	LEVEL	GENRE	WORD COUNT	AUTHOR / SERIES	PUBLISHER / DISTRIBUTOR
Red Box, The	H	RF	250+	Phonics Readers Plus	Steck-Vaughn
Red Cap	W	HF	250+	Wisler, G. Clifton	Penguin Group
Redcoats in America	T	I	1299	Vocabulary Readers	Houghton Mifflin Harcourt
Red Cowgirl Boots	F	RF	279	Rigby Flying Colors	Rigby
Red Dog	U	RF	250+	Wallace, Bill	Simon & Schuster
*Red Doll and Other Stories, The	H	F	250+	New Way Literature	Steck-Vaughn
Red Egg and Ginger	M	RF	250+	Greetings	Rigby
Red Flyer, The	K	RF	552	Springboard	Wright Group/McGraw Hill
Red Foxes	K	I	318	Pull Ahead Books	Lerner Publications
Red Hot Pet, A	L	F	250+	Rigby Gigglers	Rigby
Red Is Best	I	RF	309	Stinson, Kathy	Annick Press
Red Means Good Fortune: A Story of San Francisco's Chinatown	S	I	250+	Goldin, Barbara Diamond	Penguin Group
Red Midnight	Y	HF	250+	Mikaelsen, Ben	HarperTrophy
Red Nose Frost: A Traditional Tale From Russia	L	TL	250+	Rigby Literacy	Rigby
Red or Blue?	LB	RF	13	Ready Readers	Pearson Learning Group
Red Pajamas, The	D	F	98	Leveled Literacy Intervention/ Blue System	Heinemann
Red Planet, The	O	I	765	Leveled Readers	Houghton Mifflin Harcourt
Red Planet, The	O	I	765	Leveled Readers/CA	Houghton Mifflin Harcourt
Red Planet, The	O	I	765	Leveled Readers/TX	Houghton Mifflin Harcourt
Red Planet, The	S	I	250+	Orbit Double Takes	Pacific Learning
Red Puppy	C	RF	85	PM Plus Story Books	Rigby
Red Ribbon Rosie	M	RF	250+	Marzollo, Jean	Random House
*Red Riding Hood and the Flower in the Woods	L	TL	250+	New Way Literature	Steck-Vaughn
Red River Girl	U	HF	250+	Sommerdorf, Norma	Holiday House
Red Rose, The	E	F	127	Story Box	Wright Group/McGraw Hill
Red Scare, The	Z	I	3314	Vocabulary Readers	Houghton Mifflin Harcourt
Red Scare, The	Z	I	3314	Vocabulary Readers/CA	Houghton Mifflin Harcourt
Red Scarf Girl: Memoir of the Cultural Revolution	Z	B	250+	Jiang, Ji Li	HarperTrophy
Red Shoes, The	L	RF	250+	Sails	Rigby
Red Socks and Yellow Socks	G	F	155	Sunshine	Wright Group/McGraw Hill
Red Sox and the World Series, The	O	I	460	Vocabulary Readers	Houghton Mifflin Harcourt
Red Squirrel Hides Some Nuts	E	RF	128	PM Plus Story Books	Rigby
Red Squirrel's Adventure	H	RF	223	PM Plus Story Books	Rigby
Red Ted at the Beach	E	F	163	Storyworlds	Heinemann Educational Publishers
Red Ted Goes to School	E	RF	183	Storyworlds	Heinemann Educational Publishers
Red, White, and Blue	LB	I	21	Canizares, Susan; Chessen, Betsey	Scholastic
Red: Seeing Red All Around Us	L	I	250+	Colors	Capstone Press
Redcoats in America	T	I	1299	Vocabulary Readers/CA	Houghton Mifflin Harcourt
Redcoats in America	T	I	1299	Vocabulary Readers/TX	Houghton Mifflin Harcourt
Red-Eyed Tree Frogs	O	I	2636	Early Bird Nature Books	Lerner Publications
Reds and Blues	B	RF	57	Reading Street	Pearson
Red-Tailed Hawk, The	L	RF	197	Books For Young Learners	Richard C. Owen
Red-Tails Take Manhattan: The Story of Pale Male	T	I	250+	Literacy By Design	Rigby
Reduce	D	I	28	Conservation	Lerner Publishing
Reduce, Reuse, and Recycle	K	I	326	Early Connections	Benchmark Education
Redwall	Z	F	250+	Jacques, Brian	Avon
Reefs	T	I	250+	iOpeners	Pearson Learning Group

* Collection of short stories
# Graphic text

R

TITLE	LEVEL	GENRE	WORD COUNT	AUTHOR / SERIES	PUBLISHER / DISTRIBUTOR
Reel Heroes	X	I	250+	Boldprint	Steck-Vaughn
Reflections	I	F	110	Jonas, Ann	Morrow
Refuge Cove	W	RF	250+	Orca Soundings	Orca Book Publishers
Refugees, The	P	RF	250+	Orbit Chapter Books	Pacific Learning
Regarding the Fountain: A Tale, in Letter, of Liars and Leaks	U	F	250+	Klise, Kate	Avon
Regina's Ride	P	RF	1017	Leveled Readers	Houghton Mifflin Harcourt
Regions from Coast to Coast	O	I	250+	Literacy by Design	Rigby
Reindeer Crunch and Other Christmas Recipes	S	I	250+	Fun Food for Cool Cooks	Capstone Press
Relationships of Living Things	R	I	250+	Atwater, Mary et al.	Macmillan/McGraw Hill
Relay Race, The	H	RF	234	PM Stars	Rigby
Rella's Wish	R	TL	1207	Leveled Readers	Houghton Mifflin Harcourt
REM World	U	F	250+	Philbrick, Rodman	Scholastic
Remarkable Journey of Prince Jen, The	V	F	250+	Alexander, Lloyd	Bantam
Remarkable Pencils, The	S	F	4606	Take Two Books	Wright Group/McGraw Hill
Remarkable Robots	P	I	994	Vocabulary Readers	Houghton Mifflin Harcourt
Remarkable Robots	P	I	994	Vocabulary Readers/CA	Houghton Mifflin Harcourt
Remarkable Robots	P	I	994	Vocabulary Readers/TX	Houghton Mifflin Harcourt
Remarkable Romans, The	Y	I	2053	Leveled Readers	Houghton Mifflin Harcourt
Remarkable Romans, The	Y	I	2053	Leveled Readers/CA	Houghton Mifflin Harcourt
Rembrandt	S	B	250+	Masterpieces: Artists and Their Works	Capstone Press
Remember Not to Forget: A Memory of the Holocaust	V	I	250+	Finkelstein, Norman H.	William Morrow
Remember the Ladies: A Story About Abigail Adams	R	B	8915	Creative Minds Biographies	Carolrhoda Books
Remember the Ladies: The First Women's Rights Convention	U	I	250+	Johnston, Norma	Scholastic
Remembering the Big Quake	R	I	250+	Orbit Chapter Books	Pacific Learning
Remnants	W	SF	250+	Applegate, K. A.	Scholastic
Renaissance	Z	I	250+	Eyewitness Books	DK Publishing
Renaissance, The	W	I	250+	Orbit Chapter Books	Pacific Learning
Rent a Third Grader	O	RF	250+	Hiller, B. B.	Scholastic
Replay	T	RF	250+	Creech, Sharon	Harper Collins
Report Card, The	R	RF	250+	Clements, Andrew	Aladdin
Report to the Principal's Office	U	RF	250+	Spinelli, Jerry	Scholastic
Reptile	V	I	250+	Eyewitness Books	DK Publishing
Reptile Farm, The	I	I	228	Sun Sprouts	ETA Cuisenaire
Reptile Park, The	N	I	963	Rigby Flying Colors	Rigby
Reptiles	S	I	250+	Boldprint	Steck-Vaughn
Reptiles	M	I	250+	Exploring the Animal Kingdom	Capstone Press
Reptiles and Amphibians	R	I	250+	Explorers	Wright Group/McGraw Hill
Reptiles and Amphibians	L	I	250+	Rosen Real Readers	Rosen Publishing Group
Reptiles and Amphibians	P	I	944	Time for Kids	Teacher Created Materials
Reptiles as Pets	O	I	1109	Vocabulary Readers	Houghton Mifflin Harcourt
Reptiles as Pets	O	I	1109	Vocabulary Readers/CA	Houghton Mifflin Harcourt
Reptiles as Pets	O	I	1109	Vocabulary Readers/TX	Houghton Mifflin Harcourt
Rescue at Red Rock	U	RF	250+	WorldScapes	ETA Cuisenaire
Rescue at Sea	J	RF	250+	Storyworlds	Heinemann Educational Books
Rescue Boats	G	I	124	Mighty Machines	Capstone Press
Rescue Dogs	V	I	2617	Vocabulary Readers	Houghton Mifflin Harcourt
Rescue Dogs	V	I	2617	Vocabulary Readers/CA	Houghton Mifflin Harcourt
Rescue Dogs	V	I	2617	Vocabulary Readers/TX	Houghton Mifflin Harcourt

* Collection of short stories
\# Graphic text

TITLE	LEVEL	GENRE	WORD COUNT	AUTHOR / SERIES	PUBLISHER / DISTRIBUTOR
Rescue on Ruapehu	M	RF	250+	Rigby Literacy	Rigby
Rescue on the Outer Banks	N	HF	1724	On My Own History	Lerner Publications
Rescue!	J	RF	250+	Lighthouse	Rigby
Rescue!	J	RF	250+	Sunshine	Wright Group/McGraw Hill
Rescue!	O	RF	250+	Wildcats	Wright Group/McGraw Hill
Rescue, The	L	RF	176	Pacific Literacy	Pacific Learning
Rescue, The	H	RF	155	PM Extensions-Green	Rigby
Rescue, The	A	F	35	Springboard	Wright Group/McGraw Hill
Rescuers, The	S	F	250+	Sharp, Margery	Dell
Rescuing Mr. Black	I	RF	452	Rigby Flying Colors	Rigby
Rescuing Nelson	J	F	369	PM Collection	Rigby
Rescuing Stranded Whales	L	I	554	Reading Street	Pearson
Rescuing the Whooping Crane	S	I	1143	Leveled Readers	Houghton Mifflin Harcourt
Rescuing the Whooping Crane	S	I	1143	Leveled Readers/CA	Houghton Mifflin Harcourt
Rescuing the Whooping Crane	S	I	1143	Leveled Readers/TX	Houghton Mifflin Harcourt
Resistance	U	HF	250+	Jungman, Ann	Stone Arch Books
Respect	L	I	250+	Character Education	Red Brick Learning
Respect	L	I	250+	Everyday Character Education	Capstone Press
Respect	G	RF	163	Well-Being Series	Dominie Press
Respect the Winds	M	TL	250+	Take Two Books	Wright Group/McGraw Hill
Respecting Others	F	I	68	Citizenship	Lerner Publications
Respiratory System, The	P	I	2445	Early Bird Body Systems	Lerner Publishing
Respiratory System, The	M	I	212	Human Body Systems	Red Brick Learning
Responsibility	L	I	250+	Character Education	Red Brick Learning
Responsibility	L	I	250+	Everyday Character Education	Capstone Press
Responsible	Z+	RF	250+	Orca Soundings	Orca Book Publishers
Restless Humanity	V	I	1436	Reading Street	Pearson
Restless Spirit	Z	B	250+	Partridge, Elizabeth	Penguin Group
Return of Rinaldo, the Sly Fox	M	TL	250+	Scheffler, Ursel	North-South Books
Return of the Great Brain, The	T	RF	250+	Fitzgerald, John D.	Dell
Return of the Home Run Kid	Q	RF	250+	Christopher, Matt	Scholastic
Return of the Third-Grade Ghosthunters, The	M	RF	250+	Maccarone, Grace	Scholastic
Return of the Wolf, The	S	RF	250+	Literacy By Design	Rigby
Return of the Yellowstone Grizzly, The	S	I	2122	Leveled Readers	Houghton Mifflin Harcourt
Return of the Yellowstone Grizzly, The	S	I	2122	Leveled Readers/CA	Houghton Mifflin Harcourt
Return of the Yellowstone Grizzly, The	S	I	2122	Leveled Readers/TX	Houghton Mifflin Harcourt
Return of Wild Whoopers, The	X	I	3122	Leveled Readers	Houghton Mifflin Harcourt
Return to Gill Park	S	RF	250+	Gordon, Amy	Holiday House
Return to Howliday Inn	P	F	250+	Howe, James	Avon Camelot
Return to Titanic	Q	I	250+	Explorer Books-Pathfinder	National Geographic
Return to Titanic	P	I	250+	Explorer Books-Pioneer	National Geographic
Reunion in the Sky	Y	RF	3313	Leveled Readers	Houghton Mifflin Harcourt
Reunion in the Sky	Y	RF	3313	Leveled Readers/CA	Houghton Mifflin Harcourt
Reuse	D	I	27	Conservation	Lerner Publishing
Reuse and Recycle	I	I	118	Instant Readers	Harcourt School Publishers
Revenge of Captain Blood, The	O	F	250+	High-Fliers	Pacific Learning
Revenge of the Mummy	P	RF	250+	Parker, A. E.	Scholastic
Revenge of the Tribes	Y	I	250+	History for Young Canadians	Fitzhenry & Whiteside
Revenge of the Wannabes	X	RF	250+	Harrison, Lisi	Little, Brown & Co.
Revolution News	W	I	250+	The History News	Candlewick Press
Revolution of Sabine, The	X	HF	250+	Ain, Beth Levine	Candlewick Press
Revolution!	V	HF	3239	Leveled Readers	Houghton Mifflin Harcourt
Revolutionary Poet: A Story About Phillis Wheatley	Q	B	250+	Weidt, Maryann N.	Carolrhoda Books

* Collection of short stories
# Graphic text

TITLE	LEVEL	GENRE	WORD COUNT	AUTHOR / SERIES	PUBLISHER / DISTRIBUTOR
Revolutionary War on Wednesday	M	F	250+	Osborne, Mary Pope	Random House
Revolutionary War, The	V	I	250+	America Goes to War	Red Brick Learning
Revolutions That Shaped America	V	I	250+	Explore More	Wright Group/McGraw Hill
Reward for Work Well Done, The: Jonas Salk	Q	B	250+	High-Fliers	Pacific Learning
Rex	A	F	32	Leveled Literacy Intervention/ Orange System	Heinemann
Rex Plays Fetch	J	RF	250+	PM Plus Story Books	Rigby
Rex Runs Away	G	RF	225	On Our Way to English	Rigby
Rex to the Rescue	G	F	159	Sunshine	Wright Group/McGraw Hill
Rex's Box	D	RF	49	Reading Street	Pearson
Rex's Dance	E	F	103	Little Readers	Houghton Mifflin Harcourt
Rhinos	O	I	250+	Holmes, Kevin J.	Red Brick Learning
Rhode Island	T	I	250+	Hello U.S.A.	Lerner Publications
Rhode Island	R	I	250+	This Land Is Your Land	Compass Point Books
Rhode Island Colony, The	R	I	250+	The American Colonies	Capstone Press
Rhyme Game, The	G	RF	159	Storyteller-Setting Sun	Wright Group/McGraw Hill
Rhymes	A	I	9	Ready Readers	Pearson Learning Group
Rhyming Princess	J	F	480	Storyteller	Wright Group/McGraw Hill
Rhyming Riddles	H	I	240	Cambridge Reading	Pearson Learning Group
Rhythm and Shoes	N	I	250+	Pacific Literacy	Pacific Learning
Rhythm Is Everywhere	N	I	532	Vocabulary Readers	Houghton Mifflin Harcourt
Rhythm Is Everywhere	N	I	532	Vocabulary Readers/CA	Houghton Mifflin Harcourt
Ribbit!	A	I	7	Little Celebrations	Pearson Learning Group
Ribbon, The	C	I	46	Rise & Shine	Hampton-Brown
Ribsy	O	RF	250+	Cleary, Beverly	Hearst
Ric and Rin Run!	B	F	24	Reading Street	Pearson
Rice	L	I	132	Literacy Tree	Rigby
Rice	O	I	250+	Windows on Literacy	National Geographic
Rice - From Paddy Field to Plate	N	I	740	Springboard	Wright Group/McGraw Hill
Rice Cakes	H	F	332	Literacy 2000	Rigby
Rich and Famous Body and the Empty Checkbook, The	N	RF	250+	Wonder World	Wright Group/McGraw Hill
Rich or Poor?	W	I	250+	WorldScapes	ETA Cuisenaire
Richard M. Nixon	U	B	250+	Profiles of the Presidents	Compass Point Books
Richard M. Nixon: Thirty-seventh President	R	B	250+	Getting to Know the U.S. Presidents	Children's Press
Richard Nixon	T	B	3812	History Maker Bios	Lerner Publications
Richard Petty	Q	B	250+	NASCAR Racing	Capstone Press
Riches from Earth	S	I	250+	Navigators Science Series	Benchmark Education
Riches from Nature	K	I	382	Early Connections	Benchmark Education
Riches from the Earth	V	I	1352	Reading Street	Pearson
Richie the Greedy Mouse	I	F	179	Sunshine	Wright Group/McGraw Hill
Rick and Rosie	B	RF	28	Phonics and Friends	Hampton-Brown
Rick Is Sick	D	F	53	Green Light Readers	Harcourt
Rick's Dream Adventure	K	F	250+	World Quest Adventures	World Quest Learning
Ricky Ricotta's Mighty Robot vs. The Mecha-Monkeys From Mars	L	SF	250+	Pilkey, Dav	Scholastic
Ricky's Rat Gang	K	F	250+	I Am Reading	Kingfisher
Riddle Book	F	F	189	Reading Unlimited	Pearson Learning Group
Riddle of Redstone Castle, The	P	HF	250+	Tristars	Richard C. Owen
Riddle of Redstone Ruins, The	P	RF	250+	Tristars	Richard C. Owen
Riddle of the Anasazi, The	Z	I	1637	Leveled Readers	Houghton Mifflin Harcourt
Riddle of The Red Purse, The	L	RF	250+	Giff, Patricia Reilly	Bantam
Riddle of the Rosetta Stone, The	V	I	250+	Giblin, James Cross	HarperTrophy

* Collection of short stories
# Graphic text

TITLE	LEVEL	GENRE	WORD COUNT	AUTHOR / SERIES	PUBLISHER / DISTRIBUTOR
Riddle of the Seaplanes, The	R	RF	250+	Storyteller -Mountain Peaks	Wright Group/McGraw Hill
Riddles	E	I	51	Literacy 2000	Rigby
Riddles of the Universe	S	I	250+	Orbit Chapter Books	Pacific Learning
Ride in the Country, A	D	RF	83	Carousel Readers	Pearson Learning Group
Ride On: Bikes and Riders Who Rule	W	I	250+	Boldprint	Steck-Vaughn
Ride the Wild River	P	I	250+	Rigby Literacy	Rigby
Ride, A	LB	F	12	Sails	Rigby
Ride, Roll, and Run	F	RF	157	Windows on Literacy	National Geographic
Rides	Y	I	250+	Boldprint	Steck-Vaughn
Rides Are Fun	WB	I	N/A	Windows on Literacy	National Geographic
Rides, The	B	RF	42	Sails	Rigby
Riding	C	RF	67	Foundations	Wright Group/McGraw Hill
Riding	B	I	35	On Our Way to English	Rigby
Riding	H	I	210	Wonder World	Wright Group/McGraw Hill
Riding a Wave	V	I	250+	WorldScapes	ETA Cuisenaire
Riding Bicycles	H	I	150	Nonfiction Set 8	Literacy Footprints
Riding Freedom	P	HF	250+	Ryan, Pam Munoz	Scholastic
Riding High	K	RF	529	PM Story Books	Rigby
Riding My New Bike	E	I	132	Vocabulary Readers	Houghton Mifflin Harcourt
Riding My New Bike	E	I	132	Vocabulary Readers/CA	Houghton Mifflin Harcourt
Riding on Roller Coasters	R	I	250+	On Our Way to English	Rigby
Riding Out the Quake	U	RF	6171	Reading Street	Pearson
Riding Out the Storm	S	RF	1426	Leveled Readers	Houghton Mifflin Harcourt
Riding the Skateboard Ramps	K	RF	250+	PM Plus Story Books	Rigby
Riding the Steam Train	L	I	250+	Pacific Literacy	Pacific Learning
Riding to Craggy Rock	J	RF	386	PM Collection	Rigby
Riding to School	B	I	35	Leveled Readers	Houghton Mifflin Harcourt
Riding to School	B	I	35	Leveled Readers/CA	Houghton Mifflin Harcourt
Riding with the Camel Corps	W	HF	3451	Leveled Readers	Houghton Mifflin Harcourt
Riding with the Camel Corps	W	HF	3451	Leveled Readers/CA	Houghton Mifflin Harcourt
Riding with the Camel Corps	W	HF	3451	Leveled Readers/TX	Houghton Mifflin Harcourt
Riding with the Pony Express	T	HF	2776	Leveled Readers	Houghton Mifflin Harcourt
Riding with the Pony Express	T	HF	2776	Leveled Readers/CA	Houghton Mifflin Harcourt
Riding with the Pony Express	T	HF	2776	Leveled Readers/TX	Houghton Mifflin Harcourt
Riding with the Vaqueros	T	HF	1790	Leveled Readers	Houghton Mifflin Harcourt
Rifle, The	T	HF	250+	Paulsen, Gary	Dell
Right at Home	K	I	250+	Spyglass Books	Compass Point Books
Right Behind You	Z+	RF	250+	Giles, Gail	Little, Brown & Co.
Right Fly, The	U	RF	1878	Leveled Readers	Houghton Mifflin Harcourt
Right Match, The	E	RF	113	Dominie Math Stories	Pearson Learning Group
Right or Wrong?	O	RF	250+	Wildcats	Wright Group/McGraw Hill
Right Outside My Window	H	RF	121	Bookshop	Mondo
Right Pet, The	D	F	66	Leveled Readers	Houghton Mifflin Harcourt
Right Place for Jupiter, The	K	RF	250+	PM Story Books-Silver	Rigby
Right Place, Right Time	L	I	629	Gear Up!	Wright Group/McGraw Hill
Right Place, The	F	RF	165	In Step Readers	Rigby
Right to Rule, The	W	I	250+	WorldScapes	ETA Cuisenaire
Right to Survive, The	T	I	250+	Connectors	Pacific Learning
Righteous Revenge of Artemis Bonner, The	U	RF	250+	Myers, Walter Dean	HarperTrophy
Riley's Cake	H	RF	279	Rigby Flying Colors	Rigby
Rinaldo the Sly Fox	M	TL	250+	Scheffler, Ursel	North-South Books
Ring of Endless Light, A	W	F	250+	L'Engle, Madeleine	Dell
Ring of Fire, The	V	I	2580	Leveled Readers Social Studies	Houghton Mifflin Harcourt
Ringo's Assignment	N	F	250+	Springboard	Wright Group/McGraw Hill

R

* Collection of short stories
# Graphic text

TITLE	LEVEL	GENRE	WORD COUNT	AUTHOR / SERIES	PUBLISHER / DISTRIBUTOR
Rip Current Rescue	T	RF	250+	Reading Street	Pearson
Ripe Red Tomatoes	I	RF	191	Gear Up!	Wright Group/McGraw Hill
Ripeka's Carving	J	RF	250+	Literacy 2000	Rigby
*Rip-Roaring Russell	M	RF	250+	Hurwitz, Johanna	Penguin Group
Rip's Secret Spot	E	RF	116	Green Light Readers	Harcourt
Riptide	O	RF	250+	Weller, Frances Ward	Putnam/Penguin
Rise and Fall of the Incas, The	S	I	250+	Orbit Chapter Books	Pacific Learning
Rise and Shine, Mariko-chan	K	RF	250+	Tomioka, Chiyoko	Scholastic
Rising River, The	T	HF	2648	Leveled Readers	Houghton Mifflin Harcourt
Rising River, The	T	HF	2648	Leveled Readers/CA	Houghton Mifflin Harcourt
Rising River, The	T	HF	2648	Leveled Readers/TX	Houghton Mifflin Harcourt
Rising Stars of the NBA	P	B	250+	Layden, Joe	Scholastic
Rising Up, Falling Down	L	I	205	Spyglass Books	Compass Point Books
Rita at the Fair	C	F	32	Brand New Readers	Candlewick Press
Rita Blows Bubbles	C	F	25	Brand New Readers	Candlewick Press
Rita Moreno	K	B	250+	Leveled Readers Language Support	Houghton Mifflin Harcourt
Rita Moreno: Shining Star	M	B	593	Leveled Readers	Houghton Mifflin Harcourt
Rita Rolls	C	RF	36	Little Celebrations	Pearson Learning Group
River Apart, A	X	HF	250+	Sutherland, Robert	Fitzhenry & Whiteside
River as a Road, The	T	I	250+	Explore More	Wright Group/McGraw Hill
River Beds: Sleeping in the World's Rivers	P	RF	250+	Karwoski, Gail Langer	Sylvan Dell Publishing
River Between Us, The	X	HF	250+	Peck, Richard	Puffin Books
River Grows, The	E	I	70	Ready Readers	Pearson Learning Group
River Kept Rising, The	T	HF	2707	Leveled Readers	Houghton Mifflin Harcourt
River Kept Rising, The	T	HF	2707	Leveled Readers/CA	Houghton Mifflin Harcourt
River Kept Rising, The	T	HF	2707	Leveled Readers/TX	Houghton Mifflin Harcourt
River Life	N	I	250+	Windows on Literacy	National Geographic
River of No Return	T	RF	1845	Leveled Readers	Houghton Mifflin Harcourt
River Otter	I	I	208	Independent Readers Science	Houghton Mifflin Harcourt
River Patrol Boats	T	I	250+	Land and Sea	Capstone Press
River Race	N	HF	250+	Leveled Readers Language Support	Houghton Mifflin Harcourt
River Rafting Fun	J	RF	250+	PM Plus Story Books	Rigby
River Rapids Ride, The	J	RF	283	Sunshine	Wright Group/McGraw Hill
River Rats	O	RF	250+	Belcher, Angie	Pacific Learning
River Rescue	L	RF	250+	Reading Safari	Mondo
River Runners	M	RF	250+	Literacy Tree	Rigby
River Through the Ages	U	I	250+	Steele, Philip	Troll Associates
River Travel	R	I	1263	Vocabulary Readers	Houghton Mifflin Harcourt
River Travel	R	I	1263	Vocabulary Readers/CA	Houghton Mifflin Harcourt
River Travel	S	I	1200	Vocabulary Readers/TX	Houghton Mifflin Harcourt
River, The	J	I	222	Explorations	Eleanor Curtain Publishing
River, The	J	I	222	Explorations	Okapi Educational Materials
River, The	D	I	42	Foundations	Wright Group/McGraw Hill
River, The	R	RF	250+	Paulsen, Gary	Dell
River, The	C	I	40	Science	Outside the Box
River, The	J	I	280	Sun Sprouts	ETA Cuisenaire
Riverboat Bill	H	F	250	Take Two Books	Wright Group/McGraw Hill
Rivers	K	I	220	Take Two Books	Wright Group/McGraw Hill
Rivers & Lakes	R	I	250+	The Wonders of Our World	Crabtree
Rivers in the Rain Forest	O	I	250+	Pirotta, Saviour	Steck-Vaughn
River's Journey, A	G	I	116	Rigby Focus	Rigby
River's Journey, The	N	I	221	Windows on Literacy	National Geographic

* Collection of short stories
# Graphic text

TITLE	LEVEL	GENRE	WORD COUNT	AUTHOR / SERIES	PUBLISHER / DISTRIBUTOR
Rivers of Fire	U	F	250+	Carman, Patrick	Little, Brown & Co.
Rivers, Streams, and Lakes	M	I	250+	PM Plus Nonfiction	Rigby
Roach on the Fridge, A	N	RF	250+	Sails	Rigby
Road Builders	I	F	185	Leveled Literacy Intervention/ Blue System	Heinemann
Road Goes By, A	J	I	250+	Momentum Literacy Program	Troll Associates
Road Robber	I	F	250+	Sunshine	Wright Group/McGraw Hill
Road Through the Ages	U	I	250+	Steele, Philip	Troll Associates
Road to Freedom, A	V	HF	250+	Reading Expeditions	National Geographic
Road to Memphis, The	X	HF	250+	Taylor, Mildred D.	Penguin Group
Road to Revolution	T	I	250+	Reading Expeditions	National Geographic
Road to Revolution	W	I	2850	Vocabulary Readers	Houghton Mifflin Harcourt
Road to Revolution	W	I	2850	Vocabulary Readers/CA	Houghton Mifflin Harcourt
Road to Revolution	W	I	2850	Vocabulary Readers/TX	Houghton Mifflin Harcourt
Road to Seneca Falls, The	R	B	250+	Swain, Gwenyth	Carolrhoda Books
Road Trip, The	R	RF	250+	In Step Readers	Rigby
Road Work Ahead	I	RF	207	Little Readers	Houghton Mifflin Harcourt
Roadrunner	J	I	353	Vocabulary Readers	Houghton Mifflin Harcourt
Roadrunner	J	I	353	Vocabulary Readers/CA	Houghton Mifflin Harcourt
Roadrunners, The	M	I	441	Leveled Literacy Intervention/ Blue System	Heinemann
Roads and Bridges	I	RF	253	Alphakids	Sundance
Roald Dahl: A Life of Imagination	N	B	558	Pull Ahead- Biographies	Lerner Publications
Roald Dahl's Revolting Rhymes	R	F	250+	Dahl, Roald	Puffin/Penguin
Roanoke: The Lost Colony	T	I	250+	The Library of the Thirteen Colonies and The Lost Colony	Rosen Publishing Group
Roar Like a Tiger	E	RF	148	PM Plus Story Books	Rigby
Roaring Down the Rapids	O	RF	634	Leveled Readers	Houghton Mifflin Harcourt
Rob, Mom, and Socks	D	RF	44	Reading Street	Pearson
Robber Pig and the Ginger Bear	M	F	403	Read Alongs	Rigby
Robber Pig and the Green Eggs	M	F	250+	Read Alongs	Rigby
Robber, The	B	RF	25	Smart Starts	Rigby
Robber, The	M	RF	1255	Sunshine	Wright Group/McGraw Hill
Robber's Mask, The	S	RF	250+	Sails	Rigby
Robbers, The	I	RF	275	Sails	Rigby
Robbie Hood, Hurricane Hunter	S	B	1150	Independent Readers Science	Houghton Mifflin Harcourt
Robbie Woods and His Merry Men	N	RF	250+	High-Fliers	Pacific Learning
Robby in the River	I	RF	250+	Lighthouse	Rigby
Robe of Skulls, The	S	F	250+	French, Vivian	Candlewick Press
Robert and the Rocket	H	F	146	Waldron, Leesa	Scholastic
Robert E. Lee	U	B	250+	Amazing Americans	Wright Group/McGraw Hill
Robert E. Lee	S	B	4141	History Maker Bios	Lerner Publications
Robert E. Lee	U	B	250+	Let Freedom Ring	Red Brick Learning
Robert E. Lee	T	B	1940	Leveled Readers Social Studies	Houghton Mifflin Harcourt
Robert E. Lee	S	B	250+	Primary Source Readers	Teacher Created Materials
Robert E. Lee: Duty and Honor	Y	B	250+	The Civil War	Carus Publishing
Robert Frost: New England Poet	R	B	250+	Leveled Readers Language Support	Houghton Mifflin Harcourt
Robert Frost: The Journey of a Poet	U	B	963	Leveled Readers	Houghton Mifflin Harcourt
Robert Fulton	L	B	222	Famous People in Transportation	Red Brick Learning
Robert Goddard	L	B	203	Famous People in Transportation	Red Brick Learning
Robert Makes a Graph	H	I	160	Coulton, Mia	Kaeden Books
Robert Smalls Sails to Freedom	P	B	1861	On My Own History	Lerner Publications
Robert the Rose Horse	I	F	250+	Heilbroner, Joan	Random House

* Collection of short stories
\# Graphic text

R

TITLE	LEVEL	GENRE	WORD COUNT	AUTHOR / SERIES	PUBLISHER / DISTRIBUTOR
Roberto Clemente	M	B	250+	Rookie Biographies	Children's Press
Roberto Clemente	S	B	250+	Time for Kids	Teacher Created Materials
Roberto Clemente, Baseball Superstar	V	B	1776	Leveled Readers	Houghton Mifflin Harcourt
Roberto Clemente: A Life of Generosity	N	B	590	Pull Ahead- Biographies	Lerner Publications
Roberto Clemente: Baseball Superstar	N	B	250+	Rookie Biographies	Children's Press
Roberto's Smile	C	RF	43	Story Box	Wright Group/McGraw Hill
Robin Hood and the Silver Trophy	L	TL	250+	PM Tales and Plays-Silver	Rigby
Robin Hood Meets Little John	L	TL	250+	PM Story Books	Rigby
Robin Hood: The Tale of the Great Outlaw Hero	T	TL	250+	DK Readers	DK Publishing
Robins in the Spring	D	I	48	Bonnell, Kris	Reading Reading Books
Robinson Crusoe	P	TL	250+	Dolch, E. W.; Marguerite, P.	Scholastic
Robinson Crusoe	T	HF	250+	High-Fliers	Pacific Learning
Robocat	K	F	295	Leveled Readers	Houghton Mifflin Harcourt
Robocat Stops Crime!	J	F	323	Leveled Readers Language Support	Houghton Mifflin Harcourt
Robot Bedtime	E	F	121	Joy Starters	Pearson Learning Group
Robot Crash	H	F	185	Storyteller	Wright Group/McGraw Hill
Robot Rescue	R	SF	1566	Leveled Readers	Houghton Mifflin Harcourt
Robot Rescue	R	SF	1566	Leveled Readers/CA	Houghton Mifflin Harcourt
Robot Rescue	R	SF	1566	Leveled Readers/TX	Houghton Mifflin Harcourt
Robot Trouble	O	F	250+	On Our Way to English	Rigby
Robot Went Shopping	E	F	121	Joy Starters	Pearson Learning Group
Robot, The	B	F	49	Big Cat	Pacific Learning
Robot, The	B	F	30	Sails	Rigby
Robot, The	A	F	18	Smart Starts	Rigby
Robot-a-cise	K	F	250+	Sunshine	Wright Group/McGraw Hill
Robotics	X	I	7390	Cool Science	Lerner Publications
Robots	G	I	106	Big Cat	Pacific Learning
Robots	P	I	250+	Explorations	Eleanor Curtain Publishing
Robots	P	I	250+	Explorations	Okapi Educational Materials
Robots	K	I	157	Gear Up!	Wright Group/McGraw Hill
Robots	S	I	250+	iOpeners	Pearson Learning Group
Robots	I	I	184	Sails	Rigby
Robots' Car, The	C	F	127	Sails	Rigby
Robots, The	C	RF	96	Storyworlds	Heinemann Educational Publishers
Rock	M	I	250+	Materials	Capstone Press
Rock Art Rebel	Q	RF	10559	Cosson, M. J.	Stone Arch Books
Rock Band, The	O	RF	1797	Take Two Books	Wright Group/ McGraw Hill
Rock Basics	J	I	118	Nature Basics	Capstone Press
Rock Boss, The	G	F	257	Sails	Rigby
Rock Climbing	Q	I	250+	Extreme Sports	Red Brick Learning
Rock Climbing	O	I	250+	Sunshine	Wright Group/McGraw Hill
Rock Climbing at Yosemite National Park	T	I	250+	Explore More	Wright Group/McGraw Hill
Rock Climbing: Making It to the Top	S	I	250+	High Five Reading	Red Brick Learning
Rock Garden, The	H	RF	139	Windmill Books	Rigby
Rock Hunters	Q	I	250+	InfoQuest	Rigby
Rock in the Road, The	J	F	457	Pacific Literacy	Pacific Learning
Rock Kit, The	M	RF/I	424	Reading Street	Pearson
Rock 'n' Roll	X	I	250+	Boldprint	Steck-Vaughn
Rock Pools	I	I	250+	Momentum Literacy Program	Troll Associates
Rock Pools	G	I	266	Rigby Flying Colors	Rigby
Rock Pools, The	B	I	49	PM Starters	Rigby
Rock Records	Y	I	250+	iOpeners	Pearson Learning Group

R

* Collection of short stories
# Graphic text

TITLE	LEVEL	GENRE	WORD COUNT	AUTHOR / SERIES	PUBLISHER / DISTRIBUTOR
Rock Records	Q	I	250+	Reading Expeditions	National Geographic
Rock Star	N	RF	250+	Boyz Rule!	Mondo
Rock-a-Bye Moon	H	F	107	Pair-It Books	Steck-Vaughn
Rocket Ship, The	I	RF	250+	PM Plus Story Books	Rigby
Rocket Surpise, A	L	RF	250+	Sunshine	Wright Group/McGraw Hill
Rocket, The	F	RF	41	City Stories	Rigby
Rockets	N	I	250+	Explore Space!	Red Brick Learning
Rockets	C	I	49	Little Celebrations	Pearson Learning Group
Rockets	P	I	250+	Wonder World	Wright Group/McGraw Hill
Rockhound Hannah	J	RF	353	Pair-It Turn and Learn	Steck-Vaughn
Rockin' Reptiles	L	F	250+	Calmenson, Stephanie & Cole	Beech Tree Books
Rocking and Rolling Along	I	RF	73	Evangeline Nicholas Collection	Wright Group/McGraw Hill
Rockity Rock	C	RF	36	KinderReaders	Rigby
Rocks	F	I	112	Discovery Links	Newbridge
Rocks	R	I	2389	Early Bird Earth Systems	Lerner Publications
Rocks	L	I	157	Early Connections	Benchmark Education
Rocks	Q	I	250+	Exploring the Earth	Capstone Press
Rocks	B	I	33	Leveled Readers Science	Houghton Mifflin Harcourt
Rocks	E	I	59	Science	Harcourt School Publishers
Rocks	N	I	250+	Simply Science	Compass Point Books
Rocks	N	I	250+	Sun Sprouts	ETA Cuisenaire
Rocks	D	I	49	Voyages	SRA/McGraw Hill
Rocks	F	I	85	What Earth Is Made Of	Lerner Publications
Rocks & Minerals	R	I	250+	The Wonders of Our World	Crabtree
Rocks and Fossils	M	I	250+	Rosen Real Readers	Rosen Publishing Group
Rocks and Minerals	T	I	250+	Mission: Science	Compass Point Books
Rocks and Minerals	Q	I	1238	Science Support Readers	Houghton Mifflin Harcourt
Rocks and Minerals: The World Beneath Our Feet	T	I	250+	Pair-It Books	Steck-Vaughn
Rocks From Space	M	I	250+	Rigby Focus	Rigby
Rocks Rocks Rocks	E	I	76	Independent Readers Science	Houghton Mifflin Harcourt
Rocks, Soils and Fossils	M	I	618	Science Support Readers	Houghton Mifflin Harcourt
Rocks: Hard, Soft, Smooth, and Rough	N	I	250+	Amazing Science	Picture Window Books
Rocky Mountain Fur Trade, The	S	I	250+	The Library of the Westward Expansion	Rosen Publishing Group
Rocky Mountain National Park	N	I	389	Nonfiction Set 9	Literacy Footprints
Rocky's Road Home	L	F	629	Leveled Readers	Houghton Mifflin Harcourt
Rocky's Road Home	L	F	629	Leveled Readers/CA	Houghton Mifflin Harcourt
Rocky's Road Home	L	F	629	Leveled Readers/TX	Houghton Mifflin Harcourt
Rodeo Rocky: The Horses of Half Moon Ranch	S	RF	28600	Oldfield, Jenny	Sourcebooks
Rodeo Under the Sea	I	F	250+	Literacy by Design	Rigby
Rodeo Under the Sea	I	F	250+	On Our Way to English	Rigby
Rodeo!	R	I	1107	Leveled Readers	Houghton Mifflin Harcourt
Rodeo!	N	I	1186	Leveled Readers Social Studies	Houghton Mifflin Harcourt
Rodeo!	R	I	1107	Leveled Readers/CA	Houghton Mifflin Harcourt
Rodeo!	R	I	1107	Leveled Readers/TX	Houghton Mifflin Harcourt
Rodney, the Surfing Duck	N	F	250+	SupaDoopers	Sundance
Rodzina	Y	HF	250+	Cushman, Karen	Clarion
Rogue Elephant	R	RF	250+	Story Surfers	ETA Cuisenaire
Rogue Robot	P	F	250+	Bookweb	Rigby
Roles of Living Things	U	I	1856	Science Support Readers	Houghton Mifflin Harcourt
Roll of Thunder, Hear My Cry	W	HF	250+	Taylor, Mildred D.	Penguin Group
Roll On, Columbia	R	I	826	Independent Readers Social Studies	Houghton Mifflin Harcourt

R

TITLE	LEVEL	GENRE	WORD COUNT	AUTHOR / SERIES	PUBLISHER / DISTRIBUTOR
Roll Out the Red Rug	E	F	68	Ready Readers	Pearson Learning Group
Roll Over	F	F	220	Gerstein, Mordicai	Crown
Roll Over!	C	F	201	Peek, Merle	Clarion
Roller Blades, The	F	RF	137	Foundations	Wright Group/McGraw Hill
Roller Coaster	C	RF	45	Joy Readers	Pearson Learning Group
Roller Coaster	O	F	250+	Powell, J.	Stone Arch Books
Roller Coaster Ride	K	RF	484	PM Plus Story Books	Rigby
Roller Coaster Ride, The	G	RF	106	Carousel Readers	Pearson Learning Group
Roller Coaster, The	D	RF	115	Handprints C	Educators Publishing Service
Roller Coaster, The	B	F	34	KinderReaders	Rigby
Roller Coaster, The	I	RF	194	Sunshine	Wright Group/McGraw Hill
Roller Coasters	Q	I	250+	Wild Rides!	Capstone Press
Roller Skates!	J	RF	250+	Calmenson, Stephanie	Scholastic
Rollerama	N	RF	250+	SupaDoopers	Sundance
Rollercoaster	K	RF	250+	Rigby Literacy	Rigby
Rollercoaster	K	RF	250+	Rigby Star	Rigby
Rollercoaster Science	N	I	250+	Rigby Literacy	Rigby
Rollers and Blades	I	I	204	Take Two Books	Wright Group/McGraw Hill
Rolling	C	I	46	Sun Sprouts	ETA Cuisenaire
Rolling Right Along	S	I	250+	PM Extensions	Rigby
Rollo and Tweedy and the Ghost at Dougal Castle	K	F	250+	Allen, Laura Jean	HarperTrophy
*Roly-Poly	I	F	1227	Story Box	Wright Group/McGraw Hill
Roma Roller Skater	I	RF	238	Take Two Books	Wright Group/McGraw Hill
Roman News, The	W	I	250+	The History News	Candlewick Press
Roman Oracle, The	U	HF	250+	Sails	Rigby
Romana Acosta Banuelos	K	B	218	Leveled Readers Social Studies	Houghton Mifflin Harcourt
Romans, The	T	I	250+	Tristars	Richard C. Owen
Romare Bearden	R	I	1005	Vocabulary Readers	Houghton Mifflin Harcourt
Romare Bearden	R	I	1005	Vocabulary Readers/CA	Houghton Mifflin Harcourt
Romare Bearden	R	I	1005	Vocabulary Readers/TX	Houghton Mifflin Harcourt
Rome	W	I	250+	Primary Source Readers	Teacher Created Materials
Rome	V	I	250+	Theme Sets	National Geographic
Rome Is Burning	Y	I	1214	Leveled Readers	Houghton Mifflin Harcourt
Rome Is Burning	Y	I	1214	Leveled Readers/CA	Houghton Mifflin Harcourt
Rome: Everyday Kids Now and Then	S	HF	250+	Reading Expeditions	National Geographic
Ronald Reagan	T	B	3587	History Maker Bios	Lerner Publications
Ronald Reagan: Fortieth President	R	B	250+	Getting to Know the U.S. Presidents	Children's Press
Ronald W. Reagan	U	B	250+	Profiles of the Presidents	Compass Point Books
Roof and a Door, A	D	I	93	PM Nonfiction-Red	Rigby
Rookie of the Year	Y	RF	250+	Tunis, John R.	Harcourt
Room Decorating: Make Your Space Unique	Q	I	250+	Crafts	Capstone Press
Room for One More	G	RF	132	City Stories	Rigby
Room for Pip	E	F	175	Bookshop	Mondo
Room for the Animals?: How Urban Growth Affects Wildlife	V	I	250+	Literacy By Design	Rigby
Rooster and the Weather Vane, The	H	F	235	First Start	Troll Associates
Rooster Trouble	H	F	279	Sails	Rigby
Rooster's Gift, The	M	F	250+	Conrad, Pam	HarperCollins
Root Cellar, The	V	HF	250+	Lunn, Janet	Penguin Group
Roots	E	I	31	Parts of Plants	Lerner Publishing
Roots	H	I	121	Plant Parts	Capstone Press

R

* Collection of short stories
\# Graphic text

TITLE	LEVEL	GENRE	WORD COUNT	AUTHOR / SERIES	PUBLISHER / DISTRIBUTOR
Roots of the Blues	V	I	1293	Reading Street	Pearson
Rope Swing, The	E	RF	77	Oxford Reading Tree	Oxford University Press
Ropes of Revolution: The Tale of the Boston Tea Party	Q	HF	250+	Gunderson, J.	Stone Arch Books
Rory and Tina Go Skiiing	E	F	118	Springboard	Wright Group/McGraw Hill
Rory's Big Chance	L	RF	971	PM Plus Story Books	Rigby
Rosa and Fredo	M	F	250+	SupaDoopers	Sundance
Rosa at the Zoo	H	RF	135	Pacific Literacy	Pacific Learning
Rosa Catches a Fish	C	F	42	Brand New Readers	Candlewick Press
Rosa Loves to Walk	C	RF	57	Brand New Readers	Candlewick Press
Rosa Parks	Q	B	250+	Early Biographies	Compass Point Books
Rosa Parks	N	B	248	First Biographies	Red Brick Learning
Rosa Parks	P	B	250+	Greenfield, Eloise	HarperTrophy
Rosa Parks	S	B	3433	History Maker Bios	Lerner Publications
Rosa Parks	O	B	250+	In Step Readers	Rigby
Rosa Parks	Q	B	250+	Photo-Illustrated Biographies	Red Brick Learning
Rosa Parks: A Life of Courage	P	B	583	Pull Ahead Books	Lerner Publications
Rosa Parks: My Story	U	B	250+	Parks, Rosa	Scholastic
Rosa Plants a Tree	C	RF	29	Brand New Readers	Candlewick Press
Rosa the Painter	J	RF	394	Leveled Readers	Houghton Mifflin Harcourt
Rosa the Painter	J	RF	394	Leveled Readers/CA	Houghton Mifflin Harcourt
Rosa the Painter	J	RF	394	Leveled Readers/TX	Houghton Mifflin Harcourt
Rosalyn Yalow	W	B	2138	Leveled Readers Science	Houghton Mifflin Harcourt
Rosa's Adventure	S	TL	1403	Leveled Readers	Houghton Mifflin Harcourt
Rosa's Adventure	S	TL	1403	Leveled Readers/CA	Houghton Mifflin Harcourt
Rosa's Adventure	S	TL	1403	Leveled Readers/TX	Houghton Mifflin Harcourt
Rosa's Rebozo	M	TL	250+	On Our Way To English	Rigby
Rosa's Tonsils	K	RF	337	Foundations	Wright Group/McGraw Hill
Rose	F	F	82	Wheeler, Cindy	Alfred A. Knopf
Rose Avenue Street Sale, The	L	RF	890	InfoTrek	ETA Cuisenaire
Rose on the River, A	T	HF	250+	Storyteller -Mounatin Peaks	Wright Group/McGraw Hill
Rose Rest Home, The	K	RF	304	Sunshine	Wright Group/McGraw Hill
Rose Street Twins, The	Q	RF	250+	Reading Safari	Mondo
Roses for Anna	K	RF	250+	Rigby Literacy	Rigby
Roses for Renee	J	RF	395	Evangeline Nicholas Collection	Wright Group/McGraw Hill
Rosetta Stone, The	U	I	1089	Reading Street	Pearson
Rosie and Fred	D	RF	105	Rigby Flying Colors	Rigby
Rosie and the Bug Jar	D	RF	112	Leveled Readers	Houghton Mifflin Harcourt
Rosie and the Bug Jar	D	RF	112	Leveled Readers/CA	Houghton Mifflin Harcourt
Rosie at the Zoo	H	RF	135	Pacific Literacy	Pacific Learning
Rosie Is Cold	E	F	129	Bella and Rosie Series	Literacy Footprints
Rosie the Riveter	Z	I	250+	Colman, Penny	Crown
Rosie, the Nosy Goat	D	RF	56	Sunshine	Wright Group/McGraw Hill
Rosie: A Visiting Dog's Story	N	I	250+	Soar To Success	Houghton Mifflin Harcourt
Rosie's Big City Ballet	N	RF	250+	Giff, Patricia Reilly	Penguin Group
Rosie's Button Box	G	RF	233	Stepping Stones	Nelson/Michaels Assoc.
Rosie's House	K	RF	250+	Literacy 2000	Rigby
Rosie's Nutcracker Dreams	N	RF	250+	Giff, Patricia Reilly	Penguin Group
Rosie's Party	E	F	111	Little Readers	Houghton Mifflin Harcourt
Rosie's Pool	G	F	130	Little Readers	Houghton Mifflin Harcourt
Rosie's Story	L	RF	250+	Bookshop	Mondo
Rosie's Walk	F	F	32	Hutchins, Pat	Macmillan
*Rotating Rollerblades and Other Cases, The	O	RF	250+	Simon, Seymour	Avon
Rotten Reggie	G	RF	232	TOTTS	Tott Publications

* Collection of short stories
# Graphic text

TITLE	LEVEL	GENRE	WORD COUNT	AUTHOR / SERIES	PUBLISHER / DISTRIBUTOR
Rotten School Day	N	RF	250+	Boyz Rule!	Mondo
Rough and Smooth	H	I	172	Explorations	Eleanor Curtain Publishing
Rough and Smooth	H	I	172	Explorations	Okapi Eductional Materials
Rough Riders, The	W	B	250+	Cornerstones of Freedom	Children's Press
Rough-Face Girl, The	S	TL	250+	Martin, Rafe; Shannon, David	Scholastic
Round	C	I	40	Windmill Books	Rigby
Round and Round	C	RF	38	Story Box	Wright Group/McGraw Hill
Round and Round the Seasons Go	E	I	43	Learn to Read	Creative Teaching Press
Round and Round: The Story of Wheels	N	I	250+	Home Connection Collection	Rigby
Round Around Us	C	I	65	Bonnell, Kris	Reading Reading Books
Round Like a Circle	B	I	60	Windows on Literacy	National Geographic
Round the World	T	B	250+	High-Fliers	Pacific Learning
Route 66	O	I	696	Vocabulary Readers	Houghton Mifflin Harcourt
Route 66	O	I	696	Vocabulary Readers/CA	Houghton Mifflin Harcourt
Route 66	O	I	696	Vocabulary Readers/TX	Houghton Mifflin Harcourt
Route 66: Main Street of America	X	I	250+	Bookshop	Mondo
Row Row Row Your Boat	K	TL	160	Trapani, Iza	Charlesbridge
Row Your Boat	C	F	18	Literacy 2000	Rigby
Row Your Boat	C	F	18	Literacy Tree	Rigby
Row, Row, Row Your Boat	J	RF	250+	Bank Street	Bantam
Roxy	WB	F	N/A	Ready to Read	Pacific Learning
Roy and the Parakeet	E	F	74	Oxford Reading Tree	Oxford University Press
Roy at the Fun Park	G	RF	111	Oxford Reading Tree	Oxford University Press
Roy G. Biv	D	F	68	Story Box	Wright Group/McGraw Hill
Royal Baby-Sitters, The	J	RF	435	Sunshine	Wright Group/McGraw Hill
Royal Dinner, The	H	F	250+	Literacy Tree	Rigby
Royal Drum, The	L	TL	250+	Bookshop	Mondo
Royal Family, The	LB	F	17	Stewart, Josie; Salem, Lynn	Continental Press
Royal Goose, The	H	F	198	Ready Readers	Pearson Learning Group
Royal Mummies: Remains From Ancient Egypt, The	V	I	250+	Mummies	Capstone Press
Royal Road, The	S	RF	2407	Leveled Readers	Houghton Mifflin Harcourt
Royal Road, The	S	RF	2407	Leveled Readers/CA	Houghton Mifflin Harcourt
Royal Road, The	S	RF	2407	Leveled Readers/TX	Houghton Mifflin Harcourt
Royal Zookeeper, The	K	F	431	Early Connections	Benchmark Education
Roy's First Day	C	RF	125	InfoTrek	ETA Cuisenaire
Rubber	M	I	250+	Materials	Capstone Press
Rubber	O	I	250+	Rigby Focus	Rigby
Rubber Duck	I	F	170	Early Readers	Compass Point Books
Rubber Inventor: The Story of Charles Goodyear	S	B	912	Independent Readers Science	Houghton Mifflin Harcourt
Rubbery Arms and Baggy Bodies	O	I	250+	Sails	Rigby
Rubbish and Recycling	T	I	250+	The News	Richard C. Owen
Rube Goldberg's Silly Machines	R	B	438	Independent Readers Science	Houghton Mifflin Harcourt
Ruby and the Booker Boys	N	RF	250+	Barnes, Derrick	Scholastic
Ruby and the Ocean	J	RF	406	Gear Up!	Wright Group/McGraw Hill
Ruby and the Smoke, The	Y	F	250+	Pullman, Phillip	Laurel-Leaf Books
Ruby Holler	V	RF	250+	Creech, Sharon	HarperCollins
Ruby Red and Sky Blue	E	RF	157	Rigby Rocket	Rigby
Ruby the Copycat	K	RF	250+	Rathman, Peggy	Scholastic
Ruff and Me	C	RF	30	First Stories	Pacific Learning
Ruffles Needs Help!	L	RF	903	InfoTrek	ETA Cuisenaire
Rug Weavers	J	RF	182	Leveled Readers Language Support	Houghton Mifflin Harcourt

* Collection of short stories
\# Graphic text

R

TITLE	LEVEL	GENRE	WORD COUNT	AUTHOR / SERIES	PUBLISHER / DISTRIBUTOR
Ruler	C	I	32	Simple Tools	Lerner Publishing
Rulers of Persia	Y	I	2401	Leveled Readers	Houghton Mifflin Harcourt
Rulers of Persia	Y	I	2401	Leveled Readers/CA	Houghton Mifflin Harcourt
Rules	J	I	265	Early Connections	Benchmark Education
Rules	R	RF	250+	Lord, Cynthia	Scholastic
Rules Are Cool	H	RF	173	InfoTrek	ETA Cuisenaire
Rules for Pets	C	F	54	Joy Readers	Pearson Learning Group
Rules Have Changed, The	P	F	250+	Reading Safari	Mondo
Rules Help	C	I	69	Windows on Literacy	National Geographic
Rules of the Ride	P	RF	1023	Leveled Readers	Houghton Mifflin Harcourt
Rules of the Universe by Austin W. Itale	U	SF	250+	Vaupel, Robin	Holiday House
Rumble, Rumble, Boom!	D	I	26	Pacific Literacy	Pacific Learning
Rummage Sale, The	E	RF	81	Oxford Reading Tree	Oxford University Press
Rumpelstiltskin	J	TL	250+	Bookshop	Mondo
Rumpelstiltskin	J	TL	250+	Jumbled Tumbled Tales & Rhymes	Rigby
Rumpelstiltskin	M	TL	250+	Once Upon a Time	Wright Group/McGraw Hill
Rumpelstiltskin	K	TL	250+	PM Tales and Plays-Gold	Rigby
Rumpelstiltskin	J	TL	940	Traditional Tales	Pearson Learning Group
Rumpelstiltskin	N	TL	250+	Zelinsky, Paul O.	Scholastic
Rum-Tum-Tum	E	F	62	Story Box	Wright Group/McGraw Hill
Run Away Home. And Be Free.	R	HF	250+	McKissack, Patricia	Scholastic
Run Fast	D	I	96	Sails	Rigby
Run For It!	D	F	64	Rigby Literacy	Rigby
Run!	B	F	28	Sunshine	Wright Group/McGraw Hill
Run! Run!	C	F	64	Bookshop	Mondo
Run, Rabbit!	A	RF	14	Landman, Yael	Scholastic
Run, Rabbit, Run!	D	RF	96	PM Plus Story Books	Rigby
Run, Run, Run	B	RF	19	Joy Readers	Pearson Learning Group
Runaround Rowdy	L	RF	250+	PM Story Books	Rigby
Runaway Ball, The	K	RF	250+	Rigby Literacy	Rigby
Runaway Hank	J	RF	250+	The Wright Skills	Wright Group/McGraw Hill
Runaway Monkey	B	F	39	Stewart, Josie; Salem, Lynn	Continental Press
Runaway Ralph	O	F	250+	Cleary, Beverly	Hearst
Runaway Rascal	O	RF	250+	Baglio, Ben M.	Scholastic
Runaway Sandy	E	RF	97	Leveled Readers	Houghton Mifflin Harcourt
Runaway to Freedom: A Story of the Underground Railway	T	I	250+	Smucker, Barbara	HarperTrophy
Runaway Wheel, The	G	RF	204	Reading Safari	Mondo
Runaway Wheels, The	B	F	32	Pair-It Books	Steck-Vaughn
Running	C	RF	39	Foundations	Wright Group/McGraw Hill
Running	A	RF	31	Sun Sprouts	ETA Cuisenaire
Running	F	RF	185	Visions	Wright Group/McGraw Hill
Running for President	S	I	1167	Vocabulary Readers	Houghton Mifflin Harcourt
Running for President	S	I	1167	Vocabulary Readers/CA	Houghton Mifflin Harcourt
Running for President	S	I	1167	Vocabulary Readers/TX	Houghton Mifflin Harcourt
Running for the Bus	S	RF	250+	Literacy by Design	Rigby
Running Free: The Jami Goldman Story	P	B	250+	Literacy by Design	Rigby
Running Out of Time	W	SF	250+	Haddix, Margaret Peterson	Simon & Schuster
Running Rivals	P	RF	250+	Maddox, Jake	Stone Arch Books
Running Shoes, The	K	RF	519	PM Plus Story Books	Rigby
Rupert and the Griffin	Q	F	250+	Literacy 2000	Rigby
Rupert Goes to School	K	RF	250+	Storyteller-Lightning Bolts	Wright Group/McGraw Hill
Rupert's Ice Cream Shop	G	RF	273	Sails	Rigby

* Collection of short stories
\# Graphic text

TITLE	LEVEL	GENRE	WORD COUNT	AUTHOR / SERIES	PUBLISHER / DISTRIBUTOR
Rupert's Rainbow Ice Cream	I	RF	335	Sails	Rigby
Rural Veterinarian, A	R	I	1390	Leveled Readers	Houghton Mifflin Harcourt
Rural Veterinarian, A	R	I	1390	Leveled Readers/CA	Houghton Mifflin Harcourt
Rural Veterinarian, A	R	I	1390	Leveled Readers/TX	Houghton Mifflin Harcourt
Rush Hour	D	RF	111	Rigby Star	Rigby
Rush, Rush, Rush	E	RF	52	Ready Readers	Pearson Learning Group
Rushing for Gold	N	I	713	Leveled Readers	Houghton Mifflin Harcourt
Rushing for Gold	N	I	713	Leveled Readers/CA	Houghton Mifflin Harcourt
Rushing for Gold	N	I	713	Leveled Readers/TX	Houghton Mifflin Harcourt
*Russell and Elisa	M	RF	250+	Hurwitz, Johanna	Penguin Group
*Russell Rides Again	M	RF	250+	Hurwitz, Johanna	Penguin Group
*Russell Sprouts	M	RF	250+	Hurwitz, Johanna	Penguin Group
Russia	O	I	250+	Countries of the World	Red Brick Learning
Russia	P	I	2014	Country Explorers	Lerner Publications
Russia	Y	I	250+	Eyewitness Books	DK Publishing
Russia	Q	I	250+	First Reports: Countries	Compass Point Books
Russia ABCs: A Book About the People and Places of Russia	Q	I	250+	Country ABCs	Picture Window Books
Russia: A Question and Answer Book	P	I	250+	Questions and Answers: Countries	Capstone Press
Russian Colonies in the Americas	S	I	250+	On Deck	Rigby
Rusty the Rascal	L	RF	250+	Windows on Literacy	National Geographic
Rutherford B. Hayes	U	B	250+	Profiles of the Presidents	Compass Point Books
Rutherford B. Hayes: Nineteenth President	R	B	250+	Getting to Know the U.S. Presidents	Children's Press
Ruthie's Perfect Poem	N	RF	744	Leveled Readers	Houghton Mifflin Harcourt
Ryan Howard	P	B	250+	Amazing Athletes	Lerner Publications
Ryan's Dog Ringo	P	RF	250+	Literacy 2000	Rigby

R

* Collection of short stories
# Graphic text

TITLE	LEVEL	GENRE	WORD COUNT	AUTHOR / SERIES	PUBLISHER / DISTRIBUTOR
S.O.S.! Save Our Swamp!	I	RF	276	Pair-It Turn and Learn	Steck-Vaughn
Sabertooth Cat	I	I	120	Dinosaur and Prehistoric Animals	Capstone Press
Sabertooth Cat	N	I	250+	Extinct Monsters	Capstone Press
Saber-Toothed Cats	N	I	1520	On My Own Science	Lerner Publications
Sable	O	RF	250+	Hesse, Karen	Henry Holt & Co.
Sacagawea	U	B	250+	Amazing Americans	Wright Group/ McGraw Hill
Sacagawea	N	B	242	Leveled Readers	Houghton Mifflin Harcourt
Sacagawea	P	B	250+	Photo-Illustrated Biographies	Red Brick Learning
Sacagawea: 1788-1812	S	B	250+	American Indian Biographies	Capstone Press
Sacagawea's Journey	M	B	250+	Leveled Readers Language Support	Houghton Mifflin Harcourt
Sacajawea	N	B	250+	Biography	Benchmark Education
Sacajawea	Y	B	250+	Bruchac, Joseph	Harcourt Trade
Sacajawea: Her True Story	N	B	250+	Milton, Joyce	Scholastic
Sack Race, A	E	RF	106	New Way Blue	Steck-Vaughn
Sacks of Gold	I	F	263	Sunshine	Wright Group/McGraw Hill
Sad	D	I	18	Feelings	Lerner Publishing
Sad Monster	E	F	160	Handprints D, Set 1	Educators Publishing Service
Sadako and the Thousand Cranes	R	B	250+	Springboard	Wright Group/McGraw Hill
Sadako and the Thousand Paper Cranes	R	HF	250+	Coerr, Eleanor	Bantam
Sadie and the Snowman	L	RF	250+	Morgan, Allen	Scholastic
Sadie, Remember	L	HF	250+	Kline, Carol	Sundance
Safe at Work	D	I	99	Early Connections	Benchmark Education
Safe Harbor, A	K	I	167	Windows on Literacy	National Geographic
Safe Haven, A	U	I	2439	Reading Street	Pearson
Safe Homes	F	I	117	Reading Street	Pearson
Safe Place for Tigers, A	I	I	124	Gear Up!	Wright Group/McGraw Hill
Safe Place, The	H	TL	147	Pacific Literacy	Pacific Learning
Safe Return	Q	RF	250+	Dexter, Catherine	Candlewick Press
Safecrackers	Q	F	250+	Zucker, Jonny	Stone Arch Books
Safety	C	I	35	Interaction	Rigby
Safety at the Playground	E	I	42	Rosen Real Readers	Rosen Publishing Group
Safety Counts	C	F	52	Learn to Read	Creative Teaching Press
Safety First	F	I	195	Dominie Factivity Series	Pearson Learning Group
Safety First	C	I	131	Twig	Wright Group/McGraw Hill
Safety in Numbers	J	I	250+	Evans, Lynette	Scholastic
Safety on the School Bus	E	I	38	Rosen Real Readers	Rosen Publishing Group
Safety Signs	G	I	112	Early Connections	Benchmark Education
Sagebrush and Paintbrush: The Story of Charlie Russell, the Cowboy Artist	W	B	250+	Bookshop	Mondo
Saguaro	E	I	44	Books for Young Learners	Richard C. Owen
Saguaro Cactus	Q	I	1513	Early Bird Nature Books	Lerner Publications
Saguaro Cactus	N	I	250+	Habitats	Children's Press
Saguaro National Park	O	I	250+	A True Book	Children's Press
Sahara Special	S	RF	250+	Codell, Esme Raji	Hyperion
Sahara, The	N	I	250+	Leveled Readers	Houghton Mifflin Harcourt
Sail Away, Little Boat	K	F	383	Buell, Janet	Carolrhoda Books
Sailboat Race, The	J	F	330	Leveled Readers	Houghton Mifflin Harcourt
Sailboat Race, The	J	F	330	Leveled Readers/CA	Houghton Mifflin Harcourt
Sailboat Race, The	J	F	330	Leveled Readers/TX	Houghton Mifflin Harcourt
Sailing Adventures	S	I	250+	Dangerous Adventures	Red Brick Learning
Sailing the Stars	T	I	2187	Reading Street	Pearson

S

* Collection of short stories
# Graphic text

Storable Database at www.fountasandpinnellleveledbooks.com

TITLE	LEVEL	GENRE	WORD COUNT	AUTHOR / SERIES	PUBLISHER / DISTRIBUTOR
Sailing to a New Land	K	HF	250+	PM Plus Story Books	Rigby
Sailing to Safety	N	HF	1005	Leveled Readers	Houghton Mifflin Harcourt
Sailing to Safety	N	HF	1005	Leveled Readers/CA	Houghton Mifflin Harcourt
Sailing to Safety	N	HF	1005	Leveled Readers/TX	Houghton Mifflin Harcourt
Sailor Sam	I	RF	241	Sails	Rigby
Sailor Sam and the Balloons	I	RF	254	Sails	Rigby
Sailor Sam and the Birds	F	RF	148	Sails	Rigby
Sailor Sam and the Boots	F	RF	227	Sails	Rigby
Sailor Sam and the Captain	I	F	341	Sails	Rigby
Sailor Sam and the Coconuts	H	F	248	Sails	Rigby
Sailor Sam and the Goat	J	RF	319	Sails	Rigby
Sailor Sam Gets Lost	I	F	423	Sails	Rigby
Sailor Sam in Trouble	F	RF	186	Sails	Rigby
Sailor Sam Up the Mast	I	RF	298	Sails	Rigby
Sailors	A	RF	18	Sails	Rigby
Salad	A	F	36	Carousel Earlybirds	Pearson Learning Group
Salad Feast, A	D	RF	57	Little Readers	Houghton Mifflin Harcourt
Salad Vegetables	LB	I	15	Foundations	Wright Group/McGraw Hill
Salad Vegetables	A	I	27	Story Box	Wright Group/McGraw Hill
Salamandastron	Z	F	250+	Jacques, Brian	Ace Books
Salamanders and Alligators	M	I	710	Leveled Readers Science	Houghton Mifflin Harcourt
Salem Days: Life in a Colonial Seaport	T	I	250+	Adventures in Colonial America	Troll Associates
#Salem Witch Trials, The	U	I	250+	Graphic Library	Capstone Press
Salem Witch Trials, The	V	I	250+	Let Freedom Ring	Capstone Press
Salem Witch Trials, The	U	I	1093	Leveled Readers Social Studies	Houghton Mifflin Harcourt
Sally and the Daisy	C	RF	60	PM Story Books	Rigby
Sally and the Elephant	C	RF	50	PM Stars	Rigby
Sally and the Elephant	C	I	45	Wonder World	Wright Group/McGraw Hill
Sally and the Leaves	C	RF	55	PM Stars	Rigby
Sally and the Sparrows	E	RF	151	PM Extensions-Yellow	Rigby
Sally and the Wild Puppy	I	RF	270	Reading Street	Pearson
Sally Ride	H	B	77	Leveled Readers Social Studies	Houghton Mifflin Harcourt
Sally Ride in Space	L	B	235	Vocabulary Readers	Houghton Mifflin Harcourt
Sally Ride: Astronaut, Scientist, Teacher	M	B	250+	Biographies	Picture Window Books
Sally Spider's Accident	I	F	250+	Reading Safari	Mondo
Sally Spinner Finds a Home	K	F	250+	Reading Safari	Mondo
Sally the Great	H	RF	250+	Home Connection Collection	Rigby
Sally's Beans	D	RF	123	PM Story Books	Rigby
Sally's Big Save	M	RF	250+	Social Studies Connects	Kane Press
Sally's Friends	F	RF	128	PM Story Books	Rigby
Sally's New Shoes	B	RF	58	PM Starters	Rigby
Sally's Picture	G	RF	125	Literacy 2000	Rigby
Sally's Red Bucket	E	RF	127	PM Story Books	Rigby
Sally's Snowman	C	RF	57	PM Stars	Rigby
Sally's Spaceship	E	RF	86	Ready Readers	Pearson Learning Group
Sally's Surprise	M	RF	1918	Take Two Books	Wright Group/McGraw Hill
Sally's Surprise Garden	H	RF	148	Literacy Tree	Rigby
Salmon	N	I	250+	Bookshop	Mondo
Salmon Forest, The	Q	RF	250+	WorldScapes	ETA Cuisenaire
Salmon Story, A	G	I	132	Twig	Wright Group/McGraw Hill
*Salmon's Journey and More Northwest Coast Stories	P	TL	250+	Challenger, James Robert	Heritage House
Salt	J	I	247	Rigby Focus	Rigby
Salt	U	I	250+	Theme Sets	National Geographic

* Collection of short stories
# Graphic text

TITLE	LEVEL	GENRE	WORD COUNT	AUTHOR / SERIES	PUBLISHER / DISTRIBUTOR
Salt Caravan, The	S	I	250+	WorldScapes	ETA Cuisenaire
Salt Lick Boom Town	J	F	577	Reading Street	Pearson
Salton Sea, The	V	I	3036	Leveled Readers	Houghton Mifflin Harcourt
Salton Sea, The	V	I	3036	Leveled Readers/CA	Houghton Mifflin Harcourt
Salton Sea, The	V	I	3036	Leveled Readers/TX	Houghton Mifflin Harcourt
Saltwater Fishing	S	I	250+	The Great Outdoors	Capstone Press
Salty Dog	L	RF	250+	Rand, Gloria	Henry Holt & Co.
Salty Tale, A	O	TL	793	Gear Up!	Wright Group/ McGraw Hill
Sam	D	RF	87	Early Connections	Benchmark Education
Sam	C	RF	17	KinderReaders	Rigby
Sam and Bingo	C	RF	53	PM Plus Story Books	Rigby
Sam and Dasher	G	RF	53	Rookie Readers	Children's Press
Sam and Jack: Three Stories	C	F	65	Green Light Readers	Harcourt
Sam and Kim	O	I	250+	Pacific Literacy	Pacific Learning
Sam and Mac	H	F	146	Pair-It Turn and Learn	Steck-Vaughn
Sam and Nate	L	RF	250+	Orca Echoes	Orca Book Publishers
Sam and Papa	B	RF	65	Leveled Literacy Intervention/ Green System	Heinemann
Sam and the Bag	B	F	31	Green Light Readers	Harcourt
Sam and the Firefly	J	F	250+	Eastman, Philip D.	Random House
Sam and the Lucky Money	N	RF	250+	Soar To Success	Houghton Mifflin Harcourt
Sam and the Waves	D	RF	122	PM Plus Story Books	Rigby
Sam Bennett's New Shoes	L	RF	1339	Thermes, Jennifer	Carolrhoda Books
Sam Collier and the Founding of Jamestown	O	HF	1996	On My Own History	Lerner Publications
Sam Finds the Party	K	RF	714	Leveled Readers	Houghton Mifflin Harcourt
Sam Finds the Party	K	RF	714	Leveled Readers/CA	Houghton Mifflin Harcourt
Sam Finds the Party	K	RF	714	Leveled Readers/TX	Houghton Mifflin Harcourt
Sam Goes Riding	F	RF	121	Gear Up!	Wright Group/McGraw Hill
Sam Goes to School	E	RF	131	PM Plus Story Books	Rigby
Sam Hides Red Ted	E	RF	170	Storyworlds	Heinemann Educational Publishers
Sam Houston	N	B	248	Pebble Books	Capstone Press
Sam Houston: Soldier and Statesman	V	B	250+	Let Freedom Ring	Capstone Press
Sam King and Little Bull	L	RF	250+	Wilson, Trevor	Pearson Learning Group
Sam Plays Paddle Ball	F	F	161	PM Plus Story Books	Rigby
Sam Samurai	P	F	250+	Scieszka, Jon	Penguin Group
Sam the Big, Bad Cat	E	F	86	Big Cat	Pacific Learning
Sam the Duck	C	RF	28	Reading Street	Pearson
Sam the Garbage Hound	G	F	53	Rookie Readers	Children's Press
Sam the Minuteman	J	HF	250+	Benchley, Nathaniel	HarperTrophy
Sam the Scarecrow	F	F	143	First Start	Troll Associates
Sam Who Never Forgets	K	F	281	Rice, Eve	Morrow
Sam Writes	D	RF	62	Book Bank	Wright Group/McGraw Hill
*Sam, Sam, and Other Stories	F	F	250+	Story Steps	Rigby
Samantha Saves the Day	Q	RF	250+	The American Girls Collection	Pleasant Company
Samantha's Brother	L	RF	700	Rigby Flying Colors	Rigby
Samantha's Sea	R	I	250+	Storyteller -Whispering Pines	Wright Group/McGraw Hill
Samantha's Solar Spin	L	F	250+	Reading Safari	Mondo
Samantha's Surprise	Q	RF	250+	The American Girls Collection	Pleasant Company
Same But Different	I	RF	184	Sunshine	Wright Group/McGraw Hill
Same Idea, Different Year	M	RF	250+	Bookweb	Rigby
Same Stuff as Stars, The	V	RF	250+	Paterson, Katherine	Clarion
Same Team	C	I	44	The Candid Collection	Pearson Learning Group
Same, but Different	I	I	210	Sails	Rigby

* Collection of short stories
# Graphic text

S

TITLE	LEVEL	GENRE	WORD COUNT	AUTHOR / SERIES	PUBLISHER / DISTRIBUTOR
Same, But Different, The	Q	RF	1205	Leveled Readers	Houghton Mifflin Harcourt
Samir and Yonatan	Z	RF	250+	Carmi, Daniella	Scholastic
Sammy	B	RF	32	Urmston, Kathleen	Kaeden Books
Sammy at the Farm	C	RF	83	Urmston, Kathleen; Evans, Karen	Kaeden Books
Sammy Gets a Bath	C	RF	33	Evans, Karen	Kaeden Books
Sammy Gets a Ride	F	RF	91	Evans, Karen; Urmston, Kathleen	Kaeden Books
Sammy Keyes and the Art of Deception	T	RF	250+	Van Draanen, Wendelin	Random House
Sammy Keyes and the Curse of Moustache Mary	T	RF	250+	Van Draanen, Wendelin	Random House
Sammy Keyes and the Dead Giveaway	T	RF	250+	Van Draanen, Wendelin	Yearling
Sammy Keyes and the Hotel Thief	T	RF	250+	Van Draanen, Wendelin	Random House
Sammy Keyes and the Runaway Elf	T	RF	250+	Van Draanen, Wendelin	Random House
Sammy Keyes and the Sisters of Mercy	T	RF	250+	Van Draanen, Wendelin	Random House
Sammy Keyes and the Skeleton Man	T	RF	250+	Van Draanen, Wendelin	Random House
Sammy Loves to Run	C	RF	32	Evans, Karen	Kaeden Books
Sammy Sosa	P	B	1705	Amazing Athletes	Lerner Publications
Sammy Sosa	R	B	250+	Sports Heroes	Red Brick Learning
Sammy the Seal	H	F	250+	Hoff, Syd	HarperTrophy
Sammy's Hamburger Caper	I	F	250	Urmston, Kathleen	Kaeden Books
Sammy's Moving	F	F	166	Evans, Karen; Urmston, Kathleen	Kaeden Books
Sammy's Slippery Day	H	RF	263	Urmston, Kathleen; Urmston, Graig	Kaeden Books
Sammy's Sneeze	D	RF	69	Home Connection Collection	Rigby
Sammy's Special Day	C	RF	41	Urmston, Kathleen	Kaeden Books
Sammy's Supper	I	RF	293	Reading Unlimited	Pearson Learning Group
Samoan Song, A	O	I	250+	WorldScapes	ETA Cuisenaire
Sam's Ball	D	RF	64	Lindgren, Barbro	Morrow
Sam's Balloon	C	RF	54	PM Plus Story Books	Rigby
Sam's Big Clean-up	K	RF	287	Windmill Books	Rigby
Sam's Big Day	H	RF	74	Cat on the Mat	Oxford University Press
Sam's Cap	E	RF	78	Dominie Phonics Reader	Pearson Learning Group
Sam's Cookie	D	RF	52	Lindgren, Barbro	Morrow
Sam's Dad	L	RF	250+	Storyteller Chapter Books	Wright Group/ McGraw Hill
Sam's Dinosaur Bone	I	RF	238	Sun Sprouts	ETA Cuisenaire
Sam's Dog	D	RF	52	Sun Sprouts	ETA Cuisenaire
Sam's Glasses	M	RF	250+	Literacy 2000	Rigby
Sam's Haircut	H	RF	226	PM Plus Story Books	Rigby
Sam's Magic Moment	M	RF	250+	Rigby Literacy	Rigby
Sam's Mask	E	RF	36	Pacific Literacy	Pacific Learning
Sam's Painting	F	RF	181	PM Plus Story Books	Rigby
Sam's Pet	G	F	78	Rookie Readers	Children's Press
Sam's Picnic	D	RF	104	PM Plus Story Books	Rigby
Sam's Race	C	RF	64	PM Plus Story Books	Rigby
Sam's Seasons	E	RF	143	Pair-It Books	Steck-Vaughn
Sam's Snacks	I	F	250+	Cambridge Reading	Pearson Learning Group
Sam's Solution	K	RF	250+	Literacy 2000	Rigby
Sam's Teddy Bear	D	RF	60	Lindgren, Barbro	Morrow
Sam's Wagon	D	RF	83	Lindgren, Barbro	Morrow
Samuel de Champlain in Canada	V	B	3002	Leveled Readers	Houghton Mifflin Harcourt
Samuel de Champlain: Commander of New France	U	B	1694	Leveled Readers Social Studies	Houghton Mifflin Harcourt
Samuel Eaton's Day: A Day in the Life of a Pilgrim Boy	Q	I	250+	Waters, Kate	Scholastic
#Samuel Morse and the Telegraph	V	B	250+	Graphic Library	Capstone Press

Organized Alphabetically by Title
Storable Database at www.fountasandpinnellleveledbooks.com

* Collection of short stories
\# Graphic text

TITLE	LEVEL	GENRE	WORD COUNT	AUTHOR / SERIES	PUBLISHER / DISTRIBUTOR
Samuel's Choice	S	HF	250+	Berleth, Richard	Scholastic
Samuel's Sprout	F	RF	194	Little Celebrations	Pearson Learning Group
Samurai	T	I	250+	Warriors of History	Capstone Press
Samurai and His Daughter, The	S	TL	250+	Ciddor, Anna	Scholastic
Samurai's Daughter, The	Q	TL	250+	San Souci, Robert D.	Penguin Group
San Antonio Spurs, The	S	I	4588	Team Spirit	Norwood House Press
San Diego Chargers, The	S	I	250+	Team Spirit	Norwood House Press
San Diego Padres, The	S	I	250+	Team Spirit	Norwood House Press
San Domingo	R	I	250+	Henry, Marguerite	Scholastic
San Francisco 49ers, The	S	I	250+	Team Spirit	Norwood House Press
San Francisco Earthquake, The	U	HF	250+	Reading Expeditions	National Geographic
San Francisco Earthquake, The	Q	I	618	Vocabulary Readers	Houghton Mifflin Harcourt
San Francisco Exploratorium, The	O	I	250+	Little Celebrations	Pearson Learning Group
San Francisco Giants, The	S	I	250+	Team Spirit	Norwood House Press
San Francisco Shakes	U	I	2116	Independent Readers Science	Houghton Mifflin Harcourt
San Francisco: Then and Now	P	I	476	Independent Readers Social Studies	Houghton Mifflin Harcourt
Sand	E	RF	78	Giant Step Readers	Educational Insights
Sand	H	I	49	iOpeners	Pearson Learning Group
Sand	B	I	32	Voyages	SRA/McGraw Hill
Sand	M	I	250+	Windows on Literacy	National Geographic
Sand Castle Contest	N	RF	949	Leveled Readers	Houghton Mifflin Harcourt
Sand Castle Contest	N	RF	949	Leveled Readers/CA	Houghton Mifflin Harcourt
Sand Castle Contest	N	RF	949	Leveled Readers/TX	Houghton Mifflin Harcourt
Sand Castle Contest, The	E	RF	173	Pair-It Books	Steck-Vaughn
Sand Castle, The	G	F	257	Bella and Rosie Series	Literacy Footprints
Sand Castle, The	K	F	388	Leveled Readers	Houghton Mifflin Harcourt
Sand Castle, The	K	F	388	Leveled Readers/CA	Houghton Mifflin Harcourt
Sand Castle, The	K	F	388	Leveled Readers/TX	Houghton Mifflin Harcourt
Sand Castles	G	RF	80	Wonder World	Wright Group/McGraw Hill
Sand Castles and Guitars	J	RF	250+	Literacy by Design	Rigby
Sand on the Move: The Story of Dunes	U	I	250+	A First Book	Franklin Watts
Sand Picnic, The	E	RF	123	New Way White	Steck-Vaughn
Sandcastle, The	A	I	32	First Stories	Pacific Learning
Sandcastle, The	C	I	31	Sun Sprouts	ETA Cuisenaire
Sandcastles	J	I	419	Leveled Readers Science	Houghton Mifflin Harcourt
Sandhill Cranes	O	I	1420	Early Bird Nature Books	Lerner Publications
Sandman to the Rescue	T	RF	1758	Leveled Readers	Houghton Mifflin Harcourt
Sandra Day O'Connor	R	B	250+	Amazing Americans	Wright Group/McGraw Hill
Sandra Day O'Connor	O	I	318	Independent Readers Social Studies	Houghton Mifflin Harcourt
Sandwich Brigade, The	S	RF	3675	Reading Street	Pearson
Sandwich Hero, The	K	RF	250+	Literacy 2000	Rigby
Sandwich Person, A	G	I	63	Wonder World	Wright Group/McGraw Hill
Sandwich, The	C	RF	68	Carousel Earlybirds	Pearson Learning Group
Sandwich, The	J	RF	250+	Story Box	Wright Group/McGraw Hill
Sandwiches	D	RF	64	New Way	Steck-Vaughn
Sandwiches, Sandwiches	D	RF	54	Pair-It Books	Steck-Vaughn
Sandy	C	F	32	Ready Readers	Pearson Learning Group
Sandy Gets a Leash	D	RF	120	PM Stars	Rigby
Sandy Goes to the Vet	G	RF	187	PM Stars	Rigby
Sandy Runs Away	E	RF	102	Leveled Readers Language Support	Houghton Mifflin Harcourt
Sandy's Suitcase	K	RF	250+	Edwards, Elsy	SRA/McGraw Hill

S

* Collection of short stories
# Graphic text

TITLE	LEVEL	GENRE	WORD COUNT	AUTHOR / SERIES	PUBLISHER / DISTRIBUTOR
Sanitation Workers	M	I	703	Pull Ahead Books	Lerner Publications
Sanitation Workers: Then and Now	O	I	250+	Primary Source Readers	Teacher Created Materials
Santa Claus Doesn't Mop Floors	M	F	250+	Dadey, Debbie; Jones, Marcia Thornton	Scholastic
Santa Fe Trail, The	V	I	250+	Cornerstones of Freedom	Children's Press
Santa Fe Trail, The	Q	I	250+	On Deck	Rigby
Santa Fe Trail, The	T	I	250+	We The People	Compass Point Books
Santa Fe, Then and Now	U	I	1393	Vocabulary Readers	Houghton Mifflin Harcourt
Santana	D	I	84	Springboard	Wright Group/McGraw Hill
Santa's Secrets Revealed	P	F	1897	Solheim, James	Carolrhoda Books
Santa's Suit	E	F	154	Little Elf	Literacy Footprints
Sante Fe, Then and Now	U	I	1393	Vocabulary Readers/CA	Houghton Mifflin Harcourt
Santo and I	E	RF	135	Windows on Literacy	National Geographic
Sara Crewe	O	HF	250+	Burnett, Frances Hodgson	Scholastic
Sara Steps Over	U	F	250+	Reading Safari	Mondo
Sarah	Z+	RF	250+	Steinbeck, John	Penguin Group
Sarah and the Barking Dog	I	RF	328	PM Story Books-Orange	Rigby
Sarah and Will	H	RF	251	Alphakids	Sundance
Sarah Bishop	X	HF	250+	O'Dell, Scott	Scholastic
Sarah Morton's Day: Day in the Life of a Pilgrim Girl, A	Q	I	250+	Waters, Kate	Scholastic
Sarah Snail	E	RF	55	Voyages	SRA/McGraw Hill
Sarah Sparrow Likes Rain	F	F	77	Reading Safari	Mondo
Sarah, Plain and Tall	R	HF	250+	MacLachlan, Patricia	HarperTrophy
Sarah's Choice	K	RF	371	Reading Street	Pearson
Sarah's Pet	J	RF	250+	Storyteller-Shooting Stars	Wright Group/McGraw Hill
Sarah's Seed	E	RF	107	Literacy Tree	Rigby
Sara's Lovely Songs	I	RF	250+	Ready Readers	Pearson Learning Group
Sarny: A Life Remembered	W	HF	250+	Paulsen, Gary	Delacorte Press
Sasha's Mission	Y	HF	3229	Leveled Readers	Houghton Mifflin Harcourt
Sasha's Mission	Y	HF	3229	Leveled Readers/CA	Houghton Mifflin Harcourt
Satchel Paige	R	B	250+	Cline-Ransome, Lesa	Aladddin Paperbacks
Satellites	Y	I	250+	Cool Science	Lerner Publications
Satellites	O	I	250+	Let's See	Compass Point Books
Satellites Are Everywhere!	O	I	250+	Literacy by Design	Rigby
Saturday Adventure, The	J	RF	250+	Rigby Literacy	Rigby
Saturday Adventure, The	J	RF	250+	Rigby Rocket	Rigby
Saturday Cat, The	F	RF	167	Literacy by Design	Rigby
Saturday Club, The	K	RF	250+	Melton, Holly	Hampton-Brown
Saturday Morning	G	RF	180	Pacific Literacy	Pacific Learning
Saturday Morning Breakfast	E	RF	65	Teacher's Choice Series	Pearson Learning Group
Saturday Morning Treasure Hunt, The	R	RF	250+	Storyteller-Raging Rivers	Wright Group/McGraw Hill
Saturday Mornings	D	RF	63	Bookshop	Mondo
Saturday Night at the Dinosaur Stomp	N	F	250+	Shields, Carol Diggory	Candlewick Press
Saturday Sandwiches	I	RF	154	Evangeline Nicholas Collection	Wright Group/McGraw Hill
Saturdays and Teacakes	P	RF	250+	Laminack, Lester L.	Peachtree
Saturdays with Pop	O	RF	250+	Literacy by Design	Rigby
Saturdays with Sam	V	RF	2900	Leveled Readers/CA	Houghton Mifflin Harcourt
Saturdays with Sam	V	RF	2900	Leveled Readers	Houghton Mifflin Harcourt
Saturn	N	I	250+	A First Book	Franklin Watts
Saturn	Q	I	250+	A True Book	Children's Press
Saturn	P	I	250+	Explorer Books-Pioneer	National Geographic
Saturn	J	I	136	Exploring the Galaxy	Capstone Press
Saturn	S	I	250+	Our Solar System	Compass Point Books

* Collection of short stories
\# Graphic text

S

TITLE	LEVEL	GENRE	WORD COUNT	AUTHOR / SERIES	PUBLISHER / DISTRIBUTOR
Saturn	N	I	702	Our Universe	Lerner Publications
Saturn	Q	I	250+	The Galaxy	Capstone Press
Saturn	R	I	250+	Theme Sets	National Geographic
Saturn for My Birthday	M	RF	250+	McGranaghan, John	Sylvan Dell Publishing
Saturn: The Ring World	Q	I	250+	Explorer Books-Pathfinder	National Geographic
Saturnalia	W	RF	250+	Fleischman, Paul	HarperCollins
Saudi Arabia	O	I	1558	A Ticket to …	Carolrhoda Books
Sauk and Fox, The	R	I	1329	Reading Street	Pearson
Saul's Special Pet	J	F	250+	Leveled Readers Language Support	Houghton Mifflin Harcourt
Sausage Spy, The	G	RF	297	Sails	Rigby
Savannah's Concert	K	F	250+	Literacy by Design	Rigby
Save Our Earth	S	I	250+	iOpeners	Pearson Learning Group
Save Our Sea Turtles	M	I	801	Leveled Readers	Houghton Mifflin Harcourt
Save Our Sea Turtles	M	I	801	Leveled Readers/CA	Houghton Mifflin Harcourt
Save Our Sea Turtles	R	I	1000	Vocabulary Readers/TX	Houghton Mifflin Harcourt
Save Our Tree	D	I	56	Leveled Readers Social Studies	Houghton Mifflin Harcourt
Save Queen of Sheba	V	HF	250+	Moeri, Louise	Puffin/Penguin
Save Stan's Tree	G	F	201	Literacy by Design	Rigby
Save That Trash!	G	I	181	Ready Readers	Pearson Learning Group
Save the Birds	M	RF	250+	On Our Way To English	Rigby
Save the Everglades	R	I	250+	Stamper, Judith Bauer	Steck-Vaughn
Save the Manatee	N	I	250+	Friesinger, Alison	Random House
Save the Rain Forests	L	I	250+	Fowler, Allan	Scholastic
Save the Rain Forests	L	I	250+	Read-About Science	Children's Press
Save the River!	M	SF	250+	Pair-It Books	Steck-Vaughn
Save the Sea Turtles!	M	I	250+	Leonhardt, Alice	Steck-Vaughn
Save the Sharks	S	I	1034	Leveled Readers	Houghton Mifflin Harcourt
Save the Sharks!	S	I	1034	Leveled Readers/CA	Houghton Mifflin Harcourt
Saved from the Sea	S	I	1376	Vocabulary Readers	Houghton Mifflin Harcourt
Saved from the Sea	S	I	1376	Vocabulary Readers/CA	Houghton Mifflin Harcourt
Saved from the Sea	S	I	1376	Vocabulary Readers/TX	Houghton Mifflin Harcourt
Saving a Humpback Whale	S	RF	250+	Reading Expeditions	National Geographic
Saving America's Wild Horses	Q	I	494	Vocabulary Readers	Houghton Mifflin Harcourt
Saving an American Symbol	V	I	1870	Reading Street	Pearson
Saving Endangered Species	T	I	2193	Reading Street	Pearson
Saving Energy at Home	Q	I	250+	Rigby Focus	Rigby
Saving Frogs	Q	I	250+	Scooters	ETA Cuisenaire
Saving Grace	Z+	RF	250+	Orca Soundings	Orca Book Publishers
Saving Greedy Guts	L	RF	862	Rigby Gigglers	Rigby
Saving Hoppo	I	RF	250+	PM Plus Story Books	Rigby
Saving Money	M	I	250+	Learning About Money	Capstone Press
Saving Money	O	I	250+	Let's See	Compass Point Books
Saving Money	E	I	123	Money	Lerner Publishing
Saving Planet Earth	S	SF	1603	Leveled Readers	Houghton Mifflin Harcourt
Saving Planet Earth	S	SF	1603	Leveled Readers/CA	Houghton Mifflin Harcourt
Saving Scruffy	I	RF	212	Literacy by Design	Rigby
Saving Sea Turtles	S	I	1483	Leveled Readers	Houghton Mifflin Harcourt
Saving the Egret	W	I	2663	Vocabulary Readers	Houghton Mifflin Harcourt
Saving the Egret	W	I	2663	Vocabulary Readers/CA	Houghton Mifflin Harcourt
Saving the Egret	W	I	2663	Vocabulary Readers/TX	Houghton Mifflin Harcourt
Saving the Family Farm	U	RF	250+	Reading Expeditions	National Geographic
Saving the General	T	RF	2740	Leveled Readers	Houghton Mifflin Harcourt
Saving the General	T	RF	2740	Leveled Readers/CA	Houghton Mifflin Harcourt

* Collection of short stories
# Graphic text

TITLE	LEVEL	GENRE	WORD COUNT	AUTHOR / SERIES	PUBLISHER / DISTRIBUTOR
Saving the General	T	RF	2740	Leveled Readers/TX	Houghton Mifflin Harcourt
Saving the Liberty Bell	O	HF	1806	On My Own History	Lerner Publications
Saving the Mexican Wolves	V	I	3004	Leveled Readers	Houghton Mifflin Harcourt
Saving the Mexican Wolves	V	I	3004	Leveled Readers/CA	Houghton Mifflin Harcourt
Saving the Mexican Wolves	V	I	3004	Leveled Readers/TX	Houghton Mifflin Harcourt
Saving the Oceans	N	I	250+	Explorations	Eleanor Curtain Publishing
Saving the Oceans	N	I	250+	Explorations	Okapi Educational Materials
Saving the Park	N	RF	250+	Orbit Chapter Books	Pacific Learning
Saving the Rainforests	L	I	250+	Explorations	Eleanor Curtain Publishing
Saving the Rainforests	L	I	250+	Explorations	Okapi Eductional Materials
Saving the Sarus Crane	T	I	250+	WorldScapes	ETA Cuisenaire
Saving the Yellow Eye	P	I	250+	Darby, John	Pacific Learning
Saving the Zog	S	SF	250+	Power Up!	Steck-Vaughn
Saving Tigers	K	I	347	Springboard	Wright Group/McGraw Hill
Saving Up	G	I	189	Explorations	Eleanor Curtain Publishing
Saving Up	G	I	189	Explorations	Okapi Eductional Materials
Saving Water and Energy	L	I	790	Rigby Flying Colors	Rigby
Saving Wild One	V	RF	2109	Leveled Readers	Houghton Mifflin Harcourt
Say "Cheese"	L	RF	250+	Giff, Patricia Reilly	Bantam
Say Cheese	J	I	169	Rigby Focus	Rigby
Say Cheese!	F	RF	128	Storyteller-Moon Rising	Wright Group/McGraw Hill
Say Good Night	G	F	59	Start to Read	School Zone
Say Good Night	G	RF	155	Ziefert, Harriet	Puffin/Penguin
Say Hello	G	RF	77	Foreman, Jack & Michael	Candlewick Press
Say Hello!	A	RF	15	Rise & Shine	Hampton-Brown
Say "Hi" Up High	F	F	61	Early Readers	Compass Point Books
Say Hola, Sarah	N	RF	250+	Giff, Patricia Reilly	Bantam
Say in San Juan, A	M	I	621	Vocabulary Readers	Houghton Mifflin Harcourt
Say It with Music: A Story about Irving Berlin	S	B	8710	Creative Minds Biographies	Lerner Publications
Say It, Sign It	G	RF	169	Epstein, Elaine	Scholastic
Say Please!	H	F	83	Ross, Tony	Kane/Miller Book Publishers
Say Yes	W	RF	250+	Couloumbis, Audrey	Putnam/Penguin
Scaly Things	Q	I	250+	Explorers	Wright Group/McGraw Hill
Scams: Schemes, Cons, and Hoaxes	T	I	250+	Connectors	Pacific Learning
Scare and Dare	H	RF	284	Alphakids	Sundance
Scare for Bear, A	F	F	182	Sun Sprouts	ETA Cuisenaire
Scare in the City, A	N	RF	250+	Chanek, Sherilin	Hampton-Brown
Scarecrow	R	F	386	Rylant, Cynthia	Harcourt Brace
Scarecrow, The	C	F	31	Literacy 2000	Rigby
Scarecrow, The	D	RF	97	Little Red Readers	Sundance
Scarecrow, The	L	RF	250+	Pacific Literacy	Pacific Learning
Scarecrows	F	I	85	All About Fall	Capstone Press
Scarecrows	D	I	39	Pebble Books	Capstone Press
Scarecrow's Friends	C	F	56	Start to Read	School Zone
Scarecrow's Hair	D	F	142	Sails	Rigby
Scared	D	RF	59	Twig	Wright Group/McGraw Hill
Scared at Night	H	RF	250+	Early Transitional	Pioneer Valley
Scared Bear, The	D	F	146	InfoTrek	ETA Cuisenaire
Scared Stiff	V	F	250+	Malcolm, Jahnna N.	Scholastic
Scaredy Bears	K	F	250+	Sunshine	Wright Group/McGraw Hill
Scaredy Cat	C	F	85	Learn to Read	Creative Teaching Press
Scaredy Cat	A	RF	29	Rigby Literacy	Rigby
Scaredy Cat	A	RF	29	Rigby Star	Rigby

* Collection of short stories
\# Graphic text

S

TITLE	LEVEL	GENRE	WORD COUNT	AUTHOR / SERIES	PUBLISHER / DISTRIBUTOR
Scaredy Cat Runs Away	D	F	57	Learn to Read	Creative Teaching Press
Scaredy Dog	K	RF	250+	Thomas, Jane Resh	Hyperion
Scaredy Dog!	L	F	250+	I Am Reading	Kingfisher
Scaredy Kat: Suddenly Supernatural	R	F	250+	Kimmel, Elizabeth Cody	Little, Brown & Co.
Scare-Kid	K	F	250+	Literacy 2000	Rigby
Scary Day, The	N	RF	250+	Bennett, Jean	Pacific Learning
Scary Hair	H	F	242	Big Cat	Pacific Learning
Scary Larry	G	F	62	Rookie Readers	Children's Press
Scary Masks, The	F	RF	147	PM Photo Stories	Rigby
Scary Monster	C	F	19	Eifrig, Kate	Kaeden Books
Scary Sharks	O	I	250+	Fearsome, Scary, and Creepy Animals	Enslow Publishers, Inc.
Scary Spiders!	J	RF	198	Sunshine	Wright Group/McGraw Hill
*Scary Stories 3: More Tales to Chill Your Bones	V	TL	250+	Schwartz, Alvin	Scholastic
Scat! Said the Cat	D	F	33	Sunshine	Wright Group/McGraw Hill
Scatterbrain	T	RF	250+	Reading Street	Pearson
Scavenger Hunt, The	J	F	790	Little Dinosaur	Literacy Footprints
Scavengers and Junk Eaters	O	I	2039	Take Two Books	Wright Group/ McGraw-Hill
Schernoff Discoveries, The	T	RF	250+	Paulsen, Gary	Dell
School	D	I	50	Berger, Samantha; Chanko, Pamela	Scholastic
School Bus	LB	RF	51	Crews, Donald	Morrow
School Bus Drivers	M	I	250+	Community Helpers	Red Brick Learning
School Bus Drivers	K	I	506	Pull Ahead Books	Lerner Publications
School Bus Ride, The	G	RF	160	Little Red Readers	Sundance
School Bus, The	E	RF	60	Sunshine	Wright Group/McGraw Hill
School Concert, The	K	RF	250+	Rigby Star Plus	Rigby
School Day!	A	RF	16	Cervantes, Jesus	Scholastic
School Days	U	I	250+	Literacy 2000	Rigby
School Days in 1700	Q	I	975	Independent Readers Social Studies	Houghton Mifflin Harcourt
School Days Long Ago and Today	A	I	32	Leveled Readers Social Studies	Houghton Mifflin Harcourt
School Days, Cool Days!	J	RF	250+	Storyteller-Shooting Stars	Wright Group/McGraw Hill
School Fair, The	J	RF	250+	PM Plus Story Books	Rigby
School Fair, The	I	RF	250+	Storyworlds	Heinemann Educational Books
School in a Garden	N	I	888	Leveled Readers/TX	Houghton Mifflin Harcourt
School in Colonial America	K	I	250+	Welcome Books	Children's Press
School in Many Cultures	I	I	113	Life Around the World	Capstone Press
School in the Outback	O	I	250+	WorldScapes	ETA Cuisenaire
School Is Closed	H	F	250+	Phonics Readers Plus	Steck-Vaughn
*School Journal Part 1: Numbers 1-5	N	RF	250+	Learning Media	Richard C. Owen
*School Journal Part 2: Numbers 1-4	O	RF	250+	Learning Media	Richard C. Owen
*School Journal Part 3: Numbers 1-3	O	RF	250+	Learning Media	Richard C. Owen
School Long Ago	M	I	430	Leveled Readers/TX	Houghton Mifflin Harcourt
School Lunch	LB	RF	14	Ready Readers	Pearson Learning Group
School Mouse, The	P	F	250+	King-Smith, Dick	Hyperion
School Mural, The	L	RF	250+	Pair-It Books	Steck-Vaughn
School Newspaper	F	I	84	On Deck	Rigby
School Newspaper, The	O	I	250+	Sunshine	Wright Group/McGraw Hill
School on Stilts	U	I	250+	WorldScapes	ETA Cuisenaire
School Play Stars	N	RF	250+	Girlz Rock!	Mondo
School Play, The	G	RF	103	City Stories	Rigby

S

* Collection of short stories
# Graphic text

TITLE	LEVEL	GENRE	WORD COUNT	AUTHOR / SERIES	PUBLISHER / DISTRIBUTOR
School Principals	M	I	250+	Community Helpers	Red Brick Learning
School Recyclers	L	RF	380	Leveled Readers Science	Houghton Mifflin Harcourt
School Rules	I	F	365	Reading Street	Pearson
School Secretaries	M	I	250+	Community Helpers	Red Brick Learning
School Spirit: Suddenly Supernatural	R	F	250+	Kimmel, Elizabeth Cody	Little, Brown & Co.
School Story, The	R	RF	250+	Clements, Andrew	Aladddin Paperbacks
School Then and Now	I	I	106	Then and Now	Lerner Publications
School Today and Long Ago	H	I	110	Windows on Literacy	National Geographic
School Vacation	J	RF	113	City Kids	Rigby
School, The	E	RF	27	Burningham, John	Crowell
School: Then and Now	L	I	310	Reading Street	Pearson
Schoolchildren's Blizzard, The	L	HF	1555	On My Own History	Lerner Publications
Schools	C	I	31	We Are Alike and Different	Lerner Publishing
Schools Around the World	E	I	78	Pair-It Books	Steck-Vaughn
Schools Around the World	O	I	1065	Vocabulary Readers	Houghton Mifflin Harcourt
Schools Around the World	O	I	1065	Vocabulary Readers/CA	Houghton Mifflin Harcourt
School's Out	N	RF	250+	Hurwitz, Johanna	Scholastic
Schools Then and Now	N	I	622	Vocabulary Readers	Houghton Mifflin Harcourt
Schools Then and Now	N	I	622	Vocabulary Readers/CA	Houghton Mifflin Harcourt
Schools Then and Now	N	I	622	Vocabulary Readers/TX	Houghton Mifflin Harcourt
Schoolyard Mystery, The	L	RF	250+	Levy, Elizabeth	Scholastic
Schoolyard Snickers: Classy Jokes That Make the Grade	O	F	2222	Make Me Laugh!	Lerner Publications
Schwa Was Here, The	Y	RF	250+	Shusterman, Neal	Dutton/Penguin
Science - Just Add Salt	L	I	250+	Markle, Sandra	Scholastic
Science All Around	R	I	250+	Literacy by Design	Rigby
Science Fair Surprise, The	Q	RF	250+	Burke, Melissa Blackwell	Steck-Vaughn
Science Fair, The	I	RF	135	Reading Street	Pearson
Science Fiction Pioneer: A Story About Jules Verne	T	B	8148	Creative Minds Biographies	Carolrhoda Books
Science of Cooking, The	T	I	250+	PM Plus	Rigby
Science Outside	I	I	33	Canizares, Susan; Chessen, Betsey	Scholastic
Science Tools	E	I	52	Canizares, Susan; Chessen, Betsey	Scholastic
Scientist, The	G	I	195	Adventures in Reading	Pearson Learning Group
Scientists	I	I	56	Chanko, Pamela; Berger, Samantha	Scholastic
Scientists at Work	M	I	250+	Yellow Umbrella Books	Red Brick Learning
Scientists in Space	U	I	3502	Leveled Readers Science	Houghton Mifflin Harcourt
Scissors	D	I	51	Storyteller-Setting Sun	Wright Group/McGraw Hill
Scit, Scat, Scaredy Cat!	F	F	59	Sunshine	Wright Group/McGraw Hill
Scooter's Busy Monday	I	RF	312	Rigby Flying Colors	Rigby
Scooter's School Trip	I	RF	562	Rigby Flying Colors	Rigby
Score!: You Can Play Soccer	M	I	250+	Game Day	Picture Window Books
Scoring Points	P	RF	250+	Leveled Readers Language Support	Houghton Mifflin Harcourt
Scorpions	Z	RF	250+	Myers, Walter Dean	HarperTrophy
Scotland: A Question and Answer Book	P	I	250+	Questions & Answers: Countries	Capstone Press
Scots Pine, The	M	I	250+	Cambridge Reading	Pearson Learning Group
Scottish Fold Cats	I	I	119	Cats	Capstone Press
Scout and the River	C	F	81	Handprints B	Educators Publishing Service
Scrapbooking: Keep Your Special Memories	Q	I	250+	Crafts	Capstone Press

* Collection of short stories
# Graphic text

S

TITLE	LEVEL	GENRE	WORD COUNT	AUTHOR / SERIES	PUBLISHER / DISTRIBUTOR
Scraping the Sky	T	I	250+	Rigby Literacy	Rigby
Scrapman	N	F	250+	High-Fliers	Pacific Learning
Scrapman and Scrapcat	N	F	250+	High-Fliers	Pacific Learning
Scrapman and the Incredible Flying Machine	N	F	250+	High-Fliers	Pacific Learning
Scrappers No Easy Out	Q	RF	250+	Hughes, Dean	Aladdin
Scrappers No Fear	Q	RF	250+	Hughes, Dean	Aladdin
Scratch My Back	D	F	66	Foundations	Wright Group/McGraw Hill
Scratching's Catching!	L	F	250+	I Am Reading	Kingfisher
Scream, The	K	RF	509	Leveled Literacy Intervention/ Blue System	Heinemann
Screech!	D	RF	43	Literacy 2000	Rigby
Screw Loose	O	F	3211	Prince, A.	Stone Arch Books
Screws	Q	I	1505	Early Bird Energy Physics Books	Lerner Publishing
Screws to the Rescue	O	I	250+	Simple Machine to the Rescue	Capstone Press
Scribbler of Dreams	Z+	RF	250+	Bro, Margueritte Harmon	Fitzhenry & Whiteside
Scribe of Ancient China, A	W	HF	2134	Leveled Readers	Houghton Mifflin Harcourt
Scritch-Scratch Noise, The	J	F	337	Springboard	Wright Group/McGraw Hill
Scrubbing Machine, The	F	F	148	Story Box	Wright Group/McGraw Hill
Scruff	I	RF	250+	Rigby Rocket	Rigby
Scruffy	I	RF	250	Leveled Readers	Houghton Mifflin Harcourt
Scruffy	K	RF	250+	Parish, Peggy	HarperTrophy
Scruffy Messed It Up	G	RF	105	Literacy 2000	Rigby
Scruffy Runs Away	F	RF	187	PM Photo Stories	Rigby
Scrumptious Sundae	B	RF	18	Literacy 2000	Rigby
Scruncher Goes Wandering	M	RF	250+	Krailing, Tessa	Barron's Educational
Sculpture	L	I	250+	Little Celebrations	Pearson Learning Group
Sculpture	K	I	272	Storyteller	Wright Group/McGraw Hill
Sea and Land Animals	J	I	250+	Windows on Literacy	National Geographic
Sea Anemones	G	I	58	Ocean Life	Capstone Press
Sea Animals	K	I	250+	Little Red Readers	Sundance
Sea Animals	B	I	46	Vocabulary Readers	Houghton Mifflin Harcourt
Sea Cave	T	RF	250+	Reading Safari	Mondo
Sea Creatures	K	I	332	Gear Up!	Wright Group/McGraw Hill
Sea Giants of Dinosaur Time	P	I	1235	Meet the Dinosaurs	Lerner Publications
Sea Habitats	L	I	597	Rigby Flying Colors	Rigby
Sea Horses	O	I	2252	Early Bird Nature Books	Lerner Publications
Sea Horses	F	I	67	Ocean Life	Capstone Press
Sea Horses	J	I	90	Under the Sea	Capstone Press
Sea Jellies	Q	I	1317	Gear Up!	Wright Group/ McGraw Hill
Sea Life	I	I	143	Time for Kids	Teacher Created Materials
Sea Lights	L	I	128	Books for Young Learners	Richard C. Owen
Sea Lions	O	I	2933	Early Bird Nature Books	Lerner Publications
Sea Lions	M	I	618	Vocabulary Readers	Houghton Mifflin Harcourt
Sea Lions	M	I	618	Vocabulary Readers/CA	Houghton Mifflin Harcourt
Sea Lions	M	I	618	Vocabulary Readers/TX	Houghton Mifflin Harcourt
Sea Monsters	R	I	250+	Explorer Books-Pathfinder	National Geographic
Sea Monsters	P	I	250+	Explorer Books-Pioneer	National Geographic
Sea Monsters Don't Ride Motorcycles	M	RF	250+	Dadey, Debbie; Jones, Marcia Thornton	Scholastic
Sea of Animals, A	K	I	213	Spyglass Books	Compass Point Books
Sea of Trolls, The	X	F	250+	Farmer, Nancy	Simon Pulse
Sea Otter	H	I	106	Under the Sea	Capstone Press
Sea Otter Goes Hunting	J	RF	250+	PM Plus Story Books	Rigby
Sea Otter Inlet	O	I	250+	Godkin, Celia	Fitzhenry & Whiteside

TITLE	LEVEL	GENRE	WORD COUNT	AUTHOR / SERIES	PUBLISHER / DISTRIBUTOR
Sea Otter Rescue: The Aftermath of an Oil Spill	W	I	250+	Smith, Roland	Scholastic
Sea Otters	N	I	588	Springboard	Wright Group/ McGraw Hill
Sea Otters	L	I	406	Storyteller Nonfiction	Wright Group/McGraw Hill
Sea Snakes	I	I	66	Pebble Books	Red Brick Learning
Sea Snakes	H	I	105	Under the Sea	Capstone Press
Sea Star	R	RF	250+	Henry, Marguerite	Aladdin
Sea Star, A	E	I	82	Ready Readers	Pearson Learning Group
Sea Stars	E	I	63	Ocean Life	Capstone Press
Sea Stars	K	I	289	Sun Sprouts	ETA Cuisenaire
Sea Stars	H	I	131	Under the Sea	Capstone Press
Sea Turtle Family, The	T	SF	250+	Leveled Readers	Houghton Mifflin Harcourt
Sea Turtle Family, The	T	SF	250+	Leveled Readers/CA	Houghton Mifflin Harcourt
Sea Turtle Night	I	I	200	Ready Readers	Pearson Learning Group
Sea Turtles	O	I	1704	Early Bird Nature Books	Lerner Publications
Sea Turtles	K	I	238	Gear Up!	Wright Group/McGraw Hill
Sea Turtles	L	I	553	Leveled Readers	Houghton Mifflin Harcourt
Sea Turtles	L	I	296	Marine Life For Young Readers	Pearson Learning Group
Sea Turtles	G	I	50	Pebble Books	Red Brick Learning
Sea Turtles	L	I	489	Springboard	Wright Group/ McGraw Hill
Sea Turtles	J	I	118	Under the Sea	Capstone Press
Sea Turtles At Risk	N	I	791	Reading Street	Pearson
Sea Turtles in Danger	O	I	250+	Literacy by Design	Rigby
Sea Urchins	G	I	51	Ocean Life	Capstone Press
Sea Urchins	H	I	113	Under the Sea	Capstone Press
Sea Wall, The	K	I	251	Foundations	Wright Group/McGraw Hill
Sea Where I Swim, The	F	I	134	Voyages	SRA/McGraw Hill
Sea Wind	R	RF	250+	PM Chapter Books	Rigby
Sea, The	C	I	63	Leveled Literacy Intervention/ Blue System	Heinemann
Sea, The	A	I	20	Leveled Readers	Houghton Mifflin Harcourt
Sea, The	A	I	20	Leveled Readers/CA	Houghton Mifflin Harcourt
Seabirds	S	I	250+	A First Book	Franklin Watts
Seafaring Life, The	R	I	1558	Reading Street	Pearson
Seagull Is Clever	E	RF	98	PM Story Books	Rigby
Seagull, The	C	F	78	Story Steps	Rigby
Seahaven Squids and the Amazing Pet Wash, The	R	RF	1569	Reading Street	Pearson
Seahorses	M	I	250+	Bookshop	Mondo
Seahorses, Pipefishes, and Their Kin	T	I	250+	Animals in Order	Franklin Watts
Seal	M	I	250+	Cambridge Reading	Pearson Learning Group
Seal Who Wanted to Live, The	O	F	1000	Leveled Readers/TX	Houghton Mifflin Harcourt
Seals	G	I	42	Pebble Books	Red Brick Learning
Seals	H	I	79	Polar Animals	Capstone Press
Seals	I	I	103	Under the Sea	Red Brick Learning
Seals & Sea Lions	L	I	273	Marine Life for Young Readers	Pearson Learning Group
Seals and Sea Lions	N	I	250+	Take Two Books	Wright Group/McGraw Hill
Seals of the World	J	I	251	Vocabulary Readers	Houghton Mifflin Harcourt
Search and Discover	O	I	250+	Discovery Links	Newbridge
Search for Delicious, The	U	F	250+	Babbitt, Natalie	Farrar, Straus and Giroux
Search for Gold, The	Q	I	250+	In Step Readers	Rigby
Search for New Lands, The	S	I	250+	Literacy by Design	Rigby
Search for Oil	V	I	3343	Leveled Readers Science	Houghton Mifflin Harcourt
Search for the Lost Cave, The	M	F	250+	Woodland Mysteries	Wright Group/McGraw Hill
Search for the Sunken Treasure, The	P	SF	250+	Secret Agent Jack Stalwart	Weinstein Books

* Collection of short stories
# Graphic text

TITLE	LEVEL	GENRE	WORD COUNT	AUTHOR / SERIES	PUBLISHER / DISTRIBUTOR
Searching for Dinosaurs	U	I	2309	Reading Street	Pearson
Searching for My Father	X	RF	2703	Leveled Readers	Houghton Mifflin Harcourt
Searching for My Father	X	RF	2703	Leveled Readers/CA	Houghton Mifflin Harcourt
Searching for Sea Lions	P	I	250+	Orbit Chapter Books	Pacific Learning
Searching for Sunken Treasure	R	RF	250+	Reading Expeditions	National Geographic
Seashells	L	I	186	Marine Life For Young Readers	Pearson Learning Group
Season to Season	I	RF	322	InfoTrek	ETA Cuisenaire
Season to Season	F	I	113	Pair-It Books	Steck-Vaughn
Seasons	O	I	250+	A True Book	Children's Press
Seasons	C	I	28	Discovery World	Rigby
Seasons	B	I	24	InfoTrek	ETA Cuisenaire
Seasons	H	I	119	Instant Readers	Harcourt School Publishers
Seasons	L	I	251	Leveled Readers	Houghton Mifflin Harcourt
Seasons	A	I	28	Leveled Readers Science	Houghton Mifflin Harcourt
Seasons	L	I	251	Leveled Readers/CA	Houghton Mifflin Harcourt
Seasons	L	I	251	Leveled Readers/TX	Houghton Mifflin Harcourt
Seasons	K	I	266	Nonfiction	Literacy Footprints
Seasons	H	I	354	Science Support Readers	Houghton Mifflin Harcourt
Seasons	N	I	250+	Simply Science	Compass Point Books
Seasons	F	I	95	Spinelle, Nancy Louise	Kaeden Books
Seasons	A	I	29	Vocabulary Readers	Houghton Mifflin Harcourt
Seasons	H	I	250+	Yellow Umbrella Books	Red Brick Learning
Seasons and Weather	M	I	250+	PM Plus Nonfiction	Rigby
Seasons Around the World	K	I	353	Leveled Readers	Houghton Mifflin Harcourt
Seasons Around the World	K	I	353	Leveled Readers/CA	Houghton Mifflin Harcourt
Seasons Around the World	K	I	353	Leveled Readers/TX	Houghton Mifflin Harcourt
Seasons Change	F	I	80	Reading Street	Pearson
Seasons Come and Go	J	RF	282	InfoTrek	ETA Cuisenaire
Seasons Go 'Round	V	I	250+	Literacy By Design	Rigby
Seasons of the Year	J	I	176	Patterns in Nature	Capstone Press
Seasons of the Year, The	L	I	332	Leveled Readers	Houghton Mifflin Harcourt
Seasons of the Year, The	L	I	332	Leveled Readers/CA	Houghton Mifflin Harcourt
Seasons of the Year, The	L	I	332	Leveled Readers/TX	Houghton Mifflin Harcourt
Seasons Project	H	I	218	Sun Sprouts	ETA Cuisenaire
Seasons, The	D	I	84	Early Connections	Benchmark Education
Seasons, The	J	I	193	Phonics Readers	Compass Point Books
Seasons, The	C	RF	84	Rigby Focus	Rigby
Seat Belt for Joey, A	D	F	94	On Our Way to English	Rigby
Seat Belt Song, The	K	RF	505	PM Collection	Rigby
Seattle Mariners, The	S	I	250+	Team Spirit	Norwood House Press
Seattle Seahawks, The	S	I	250+	Team Spirit	Norwood House Press
Seawall	O	RF	250+	PM Collection	Rigby
Seaward	X	F	250+	Cooper, Susan	Simon & Schuster
Seb & Sasha	U	RF	250+	Book Blazers	ETA Cuisenaire
Sebastian	G	F	162	Alphakids	Sundance
Secession: The Southern States Leave the Union	V	I	250+	Let Freedom Ring	Red Brick Learning
Second Birthday, A	L	I	250+	Greetings	Rigby
Second Chance	N	RF	250+	Kroll, Stephen	Avon Camelot
Second Chance, A	M	RF	250+	Rigby Flying Colors	Rigby
Second Grade - Friends Again!	M	RF	250+	Cohen, Miriam	Scholastic
Second Mrs. Giaconda, The	T	HF	250+	Konigsburg, E. L.	Language for Learning Assoc.
Second Story Sally	N	RF	250+	SupaDoopers	Sundance

TITLE	LEVEL	GENRE	WORD COUNT	AUTHOR / SERIES	PUBLISHER / DISTRIBUTOR
Second Summer of the Sisterhood, The	Z+	RF	250+	Pearson, Mary E	Harcourt Trade
Second-Grade Friends	M	RF	250+	Cohen, Miriam	Scholastic
Second-Grade Star	N	RF	250+	Alberts, Nancy	Scholastic
Secondhand Sneakers, The	M	F	250+	Literacy by Design	Rigby
Secondhand Star	L	RF	250+	Macdonald, Maryann	Hyperion
Secret	G	RF	114	Instant Readers	Harcourt School Publishers
Secret Agent Heroes	N	RF	250+	Boyz Rule!	Mondo
Secret at the Polk Street School, The	M	RF	250+	Giff, Patricia Reilly	Bantam
Secret Camera, A	Q	RF	250+	Tristars	Richard C. Owen
Secret Cave, The	I	RF	250+	PM Plus Story Books	Rigby
Secret Code, The	G	RF	69	Rookie Readers	Children's Press
Secret Cupboard, The	O	F	250+	Tristars	Richard C. Owen
Secret Fishing Gear, The	K	RF	508	Springboard	Wright Group/McGraw Hill
Secret Friend, The	E	RF	196	Little Celebrations	Pearson Learning Group
Secret Friend, The	E	RF	189	Little Readers	Houghton Mifflin Harcourt
Secret Garden, The	U	RF	250+	Burnett, Frances H.	Scholastic
Secret Hideaway, The	K	RF	618	PM Collection	Rigby
Secret History of Giants or the Codex Giganticum, The	Y	F	250+	Berk, Ari	Candlewick Press
Secret Inside the Log, The	J	RF	361	Leveled Readers	Houghton Mifflin Harcourt
Secret Inside the Log, The	J	RF	361	Leveled Readers/CA	Houghton Mifflin Harcourt
Secret Land of the Past	N	F	250+	Schlein, Miriam	Scholastic
Secret Language of Girls, The	V	RF	250+	Dowell, Frances O'Roark	Aladddin Paperbacks
Secret Life of Amanda K. Woods, The	T	RF	250+	Cameron, Ann	Scholastic
Secret Life of Trees, The	M	I	250+	DK Readers	DK Publishing
Secret Lives of Mr. and Mrs. Smith, The	K	F	395	Sunshine	Wright Group/McGraw Hill
Secret Message, The	E	RF	68	Literacy Tree	Rigby
Secret Message, The	J	RF	427	PM Math Readers	Rigby
Secret Missions	U	I	250+	Connectors	Pacific Learning
Secret Notes	G	RF	214	Sun Sprouts	ETA Cuisenaire
Secret of Bunratty Castle, The	Q	F	250+	Action Packs	Rigby
Secret of Foghorn Island, The	L	F	250+	Step into Reading	Random House
Secret of Iguando, The	V	F	250+	Bookshop	Mondo
Secret of Kiribu Tapu Lagoon, The	S	I	250+	Literacy 2000	Rigby
Secret of NIMH, The	V	F	250+	O'Brien, Robert C.	Scholastic
Secret of Robber's Cave, The	Q	RF	250+	Gregory, Kristiana	Scholastic
Secret of Silk, The	K	I	234	Rigby Focus	Rigby
Secret of Spooky House, The	J	F	352	Sunshine	Wright Group/McGraw Hill
Secret of the Flying Cows, The	O	RF	250+	Klooz	Stone Arch Books
Secret of the Monster Book, The	M	F	250+	Woodland Mysteries	Wright Group/McGraw Hill
Secret of the Old Oak Trunk, The	M	F	250+	Woodland Mysteries	Wright Group/McGraw Hill
Secret of the Sacred Temple, The	P	SF	250+	Secret Agent Jack Stalwart	Weinstein Books
Secret of the Seal, The	P	RF	250+	Davis, Deborah	Alfred A. Knopf
Secret of the Silver Shoes, The	Q	F	250+	Massie, Elizabeth	Steck-Vaughn
Secret of the Song, The	M	F	250+	Woodland Mysteries	Wright Group/McGraw Hill
Secret of the Stone House, The	T	F	250+	From Many Peoples	Fitzhenry & Whiteside
Secret of the Three Treasures	Q	RF	250+	Simner, Janni Lee	Holiday House
Secret on the Wall, The	S	HF	250+	Power Up!	Steck-Vaughn
Secret Recipe	I	I	182	Sun Sprouts	ETA Cuisenaire
Secret Room, The	T	F	250+	Townson, H.	Stone Arch Books
Secret Santa, The	K	RF	250+	Wallace, Carol	Holiday House
Secret Secret Passage, The	P	RF	250+	Parker, A. E.	Scholastic
Secret Silver Lining, A	Q	RF	250+	Ragged Island Mysteries	Wright Group/McGraw Hill
Secret Soccer Ball Maker, The	G	RF	191	Take Two Books	Wright Group/McGraw Hill

S

* Collection of short stories
\# Graphic text

| --- | --- | --- | --- | --- | --- |
Secret Soldier, The	R	TL	250+	WorldScapes	ETA Cuisenaire
Secret Soldier, The: The Story of Deborah Sampson	O	B	250+	McGovern, Ann	Scholastic
Secret Soup	E	RF	51	Literacy 2000	Rigby
Secret Valentine	G	F	223	First Start	Troll Associates
Secret Valley, The	O	HF	250+	Bulla, Clyde Robert	Scholastic
Secret, The	N	RF	250+	PM Collection	Rigby
Secret, The	K	TL	250+	Rigby Star Plus	Rigby
Secret, The: A Traditional Tale From Wales	K	TL	250+	Rigby Literacy	Rigby
Secrets in the Fire	Z	HF	250+	Mankell, Henning	Annick Press
Secrets in the Sea	O	I	798	Vocabulary Readers	Houghton Mifflin Harcourt
Secrets in the Sea	O	I	798	Vocabulary Readers/CA	Houghton Mifflin Harcourt
Secrets in the Shadows	Z+	RF	250+	Brashares, Ann	Random House
Secrets of Coral Reefs, The	U	I	250+	Jean-Michel Cousteau Presents	London Town Press
Secrets of Kelp Forests, The	U	I	250+	Jean-Michel Cousteau Presents	London Town Press
Secrets of Rapa Nui, The	Z	I	2362	Leveled Readers	Houghton Mifflin Harcourt
Secrets of the Desert	Q	I	250+	Literacy 2000	Rigby
Secrets of the Fun Park	O	I	250+	Home Connection Collection	Rigby
Secrets of the Mummies	W	I	250+	DK Readers	DK Publishing
Secrets of the Rain Forest	O	I	250+	Myers, Edward	Pearson Learning Group
Secrets of the Seahorse	H	I	228	In Step Readers	Rigby
Secrets of the Shipwreck, The	Q	RF	250+	Reading Safari	Mondo
Secrets of the Sky	U	I	250+	InfoQuest	Rigby
Secrets of Tidepools, The	U	I	250+	Jean-Michel Cousteau Presents	London Town Press
Secrets of Tropical Rainforests, The	U	I	250+	Wild Life Series	London Town Press
Sector 7	WB	F	N/A	Wiesner, David	Clarion
Security Guards	M	I	250+	Community Helpers	Red Brick Learning
Sedimentary Rocks	Q	I	250+	On Deck	Rigby
See for Your Self	O	B	250+	Meet the Author	Richard C. Owen
See How It Grows	C	I	34	Learn to Read	Creative Teaching Press
See How They Run: Campaign Dreams, Election Schemes, and the Race to the White House	U	I	250+	Goodman, Susan E.	Bloomsbury Children's Books
See Me	WB	I	N/A	Vocabulary Readers	Houghton Mifflin Harcourt
See Me Reading	D	RF	35	Ray's Readers	Outside the Box
See Me Work	B	I	71	Literacy by Design	Rigby
See No Evil	Y	RF	250+	Orca Currents	Orca Book Publishers
See Our Show	C	RF	38	Rigby Focus	Rigby
See the Boats Go!	D	RF	42	Windows on Literacy	National Geographic
See the Ocean	B	RF	26	Science	Outside the Box
See the Seasons	B	I	16	Instant Readers	Harcourt School Publishers
See the Shapes	B	I	37	Rigby Focus	Rigby
See the Trees	D	I	108	Vocabulary Readers	Houghton Mifflin Harcourt
See the Trees	D	I	108	Vocabulary Readers/CA	Houghton Mifflin Harcourt
See You in Second Grade	J	RF	250+	Cohen, Miriam	Bantam
See You Later, Gladiator	P	F	250+	Scieszka, Jon	Penguin Group
See You Tomorrow, Charles	J	RF	250+	Cohen, Miriam	Bantam
Seed for Sid, A	E	F	131	Leveled Readers	Houghton Mifflin Harcourt
Seed for Sid, A	E	F	131	Leveled Readers/CA	Houghton Mifflin Harcourt
Seed for Sid, A	E	F	131	Leveled Readers/TX	Houghton Mifflin Harcourt
Seed Is a Promise, A	O	I	250+	Merrill, Claire	Scholastic
Seed Song, The	E	I	41	Learn to Read	Creative Teaching Press
Seed Surprise	E	RF	67	Seedlings	Continental Press
Seed, The	D	I	51	Sunshine	Wright Group/McGraw Hill

* Collection of short stories
# Graphic text

TITLE	LEVEL	GENRE	WORD COUNT	AUTHOR / SERIES	PUBLISHER / DISTRIBUTOR
Seed, The	LB	I	14	Wonder World	Wright Group/McGraw Hill
*Seedfolks	W	RF	250+	Fleishman, Paul	HarperTrophy
Seeds	E	I	30	Parts of Plants	Lerner Publishing
Seeds	J	I	210	Pebble Books	Capstone Press
Seeds	H	I	124	Plant Parts	Capstone Press
Seeds	I	I	351	Rigby Flying Colors	Rigby
Seeds	B	I	30	Rise & Shine	Hampton-Brown
Seeds	K	I	250+	Sunshine	Wright Group/McGraw Hill
Seeds and Plants	H	I	173	Dominie Factivity Series	Pearson Learning Group
Seeds Grow	I	I	90	Sunshine	Wright Group/McGraw Hill
Seeds Grow into Plants	G	I	78	Windows on Literacy	National Geographic
Seeds on the Move	H	I	113	Explorations	Eleanor Curtain Publishing
Seeds on the Move	H	I	113	Explorations	Okapi Eductional Materials
Seeds, Seeds, Seeds	E	I	96	Sunshine	Wright Group/McGraw Hill
Seeing	K	I	149	Pebble Books	Capstone Press
Seeing	E	I	79	Senses	Lerner Publishing
Seeing	M	I	250+	The Senses	Capstone Press
Seeing and Hearing Well	M	I	674	Pull Ahead Books	Lerner Publications
Seeing Earth from Space	Y	I	250+	Lauber, Patricia	Scholastic
Seeing Eye to Eye	U	I	250+	Power Up!	Steck-Vaughn
Seeing Is Believing	K	I	320	Yellow Umbrella Books	Red Brick Learning
Seeing Is Not Believing	U	I	250+	iOpeners	Pearson Learning Group
Seeing Sayings	N	RF	866	Leveled Readers	Houghton Mifflin Harcourt
Seeing Sayings	N	RF	866	Leveled Readers/CA	Houghton Mifflin Harcourt
Seeing Sayings	N	RF	866	Leveled Readers/TX	Houghton Mifflin Harcourt
Seeing Stars	L	RF	801	Leveled Readers	Houghton Mifflin Harcourt
Seeing Stars	L	RF	801	Leveled Readers/CA	Houghton Mifflin Harcourt
Seeing Stone, The	Y	F	250+	Crossley-Holland, Kevin	Scholastic
Seeing the Circle	O	B	250+	Meet The Author	Richard C. Owen
Seeing the School Doctor	K	RF	167	City Kids	Rigby
Seeing the Sky	M	RF	250+	Windows on Literacy	National Geographic
Seeing Things Up Close	F	I	72	Windows on Literacy	National Geographic
Seeing with Heat	R	I	436	Independent Readers Science	Houghton Mifflin Harcourt
Seekers of Truth	U	B	250+	Real Lives	Troll Associates
Seeking Freedom	Y	I	2207	Leveled Readers	Houghton Mifflin Harcourt
Seeking Freedom	Y	I	2207	Leveled Readers/CA	Houghton Mifflin Harcourt
Seems, The: The Glitch in Sleep	V	F	250+	Hulme, John & Wexler, Michael	Bloomsbury Children's Books
Sees Behind Trees	T	HF	250+	Dorris, Michael	Language for Learning Assoc.
Seesaw, The	C	RF	100	Emergent	Pioneer Valley
Seesaw, The	C	F	46	Voyages	SRA/McGraw Hill
See-saw, The	A	F	24	Big Cat	Pacific Learning
See-Saw, The	D	RF	87	Storyworlds	Heinemann Educational Publishers
Seiko the Watchdog	M	F	250+	Storyteller Summer Skies	Wright Group/McGraw Hill
Selchie's Seed, The	W	F	250+	Oppenheim, Shulamith Levey	Harcourt Brace
Selena Who Speaks in Silence	J	RF	311	Evangeline Nicholas Collection	Wright Group/McGraw Hill
Self Portrait	O	B	250+	Meet the Author	Richard C. Owen
Self-Discipline	N	I	250+	Character Education	Red Brick Learning
Self-Discipline	M	I	250+	Everyday Character Education	Capstone Press
Selfish Dog, The	D	F	109	Storyworlds	Heinemann Educational Publishers
Selfish Giant, The	L	F	250+	Literacy 2000	Rigby

Organized Alphabetically by Title
Storable Database at www.fountasandpinnellleveledbooks.com

* Collection of short stories
\# Graphic text

TITLE	LEVEL	GENRE	WORD COUNT	AUTHOR / SERIES	PUBLISHER / DISTRIBUTOR
Self-Propelled Howitzers: The M109A6 Paladins	T	I	250+	War Machines	Capstone Press
Self-Respect	M	I	250+	Character Education	Red Brick Learning
Selling Things	A	I	20	Leveled Readers	Houghton Mifflin Harcourt
Selling Things	A	I	20	Leveled Readers/CA	Houghton Mifflin Harcourt
Selu and Kana Ti	K	TL	250+	Folk Tales	Mondo
Seminole Indians, The	P	I	250+	Native Peoples	Red Brick Learning
Seminole, The	R	I	250+	First Reports	Compass Point Books
Seminole, The: Patchworkers of the Everglades	R	I	250+	America's First Peoples	Capstone Press
Seminoles, The	T	I	4470	Native American Stories	Lerner Publications
Semitrucks	M	I	250+	Horsepower	Capstone Press
Semitrucks	H	I	114	Mighty Machines	Capstone Press
Sending Messages	B	I	49	Wonder World	Wright Group/McGraw Hill
Sending Signals	H	I	163	Literacy Tree	Rigby
Seneca Chief, Army General: A Story about Ely Parker	S	B	8687	Creative Minds Biographies	Lerner Publications
Senor Armadillo's Letter	E	F	156	Joy Starters	Pearson Learning Group
Senor Armadillo's Shoes	F	F	188	Joy Starters	Pearson Learning Group
Sensational Seasons	Q	I	705	Reading Street	Pearson
Sense of Place, A	Q	I	250+	Orbit Collections	Pacific Learning
Sense of Taste, The	O	I	250+	A True Book	Children's Press
Senses	E	I	66	Voyages	SRA/McGraw Hill
Senses at the Seashore	I	I	123	Shelley Rotner's Early Childhood	Millbrook Press
Senses in the City	I	I	152	Shelley Rotner's Early Childhood Library	Millbrook Press
Separate Ways	L	RF	833	PM Plus Story Books	Rigby
Separate Worlds	Q	I	858	Vocabulary Readers	Houghton Mifflin Harcourt
Separate Worlds	Q	I	858	Vocabulary Readers/CA	Houghton Mifflin Harcourt
Separate Worlds	Q	I	858	Vocabulary Readers/TX	Houghton Mifflin Harcourt
September 11, 2001	U	I	250+	Cornerstones of Freedom	Children's Press
September 11, 2001 Attack on New York City	Z	I	250+	Hampton, Wilborn	Candlewick Press
Sequoyah	S	B	3594	History Maker Bios	Lerner Publications
Sequoyah	O	B	865	Leveled Readers Social Studies	Houghton Mifflin Harcourt
Sequoyah	Q	B	1340	Vocabulary Readers	Houghton Mifflin Harcourt
Sequoyah	Q	B	1340	Vocabulary Readers/CA	Houghton Mifflin Harcourt
Serena and Venus Williams	T	B	250+	Sports Heroes	Red Brick Learning
Serpent on My Skin	O	F	250+	The Adventures of Sam X	Stone Arch Books
Serpent's Children, The	W	HF	250+	Yep, Laurence	HarperTrophy
Serves Two Hundred	S	RF	2585	Leveled Readers	Houghton Mifflin Harcourt
Serves Two Hundred	S	RF	2585	Leveled Readers/CA	Houghton Mifflin Harcourt
Serves Two Hundred	S	RF	2585	Leveled Readers/TX	Houghton Mifflin Harcourt
Serving the Community	K	I	250+	Windows on Literacy	National Geographic
Set in Stone	L	I	250+	Yellow Umbrella Books	Red Brick Learning
Sets of Picture Cards	J	RF	260	PM Math Readers	Rigby
Sets: Sorting into Groups	L	I	250+	Exploring Math	Capstone Press
Setting the Table	A	I	32	Leveled Literacy Intervention/ Orange System	Heinemann
Seven	H	RF	131	Early Connections	Benchmark Education
Seven Big Bubbles	F	RF	94	Gear Up!	Wright Group/McGraw Hill
Seven Blind Mice	K	TL	250+	Young, Ed	Puffin Books
Seven Chinese Brothers, The	P	TL	250+	Mahy, Margaret	Scholastic
Seven Continents	L	I	202	Windows on Literacy	National Geographic
Seven Continents, The	M	I	250+	Rigby Star Quest	Rigby
Seven Cool Cats	F	F	97	Seedlings	Continental Press
Seven Fables, Seven Truths	R	TL	250+	Pair-It Books	Steck-Vaughn

S

* Collection of short stories
# Graphic text

TITLE	LEVEL	GENRE	WORD COUNT	AUTHOR / SERIES	PUBLISHER / DISTRIBUTOR
Seven Fat Cats	G	F	152	The Story Basket	Wright Group/McGraw Hill
Seven Foolish Fishermen	K	TL	250+	PM Tales and Plays-Gold	Rigby
Seven in a Line	F	I	138	PM Math Readers	Rigby
Seven Kisses in a Row	O	RF	250+	MacLachlan, Patricia	HarperCollins
Seven Little Ducks	F	TL	190	PM Readalongs	Rigby
Seven Little Kids, The	G	TL	363	Folk Tales	Pioneer Valley
Seven Little Monsters	H	F	55	Sendak, Maurice	HarperCollins
Seven Natural Wonders of the World	S	I	250+	Literacy by Design	Rigby
Seven Natural Wonders, The	Q	I	250+	Navigators Social Studies Series	Benchmark Education
Seven Spools of Thread: A Kwanzaa Story	N	TL	250+	Medearis, Angela Shelf	Scholastic
Seven Stones of Sligo	O	TL	250+	PM Collection	Rigby
*Seven Strange and Ghostly Tales	Y	F	250+	Jacques, Brian	Penguin Group
Seven Treasure Hunts, The	M	RF	250+	Byars, Betsy	HarperTrophy
Seventh Grade Weirdo	S	RF	250+	Wardlaw, Lee	Scholastic
Seventh Tower, The: The Fall	W	F	250+	Nix, Garth	Scholastic
Sewer Rats	V	RF	250+	Orca Currents	Orca Book Publishers
Sewers and the Rats That Love Them: The Disgusting Story Behind Where It All Goes	S	I	250+	Sanitation Investigation	Capstone Press
Sewing Machine, The	Q	I	250+	Great Inventions	Capstone Press
Shabanu: Daughter of the Wind	Z	RF	250+	Staples, Suzanne Fisher	Random House
Shackleton Expedition, The	S	I	250+	Fine, Jil	Children's Press
Shades of Gray	W	HF	250+	Reeder, Carolyn	Avon Camelot
Shadow Dance	D	RF	66	Little Celebrations	Pearson Learning Group
Shadow in the Dark, The	W	F	250+	Dark Man	Ransom
Shadow of a Bull	U	RF	250+	Wojciechowska, Maia	Simon & Schuster
Shadow of a Doubt	Z	RF	250+	Rottman, S.L.	Peachtree
Shadow of the Wolf	N	I	250+	Whelan, Gloria	Random House
Shadow Over Second	M	RF	250+	Christopher, Matt	Little, Brown & Co.
Shadow Play	WB	I	N/A	Windows on Literacy	National Geographic
Shadow Puppets	H	I	163	Alphakids	Sundance
Shadow Puppets	K	I	236	Rigby Focus	Rigby
Shadow Thieves, The	X	F	250+	Ursu, Anne	Aladddin Paperbacks
Shadow: The Puppy Place	N	RF	250+	Miles, Ellen	Scholastic
Shadows	F	I	110	Independent Readers Science	Houghton Mifflin Harcourt
Shadows	D	RF	35	Literacy 2000	Rigby
Shadows	J	I	250+	Otto, Carolyn B.	Scholastic
Shadows	E	RF	190	Visions	Wright Group/McGraw Hill
Shadows	F	I	130	Wonder World	Wright Group/McGraw Hill
*Shadows & Moonshine	V	TL	250+	Aiken, Joan	David R. Godine
Shadows and Shade	J	I	250+	Explorations	Eleanor Curtain Publishing
Shadows and Shade	J	I	250+	Explorations	Okapi Educational Materials
*Shady Deal, The: Tales of Cleverness and Cunning	Q	TL	250+	Literacy 2000	Rigby
Shag Goes Fishing, The	E	RF	51	Ready to Read	Pacific Learning
Shaggy	C	RF	23	Windows on Literacy	National Geographic
Shaggy Sheep, The	J	RF	301	Wonders	Hampton-Brown
Shaji in New York	T	RF	1906	Leveled Readers	Houghton Mifflin Harcourt
Shake Rattle and Roll	U	I	250+	Rigby Literacy	Rigby
Shake, Rumble, and Roll	Q	I	250+	InfoQuest	Rigby
Shakespeare Stealer, The	X	HF	250+	Blackwood, Gary	Scholastic
Shamus	J	F	386	Sails	Rigby
Shane	V	HF	250+	Schaefer, Jack	Random House
Shane and Ned	E	F	52	Windmill Books	Rigby
Shanghai Shadows	Z	HF	250+	Ruby, Lois	Holiday House

* Collection of short stories
# Graphic text

TITLE	LEVEL	GENRE	WORD COUNT	AUTHOR / SERIES	PUBLISHER / DISTRIBUTOR
Shape Explorers, The	P	RF	250+	In Step Readers	Rigby
Shape in the Dark, The: A Story of Hadrian's Wall	Z	HF	2603	Leveled Readers	Houghton Mifflin Harcourt
Shape Maker, The	A	RF	24	Harry's Math Books	Outside the Box
Shape of Things, The	I	I	140	Dodds, Dayle Ann	Candlewick Press
Shape of Things, The	K	I	124	Spyglass Books	Compass Point Books
Shape Parade	B	F	23	Gear Up!	Wright Group/McGraw Hill
Shape Search	H	I	260	InfoTrek	ETA Cuisenaire
Shape Story, A	D	RF	56	Seedlings	Continental Press
Shape Walk	C	RF	25	Little Celebrations	Pearson Learning Group
Shapes	J	I	196	Beginning to Learn About	Steck-Vaughn
Shapes	LB	I	12	Big Cat	Pacific Learning
Shapes	D	I	98	Carousel Readers	Pearson Learning Group
Shapes	B	I	19	Discovery World	Rigby
Shapes	B	I	40	Early Connections	Benchmark Education
Shapes	B	I	64	On Our Way to English	Rigby
Shapes	C	I	30	Rise & Shine	Hampton-Brown
Shapes	B	I	29	Shutterbug Books	Steck-Vaughn
Shapes	A	I	16	Time for Kids	Teacher Created Materials
Shapes	A	I	24	Urmston, Kathleen; Evans, Karen	Kaeden Books
Shapes	C	I	31	Visions	Wright Group/McGraw Hill
Shapes Around the World	M	I	250+	On Our Way to English	Rigby
Shapes at the Beach	D	I	46	Rosen Real Readers	Rosen Publishing Group
Shapes at the Mall	B	I	41	InfoTrek	ETA Cuisenaire
Shapes Everywhere	E	I	82	Early Connections	Benchmark Education
Shapes in My World	D	I	47	Visions	Wright Group/McGraw Hill
Shapes in the City	K	I	191	Twig	Wright Group/McGraw Hill
Shapes in the Sky: A Book About Clouds	M	I	250+	Amazing Science	Picture Window Books
Shapes of Water, The: Stories About Patterns and Shapes	N	I	250+	Orbit Chapter Books	Pacific Learning
Shapes on the Seashore	B	I	30	Big Cat	Pacific Learning
Shapes with a Rope	F	I	153	PM Math Readers	Rigby
Shapes: Discovering Flats and Solids	L	I	250+	Exploring Math	Capstone Press
Shaping Earth's Surface	R	I	1811	Science Support Readers	Houghton Mifflin Harcourt
Shaping of the Continents, The	V	I	2960	Reading Street	Pearson
Shaping the Earth	L	I	233	Rigby Focus	Rigby
Shar	D	RF	113	Sails	Rigby
Share Bear	D	F	96	Sun Sprouts	ETA Cuisenaire
Sharing	C	RF	33	Harry's Math Books	Outside the Box
Sharing	C	I	107	Leveled Readers	Houghton Mifflin Harcourt
Sharing	C	I	107	Leveled Readers/CA	Houghton Mifflin Harcourt
Sharing	C	I	107	Leveled Readers/TX	Houghton Mifflin Harcourt
Sharing	C	RF	24	Literacy 2000	Rigby
Sharing a Dream	O	B	913	Leveled Readers	Houghton Mifflin Harcourt
Sharing a Dream	O	B	913	Leveled Readers/CA	Houghton Mifflin Harcourt
Sharing a Dream	O	B	913	Leveled Readers/TX	Houghton Mifflin Harcourt
Sharing a Room	K	RF	425	Gear Up!	Wright Group/McGraw Hill
Sharing Danny's Dad	G	RF	89	Little Celebrations	Pearson Learning Group
Sharing Homes	D	I	41	Hiris, Monica	Kaeden Books
Sharing Time	D	RF	113	Carousel Readers	Pearson Learning Group
Shark	W	I	250+	Eyewitness Books	DK Publishing
Shark	B	I	69	Vocabulary Readers	Houghton Mifflin Harcourt
Shark	B	I	69	Vocabulary Readers/CA	Houghton Mifflin Harcourt

* Collection of short stories
# Graphic text

TITLE	LEVEL	GENRE	WORD COUNT	AUTHOR / SERIES	PUBLISHER / DISTRIBUTOR
Shark	B	I	69	Vocabulary Readers/TX	Houghton Mifflin Harcourt
Shark Attack!	K	I	301	Explorations	Eleanor Curtain Publishing
Shark Attack!	K	I	301	Explorations	Okapi Eductional Materials
Shark Attack!: Bethany Hamilton's Story of Survival	S	I	250+	True Tales of Survival	Capstone Press
Shark in a Sack	C	F	65	Sunshine	Wright Group/McGraw Hill
Shark in School	N	RF	250+	Giff, Patricia Reilly	Bantam
Shark Lady: The Adventures of Eugenie Clark	O	B	250+	McGovern, Ann	Scholastic
Shark Park	Q	RF	250+	Story Surfers	ETA Cuisenaire
Shark Tales	R	I	250+	Explorer Books-Pathfinder	National Geographic
Shark Tales	P	I	250+	Explorer Books-Pioneer	National Geographic
Shark with No Teeth, The	J	F	250+	Storyworlds	Heinemann Educational Books
Shark!	L	I	479	Leveled Readers Science	Houghton Mifflin Harcourt
Shark!: The Truth Behind the Terror	T	I	250+	High Five Reading	Red Brick Learning
Sharks	N	I	250+	Bookshop	Mondo
Sharks	O	I	250+	First Reports	Compass Point Books
Sharks	M	I	250+	Gibbons, Gail	Holiday House
Sharks	O	I	250+	Holmes, Kevin J.	Red Brick Learning
Sharks	R	I	1102	Leveled Readers	Houghton Mifflin Harcourt
Sharks	R	I	1102	Leveled Readers/CA	Houghton Mifflin Harcourt
Sharks	R	I	1102	Leveled Readers/TX	Houghton Mifflin Harcourt
Sharks	G	I	42	Pebble Books	Red Brick Learning
Sharks	H	I	155	Ready Readers	Pearson Learning Group
Sharks	M	I	250+	Rigby Rocket	Rigby
Sharks	T	I	250+	Simon, Seymour	HarperTrophy
Sharks	S	I	250+	Story Surfers	ETA Cuisenaire
Sharks	P	I	250+	Tristars	Richard C. Owen
Sharks	I	I	84	Under the Sea	Capstone Press
Sharks	L	I	238	Wonder World	Wright Group/McGraw Hill
Sharks and Rays	Q	I	250+	Explorers	Wright Group/McGraw Hill
Sharks and Rays	L	I	250+	Marine Life For Young Readers	Pearson Learning Group
Sharks Under Attack	S	I	1055	Leveled Readers	Houghton Mifflin Harcourt
Sharks Under Attack	S	I	1055	Leveled Readers/CA	Houghton Mifflin Harcourt
Sharon the Shark	I	F	266	Supersonics	Rigby
Shaun White	P	B	1931	Amazing Athletes	Lerner Publications
Shawl, The	R	RF	250+	Book Blazers	ETA Cuisenaire
Shawnee, The	R	I	250+	First Reports	Compass Point Books
She Said	C	RF	35	Ready Readers	Pearson Learning Group
Sheeba	L	F	250+	Noonan, Diana	Pearson Learning Group
Sheep	L	I	250+	PM Animal Facts: Purple	Rigby
Sheep Have Lambs	M	I	250+	Animals and Their Young	Compass Point Books
Sheep in a Jeep	G	F	83	Shaw, Nancy	Houghton Mifflin Harcourt
Sheep on the Farm	G	I	66	Pebble Books	Capstone Press
Sheep Sheep Sheep	J	TL	250+	Redhead, Janet Slater	Steck-Vaughn
Sheepdog in the Snow	Q	RF	250+	Baglio, Ben M.	Scholastic
Sheepdog Max	F	F	171	Sun Sprouts	ETA Cuisenaire
Sheep's Bell	C	RF	37	Ready Readers	Pearson Learning Group
Sheila Rae, the Brave	K	F	250+	Henkes, Kevin	Scholastic
Shelf Life	Y	RF	250+	Paulsen, Gary	Simon & Schuster
Shell	W	I	250+	Eyewitness Books	DK Publishing
She'll Be Coming Around the Mountain	J	RF	250+	Bank Street	Bantam
She'll Be Coming Around the Mountain	E	F	250+	Learn to Read	Creative Teaching Press
She'll Be Coming Around the Mountain	J	TL	250+	Traditional Songs	Picture Window Books

Organized Alphabetically by Title
Storable Database at www.fountasandpinnellleveledbooks.com

* Collection of short stories
\# Graphic text

TITLE	LEVEL	GENRE	WORD COUNT	AUTHOR / SERIES	PUBLISHER / DISTRIBUTOR
Shell Homes	I	I	163	Sails	Rigby
Shell Shopping	F	RF	145	Ready Readers	Pearson Learning Group
Shell-Flower	S	B	1761	Leveled Readers	Houghton Mifflin Harcourt
Shell-Flower and the Strangers	R	B	250+	Leveled Readers	Houghton Mifflin Harcourt
Shells	F	I	246	Rigby Flying Colors	Rigby
Shells	A	I	34	Rigby Literacy	Rigby
Shells	E	I	133	Sails	Rigby
Shells	B	I	39	Seedlings	Continental Press
Shelter	I	I	60	Canizares, Susan; Moreton, Daniel	Scholastic
*Shelter Dogs: Amazing Stories of Adopted Strays	P	I	250+	Kehret, Peg	Albert Whitman & Co.
Shep the Sheep of Caladeen	K	F	829	Appleton-Smith, Laura	Flyleaf Publishing
Sheriffs and Deputy Sheriffs	S	I	250+	Law Enforcement	Capstone Press
Sherlock Holmes and the Baker Street Irregulars: The Fall of the Amazing Zalindas	V	HF	250+	Mack, Tracy & Citrin, Michael	Orchard Books
Sherlock Hounds: Our Heroic Search and Rescue Dogs	S	I	250+	Bookshop	Mondo
Sherman Shoots . . .	B	RF	16	Ray's Readers	Outside the Box
Sherpa Guide, A	N	I	610	Vocabulary Readers	Houghton Mifflin Harcourt
Sherpa Guide, A	N	I	610	Vocabulary Readers/CA	Houghton Mifflin Harcourt
Sherpa Guide, A	N	I	610	Vocabulary Readers/TX	Houghton Mifflin Harcourt
Sheryl Swoopes	R	B	250+	Sports Heroes	Red Brick Learning
She's Got Game!	U	I	250+	Boldprint	Steck-Vaughn
Shetland Pony, The	R	I	250+	Horses	Capstone Press
Shh! We're Writing the Constitution	T	I	250+	Fritz, Jean	G.P. Putnam's Sons
SHHH	F	RF	66	Henkes, Kevin	Greenwillow
Shhhh!	G	F	68	Kline, Suzy	Whitman
Shifter Karts: High-Speed Go-Karts	M	I	250+	Horsepower	Capstone Press
Shifting Ground	S	HF	250+	Power Up!	Steck-Vaughn
Shifting Perspectives	V	I	250+	InfoQuest	Rigby
Shifting Sands	R	I	250+	InfoQuest	Rigby
Shifting Society, A	V	I	2439	Reading Street	Pearson
Shifty Shark, The	P	F	250+	Tristars	Richard C. Owen
Shih Tzus	R	I	250+	All About Dogs	Capstone Press
Shih Tzus	I	I	162	Dogs	Capstone Press
Shiloh	R	RF	250+	Naylor, Phyllis Reynolds	Bantam
Shimmer of Butterflies, A	U	I	250+	Wild Life Series	London Town Press
Shine Sun	F	RF	115	Rookie Readers	Children's Press
Shingo's Grandfather	K	RF	370	Sunshine	Wright Group/McGraw Hill
*Shining Blue Planet and Other Cases, The	O	RF	250+	Simon, Seymour	Avon
Shintaro's Umbrellas	I	RF	95	Books for Young Learners	Richard C. Owen
Ship in a Bottle, The	Q	RF	250+	Ragged Island Mysteries	Wright Group/McGraw Hill
Ship Is Coming!, A	M	RF	250+	On Our Way to English	Rigby
Ships	L	I	275	Wonder World	Wright Group/McGraw Hill
Ships at Sea	K	I	250+	PM Plus	Rigby
Shipwreck at the Bottom of the World	Y	I	250+	Armstrong, Jennifer	Crown Publishers, Inc.
Shipwreck in the South China Sea	R	I	250+	On Our Way to English	Rigby
Shipwreck Saturday	K	RF	250+	Cosby, Bill	Scholastic
Shipwreck Search: Discovery of the H.L. Hunley	N	I	1809	On My Own History	Lerner Publications
Shipwreck! Debbie Kiley's Story of Survival	S	I	250+	True Tales of Survival	Capstone Press
Shipwrecked!	Q	F	250+	Bookweb	Rigby
Shirley Chisholm	S	B	1396	Leveled Readers	Houghton Mifflin Harcourt

* Collection of short stories
# Graphic text

S

TITLE	LEVEL	GENRE	WORD COUNT	AUTHOR / SERIES	PUBLISHER / DISTRIBUTOR
Shirley Chisholm	S	B	1396	Leveled Readers/CA	Houghton Mifflin Harcourt
Shirley Chisholm	S	B	1396	Leveled Readers/TX	Houghton Mifflin Harcourt
Shivers	R	I	250+	Boldprint	Steck-Vaughn
Shoe	K	RF	250+	Literacy by Design	Rigby
Shoe	K	RF	250+	Rigby Literacy	Rigby
Shoe Grabber, The	I	F	260	Read Alongs	Rigby
Shoe Town	G	F	134	Green Light Readers	Harcourt
Shoe, A	A	F	24	Sails	Rigby
Shoebag	P	F	250+	James, Mary	Scholastic
Shoeless Joe & Me	T	F	250+	Gutman, Dan	Harper Trophy
Shoemaker and the Elves, The	J	TL	250+	Sunshine	Wright Group/McGraw Hill
Shoes	D	F	79	Book Bank	Wright Group/McGraw Hill
Shoes	A	RF	16	Little Celebrations	Pearson Learning Group
Shoes	B	RF	40	Little Readers	Houghton Mifflin Harcourt
Shoes	D	RF	150	Sun Sprouts	ETA Cuisenaire
Shoes	F	I	73	Talk About Books	Pearson Learning Group
Shoes	D	I	150	Winthrop, Elizabeth	HarperTrophy
Shoes for Everyone: A Story About Jan Matzeliger	R	B	250+	Mitchell, Barbara	Carolrhoda Books
Shoes Through the Ages	Q	I	250+	Brill, Marlene Targ	Steck-Vaughn
Shoes, Shoes, Shoes	H	RF	274	Real Kids Readers	Millbrook Press
Shoeshine Girl	N	RF	250+	Bulla, Clyde Robert	HarperTrophy
Shoeshine Girl	S	HF	1731	Leveled Readers	Houghton Mifflin Harcourt
Shoeshine Girl	S	HF	1731	Leveled Readers/CA	Houghton Mifflin Harcourt
Shonto Begay: His Life and Work	Y	B	2196	Leveled Readers	Houghton Mifflin Harcourt
Shoo Fly	D	RF	76	Sun Sprouts	ETA Cuisenaire
Shoo!	E	RF	191	Rigby Rocket	Rigby
Shoo!	C	F	37	Sunshine	Wright Group/McGraw Hill
Shoo, Crow! Shoo!	F	F	41	Early Readers	Compass Point Books
Shoo, Fly	B	F	31	Science	Outside the Box
Shoo, Fly	J	RF	336	Storyteller	Wright Group/McGraw Hill
Shoo, Fly Guy!	I	F	250+	Arnold, Tedd	Scholastic
Shoo, Fly!	B	RF	24	Story Box	Wright Group/McGraw Hill
*Shoo, Shoo, Shoo! and Other Stories	H	F	239	Story Steps	Rigby
Shoo, Spider!	I	RF	250+	Scooters	ETA Cuisenaire
Shoot of Corn, A	L	RF	250+	Cambridge Reading	Pearson Learning Group
Shooting Star, The	M	RF	661	PM Collection	Rigby
Shooting Stars	R	RF	250+	Costello, Emily	Dell
Shooting the Sun: A Chinese Myth	L	TL	509	Springboard	Wright Group/ McGraw Hill
Shopping	E	RF	170	Handprints C	Educators Publishing Service
Shopping	C	I	41	Interaction	Rigby
Shopping	J	I	254	Leveled Readers	Houghton Mifflin Harcourt
Shopping	D	RF	26	Literacy 2000	Rigby
Shopping	C	I	78	Little Red Readers	Sundance
Shopping	E	I	45	Read-More Books	Pearson Learning Group
Shopping	B	RF	31	Rigby Star	Rigby
Shopping	A	F	25	Sails	Rigby
Shopping	E	RF	101	Storyteller-Setting Sun	Wright Group/McGraw Hill
Shopping	J	RF	250+	Sunshine	Wright Group/McGraw Hill
Shopping	LB	RF	15	Sunshine	Wright Group/McGraw Hill
Shopping	D	RF	44	Sunshine	Wright Group/McGraw Hill
Shopping at the Mall	G	RF	145	Urmston, Kathleen; Evans, Karen	Kaeden Books

* Collection of short stories
# Graphic text

TITLE	LEVEL	GENRE	WORD COUNT	AUTHOR / SERIES	PUBLISHER / DISTRIBUTOR
Shopping at the Supermarket	B	I	46	Foundations	Wright Group/McGraw Hill
Shopping Day	D	I	44	Vocabulary Readers	Houghton Mifflin Harcourt
Shopping for School	C	RF	33	Visions	Wright Group/McGraw Hill
Shopping in Many Cultures	I	I	92	Life Around the World	Capstone Press
Shopping List, The	F	RF	153	Rigby Flying Colors	Rigby
Shopping List, The	I	F	284	Storyteller	Wright Group/McGraw Hill
Shopping List, The	G	I	120	Windows on Literacy	National Geographic
Shopping Mall, The	B	I	44	PM Starters	Rigby
Shopping Trip, A	D	RF	84	InfoTrek	ETA Cuisenaire
Shopping with a Crocodile	L	F	250+	Pacific Literacy	Pacific Learning
Shopping with Dad	C	RF	43	Home Connection Collection	Rigby
Shopping with Dad	C	RF	72	Windows on Literacy	National Geographic
Shopping with Grandma	F	RF	162	PM Photo Stories	Rigby
Shopping with the Meanies	H	F	225	The Story Basket	Wright Group/McGraw Hill
Shores of Freedom	S	I	250+	InfoQuest	Rigby
Short and Tall: An Animal Opposites Book	J	I	250+	Animal Opposites	Capstone Press
Shortest Kid in the World	K	RF	250+	Bliss, Corinne Demas	Random House
Shortstop from Tokyo	P	RF	250+	Christopher, Matt	Little, Brown & Co.
Shorty	M	RF	250+	Literacy 2000	Rigby
Shoshones, The	T	I	3888	Native American Stories	Lerner Publications
Shosun's Mistake	N	I	250+	Sails	Rigby
Shots	I	RF	90	City Kids	Rigby
Should Kids Play Video Games?	T	I	250+	Bookshop	Mondo
Should There Be Presidential Term Limits?	V	I	250+	Bookshop	Mondo
Should There Be Space Exploration?	U	I	250+	Bookshop	Mondo
Should There Be Zoos?: A Persuasive Text	S	I	250+	Bookshop	Mondo
Should This Have Happened?	Q	I	250+	Sails	Rigby
Should We Drill for Oil in Protected Areas?	W	I	250+	Bookshop	Mondo
Should We Have Pets?	N	I	250+	Bookshop	Mondo
Should You Ever?	I	F	69	Tiger Cub	Peguis
Shoveling Snow	F	RF	109	Cummings, Pat	Scholastic
Show and Tell	E	RF	214	Alphakids	Sundance
Show and Tell	K	RF	201	City Kids	Rigby
Show and Tell	G	RF	190	First Start	Troll Associates
Show and Tell	B	F	20	Leveled Readers	Houghton Mifflin Harcourt
Show and Tell	A	F	20	Leveled Readers/CA	Houghton Mifflin Harcourt
Show and Tell	A	RF	32	Little Books	Sadlier-Oxford
Show and Tell	I	RF	201	Little Celebrations	Pearson Learning Group
Show and Tell	F	RF	111	Little Red Readers	Sundance
Show and Tell	H	RF	407	Real Kids Readers	Millbrook Press
Show Me a Snake Hole	L	RF	250+	Frederick, Shirley	Hampton-Brown
Show Must Go On!, The	L	RF	586	Leveled Readers	Houghton Mifflin Harcourt
Show of Hands, A	L	I	250+	Rigby Literacy	Rigby
Show Time at the Polk Street School	M	RF	250+	Giff, Patricia Reilly	Bantam
Show Us Your Wings	G	I	132	Yellow Umbrella Books	Red Brick Learning
Show What You Can Do	R	RF	250+	In Step Readers	Rigby
Show, The	A	RF	40	Leveled Literacy Intervention/Orange System	Heinemann
Show, The	A	RF	25	Leveled Readers	Houghton Mifflin Harcourt
Show, The	A	RF	25	Leveled Readers/CA	Houghton Mifflin Harcourt
Show, The	A	F	24	Sails	Rigby
Show-and-Tell	H	RF	205	Cambridge Reading	Pearson Learning Group
Show-and-Tell	J	RF	220	Foundations	Wright Group/McGraw Hill
Show-and-Tell Frog, The	J	F	250+	Oppenheim, Joanna	Bantam

S

TITLE	LEVEL	GENRE	WORD COUNT	AUTHOR / SERIES	PUBLISHER / DISTRIBUTOR
Show-and-Tell Sam	F	F	92	Rookie Readers	Children's Press
Show-and-Tell War, The	N	RF	250+	Smith, Janice Lee	HarperTrophy
Show-Off Frog	L	F	907	Pair-It Turn and Learn	Steck-Vaughn
Shredderman: Attack of the Tigger	R	RF	250+	Van Draanen, Wendelin	Scholastic
Shredderman: Secret Identity	R	RF	250+	Van Draanen, Wendelin	Scholastic
Shrewbettina Goes to Work	WB	F	N/A	Goodall, John	McElderry
Shrimp	H	I	95	Under the Sea	Capstone Press
Shugg's Pet Octopus	M	F	250+	Rigby Gigglers	Rigby
Shush!	D	RF	29	Pacific Literacy	Pacific Learning
Shut the Door	D	RF	46	Visions	Wright Group/McGraw Hill
Shy Ana	I	RF	196	Reading Street	Pearson
Shy People's Picnic, The	M	F	250+	Little Celebrations	Pearson Learning Group
Si Won's Victory	M	RF	250+	Little Celebrations	Pearson Learning Group
Siamese Cats	I	I	117	Cats	Capstone Press
Siberian Huskies	I	I	134	Dogs	Capstone Press
Siberian Survivor	R	I	250+	Explorer Books-Pathfinder	National Geographic
Siberian Survivor	P	I	250+	Explorer Books-Pioneer	National Geographic
Sick Bear, The	D	RF	61	Joy Readers	Pearson Learning Group
Sick Day, A	I	RF	331	InfoTrek	ETA Cuisenaire
Sick in Bed	F	RF	109	Little Red Readers	Sundance
Sick Rooster, The	I	F	265	Sails	Rigby
Sid and Sam	E	RF	120	Buck, Nola	HarperTrophy
Siddhartha Gautama: The Buddha	X	B	250+	Primary Source Readers	Teacher Created Materials
Side by Side	M	I	250+	Explorations	Eleanor Curtain Publishing
Side by Side	M	I	250+	Explorations	Okapi Educational Materials
Sidekick, The	L	F	1309	Reading Street	Pearson
Sidetrack Sam	K	RF	250+	Literacy 2000	Rigby
Sidewalk Story	N	RF	250+	Mathis, Sharon Bell	Penguin Group
Sidewalk, The	A	RF	32	Leveled Literacy Intervention/ Orange System	Heinemann
*Sideways Arithmetic from Wayside School	S	I	250+	Sachar, Louis	Scholastic
*Sideways Stories from Wayside School	P	F	250+	Sachar, Louis	Hearst
Sierra	Q	I	250+	Siebert, Diane	HarperCollins
Sieur de La Salle	Q	B	250+	Biographies-Great Explorers	Capstone Press
Sight, The	Z	F	250+	Clement-Davies, David	Penguin Group
Sights and Sounds of New York City's Chinatown, The	M	I	507	Reading Street	Pearson
Sigmond Slitherforth	O	F	250+	Wonder World	Wright Group/McGraw Hill
Sign of the Beaver	T	HF	250+	Speare, Elizabeth George	Bantam
Sign of the Chrysanthemum, The	U	RF	250+	Paterson, Katherine	HarperTrophy
Signs	G	RF	127	Breakthrough	Longman
Signs	F	I	40	Canizares, Susan; Chanko, Pamela	Scholastic
Signs	C	I	40	Carousel Earlybirds	Pearson Learning Group
Signs	B	I	24	Literacy 2000	Rigby
Signs	C	I	35	Little Celebrations	Pearson Learning Group
Signs	E	I	131	Twig	Wright Group/McGraw Hill
Signs	LB	I	21	Yellow Umbrella Books	Red Brick Learning
Signs All Around	E	RF	90	InfoTrek	ETA Cuisenaire
Signs All Around Us	G	I	165	Gear Up!	Wright Group/McGraw Hill
Signs All Around Us	M	I	900	Vocabulary Readers	Houghton Mifflin Harcourt
Signs All Around Us	M	I	900	Vocabulary Readers/CA	Houghton Mifflin Harcourt
Signs Are Everywhere	J	I	276	Vocabulary Readers	Houghton Mifflin Harcourt
Signs Are Everywhere	J	I	276	Vocabulary Readers/CA	Houghton Mifflin Harcourt

* Collection of short stories
# Graphic text

TITLE	LEVEL	GENRE	WORD COUNT	AUTHOR / SERIES	PUBLISHER / DISTRIBUTOR
Signs Are Everywhere	J	I	276	Vocabulary Readers/TX	Houghton Mifflin Harcourt
Signs in Our Neighborhood	I	RF	191	InfoTrek	ETA Cuisenaire
Signs of Spring	H	F	250+	Bookshop	Mondo
Signs on the Way	F	I	106	Windows on Literacy	National Geographic
Signs, Songs, and Symbols of America	S	I	1278	Reading Street	Pearson
Silent Boy, The	Y	RF	250+	Lowry, Lois	Houghton Mifflin Harcourt
Silent Hero, The	O	I	250+	Shea, George	Random House
Silent Sam	G	RF	146	Bebop Books	Lee & Low Books Inc.
Silent to the Bone	V	RF	250+	Konigsburg, E. L.	Atheneum
Silent World, A	L	RF	250+	Literacy 2000	Rigby
Silk	U	I	250+	Theme Sets	National Geographic
Silk Road, The	V	I	1594	Leveled Readers	Houghton Mifflin Harcourt
Silk Road, The	V	I	1594	Leveled Readers/CA	Houghton Mifflin Harcourt
Silk Route, The	U	HF	250+	Major, John S.	HarperCollins
Silk Umbrellas	S	RF	250+	Marsden, Carolyn	Candlewick Press
Silkworm Moths	P	I	1375	Early Bird Nature Books	Lerner Publishing
Silkworms	L	I	328	Explorations	Eleanor Curtain Publishing
Silkworms	L	I	328	Explorations	Okapi Eductional Materials
Silkworms	P	I	250+	Life Cycles	Capstone Press
Silkworms	N	I	250+	Take Two Books	Wright Group/McGraw Hill
Silly Aunt Tilly	H	F	176	Instant Readers	Harcourt School Publishers
Silly Billys	H	F	250+	Sunshine	Wright Group/McGraw Hill
Silly Cat	C	F	48	Sails	Rigby
Silly Cat Tricks	D	F	83	Teacher's Choice Series	Pearson Learning Group
Silly Clown	B	RF	35	Sails	Rigby
Silly Old Possum	C	RF	41	Story Box	Wright Group/McGraw Hill
Silly Sally	C	RF	24	Rookie Readers	Children's Press
Silly Supper, The	J	RF	250+	The Wright Skills	Wright Group/McGraw Hill
Silly Tilly's Valentine	K	F	250+	Hoban, Lillian	HarperTrophy
Silly Times with Two Silly Trolls	I	F	250+	Jewell, Nancy	HarperTrophy
Silly Tricks	B	F	30	Sails	Rigby
Silly Willy	M	RF	250+	Bookshop	Mondo
Silly Willy and Silly Billy	J	F	221	Foundations	Wright Group/McGraw Hill
Silver	N	RF	250+	Whelan, Gloria	Random House
Silver and Prince	L	RF	250+	PM Story Books-Silver	Rigby
Silver and Stripes	K	F	1187	Reading Street	Pearson
Silver Donkey	V	HF	250+	Hartnett, Sonya	Candlewick Press
Silver Horn, The	S	F	250+	Bookshop	Mondo
Silver Pony, The	WB	F	N/A	Ward, Lynd	Houghton Mifflin Harcourt
Silverwing: How One Small Bat Became a Noble Hero	U	F	250+	Oppel, Kenneth	Simon & Schuster
Silvia Hops Home	E	RF	163	On Our Way to English	Rigby
Silvia's Soccer Game	F	RF	138	Ready Readers	Pearson Learning Group
Simon and the Aliens	N	SF	250+	SupaDoopers	Sundance
Simon Bolivar	W	B	1858	Leveled Readers Social Studies	Houghton Mifflin Harcourt
Simone's Travels	L	RF	1297	Reading Street	Pearson
Simon's Big Challenge	Q	RF	250+	Pair-It Books	Steck-Vaughn
Simon's Scoop	N	RF	250+	Literacy by Design	Rigby
Simon's Sea Monster	I	RF	250+	Reading Safari	Mondo
Simple Machines	L	I	250+	Early Connections	Benchmark Education
Simple Machines	Q	I	250+	Rosen Real Readers	Rosen Publishing Group
Simple Machines	O	I	250+	Windows on Literacy	National Geographic
Simple Machines at Work	L	I	399	Reading Street	Pearson
Simple Machines in Compound Machines	P	I	856	Reading Street	Pearson

S

* Collection of short stories
# Graphic text

TITLE	LEVEL	GENRE	WORD COUNT	AUTHOR / SERIES	PUBLISHER / DISTRIBUTOR
Simple Solution	I	RF	250+	Literacy Tree	Rigby
Simple System, A	V	I	250+	WorldScapes	ETA Cuisenaire
Simply Alice	V	RF	250+	Naylor, Phyllis Reynolds	Simon & Schuster
Simply Sam	E	RF	69	Voyages	SRA/McGraw Hill
Sing a Song	E	F	154	Story Box	Wright Group/McGraw Hill
Sing Down the Moon	T	HF	250+	O'Dell, Scott	Language for Learning Assoc.
Sing for Your Father, Su Phan	W	HF	250+	Pevsner, Stella; Tang, Fay	Bantam
Sing for Your Supper	P	HF	250+	High-Fliers	Pacific Learning
*Sing to the Moon	K	F	2448	Story Box	Wright Group/McGraw Hill
Singer and the First Lady, The	T	I	1488	Vocabulary Readers	Houghton Mifflin Harcourt
Singer and the First Lady, The	T	I	1488	Vocabulary Readers/CA	Houghton Mifflin Harcourt
*Singing Drum, The	T	TL	250+	Literacy 2000	Rigby
Singing Duck, The	I	F	391	Leveled Literacy Intervention/ Blue System	Heinemann
Singing Giant, The	H	F	250+	Rigby Star	Rigby
Singing Giant, The: A Play	H	F	250+	Rigby Star	Rigby
Singing Giant, The: A Play	H	F	250+	Rigby Literacy	Rigby
Singing Giant, The: A Story	H	F	250+	Rigby Literacy	Rigby
Singing Princess, The	K	F	250+	Literacy by Design	Rigby
Singing Princess, The	K	F	250+	Rigby Literacy	Rigby
Singing Robins	K	I	397	Pull Ahead Books	Lerner Publications
Single Shard, A	U	HF	250+	Park, Linda Sue	Clarion
Sing-Song Tree, The	L	I	250+	Sunshine	Wright Group/McGraw Hill
Sink or Float	F	I	91	Instant Readers	Harcourt School Publishers
Sink or Float?	C	I	36	Independent Readers Science	Houghton Mifflin Harcourt
Sink or Float?	E	I	112	Learn to Read	Creative Teaching Press
Sink or Float?	E	I	159	Vocabulary Readers	Houghton Mifflin Harcourt
Sink or Float?	E	I	159	Vocabulary Readers/CA	Houghton Mifflin Harcourt
Sink or Float?	E	I	159	Vocabulary Readers/TX	Houghton Mifflin Harcourt
#Sinking of the Titanic, The	S	I	250+	Graphic Library	Capstone Press
Sione Went Fishing	I	RF	225	Sunshine	Wright Group/McGraw Hill
Sione's Talo	H	TL	164	Nelisi, Lino	Scholastic
Sioux Indians, The	P	I	250+	Native Peoples	Red Brick Learning
Sioux, The	R	I	250+	First Reports	Compass Point Books
Sioux, The	T	I	4485	Native American Stories	Lerner Publications
Sioux, The: Nomadic Buffalo Hunters	R	I	250+	America's First Peoples	Capstone Press
Sir Arthur	P	B	250+	Apte, Sunita	Scholastic
Sir Cumference and the Dragon of Pi	Q	HF	250+	Neuschwander, Cindy	Charlesbridge
Sir Cumference and the First Round Table	Q	HF	250+	Neuschwander, Cindy	Charlesbridge
Sir Cumference and the Great Knight of Angleland	Q	HF	250+	Neuschwander, Cindy	Charlesbridge
Sir Cumference and the Isle of Immeter	Q	HF	250+	Neuschwander, Cindy	Charlesbridge
Sir Cumference and the Sword in the Cone	Q	HF	250+	Neuschwander, Cindy	Scholastic
Sir Down, Dog	G	RF	192	Sun Sprouts	ETA Cuisenaire
Sir Edmund Hillary	R	I	1437	Vocabulary Readers	Houghton Mifflin Harcourt
Sir Edmund Hillary	R	B	1437	Vocabulary Readers/CA	Houghton Mifflin Harcourt
Sir Hans Sloane	O	B	766	Leveled Readers	Houghton Mifflin Harcourt
Sir Hans Sloane	O	B	766	Leveled Readers/CA	Houghton Mifflin Harcourt
Sir Hans Sloane	O	B	766	Leveled Readers/TX	Houghton Mifflin Harcourt
Sir Tom	T	HF	1617	Reading Street	Pearson
Sir Walter Raleigh	S	B	3532	History Maker Bios	Lerner Publications
Sister	W	RF	250+	Greenfield, Eloise	HarperCollins
Sister Anne's Hands	R	HF	250+	Lorbiecki, Marybeth	Puffin Books

S

* Collection of short stories
# Graphic text

TITLE	LEVEL	GENRE	WORD COUNT	AUTHOR / SERIES	PUBLISHER / DISTRIBUTOR
Sister Ella	Q	HF	250+	High-Fliers	Pacific Learning
Sister Spider Knows	W	RF	250+	Fogelin, Adrian	Peachtree
Sister Tricksters	S	TL	250+	San Souci, Robert D.	August House Publishers
Sisterhood of the Traveling Pants, The	Z+	RF	250+	Schraff, Anne	Townsend Press
Sisters	F	I	63	Families	Capstone Press
Sisters	B	I	28	Pebble Books	Capstone Press
Sisters	E	I	77	Talk About Books	Pearson Learning Group
Sisters Against Slavery: A Story about Sarah and Angelina Grimke	S	B	8509	Creative Minds Biographies	Lerner Publications
Sisters and Brothers	A	I	15	Vocabulary Readers	Houghton Mifflin Harcourt
Sisters and Brothers	A	I	15	Vocabulary Readers/CA	Houghton Mifflin Harcourt
Sisters Club, The	P	RF	250+	McDonald, Megan	Pleasant Company Publications
Sisters Grimm, The	U	F	250+	Buckley, Michael	Scholastic
Sisters Play Soccer	R	RF	1426	Leveled Readers	Houghton Mifflin Harcourt
Sisters Play Soccer	R	RF	1426	Leveled Readers/CA	Houghton Mifflin Harcourt
Sisters Play Soccer	R	RF	1426	Leveled Readers/TX	Houghton Mifflin Harcourt
Sit, Ned!	D	RF	67	Leveled Readers	Houghton Mifflin Harcourt
Sit, Pig!	A	RF	20	Vocabulary Readers	Houghton Mifflin Harcourt
Sit, Sam	F	RF	165	Early Connections	Benchmark Education
Sitting	E	F	46	Literacy 2000	Rigby
Sitting Bull	S	B	250+	History Maker Bios	Lerner Publications
Sitting Bull	N	B	217	Pebble Books	Capstone Press
Sitting Bull	R	B	250+	Primary Source Readers	Teacher Created Materials
Sitting Bull	N	B	250+	Rookie Biographies	Children's Press
Sitting Pretty	L	RF	533	Gear Up!	Wright Group/ McGraw Hill
Six Cats	C	RF	50	Joy Readers	Pearson Learning Group
Six Empty Pockets	F	RF	85	Rookie Readers	Children's Press
Six Fat Cubs	D	F	52	Reading Street	Pearson
Six Fine Fish	F	F	252	Ready Readers	Pearson Learning Group
Six Foolish Fishermen	L	TL	715	Elkin, Benjamin	Children's Press
Six Go By	C	F	24	Ready Readers	Pearson Learning Group
Six Legs	B	I	34	Harry's Math Books	Outside the Box
Six Little Chicks	F	F	227	Sun Sprouts	ETA Cuisenaire
Six Pieces of Cake	C	RF	40	Harry's Math Books	Outside the Box
Six Silly Brothers	K	TL	616	Sun Sprouts	ETA Cuisenaire
Six Silly Foxes	G	F	147	Green Light Readers	Harcourt
Six Things to Make	L	I	250+	Bookshop	Mondo
Six Under the Sea	E	I	158	PM Math Readers	Rigby
Six Voyages of Pleasant Fieldmouse, The	R	F	250+	Wahl, Jan	Tom Doherty
Six Wet Pets	B	F	31	Leveled Readers Language Support	Houghton Mifflin Harcourt
Six-Dinner Sid	L	F	250+	Moore, Inga	Scholastic
*Sixteen Short Stories by Outstanding Writers	Z	RF	250+	Gallo, Donald R.	Dell
Sixth Grade Can Really Kill You	S	RF	250+	DeClements, Barthe	Scholastic
Sixth Grade Secrets	S	RF	250+	Sachar, Louis	Scholastic
Sixth-Grade Sleepover	R	RF	250+	Bunting, Eve	Scholastic
Size: Many Ways to Measure	L	I	250+	Exploring Math	Capstone Press
Sizes	C	I	32	Discovery World	Rigby
Sizewise	S	I	250+	The News	Richard C. Owen
Skate Jam, The	P	RF	250+	Orbit Double Takes	Pacific Learning
Skateboard Bill	J	RF	79	Voyages	SRA/McGraw Hill
Skateboard City	Q	RF	250+	Power Up!	Steck-Vaughn
Skateboard for Alex, A	I	F	229	Javernick, Ellen	Kaeden Books

* Collection of short stories
# Graphic text

S

TITLE	LEVEL	GENRE	WORD COUNT	AUTHOR / SERIES	PUBLISHER / DISTRIBUTOR
Skateboard Power	P	RF	1298	Zucker, Jonny	Stone Arch Books
Skateboard Tough	Q	RF	250+	Christopher, Matt	Little, Brown & Co.
Skateboarder, The	I	I	175	Sun Sprouts	ETA Cuisenaire
Skateboarder's Club, The	O	RF	250+	On Our Way to English	Rigby
Skateboarding	F	RF	147	Developing Books	Pioneer Valley
Skateboarding	N	I	463	Gear Up!	Wright Group/ McGraw Hill
Skateboarding	M	I	250+	Horsepower	Capstone Press
Skateboarding	C	RF	35	Lowe, Diane	Kaeden Books
Skateboarding	H	I	106	Nonfiction	Literacy Footprints
Skateboarding	O	I	250+	PM Nonfiction-Emerald	Rigby
Skateboarding	Q	I	250+	X-Sports	Capstone Press
Skateboarding Greats: Champs of the Ramps	Q	I	250+	Skateboarding	Red Brick Learning
Skateboarding History: From the Backyard to the Big Time	Q	I	250+	Skateboarding	Red Brick Learning
Skateboards: Designs and Equipment	Q	I	250+	Skateboarding	Red Brick Learning
Skatepark Challenge	P	RF	4116	Maddox, Jake	Stone Arch Books
Skateparks: Grab Your Skateboard	Q	I	250+	Skateboarding	Red Brick Learning
Skater Chicks	N	RF	250+	Girlz Rock!	Mondo
Skates for Luke	I	RF	346	PM Story Books-Orange	Rigby
Skates of Uncle Richard, The	P	RF	250+	Fenner, Carol	Random House
Skateway to Freedom	V	HF	250+	Alma, Ann	Orca Book Publishers
Skating	B	F	35	Foundations	Wright Group/McGraw Hill
Skating	C	F	52	Story Box	Wright Group/McGraw Hill
Skating at Rainbow Lake	J	RF	250+	PM Story Books-Silver	Rigby
Skating on Thin Ice	G	F	130	First Start	Troll Associates
Skating to Fame	Q	I	524	Vocabulary Readers	Houghton Mifflin Harcourt
Skating Trail, The	I	RF	250+	PM Plus Story Books	Rigby
Skating Whiz	E	RF	40	Visions	Wright Group/McGraw Hill
Skeeter	N	RF	250+	PM Chapter Books	Rigby
Skeletal System, The	P	I	2167	Early Bird Body Systems	Lerner Publishing
Skeletal System, The	K	I	166	Human Body Systems	Red Brick Learning
Skeleton and Muscles, The	P	I	690	Time for Kids	Teacher Created Materials
Skeleton Key	X	SF	250+	Horowitz, Anthony	Speak
Skeleton Man	V	F	250+	Bruchac, Joseph	Scholastic
Skeleton on the Bus, The	J	F	250+	Literacy 2000	Rigby
Skeletons	I	I	98	Storyteller	Wright Group/McGraw Hill
Skeletons Don't Play Tubas	M	F	250+	Dadey, Debbie; Jones, Marcia Thornton	Scholastic
Skeletons Inside and Out	S	I	250+	iOpeners	Pearson Learning Group
Ski Lesson, The	H	I	155	Storyteller-Moon Rising	Wright Group/McGraw Hill
Ski Race, The	F	RF	155	Springboard	Wright Group/McGraw Hill
Ski School	LB	RF	34	Little Books for Early Readers	University of Maine
Skier, The	B	RF	48	PM Starters	Rigby
Skimper-Scamper	G	F	208	Instant Readers	Harcourt Trade
Skin	F	I	97	Literacy 2000	Rigby
Skin	T	I	250+	Theme Sets	National Geographic
Skin I'm in, The	W	RF	250+	Flake, Sharon G.	Hyperion
Skin, Skin	E	I	44	Wonder World	Wright Group/McGraw Hill
Skinny-Bones	P	RF	250+	Park, Barbara	Random House
Skip Count Song, The	F	I	84	Learn to Read	Creative Teaching Press
Skipper's Balloon	E	RF	62	Oxford Reading Tree	Oxford University Press
Skipper's Birthday	E	RF	64	Oxford Reading Tree	Oxford University Press
Skipper's Idea	E	RF	81	Oxford Reading Tree	Oxford University Press
Skipper's Laces	E	RF	66	Oxford Reading Tree	Oxford University Press

* Collection of short stories
# Graphic text

TITLE	LEVEL	GENRE	WORD COUNT	AUTHOR / SERIES	PUBLISHER / DISTRIBUTOR
Skirt, The	N	RF	250+	Soto, Gary	Bantam
Skittles and Skullbones	J	F	250+	Supersonics	Rigby
Skull of Truth, The	T	F	250+	Coville, Bruce	Harcourt
Skunk Cooks Soup	G	F	299	Leveled Readers	Houghton Mifflin Harcourt
Skunk Cooks Soup	G	F	299	Leveled Readers/CA	Houghton Mifflin Harcourt
Skunk Cooks Soup	G	F	299	Leveled Readers/TX	Houghton Mifflin Harcourt
Skunk with No Stripes, The	H	F	333	Leveled Literacy Intervention/ Green System	Heinemann
Skunks	M	I	250+	PM Animal Facts: Gold	Rigby
Skunks	H	I	111	Seedlings	Continental Press
Sky	N	RF	506	Leveled Readers	Houghton Mifflin Harcourt
Sky Bikers	O	F	250+	Norman, Tony	Stone Arch Books
Sky Boys: How They Built the Empire State Building	Q	HF	250+	Hopkinson, Deborah & Ransome, James E.	Schwartz & Wade Books
Sky Changes	M	I	250+	PM Plus Nonfiction	Rigby
Sky Colors	G	I	147	Shutterbug Books	Steck-Vaughn
Sky Dogs	U	RF	250+	Yolen, Jane	Harcourt Brace
Sky High	L	F	619	Pair-It Books	Steck-Vaughn
Sky Is Falling Down, The	D	TL	101	Joy Readers	Pearson Learning Group
Sky Is Falling, The	F	TL	186	Folk Tales	Pioneer Valley
Sky Is Falling, The	I	F	181	Storyteller-Setting Sun	Wright Group/McGraw Hill
Sky Rider	O	RF	250+	Belcher, Angie	Pacific Learning
Sky Time	F	F	366	Phonics and Friends	Hampton-Brown
Sky Watch	Q	I	250+	Explorers	Wright Group/McGraw Hill
Sky Watchers	G	RF	172	Windows on Literacy	National Geographic
Sky, The	LB	I	16	Handprints A	Educators Publishing Service
Sky, The	A	I	40	Leveled Literacy Intervention/ Green System	Heinemann
SkyFire	J	F	250+	Asch, Frank	Scholastic
Sky-High Dreams	Q	HF	1123	Leveled Readers	Houghton Mifflin Harcourt
Sky-High Dreams	Q	HF	1123	Leveled Readers/CA	Houghton Mifflin Harcourt
Sky-High Dreams	Q	HF	1123	Leveled Readers/TX	Houghton Mifflin Harcourt
Skylark	R	HF	250+	MacLachlan, Patricia	HarperTrophy
Sky's the Limit, The	P	I	250+	Orbit Chapter Books	Pacific Learning
Sky's the Limit, The	Q	RF	250+	Wildcats	Wright Group/McGraw Hill
Sky's the Limit, The: Naturally Funny Jokes	O	F	1731	Make Me Laugh!	Lerner Publications
SkyScraper, The	K	I	252	Little Red Readers	Sundance
Skyscrapers	O	I	250+	Simon, Seymour	Chronicle Books
Slake's Limbo	Y	RF	250+	Holman, Felice	Aladdin
Slam	Z+	RF	250+	Hornby, Nick	G.P. Putnam's Sons
Slam Dunk Sanchez	G	RF	238	Sunshine	Wright Group/McGraw Hill
Slam Dunk Saturday	M	RF	250+	Marzollo, Jean	Random House
Slam!	W	RF	250+	Myers, Walter Dean	Scholastic
Slapshot!	W	I	250+	Boldprint	Steck-Vaughn
Slave Dancer, The	Y	HF	250+	Fox, Paula	Random House
Slave Trade in Early America, The	V	I	250+	Let Freedom Ring	Capstone Press
Slavery in America	T	I	250+	Primary Source Readers	Teacher Created Materials
Sled Dog Morning, A	I	RF	310	Appleton-Smith, Laura	Flyleaf Publishing
Sled, The	D	RF	84	Leveled Readers Language Support	Houghton Mifflin Harcourt
Sledding	C	F	34	Brand New Readers	Candlewick Press
Sledding	A	F	58	Leveled Readers	Houghton Mifflin Harcourt
Sledding	A	F	58	Leveled Readers/CA	Houghton Mifflin Harcourt

S

* Collection of short stories
# Graphic text

TITLE	LEVEL	GENRE	WORD COUNT	AUTHOR / SERIES	PUBLISHER / DISTRIBUTOR
Sledding	A	F	58	Leveled Readers/TX	Houghton Mifflin Harcourt
Sledding Adventures, The	F	F	186	Arctic Stories	Pioneer Valley
Sleep Tight	H	RF	163	Cambridge Reading	Pearson Learning Group
Sleep Tight Spaceboy	G	F	112	Spaceboy	Literacy Footprints
Sleepers, Wake	T	SF	250+	Jacobs, Paul Samuel	Language for Learning Assoc.
Sleeping	I	RF	114	Book Bank	Wright Group/McGraw Hill
Sleeping	E	I	43	Literacy 2000	Rigby
Sleeping Animals	H	I	194	Alphakids	Sundance
Sleeping Beauty	K	TL	250+	Enrichment	Wright Group/McGraw Hill
Sleeping Beauty, The	L	TL	250+	PM Tales and Plays-Silver	Rigby
Sleeping Out	D	RF	49	Story Box	Wright Group/McGraw Hill
Sleeping, Dreaming	P	I	250+	Wonder World	Wright Group/McGraw Hill
Sleep-Over Mouse	D	F	63	My First Reader	Grolier Press
Sleepover Party, The	I	RF	330	Adams, Lorraine; Bruvold, Lynn	Eagle Crest Books
Sleepover, The	N	RF	250+	Girlz Rock!	Mondo
Sleepover, The	H	RF	297	Leveled Readers	Houghton Mifflin Harcourt
Sleepover, The	F	RF	261	Rigby Flying Colors	Rigby
Sleepovers	V	I	250+	10 Things You Need to Know About	Capstone Press
Sleepwalker	O	RF	1920	Powell, J.	Stone Arch Books
Sleepy Bear	E	I	153	Foundations	Wright Group/McGraw Hill
Sleepy Bear	F	I	80	Literacy 2000	Rigby
Sleepy Dog	D	F	118	Ziefert, Harriet	Random House
Sleepy Polar Bear	H	F	97	Hiris, Monica	Kaeden Books
Sleepy Tiger	B	F	41	Sails	Rigby
Sleepy Zoo	B	F	58	Sun Sprouts	ETA Cuisenaire
Sleepyville Wakes Up	T	HF	3021	Reading Street	Pearson
Slice of Pizza, A	I	RF	175	Twig	Wright Group/McGraw Hill
Slide and Slurp, Scratch and Burp: More About Verbs	O	I	287	Words Are CATegorical	Millbrook Press
Slides	D	I	58	Pacific Literacy	Pacific Learning
Sliding into Home	T	RF	250+	Butler, Dori Hillestad	Peachtree
Slim Shorty and the Mules	L	RF	411	Reading Unlimited	Pearson Learning Group
Slimy Skin	B	I	37	Sails	Rigby
Slinky Scaly Snakes!	K	I	250+	DK Readers	DK Publishing
Slip and Slide	K	I	215	Spyglass Books	Compass Point Books
Slippery Planet, The	L	F	250+	Cambridge Reading	Pearson Learning Group
Slippery Slope, The	V	F	250+	Snicket, Lemony	Scholastic
Slippery, Sloppery Spaghetti	H	RF	250+	Home Connection Collection	Rigby
Slipping	X	F	250+	Bell, Cathleen Davitt	Bloomsbury Children's Books
Slither and Slide	H	I	112	Gear Up!	Wright Group/McGraw Hill
Slither McCreep and His Brother, Joe	K	RF	250+	Johnston, Tony	Harcourt Brace
Slithery Snakes and Unicorns	I	F	289	Sunshine	Wright Group/McGraw Hill
Sloppy Copy Slipup, The	P	RF	250+	DiSalvo, DyAnne	Holiday House
Sloppy Tiger and the Party	I	F	293	Sunshine	Wright Group/McGraw Hill
Sloppy Tiger Bedtime	I	F	320	Sunshine	Wright Group/McGraw Hill
Slow and Fast	B	I	31	Handprints A	Educators Publishing Service
Slow Changes on Earth	Q	I	1394	Science Support Readers	Houghton Mifflin Harcourt
Slow Changes on Earth	Q	I	250+	Windows on Literacy	National Geographic
Slow Poke Snail	G	RF	117	Instant Readers	Harcourt School Publishers
Slow Race, The	I	RF	337	InfoTrek	ETA Cuisenaire

* Collection of short stories
\# Graphic text

S

TITLE	LEVEL	GENRE	WORD COUNT	AUTHOR / SERIES	PUBLISHER / DISTRIBUTOR
Sludge and Slime: Oil Spills in Our World	O	I	250+	On Deck	Rigby
Sluefoot Sue's Wild Ride	T	F	1831	Leveled Readers	Houghton Mifflin Harcourt
Slug and Bug	B	F	42	Leveled Readers Language Support	Houghton Mifflin Harcourt
Slug Is Born, A	F	I	131	Sails	Rigby
Slug Makes a House	F	F	219	Rigby Rocket	Rigby
Slug the Sea Monster	H	F	250+	Storyworlds	Heinemann Educational Books
Slugs	O	I	1282	Early Bird Nature Books	Lerner Publishing
Slugs and Snails	N	I	250+	Bookshop	Mondo
Slugs and Snails	P	I	250+	Mini Pets	Steck-Vaughn
Slugs and Snails	H	I	132	Wonder World	Wright Group/McGraw Hill
Slumber Party Organizer, The	P	I	250+	Sunshine	Wright Group/McGraw Hill
Slump, The	N	RF	250+	Kroll, Stephen	Avon Camelot
Slurp! Burp!	E	F	107	Rigby Rocket	Rigby
Sly Fox and Little Red Hen	K	TL	250+	PM Tales and Plays-Purple	Rigby
Sly Fox and Red Hen	F	TL	314	Hunia, Fran	Ladybird Books
Sly Squirrel's Tall Tales	L	F	1162	InfoTrek	ETA Cuisenaire
Small and Large	E	I	89	iOpeners	Pearson Learning Group
Small Baby Raccoon, A	G	RF	104	Ready Readers	Pearson Learning Group
Small Bad Wolf	K	F	250+	I Am Reading	Kingfisher
Small Pig	I	F	250+	Lobel, Arnold	HarperTrophy
Small Rabbit Goes Visiting	H	F	445	Book Bank	Wright Group/McGraw Hill
Small Sailboat, A	I	RF	135	Books for Young Learners	Richard C. Owen
Small Screen	S	I	250+	Boldprint	Steck-Vaughn
Small Steps	Z	RF	250+	Sachar, Louis	Delacorte Press
Small Steps: The Year I Got Polio	U	B	250+	Kehret, Peg	Albert Whitman & Co.
Small Treasures	F	RF	52	Gibson, Akimi	Scholastic
Small Trip, A	G	RF	103	Reading Street	Pearson
Small Wolf	J	HF	250+	Benchley, Nathaniel	HarperTrophy
Small World, A	H	RF	146	Sunshine	Wright Group/McGraw Hill
Smallest Cow in the World, The	K	RF	250+	Paterson, Katherine	HarperTrophy
Smallest Dinosaurs, The	P	I	1115	Meet the Dinosaurs	Lerner Publications
Smallest Horses, The	J	RF	250+	PM Plus Story Books	Rigby
Smallest Tree, The	K	F	250+	Literacy 2000	Rigby
Smart Dog	N	RF	2182	Reading Street	Pearson
Smart Mouse, The	K	TL	597	Leveled Readers	Houghton Mifflin Harcourt
Smart Mouse, The	K	TL	597	Leveled Readers/CA	Houghton Mifflin Harcourt
Smart Mouse, The	K	TL	597	Leveled Readers/TX	Houghton Mifflin Harcourt
Smart Pigs	H	RF	102	Stewart, Josie	Continental Press
Smartest Bear and His Brother Oliver, The	N	F	250+	Bach, Alice	Bantam
Smartest Dinosaurs, The	P	I	1195	Meet the Dinosaurs	Lerner Publications
Smartest Man in Ireland, The	S	F	250+	Hunter, Mollie	Harcourt BraceHarcourt Brace
Smartest One in Class, The	H	RF	68	City Stories	Rigby
Smarty Pants	E	F	116	Story Box	Wright Group/McGraw Hill
Smasher	O	RF	250+	King-Smith, Dick	Random House
Smashing Scroll, The	T	F	799	Dahl, Michael	Stone Arch Books
Smelling	I	I	111	Pebble Books	Red Brick Learning
Smelling	E	I	88	Senses	Lerner Publishing
Smelling	M	I	250+	The Senses	Capstone Press
Smelling!	H	I	146	Sails	Rigby
Smells	A	RF	40	Leveled Literacy Intervention/ Green System	Heinemann

S

* Collection of short stories
# Graphic text

TITLE	LEVEL	GENRE	WORD COUNT	AUTHOR / SERIES	PUBLISHER / DISTRIBUTOR
Smells All Around Us	G	I	202	PM Science Readers	Rigby
Smells Good!	H	I	216	PM Science Readers	Rigby
Smelly Armor	J	F	282	Story Box	Wright Group/McGraw Hill
Smelly Skunks	H	I	147	Sails	Rigby
Smile	D	F	38	Read-Alongs	Rigby
Smile and Say "Cheetah"	I	RF	200	World Quest Adventures	World Quest Learning
Smile if You Like Circles	J	I	250+	Phonics Readers Plus	Steck-Vaughn
Smile! Said Dad	D	RF	66	Pacific Literacy	Pacific Learning
Smile, Baby!	F	RF	165	Little Readers	Houghton Mifflin Harcourt
Smile, The	D	RF	53	Pacific Literacy	Pacific Learning
Smile, The	K	RF	253	Read Alongs	Rigby
Smiles	F	RF	366	Visions	Wright Group/McGraw Hill
Smiling Salad, A	C	RF	32	Pair-It Books	Steck-Vaughn
Smiling Stan, the Pedicab Man	E	RF	121	Joy Readers	Pearson Learning Group
Smith: John Smith and the Settlement of Jamestown	U	B	250+	Exploring the World	Compass Point Books
Smiths and Their Animals, The	J	RF	468	Leveled Readers	Houghton Mifflin Harcourt
Smiths and Their Animals, The	J	RF	468	Leveled Readers/CA	Houghton Mifflin Harcourt
Smiths and Their Animals, The	J	RF	468	Leveled Readers/TX	Houghton Mifflin Harcourt
Smog, Dust, and Toads	R	I	250+	Orbit Chapter Books	Pacific Learning
Smoke Jumpers	I	I	199	On Deck	Rigby
Smokejumpers: Battling the Forest Flames	T	I	250+	High Five Reading	Red Brick Learning
Smokey the Dragon	M	F	250+	Bennett, Jean	Pearson Learning Group
Smokie	E	RF	47	Carousel Readers	Pearson Learning Group
Smoking Mountain, The: The Story of Popocatepetl and Iztaccihuatl	W	TL	2393	Graphic Myths and Legends	Lerner Publications
Smoky the Cow Horse	S	RF	250+	James, Will	Scholastic
Smooth and Rough	K	I	250+	Animal Opposites	Capstone Press
Smooth or Rough?	D	I	49	Rigby Focus	Rigby
Smudge-Face: A Native American Cinderella Tale	M	TL	580	Leveled Readers	Houghton Mifflin Harcourt
Smushy Bus, The	L	F	744	Helakoski, Leslie	Millbrook Press
Snack for Gilbert, A	B	RF	28	Gilbert the Pig	Pioneer Valley
Snack for Roberto, A	D	RF	82	Early Emergent, Set 2	Pioneer Valley
Snack Time	G	RF	59	City Kids	Rigby
Snack Time	B	RF	48	InfoTrek	ETA Cuisenaire
Snack Time	A	I	19	Vocabulary Readers	Houghton Mifflin Harcourt
Snack Time	A	I	19	Vocabulary Readers/CA	Houghton Mifflin Harcourt
Snack Time Around the World	M	I	250+	Meals Around the World	Picture Window Books
Snacks	D	RF	19	Joy Readers	Pearson Learning Group
Snacks for Healthy Teeth	H	I	136	Healthy Teeth	Capstone Press
Snaggle Doodles	M	RF	250+	Giff, Patricia Reilly	Bantam
Snail Girl	H	RF	250+	Momentum Literacy Program	Troll Associates
Snail Hits the Trail	K	F	1107	Appleton-Smith, Laura	Flyleaf Publishing
Snail Race, The	H	F	223	Springboard	Wright Group/McGraw Hill
Snail Saves the Day	G	F	76	Stadler, John	HarperCollins
Snail That Snored, The	I	F	250+	Phonics Readers Plus	Steck-Vaughn
Snail Trail to 100	J	RF	212	PM Math Readers	Rigby
Snail Trail, The	I	F	243	Sunshine	Wright Group/McGraw Hill
Snail, The	B	I	75	Rigby Flying Colors	Rigby
Snails	A	I	40	First Stories	Pacific Learning
Snails	E	I	67	Foundations	Wright Group/McGraw Hill
Snails	O	I	250+	Holmes, Kevin J.	Red Brick Learning
Snails and Slugs	E	I	54	Sun Sprouts	ETA Cuisenaire

* Collection of short stories
# Graphic text

TITLE	LEVEL	GENRE	WORD COUNT	AUTHOR / SERIES	PUBLISHER / DISTRIBUTOR
Snails in School	H	I	181	Discovery Links	Newbridge
Snake Alarm	M	RF	250+	Krailing, Tessa	Barron's Educational
Snake and the Birds	J	F	420	Sails	Rigby
Snake at the Lake	J	F	250+	The Wright Skills	Wright Group/McGraw Hill
Snake Gets Lost	H	F	259	Springboard	Wright Group/McGraw Hill
Snake Goes Away	C	F	55	Literacy by Design	Rigby
Snake Goes Away	C	F	55	Rigby Literacy	Rigby
Snake Hunts for Lunch	E	RF	115	Hoenecke, Karen	Kaeden Books
Snake Is Going Away!	C	F	57	Rigby Star	Rigby
Snake Safari	Q	I	250+	Explorer Books-Pathfinder	National Geographic
Snake Safari	P	I	250+	Explorer Books-Pioneer	National Geographic
Snake Slithers, A	H	I	82	Reading Unlimited	Pearson Learning Group
Snake That Couldn't Hiss, The	I	F	250+	Storyworlds	Heinemann Educational Books
Snake!	M	RF	641	Sunshine	Wright Group/McGraw Hill
Snake, The	O	I	250+	Crewe, Sabrina	Steck-Vaughn
Snake, The	A	F	30	Sails	Rigby
Snakebite	J	RF	271	Story Box	Wright Group/McGraw Hill
Snakes	E	I	37	All About Pets	Capstone Press
Snakes	Q	I	250+	Explorers	Wright Group/McGraw Hill
Snakes	O	I	250+	First Reports	Compass Point Books
Snakes	K	I	259	Foundations	Wright Group/McGraw Hill
Snakes	F	I	98	Life Cycles	Lerner Publications
Snakes	I	I	208	Momentum Literacy Program	Troll Associates
Snakes	H	I	145	Nonfiction	Literacy Footprints
Snakes	I	I	242	Sails	Rigby
Snakes	S	I	250+	Simon, Seymour	Scholastic
Snakes	J	I	448	Sunshine	Wright Group/McGraw Hill
Snakes	J	I	450	Time for Kids	Teacher Created Materials
Snakes	LB	I	25	Twig	Wright Group/McGraw Hill
Snakes	E	I	37	Visions	Wright Group/McGraw Hill
Snakes	L	I	252	Wonder World	Wright Group/McGraw Hill
Snakes and Lizards	I	I	205	Yellow Umbrella Books	Red Brick Learning
Snake's Big Mouth	H	F	199	Gear Up!	Wright Group/McGraw Hill
Snake's Dinner	E	F	156	Alphakids	Sundance
Snake's Sore Head	F	F	139	Storyteller-Moon Rising	Wright Group/McGraw Hill
Snakes That Rattle	I	I	374	Sails	Rigby
Snakes!	L	I	250+	Recht Penner, Lucille	Random House
Snakes!: Deadly Predators or Harmless Pets?	S	I	250+	High Five Reading	Red Brick Learning
Snakes: Cold-Blooded Crawlers	M	I	250+	The Wild World of Animals	Red Brick Learning
Snap Happy	E	RF	164	Rigby Rocket	Rigby
Snap Likes Ginger Cookies	E	F	63	Gosset, Rachel	Scholastic
Snap!	B	F	50	Leveled Literacy Intervention/ Green System	Heinemann
Snap!	B	F	31	Sunshine	Wright Group/McGraw Hill
Snap! Splash!	G	I	48	Pacific Literacy	Pacific Learning
Snap! Splat!	C	F	25	Sunshine	Wright Group/McGraw Hill
Snap, Crackle, and Flow	U	I	250+	Navigators Science Series	Benchmark Education Company
Snapshots	D	RF	20	Bebop Books	Lee & Low Books Inc.
Snarf Attack: Underfoodle and the Secret of Life: The Riot Brothers Tell All	O	RF	250+	Amato, Mary	Holiday House
Snarling Suspect, The	O	RF	250+	Klooz	Stone Arch Books
Sneakers	K	I	388	Sunshine	Wright Group/McGraw Hill

TITLE	LEVEL	GENRE	WORD COUNT	AUTHOR / SERIES	PUBLISHER / DISTRIBUTOR
Sneakers! Sneakers!	F	F	49	Little Celebrations	Pearson Learning Group
Sneaky Salamanders	L	I	370	Pull Ahead Books	Lerner Publications
Sneeze, The	C	F	85	Sails	Rigby
Sneezes	F	RF	36	Literacy 2000	Rigby
Sneezles, The	L	F	1262	Big Cat	Pacific Learning
Snickers	I	RF	250+	Momentum Literacy Program	Troll Associates
Snick-Snack Sniffle-Nose	H	F	187	Supersonics	Rigby
Sniffer's Golden Nose	L	F	250+	I Am Reading	Kingfisher
Sniffy	F	RF	290	Rigby Rocket	Rigby
Snip, Snap	I	F	250+	Sunshine	Wright Group/McGraw Hill
Snip-Snap, Clickety-Click	C	F	54	Little Celebrations	Pearson Learning Group
Snitch	T	RF	250+	Orca Soundings	Orca Book Publishers
Snorkeling	I	RF	233	Leveled Readers Language Support	Houghton Mifflin Harcourt
Snot Stew	P	F	250+	Wallace, Bill	Pocket Books
Snow	E	I	28	Book Bank	Wright Group/McGraw Hill
Snow	B	I	29	Discovery Links	Newbridge
Snow	B	I	33	Hoenecke, Karen	Kaeden Books
Snow	I	RF	237	Sails	Rigby
Snow	C	RF	47	Science	Outside the Box
Snow	D	I	21	Sunshine	Wright Group/McGraw Hill
Snow	A	I	11	Vocabulary Readers	Houghton Mifflin Harcourt
Snow	K	I	370	Yellow Umbrella Books	Red Brick Learning
Snow	H	RF	217	Young Writers' World	Nelson/Michaels Assoc.
Snow and Ice	G	I	340	Sails	Rigby
Snow Baby, The	F	RF	337	Easy Stories	Norwood House Press
Snow Baby, The: The Arctic Childhood of Admiral Robert E. Peary's Daring Daughter	X	B	250+	Kirkpatrick, Katherine	Holiday House
Snow Bright and the Seven Sumos	M	F	250+	SupaDoopers	Sundance
Snow Bright and the Tooth Magician	M	F	250+	SupaDoopers	Sundance
Snow Cover	C	RF	29	Little Celebrations	Pearson Learning Group
Snow Daughter, The	L	TL	505	Sunshine	Wright Group/McGraw Hill
Snow Day	I	RF	250+	Bliss, Corinne Demas	Random House
Snow Goes to Town	L	F	250+	Literacy 2000	Rigby
Snow in the Kitchen	L	RF	250+	Cambridge Reading	Pearson Learning Group
Snow Is Cold	C	I	47	Little Readers	Houghton Mifflin Harcourt
Snow Joe	D	RF	59	Rookie Readers	Children's Press
Snow on the Hill	H	RF	213	PM Extensions-Green	Rigby
Snow Queen, The	U	TL	250+	Lewis, Naomi	Candlewick Press
Snow Rescue	K	RF	250+	Reading Safari	Mondo
Snow Treasure	R	HF	250+	McSwigan, Marie	Scholastic
Snow Walk	LB	RF	32	Reading Corners	Pearson Learning Group
Snow Walker, The	L	HF	250+	Wetterer, Margaret K. & Charles M.	Carolrhoda Books
Snow White and Rose Red	K	TL	250+	Hunia, Fran	Ladybird Books
Snow White and the Seven Dwarfs	I	TL	250+	Enrichment	Wright Group/McGraw Hill
Snow White and the Seven Dwarfs	K	TL	250+	PM Tales and Plays-Gold	Rigby
Snow, The	G	RF	112	Burningham, John	Crowell
Snow, The	B	F	36	Sails	Rigby
Snow, The	D	RF	36	Sunshine	Wright Group/McGraw Hill
Snowball Attack	N	RF	250+	Girlz Rock!	Mondo
Snowball Fight	WB	RF	N/A	Rigby Literacy	Rigby
Snowball Fight!	D	RF	35	Wonder World	Wright Group/McGraw Hill
Snowball War, The	K	RF	250+	Chardiet, Bernice	Scholastic

* Collection of short stories
# Graphic text

S

TITLE	LEVEL	GENRE	WORD COUNT	AUTHOR / SERIES	PUBLISHER / DISTRIBUTOR
Snowball, The	G	F	92	Armstrong, Jennifer	Random House
Snowball, the White Mouse	G	RF	223	PM Plus Story Books	Rigby
Snowball: The Puppy Place	N	RF	250+	Miles, Ellen	Scholastic
Snowboard Maverick	S	RF	250+	Christopher, Matt	Norwood House Press
Snowboard Showdown	R	RF	250+	Christopher, Matt	Norwood House Press
Snowboarding	A	I	37	Nonfiction	Literacy Footprints
Snowboarding	M	I	250+	To the Extreme	Capstone Press
Snowboarding	Q	I	250+	X-Sports	Capstone Press
Snowboarding Diary	O	I	250+	PM Nonfiction-Emerald	Rigby
Snowboarding for Fun!	S	I	250+	Sports for Fun	Compass Point Books
Snowbound!	T	RF	250+	Power Up!	Steck-Vaughn
Snowdrops for Cousin Ruth	S	RF	250+	Katz, Susan	Simon & Schuster
Snowflakes	H	I	110	All About Winter	Capstone Press
Snowflakes	F	RF	80	Seedlings	Continental Press
Snowflakes	D	RF	49	Urmston, Kathleen; Evans, Karen	Kaeden Books
Snowman	LB	RF	14	Smart Starts	Rigby
Snowman	A	RF	19	Story Box	Wright Group/McGraw Hill
Snowman	C	RF	21	Sunshine	Wright Group/McGraw Hill
Snowman Day	B	RF	72	First Stories	Pacific Learning
Snowman Mystery, The	I	RF	200	InfoTrek	ETA Cuisenaire
Snowman, A	C	I	59	Foundations	Wright Group/McGraw Hill
Snowman, The	WB	F	N/A	Briggs, Raymond	Random House
Snowman, The	B	RF	76	Leveled Readers Emergent	Houghton Mifflin Harcourt
Snowman, The	E	RF	76	Oxford Reading Tree	Oxford University Press
Snowman, The	B	F	30	Sails	Rigby
Snowman, The	B	I	32	Story Steps	Rigby
Snowman, The	C	RF	33	Gear Up!	Wright Group/McGraw Hill
Snowmobile Racing	S	I	250+	Motor Sports	Red Brick Learning
Snowmobiles	M	I	250+	Horsepower	Capstone Press
Snowmobiles	Q	I	250+	Wild Rides!	Red Brick Learning
Snowmobiling	S	I	250+	The Great Outdoors	Red Brick Learning
Snowplows	I	I	127	Mighty Machines	Capstone Press
Snowplows	L	I	450	Pull Ahead Books	Lerner Publications
Snowshoe Thompson	K	HF	250+	Levinson, N. Smiler	HarperTrophy
Snowstorm, The	H	F	231	Arctic Stories	Pioneer Valley
Snowy	B	I	24	Weather	Lerner Publications
Snowy Day, A	G	I	232	Leveled Readers	Houghton Mifflin Harcourt
Snowy Day, A	G	I	232	Leveled Readers/CA	Houghton Mifflin Harcourt
Snowy Day, A	G	I	232	Leveled Readers/TX	Houghton Mifflin Harcourt
Snowy Day, A	E	I	54	Pebble Books	Capstone Press
Snowy Day, A	E	I	112	Weather	Lerner Publishing
Snowy Day, The	J	RF	319	Keats, Ezra Jack	Scholastic
Snowy Days	I	I	163	Literacy by Design	Rigby
Snowy Gets a Wash	E	RF	181	PM Extensions-Yellow	Rigby
Snowy Owls	H	I	124	Polar Animals	Capstone Press
Snowy the Polar Teddy	B	F	28	Reading Safari	Mondo
Snug as a Bug	C	F	76	Literacy by Design	Rigby
Snuggle Up	F	RF	125	Harrison, P.; Worthington, Denise	Continental Press
So Big!	B	F	63	Leveled Literacy Intervention/ Orange System	Heinemann
So Do I	D	RF	49	Teacher's Choice Series	Pearson Learning Group
So Far From the Bamboo Grove	V	HF	250+	Watkins, Yoko Kawashima	William Morrow

S

* Collection of short stories
# Graphic text

TITLE	LEVEL	GENRE	WORD COUNT	AUTHOR / SERIES	PUBLISHER / DISTRIBUTOR
So Long Stinky Queen	M	RF	250+	First Flight	Fitzhenry & Whiteside
So Many Birthdays	I	RF	250+	Momentum Literacy Program	Troll Associates
So Many Circles	C	I	36	Yellow Umbrella Books	Red Brick Learning
So Many Houses	D	I	79	Rookie Readers	Children's Press
So Many Legs	E	F	110	In Step Readers	Rigby
So Many Snakes	I	I	152	Rosen Real Readers	Rosen Publishing Group
So Many Sounds	F	I	153	Vocabulary Readers	Houghton Mifflin Harcourt
So Many Sounds	F	I	153	Vocabulary Readers/CA	Houghton Mifflin Harcourt
So Many Sounds	F	I	153	Vocabulary Readers/TX	Houghton Mifflin Harcourt
So Many Strawberries	E	RF	75	Books for Young Learners	Richard C. Owen
So Many Things to Do	A	RF	21	Home Connection Collection	Rigby
So Much	I	RF	250+	Cooke, Trish	Candlewick Press
So Much to Do	H	RF	250+	On Our Way to English	Rigby
So Much to Tell You	Z+	RF	250+	Marsden, John	Lothian Books
So Sleepy	D	RF	33	Books for Young Learners	Richard C. Owen
So That's What It Is!	F	I	133	Rigby Literacy	Rigby
So What?	I	RF	250+	Cohen, Miriam	Bantam
So You Want to Be a Teacher?	L	I	715	Springboard	Wright Group/McGraw Hill
So You Want to Be a Writer?	O	I	250+	Springboard	Wright Group/ McGraw-Hill
So You Want to Be an Inventor?	P	I	250+	St. George, Judith; Small, David	Philomel/Penguin
So You Want to Move a Building?	M	I	380	Pacific Literacy	Pacific Learning
So You Want to Work in Publishing?	W	I	2842	Vocabulary Readers	Houghton Mifflin Harcourt
So You Want to Work in Publishing?	W	I	2842	Vocabulary Readers/CA	Houghton Mifflin Harcourt
So, So Sam	G	RF	107	TOTTS	Tott Publications
Soap Soup and Other Verses	K	TL	250+	Kuskin, Karla	HarperTrophy
Soap Story, A	H	RF	95	City Stories	Rigby
Soaring Bald Eagles	K	I	377	Pull Ahead Books	Lerner Publications
Soaring without an Engine	Q	I	1154	Take Two Books	Wright Group/ McGraw Hill
Soccer	S	I	250+	Boldprint	Steck-Vaughn
Soccer	M	I	250+	Little Celebrations	Pearson Learning Group
Soccer	K	I	250+	On Deck	Rigby
Soccer	E	I	78	Sun Sprouts	ETA Cuisenaire
Soccer	K	I	270	Take Two Books	Wright Group/McGraw Hill
Soccer	G	I	189	Vocabulary Readers	Houghton Mifflin Harcourt
Soccer	G	I	189	Vocabulary Readers/CA	Houghton Mifflin Harcourt
Soccer	G	I	189	Vocabulary Readers/TX	Houghton Mifflin Harcourt
Soccer at the Park	E	RF	131	PM Extensions-Yellow	Rigby
Soccer Cousins	K	RF	250+	Marzollo, Jean	Scholastic
Soccer for Fun	S	I	250+	Sports for Fun	Compass Point Books
Soccer Fun!	N	RF	661	Leveled Readers	Houghton Mifflin Harcourt
Soccer Game	B	F	21	Reading Street	Pearson
Soccer Game!	F	RF	63	Maccarone, Grace	Scholastic
Soccer Game, The	F	RF	278	Leveled Literacy Intervention/ Green System	Heinemann
Soccer Halfback	S	RF	250+	Christopher, Matt	Norwood House Press
Soccer Hero	Q	RF	250+	Christopher, Matt	Little, Brown & Co.
Soccer Mania!	M	RF	250+	Tamar, Erika	Random House
Soccer Sam	C	RF	70	Handprints B	Educators Publishing Service
Soccer Sam	M	RF	250+	Marzollo, Jean	Random House
Soccer Scoop	S	RF	250+	Christopher, Matt	Norwood House Press
Soccer Showdown	Q	F	1720	Zucker, Jonny	Stone Arch Books
Soccer Sisters	R	RF	1541	Leveled Readers	Houghton Mifflin Harcourt
Soccer Sisters	R	RF	1541	Leveled Readers/CA	Houghton Mifflin Harcourt

S

* Collection of short stories
\# Graphic text

TITLE	LEVEL	GENRE	WORD COUNT	AUTHOR / SERIES	PUBLISHER / DISTRIBUTOR
Soccer Sisters	R	RF	1541	Leveled Readers/TX	Houghton Mifflin Harcourt
Soccer Song	F	RF	157	Green Light Readers	Harcourt
Soccer Star, The	F	RF	190	Windows on Literacy	National Geographic
Soccer Stars, Best Friend Face-off	R	RF	250+	Costello, Emily	Dell
Soccer: Get in the Game!	S	I	250+	Explore More	Wright Group/McGraw Hill
*Sock Gobbler and Other Stories, The	M	F	250+	Learning Media	Pacific Learning
Socks	C	RF	40	Bonnell, Kris	Reading Reading Books
Socks	O	RF	250+	Cleary, Beverly	Avon
Socks	B	RF	21	Ready Readers	Pearson Learning Group
Socks	D	RF	250+	Rigby Literacy	Rigby
Socks	LB	RF	21	Smart Starts	Rigby
Socks Off	H	RF	177	Alphakids	Sundance
Socrates: Greek Philosopher	X	B	250+	Primary Source Readers	Teacher Created Materials
Sod Houses on the Great Plains	N	I	250+	Rounds, Glen	Holiday House
Soda Pop	A	RF	26	Bonnell, Kris	Reading Reading Books
Soddies	M	I	250+	Twig	Wright Group/McGraw Hill
Soft and Hard	B	I	40	Explorations	Eleanor Curtain Publishing
Soft and Hard	B	I	40	Explorations	Okapi Educational Materials
Soft and Hard: An Animal Opposites Book	J	I	250+	Animal Opposites	Capstone Press
Soil	R	I	2027	Early Bird Earth Systems	Lerner Publications
Soil	Q	I	250+	Exploring the Earth	Capstone Press
Soil	N	I	250+	Simply Science	Compass Point Books
Soil	F	I	93	What Earth Is Made Of	Lerner Publications
Soil	K	I	381	Windows on Literacy	National Geographic
Soil - It Takes All Kinds	O	I	250+	InfoTrek	ETA Cuisenaire
Soil Basics	J	I	140	Nature Basics	Capstone Press
Soil on the Move	O	I	250+	InfoTrek	ETA Cuisenaire
Soil: A Resource Our World Depends On	V	I	250+	Managing Our Resources	Heinemann
Sojourner Truth	T	B	250+	Amazing Americans	Wright Group/McGraw Hill
Sojourner Truth	Q	B	250+	Early Biographies	Compass Point Books
Sojourner Truth	M	B	250+	Famous Americans	Red Brick Learning
Sojourner Truth	S	B	4018	History Maker Bios	Lerner Publications
Sojourner Truth	U	B	250+	Let Freedom Ring	Red Brick Learning
Sojourner Truth	P	B	1551	On My Own Biography	Lerner Publications
Sojourner Truth	P	B	250+	Photo-Illustrated Biographies	Red Brick Learning
Sojourner Truth, Speaker for Equal Rights	O	B	374	Independent Readers Social Studies	Houghton Mifflin Harcourt
Sojourner Truth: Ain't I a Woman?	V	B	250+	McKissack, Fredrick & Patricia	Scholastic
Sojourner Truth: Early Abolitionist	P	B	250+	On Deck	Rigby
Sojourner Truth: Freedom Fighter	P	B	250+	Great African Americans	Capstone Press
Solar Energy	V	I	2068	Leveled Readers Science	Houghton Mifflin Harcourt
Solar Power	X	I	250+	Energy at Work	Capstone Press
Solar Storms	R	I	250+	Rosen Real Readers	Rosen Publishing Group
Solar System and Beyond, The	V	I	2234	Reading Street	Pearson
Solar System Sights	R	I	250+	In Step Readers	Rigby
Solar System Sights	R	I	250+	Literacy by Design	Rigby
Solar System, The	Q	I	250+	A True Book	Children's Press
Solar System, The	N	I	714	Our Universe	Lerner Publications
Solar System, The	S	I	2061	Science Support Readers	Houghton Mifflin Harcourt
Solar System, The	N	I	250+	Simply Science	Compass Point Books
Solar System, The	Q	I	250+	The Galaxy	Capstone Press
Solar System, The	U	I	250+	The Heinle Reading Library	Thomson Learning
Solar System, The	O	I	607	Time for Kids	Teacher Created Materials
Solar-Powered Sam	J	F	148	Books for Young Learners	Richard C. Owen

S

* Collection of short stories
# Graphic text

TITLE	LEVEL	GENRE	WORD COUNT	AUTHOR / SERIES	PUBLISHER / DISTRIBUTOR
Soldier Boy	T	HF	250+	Burks, Brian	Harcourt Trade
Soldier's Heart	V	HF	250+	Paulsen, Gary	Random House
Solid or Not?	G	I	113	Early Connections	Benchmark Education
Solid Shapes	K	I	372	Yellow Umbrella Books	Red Brick Learning
Solid, Liquid, Gas: What Is Matter?	R	I	250+	Rosen Real Readers	Rosen Publishing Group
Solids, Liquids and Gases	K	I	361	Science Support Readers	Houghton Mifflin Harcourt
Solids, Liquids, and Gases	J	I	119	Nature Basics	Capstone Press
Solids, Liquids, Gases	N	I	250+	Simply Science	Compass Point Books
Solitary Blue, A	W	RF	250+	Voigt, Cynthia	Scholastic
Solo Flyer	L	RF	605	PM Collection	Rigby
Solo Girl	M	RF	250+	Pinkey, Andrea Davis	Hyperion
Solve It!	K	RF	250+	Goldish, Meish	Scholastic
Solve This!	M	F	250+	Storyteller- Lightning Bolts	Wright Group/ McGraw Hill
Solving Problems	G	RF	246	InfoTrek	ETA Cuisenaire
Somalia	O	I	250+	Countries of the World	Red Brick Learning
Some Birds Can Fly	B	I	48	Sails	Rigby
Some Birds Cannot Fly	B	I	48	Sails	Rigby
Some Days Are Like That	D	RF	69	Teacher's Choice Series	Pearson Learning Group
Some Dog!	O	RF	250+	PM Collection	Rigby
Some Dogs Don't	B	F	29	Tiger Cub	Peguis
Some Friend	R	RF	250+	Warner, Sally	Alfred A. Knopf
Some Kids Are Blind	J	I	134	Understanding Differences	Red Brick Learning
Some Kids Are Blind	J	I	122	Understanding Differences	Capstone Press
Some Kids Are Deaf	J	I	158	Understanding Differences	Red Brick Learning
Some Kids Are Deaf	J	I	152	Understanding Differences	Capstone Press
Some Kids Have Autism	M	I	154	Understanding Differences	Capstone Press
Some Kids Use Wheelchairs	I	I	123	Understanding Differences	Red Brick Learning
Some Kids Use Wheelchairs	I	I	121	Understanding Differences	Capstone Press
Some Kids Wear Leg Braces	J	I	144	Understanding Differences	Red Brick Learning
Some Kids Wear Leg Braces	J	I	142	Understanding Differences	Capstone Press
Some Machines Are Enormous	J	I	250+	Bookshop	Mondo
*Some of the Kinder Planets	U	SF	250+	Wynne-Jones, Tim	Penguin Group
Some People	D	I	50	Reading Corners	Pearson Learning Group
Some Snakes	J	I	118	Voyages	SRA/McGraw Hill
Some Things Float	C	I	41	Windows on Literacy	National Geographic
Some Things Go Together	C	RF	133	Twig	Wright Group/McGraw Hill
Some Things Keep Changing	M	I	250+	Explorations	Eleanor Curtain Publishing
Some Things Keep Changing	M	I	250+	Explorations	Okapi Educational Materials
Some Things Push and Some Things Pull	D	I	42	Dominie Factivity Series	Pearson Learning Group
Somebody Moved in Next Door	Q	RF	250+	PM Chapter Books	Rigby
Someday a Tree	P	RF	250+	Bunting, Eve	Clarion
Someday Cyril	N	RF	250+	Gershator, Phillis	Mondo
*Somehow Tenderness Survives: Stories of Southern Africa	Z	HF	250+	Rochman, Hazel	HarperTrophy
Someone Is Following Pip Ramsey	N	RF	250+	Roy, Ron	Random House
Someone to Count On	T	RF	250+	Hermes, Patricia	Language for Learning Assoc.
Something Beautiful	L	RF	250+	Wyeth, Sharon Dennis	Random House
Something Else	L	F	250+	Cave, Kathryn	Mondo
Something Everyone Needs	J	RF	250+	Ready Readers	Pearson Learning Group
Something Evil	T	SF	250+	Orme, David	Stone Arch Books
Something Fishy	B	RF	36	Rigby Rocket	Rigby
Something for Everyone	R	RF	1371	Leveled Readers	Houghton Mifflin Harcourt
Something Girl	Z	RF	250+	Orca Soundings	Orca Book Publishers

S

* Collection of short stories
# Graphic text

TITLE	LEVEL	GENRE	WORD COUNT	AUTHOR / SERIES	PUBLISHER / DISTRIBUTOR
*Something Is There and Other Stories	J	F	250+	Story Steps	Rigby
Something is Waiting	J	I	94	Literacy Tree	Rigby
Something Nasty	I	F	250+	Popcorn	Sundance
Something New	D	I	72	Little Celebrations	Pearson Learning Group
Something Noise, The	J	RF	276	Windmill Books	Rigby
Something Queer at the Ball Park	N	RF	250+	Levy, Elizabeth	Bantam
Something Queer at the Haunted School	N	RF	250+	Levy, Elizabeth	Bantam
Something Queer at the Lemonade Stand	N	RF	250+	Levy, Elizabeth	Bantam
Something Queer at the Library	N	RF	250+	Levy, Elizabeth	Bantam
Something Queer at the Scary Movie	N	RF	250+	Levy, Elizabeth	Hyperion
Something Queer in Outer Space	N	RF	250+	Levy, Elizabeth	Hyperion
Something Queer in the Cafeteria	N	RF	250+	Levy, Elizabeth	Hyperion
Something Queer in the Wild West	N	RF	250+	Levy, Elizabeth	Hyperion
Something Queer Is Going On	N	RF	250+	Levy, Elizabeth	Bantam
Something Queer on Vacation	N	RF	250+	Levy, Elizabeth	Bantam
Something Rotten at Village Market	U	RF	250+	Power Up!	Steck-Vaughn
Something Slimy on Primrose Drive	R	F	9739	Wallace, Karen	Stone Arch Books
Something Soft for Danny Bear	M	F	493	Literacy 2000	Rigby
Something Special	J	I	207	Vocabulary Readers	Houghton Mifflin Harcourt
Something Special	J	I	207	Vocabulary Readers/CA	Houghton Mifflin Harcourt
Something Special for Miss Margery	J	F	250+	Voyages	SRA/McGraw Hill
Something to Do	P	RF	1455	Reading Street	Pearson
Something to Munch	E	RF	58	Ready Readers	Pearson Learning Group
Something to Share	D	RF	98	Carousel Readers	Pearson Learning Group
Something Upstairs	T	RF	250+	Avi	Language for Learning Assoc.
Something Very Sorry	R	RF	250+	Bohlmeijer, Arno	Putnam/Penguin
Something's Different	N	I	294	Shelley Rotner's Early Childhood	Millbrook Press
Sometimes	E	F	70	Green Light Readers	Harcourt
Sometimes	B	RF	18	Literacy 2000	Rigby
Sometimes	A	I	28	On Our Way to English	Rigby
Sometimes	C	RF	25	Wonder World	Wright Group/McGraw Hill
Sometimes . . .	F	RF	31	City Stories	Rigby
Sometimes . . .	B	RF	25	Home Connection Collection	Rigby
Sometimes Bad Things Happen	J	I	137	Shelley Rotner's Early Childhood	Millbrook Press
Sometimes I Feel Like a Storm Cloud	M	RF	250+	Bookshop	Mondo
Sometimes I Share	H	RF	108	Ziefert, Harriet	HarperCollins
Sometimes I'm Silly	C	RF	24	Visions	Wright Group/McGraw Hill
Sometimes Things Change	G	I	71	Rookie Readers	Children's Press
Somewhere	J	TL	93	Bookshop	Mondo
Somewhere in the Darkness	X	RF	250	Myers, Walter Dean	Scholastic
Somewhere in the Universe	I	I	167	Literacy Tree	Rigby
Son of Liberty, A Novel of the American Revolution	V	HF	250+	Massie, Elizabeth	Tom Doherty
Son of the Mob	Z+	RF	250+	Korman, Gordon	Hyperion
Son of the Mob	Z+	RF	250+	Schraff, Anne	Townsend Press
Song for Summer, A	Z+	HF	250+	Korman, Gordon	Hyperion
Song Heard 'Round the World, A	T	I	1331	Leveled Readers	Houghton Mifflin Harcourt
Song Heard 'Round the World, A	T	I	1331	Leveled Readers/CA	Houghton Mifflin Harcourt
Song Heard 'Round the World, A	T	I	1331	Leveled Readers/TX	Houghton Mifflin Harcourt
Song Lee and the Hamster Hunt	L	RF	250+	Kline, Suzy	Penguin Group
Song Lee and the Leech Man	L	RF	250+	Kline, Suzy	Penguin Group
Song Lee in Room 2B	L	RF	250+	Kline, Suzy	Penguin Group
Song Makers Go to Salem, The	N	RF	2177	Reading Street	Pearson

S

* Collection of short stories
# Graphic text

TITLE	LEVEL	GENRE	WORD COUNT	AUTHOR / SERIES	PUBLISHER / DISTRIBUTOR
Song of the Giraffe	O	RF	250+	Jacobs, Shannon K.	Little, Brown & Co.
Song of the Mantis, The	S	I	250+	Literacy 2000	Rigby
Song of the Stranger	T	RF	250+	Tung, Angela	Lowell House
Song of the Trees	R	HF	250+	Taylor, Mildred	Bantam
Song Quest	W	F	250+	Roberts, Katherine	Scholastic
Songbird, The	B	F	39	Ray's Readers	Outside the Box
Songs for the People	P	B	871	Leveled Readers	Houghton Mifflin Harcourt
Songs for the People	P	B	871	Leveled Readers/CA	Houghton Mifflin Harcourt
Songs for the People	P	B	871	Leveled Readers/TX	Houghton Mifflin Harcourt
Sonny Gets Lost	G	RF	197	Springboard	Wright Group/McGraw Hill
Sons of Liberty	Y	RF	250+	Griffin, Adele	Hyperion
Sonya's Guide Dog	H	I	134	Gear Up!	Wright Group/McGraw Hill
Sophie Hits Six	M	F	250+	King-Smith, Dick	Candlewick Press
Sophie in the Saddle	M	F	250+	King-Smith, Dick	Candlewick Press
Sophie Is Seven	M	F	250+	King-Smith, Dick	Candlewick Press
Sophie's Box	G	F	174	Cambridge Reading	Pearson Learning Group
Sophie's Chicken	H	RF	107	Tadpoles	Rigby
Sophie's Lucky	M	F	250+	King-Smith, Dick	Candlewick Press
Sophie's Singing Mother	J	RF	313	Jellybeans	Rigby
Sophie's Snail	M	F	250+	King-Smith, Dick	Candlewick Press
Sophie's Tom	M	F	250+	King-Smith, Dick	Candlewick Press
Sophie's Wheels	H	RF	137	Pearson, Debora	Annick Press
Sor Juana Inez de la Cruz	O	B	693	Leveled Readers Social Studies	Houghton Mifflin Harcourt
Sorting Color	J	I	327	Sorting	Capstone Press
Sorting it Out	R	I	250+	Ribgy Literacy	Rigby
Sorting Leaves	D	I	66	PM Math Readers	Rigby
Sorting Money	K	I	348	Sorting	Capstone Press
Sorting My Money	J	I	209	Early Connections	Benchmark Education
Sorting Size	K	I	337	Sorting	Capstone Press
Sorting Toys	J	I	357	Sorting	Capstone Press
Sort-of-Difficult Origami	R	I	250+	Origami	Capstone Press
SOS on the Inca Trail	P	RF	250+	WorldScapes	ETA Cuisenaire
SOS Titanic	V	HF	250+	Bunting, Eve	Harcourt Trade
SOS!: Rescue Heroes	R	I	250+	Boldprint	Steck-Vaughn
Sound	Q	I	2236	Early Bird Energy	Lerner Publishing
Sound	P	I	250+	Our Physical World	Capstone Press
Sound	N	I	250+	Windows on Literacy	National Geographic
Sound of Colors, The: A Journey of the Imagination	R	F	250+	Liao, Jimmy	Little, Brown & Co.
Sound, Heat & Light: Energy at Work	L	I	250+	Berger, Melvin	Scholastic
Sound: Loud, Soft, High, and Low	M	I	250+	Amazing Science	Picture Window Books
Sounder	T	RF	250+	Armstrong, William	Scholastic
Sounds	F	I	109	Big Cat	Pacific Learning
Sounds	J	I	200	Early Connections	Benchmark Education
Sounds	N	I	250+	Lighthouse	Rigby
Sounds All Around	G	I	153	Discovery Links	Newbridge
Sounds All Around	A	I	28	Independent Readers Science	Houghton Mifflin Harcourt
Sounds All Around	L	I	411	Springboard	Wright Group/ McGraw Hill
Sounds All Around Us	K	I	168	Phonics Readers	Compass Point Books
Sounds Around Us, The	C	I	22	Rosen Real Readers	Rosen Publishing Group
Sounds in the Night	F	RF	126	Visions	Wright Group/McGraw Hill
Sounds like Music	R	I	250+	Orbit Chapter Books	Pacific Learning
Sounds of Music, The	G	I	140	Leveled Readers Science	Houghton Mifflin Harcourt

S

* Collection of short stories
# Graphic text

TITLE	LEVEL	GENRE	WORD COUNT	AUTHOR / SERIES	PUBLISHER / DISTRIBUTOR
Soup	A	RF	24	Handprints A	Educators Publishing Service
Soup	A	I	17	Little Celebrations	Pearson Learning Group
Soup	Q	HF	250+	Peck, Robert Newton	Bantam
Soup	I	F	250+	Sunshine	Wright Group/McGraw Hill
Soup Can Telephone	I	I	190	Wonder World	Wright Group/McGraw Hill
Soup Fit for a King	J	RF	250+	Sunshine	Wright Group/McGraw Hill
Soup for Snail	E	F	61	Leveled Readers Language Support	Houghton Mifflin Harcourt
South Africa	O	I	250+	Countries of the World	Red Brick Learning
South Africa	P	I	2059	Country Explorers	Lerner Publications
South Africa	Q	I	250+	First Reports: Countries	Compass Point Books
South Africa: A Question and Answer Book	P	I	250+	Question and Answer Countries	Capstone Press
South America	N	I	250+	Continents	Capstone Press
South America	N	I	446	Pull Ahead Books	Lerner Publications
South Carolina	T	I	250+	Hello U.S.A.	Lerner Publications
South Carolina	T	I	250+	Theme Sets	National Geographic
South Carolina	R	I	250+	This Land Is Your Land	Compass Point Books
South Carolina Colony, The	R	I	250+	The American Colonies	Capstone Press
South Dakota	T	I	250+	Hello U.S.A.	Lerner Publications
South Dakota	R	I	250+	This Land Is Your Land	Compass Point Books
South Korea	O	I	250+	Countries of the World	Red Brick Learning
South Pole Bound	O	RF	788	Leveled Readers	Houghton Mifflin Harcourt
Southeast Indians, The: Daily Life in the 1500s	O	I	250+	Native American Life	Capstone Press
Southern Sounds	S	I	2194	Independent Readers Social Studies	Houghton Mifflin Harcourt
Southwest Indians, The: Daily Life in the 1500s	O	I	250+	Native American Life	Capstone Press
Southwest's History, The	Y	I	2847	Vocabulary Readers/CA	Houghton Mifflin Harcourt
Southwest's History, The	Y	I	2847	Vocabulary Readers	Houghton Mifflin Harcourt
Souvenirs	K	RF	179	Literacy 2000	Rigby
Space	H	I	100	Sunshine	Wright Group/McGraw Hill
Space	R	I	250+	Worldwise	Franklin Watts
Space Aliens in Our School	D	F	45	Joy Readers	Pearson Learning Group
Space Animals	P	I	474	Independent Readers Science	Houghton Mifflin Harcourt
Space Ant	F	F	194	Rigby Star	Rigby
Space Ant Goes Home	F	F	194	Rigby Literacy	Rigby
Space Ark, The	B	SF	20	Sunshine	Wright Group/McGraw Hill
Space Boots	L	SF	250+	Rigby Rocket	Rigby
Space Cat	K	F	250+	Sails	Rigby
Space Commander: Eileen Collins	U	B	250+	Leveled Readers Language Support	Houghton Mifflin Harcourt
Space Disasters	W	I	7416	Disasters Up Close	Lerner Publications
Space Dog and Roy	L	F	250+	Standiford, Natalie	Random House
Space Dog and the Pet Show	L	F	250+	Standiford, Natalie	Random House
Space Dog in Trouble	L	F	250+	Standiford, Natalie	Random House
Space Dog the Hero	L	F	250+	Standiford, Natalie	Random House
Space Exploration	S	I	250+	Navigators Science Series	Benchmark Education
Space Exploration	S	I	250+	Our Solar System	Compass Point Books
Space Exploration	R	I	1133	Time for Kids	Teacher Created Materials
Space Explorers	O	I	724	Gear Up!	Wright Group/ McGraw Hill
Space Fairy	H	F	182	Galaxy Girl	Literacy Footprints
Space Fort, The	D	F	108	Galaxy Girl	Literacy Footprints
Space Games	O	SF	1939	Orme, David	Stone Arch Books
Space Is an Amazing Place	G	RF	182	Windows on Literacy	National Geographic

S

* Collection of short stories
# Graphic text

TITLE	LEVEL	GENRE	WORD COUNT	AUTHOR / SERIES	PUBLISHER / DISTRIBUTOR
Space Journey	A	F	19	Sunshine	Wright Group/McGraw Hill
Space Junk	Q	RF	250+	Sails	Rigby
Space Junk	M	I	250+	The Solar System	Capstone Press
Space Junk	O	RF	250+	Wildcats	Wright Group/McGraw Hill
Space Mail	R	RF	250+	On Our Way to English	Rigby
Space Math	R	I	250+	Rosen Real Readers	Rosen Publishing Group
Space Missions	N	I	250+	Explore Space!	Red Brick Learning
Space Monster Saves the Day	J	F	871	Spaceboy	Literacy Footprints
Space Monster's Birthday Party	H	F	257	Galaxy Girl	Literacy Footprints
Space Odyssey	R	SF	250+	Take Two Books	Wright Group/McGraw Hill
Space Pirates	O	SF	1967	Orme, David	Stone Arch Books
Space Play	V	F	250+	Power Up!	Steck-Vaughn
Space Program, The	V	F	250+	Bookshop	Mondo
Space Quest	O	I	250+	Discovery World	Rigby
Space Race	F	RF	196	Rigby Rocket	Rigby
Space Race	J	F	213	Sunshine	Wright Group/McGraw Hill
Space Robots	N	I	250+	Explore Space!	Red Brick Learning
Space Rock	L	F	250+	Buller, Jon	Random House
Space Rocks: A Look at Asteroids and Comets	M	I	250+	Rosen Real Readers	Rosen Publishing Group
Space Sailors	I	I	181	On Our Way to English	Rigby
Space Shuttle, The	G	I	104	Nonfiction	Literacy Footprints
Space Shuttle, The	D	I	45	Sunshine	Wright Group/McGraw Hill
Space Shuttle, The	R	I	1308	Vocabulary Readers	Houghton Mifflin Harcourt
Space Shuttle, The	R	I	1308	Vocabulary Readers/CA	Houghton Mifflin Harcourt
Space Shuttle, The	R	I	1308	Vocabulary Readers/TX	Houghton Mifflin Harcourt
Space Shuttles	N	I	250+	Explore Space!	Red Brick Learning
Space Shuttles	M	I	250+	The Solar System	Capstone Press
Space Station	Q	I	250+	Orbit Double Takes	Pacific Learning
Space Station Orion	L	F	250+	Rigby Literacy	Rigby
*Space Station Plot and Other Cases, The	O	RF	250+	Simon, Seymour	Avon
Space Station: Accident on Mir	T	I	250+	DK Readers	DK Publishing
Space Stations	Q	I	250+	A True Book	Children's Press
Space Stations	N	I	250+	Explore Space!	Red Brick Learning
Space Stations	O	I	250+	Take Two Books	Wright Group/McGraw Hill
Space Suits	N	I	250+	Explore Space!	Red Brick Learning
Space Tourism	M	I	250+	The Solar System	Capstone Press
Space Trace, The	T	F	250+	Reading Safari	Mondo
Space Travel	U	I	250+	The Heinle Reading Library	Thomson Learning
Space Walk	J	I	281	Reading Street	Pearson
Space Walks	N	I	250+	Explore Space!	Red Brick Learning
Space Wardrobe	W	I	1501	Independent Readers Science	Houghton Mifflin Harcourt
Space Wreck	O	SF	250+	Orme, David	Stone Arch Books
Space Zoo, The	J	F	612	Spaceboy	Literacy Footprints
Space, Stars, and Planets	J	I	332	Sails	Rigby
Spaceboy Finds a Friend	E	F	94	Spaceboy	Literacy Footprints
Spaceboy Plays Hide and Seek	D	F	80	Spaceboy	Literacy Footprints
Spacejacked!	Q	F	250+	Story Surfers	ETA Cuisenaire
Spaceship	B	I	27	Hoenecke, Karen	Kaeden Books
Spaceship Earth	T	I	250+	Science Readers	Teacher Created Materials
Spaceship One: Making Dreams Come True	T	I	250+	High Five Reading	Red Brick Learning
Spaghetti Party, The	K	RF	250+	Bank Street	Bantam
Spaghetti! Spaghetti!	G	RF	85	Book Bank	Wright Group/McGraw Hill
Spain: A Question and Answer Book	P	I	250+	Question and Answer Countries	Capstone Press
Spanish Colonies in the Americas	S	I	250+	On Deck	Rigby

* Collection of short stories
\# Graphic text

S

TITLE	LEVEL	GENRE	WORD COUNT	AUTHOR / SERIES	PUBLISHER / DISTRIBUTOR
Spanish Conquests in the Americas	X	I	2534	Reading Street	Pearson
Spanish Mustang, The	R	I	250+	Horses	Capstone Press
Spanish Omelette	L	RF	250+	PM Story Books-Silver	Rigby
Spanish-American War, The	V	I	250+	America Goes to War	Red Brick Learning
Spanish-American War, The	W	I	250+	Cornerstones of Freedom	Children's Press
Sparky's Bone	F	F	273	Ready Readers	Pearson Learning Group
Sparrow's Gift, The	L	TL	250+	On Our Way to English	Rigby
Sparrows, The	F	I	60	Books for Young Learners	Richard C. Owen
Speak	Z	RF	250+	Anderson, Laurie Halse	Penguin Group
Speak Up!	F	F	194	Sunshine	Wright Group/McGraw Hill
Speak Your Mind	U	I	250+	Sails	Rigby
Speaking in Sign	O	I	778	Vocabulary Readers	Houghton Mifflin Harcourt
Speaking in Sign	O	I	778	Vocabulary Readers/CA	Houghton Mifflin Harcourt
Speaking Out	T	I	250+	Power Up!	Steck-Vaughn
Special Beach Day	I	RF	215	Reading Street	Pearson
Special Buildings	M	I	555	Reading Street	Pearson
Special Cake, The	K	RF	250+	Cambridge Reading	Pearson Learning Group
Special Clothes	J	RF	411	Leveled Readers	Houghton Mifflin Harcourt
Special Day, A	E	RF	92	Windows on Literacy	National Geographic
Special Days, Special Food	J	I	306	Reading Street	Pearson
Special Delivery	B	F	54	Bookshop	Mondo
Special Effects	P	I	250+	Wildcats	Wright Group/McGraw Hill
Special Festival, A	M	RF	1070	Reading Street	Pearson
Special Foods, Special Places	WB	I	N/A	Windows on Literacy	National Geographic
Special Friend, A	F	RF	80	Carousel Readers	Pearson Learning Group
Special Garden, A	G	I	183	PM Science Readers	Rigby
Special Gifts	M	RF	250+	Rylant, Cynthia	Aladdin
Special Guests	I	F	414	Springboard	Wright Group/McGraw Hill
Special Night, A	U	HF	2340	Leveled Readers	Houghton Mifflin Harcourt
Special Night, A	U	HF	2340	Leveled Readers/CA	Houghton Mifflin Harcourt
Special Night, A	U	HF	2340	Leveled Readers/TX	Houghton Mifflin Harcourt
Special Places	E	RF	96	Rigby Literacy	Rigby
Special Places at School	J	I	250+	Explorations	Eleanor Curtain Publishing
Special Places at School	J	I	250+	Explorations	Okapi Educational Materials
Special Present, The	L	RF	250+	Take Two Books	Wright Group/McGraw Hill
Special Ride, The	K	RF	647	PM Collection	Rigby
Special Saris	N	RF	1677	Take Two Books	Wright Group/McGraw Hill
Special Stories	J	I	189	Vocabulary Readers	Houghton Mifflin Harcourt
Special Table, The	J	RF	450	Gear Up!	Wright Group/McGraw Hill
Special Talents: Extraordinary Lives	P	B	2021	Reading Street	Pearson
Special Things	G	RF	128	Literacy 2000	Rigby
Special Tools	J	I	266	Vocabulary Readers	Houghton Mifflin Harcourt
Special Tools	J	I	266	Vocabulary Readers/CA	Houghton Mifflin Harcourt
Special Tools	J	I	266	Vocabulary Readers/TX	Houghton Mifflin Harcourt
Special Tricks	L	I	320	Sails	Rigby
Special Trip, A	O	RF	910	Leveled Readers Science	Houghton Mifflin Harcourt
Specs	J	B	250+	Ready Set Read	Steck-Vaughn
Spectacular Stone Soup	L	RF	250+	Giff, Patricia Reilly	Yearling
Speech, The	P	RF	250+	Leveled Readers Language Support	Houghton Mifflin Harcourt
Speeches on the Air	Z	I	2358	Leveled Readers	Houghton Mifflin Harcourt
Speed Boat, The	C	RF	170	Sunshine	Wright Group/McGraw Hill
Speed of Light	S	F	250+	Story Surfers	ETA Cuisenaire
Speed Racer	F	RF	74	Leveled Readers Science	Houghton Mifflin Harcourt

S

* Collection of short stories
# Graphic text

TITLE	LEVEL	GENRE	WORD COUNT	AUTHOR / SERIES	PUBLISHER / DISTRIBUTOR
Speed Star	Q	F	1608	Zucker, Jonny	Stone Arch Books
Speedboats	M	I	250+	Horsepower	Capstone Press
*Speeding Sleigh and Other Cases, The	O	RF	250+	Simon, Seymour	Avon
Speedway Switch	Q	RF	5269	Maddox, Jake	Stone Arch Books
Speedway, The	B	RF	43	InfoTrek	ETA Cuisenaire
Speedy Bee	D	F	106	PM Plus Story Books	Rigby
Speedy Bee's Dance	E	F	166	PM Stars	Rigby
Speedy Cheetahs	K	I	379	Pull Ahead Books	Lerner Publications
*Speedy Pasta and Other Cases, The	O	RF	250+	Simon, Seymour	Avon
*Speedy Snake and Other Cases, The	O	RF	250+	Simon, Seymour	Avon
*Speedy Soapbox Car and Other Cases, The	O	RF	250+	Simon, Seymour	Avon
Spell Casters, Phoebe's Fortune	R	F	250+	Warriner, Holly	Aladdin
Spellbound	W	F	250+	Dale, Anna	Bloomsbury Children's Books
Spelling Bee, The	R	RF	1753	Reading Street	Pearson
Spelling Contest, The	M	RF	986	Leveled Readers	Houghton Mifflin Harcourt
Spelling Contest, The	M	RF	986	Leveled Readers/CA	Houghton Mifflin Harcourt
Spelling It Out	L	F	688	Rigby Gigglers	Rigby
Spencer School Sleepover, The	M	RF	250+	Sunshine	Wright Group/McGraw Hill
Spending Money	L	I	250+	Learning About Money	Capstone Press
Spending Money	O	I	250+	Let's See	Compass Point Books
Spending Money	E	I	102	Money	Lerner Publishing
Spheres	K	I	260	3-D Shapes	Capstone Press
Sphynx Cats	I	I	122	Cats	Capstone Press
Spices	U	I	250+	Theme Sets	National Geographic
Spicy-Herby Day, A	G	RF	117	Evangeline Nicholas Collection	Wright Group/McGraw Hill
Spider	D	F	43	Sunshine	Wright Group/McGraw Hill
Spider and Buffalo	N	I	250+	Storyteller	Wright Group/McGraw Hill
Spider and the King, The	L	TL	250+	Literacy 2000	Rigby
Spider Bank, The	L	I	250+	Story Steps	Rigby
Spider Boy	R	RF	250+	Fletcher, Ralph	Bantam
Spider Can't Fly	G	F	149	Book Bank	Wright Group/McGraw Hill
Spider Homes	D	I	97	Sails	Rigby
Spider in My Bedroom, A	K	RF	477	PM Plus Story Books	Rigby
Spider Kane and the Mystery at Jumbo Nightcrawler's	O	F	250+	Osborne, Mary Pope	Random House
Spider Kane and the Mystery Under the May-Apple	O	F	250+	Osborne, Mary Pope	Random House
Spider Legs	D	I	52	Twig	Wright Group/McGraw Hill
Spider Man	M	I	250+	Literacy 2000	Rigby
Spider Night	K	F	250+	Kunari, Anna	Hampton-Brown
Spider Plant, The	I	I	222	Rigby Flying Colors	Rigby
Spider Power	O	I	947	Springboard	Wright Group/ McGraw-Hill
Spider Relatives	Q	I	250+	Literacy 2000	Rigby
Spider Soup	J	F	556	Rigby Gigglers	Rigby
Spider Spins	D	F	36	Ray's Readers	Outside the Box
Spider, Spider	D	F	70	Sunshine	Wright Group/McGraw Hill
Spider, The	O	I	250+	Crewe, Sabrina	Steck-Vaughn
Spider, The	B	F	36	Sails	Rigby
Spiders	M	I	250+	Bookshop	Mondo
Spiders	G	I	99	Bugs, Bugs, Bugs	Red Brick Learning
Spiders	E	I	53	Discovery Links	Newbridge
Spiders	R	I	250+	Explorer Books-Pathfinder	National Geographic
Spiders	P	I	250+	Explorer Books-Pioneer	National Geographic

* Collection of short stories
# Graphic text

TITLE	LEVEL	GENRE	WORD COUNT	AUTHOR / SERIES	PUBLISHER / DISTRIBUTOR
Spiders	O	I	250+	Holmes, Kevin J.	Red Brick Learning
Spiders	P	I	250+	Mini Pets	Steck-Vaughn
Spiders	N	I	250+	Minibeasts	Franklin Watts
Spiders	O	I	250+	Nature's Friends	Compass Point Books
Spiders	H	I	153	Nonfiction	Literacy Footprints
Spiders	C	I	98	Vocabulary Readers	Houghton Mifflin Harcourt
Spiders	C	I	98	Vocabulary Readers/CA	Houghton Mifflin Harcourt
Spiders	E	I	75	Wonder World	Wright Group/McGraw Hill
Spiders and the Web	K	I	187	Animal Homes	Capstone Press
Spiders and Their Webs	I	I	162	Sunshine	Wright Group/McGraw Hill
Spiders Are Special Animals	J	I	166	Sunshine	Wright Group/McGraw Hill
Spiders Everywhere	D	F	36	Books for Young Learners	Richard C. Owen
Spiders in Space	I	F	242	Sunshine	Wright Group/McGraw Hill
Spiders Spin Silk	J	I	183	Windows on Literacy	National Geographic
Spider's Web	N	I	250+	Back, Christine	Silver Burdett Press
Spider's Web	B	RF	31	Sails	Rigby
Spider's Web, A	L	I	323	Wonder World	Wright Group/McGraw Hill
Spiders!	J	I	185	Rosen Real Readers	Rosen Publishing Group
Spiders, Spiders Everywhere!	D	RF	80	Learn to Read	Creative Teaching Press
Spiders, The	S	RF	250+	Sails	Rigby
Spies Go Shopping	I	RF	323	Sails	Rigby
Spies on the Devil's Belt	W	HF	250+	Haynes, Betsy	Scholastic
Spies! Real People, Real Stories	T	I	250+	High Five Reading	Red Brick Learning
Spies, The	A	RF	24	Sails	Rigby
Spike and the Concert	L	RF	250+	Cambridge Reading	Pearson Learning Group
Spikes, Scales, and Armor	H	I	185	Sails	Rigby
Spin Off	Q	F	1663	Zucker, Jonny	Stone Arch Books
Spin, Weave, Knit, and Knot	P	I	250+	PM Extensions	Rigby
Spinach-Eating Machine, The	K	F	536	Springboard	Wright Group/McGraw Hill
Spines, Stings, and Teeth	K	I	274	Big Cat	Pacific Learning
Spinning Snake, A	F	RF	156	Sunshine	Wright Group/McGraw Hill
Spinning Spiders	L	I	320	Pull Ahead Books	Lerner Publications
Spinning Top	I	I	182	Wonder World	Wright Group/McGraw Hill
Spinning Tops	G	RF	201	PM Photo Stories	Rigby
Spiny Sea Stars	L	I	452	Pull Ahead Books	Lerner Publications
Spirit of Hope	N	F	250+	Bookshop	Mondo
Spirit of St. Louis, The	V	I	250+	Cornerstones of Freedom	Children's Press
Spirit Quest	S	RF	250+	Sharpe, Susan	Scholastic
Splash	C	F	34	Foundations	Wright Group/McGraw Hill
Splash!	A	I	35	Bebop Books	Lee & Low Books Inc.
Splash!	H	F	250+	Green Light Readers	Harcourt
Splash!	E	RF	85	Joy Readers	Pearson Learning Group
Splash!	A	RF	21	Leveled Readers	Houghton Mifflin Harcourt
Splash!	E	RF	85	Leveled Readers Language Support	Houghton Mifflin Harcourt
Splash!	A	RF	21	Leveled Readers/CA	Houghton Mifflin Harcourt
Splash!	D	I	31	Little Celebrations	Pearson Learning Group
Splash!	D	RF	63	New Way Red	Steck-Vaughn
Splash!	D	F	35	Sun Sprouts	ETA Cuisenaire
Splashing Dad	C	RF	37	Early Emergent	Pioneer Valley
Splashy Fins, Flashy Skins: Deep-Sea Rhymes to Make You Grin	M	I	423	Silly Millies	Millbrook Press
Splatter	N	RF	250+	Orbit Chapter Books	Pacific Learning
Splinters	T	RF	250+	Sails	Rigby

* Collection of short stories
\# Graphic text

TITLE	LEVEL	GENRE	WORD COUNT	AUTHOR / SERIES	PUBLISHER / DISTRIBUTOR
Splish Splash!	B	RF	28	Windmill Books	Wright Group/McGraw Hill
Splish! Splash!	D	F	45	Little Celebrations	Pearson Learning Group
Splish! Splash!: A Book About Rain	M	I	250+	Amazing Science	Picture Window Books
Splishy-Sploshy	E	F	127	Story Basket	Wright Group/McGraw Hill
Splitzaroni	P	SF	1743	White, K.I.	Stone Arch Books
Splosh	C	F	47	Story Box	Wright Group/McGraw Hill
Spoiled Rotten	L	RF	250+	DeClements, Barthe	Hyperion
Spoiled Rotten	S	RF	250+	Orca Currents	Orca Book Publishers
Sponges	I	I	102	Under the Sea	Capstone Press
Spooky House	R	RF	250+	Sails	Rigby
Spooky Pet	B	RF	24	Smart Starts	Rigby
Spooky Riddles	I	TL	182	Brown, Marc	Random House
Spooky Spine Chillers	W	I	250+	DK Readers	DK Publishing
Spooky Swamp Sound, The	G	F	179	Sunshine	Wright Group/McGraw Hill
Spooky Tail of Prewitt Peacock, The	M	F	250+	Peet, Bill	Houghton Mifflin Harcourt
Sport Rules	S	I	250+	The News	Richard C. Owen
Sports and Motion	Q	I	1474	Vocabulary Readers	Houghton Mifflin Harcourt
Sports and Motion	Q	I	1474	Vocabulary Readers/CA	Houghton Mifflin Harcourt
Sports and Motion	Q	I	1474	Vocabulary Readers/TX	Houghton Mifflin Harcourt
Sports Are Fun	B	I	21	Pair-It Books	Steck-Vaughn
Sports Around the World	I	I	192	Early Connections	Benchmark Education
Sports Around the World	I	I	145	Shutterbug Books	Steck-Vaughn
Sports Bag	F	I	147	Sun Sprouts	ETA Cuisenaire
Sports Bloopers	P	I	250+	Hollander, Phyllis & Zander	Scholastic
Sports Cars	M	I	250+	Horsepower	Capstone Press
Sports Cars	W	I	6306	Motor Mania	Lerner Publications
Sports Day	C	RF	24	Home Connection Collection	Rigby
Sports Day	B	RF	39	Rigby Rocket	Rigby
Sports for All	Q	I	250+	Explorers	Wright Group/McGraw Hill
Sports for You	S	I	250+	The News	Richard C. Owen
*Sports Hall of Fame	O	B	250+	Bookshop	Mondo
Sports Heroes	R	I	250+	PM Nonfiction-Ruby	Rigby
Sports Legends	O	B	250+	Navigators Biography Series	Benchmark Education
Sports Math	S	I	250+	Navigators Math Series	Benchmark Education Company
Sports Matters: A Magazine for Kids	L	I	250+	Rigby Literacy	Rigby
Sports Mysteries: Case of the Basketball Video	P	RF	250+	Edwards, T. J.	Scholastic
Sports Mysteries: Case of the Missing Pitcher	P	RF	250+	Edwards, T. J.	Scholastic
Sports News	S	RF	250+	Sails	Rigby
Sports of the First Americans	T	I	1590	Leveled Readers Social Studies	Houghton Mifflin Harcourt
Sports on the Edge	P	I	250+	Literacy by Design	Rigby
Sports on Wheels	R	I	250+	PM Nonfiction-Ruby	Rigby
Sports Planet: Sports Played Around the World	R	I	250+	Power Up!	Steck-Vaughn
Sports Skills	S	I	250+	Sunshine	Wright Group/McGraw Hill
Sports Technology	Y	I	7338	Cool Science	Lerner Publications
Sports Technology	R	I	250+	PM Nonfiction-Ruby	Rigby
Sportsmanship	M	I	250+	Character Education	Red Brick Learning
Spot	B	RF	62	Springboard	Wright Group/McGraw Hill
Spot That Cat!	J	I	208	Story Box	Wright Group/McGraw Hill
Spot the Sporty Puppy	L	RF	250+	Dale, Jenny	Aladdin
Spots	A	I	24	Gear Up!	Wright Group/McGraw Hill
Spots	A	I	32	Leveled Literacy Intervention/ Orange System	Heinemann
Spots	E	RF	48	Literacy 2000	Rigby

* Collection of short stories
\# Graphic text

TITLE	LEVEL	GENRE	WORD COUNT	AUTHOR / SERIES	PUBLISHER / DISTRIBUTOR
Spots	E	RF	116	Real Kids Readers	Millbrook Press
Spots	I	I	226	Sails	Rigby
Spots	LB	RF	27	Smart Starts	Rigby
Spots	C	I	41	Sunshine	Wright Group/McGraw Hill
Spots	B	F	31	Visions	Wright Group/McGraw Hill
Spots	B	I	62	Vocabulary Readers	Houghton Mifflin Harcourt
Spots	B	I	62	Vocabulary Readers/CA	Houghton Mifflin Harcourt
Spots	B	I	62	Vocabulary Readers/TX	Houghton Mifflin Harcourt
Spots and Other Lumps and Bumps	S	I	250+	High-Fliers	Pacific Learning
Spots and Stripes	A	I	24	Rosen Real Readers	Rosen Publishing Group
Spot's Birthday Party	I	F	97	Hill, Eric	Putnam/Penguin
Spot's First Christmas	J	RF	102	Hill, Eric	Putnam/Penguin
Spot's First Walk	G	F	63	Hill, Eric	Putnam/Penguin
Spots or Stripes?	B	I	24	Shutterbug Books	Steck-Vaughn
Spots!	E	RF	55	Oxford Reading Tree	Oxford University Press
Spots, Feathers and Curly Tails	C	I	42	Tafuri, Nancy	Morrow
Spotted Beetles: Ladybugs in Your Backyard	M	I	250+	Backyard Bugs	Picture Window Books
*Spotted Pony, The: A Collection of Hanukkah Stories	U	TL	250+	Kimmel, Eric A.	Holiday House
Spraying Skunks	K	I	391	Pull Ahead Books	Lerner Publications
Spray-Paint Mystery, The	O	RF	250+	Medearis, Angela Shelf	Scholastic
Spread the Word	N	I	693	Vocabulary Readers	Houghton Mifflin Harcourt
Spread the Word	N	I	693	Vocabulary Readers/CA	Houghton Mifflin Harcourt
Spreading the Word	Q	I	250+	Wildcats	Wright Group/McGraw Hill
Spring	C	I	47	Carousel Readers	Pearson Learning Group
Spring	C	I	34	Gear Up!	Wright Group/McGraw Hill
Spring	I	I	142	Pebble Books	Capstone Press
Spring	E	I	49	Seasons	Lerner Publishing
Spring	E	I	58	Sunshine	Wright Group/McGraw Hill
Spring Festivals Around the World	P	I	250+	Literacy by Design	Rigby
Spring Fever!	T	F	250+	Lerangis, Peter	Language for Learning Assoc.
Spring Has Sprung	K	I	250+	Spyglass Books	Compass Point Books
Spring in the City	M	F	761	Leveled Readers	Houghton Mifflin Harcourt
Spring in the City	B	I	46	Leveled Readers Emergent	Houghton Mifflin Harcourt
Spring Is Coming	C	I	30	Bonnell, Kris	Reading Reading Books
Spring Is Here	C	RF	62	Gear Up!	Wright Group/McGraw Hill
Spring Pops Up	C	I	26	Instant Readers	Harcourt School Publishers
Spring Rain	A	I	24	Vocabulary Readers	Houghton Mifflin Harcourt
Spring Rose, Winter Bear	H	I	218	Reading Street	Pearson
Spring Shower	D	RF	105	In Step Readers	Rigby
Spring Snow	D	RF	48	Little Books for Early Readers	University of Maine
Spring, Summer, Fall, Winter	G	I	64	Windows on Literacy	National Geographic
Springs	F	I	142	Alphakids	Sundance
Springs	M	I	245	Books for Young Learners	Richard C. Owen
Springtime Rock and Roll, The	H	F	249	Literacy Tree	Rigby
Sprint Cars	M	I	250+	Horsepower	Capstone Press
Sprint Cars	Q	I	250+	Wild Rides!	Capstone Press
Spy	X	I	250+	Eyewitness Books	DK Publishing
Spy Basics	U	I	250+	Spies	Capstone Press
Spy Cat	S	F	250+	Kehret, Peg	Puffin/Penguin
Spy Danny	I	F	230	Coulton, Mia	Maryruth Books
Spy Down the Street, The	M	F	250+	Woodland Mysteries	Wright Group/McGraw Hill
Spy Gear	U	I	250+	Spies	Capstone Press

* Collection of short stories
# Graphic text

Organized Alphabetically by Title **553**
Storable Database at www.fountasandpinnellleveledbooks.com

TITLE	LEVEL	GENRE	WORD COUNT	AUTHOR / SERIES	PUBLISHER / DISTRIBUTOR
Spy in the Attic, The	M	RF	250+	Scheffler, Ursel	North-South Books
Spy in the White House, A	N	RF	250+	Roy, Ron	Scholastic
Spy Manual	M	I	250+	Sails	Rigby
Spy Maps	N	F	250+	Sails	Rigby
Spy on Third Base, The	M	RF	250+	Christopher, Matt	Little, Brown & Co.
Spy School	J	F	477	Sails	Rigby
Spy Skills	U	I	250+	Spies	Capstone Press
Spy Technology	X	I	7165	Cool Science	Lerner Publications
Spy Tools	L	I	335	Sails	Rigby
Spy!	Y	I	250+	Myers, Anna	Walker & Company
Spy, The	B	RF	30	Sails	Rigby
Spycatcher	N	RF	250+	Damian Drooth Supersleuth	Stone Arch Books
Spymail	T	RF	250+	Sails	Rigby
Spyology: The Complete Book of Spycraft	X	I	250+	Blake, Spencer	Candlewick Press
Squanto	S	B	250+	Amazing Americans	Wright Group/McGraw Hill
Squanto and the First Thanksgiving	L	HF	250+	Celsi, Teresa	Steck-Vaughn
Squanto and the First Thanksgiving	N	I	1371	On My Own Holidays	Lerner Publications
Squanto: Friend of the Pilgrims	O	B	250+	Bulla, Clyde Robert	Scholastic
Square	B	I	32	Shapes	Lerner Publications
Squares	B	I	27	Harry's Math Books	Outside the Box
Squares Around Town	J	I	292	Shapes Around Town	Capstone Press
Squares Everywhere	C	I	26	Discovery Links	Newbridge
Squares: Seeing Squares All Around Us	K	I	183	Shapes	Capstone Press
Squash in the Schoolyard	N	I	1100	Vocabulary Readers/TX	Houghton Mifflin Harcourt
Squashed	U	RF	250+	Bauer, Joan	Speak
Squeaking Bats	K	I	319	Pull Ahead Books	Lerner Publications
Squeaky Car, The	G	RF	200	New Way Green	Steck-Vaughn
Squeaky Clean	C	RF	29	Stewart, Josie	Continental Press
Squid Monster	T	RF	250+	Sails	Rigby
Squids	I	I	129	Under the Sea	Capstone Press
Squiggles and Strokes	U	I	250+	Bookweb	Rigby
Squire Takes a Wife, A	J	F	250+	Ready Set Read	Steck-Vaughn
Squirrel Monkeys	I	I	402	Sails	Rigby
Squirrel School	A	F	28	Springboard	Wright Group/McGraw Hill
Squirrels	I	I	250+	Pebble Books	Red Brick Learning
Squirrels	F	RF	109	Ready Readers	Pearson Learning Group
Squirrels	N	I	460	Storyteller Nonfiction	Wright Group/McGraw Hill
Squirrels and Their Nests	J	I	130	Animal Homes	Capstone Press
Squirrels in the School	Q	RF	250+	Baglio, Ben M.	Scholastic
Squirrel's World	K	F	250+	Moser, Lisa	Candlewick Press
Squirrels: Furry Scurriers	M	I	250+	The Wild World of Animals	Red Brick Learning
Ssh, Don't Wake the Baby	F	RF	135	Voyages	SRA/McGraw Hill
Sss Snakes	C	I	48	Bonnell, Kris	Reading Reading Books
Sssh!	C	RF	49	Book Bank	Wright Group/McGraw Hill
St. Lawrence Seaway, The	O	I	371	Independent Readers Social Studies	Houghton Mifflin Harcourt
St. Louis Cardinals, The	S	I	250+	Team Spirit	Norwood House Press
St. Louis Rams, The	S	I	250+	Team Spirit	Norwood House Press
St. Louis, Gateway to the West	W	I	2714	Vocabulary Readers	Houghton Mifflin Harcourt
St. Louis, Gateway to the West	W	I	2714	Vocabulary Readers/CA	Houghton Mifflin Harcourt
St. Louis, Gateway to the West	W	I	2714	Vocabulary Readers/TX	Houghton Mifflin Harcourt
St. Louis, Missouri	Q	I	250+	Theme Sets	National Geographic
St. Patrick's Day	Q	I	250+	Holiday Histories	Heinemann Library
St. Patrick's Day	J	I	136	Holidays and Celebrations	Capstone Press

* Collection of short stories
\# Graphic text

S

TITLE	LEVEL	GENRE	WORD COUNT	AUTHOR / SERIES	PUBLISHER / DISTRIBUTOR
St. Patrick's Day	M	I	250+	Holidays and Celebrations	Picture Window Books
St. Patrick's Day	P	I	250+	Let's See	Compass Point Books
Stables Are for Horses	I	I	66	Windmill Books	Wright Group/McGraw Hill
Stacey and the Haunted Masquerade	O	RF	250+	Martin, Ann M.	Scholastic
Stacey and the Missing Ring	O	RF	250+	Martin, Ann M.	Scholastic
Stacey and the Mystery at the Mall	O	RF	250+	Martin, Ann M.	Scholastic
Stacey and the Mystery Money	O	RF	250+	Martin, Ann M.	Scholastic
Stacy Says Good-Bye	L	RF	250+	Giff, Patricia Reilly	Bantam
Stage Fright	N	RF	250+	Martin, Ann M.	Scholastic
Stage Fright	O	RF	250+	Orbit Double Takes	Pacific Learning
Stagecoach Travel	Q	I	916	Vocabulary Readers	Houghton Mifflin Harcourt
Stagecoach Travel	Q	I	916	Vocabulary Readers/CA	Houghton Mifflin Harcourt
Stagecoach Travel	Q	I	916	Vocabulary Readers/TX	Houghton Mifflin Harcourt
Stagecoach Years, The	P	I	250+	Rigby Flying Colors	Rigby
Staircase to the Sky	E	RF	133	Visions	Wright Group/McGraw Hill
Stallion in Spooky Hollow	Q	RF	250+	Baglio, Ben M.	Scholastic
Stallion's Call, The	E	F	77	Salem, Lynn; Stewart, Josie	Continental Press
Stamping Art: Imprint Your Designs	Q	I	250+	Crafts	Capstone Press
Stamping for Fun!	S	I	250+	For Fun! Crafts	Compass Point Books
Stamps	G	I	58	Wonder World	Wright Group/McGraw Hill
Stan Packs	E	RF	84	Ready Readers	Pearson Learning Group
Stan the Hot Dog Man	K	RF	250+	Kessler, Ethel & Leonard	HarperTrophy
Stand Tall	U	RF	250+	Bauer, Joan	Penguin Group
Standing in the Light	U	HF	250+	Dear America	Scholastic
Standing Stones	X	I	250+	WorldScapes	ETA Cuisenaire
*Standing Tall: The Stories of Ten Hispanic Americans	X	B	250+	Palacios, Argentina	Scholastic
Stanley	I	F	250+	Hoff, Syd	HarperTrophy
Stanley and the Class Pet	K	F	250+	Saltzberg, Barney	Candlewick Press
Stanley and the Magic Lamp	N	F	250+	Brown, Jeff	HarperTrophy
Star	M	RF	250+	Simon, Jo Ann	Random House
Star and Patches	K	RF	440	PM Plus Story Books	Rigby
Star Boy's Surprise	K	F	647	Big Cat	Pacfic Learning
Star Discovered, A: Lucky Foot Stable Series	R	RF	33427	Dawson, JoAnn S.	Sourcebooks
Star Fisher, The	S	RF	250+	Yep, Lawrence	Scholastic
Star Garden, The	L	I	862	Sun Sprouts	ETA Cuisenaire
Star Gazing	L	I	573	Explorations	Eleanor Curtain Publishing
Star Gazing	L	I	573	Explorations	Okapi Eductional Materials
Star Gazing in Our Solar System	J	I	202	Independent Readers Science	Houghton Mifflin Harcourt
Star of Wonder: Lucky Foot Stable Series	R	RF	32540	Dawson, JoAnn S.	Sourcebooks
Star Pictures	K	I	96	Books for Young Learners	Richard C. Owen
Star Pictures	D	I	43	iOpeners	Pearson Learning Group
Star Struck	O	F	250+	High-Fliers	Pacific Learning
Star Thief	P	RF	250+	Orbit Chapter Books	Pacific Learning
Star Tracks	R	I	2014	Reading Street	Pearson
Starfish	I	I	237	Sails	Rigby
Starfish & Urchins	L	I	322	Marine Life For Young Readers	Pearson Learning Group
Starfishers to the Rescue	M	SF	250+	Dreyer, Ellen	Pearson Learning Group
Stargazers	C	F	83	Galaxy Girl	Literacy Footprints
Stargazer's Club, The	O	RF	812	Leveled Readers	Houghton Mifflin Harcourt
Stargazer's Club, The	O	RF	812	Leveled Readers/CA	Houghton Mifflin Harcourt
Stargirl	V	RF	250+	Spinelli, Jerry	Alfred A. Knopf
Starring First Grade	J	RF	250+	Cohen, Miriam	Bantam
Starring Grace	O	RF	250+	Hoffman, Mary	Puffin Books

S

* Collection of short stories
# Graphic text

TITLE	LEVEL	GENRE	WORD COUNT	AUTHOR / SERIES	PUBLISHER / DISTRIBUTOR
Starring Rosie	N	RF	250+	Giff, Patricia Reilly	Penguin Group
Stars	Q	I	250+	A True Book	Children's Press
Stars	H	I	181	Discovery Links	Newbridge
Stars	I	I	137	Exploring the Galaxy	Capstone Press
Stars	N	I	835	Our Universe	Lerner Publications
Stars	P	I	250+	Reading Expeditions	National Geographic
Stars	H	I	99	Space	Lerner Publications
Stars	G	I	105	Sunshine	Wright Group/McGraw Hill
Stars	Q	I	250+	The Galaxy	Red Brick Learning
Stars	I	I	181	Yellow Umbrella Books	Red Brick Learning
Stars and Planets	Z	I	250+	Stott, Carole	Scholastic
Stars Around Town	J	I	334	Shapes Around Town	Capstone Press
Stars in the Sky	F	I	161	In Step Readers	Rigby
Stars in the Sky	F	I	153	Literacy by Design	Rigby
Stars in the Sky	I	I	207	PM Science Readers	Rigby
Stars of the Show	L	RF	426	Rigby Flying Colors	Rigby
Stars, The	K	I	102	Out In Space	Red Brick Learning
Stars: Seeing Stars All Around Us	J	I	193	Shapes	Capstone Press
Starshine	H	F	224	Sunshine	Wright Group/McGraw Hill
Starship Rescue	Q	SF	3859	Breslin, T.	Stone Arch Books
Star-Spangled Banner in Translation, The: What It Really Means	V	I	250+	Kids' Translations	Capstone Press
Star-Spangled Banner, The	O	I	1575	On My Own History	Lerner Publications
Starstruck!	M	RF	250+	Bookweb	Rigby
Start and Stop	F	I	49	The Way Things Move	Red Brick Learning
Start of the American Revolutionary War, The: Paul Revere Rides at Midnight	S	I	250+	Headlines from History	Rosen Publishing Group
Starting a Business	S	I	596	Vocabulary Readers	Houghton Mifflin Harcourt
Starting a Rock Collection	T	I	250+	Independent Readers Science	Houghton Mifflin Harcourt
Starting Points	Y	I	250+	iOpeners	Pearson Learning Group
Starting School	E	RF	97	Voyages	SRA/McGraw Hill
State Plants of the United States	K	I	286	Springboard	Wright Group/McGraw Hill
State Quarters	N	I	632	Vocabulary Readers	Houghton Mifflin Harcourt
State Quarters	N	I	632	Vocabulary Readers/CA	Houghton Mifflin Harcourt
State Quarters	N	I	632	Vocabulary Readers/TX	Houghton Mifflin Harcourt
Stateswoman to the World: A Story About Eleanor Roosevelt	R	B	8674	Creative Minds Biographies	Carolrhoda Books
Statue of Liberty, The	S	I	250+	A True Book	Children's Press
Statue of Liberty, The	N	I	250+	American Symbols	Capstone Press
Statue of Liberty, The	Q	I	250+	Let's See	Compass Point Books
Statue of Liberty, The	Q	I	250+	National Landmarks	Red Brick Learning
Statue of Liberty, The	J	I	250+	Penner, Lucille	Random House
Statue of Liberty, The	P	I	580	Pull Ahead Books	Lerner Publications
Statue of Liberty, The	V	I	250+	The Heinle Reading Library	Thomson Learning
Statue of Liberty, The: From Paris to New York City	P	I	250+	On Our Way to English	Rigby
Statue of Liberty, The: From Paris to New York City	N	I	390	Reading Street	Pearson
Statues Across America	K	I	293	Vocabulary Readers	Houghton Mifflin Harcourt
Stay Away from Simon!	O	RF	250+	Carrick, Carol	Clarion
Stay Away!	E	I	71	Explorations	Eleanor Curtain Publishing
Stay Away!	E	I	71	Explorations	Okapi Educational Materials
Stay Clear!: What You Should Know about Skin Care	V	I	7457	Health Zone	Lerner Publications

* Collection of short stories
# Graphic text

S

TITLE	LEVEL	GENRE	WORD COUNT	AUTHOR / SERIES	PUBLISHER / DISTRIBUTOR
Stay Cool	E	F	134	Start to Read	School Zone
Stay Fit!: How You Can Get in Shape	U	I	6630	Health Zone	Lerner Publications
Stay Safe!	E	I	122	Literacy by Design	Rigby
Stay Safe!: How You Can Keep Out of Harm's Way	Y	I	6926	Health Zone	Lerner Publications
Stay! Keeper's Story	U	F	250+	Lowry, Lois	Random House
Staying Clean	M	I	746	Pull Ahead Books	Lerner Publications
Staying Cool in the Heat	Q	I	969	Leveled Readers	Houghton Mifflin Harcourt
Staying Cool in the Heat	Q	I	969	Leveled Readers/CA	Houghton Mifflin Harcourt
Staying Cool in the Heat	Q	I	969	Leveled Readers/TX	Houghton Mifflin Harcourt
Staying Happy	N	I	611	Pull Ahead Books	Lerner Publications
Staying Healthy	W	I	250+	iOpeners	Pearson Learning Group
Staying Healthy	I	I	248	Time for Kids	Teacher Created Materials
Staying Healthy	LB	I	7	Windows on Literacy	National Geographic
Staying Healthy in Space	I	I	291	Leveled Readers/CA	Houghton Mifflin Harcourt
Staying Healthy in Space	I	I	291	Leveled Readers/TX	Houghton Mifflin Harcourt
Staying Healthy in Space	I	I	291	Leveled Readers	Houghton Mifflin Harcourt
Staying Healthy: Eating Right	O	I	250+	McGinty, Alice B.	Franklin Watts
Staying Nine	O	RF	250+	Conrad, Pam	HarperTrophy
Staying Power: Tales of Survival	S	I	250+	Kids Discover Reading	Wright Group/McGraw Hill
Staying Safe in Emergencies	L	I	446	Pull Ahead Books	Lerner Publications
Staying Safe in the Water	F	I	264	Rigby Flying Colors	Rigby
Staying Well	F	I	154	Early Connections	Benchmark Education
Staying with Big Bill	F	F	207	Sails	Rigby
Staying with Grandma Norma	F	RF	168	Salem, Lynn; Stewart, Josie	Continental Press
Steal Away . . . to Freedom	Z	RF	250+	Armstrong, Jennifer	Scholastic
Steal Away Home	V	HF	250+	Ruby, Lois	Aladdin
Stealing Freedom	U	HF	250+	Carbone, Lisa	Random House
Stealing Home: The Story of Jackie Robinson	V	B	250+	Denenberg, Barry	Scholastic
Stealth Attack Fighters: The F-117A Nighthawks	V	I	250+	War Planes	Capstone Press
Stealth Bombers: The B-2 Spirits	U	I	250+	War Planes	Capstone Press
Steam Engine, The: Fueling the Industrial Revolution	R	I	250+	On Deck	Rigby
Steam Power	L	I	308	Rigby Focus	Rigby
Steel Eyes	T	F	250+	Zucker, Jonny	Stone Arch Books
Stegosaurus	I	I	126	Dinosaur and Prehistoric Animals	Capstone Press
Stella	E	RF	57	Storyteller-Moon Rising	Wright Group/McGraw Hill
Stems	E	I	30	Parts of Plants	Lerner Publishing
Stems	K	I	231	Pebble Books	Capstone Press
Stems	I	I	122	Plant Parts	Capstone Press
Stencils, Prints, and Special Effects: How to Create Models, Cards, Decorations, and Pictures With a Difference	Q	I	250+	Bookshop	Mondo
Step Fourth, Mallory!	O	RF	17656	Friedman, Laurie	Carolrhoda Books
Step On It!	L	F	356	Gear Up!	Wright Group/ McGraw Hill
Stephen Hawking	V	B	2515	Leveled Readers Science	Houghton Mifflin Harcourt
Stepping Back in Time	W	RF	2045	Leveled Readers	Houghton Mifflin Harcourt
Stepping on the Cracks	V	HF	250+	Hahn, Mary Downing	Avon
Stepping Stones	C	F	42	Sunshine	Wright Group/McGraw Hill
Stepping Through Time	N	I	250+	Rigby Literacy	Rigby
Steps	W	I	250+	Boldprint	Steck-Vaughn
Steps, The	T	RF	250+	Cohn, Rachel	Simon & Schuster

TITLE	LEVEL	GENRE	WORD COUNT	AUTHOR / SERIES	PUBLISHER / DISTRIBUTOR
Sterkarm Handshake, The	Z	F	250+	Price, Susan	Scholastic
Steve Nash	P	B	2062	Amazing Athletes	Lerner Publications
Steve's Room	G	RF	171	Ready Readers	Pearson Learning Group
Stew for Egor's Mom, A	G	F	162	Ready Readers	Pearson Learning Group
Stick Insects: Masters of Defense	U	I	250+	Insect World: Masters of Defense	Lerner Publications
Stick to It!: The Story of Wilma Rudolph	M	B	250+	Spyglass Books	Compass Point Books
Sticks and Stones	W	I	250+	Boldprint	Steck-Vaughn
Sticks and Stones	W	I	250+	Boldprint	Steck-Vaughn
Sticks and Stones	Z+	RF	250+	Orca Soundings	Orca Book Publishers
Sticks and Stones, Bobbie Bones	P	RF	250+	Roberts, Brenda C.	Scholastic
Sticky Problem, A	J	RF	488	In Step Readers	Rigby
Sticky Rice with Mango	H	I	191	In Step Readers	Rigby
Sticky Stanley	F	F	97	First Start	Troll Associates
Still Around!	N	I	250+	Rigby Literacy	Rigby
Still Standing	O	I	388	Independent Readers Science	Houghton Mifflin Harcourt
Stingers	A	I	24	Sails	Rigby
Stingrays	I	I	126	Wonder World	Wright Group/McGraw Hill
Stink and the Great Guinea Pig Express	M	RF	250+	McDonald, Megan	Candlewick Press
Stink and the Incredible Super-Galactic Jawbreaker	M	RF	250+	McDonald, Megan	Candlewick Press
Stink and the World's Worst Super-Stinky Sneakers	M	RF	250+	McDonald, Megan	Candlewick Press
Stink: The Incredible Shrinking Kid	M	RF	250+	McDonald, Megan	Candlewick Press
Stinkers!	I	I	215	Sails	Rigby
Stinky and Successful: The Riot Brothers Never Stop	P	RF	250+	Amato, Mary	Holiday House
Stinky Skunk, The	L	F	556	Leveled Readers	Houghton Mifflin Harcourt
Stinky Skunk, The	L	F	556	Leveled Readers/CA	Houghton Mifflin Harcourt
Stinky Skunk, The	L	F	556	Leveled Readers/TX	Houghton Mifflin Harcourt
Stitches	G	RF	250+	Ziefert, Harriet	Puffin/Penguin
Stock Cars	M	I	250+	Horsepower	Capstone Press
Stock Cars	H	I	130	Mighty Machines	Capstone Press
Stock Cars	W	I	5618	Motor Mania	Lerner Publications
Stock Cars	N	I	514	Pull Ahead Books	Lerner Publications
Stock Cars	T	I	250+	The World's Fastest	Red Brick Learning
Stolen Sun, The	N	TL	250+	WorldScapes	ETA Cuisenaire
Stolen Words	Y	RF	3372	Leveled Readers	Houghton Mifflin Harcourt
Stolen Words	Y	RF	3372	Leveled Readers/CA	Houghton Mifflin Harcourt
Stomach Full of Stones, A	J	I	412	Sails	Rigby
Stomachs	N	I	250+	Sails	Rigby
Stomp It!: Board Sports and Riders Who Rip	V	I	250+	Boldprint	Steck-Vaughn
Stone Cutter, The	H	TL	276	Big Cat	Pacific Learning
Stone Dragon: The Great Wall of China	N	I	250+	In Step Readers	Rigby
Stone Fox	P	RF	250+	Gardiner, John Reynolds	HarperTrophy
Stone Hat, The	M	RF	849	Books for Young Learners	Richard C. Owen
Stone in My Hand, A	W	RF	250+	Clinton, Cathryn	Candlewick Press
Stone in the Road, A	L	TL	250+	Bookshop	Mondo
Stone Is Strong	M	I	250+	Yellow Umbrella Books	Red Brick Learning
Stone Mouse, The	K	F	250+	Lighthouse	Rigby
Stone Soup	I	TL	555	Leveled Literacy Intervention/ Green System	Heinemann
Stone Soup	J	TL	932	McGovern, Ann	Scholastic
Stone Soup	J	TL	250+	PM Tales and Plays-Turquoise	Rigby
Stone Soup	H	TL	250+	Rigby Literacy	Rigby

S

* Collection of short stories
# Graphic text

TITLE	LEVEL	GENRE	WORD COUNT	AUTHOR / SERIES	PUBLISHER / DISTRIBUTOR
*Stone Soup and Other Stories	L	TL	250+	New Way Literature	Steck-Vaughn
Stone Soup, A Traditional Tale	H	TL	250+	Rigby Star	Rigby
Stone Works	K	I	124	Wonder World	Wright Group/McGraw Hill
Stonehenge	X	I	250+	The Unexplained	Capstone Press
Stonehenge: Mystery Unsolved?	U	I	1754	Leveled Readers	Houghton Mifflin Harcourt
Stonehenge: Still a Mystery	T	I	250+	Leveled Readers Language Support	Houghton Mifflin Harcourt
Stones in Water	X	RF	250+	Napoli, Donna Jo	Puffin/Penguin
Stones of the Sky	N	TL	250+	Windows on Literacy	National Geographic
Stonewall Jackson: Spirit of the South	Y	B	250+	The Civil War	Carus Publishing
Stop	C	F	54	Story Box	Wright Group/McGraw Hill
Stop and Go, Yes and No: What Is an Antonym?	O	I	303	Words Are CATegorical	Millbrook Press
Stop Going Cock-a-Doodle-Doo	E	F	146	Sails	Rigby
Stop Knitting, Nina!	I	F	250+	Home Connection Collection	Rigby
Stop Teasing Taylor!	I	RF	490	We Both Read	Treasure Bay
Stop That	C	F	41	Ready Readers	Pearson Learning Group
Stop That Noise!	A	F	21	KinderReaders	Rigby
Stop That Noise!	C	RF	21	Pacific Literacy	Pacific Learning
Stop That Noise!	K	RF	1183	Real Kids Readers	Millbrook Press
Stop That Rabbit	G	F	168	First Start	Troll Associates
Stop That Robot!	WB	F	N/A	Big Cat	Pacific Learning
Stop the Car!	G	RF	179	Lighthouse	Rigby
Stop Thief!	J	TL	250+	Lighthouse	Ginn & Co.
Stop!	C	F	68	Literacy by Design	Rigby
Stop!	B	RF	90	PM Starters	Rigby
Stop!	A	RF	12	Ready Readers	Pearson Learning Group
Stop!	C	RF	31	Wonder World	Wright Group/McGraw Hill
*Stop! And Other Stories	E	F	161	Story Steps	Rigby
Stop, Look, and Listen	C	RF	71	Lighthouse	Rigby
Stop, Look, and Listen	G	RF	102	Literacy Tree	Rigby
Stop, Quinn, Stop	D	F	66	Reading Street	Pearson
Stop, Stop	M	F	250+	Hurd, Edith Thacher	HarperCollins
Store Clerks: Then and Now	M	I	250+	Primary Source Readers	Teacher Created Materials
Stores	C	RF	66	Carousel Readers	Pearson Learning Group
Stories	C	RF	43	Learn to Read	Creative Teaching Press
*Stories for Children	V	TL	250+	Singer, Isaac Bashevis	Farrar, Straus and Giroux
*Stories From the Days of Christopher Columbus	U	HF	250+	Young, Richard; Young, Judy Dockery	August House Publishers
Stories From the Underground Railroad	R	I	250+	Explorer Books-Pathfinder	National Geographic
Stories From the Underground Railroad	Q	I	250+	Explorer Books-Pioneer	National Geographic
*Stories Huey Tells, The	N	RF	250+	Cameron, Ann	Alfred A. Knopf
Stories in Stone	M	I	250+	Pacific Literacy	Pacific Learning
Stories in Stone: The World of Animal Fossils	U	I	250+	A First Book	Franklin Watts
*Stories Julian Tells, The	N	RF	250+	Cameron, Ann	Alfred A. Knopf
*Stories of Sherlock Holmes	V	RF	250+	High-Fliers	Pacific Learning
*Stories of the North	Y	RF	250+	London, Jack	Scholastic
Stories to Tell	Q	F	250+	Reading Safari	Mondo
Storm at Coldwater Creek	M	HF	250+	Sunshine	Wright Group/McGraw Hill
Storm at Sea, A	R	HF	1145	Leveled Readers	Houghton Mifflin Harcourt
Storm Book, The	P	I	250+	Zolotow, Charlotte	HarperCollins
Storm Chasers	R	I	1371	Leveled Readers	Houghton Mifflin Harcourt
Storm Chasers	R	I	1371	Leveled Readers/CA	Houghton Mifflin Harcourt
Storm Chasers	L	RF	250+	Navigators Fiction Series	Benchmark Education

S

TITLE	LEVEL	GENRE	WORD COUNT	AUTHOR / SERIES	PUBLISHER / DISTRIBUTOR
Storm Chasers: On the Trail of Deadly Tornadoes	S	I	250+	High Five Reading	Red Brick Learning
Storm Danger!	S	I	1739	Reading Street	Pearson
Storm in the Night	N	RF	250+	Stolz, Mary	HarperCollins
Storm Is Coming, A	H	I	172	Explorations	Eleanor Curtain Publishing
Storm Is Coming, A	H	I	172	Explorations	Okapi Eductional Materials
Storm on the Beach, A	I	RF	72	Book Bank	Wright Group/McGraw Hill
Storm Surfer	P	RF	250+	Maddox, Jake	Stone Arch Books
Storm Thief	X	SF	250+	Wooding, Chris	Scholastic
Storm!	E	I	49	Wonder World	Wright Group/McGraw Hill
Storm!	N	RF	250+	Wonder World	Wright Group/McGraw Hill
Storm, The	G	RF	75	Books for Young Learners	Richard C. Owen
Storm, The	A	I	24	Davidson, Avelyn	Scholastic
Storm, The	E	RF	71	Foundations	Wright Group/McGraw Hill
Storm, The	D	RF	30	Gear Up!	Wright Group/McGraw Hill
Storm, The	E	F	154	Leveled Literacy Intervention/ Green System	Heinemann
Storm, The	D	I	71	Leveled Readers	Houghton Mifflin Harcourt
Storm, The	D	I	71	Leveled Readers/CA	Houghton Mifflin Harcourt
Storm, The	E	RF	33	Literacy 2000	Rigby
Storm, The	C	RF	29	Story Box	Wright Group/McGraw Hill
Storm, The	B	I	19	Sunshine	Wright Group/McGraw Hill
Storm, The	C	I	28	Voyages	SRA/McGraw Hill
Stormbreaker	Z	RF	250+	Horowitz, Anthony	Scholastic
Storms	N	I	250+	PM Plus Story Books	Rigby
Storms	H	I	284	Sails	Rigby
Storms	N	I	250+	Windows on Literacy	National Geographic
Storms!	L	I	359	Pair-It Books	Steck-Vaughn
Stormy Seas: A Story from the Shetland Islands	R	RF	250+	Reading Expeditions	National Geographic
Stormy Weather	O	I	250+	Navigators Science Series	Benchmark Education
Stormy Weather	H	I	208	PM Science Readers	Rigby
Stormy Weather	S	I	1618	Reading Street	Pearson
Stormy Weather	G	I	88	Twig	Wright Group/McGraw Hill
Stormy, Misty's Foal	R	RF	250+	Henry, Marguerite	Aladdin
Story Box, The	K	RF	592	Leveled Readers	Houghton Mifflin Harcourt
Story of a Book, The	L	I	250+	Take Two Books	Wright Group/McGraw Hill
Story of a Girl	Z+	RF	250+	Zarr, Sara	Little, Brown & Co.
Story of Alexander Graham Bell, Inventor of the Telephone	O	B	250+	Davidson, Margaret	Scholastic
Story of Amy Johnson, The: Pioneering Woman Navigator	R	B	250+	Literacy 2000	Rigby
Story of Anne and Maud, The	W	B	1926	Leveled Readers	Houghton Mifflin Harcourt
Story of Anne and Maud, The	W	B	1926	Leveled Readers/CA	Houghton Mifflin Harcourt
Story of Atlas, The	Q	TL	776	Sun Sprouts	ETA Cuisenaire
Story of Benjamin Franklin, Amazing American	O	B	250+	Davidson, Margaret	Scholastic
Story of Big Bess Call, The	M	TL	250+	Sunshine	Wright Group/McGraw Hill
Story of Books, The	O	I	250+	Sunshine	Wright Group/McGraw Hill
Story of Bunker's Cove	R	I	250+	Leveled Readers Language Support	Houghton Mifflin Harcourt
Story of Cars, The	M	I	250+	Pair-It Turn and Learn	Steck-Vaughn
Story of Cheese, The	K	I	221	Pair-It Turn and Learn	Steck-Vaughn
Story of Chicken Licken	I	TL	250+	Ormerod, Jan	Lothrop
Story of Communication, The	L	I	444	Reading Street	Pearson
Story of Corn, The	H	I	171	Ready Readers	Pearson Learning Group

* Collection of short stories
# Graphic text

TITLE	LEVEL	GENRE	WORD COUNT	AUTHOR / SERIES	PUBLISHER / DISTRIBUTOR
Story of Doña Chila, The	P	B	250+	Moore, Eva	Scholastic
Story of Dorothea Lange, The	U	B	1954	Leveled Readers	Houghton Mifflin Harcourt
Story of Dorothea Lange, The	U	B	1954	Leveled Readers/CA	Houghton Mifflin Harcourt
Story of Dorothea Lange, The	U	B	1954	Leveled Readers/TX	Houghton Mifflin Harcourt
Story of Ferdinand, The	K	F	250+	Leaf, Munro	Viking
Story of Flight, The	T	I	2357	Reading Street	Pearson
Story of Frog Belly Rat Bone, The	N	F	250+	Ering, Timothy Basil	Candlewick Press
Story of George Washington Carver, The	Q	B	250+	Moore, Eva	Bantam
Story of Geronimo, The	T	B	250+	Cornerstones of Freedom	Children's Press
Story of Harriet Tubman, The: Conductor of the Underground Railroad	S	B	250+	McMullan, Kate	Scholastic
Story of Harriet Tubman, The: Freedom Train	T	B	250+	Sterling, Dorothy	Bantam
Story of High Street, The	WB	RF	N/A	Goodall, John S.	Andre Deutsch
Story of Hungbu and Nolbu, The	K	TL	250+	Bookshop	Mondo
Story of Jackie Robinson, The: Bravest Man in Baseball	O	B	250+	Davidson, Margaret	Scholastic
Story of Jeans, The	M	I	250+	Discovery World	Rigby
Story of Juan Bobo, The	D	TL	58	Leveled Readers Language Support	Houghton Mifflin Harcourt
Story of Jumping Mouse, The	P	TL	250+	Steptoe, John	HarperTrophy
Story of Laura Ingalls Wilder, Pioneer Girl, The	Q	B	250+	Stine, Megan	Bantam
Story of Libraries, The	V	I	2145	Reading Street	Pearson
Story of Money, The	J	I	250+	On Our Way to English	Rigby
Story of Muhammad Ali: Heavyweight Champion of the World, The	S	B	250+	Denenberg, Barry	Dell
Story of My Life, The	X	B	250+	Keller, Helen	Bantam
Story of My Life, The	P	B	250+	Leveled Readers Language Support	Houghton Mifflin Harcourt
Story of Orange Juice, The	M	I	250+	Yellow Umbrella Books	Red Brick Learning
Story of Oskar Schindler, The	Z	B	2470	Leveled Readers	Houghton Mifflin Harcourt
Story of Pathos	S	HF	4191	Take Two Books	Wright Group/ McGraw Hill
Story of Pluto, The	S	I	2306	Leveled Readers Science	Houghton Mifflin Harcourt
Story of Pocahontas, The	M	B	250+	DK Readers	DK Publishing
Story of Ruby Bridges, The	O	B	250+	Coles, Robert	Scholastic
Story of Running Water, The	J	TL	287	Cambridge Reading	Pearson Learning Group
Story of Sacagawea, The	O	B	250+	Rosen Real Readers	Rosen Publishing Group
Story of Small Fry, The	P	I	250+	Action Packs	Rigby
Story of Sue, The: T Rex	X	I	2391	Independent Readers Science	Houghton Mifflin Harcourt
Story of the Blues, The	U	I	1357	Vocabulary Readers	Houghton Mifflin Harcourt
Story of the Blues, The	U	I	1357	Vocabulary Readers/CA	Houghton Mifflin Harcourt
Story of the Lonely Tree, The	H	RF	207	Take Two Books	Wright Group/McGraw Hill
Story of the Mayflower Compact, The	T	I	250+	Cornerstones of Freedom	Children's Press
Story of the Mexican Jumping Bean, The	M	TL	250+	Story Vines	Wright Group/McGraw Hill
Story of the Persian Gulf War, The	W	I	250+	Cornerstones of Freedom	Children's Press
Story of the Pony Express, The	P	I	250+	Windows on Literacy	National Geographic
Story of the Sinking of the Battleship Maine, The	W	I	250+	Cornerstones of Freedom	Children's Press
Story of the Surrender at Yorktown, The	V	I	250+	Cornerstones of Freedom	Children's Press
Story of the Three Kingdoms, The	O	TL	250+	Myers, Walter Dean	Harper Collins
Story of the White House, The	S	I	250+	Waters, Kate	Scholastic
Story of the Women's Movement, The	V	I	250+	Cornerstones of Freedom	Children's Press
Story of Thomas Alva Edison, Inventor, The	R	B	250+	Davidson, Margaret	Scholastic
Story of Walt Disney, Maker of Magical Worlds, The	O	B	250+	Selden, Bernice	Bantam

* Collection of short stories
# Graphic text

S

TITLE	LEVEL	GENRE	WORD COUNT	AUTHOR / SERIES	PUBLISHER / DISTRIBUTOR
Story of Waltzing Matilda, The	V	I	2872	Independent Readers Social Studies	Houghton Mifflin Harcourt
Story of Water, The: A Moving Adventure	R	I	250+	Literacy by Design	Rigby
Story of William Tell, The	M	TL	250+	PM Story Books-Silver	Rigby
Story of Writing, The	V	I	1880	Reading Street	Pearson
Story of You, The	M	I	482	Sunshine	Wright Group/McGraw Hill
Story Sticks	F	I	58	Instant Readers	Harcourt School Publishers
Story Teller's Story, A	O	B	250+	Meet The Author	Richard C. Owen
Story Time	C	RF	32	Ready Readers	Pearson Learning Group
Story, a Story, A: An African Tale	M	TL	250+	Haley, Gail E.	Aladdin
Storyteller Quilts	R	I	250+	Storyteller -Raging Rivers	Wright Group/McGraw Hill
Storyteller, The	L	RF	1071	Leveled Readers/TX	Houghton Mifflin Harcourt
Storytellers	L	I	506	Storyteller Nonfiction	Wright Group/McGraw Hill
Storyteller's Beads, The	Y	RF	250+	Kurtz, Jane	Harcourt Trade
Storyteller's Journey, A	Q	I	250+	Bookweb	Rigby
Storytelling	O	I	955	Gear Up!	Wright Group/ McGraw Hill
Storytelling Around the World	Q	I	1269	Vocabulary Readers	Houghton Mifflin Harcourt
Storytelling Around the World	P	I	573	Vocabulary Readers	Houghton Mifflin Harcourt
Storytelling Around the World	Q	I	1269	Vocabulary Readers/CA	Houghton Mifflin Harcourt
Storytelling Through the Years	Q	I	930	Vocabulary Readers	Houghton Mifflin Harcourt
Storytelling Through the Years	Q	I	930	Vocabulary Readers/CA	Houghton Mifflin Harcourt
Storytelling Through the Years	Q	I	930	Vocabulary Readers/TX	Houghton Mifflin Harcourt
Stowaway	W	HF	250+	Hesse, Karen	Simon & Schuster
Straight from the Horse's Mouth	P	I	250+	Sunshine	Wright Group/McGraw Hill
Straight Line Wonder, The	J	F	250+	Bookshop	Mondo
Stranded in Boringsville	T	RF	250+	Bateson, Catherine	Holiday House
Stranded in the Desert	R	RF	250+	Reading Safari	Mondo
Stranded in the Snow!: Eric LeMarque's Story of Survival	R	I	250+	True Tales of Survival	Capstone Press
Stranded!: Amy Racina's Story of Survival	S	I	250+	True Tales of Survival	Capstone Press
Stranded!: Amy Racina's Story of Survival	S	I	250+	True Tales of Survival	Capstone Press
Strange Animals	N	I	250+	Windows on Literacy	National Geographic
Strange Bird, A	P	F	1024	Leveled Readers	Houghton Mifflin Harcourt
Strange Case of Dr. Jekyll and Mr. Hyde, The	Z+	F	250+	Stevenson, Robert Louis	Penguin Group
*Strange Clues and Other Cases, The	O	RF	250+	Simon, Seymour	Avon
Strange Creatures	N	SF	250+	Orbit Chapter Books	Pacific Learning
Strange Day at the Zoo, A	M	F	1398	Take Two Books	Wright Group/McGraw Hill
Strange Day in Mayville, A	L	TL	250+	Leveled Readers Language Support	Houghton Mifflin Harcourt
Strange Jobs	Q	I	250+	Sunshine	Wright Group/McGraw Hill
Strange Life of Undersea Vents, The	W	I	2522	Leveled Readers	Houghton Mifflin Harcourt
Strange Meetings	Q	F	250+	Literacy 2000	Rigby
*Strange Museum and Other Cases, The	O	RF	250+	Simon, Seymour	Avon
Strange Plants	E	I	30	Books for Young Learners	Richard C. Owen
Strange Plants	J	I	433	Leveled Readers Science	Houghton Mifflin Harcourt
Strange Plants	O	I	250+	Windows on Literacy	National Geographic
Strange Rocks	U	I	2135	Leveled Readers Science	Houghton Mifflin Harcourt
Strange Shoe, The	L	TL	250+	PM Tales and Plays-Silver	Rigby
Strange Sports with Weird Gear	S	I	1454	Reading Street	Pearson
Strange Things	L	RF	289	Books for Young Learners	Richard C. Owen
Stranger at the Window	U	RF	250+	Alcock, Vivien	Houghton Mifflin Harcourt
Stranger Came Ashore, A	U	F	250+	Hunter, Mollie	HarperTrophy
Stranger With My Face	Y	RF	250+	Duncan, Lois	Laurel-Leaf Books
Stranger's Gift, The	L	TL	250+	Literacy 2000	Rigby

Organized Alphabetically by Title
Storable Database at www.fountasandpinnellleveledbooks.com

* Collection of short stories
# Graphic text

TITLE	LEVEL	GENRE	WORD COUNT	AUTHOR / SERIES	PUBLISHER / DISTRIBUTOR
Strangest Rock on Earth, The	Q	RF	250+	Pair-It Books	Steck-Vaughn
Stravaganza: City of Flowers	Z+	F	250+	Hoffman, Mary	Bloomsbury Children's Books
Stravaganza: City of Masks	Z+	F	250+	Hoffman, Mary	Bloomsbury Children's Books
Stravaganza: City of Secrets	Z+	F	250+	Hoffman, Mary	Bloomsbury Children's Books
Stravaganza: City of Stars	Z+	F	250+	Hoffman, Mary	Bloomsbury Children's Books
Straw House, The	E	TL	241	Storyworlds	Heinemann Educational Publishers
Strawberries	C	I	37	Little Books for Early Readers	University of Maine
Strawberry Hill	Y	RF	250+	LaFaye, A.	Simon & Schuster
Strawberry Jam	E	RF	77	Oxford Reading Tree	Oxford University Press
Strawberry Picking	J	RF	250+	Cambridge Reading	Pearson Learning Group
Strawberry Pie	E	RF	138	Windows on Literacy	National Geographic
Strawberry Pop and Soda Crackers	K	RF	396	Little Celebrations	Pearson Learning Group
Stray Dog, The	J	RF	205	Simont, Marc	Scholastic
Stray, The	R	RF	250+	King-Smith, Dick	Alfred A. Knopf
Streak, The	N	RF	250+	Kroll, Stephen	Avon Camelot
Stream, The	C	RF	24	Science	Outside the Box
Stream, The	F	F	43	Voyages	SRA/McGraw Hill
Street Action	O	I	250+	Wildcats	Wright Group/McGraw Hill
Street Musicians	J	RF	283	Sunshine	Wright Group/McGraw Hill
Street Performers	I	I	270	Vocabulary Readers	Houghton Mifflin Harcourt
Street Performers	I	I	270	Vocabulary Readers/CA	Houghton Mifflin Harcourt
Street Skating: Grinds and Grabs	Q	I	250+	Skateboarding	Capstone Press
Street Sweepers	I	I	138	Mighty Machines	Capstone Press
Streets of Gold	U	HF	1933	Leveled Readers	Houghton Mifflin Harcourt
Streetsweeper, The	M	RF	250+	Bookweb	Rigby
Strega Nona	K	TL	250+	DePaola, Tomie	Scholastic
Strength and Stability	O	I	250+	InfoTrek	ETA Cuisenaire
Strength in Numbers	O	I	250+	InfoQuest	Rigby
Strider	R	RF	250+	Cleary, Beverly	HarperCollins
Strike	O	I	250+	Pacific Literacy	Pacific Learning
Strike Fighters: The F/A-18E/F Super Hornets	V	I	250+	War Planes	Capstone Press
Strike Four!	H	RF	250+	Ziefert, Harriet	Puffin/Penguin
Strike Me Down with a Stringbean	L	F	404	Read Alongs	Rigby
Strike Now!	W	HF	250+	Reading Expeditions	National Geographic
Strike Out!	M	RF	250+	Howard, Tristan	Scholastic
String Food	K	I	250+	Home Connection Collection	Rigby
String Performers	J	I	250+	Home Connection Collection	Rigby
String Things	G	I	165	Springboard	Wright Group/McGraw Hill
Strings	C	I	53	Storyteller-First Snow	Wright Group/McGraw Hill
Strings, Ropes, and Cables	I	I	250+	Home Connection Collection	Rigby
Striped Ice Cream	N	RF	250+	Lexau, Joan M.	Scholastic
Stripes	WB	I	N/A	Big Cat	Pacific Learning
Stripes	B	I	24	Explorations	Eleanor Curtain Publishing
Stripes	B	I	24	Explorations	Okapi Educational Materials
Stripes	LB	I	28	Twig	Wright Group/McGraw Hill
Stripes and Spots	A	I	32	Sails	Rigby
Stroll and Walk, Babble and Talk: More about Synonyms	O	I	238	Cleary, Brian P.	Millbrook Press
Strongest Animal, The	F	RF	58	Books for Young Learners	Richard C. Owen

S

* Collection of short stories
# Graphic text

Storable Database at www.fountasandpinnellleveledbooks.com

TITLE	LEVEL	GENRE	WORD COUNT	AUTHOR / SERIES	PUBLISHER / DISTRIBUTOR
Strongest One of All, The	H	TL	222	Instant Readers	Harcourt School Publishers
Struggle for Higher Education, The	Y	I	2321	Reading Street	Pearson
Strum Family Band, The	J	RF	250+	The Story Basket	Wright Group/McGraw Hill
Stuart Goes to School	M	F	250+	Pennypacker, Sara	Scholastic
Stuart Little	R	F	250+	White, E. B.	HarperTrophy
Stuart's Cape	M	F	250+	Pennypacker, Sara	Scholastic
Stuart's Moon Suit	R	RF	1075	Reading Street	Pearson
Stubborn Goat, The	I	F	212	Alphakids	Sundance
Stuck at Camp	S	RF	2198	Leveled Readers	Houghton Mifflin Harcourt
Stuck at Camp	S	RF	2198	Leveled Readers/CA	Houghton Mifflin Harcourt
Stuck at Camp	S	RF	2198	Leveled Readers/TX	Houghton Mifflin Harcourt
Stuck at the End of the Ice Age	Z	I	1877	Leveled Readers	Houghton Mifflin Harcourt
Stuck in Neutral	Z	RF	250+	Trueman, Terry	HarperCollins
Stuck in the Ice	M	I	250+	Leveled Readers Language Support	Houghton Mifflin Harcourt
Stuck in the Muck	E	F	139	Spinelle, Nancy Louise	Kaeden Books
Stuck in the Mud	E	RF	120	Lighthouse	Rigby
Stuck in the Tar Pits	W	I	250+	Independent Readers Science	Houghton Mifflin Harcourt
Stuck on an Island	H	RF	181	Sunshine	Wright Group/McGraw Hill
Studying a Glacier	M	I	501	Leveled Readers Science	Houghton Mifflin Harcourt
Studying the Past	T	I	512	Vocabulary Readers	Houghton Mifflin Harcourt
Stuffed	T	RF	250+	Orca Soundings	Orca Book Publishers
Stuk's Village	S	HF	1553	Reading Street	Pearson
Stump Hill	K	RF	627	Early Connections	Benchmark Education
Stumptown Kid	W	HF	250+	Gorman, Carol & Findley, Ron J.	Peachtree
Stumpy's Secret	P	RF	250+	Hager, Mandy	Pacific Learning
Stunt Planes	Q	I	250+	Wild Rides!	Capstone Press
Sturdy Turtles	L	I	399	Pull Ahead Books	Lerner Publications
Stuyvesant, Peter: New Amsterdam and the Origins of New York	W	B	250+	Power Plus	Rosen Publishing Group
Style All Her Own, A	K	RF	737	Friedman, Laurie	Carolrhoda Books
Sub, The	P	RF	250+	Peterson, P. J.	Puffin/Penguin
Submarines	T	I	250+	Land and Sea	Capstone Press
Submarines	J	I	118	Mighty Machines	Capstone Press
Submarines	V	I	4440	Military Hardware in Action	Lerner Publications
Submarines	N	I	389	Pull Ahead Books	Lerner Publications
Submarines	O	I	250+	Rigby Flying Colors	Rigby
Sub-Saharan Africa	W	I	250+	Primary Source Readers	Teacher Created Materials
Subtle Knife, The	Z	F	250+	Pullman, Philip	Ballantine Books
Subtraction Fun	K	I	250+	Yellow Umbrella Books	Capstone Press
Subway Mouse, The	L	F	250+	Reid, Barbara	Scholastic
Sudden Impact	T	RF	250+	Orca Soundings	Orca Book Publishers
Sudden Secrets	N	RF	250+	Rigby Literacy	Rigby
Sudden Storm, A	S	RF	250+	Power Up!	Steck-Vaughn
Sue and Drew	I	RF	440	Reading Street	Pearson
Sue Hendrickson	M	B	631	Leveled Readers	Houghton Mifflin Harcourt
Sue Hendrickson	M	B	631	Leveled Readers/CA	Houghton Mifflin Harcourt
Sue Hendrickson	M	B	631	Leveled Readers/TX	Houghton Mifflin Harcourt
Sue Hendrickson: Fossil Hunter	L	B	671	Leveled Readers	Houghton Mifflin Harcourt
Sue Hendrickson: Fossil Hunter	L	B	671	Leveled Readers/CA	Houghton Mifflin Harcourt
Sue Hendrickson: Fossil Hunter	L	B	671	Leveled Readers/TX	Houghton Mifflin Harcourt
Sue Hendrickson: Modern Adventurer	R	B	250+	Explore More	Wright Group/McGraw Hill
Sue Likes Blue	G	RF	131	Start to Read	School Zone
Sue's Hummingbird	M	RF	893	Reading Street	Pearson

* Collection of short stories
\# Graphic text

S

TITLE	LEVEL	GENRE	WORD COUNT	AUTHOR / SERIES	PUBLISHER / DISTRIBUTOR
Sugar and Spice and All Things Nice	L	I	250+	Storyteller Chapter Books	Wright Group/ McGraw Hill
Sugar Bush, The	K	I	250+	Greetings	Rigby
Sugar Cakes Cyril	M	RF	4022	Gershator, Phillis	Mondo
Sugar Gliders	O	I	2266	Early Bird Nature Books	Lerner Publications
Sugar Snow	J	HF	250+	Wilder, Laura Ingalls	HarperCollins
Sugaring Season (Making Maple Syrup)	S	I	250+	Burns, Diane	Carolrhoda Books
Sugaring Time	S	I	250+	Lasky, Kathryn	Macmillan
Sugaring Weather	R	HF	1449	Leveled Readers	Houghton Mifflin Harcourt
Sugaring Weather	R	HF	1449	Leveled Readers/CA	Houghton Mifflin Harcourt
Sugaring Weather	R	HF	1449	Leveled Readers/TX	Houghton Mifflin Harcourt
Sugaring-Off Party, The	Q	RF	1683	London, Jonathan	Fitzhenry & Whiteside
Suitcase	N	RF	250+	Walter, Mildred Pitts	Scholastic
Suki and the Case of the Lost Bunnies	K	RF	250+	Ready Readers	Pearson Learning Group
Sulky Simon	J	RF	246	Windmill Books	Rigby
Sultan's Challenge, The	N	TL	250+	WorldScapes	ETA Cuisenaire
Summer	B	RF	45	Leveled Readers Language Support	Houghton Mifflin Harcourt
Summer	I	I	178	Pebble Books	Capstone Press
Summer	E	I	53	Seasons	Lerner Publishing
Summer	E	I	73	Sunshine	Wright Group/McGraw Hill
Summer at Cove Lake	G	RF	288	Ready Readers	Pearson Learning Group
Summer Ball	V	RF	250+	Lupica, Mike	Philomel Books
Summer Camp	J	RF	182	City Kids	Rigby
Summer Camp	A	F	25	Leveled Readers	Houghton Mifflin Harcourt
Summer Camp	A	F	25	Leveled Readers/CA	Houghton Mifflin Harcourt
Summer Day, A	C	I	74	Leveled Readers	Houghton Mifflin Harcourt
Summer Fun	E	RF	30	Literacy 2000	Rigby
Summer Fun	J	I	261	Spyglass Books	Compass Point Books
Summer I Shrank My Grandmother, The	Q	F	250+	Woodruff, Elvira	Bantam
Summer in Antarctica	M	I	250+	Explorations	Eleanor Curtain Publishing
Summer in Antarctica	M	I	250+	Explorations	Okapi Educational Materials
Summer in the South, A	Q	F	250+	Marshall, James	Houghton Mifflin Harcourt
*Summer Life, A	Z	RF	250+	Soto, Gary	Bantam
Summer Mail	W	RF	3361	Leveled Readers	Houghton Mifflin Harcourt
Summer of Baseball Parks, The	K	RF	690	Leveled Readers	Houghton Mifflin Harcourt
Summer of Baseball Parks, The	K	RF	690	Leveled Readers/CA	Houghton Mifflin Harcourt
Summer of Baseball Parks, The	K	RF	690	Leveled Readers/TX	Houghton Mifflin Harcourt
Summer of Hurricane Andrew, The	O	RF	1259	Reading Street	Pearson
Summer of My German Soldier	Z	HF	250+	Greene, Bette	Dell
Summer of Secrets	Z	RF	250+	Langan, Paul	Townsend Press
Summer of the Great-Grandmother, The	Z	B	250+	L'Engle, Madeleine	HarperCollins
Summer of the Swans, The	U	RF	250+	Byars, Betsy	Penguin Group
Summer Party, The	O	RF	250+	On Our Way to English	Rigby
Summer Rays	V	RF	3077	Leveled Readers	Houghton Mifflin Harcourt
Summer Reading Is Killing Me!	P	F	250+	Scieszka, Jon	Penguin Group
Summer Sabotage	Q	RF	250+	Reading Safari	Mondo
Summer Sands	M	RF	839	Evangeline Nicholas Collection	Wright Group/McGraw Hill
Summer School! What Genius Thought That Up?	R	RF	250+	Winkler, Henry and Oliver, Lin	Grosset & Dunlap
Summer Sun Risin'	N	RF	355	Bebop Books	Lee & Low Books Inc.
Summer Switch	R	F	250+	Rodgers, Mary	HarperTrophy
Summer to Die, A	T	RF	250+	Lowry, Lois	Dell
Summer Trips	I	I	272	Visions	Wright Group/McGraw Hill
Summer Trouble	P	RF	1603	Zucker, Jonny	Stone Arch Books

* Collection of short stories
# Graphic text

TITLE	LEVEL	GENRE	WORD COUNT	AUTHOR / SERIES	PUBLISHER / DISTRIBUTOR
Summer Wheels	O	B	250+	Bunting, Eve	Harcourt Trade
Summer with the Grandparents	S	RF	3324	Reading Street	Pearson
Summer with Uncle Vince	Q	F	1497	Leveled Readers	Houghton Mifflin Harcourt
Summer with Uncle Vince	Q	F	1497	Leveled Readers/CA	Houghton Mifflin Harcourt
Summer with Uncle Vince	Q	F	1497	Leveled Readers/TX	Houghton Mifflin Harcourt
Summertime in the Big Woods	J	HF	250+	Wilder, Laura Ingalls	HarperCollins
Summing Up Sport	U	I	250+	News Extra	Richard C. Owen
Sun	S	I	250+	Our Solar System	Compass Point Books
Sun	H	I	131	Space	Lerner Publications
Sun	Q	I	250+	The Galaxy	Red Brick Learning
Sun & Spoon	R	RF	250+	Henkes, Kevin	Penguin Group
Sun Above and the River Below, The	P	TL	250+	Literacy by Design	Rigby
Sun and the Moon, The	C	RF	41	PM Stars	Rigby
Sun and the Wind, The	E	TL	173	Storyworlds	Heinemann Educational Publishers
Sun Flower, A	B	RF	42	Foundations	Wright Group/McGraw Hill
Sun Power	P	I	250+	Rigby Focus	Rigby
Sun Power	G	I	79	Windows on Literacy	National Geographic
Sun Racers	M	I	749	Rigby Flying Colors	Rigby
Sun Shines on Me, The	B	I	34	Science	Outside the Box
*Sun Smile	I	F	250+	Story Box	Wright Group/McGraw Hill
Sun Up, Sun Down	H	I	148	Independent Readers Science	Houghton Mifflin Harcourt
Sun Up, Sun Down: The Story of Day and Night	Q	I	250+	Science Works	Picture Window Books
Sun, a Flower, A	LB	I	42	Foundations	Wright Group/McGraw Hill
Sun, Earth, and Moon	L	I	391	Vocabulary Readers	Houghton Mifflin Harcourt
Sun, Earth, and Moon	L	I	391	Vocabulary Readers/CA	Houghton Mifflin Harcourt
Sun, Moon, Earth	E	I	53	Leveled Readers Science	Houghton Mifflin Harcourt
Sun, Rain, and Snow	B	I	72	Leveled Readers Emergent	Houghton Mifflin Harcourt
Sun, The	E	I	42	Discovery Links	Newbridge
Sun, The	R	I	250+	Explorer Books-Pathfinder	National Geographic
Sun, The	P	I	250+	Explorer Books-Pioneer	National Geographic
Sun, The	I	I	183	Exploring the Galaxy	Capstone Press
Sun, The	D	I	119	Leveled Readers	Houghton Mifflin Harcourt
Sun, The	N	I	573	Leveled Readers Science	Houghton Mifflin Harcourt
Sun, The	D	I	119	Leveled Readers/CA	Houghton Mifflin Harcourt
Sun, The	D	I	119	Leveled Readers/TX	Houghton Mifflin Harcourt
Sun, The	N	I	250+	Literacy 2000	Rigby
Sun, The	N	I	956	Our Universe	Lerner Publications
Sun, The	K	I	135	Out In Space	Red Brick Learning
Sun, The	B	I	32	Rigby Focus	Rigby
Sun, The	N	I	250+	Windows on Literacy	National Geographic
Sun, The	J	I	219	Wonder World	Wright Group/McGraw Hill
Sun, The	E	I	66	Yellow Umbrella Books	Red Brick Learning
Sun, the Wind & Tashira, The	J	TL	371	Folk Tales	Mondo
Sun, the Wind, and the Rain, The	G	RF	170	PM Plus Nonfiction	Rigby
Sunburn	J	RF	176	City Kids	Rigby
Sunburn	B	I	48	Prokopchak, Ann	Kaeden Books
Sunday Horse	N	RF	250+	Literacy Tree	Rigby
Sunflower	E	I	55	Joy Starters	Pearson Learning Group
Sunflower	N	I	250+	Life Cycles	Creative Teaching Press
Sunflower Seeds	D	I	48	Story Box	Wright Group/McGraw Hill
Sunflower That Went Flop, The	K	F	637	Story Box	Wright Group/McGraw Hill
Sunflower, The	C	I	27	Pacific Literacy	Pacific Learning
Sunflowers	E	I	33	Books for Young Learners	Richard C. Owen

* Collection of short stories
# Graphic text

TITLE	LEVEL	GENRE	WORD COUNT	AUTHOR / SERIES	PUBLISHER / DISTRIBUTOR
Sunflowers	D	I	35	Pebble Books	Capstone Press
Sunjata: Warrior King of Mali	U	TL	3046	Graphic Myths and Legends	Lerner Publications
Sunken Treasure	P	I	250+	Gibbons, Gail	Houghton Mifflin Harcourt
Sunny	C	I	26	Weather	Lerner Publications
Sunny Day, A	E	I	65	Pebble Books	Capstone Press
Sunny Day, A	E	I	90	Weather	Lerner Publishing
Sunny-Side Up	M	RF	250+	Giff, Patricia Reilly	Bantam
Sunrise	C	F	46	Literacy 2000	Rigby
Sunrise Over Fallujah	Z+	RF	250+	Myers, Walter Dean	Scholastic
Sun's Family of Planets, The	L	I	250+	Read-About Science	Children's Press
Sun's Magic, The	B	I	28	Seedlings	Continental Press
Sun's Strength, The: An Ancient Chinese Myth	W	TL	1972	Leveled Readers	Houghton Mifflin Harcourt
Sunset of the Sabertooth	M	F	250+	Osborne, Mary Pope	Random House
Sunset Pond, The	J	RF	433	Appleton-Smith, Laura	Flyleaf Publishing
Sunsets of Miss Olivia Wiggins, The	Q	RF	250+	Laminack, Lester L.	Peachtree
Sunshine	WB	RF	N/A	Ormerod, Jan	Lothrop, Lee & Shepard
Sunshine	L	I	307	Weather	Capstone Press
Sunshine Street	H	RF	110	Sunshine	Wright Group/McGraw Hill
Sunshine, Moonshine	E	RF	128	Armstrong, Jennifer	Random House
Sunshine, the Black Cat	G	RF	143	Carousel Readers	Pearson Learning Group
Sunshine: A Book About Sunlight	M	I	250+	Amazing Science	Picture Window Books
Super Amos	R	RF	250+	Paulsen, Gary	Bantam
Super Animals	F	I	149	Leveled Readers Science	Houghton Mifflin Harcourt
Super Ben	C	RF	33	Big Cat	Pacific Learning
Super Bob and the Birthday Surprise	K	F	525	Rigby Gigglers	Rigby
Super Bob and the Howling Bucket	K	F	250+	Rigby Gigglers	Rigby
Super Car	B	F	21	Rigby Rocket	Rigby
Super Danny	C	F	35	Coulton, Mia	Maryruth Books
Super Fox	G	F	265	Leveled Literacy Intervention/ Blue System	Heinemann
Super Hero	B	RF	33	Sunshine	Wright Group/McGraw Hill
#Super Hero ABC	Q	F	250+	McLeod, Bob	Harper Collins
Super Parrot	J	RF	250+	Real Reading	Steck-Vaughn
Super Pig's Adventures	E	F	133	New Way Blue	Steck-Vaughn
Super Sandwich	E	I	72	Little Red Readers	Sundance
Super Sculptures	J	I	282	Big Cat	Pacific Learning
Super Shake, The	M	F	250+	Reading Safari	Mondo
Super Shopping	D	RF	41	Rigby Literacy	Rigby
Super Shopping	D	RF	56	Rigby Star	Rigby
Super Smile Shop, The	H	F	254	Story Basket	Wright Group/McGraw Hill
Super Soccer Freak Show	Q	F	250+	Wiley & Grampa's Creature Features	Little, Brown & Co.
Super Space Stations	M	I	250+	Rosen Real Readers	Rosen Publishing Group
Super Storms	M	I	250+	Simon, Seymour	Chronicle Books
Super Strawberries	I	I	344	Rigby Flying Colors	Rigby
Super Supermarket Plan, The	J	RF	250+	Home Connection Collection	Rigby
Super Suzy	J	RF	323	InfoTrek	ETA Cuisenaire
Super Terrific Me!	D	RF	64	Early Learning Modules	Steck-Vaughn
Super Winter Survivors	U	I	250+	Literacy by Design	Rigby
Superbikes	M	I	250+	Horsepower	Capstone Press
Superbikes	T	I	250+	The World's Fastest	Red Brick Learning
Supercharged Infield	P	RF	250+	Christopher, Matt	Little, Brown & Co.
Supercomputer Pizzas	M	F	250+	Bookweb	Rigby
SuperCroc	Q	I	250+	Explorer Books-Pathfinder	National Geographic

* Collection of short stories
# Graphic text

S

TITLE	LEVEL	GENRE	WORD COUNT	AUTHOR / SERIES	PUBLISHER / DISTRIBUTOR
SuperCroc	P	I	250+	Explorer Books-Pioneer	National Geographic
SuperCroc Found	N	I	1752	On My Own History	Lerner Publications
Supercross	W	I	6107	Motor Mania	Lerner Publications
Supercross Motorcylces	N	I	442	Pull Ahead Books	Lerner Publications
Supercross Racing	Q	I	250+	Dirt Bikes	Capstone Press
Super-Duper Sandwich, The	I	F	202	Books for Young Learners	Richard C. Owen
Super-Duper Shoes	H	RF	82	Rigby Star	Rigby
Super-Duper Sunflower Seeds, The	I	F	389	Book Bank	Wright Group/McGraw Hill
Superfudge	Q	RF	250+	Blume, Judy	Bantam
Superheroes Save the Day	J	F	714	Leveled Readers	Houghton Mifflin Harcourt
Superheroes Save the Day	J	F	714	Leveled Readers/CA	Houghton Mifflin Harcourt
Superheroes Save the Day	J	F	714	Leveled Readers/TX	Houghton Mifflin Harcourt
Superheroes to the Rescue	J	F	735	Leveled Readers	Houghton Mifflin Harcourt
Superheroes to the Rescue	J	F	735	Leveled Readers/CA	Houghton Mifflin Harcourt
Superheroes to the Rescue	J	F	735	Leveled Readers/TX	Houghton Mifflin Harcourt
Superkids	H	F	165	Sunshine	Wright Group/McGraw Hill
Supermarket Chase, The	K	RF	438	Sunshine	Wright Group/McGraw Hill
Supermarket Managers	M	I	250+	Community Helpers	Red Brick Learning
Supermarket on Mars	B	F	38	Rigby Rocket	Rigby
Supermarket, The	K	I	263	Pebble Books	Capstone Press
Supernaturalist, The	W	SF	250+	Colfer, Eoin	Hyperion
Supernova	N	RF	250+	PM Collection	Rigby
Supersonic Fighters: The F-16 Fighting Falcons	V	I	250+	War Planes	Capstone Press
Superstars	I	F	252	Sunshine	Wright Group/McGraw Hill
Super-tuned!	N	RF	250+	PM Collection	Rigby
Supper for Cal	H	RF	189	Leveled Readers	Houghton Mifflin Harcourt
Supreme Court of the United States, The	W	I	250+	American Civics	Red Brick Learning
Supreme Court, The	S	I	250+	A True Book	Children's Press
Supreme Court, The	Q	I	527	Vocabulary Readers	Houghton Mifflin Harcourt
Supreme Court, The	Q	I	527	Vocabulary Readers/CA	Houghton Mifflin Harcourt
Supreme Court, The	Q	I	527	Vocabulary Readers/TX	Houghton Mifflin Harcourt
Surf Carnival, The	K	RF	434	PM Story Books	Rigby
Surf Girls	N	RF	250+	Girlz Rock!	Mondo
Surfer, The	D	RF	40	Wonder World	Wright Group/McGraw Hill
Surfing the Information Highway	H	I	137	Wonder World	Wright Group/McGraw Hill
Surf's Up	P	RF	250+	Wildcats	Wright Group/McGraw Hill
Surprise Box, The	I	RF	250+	Voyages	SRA/McGraw Hill
Surprise Cake	C	F	32	Literacy 2000	Rigby
Surprise Dinner, The	L	RF	680	PM Collection	Rigby
Surprise Feast, The	O	I	250+	Rigby Focus	Rigby
Surprise for Jake	D	RF	80	Windows on Literacy	National Geographic
Surprise for Mom	E	RF	101	Urmston, Kathleen; Evans, Karen	Kaeden Books
Surprise for Mom, A	E	I	177	Leveled Literacy Intervention/ Green System	Heinemann
Surprise for Ms. Green, A	J	RF	393	Leveled Readers	Houghton Mifflin Harcourt
Surprise for Ms. Green, A	J	RF	393	Leveled Readers/CA	Houghton Mifflin Harcourt
Surprise for Ms. Green, A	J	RF	393	Leveled Readers/TX	Houghton Mifflin Harcourt
Surprise for Roxy, A	D	F	107	Leveled Literacy Intervention/ Blue System	Heinemann
Surprise for the Bears, A	M	RF	966	Leveled Readers	Houghton Mifflin Harcourt
Surprise for the Bears, A	M	RF	966	Leveled Readers/CA	Houghton Mifflin Harcourt
Surprise for the Bears, A	M	RF	966	Leveled Readers/TX	Houghton Mifflin Harcourt

S

* Collection of short stories
\# Graphic text

TITLE	LEVEL	GENRE	WORD COUNT	AUTHOR / SERIES	PUBLISHER / DISTRIBUTOR
Surprise for the Big Bad Wolf, A	L	F	562	Leveled Literacy Intervention/ Blue System	Heinemann
Surprise for Zack, A	I	RF	250+	PM Plus Story Books	Rigby
Surprise from the Sky	I	F	295	Windmill Books	Rigby
Surprise Invitation, The	J	RF	250+	PM Plus Story Books	Rigby
Surprise Moon	I	RF	206	Bebop Books	Lee & Low Books Inc.
Surprise Party	E	F	94	Bella and Rosie Series	Literacy Footprints
Surprise Party	K	I	333	Hutchins, Pat	Macmillan
Surprise Party, The	I	F	192	New Way Green	Steck-Vaughn
Surprise Party, The	J	RF	250+	Prager, Annabelle	Random House
Surprise Pet, A	C	F	54	Leveled Readers Language Support	Houghton Mifflin Harcourt
Surprise Snow, The	K	RF	545	Leveled Readers	Houghton Mifflin Harcourt
*Surprise Visit, The	G	F	250+	New Way Blue	Steck-Vaughn
Surprise!	M	RF	882	Gear Up!	Wright Group/McGraw Hill
Surprise!	I	RF	168	Little Celebrations	Pearson Learning Group
Surprise!	D	RF	28	My First Reader	Grolier Press
Surprise!	H	RF	434	Real Kids Readers	Millbrook Press
Surprise!	D	F	28	Story Steps	Rigby
Surprise, The	E	F	225	Leveled Literacy Intervention/ Green System	Heinemann
Surprise, The	H	F	124	Literacy 2000	Rigby
Surprise, The	G	RF	199	Rigby Flying Colors	Rigby
Surprise, The	D	RF	101	Springboard	Wright Group/McGraw Hill
Surprise, The	A	F	14	Story Box	Wright Group/McGraw Hill
Surprising Myself	O	B	250+	Meet The Author	Richard C. Owen
Surprising Sharks	N	I	250+	Read and Wonder	Candlewick Press
Surprising Swimmers: Nature's Most Amazing Animals	R	I	250+	Fredericks, Anthony D.	NorthWord Press
Surprising World of Plants, The	T	I	250+	Pair-It Books	Steck-Vaughn
Surrender	Z+	RF	250+	Hartnett, Sonya	Candlewick Press
Surrender at Appomattox, The	U	I	1530	Leveled Readers Social Studies	Houghton Mifflin Harcourt
Surrender at Yorktown	P	I	250+	Leveled Readers	Houghton Mifflin Harcourt
Surrender at Yorktown	S	I	600	Leveled Readers Social Studies	Houghton Mifflin Harcourt
Survival Animal Adaptations	V	I	250+	iOpeners	Pearson Learning Group
Survival at Plymouth Colony	V	I	2316	Vocabulary Readers	Houghton Mifflin Harcourt
Survival at Plymouth Colony	V	I	2316	Vocabulary Readers/CA	Houghton Mifflin Harcourt
Survival at Plymouth Colony	V	I	2316	Vocabulary Readers/TX	Houghton Mifflin Harcourt
Survival Fun	T	I	250+	High-Fliers	Pacific Learning
Survival in Cyberspace	T	SF	250+	Storyteller - Whispering Pines	Wright Group/McGraw Hill
Survival in the Storm	X	HF	250+	Janke, Katelan	Scholastic
Survival of Fish, The	M	I	946	Sunshine Science	Wright Group/McGraw Hill
Survive	N	RF	250+	Buckton, Chris	Stone Arch Books
Survive!	Q	RF	250+	Wildcats	Wright Group/McGraw Hill
Surviving Hitler: A Boy in the Nazi Death Camps	Y	B	250+	Warren, Andrea	Harper Trophy
Surviving in the Tundra	N	I	747	Springboard	Wright Group/McGraw Hill
Surviving in the Wild	N	I	250+	Rigby Literacy	Rigby
Surviving Jamestown: The Adventures of Young Sam Collier	W	HF	250+	Karwaski, Gail Langer	Peachtree
Surviving the Applewhites	T	RF	250+	Tolan, Stephanie S.	Scholastic
Surviving the Odds	P	I	250+	WorldScapes	ETA Cuisenaire
Surviving the Weather: Animals in Their Environments	R	I	1905	Reading Street	Pearson

* Collection of short stories
# Graphic text

S

TITLE	LEVEL	GENRE	WORD COUNT	AUTHOR / SERIES	PUBLISHER / DISTRIBUTOR
Survivors	X	I	250+	Boldprint	Steck-Vaughn
Survivors in the Frozen North	L	RF	250+	PM Plus Story Books	Rigby
Survivors, The	U	F	250+	Book Blazers	ETA Cuisenaire
Susan B. Anthony	Q	B	250+	Early Biographies	Compass Point Books
Susan B. Anthony	S	B	3840	History Maker Bios	Lerner Publications
Susan B. Anthony	N	B	237	Pebble Books	Capstone Press
Susan B. Anthony	P	B	250+	Photo-Illustrated Biographies	Red Brick Learning
Susan B. Anthony	Q	B	796	Time for Kids	Teacher Created Materials
Susan B. Anthony and Elizabeth Cady Stanton	V	B	250+	Amazing Americans	Wright Group/ McGraw Hill
Susan B. Anthony, Fighter for Women's Rights	N	I	381	Independent Readers Social Studies	Houghton Mifflin Harcourt
Susan B. Anthony: A Life of Fairness	O	B	532	Pull Ahead Books	Lerner Publications
Susan B. Anthony: Champion of Women's Rights	R	B	250+	Monsell, Helen Albee	Simon & Schuster
Susanna of the Alamo	T	B	250+	Jakes, John	Language for Learning Assoc.
Susan's Missing Painting	L	RF	757	Reading Street	Pearson
Susie Goes Shopping	F	F	194	First Start	Troll Associates
Suspense…	Y	I	250+	Boldprint	Steck-Vaughn
Suzie Ridinghood	R	RF	250+	Reading Safari	Mondo
Swamp Explorer	R	I	250+	On Our Way to English	Rigby
Swamp Hen	F	I	59	Pacific Literacy	Pacific Learning
Swamp Monsters	K	F	250+	Christian, Mary Blount	Puffin/Penguin
Swamp of the Hideous Zombies	M	F	250+	Hayes, Geoffrey	Random House
Swamp Stomp	T	RF	250+	Power Up!	Steck-Vaughn
Swampland	N	I	250+	Habitats	Children's Press
Swan Family, The	F	RF	172	PM Plus Story Books	Rigby
Swan Kingdom, The	Z	F	250+	Marriott, Zoe	Candlewick Press
Swan Kingdom, The	Z	F	250+	Marriott, Zoe	Candlewick Press
Swans	D	I	53	Joy Readers	Pearson Learning Group
Swan's Child, The	X	F	250+	Kuyper, Sjoerd	Holiday House
Swat it!	D	F	46	Bauer, Roger	Kaeden Books
SWAT Teams	S	I	250+	Law Enforcement	Capstone Press
Swat Teams	S	I	250+	Line of Duty	Capstone Press
Sweet Bees	F	RF	96	Gear Up!	Wright Group/McGraw Hill
Sweet Clara and the Freedom Quilt	S	HF	250+	Hopkinson, Deborah	Scholastic
Sweet Face's Adventure	K	F	250+	Jasper the Cat	Pioneer Valley
Sweet Mangoes: A Tale from India	M	TL	250+	In Step Readers	Rigby
Sweet Memories Still	Q	RF	250+	Kinsey-Warnock, Natalie	Bantam
Sweet or Sour?	I	I	177	Sunshine	Wright Group/McGraw Hill
Sweet Potato Pie	E	RF	72	Rockwell, Anne	Random House
Sweet to Eat	I	RF	105	Pacific Literacy	Pacific Learning
Sweetest Present, The	E	F	80	Leveled Readers	Houghton Mifflin Harcourt
Sweethearts	Z+	RF	250+	Zarr, Sara	Little, Brown & Co.
Swift Rivers	W	RF	250+	Meigs, Cornelia	Walker & Company
Swift Thief: The Adventure of Velociraptor	N	I	250+	Dinosaur World	Picture Window Books
Swiftly Tilting Planet, A	V	F	250+	L'Engle, Madeleine	Bantam
Swim!	A	I	31	Leveled Literacy Intervention/ Green System	Heinemann
Swim, Climb, and Fly	B	I	30	Sails	Rigby
Swimming	C	RF	65	Carousel Readers	Pearson Learning Group
Swimming	A	I	24	Leveled Readers	Houghton Mifflin Harcourt
Swimming	A	I	24	Leveled Readers/CA	Houghton Mifflin Harcourt
Swimming Across the Pool	J	RF	250+	PM Plus Story Books	Rigby

* Collection of short stories
# Graphic text

S

TITLE	LEVEL	GENRE	WORD COUNT	AUTHOR / SERIES	PUBLISHER / DISTRIBUTOR
Swimming for Fun	S	I	250+	Sports for Fun	Compass Point Books
Swimming Lessons	H	RF	178	Handprints D	Educators Publishing Service
Swimming Lessons	W	RF	2005	Leveled Readers	Houghton Mifflin Harcourt
Swimming Lessons	I	I	200	Storyteller Nonfiction	Wright Group/McGraw Hill
Swimming Pool, The	C	RF	29	Visions	Wright Group/McGraw Hill
Swimming Safely	T	I	2315	Reading Street	Pearson
Swimming Salmon	L	I	393	Pull Ahead Books	Lerner Publications
Swimming Silently	T	SF	2811	Leveled Readers	Houghton Mifflin Harcourt
Swimming Silently	T	SF	2811	Leveled Readers/CA	Houghton Mifflin Harcourt
Swimming with a Dragon	H	RF	230	PM Plus Story Books	Rigby
Swimming with Dolphins	M	I	810	Big Cat	Pacific Learning
Swimming with Dolphins	R	I	1715	Reading Street	Pearson
Swimming with Sharks	N	B	250+	In Step Readers	Rigby
Swimmy	M	F	250+	Lionni, Leo	Scholastic
Swing	A	RF	18	Story Box	Wright Group/McGraw Hill
Swing Dancing	S	I	250+	Dance	Capstone Press
Swing, Swing, Swing	C	F	93	Tuchman, G.; Dieterichs, S.	Scholastic
Swiped	Q	RF	250+	Orca Currents	Orca Book Publishers
Switch It On	S	I	250+	InfoQuest	Rigby
Switcharound	R	RF	250+	Lowry, Lois	Random House
Switzerland	O	I	250+	Countries of the World	Red Brick Learning
Switzerland	B	I	36	Nonfiction Set 2	Literacy Footprints
Swivelhead	P	F	250+	High-Fliers	Pacific Learning
Swoop!	I	RF	250+	PM Plus Story Books	Rigby
Sword in the Stone, The	J	TL	250+	Maccarone, Grace	Scholastic
*Sword of the Samurai: Adventure Stories From Japan	S	HF	250+	Kimmel, Eric A.	HarperCollins
Swords	U	I	250+	Boos, Ben	Candlewick Press
Sybil Ludington's Midnight Ride	N	HF	1851	On My Own History	Lerner Publications
Sydney - Where Biscuits Go Surfing	R	RF	250+	Coy, Michael	Scholastic
Sydney and the Kangaroo	J	F	250+	Rigby Rocket	Rigby
Sylvia Earle and the Deep Ocean	T	B	1370	Leveled Readers	Houghton Mifflin Harcourt
Sylvia Earle and the Deep Ocean	T	B	1370	Leveled Readers/CA	Houghton Mifflin Harcourt
Sylvia Earle, First Lady of the Sea	G	B	98	Independent Readers Science	Houghton Mifflin Harcourt
Symbols of Freedom	O	I	250+	Windows on Literacy	National Geographic
Symmetry in Our World	O	I	250+	Early Connections	Benchmark Education
Symphony of Whales, A	P	RF	250+	Schuch, Steve	Scholastic
Synchro Swans	T	I	250+	WorldScapes	ETA Cuisenaire
Syria: A Question and Answer Book	P	I	250+	Question and Answer Countries	Capstone Press

* Collection of short stories
# Graphic text

TITLE	LEVEL	GENRE	WORD COUNT	AUTHOR / SERIES	PUBLISHER / DISTRIBUTOR
T. J.'s Tree	G	RF	77	Literacy 2000	Rigby
T. Rex	M	I	250+	Read and Wonder	Candlewick Press
T. Rex Trek	L	F	594	Springboard	Wright Group/ McGraw Hill
T. Rex Troy Tells the Tale	M	F	250+	Springboard	Wright Group/McGraw Hill
T. Rex: The Adventure of Tyrannosaurus Rex	N	I	250+	Dinosaur World	Picture Window Books
Tabby	WB	RF	N/A	Aliki	HarperCollins
Tabby Cat at Night	B	RF	39	Brand New Readers	Candlewick Press
Tabby Cat's Scarf	D	RF	41	Brand New Readers	Candlewick Press
Tabby in the Tree	F	RF	200	PM Story Books	Rigby
Table for Two	L	TL	250+	Little Celebrations	Pearson Learning Group
Tactical Fighters: The F-15 Eagles	V	I	250+	War Planes	Capstone Press
Tadpole Diary	O	I	250+	Literacy Tree	Rigby
Tag-Along Tim	J	RF	358	Leveled Readers	Houghton Mifflin Harcourt
Tag-Along Tim	J	RF	358	Leveled Readers/CA	Houghton Mifflin Harcourt
Tag-Along Tim	J	RF	358	Leveled Readers/TX	Houghton Mifflin Harcourt
Taiga Biome, The	U	I	3085	Reading Street	Pearson
Tail of Emily Windsnap, The	T	F	250+	Kessler, Liz	Candlewick Press
Tails	B	I	33	Animal Traits	Lerner Publications
Tails	B	I	42	Book Bank	Wright Group/McGraw Hill
Tails	E	I	59	Bookshop	Mondo
Tails	E	I	59	Discovery Links	Newbridge
Tails	C	I	69	Explorations	Eleanor Curtain Publishing
Tails	C	I	69	Explorations	Okapi Educational Materials
Tails	D	I	108	Leveled Literacy Intervention/ Blue System	Heinemann
Tails	F	I	47	Literacy 2000	Rigby
Tails	B	I	49	Sails	Rigby
Tails	I	I	170	Sunshine	Wright Group/McGraw Hill
Tails	D	I	115	Vocabulary Readers	Houghton Mifflin Harcourt
Tails	D	I	115	Vocabulary Readers/CA	Houghton Mifflin Harcourt
Tails	D	I	52	Wonder World	Wright Group/McGraw Hill
Tails and Claws	C	I	65	Wonder World	Wright Group/McGraw Hill
Tails Can Tell	I	I	346	Wonder World	Wright Group/McGraw Hill
Tails, Tails, Tails	E	I	131	Sails	Rigby
Take a Backyard Bird Walk	U	I	250+	Take a Walk Books	Stillwater Publishing
Take a Bite	C	F	19	Little Celebrations	Pearson Learning Group
Take a Bow, Jody	D	RF	78	Eaton, Audrey; Kennedy, Jane	Continental Press
Take a Chance	X	RF	2464	Leveled Readers	Houghton Mifflin Harcourt
Take a City Nature Walk	U	I	250+	Take a Walk Books	Stillwater Publishing
Take a Guess	C	F	45	Little Celebrations	Pearson Learning Group
Take a Guess	G	I	202	Shutterbug Books	Steck-Vaughn
Take a Guess: A Look at Estimation	K	I	164	Spyglass Books	Compass Point Books
Take a Look	N	I	250+	Wildcats	Wright Group/McGraw Hill
Take a Look at My Family	F	RF	155	Phonics and Friends	Hampton-Brown
Take a Ride	F	I	105	Gear Up!	Wright Group/McGraw Hill
Take a Seat!	L	I	346	Gear Up!	Wright Group/ McGraw Hill
Take a Stand! What You Can Do about Bullying	V	I	7438	Health Zone	Lerner Publications
Take a Tree Walk	U	I	250+	Take a Walk Books	Stillwater Publishing
Take a Trip to China	L	I	301	Vocabulary Readers	Houghton Mifflin Harcourt
Take a Trip to China	L	I	301	Vocabulary Readers/CA	Houghton Mifflin Harcourt
Take a Trip to China	L	I	301	Vocabulary Readers/TX	Houghton Mifflin Harcourt
Take a Walk with Butterflies and Dragonflies	U	I	250+	Take a Walk Books	Stillwater Publishing
Take Away	E	I	81	Yellow Umbrella Books	Red Brick Learning
Take Care of Our Earth	M	I	250+	Pair-It Books	Steck-Vaughn

* Collection of short stories
# Graphic text

TITLE	LEVEL	GENRE	WORD COUNT	AUTHOR / SERIES	PUBLISHER / DISTRIBUTOR
Take Care Out There	Q	I	250+	Orbit Collections	Pacific Learning
Take Me Out to the Ballpark	K	RF	711	Leveled Readers	Houghton Mifflin Harcourt
Take Me Out to the Ballpark	K	RF	711	Leveled Readers/CA	Houghton Mifflin Harcourt
Take Me Out to the Ballpark	K	RF	711	Leveled Readers/TX	Houghton Mifflin Harcourt
Take Me to Your Leader!	L	SF	888	Rigby Gigglers	Rigby
Take the Subway	F	I	111	Vocabulary Readers	Houghton Mifflin Harcourt
Take Two	G	RF	228	PM Math Stories	Rigby
Take-away Puppy, The	G	RF	248	PM Math Stories	Rigby
Takeaway!	G	F	40	Book Bus	Creative Edge
Taken by the Wind	M	RF	250+	Wahman, Joe	Wright Group/McGraw Hill
Taking Care of a Hamster	D	I	65	Leveled Readers Science	Houghton Mifflin Harcourt
Taking Care of Animals	R	I	1343	Leveled Readers	Houghton Mifflin Harcourt
Taking Care of Animals	R	I	1343	Leveled Readers/CA	Houghton Mifflin Harcourt
Taking Care of Animals	R	I	1343	Leveled Readers/TX	Houghton Mifflin Harcourt
Taking Care of Babies	I	I	117	Sails	Rigby
Taking Care of Baby	G	I	159	Discovery Links	Newbridge
Taking Care of Farm Animals	WB	I	N/A	Windows on Literacy	National Geographic
Taking Care of Meli	F	I	205	Leveled Literacy Intervention/ Blue System	Heinemann
Taking Care of My Ears	G	I	137	Keeping Healthy	Capstone Press
Taking Care of My Eyes	G	I	131	Keeping Healthy	Capstone Press
Taking Care of My Hair	G	I	118	Keeping Healthy	Capstone Press
Taking Care of My Hands and Feet	G	I	102	Keeping Healthy	Capstone Press
Taking Care of My Skin	G	I	122	Keeping Healthy	Capstone Press
Taking Care of My Teeth	G	I	125	Keeping Healthy	Capstone Press
Taking Care of Our World	H	I	137	Rosen Real Readers	Rosen Publishing Group
Taking Care of Our World	E	I	137	Visions	Wright Group/McGraw Hill
Taking Care of Ourselves	J	I	250+	PM Plus Nonfiction	Rigby
Taking Care of Pets	B	I	55	Yellow Umbrella Books	Red Brick Learning
Taking Care of Rosie	E	RF	61	Salem, Lynn; Stewart, Josie	Continental Press
Taking Care of Terrific	S	RF	250+	Lowry, Lois	Dell
Taking Care of the Earth	N	I	1274	Reading Street	Pearson
Taking Care of Yoki	R	RF	250+	Campbell, Barbara	HarperTrophy
Taking It to the Extreme	O	I	971	Leveled Readers	Houghton Mifflin Harcourt
Taking It to the Extreme	O	I	971	Leveled Readers/CA	Houghton Mifflin Harcourt
Taking Jason to Grandma's	F	RF	118	Book Bank	Wright Group/McGraw Hill
Taking Liberty	X	HF	250+	Rinaldi, Ann	Simon & Schuster
Taking Our Photo	E	RF	132	Voyages	SRA/McGraw Hill
Taking Photographs	M	I	788	Early Connections	Benchmark Education
Taking Pictures	E	RF	137	Alphakids	Sundance
Taking Pictures	A	F	20	Leveled Readers	Houghton Mifflin Harcourt
Taking Pictures	A	F	20	Leveled Readers/CA	Houghton Mifflin Harcourt
Taking Sides	S	RF	250+	Soto, Gary	Harcourt Trade
Taking to the Air	Q	I	250+	Literacy Tree	Rigby
Taking Turns	E	RF	177	Rigby Flying Colors	Rigby
Taking You Places: A Book About Bus Drivers	H	I	127	Community Workers	Picture Window Books
Tale of Cowboy	A	RF	31	Reading Unlimited	Pearson Learning Group
Tale of Cowboy Roy, The	H	F	185	Ready Readers	Pearson Learning Group
Tale of Despereaux, The	U	F	250+	DiCamillo, Kate	Candlewick Press
Tale of Peter Rabbit, The	L	TL	250+	Potter, Beatrix	Scholastic
Tale of Sir Spiffing Biffing, The	M	F	250+	Rigby Rocket	Rigby
Tale of the Christmas Mouse	H	F	97	First Start	Troll Associates
Tale of the Golden Goose, The	L	TL	250+	Behr, Alexandra	Hampton-Brown
Tale of the Swamp Rat	T	F	250+	Crocker, Carter	Philomel Books

* Collection of short stories
# Graphic text

TITLE	LEVEL	GENRE	WORD COUNT	AUTHOR / SERIES	PUBLISHER / DISTRIBUTOR
Tale of the Turnip, The	I	TL	250+	PM Traditional Tales-Orange	Rigby
Tale of Travelers	O	TL	250+	Literacy by Design	Rigby
Tale of Veruschka Babuschka, The	M	TL	250+	Literacy 2000	Rigby
Talent Contest, The	K	RF	250+	PM Story Books-Silver	Rigby
Talent Night at School	F	RF	102	Little Red Readers	Sundance
Talent Show	N	RF	250+	Girlz Rock!	Mondo
Talent Show	E	F	227	Leveled Literacy Intervention/ Green System	Heinemann
Talent Show from the Black Lagoon, The	N	F	250+	Thayler, Mike	Scholastic
Talented Alex	O	RF	772	Leveled Readers	Houghton Mifflin Harcourt
Tales for Hard Times: A Story About Charles Dickens	R	B	8559	Creative Minds Biographies	Carolrhoda Books
Tales from Gull Island	U	RF	250+	Power Up!	Steck-Vaughn
Tales from Near and Far	P	TL	250+	Literacy by Design	Rigby
*Tales from the Homeplace: Adventures of a Texas Farm Girl	S	RF	250+	Burandt, Harriet; Dale, Shelley	Bantam
Tales from the Odyssey	Z	TL	3197	Leveled Readers	Houghton Mifflin Harcourt
Tales from the Odyssey	Z	TL	3197	Leveled Readers/CA	Houghton Mifflin Harcourt
*Tales from the Underground Railroad	S	HF	250+	Connell, Kate	Steck-Vaughn
Tales from the Waterhole	L	F	250+	Candlewick Sparks	Candlewick Press
Tales Mummies Tell	W	I	250+	Lauber, Patricia	Scholastic
Tales of a Fourth Grade Nothing	Q	RF	250+	Blume, Judy	Bantam
*Tales of Amanda Pig	L	F	250+	Van Leeuwen, Jean	Puffin/Penguin
Tales of Hercules	U	TL	1315	Leveled Readers	Houghton Mifflin Harcourt
Tales of Hercules	U	TL	1315	Leveled Readers/CA	Houghton Mifflin Harcourt
Tales of Olga da Polga, The	P	F	250+	Bond, Michael	Houghton Mifflin Harcourt
*Tales of Oliver Pig	L	F	250+	Van Leeuwen, Jean	Puffin/Penguin
Tales of Real Escape	X	B	250+	Dowswell, Paul	Scholastic
*Tales of the Full Moon	R	TL	250+	Hart, Sue	Fulcrum Publishing
Tales, Fables and Rhymes	N	I	250+	Tristars	Richard C. Owen
Talk About a Family	O	RF	250+	Greenfield, Eloise	HarperTrophy
Talk Back	U	I	250+	The News	Richard C. Owen
Talk! Talk! Talk!	N	I	50	Little Celebrations	Pearson Learning Group
Talk, Talk, Talk	C	RF	56	Literacy 2000	Rigby
Talkin' About Bessie: The Story of Aviator Elizabeth Coleman	S	B	250+	Grimes, Nikki	Scholastic
Talking Earth, The	U	RF	250+	George, Jean Craighead	HarperTrophy
Talking Eggs, The	P	TL	250+	San Souci, Robert D.	Scholastic
Talking to Faith Ringgold	S	B	250+	Ringgold, Faith; Freeman, Linda; Roucher, Nancy	Crown
Talking to Our Friends	F	I	138	Rigby Focus	Rigby
Talking to the Animals	J	F	360	InfoTrek	ETA Cuisenaire
Talking Yam, The	I	F	340	Little Readers	Houghton Mifflin Harcourt
Tall	I	I	249	Sails	Rigby
Tall Stories About Snakes	G	I	141	Voyages	SRA/McGraw Hill
Tall Tails: Cross-Country with Lewis and Clark	Q	F	250+	Smith, Donna	Scholastic
*Tall Tale and Other Cases, The	O	RF	250+	Simon, Seymour	Avon
Tall Tale of John Henry, The	N	TL	250+	Neufeld, David	Scholastic
Tall Tale to Tell, A	O	I	860	Independent Readers Social Studies	Houghton Mifflin Harcourt
Tall Tale Tuesday	M	RF	825	Leveled Readers	Houghton Mifflin Harcourt
Tall Tale Tuesday	M	RF	825	Leveled Readers/CA	Houghton Mifflin Harcourt
Tall Tale Tuesday	M	RF	825	Leveled Readers/TX	Houghton Mifflin Harcourt
Tall Tales	I	RF	139	Literacy Tree	Rigby

* Collection of short stories
\# Graphic text

TITLE	LEVEL	GENRE	WORD COUNT	AUTHOR / SERIES	PUBLISHER / DISTRIBUTOR
Tall Tales	O	RF	250+	PM Collection	Rigby
Tall Tales	O	TL	615	Vocabulary Readers	Houghton Mifflin Harcourt
Tall Things	D	I	83	PM Nonfiction-Red	Rigby
Tall Tony	K	RF	383	Leveled Readers	Houghton Mifflin Harcourt
Talladega Superspeedway	S	I	250+	NASCAR Racing	Capstone Press
Tallahassee Higgins	T	RF	250+	Hahn, Mary Downing	Clarion Books
Taller and Smaller	D	F	29	Sun Sprouts	ETA Cuisenaire
Taller Than Molly	C	F	43	Harry's Math Books	Outside the Box
Tallest Boy in the Class, The	J	RF	396	Leveled Readers Language Support	Houghton Mifflin Harcourt
Tallest Sunflower, The	I	I	250+	Counters & Seekers	Steck-Vaughn
Tallest Tower, The	M	F	250+	Bookweb	Rigby
Tallest Tower, The	J	HF	304	Leveled Readers	Houghton Mifflin Harcourt
Tallest Tower, The	J	HF	304	Leveled Readers/CA	Houghton Mifflin Harcourt
Tallest Tower, The	J	HF	304	Leveled Readers/TX	Houghton Mifflin Harcourt
Tallgrass Prairie, The	P	I	873	Gear Up!	Wright Group/ McGraw Hill
Tally Charts	K	I	250+	Making Graphs	Capstone Press
Tam and Sam Go to the Zoo	B	RF	32	Reading Street	Pearson
Tam and Sam in the Orange Grove	D	RF	36	Reading Street	Pearson
Tam at the Beach	B	RF	29	Reading Street	Pearson
Tame and Wild	I	I	180	Sails	Rigby
Tame and Wild	L	I	306	Spyglass Books	Compass Point Books
Tamika and the Wisdom Rings	O	RF	250+	Yarbrough, Camille	Random House
Taming the Star Runner	Z	RF	250+	Hinton, S. E.	Laurel-Leaf Books
Tammy Toodlepepper Paints the Town	I	RF	250+	Reading Safari	Mondo
Tammy Toodlepepper to the Rescue	T	F	250+	Reading Safari	Mondo
Tammy Toodlepepper, Collector	P	RF	250+	Reading Safari	Mondo
Tammy's Goal	N	RF	921	Leveled Readers	Houghton Mifflin Harcourt
Tammy's Goal	N	RF	921	Leveled Readers/CA	Houghton Mifflin Harcourt
Tammy's Goal	N	RF	921	Leveled Readers/TX	Houghton Mifflin Harcourt
Tampa Bay Buccaneers, The	S	I	250+	Team Spirit	Norwood House Press
Tampa Bay Rays, The	S	I	250+	Team Spirit	Norwood House Press
Tangerine	U	RF	250+	Bloor, Edward	Scholastic
Tangle Wreck	W	F	250+	Winterson, Jeanette	Bloomsbury Children's Books
Tangled Threads: A Hmong Girl's Story	Z	RF	250+	Shea, Pegi Deitz	Clarion
Tania's Tooth	I	RF	131	Sunshine	Wright Group/McGraw Hill
Tanks	H	I	102	Mighty Machines	Capstone Press
Tanks	V	I	4716	Military Hardware in Action	Lerner Publications
Tanks	N	I	386	Pull Ahead Books	Lerner Publications
Tanya on Track	U	RF	1978	Leveled Readers	Houghton Mifflin Harcourt
Tap Dancing	S	I	250+	Dance	Capstone Press
Tap into Sap	O	I	250+	InfoQuest	Rigby
Tapping Tale, The	E	RF	93	Green Light Readers	Harcourt
Tar Beach	P	HF	250+	Ringgold, Faith	Crown
Tarantula	K	I	144	Alphakids	Sundance
Tarantula in My Purse, The	S	B	250+	George, Jean Craighead	HarperCollins
Tarantula Power!	N	RF	250+	Nagda, Ann Whitehead	Holiday House
Tarantulas	O	I	1708	Early Bird Nature Books	Lerner Publications
Tarantulas	K	I	97	Pebble Books	Red Brick Learning
Tarantulas Are Spiders	F	I	39	Bookshop	Mondo
Tarantulas!	K	I	250+	On Our Way to English	Rigby
Tasmanian Devils	P	I	2075	Animal Scavengers	Lerner Publishing
Tasmanian Devils	R	I	250+	Orbit Chapter Books	Pacific Learning

* Collection of short stories
# Graphic text

TITLE	LEVEL	GENRE	WORD COUNT	AUTHOR / SERIES	PUBLISHER / DISTRIBUTOR
Tasmanian Devils	M	I	250+	PM Animal Facts: Gold	Rigby
Tasmanian Tiger	N	I	250+	Extinct Monsters	Capstone Press
Taste Bud Travels	O	I	250+	Bookweb	Rigby
Taste of America	T	I	250+	iOpeners	Pearson Learning Group
Taste of Blackberries, A	S	RF	250+	Smith, Doris Buchanan	Scholastic
Taste of Salt: The Story of Modern Haiti	W	I	250+	Temple, Frances	HarperTrophy
Taste of the Domincan Republic, A	S	I	675	Vocabulary Readers	Houghton Mifflin Harcourt
Taste of the Dominican Republic, A	S	I	675	Vocabulary Readers/CA	Houghton Mifflin Harcourt
Taste Sensation	E	I	115	Visions	Wright Group/McGraw Hill
Taste Test, The	G	I	215	PM Science Readers	Rigby
Tasting	I	I	141	Pebble Books	Red Brick Learning
Tasting	E	I	79	Senses	Lerner Publishing
Tasting	M	I	250+	The Senses	Capstone Press
Tasty Bug, A	D	I	50	Little Celebrations	Pearson Learning Group
Tattercoat and the Magical Flute, A Cinderella Tale from England	M	TL	692	Leveled Readers Language Support	Houghton Mifflin Harcourt
Tattercoat, A Cinderella Tale from England	N	TL	692	Leveled Readers	Houghton Mifflin Harcourt
Taxi, The	C	F	45	Joy Readers	Pearson Learning Group
T-Ball	D	RF	35	Visions	Wright Group/McGraw Hill
Tchin the Storyteller	N	B	269	Vocabulary Readers	Houghton Mifflin Harcourt
Tea	K	I	267	Wonder World	Wright Group/McGraw Hill
Tea Leaves	O	RF	250+	Bookshop	Mondo
Tea Overboard! The Boston Tea Party	V	I	1753	Leveled Readers	Houghton Mifflin Harcourt
Tea Party	C	RF	38	Carousel Readers	Pearson Learning Group
Tea Party, The	C	F	76	Storyteller-First Snow	Wright Group/McGraw Hill
Teach Us, Amelia Bedelia	L	F	250+	Parish, Peggy	Scholastic
Teacher	C	I	22	Work People Do	Lerner Publishing
Teacher from the Black Lagoon, The	K	F	250+	Thaler, Mike	Scholastic
Teacher Named Confucius, A	W	I	2106	Leveled Readers	Houghton Mifflin Harcourt
Teacher Named Confucius, A	W	I	2106	Leveled Readers/CA	Houghton Mifflin Harcourt
Teacher Talk	H	RF	68	City Stories	Rigby
Teacher, The	G	I	155	PM Nonfiction-Blue	Rigby
Teachers	M	I	250+	Community Helpers	Red Brick Learning
Teachers	L	I	250+	Community Workers	Compass Point Books
Teachers	J	I	547	Pull Ahead Books	Lerner Publications
Teachers at Our School	I	RF	115	City Kids	Rigby
Teacher's Funeral, The	V	HF	250+	Peck, Richard	Puffin Books
Teacher's Pet	L	F	250+	Dicks, Terrance	Scholastic
Teacher's Pet	O	RF	250+	Hurwitz, Johanna	Scholastic
Teachers: Then and Now	O	I	250+	Primary Source Readers	Teacher Created Materials
Team of Two, A	P	I	566	Vocabulary Readers	Houghton Mifflin Harcourt
Team Player, The	S	RF	1115	Leveled Readers	Houghton Mifflin Harcourt
Team Players	Q	I	555	Vocabulary Readers	Houghton Mifflin Harcourt
Team Sports	B	I	23	Twig	Wright Group/McGraw Hill
Team Supper, The	X	RF	3216	Leveled Readers	Houghton Mifflin Harcourt
Team Supper, The	X	RF	3216	Leveled Readers/CA	Houghton Mifflin Harcourt
Team Work	C	F	112	Leveled Readers	Houghton Mifflin Harcourt
Team Work	C	F	112	Leveled Readers/CA	Houghton Mifflin Harcourt
Teaming Up	R	I	250+	Power Up!	Steck-Vaughn
Teammates	S	B	250+	Golenbock, Peter	Harcourt Brace
Teamwork	L	RF	929	PM Plus Story Books	Rigby
Teamwork	F	I	148	Yellow Umbrella Books	Capstone Press
Teamwork Saves the Day	K	RF	250+	On Our Way to English	Rigby
Tearing Down the Kingdom	P	I	250+	Rigby Literacy	Rigby

* Collection of short stories
\# Graphic text

TITLE	LEVEL	GENRE	WORD COUNT	AUTHOR / SERIES	PUBLISHER / DISTRIBUTOR
Tears of a Tiger	Z	RF	250+	Draper, Sharon M.	Simon & Schuster
Teasing Dad	F	RF	158	PM Extensions-Blue	Rigby
Teasing Mom	H	RF	239	PM Plus Story Books	Rigby
Tec and the Hole	B	RF	28	Big Cat	Pacific Learning
Technology Today	J	I	166	Early Connections	Benchmark Education
Technology: Past and Present	K	I	250+	Literacy by Design	Rigby
Technosports	P	I	250+	Bookweb	Rigby
Tecumseh	V	B	250+	Cornerstones of Freedom	Children's Press
Tecumseh	S	B	3702	History Maker Bios	Lerner Publications
Tecumseh: Shawnee Leader	V	B	250+	Let Freedom Ring	Capstone Press
Tedd & Huggly	C	F	47	Canizares, Susan; Berger, Samantha	Scholastic
Teddy Bear for Sale	G	F	152	Herman, Gail	Scholastic
Teddy Bear, Teddy Bear	E	F	38	Tiger Cub	Peguis
Teddy Bear, The	B	I	56	Rigby Flying Colors	Rigby
Teddy Bears	I	I	180	Purkis, Sallie	Nelson/Michaels Assoc.
Teddy Bears at School!	I	RF	304	InfoTrek	ETA Cuisenaire
Teddy Bears Cure a Cold	K	F	240	Gretz, Susanna	Scholastic
Teddy Bear's Picnic	D	F	66	PM Plus Story Books	Rigby
Teddy's Sticky Mess	K	F	639	Sun Sprouts	ETA Cuisenaire
Ted's Letter	E	RF	76	Dominie Phonics Reader	Pearson Learning Group
Ted's Red Ball	G	F	131	Supersonics	Rigby
Ted's Red Sled	D	RF	69	Ready Readers	Pearson Learning Group
Tee Off	U	I	250+	WorldScapes	ETA Cuisenaire
Tee-Ball	C	RF	53	Little Celebrations	Pearson Learning Group
Teen's Guide to Working, A	X	I	250+	Power Up!	Steck-Vaughn
Teens in South Africa	Z+	I	250+	Global Connections	Compass Point Books
Teeny Tiny	I	TL	250+	Bennett, Jill	Putnam/Penguin
Teeny Tiny	H	TL	250+	Rigby Literacy	Rigby
Teeny Tiny Taste, A	H	RF	112	City Stories	Rigby
Teeny Tiny Tina	C	F	34	Literacy 2000	Rigby
Teeny Tiny Woman, The	F	TL	250+	O'Connor, Jane	Random House
Teeny Tiny Woman, The	J	TL	369	Seuling, Barbara	Scholastic
Teeny-Tiny Woman, The	H	TL	231	Ziefert, Harriet	Puffin/Penguin
Teeter-Totter, The	C	TL	35	Joy Readers	Pearson Learning Group
Teeth	N	I	250+	Literacy By Design	Rigby
Teeth	N	I	250+	Rigby Literacy	Rigby
Teeth	D	I	71	Story Box	Wright Group/McGraw Hill
Teeth	K	I	470	Sunshine	Wright Group/McGraw Hill
Teeth	J	I	188	Take Two Books	Wright Group/McGraw Hill
Teeth	C	I	26	Wonder World	Wright Group/McGraw Hill
Telephone	S	I	250+	Theme Sets	National Geographic
Telephone, The	P	I	250+	Great Inventions	Red Brick Learning
Telephone, The	J	I	167	Reading Street	Pearson
Telephone, The: A Great Invention	J	I	165	Leveled Readers Social Studies	Houghton Mifflin Harcourt
Telephones	O	I	250+	Let's See	Compass Point Books
Telephones Through Time	N	I	654	Reading Street	Pearson
Telescope, The; Looking into Space	R	I	250+	On Deck	Rigby
Television	O	I	250+	Let's See	Compass Point Books
Television	S	I	250+	Theme Sets	National Geographic
Television Drama	Q	RF	250+	Literacy 2000	Rigby
Television, The	Q	I	250+	Great Inventions	Capstone Press
Television, The: Window to the World	R	I	250+	On Deck	Rigby
Tell	Y	RF	250+	Orca Soundings	Orca Book Publishers

* Collection of short stories
# Graphic text

TITLE	LEVEL	GENRE	WORD COUNT	AUTHOR / SERIES	PUBLISHER / DISTRIBUTOR
Tell All About It	A	F	27	Leveled Readers	Houghton Mifflin Harcourt
Tell All About It	A	F	27	Leveled Readers/CA	Houghton Mifflin Harcourt
Tell It in Code	I	I	166	Vocabulary Readers	Houghton Mifflin Harcourt
Tell It in Code	L	I	166	Vocabulary Readers/CA	Houghton Mifflin Harcourt
Tell It to a Friend	K	I	250+	Home Connection Collection	Rigby
Tell Me a Story	R	I	250+	InfoQuest	Rigby
Tell Me a Story	O	B	250+	Meet The Author	Richard C. Owen
Tell Me a Story	J	RF	236	Voyages	SRA/McGraw Hill
Tell Me a Story, Grandpa	L	RF	250+	Little Celebrations	Pearson Learning Group
Tell Me a Story, Mama	L	RF	250+	Johnson, Angela	Scholastic
Tell Me About Turtles	D	I	31	Rosen Real Readers	Rosen Publishing Group
Tell Me No Lies	Q	RF	250+	Ragged Island Mysteries	Wright Group/McGraw Hill
Tell Me Why Planes Have Wings	O	I	250+	Whiz Kids	Franklin Watts
Tell Them We Remember	Y	I	250+	Bachrach, Susan D.	Little, Brown & Co.
Tell Us a Tale, Hans!: The Life of Hans Christian Andersen	R	B	250+	Bookshop	Mondo
Telling Stories Through Art	N	I	250+	Take Two Books	Wright Group/McGraw Hill
Telling the Truth	H	RF	229	PM Stars	Rigby
Telling Time Through the Ages	Q	I	250+	Navigators Social Studies Series	Benchmark Education
Tell-tale	H	RF	250+	Story Box	Wright Group/McGraw Hill
Temperate Climate	R	I	250+	Theme Sets	National Geographic
Temperate Forests	Q	I	250+	Ecosystems	Red Brick Learning
Temperate Forests	S	I	250+	Theme Sets	National Geographic
Temperature	P	I	250+	Our Physical World	Capstone Press
Temperature: Heating Up and Cooling Down	M	I	250+	Amazing Science	Picture Window Books
Ten Apples Up on Top	J	F	250+	LeSieg, Theo	Random House
Ten Bears in My Bed	G	F	252	Mack, Stan	Pantheon
Ten Black Dots	I	I	176	Crews, Donald	Greenwillow
Ten Blue Things	F	I	193	InfoTrek	ETA Cuisenaire
Ten Cats Have Hats: A Counting Book	E	F	89	Marzollo, Jean	Scholastic
Ten Crazy Caterpillars	C	F	40	Voyages	SRA/McGraw Hill
Ten Easy Tips for Staying Safe	L	I	250+	Rosen Real Readers	Rosen Publishing Group
Ten Frogs for the Pond	F	I	193	PM Math Readers	Rigby
Ten Happy Elephants	I	F	201	Sunshine	Wright Group/McGraw Hill
Ten Little Bears	G	F	211	Reading Unlimited	Pearson Learning Group
Ten Little Caterpillars	F	F	102	Literacy 2000	Rigby
Ten Little Chickens	F	RF	170	InfoTrek	ETA Cuisenaire
Ten Little Garden Snails	H	F	101	PM Story Books	Rigby
Ten Little Men	E	F	38	Literacy 2000	Rigby
Ten Loopy Caterpillars	I	F	191	Jellybeans	Rigby
Ten Minutes Till Bedtime	LB	RF	16	Rathmann, Peggy	Putnam/Penguin
Ten O'Clock Club, The	N	F	250+	York, Carol Beach	Scholastic
Ten Oni Drummers	M	F	157	Bebop Books	Lee & Low Books Inc.
Ten Red Sleds	D	RF	82	Reading Street	Pearson
Ten Sleepy Sheep	G	F	65	Keller, Holly	Greenwillow
Ten Traveling Tigers	H	F	165	Little Readers	Houghton Mifflin Harcourt
*Ten True Animal Rescues	O	I	250+	Betancourt, Jeanne	Scholastic
Ten Yellow Buses	H	RF	146	Twig	Wright Group/McGraw Hill
Ten, Nine, Eight	H	RF	59	Bang, Molly	Scholastic
Ten-Book Summer	T	RF	250+	Power Up!	Steck-Vaughn
Tenement Writer, The: An Immigrant's Story	T	I	250+	Sonder, Ben	Steck-Vaughn
Ten-Gallon Hat, The	K	F	250+	Voyages	SRA/McGraw Hill
Tennessee	T	I	250+	Hello U.S.A.	Lerner Publications
Tennessee	R	I	250+	This Land Is Your Land	Compass Point Books

T

* Collection of short stories
# Graphic text

TITLE	LEVEL	GENRE	WORD COUNT	AUTHOR / SERIES	PUBLISHER / DISTRIBUTOR
Tennessee Summer	R	RF	2198	Leveled Readers	Houghton Mifflin Harcourt
Tennessee Titans, The	S	I	250+	Team Spirit	Norwood House Press
Tennessee Tornado, The: Wilma Rudolph	T	B	2097	Leveled Readers	Houghton Mifflin Harcourt
Tennis	K	I	250+	On Deck	Rigby
Tennis Ace	N	RF	250+	Boyz Rule!	Mondo
Tennis Lessons	M	RF	250+	Rigby Flying Colors	Rigby
Tennis Match, The	D	F	85	Springboard	Wright Group/McGraw Hill
Ten-Second Race, The	F	F	102	Learn to Read	Creative Teaching Press
Tent, The	V	RF	250+	Paulsen, Gary	Bantam
Tents	I	RF	175	Reading Unlimited	Pearson Learning Group
Tents	I	I	319	Sails	Rigby
Teotihuacan: Designing an Ancient Mexican City	T	I	250+	Math for the Real World	Rosen Publishing Group
Termites	I	RF	130	Books for Young Learners	Richard C. Owen
Termites	I	I	72	Pebble Books	Red Brick Learning
Termites	I	I	226	Sails	Rigby
Termites: Hardworking Insect Families	T	I	2520	Insect World	Lerner Publications
Terra-Cotta Army	P	I	920	Vocabulary Readers	Houghton Mifflin Harcourt
Terra-Cotta Army	P	I	920	Vocabulary Readers/CA	Houghton Mifflin Harcourt
Terrible Armadillo	I	F	229	Jellybeans	Rigby
Terrible Fright, A	K	TL	291	Story Box	Wright Group/McGraw Hill
Terrible Power of House Rabbit, The	O	F	250+	High-Fliers	Pacific Learning
*Terrible Test Mark and Other Cases, The	O	RF	250+	Simon, Seymour	Avon
Terrible Tiger	G	F	124	Rigby Literacy	Rigby
Terrible Tiger	G	F	133	Rigby Star	Rigby
*Terrible Tiger and Sleeping Beauty	L	TL	250+	New Way Literature	Steck-Vaughn
Terrible Tiger, The	G	F	140	Sunshine	Wright Group/McGraw Hill
Terrible Times	U	F	250+	Ardagh, Philip	Scholastic
Terrible Twos	E	RF	86	Tadpoles	Rigby
Terrific Shoes	C	RF	19	Ready Readers	Pearson Learning Group
Terrific Trees	K	I	250+	Rigby Literacy	Rigby
Terror at Turtle Mountain	W	HF	250+	Draper, Penny	Fitzhenry & Whiteside
Terror Bird	N	I	250+	Extinct Monsters	Capstone Press
Terror in the Towers	O	I	250+	Kerson, Adrian	Random House
Terror of the Pink Dodo Balloons, The	O	F	250+	David, Lawrence	Puffin/Penguin
Terror World	Q	F	1350	Norman, Tony	Stone Arch Books
Tess and Paddy	J	RF	242	Sunshine	Wright Group/McGraw Hill
Tess and the Cat	D	RF	81	Sun Sprouts	ETA Cuisenaire
Test of Time, The	R	I	250+	InfoQuest	Rigby
Texas	T	I	250+	Hello U.S.A.	Lerner Publications
Texas	S	I	250+	Land of Liberty	Red Brick Learning
Texas	Q	I	250+	One Nation	Capstone Press
Texas	R	I	250+	This Land Is Your Land	Compass Point Books
Texas Rangers, The	S	I	250+	Team Spirit	Norwood House Press
Textiles from Around the World	Q	I	851	Leveled Readers	Houghton Mifflin Harcourt
Textiles from Around the World	Q	I	851	Leveled Readers/CA	Houghton Mifflin Harcourt
Textiles from Around the World	Q	I	851	Leveled Readers/TX	Houghton Mifflin Harcourt
Thailand	O	I	250+	Countries of the World	Red Brick Learning
Thank You	J	I	250+	Ready to Read	Pacific Learning
Thank You!	D	I	41	Chessen, Betsey; Chanko, Pamela	Scholastic
Thank You, Amelia Bedelia	L	F	250+	Little Readers	Houghton Mifflin Harcourt
Thank You, Jackie Robinson	P	B	250+	Cohen, Barbara	Scholastic
Thank You, Nicky!	F	F	119	Ziefert, Harriet	Penguin Group
Thank You, Sandra Cisneros	N	RF	250+	Leveled Readers	Houghton Mifflin Harcourt

* Collection of short stories
# Graphic text

TITLE	LEVEL	GENRE	WORD COUNT	AUTHOR / SERIES	PUBLISHER / DISTRIBUTOR
Thankful for My Family	V	HF	2609	Leveled Readers	Houghton Mifflin Harcourt
Thankful for My Family	V	HF	2609	Leveled Readers/CA	Houghton Mifflin Harcourt
Thanks to Sandra Cisneros	O	RF	940	Leveled Readers Language Support	Houghton Mifflin Harcourt
Thanksgiving	Q	I	250+	Celebrate!	Capstone Press
Thanksgiving	E	I	95	Fiesta Holiday Series	Pearson Learning Group
Thanksgiving	B	F	40	First Stories	Pacific Learning
Thanksgiving	K	I	250+	Holidays and Celebrations	Picture Window Books
Thanksgiving	J	I	181	Holidays and Celebrations	Capstone Press
Thanksgiving	O	I	250+	Holidays and Festivals	Compass Point Books
Thanksgiving	P	I	250+	Let's See	Compass Point Books
Thanksgiving	F	F	75	Urmston, Kathleen; Evans, Karen	Kaeden Books
Thanksgiving Day	M	I	250+	Holiday Histories	Heinemann Library
Thanksgiving Day	H	I	218	Literacy by Design	Rigby
Thanksgiving Day	L	I	132	National Holidays	Red Brick Learning
Thanksgiving Day	LB	I	12	Shutterbug Books	Steck-Vaughn
Thanksgiving: Why We Celebrate It the Way We Do	P	I	250+	Hintz, Martin & Kate	Red Brick Learning
Thao Kham, the Pebble Shooter	M	TL	250+	Story Vines	Wright Group/McGraw Hill
That Bear Is Back!	K	F	493	Rigby Gigglers	Rigby
That Cat	D	I	52	Bonnell, Kris	Reading Reading Books
That Cat	B	RF	56	First Stories	Pacific Learning
That Cat!	G	RF	146	Ready Readers	Pearson Learning Group
That Cat!	I	RF	418	Real Kids Readers	Millbrook Press
That Dog!	G	RF	213	Foundations	Wright Group/McGraw Hill
That Fat Hat	K	F	250+	Barkan, Joanne	Scholastic
That Fly	C	F	26	Ready Readers	Pearson Learning Group
That Is Math!	E	I	84	On Our Way to English	Rigby
That Is Not My Hat!	K	RF	1418	Real Kids Readers	Millbrook Press
That Is Symmetry!	G	I	190	On Our Way to English	Rigby
That Looks Different!	K	I	227	Windows on Literacy	National Geographic
That Old House	K	F	250+	Rigby Literacy	Rigby
That Pig Can't Do a Thing	F	F	83	Ready Readers	Pearson Learning Group
That Wild Berries Should Grow	U	HF	250+	Whelan, Gloria	Eerdman's Books for Young Readers
*That's a Laugh: Four Funny Fables	M	TL	250+	Literacy 2000	Rigby
That's a Wacky Idea	R	I	1500	Vocabulary Readers	Houghton Mifflin Harcourt
That's a Wacky Idea	R	I	1500	Vocabulary Readers/CA	Houghton Mifflin Harcourt
That's a Wacky Idea	R	I	1500	Vocabulary Readers/TX	Houghton Mifflin Harcourt
That's About Right: A Book About Estimating	S	I	250+	On Our Way to English	Rigby
That's Dangerous	D	F	71	Voyages	SRA/McGraw Hill
That's Determination!	L	RF	250+	Rigby Literacy	Rigby
That's Disgusting!	Y	I	250+	Boldprint	Steck-Vaughn
That's Easy	F	F	205	Handprints D, Set 1	Educators Publishing Service
That's Exercise	D	RF	59	Gear Up!	Wright Group/McGraw Hill
That's Fair, Bear	H	F	250+	Sun Sprouts	ETA Cuisenaire
That's Hard, That's Easy	H	RF	393	Real Kids Readers	Millbrook Press
That's HOT!	L	I	250+	Spyglass Books	Compass Point Books
That's It!	S	I	250+	Orbit Collections	Pacific Learning
That's Mine!	LB	RF	15	Rigby Literacy	Rigby
That's Mine!	LB	RF	15	Rigby Star	Rigby
That's Not All	G	F	105	Start to Read	School Zone
That's Not My Hobby!	J	RF	250+	Rigby Literacy	Rigby

* Collection of short stories
# Graphic text

TITLE	LEVEL	GENRE	WORD COUNT	AUTHOR / SERIES	PUBLISHER / DISTRIBUTOR
That's Not My Hobby!	J	RF	250+	Rigby Star	Rigby
That's Not Our Dog	I	RF	250+	PM Plus Story Books	Rigby
That's Our Custodian!	M	I	992	That's Our School	Millbrook Press
That's Our Librarian!	M	I	734	That's Our School	Millbrook Press
That's Our Nurse!	M	I	866	That's Our School	Millbrook Press
That's Our Principal!	M	I	593	That's Our School	Millbrook Press
That's Our Teacher!	M	I	608	That's Our School	Millbrook Press
That's Really Weird!	K	F	129	Read Alongs	Rigby
That's Some Sun!	O	I	250+	Literacy By Design	Rigby
That's the Life!	I	RF	216	Storyteller	Wright Group/McGraw Hill
That's Us	G	I	172	Sails	Rigby
That's Working Together!	G	I	235	Shutterbug Books	Steck-Vaughn
The Great Divide	N	I	347	Yellow Umbrella Books	Red Brick Learning
Theater Actors: Then and Now	Q	I	250+	Primary Source Readers	Teacher Created Materials
Theater, The	P	I	840	Leveled Readers	Houghton Mifflin Harcourt
Theater, The	P	I	840	Leveled Readers/CA	Houghton Mifflin Harcourt
Theft in Time, A: Timedetectors II	V	HF	250+	Action Packs	Rigby
Then & Now	C	I	60	Berger, Samantha; Moreton, Daniel	Scholastic
Then Again, Maybe I Won't	T	RF	250+	Blume, Judy	Language for Learning Assoc.
Then and Now	J	I	250+	Discovery World	Rigby
Then and Now	J	RF	250+	Early Connections	Benchmark Education
Then and Now	H	I	250+	iOpeners	Pearson Learning Group
Then and Now	H	I	241	Rigby Rocket	Rigby
Theodore	D	F	35	Ray's Readers	Outside the Box
Theodore Roosevelt	R	B	250+	Amazing Americans	Wright Group/McGraw Hill
Theodore Roosevelt	S	B	3356	History Maker Bios	Lerner Publications
Theodore Roosevelt	N	B	208	Pebble Books	Capstone Press
Theodore Roosevelt	P	B	250+	Photo-Illustrated Biographies	Red Brick Learning
Theodore Roosevelt	U	B	250+	Profiles of the Presidents	Compass Point Books
#Theodore Roosevelt: Bear of a President	R	B	250+	Graphic Library	Capstone Press
Theodore Roosevelt: Friend of Nature	P	B	756	Leveled Readers	Houghton Mifflin Harcourt
Theodore Roosevelt: Twenty-sixth President	R	B	250+	Getting to Know the U.S. Presidents	Children's Press
Theodosia and the Serpents of Chaos	X	F	250+	LaFeuers, R.L.	Houghton Mifflin Harcourt
Therapy Dogs to the Rescue	L	I	250+	Rigby Literacy	Rigby
There Are Mice in Our School	I	RF	95	City Kids	Rigby
There Are No Polar Bears Down There	G	I	48	Voyages	SRA/McGraw Hill
There Are Spots On . . .	LB	I	14	Little Books for Early Readers	University of Maine
There Are Things I Don't Know	P	RF	250+	On Our Way To English	Rigby
There Goes Peanut Butter!	C	RF	22	Ketch, Ann	Kaeden Books
There Is a Planet	C	I	52	Sunshine	Wright Group/McGraw Hill
There Is a Town	D	RF	116	Herman, Gail	Random House
There Is No Water	J	RF	250+	Home Connection Collection	Rigby
There She Blows!	T	I	250+	Orbit Chapter Books	Pacific Learning
There Stood Our Dog	I	F	250+	Voyages	SRA/McGraw Hill
There Was a Crooked Man	E	F	40	Sunshine	Wright Group/McGraw Hill
There Was a Mouse	D	RF	77	Books for Young Learners	Richard C. Owen
There's a Bear in My Chair	H	F	193	Magoun, James	Kaeden Books
There's a Boy in the Girls' Bathroom	Q	RF	250+	Sachar, Louis	Alfred A. Knopf
*There's a Carrot in My Ear and Other Noodle Tails	J	TL	250+	Schwartz, Alvin	HarperTrophy
There's a Dinosaur!	L	I	250+	Stone, Evelyn	Hampton-Brown

TITLE	LEVEL	GENRE	WORD COUNT	AUTHOR / SERIES	PUBLISHER / DISTRIBUTOR
There's a Dog in the Yard	I	I	119	City Kids	Rigby
There's a Frog in My Oatmeal!	J	F	250+	Scooters	ETA Cuisenaire
There's a Frog in My Sleeping Bag	R	RF	250+	Clymer, Susan	Scholastic
There's a Hamster in My Lunchbox	R	RF	250+	Clymer, Susan	Scholastic
There's a Hippopotamus Under My Bed	J	F	250+	Thaler, Mike	Avon
There's a Monster in the Tree	E	F	250+	Learn to Read	Creative Teaching Press
There's a Mouse in the House	B	F	42	Bookshop	Mondo
There's a Nightmare in My Closet	I	F	153	Mayer, Mercer	Penguin Group
There's a Rainbow in the River	L	RF	250+	Home Connection Collection	Rigby
There's a Ship Outside My Window	O	RF	250+	PM Collection	Rigby
There's a Tarantula in My Homework	R	RF	250+	Clymer, Susan	Scholastic
There's an Alligator Under My Bed	J	RF	250+	Mayer, Mercer	Penguin Group
There's an Owl in the Shower	Q	RF	250+	George, Jean Craighead	HarperCollins
There's No One Like Me!	D	I	80	Sunshine	Wright Group/McGraw Hill
There's No Place Like Home	R	I	250+	Hill, David	Pacific Learning
There's No Place Like Home!	Q	I	250+	Rigby Literacy	Rigby
There's Something in My Attic	J	RF	258	Mayer, Mercer	Penguin Group
Thermometer	C	I	32	Simple Tools	Lerner Publishing
These Lands Are Ours: Tecumseh's Fight For the Old Northwest	T	B	250+	Connell, Kate	Steck-Vaughn
These Legs	C	I	42	Foundations	Wright Group/McGraw Hill
These Old Rags	M	RF	352	Evangeline Nicholas Collection	Wright Group/McGraw Hill
Theseus and the Minotaur	S	I	250+	High-Fliers	Pacific Learning
Theseus and the Minotaur	W	I	250+	World Mythology	Capstone Press
They All Ran Away	C	F	82	Lighthouse	Rigby
They Are Sick	C	RF	39	Reading Street	Pearson
They Call Me . . .	D	I	31	The Candid Collection	Pearson Learning Group
They Came From Center Field	R	RF	250+	Gutman, Dan	Scholastic
They Changed the World	R	I	250+	iOpeners	Pearson Learning Group
They Changed the World	Q	I	250+	Orbit Chapter Books	Pacific Learning
They Help Animals	C	RF	33	Reading Street	Pearson
They Led the Way	N	B	551	Yellow Umbrella Books	Red Brick Learning
*They Led the Way: 14 American Women	O	B	250+	Johnston, Johanna	Scholastic
They Shall Be Heard: Susan B. Anthony & Elizabeth Cady Stanton	T	B	250+	Connell, Kate	Steck-Vaughn
They Survived Mount St. Helens!	O	I	250+	Stine, Megan	Random House
They Worked Together	O	I	250+	iOpeners	Pearson Learning Group
*Thief in the Village, A	V	RF	250+	Berry, James	Puffin/Penguin
Thief Lord, The	V	F	250+	Funke, Cornelia	Scholastic
Thief of Hearts	V	RF	250+	Yep, Laurence	HarperCollins
Thief Queen's Daughter, The	X	F	250+	Haydon, Elizabeth	Tom Doherty
Thing in the Log, The	H	RF	81	Reading Unlimited	Pearson Learning Group
Things Birds Eat, The	C	I	38	Chessen, Betsey	Scholastic
Things Can Change	B	I	27	Leveled Readers Science	Houghton Mifflin Harcourt
Things Change	M	I	569	Bourne, Phyllis Montenegro	Hampton-Brown
Things Don't Change Much	L	RF	250+	Home Connection Collection	Rigby
Things I Can Do	B	F	47	Leveled Readers	Houghton Mifflin Harcourt
Things I Can Do	B	F	47	Leveled Readers/CA	Houghton Mifflin Harcourt
Things I Can Do	B	I	36	Little Readers	Houghton Mifflin Harcourt
Things I Can Do	B	I	36	Little Red Readers	Sundance
Things I Do for Fun	B	I	36	Little Red Readers	Sundance
Things I Do with My Friends	B	I	35	Little Red Readers	Sundance
Things I Like	D	F	42	Browne, Anthony	Random House
Things I Like	C	RF	42	Carousel Earlybirds	Pearson Learning Group

Organized Alphabetically by Title
Storable Database at www.fountasandpinnellleveledbooks.com

* Collection of short stories
\# Graphic text

T

TITLE	LEVEL	GENRE	WORD COUNT	AUTHOR / SERIES	PUBLISHER / DISTRIBUTOR
Things I Like	C	I	39	Little Readers	Houghton Mifflin Harcourt
Things I Like	B	RF	25	Storyteller	Wright Group/McGraw Hill
Things I Like Doing	A	I	24	Early Connections	Benchmark Education
Things I Like to Do	C	RF	63	Carousel Earlybirds	Pearson Learning Group
Things I Like to Do	C	RF	58	Foundations	Wright Group/McGraw Hill
Things I Like to Do	B	F	56	Leveled Readers	Houghton Mifflin Harcourt
Things I Like to Do	B	F	56	Leveled Readers/CA	Houghton Mifflin Harcourt
Things I Need	A	I	21	On Our Way to English	Rigby
Things I See	A	I	28	Leveled Readers Emergent	Houghton Mifflin Harcourt
Things Not Seen	V	F	250+	Clements, Andrew	Scholastic
Things on Wheels	C	I	69	Little Red Readers	Sundance
Things People Do for Fun	H	I	124	Foundations	Wright Group/McGraw Hill
Things People Do, The	W	I	250+	Story Surfers	ETA Cuisenaire
Things That Drag Behind	D	I	42	Teacher's Choice Series	Pearson Learning Group
Things That Fly	B	I	72	Leveled Literacy Intervention/ Blue System	Heinemann
Things That Go Fast	A	I	39	Leveled Literacy Intervention/ Orange System	Heinemann
Things That Go: A Traveling Alphabet	L	I	250+	Reit, Seymour	Bantam
Things That Help Me	C	I	18	Pacific Literacy	Pacific Learning
Things That Melt	G	I	84	Leveled Readers Science	Houghton Mifflin Harcourt
Things That People Make	N	I	250+	Explorations	Eleanor Curtain Publishing
Things That People Make	N	I	250+	Explorations	Okapi Educational Materials
Things That Protect You	D	RF	51	Foundations	Wright Group/McGraw Hill
Things That Sting	G	I	84	Gear Up!	Wright Group/McGraw Hill
Things to Do	G	I	170	Time for Kids	Teacher Created Materials
Things to Make	H	I	198	Time for Kids	Teacher Created Materials
Things to Read	LB	I	18	Little Books for Early Readers	University of Maine
Things to See in Maine	LB	I	14	Little Books for Early Readers	University of Maine
Things With Wings	J	I	267	Storyteller Nonfiction	Wright Group/McGraw Hill
Things You Either Hate or Love	Z+	RF	250+	Lowry, Brigid	Holiday House
Think Again!	M	TL	1207	Big Cat	Pacific Learning
Think and Be Safe	H	I	211	InfoTrek	ETA Cuisenaire
Think Before You Speak	S	RF	1904	Leveled Readers	Houghton Mifflin Harcourt
Think Before You Speak	S	RF	1904	Leveled Readers/CA	Houghton Mifflin Harcourt
Think Before You Speak	S	RF	1904	Leveled Readers/TX	Houghton Mifflin Harcourt
Think Like a Photographer! (and shoot better pictures)	W	I	250+	Bookshop	Mondo
Think Like a Scientist	Q	I	250+	Burke, Melissa Blackwell	Steck-Vaughn
Think of an Eel	N	I	250+	Read and Wonder	Candlewick Press
Think, Think, Think: Learning About Your Brain	M	I	250+	Amazing Body	Picture Window Books
Thinking About Ants	L	I	250+	Bookshop	Mondo
Third Grade Bullies	N	RF	250+	Levy, Elizabeth	Hyperion
Third Grade Stars	P	RF	250+	Ransom, Candice	Troll Associates
Third Grade Wedding Bells?	N	RF	250+	McKenna, Colleen O'Shaughnessy	Holiday House
Thirsty Cats, The	D	F	98	Springboard	Wright Group/McGraw Hill
Thirteen	R	RF	250+	Ransom, Candice	Scholastic
Thirteen Colonies, The	T	I	250+	Reading Expeditions	National Geographic
Thirty-Nine Steps, The	Z+	RF	250+	Buchan, John	Penguin Group
This and That	D	RF	22	Home Connection Collection	Rigby
This Can't Be Happening at Macdonald Hall	S	RF	250+	Korman, Gordon	Scholastic
This Desert	C	I	37	Little Celebrations	Pearson Learning Group

T

* Collection of short stories
# Graphic text

TITLE	LEVEL	GENRE	WORD COUNT	AUTHOR / SERIES	PUBLISHER / DISTRIBUTOR
This Farm	C	I	39	Yellow Umbrella Books	Red Brick Learning
This Food Grows Here	A	I	16	Windows on Literacy	National Geographic
This Fox and That Fox	E	RF	78	Reading Street	Pearson
This Game	B	I	63	Carousel Earlybirds	Pearson Learning Group
This Gecko	E	I	57	Twig	Wright Group/McGraw Hill
This Gum For Hire: A Chet Gecko Mystery	R	F	250+	Hale, Bruce	Harcourt, Inc.
This Hat	D	RF	52	Little Celebrations	Pearson Learning Group
This Is a Fish	B	I	49	Springboard	Wright Group/McGraw Hill
This Is a Forest	A	I	32	In Step Readers	Rigby
This Is an Island	D	RF	46	Windows on Literacy	National Geographic
This Is for Me	B	F	42	Sails	Rigby
This Is George	I	I	86	Pair-It Turn and Learn	Steck-Vaughn
This Is Lobstering	A	I	27	Little Books for Early Readers	University of Maine
This Is Me	E	RF	70	Rigby Literacy	Rigby
This Is Me	D	RF	70	Rigby Star Quest	Rigby
This Is Me	B	I	70	Sun Sprouts	ETA Cuisenaire
This Is Me	B	I	27	Time for Kids	Teacher Created Materials
This Is Me and Where I Am	G	RF	111	Fitzgerald, Joanne	Fitzhenry & Whiteside
This Is Me!	A	I	23	Gear Up!	Wright Group/McGraw Hill
This Is Me!	B	I	44	InfoTrek	ETA Cuisenaire
This Is Me! Mel B.!	R	B	250+	High-Fliers	Pacific Learning
This Is My Family	D	RF	77	On Our Way to English	Rigby
This Is My Family	D	I	36	Read-More Books	Pearson Learning Group
This Is My Friend	C	RF	77	Foundations	Wright Group/McGraw Hill
This Is My Home	C	F	51	Joy Readers	Pearson Learning Group
This Is My House	L	I	250+	Dorros, Arthur	Scholastic
This Is My Street	I	RF	229	Windows on Literacy	National Geographic
This Is Our House	K	RF	250+	Rosen, Michael	Candlewick Press
This Is the Bear	I	F	211	Hayes, Sarah & Craig	Harper & Row
This Is the House That Bjorn…	I	RF	172	Tiger Cub	Peguis
This Is the Place for Me	I	F	250+	Cole, Joanna	Scholastic
This Is the Plate	D	RF	28	Little Celebrations	Pearson Learning Group
This Is the Register	F	RF	81	Cambridge Reading	Pearson Learning Group
This Is the Seed	I	F	171	Little Celebrations	Pearson Learning Group
This Is the Seed	D	RF	115	Seedlings	Continental Press
This Is the Tree: A Story of the Baobab	O	I	332	Moss, Miriam	Kane/Miller Book Publishers
This Is the Way	F	RF	200	Learn to Read	Creative Teaching Press
This Is the Way We Go to School	T	RF	2879	Reading Street	Pearson
This Is Water	B	I	24	Bookshop	Mondo
This Is What I Did	Z+	RF	250+	Ellis, Ann Dee	Little, Brown & Co.
This Land Is Our Land	O	I	781	Reading Street	Pearson
This Land Is Your Land: America's National Parks	S	I	250+	Explore More	Wright Group/McGraw Hill
This Little Boy	J	I	308	Springboard	Wright Group/McGraw Hill
This Little Critter	D	I	98	Springboard	Wright Group/McGraw Hill
This Little Pig	D	F	43	Seedlings	Continental Press
This Little Seed	E	I	58	Rigby Focus	Rigby
This Mouth	D	I	64	Wonder World	Wright Group/McGraw Hill
This Old Car	H	RF	79	Voyages	SRA/McGraw Hill
This One Can Run	B	I	34	Science	Outside the Box
This Piece or That Piece?	E	F	88	Leveled Readers	Houghton Mifflin Harcourt
This Place Is Dry	R	I	250+	Cobb, Vicki	Walker & Company
This Place Is Wet	R	I	250+	Cobb, Vicki	Walker & Company

* Collection of short stories
\# Graphic text

TITLE	LEVEL	GENRE	WORD COUNT	AUTHOR / SERIES	PUBLISHER / DISTRIBUTOR
This Room Is a Mess!	I	RF	250+	Ready Readers	Pearson Learning Group
This Tail Belongs to . . .	B	I	24	Science	Outside the Box
This Tall	B	RF	41	Foundations	Wright Group/McGraw Hill
This Way to School	H	I	170	Gear Up!	Wright Group/McGraw Hill
This Year's Play	N	F	250+	Springboard	Wright Group/ McGraw Hill
Thistle and the Shell of Laughter: The Fairy Chronicles	Q	F	12190	Sweet, J.H.	Sourcebooks
Thomas Adams Invents Chewing Gum	N	B	417	Reading Street	Pearson
Thomas Alva Edison: Great Inventor	Q	B	250+	Levinson, Nancy Smiler	Scholastic
Thomas Edison	P	B	250+	Early Biographies	Compass Point Books
Thomas Edison	N	B	196	First Biographies	Capstone Press
Thomas Edison	S	B	3651	History Maker Bios	Lerner Publications
Thomas Edison	T	B	250+	In Their Own Words	Scholastic
Thomas Edison	P	B	250+	Photo-Illustrated Biographies	Red Brick Learning
Thomas Edison	K	B	145	Windows on Literacy	National Geographic
Thomas Edison and the Light Bulb	Q	B	619	Independent Readers Science	Houghton Mifflin Harcourt
Thomas Edison and the Pioneers of Electromagnetism	U	B	250+	Science Readers	Teacher Created Materials
Thomas Edison: Inventor with a Lot of Bright Ideas	R	B	250+	Getting to Know the World's Greatest Inventors and Scientists	Children's Press
Thomas Had a Temper	F	RF	139	Alphakids	Sundance
Thomas Jefferson	T	B	250+	Amazing Americans	Wright Group/McGraw Hill
Thomas Jefferson	Q	B	250+	Early Biographies	Compass Point Books
Thomas Jefferson	N	B	198	First Biographies	Capstone Press
Thomas Jefferson	S	B	3374	History Maker Bios	Lerner Publications
Thomas Jefferson	N	B	157	Independent Readers Social Studies	Houghton Mifflin Harcourt
Thomas Jefferson	V	B	250+	Let Freedom Ring	Capstone Press
Thomas Jefferson	Q	B	250+	Photo-Illustrated Biographies	Red Brick Learning
Thomas Jefferson	U	B	250+	Primary Source Readers	Teacher Created Materials
Thomas Jefferson	U	B	250+	Profiles of the Presidents	Compass Point Books
Thomas Jefferson and the Louisiana Purchase	Q	B	250+	On Deck	Rigby
Thomas Jefferson: A Life of Patriotism	O	B	557	Pull Ahead Books	Lerner Publications
Thomas Jefferson: Author, Inventor, President	N	B	250+	Rookie Biographies	Children's Press
Thomas Jefferson: Man with a Vision	U	B	250+	Crisman, Ruth	Scholastic
Thomas Jefferson: Third President	R	B	250+	Getting to Know the U.S. Presidents	Children's Press
Thomas Peters, A Remarkable Man	U	B	2255	Leveled Readers/CA	Houghton Mifflin Harcourt
Thomas Peters, A Remarkable Man	U	B	2255	Leveled Readers/TX	Houghton Mifflin Harcourt
Thomas Peters, A Remarkable Man	U	B	2255	Leveled Readers	Houghton Mifflin Harcourt
Thomas Tries Something New	L	F	570	Springboard	Wright Group/McGraw Hill
Those Amazingly Useful Ears	O	I	250+	Frederick, Shirley	Hampton-Brown
Those Birds!	K	RF	250+	Storyteller-Lightning Bolts	Wright Group/McGraw Hill
Those Tricky Animals	M	I	250+	Literacy Tree	Rigby
Thoughts, Pictures, and Words	O	B	250+	Meet The Author	Richard C. Owen
Thousand Words, A	O	RF	688	Leveled Readers	Houghton Mifflin Harcourt
Thousand Words, A	O	RF	688	Leveled Readers/CA	Houghton Mifflin Harcourt
Thousand Words, A	O	RF	688	Leveled Readers/TX	Houghton Mifflin Harcourt
Threads of Deceit	U	RF	250+	High-Fliers	Pacific Learning
Three Bears' Christmas, The	J	F	250+	Duval, Kathy	Holiday House
Three Bears, The	E	TL	201	Fairy Tales and Folklore	Norwood House Press
Three Bears, The	G	TL	344	Folk Tales	Pioneer Valley
Three Bears, The	K	TL	873	Galdone, Paul	Clarion

* Collection of short stories
# Graphic text

TITLE	LEVEL	GENRE	WORD COUNT	AUTHOR / SERIES	PUBLISHER / DISTRIBUTOR
Three Bears, The	E	TL	116	Leveled Literacy Intervention/ Green System	Heinemann
Three Bears, The	D	F	101	Lighthouse	Rigby
Three Bears, The	I	TL	250+	Tiger Cub	Peguis
Three Big Cities	N	I	535	Springboard	Wright Group/ McGraw Hill
Three Billy Goats Gruff	I	TL	250+	Sunshine	Wright Group/McGraw Hill
Three Billy Goats Gruff	I	TL	536	Traditional Tales	Pearson Learning Group
Three Billy Goats Gruff, The	K	TL	250+	Asbjornsen, P. C.; Moe, J. E.	Harcourt School Publishers
Three Billy Goats Gruff, The	I	TL	549	Brown, Marcia	Harcourt School Publishers
Three Billy Goats Gruff, The	F	TL	250+	Folk Tales	Pioneer Valley
Three Billy Goats Gruff, The	I	TL	250+	Literacy Tree	Rigby
Three Billy Goats Gruff, The	G	TL	140	Little Readers	Houghton Mifflin Harcourt
Three Billy Goats Gruff, The	H	TL	250+	New Way Green	Steck-Vaughn
Three Billy Goats Gruff, The	I	TL	450	PM Traditional Tales-Orange	Rigby
Three Billy Goats Gruff, The	G	TL	250+	Shapiro, Sara	Scholastic
Three Billy Goats Gruff, The	I	F	250+	Southgate, Vera	Ladybird Books
Three Billy Goats Gruff, The	K	TL	478	Stevens, Janet	Harcourt School Publishers
Three Billy Goats, The	J	TL	532	Leveled Literacy Intervention/ Green System	Heinemann
Three Billy Goats, The	E	TL	133	Storyworlds	Heinemann Educational Publishers
Three Blind Mice Mystery, The	L	F	250+	Krensky, Stephen	Bantam
Three Brothers, The	M	TL	250+	Rigby Flying Colors	Rigby
*Three By the Sea	J	RF	250+	Marshall, Edward	Puffin/Penguin
Three Cheers for Hippo	G	F	90	Stadler, John	HarperCollins
Three Days on a River in a Red Canoe	K	I	250+	Williams, Vera B.	Scholastic
Three Ducks Went Wandering	K	F	250+	Roy, Ron	Clarion
Three Friends or Two?	S	RF	1940	Leveled Readers	Houghton Mifflin Harcourt
Three Friends or Two?	S	RF	1940	Leveled Readers/CA	Houghton Mifflin Harcourt
Three Funny Tales	K	TL	900	Springboard	Wright Group/McGraw Hill
Three Goats, The	E	TL	220	Fairy Tales and Folklore	Norwood House Press
Three Goats, The	F	TL	128	Storyteller-Setting Sun	Wright Group/McGraw Hill
Three Hedgehogs, The	K	F	552	Rigby Gigglers	Rigby
Three Investigators, The Mystery of the Fiery Eye	Y	RF	250+	Arthur, Robert	Random House
Three Jars Full	F	I	89	Rigby Focus	Rigby
Three Kinds of Bears	Q	I	3256	Leveled Readers Science	Houghton Mifflin Harcourt
Three Kittens	G	F	116	Ginsburg, Mirra	Crown
Three Little Ducks	E	F	102	Story Box	Wright Group/McGraw Hill
Three Little Kittens	H	TL	164	Ready Readers	Pearson Learning Group
Three Little Monkeys	E	F	36	Sunshine	Wright Group/McGraw Hill
Three Little Pigs	L	TL	919	Galdone, Paul	Houghton Mifflin Harcourt
Three Little Pigs	H	TL	39	Hunia, Fran	Ladybird Books
Three Little Pigs	L	TL	250+	Once Upon a Time	Wright Group/McGraw Hill
Three Little Pigs	C	TL	39	Sunshine	Wright Group/McGraw Hill
Three Little Pigs and a Big Bad Wolf	F	TL	267	Leveled Literacy Intervention/ Green System	Heinemann
Three Little Pigs and One Big Pig	E	TL	123	Ready Readers	Pearson Learning Group
Three Little Pigs Wise Up and the Princess, the Prince, and the Vegetables, The	M	F	250+	Navigators Fiction Series	Benchmark Education
Three Little Pigs, The	F	TL	274	Alphakids	Sundance
Three Little Pigs, The	E	TL	189	Fairy Tales and Folklore	Norwood House Press
Three Little Pigs, The	C	TL	99	Folk Tales	Pioneer Valley
Three Little Pigs, The	I	TL	250+	Literacy 2000	Rigby

* Collection of short stories
\# Graphic text

T

TITLE	LEVEL	GENRE	WORD COUNT	AUTHOR / SERIES	PUBLISHER / DISTRIBUTOR
Three Little Pigs, The	G	TL	250+	Little Readers	Houghton Mifflin Harcourt
Three Little Pigs, The	L	TL	250+	Marshall, James	Scholastic
Three Little Pigs, The	H	TL	392	New Way Blue	Steck-Vaughn
Three Little Pigs, The	I	TL	523	PM Traditional Tales-Orange	Rigby
Three Little Pigs, The	H	TL	346	Reading Corners	Pearson Learning Group
Three Little Pigs, The	H	TL	276+	Reading Unlimited	Pearson Learning Group
Three Little Pigs, The	I	TL	568	Traditional Tales	Pearson Learning Group
Three Little Pigs, The	G	TL	250+	We Both Read	Treasure Bay
Three Little Pigs, The	I	TL	250+	Ziefert, Harriet	Puffin/Penguin
Three Little Witches	G	F	189	First Start	Troll Associates
Three Little Wolves and the Big Bad Pig, The	O	TL	250+	Trivizas, Eugene	Scholastic
Three Lives to Live	T	F	250+	Lindbergh, Anne	Little, Brown & Co.
Three Magicians, The	K	F	250+	Literacy 2000	Rigby
*Three More Stories You Can Read to Your Cat	L	F	250+	Miller, Sara Swan	Houghton Mifflin Harcourt
*Three More Stories You Can Read to Your Dog	L	F	250+	Miller, Sara Swan	Houghton Mifflin Harcourt
Three Muddy Monkeys	F	F	180	Foundations	Wright Group/McGraw Hill
Three Names of Me	N	RF	250+	Cummings, Mary	Albert Whitman & Co.
Three Naughty Ostriches	J	F	369	Springboard	Wright Group/McGraw Hill
Three of the Greats	M	B	360	Reading Street	Pearson
Three Pigs	G	F	126	Gear Up!	Wright Group/McGraw Hill
Three Pigs, The	D	TL	113	Leveled Literacy Intervention/ Green System	Heinemann
Three R's, The	U	RF	3211	Leveled Readers	Houghton Mifflin Harcourt
Three R's, The	U	RF	3211	Leveled Readers/CA	Houghton Mifflin Harcourt
Three R's, The	U	RF	3211	Leveled Readers/TX	Houghton Mifflin Harcourt
Three Ships for Columbus	N	I	250+	Stories of America	Steck-Vaughn
Three Sillies, The	L	F	250+	Literacy 2000	Rigby
Three Silly Cowboys, The	H	F	213	Ready Readers	Pearson Learning Group
Three Silly Monkeys	E	F	150	Foundations	Wright Group/McGraw Hill
Three Silly Monkeys Go Fishing	I	F	163	Foundations	Wright Group/McGraw Hill
Three Sisters, The	J	I	313	Vocabulary Readers	Houghton Mifflin Harcourt
Three Sisters, The	J	I	313	Vocabulary Readers/CA	Houghton Mifflin Harcourt
Three Sisters, The	J	I	313	Vocabulary Readers/TX	Houghton Mifflin Harcourt
Three Smart Pals	L	RF	250+	Rocklin, Joanne	Scholastic
*Three Stories You Can Read to Your Cat	K	F	250+	Miller, Sara Swan	Houghton Mifflin Harcourt
*Three Stories You Can Read to Your Dog	K	F	250+	Miller, Sara Swan	Houghton Mifflin Harcourt
*Three Stories You Can Read to Your Teddy Bear	L	F	250+	Miller, Sara Swan	Houghton Mifflin Harcourt
Three Twentieth-Century Dictators	Y	B	250+	Navigators Biography Series	Benchmark Education
*Three Up a Tree	J	RF	250+	Marshall, James	Puffin/Penguin
Three White Sheep	B	F	20	Ready Readers	Pearson Learning Group
Three Wishes	L	F	250+	Popcorn	Sundance
Three Wishes	H	TL	250+	Ready Readers	Pearson Learning Group
Three Wishes: Palestinian and Israeli Children Speak	Z	I	250+	Ellis, Deborah	Groundwood Books
Three Wishes, The	L	TL	250+	Bookshop	Mondo
*Three Wishes, The	O	TL	250+	Literacy 2000	Rigby
Three Wishes, The	I	TL	250+	Storyworlds	Heinemann Educational Books
Three Wishes, The	K	TL	501	Sunshine	Wright Group/McGraw Hill
Three Women Reporters	X	I	2956	Vocabulary Readers	Houghton Mifflin Harcourt
Three Women Reporters	X	I	2956	Vocabulary Readers/CA	Houghton Mifflin Harcourt
Three Women Reporters	X	I	2956	Vocabulary Readers/TX	Houghton Mifflin Harcourt
Three-Horn: The Adventure of Triceratops	N	I	250+	Dinosaur World	Picture Window Books

* Collection of short stories
# Graphic text

TITLE	LEVEL	GENRE	WORD COUNT	AUTHOR / SERIES	PUBLISHER / DISTRIBUTOR
Three-Legged Race, The	H	RF	202	Windmill Books	Rigby
Three-Toed Sloths	O	I	926	Springboard	Wright Group/ McGraw-Hill
Threw and Through	K	F	255	Sunshine	Wright Group/McGraw Hill
Thrill of the Ride, The	Q	I	250+	Power Up!	Steck-Vaughn
Thrill Rides!: All About Roller Coasters	V	I	250+	Bookshop	Mondo
Thrills at the Fair	J	RF	250+	The Wright Skills	Wright Group/McGraw Hill
Thrills on the Water	M	I	445	Sails	Rigby
Through Grandpa's Eyes	P	RF	250+	MacLachlan, Patricia	HarperTrophy
Through My Eyes	X	B	250+	Bridges, Ruby	Scholastic
Through the Cell Wall	Z	I	2080	Independent Readers Science	Houghton Mifflin Harcourt
Through the Day	C	I	76	Rigby Literacy	Rigby
Through the Eyes of Your Ancestors: A Step-by-Step Guide to Uncovering Your Family's History	V	I	250+	Taylor, Maureen	Houghton Mifflin Harcourt
Through the Fence	Q	F	1862	Take Two Books	Wright Group/ McGraw-Hill
Through the Garden Door	M	F	250+	Reeves, Barbara	Pearson Learning Group
Through the Medicine Cabinet	N	F	250+	The Zack Files	Grossett & Dunlap
Throw-Away Pets	N	RF	250+	Duffey, Betsy	Puffin/Penguin
Throwing Parties	V	I	250+	10 Things You Need To Know About	Capstone Press
*Throwing Shadows	T	RF	250+	Konigsburg, E. L.	Language for Learning Assoc.
Thumb in the Box, The	S	RF	250+	Roberts, Ken	Groundwood Books
Thumb on a Diamond	S	RF	250+	Roberts, Ken	Groundwood Books
Thumbelina	K	TL	807	Tales from Hans Andersen	Wright Group/McGraw Hill
Thumbprint Critters	D	I	27	Little Celebrations	Pearson Learning Group
Thumper's Sore Paw	F	RF	136	Springboard	Wright Group/McGraw Hill
Thumpety-Rah!	G	F	98	Sunshine	Wright Group/McGraw Hill
Thump-Thump: Learning About Your Heart	M	I	250+	Amazing Body	Picture Window Books
Thunder and Lightning	K	I	250+	Pfeffer, Wendy	Scholastic
Thunder at Gettysburg	S	I	250+	Gauch, Patricia Lee	Bantam
Thunder Rolling in the Mountains	U	HF	250+	O'Dell, Scott; Hall, Elizabeth	Bantam
Thunder Valley	T	RF	250+	Paulsen, Gary	Bantam
Thunderbowl	Z+	RF	250+	Orca Soundings	Orca Book Publishers
Thunderstorm Is Coming!, A	I	I	130	Vocabulary Readers	Houghton Mifflin Harcourt
Thunderstorms	O	I	250+	A True Book	Children's Press
Thunderstorms	M	I	501	Pull Ahead Books	Lerner Publications
Thurgood Marshall	U	B	250+	Amazing Americans	Wright Group/McGraw Hill
Thurgood Marshall	S	B	1264	Leveled Readers	Houghton Mifflin Harcourt
Thurgood Marshall	S	B	1264	Leveled Readers/CA	Houghton Mifflin Harcourt
Thurgood Marshall	S	B	1264	Leveled Readers/TX	Houghton Mifflin Harcourt
Thurgood Marshall	L	B	250+	Pebble Books	Red Brick Learning
Thurgood Marshall	P	B	250+	Photo-Illustrated Biographies	Red Brick Learning
Thurgood Marshall and Civil Rights	V	B	2540	Independent Readers Social Studies	Houghton Mifflin Harcourt
Thurgood Marshall: Civil Rights Champion	P	B	250+	Great African Americans	Capstone Press
Thurgood Marshall: First Black Supreme Court Justice	N	B	250+	Rookie Biographies	Children's Press
THWONK	Y	F	250+	Bauer, Joan	Speak
Tick Tock World Clocks	F	I	43	iOpeners	Pearson Learning Group
Tick, Tock, Check the Clock!	C	F	64	Literacy by Design	Rigby
Ticket to Canada	U	RF	1904	Leveled Readers	Houghton Mifflin Harcourt
Tickle-Bugs, The	J	F	250+	Literacy 2000	Rigby
Tick-Tock	C	RF	53	Story Box	Wright Group/McGraw Hill
Tic-Tac-Toe Three in a Row	H	RF	132	Stamper, Judith Bauer	Scholastic

T

* Collection of short stories
# Graphic text

TITLE	LEVEL	GENRE	WORD COUNT	AUTHOR / SERIES	PUBLISHER / DISTRIBUTOR
Tide Pool, The	B	I	57	Leveled Literacy Intervention/ Blue System	Heinemann
Tide Pools	K	I	388	Leveled Readers	Houghton Mifflin Harcourt
Tide Pools	K	I	388	Leveled Readers/CA	Houghton Mifflin Harcourt
Tide Pools	K	I	388	Leveled Readers/TX	Houghton Mifflin Harcourt
Tides	I	I	210	Wonder World	Wright Group/McGraw Hill
Tides of Change	V	I	250+	InfoQuest	Rigby
Tidy the Clown	H	F	240	InfoTrek	ETA Cuisenaire
Tidy Titch	I	RF	231	Hutchins, Pat	Morrow
Tie, The	O	I	819	Vocabulary Readers	Houghton Mifflin Harcourt
Tie, The	O	I	819	Vocabulary Readers/CA	Houghton Mifflin Harcourt
Ties That Bind, Ties That Break	X	HF	250+	Namioka, Lensey	Delacorte Press
Tig in the Dumps	M	RF	1229	Big Cat	Pacific Learning
Tig the Talented Pig	B	F	50	Reading Street	Pearson
Tiger & the Mad Millionaire, The	L	F	250+	Voyages	SRA/McGraw Hill
Tiger and Monkey	D	F	92	Sails	Rigby
Tiger and the Jackal, The	I	TL	250+	Storyworlds	Heinemann Educational Books
Tiger Cub Grows Up, A	J	I	684	Baby Animals	Carolrhoda Books
Tiger Dave	G	F	33	Books for Young Learners	Richard C. Owen
Tiger Dreams	J	RF	193	Cambridge Reading	Pearson Learning Group
Tiger Eyes	W	RF	250+	Blume, Judy	Bantam
Tiger Hunt	J	RF	250+	Rigby Literacy	Rigby
Tiger Is a Scaredy Cat	F	F	220	Phillips, Joan	Random House
Tiger Rising, The	T	RF	250+	DiCamillo, Kate	Candlewick Press
Tiger Runs Away	G	RF	213	PM Extensions-Blue	Rigby
Tiger Shark	J	I	136	Sharks	Capstone Press
Tiger Tales	O	F	250+	Little Celebrations	Pearson Learning Group
Tiger Threat	U	RF	250+	Orca Sports	Orca Book Publishers
Tiger Trek	P	I	250+	WorldScapes	ETA Cuisenaire
Tiger Turcotte Takes on the Know-It-All	M	RF	4908	Flood, Pansie Hart	Carolrhoda Books
Tiger Woods	P	B	1617	Amazing Athletes	Lerner Publications
Tiger Woods	N	B	250+	Biography	Benchmark Education
Tiger Woods	Q	B	1081	Leveled Readers	Houghton Mifflin Harcourt
Tiger Woods	Q	B	1081	Leveled Readers/CA	Houghton Mifflin Harcourt
Tiger Woods	Q	B	1081	Leveled Readers/TX	Houghton Mifflin Harcourt
Tiger Woods	R	B	250+	Sports Heroes	Red Brick Learning
Tiger Woods: An American Master	R	B	250+	Edwards, Nicholas	Scholastic
Tiger Woods: Unbeatable!	X	B	2056	Leveled Readers	Houghton Mifflin Harcourt
Tiger, the Man, and the Jackal, The	K	F	520	Leveled Readers	Houghton Mifflin Harcourt
Tiger, Tiger	C	F	55	PM Story Books	Rigby
Tigers	O	I	1462	Early Bird Nature Books	Lerner Publications
Tigers	I	I	324	Sails	Rigby
Tiger's Apprentice, The	T	F	250+	Yep, Laurence	Harper Trophy
Tigers at Twilight	M	F	250+	Osborne, Mary Pope	Random House
Tiger's Blood	T	F	250+	Yep, Laurence	Harper Trophy
Tiger's Clock	C	F	28	Learn to Read	Creative Teaching Press
Tiger's Promise, Based on a Folktale from India, The	J	TL	250+	Leveled Readers Language Support	Houghton Mifflin Harcourt
Tiger's Tale	L	F	1443	Big Cat	Pacific Learning
Tiger's Tummy Ache	I	TL	220	Ready Readers	Pearson Learning Group
Tigers, Elephants, and Giraffes	A	I	18	Vocabulary Readers	Houghton Mifflin Harcourt
Tigers: Striped Stalkers	M	I	250+	The Wild World of Animals	Red Brick Learning
Tight End	T	RF	250+	Christopher, Matt	Little, Brown & Co.

TITLE	LEVEL	GENRE	WORD COUNT	AUTHOR / SERIES	PUBLISHER / DISTRIBUTOR
Tikki Tikki Tembo	N	TL	250+	Mosel, Arlene	Scholastic
Tiling with Shapes	L	I	371	Yellow Umbrella Books	Red Brick Learning
Till's Christmas	R	RF	250+	Thacker, Nola	Scholastic
Tiltawhirl John	U	RF	250+	Paulsen, Gary	Penguin Group
Tim and the Tooth Fairy	I	RF	250+	Rigby Rocket	Rigby
Tim Berners-Lee: Spinning the World Wide Web	W	B	250+	Explore More	Wright Group/McGraw Hill
Tim Does It Again	K	RF	250+	Rigby Gigglers	Rigby
Timber Box, The	M	TL	250+	Enrichment	Wright Group/McGraw Hill
Time	A	RF	31	Davidson, Avelyn	Scholastic
Time	Q	RF	1841	Take Two Books	Wright Group/ McGraw Hill
Time and Again	P	SF	10061	Childs, Rob	Stone Arch Books
Time Apart, A	T	RF	250+	Stanley, Diane	William Morrow
Time Benders	T	SF	250+	Paulsen, Gary	Bantam
Time Capsule	Q	F	250+	Bookweb	Rigby
Time Capsule, The	M	SF	257	Book Bank	Wright Group/McGraw Hill
Time Capsule, The	J	RF	250+	Reading Safari	Mondo
Time Flies	R	I	250+	Literacy 2000	Rigby
Time Flies	WB	F	N/A	Rohmann, Eric	Crown
Time for a Bath	D	RF	60	Mader, Jan	Kaeden Books
Time for a Change	C	RF	31	Pacific Literacy	Pacific Learning
Time for a Family	K	I	108	Literacy Tree	Rigby
Time for a Party	F	I	111	Discovery World	Rigby
Time for Andrew	S	F	250+	Hahn, Mary	Avon Camelot
Time for Bed	C	RF	31	Rigby Rocket	Rigby
Time for Bed	C	RF	27	Rosen Real Readers	Rosen Publishing Group
Time for Bed	B	RF	28	Science	Outside the Box
Time for Bed	C	RF	28	Smart Starts	Rigby
Time for Bed, Little Bear	I	F	303	Story Basket	Wright Group/McGraw Hill
Time for Bed?	H	RF	256	Real Kids Readers	Millbrook Press
Time for Breakfast	B	RF	25	Gear Up!	Wright Group/McGraw Hill
Time for Breakfast!	A	F	20	Leveled Readers	Houghton Mifflin Harcourt
Time for Breakfast!	A	F	20	Leveled Readers/CA	Houghton Mifflin Harcourt
Time for Carter to Barter	J	RF	494	Gear Up!	Wright Group/McGraw Hill
Time for Dinner	B	I	38	PM Starters	Rigby
Time for Dinner	LB	F	15	Smart Starts	Rigby
Time for Lunch	D	F	122	Leveled Literacy Intervention/ Green System	Heinemann
Time for Lunch	B	RF	28	Ready Readers	Pearson Learning Group
Time for Lunch!	I	F	250+	Rigby Rocket	Rigby
Time for Play	D	RF	85	PM Plus Nonfiction	Rigby
Time for Sale	Q	F	250+	Literacy 2000	Rigby
Time for School	A	I	32	At School Series	Pioneer Valley
Time for Sleep!	D	F	62	Sunshine	Wright Group/McGraw Hill
Time for Soup!	LB	I	12	Vocabulary Readers	Houghton Mifflin Harcourt
Time for Tacos	B	RF	26	Bebop Books	Lee & Low Books Inc.
Time for Tea	B	RF	20	Phonics and Friends	Hampton-Brown
Time Garden, The	T	F	250+	Eager, Edward	Harcourt
Time Line of the American Revolution, A	R	I	250+	Rosen Real Readers	Rosen Publishing Group
Time Lines: 1900-2000	O	I	250+	Windows on Literacy	National Geographic
*Time Machine and Other Cases, The	O	RF	250+	Simon, Seymour	Avon
Time Machine, The	Z	SF	250+	Wells, H. G.	Scholastic
Time of Angels, A	W	F	250+	Hesse, Karen	Hyperion

T

* Collection of short stories
# Graphic text

TITLE	LEVEL	GENRE	WORD COUNT	AUTHOR / SERIES	PUBLISHER / DISTRIBUTOR
Time of Change, A: Women in the Early Twentieth Century	S	I	1877	Reading Street	Pearson
Time Song, The	G	I	99	Learn to Read	Creative Teaching Press
Time Spinner	S	F	250+	Bookshop	Mondo
Time to Celebrate!	M	I	250+	iOpeners	Pearson Learning Group
Time to Eat	B	RF	27	Reading Street	Pearson
Time to Eat	LB	I	3	Windows on Literacy	National Geographic
Time to Estimate	L	I	250+	Yellow Umbrella Books	Capstone Press
Time to Go	D	RF	89	Literacy by Design	Rigby
Time to Go	D	F	89	On Our Way to English	Rigby
Time to Play!	C	RF	70	InfoTrek	ETA Cuisenaire
Time to Sleep	C	I	52	Independent Readers Science	Houghton Mifflin Harcourt
Time to Sleep	B	I	44	Sails	Rigby
Time to Sleep, A	I	I	239	Sails	Rigby
Time to Tell Time	L	I	116	Spyglass Books	Compass Point Books
Time to Unite, A	V	I	1327	Vocabulary Readers	Houghton Mifflin Harcourt
Time to Unite, A	V	I	1327	Vocabulary Readers/CA	Houghton Mifflin Harcourt
Time-Travel: Pioneer Community	O	SF	250+	InfoTrek	ETA Cuisenaire
Time-Travel: Pioneer Tools	O	SF	250+	InfoTrek	ETA Cuisenaire
Time Travelers: Adventures in Archaeology	W	I	250+	PM Collection	Rigby
Time Warp, The	N	SF	1684	Take Two Books	Wright Group/McGraw Hill
Timedetectors	V	SF	250+	Literacy 2000	Rigby
Timedetectors	N	SF	250+	SupaDoopers	Sundance
Timekeepers, The	Y	I	3385	Leveled Readers	Houghton Mifflin Harcourt
Timekeepers, The	Y	I	3385	Leveled Readers/CA	Houghton Mifflin Harcourt
Timeline of Electricity	S	I	948	Leveled Readers Science	Houghton Mifflin Harcourt
Time's Up!	L	F	250+	Sunshine	Wright Group/McGraw Hill
Time-Travel: Pioneer Children	O	SF	250+	InfoTrek	ETA Cuisenaire
Time-Travel: Pioneer Food	O	SF	250+	InfoTrek	ETA Cuisenaire
Timid Boy and Mama Bear, A Pueblo Legend	L	TL	543	Leveled Readers	Houghton Mifflin Harcourt
Timid Boy and Mama Bear, A Pueblo Legend	L	TL	543	Leveled Readers/CA	Houghton Mifflin Harcourt
Timid Boy and Mama Bear, A Pueblo Legend	L	TL	543	Leveled Readers/TX	Houghton Mifflin Harcourt
Timmy	E	RF	54	Literacy 2000	Rigby
Timmy Tries	C	RF	22	Little Celebrations	Pearson Learning Group
Timothy Whuffenpuffen-Whippersnapper	S	F	250+	Literacy 2000	Rigby
Timothy's Five-City Tour	M	F	250+	Pair-It Books	Steck-Vaughn
Tim's Bedtime	J	F	250+	Supersonics	Rigby
Tim's Favorite Toy	F	RF	202	PM Extensions-Blue	Rigby
Tim's Garden	C	RF	31	Reading Street	Pearson
Tim's Paintings	A	RF	33	Smart Starts	Rigby
Tim's Pig	B	F	41	Leveled Readers	Houghton Mifflin Harcourt
Tim's Pig Eats	B	F	39	Leveled Readers Language Support	Houghton Mifflin Harcourt
Tim's Pumpkin	I	RF	250+	Home Connection Collection	Rigby
Tin Can Man, The	E	RF	105	Real Kids Readers	Millbrook Press
Tin Lizzy	M	RF	425	Windmill Books	Rigby
Tin Treasures	J	I	250+	Greetings	Rigby
Tina and the Statue of Liberty	M	F	965	In Step Readers	Rigby
Tina's Taxi	F	RF	83	Franco, Betsy	Scholastic
Tiny and the Big Wave	F	RF	163	PM Extensions-Yellow	Rigby
Tiny Baby Kangaroos	L	I	296	Leveled Readers	Houghton Mifflin Harcourt
Tiny Baby Kangaroos	L	I	296	Leveled Readers/CA	Houghton Mifflin Harcourt
Tiny Baby Kangaroos	L	I	296	Leveled Readers/TX	Houghton Mifflin Harcourt
Tiny Christmas Elf, The	G	F	173	First Start	Troll Associates

T

* Collection of short stories
# Graphic text

TITLE	LEVEL	GENRE	WORD COUNT	AUTHOR / SERIES	PUBLISHER / DISTRIBUTOR
Tiny Creatures	J	I	250+	Discovery World	Rigby
Tiny Dinosaurs	L	RF	250+	PM Story Books	Rigby
Tiny Island Fever	P	F	250+	Scooters	ETA Cuisenaire
Tiny Little Woman, The	D	F	74	Joy Readers	Pearson Learning Group
Tiny Teddies' Picnic, The	D	RF	103	PM Photo Stories	Rigby
Tiny Woman's Coat, The	H	F	147	Sunshine	Wright Group/McGraw Hill
Tiny Workers: Ants in Your Backyard	M	I	250+	Backyard Bugs	Picture Window Books
Tiny's Big Adventure	J	F	234	Waddell, Martin	Candlewick Press
Tippu	K	F	250+	Soar To Success	Houghton Mifflin Harcourt
Tiptoe Round the Corner	H	F	96	Voyages	SRA/McGraw Hill
Tires	F	RF	180	Foundations	Wright Group/McGraw Hill
Titan Clash	V	RF	250+	Orca Sports	Orca Book Publishers
Titanic	S	HF	250+	Duey, Kathleen; Bale, Karen A.	Simon & Schuster
Titanic Crossing	R	HF	250+	Williams, Barbara	Scholastic
Titanic Disaster at Sea	U	I	250+	Jenkins, Martin	Candlewick Press
Titanic Disaster Inquiry, The	Y	I	2862	Vocabulary Readers	Houghton Mifflin Harcourt
Titanic Disaster Inquiry, The	Y	I	2862	Vocabulary Readers/CA	Houghton Mifflin Harcourt
Titanic Sinks!, The	T	I	250+	Conklin, Thomas	Random House
Titanic, The	V	I	250+	Cornerstones of Freedom	Children's Press
Titanic, The	O	I	727	Rigby Flying Colors	Rigby
Titanic, The: An Interactive History Adventure	T	HF	250+	You Choose Books	Capstone Press
Titanic, The: Lost . . . and Found	N	I	250+	Donnelly, Judy	Random House
Titan's Curse, The	W	F	250+	Riordan, Rick	Hyperion
Titch	G	RF	121	Hutchins, Pat	Penguin Group
Title IX	Y	I	2959	Leveled Readers	Houghton Mifflin Harcourt
Title IX	Y	I	2959	Leveled Readers/CA	Houghton Mifflin Harcourt
Title IX	Y	I	2959	Leveled Readers/TX	Houghton Mifflin Harcourt
Title Run	W	RF	250+	Redline Racing Series	Fitzhenry & Whiteside
Tittle-Tattle Goose	E	F	117	Story Box	Wright Group/McGraw Hill
To Bathe a Boa	L	F	297	Kudrna, C. Imbior	Carolrhoda Books
To Be a Kid	I	I	124	Ajmera, Maya & Ivanko, John D.	Charlesbridge
To Be a Slave	Z	I	250+	Lester, Julius	Dial/Penguin
To Be Free	T	HF	250+	Power Up!	Steck-Vaughn
To Be Tall	D	RF	42	Dominie Math Stories	Pearson Learning Group
To Build or Not to Build?	X	RF	3029	Leveled Readers	Houghton Mifflin Harcourt
To Build or Not To Build?	X	RF	3029	Leveled Readers/CA	Houghton Mifflin Harcourt
To Catch a Mermaid	S	F	250+	Selfors, Suzanne	Little, Brown & Co.
To Fly with the Swallows: A Story of Old California	S	I	250+	deRuiz, Dana Catharine	Steck-Vaughn
To JJ From CC	P	RF	250+	Literacy 2000	Rigby
To Kill a Mockingbird	Z	HF	250+	Lee, Harper	Warner Books
To Market, To Market	Q	I	1245	Reading Street	Pearson
To Market, to Market	I	TL	393	Story Box	Wright Group/McGraw Hill
To New York	D	RF	32	Story Box	Wright Group/McGraw Hill
To Reach the Top	R	I	250+	Power Up!	Steck-Vaughn
To Root, to Toot, to Parachute: What Is a Verb?	O	I	382	Words Are CATegorical	Millbrook Press
To School	A	F	22	Sunshine	Wright Group/McGraw Hill
To Space and Back	T	I	250+	Ride, Sally	Beech Tree Books
To Stand Forever	T	HF	250+	Literacy by Design	Rigby
To Tell the Truth, A Native American Cinderella Tale	L	TL	250+	Leveled Readers Language Support	Houghton Mifflin Harcourt
To the Beach	D	RF	43	Urmston, Kathleen; Evans, Karen	Kaeden Books
To the Moon and Beyond	S	I	250+	Sunshine	Wright Group/McGraw Hill
To the Moon!	S	SF	1767	Reading Street	Pearson

* Collection of short stories
# Graphic text

TITLE	LEVEL	GENRE	WORD COUNT	AUTHOR / SERIES	PUBLISHER / DISTRIBUTOR
To the Ocean	C	I	26	Twig	Wright Group/McGraw Hill
To the Point: A Story About E.B. White	R	B	6638	Creative Minds Biographies	Carolrhoda Books
To the Rescue	P	I	250+	InfoQuest	Rigby
To the Rescue	T	I	250+	WorldScapes	ETA Cuisenaire
To the Space Station	D	F	89	Springboard	Wright Group/McGraw Hill
To the Top of Mount Everest	T	I	2432	Leveled Readers Science	Houghton Mifflin Harcourt
To the Top!: Climbing the World's Highest Mountain	N	B	250+	Kramer, Sydelle	Random House
To Town	F	F	148	Story Box	Wright Group/McGraw Hill
To Trade or Not to Trade	T	I	250+	On Our Way to English	Rigby
To Work	C	RF	43	Sunshine	Wright Group/McGraw Hill
Toad for Tuesday, A	O	F	250+	Erickson, Russell E.	Beech Tree Books
Toad Takes Off	I	F	216	Schade, Susan; Buller, John	Random House
Toad's Birthday	E	F	135	Leveled Readers	Houghton Mifflin Harcourt
Toad's Birthday	E	F	135	Leveled Readers/CA	Houghton Mifflin Harcourt
Toad's Birthday	E	F	135	Leveled Readers/TX	Houghton Mifflin Harcourt
Toast	C	RF	82	First Stories	Pacific Learning
Toast for Mom	I	RF	250+	Ready Readers	Pearson Learning Group
Toby and B. J.	I	F	307	PM Story Books-Orange	Rigby
Toby and the Accident	J	F	329	PM Story Books	Rigby
Toby and the Big Red Van	I	F	291	PM Story Books-Orange	Rigby
Toby and the Big Tree	I	F	298	PM Story Books-Orange	Rigby
Toby at Stony Bay	J	F	494	PM Story Books	Rigby
Toby Tomato	D	F	54	Little Celebrations	Pearson Learning Group
Toby's Great Day	I	RF	190	Reading Safari	Mondo
Toby's Vacation	R	RF	1596	Reading Street	Pearson
Today	I	RF	151	Early Connections	Benchmark Education
Today and Long Ago	F	I	125	Rigby Star Quest	Rigby
Today I Got Yelled At	J	RF	174	City Kids	Rigby
Today Is Monday	E	TL	103	Instant Readers	Harcourt School Publishers
Today: August 17, 1929	O	F	250+	Tristars	Richard C. Owen
Today's Weather Is . . . A Book of Experiments	O	I	250+	Bookshop	Mondo
Todd's Teacher	F	RF	200+	Cherrington, Janelle	Scholastic
Todd's Tomatoes	J	RF	480	Leveled Readers	Houghton Mifflin Harcourt
Todd's Tomatoes	J	RF	480	Leveled Readers/CA	Houghton Mifflin Harcourt
Toenails	E	I	83	Voyages	SRA/McGraw Hill
Toes	L	I	250+	Sunshine	Wright Group/McGraw Hill
Together	C	RF	37	Sunshine	Wright Group/McGraw Hill
Together and Apart	D	I	33	Shutterbug Books	Steck-Vaughn
Together for Thanksgiving	I	I	154	Reading Street	Pearson
Toilet Paper Tigers, The	Q	RF	250+	Korman, Gordon	Bantam
Tokyo Japan's Capital	J	I	208	In Step Readers	Rigby
Tolerance	L	I	250+	Character Education	Red Brick Learning
Tolerance	M	I	250+	Everyday Character Education	Capstone Press
Toliver's Secret	T	HF	250+	Brady, Esther Wood	Alfred A. Knopf
Tom	A	RF	24	Leveled Literacy Intervention/Orange System	Heinemann
Tom and His Tractor	C	RF	27	Cat on the Mat	Oxford University Press
Tom and Pam	E	RF	69	Reading Street	Pearson
Tom Brady	P	B	1599	Amazing Athletes	Lerner Publications
Tom Edison's Bright Idea	N	B	250+	Keller, Jack	Steck-Vaughn
Tom Gets Fit	D	RF	150	New Way Red	Steck-Vaughn
Tom Is Brave	D	RF	57	PM Story Books	Rigby

* Collection of short stories
# Graphic text

TITLE	LEVEL	GENRE	WORD COUNT	AUTHOR / SERIES	PUBLISHER / DISTRIBUTOR
Tom Sawyer	J	B	250+	Jumbled Tumbled Tales & Rhymes	Rigby
Tom the TV Cat	J	F	250+	Heilbroner, Joan	Random House
Tom Thumb	E	TL	296	Fairy Tales and Folklore	Norwood House Press
Tom Turtle	D	F	87	Hill, Christopher	Ginn & Co.
*Tom, Babette & Simon	T	F	250+	Avi	Avon
Tom, the Dragon	M	F	522	New Way Orange	Steck-Vaughn
Tomahawk Beckwourth	T	B	250+	High-Fliers	Pacific Learning
Tomato Picking Day	L	I	250+	Take Two Books	Wright Group/McGraw Hill
Tomato Rose	I	RF	250+	Phonics Readers Plus	Steck-Vaughn
Tomatoes	M	I	250+	Take Two Books	Wright Group/McGraw Hill
Tomatoes and Bricks	E	RF	126	Windmill Books	Wright Group/McGraw Hill
Tomatoes Everywhere	J	I	162	On Our Way to English	Rigby
Tomb of Nebamun, The	S	I	250+	Cambridge Reading	Pearson Learning Group
Tomb Raiders	U	I	250+	High-Fliers	Pacific Learning
Tomie dePaola	L	B	196	First Biographies	Red Brick Learning
Tommy Douglas	X	B	250+	The Canadians	Fitzhenry & Whiteside
Tommy Snake's Problem	H	F	328	TOTTS	Tott Publications
Tommy Thompson's Ship of Gold	P	I	685	Leveled Readers	Houghton Mifflin Harcourt
Tommy's Treasure	I	RF	232	Literacy 2000	Rigby
Tommy's Tummy Ache	C	F	20	Literacy 2000	Rigby
Tomoko's Playhouse	D	RF	82	Reading Safari	Mondo
Tomorrow's Energy	Q	I	250+	Orbit Chapter Books	Pacific Learning
Tomorrow's Wizard	R	F	250+	MacLachlan, Patricia	Scholastic
Tom's Box	I	F	250+	Cambridge Reading	Pearson Learning Group
Tom's Friend	M	RF	250+	Voyages	SRA/McGraw Hill
Tom's Midnight Garden	V	F	250+	Pearce, Philippa	HarperTrophy
Tom's Ride	G	RF	185	PM Plus Story Books	Rigby
Tom's Rubber Band	E	RF	82	Sunshine	Wright Group/McGraw Hill
Tom's Trousers	G	RF	173	Storyteller-Night Crickets	Wright Group/McGraw Hill
Tom-Ti-Ra and the Mysterious Noise	B	F	26	Book Bus	Creative Edge
Tongue Twister Prize, The	J	RF	331	Little Books	Sadlier-Oxford
Tongues	H	I	223	Sails	Rigby
Tongues Are for Tasting, Licking, Tricking	L	I	250+	Literacy 2000	Rigby
Tonight on the Titanic	M	F	250+	Osborne, Mary Pope	Random House
Toning the Sweep	Z	RF	250+	Johnson, Angela	Scholastic
Tony and the Butterfly	J	RF	250+	Literacy Tree	Rigby
Tony Hawk	P	B	1640	Amazing Athletes	Lerner Publications
Tony Hawk	U	B	250+	The Heinle Reading Library	Thomson Learning
Tony Hawk: Skateboarding Legend	Q	I	250+	Skateboarding	Capstone Press
Tony's Dad	J	RF	399	Sails	Rigby
Tony's Taxi	LB	I	7	Reading Street	Pearson
Tony's Trail	S	RF	2333	Leveled Readers	Houghton Mifflin Harcourt
Tony's Trail	S	RF	2333	Leveled Readers/CA	Houghton Mifflin Harcourt
Too Big for Me	D	F	70	Story Box	Wright Group/McGraw Hill
Too Big for Me!	C	RF	90	First Stories	Pacific Learning
Too Big to Play	E	RF	162	Bonnell, Kris	Reading Reading Books
Too Busy for Pets!	J	RF	472	Sunshine	Wright Group/McGraw Hill
Too Fast	A	F	36	Reading Corners	Pearson Learning Group
Too High!	D	RF	66	Ready Readers	Pearson Learning Group
Too Hot to Handle	Q	RF	250+	Christopher, Matt	Little, Brown & Co.
Too Hot!	C	RF	39	Lighthouse	Rigby
Too Late!	G	F	226	Foundations	Wright Group/McGraw Hill
Too Little	E	RF	119	Foundations	Wright Group/McGraw Hill

* Collection of short stories
# Graphic text

TITLE	LEVEL	GENRE	WORD COUNT	AUTHOR / SERIES	PUBLISHER / DISTRIBUTOR
Too Little	D	RF	83	Sun Sprouts	ETA Cuisenaire
Too Many Animals	G	F	111	Alphakids	Sundance
Too Many Babas	K	TL	250+	Croll, Carolyn	HarperTrophy
Too Many Babas	K	TL	250+	Little Readers	Houghton Mifflin Harcourt
Too Many Balloons	D	RF	182	Rookie Readers	Children's Press
*Too Many Bones	G	F	125	New Way Blue	Steck-Vaughn
Too Many Cars	LB	RF	15	Hartley, Susan; Armstrong, Shane	Scholastic
Too Many Clothes	C	RF	24	Literacy 2000	Rigby
Too Many Dogs	B	F	28	Dominie Math Stories	Pearson Learning Group
Too Many Mice	J	F	250+	Bank Street	Bantam
Too Many Nuts	H	RF	132	Books for Young Learners	Richard C. Owen
Too Many Pets	D	RF	93	Rigby Rocket	Rigby
Too Many Puppies	J	RF	250+	Brewster, Patience	Scholastic
Too Many Rabbits	J	RF	250+	Parish, Peggy	Bantam
Too Many Signs!	L	RF	978	Leveled Readers	Houghton Mifflin Harcourt
Too Many Signs!	L	RF	978	Leveled Readers/CA	Houghton Mifflin Harcourt
Too Many Signs!	L	RF	978	Leveled Readers/TX	Houghton Mifflin Harcourt
Too Many Steps	J	RF	424	Foundations	Wright Group/McGraw Hill
Too Many Tamales	M	RF	250+	Soto, Gary	Putnam/Penguin
Too Many Teeth	L	F	487	Leveled Literacy Intervention/Blue System	Heinemann
Too Many Tickets	N	RF	250+	On Our Way to English	Rigby
Too Much	B	RF	27	Teacher's Choice Series	Pearson Learning Group
Too Much Ketchup	D	F	30	Ready Readers	Pearson Learning Group
Too Much Magic	R	F	250+	Sterman, Betsy & Samuel	HarperTrophy
Too Much Noise	H	TL	340	Literacy 2000	Rigby
Too Much Noise	J	TL	250+	McGovern, Ann	Scholastic
Too Much Stuff	B	F	75	Leveled Literacy Intervention/Green System	Heinemann
Too Much Stuff!	M	RF	250+	Literacy by Design	Rigby
*Too Much Talk and Other Stories	J	TL	250+	New Way Literature	Steck-Vaughn
Too Much Talk!	I	TL	250+	Rigby Star	Rigby
Too Much Trouble for Grandpa	K	F	250+	Lewis, Rob	Mondo
Too Much Trouble for Grandpa	J	F	250+	Sokoloff, Myka-Lynne	Sadlier-Oxford
Too Small Jill	J	RF	306	Little Books	Sadlier-Oxford
Too Small!	I	RF	245	InfoTrek	ETA Cuisenaire
Too Soon to Say Goodbye	S	RF	250+	Kent, Deborah	Scholastic
Too Tall	J	F	423	Leveled Literacy Intervention/Green System	Heinemann
Too-Good-to-Be-True Shoes	O	F	250+	High-Fliers	Pacific Learning
Tool Box, The	H	RF	144	Rockwell, Anne	Macmillan
Tools and Gadgets	T	I	250+	Historic Communities	Crabtree
Tools Can Help Us See	G	I	107	Windows on Literacy	National Geographic
Tools Measure Weather	I	I	145	Windows on Literacy	National Geographic
Tools of Investigators, The	M	I	575	Vocabulary Readers	Houghton Mifflin Harcourt
Tools of Investigators, The	M	I	575	Vocabulary Readers/CA	Houghton Mifflin Harcourt
Tools Scientists Use	K	I	184	Windows on Literacy	National Geographic
Tools to Use	D	I	42	Little Red Readers	Sundance
Toot! Toot!	LB	F	21	Joy Readers	Pearson Learning Group
Toot, Toot	C	I	47	Wildsmith, Brian	Oxford University Press
Too-Tall Paul, Too-Small Paul	H	RF	325	Real Kids Readers	Millbrook Press
Tooter Pepperday	L	RF	250+	Spinelli, Jerry	Random House
Tooth Fairy Tells All, The	K	F	513	Silly Millies	Millbrook Press

TITLE	LEVEL	GENRE	WORD COUNT	AUTHOR / SERIES	PUBLISHER / DISTRIBUTOR
Tooth Fairy, The	WB	F	N/A	Collington, Peter	Wright Group/McGraw Hill
Tooth Fairy, The	D	F	57	My First Reader	Grolier Press
Tooth on the Loose	H	RF	235	Literacy by Design	Rigby
Tooth Race, The	I	RF	250+	Little Readers	Houghton Mifflin Harcourt
Tooth Trouble	L	RF	250+	Klein, Abby	Scholastic
Toothbrush Tale	G	F	117	New Way Blue	Steck-Vaughn
Toothless!	M	F	250+	Rigby Gigglers	Rigby
Toothpaste Millionaire, The	T	RF	250+	Merrill, Jean	Houghton Mifflin Harcourt
Toothwalkers	N	I	250+	Sails	Rigby
Too-Tight Shoes	I	RF	170	Evangeline Nicholas Collection	Wright Group/McGraw Hill
Top Cat	O	I	250+	Byars, Betsy	Penguin Group
Top Cat	K	F	250+	Story Steps	Rigby
Top Dinosaurs	I	I	176	Big Cat	Pacific Learning
Top Hat, the Detective	O	RF	1364	Reading Street	Pearson
Top of the World, The: Climbing Mount Everest	R	I	250+	Jenkins, Steve	Houghton Mifflin Harcourt
Top Secret: The World of Spies	Y	I	250+	Boldprint	Steck-Vaughn
*Top Ten Shakespeare Stories	Z	HF	250+	Terry, Deary	Scholastic
Torn Thread	W	HF	250+	Isaacs, Anne	Scholastic
Tornado	O	I	250+	Byars, Betsy	HarperTrophy
Tornado	T	I	250+	Kramer, Stephen	Lerner Publishing
Tornado	E	I	37	Spinelle, Nancy Louise	Kaeden Books
Tornado Chasers	T	RF	1520	Independent Readers Science	Houghton Mifflin Harcourt
Tornado Tony	H	RF	182	Well-Being Series	Pearson Learning Group
Tornado Warning!	N	I	545	Gear Up!	Wright Group/ McGraw Hill
Tornado Watch	O	I	250+	In Step Readers	Rigby
Tornado Watch	O	I	250+	Literacy by Design	Rigby
Tornado!	R	RF	1470	Leveled Readers Social Studies	Houghton Mifflin Harcourt
Tornado, The	L	RF	250+	PM Story Books	Rigby
Tornadoes	W	I	250+	Disasters Up Close	Lerner Publications
Tornadoes	S	I	250+	Natural Disasters	Capstone Press
Tornadoes	M	I	664	Pull Ahead Books	Lerner Publications
Tornadoes	S	I	250+	Theme Sets	National Geographic
Tornadoes	O	I	250+	Weather Update	Capstone Press
Tornadoes and Hurricanes	L	I	393	Time for Kids	Teacher Created Materials
Tornadoes!	N	I	250+	Hopping, Lorraine Jean	Scholastic
Toronto Blue Jays, The	S	I	250+	Team Spirit	Norwood House Press
Tortilla Factory, The	M	RF	1175	Reading Street	Pearson
Tortillas	E	RF	71	Gonzalez-Jensen, Margarita	Scholastic
Tortoise and the Hare Race Again, The	N	TL	250+	Bernstein, Dan	Holiday House
Tortoise and the Hare, The	H	TL	148	Cambridge Reading	Pearson Learning Group
*Tortoise Shell and Other African Stories, The	N	TL	250+	Smith, Geof	Scholastic
Tossed Salad	C	I	28	Twig	Wright Group/McGraw Hill
Total Eclipse of the Sun	W	I	250+	Independent Readers Science	Houghton Mifflin Harcourt
Totara Tree, The	M	RF	391	Book Bank	Wright Group/McGraw Hill
Totem Poles	D	I	46	Leveled Readers Social Studies	Houghton Mifflin Harcourt
Totem Poles	L	I	246	Twig	Wright Group/McGraw Hill
Totem Poles of North America	D	I	42	Leveled Readers Social Studies	Houghton Mifflin Harcourt
Touch	C	I	39	Twig	Wright Group/McGraw Hill
Touch It!	E	I	61	Shutterbug Books	Steck-Vaughn
*Touch of Gold and Other Stories, The	M	TL	250+	Lane, Sheila; Kemp, Marion	Wood Lock Educational
Touch of Sepia, A	M	RF	250+	Voyages	SRA/McGraw Hill
Touch the Earth	L	RF	250+	Bookshop	Mondo
Touch the Moon	H	F	238	Gear Up!	Wright Group/McGraw Hill
Touchdown for Tommy	Q	RF	250+	Christopher, Matt	Little, Brown & Co.

* Collection of short stories
# Graphic text

TITLE	LEVEL	GENRE	WORD COUNT	AUTHOR / SERIES	PUBLISHER / DISTRIBUTOR
Touchdown!: You Can Play Football	M	I	250+	Game Day	Picture Window Books
Touching	J	I	142	Pebble Books	Capstone Press
Touching	E	I	92	Senses	Lerner Publishing
Touching	M	I	250+	The Senses	Capstone Press
Touching Spirit Bear	Y	F	250+	Mikaelsen, Ben	HarperCollins
Tough Choices	W	RF	250+	Power Up!	Steck-Vaughn
Tough Nut to Crack, A	Q	RF	250+	Birdseye, Tom	Holiday House
Tough Times	S	I	970	Vocabulary Readers	Houghton Mifflin Harcourt
Tough Times	S	I	970	Vocabulary Readers/CA	Houghton Mifflin Harcourt
Tough Times	S	I	970	Vocabulary Readers/TX	Houghton Mifflin Harcourt
Tough Trails	U	RF	250+	Orca Soundings	Orca Book Publishers
Touring the Cities of the World	U	I	250+	Explore More	Wright Group/McGraw Hill
Tournament Trouble	R	RF	250+	Costello, Emily	Dell
Tow Trucks	I	I	132	Mighty Machines	Capstone Press
Tow Trucks	L	I	493	Pull Ahead Books	Lerner Publications
Tower, The	A	RF	40	InfoTrek	ETA Cuisenaire
Tower, The	P	SF	250+	Orbit Double Takes	Pacific Learning
Towers	M	I	250+	Rigby Literacy	Rigby
Town Auction, The	M	RF	866	Leveled Readers	Houghton Mifflin Harcourt
Town Auction, The	M	RF	866	Leveled Readers/CA	Houghton Mifflin Harcourt
Town Auction, The	M	RF	866	Leveled Readers/TX	Houghton Mifflin Harcourt
Town in Trouble, A	P	F	1019	Leveled Readers	Houghton Mifflin Harcourt
Town Mouse and Country Mouse	E	TL	170	Folk Tales	Pioneer Valley
Town Mouse and Country Mouse	K	TL	250+	PM Tales and Plays-Purple	Rigby
Town Mouse and Country Mouse	I	TL	276	Sun Sprouts	ETA Cuisenaire
Town Mouse and Country Mouse, The	I	TL	172	Aesop	Wright Group/McGraw Hill
Town Mouse and the Country Mouse, The	F	TL	203	Storyworlds	Heinemann Educational Publishers
Toxic Waste: Chemical Spills in Our World	R	I	250+	On Deck	Rigby
Toy Box, A	LB	I	19	Literacy 2000	Rigby
Toy Box, The	B	I	49	PM Plus Starters	Rigby
Toy Box, The	LB	RF	14	Ready Readers	Pearson Learning Group
Toy Box, The	B	RF	49	Sun Sprouts	ETA Cuisenaire
Toy Farm, The	I	RF	311	PM Story Books-Orange	Rigby
Toy for Vik, A	C	RF	66	Rigby Rocket	Rigby
Toy Maker, The	B	RF	31	Ray's Readers	Outside the Box
Toy Models	A	I	40	Early Connections	Benchmark Education
Toy Shop, The	L	RF	250+	Book Project	Sundance
Toy Store	B	F	37	Reading Street	Pearson
Toy Store, The	B	RF	55	Leveled Readers Emergent	Houghton Mifflin Harcourt
Toy Tooth, The	I	RF	250+	Rigby Literacy	Rigby
Toy Town	C	I	36	Home Connection Collection	Rigby
Toy Trouble	H	F	250+	Bookshop	Mondo
Toymil and the Bear	I	RF	233	Story Box	Wright Group/McGraw Hill
Toys	B	RF	37	Foundations	Wright Group/McGraw Hill
Toys	A	RF	30	Leveled Literacy Intervention/Orange System	Heinemann
Toys	E	I	76	Talk About Books	Pearson Learning Group
Toys	D	RF	106	Tiger Cub	Peguis
Toys	C	I	41	Windows on Literacy	National Geographic
Toys and Games Then and Now	H	I	111	Then and Now	Lerner Publications
Toys and Play	F	RF	194	PM Plus Nonfiction	Rigby
Toys Can Move	LB	I	7	Windows on Literacy	National Geographic
Toys Long Ago	D	I	54	Yellow Umbrella Books	Red Brick Learning

* Collection of short stories
# Graphic text

TITLE	LEVEL	GENRE	WORD COUNT	AUTHOR / SERIES	PUBLISHER / DISTRIBUTOR
Toys' Party, The	F	F	48	Oxford Reading Tree	Oxford University Press
Toys' Picnic, The	B	RF	67	First Stories	Pacific Learning
Toys with Wheels	C	I	41	Home Connection Collection	Rigby
Toys, Then and Now	G	I	108	Take Two Books	Wright Group/McGraw Hill
Toytown Bus Helps Out, The	E	F	125	PM Stars	Rigby
Toytown Fire Engine, The	D	F	105	PM Plus Story Books	Rigby
Toytown Helicopter, The	D	F	97	PM Plus Story Books	Rigby
Toytown Race Car, The	F	F	188	PM Plus Story Books	Rigby
Toytown Rescue, The	D	F	100	PM Plus Story Books	Rigby
Tracey and the Sun	M	F	250+	Sails	Rigby
Tracing the Anasazi	P	I	830	Independent Readers Social Studies	Houghton Mifflin Harcourt
Tracing the Harlem Renaissance	W	I	1965	Vocabulary Readers	Houghton Mifflin Harcourt
Tracing the Harlem Renaissance	W	I	1965	Vocabulary Readers/CA	Houghton Mifflin Harcourt
Track	K	I	250+	On Deck	Rigby
Track and Field	M	I	788	Springboard	Wright Group/McGraw Hill
Tracker	T	RF	250+	Paulsen, Gary	Scholastic
Trackers of Dynamic Earth	S	B	250+	Navigators Biography Series	Benchmark Education
Tracking Our Class Garden	O	RF	2522	Reading Street	Pearson
Tracking the Caribou	O	I	250+	Lighthouse	Ginn & Co.
Tracking Triple Seven	Z	RF	250+	Bastedo, Jamie	Fitzhenry & Whiteside
Tracking with Uncle Joe	K	RF	653	Appleton-Smith, Laura	Flyleaf Publishing
Tracks	C	I	25	Sunshine	Wright Group/McGraw Hill
Tracks	C	I	49	Twig	Wright Group/McGraw Hill
Tracks	L	I	250+	Voyages	SRA/McGraw Hill
Tracks in the Sand	I	I	125	Levin, Amy	Scholastic
Tracks in the Sand	H	I	190	Sails	Rigby
Tracks in the Sand	L	I	250+	Sunshine	Wright Group/McGraw Hill
Tracks in the Snow	E	I	207	Sails	Rigby
Tracks on the Ground	N	I	250+	Pacific Literacy	Pacific Learning
Tractor Trailers	N	I	250+	Transportation	Red Brick Learning
Tractors	M	I	250+	Transportation	Compass Point Books
Trading Places	L	RF	1063	Rigby Flying Colors	Rigby
Trading Talents	S	RF	1952	Leveled Readers	Houghton Mifflin Harcourt
Trading Talents	S	RF	1952	Leveled Readers/CA	Houghton Mifflin Harcourt
Trading Talents	S	RF	1952	Leveled Readers/TX	Houghton Mifflin Harcourt
Tradition of the Harvest, The	P	RF	250+	Leveled Readers Language Support	Houghton Mifflin Harcourt
Traditional Crafts of Mexico	Q	I	1053	Reading Street	Pearson
Traffic	A	I	28	Leveled Literacy Intervention/ Green System	Heinemann
Traffic	A	I	30	Lighthouse	Rigby
Traffic Jam	F	RF	55	City Stories	Rigby
Traffic Jam	C	RF	76	First Stories	Pacific Learning
Traffic Jam	E	RF	133	Harper, Leslie	Kaeden Books
Traffic Jam	D	RF	18	Little Red Readers	Sundance
Traffic Jam	LB	RF	18	Voyages	SRA/McGraw Hill
Traffic Jam, The	A	RF	33	Handprints B	Educators Publishing Service
Traffic Light Rap	I	RF	261	Sun Sprouts	ETA Cuisenaire
Traffic Light Sandwich	H	I	87	Wonder World	Wright Group/McGraw Hill
Trail Home, The	S	RF	2004	Leveled Readers	Houghton Mifflin Harcourt
Trail of Bones	U	SF	250+	Williams, Mark London	Candlewick Press
Trail of Tears, 1838, The	V	I	250+	Let Freedom Ring	Capstone Press

* Collection of short stories
\# Graphic text

TITLE	LEVEL	GENRE	WORD COUNT	AUTHOR / SERIES	PUBLISHER / DISTRIBUTOR
Trailblazers!	O	RF	250+	Action Packs	Rigby
Train	V	I	250+	Eyewitness Books	DK Publishing
Train Ride	C	RF	15	Bebop Books	Lee & Low Books Inc.
Train Ride Story, The	I	F	189	Sunshine	Wright Group/McGraw Hill
Train Ride, The	D	RF	127	In Step Readers	Rigby
Train Ride, The	C	F	29	Literacy 2000	Rigby
Train that Ran Away	I	F	32	Jellybeans	Rigby
Train Time	L	I	250+	Baehr, Lisa	Hampton-Brown
Train to the West?	O	I	279	Vocabulary Readers	Houghton Mifflin Harcourt
Train Trip, A	L	I	172	Vocabulary Readers	Houghton Mifflin Harcourt
Train Wreck	S	HF	250+	Duey, Kathleen; Bale, Karen A.	Simon & Schuster
Train Wreck!	T	I	2383	Reading Street	Pearson
Train, Car, Boat, Plane	E	RF	180	Leveled Readers	Houghton Mifflin Harcourt
Train, Car, Boat, Plane	E	RF	180	Leveled Readers/CA	Houghton Mifflin Harcourt
Train, The	C	I	38	Gear Up!	Wright Group/McGraw Hill
Train, The	C	RF	27	Visions	Wright Group/McGraw Hill
Training a Dog	M	I	591	Vocabulary Readers	Houghton Mifflin Harcourt
Training a Dog	M	I	591	Vocabulary Readers/CA	Houghton Mifflin Harcourt
Training a Guide Dog	N	I	250+	Literacy by Design	Rigby
Training a Police Dog	G	I	103	Vocabulary Readers	Houghton Mifflin Harcourt
Training for Space	T	I	508	Vocabulary Readers	Houghton Mifflin Harcourt
Training for the Olympics	T	I	1381	Independent Readers Science	Houghton Mifflin Harcourt
Training My Dog	L	I	917	Leveled Readers Science	Houghton Mifflin Harcourt
Training Peanut	M	RF	1278	Reading Street	Pearson
Trains	H	I	250+	Albanese, Rachel	Scholastic
Trains	Q	I	250+	Literacy 2000	Rigby
Trains	H	I	122	Mighty Machines	Capstone Press
Trains	K	I	339	Pull Ahead Books	Lerner Publications
Trains	E	I	137	Sails	Rigby
Trains	F	I	146	Springboard	Wright Group/McGraw Hill
Trains	T	I	250+	The World's Fastest	Red Brick Learning
Trains	A	I	36	Vocabulary Readers	Houghton Mifflin Harcourt
Trains	A	I	36	Vocabulary Readers/CA	Houghton Mifflin Harcourt
Trains	A	I	36	Vocabulary Readers/TX	Houghton Mifflin Harcourt
Trains and How They Work	Q	I	895	Time for Kids	Teacher Created Materials
Trains of the Past	M	I	250+	On Deck	Rigby
Trains on the Rails	K	I	250+	PM Plus	Rigby
Train Trip, A	L	I	172	Vocabulary Readers/CA	Houghton Mifflin Harcourt
Traitor Game, The	Z+	F	250+	Collins, B.R.	Bloomsbury Children's Books
Traitor: The Case of Benedict Arnold	X	B	250+	Fritz, Jean	Putnam/Penguin
Transcontinental Railroad, The	V	I	250+	Cornerstones of Freedom	Children's Press
Transcontinental Railroad, The	T	I	250+	Navigators Social Studies Series	Benchmark Education
Transcontinental Railroad, The	S	I	250+	The Library of the Westward Expansion	Rosen Publishing Group
Transcontinental Railroad, The: Connecting America	S	I	250+	Explore More	Wright Group/McGraw Hill
Transforming Trash	S	I	250+	Orbit Chapter Books	Pacific Learning
Transportation	C	I	17	We Are Alike and Different	Lerner Publishing
Transportation Firsts	T	I	250+	High-Fliers	Pacific Learning
Transportation in Many Cultures	I	I	89	Life Around the World	Capstone Press
Transportation Museum, The	C	I	79	Little Red Readers	Sundance
Transportation Then and Now	I	I	123	Then and Now	Lerner Publications
Transportation Through Time	Q	I	250+	Rigby Focus	Rigby

* Collection of short stories
# Graphic text

TITLE	LEVEL	GENRE	WORD COUNT	AUTHOR / SERIES	PUBLISHER / DISTRIBUTOR
Transportation Time Line, A	P	I	250+	Discovery World	Rigby
Transportation Yesterday and Today	M	I	659	Relf, Coco	Harcourt School Publishers
Transportation: Going, Going, Gone	R	I	250+	Kids Discover Reading	Wright Group/McGraw Hill
Trapp Family Singers, The	X	B	2962	Leveled Readers	Houghton Mifflin Harcourt
Trapp Family Singers, The	X	B	2962	Leveled Readers/CA	Houghton Mifflin Harcourt
Trapped	T	F	250+	Moloney, James	Stone Arch Books
Trapped by a Teacher	Q	RF	250+	Action Packs	Rigby
Trapped Genie, The	M	F	250+	Tristars	Richard C. Owen
Trapped in a Canyon!: Aron Ralston's Story of Survival	R	I	250+	True Tales of Survival	Capstone Press
Trapped in Space	P	SF	250+	Johnson, David	Stone Arch Books
Trapped!	N	RF	250+	High-Fliers	Pacific Learning
Trapped!	L	RF	250+	New Way Literature	Steck-Vaughn
Trapped!	O	RF	250+	SupaDoopers	Sundance
Trash	I	I	242	Springboard	Wright Group/McGraw Hill
Trash	H	I	154	Sun Sprouts	ETA Cuisenaire
Trash	H	F	130	Sunshine	Wright Group/McGraw Hill
Trash Art	LB	I	18	Shutterbug Books	Steck-Vaughn
Trash Can Band, The	J	RF	252	Little Books	Sadlier-Oxford
Trash with Dash	T	I	250+	Power Up!	Steck-Vaughn
Travel in the U.S.A., Then & Now	P	I	739	Time for Kids	Teacher Created Materials
Travel Money, U.S.A.	I	I	245	Early Connections	Benchmark Education
Travel Smart	P	I	250+	iOpeners	Pearson Learning Group
Travel Team	X	RF	250+	Lupica, Mike	Puffin Books
Travelers and the Bear, The	M	TL	250+	Literacy by Design	Rigby
Travelers and Traders	Q	I	250+	Explorers	Wright Group/McGraw Hill
Traveling	C	F	86	Foundations	Wright Group/McGraw Hill
Traveling Across Australia	O	I	250+	Windows on Literacy	National Geographic
Traveling Animals	M	I	381	Sails	Rigby
Traveling Around the City	M	I	387	Rigby Flying Colors	Rigby
Traveling by Train	O	I	485	Leveled Readers Social Studies	Houghton Mifflin Harcourt
Traveling Guitar, The	O	RF	674	Leveled Readers	Houghton Mifflin Harcourt
Traveling in America	O	I	250+	On Our Way to English	Rigby
Traveling Ted's Postcards	C	F	161	Little Celebrations	Pearson Learning Group
Travels and Travails	U	B	250+	High-Fliers	Pacific Learning
Travels of Alvar Nunez Cebeza de Vaca, The	X	B	3751	Leveled Readers Social Studies	Houghton Mifflin Harcourt
Travels of Marco Polo, The	T	I	250+	Explorers & Exploration	Steck-Vaughn
Travels of Marco Polo, The	S	B	250+	WorldScapes	ETA Cuisenaire
Travels with Rainie Marie	S	B	250+	Martin, Patricia	Hyperion
Travis Pastrana	P	B	1818	Amazing Athletes	Lerner Publications
Travis Pastrana: Motocross Legend	Q	B	250+	Dirt Bikes	Capstone Press
Treasure Cave, The	L	F	250+	Cambridge Reading	Pearson Learning Group
Treasure Hunt	O	I	250+	Early Connections	Benchmark Education
Treasure Hunt	LB	F	14	Smart Starts	Rigby
Treasure Hunt, The	I	RF	350	InfoTrek	ETA Cuisenaire
Treasure Hunt, The	K	RF	250+	Literacy by Design	Rigby
Treasure Hunting	M	RF	250+	Literacy 2000	Rigby
Treasure Hunting: Looking for Lost Riches	S	I	250+	High Five Reading	Red Brick Learning
Treasure in the Attic	G	RF	153	Seedlings	Continental Press
Treasure Island	W	HF	250+	High-Fliers	Pacific Learning
Treasure Island	Z	HF	250+	Stevenson, Robert Lewis	Scholastic
Treasure Island, A	F	RF	177	PM Plus Story Books	Rigby
Treasure Lost at Sea: The Nuestra Senora de Atocha	T	I	250+	Rigby Literacy	Rigby

* Collection of short stories
# Graphic text

T

TITLE	LEVEL	GENRE	WORD COUNT	AUTHOR / SERIES	PUBLISHER / DISTRIBUTOR
Treasure Map, The	B	F	32	Harry's Math Books	Outside the Box
Treasure Map, The	L	F	306	Leveled Readers	Houghton Mifflin Harcourt
Treasure Map, The	L	F	306	Leveled Readers/CA	Houghton Mifflin Harcourt
Treasure Map, The	L	F	306	Leveled Readers/TX	Houghton Mifflin Harcourt
Treasure of Alpheus Winterborn, The	S	F	250+	Bellairs, John	Penguin Group
Treasure of El Patrón, The	T	RF	250+	Paulsen, Gary	Bantam
Treasure of the Lost Lagoon, The	K	F	250+	Hayes, Geoffrey	Random House
Treasure on Fraser Street, The	K	RF	250+	Home Connection Collection	Rigby
Treasure!	J	RF	250+	Phonics Readers Plus	Steck-Vaughn
Treasure, The	B	RF	31	Sails	Rigby
Treasures	L	RF	263	Books for Young Learners	Richard C. Owen
Treasures	T	I	250+	Connectors	Pacific Learning
Treasures from the Sea	U	I	250+	Connectors	Pacific Learning
Treasures in the Dust	U	HF	250+	Porter, Tracey	HarperTrophy
*Treasury of Pirate Stories, A	S	F	250+	Bradman, Tony	Kingfisher
Treat Me Right!	Q	I	250+	Kids Talk	Picture Window Books
Treat, The	E	F	96	Leveled Readers Language Support	Houghton Mifflin Harcourt
Tree	W	I	250+	Eyewitness Books	DK Publishing
Tree Branch, The	WB	RF	N/A	Instant Readers	Harcourt School Publishers
Tree by Leaf	V	F	250+	Voigt, Cynthia	Simon & Schuster
Tree Can Be, A	E	I	74	Nayer, Judy	Scholastic
Tree Falls Down, A	M	F	250+	Orbit Double Takes	Pacific Learning
Tree Fell Over the River, A	C	RF	72	Little Red Readers	Sundance
Tree for All Seasons, A	B	I	24	Independent Readers Science	Houghton Mifflin Harcourt
Tree for All Seasons, A	B	I	24	Science Support Readers	Houghton Mifflin Harcourt
Tree for Spring, A	G	RF	186	PM Collection	Rigby
Tree Fort Adventure	H	RF	219	Adams, Lorraine; Bruvold, Lynn	Eagle Crest Books
Tree Fort, The	G	RF	182	Adams, Lorraine; Bruvold, Lynn	Eagle Crest Books
Tree Fort, The	H	RF	160	Early Transitional	Pioneer Valley
Tree Frogs	J	I	87	Pebble Books	Red Brick Learning
Tree Horse, A	H	RF	220	PM Plus Story Books	Rigby
Tree House Fun	G	RF	165	First Start	Troll Associates
Tree House, The	N	RF	250+	Boyz Rule!	Mondo
Tree House, The	E	RF	25	Brown, Roberta; Carey, Sue	Scholastic
Tree House, The	I	RF	322	Explorations	Eleanor Curtain Publishing
Tree House, The	I	RF	322	Explorations	Okapi Eductional Materials
Tree House, The	F	F	198	Leveled Literacy Intervention/ Green System	Heinemann
Tree House, The	A	F	20	Leveled Readers	Houghton Mifflin Harcourt
Tree House, The	A	F	20	Leveled Readers/CA	Houghton Mifflin Harcourt
Tree House, The	B	F	30	Story Box	Wright Group/McGraw Hill
Tree House, The	B	RF	32	Sunshine	Wright Group/McGraw Hill
Tree Is a Home, A	H	I	203	Learn to Read	Creative Teaching Press
Tree Is a Home, A	I	I	135	Pacific Literacy	Pacific Learning
Tree Is My Home, A	G	RF	114	Leveled Readers Science	Houghton Mifflin Harcourt
Tree of Birds	J	F	250+	Leveled Readers Language Support	Houghton Mifflin Harcourt
Tree of Life, The	M	I	502	Springboard	Wright Group/ McGraw Hill
Tree Stump, The	B	TL	34	Little Celebrations	Pearson Learning Group
Tree With Eyes, The	O	F	250+	The Adventures of Sam X	Stone Arch Books
Tree, The	G	I	94	Alphakids	Sundance
Tree, The	F	RF	101	Sunshine	Wright Group/McGraw Hill
Tree, the Trunk, and the Tuba, The	Q	RF	250+	Literacy 2000	Rigby

* Collection of short stories
# Graphic text

T

TITLE	LEVEL	GENRE	WORD COUNT	AUTHOR / SERIES	PUBLISHER / DISTRIBUTOR
Treehouse	D	I	43	Hoenecke, Karen	Kaeden Books
Treehouse Club, The	F	RF	158	Home Connection Collection	Rigby
Treehouse Club, The	N	RF	250+	Navigators Fiction Series	Benchmark Education
Trees	L	I	158	Bookshop	Mondo
Trees	K	I	388	Early Connections	Benchmark Education
Trees	J	I	124	Literacy 2000	Rigby
Trees	H	I	194	Momentum Literacy Program	Troll Associates
Trees	G	I	351	Sails	Rigby
Trees	H	I	28	Sun Sprouts	ETA Cuisenaire
Trees	A	I	28	Twig	Wright Group/McGraw Hill
Trees	G	I	149	Vocabulary Readers	Houghton Mifflin Harcourt
Trees	G	I	149	Vocabulary Readers/CA	Houghton Mifflin Harcourt
Trees	G	I	149	Vocabulary Readers/TX	Houghton Mifflin Harcourt
Trees and Leaves	F	I	33	iOpeners	Pearson Learning Group
Trees and Leaves	S	I	250+	Nature Club	Troll Associates
Trees and Plants in the Rain Forest	O	I	250+	Pirotta, Saviour	Steck-Vaughn
Trees Are Special	I	I	85	Sunshine	Wright Group/McGraw Hill
Trees Are Terrific!	G	I	123	Yellow Umbrella Books	Red Brick Learning
Trees Belong to Everyone	L	I	250+	Literacy 2000	Rigby
Trees for Life	L	I	768	Sun Sprouts	ETA Cuisenaire
Tree's Life, A	J	I	102	Windows on Literacy	National Geographic
Trees Please!	L	I	250+	Storyteller Chapter Books	Wright Group/ McGraw Hill
Trek to the Top	N	I	655	Reading Street	Pearson
Trek, The	I	RF	158	Jonas, Ann	Greenwillow
Trekking in Nepal	S	I	250+	WorldScapes	ETA Cuisenaire
Trent and Grace Make a Home	D	F	100	Springboard	Wright Group/McGraw Hill
Trevor from Trinidad	Q	RF	1685	Leveled Readers	Houghton Mifflin Harcourt
Trevor's New Home	O	RF	250+	Leveled Readers Language Support	Houghton Mifflin Harcourt
Trial by Jury	R	I	1357	Vocabulary Readers	Houghton Mifflin Harcourt
Trial by Jury	R	I	1357	Vocabulary Readers/CA	Houghton Mifflin Harcourt
Triangle	B	I	34	Shapes	Lerner Publications
Triangle Fire, The: Hannah's Diary	Q	HF	250+	Orbit Chapter Books	Pacific Learning
Triangles	I	I	178	Shapes	Red Brick Learning
Triangles Around Town	J	I	271	Shapes Around Town	Capstone Press
Triathlon	Q	I	250+	Extreme Sports	Red Brick Learning
Triathlon	N	I	423	Nonfiction	Literacy Footprints
Triathlon Team, The	H	RF	352	Rigby Flying Colors	Rigby
Tribes	Z+	RF	250+	Slade, Arthur	Random House
Triceratops	I	I	139	Dinosaur and Prehistoric Animals	Capstone Press
Triceratops and the Crocodiles, The	I	HF	250+	PM Plus Story Books	Rigby
Triceratops on the Farm	L	F	208	Wesley & the Dinosaurs	Wright Group/McGraw Hill
Trick of the Tale	T	TL	250+	Matthews, John and Caitlin	Candlewick Press
Trick or Treat Halloween	F	RF	131	First Start	Troll Associates
Trick, The	J	TL	550	Leveled Readers/TX	Houghton Mifflin Harcourt
Trick, The	F	RF	65	New Way Red	Steck-Vaughn
Tricking the Eye	U	I	2024	Reading Street	Pearson
Tricking the Tiger	J	TL	250+	PM Plus Story Books	Rigby
Tricking Tracy	F	RF	125	Tadpoles	Rigby
Tricks	I	I	218	Sun Sprouts	ETA Cuisenaire
Tricks to Doing Magic	Q	I	2054	Reading Street	Pearson
Trickster Ghost, The	O	F	250+	Showell, E.	Scholastic
Tricksters	M	RF	250+	SupaDoopers	Sundance

* Collection of short stories
\# Graphic text

TITLE	LEVEL	GENRE	WORD COUNT	AUTHOR / SERIES	PUBLISHER / DISTRIBUTOR
Tricksters of Fringle, The	P	I	250+	Sails	Rigby
Tricksters, The	D	F	49	Ray's Readers	Outside the Box
Tricky Insects and Other Fun Creatures	K	I	250+	Spyglass Books	Compass Point Books
Tricky Rabbit	I	TL	198	Books for Young Learners	Richard C. Owen
Tricky Sticky Problem, The	H	RF	71	Pacific Literacy	Pacific Learning
Triffic the Extraordinary Pig	R	F	250+	King-Smith, Dick	Bantam
Trilobites	K	I	141	Books for Young Learners	Richard C. Owen
Trino's Choice	Y	RF	250+	Bertrand, Diane Gonzales	Pinata Books
Trino's Time	Y	RF	250+	Bertrand, Diane Gonzales	Pinata Books
Trip Across the Country, A	C	RF	47	Independent Readers Social Studies	Houghton Mifflin Harcourt
Trip Around the Gulf of Mexico, A	M	I	250+	People, Spaces & Places	Rand McNally
Trip by Train, A	J	RF	298	InfoTrek	ETA Cuisenaire
Trip into Space, A	I	I	129	Little Red Readers	Sundance
Trip into Space, A	H	I	79	Story Steps	Rigby
Trip of a Lifetime, The	S	RF	250+	Reading Safari	Mondo
Trip on the Erie Canal, A	L	RF	260	Independent Readers Social Studies	Houghton Mifflin Harcourt
Trip Through Africa, A	O	I	971	Vocabulary Readers	Houghton Mifflin Harcourt
Trip Through Africa, A	O	I	971	Vocabulary Readers/CA	Houghton Mifflin Harcourt
Trip Through Our Solar System, A	L	I	250+	Rosen Real Readers	Rosen Publishing Group
Trip Through the Airport, A	L	I	250+	Rigby Literacy	Rigby
Trip Through Time, A	M	I	357	Gear Up!	Wright Group/ McGraw Hill
Trip to a Pond	B	RF	33	Leveled Readers Science	Houghton Mifflin Harcourt
Trip to Freedom	M	B	250+	Greetings	Rigby
Trip to Japan, A	M	I	250+	Rosen Real Readers	Rosen Publishing Group
Trip to the Aquarium, A	LB	RF	18	Kloes, Carol	Kaeden Books
Trip to the Beach, A	F	F	258	Bella and Rosie Series	Literacy Footprints
Trip to the Beach, A	E	I	44	iOpeners	Pearson Learning Group
Trip to the Capitol, A	S	I	1043	Reading Street	Pearson
Trip to the City, A	E	F	119	Bookshop	Mondo
Trip to the Dentist, A	I	I	196	Rosen Real Readers	Rosen Publishing Group
Trip to the Doctor, A	B	I	36	Windows on Literacy	National Geographic
Trip to the Fire Station	K	I	182	Rosen Real Readers	Rosen Publishing Group
Trip to the Fire Station	A	I	25	Vocabulary Readers	Houghton Mifflin Harcourt
Trip to the Fire Station	A	I	25	Vocabulary Readers/CA	Houghton Mifflin Harcourt
Trip to the Laundromutt, A	H	F	229	Leveled Literacy Intervention/ Green System	Heinemann
Trip to the Park, The	H	RF	277	Foundations	Wright Group/McGraw Hill
Trip to the Post Office, A	I	I	191	Rosen Real Readers	Rosen Publishing Group
Trip to the Rock	B	F	90	Leveled Readers	Houghton Mifflin Harcourt
Trip to the Rock	B	F	90	Leveled Readers/CA	Houghton Mifflin Harcourt
Trip to the Rock	B	F	90	Leveled Readers/TX	Houghton Mifflin Harcourt
Trip to the Station, A	I	I	241	Rosen Real Readers	Rosen Publishing Group
Trip to the Video Store, A	H	RF	203	Foundations	Wright Group/McGraw Hill
Trip to the Zoo, A	C	RF	78	Carousel Readers	Pearson Learning Group
Trip to the Zoo, A	F	I	93	Independent Readers Science	Houghton Mifflin Harcourt
Trip to the Zoo, A	F	I	112	Rosen Real Readers	Rosen Publishing Group
Trip with Grandma, A	K	F	727	Ohi, Ruth	Annick Press
Trip, The	E	F	224	Leveled Literacy Intervention/ Blue System	Heinemann
Trip, The	E	F	108	Ready Readers	Pearson Learning Group
Triple Rotten Day, The	L	RF	250+	Seuling, Barbara	Scholastic

TITLE	LEVEL	GENRE	WORD COUNT	AUTHOR / SERIES	PUBLISHER / DISTRIBUTOR
Triplet Trouble and the Bicycle Race	L	RF	250+	Dadey, Debbie; Jones, Marcia Thornton	Scholastic
Triplet Trouble and the Class Trip	L	RF	250+	Dadey, Debbie; Jones, Marcia Thornton	Scholastic
Triplet Trouble and the Cookie Contest	L	RF	250+	Dadey, Debbie; Jones, Marcia Thornton	Scholastic
Triplet Trouble and the Field Day Disaster	L	RF	250+	Dadey, Debbie; Jones, Marcia Thornton	Scholastic
Triplet Trouble and the Pizza Party	L	RF	250+	Dadey, Debbie; Jones, Marcia Thornton	Scholastic
Triplet Trouble and the Red Heart Race	L	RF	250+	Dadey, Debbie; Jones, Marcia Thornton	Scholastic
Triplet Trouble and the Runaway Reindeer	L	RF	250+	Dadey, Debbie; Jones, Marcia Thornton	Scholastic
Triplet Trouble and the Talent Show Mess	L	RF	250+	Dadey, Debbie; Jones, Marcia Thornton	Scholastic
Tristan & Isolde: The Warrior and the Princess	X	TL	3189	Graphic Myths and Legends	Lerner Publications
Tri-State Tornado, The	V	HF	250+	Reading Expeditions	National Geographic
Triumph on Everest: A Photobiography of Sir Edmund Hillary	W	B	250+	Coburn, Broughton	National Geographic
Trixie	L	RF	250+	Voyages	SRA/McGraw Hill
Trixie and the Cyber Pet	M	F	250+	Krailing, Tessa	Barron's Educational
Trixie's Summer	J	RF	250+	PM Plus Story Books	Rigby
Trog	J	F	432	Sunshine	Wright Group/McGraw Hill
Trojan Horse, The	N	I	250+	Literacy 2000	Rigby
Trojan Horse, The: How the Greeks Won the War	Q	HF	250+	Little, Emily	Random House
Trojan Horse: The World's Greatest Adventure	W	HF	250+	DK Readers	DK Publishing
Troll from the Mill, The	C	F	35	Rigby Star	Rigby
Troll Tricks	H	TL	250+	Phonics Readers	Scholastic
Trolley Ride	A	I	16	Vocabulary Readers	Houghton Mifflin Harcourt
Trolley Ride, The	C	F	87	Tadpoles	Rigby
Trolls Don't Ride Roller Coasters	M	F	250+	Dadey, Debbie; Jones, Marcia Thornton	Scholastic
Troll's Story, The	K	TL	250+	Reading Safari	Mondo
Trong's Hero	H	RF	282	In Step Readers	Rigby
Troop of Little Dinosaurs, A	J	HF	250+	PM Story Books	Rigby
Tropical Climate	R	I	250+	Theme Sets	National Geographic
Tropical Rain Forest and You	P	I	1192	Reading Street	Pearson
Tropical Rain Forests	O	I	250+	A True Book	Children's Press
Tropical Rain Forests	S	I	250+	Theme Sets	National Geographic
Tropical Rainforests	N	I	250+	Habitats of the World	Pearson Learning Group
Trouble	E	RF	113	Teacher's Choice Series	Pearson Learning Group
Trouble Dolls	P	F	250+	Buffett, Jimmy; Savannah, Jane	Harcourt School Publishers
Trouble for Jasper	J	F	659	Jasper the Cat	Pioneer Valley
Trouble in a Tree	C	F	36	Bonnell, Kris	Reading Reading Books
Trouble in Space	M	I	723	Leveled Readers	Houghton Mifflin Harcourt
Trouble in Space	M	I	723	Leveled Readers/CA	Houghton Mifflin Harcourt
Trouble in Space	M	I	723	Leveled Readers/TX	Houghton Mifflin Harcourt
Trouble in the Ark	J	F	119	Rose, Gerald	Oxford University Press
Trouble in the Sandbox	J	RF	318	Foundations	Wright Group/McGraw Hill
Trouble Is My Beeswax: A Chet Gecko Mystery	R	F	250+	Hale, Bruce	Harcourt, Inc.
Trouble on a Trip to the Moon	M	I	723	Leveled Readers	Houghton Mifflin Harcourt
Trouble on a Trip to the Moon	M	I	723	Leveled Readers/CA	Houghton Mifflin Harcourt

T

* Collection of short stories
# Graphic text

TITLE	LEVEL	GENRE	WORD COUNT	AUTHOR / SERIES	PUBLISHER / DISTRIBUTOR
Trouble on a Trip to the Moon	M	I	723	Leveled Readers/TX	Houghton Mifflin Harcourt
Trouble on the Farm: How Farmers Meet the Challenges of Nature	U	I	250+	Literacy by Design	Rigby
Trouble on the Trail	M	RF	250+	On Our Way to English	Rigby
Trouble on the Walking Path	J	F	250+	Reading Safari	Mondo
Trouble River	S	HF	250+	Byars, Betsy	Scholastic
Trouble Under the Big Top	O	RF	250+	Klooz	Stone Arch Books
Trouble with Babies, The	Q	RF	250+	Freeman, Martha	Holiday House
Trouble with Buster, The	N	RF	250+	Lorimer, Janet	Scholastic
Trouble with Cats, The	Q	RF	250+	Freeman, Martha	Holiday House
Trouble with Heathrow, The	I	RF	173	Sunshine	Wright Group/McGraw Hill
Trouble with Herbert, The	L	F	1830	Eyles, Heather	Mondo
Trouble with Liberty, The	Y	RF	250+	Orca Soundings	Orca Book Publishers
Trouble with Oatmeal, The	O	RF	250+	PM Collection	Rigby
Trouble with Parents, The	N	RF	250+	SupaDoopers	Sundance
Trouble with Patrick, The	O	RF	250+	Action Packs	Rigby
Trouble with Triplets	M	RF	829	Leveled Readers	Houghton Mifflin Harcourt
Trouble with Triplets	M	RF	829	Leveled Readers/CA	Houghton Mifflin Harcourt
Trouble with Triplets	M	RF	829	Leveled Readers/TX	Houghton Mifflin Harcourt
Trouble with Tuck, The	R	RF	250+	Taylor, Theodore	Avon
Trouble with Twins, The	Q	RF	250+	Freeman, Martha	Holiday House
Troublemaker	M	RF	250+	SupaDoopers	Sundance
Troubles with Bubbles	E	F	89	New Reader Series	Bungalo Books
Troubling a Star	V	F	250+	L'Engle, Madeleine	Dell
Trout Summer	T	RF	250+	Conly, Jane Leslie	Scholastic
Troy's Cake	I	F	289	Gear Up!	Wright Group/McGraw Hill
Troy's Cold	J	F	302	Gear Up!	Wright Group/McGraw Hill
Troy's Flying Machine	K	F	373	Gear Up!	Wright Group/ McGraw Hill
Truck	LB	I	43	Crews, Donald	Scholastic
Truck Is Stuck, The	B	RF	23	Ready Readers	Pearson Learning Group
Truck Parade, The	K	RF	483	PM Plus Story Books	Rigby
Truck Stop, The	LB	RF	25	Kloes, Carol	Kaeden Books
Truck, The	C	F	77	Sails	Rigby
Trucker	P	RF	250+	Beale, Fleur	Pacific Learning
Trucks	A	RF	56	Bookshop	Mondo
Trucks	E	I	196	Foundations	Wright Group/McGraw Hill
Trucks	B	I	75	Leveled Literacy Intervention/ Green System	Heinemann
Trucks	C	I	38	Literacy 2000	Rigby
Trucks	A	I	35	Little Books for Early Readers	University of Maine
Trucks	C	I	27	Pebble Books	Capstone Press
Trucks	D	I	147	Sails	Rigby
Trucks	C	I	37	Stenger, Lisa	Kaeden Books
Trucks	T	I	250+	The World's Fastest	Red Brick Learning
Trucks	C	I	24	Twig	Wright Group/McGraw Hill
Trucks	C	I	81	Vocabulary Readers	Houghton Mifflin Harcourt
Trucks	C	I	81	Vocabulary Readers/CA	Houghton Mifflin Harcourt
Trucks and Other Big Machines	C	I	79	Springboard	Wright Group/McGraw Hill
Trucks on the Road	K	I	250+	PM Plus	Rigby
Trucks, The	B	F	36	Sails	Rigby
Truckster	F	F	194	Instant Readers	Harcourt School Publishers
True Confessions	S	RF	250+	Tashjian, Janet	Scholastic
True Confessions of Charlotte Doyle, The	V	HF	250+	Avi	Avon
True Cortez, A	P	RF	685	Leveled Readers	Houghton Mifflin Harcourt

* Collection of short stories
\# Graphic text

TITLE	LEVEL	GENRE	WORD COUNT	AUTHOR / SERIES	PUBLISHER / DISTRIBUTOR
*True Crimes and How They Were Solved	Z	I	250+	Larsen, Anita	Scholastic
True Meaning of Cleavage, The	Z+	RF	250+	Fredericks, Mariah	Simon & Schuster
True North	Y	F	3229	Leveled Readers	Houghton Mifflin Harcourt
True North	Y	F	3229	Leveled Readers/CA	Houghton Mifflin Harcourt
True or False?	G	I	119	Ready Readers	Pearson Learning Group
True Stories about Abraham Lincoln	O	B	250+	Gross, Ruth Belov	Scholastic
True Story of Balto, The	L	I	250+	Standiford, Natalie	Random House
True Story of the 3 Little Pigs!, The	Q	TL	250+	Scieszka, Jon	Puffin/Penguin
True Story of the Three Little Pigs, The	Q	TL	250+	Scieszka, Jon	Scholastic
True Talents	Y	F	250	Lubar, David	Tom Doherty
*True-Life Treasure Hunts	N	I	250+	Donnelly, Judy	Random House
Truman's Aunt Farm	K	F	250+	Soar To Success	Houghton Mifflin Harcourt
Trumpet of the Swan, The	R	F	250+	White, E. B.	Scholastic
Trumpeter of Krakow, The	Z	HF	250+	Kelly, Eric P.	Aladdin
Trunks, Humps, and Tails	I	I	298	Sails	Rigby
Truth	Z+	RF	250+	Orca Soundings	Orca Book Publishers
Truth About Great White Sharks, The	U	I	250+	Cerullo, Mary	Scholastic
Truth About Red Allen, The	S	RF	250+	Power Up!	Steck-Vaughn
Truth About Rodents, The	R	I	912	Vocabulary Readers	Houghton Mifflin Harcourt
Truth About Rodents, The	R	I	912	Vocabulary Readers/CA	Houghton Mifflin Harcourt
Truth About Rodents, The	R	I	912	Vocabulary Readers/TX	Houghton Mifflin Harcourt
Truth About the Moon, The	M	TL	250+	Bess, Clayton	Houghton Mifflin Harcourt
Truth About Truman School, The	X	RF	250+	Butler, Dori Hillestad	Albert Whitman & Co.
Truth and Salsa	W	RF	250+	Lowery, Linda	Peachtree
Try Again, Emma	I	RF	250+	Lighthouse	Rigby
Try Again, Hannah	G	RF	228	PM Extensions-Green	Rigby
Try It	D	RF	49	Reading Corners	Pearson Learning Group
Try It!	T	I	250+	iOpeners	Pearson Learning Group
Try This!	I	I	250+	Rigby Literacy	Rigby
Try to Be a Brave Girl, Sarah	F	RF	102	Windmill Books	Wright Group/McGraw Hill
Try Your Best	F	RF	190	Green Light Readers	Harcourt
T-Shirt Triplets, The	L	RF	344	Literacy 2000	Rigby
T-Shirts	F	RF	112	Pacific Literacy	Pacific Learning
Tsunami	Z	I	2393	Leveled Readers	Houghton Mifflin Harcourt
Tsunami Survival Stories	O	I	770	Springboard	Wright Group/ McGraw Hill
Tsunami!	Q	I	784	Independent Readers Science	Houghton Mifflin Harcourt
Tsunami! Wave of Destruction	T	I	250+	Sails	Rigby
Tsunami!: Deadly Wall of Water	S	I	250+	High Five Reading	Red Brick Learning
Tsunamis	W	I	250+	Disasters Up Close	Lerner Publications
Tsunamis	M	I	737	Pull Ahead Books	Lerner Publications
Tuba Lessons	WB	RF	N/A	Bartlett, T. C.; Monique, Felix	Harcourt School Publishers
Tubes in My Ears: My Trip to the Hospital	K	I	250+	Bookshop	Mondo
Tuck Everlasting	W	F	250+	Babbitt, Natalie	Farrar, Straus and Giroux
Tucker Finds Adventure	J	F	250+	Fletcher, Rusty	Pearson Learning Group
Tucket's Gold	U	HF	250+	Paulsen, Gary	Bantam
Tucket's Ride	U	HF	250+	Paulsen, Gary	Bantam
Tuesday	WB	F	N/A	Wiesner, David	Clarion
Tug of War	I	TL	250+	Folk Tales	Wright Group/McGraw Hill
Tug of War, The	G	F	194	Story Steps	Rigby
Tug of War, The	I	TL	250+	Storyworlds	Heinemann Educational Books
Tugboats	I	I	116	Mighty Machines	Capstone Press
Tugboats	O	I	250+	Transportation	Red Brick Learning

T

* Collection of short stories
# Graphic text

TITLE	LEVEL	GENRE	WORD COUNT	AUTHOR / SERIES	PUBLISHER / DISTRIBUTOR
Tug-of-War	C	F	68	Leveled Literacy Intervention/ Blue System	Heinemann
Tug-of-War, The	L	TL	648	Rigby Flying Colors	Rigby
Tuk Becomes a Hunter	N	TL	838	Leveled Readers	Houghton Mifflin Harcourt
Tuk Becomes a Hunter	N	TL	838	Leveled Readers/CA	Houghton Mifflin Harcourt
Tuk Becomes a Hunter	N	TL	838	Leveled Readers/TX	Houghton Mifflin Harcourt
Tuk the Hunter	N	TL	1077	Leveled Readers	Houghton Mifflin Harcourt
Tuk the Hunter	N	TL	1077	Leveled Readers/CA	Houghton Mifflin Harcourt
Tuk the Hunter	N	TL	1077	Leveled Readers/TX	Houghton Mifflin Harcourt
Tulips	F	I	102	Life Cycles	Lerner Publications
Tulips for Annie's Mother	O	HF	781	Reading Street	Pearson
Tulips for Dad	J	RF	250+	Cambridge Reading	Pearson Learning Group
Tulips for My Teacher	G	RF	209	PM Photo Stories	Rigby
Tullian Trouble	T	SF	250+	Sails	Rigby
Tumbleweed Stew	J	TL	250+	Crummel, Susan Stevens	Harcourt
Tumbleweed Stew	J	TL	250+	Green Light Readers	Harcourt
Tummy Ache	J	RF	104	Sunshine	Wright Group/McGraw Hill
Tundra	Q	I	250+	First Reports	Compass Point Books
Tuning Up	O	B	250+	Meet the Author	Richard C. Owen
Tunnel, The	B	F	30	Sails	Rigby
Tunneling Earthworms	L	I	457	Pull Ahead Books	Lerner Publications
Tunnels	M	I	250+	Explorations	Eleanor Curtain Publishing
Tunnels	M	I	250+	Explorations	Okapi Educational Materials
Tunnels	W	F	250+	Gordon, Roderick & Williams, Brian	Scholastic
Tunnels	I	I	179	Sails	Rigby
Tunnels	L	I	262	Windows on Literacy	National Geographic
Tupac Shakur	Z	B	250+	Rock Music Library	Capstone Press
Turbulence Ahead	Q	I	250+	InfoQuest	Rigby
Turkey	E	F	106	Sails	Rigby
Turkey That Ate My Father, The	Q	F	250+	Marney, Dean	Scholastic
Turkey Trouble	M	RF	250+	Giff, Patricia Reilly	Bantam
Turkey, The	B	F	30	Sails	Rigby
Turkey: Between Europe and Asia	Y	I	3597	Leveled Readers Social Studies	Houghton Mifflin Harcourt
Turkeys on the Farm	I	I	94	Pebble Books	Red Brick Learning
Turkeys' Side of It, The	N	RF	250+	Smith, Janice Lee	HarperTrophy
Turn Homeward, Hannalee	T	HF	250+	Beatty, Patricia	William Morrow
Turn It Down!	U	I	250+	iOpeners	Pearson Learning Group
Turn on a Faucet	L	I	238	Windows on Literacy	National Geographic
Turn Up the Radio	R	I	795	Independent Readers Social Studies	Houghton Mifflin Harcourt
Turning the Tide for Turtles	P	I	250+	Literacy by Design	Rigby
Turnip, The	F	TL	250+	Ziefert, Harriet	Puffin/Penguin
Turtle and Hare	D	TL	94	Leveled Readers	Houghton Mifflin Harcourt
Turtle and Hare	D	TL	94	Leveled Readers/CA	Houghton Mifflin Harcourt
Turtle and Hare	D	TL	94	Leveled Readers/TX	Houghton Mifflin Harcourt
Turtle and Snake	E	F	145	Sails	Rigby
Turtle Flies South	K	F	250+	Literacy 2000	Rigby
Turtle in the Sun, A	C	F	38	Bonnell, Kris	Reading Reading Books
Turtle Nest	H	I	85	Books for Young Learners	Richard C. Owen
Turtle Tale	J	F	250+	Asch, Frank	Scholastic
Turtle Talk	I	I	217	Storyteller-Setting Sun	Wright Group/McGraw Hill
Turtle Trouble	E	RF	157	Seedlings	Continental Press
Turtle Trouble	S	I	250+	WorldScapes	ETA Cuisenaire

TITLE	LEVEL	GENRE	WORD COUNT	AUTHOR / SERIES	PUBLISHER / DISTRIBUTOR
Turtle, The	D	I	68	Foundations	Wright Group/McGraw Hill
Turtles	S	I	250+	A First Book	Franklin Watts
Turtles	E	I	41	All About Pets	Capstone Press
Turtles and Hatchlings	B	I	33	Animal Families	Lerner Publications
Turtle's Big Race	J	TL	250+	Pair-It Books	Steck-Vaughn
Turtle's Boat	C	F	48	Gear Up!	Wright Group/McGraw Hill
Turtle's Small Pond	J	TL	572	Leveled Readers	Houghton Mifflin Harcourt
Turtles Take Their Time	L	I	250+	Read-About Science	Children's Press
Turtle's Trouble	D	F	110	Sails	Rigby
Turtles, Tortoises, and Terrapins	N	I	250+	Storyteller Summer Skies	Wright Group/McGraw Hill
Tut, Tut	P	F	250+	Scieszka, Jon	Penguin Group
Tutankhamen's Gift	R	I	250+	Sabuda, Robert	Simon & Schuster
Tuti's Play	H	RF	134	Bebop Books	Lee & Low Books Inc.
Tut's Mummy: Lost and Found	P	I	250+	Donnelly, Judy	Random House
Tuttle's Shell	K	F	250+	Bookshop	Mondo
TV Kid, The	R	RF	250+	Byars, Betsy	Puffin/Penguin
TV Kid, The	R	B	1199	Leveled Readers	Houghton Mifflin Harcourt
TV Kid, The	R	B	1199	Leveled Readers/CA	Houghton Mifflin Harcourt
TV Kid, The	R	B	1199	Leveled Readers/TX	Houghton Mifflin Harcourt
TV Reporters	M	I	250+	Community Helpers	Red Brick Learning
TV Takeover: Questioning Television	S	I	250+	Media Literacy	Capstone Press
TV Time-Out	M	RF	250+	Sunshine	Wright Group/McGraw Hill
Tweedle Dee Dee	G	TL	241	Voake, Charlotte	Candlewick Press
Tweedle-De-Dee Tumbleweed	G	F	103	Reese, Bob	Children's Press
Twelve Balloons for the Clown	J	RF	404	PM Math Readers	Rigby
Twelve Dancing Princesses	M	I	250+	Enrichment	Wright Group/McGraw Hill
Twelve Travelers, Twenty Horses	U	HF	250+	Robinet, Harriette Gillem	Aladddin Paperbacks
Twenty Steps to the Treasure	H	RF	194	PM Math Readers	Rigby
Twenty-Four-Hour Challenge, The	M	RF	727	In Step Readers	Rigby
Twenty-One Balloons, The	V	SF	250+	DuBois, William	Scholastic
Twice as Nice	L	I	691	Sun Sprouts	ETA Cuisenaire
Twiddle Twins' Haunted House, The	L	F	1141	Goldsmith, Howard	Mondo
Twiddle Twins' Music Box Mystery, The	L	F	250+	Goldsmith, Howard	Mondo
Twiddle Twins' Single Footprint Mystery, The	L	F	250+	Goldsmith, Howard	Mondo
Twiga and the Moon	I	F	250+	Storyworlds	Heinemann Educational Books
Twilight	Z+	F	250+	Meyer, Stephanie	Little, Brown & Co.
Twilight in Grace Falls	W	RF	250+	Honeycutt, Natalie	Avon
Twilight of the Wolves	V	F	7348	Reading Street	Pearson
Twilight: Warriors, The New Prophecy	U	F	250+	Hunter, Erin	Harper Trophy
Twinkie Squad, The	S	RF	250+	Korman, Gordon	Scholastic
Twinkle, Twinkle, Little Star	L	TL	250+	Trapani, Iza	Charlesbridge
Twins	H	I	113	Vocabulary Readers	Houghton Mifflin Harcourt
Twins This and That, The	J	F	494	Appleton-Smith, Laura	Flyleaf Publishing
Twins, The	H	RF	250+	Early Transitional, Set 1	Pioneer Valley
Twisted Window, The	Z+	RF	250+	Duncan, Lois	Laurel-Leaf Books
Twister Trap, The	T	F	250+	Dahl, Michael	Stone Arch Books
Twisters	M	I	250+	Early Connections	Benchmark Education
Twisters and Other Terrible Storms	R	I	250+	Osborne, Will; Osborne, Mary Pope	Random House
Twisters and Other Wind Storms	P	I	250+	Wildcats	Wright Group/McGraw Hill
Twisters!	M	I	250+	DK Readers	DK Publishing
Twisting Up a Storm	S	I	250+	Duksta, Cheryl	Pacific Learning
Twits, The	S	F	250+	Dahl, Roald	Penguin Group

* Collection of short stories
# Graphic text

T

TITLE	LEVEL	GENRE	WORD COUNT	AUTHOR / SERIES	PUBLISHER / DISTRIBUTOR
Two	E	RF	84	Carousel Readers	Pearson Learning Group
Two	A	I	17	Little Celebrations	Pearson Learning Group
Two African Countries	Q	I	250+	High-Fliers	Pacific Learning
Two Against the Mississippi	T	HF	2187	Leveled Readers	Houghton Mifflin Harcourt
Two Against the Mississippi	T	HF	2187	Leveled Readers/CA	Houghton Mifflin Harcourt
Two Against the Mississippi	T	HF	2187	Leveled Readers/TX	Houghton Mifflin Harcourt
Two and Three	B	RF	45	Reading Street	Pearson
Two Baby Elephants	I	F	240	Lighthouse	Rigby
Two Baskets	E	RF	181	Bookshop	Mondo
Two Bear Cubs	H	F	89	Jonas, Ann	Morrow
Two by Two	G	TL	88	Cambridge Reading	Pearson Learning Group
Two Can Do It!	C	RF	32	Canizares, Susan; Chessen, Betsey	Scholastic
Two Cities: Traveling Through Place Value	S	I	250+	In Step Readers	Rigby
Two Class Trips	N	RF	250+	InfoTrek	ETA Cuisenaire
Two Cold Ears	O	B	560	Leveled Readers	Houghton Mifflin Harcourt
Two Crazy Pigs	I	F	250+	Nagel, Karen Berman	Scholastic
Two Eyes, a Nose, and a Mouth	I	I	169	Grobel Intrater, Roberta	Scholastic
Two Eyes, Two Ears	D	I	83	PM Nonfiction-Red	Rigby
*Two Fables of Aesop to Read and Tell	J	TL	411	Books for Young Learners	Richard C. Owen
Two Feet	F	RF	129	Pescoe, Gwen	Educational Insights
Two Foolish Cats, The	K	F	250+	Literacy 2000	Rigby
Two Foot Punch	Y	RF	250+	Orca Sports	Orca Book Publishers
Two Giants, The	K	TL	250+	Storyworlds	Heinemann Educational Books
Two Great Rivers	S	I	1893	Reading Street	Pearson
Two Halves and Four Quarters	I	RF	250	PM Math Readers	Rigby
Two Heads Are Better Than One	Q	RF	250+	Mazer, Anne	Scholastic
Two Heroes	I	F	282	Leveled Readers	Houghton Mifflin Harcourt
Two Heroes	I	F	282	Leveled Readers/CA	Houghton Mifflin Harcourt
Two Heroes	I	F	282	Leveled Readers/TX	Houghton Mifflin Harcourt
Two Homes	G	RF	166	Masurel, Claire	Candlewick Press
Two Hungry Hippos	M	I	250+	Early Connections	Benchmark Education
Two Imporant Debates	X	I	2805	Vocabulary Readers/CA	Houghton Mifflin Harcourt
Two Imporant Debates	X	I	2805	Vocabulary Readers/TX	Houghton Mifflin Harcourt
Two Important Debates	X	I	2805	Vocabulary Readers	Houghton Mifflin Harcourt
Two Is a Pair	E	I	78	Teacher's Choice Series	Pearson Learning Group
Two Labors of Hercules	P	TL	956	Gear Up!	Wright Group/ McGraw Hill
Two Languages	K	I	202	Vocabulary Readers	Houghton Mifflin Harcourt
Two Little Birds and Other Stories	D	RF	60	Story Steps	Rigby
Two Little Chicks	C	F	32	KinderReaders	Rigby
Two Little Dogs	E	F	74	Story Box	Wright Group/McGraw Hill
Two Little Ducks Get Lost	F	F	178	PM Plus Story Books	Rigby
Two Little Goldfish	I	RF	344	PM Story Books-Orange	Rigby
Two Little Houses	H	RF	252	InfoTrek	ETA Cuisenaire
Two Little Mice, The	I	F	163	Literacy 2000	Rigby
Two Loves of Will Shakespeare, The	Z+	RF	250+	Lawlor, Laurie	Holiday House
Two More	LB	F	16	Voyages	SRA/McGraw Hill
Two of Us, The	C	I	135	Vocabulary Readers	Houghton Mifflin Harcourt
Two of Us, The	C	I	135	Vocabulary Readers/CA	Houghton Mifflin Harcourt
Two Ogres, The	F	F	116	Joy Readers	Pearson Learning Group
Two Plus One Goes A.P.E.	L	RF	250+	Springstubb, Tricia	Scholastic
Two Plus Two	E	RF	44	Teacher's Choice Series	Pearson Learning Group
Two Points	B	RF	40	Kennedy, Jane.; Eaton, Audrey	Continental Press

* Collection of short stories
# Graphic text

TITLE	LEVEL	GENRE	WORD COUNT	AUTHOR / SERIES	PUBLISHER / DISTRIBUTOR
Two Red Tugs	L	F	547	PM Story Books	Rigby
Two Runaways, The	M	RF	250+	Woodland Mysteries	Wright Group/McGraw Hill
Two Sides of Mining, The	X	I	1907	Reading Street	Pearson
*Two Silly Trolls	J	F	250+	Jewell, Nancy	HarperTrophy
Two Sisters Play Tennis	J	I	327	Leveled Readers	Houghton Mifflin Harcourt
Two Sisters Play Tennis	J	I	327	Leveled Readers/CA	Houghton Mifflin Harcourt
Two Sisters Play Tennis	J	I	327	Leveled Readers/TX	Houghton Mifflin Harcourt
Two Stupid Cats	G	F	140	Sunshine	Wright Group/McGraw Hill
Two Sweet Peas	M	RF	250+	Bebop Books	Lee & Low Books Inc.
Two Teams	H	I	146	Leveled Literacy Intervention/ Green System	Heinemann
Two Tickets to Freedom: The True Story of Ellen and William Craft	S	HF	250+	Freedman, Florence	Scholastic
Two Tooth Fairies	L	F	1043	InfoTrek	ETA Cuisenaire
Two Traditions of Dance	P	I	382	Vocabulary Readers	Houghton Mifflin Harcourt
Two Travelers and Bear	L	TL	610	Rigby Flying Colors	Rigby
*Two Tricky Tales	L	TL	250+	Pacific Literacy	Pacific Learning
Two Turtles	LB	RF	13	Ready Readers	Pearson Learning Group
Two Week Diary	H	RF	208	Sun Sprouts	ETA Cuisenaire
Two Women Astronauts	S	B	1353	Reading Street	Pearson
Two Worlds Meet: The Travels of Francisco de Coronado	T	B	250+	On Our Way to English	Rigby
Two Yellow Eyes	F	F	211	Sun Sprouts	ETA Cuisenaire
Two-Part Invention	Z	B	250+	L'Engle, Madeleine	HarperCollins
Two-Star Day	O	RF	446	Leveled Readers	Houghton Mifflin Harcourt
Two-Timer	I	RF	465	Rigby Flying Colors	Rigby
Tye May and the Magic Brush	M	TL	250+	Bang, Molly Garrett	Mulberry Books
Tygrine Cat, The	W	F	250+	Iserles, Inbali	Candlewick Press
Tyler Toad and Thunder	M	F	250+	Crowe, Robert	Dutton/Penguin
Tyler's Train	C	RF	42	Little Celebrations	Pearson Learning Group
Types of Trees	D	I	29	Vocabulary Readers	Houghton Mifflin Harcourt
Tyrannosaurus Rex	O	I	250+	A True Book	Children's Press
Tyrannosaurus Rex	I	I	117	Dinosaur and Prehistoric Animals	Capstone Press
Tyrannosaurus Rex	N	I	250+	Discovering Dinosaurs	Capstone Press
Tyrannosaurus Rex	M	I	250+	Prehistoric Creatures Then and Now	Steck-Vaughn
Tyrannosaurus the Terrible	L	F	182	Wesley & the Dinosaurs	Wright Group/McGraw Hill
Ty's One-man Band	L	RF	250+	Walter, Mildred Pitts	Scholastic

T

* Collection of short stories
# Graphic text

TITLE	LEVEL	GENRE	WORD COUNT	AUTHOR / SERIES	PUBLISHER / DISTRIBUTOR
U.S. Air Force Space Command, The	S	I	250+	The U.S. Armed Forces	Capstone Press
U.S. Air Force Special Forces: Pararescue	V	I	250+	Warfare and Weapons	Capstone Press
U.S. Air Force Special Operations	Y	I	8537	U.S. Armed Forces	Lerner Publications
U.S. Air Force Spy Planes	R	I	250+	Military Vehicles	Capstone Press
U.S. Air Force Thunderbirds, The	S	I	250+	The U.S. Armed Forces	Capstone Press
U.S. Air Force, The	M	I	142	Military Branches	Capstone Press
U.S. Air Force, The	Q	I	7489	U.S. Armed Forces	Lerner Publications
U.S. Airforce, The	S	I	250+	The U.S. Armed Forces	Capstone Press
U.S. Army at War, The	V	I	250+	On the Front Lines	Capstone Press
U.S. Army Golden Knights, The	S	I	250+	The U.S. Armed Forces	Capstone Press
U.S. Army Humvees	R	I	250+	Military Vehicles	Capstone Press
U.S. Army Infantry Fighting Vehicles	R	I	250+	Millitary Vehicles	Capstone Press
U.S. Army National Guard, The	S	I	250+	The U.S. Armed Forces	Capstone Press
U.S. Army Rangers, The	S	I	250+	The U.S. Armed Forces	Capstone Press
U.S. Army Special Operations Forces	Y	I	7169	U.S. Armed Forces	Lerner Publications
U.S. Army, The	M	I	121	Military Branches	Capstone Press
U.S. Army, The	S	I	250+	The U.S. Armed Forces	Capstone Press
U.S. Army, The	Y	I	7218	U.S. Armed Forces	Lerner Publications
U.S. Border Patrol, The: Guarding the Nation	S	I	250+	Line of Duty	Capstone Press
U.S. Coast Guard Cutters	Q	I	250+	Military Vehicles	Capstone Press
U.S. Coast Guard, The	M	I	137	Military Branches	Capstone Press
U.S. Coast Guard, The	Y	I	6397	U.S. Armed Forces	Lerner Publications
U.S. Congress, The	Q	I	250+	Let's See	Compass Point Books
U.S. Constitution, The	M	I	149	Allen, Kathy	Capstone Press
U.S. Constitution, The	O	I	250+	Our Government	Capstone Press
U.S. Constitution, The	M	I	138	Pebble Plus	Capstone Press
U.S. Constitution, The	T	I	250+	We The People	Compass Point Books
U.S. Marine Corps Assault Vehicles	R	I	250+	Millitary Vehicles	Capstone Press
U.S. Marine Corps at War, The	V	I	250+	On the Front Lines	Capstone Press
U.S. Marine Corps Combat Jets	R	I	250+	Millitary Vehicles	Capstone Press
U.S. Marine Corps, The	M	I	143	Military Branches	Capstone Press
U.S. Marine Corps, The	S	I	250+	The U.S. Armed Forces	Capstone Press
U.S. Marine Corps, The	Y	I	6650	U.S. Armed Forces	Lerner Publications
U.S. Marine Expeditionary Units	S	I	250+	The U.S. Armed Forces	Capstone Press
U.S. Marshals Service, The: Catching Fugitives	S	I	250+	Line of Duty	Capstone Press
U.S. Naval Special Warfare Forces	Y	I	7871	U.S. Armed Forces	Lerner Publications
U.S. Navy Cruisers	R	I	250+	Millitary Vehicles	Capstone Press
U.S. Navy Destroyers	R	I	250+	Millitary Vehicles	Capstone Press
U.S. Navy Special Forces: Seal Teams	V	I	250+	Warfare and Weapons	Capstone Press
U.S. Navy, The	M	I	131	Military Branches	Capstone Press
U.S. Navy, The	S	I	250+	The U.S. Armed Forces	Capstone Press
U.S. Navy, The	Y	I	7664	U.S. Armed Forces	Lerner Publications
U.S. Secret Service, The: Protecting Our Leaders	S	I	250+	Line of Duty	Capstone Press
U.S. Supreme Court, The	Q	I	250+	Let's See	Compass Point Books
UFOs	X	I	250+	The Unexplained	Capstone Press
UFOs	Z	I	7472	The Unexplained	Lerner Publications
Ugh! A Bug!	F	I	108	Silly Millies	Millbrook Press
Uglies	Z	SF	250+	Westerfeld, Scott	Simon Pulse
Ugly Duckling, The	I	TL	359	Folk Tales	Pioneer Valley
Ugly Duckling, The	J	TL	563	Leveled Literacy Intervention/ Blue System	Heinemann
Ugly Duckling, The	I	TL	250+	Literacy 2000	Rigby

U

TITLE	LEVEL	GENRE	WORD COUNT	AUTHOR / SERIES	PUBLISHER / DISTRIBUTOR
Ugly Duckling, The	J	TL	452	PM Tales and Plays-Turquoise	Rigby
Ugly Duckling, The	E	TL	148	Rigby Rocket	Rigby
Ugly Duckling, The	F	TL	246	Storyworlds	Heinemann Educational Publishers
Ugly Duckling, The	J	TL	558	Tales from Hans Andersen	Wright Group/McGraw Hill
Ugly Mug	P	RF	250+	Joseph, Vivienne	Pacific Learning
Ugly Pugsy	O	F	250+	Bookweb	Rigby
Ugly Vegetables, The	L	RF	250+	Lin, Grace	Charlesbridge
Uh-Oh!	D	RF	62	Literacy by Design	Rigby
Uh-Oh!	D	RF	62	Rigby Literacy	Rigby
Uh-Oh! Said the Crow	J	F	250+	Oppenheim, Joanna	Bantam
Ukraine	Q	I	250+	Theme Sets	National Geographic
Ultimate Field Trip 1: Adventures in the Amazon Rain Forest	S	I	250+	Goodman, Susan E.	Simon & Schuster
Ultimate Weapon: The Race to Develop the Atomic Bomb, The	Z	I	250+	Sullivan, Edward T.	Holiday House
Ulysses S. Grant	S	B	3899	History Maker Bios	Lerner Publications
Ulysses S. Grant	U	B	250+	Let Freedom Ring	Red Brick Learning
Ulysses S. Grant	S	B	250+	Primary Source Readers	Teacher Created Materials
Ulysses S. Grant	U	B	250+	Profiles of the Presidents	Compass Point Books
Ulysses S. Grant: Confident Leader and Hero	Y	B	250+	The Civil War	Carus Publishing
Ulysses S. Grant: Eighteenth President	R	B	250+	Getting to Know the U.S. Presidents	Children's Press
Umbrella	C	F	73	Story Box	Wright Group/McGraw Hill
Umbrella, The	N	TL	250+	Brett, Jan	Scholastic
Umbrellas	L	I	430	Sunshine	Wright Group/McGraw Hill
Unbelievable Johnny Appleseed, The	N	B	250+	Leveled Readers Language Support	Houghton Mifflin Harcourt
Unbelievable!	T	I	250+	Boldprint	Steck-Vaughn
Unbelievable!	K	SF	250+	Shulman, Lisa	Hampton-Brown
Uncertain Princess, The	J	F	479	InfoTrek	ETA Cuisenaire
Uncharted Waters	T	RF	250+	Bulion, Leslie	Peachtree
Unclaimed Treasures	X	RF	250+	MacLachlan, Patricia	HarperTrophy
Uncle Buncle's House	C	RF	56	Sunshine	Wright Group/McGraw Hill
Uncle Carlos's Barbecue	H	RF	207	Foundations	Wright Group/McGraw Hill
Uncle Elephant	J	F	1784	Lobel, Arnold	HarperCollins
Uncle Elephant and Uncle Tiger	D	TL	77	Joy Readers	Pearson Learning Group
Uncle Jed's Barbershop	S	RF	250+	Mitchell, Margaree King	Scholastic
Uncle Jim	G	RF	127	Windmill Books	Rigby
Uncle Joe	H	F	149	Pacific Literacy	Pacific Learning
Uncle Rabbit	N	TL	890	Leveled Readers	Houghton Mifflin Harcourt
Uncle Rabbit	N	TL	890	Leveled Readers/CA	Houghton Mifflin Harcourt
Uncle Rabbit	N	TL	890	Leveled Readers/TX	Houghton Mifflin Harcourt
Uncle Tease	N	RF	250+	Literacy Tree	Rigby
Uncle Ted and the Hiccups	I	RF	281	Sails	Rigby
Uncle Ted Is Tricky!	F	RF	224	Sails	Rigby
Uncle Ted's Big Jump	I	F	448	Sails	Rigby
Uncle Ted's Teeth	F	RF	211	Sails	Rigby
Uncle Timi's Sleep	G	RF	102	Pacific Literacy	Pacific Learning
Uncles	F	I	44	Families	Capstone Press
Uncles	D	I	36	Pebble Books	Capstone Press
Uncle's Bakery	H	RF	81	Early Readers	Compass Point Books
Uncle's Clever Tricks	D	RF	61	Joy Readers	Pearson Learning Group

* Collection of short stories
\# Graphic text

U

TITLE	LEVEL	GENRE	WORD COUNT	AUTHOR / SERIES	PUBLISHER / DISTRIBUTOR
Uncommon Revolutionary: A Story About Thomas Paine	R	B	8127	Creative Minds Biographies	Carolrhoda Books
Uncovering Classical Athens	X	I	3004	Reading Street	Pearson
Uncovering the Past	M	I	478	Leveled Readers	Houghton Mifflin Harcourt
Uncovering the Past	M	I	478	Leveled Readers/CA	Houghton Mifflin Harcourt
Uncovering the Past	M	I	478	Leveled Readers/TX	Houghton Mifflin Harcourt
Uncovering the Secrets of Ancient Egypt	Y	I	2309	Reading Street	Pearson
Under a Full Moon	D	F	65	Leveled Readers	Houghton Mifflin Harcourt
Under a Microscope	H	I	254	Sunshine	Wright Group/McGraw Hill
Under Construction	S	I	250+	Kids Discover Reading	Wright Group/McGraw Hill
Under Lock and Key	O	RF	250+	Literacy by Design	Rigby
Under Lock and Key	O	RF	250+	On Our Way To English	Rigby
Under My Bed	D	F	49	Literacy 2000	Rigby
Under My Bed	C	F	49	Little Celebrations	Pearson Learning Group
Under My Nose	O	B	250+	Meet The Author	Richard C. Owen
Under My Sombrero	F	F	79	Books for Young Learners	Richard C. Owen
Under One Rock Bugs, Slugs and other Ughs	O	I	950	Sharing Nature with Children	Dawn Publications
Under the Banyan Tree	X	RF	250+	DePalma, Toni	Holiday House
Under the Bed	A	RF	28	Smart Starts	Rigby
Under the Big Top	E	I	103	Twig	Wright Group/McGraw Hill
Under the Blood-Red Sun	W	HF	250+	Salisbury, Graham	Bantam
Under the Bright Lights	R	I	466	Vocabulary Readers	Houghton Mifflin Harcourt
Under the City	K	I	206	Sunshine	Wright Group/McGraw Hill
Under the Ground	LB	I	12	Animal Homes	Lerner Publications
Under the Ground	C	I	42	Foundations	Wright Group/McGraw Hill
Under the Ground	B	I	28	Gear Up!	Wright Group/McGraw Hill
Under the Ground	P	I	250+	Literacy 2000	Rigby
Under the Ground	K	I	250+	Pluckrose, Henry	Franklin Watts
Under the Ground	B	I	44	Sails	Rigby
Under the Ground	Q	I	250+	Wildcats	Wright Group/McGraw Hill
Under the Hood	S	I	250+	NASCAR Racing	Capstone Press
Under the Ice	C	I	88	Sails	Rigby
Under the Leaf	D	F	100	Sails	Rigby
Under the Microscope	H	I	164	Sails	Rigby
Under the Ocean	U	I	250+	The Natural World	Scholastic
Under the Ocean	T	I	614	Vocabulary Readers	Houghton Mifflin Harcourt
Under the Old Oak Tree	G	F	205	Seedlings	Continental Press
Under the Royal Palms	V	B	250+	Ada, Alma Flor	Scholastic
Under the Sea with Gogool and Googolplex	L	SF	250+	Orca Echoes	Orca Book Publishers
Under the Sky	C	I	44	Learn to Read	Creative Teaching Press
Under the Umbrella	C	RF	60	Phonics and Friends	Hampton-Brown
Under Water	A	I	35	Twig	Wright Group/McGraw Hill
Under Wraps	U	I	250+	Goldish, Meish	Scholastic
Under, Over, By the Clover: What Is a Preposition?	O	I	200	Words Are CATegorical	Millbrook Press
Undercover Tailback	Q	RF	250+	Christopher, Matt	Scholastic
Underfoot	N	I	250+	Look Once Look Again	Creative Teaching Press
Underground	C	I	31	Twig	Wright Group/McGraw Hill
Underground and All Around	N	I	250+	Rigby Literacy	Rigby
Underground Homes	L	I	693	Rigby Flying Colors	Rigby
Underground Homes	N	I	800	Vocabulary Readers	Houghton Mifflin Harcourt
Underground Homes	N	I	800	Vocabulary Readers/CA	Houghton Mifflin Harcourt
Underground Railroad, The	V	I	250+	Bial, Raymond	Houghton Mifflin Harcourt

U

* Collection of short stories
# Graphic text

TITLE	LEVEL	GENRE	WORD COUNT	AUTHOR / SERIES	PUBLISHER / DISTRIBUTOR
Underground Railroad, The	V	I	250+	Cornerstones of Freedom	Children's Press
Underground Railroad, The	N	I	250+	Twig	Wright Group/McGraw Hill
Underground Railroad, The: An Interactive History Adventure	T	HF	250+	You Choose Books	Capstone Press
Underground Railroad, The: Bringing Slaves North to Freedom	V	I	250+	Let Freedom Ring	Capstone Press
Underground Rescue	W	RF	2180	Leveled Readers	Houghton Mifflin Harcourt
Undersea World	V	I	250+	Boldprint	Steck-Vaughn
Understanding Global Warming	X	I	11190	Saving Our Living Earth	Lerner Publications
Understanding Newton's Laws	Y	I	2888	Leveled Readers Science	Houghton Mifflin Harcourt
Understudies	P	RF	250+	Bookweb	Rigby
Underwater	I	I	100	Start to Read	School Zone
Underwater	T	I	250+	The News	Richard C. Owen
Underwater Animals	Q	I	250+	Explorers	Wright Group/McGraw Hill
Underwater Journey	F	I	60	Sunshine	Wright Group/McGraw Hill
Underwater Spiders	I	I	223	Sails	Rigby
Underwater with Jacques Cousteau	L	B	633	Leveled Readers Science	Houghton Mifflin Harcourt
Undone	Z+	RF	250+	Taylor, Brooke	Walker & Company
Undying Glory: The Story of the Massachusetts 54th Regiment	U	HF	250+	Cox, Clinton	Scholastic
Unexpected Hero, An	W	RF	2407	Leveled Readers	Houghton Mifflin Harcourt
Unexpected Music	V	I	2742	Reading Street	Pearson
Unexpected Treasure	Q	RF	250+	Ragged Island Mysteries	Wright Group/McGraw Hill
Unhappy Troll, The	D	F	47	Ray's Readers	Outside the Box
Unicorns Don't Give Sleigh Rides	M	F	250+	Dadey, Debbie; Jones, Marcia Thornton	Scholastic
Uninvited Guests	S	I	250+	Sails	Rigby
United Nations, The	R	I	250+	Rigby Focus	Rigby
United States ABCs, The: A Book About the People and Places of the United States	Q	I	250+	Country ABCs	Picture Window Books
United States and Russian Space Race, The	V	I	3331	Reading Street	Pearson
United States Constitution, The	V	I	250+	Let Freedom Ring	Red Brick Learning
United States Goes West, The	T	I	1285	Reading Street	Pearson
United States Holocaust Memorial Museum, The	W	I	250+	Cornerstones of Freedom	Children's Press
United States Marshals Service	S	I	250+	Law Enforcement	Capstone Press
United States, The	Q	I	250+	First Reports: Countries	Compass Point Books
United States, The: A Question and Answer Book	P	I	250+	Questions & Answers: Countries	Capstone Press
United States, The: Region by Region	S	I	250+	Pair-It Books	Steck-Vaughn
*Universal Solvent and Other Cases, The	O	RF	250+	Simon, Seymour	Avon
Universe, The	Q	I	250+	Pair-It Books	Steck-Vaughn
Unlocking the Secrets of Your Amazing Brain	W	I	250+	Explore More	Wright Group
Unmaking of Duncan Veerick, The	X	RF	250+	Levin, Betty	Front Street
Unseen by the Eye	T	I	250+	Connectors	Pacific Learning
Unsinkable Madame C. J. Walker, The	Y	B	3573	Leveled Readers	Houghton Mifflin Harcourt
"Unsinkable" Titanic, The	S	I	1403	Reading Street	Pearson
Unsung American Hero, An	U	B	2605	Leveled Readers	Houghton Mifflin Harcourt
Unsung American Hero, An	U	B	2605	Leveled Readers/CA	Houghton Mifflin Harcourt
Unsung American Hero, An	U	B	2605	Leveled Readers/TX	Houghton Mifflin Harcourt
Until We Got Princess	E	RF	94	Bookshop	Mondo
Until We Meet Again	Z	RF	250+	Schraff, Anne	Townsend Press
Untold Story, The	W	I	250+	WorldScapes	ETA Cuisenaire

* Collection of short stories
\# Graphic text

U

TITLE	LEVEL	GENRE	WORD COUNT	AUTHOR / SERIES	PUBLISHER / DISTRIBUTOR
Unusual Coin, The	O	F	951	Leveled Readers	Houghton Mifflin Harcourt
Unusual Creepy-Crawlies	N	I	801	Springboard	Wright Group/McGraw Hill
Unusual Machines	J	I	229	Little Red Readers	Sundance
Unusual Recipe Competition, The	N	RF	250+	Springboard	Wright Group/McGraw Hill
Unusual Show, An	H	F	63	Blonder, Ellen	Scholastic
Unusual Spiders	N	I	250+	Take Two Books	Wright Group/McGraw Hill
Unvisibles, The	T	F	250+	Whybrow, Ian	Holiday House
Up and Away	Q	I	250+	Explorers	Wright Group/McGraw Hill
Up and Away	S	RF	250+	Reading Safari	Mondo
Up and Away!: Taking a Flight	N	RF	250+	Bookshop	Mondo
Up and Away, Curious George!	A	F	22	Leveled Readers/CA	Houghton Mifflin Harcourt
Up and Away, Curious George!	A	F	22	Leveled Readers	Houghton Mifflin Harcourt
Up and Down	C	RF	92	Handprints C, Set 1	Educators Publishing Service
Up and Down	B	I	25	Little Books for Early Readers	University of Maine
Up and Down	D	RF	99	New Way Red	Steck-Vaughn
Up and Down	C	I	81	PM Plus Nonfiction	Rigby
Up and Down	C	RF	68	Rigby Literacy	Rigby
Up and Down	D	I	102	Sails	Rigby
Up and Down	E	RF	79	Storyteller-Setting Sun	Wright Group/McGraw Hill
Up and Down	I	I	213	Where Words	Capstone Press
Up and Down on the Playground	B	RF	22	Bonnell, Kris	Reading Reading Books
Up and Under	D	I	97	Sails	Rigby
Up and Up	WB	RF	N/A	Hughes, Shirley	Lothrop, Lee & Shepard
Up Before Daybreak: Cotton and People in America	Y	I	250+	Hopkinson, Deborah	Scholastic
Up Close	G	I	123	Discovery Links	Newbridge
Up Cloudy Mountain	S	RF	250+	Sails	Rigby
Up High in the Mountains	N	RF	250+	Wildcats	Wright Group/McGraw Hill
Up in a Tree	D	RF	111	Leveled Literacy Intervention/ Green System	Heinemann
Up in a Tree	C	RF	47	Sunshine	Wright Group/McGraw Hill
Up in the Air	P	I	250+	Wildcats	Wright Group/McGraw Hill
Up in the Sky	B	I	56	PM Plus Starters	Rigby
Up the Amazon	Q	I	250+	Windows on Literacy	National Geographic
Up the Down Staircase	Z+	RF	250+	Kaufman, Bel	HarperCollins
Up the Haystack	H	RF	251	Bookshop	Mondo
Up the Hill	LB	RF	16	Handprints A	Educators Publishing Service
Up the Tree	B	RF	38	First Stories	Pacific Learning
Up the Tree	D	RF	41	New Way Red	Steck-Vaughn
Up the Tree	B	RF	41	Rigby Rocket	Rigby
Up They Go	B	RF	30	Ready Readers	Pearson Learning Group
Up to the Challenge	S	I	250+	Connectors	Pacific Learning
Up Went Edmond	D	F	26	Pacific Literacy	Pacific Learning
Up Went the Goat	C	F	38	Start to Read	School Zone
Up, Down, and All Around	D	I	44	Windows on Literacy	National Geographic
Up, Over, and Down	LB	F	24	Reading Safari	Mondo
Up, Up and Away	M	I	250+	Yellow Umbrella Books	Red Brick Learning
Up, Up, and Away	B	I	40	Lighthouse	Rigby
Up, Up, and Away	T	I	1870	Reading Street	Pearson
Up, Up, and Away	M	I	250+	Twig	Wright Group/McGraw Hill
Up, Up, and Away!	Q	I	1113	Leveled Readers	Houghton Mifflin Harcourt

* Collection of short stories
# Graphic text

U

TITLE	LEVEL	GENRE	WORD COUNT	AUTHOR / SERIES	PUBLISHER / DISTRIBUTOR
Up, Up, and Away!	Q	I	1113	Leveled Readers/CA	Houghton Mifflin Harcourt
Up, Up, and Away!	Q	I	1113	Leveled Readers/TX	Houghton Mifflin Harcourt
Up, Up, and Away: The Story of Amelia Earhart	F	B	42	Canizares, Susan; Chanko, Pamela	Scholastic
Ups and Downs of Carl Davis III, The	T	RF	250+	Guy, Rosa	Language for Learning Assoc.
Upside Down	B	I	36	Sails	Rigby
Upside-Down Elephant, The	K	RF	396	Leveled Readers	Houghton Mifflin Harcourt
Upside-Down Life, An	I	I	199	Sails	Rigby
Upside-Down Reader, The	L	F	250+	Gruber, Wolfram	North-South Books
Upside-Down Voyage, The	S	HF	250+	Bookshop	Mondo
Upstairs Mouse, Downstairs Mole	L	F	250+	Wong, Herbert Yee	Houghton Mifflin Harcourt
Upstate Autumn	R	RF	1676	Leveled Readers	Houghton Mifflin Harcourt
Uranus	Q	I	250+	A True Book	Children's Press
Uranus	J	I	136	Exploring the Galaxy	Capstone Press
Uranus	S	I	250+	Our Solar System	Compass Point Books
Uranus	N	I	792	Our Universe	Lerner Publications
Uranus	Q	I	250+	The Galaxy	Red Brick Learning
Urban Wildlife	R	I	1212	Leveled Readers	Houghton Mifflin Harcourt
Ursus Travels	N	F	1066	Leveled Readers	Houghton Mifflin Harcourt
Ursus Travels	N	F	1066	Leveled Readers/CA	Houghton Mifflin Harcourt
Ursus Travels	N	F	1066	Leveled Readers/TX	Houghton Mifflin Harcourt
Ursus, the Traveling Bear	N	F	1038	Leveled Readers	Houghton Mifflin Harcourt
Ursus, the Traveling Bear	N	F	1038	Leveled Readers/CA	Houghton Mifflin Harcourt
Ursus, the Traveling Bear	N	F	1038	Leveled Readers/TX	Houghton Mifflin Harcourt
US and A	R	I	3003	Take Two Books	Wright Group/ McGraw Hill
Us and Uncle Fraud	S	RF	250+	Lowry, Lois	Houghton Mifflin Harcourt
Usborne Book of Inventors, The: From DaVinci to Biro	X	B	250+	Reid, Struan; Fara, Patricia	Scholastic
Usborne Book of Scientists, The: From Archimedes to Einstein	X	B	250+	Reid, Struan; Fara, Patricia	Scholastic
Use Your Beak!	F	RF	106	Erickson, Betty	Continental Press
Using a Beak	M	I	250+	Sails	Rigby
Using a Microscope	H	I	182	Rigby Focus	Rigby
Using a Tail	M	I	250+	Sails	Rigby
Using Color	J	I	249	Explorations	Okapi Educational Materials
Using Color	J	I	249	Explorations	Eleanor Curtain Publishing
Using Leaves	H	I	176	Sails	Rigby
Using Magnets	F	I	160	Early Connections	Benchmark Education
Using Nature's Gifts	K	I	250+	People, Spaces & Places	Rand McNally
Using Numbers at Work	C	I	75	Early Connections	Benchmark Education
Using Resources	K	I	624	Science Support Readers	Houghton Mifflin Harcourt
Using Rocks	C	I	62	Explorations	Eleanor Curtain Publishing
Using Rocks	C	I	62	Explorations	Okapi Educational Materials
Using Rocks	K	I	167	Windows on Literacy	National Geographic
Using Special Talents	T	I	2350	Reading Street	Pearson
Using the Library	L	I	291	Wonder World	Wright Group/McGraw Hill
Using the River	M	I	250+	Rigby Literacy	Rigby
Using the River	M	I	250+	Rigby Star Quest	Rigby
Using Tools	C	I	30	Discovery Links	Newbridge
Using Tools at Work	E	I	118	Early Connections	Benchmark Education
Using Wheels	G	I	115	Little Red Readers	Sundance
Using Your Safety Senses	K	I	413	Leveled Readers Science	Houghton Mifflin Harcourt

U

* Collection of short stories
\# Graphic text

TITLE	LEVEL	GENRE	WORD COUNT	AUTHOR / SERIES	PUBLISHER / DISTRIBUTOR
Using Your Senses at School	F	I	37	Windows on Literacy	National Geographic
Utah	T	I	250+	Hello U.S.A.	Lerner Publications
Utah	R	I	250+	This Land Is Your Land	Compass Point Books
Utah Jazz, The	S	I	250+	Team Spirit	Norwood House Press
Utes, The	P	I	250+	Native Peoples	Red Brick Learning
Utterly Me, Clarice Bean	O	RF	250+	Child, Lauren	Candlewick Press

* Collection of short stories
# Graphic text

U

TITLE	LEVEL	GENRE	WORD COUNT	AUTHOR / SERIES	PUBLISHER / DISTRIBUTOR
Vacation at Lighthouse Rock	L	RF	897	PM Plus Story Books	Rigby
Vacation for MM Mouse, A	I	F	275	Sails	Rigby
Vacation Journal, A	M	B	250+	Discovery World	Rigby
Vacation on Earth	P	F	250+	Scooters	ETA Cuisenaire
Vacation Under the Volcano	M	F	250+	Osborne, Mary Pope	Random House
Vacation, The	C	RF	94	Emergent	Pioneer Valley
Vacation, The	B	F	30	Sails	Rigby
Vacations	B	RF	22	Smart Starts	Rigby
Vagabond Crabs	J	I	117	Literacy 2000	Rigby
Valentine Star, The	M	RF	250+	Giff, Patricia Reilly	Bantam
Valentine's Checkup	C	RF	45	Little Books	Sadlier-Oxford
Valentine's Day	E	I	132	Fiesta Holiday Series	Pearson Learning Group
Valentine's Day	Q	I	250+	Holiday Histories	Heinemann Library
Valentine's Day	J	I	109	Holidays and Celebrations	Capstone Press
Valentine's Day	M	I	250+	Holidays and Celebrations	Picture Window Books
Valentine's Day	O	I	250+	Holidays and Festivals	Compass Point Books
Valentine's Day	P	I	250+	Let's See	Compass Point Books
Valentine's Day	C	F	49	Story Box	Wright Group/McGraw Hill
Valentine's Day Is…	M	I	250+	Gibbons, Gail	Holiday House
Valentines for Little Fox	G	F	249	Handprints D	Educators Publishing Service
Valentines: Cards and Crafts from the Heart	Q	I	250+	Crafts	Capstone Press
Valley Forge	S	I	250+	Ammon, Richard	Scholastic
Valley Forge	X	I	3045	Vocabulary Readers	Houghton Mifflin Harcourt
Valley Forge	X	I	3045	Vocabulary Readers/CA	Houghton Mifflin Harcourt
Valley Forge	X	I	3045	Vocabulary Readers/TX	Houghton Mifflin Harcourt
Valley of Hope	T	RF	250+	Reading Safari	Mondo
Valleys	J	I	294	Landforms	Lerner Publications
Vampire Bats, Bookworms, and Clothes Moths	M	I	778	Springboard	Wright Group/McGraw Hill
Vampire Trouble	L	F	250+	Dadey, Debbie; Jones, Marcia Thornton	Scholastic
Vampire Who Came for Christmas, The	Q	F	250+	Regan, Diane Curtis	Bantam
Vampires	X	I	4943	Monster Chronicles	Lerner Publications
Vampires Don't Wear Polka Dots	M	F	250+	Dadey, Debbie; Jones, Marcia Thornton	Scholastic
Van Gogh	Z	B	250+	Eyewitness Books	DK Publishing
Van Gogh	S	B	250+	Masterpieces: Artists and Their Works	Red Brick Learning
Van Gogh Cafe, The	S	RF	250+	Rylant, Cynthia	Harcourt School Publishers
Van, The	C	F	55	Georgie Giraffe	Literacy Footprints
Van, The	B	RF	48	Phonics and Friends	Hampton-Brown
Vanished	Z	I	6364	The Unexplained	Lerner Publications
Vanished!	S	I	250+	Bookweb	Rigby
Vanished!: The Mysterious Disappearance of Amelia Earhart	P	B	250+	Kulling, Monica	Random House
Vanishing Cultures	R	I	250+	Explorer Books-Pathfinder	National Geographic
Vanishing Cultures	P	I	250+	Explorer Books-Pioneer	National Geographic
Vegetable Garden, The	A	I	21	Leveled Readers	Houghton Mifflin Harcourt
Vegetable Garden, The	A	I	21	Leveled Readers/CA	Houghton Mifflin Harcourt
Vegetable Group, The	H	I	88	The Food Guide Pyramid	Capstone Press
Vegetable Soup	C	RF	60	Bonnell, Kris	Reading Reading Books
Vegetable Soup	E	F	67	Leveled Readers	Houghton Mifflin Harcourt
Vegetable Soup	G	RF	84	Morris, Ann	Scholastic
Vegetable Soup	A	I	24	Vocabulary Readers	Houghton Mifflin Harcourt

* Collection of short stories
# Graphic text

V

TITLE	LEVEL	GENRE	WORD COUNT	AUTHOR / SERIES	PUBLISHER / DISTRIBUTOR
Vegetables	F	I	85	Food Groups	Lerner Publications
Vegetables	H	I	180	Sun Sprouts	ETA Cuisenaire
Vegetables	LB	I	7	Windows on Literacy	National Geographic
Vegetables and How They Grow	F	I	86	Rosen Real Readers	Rosen Publishing Group
Vegetables Around the World	O	I	709	Vocabulary Readers	Houghton Mifflin Harcourt
Vegetables Around the World	O	I	709	Vocabulary Readers/CA	Houghton Mifflin Harcourt
Vegetables We Eat	M	I	250+	Gibbons, Gail	Holiday House
Vegetarians	K	I	216	Take Two Books	Wright Group/McGraw Hill
Vehicles	B	I	60	Nonfiction Set 2	Literacy Footprints
Vehicles for Fun and Sports	K	I	439	PM Plus	Rigby
Vehicles in the Air	K	I	436	PM Plus	Rigby
Velveteen Rabbit, The	Q	F	250+	Williams, Margery	Hearst
Venezuela	O	I	1699	A Ticket to …	Carolrohoda Books
Venezuela	P	I	2300	Country Explorers	Lerner Publications
Venezuela: A Question and Answer Book	P	I	250+	Question and Answer Countries	Capstone Press
Venus	Q	I	250+	A True Book	Children's Press
Venus	J	I	118	Exploring the Galaxy	Capstone Press
Venus	S	I	250+	Our Solar System	Compass Point Books
Venus	N	I	732	Our Universe	Lerner Publications
Venus	Q	I	250+	The Galaxy	Capstone Press
Venus	Q	I	250+	Vogt, Gregory L.	Millbrook Press
Venus	W	I	250+	World Mythology	Capstone Press
Venus & Serena Williams	P	B	1536	Amazing Athletes	Lerner Publications
Venus and Serena Williams: The Smashing Sisters	R	B	250+	High Five Reading	Red Brick Learning
Venus and the Comets	O	RF	10650	Tamar, Erika	Darby Creek Publishing
Venus Flytraps	Q	I	1980	Early Bird Nature Books	Lerner Publications
Venus: The Flytrap Who Wouldn't Eat Flies	M	F	601	Leveled Literacy Intervention/ Blue System	Heinemann
Vermont	T	I	250+	Hello U.S.A.	Lerner Publications
Vermont	R	I	250+	This Land Is Your Land	Compass Point Books
Vert Skating: Mastering the Ramp	Q	I	250+	Skateboarding	Capstone Press
Very Best Fish, The	N	RF	250+	Leveled Readers Language Support	Houghton Mifflin Harcourt
Very Big	D	I	49	Ready Readers	Pearson Learning Group
Very Big Potato, The	H	RF	250+	Cherrington, Janelle	Scholastic
Very Boastful Kangaroo, The	I	F	232	Green Light Readers	Harcourt
Very Busy Hen, The	D	F	123	Leveled Literacy Intervention/ Green System	Heinemann
Very Busy Spider, The	I	F	263	Carle, Eric	Philomel/Penguin
Very Funny Act, A	H	RF	181	Home Connection Collection	Rigby
Very Good Idea, A	J	RF	448	Springboard	Wright Group/McGraw Hill
Very Greedy Dog, The	H	TL	228	Aesop's Fables	Pearson Learning Group
Very Happy Birthday, A	M	RF	1017	Jellybeans	Rigby
Very Hungry Caterpillar, The	J	F	237	Carle, Eric	Philomel/Penguin
Very Long Night, The	I	RF	252	Dominie Math Stories	Pearson Learning Group
Very Nice Lunch, A	D	F	115	Leveled Readers	Houghton Mifflin Harcourt
Very Nice Lunch, A	D	F	115	Leveled Readers/CA	Houghton Mifflin Harcourt
Very Silly School, A	G	F	200+	Cherrington, Janelle	Scholastic
Very Special Birthdays	L	I	404	Reading Street	Pearson
Very Special Effects: Computers in Filmmaking	U	I	2087	Reading Street	Pearson
Very Special Gift, A	T	HF	3082	Reading Street	Pearson
Very Special Kwanzaa, A	O	I	250+	Chocolate, Deborah M. Newton	Scholastic
Very Strange Dollhouse, A	L	F	250+	Dussling, Jennifer	Grossett & Dunlap

V

TITLE	LEVEL	GENRE	WORD COUNT	AUTHOR / SERIES	PUBLISHER / DISTRIBUTOR
Very Strong Baby, The	E	F	74	Joy Readers	Pearson Learning Group
Very Thin Cat of Alloway Road, The	L	RF	250+	Literacy 2000	Rigby
Veterans Day	J	I	101	American Holidays	Lerner Publications
Veterans Day	K	I	250+	Cotton, Jaqueline S.	Scholastic
Veterans Day	Q	I	250+	Holiday Histories	Heinemann Library
Veterans Day	N	I	555	Leveled Readers Social Studies	Houghton Mifflin Harcourt
Veterans Day	L	I	96	National Holidays	Red Brick Learning
Veterans Day	N	I	1574	On My Own Holidays	Lerner Publications
Veterinarians	L	I	250+	Community Helpers	Red Brick Learning
Veterinarians	M	I	250+	Community Workers	Compass Point Books
Vibrations	H	I	38	The Way Things Move	Red Brick Learning
Vicar of Nibbleswick, The	O	RF	250+	Dahl, Roald	Puffin/Penguin
Vicky the High Jumper	K	I	250+	Literacy 2000	Rigby
Vicky's Box	J	F	412	Cambridge Reading	Pearson Learning Group
Victor and the Computer Cat	F	RF	92	Oxford Reading Tree	Oxford University Press
Victor and the Kite	F	RF	84	Oxford Reading Tree	Oxford University Press
Victor and the Martian	H	RF	109	Oxford Reading Tree	Oxford University Press
Victor and the Sail-cart	H	RF	94	Oxford Reading Tree	Oxford University Press
Victor Makes a TV	H	F	85	Reading Unlimited	Pearson Learning Group
Victor Sews	P	RF	1323	Leveled Readers	Houghton Mifflin Harcourt
Victor Takes a Sewing Class	N	RF	250+	Leveled Readers Language Support	Houghton Mifflin Harcourt
Victor the Champion	G	RF	102	Oxford Reading Tree	Oxford University Press
Victor the Hero	H	RF	103	Oxford Reading Tree	Oxford University Press
Video Game	F	RF	109	Alphakids	Sundance
Video Game, The	C	RF	94	InfoTrek	ETA Cuisenaire
Video Games	U	I	250+	Boldprint	Steck-Vaughn
Video Games: From Start to Finish	R	I	250+	Power Up!	Steck-Vaughn
Vietnam	O	I	2179	A Ticket to …	Carolrohoda Books
Vietnam	O	I	250+	Countries of the World	Red Brick Learning
Vietnam	P	I	2092	Country Explorers	Lerner Publications
Vietnam	Q	I	250+	First Reports: Countries	Compass Point Books
Vietnam	Q	I	250+	Theme Sets	National Geographic
Vietnam Veterans Memorial, The	Q	I	250+	National Landmarks	Red Brick Learning
Vietnam Women's Memorial, The	W	I	250+	Cornerstones of Freedom	Children's Press
Vietnam: A Question and Answer Book	P	I	250+	Question and Answer Countries	Capstone Press
View from Above, A	M	I	250+	Rigby Literacy	Rigby
View from Saturday, The	U	RF	250+	Konigsburg, E. L.	Atheneum
Viking	X	I	250+	Eyewitness Books	DK Publishing
Viking It and Liking It	P	F	250+	Scieszka, Jon	Penguin Group
Viking Longship, The	U	I	1515	Vocabulary Readers	Houghton Mifflin Harcourt
Viking Longship, The	U	I	1515	Vocabulary Readers/CA	Houghton Mifflin Harcourt
Viking Ships at Sunrise	M	F	250+	Osborne, Mary Pope	Random House
Vikings	T	I	250+	Warriors of History	Capstone Press
Vikings in North America, The	Y	I	3212	Vocabulary Readers	Houghton Mifflin Harcourt
Vikings in North America, The	Y	I	3212	Vocabulary Readers/CA	Houghton Mifflin Harcourt
Vikings, The	Q	I	250+	High-Fliers	Pacific Learning
Vikings, The	S	I	250+	Journey Into Civilization	Chelsea House
Vile Village, The	V	F	250+	Snicket, Lemony	Scholastic
Village by the Sea, The	U	RF	250+	Fox, Paula	Bantam
Villains	S	I	250+	Boldprint	Steck-Vaughn
Violet Raines Almost Got Struck by Lightning	T	RF	250+	Haworth, Danette	Walker & Co.
Virginia	T	I	250+	Hello U.S.A.	Lerner Publications
Virginia	T	I	250+	Theme Sets	National Geographic

V

* Collection of short stories
\# Graphic text

TITLE	LEVEL	GENRE	WORD COUNT	AUTHOR / SERIES	PUBLISHER / DISTRIBUTOR
Virginia	R	I	250+	This Land Is Your Land	Compass Point Books
Virginia Colony, The	R	I	250+	The American Colonies	Capstone Press
Virginia Opossums	K	I	418	Springboard	Wright Group/ McGraw Hill
Virtual Fred	O	SF	250+	Courtney, Vincent	Random House
Virtually True: Questioning Online Media	S	I	250+	Media Literacy	Capstone Press
Vision of Beauty: The Story of Sarah Breedlove Walker	U	B	250+	Lasky, Kathryn	Candlewick Press
Visit from Aunt Bee, A	C	RF	58	Leveled Literacy Intervention/ Orange System	Heinemann
Visit to a Butterfly Greenhouse, A	J	I	170	Reading Street	Pearson
Visit to a Farm, A	I	I	322	Time for Kids	Teacher Created Materials
Visit to a Museum	N	I	306	Leveled Readers Social Studies	Houghton Mifflin Harcourt
Visit to a Publisher, A	K	I	325	Time for Kids	Teacher Created Materials
Visit to a Pueblo, A	K	I	129	Vocabulary Readers	Houghton Mifflin Harcourt
Visit to an Automobile Factory, A	J	I	325	Time for Kids	Teacher Created Materials
Visit to Antarctica, A	R	I	1162	Leveled Readers	Houghton Mifflin Harcourt
Visit to Antarctica, A	R	I	1162	Leveled Readers/CA	Houghton Mifflin Harcourt
Visit to Antarctica, A	R	I	1162	Leveled Readers/TX	Houghton Mifflin Harcourt
Visit to Cousin Boris	I	F	250+	Popcorn	Sundance
Visit to Dr. Jane, A	D	RF	116	Joy Starters	Pearson Learning Group
Visit to the Airport, A	H	I	105	A Visit to…	Red Brick Learning
Visit to the Andes, A	O	I	865	Vocabulary Readers	Houghton Mifflin Harcourt
Visit to the Andes, A	O	I	865	Vocabulary Readers/CA	Houghton Mifflin Harcourt
Visit to the Animal Shelter, The	J	I	367	InfoTrek	ETA Cuisenaire
Visit to the Apple Orchards, A	H	I	114	A Visit to…	Red Brick Learning
Visit to the City, A	C	RF	64	Leveled Literacy Intervention/ Green System	Heinemann
Visit to the City, A	D	I	54	Vocabulary Readers	Houghton Mifflin Harcourt
Visit to the Dentist's Office, A	H	I	116	A Visit to…	Red Brick Learning
Visit to the Doctor, A	A	I	28	Little Books for Early Readers	University of Maine
Visit to the Dominican Republic, A	N	I	601	Vocabulary Readers	Houghton Mifflin Harcourt
Visit to the Dominican Republic, A	N	I	601	Vocabulary Readers/CA	Houghton Mifflin Harcourt
Visit to the Dominican Republic, A	N	I	601	Vocabulary Readers/TX	Houghton Mifflin Harcourt
Visit to the Library, A	E	I	109	Foundations	Wright Group/McGraw Hill
Visit to the Library, A	F	I	140	Springboard	Wright Group/McGraw Hill
Visit to the Planetarium, A	M	I	250+	Burke, Melissa Blackwell	Houghton Mifflin Harcourt
Visit to the Police Station, A	I	I	115	A Visit to…	Capstone Press
Visit to the Statue of Liberty, A	G	I	77	Independent Readers Social Studies	Houghton Mifflin Harcourt
Visit to Vancouver Island, A	O	RF	1261	Leveled Readers Social Studies	Houghton Mifflin Harcourt
Visiting a Park	A	I	20	Vocabulary Readers	Houghton Mifflin Harcourt
Visiting a Park	A	I	20	Vocabulary Readers/CA	Houghton Mifflin Harcourt
Visiting a Village	T	I	250+	Kalman, Bobbie	Scholastic
Visiting Grandma and Grandpa	G	RF	136	Carousel Readers	Pearson Learning Group
Visiting Grandma and Grandpa	A	I	24	Leveled Readers	Houghton Mifflin Harcourt
Visiting Grandma and Grandpa	A	I	24	Leveled Readers/CA	Houghton Mifflin Harcourt
Visiting the Eagle Hotel	M	I	250+	Rigby Literacy	Rigby
Visiting the Police Station	I	I	200	Rosen Real Readers	Rosen Publishing Group
Visiting the Vet	H	I	259	Foundations	Wright Group/McGraw Hill
Visiting the Vet	H	I	140	Sun Sprouts	ETA Cuisenaire
Visiting the Zoo	A	RF	26	Leveled Readers	Houghton Mifflin Harcourt
Visiting the Zoo	A	RF	26	Leveled Readers/CA	Houghton Mifflin Harcourt
Visitor, The	I	F	250+	Popcorn	Sundance
Visitors	E	RF	46	Literacy 2000	Rigby

* Collection of short stories
# Graphic text

V

TITLE	LEVEL	GENRE	WORD COUNT	AUTHOR / SERIES	PUBLISHER / DISTRIBUTOR
Viva America	U	I	2222	Reading Street	Pearson
Viva Mexico	L	I	432	Leveled Readers Social Studies	Houghton Mifflin Harcourt
Viva México!: A Story of Benito Juárez and Cinco de Mayo	Q	B	250+	Stories of America	Steck-Vaughn
Vlad the Impaler: The Real Count Dracula	Y	HF	250+	Goldberg, Enid A., Itzkowitz, Norman	Scholastic
Voice for Equality, A	S	B	1263	Leveled Readers	Houghton Mifflin Harcourt
Voice for Equality, A	S	B	1263	Leveled Readers/CA	Houghton Mifflin Harcourt
Voice for Equality, A	S	B	1263	Leveled Readers/TX	Houghton Mifflin Harcourt
Voice for the Animals, A	S	I	250+	Navigators Social Studies Series	Benchmark Education Company
Voice of Freedom	X	I	2235	Leveled Readers	Houghton Mifflin Harcourt
Voice of Freedom	X	I	2235	Leveled Readers/CA	Houghton Mifflin Harcourt
Voice of Freedom: A Story About Frederick Douglass	R	B	8445	Creative Minds Biographies	Carolrhoda Books
Voice of Her Own, A: The Story of Phillis Wheately, Slave Poet	S	B	250	Lasky, Kathryn	Candlewick Press
Voice of the People, The: American Democracy in Action	V	I	250+	Maestro, Betsy & Giulio	William Morrow
Voice of the Pioneer: Carrie Chapman Catt	R	B	1916	Leveled Readers Social Studies	Houghton Mifflin Harcourt
Voices	S	RF	250+	Book Blazers	ETA Cuisenaire
Voices From the Civil War	U	I	250+	Navigators Social Studies Series	Benchmark Education
Voices in St. Augustine	R	F	250+	Wood, Jane R.	Bluefish Bay Publishing
Volcanic Eruption!: Susan Ruff and Bruce Nelson's Story of Survival	R	I	250+	True Tales of Survival	Capstone Press
Volcano	U	I	250+	Lauber, Patricia	Scholastic
Volcano	C	I	44	Science	Outside the Box
Volcano Awakes!, The	S	I	250+	Sails	Rigby
Volcano Goddess Will See You Now, The	N	F	250+	The Zack Files	Grossett & Dunlap
Volcano Man	N	I	250+	On Our Way to English	Rigby
Volcano Project	M	I	677	Sun Sprouts	ETA Cuisenaire
Volcano Woman	M	TL	250+	Cambridge Reading	Pearson Learning Group
Volcano!	R	I	250+	Explorer Books-Pathfinder	National Geographic
Volcano!	P	I	250+	Explorer Books-Pioneer	National Geographic
Volcano! Sleeping Giants Awake	U	I	250+	Explore More	Wright Group/McGraw Hill
Volcanoes	O	I	250+	A True Book	Children's Press
Volcanoes	W	I	250+	Disasters Up Close	Lerner Publications
Volcanoes	N	I	250+	Early Connections	Benchmark Education
Volcanoes	T	I	250+	Earth Science	Franklin Watts
Volcanoes	N	I	250+	Earthforms	Capstone Press
Volcanoes	Q	I	250+	Explorers	Wright Group/McGraw Hill
Volcanoes	N	I	679	Gear Up!	Wright Group/McGraw Hill
Volcanoes	V	I	250+	iOpeners	Pearson Learning Group
Volcanoes	M	I	626	Pull Ahead Books	Lerner Publications
Volcanoes	P	I	250+	Reading Expeditions	National Geographic
Volcanoes	L	I	250+	Sunshine	Wright Group/McGraw Hill
Volcanoes	R	I	250+	The Wonders of Our World	Crabtree
Volcanoes	M	I	387	Time for Kids	Teacher Created Materials
Volcanoes	Q	I	250+	Windows on Literacy	National Geographic
Volcanoes	Q	I	250+	Worldwise	Franklin Watts
Volcanoes and Earthquakes	T	I	250+	Lauber, Patricia	Language for Learning Assoc.
Volcanoes and Geysers	O	I	250+	PM Plus Story Books	Rigby
Volcanoes and Other Natural Disasters	R	I	250+	DK Readers	DK Publishing

* Collection of short stories
\# Graphic text

V

TITLE	LEVEL	GENRE	WORD COUNT	AUTHOR / SERIES	PUBLISHER / DISTRIBUTOR
Volcanoes Around the World	O	I	380	Vocabulary Readers	Houghton Mifflin Harcourt
Volcanoes Inside and Out	N	I	1784	On My Own Science	Lerner Publications
Volcanoes National Park	S	I	1396	Leveled Readers Science	Houghton Mifflin Harcourt
Volcanoes: When a Mountain Explodes	S	I	250+	High Five Reading	Red Brick Learning
Volleyball for Fun!	S	I	250+	Sports for Fun!	Compass Point Books
Vote for Larry	Z+	RF	250+	Tashjian, Janet	Henry Holt & Co.
Vote!: The Complicated Life of Claudia Cristina Cortez	S	RF	250+	Gallagher, Diana G.	Stone Arch Books
Voting and Elections	Q	I	250+	Let's See	Compass Point Books
Voyage Across the Pacific	S	I	1250	Leveled Readers	Houghton Mifflin Harcourt
Voyage into Space	J	F	250+	Storyworlds	Heinemann Educational Books
Voyage of Mae Jemison, The	H	B	46	Canizares, Susan; Berger, Samantha	Scholastic
Voyage of Patience Goodspeed, The	U	HF	250+	Frederick, Heather Vogel	Simon & Schuster
Voyage of the Clowns, The	J	F	250+	The Wright Skills	Wright Group/McGraw Hill
Voyage of the Fram, The	R	I	611	Vocabulary Readers	Houghton Mifflin Harcourt
Voyage of the Frog, The	S	RF	250+	Paulsen, Gary	Bantam
Voyage to Antartica	T	I	2505	Leveled Readers Science	Houghton Mifflin Harcourt
Voyage to California	R	HF	1428	Leveled Readers	Houghton Mifflin Harcourt
Voyage to California	R	HF	1428	Leveled Readers/CA	Houghton Mifflin Harcourt
Voyage to California	R	HF	1428	Leveled Readers/TX	Houghton Mifflin Harcourt
Voyage, The	M	F	250+	Pair-It Books	Steck-Vaughn
Voyager: An Adventure Through Space	Q	I	250+	Gustafson, John	Scholastic
Vroom!	G	F	167	Rigby Literacy	Rigby
Vroom!	G	F	169	Rigby Star	Rigby
Vulpes the Red Fox	T	F	250+	George, Jean Craighead	Puffin/Penguin
Vultures	P	I	1513	Animal Scavengers	Lerner Publishing
Vultures	O	I	1509	Early Bird Nature Books	Lerner Publishing
Vultures on Vacation	C	F	36	Ready Readers	Pearson Learning Group

V

TITLE	LEVEL	GENRE	WORD COUNT	AUTHOR / SERIES	PUBLISHER / DISTRIBUTOR
W.E.B. DuBois and the Fight for a Just Society	R	B	904	Leveled Readers Social Studies	Houghton Mifflin Harcourt
Wackiest White House Pets	R	RF	250+	Davis, Gibbs	Scholastic
Wacky Jacks	L	RF	250+	Adler, David A.	Random House
Wacky Museums and Roadside Sights	Q	I	250+	Power Up!	Steck-Vaughn
Wacky Plant Cycles	O	I	250+	Bookshop	Mondo
Wacky Trees	S	I	250+	Plants and Fungi	Franklin Watts
Wacky Wheels	N	I	250+	Pacific Literacy	Pacific Learning
Wading Birds	L	I	446	Pull Ahead Books	Lerner Publications
Wagon Ride, The	E	RF	115	Teacher's Choice Series	Pearson Learning Group
Wagon Wheels	K	HF	250+	Brenner, Barbara	HarperTrophy
Wagon, The	H	RF	78	Reading Unlimited	Pearson Learning Group
Wainscott Weasel, The	T	F	250+	Seidler, Tor	HarperCollins
Wait for Me	C	RF	75	Little Books	Sadlier-Oxford
Wait for Me	D	RF	185	Visions	Wright Group/McGraw Hill
Wait for Your Turn!	H	RF	141	Teacher's Choice Series	Pearson Learning Group
Wait Skates	G	RF	58	Rookie Readers	Children's Press
Wait Till Helen Comes	U	F	250+	Hahn, Mary Downing	Houghton Mifflin Harcourt
Wait Until Next Year	V	RF	2226	Leveled Readers	Houghton Mifflin Harcourt
Waiting	G	RF	59	Literacy 2000	Rigby
Waiting	A	RF	28	Story Box	Wright Group/McGraw Hill
Waiting	E	RF	75	Voyages	SRA/McGraw Hill
Waiting Alligators	K	I	445	Pull Ahead Books	Lerner Publications
Waiting for a Frog	G	RF	124	Coats, Glenn	Kaeden Books
Waiting for Aunt Ro	Q	RF	1267	Leveled Readers	Houghton Mifflin Harcourt
Waiting for Aunt Ro	Q	RF	1267	Leveled Readers/CA	Houghton Mifflin Harcourt
Waiting for Aunt Ro	Q	RF	1267	Leveled Readers/TX	Houghton Mifflin Harcourt
Waiting for Granny	F	RF	179	Leveled Readers Language Support	Houghton Mifflin Harcourt
Waiting for the Rain	J	RF	307	Foundations	Wright Group/McGraw Hill
Waiting in Line	F	RF	74	City Stories	Rigby
Wake Me in Spring	J	F	301	Preller, James	Scholastic
Wake Up Ginger	C	F	70	Bookshop	Mondo
Wake Up Mom!	C	RF	94	Sunshine	Wright Group/McGraw Hill
Wake Up!	F	RF	104	Gear Up!	Wright Group/McGraw Hill
Wake Up!	C	F	62	Story Steps	Rigby
Wake Up, Dad	C	RF	67	PM Story Books	Rigby
Wake Up, Emily, It's Mother's Day	M	RF	250+	Giff, Patricia Reilly	Yearling
Wake Up, Scooterville	K	RF	250+	Stamper, Judith Bauer	Scholastic
Wake Up, Sleepyheads!	F	RF	35	Little Books	Sadlier-Oxford
Wake Up, Sun!	E	F	250+	Harrison, David	Random House
Wake Up, Wake Up!	D	F	110	Wildsmith, Brian & Rebecca	Scholastic
Wake Up, Young Soldier	R	I	864	Independent Readers Social Studies	Houghton Mifflin Harcourt
Wakeboarding	M	I	250+	To the Extreme	Capstone Press
Wake-Up, Baby!	J	F	209	Oppenheim, Joanna	Bantam
Waking Up	A	F	50	Leveled Literacy Intervention/Green System	Heinemann
Waking Up	H	RF	250+	Seese, Ellen	Kaeden Books
Wali Dad's Gift	P	TL	1003	Leveled Readers	Houghton Mifflin Harcourt
Wali Dad's Gifts	P	TL	1003	Leveled Readers/CA	Houghton Mifflin Harcourt
Wali Dad's Gifts	P	TL	1003	Leveled Readers/TX	Houghton Mifflin Harcourt
Walk Across America, A	T	I	250+	Literacy by Design	Rigby
Walk Around the City, A	L	I	435	Reading Street	Pearson

W

* Collection of short stories
# Graphic text

TITLE	LEVEL	GENRE	WORD COUNT	AUTHOR / SERIES	PUBLISHER / DISTRIBUTOR
Walk at Night, A	G	RF	198	Leveled Literacy Intervention/ Green System	Heinemann
Walk at the Farm, A	J	F	618	Gilbert the Pig	Pioneer Valley
Walk for Jasper, A	D	RF	87	Jasper the Cat	Pioneer Valley
Walk for Pickles, A	D	RF	82	Pickles the Dog Series	Pioneer Valley
Walk in Antarctica, A	E	F	118	Reading Street	Pearson
Walk in My Woods, A	D	I	83	Independent Readers Science	Houghton Mifflin Harcourt
*Walk in My World, A	Y	RF	250+	Mazer, Anne	Persea Books
Walk in the Boreal Forest, A	T	I	2143	Biomes of North America	Lerner Publications
Walk in the Deciduous Forest, A	T	I	1959	Biomes of North America	Lerner Publications
Walk in the Desert, A	T	I	2115	Biomes of North America	Lerner Publications
Walk in the Mountains, A	K	I	373	Reading Street	Pearson
Walk in the Park, A	C	I	57	Dominie Factivity Series	Pearson Learning Group
Walk in the Prairie, A	T	I	2207	Biomes of North America	Lerner Publications
Walk in the Rain Forest, A	T	I	2124	Biomes of North America	Lerner Publications
Walk in the Rain Forest, A	L	RF	1005	InfoTrek	ETA Cuisenaire
Walk in the Rain, A	B	RF	28	Pair-It Books	Steck-Vaughn
Walk in the Tundra, A	T	I	2168	Biomes of North America	Lerner Publications
Walk in the Woods, A	F	F	212	Leveled Readers	Houghton Mifflin Harcourt
Walk in the Woods, A	A	RF	20	Leveled Readers	Houghton Mifflin Harcourt
Walk in the Woods, A	A	RF	20	Leveled Readers/CA	Houghton Mifflin Harcourt
Walk Tall	N	I	250+	Pacific Literacy	Pacific Learning
Walk Through a Rainforest, A: Life in the Ituri Forest of Zaire	V	RF	250+	Jenike, David & Mark	HarperCollins
Walk Through History on the Freedom Trail	Q	I	828	Leveled Readers Social Studies	Houghton Mifflin Harcourt
Walk Two Moons	W	RF	250+	Creech, Sharon	HarperCollins
Walk with a Wolf	N	RF	250+	Read and Wonder	Candlewick Press
Walk with Dad, A	C	I	59	Bonnell, Kris	Reading Reading Books
Walk With Grandpa, A	L	RF	388	Read Alongs	Rigby
Walk with John Muir, A	U	B	2237	Independent Readers Social Studies	Houghton Mifflin Harcourt
Walk with Meli, A	E	RF	200	Leveled Literacy Intervention/ Green System	Heinemann
Walk, Ride, Run	D	RF	116	PM Plus Story Books	Rigby
Walk, The	B	RF	29	Early Emergent	Pioneer Valley
Walk, The	G	RF	129	Reading Unlimited	Pearson Learning Group
Walkathon, The	K	RF	250+	PM Story Books-Silver	Rigby
Walker's Crossing	X	RF	250+	Naylor, Phyllis Reynolds	Aladdin
Walking	M	I	250+	Literacy 2000	Rigby
Walking by the Rio	K	RF	118	Books for Young Learners	Richard C. Owen
Walking for Freedom: The Montgomery Bus Boycott	R	I	250+	Kelso, Richard	Steck-Vaughn
Walking Home Alone	J	RF	327	Books for Young Learners	Richard C. Owen
Walking in the Autumn	H	I	206	PM Nonfiction-Green	Rigby
Walking in the Forest	E	RF	39	Reading Street	Pearson
Walking in the Jungle	E	RF	113	Little Red Readers	Sundance
Walking in the Spring	H	I	168	PM Nonfiction-Green	Rigby
Walking in the Summer	H	I	233	PM Nonfiction-Green	Rigby
Walking in the Winter	H	I	251	PM Nonfiction-Green	Rigby
Walking on the Moon	N	I	250+	Explore Space!	Red Brick Learning
Walking the Choctaw Road	Y	TL	250+	Tingle, Tim	Cinco Puntos Press
Walking the Dog	D	RF	69	Sun Sprouts	ETA Cuisenaire
Walking the Dogs	H	RF	80	City Stories	Rigby

W

* Collection of short stories
# Graphic text

TITLE	LEVEL	GENRE	WORD COUNT	AUTHOR / SERIES	PUBLISHER / DISTRIBUTOR
Walking the Road to Freedom: A Story About Sojourner Truth	R	B	7713	Creative Minds Biographies	Carolrhoda Books
Walking the Road to Freedom: A Story About Sojourner Truth	R	B	250+	Ferris, Jeri	Dell
Walking to School	C	RF	38	Voyages	SRA/McGraw Hill
Walking Up Walls	I	I	140	Windows on Literacy	National Geographic
Walking, Walking	C	I	32	Twig	Wright Group/McGraw Hill
Walkingsticks	I	I	89	Bugs, Bugs, Bugs	Capstone Press
Walkingsticks	I	I	83	Pebble Books	Red Brick Learning
Wall of Names, A: The Story of the Vietnam Veterans Memorial	P	I	250+	Donnelly, Judy	Random House
Wall, The	P	HF	250+	Bunting, Eve	Clarion
Wall: Growing Up Behind the Iron Curtain, The	Y	I	250+	Sis, Peter	Farrar, Straus and Giroux
Walls of the World	X	I	250+	iOpeners	Pearson Learning Group
Walruses	I	I	55	Pebble Books	Red Brick Learning
Walruses	H	I	117	Under the Sea	Capstone Press
Walruses	N	I	250+	World of Mammals	Capstone Press
Walt Disney	P	B	250+	Photo-Illustrated Biographies	Red Brick Learning
Walt Disney's World	G	I	96	Leveled Readers Social Studies	Houghton Mifflin Harcourt
Walter and the Food Fair	O	RF	1046	Leveled Readers/TX	Houghton Mifflin Harcourt
Walter and the Inventor's Garden	L	F	250+	Pacific Literacy	Pacific Learning
Walter Hottle Bottle	L	RF	250+	Voyages	SRA/McGraw Hill
Walter the Warlock	M	F	250+	Hautzig, Deborah	Random House
Walter, the Water Taxi	F	F	140	Springboard	Wright Group/McGraw Hill
Walter's Worries	L	F	250+	Pacific Literacy	Pacific Learning
*Waltur Buys a Pig in a Poke and Other Stories	K	F	250+	Gregorich, Barbara	Houghton Mifflin Harcourt
Wampanoag, The: The People of the First Light	S	I	250+	American Indian Nations	Capstone Press
Wampum Beads	P	I	526	Springboard	Wright Group/ McGraw Hill
Wand in the Word, The: Conversations with Writers of Fantasy	X	I	250+	Marcus, Leonard S.	Candlewick Press
Wanderer, The	V	RF	250+	Creech, Sharon	HarperCollins
Wanted . . . Mud Blossom	P	RF	250+	Byars, Betsy	Dell
Wanted Dead or Alive: The True Story of Harriet Tubman	P	B	250+	McGovern, Ann	Scholastic
War and Peace	U	I	250+	Kids Discover Reading	Wright Group/McGraw Hill
War Comes to Willy Freeman	U	HF	250+	Collier, James & Christopher	Dell
*War Dog Heroes: True Stories of Dog Courage in Wartime	S	I	250+	Sanderson, Jeannette	Scholastic
War Heroes	V	B	250+	Storyteller -Mountain Peaks	Wright Group/McGraw Hill
War in the Middle East, A Reporter's Story: Black September and the Yom Kippur War	Z	I	250+	Hampton, Wilborn	Candlewick Press
War of 1812, The	S	I	250+	A First Book	Franklin Watts
War of 1812, The	V	I	250+	America Goes to War	Red Brick Learning
War of 1812, The	V	I	250+	Let Freedom Ring	Capstone Press
War of 1812, The	U	I	250+	Primary Source Readers	Teacher Created Materials
War of the Roses, The	U	HF	250+	Reading Expeditions	National Geographic
War of the Witches	Z+	F	250+	Carranza, Maite	Bloomsbury
War of the Worlds, The	Z	SF	250+	Wells, H. G.	Tom Doherty
War Shirt, The	M	RF	250+	Greetings	Rigby
War Torn	U	RF	250+	Power Up!	Steck-Vaughn
War With Grandpa, The	S	RF	250+	Smith, Robert Kimmel	Bantam
Warm and Fuzzy	I	F	270	Reading Street	Pearson
Warm Clothes	C	I	51	Preparing for Winter	Capstone Press
Warming Up! Cooling Off!	I	I	553	Sunshine	Wright Group/McGraw Hill

* Collection of short stories
# Graphic text

W

TITLE	LEVEL	GENRE	WORD COUNT	AUTHOR / SERIES	PUBLISHER / DISTRIBUTOR
Warning Lights in the Dark	L	I	393	Rigby Flying Colors	Rigby
Warning: Volcano!: The Story of Mount St. Helens	O	I	250+	Rosen Real Readers	Rosen Publishing Group
Warren G. Harding	U	B	250+	Profiles of the Presidents	Compass Point Books
Warren G. Harding: Twenty-ninth President	R	B	250+	Getting to Know the U.S. Presidents	Children's Press
Warrior Queens	V	I	250+	WorldScapes	ETA Cuisenaire
Warriors	X	I	250+	Boldprint	Steck-Vaughn
Warships	V	I	4310	Military Hardware in Action	Lerner Publications
Warships	N	I	441	Pull Ahead Books	Lerner Publications
Warthogs	O	I	250+	Holmes, Kevin J.	Red Brick Learning
Warton and the King of the Skies	O	F	250+	Erickson, Russell E.	Houghton Mifflin Harcourt
Wash Day	E	RF	94	Real Kids Readers	Millbrook Press
Wash Day	A	RF	35	Voyages	SRA/McGraw Hill
Wash Your Hands!	J	F	246	Ross, Tony	Kane/Miller Book Publishers
Washing	E	RF	150	Foundations	Wright Group/McGraw Hill
Washing Our Dog	H	RF	120	Alphakids	Sundance
Washing the Dishes	D	RF	111	Rigby Flying Colors	Rigby
Washing the Dog	G	I	84	Little Readers	Houghton Mifflin Harcourt
Washing the Dog	G	I	84	Little Red Readers	Sundance
Washing the Elephant	B	F	35	Lighthouse	Rigby
Washington	T	I	250+	Hello U.S.A.	Lerner Publications
Washington	R	I	250+	This Land Is Your Land	Compass Point Books
Washington Is Burning	O	HF	1851	On My Own History	Lerner Publications
Washington Monument, The	Q	I	250+	National Landmarks	Red Brick Learning
Washington Monument, The	P	I	535	Pull Ahead Books	Lerner Publications
Washington Nationals, The	S	I	250+	Team Spirit	Norwood House Press
Washington Redskins, The	S	I	250+	Team Spirit	Norwood House Press
Washington, D.C.	T	I	250+	Hello U.S.A.	Lerner Publications
Washington, D.C.	F	I	113	Reading Street	Pearson
Washington, D.C.	L	I	163	Rosen Real Readers	Rosen Publishing Group
Washington, D.C.	R	I	250+	This Land Is Your Land	Compass Point Books
Washington, D.C.	K	I	187	Windows on Literacy	National Geographic
Washington, D.C.: A Scrapbook	Q	I	250+	Benson, Laura Lee	Charlesbridge
Wasps	H	I	112	Bugs, Bugs, Bugs!	Capstone Press
Wasps	I	I	59	Pebble Books	Red Brick Learning
Waste Not: Time to Recycle	K	I	250+	Spyglass Books	Compass Point Books
Waste of Space, A	M	RF	250+	SupaDoopers	Sundance
Waste Watchers	T	RF	250+	Reading Expeditions	National Geographic
Watch by the Sea, The	L	RF	250+	Cambridge Reading	Pearson Learning Group
Watch Girl, The	S	SF	2280	Leveled Readers	Houghton Mifflin Harcourt
Watch Girl, The	S	SF	2280	Leveled Readers/CA	Houghton Mifflin Harcourt
Watch Girl, The	S	SF	2280	Leveled Readers/TX	Houghton Mifflin Harcourt
Watch It Grow	K	I	243	Spyglass Books	Compass Point Books
Watch Me	E	RF	151	Handprints C	Educators Publishing Service
Watch Me Grow!	I	I	296	InfoTrek	ETA Cuisenaire
Watch Me Zoom	C	RF	45	Windmill Books	Rigby
Watch Out	B	F	44	Bookshop	Mondo
Watch Out for Trash Cans!	G	F	278	Sails	Rigby
Watch Out!	C	F	27	Literacy 2000	Rigby
Watch Out!	M	I	504	Reading Street	Pearson
Watch Out! Polar Bears!	L	I	602	Leveled Readers	Houghton Mifflin Harcourt

W

TITLE	LEVEL	GENRE	WORD COUNT	AUTHOR / SERIES	PUBLISHER / DISTRIBUTOR
Watch Out! Polar Bears!	L	I	602	Leveled Readers/CA	Houghton Mifflin Harcourt
Watch Out! Polar Bears!	L	I	602	Leveled Readers/TX	Houghton Mifflin Harcourt
Watch Out, Man-Eating Snake	L	RF	250+	Giff, Patricia Reilly	Bantam
Watch Out, William!	I	F	250+	I Am Reading	Kingfisher
Watch the Sky	D	I	41	Windows on Literacy	National Geographic
Watcher, The	Z	RF	250+	Howe, James	Simon & Schuster
Watchers: I.D.	V	SF	250+	Lerangis, Peter	Scholastic
Watchers: Island	V	SF	250+	Lerangis, Peter	Scholastic
Watchers: Lab 6	V	SF	250+	Lerangis, Peter	Scholastic
Watchers: Last Stop	V	SF	250+	Lerangis, Peter	Scholastic
Watchers: Rewind	V	SF	250+	Lerangis, Peter	Scholastic
Watchers: War	V	SF	250+	Lerangis, Peter	Scholastic
Watching Chimps	Q	I	250+	Explorer Books-Pathfinder	National Geographic
Watching Chimps	P	I	250+	Explorer Books-Pioneer	National Geographic
Watching Clouds	H	I	201	PM Science Readers	Rigby
Watching Every Drop	M	I	250+	Home Connection Collection	Rigby
Watching Josh	Q	RF	250+	Ragged Island Mysteries	Wright Group/McGraw Hill
Watching the Game	G	RF	210	Momentum Literacy Program	Troll Associates
Watching the Weather	G	I	142	Discovery Links	Newbridge
Watching the Whales	L	RF	267	Foundations	Wright Group/McGraw Hill
Watching TV	E	RF	89	Foundations	Wright Group/McGraw Hill
Watching TV	B	RF	18	Sunshine	Wright Group/McGraw Hill
Water	C	RF	20	Carousel Readers	Pearson Learning Group
Water	E	I	99	Early Connections	Benchmark Education
Water	C	I	12	Geography	Lerner Publishing
Water	B	I	28	Literacy 2000	Rigby
Water	B	I	24	Little Celebrations	Pearson Learning Group
Water	J	I	250+	Momentum Literacy Program	Troll Associates
Water	K	I	211	Nonfiction	Literacy Footprints
Water	G	I	126	On Our Way to English	Rigby
Water	B	I	36	Science	Outside the Box
Water	C	I	48	Seedlings	Continental Press
Water	N	I	250+	Simply Science	Compass Point Books
Water	B	RF	33	Sunshine	Wright Group/McGraw Hill
Water	Q	I	250+	Theme Sets	National Geographic
Water	D	I	54	Time for Kids	Teacher Created Materials
Water	H	I	89	What Earth Is Made Of	Lerner Publications
Water	J	I	164	Windows on Literacy	National Geographic
Water	H	I	94	Wonder World	Wright Group/McGraw Hill
Water	A	I	21	Yellow Umbrella Books	Red Brick Learning
Water All Around	C	I	26	Leveled Readers Science	Houghton Mifflin Harcourt
Water All Around the Earth	P	I	250+	On Our Way to English	Rigby
Water and Wind	N	I	250+	PM Plus Story Books	Rigby
Water Animals	P	I	250+	Animals Are Amazing	Carus Publishing Company
Water as a Gas	L	I	127	Pebble Books	Capstone Press
Water as a Liquid	I	I	141	Pebble Books	Red Brick Learning
Water as a Solid	J	I	113	Pebble Books	Red Brick Learning
Water at Work	K	I	159	Instant Readers	Harcourt School Publishers
Water Balloons	C	F	26	Brand New Readers	Candlewick Press
Water Basics	J	I	131	Nature Basics	Capstone Press
Water Boatman, The	F	I	44	Pacific Literacy	Pacific Learning
Water Buffalo Days	P	B	250+	Huynh, Quong Nhuong	HarperTrophy
Water Bugs	I	I	76	Pebble Books	Red Brick Learning
Water Caller, The	T	SF	250+	Power Up!	Steck-Vaughn

* Collection of short stories
\# Graphic text

W

TITLE	LEVEL	GENRE	WORD COUNT	AUTHOR / SERIES	PUBLISHER / DISTRIBUTOR
Water Can Be . . .	B	I	17	Science	Outside the Box
Water Can Change	K	I	138	Windows on Literacy	National Geographic
Water Changes	C	I	36	Discovery Links	Newbridge
Water Changes	D	I	25	Instant Readers	Harcourt School Publishers
Water Cycle of Africa, The	U	I	1453	Reading Street	Pearson
Water Cycle, The	T	I	250+	Earth Science	Franklin Watts
Water Cycle, The	N	I	647	Gear Up!	Wright Group/ McGraw Hill
Water Cycle, The	J	I	296	Instant Readers	Harcourt School Publishers
Water Cycle, The	L	I	146	Pebble Books	Capstone Press
Water Cycle, The	S	I	1209	Science Support Readers	Houghton Mifflin Harcourt
Water Cycle, The	J	I	113	Water	Lerner Publications
Water Cycle, The	J	I	250+	Yellow Umbrella Books	Capstone Press
Water Falling	D	I	41	Literacy 2000	Rigby
Water Fight, The	E	RF	64	Oxford Reading Tree	Oxford University Press
Water for Life	T	I	250+	WorldScapes	ETA Cuisenaire
Water for the World	M	I	250+	Home Connection Collection	Rigby
Water Goes Up! Water Goes Down!	K	I	299	Early Connections	Benchmark Education
Water Hole, The	B	I	48	Sails	Rigby
*Water Lilies and Other Stories	L	TL	250+	New Way Literature	Steck-Vaughn
Water Monsters	Z	I	250+	Unsolved Mysteries	Steck-Vaughn
Water Moves	C	I	39	Explorations	Eleanor Curtain Publishing
Water Moves	C	I	39	Explorations	Okapi Educational Materials
Water Park, The	D	F	123	Georgie Giraffe	Literacy Footprints
Water Park, The	A	RF	24	Sails	Rigby
Water Patrol, The: Saving Surfers' Lives in Big Waves	Q	I	250+	High Five Reading	Capstone Press
Water Power	J	I	86	Windows on Literacy	National Geographic
Water Resources	T	I	1862	Science Support Readers	Houghton Mifflin Harcourt
Water Scientists	T	B	250+	Science Readers	Teacher Created Materials
Water Toys, The	C	RF	58	Adams, Lorraine; Bruvold, Lynn	Eagle Crest Books
Water Wise	R	I	250+	InfoQuest	Rigby
Water Wise	N	I	250+	iOpeners	Pearson Learning Group
Water Wonders of the World: From Killer Waves to Monsters of the Deep	W	I	250+	Bookshop	Mondo
Water! Water!	F	I	186	Story Basket	Wright Group/McGraw Hill
Water! Water!	C	I	33	Sunshine	Wright Group/McGraw Hill
Water, Ice, and Steam	I	I	143	Rosen Real Readers	Rosen Publishing Group
Water, Land, and Air	H	I	76	Windows on Literacy	National Geographic
Water, The	B	F	36	Sails	Rigby
Water, Water	B	I	48	Rigby Literacy	Rigby
Water, Water	C	F	112	Sails	Rigby
Water, Water Everywhere	F	RF	61	Books for Young Learners	Richard C. Owen
Water, Water Everywhere!	C	I	27	Leveled Readers Science	Houghton Mifflin Harcourt
Water: A Natural Resource	P	I	250+	Rigby Focus	Rigby
Water: A Resource Our World Depends On	V	I	250+	Managing Our Resources	Heinemann
Water: Liquid, Solid, Gas	M	I	240	Twig	Wright Group/McGraw Hill
Water: Up, Down, and All Around	M	I	250+	Amazing Science	Picture Window Books
Waterbirds	P	I	250+	InfoQuest	Rigby
Waterbirds	H	I	200	Rigby Flying Colors	Rigby
Watercolor	Z	I	250+	Eyewitness Books	DK Publishing
Watercolors	K	I	369	Vocabulary Readers	Houghton Mifflin Harcourt
Watercolors	K	I	369	Vocabulary Readers/CA	Houghton Mifflin Harcourt
Waterfalls, Glaciers, and Avalanches	M	I	250+	PM Plus Nonfiction	Rigby
Waterhole	K	I	149	Planet Earth	Rigby

TITLE	LEVEL	GENRE	WORD COUNT	AUTHOR / SERIES	PUBLISHER / DISTRIBUTOR
Waterhole, The	L	F	250+	Sunshine	Wright Group/McGraw Hill
Watermelon	J	I	61	Books for Young Learners	Richard C. Owen
Watermelon	E	I	81	Rise & Shine	Hampton-Brown
Watermelon for Lunch	G	F	196	Leveled Readers	Houghton Mifflin Harcourt
Watermelon, The	D	RF	80	Joy Readers	Pearson Learning Group
Watermelons	WB	I	N/A	Windows on Literacy	National Geographic
Water-Powered Mills	R	I	250+	Theme Sets	National Geographic
Water's Journey	G	I	114	Instant Readers	Harcourt School Publishers
Watership Down	Y	F	250+	Adams, Richard	Avon
Waterstone, The	X	F	250+	Rupp, Rebecca	Candlewick Press
Watsons Go to Birmingham - 1963, The	U	HF	250+	Curtis, Christopher Paul	Bantam
Wave Warrior	W	RF	250+	Orca Soundings	Orca Book Publishers
Waves	E	F	70	Voyages	SRA/McGraw Hill
Waves and Rays	Y	I	2452	Independent Readers Science	Houghton Mifflin Harcourt
Waves: The Changing Surface of the Sea	J	I	204	Wonder World	Wright Group/McGraw Hill
Waving Sheep, The	H	F	252	PM Story Books	Rigby
Wax Man, The	I	TL	250+	Loya, Olga	Scholastic
Wax Museum	L	I	250+	Cook, Donald	Grossett & Dunlap
Way Down Deep	U	RF	250+	White, Ruth	Farrar, Straus and Giroux
Way Down South	F	F	109	Learn to Read	Creative Teaching Press
Way Home, A	X	RF	3493	Leveled Readers	Houghton Mifflin Harcourt
Way Home, A	X	RF	3493	Leveled Readers/CA	Houghton Mifflin Harcourt
Way I Go to School, The	B	I	53	PM Starters	Rigby
Way Things Were, The	D	I	39	iOpeners	Pearson Learning Group
Way to Go	E	RF	138	Bookshop	Mondo
Way West, The: Journal of a Pioneer Woman	R	B	250+	Knight, Amelia Stewart	Simon & Schuster
Way with Words, A	R	I	250+	InfoQuest	Rigby
Wayne's Box	E	F	114	Cambridge Reading	Pearson Learning Group
Wayra's Gift: A Story from Peru	S	RF	250+	Reading Expeditions	National Geographic
Ways Things Move	I	I	98	Forces and Motion	Lerner Publications
Ways to Go	D	RF	37	Early Readers	Compass Point Books
Ways We Communicate	E	I	96	Yellow Umbrella Books	Red Brick Learning
*Wayside School Gets a Little Stranger	P	F	250+	Sachar, Louis	Avon Camelot
*Wayside School Is Falling Down	P	F	250+	Sachar, Louis	Avon
Wayward Satellite, The	T	SF	250+	Take Two Books	Wright Group/McGraw Hill
We All Help	C	RF	56	InfoTrek	ETA Cuisenaire
We All Play Sports	C	I	26	Pacific Literacy	Pacific Learning
We All Scream For Ice Cream	I	I	219	Early Connections	Benchmark Education
We Are a Big Family	A	RF	28	Leveled Readers Emergent	Houghton Mifflin Harcourt
We Are All Alike	M	I	250+	Early Connections	Benchmark Education
We Are All Alike We Are All Different	F	I	250+	The Cheltenham Elementary School Kindergartners	Scholastic
We Are Best Friends	H	RF	629	Aliki	Morrow
We Are Firefighters	I	I	67	Vocabulary Readers	Houghton Mifflin Harcourt
We Are Painting	A	RF	38	Alexander, Francie	Scholastic
We Are Playing	B	RF	19	Rigby Literacy	Rigby
We Are Singing	B	RF	26	Ready Readers	Pearson Learning Group
We Are Twins	A	I	24	Little Books for Early Readers	University of Maine
We Are Up Here	B	I	74	Rigby Flying Colors	Rigby
We Are We Going?	F	RF	211	InfoTrek	ETA Cuisenaire
We Are Working	C	I	63	On Our Way to English	Rigby
We Can	A	F	21	KinderReaders	Rigby
We Can Be Helpers!	G	RF	231	On Our Way to English	Rigby
We Can Do It!	LB	RF	19	Rigby Focus	Rigby

* Collection of short stories
# Graphic text

TITLE	LEVEL	GENRE	WORD COUNT	AUTHOR / SERIES	PUBLISHER / DISTRIBUTOR
We Can Eat the Plants	C	RF	38	Learn to Read	Creative Teaching Press
We Can Fan	C	RF	44	Reading Street	Pearson
We Can Help the Earth	K	I	212	Pair-It Turn and Learn	Steck-Vaughn
We Can Make Graphs	D	I	58	Learn to Read	Creative Teaching Press
We Can Make Pizza	A	I	30	Little Books for Early Readers	University of Maine
We Can Measure!	H	RF	180	On Our Way to English	Rigby
We Can Play	E	RF	58	TOTTS	Tott Publications
We Can Recycle	I	I	231	Independent Readers Science	Houghton Mifflin Harcourt
We Can Recycle	B	I	28	Leveled Readers Science	Houghton Mifflin Harcourt
We Can Run	C	RF	77	PM Starters	Rigby
We Can See Three	C	I	73	PM Math Readers	Rigby
We Can Share at School	B	RF	35	Learn to Read	Creative Teaching Press
We Can Share It	H	F	140	Little Celebrations	Pearson Learning Group
We Care	E	RF	144	InfoTrek	ETA Cuisenaire
We Care for Our School	I	I	134	Wonder World	Wright Group/McGraw Hill
We Clean Up	B	I	38	InfoTrek	ETA Cuisenaire
We Clean Up!	D	RF	35	Home Connection Collection	Rigby
We Dance	C	I	30	Pacific Literacy	Pacific Learning
We Dress Up	B	RF	56	PM Plus Starters	Rigby
We Eat Rice	C	RF	46	Bebop Books	Lee & Low Books Inc.
We Get Squished!	B	F	31	First Stories	Pacific Learning
We Go Out	A	I	41	PM Starters	Rigby
We Go Shopping	B	I	35	Explorations	Okapi Eductional Materials
We Go Shopping	B	I	35	Explorations	Eleanor Curtain Publishing
We Go to Grandma's House	C	I	63	Windows on Literacy	National Geographic
We Go to School	B	RF	27	Carousel Earlybirds	Pearson Learning Group
We Got an Idea!	T	I	250+	Rigby Literacy	Rigby
We Honor America	H	I	132	Rosen Real Readers	Rosen Publishing Group
We Just Moved!	I	F	250+	Krensky, Stephen	Scholastic
We Like	C	RF	42	Foundations	Wright Group/McGraw Hill
We Like Apples	A	I	30	InfoTrek	ETA Cuisenaire
We Like Apples	A	RF	35	Leveled Readers	Houghton Mifflin Harcourt
We Like Apples	A	RF	35	Leveled Readers/CA	Houghton Mifflin Harcourt
We Like Fish	D	I	109	PM Starters	Rigby
We Like Fruit	B	I	31	Big Cat	Pacific Learning
We Like Fruit	B	RF	33	Lee, Millen	Scholastic
We Like Fruit!	A	RF	24	In Step Readers	Rigby
We Like Hats	B	F	38	Bella and Rosie Series	Literacy Footprints
We Like Pie!	A	RF	28	Leveled Readers Emergent	Houghton Mifflin Harcourt
We Like Puddles	C	RF	51	Kolodny, Cynthia	Kaeden Books
We Like School	A	I	23	Gear Up!	Wright Group/McGraw Hill
We Like Summer!	C	RF	41	Blevins, Wiley	Scholastic
We Like the Beach	B	I	34	Bonnell, Kris	Reading Reading Books
We Like the Sun	C	RF	30	Pair-It Books	Steck-Vaughn
We Like to Graph	C	I	48	Coulton, Mia	Kaeden Books
We Like to Play	C	RF	70	Tarlow, Ellen	Scholastic
We Like to Play!	A	I	28	Leveled Readers Emergent	Houghton Mifflin Harcourt
We Live Here	B	RF	25	Salzman, Gabriel	Scholastic
We Live Here Too!	Q	I	250+	Kids Talk	Picture Window Books
We Live in North America	M	I	250+	Yellow Umbrella Books	Red Brick Learning
We Look at Dinosaurs	E	I	62	Reading Street	Pearson
We Love Pets	A	I	24	Bonnell, Kris	Reading Reading Books
We Love Recess	C	I	63	Fiesta Series	Pearson Learning Group
We Love the Farm	C	RF	54	Lighthouse	Rigby

* Collection of short stories
# Graphic text

W

TITLE	LEVEL	GENRE	WORD COUNT	AUTHOR / SERIES	PUBLISHER / DISTRIBUTOR
We Love You, Ms. Pinkerville	L	RF	808	Leveled Readers	Houghton Mifflin Harcourt
We Love You, Ms. Pinkerville	L	RF	808	Leveled Readers/CA	Houghton Mifflin Harcourt
We Love You, Ms. Pinkerville	L	RF	808	Leveled Readers/TX	Houghton Mifflin Harcourt
We Made a Dragon	K	I	628	Explorations	Eleanor Curtain Publishing
We Made a Dragon	K	I	628	Explorations	Okapi Eductional Materials
We Made a Quilt Today	I	RF	237	InfoTrek	ETA Cuisenaire
We Make Cookies	E	RF	48	Pair-It Books	Steck-Vaughn
We Make Music	D	F	44	Literacy 2000	Rigby
We Make Patterns	B	RF	30	Gear Up!	Wright Group/McGraw Hill
We Make Pizza	C	RF	37	Carousel Readers	Pearson Learning Group
We Need a New School	F	RF	151	Developing Books Set 4	Pioneer Valley
We Need Auto Mechanics	I	I	79	Pebble Books	Red Brick Learning
We Need Child Care Workers	E	I	58	Helpers in Our community	Red Brick Learning
We Need Construction Workers	I	I	59	Helpers in Our Community	Red Brick Learning
We Need Custodians	E	I	33	Pebble Books	Capstone Press
We Need Dentists	H	I	54	Pebble Books	Red Brick Learning
We Need Directions!	I	I	250+	Rookie Read-About Geography	Children's Press
We Need Doctors	H	I	42	Pebble Books	Red Brick Learning
We Need Farmers	H	I	45	Pebble Books	Red Brick Learning
We Need Fire Fighters	G	I	64	Pebble Books	Red Brick Learning
We Need Garbage Collectors	I	I	77	Helpers in Our Community	Red Brick Learning
We Need Insects	N	I	250+	iOpeners	Pearson Learning Group
We Need Librarians	I	I	78	Pebble Books	Red Brick Learning
We Need Mail Carriers	G	I	61	Pebble Books	Red Brick Learning
We Need Nurses	H	I	65	Pebble Books	Red Brick Learning
We Need Pharmacists	I	I	81	Pebble Books	Red Brick Learning
We Need Plumbers	I	I	107	Pebble Books	Red Brick Learning
We Need Police Officers	G	I	59	Pebble Books	Red Brick Learning
We Need Principals	E	I	53	Pebble Books	Capstone Press
We Need Rain	B	I	21	Shutterbug Books	Steck-Vaughn
We Need School Bus Drivers	G	I	112	Pebble Books	Capstone Press
We Need Teachers	E	I	38	Pebble Books	Capstone Press
We Need the Sun	G	I	202	PM Science Readers	Rigby
We Need Trees	C	I	33	Hoenecke, Karen	Kaeden Books
We Need Veterinarians	G	I	48	Pebble Books	Red Brick Learning
We Need Water	I	I	99	Pebble Books	Red Brick Learning
We Need Water	D	I	26	Science	Outside the Box
We Need Zoo Keepers	H	I	72	Helpers in Our Community	Red Brick Learning
We Play Music	A	RF	20	Bebop Books	Lee & Low Books Inc.
We Play Together	A	RF	22	Blevins, Wiley	Scholastic
We Read	A	I	20	Blevins, Wiley	Scholastic
We Remember the Holocaust	Y	I	250+	Adler, David A.	Henry Holt & Co.
We Ride	C	I	55	Bonnell, Kris	Reading Reading Books
We Ride	B	I	40	Carousel Earlybirds	Pearson Learning Group
We Ride!	A	I	31	Vocabulary Readers	Houghton Mifflin Harcourt
We Scream for Ice Cream	K	RF	250+	Chardiet, Bernice; Maccarone, Grace	Scholastic
We See Them Grow	F	RF	73	Reading Street	Pearson
We Shall Not Be Moved	Z	I	250+	Dash, Joan	Scholastic
We Shall Overcome	V	I	1593	Reading Street	Pearson
We Ski	B	I	35	Storyteller-First Snow	Wright Group/McGraw Hill
We Trust Gabriella	S	RF	1503	Leveled Readers	Houghton Mifflin Harcourt
We Trust Gabriella	S	RF	1503	Leveled Readers/CA	Houghton Mifflin Harcourt
We Use Honey	H	I	120	Reading Street	Pearson

W

* Collection of short stories
\# Graphic text

TITLE	LEVEL	GENRE	WORD COUNT	AUTHOR / SERIES	PUBLISHER / DISTRIBUTOR
We Use Numbers	J	I	298	Early Connections	Benchmark Education
We Use Water	C	I	48	Early Connections	Benchmark Education
We Use Water	E	I	89	Water	Lerner Publications
We Use Water	B	I	42	Windows on Literacy	National Geographic
We Want Jobs!: A Story of the Great Depression	R	I	250+	Norrell, Robert J.	Steck-Vaughn
We Want That	F	RF	158	Visions	Wright Group/McGraw Hill
We Want Watermelon	B	RF	49	Phonics and Friends	Hampton-Brown
We Went Flying	C	RF	40	Carousel Earlybirds	Pearson Learning Group
We Went to the Zoo	B	I	32	Little Red Readers	Sundance
We Were There, Too!: Young People in U.S. History	Y	B	250+	Hoose, Phillip	Farrar, Straus and Giroux
We Wrote to Grandma	H	RF	239	Momentum Literacy Program	Troll Associates
Weather	C	I	54	Chanko, Pamela; Moreton, Daniel	Scholastic
Weather	E	I	138	Early Connections	Benchmark Education
Weather	M	I	250+	Explorations	Okapi Educational Materials
Weather	M	I	250+	Explorations	Eleanor Curtain Publishing
Weather	O	I	250+	Fleisher, Julian	Scholastic
Weather	N	I	250+	Literacy 2000	Rigby
Weather	B	I	23	On Our Way to English	Rigby
Weather	I	I	347	Science Support Readers	Houghton Mifflin Harcourt
Weather	T	I	2887	Science Support Readers	Houghton Mifflin Harcourt
Weather	S	I	250+	Simon, Seymour	Smithsonian
Weather	N	I	250+	Simply Science	Compass Point Books
Weather	LB	I	14	Smart Starts	Rigby
Weather	E	I	50	Time for Kids	Teacher Created Materials
Weather	E	I	39	Vocabulary Readers/TX	Houghton Mifflin Harcourt
Weather Alert!	N	I	314	Independent Readers Social Studies	Houghton Mifflin Harcourt
Weather Alert!	T	I	250+	Sails	Rigby
Weather and Climate	S	I	250+	Pair-It Books	Steck-Vaughn
Weather Box, The	N	F	250+	On Our Way to English	Rigby
Weather Chart, The	B	I	24	Sunshine	Wright Group/McGraw Hill
Weather Days	A	I	24	Vocabulary Readers	Houghton Mifflin Harcourt
Weather Drum, The	M	TL	250+	Cambridge Reading	Pearson Learning Group
Weather Engine, The	V	I	250+	InfoQuest	Rigby
Weather Forecast, The	I	F	272	Story Box	Wright Group/McGraw Hill
Weather Forecasting	Q	I	250+	Wonder World	Wright Group/McGraw Hill
Weather in the City	B	I	64	Windows on Literacy	National Geographic
Weather or Not	M	I	415	Reading Street	Pearson
Weather Report	B	I	32	Big Cat	Pacific Learning
Weather Report, The	E	I	119	Rosen Real Readers	Rosen Publishing Group
Weather Scientists	S	B	250+	Science Readers	Teacher Created Materials
Weather Today	H	RF	129	Windows on Literacy	National Geographic
Weather Watch	N	I	624	Wonders!	Hampton-Brown
Weather Watcher, The	K	I	245	Spyglass Books	Compass Point Books
Weather Watchers	N	I	677	Leveled Readers	Houghton Mifflin Harcourt
Weather Watchers	N	I	677	Leveled Readers/CA	Houghton Mifflin Harcourt
Weather Watching	Q	I	250+	Explorers	Wright Group/McGraw Hill
Weather Watching	L	I	339	Rigby Focus	Rigby
Weather Wise	L	I	250+	Spyglass Books	Compass Point Books
Weather Words	F	I	174	In Step Readers	Rigby
Weather Words and What They Mean	R	I	250+	Gibbons, Gail	Scholastic
Weather Works	T	I	250+	The News	Richard C. Owen
Weather, The	A	I	21	On Our Way to English	Rigby

* Collection of short stories
# Graphic text

Storable Database at www.fountasandpinnellleveledbooks.com

W

TITLE	LEVEL	GENRE	WORD COUNT	AUTHOR / SERIES	PUBLISHER / DISTRIBUTOR
Weathering the Storm	W	RF	2125	Leveled Readers	Houghton Mifflin Harcourt
Weatherworks	S	I	250+	Navigators How-to Series	Benchmark Education
Weaver's Gift, The	K	RF	269	Leveled Readers	Houghton Mifflin Harcourt
Weavers of the World	K	I	246	Gear Up!	Wright Group/McGraw Hill
Weaving	K	I	256	Vocabulary Readers	Houghton Mifflin Harcourt
Weaving	K	I	256	Vocabulary Readers/CA	Houghton Mifflin Harcourt
Weaving	K	I	256	Vocabulary Readers/TX	Houghton Mifflin Harcourt
*Weaving Contest, The	O	TL	250+	Literacy 2000	Rigby
Web at Dragonfly Pond, The	P	RF	1970	Sharing Nature with Children	Dawn Publications
Webcam Scam	Q	RF	250+	Powell, J.	Stone Arch Books
Webster's Great Pond	N	I	250+	Rigby Literacy	Rigby
Wedding Day Disaster	M	RF	250+	SupaDoopers	Sundance
Wedding, The	F	RF	50	Literacy 2000	Rigby
Wedding, The	J	RF	250+	Sunshine	Wright Group/McGraw Hill
Wedges to the Rescue	O	I	250+	Simple Machine to the Rescue	Capstone Press
Wednesday Wars, The	X	HF	250+	Schmidt, Gary D.	Clarion Books
Wee Whopper	H	F	181	Windmill Books	Rigby
Wee Willie Winkie	D	RF	34	Seedlings	Continental Press
Weedy Sea Dragons	G	I	106	Seedlings	Continental Press
Week in the Woods, A	T	RF	250+	Clements, Andrew	Simon & Schuster
Week of Surprises, A	F	RF	138	Leveled Readers Language Support	Houghton Mifflin Harcourt
Week of the Jellyhoppers, The	R	F	250+	Literacy 2000	Rigby
Week with Aunt Bea, A	D	RF	62	Bookshop	Mondo
Week, A	F	I	111	Calendars	Lerner Publications
Week, A	H	I	115	The Calendar	Capstone Press
Weekend Project, The	K	RF	722	InfoTrek	ETA Cuisenaire
Weight Lifting	Q	I	250+	Extreme Sports	Red Brick Learning
Weird and Wacky Inventions	O	I	250+	Tristars	Richard C. Owen
Weird Chemistry: Kitchen Creations	S	I	250+	Explore More	Wright Group/McGraw Hill
Weird Physics: Feel the Force	V	I	250+	Explore More	Wright Group/McGraw Hill
Weird Walkers	R	I	250+	Fredericks, Anthony D.	NorthWord Press
Weird Weather	N	I	250+	Rigby Rocket	Rigby
Weird, Wacky & Wonderful, Amazing World Records	Q	I	250+	Story Surfers	ETA Cuisenaire
Welcome Home	L	I	250+	Early Connections	Benchmark Education
Welcome Home!	L	RF	1133	InfoTrek	ETA Cuisenaire
Welcome to Brazil	M	I	250+	Spyglass Books	Compass Point Books
Welcome to Canada	M	I	250+	Spyglass Books	Compass Point Books
Welcome to Hong Kong!	J	I	174	Vocabulary Readers	Houghton Mifflin Harcourt
Welcome to Japan	M	I	250+	Spyglass Books	Compass Point Books
Welcome to Kenya	M	I	250+	Spyglass Books	Compass Point Books
Welcome to Mexico	M	I	250+	Spyglass Books	Compass Point Books
Welcome to Our School	G	RF	101	Leveled Readers Social Studies	Houghton Mifflin Harcourt
Welcome to Russia	M	I	250+	Spyglass Books	Compass Point Books
Welcome to the Bakery	J	I	122	Vocabulary Readers	Houghton Mifflin Harcourt
Welcome to the Globe: The Story of Shakespeare's Theater	V	I	250+	DK Readers	DK Publishing
Welcome to the Outback	T	RF	250+	Reading Safari	Mondo
Welcome to the White House	F	I	106	Independent Readers Social Studies	Houghton Mifflin Harcourt
Welcome to the Zigzag Zoo	B	F	42	Phonics and Friends	Hampton-Brown
Welcome, Wilma	O	F	667	Leveled Readers	Houghton Mifflin Harcourt
Welcoming New Neighbors	M	I	916	Vocabulary Readers	Houghton Mifflin Harcourt

* Collection of short stories
# Graphic text

W

TITLE	LEVEL	GENRE	WORD COUNT	AUTHOR / SERIES	PUBLISHER / DISTRIBUTOR
Welcoming New Neighbors	M	I	916	Vocabulary Readers/CA	Houghton Mifflin Harcourt
Well Done, Sam	I	RF	250+	Cambridge Reading	Pearson Learning Group
*Well I Never	K	F	2517	Story Box	Wright Group/McGraw Hill
We'll Never Forget You, Roberto Clemente	Q	B	250+	Engel, Trudie	Scholastic
We'll Race You, Henry: A Story About Henry Ford	R	B	5706	Creative Minds Biographies	Carolrhoda Books
Well, The	T	HF	250+	Taylor, Mildred D.	Puffin/Penguin
Well-fed Bear, The	E	F	35	Literacy 2000	Rigby
Well-Trained Dog, A	M	RF	797	Leveled Readers	Houghton Mifflin Harcourt
Well-Trained Dog, A	M	RF	797	Leveled Readers/CA	Houghton Mifflin Harcourt
Well-Trained Dog, A	M	RF	797	Leveled Readers/TX	Houghton Mifflin Harcourt
Welly Dancing	F	RF	158	Rigby Rocket	Rigby
Welsh Lamb, A	L	RF	250+	Cambridge Reading	Pearson Learning Group
Wemberly Worried	L	F	250+	Henkes, Kevin	Scholastic
Wendy Worm's Adventure	I	F	286	Springboard	Wright Group/McGraw Hill
We're a Team!	H	RF	100	City Stories	Rigby
We're Going Camping	J	I	111	Windows on Literacy	National Geographic
We're Going on a Bear Hunt	I	TL	363	Rosen, Michael	Macmillan
We're Going on a Nature Hunt	I	RF	250+	Metzger, Steve	Scholastic
We're Going on a Picnic	H	RF	250+	Cambridge Reading	Pearson Learning Group
We're in Big Trouble, Black Board Bear	I	F	250+	Alexander, Martha	Dial/Penguin
We're Just Looking	E	RF	115	Seedlings	Continental Press
We're Off to Thunder Mountain	L	RF	250+	Bookshop	Mondo
Werewolf Chronicles, The	T	F	250+	Philbrick, Rodman; Harnett, Lynn	Scholastic
Werewolves	X	I	5026	Monster Chronicles	Lerner Publications
Werewolves Don't Go to Summer Camp	M	F	250+	Dadey, Debbie; Jones, Marcia Thornton	Scholastic
Weslandia	P	F	250+	Fleischman, Paul	Candlewick Press
West Side Kids: Don't Call Me Slob-o	R	RF	250+	Orgel, Doris	Hyperion
West Side Kids: The Big Idea	R	RF	250+	Schecter, Ellen	Hyperion
West Side Kids: The Pet Sitters	R	RF	250+	Schecter, Ellen	Hyperion
West Virginia	T	I	250+	Hello U.S.A.	Lerner Publications
West Virginia	R	I	250+	This Land Is Your Land	Compass Point Books
West Virginia: Facts and Symbols	O	I	250+	Feeney, Kathy	Red Brick Learning
Westing Game, The	V	RF	250+	Raskin, Ellen	Penguin Group
Westward Expansion: An Interactive History Adventure	V	HF	250+	You Choose Books	Capstone Press
Westward Ho!	T	I	250+	Carlson, Laurie	Chicago Review Press
Westward Ho!	T	I	250+	Kids Discover Reading	Wright Group/McGraw Hill
Wet and Dry: An Animal Opposites Book	K	I	250+	Animal Opposites	Capstone Press
Wet Day at School, A	J	RF	130	Sunshine	Wright Group/McGraw Hill
Wet Grass	H	RF	188	Story Box	Wright Group/McGraw Hill
Wet Paint	E	F	92	Storyteller-Setting Sun	Wright Group/McGraw Hill
Wet Weather Camping	J	RF	250+	PM Plus Story Books	Rigby
Wet World	N	RF	250+	Boyz Rule!	Mondo
Wetland	F	I	92	Habitats	Lerner Publications
Wetland Adventure	R	RF	250+	Reading Expeditions	National Geographic
Wetland Birds	J	I	219	Sun Sprouts	ETA Cuisenaire
Wetland Home, A	Q	I	250+	Sunshine	Wright Group/McGraw Hill
Wetland Plants	N	I	250+	Life in the World's Biomes	Capstone Press
Wetlanders	U	RF	250+	Reading Expeditions	National Geographic
Wetlands	Q	I	250+	Ecosystems	Red Brick Learning
Wetlands	Q	I	250+	First Reports	Compass Point Books

* Collection of short stories
# Graphic text

TITLE	LEVEL	GENRE	WORD COUNT	AUTHOR / SERIES	PUBLISHER / DISTRIBUTOR
Wetlands	K	I	175	Rigby Focus	Rigby
Wetlands	S	I	250+	Theme Sets	National Geographic
We've Got Mail! Sending Mail in the United States from Past to Present	Q	I	250+	Literacy by Design	Rigby
Whale	V	I	250+	Eyewitness Books	DK Publishing
Whale in the Well, The	H	F	163	Rigby Star	Rigby
Whale Is Not a Fish, A: And Other Animal Mix-ups	P	I	250+	Berger, Melvin	Scholastic
Whale Music	N	RF	771	Leveled Readers	Houghton Mifflin Harcourt
Whale Rescue	K	I	254	In Step Readers	Rigby
Whale Shark	J	I	136	Sharks	Capstone Press
Whale Songs	K	I	173	Vocabulary Readers	Houghton Mifflin Harcourt
Whale Songs	K	I	173	Vocabulary Readers/CA	Houghton Mifflin Harcourt
Whale Tales	N	I	250+	Orbit Chapter Books	Pacific Learning
Whale Talk	Z+	RF	250+	Crutcher, Chris	Random House
Whale Watch	B	I	27	Ready Readers	Pearson Learning Group
Whale Watchers, The	E	F	63	Windmill Books	Rigby
Whale Watching	J	I	250+	Pacific Literacy	Pacific Learning
Whale! Nantucket Whaling Days	S	I	2363	Independent Readers Social Studies	Houghton Mifflin Harcourt
Whale, The	O	I	250+	Crewe, Sabrina	Steck-Vaughn
Whales	O	I	250+	Bookshop	Mondo
Whales	O	I	1664	Early Bird Nature Books	Lerner Publishing
Whales	G	I	150	Foundations	Wright Group/McGraw Hill
Whales	O	I	250+	Holmes, Kevin J.	Red Brick Learning
Whales	I	I	45	Pebble Books	Red Brick Learning
Whales	N	I	250+	PM Animal Facts: Silver	Rigby
Whales	O	I	250+	Simon, Seymour	Houghton Mifflin Harcourt
Whales	O	I	250+	Soar To Success	Houghton Mifflin Harcourt
Whales	I	I	102	Under the Sea	Capstone Press
Whales	M	I	333	Wonder World	Wright Group/McGraw Hill
Whales - The Gentle Giants	L	I	250+	Milton, Joyce	Random House
Whales and Other Animal Wonders	P	I	1555	Reading Street	Pearson
Whales in the Ocean	D	I	35	Rosen Real Readers	Rosen Publishing Group
Whales of the World	U	I	1500	Leveled Readers/TX	Houghton Mifflin Harcourt
Whales on Stilts	S	SF	250+	Anderson, M. T.	Harcourt Achieve
Whales on the Move	N	I	250+	Little Celebrations	Pearson Learning Group
Whales' Song, The	N	I	250+	Sheldon, Dyan	Penguin Group
Whale's Year, The	J	I	212	Lighthouse	Rigby
Whales: Giants of the Deep	M	I	250+	The Wild World of Animals	Red Brick Learning
What a Bad Dog!	D	RF	52	Oxford Reading Tree	Oxford University Press
What a Birthday!	G	RF	138	Leveled Readers Language Support	Houghton Mifflin Harcourt
What a Cat Can Do	B	RF	63	Literacy by Design	Rigby
What a Catch!	G	RF	118	Instant Readers	Harcourt School Publishers
What a Catch!	E	RF	91	Rigby Rocket	Rigby
What a Century!	V	I	250+	InfoQuest	Rigby
What a Clown!	A	F	18	Rigby Rocket	Rigby
What a Day!	K	RF	621	Miranda, Anne	Hampton-Brown
What a Dog!	F	RF	134	First Start	Troll Associates
What a Dog!	H	RF	223	Story Basket	Wright Group/McGraw Hill
What a Funny Thing to Do	K	RF	236	Stepping Stones	Nelson/Michaels Assoc.
What a Great Idea!	L	RF	250+	Home Connection Collection	Rigby
What a Great Idea!	S	I	1390	Reading Street	Pearson

W

Organized Alphabetically by Title
Storable Database at www.fountasandpinnellleveledbooks.com

* Collection of short stories
\# Graphic text

TITLE	LEVEL	GENRE	WORD COUNT	AUTHOR / SERIES	PUBLISHER / DISTRIBUTOR
What a Great Idea! Inventions That Changed the World	V	I	250+	Tomecek, Stephen M.	Scholastic
What a Haircut!	J	RF	250+	Voyages	SRA/McGraw Hill
What a Hamster Needs	C	I	46	Leveled Readers Science	Houghton Mifflin Harcourt
What a Job!	M	I	250+	Rigby Literacy	Rigby
What a Load of Garbage	L	I	250+	Lighthouse	Rigby
What a Load of Rubbish	L	I	250+	Lighthouse	Ginn & Co.
What a Mess!	C	RF	79	Bookshop	Mondo
*What a Mess!	G	RF	124	New Way Blue	Steck-Vaughn
What a Mess!	LB	RF	14	Smart Starts	Rigby
What a Mess!	C	RF	51	Story Box	Wright Group/McGraw Hill
What a Noise!	I	RF	165	Pacific Literacy	Pacific Learning
What a Nose!	H	I	154	Sails	Rigby
What a Plant!	S	I	250+	Sunshine	Wright Group/McGraw Hill
What a School	F	RF	100	Salem, Lynn; Stewart, Josie	Continental Press
What a Shower!	B	RF	23	Instant Readers	Harcourt School Publishers
What a Spelling Test!	I	F	123	City Stories	Rigby
What a Street!	B	RF	28	Bebop Books	Lee & Low Books Inc.
What a Tale!	C	RF	38	Wildsmith, Brian	Oxford University Press
What a Trip, Amber Brown	L	RF	250+	Danziger, Paula	Puffin/Penguin
What a Waste	H	I	180	Sun Sprouts	ETA Cuisenaire
What a Wedding!	N	I	250+	Sails	Rigby
What a Week!	C	RF	36	Home Connection Collection	Rigby
What a Week!	C	RF	64	Rigby Literacy	Rigby
What a Week!	C	RF	89	Rigby Star	Rigby
What a Wonderful Idea	O	RF	1059	Leveled Readers	Houghton Mifflin Harcourt
What a Year	N	RF	250+	DePaola, Tomie	Penguin Group
What About Bennie?	H	RF	124	Literacy Tree	Rigby
What Am I Eating?	X	I	3086	Vocabulary Readers	Houghton Mifflin Harcourt
What Am I Eating?	X	I	3086	Vocabulary Readers/CA	Houghton Mifflin Harcourt
What Am I Going to Be?	H	RF	111	Storyteller-Moon Rising	Wright Group/McGraw Hill
What Am I Made Of?	N	I	250+	Bennett, David	Scholastic
What Am I?	I	I	100	Foundations	Wright Group/McGraw Hill
What Am I?	B	RF	50	Handprints B	Educators Publishing Service
What Am I?	LB	RF	16	Just Beginning	Pearson Learning Group
What Am I?	E	RF	250+	Let's Play	Norwood House Press
What Am I?	D	I	111	Leveled Literacy Intervention/Green System	Heinemann
What Am I?	C	I	146	Rigby Flying Colors	Rigby
What Am I?	D	I	51	Story Steps	Rigby
What Am I?	F	I	100	Sun Sprouts	ETA Cuisenaire
What Am I?	G	I	124	Sunshine	Wright Group/McGraw Hill
What Am I?	C	I	51	Williams, Deborah	Kaeden Books
What Am I? An Animal Guessing Game	L	F	250+	Trapani, Iza	Charlesbridge
What Am I? Weird and Wonderful Sea Animals	L	I	470	Explorations	Eleanor Curtain Publishing
What Am I? Weird and Wonderful Sea Animals	L	I	470	Explorations	Okapi Eductional Materials
What An Adventure!	K	I	305	Reading Street	Pearson
What Ancient Astronomers Knew	U	I	2852	Leveled Readers Science	Houghton Mifflin Harcourt
What Angela Needs	K	RF	250+	Voyages	SRA/McGraw Hill
What Animal Lives Here?	H	I	250+	Woolley, M.; Pigdon, K.	Mondo
What Animals Do You See?	F	RF	100	Reading Street	Pearson
What Animals Do You See?	C	I	50	Read-More Books	Pearson Learning Group
What Animals Eat	D	I	112	Leveled Readers	Houghton Mifflin Harcourt

* Collection of short stories
# Graphic text

W

TITLE	LEVEL	GENRE	WORD COUNT	AUTHOR / SERIES	PUBLISHER / DISTRIBUTOR
What Animals Eat	D	I	112	Leveled Readers/CA	Houghton Mifflin Harcourt
What Animals Eat	E	I	75	Little Red Readers	Sundance
What Are Baby Koalas Called?	N	I	250+	Why In the World?	Capstone Press
What Are Caves?	K	I	108	Pebble Books	Red Brick Learning
What Are Deserts?	K	I	105	Pebble Books	Capstone Press
What Are Forests?	K	I	114	Pebble Books	Capstone Press
What Are Friends For?	C	I	32	Little Celebrations	Pearson Learning Group
What Are Friends For?	C	I	33	Rosen Real Readers	Rosen Publishing Group
What Are Inclined Planes?	M	I	70	Pebble Books	Red Brick Learning
What Are Lakes?	K	I	92	Pebble Books	Red Brick Learning
What Are Levers?	M	I	66	Pebble Books	Red Brick Learning
What Are Mountains?	K	I	70	Pebble Books	Capstone Press
What Are My Chances?	J	I	393	Early Connections	Benchmark Education
What Are Oceans?	K	I	97	Pebble Books	Capstone Press
What Are Pulleys?	M	I	88	Pebble Books	Red Brick Learning
What Are Purple Elephants Good For?	H	F	136	Reading Corners	Pearson Learning Group
What Are Rivers?	K	I	111	Pebble Books	Red Brick Learning
What Are Screws?	M	I	65	Pebble Books	Red Brick Learning
What Are Volcanoes?	K	I	108	Pebble Books	Red Brick Learning
What Are We Doing?	A	F	21	KinderReaders	Rigby
What Are Wedges?	M	I	60	Pebble Books	Red Brick Learning
What Are Wheels and Axles?	M	I	70	Pebble Books	Red Brick Learning
*What Are You Afraid Of?: Stories About Phobias	Z+	RF	250+	Gallo, Donald	Candlewick Press
What Are You Called?	C	I	66	Voyages	SRA/McGraw Hill
What Are You Doing?	D	RF	101	Foundations	Wright Group/McGraw Hill
What Are You Figuring Now?	R	B	250+	Ferris, Jeri	Scholastic
What Are You Figuring Now? A Story About Benjamin Banneker	R	B	7346	Creative Minds Biographies	Carolrhoda Books
What Are You Going to Buy?	F	F	180	Read Alongs	Rigby
What Are You Waiting For?	E	RF	48	Silly Millies	Millbrook Press
What Are You?	A	F	27	Literacy 2000	Rigby
What Bear Cubs Like to Do	I	I	83	Little Books	Sadlier-Oxford
What Bears Like	A	I	21	Cherrington, Janelle	Scholastic
What Birds Eat	B	I	60	Sails	Rigby
What Blows in the Wind?	A	RF	36	Science	Outside the Box
What Boo and I Do	G	I	171	Bebop Books	Lee & Low Books Inc.
What Came Out of My Bean?	H	RF	158	Book Bank	Wright Group/McGraw Hill
What Can a Diver See?	D	I	44	Windows on Literacy	National Geographic
What Can Bugs Do?	A	I	24	Bonnell, Kris	Reading Reading Books
What Can Change?	G	I	96	Discovery Links	Newbridge
What Can Float?	B	I	27	Ready Readers	Pearson Learning Group
What Can Float?	C	I	32	Windmill Books	Rigby
What Can Fly?	B	I	29	Discovery Links	Newbridge
What Can Fly?	C	I	33	Joy Readers	Pearson Learning Group
What Can Fly?	B	I	28	Literacy 2000	Rigby
What Can Fly?	A	I	31	Nonfiction	Literacy Footprints
What Can Go Fast?	B	I	37	Little Red Readers	Sundance
What Can Hurt?	C	I	30	Windmill Books	Rigby
What Can I Buy?	E	RF	66	InfoTrek	ETA Cuisenaire
What Can I Buy?	F	RF	156	Moriarty, Julie	Scholastic
What Can I Buy?	C	I	33	Rosen Real Readers	Rosen Publishing Group
What Can I Do Today?	A	I	20	Windows on Literacy	National Geographic
What Can I Do?	C	I	42	Foundations	Wright Group/McGraw Hill
What Can I Do?	C	RF	61	Gear Up!	Wright Group/McGraw Hill

* Collection of short stories
\# Graphic text

W

TITLE	LEVEL	GENRE	WORD COUNT	AUTHOR / SERIES	PUBLISHER / DISTRIBUTOR
What Can I Do?	H	I	250+	Greetings	Rigby
What Can I Do?	C	I	42	Read-More Books	Pearson Learning Group
What Can I Read?	A	RF	28	Carousel Earlybirds	Pearson Learning Group
What Can I See?	C	I	42	Foundations	Wright Group/McGraw Hill
What Can I See?	B	RF	36	Storyteller	Wright Group/McGraw Hill
What Can It Be?	N	I	250+	Early Connections	Benchmark Education
What Can It Be?	F	I	113	Storyteller-First Snow	Wright Group/McGraw Hill
What Can Jigarees Do?	A	F	22	Story Box	Wright Group/McGraw Hill
What Can Jump?	C	I	78	Sails	Rigby
What Can Jump?	B	I	28	Shutterbug Books	Steck-Vaughn
What Can Jump?	A	I	32	Windmill Books	Rigby
What Can Rosa Paint?	J	RF	383	Leveled Readers	Houghton Mifflin Harcourt
What Can Rosa Paint?	J	RF	383	Leveled Readers/CA	Houghton Mifflin Harcourt
What Can Rosa Paint?	J	RF	383	Leveled Readers/TX	Houghton Mifflin Harcourt
What Can She Do?	A	I	21	Little Books for Early Readers	University of Maine
What Can Sing?	D	I	65	Sun Sprouts	ETA Cuisenaire
What Can Swim?	B	I	30	Windmill Books	Rigby
What Can This Animal Do?	B	I	28	Foundations	Wright Group/McGraw Hill
What Can We Do Today?	G	RF	146	Carousel Readers	Pearson Learning Group
What Can We Do?	J	RF	439	Leveled Readers Social Studies	Houghton Mifflin Harcourt
What Can We Make?	E	I	115	InfoTrek	ETA Cuisenaire
What Can We Smell?	C	I	44	Windmill Books	Rigby
What Can You Be?	C	I	166	Tiger Cub	Peguis
What Can You Do with a Ball of String?	G	RF	250+	Home Connection Collection	Rigby
What Can You Do with an Elephant House?	R	I	250+	Gaynor, Miriam; Goodwin, A.	Pacific Learning
What Can You Do?	C	I	59	Tiger Cub	Peguis
What Can You Do?	A	I	18	Vocabulary Readers	Houghton Mifflin Harcourt
What Can You Do? A Book About Discovering What You Do Well	J	I	196	Shelley Rotner's Early Childhood	Millbrook Press
What Can You Hear?	D	I	80	Tiger Cub	Peguis
What Can You Make?	B	I	22	Ready Readers	Pearson Learning Group
What Can You Measure With a Lollipop?	H	I	159	Early Connections	Benchmark Education
What Can You See on Farms?	A	I	28	Gear Up!	Wright Group/McGraw Hill
What Can You See?	C	I	25	Literacy 2000	Rigby
What Can You See?	C	RF	31	Rigby Literacy	Rigby
What Can You See?	B	I	31	Tiger Cub	Peguis
What Can You See?	C	I	43	Vocabulary Readers	Houghton Mifflin Harcourt
What Can You Taste?	B	I	45	Windmill Books	Rigby
What Cat Is That?	J	RF	250+	Real Reading	Steck-Vaughn
What Causes Forest Fires?	N	I	868	Leveled Readers Science	Houghton Mifflin Harcourt
What Changes Our Earth?	K	I	273	People, Spaces & Places	Rand McNally
What Color Is It?	B	I	29	Properties of Matter	Lerner Publications
What Color Is the Sky?	F	I	74	Windows on Literacy	National Geographic
What Comes First?	C	I	56	Bookshop	Mondo
What Comes from a Cow?	G	I	85	Sunshine	Wright Group/McGraw Hill
What Comes from Eggs?	B	I	74	Bookshop	Mondo
What Comes in Groups?	F	I	133	Shutterbug Books	Steck-Vaughn
What Comes in Threes?	C	F	41	Learn to Read	Creative Teaching Press
What Comes in Twos?	D	I	125	Early Connections	Benchmark Education
What Comes Next?	J	I	250+	Early Connections	Benchmark Education
What Comes Out at Night?	B	I	48	Little Red Readers	Sundance
What Computers Do	I	I	186	Yellow Umbrella Books	Red Brick Learning
What Could I Be?	C	RF	64	Foundations	Wright Group/McGraw Hill
What Could It Be?	B	RF	19	Instant Readers	Harcourt School Publishers

TITLE	LEVEL	GENRE	WORD COUNT	AUTHOR / SERIES	PUBLISHER / DISTRIBUTOR
What Daddies Do Best	F	F	113	Numeroff, Laura Joffe	Simon & Schuster
What Damian Didn't Know About Dinosaurs	J	RF	250+	Rigby Rocket	Rigby
What Day Is It?	D	F	79	Green Light Readers	Harcourt
What Did Ben Want?	A	RF	28	Smart Starts	Rigby
What Did I Forget?	D	RF	43	Teacher's Choice Series	Pearson Learning Group
What Did I Use?	C	I	65	Discovery World	Rigby
What Did Kim Catch?	C	RF	48	Literacy 2000	Rigby
What Did They Drive?	D	RF	73	Windows on Literacy	National Geographic
What Did They Want?	C	RF	28	Smart Starts	Rigby
What Did You Bring?	B	I	23	Ready Readers	Pearson Learning Group
What Did You Eat Today?	L	F	250+	Literacy Tree	Rigby
What Did You Lose, Santa?	WB	F	N/A	Amoss, Berthe	Harper & Row
What Dinah Saw	M	F	250+	Lighthouse	Rigby
What Dinosaurs Ate	F	I	44	Planet Earth	Rigby
What Do Animals Do?	E	I	29	Little Red Readers	Sundance
What Do Archaeologists Do?	W	I	2557	Reading Street	Pearson
What Do Artists Use?	F	I	31	Canizares, Susan; Berger, Samantha	Scholastic
What Do Cats Like?	B	I	19	Bonnell, Kris	Reading Reading Books
*What Do Fish Have To Do With Anything?	W	RF	250+	Avi	Candlewick Press
What Do I See in the Garden?	F	I	108	Wonder World	Wright Group/McGraw Hill
What Do I See?	A	I	18	Gear Up!	Wright Group/McGraw Hill
What Do I See?	A	I	32	Literacy by Design	Rigby
What Do I See?	B	I	28	Twig	Wright Group/McGraw Hill
What Do I Use?	D	I	57	Scooters	ETA Cuisenaire
What Do I Wear?	J	I	40	Leveled Readers Social Studies	Houghton Mifflin Harcourt
What Do Insects Do?	A	I	24	Canizares, Susan; Chanko, Pamela	Scholastic
What Do Pets Need?	E	I	106	Early Connections	Benchmark Education
What Do Pets Need?	E	I	67	Windows on Literacy	National Geographic
What Do Scientists Do?	H	I	79	Discovery Links	Newbridge
What Do Scientists Do?	O	I	1576	Gear Up!	Wright Group/ McGraw Hill
What Do Scientists Do?	B	I	24	Twig	Wright Group/McGraw Hill
What Do We Have to Get?	E	RF	117	Ready Readers	Pearson Learning Group
What Do We Have?	C	F	28	Step-By-Step Series	Pearson Learning Group
What Do We Like Best?	E	I	90	InfoTrek	ETA Cuisenaire
What Do We Measure?	I	I	157	Gear Up!	Wright Group/McGraw Hill
What Do We Need?	F	I	147	On Our Way to English	Rigby
What Do You Do at the Zoo?	G	RF	182	Silly Millies	Millbrook Press
What Do You Do on a Farm?	F	F	188	Silly Millies	Millbrook Press
What Do You Do?	G	F	125	Little Celebrations	Pearson Learning Group
What Do You Do?	E	I	162	Tiger Cub	Peguis
What Do You Have?	C	I	165	Tiger Cub	Peguis
What Do You Have?	C	I	88	Windmill Books	Rigby
What Do You Hear When Cows Sing?	J	F	250+	Maestro, Marco & Giulio	HarperTrophy
What Do You Hear?	D	I	60	Windmill Books	Rigby
What Do You Know About Dolphins?	J	I	137	Windows on Literacy	National Geographic
What Do You Like to Eat?	D	I	99	Foundations	Wright Group/McGraw Hill
What Do You Like to Wear?	D	I	50	Read-More Books	Pearson Learning Group
What Do You Like?	B	I	52	Little Books for Early Readers	University of Maine
What Do You Like?	B	RF	52	Storyteller	Wright Group/McGraw Hill
What Do You Play?	A	I	25	Science	Outside the Box
What Do You See at the Pet Store?	C	I	27	Read-More Books	Pearson Learning Group
What Do You See by the Sea?	A	I	14	Little Books	Sadlier-Oxford

W

* Collection of short stories
# Graphic text

TITLE	LEVEL	GENRE	WORD COUNT	AUTHOR / SERIES	PUBLISHER / DISTRIBUTOR
What Do You See?	B	I	20	Carousel Readers	Pearson Learning Group
What Do You See?	F	F	89	Learn to Read	Creative Teaching Press
What Do You See?	B	I	67	On Our Way to English	Rigby
What Do You See?	A	RF	71	Phonics and Friends	Hampton-Brown
What Do You See?	E	I	71	Science	Harcourt School Publishers
What Do You See?	C	I	35	Windmill Books	Rigby
What Do You See?	D	I	78	Windows on Literacy	National Geographic
What Do You See? A Book About the Seasons	D	I	92	Shapiro, Sara	Scholastic
What Do You Think?	U	I	250+	Sails	Rigby
What Do You Think?	O	I	250+	Wildcats	Wright Group/McGraw Hill
What Do You Touch?	C	I	50	Windmill Books	Rigby
What Do You Want That For?	E	RF	149	Lighthouse	Rigby
What Does a Detective Do?	H	RF	128	Reading Street	Pearson
What Does a Firefighter Do?	G	I	136	Yellow Umbrella Books	Red Brick Learning
What Does a Garden Need?	G	I	118	Discovery Links	Newbridge
What Does a Governor Do?	L	I	288	Independent Readers Social Studies	Houghton Mifflin Harcourt
What Does an Electrician Do?	T	I	1322	Independent Readers Science	Houghton Mifflin Harcourt
What Does Greedy Cat Like?	C	RF	35	Pacific Literacy	Pacific Learning
What Does It Do?	J	I	198	Ready Set Read	Steck-Vaughn
What Does Lucy Like?	A	RF	11	Little Books	Sadlier-Oxford
What Else?	I	RF	154	Sunshine	Wright Group/McGraw Hill
What Every Girl (except me) Knows	V	RF	250+	Baskin, Nora Raleigh	Little, Brown & Co.
What Feels Cold?	B	I	30	Windmill Books	Rigby
What Feels Hot?	A	I	28	Windmill Books	Rigby
What Feels Sticky?	B	I	26	Windmill Books	Rigby
What Fell Out?	D	RF	32	Carousel Readers	Pearson Learning Group
What Floats?	D	I	46	Sun Sprouts	ETA Cuisenaire
What Floats?	C	I	16	Twig	Wright Group/McGraw Hill
What Floats? What Sinks?	J	I	185	Early Connections	Benchmark Education
What Fun!	F	F	250+	Sun Sprouts	ETA Cuisenaire
What Game Shall We Play?	H	F	306	Hutchins, Pat	Sundance
What Gives You Goose Bumps?	H	RF	140	Home Connection Collection	Rigby
What Goes Around and Around?	B	I	46	Windmill Books	Rigby
What Goes Fast?	B	I	42	InfoTrek	ETA Cuisenaire
What Goes in the Bathtub?	C	RF	31	Literacy 2000	Rigby
What Goes into a Salad?	C	RF	22	Home Connection Collection	Rigby
What Goes Together?	A	I	28	Leveled Readers Science	Houghton Mifflin Harcourt
What Goes Up and Down?	C	I	40	Windmill Books	Rigby
What Goes Up High?	A	I	38	Windmill Books	Rigby
What Goes Up?	B	I	42	Rigby Literacy	Rigby
What Grows From a Tree?	I	I	250+	Yellow Umbrella Books	Red Brick Learning
What Grows Here?	C	I	37	Windows on Literacy	National Geographic
What Grows on Trees?	E	I	49	Start to Read	School Zone
What Grows There	P	I	448	Independent Readers Social Studies	Houghton Mifflin Harcourt
What Grows?	B	I	21	Rigby Focus	Rigby
What Grows?	A	I	15	Shutterbug Books	Steck-Vaughn
What Hangs from the Tree?	C	I	42	Questions & Answers	Pearson Learning Group
What Happened at the Boston Tea Party?	Q	I	250+	Rosen Real Readers	Rosen Publishing Group
What Happened on Maple Street?	Q	RF	1252	Leveled Readers	Houghton Mifflin Harcourt
What Happened on Maple Street?	Q	RF	1252	Leveled Readers/CA	Houghton Mifflin Harcourt
What Happened on Maple Street?	Q	RF	1252	Leveled Readers/TX	Houghton Mifflin Harcourt
What Happened to Aunt Cordelia?	J	RF	250+	Voyages	SRA/McGraw Hill

W

TITLE	LEVEL	GENRE	WORD COUNT	AUTHOR / SERIES	PUBLISHER / DISTRIBUTOR
What Happened to Bodie?	T	I	250+	Rigby Literacy	Rigby
What Happened to Cass McBride?	Z+	RF	250+	Giles, Gail	Little, Brown & Co.
What Happened to Humpty Dumpty?	D	F	74	Reading Safari	Mondo
What Happened to Lani Garver	Z+	RF	250+	Plum-Ucci, Carol	Harcourt Trade
What Happened?	G	I	60	Learn to Read	Creative Teaching Press
What Happens at the Bank?	K	I	388	Leveled Readers Social Studies	Houghton Mifflin Harcourt
What Happens When You Recycle?	K	I	215	Discovery World	Rigby
What Has Changed?	A	I	18	Windows on Literacy	National Geographic
What Has Changed?	K	I	250+	Yellow Umbrella Books	Red Brick Learning
What Has Spots?	B	I	29	Literacy 2000	Rigby
What Has Stripes?	C	I	25	Ballinger, Margaret	Scholastic
What Has Three Branches?	N	I	323	Leveled Readers	Houghton Mifflin Harcourt
What Has Three Branches?	N	I	323	Leveled Readers/CA	Houghton Mifflin Harcourt
What Has Wheels?	A	I	28	Hoenecke, Karen	Kaeden Books
What Has Wings?	H	RF	250+	Momentum Literacy Program	Troll Associates
What Hatches?	J	I	250+	Yellow Umbrella Books	Capstone Press
What Hearts	S	RF	250+	Brooks, Bruce	Language for Learning Assoc.
What Helps a Bird to Fly?	F	I	95	Birds Series	Pearson Learning Group
What I Left on My Plate	C	RF	54	Teacher's Choice Series	Pearson Learning Group
What I Like at School	C	I	64	Little Red Readers	Sundance
What I Like to Wear	D	I	93	Home Connection Collection	Rigby
What I See	A	RF	46	Green Light Readers	Harcourt
What I Want to Be	J	RF	377	Leveled Readers	Houghton Mifflin Harcourt
What I Want to Be	J	RF	377	Leveled Readers/CA	Houghton Mifflin Harcourt
What I Want to Be	J	RF	377	Leveled Readers/TX	Houghton Mifflin Harcourt
What I Wear	D	RF	76	Sun Sprouts	ETA Cuisenaire
What I Would Do	I	RF	173	Read Alongs	Rigby
What I'd Like to Be	F	I	112	Little Red Readers	Sundance
What If . . .	E	RF	57	Teacher's Choice Series	Pearson Learning Group
What if You Get Lost?	D	I	40	Rosen Real Readers	Rosen Publishing Group
What If...?	F	RF	118	InfoTrek	ETA Cuisenaire
What If?	C	F	41	Little Celebrations	Pearson Learning Group
What in the World Is the World Wide Web?	S	I	250+	Orbit Chapter Books	Pacific Learning
What Is a Bird?	H	I	71	Pebble Books	Red Brick Learning
What Is a Family?	J	I	250+	Spyglass Books	Compass Point Books
What Is a Fish?	H	I	77	Pebble Books	Red Brick Learning
What Is a Fly?	M	I	561	Sunshine	Wright Group/McGraw Hill
What Is a Food Chain?	G	I	71	Instant Readers	Harcourt School Publishers
What Is a Frog?	K	I	333	Springboard	Wright Group/McGraw Hill
What Is a Government?	W	I	250+	iOpeners	Pearson Learning Group
What Is a Huggles?	B	F	41	Sunshine	Wright Group/McGraw Hill
What Is a Hundred?	L	I	409	Yellow Umbrella Books	Red Brick Learning
What Is a Mammal?	I	I	70	Pebble Books	Red Brick Learning
What Is a Mammal?	F	I	102	Rosen Real Readers	Rosen Publishing Group
What Is a Map?	H	I	250+	Yellow Umbrella Books	Red Brick Learning
What Is a Mountain?	I	I	231	Rosen Real Readers	Rosen Publishing Group
What Is a Park?	H	I	138	Discovery World	Rigby
What Is a Park?	J	I	230	People, Spaces & Places	Rand McNally
What Is a Poem?	G	I	69	Vocabulary Readers	Houghton Mifflin Harcourt
What Is a Rainbow?	H	I	115	Rosen Real Readers	Rosen Publishing Group
What Is a Reptile?	M	I	183	Now I Know	Troll Associates
What Is a Reptile?	I	I	67	Pebble Books	Red Brick Learning
What Is an Amphibian?	K	I	85	Pebble Books	Red Brick Learning

W

* Collection of short stories
\# Graphic text

TITLE	LEVEL	GENRE	WORD COUNT	AUTHOR / SERIES	PUBLISHER / DISTRIBUTOR
What Is an Elephant?	H	TL	165	Story Box	Wright Group/McGraw Hill
What Is an Insect?	H	I	57	Pebble Books	Red Brick Learning
What Is an Insect?	A	I	36	Yellow Umbrella Books	Red Brick Learning
What Is at the Top?	E	F	197	Ready Readers	Pearson Learning Group
What Is Bat?	G	F	136	Literacy 2000	Rigby
What Is Being Moved?	WB	RF	N/A	Windows on Literacy	National Geographic
What Is Big?	D	RF	72	Armstrong, Shane; Hartley, Susan	Scholastic
What Is Blue?	C	I	31	Carousel Earlybirds	Pearson Learning Group
What Is CGI?	L	I	285	Big Cat	Pacific Learning
What Is Congress?	P	I	628	Leveled Readers Social Studies	Houghton Mifflin Harcourt
What Is Delicious?	C	I	25	Windmill Books	Rigby
What Is Democracy?	Q	I	250+	Rigby Focus	Rigby
What Is Elephant's Present?	C	F	43	Reading Safari	Mondo
What Is Enormous?	B	I	33	Windmill Books	Rigby
What Is Fast?	A	I	30	Windmill Books	Rigby
What Is Fierce?	B	I	32	Windmill Books	Rigby
What Is Fun?	C	I	34	Windmill Books	Rigby
What Is Gravity?	L	I	250+	On Our Way to English	Rigby
What Is Green Technology?	W	I	2318	Leveled Readers	Houghton Mifflin Harcourt
What Is Green Technology?	W	I	2318	Leveled Readers/CA	Houghton Mifflin Harcourt
What Is Green?	B	I	30	Carousel Earlybirds	Pearson Learning Group
What Is He Looking For?	A	F	42	KinderReaders	Rigby
What Is He?	B	F	35	Rigby Star	Rigby
What Is Hidden?	B	I	27	Little Celebrations	Pearson Learning Group
What Is Hiding?	C	I	116	Rigby Flying Colors	Rigby
What Is in Space?	C	I	41	Sunshine Science	Wright Group/McGraw Hill
What Is in Space?	B	I	35	Yellow Umbrella Books	Red Brick Learning
What Is in the Box?	D	RF	51	Instant Readers	Harcourt School Publishers
What Is In the Box?	B	RF	30	Rigby Rocket	Rigby
What Is in the Closet?	E	F	107	Story Box	Wright Group/McGraw Hill
What Is in the Sky?	J	I	174	Phonics Readers	Compass Point Books
What Is in the Sky?	B	I	32	Rosen Real Readers	Rosen Publishing Group
What Is in the Wind?	L	I	472	Leveled Readers	Houghton Mifflin Harcourt
What Is in the Wind?	L	TL	472	Leveled Readers/CA	Houghton Mifflin Harcourt
What Is in the Wind?	L	I	472	Leveled Readers/TX	Houghton Mifflin Harcourt
What Is It Called?	D	RF	48	Reading Unlimited	Pearson Learning Group
What Is It Like Today?	D	I	102	On Our Way to English	Rigby
What Is It Made Of?	J	I	250+	Independent Readers Science	Houghton Mifflin Harcourt
What Is It Made Of?	D	I	107	InfoTrek	ETA Cuisenaire
What Is It Made Of?	D	I	119	PM Science Readers	Rigby
What Is It?	F	I	135	Foundations	Wright Group/McGraw Hill
What Is It?	G	I	69	iOpeners	Pearson Learning Group
What Is It?	B	F	35	Rigby Literacy	Rigby
What Is It?	B	RF	16	Rigby Rocket	Rigby
What Is It?	E	I	69	Storyteller-First Snow	Wright Group/McGraw Hill
What Is It? Said the Dog	H	F	256	Allen, Margaret Buell	Ginn & Co.
What Is Little?	LB	I	22	Rise & Shine	Hampton-Brown
What Is Matter?	L	I	250+	Early Connections	Benchmark Education
What Is Money?	M	I	250+	Learning About Money	Capstone Press
What Is Noisy?	B	I	31	Windmill Books	Rigby
What Is Old?	C	I	32	Windmill Books	Rigby
What Is Red?	B	I	27	Carousel Earlybirds	Pearson Learning Group
What Is Red?	B	I	30	Literacy 2000	Rigby

W

TITLE	LEVEL	GENRE	WORD COUNT	AUTHOR / SERIES	PUBLISHER / DISTRIBUTOR
What Is Scary?	B	I	31	Windmill Books	Rigby
What Is Slippery?	C	I	26	Windmill Books	Rigby
What Is Slow?	C	I	29	Windmill Books	Rigby
What Is Soft?	C	I	30	Windmill Books	Rigby
What Is Tall?	B	I	30	Windmill Books	Rigby
What Is That Ball Made From?	J	I	259	Take Two Books	Wright Group/McGraw Hill
What Is That?	F	RF	54	Pair-It Turn and Learn	Steck-Vaughn
What Is That?	C	I	61	Ready Readers	Pearson Learning Group
What Is That? Said the Cat	F	F	118	Maccarone, Grace	Scholastic
What Is the Media?	T	I	2493	Independent Readers Social Studies	Houghton Mifflin Harcourt
What Is the U.S. Constitution?	R	I	250+	Rosen Real Readers	Rosen Publishing Group
What Is the Weather Today?	B	I	49	Leveled Readers Science	Houghton Mifflin Harcourt
What Is the Weather Today?	H	I	250+	Momentum Literacy Program	Troll Associates
What Is This Skeleton?	C	I	48	Sunshine Science	Wright Group/McGraw Hill
What Is This?	A	I	29	KinderReaders	Rigby
What Is This?	A	I	25	Little Books for Early Readers	University of Maine
What Is This?	C	I	28	Ready Readers	Pearson Learning Group
What Is This?	A	I	25	Tiger Cub	Peguis
What Is Under the Hat?	B	F	29	Ready Readers	Pearson Learning Group
What Is Up When You Are Down?	E	I	65	Rookie Readers	Children's Press
What Is Very Long?	C	I	85	Leveled Literacy Intervention/ Orange System	Heinemann
What Is Water?	E	I	71	Water	Lerner Publications
What Is Wet?	A	I	32	Literacy by Design	Rigby
What Is White?	B	I	26	Carousel Earlybirds	Pearson Learning Group
What Is Yellow?	B	I	26	Carousel Earlybirds	Pearson Learning Group
What Is Young?	C	I	31	Windmill Books	Rigby
What Jamie Saw	T	RF	250+	Coman, Carolyn	Penguin Group
What Jessie Really Likes	C	RF	59	Lighthouse	Rigby
What Joe Hamster Finds	J	F	250+	Sunshine	Wright Group/McGraw Hill
What Joy Found	L	RF	250+	Ready Readers	Pearson Learning Group
What Keeps Them Warm?	L	I	156	Pacific Literacy	Pacific Learning
What Kind of Animals?	D	I	37	Leveled Readers Science	Houghton Mifflin Harcourt
What Kind of Babysitter Is This?	L	RF	250+	Johnson, Dolores	Scholastic
What Kind of Day?	D	I	67	Pair-It Turn and Learn	Steck-Vaughn
What Kind of Dog Am I?	C	I	21	Twig	Wright Group/McGraw Hill
What Kind of Sound?	G	I	110	Pair-It Turn and Learn	Steck-Vaughn
What Kind of Sound?	B	I	25	Yellow Umbrella Books	Red Brick Learning
What Lays Eggs?	I	I	216	Momentum Literacy Program	Troll Associates
What Lays Eggs?	D	I	56	Storyteller Nonfiction	Wright Group/McGraw Hill
What Lived in That Shell?	N	I	575	Springboard	Wright Group/ McGraw Hill
What Lives in a Rotting Log?	L	I	465	Springboard	Wright Group/ McGraw Hill
What Lives in a Swamp?	B	I	36	Windows on Literacy	National Geographic
What Lives in a Tide Pool?	J	I	187	Windows on Literacy	National Geographic
What Lives on a Prairie?	N	I	250+	Rosen Real Readers	Rosen Publishing Group
What Made Teddalik Laugh	M	TL	250+	Folk Tales	Wright Group/McGraw Hill
What Made This?	B	I	21	Science	Outside the Box
What Magnets Can Do	K	I	250+	Fowler, Allan	Scholastic
What Makes a Bird a Bird?	O	I	250+	Garelick, May	Mondo
What Makes a Community?	P	I	250+	Reading Expeditions	National Geographic
What Makes a Garden Grow?	E	I	83	Independent Readers Science	Houghton Mifflin Harcourt
What Makes a Shadow?	B	I	27	Leveled Readers Science	Houghton Mifflin Harcourt
What Makes a Tiger Hard to See?	I	I	253	Windows on Literacy	National Geographic

W

* Collection of short stories
\# Graphic text

TITLE	LEVEL	GENRE	WORD COUNT	AUTHOR / SERIES	PUBLISHER / DISTRIBUTOR
What Makes Great Athletes	T	I	2156	Reading Street	Pearson
What Makes It Go?	C	I	29	iOpeners	Pearson Learning Group
What Makes It Work?	U	I	3412	Take Two Books	Wright Group/McGraw Hill
What Makes Light?	F	I	119	Sunshine	Wright Group/McGraw Hill
What Makes Me Healthy?	H	I	132	Windows on Literacy	National Geographic
What Makes Ten?	D	I	34	Yellow Umbrella Books	Red Brick Learning
What Makes You Cough, Sneeze, Burp, Hiccup, Blink, Yawn, Sweat, and Shiver?	P	I	250+	My Health	Franklin Watts
What Mommies Do Best	F	F	113	Numeroff, Laura Joffe	Simon & Schuster
What My Dog Knows	L	RF	866	Leveled Readers Science	Houghton Mifflin Harcourt
What Mynah Bird Saw	F	TL	90	Sunshine	Wright Group/McGraw Hill
What Needs the Sun	B	I	65	Literacy by Design	Rigby
What Next, Baby Bear?	L	F	313	Murphy, Jill	Dial/Penguin
What Next?	F	F	277	Story Basket	Wright Group/McGraw Hill
What on Earth?	I	F	133	Sunshine	Wright Group/McGraw Hill
What People Do	E	I	113	Early Connections	Benchmark Education
What People Do	H	I	148	Little Red Readers	Sundance
What People Wore During the American Revolution	T	I	250+	Clothing, Costumes and Uniforms Throughout American History	Rosen Publishing Group
What People Wore During the Westward Expansion	T	I	250+	Clothing, Costumes and Uniforms Throughout American History	Rosen Publishing Group
What People Wore in Colonial America	T	I	250+	Clothing, Costumes and Uniforms Throughout American History	Rosen Publishing Group
What People Wore in Early America	T	I	250+	Clothing, Costumes and Uniforms Throughout American History	Rosen Publishing Group
What Plant Is This?	B	I	22	Windows on Literacy	National Geographic
What Plants and Animals Need	K	I	200	Phonics Readers	Compass Point Books
What Plays Music?	C	I	36	Questions & Answers	Pearson Learning Group
What Pushes? What Pulls?	I	I	141	Early Connections	Benchmark Education
What Rhymes With . . .	A	I	9	Ready Readers	Pearson Learning Group
What Rhymes With Cat?	LB	F	4	Ready Readers	Pearson Learning Group
What Road to Follow?	T	HF	1365	Leveled Readers	Houghton Mifflin Harcourt
What Road to Follow?	T	HF	1365	Leveled Readers/CA	Houghton Mifflin Harcourt
What School Was Like Long Ago	K	I	499	Leveled Readers/TX	Houghton Mifflin Harcourt
What Season Is It?	F	I	79	Leveled Readers Social Studies	Houghton Mifflin Harcourt
What Season Is This?	C	I	24	Wonder World	Wright Group/McGraw Hill
What Shall I Do?	M	RF	584	Sunshine	Wright Group/McGraw Hill
What Shall I Wear?	E	I	58	Book Bank	Wright Group/McGraw Hill
What Shall Workers Do?	W	I	2287	Independent Readers Social Studies	Houghton Mifflin Harcourt
What Shape Is It?	B	I	35	Properties of Matter	Lerner Publications
What Shape Is Water?	G	I	188	Sun Sprouts	ETA Cuisenaire
What Should I Wear?	C	RF	70	Lighthouse	Rigby
What Should We Wear?	F	I	50	iOpeners	Pearson Learning Group
What Smells Good?	C	I	26	Windmill Books	Rigby
What Some People Will Do	T	RF	250+	Power Up!	Steck-Vaughn
What the Dickens	W	F	250+	Maguire, Gregory	Candlewick Press
What the Dinosaurs Saw	I	I	123	Schlein, Miriam	Scholastic
What the Dog Saw	G	F	131	Reading Street	Pearson
What the King Likes	B	F	32	Sun Sprouts	ETA Cuisenaire

W

* Collection of short stories
\# Graphic text

TITLE	LEVEL	GENRE	WORD COUNT	AUTHOR / SERIES	PUBLISHER / DISTRIBUTOR
What the President Did Today	O	I	785	Leveled Readers	Houghton Mifflin Harcourt
What the President Did Today	O	I	785	Leveled Readers/CA	Houghton Mifflin Harcourt
What the President Does	O	I	817	Leveled Readers	Houghton Mifflin Harcourt
What the President Does	O	I	817	Leveled Readers/CA	Houghton Mifflin Harcourt
What They Found: Love on 145th Street	Z+	RF	250+	Myers, Walter Dean	Wendy Lamb Books
What Things Go Together	LB	RF	26	Literacy 2000	Rigby
What Tigers Do	A	I	18	Bonnell, Kris	Reading Reading Books
What Time Is It?	B	RF	48	Instant Readers	Harcourt School Publishers
What Time Is It?	W	I	35	iOpeners	Pearson Learning Group
What Time Is It?	D	I	43	Learn to Read	Creative Teaching Press
What Time Is It?	D	I	53	Little Celebrations	Pearson Learning Group
What Time Is It?	D	RF	65	Moriarty, Julie	Scholastic
What Time Is It?	B	I	48	Rosen Real Readers	Rosen Publishing Group
What Time Is It?	I	I	189	Shutterbug Books	Steck-Vaughn
What Time Is It?	H	I	207	Springboard	Wright Group/McGraw Hill
What Time Is It?	E	RF	136	Teacher's Choice Series	Pearson Learning Group
What to Do About Alice?	R	B	250+	Kerley, Barbara	Scholastic
What to Do About Woolsey?	I	RF	250+	Literacy by Design	Rigby
What to Do in an Emergency	J	I	391	Reading Street	Pearson
What to Wear?	D	RF	42	Harry's Math Books	Outside the Box
What Tommy Did	E	RF	125	Literacy 2000	Rigby
What Was That?	E	RF	66	Leveled Readers	Houghton Mifflin Harcourt
What Was That?	H	RF	250+	Scooters	ETA Cuisenaire
What Was This?	F	I	53	Wonder World	Wright Group/McGraw Hill
What We Do at School	A	F	31	Bookshop	Mondo
What We Like	B	RF	43	Early Connections	Benchmark Education
What We Like	D	RF	71	Little Red Readers	Sundance
What Were Castles For?	R	I	250+	Usborne Starting Point History	EDC Publishing
What Will Alex Do?	C	F	75	Abbatiello, Toya	Kaeden Books
What Will Float?	G	I	224	Sunshine	Wright Group/McGraw Hill
What Will I Be?	D	I	104	Early Connections	Benchmark Education
What Will the Weather Be?	O	I	250+	DeWitt, Lynda	HarperTrophy
What Will the Weather Be?	H	I	207	Rigby Literacy	Rigby
What Will You Pack?	B	RF	35	Ready Readers	Pearson Learning Group
What Would Joey Do?	T	RF	250+	Gantos, Jack	Farrar, Straus and Giroux
What Would the Zoo Do?	D	F	59	Salem, Lynn	Continental Press
What Would You Do?	G	RF	160	Sunshine	Wright Group/McGraw Hill
What Would You Do?	M	I	392	Vocabulary Readers	Houghton Mifflin Harcourt
What Would You Like?	D	F	52	Sunshine	Wright Group/McGraw Hill
What You See Is What You Get	I	F	192	McLenighan, Valjean	Pearson Learning Group
Whatcha Got?	M	RF	250+	Social Studies Connects	The Kane Press
Whatever Am I Going to Do Now?	M	RF	250+	Little Celebrations	Pearson Learning Group
Whatever Happened to Janie?	Y	RF	250+	Cooney, Caroline B.	Laurel-Leaf Books
Whatever Will These Become?	E	I	47	Literacy 2000	Rigby
Whatever Will These Become?	E	I	47	Literacy Tree	Rigby
Whatever!: The Complicated Life of Claudia Cristina Cortez	S	RF	250+	Gallagher, Diana G.	Stone Arch Books
What's Alike?	WB	I	N/A	Windows on Literacy	National Geographic
What's Alive?	D	I	53	Discovery Links	Newbridge
What's Around the Corner?	H	RF	90	Literacy Tree	Rigby
What's Behind This Door?	B	I	43	Twig	Wright Group/McGraw Hill
What's Best for Red?	K	RF	444	Eggers, Casey	Hampton-Brown
What's Black and White and Moos?	E	I	78	Twig	Wright Group/McGraw Hill
What's Cooking, Jenny Archer?	M	RF	250+	Conford, Ellen	Little, Brown & Co.

Organized Alphabetically by Title
Storable Database at www.fountasandpinnellleveledbooks.com

* Collection of short stories
\# Graphic text

W

TITLE	LEVEL	GENRE	WORD COUNT	AUTHOR / SERIES	PUBLISHER / DISTRIBUTOR
What's Cooking?	H	RF	287	Bookshop	Mondo
What's Cooking?	Q	I	250+	Orbit Chapter Books	Pacific Learning
What's for Breakfast?	C	F	36	Big Cat	Pacific Learning
What's for Dinner, Dad?	K	RF	459	Sunshine	Wright Group/McGraw Hill
What's for Dinner?	B	I	35	Hoenecke, Karen	Kaeden Books
What's for Dinner?	B	I	38	Sails	Rigby
What's for Dinner?	E	RF	112	Seedlings	Continental Press
What's for Dinner?	Q	I	250+	Sunshine	Wright Group/McGraw Hill
What's for Lunch	E	F	91	New Way Red	Steck-Vaughn
What's for Lunch?	C	F	48	Carle, Eric	Scholastic
What's for Lunch?	H	F	169	Ready Readers	Pearson Learning Group
What's for Lunch?	D	I	49	Rise & Shine	Hampton-Brown
What's for Lunch?	B	F	36	Story Box	Wright Group/McGraw Hill
What's for Lunch?	A	I	30	Vocabulary Readers	Houghton Mifflin Harcourt
What's Going On?	C	RF	21	Learn to Read	Creative Teaching Press
What's Going On?	H	RF	377	Real Kids Readers	Millbrook Press
What's Happening?: A Book of Explanations	Q	I	250+	Bookshop	Mondo
What's in a Name?	P	I	1151	Reading Street	Pearson
What's in a Name?: A Story about George Eliot	T	B	250+	PM Chapter Books	Rigby
What's in a Park?	G	I	46	Chessen, Betsey; Chanko, Pamela	Scholastic
What's in Here?	E	I	122	Sun Sprouts	ETA Cuisenaire
What's in My Pocket	F	I	72	Learn to Read	Creative Teaching Press
What's in Orbit?	S	I	250+	Take Two Books	Wright Group/McGraw Hill
What's in the Bag?	E	HF	98	Visions	Wright Group/McGraw Hill
What's in the Box?	B	I	24	Rigby Literacy	Rigby
What's in the Woods?	J	RF	250+	The Wright Skills	Wright Group/McGraw Hill
What's in This Egg?	A	F	16	Sunshine	Wright Group/McGraw Hill
What's Inside?	C	I	35	Big Cat	Pacific Learning
What's Inside?	G	I	50	Foundations	Wright Group/McGraw Hill
What's Inside?	LB	RF	47	Hoenecke, Karen	Kaeden Books
What's Inside?	E	I	37	Sunshine	Wright Group/McGraw Hill
What's Inside?	H	I	138	Windows on Literacy	National Geographic
What's Inside?	K	I	238	Wonder World	Wright Group/McGraw Hill
What's It For?	D	I	47	Visions	Wright Group/McGraw Hill
What's It Like to Be a Fish?	L	I	250+	Little Readers	Houghton Mifflin Harcourt
What's It Made Of?	E	I	131	Rigby Star Quest	Rigby
What's Living at Your Place?	Q	I	250+	Orbit Chapter Books	Pacific Learning
What's Missing?	K	I	252	Book Bank	Wright Group/McGraw Hill
What's Missing?	D	RF	102	Spinelle, Nancy Louise	Kaeden Books
What's Money All About?	R	I	1344	Reading Street	Pearson
What's My Job?	B	I	25	Windows on Literacy	National Geographic
What's New at the Zoo?	H	F	151	Instant Readers	Harcourt School Publishers
What's New with Dinosaur Fossils?	V	I	2566	Reading Street	Pearson
What's New?	T	I	250+	Sails	Rigby
What's on My Farm?	B	RF	38	Rise & Shine	Hampton-Brown
What's on the Road?	B	I	34	Windows on Literacy	National Geographic
What's on the Ships?	G	I	170	Windows on Literacy	National Geographic
What's on the Truck?	I	I	137	Windows on Literacy	National Geographic
What's on Your T-Shirt?	C	RF	64	Carousel Readers	Pearson Learning Group
What's Poisoning the Garden?	U	RF	250+	Reading Expeditions	National Geographic
What's Round?	LB	I	14	Discovery Links	Newbridge
What's So Funny?	R	I	250+	Boldprint	Steck-Vaughn
What's That Noise?	I	RF	250+	Rigby Rocket	Rigby
What's That Noise?	B	RF	23	Science	Outside the Box

TITLE	LEVEL	GENRE	WORD COUNT	AUTHOR / SERIES	PUBLISHER / DISTRIBUTOR
What's That Smell?	H	RF	56	Pacific Literacy	Pacific Learning
What's That?	C	RF	27	Carousel Earlybirds	Pearson Learning Group
What's That?	I	F	250+	Popcorn	Sundance
What's That?	B	RF	33	Sunshine	Wright Group/McGraw Hill
What's That?	C	F	28	The Book Project	Sundance
What's the Address?	L	I	186	iOpeners	Pearson Learning Group
What's the Big Idea, Ben Franklin?	O	B	250+	Fritz, Jean	Scholastic
What's the Difference?	P	I	250+	Literacy by Design	Rigby
What's the Difference?	Q	I	250+	Orbit Collections	Pacific Learning
What's the Matter in Mr. Whiskers' Room?	P	I	250+	Ross, Michael Elsohn	Candlewick Press
What's the Matter with Herbie Jones?	N	RF	250+	Kline, Suzy	Penguin Group
What's the Matter, Kelly Beans?	N	RF	250+	Enderle, Judith R.; Tessler, S. G.	Candlewick Press
What's the Problem?	Q	I	250+	Orbit Collections	Pacific Learning
What's the Time	F	RF	74	Cambridge Reading	Pearson Learning Group
What's the Time Mr. Wolf?	C	F	49	Windmill Books	Wright Group/McGraw Hill
What's the Time?	H	I	217	Sun Sprouts	ETA Cuisenaire
What's the Weather Like Today?	D	I	119	Learn to Read	Creative Teaching Press
What's the Weather?	B	RF	21	Cali, Jennifer	Scholastic
What's This Matter?	F	I	88	Independent Readers Science	Houghton Mifflin Harcourt
What's This Spider Doing?	E	I	89	Story Steps	Rigby
What's This?	N	I	250+	Literacy 2000	Rigby
What's This?	L	I	462	Sun Sprouts	ETA Cuisenaire
What's Under My Bed?	C	RF	18	Visions	Wright Group/McGraw Hill
What's Under the Ocean	H	I	108	Now I Know	Troll Associates
What's Underground?	I	I	207	Big Cat	Pacific Learning
What's Underneath?	K	I	200	Discovery World	Rigby
What's Up?	E	RF	26	Instant Readers	Harcourt School Publishers
What's Up?	B	I	26	Pacific Literacy	Pacific Learning
What's Up?: Watching the Night Sky	L	I	250+	Rigby Literacy	Rigby
What's With Wulf?	Q	F	250+	Extreme Monsters	Penny Candy Press
What's Wrong With Gilbert?	J	F	664	Gilbert the Pig	Pioneer Valley
What's Your Angle, Pythagoras?	S	HF	250+	Ellis, Julie	Scholastic
What's Your Opinion?	Q	I	250+	Sails	Rigby
What's Your Source? Questioning the News	T	I	250+	Media Literacy	Capstone Press
What's Your Story?	WB	RF	N/A	Voyages	SRA/McGraw Hill
What's Zero?	I	I	250+	Yellow Umbrella Books	Red Brick Learning
Wheat	D	I	52	Canizares, Susan; Chanko, Pamela	Scholastic
Wheat We Eat, The	K	I	250+	Rookie Read About Science	Children's Press
Wheel, The	C	RF	102	Joy Readers	Pearson Learning Group
Wheelbarrow Garden, The	H	RF	231	PM Plus Story Books	Rigby
Wheels	B	I	39	Big Cat	Pacific Learning
Wheels	D	I	69	Cobb, Annie	Random House
Wheels	C	I	29	Discovery Links	Newbridge
Wheels	E	I	93	Explorations	Eleanor Curtain Publishing
Wheels	E	I	93	Explorations	Okapi Educational Materials
Wheels	H	I	129	Gear Up!	Wright Group/McGraw Hill
Wheels	A	I	32	Leveled Literacy Intervention/ Orange System	Heinemann
Wheels	C	I	27	Literacy 2000	Rigby
Wheels	E	RF	62	Nayer, Judy	Scholastic
Wheels	D	I	49	Rise & Shine	Hampton-Brown
Wheels	B	F	25	Sails	Rigby
Wheels	D	I	33	Sun Sprouts	ETA Cuisenaire

W

* Collection of short stories
\# Graphic text

TITLE	LEVEL	GENRE	WORD COUNT	AUTHOR / SERIES	PUBLISHER / DISTRIBUTOR
Wheels	C	I	39	Sunshine	Wright Group/McGraw Hill
Wheels	D	RF	27	Voyages	SRA/McGraw Hill
Wheels	D	I	33	Windows on Literacy	National Geographic
Wheels and Axles	Q	I	1689	Early Bird Energy Physics Books	Lerner Publishing
Wheels and Axles to the Rescue	O	I	250+	Simple Machine to the Rescue	Capstone Press
Wheels Around	T	I	250+	The News	Richard C. Owen
Wheels Around Us	P	I	250+	Windows on Literacy	National Geographic
Wheels on the Bike Go Round and Round, The	T	I	2241	Reading Street	Pearson
Wheels on the Bus	I	TL	362	Kovalski, Mary Ann	Little, Brown & Co.
Wheels on the Bus, The	J	TL	250+	Traditional Songs	Picture Window Books
Wheels on the Racecar, The	I	F	250+	Zane, Alexander	Scholastic
When a Storm Comes	J	I	172	Windows on Literacy	National Geographic
When Arthur Wouldn't Sleep	I	F	280	Big Cat	Pacific Learning
When Baby Is Happy	D	RF	52	Joy Starters	Pearson Learning Group
When Birds Get Flu and Cows Go Mad!	W	I	250+	24/7 Science Behind the Scenes	Scholastic
When Bob Woke Up Late	G	RF	139	Ready Readers	Pearson Learning Group
When Children Worked	N	I	292	Independent Readers Social Studies	Houghton Mifflin Harcourt
When Cultures Meet	R	I	250+	Reading Expeditions	National Geographic
When Dad Came Home	F	RF	46	Literacy 2000	Rigby
When Dad Got Lost	F	RF	113	City Stories	Rigby
When Dad Went Fishing	H	RF	250+	Cambridge Reading	Pearson Learning Group
When Dad Went to Daycare	H	RF	211	Sunshine	Wright Group/McGraw Hill
When Day Turned to Night: April 14, 1935	T	I	250+	Rigby Literacy	Rigby
When Do Cars Stop?	C	I	62	Questions & Answers	Pearson Learning Group
When Do You Feel?	F	I	132	Twig	Wright Group/McGraw Hill
When Enviornments Change	R	I	1093	Science Support Readers	Houghton Mifflin Harcourt
When Goldilocks Went to the House of the Bears	F	TL	156	Bookshop	Mondo
When Goldilocks Went to the House of the Bears	E	TL	165	Tiger Cub	Peguis
When Grandma Visits Me	D	F	113	Dominie Readers	Pearson Learning Group
When Grandpa Was a Boy	C	RF	93	Leveled Readers	Houghton Mifflin Harcourt
When Grandpa Was a Boy	C	RF	93	Leveled Readers/CA	Houghton Mifflin Harcourt
When Grandpa Was a Boy	C	RF	93	Leveled Readers/TX	Houghton Mifflin Harcourt
When Grandpa Was Young	L	I	250+	Rigby Focus	Rigby
When Hitler Stole Pink Rabbit	X	HF	250+	Kerr, Judith	Scholastic
When I Broke the Office Window	L	RF	257	City Kids	Rigby
When I First Came to This Land	K	TL	250+	Ziefert, Harriet	Scholastic
When I Forgot	N	RF	250+	Orbit Chapter Books	Pacific Learning
When I Get Bigger	K	RF	205	Mayer, Mercer	Donovan
When I Go See Gram	G	RF	123	Ready Readers	Pearson Learning Group
When I Go to Grandma's House	K	RF	199	Cleary, Brian	Kaeden Books
When I Grow Up	B	RF	58	Lighthouse	Rigby
When I Grow Up	F	RF	63	Rhythm 'N' Rhyme Readers	Pearson Learning Group
When I Grow Up	D	RF	112	Rigby Rocket	Rigby
When I Grow Up	C	RF	38	Rise & Shine	Hampton-Brown
When I Look Up	B	RF	55	Foundations	Wright Group/McGraw Hill
When I Looked Out My Window	H	RF	215	Springboard	Wright Group/McGraw Hill
When I Play	C	RF	31	Literacy 2000	Rigby
When I Pretend	C	RF	40	Literacy 2000	Rigby
When I Turned Six	I	HF	150	Voyages	SRA/McGraw Hill
When I Visit My Cousin	E	I	67	Independent Readers Social Studies	Houghton Mifflin Harcourt

* Collection of short stories
# Graphic text

W

TITLE	LEVEL	GENRE	WORD COUNT	AUTHOR / SERIES	PUBLISHER / DISTRIBUTOR
When I Was a Baby	C	I	101	Gear Up!	Wright Group/McGraw Hill
When I Was a Baby	D	I	64	Rigby Rocket	Rigby
When I Was Little	B	I	79	Leveled Readers	Houghton Mifflin Harcourt
When I Was Little	B	I	79	Leveled Readers/CA	Houghton Mifflin Harcourt
When I Was Sick	D	RF	62	Explorations	Eleanor Curtain Publishing
When I Was Sick	D	I	62	Explorations	Okapi Educational Materials
When I Was Sick	F	RF	53	Literacy 2000	Rigby
When I Was Young and Wild Bill's Secret Wish	P	RF	250+	Orbit Chapter Books	Pacific Learning
When I Was Your Age: Original Stories About Growing Up (Vol. 1)	W	B	250+	Ehrlich, Amy (Ed.)	Candlewick Press
When I'm Older	F	RF	156	Literacy 2000	Rigby
When It Rains	C	RF	39	Foundations	Wright Group/McGraw Hill
When It Rains	F	I	106	Frankford, Marilyn	Kaeden Books
When It Rains	E	RF	36	Voyages	SRA/McGraw Hill
When It Rains . . .	C	I	37	Teacher's Choice Series	Pearson Learning Group
When It Rains, It Pours	S	I	250+	WorldScapes	ETA Cuisenaire
When It Snowed	C	RF	33	Home Connection Collection	Rigby
When Itchy Witchy Sneezes	C	F	39	Sunshine	Wright Group/McGraw Hill
When Jessie Came Across the Sea	S	HF	250+	Hest, Amy	Candlewick Press
When Johnny Went Marching: Young Americans Fight the Civil War	Y	I	250+	Wisler, B. Clifton	HarperCollins
When Jose Hits That Ball	G	RF	45	Pacific Literacy	Pacific Learning
When Justice Failed: The Fred Korematsu Story	U	B	250+	Chin, Steven A.	Steck-Vaughn
When Lana Was Absent	F	RF	78	Tadpoles	Rigby
When Lincoln Was a Boy	E	I	132	Twig	Wright Group/McGraw Hill
When Marian Sang	R	B	250+	Ryan, Pam Munoz	Scholastic
When Mr. Quinn Snored	C	F	31	Little Books	Sadlier-Oxford
When My Dad Came to School	M	RF	230	City Kids	Rigby
When My Name Was Keoko	Y	HF	250+	Park, Linda Sue	Dell Yearling
When Plague Strikes	Z	I	250+	Giblin, James Cross	HarperCollins
When Robins Sing	H	I	238	Twig	Wright Group/McGraw Hill
When She Was Good	Z	RF	250+	Mazer, Norma Fox	Scholastic
When Sophie Gets Angry - Really, Really Angry . . .	K	RF	166	Bang, Molly	Scholastic
When Spring Comes	D	I	23	Windows on Literacy	National Geographic
When the Beginning Began: Stories About God, the Creatures, and Us	U	TL	250+	Lester, Julius	Harcourt Brace
When the Circus Came to Town	R	RF	250+	Horvath, Polly	Sunburst
When the Circus Comes to Town	A	I	40	Little Red Readers	Sundance
When the Cookernup Store Burned Down	K	F	250+	Sunshine	Wright Group/McGraw Hill
When the Disaster's Over	U	I	2566	Reading Street	Pearson
When the Earth Was Bare	P	TL	250+	Voyages	SRA/McGraw Hill
*When the Giants Came to Town	L	F	250+	Leonard, Marcia	Scholastic
When the King Rides By	J	F	247	Bookshop	Mondo
When the Moon Was Blue	I	F	174	Literacy 2000	Rigby
When the Rain Comes	C	I	54	Windows on Literacy	National Geographic
When the Sun Goes Down	G	I	109	Wonder World	Wright Group/McGraw Hill
When the Tide Goes Out	D	I	74	Story Steps	Rigby
When the Toy Shop Shuts	WB	F	N/A	The Book Project	Sundance
When the Tripods Came	V	F	250+	Christopher, John	Aladdin
When the Truck Got Stuck!	M	RF	250+	Cowley, Joy	Pacific Learning
When the TV Broke	H	RF	209	Ziefert, Harriet	Puffin/Penguin
When the Volcano Erupted	J	F	262	PM Collection	Rigby
When the Water Closes Over My Head	R	RF	250+	Napoli, Donna	Puffin/Penguin

W

* Collection of short stories
# Graphic text

TITLE	LEVEL	GENRE	WORD COUNT	AUTHOR / SERIES	PUBLISHER / DISTRIBUTOR
When the Wind Blows	G	I	107	Rigby Focus	Rigby
When the Wolves Returned: Restoring Nature's Balance in Yellowstone	S	I	250+	Patent, Dorothy Hinshaw	Walker & Company
When They Were Little Like Me	E	I	70	Leveled Readers Social Studies	Houghton Mifflin Harcourt
When Tony Got Lost at the Zoo	L	RF	122	City Kids	Rigby
When Tsunamis Strike	T	I	1836	Vocabulary Readers	Houghton Mifflin Harcourt
When Tsunamis Strike	T	I	1836	Vocabulary Readers/CA	Houghton Mifflin Harcourt
When We Are Big	E	RF	123	Ready Readers	Pearson Learning Group
When Will I Read?	I	RF	250+	Cohen, Miriam	Bantam
When Will We Be Sisters?	K	RF	250+	Kroll, Virginia	Scholastic
When Willard Met Babe Ruth	R	HF	250+	Hall, Donald	Voyager Books
When You Were a Baby	G	RF	104	Jonas, Ann	Morrow
When Zachary Beaver Came to Town	Y	RF	250+	Holt, Kimberly Willis	Dell Yearling
Where Am I?	C	RF	34	Pair-It Turn and Learn	Steck-Vaughn
Where and Why?	C	RF	28	Learn to Read	Creative Teaching Press
Where Are All the Bats?	F	RF	105	Reading Street	Pearson
Where Are My Socks?	D	RF	42	Pacific Literacy	Pacific Learning
Where Are the Babies?	B	I	8	PM Starters	Rigby
Where are the Baby Chicks?	D	F	64	Gilbert the Pig	Pioneer Valley
Where Are the Bears?	K	F	250+	Winters, Kay	Bantam
Where Are the Car Keys?	B	RF	36	Windmill Books	Wright Group/McGraw Hill
Where Are The Dinosaurs?	B	I	60	Bookshop	Mondo
Where Are the Eggs?	F	I	152	Discovery Links	Newbridge
Where Are the Monkeys?	G	RF	217	On Our Way to English	Rigby
Where Are the Seeds?	D	I	67	Wonder World	Wright Group/McGraw Hill
Where Are the Sunhats?	D	RF	130	PM Story Books	Rigby
Where Are the Wolves?	R	I	250+	Motil, Rebecca	Scholastic
Where Are They Going?	C	F	42	Story Box	Wright Group/McGraw Hill
Where Are They Going?	C	I	38	Windows on Literacy	National Geographic
Where Are They?	C	RF	24	Humphrey, Kiesha	Scholastic
Where Are They?	D	RF	98	Rigby Literacy	Rigby
Where Are They?	B	I	98	Rosen Real Readers	Rosen Publishing Group
Where Are We Going?	C	RF	70	In Step Readers	Rigby
Where Are We?	B	RF	72	Early Emergent	Pioneer Valley
Where Are You Going, Aja Rose?	D	RF	100	Sunshine	Wright Group/McGraw Hill
Where Are You Going, Little Mouse?	H	F	148	Kraus, Robert	Greenwillow
Where Are You Going?	B	F	42	KinderReaders	Rigby
Where Are You Going?	D	RF	66	Learn to Read	Creative Teaching Press
Where Are You, Mouse?	E	RF	170	Sails	Rigby
Where Babies Play	C	F	36	Instant Readers	Harcourt School Publishers
Where Can a Hippo Hide?	D	F	41	Ready Readers	Pearson Learning Group
Where Can I Play?	C	RF	45	Windows on Literacy	National Geographic
Where Can I Write?	C	RF	42	Early Emergent	Pioneer Valley
Where Can It Be?	E	RF	83	Jonas, Ann	Morrow
Where Can Kitty Sleep?	B	RF	15	Windmill Books	Wright Group/McGraw Hill
Where Can Louis Sleep?	D	I	75	Bonnell, Kris	Reading Reading Books
Where Can Pussy Sleep?	B	RF	15	Windmill Books	Wright Group/McGraw Hill
Where Can Teddy Go?	E	RF	141	Foundations	Wright Group/McGraw Hill
Where Can We Go from Here?	F	I	54	Spinelle, Nancy Louise	Kaeden Books
Where Can We Put an Elephant?	B	F	48	Windmill Books	Wright Group/McGraw Hill
Where Can You Shop?	C	I	82	Windows on Literacy	National Geographic
Where Did All the Water Go?	F	I	139	PM Plus Nonfiction	Rigby
Where Did It Go?	F	F	216	Learn to Read	Creative Teaching Press
Where Did the Maya Go?	P	F	250+	Action Packs	Rigby

TITLE	LEVEL	GENRE	WORD COUNT	AUTHOR / SERIES	PUBLISHER / DISTRIBUTOR
Where Did the Maya Go?	T	F	250+	WorldScapes	ETA Cuisenaire
Where Did They Go?	D	RF	102	Teacher's Choice Series	Pearson Learning Group
Where Dinosaurs Walked	K	I	189	Phonics Readers	Compass Point Books
Where Do All the Birds Go?	M	RF	250+	Wonder World	Wright Group/McGraw Hill
Where Do Animals Live?	F	I	187	Bookshop	Mondo
Where Do Birds Live?	C	I	57	Chessen, Betsy	Scholastic
Where Do Bugs Live?	D	I	33	Pair-It Books	Steck-Vaughn
Where Do Frogs Come From?	H	I	144	Green Light Readers	Harcourt
Where Do I Live?	C	I	29	Visions	Wright Group/McGraw Hill
Where Do I Sleep?	M	RF	250+	Wonder World	Wright Group/McGraw Hill
Where Do Monsters Live?	C	F	56	Learn to Read	Creative Teaching Press
Where Do Plants Grow?	D	I	28	iOpeners	Pearson Learning Group
Where Do Puddles Go?	J	I	250+	Rookie Read-About Science	Children's Press
Where Do Snakes Live?	G	I	251	Sails	Rigby
Where Do the Puddles Go?	L	I	170	Windows on Literacy	National Geographic
Where Do They Go?	B	I	43	InfoTrek	ETA Cuisenaire
Where Do They Go?	D	RF	66	Rigby Literacy	Rigby
Where Do They Live?	Q	I	250+	Orbit Collections	Pacific Learning
Where Do They Live?	C	I	45	Ready Readers	Pearson Learning Group
Where Do We Go?	B	RF	22	Ready Readers	Pearson Learning Group
Where Do You Live?	N	I	250+	People, Spaces & Places	Rand McNally
Where Do You Live?	C	I	68	Tiger Cub	Peguis
Where Do You Live?	L	I	250+	Twig	Wright Group/McGraw Hill
Where Do You Live?	I	I	68	Windows on Literacy	National Geographic
Where Do You Play?	D	I	131	Twig	Wright Group/McGraw Hill
Where Do You Think You're Going, Christopher Columbus?	S	B	250+	Fritz, Jean	Putnam/Penguin
Where Does a Leopard Hide?	C	I	108	Foundations	Wright Group/McGraw Hill
Where Does All the Garbage Go?	K	I	250+	Twig	Wright Group/McGraw Hill
Where Does Breakfast Come From?	H	I	170	Discovery World	Rigby
Where Does Breakfast Come From?	E	I	56	iOpeners	Pearson Learning Group
Where Does Energy Come From?	J	I	245	Leveled Readers Social Studies	Houghton Mifflin Harcourt
Where Does Food Come From?	H	RF	298	InfoTrek	ETA Cuisenaire
Where Does Food Come From?	I	I	169	PM Plus Nonfiction	Rigby
Where Does Food Come From?	G	I	361	Shelley Rotner's Early Childhood	Millbrook Press
Where Does Food Grow?	D	I	43	Blevins, Wiley	Scholastic
Where Does Garbage Go?	K	I	250+	Soar To Success	Houghton Mifflin Harcourt
Where Does It Go?	C	I	61	Questions & Answers	Pearson Learning Group
Where Does It Park?	C	I	51	Canizares, Susan	Scholastic
Where Does Lightning Come From?	N	I	250+	Why In the World?	Capstone Press
Where Does Mrs. Brown Live?	J	I	159	Springboard	Wright Group/McGraw Hill
Where Does Rain Come From?	N	I	250+	Rosen Real Readers	Rosen Publishing Group
Where Does the Butterfly Go When It Rains?	K	RF	250+	Bookshop	Mondo
Where Does the Garbage Go?	M	I	250+	Soar To Success	Houghton Mifflin Harcourt
Where Does the Mail Go?	F	I	115	Yellow Umbrella Books	Red Brick Learning
Where Does the Rabbit Hop?	E	I	71	Ready Readers	Pearson Learning Group
Where Does the Teacher Sleep?	C	F	50	Gibson, Kathleen	Continental Press
Where Does the Water Go?	L	I	189	Windows on Literacy	National Geographic
Where Does the Wind Go?	M	I	95	Bookshop	Mondo
Where Have All the Pandas Gone?	R	I	250+	Berger, Melvin & Gilda	Scholastic
Where I Live	B	RF	36	Carousel Earlybirds	Pearson Learning Group
Where I Live	C	RF	35	Pacific Literacy	Pacific Learning
Where I'd Like to Be	S	RF	250+	Dowell, Frances O'Roark	Aladdin
Where in the World Is the Perfect Family?	P	RF	250+	Hest, Amy	Penguin Group

* Collection of short stories
\# Graphic text

W

TITLE	LEVEL	GENRE	WORD COUNT	AUTHOR / SERIES	PUBLISHER / DISTRIBUTOR
Where in the World?	D	I	41	Nelson, May	Scholastic
Where Is a Bear?	A	I	36	Bonnell, Kris	Reading Reading Books
Where Is Benny Button?	B	RF	16	Reading Safari	Mondo
Where Is Blackbeard's Ship?	O	I	286	Vocabulary Readers	Houghton Mifflin Harcourt
Where Is Cow's Lunch?	H	RF	321	Leveled Readers	Houghton Mifflin Harcourt
Where Is Cow's Lunch?	H	RF	321	Leveled Readers/CA	Houghton Mifflin Harcourt
Where Is Cow's Lunch?	H	RF	321	Leveled Readers/TX	Houghton Mifflin Harcourt
Where Is Curly?	D	F	69	Rigby Literacy	Rigby
Where Is Curly?	D	F	88	Rigby Star	Rigby
Where Is Daniel?	E	RF	135	Carousel Readers	Pearson Learning Group
Where Is Eric?	I	F	193	Munoz, Isabel	Scholastic
Where Is Eric?	C	RF	29	Rigby Literacy	Rigby
Where Is Fluffy?	E	RF	98	Adams, Lorraine; Bruvold, Lynn	Eagle Crest Books
Where Is Gabby?	B	RF	21	Early Emergent	Pioneer Valley
Where Is Gus-Gus?	L	RF	861	Leveled Readers	Houghton Mifflin Harcourt
Where Is Gus-Gus?	L	RF	861	Leveled Readers/CA	Houghton Mifflin Harcourt
Where Is Gus-Gus?	L	RF	861	Leveled Readers/TX	Houghton Mifflin Harcourt
Where Is Hannah?	D	RF	141	PM Extensions-Red	Rigby
Where Is Happy Monkey?	C	F	46	Joy Readers	Pearson Learning Group
Where Is Hoppy?	K	RF	250+	Literacy by Design	Rigby
Where Is It Going?	A	I	20	Windows on Literacy	National Geographic
Where Is It Safe to Play?	D	I	103	PM Plus Nonfiction	Rigby
Where Is it?	D	RF	250+	Book Bus	Creative Edge
Where Is It?	LB	I	8	Reading Street	Pearson
Where Is It?	B	RF	21	Ready Readers	Pearson Learning Group
Where Is It?	D	RF	32	Rookie Readers	Children's Press
Where Is It?	F	I	32	Tiger Cub	Peguis
Where Is Jake?	E	RF	35	My First Reader	Grolier Press
Where Is Jodi?	I	RF	315	Springboard	Wright Group/McGraw Hill
Where Is Joe?	K	I	146	Rigby Star Quest	Rigby
Where Is Kate's Skate?	D	RF	46	KinderReaders	Rigby
Where Is Kazam?	D	F	31	Brand New Readers	Candlewick Press
Where Is Little Bo Peep?	E	F	127	Rigby Rocket	Rigby
Where Is Lunch?	B	F	25	Pacific Literacy	Pacific Learning
Where Is Marco?	C	F	75	Bookshop	Mondo
Where Is Matt's Cap?	F	RF	107	Plass, Beverly	Kaeden Books
Where Is Max?	D	RF	62	Rookie Readers	Children's Press
Where Is Max?	C	F	54	Sun Sprouts	ETA Cuisenaire
Where Is Miss Pool?	D	RF	55	Pacific Literacy	Pacific Learning
Where Is Muffin?	F	RF	298	Haight, Angela	Kaeden Books
Where Is My Ball?	B	F	24	The Book Project	Sundance
Where Is My Bear?	C	RF	73	Springboard	Wright Group/McGraw Hill
Where Is My Bone?	C	F	42	Sunshine	Wright Group/McGraw Hill
Where Is My Book?	B	RF	81	InfoTrek	ETA Cuisenaire
Where Is My Cat?	D	RF	102	Handprints C, Set 1	Educators Publishing Service
Where Is My Caterpillar?	H	F	277	Wonder World	Wright Group/McGraw Hill
Where Is My Continent?	J	I	131	Where Am I?	Lerner Publications
Where Is My Country?	I	I	122	Where Am I?	Lerner Publications
Where Is My Dinosaur?	D	RF	119	Rigby Flying Colors	Rigby
Where Is My Grandma?	C	RF	74	Foundations	Wright Group/McGraw Hill
Where Is My Home?	E	I	118	Where Am I?	Lerner Publications
Where Is My Pencil?	C	RF	34	Little Celebrations	Pearson Learning Group
Where Is My Pet?	A	RF	34	Smart Starts	Rigby

* Collection of short stories
# Graphic text

W

TITLE	LEVEL	GENRE	WORD COUNT	AUTHOR / SERIES	PUBLISHER / DISTRIBUTOR
Where Is My Puppy?	B	RF	33	Bebop Books	Lee & Low Books Inc.
Where Is My Spider?	H	RF	225	Story Box	Wright Group/McGraw Hill
Where Is My State?	H	I	136	Where Am I?	Lerner Publications
Where Is My Teacher?	B	I	43	Little Books for Early Readers	University of Maine
Where Is My Town?	G	I	109	Where Am I?	Lerner Publications
Where Is Nancy?	E	RF	56	Literacy 2000	Rigby
Where Is Patch?	B	RF	31	Rigby Star	Rigby
Where Is Patch?	C	RF	73	Springboard	Wright Group/McGraw Hill
Where Is Peanut?	D	RF	71	Emergent Set 4	Pioneer Valley
Where Is Sam?	B	RF	40	Springboard	Wright Group/McGraw Hill
Where Is Santa?	E	F	158	Little Elf	Literacy Footprints
Where Is She?	A	I	35	Little Books for Early Readers	University of Maine
Where Is Skunk?	D	F	65	Story Box	Wright Group/McGraw Hill
Where Is Tabby Cat?	C	RF	37	Brand New Readers	Candlewick Press
Where Is Teddy's Head?	A	RF	27	Windmill Books	Wright Group/McGraw Hill
Where Is the Bear?	K	F	250+	Nims, Bonnie	Whitman
Where Is the Big Cat?	E	RF	90	Bonnell, Kris	Reading Reading Books
Where Is the Cat?	A	RF	55	On Our Way to English	Rigby
Where Is the Cat?	C	I	28	Read-More Books	Pearson Learning Group
Where Is the Crab?	C	I	30	Vocabulary Readers	Houghton Mifflin Harcourt
Where Is the Dog Collar?	S	F	1449	Leveled Readers	Houghton Mifflin Harcourt
Where Is the Dog Collar?	S	F	1449	Leveled Readers/CA	Houghton Mifflin Harcourt
Where Is the Dog?	A	I	18	Vocabulary Readers	Houghton Mifflin Harcourt
Where Is the Ladybug Going?	D	I	53	Bonnell, Kris	Reading Reading Books
Where Is the Milk?	D	RF	87	Foundations	Wright Group/McGraw Hill
Where Is the Party?	E	F	121	Sails	Rigby
Where Is the Queen?	H	F	109	Ready Readers	Pearson Learning Group
Where Is the School Bus?	D	RF	40	Carousel Readers	Pearson Learning Group
Where Is the Snake?	C	F	60	The Book Project	Sundance
Where Is the Spy?	D	F	138	Sails	Rigby
Where Is the Sun?	D	I	70	Leveled Readers Science	Houghton Mifflin Harcourt
Where Is the Wind?	C	F	69	Big Cat	Pacific Learning
Where Is Water?	C	I	36	Twig	Wright Group/McGraw Hill
Where Is Water?	E	I	79	Water	Lerner Publications
Where Is White Rabbit?	K	RF	250+	Pacific Literacy	Pacific Learning
Where Is Your Home?	I	I	126	Phonics Readers	Compass Point Books
Where Is Zig?	D	F	63	Leveled Readers	Houghton Mifflin Harcourt
Where Jeans Come From	K	I	250+	Ready Readers	Pearson Learning Group
Where on Earth?	P	I	1581	Big Cat	Pacific Learning
Where People Live	J	RF	259	Early Connections	Benchmark Education
*Where the Flame Trees Bloom	U	B	250+	Ada, Alma Flor	Simon & Schuster
Where the Great Hawk Flies	U	HF	250+	Ketchum, Liza	Scholastic
Where the Ground Meets the Sky	Y	HF	250+	Davies, Jacqueline	Marshall Cavendish
Where the Lilies Bloom	Y	RF	250+	Cleavers, Vera & Bill	HarperTrophy
Where the Money Is	S	I	250+	WorldScapes	ETA Cuisenaire
Where the Red Fern Grows	X	RF	250+	Rawls, Wilson	Bantam
Where the River Runs: A Portrait of a Refugee Family	W	B	250+	Graff, Nancy Price	Scholastic
Where the Wild Things Are	J	F	339	Sendak, Maurice	Harper & Row
Where There Was Smoke	M	I	250+	Martinucci, Suzanne	Scholastic
Where Things Grow	C	I	81	Leveled Literacy Intervention/ Green System	Heinemann
Where to Buy It	B	I	45	Rosen Real Readers	Rosen Publishing Group
Where to Look for a Dinosaur	O	F	250+	Most, Bernard	Harcourt Brace

Organized Alphabetically by Title
Storable Database at www.fountasandpinnellleveledbooks.com

* Collection of short stories
# Graphic text

W

TITLE	LEVEL	GENRE	WORD COUNT	AUTHOR / SERIES	PUBLISHER / DISTRIBUTOR
Where Was Atlantis?	Z	I	250+	Unsolved Mysteries	Steck-Vaughn
Where Was Patrick Henry on the 29th of May?	R	B	250+	Fritz, Jean	Scholastic
Where We Live	C	I	34	Vocabulary Readers	Houghton Mifflin Harcourt
Where Will I Sit?	F	RF	78	Teacher's Choice Series	Pearson Learning Group
Where Will You Sleep Tonight?	C	I	77	Foundations	Wright Group/McGraw Hill
Where?	D	I	119	Yellow Umbrella Books	Red Brick Learning
Where's Al?	D	F	49	Barton, Byron	Houghton Mifflin Harcourt
Where's Baby Tom?	D	RF	91	Book Bank	Wright Group/McGraw Hill
Where's Bear?	C	F	41	Windmill Books	Wright Group/McGraw Hill
Where's Cupcake?	D	RF	71	Little Readers	Houghton Mifflin Harcourt
Where's Grandma?	M	F	250+	Literacy by Design	Rigby
Where's Henry?	F	RF	112	Home Connection Collection	Rigby
Where's Little Mole?	C	F	43	Little Celebrations	Pearson Learning Group
Where's Lulu?	I	RF	250+	Hooks, William H.	Bantam
Where's My Backpack?	C	RF	27	Little Celebrations	Pearson Learning Group
Where's My Daddy?	F	F	87	Watanabe, Shigeo	Putnam/Penguin
Where's My Snack?	I	RF	250+	Sunshine	Wright Group/McGraw Hill
Where's My Teddy?	I	F	221	Alborough, Jez	Candlewick Press
Where's My Yellow Yo-Yo?	B	RF	36	Phonics and Friends	Hampton-Brown
Where's Our Car?	D	RF	69	Rigby Star	Rigby
Where's Spot?	E	F	65	Hill, Eric	Putnam/Penguin
Where's Sylvester's Bed?	F	RF	78	Wonder World	Wright Group/McGraw Hill
Where's the Baby?	E	RF	139	Alphakids	Sundance
Where's the Bus?	L	F	250+	Sunshine	Wright Group/McGraw Hill
Where's the Dog?	B	RF	36	Windmill Books	Rigby
Where's the Egg Cup?	B	RF	25	Windmill Books	Wright Group/McGraw Hill
Where's the Fish?	B	F	39	Gomi, Taro	Morrow
Where's the Frog?	D	I	46	Discovery Links	Newbridge
Where's the Halloween Treat?	C	RF	102	Ziefert, Harriet	Penguin Group
Where's the Puppy?	D	RF	70	Dwight, Laura	Checkerboard
Where's the Snow?	G	RF	142	Erickson, Betty	Continental Press
Where's Tim?	C	F	38	Sunshine	Wright Group/McGraw Hill
Where's Tony?	J	RF	114	City Kids	Rigby
Where's Your Lunch?	G	RF	243	InfoTrek	ETA Cuisenaire
Where's Your Tooth?	C	RF	53	Learn to Read	Creative Teaching Press
Wherever the Wind Takes Us	O	RF	1934	Take Two Books	Wright Group/ McGraw-Hill
Which Animal Is That?	I	I	250+	Momentum Literacy Program	Troll Associates
Which Animal?	B	I	14	Foundations	Wright Group/McGraw Hill
Which Baby Animal?	I	I	250+	Scooters	ETA Cuisenaire
Which Clothes Do You Wear?	C	I	49	Foundations	Wright Group/McGraw Hill
Which Comes First?	J	I	250+	Voyages	SRA/McGraw Hill
Which Does not Belong?	A	I	35	Shutterbug Books	Steck-Vaughn
Which Egg Is Mine?	D	F	65	Rise & Shine	Hampton-Brown
Which Hat Today?	E	RF	94	Gosset, Rachel; Ballinger, Margaret	Scholastic
Which Holiday Is It?	I	I	110	Phonics Readers	Compass Point Books
Which House?	I	I	231	Scooters	ETA Cuisenaire
Which Insects Live Here?	J	I	129	Rigby Literacy	Rigby
Which Is Better?	G	I	104	Pair-It Turn and Learn	Steck-Vaughn
Which Is Different?	B	I	28	Rigby Star Quest	Rigby
Which Is Heavier?	D	I	51	Questions & Answers	Pearson Learning Group
Which Juice Would You Like?	C	F	28	Step-By-Step Series	Pearson Learning Group
Which One Does Not Belong?	B	I	20	Windows on Literacy	National Geographic
Which One Is It?	D	I	48	InfoTrek	ETA Cuisenaire

W

TITLE	LEVEL	GENRE	WORD COUNT	AUTHOR / SERIES	PUBLISHER / DISTRIBUTOR
Which One Is Which?	G	I	187	Sunshine	Wright Group/McGraw Hill
Which Toys?	D	I	40	Home Connection Collection	Rigby
Which Way Home?	C	RF	26	Little Celebrations	Pearson Learning Group
Which Way, Jack?	O	F	250+	Action Packs	Rigby
Which Way, Wendy	M	RF	250+	Social Studies Connects	The Kane Press
Which Wheels Are Best?	M	I	250+	Scooters	ETA Cuisenaire
Which Witch?	S	F	250+	Ibbotson, Eva	Puffin/Penguin
While We Sleep	J	I	387	Gear Up!	Wright Group/McGraw Hill
Whipping Boy, The	R	F	250+	Fleischman, Sid	Troll Associates
Whirligig	Y	RF	250+	Fleischman, Paul	Laurel-Leaf Books
Whiskers	B	RF	24	Gear Up!	Wright Group/McGraw Hill
Whiskers	C	I	32	Wonder World	Wright Group/McGraw Hill
Whisker's Excuses	L	F	540	Springboard	Wright Group/ McGraw Hill
Whisper	R	TL	1000	Leveled Readers/TX	Houghton Mifflin Harcourt
Whisper and Shout	C	I	92	Twig	Wright Group/McGraw Hill
Whisper of the Stars, The	R	I	250+	WorldScapes	ETA Cuisenaire
Whispering Mountain, The	Y	F	250+	Aiken, Joan	Tom Doherty
Whistle for Willie	L	RF	380	Keats, Ezra Jack	Penguin Group
Whistle Like a Bird	D	RF	53	Pair-It Books	Steck-Vaughn
Whistle Tooth, The	H	RF	188	Storyteller-Night Crickets	Wright Group/McGraw Hill
Whistler's Hollow	T	HF	250+	Dadey, Debbie	Bloomsbury Children's Books
Whistling Wings	N	F	1002	Goering, Laura	Sylvan Dell Publishing
White Bird	N	RF	250+	Bulla, Clyde Robert	Random House
White Dragon: Anna Allen in the Face of Danger	R	I	1253	Leveled Readers	Houghton Mifflin Harcourt
White Elephants	L	RF	250+	Sunshine	Wright Group/McGraw Hill
White Elephants and Yellow Jackets	O	I	250+	Action Packs	Rigby
White Fang	Y	RF	250+	London, Jack	Scholastic
White Horse, The	K	F	250+	Literacy 2000	Rigby
White House, The	N	I	250+	American Symbols	Capstone Press
White House, The	V	I	250+	Cornerstones of Freedom	Children's Press
White House, The	Q	I	250+	Let's See	Compass Point Books
White House, The	P	I	619	Pull Ahead Books	Lerner Publications
White Jaguar, The	U	RF	250+	WorldScapes	ETA Cuisenaire
White Mountain, The	V	F	250+	Christopher, John	Aladdin
White Mountain, The	Q	I	1079	Leveled Readers	Houghton Mifflin Harcourt
White Mountain, The	Q	I	1079	Leveled Readers/CA	Houghton Mifflin Harcourt
White Paw, Black Paw	C	F	41	KinderReaders	Rigby
White Wednesday	H	RF	321	Literacy 2000	Rigby
White White Snow, The	C	I	60	Bonnell, Kris	Reading Reading Books
White Wolf	S	F	250+	Branford, Henrietta	Candlewick Press
White Wolf, The	N	RF	250+	A to Z Mysteries	Random House
White: Seeing White All Around Us	L	I	250+	Colors	Capstone Press
Whitemen	W	HF	250+	High-Fliers	Pacific Learning
Whiteout	N	RF	1029	Leveled Readers	Houghton Mifflin Harcourt
White-Tailed Deer	O	I	1849	Early Bird Nature Books	Lerner Publishing
White-Tailed Deer, The	R	I	250+	Wildlife of North America	Red Brick Learning
Whitewater Rafting	G	I	66	Nonfiction Set 4	Literacy Footprints
Whitewater Scrubs	O	RF	4067	McEwan, Jamie	Darby Creek Publishing
Whizz! Click!	L	RF	285	Pacific Literacy	Pacific Learning
Who Am I ?	D	I	81	Rise & Shine	Hampton-Brown
Who Am I?	E	I	64	Christensen, Nancy	Scholastic
Who Am I?	S	I	250+	Orbit Collections	Pacific Learning

W

* Collection of short stories
\# Graphic text

TITLE	LEVEL	GENRE	WORD COUNT	AUTHOR / SERIES	PUBLISHER / DISTRIBUTOR
Who Am I?	B	F	32	The Book Project	Sundance
Who Are the Three Musketeers?	V	I	1710	Vocabulary Readers	Houghton Mifflin Harcourt
Who Are the Three Musketeers?	V	I	1710	Vocabulary Readers/CA	Houghton Mifflin Harcourt
Who Are We?	C	RF	30	Home Connection Collection	Rigby
Who Are You?	C	RF	55	Book Bank	Wright Group/McGraw Hill
Who Ate the Broccoli?	E	F	42	Little Readers	Houghton Mifflin Harcourt
Who Ate the Pizza?	C	RF	59	Foundations	Wright Group/McGraw Hill
Who Builds?	I	I	97	Yellow Umbrella Books	Red Brick Learning
Who Came By Here?	C	RF	31	Rise & Shine	Hampton-Brown
Who Came Out?	F	F	45	Ready Readers	Pearson Learning Group
Who Can Be a Hero?	A	I	41	Leveled Readers Social Studies	Houghton Mifflin Harcourt
Who Can Be an Astronaut?	U	I	1484	Vocabulary Readers	Houghton Mifflin Harcourt
Who Can Be an Astronaut?	U	I	1484	Vocabulary Readers/CA	Houghton Mifflin Harcourt
Who Can Be President?	R	I	1310	Leveled Readers	Houghton Mifflin Harcourt
Who Can Be President?	R	I	1310	Leveled Readers/CA	Houghton Mifflin Harcourt
Who Can Curly See?	LB	F	16	Rigby Star	Rigby
Who Can Fix the Computer?	G	RF	178	Handprints D	Educators Publishing Service
Who Can Help?	F	I	93	Gear Up!	Wright Group/McGraw Hill
Who Can Help?	L	I	588	Reading Street	Pearson
Who Can Hop?	C	I	35	Questions & Answers	Pearson Learning Group
Who Can Play?	B	RF	26	Sun Sprouts	ETA Cuisenaire
Who Can Read?	C	RF	72	Handprints C	Educators Publishing Service
Who Can See the Camel?	C	RF	70	Story Box	Wright Group/McGraw Hill
Who Can Wiggle?	A	I	33	Bonnell, Kris	Reading Reading Books
Who Can?	B	RF	35	Bookshop	Mondo
Who Cleans the Museum?	I	RF	85	Books for Young Learners	Richard C. Owen
Who Cracked the Liberty Bell? And Other Questions About the American Revolution	R	I	250+	Roop, Peter & Connie	Scholastic
Who Cried for Pie?	D	F	86	First Start	Troll Associates
Who Did It?	H	RF	206	Storyworlds	Heinemann Educational Books
Who Do I Look Like?	G	RF	143	Rookie Readers	Children's Press
Who Eats What?	N	I	697	Leveled Readers Science	Houghton Mifflin Harcourt
Who Eats What?	T	I	250+	The News	Richard C. Owen
Who Fed the Chickens?	C	F	14	Little Celebrations	Pearson Learning Group
Who Goes in the Water?	D	I	77	Bonnell, Kris	Reading Reading Books
Who Goes Out on Halloween?	G	RF	163	Alexander, Sue	Bantam
Who Goes to School?	E	RF	298	Easy Stories	Norwood House Press
Who Grows Up in the Desert?: A Book About Desert Animals and Their Offspring	L	I	250+	Who Grows Up Here?	Picture Window Books
Who Grows Up in the Forest?: A Book About Forest Animals and Their Offspring	L	I	250+	Who Grows Up Here?	Picture Window Books
Who Grows Up in the Ocean?: A Book About Ocean Animals and Their Offspring	L	I	250+	Who Grows Up Here?	Picture Window Books
Who Grows Up in the Rain Forest?: A Book About Rain Forest Animals and Their Offspring	L	I	250+	Who Grows Up Here?	Picture Window Books
Who Grows Up in the Snow?: A Book About Polar Animals and Their Offspring	L	I	250+	Who Grows Up Here?	Picture Window Books
Who Grows Up on the Farm?: A Book About Farm Animals and Their Offspring	K	L	250+	Who Grows Up Here?	Picture Window Books
Who Has a Hump?	B	F	24	Bonnell, Kris	Reading Reading Books
Who Has a Tail?	G	I	186	Ready Readers	Pearson Learning Group

* Collection of short stories
# Graphic text

W

TITLE	LEVEL	GENRE	WORD COUNT	AUTHOR / SERIES	PUBLISHER / DISTRIBUTOR
Who Has More?	B	I	55	Shutterbug Books	Steck-Vaughn
Who Has Wings?	C	I	30	Questions & Answers	Pearson Learning Group
Who Hid?	B	RF	25	Leber, Nancy	Scholastic
Who Is a Friend?	F	I	191	Yellow Umbrella Books	Capstone Press
Who Is Asleep?	A	I	32	Springboard	Wright Group/McGraw Hill
Who Is Carrie?	W	HF	250+	Collier, James & Christopher	Bantam
Who Is Coming?	E	RF	28	Rookie Readers	Children's Press
Who Is Hungry?	D	I	134	Rigby Flying Colors	Rigby
Who Is in Your Family?	F	I	229	Vocabulary Readers	Houghton Mifflin Harcourt
Who Is in Your Family?	F	I	229	Vocabulary Readers/CA	Houghton Mifflin Harcourt
Who Is in Your Family?	F	I	229	Vocabulary Readers/TX	Houghton Mifflin Harcourt
Who Is Maria Tallchief?	R	B	250+	Who Was..?	Grosset & Dunlap
Who Is Ready?	C	RF	36	Ready Readers	Pearson Learning Group
Who Is Taller?	C	RF	26	Learn to Read	Creative Teaching Press
Who Is Taller?	F	I	163	Sun Sprouts	ETA Cuisenaire
Who Is the Robot?	C	RF	67	Pacific Literacy	Pacific Learning
Who Is the Tallest?	F	I	91	Alphakids	Sundance
Who Is the Tallest?	D	RF	46	Sunshine	Wright Group/McGraw Hill
Who Is Who?	D	RF	115	Rookie Readers	Children's Press
Who Keeps Us Safe?	B	I	28	Yellow Umbrella Books	Red Brick Learning
Who Killed Mr. Boddy?	P	RF	250+	Parker, A. E.	Scholastic
Who Laid These Eggs?	C	I	62	Little Celebrations	Pearson Learning Group
Who Lays Eggs?	G	I	132	Twig	Wright Group/McGraw Hill
Who Likes Ice Cream?	A	F	15	Literacy 2000	Rigby
Who Likes It Hot?	K	F	250+	Bookshop	Mondo
Who Likes the Cold?	A	I	29	Twig	Wright Group/McGraw Hill
Who Likes the Night?	G	RF	250+	Phonics and Friends	Hampton-Brown
Who Likes to Swim?	D	I	100	Teacher's Choice Series	Pearson Learning Group
Who Likes Water?	B	F	35	KinderReaders	Rigby
Who Lives at the Zoo?	LB	I	11	Windows on Literacy	National Geographic
Who Lives Here?	C	I	62	Learn to Read	Creative Teaching Press
Who Lives Here?	F	I	100	Leveled Readers Science	Houghton Mifflin Harcourt
Who Lives Here?	I	I	230	Little Readers	Houghton Mifflin Harcourt
Who Lives Here?	C	I	42	Questions & Answers	Pearson Learning Group
Who Lives Here?	D	RF	102	Reed, Janet	Scholastic
Who Lives Here?	C	I	28	Story Box	Wright Group/McGraw Hill
Who Lives Here?	F	I	185	Storyteller Nonfiction	Wright Group/McGraw Hill
Who Lives Here?	B	I	43	Windows on Literacy	National Geographic
Who Lives in a Tree?	B	I	46	Canizares, Susan; Moreton, Daniel	Scholastic
Who Lives in a Tree?	C	I	43	Discovery Links	Newbridge
Who Lives in the Arctic?	B	I	48	Canizares, Susan; Chanko, Pamela	Scholastic
Who Lives in the Sea?	B	I	69	Bookshop	Mondo
Who Lives in the Woods?	F	I	110	Pair-It Books	Steck-Vaughn
Who Lives in this Hole?	C	I	25	Twig	Wright Group/McGraw Hill
Who Lives on a Farm?	B	I	36	Story Steps	Rigby
Who Looks After Me?	M	I	250+	Literacy 2000	Rigby
Who Looks After Me?	B	I	20	Windows on Literacy	National Geographic
Who Looks After Our World?	E	I	45	Home Connection Collection	Rigby
Who Loves Getting Wet?	I	F	204	Sunshine	Wright Group/McGraw Hill
Who Made That?	C	RF	31	Ready Readers	Pearson Learning Group
Who Made These Tracks?	B	I	24	Literacy 2000	Rigby
Who Made These Tracks?	D	I	45	Teacher's Choice Series	Pearson Learning Group

Organized Alphabetically by Title
Storable Database at www.fountasandpinnellleveledbooks.com

* Collection of short stories
\# Graphic text

W

Who Makes the Rules?	M	I	250+	Schafer, Lola M.	Benchmark Education
Who Needs Math?	K	RF	349	Story Box	Wright Group/McGraw Hill
Who Needs Plants?	F	I	97	Yellow Umbrella Books	Red Brick Learning
Who Needs Rooster?	G	F	223	Literacy by Design	Rigby
Who Needs Teeth?	I	I	116	Phonics Readers	Compass Point Books
Who Owns Kelly Paddik?	Y	RF	250+	Orca Soundings	Orca Book Publishers
Who Passed Through?	K	RF	380	Leveled Readers	Houghton Mifflin Harcourt
Who Pushed Humpty?	K	TL	250+	Literacy 2000	Rigby
Who Put That Hair in My Toothbrush?	V	RF	250+	Spinelli, Jerry	Little, Brown & Co.
Who Put the Butter in Butterfly?	Y	I	250+	Feldman, David	Harper Collins
Who Reads?	B	I	25	Teacher's Choice Series	Pearson Learning Group
Who Really Killed Cock Robin?	U	RF	250+	George, Jean Craighead	HarperTrophy
Who Rides the Bus?	C	RF	19	Little Celebrations	Pearson Learning Group
Who Sank the Boat?	K	F	219	Allen, Pamela	Coward
Who Says?	D	F	36	My First Reader	Grolier Press
Who Says?	C	I	49	Twig	Wright Group/McGraw Hill
Who Shot the Movies?	T	I	250+	The News	Richard C. Owen
Who Shot the President?: The Death of John F. Kennedy	P	I	250+	Donnelly, Judy	Random House
Who Should...?	F	RF	149	InfoTrek	ETA Cuisenaire
Who Spilled the Beans?	E	F	87	Story Basket	Wright Group/McGraw Hill
Who Stole the Cookies?	F	F	153	All Aboard Reading	Grosset & Dunlap
Who Stole the Fish?	H	F	250+	Cambridge Reading	Pearson Learning Group
Who Stole the Tiger's Eye?	Q	F	250+	Sunshine	Wright Group/McGraw Hill
Who Stole the Wizard of Oz?	P	RF	250+	Avi	Alfred A. Knopf
Who the Man	X	RF	250+	Lynch, Chris	HarperCollins
Who Took Our Cake?	E	RF	98	Rigby Focus	Rigby
Who Took the Cake?	C	RF	32	First Stories	Pacific Learning
Who Took the Cookies from the Cookie Jar?	D	F	81	Learn to Read	Creative Teaching Press
Who Took the Farmer's Hat?	I	F	340	Nodset, Joan	Scholastic
Who Took the Teacher's Scissors?	F	F	175	Springboard	Wright Group/McGraw Hill
Who Uses These Tools?	B	I	23	Twig	Wright Group/McGraw Hill
Who Wants a Ride?	I	RF	214	Bernard, Robin	Scholastic
Who Wants Arthur?	J	F	250+	Leveled Readers Language Support	Houghton Mifflin Harcourt
Who Wants One?	I	F	212	Serfozo, Mary	Macmillan
Who Wants to Live in My House?	D	RF	60	Book Bank	Wright Group/McGraw Hill
Who Wants to See the Doctor?	F	I	116	Adventures in Reading	Pearson Learning Group
Who Was Albert Einstein?	R	B	250+	Who Was...?	Grosset & Dunlap
Who Was Ben Franklin?	S	B	250+	Fradin, Dennis Brindell	Grossett & Dunlap
Who Was Betsy Ross?	M	B	250+	Rosen Real Readers	Rosen Publishing Group
Who Was Harriet Tubman?	R	B	250+	Who Was...?	Grosset & Dunlap
Who Was Harry Houdini?	R	B	250+	Who Was...?	Grosset & Dunlap
Who Was Helen Keller?	Q	B	250+	Who Was...?	Grossett & Dunlap
Who Was Johnny Appleseed?	Q	B	250+	Who Was...?	Grossett & Dunlap
Who Was Marco Polo?	R	B	250+	Who Was...?	Grosset & Dunlap
Who Was Marjorie Harris Carr?	O	B	597	Leveled Readers Science	Houghton Mifflin Harcourt
Who Was Paul Revere?	M	B	250+	Rosen Real Readers	Rosen Publishing Group
Who Was Poor Richard? Colonials to Remember	V	I	2615	Independent Readers Social Studies	Houghton Mifflin Harcourt
Who Wears This Hat?	B	I	42	Windmill Books	Wright Group/McGraw Hill
Who Wears This Hat?	H	I	139	Windows on Literacy	National Geographic
Who Were the Beatles?	R	B	250+	Who Was...?	Grosset & Dunlap
Who Were the First People?	R	I	250+	Usborne Starting Point History	EDC Publishing

* Collection of short stories
# Graphic text

W

TITLE	LEVEL	GENRE	WORD COUNT	AUTHOR / SERIES	PUBLISHER / DISTRIBUTOR
Who Were the Romans?	R	I	250+	Usborne Starting Point History	EDC Publishing
Who Were the Vikings?	R	I	250+	Usborne Starting Point History	EDC Publishing
Who Were the Wright Brothers?	W	B	3260	Vocabulary Readers	Houghton Mifflin Harcourt
Who Were the Wright Brothers?	W	B	3260	Vocabulary Readers/CA	Houghton Mifflin Harcourt
Who Will Be My Friends?	F	RF	205	Hoff, Syd	HarperTrophy
Who Will Be My Mother?	E	F	156	Story Box	Wright Group/McGraw Hill
Who Will Help Me?	C	RF	53	Home Connection Collection	Rigby
Who Will Help?	B	RF	20	Carousel Readers	Pearson Learning Group
Who Will Help?	D	TL	93	Learn to Read	Creative Teaching Press
Who Will Help?	F	RF	74	New Way Red	Steck-Vaughn
Who Will Look Out for Danny?	S	RF	250+	Action Packs	Rigby
Who Will Marry Maisie?	G	F	250+	Rigby Rocket	Rigby
Who Will Use This?	H	I	154	Rigby Literacy	Rigby
Who Will Win the Race?	D	RF	53	Sunshine	Wright Group/McGraw Hill
Who Will Win?	H	RF	234	In Step Readers	Rigby
Who Works at the Beach?	G	I	102	Windows on Literacy	National Geographic
Who Works at the Supermarket?	K	I	325	Springboard	Wright Group/McGraw Hill
Who Works at the Zoo?	D	I	31	Windows on Literacy	National Geographic
Who Works Here?	D	I	57	Questions & Answers	Pearson Learning Group
Who You Are on the Inside	G	I	126	Shutterbug Books	Steck-Vaughn
Who?	E	F	46	Storyteller-Setting Sun	Wright Group/McGraw Hill
Whole Days Outdoors	O	B	250+	Meet the Author	Richard C. Owen
Whole World in One City, A	O	RF	1185	Reading Street	Pearson
Who'll Hold the Baby?	F	RF	181	Voyages	SRA/McGraw Hill
Whoops	I	F	250+	Supersonics	Rigby
Whoops!	E	RF	49	Little Celebrations	Pearson Learning Group
Whoops!	E	RF	147	Rigby Rocket	Rigby
Whoops! It Works!	O	I	250+	Lopez, Orlando	Pearson Learning Group
Whoosh! The Story of Snowboarding	M	I	250+	Literacy by Design	Rigby
Who's a Pest?	J	F	250+	Bonsall, Crosby	HarperTrophy
Who's Afraid of Shadows?	I	RF	219	Talking Point Series	Pearson Learning Group
Who's Afraid of the Big, Bad Bully?	K	RF	250+	Slater, Teddy	Scholastic
Who's Afraid of the Dark?	I	RF	250+	Bonsall, Crosby	HarperTrophy
Who's Afraid?	I	RF	165	Reading Unlimited	Pearson Learning Group
Who's at School?	A	I	36	Rosen Real Readers	Rosen Publishing Group
Who's Behind the Door at My House?	G	RF	184	Salmon, Michael	Steck-Vaughn
Who's Behind the Door at My School?	G	RF	187	Salmon, Michael	Steck-Vaughn
Who's Coming for a Ride?	B	F	25	Literacy 2000	Rigby
Who's Going to Lick the Bowl?	C	RF	18	Story Box	Wright Group/McGraw Hill
Who's Hiding There?	I	RF	242	Pair-It Books	Steck-Vaughn
Who's Hiding?	D	I	51	Learn to Read	Creative Teaching Press
Who's Hiding?	F	F	26	Onishi, Satoru	Kane/Miller Book Publishers
Who's in Love with Arthur?	M	F	250+	Brown, Marc	Little, Brown & Co.
Who's in the Jungle?	F	I	116	Ready Readers	Pearson Learning Group
Who's in the Nest?	E	F	75	Start to Read	School Zone
Who's in the Shed?	I	F	202	Literacy Tree	Rigby
Who's Looking After the Baby?	H	RF	127	Foundations	Wright Group/McGraw Hill
Who's That Stepping on Plymouth Rock?	R	HF	250+	Fritz, Jean	Putnam/Penguin
Who's the Alien?	M	SF	250+	Rigby Gigglers	Rigby
Who's the Boss?	J	F	647	Jasper the Cat	Pioneer Valley
Who's There?	B	F	49	Bookshop	Mondo
Who's There?	E	F	92	Story Box	Wright Group/McGraw Hill
Whose Birthday Is It Today?	C	RF	50	Book Bank	Wright Group/McGraw Hill

W

* Collection of short stories
\# Graphic text

TITLE	LEVEL	GENRE	WORD COUNT	AUTHOR / SERIES	PUBLISHER / DISTRIBUTOR
Whose Bones?	B	I	28	Fernandez, Queta	Scholastic
Whose Ears Are These?: A Look at Animal Ears - Short, Flat, and Floppy	M	I	250+	Whose Is It? Science	Picture Window Books
Whose Egg Is This?	E	F	99	Story Steps	Rigby
Whose Eggs Are These?	E	RF	125	Sunshine	Wright Group/McGraw Hill
Whose Eyes Are These?: A Look at Animal Eyes - Big, Round, and Narrow	M	I	250+	Whose Is It? Science	Picture Window Books
Whose Feet Are These? A Look at Hooves, Paws, and Claws	M	I	250+	Whose Is It? Science	Picture Window Books
Whose Footprints?	D	I	125	Lighthouse	Rigby
Whose Forest Is It?	C	RF	45	Learn to Read	Creative Teaching Press
Whose Hooves?	I	I	132	Gear Up!	Wright Group/McGraw Hill
Whose Legs Are These?: A Look at Animal Legs - Kicking, Running, and Hopping	M	I	250+	Whose Is It? Science	Picture Window Books
Whose List Is This?	C	F	14	Little Celebrations	Pearson Learning Group
Whose Mouse Are You?	H	F	98	Kraus, Robert	Macmillan
Whose Mouth Is This?: A Look at Bills, Suckers, and Tubes	M	I	250+	Whose Is It? Science	Picture Window Books
Whose Nose Is This?: A Look at Beaks, Snouts, and Trunks	M	I	250+	Whose Is It? Science	Picture Window Books
Whose Shoes?	K	RF	250+	Sunshine	Wright Group/McGraw Hill
Whose Shoes?	D	I	84	Twig	Wright Group/McGraw Hill
Whose Side Are You On?	K	TL	250+	Cisco, Cheyenne	Sadlier-Oxford
Whose Side Are You On?	Q	RF	250+	Moore, Emily	Bantam
Whose Skin Is This?: A Look at Animal Skin - Scaly, Furry, and Prickly	M	I	250+	Whose Is It? Science	Picture Window Books
Whose Tail Is This?: A Look at Tails - Swishing, Wiggling, and Rattling	M	I	250+	Whose Is It? Science	Picture Window Books
Whose Tracks?	B	I	14	Little Celebrations	Pearson Learning Group
Whose Way Today?	M	RF	683	Leveled Readers	Houghton Mifflin Harcourt
Why Animals Never Got Fire: A Story of the Coeur d'Alene Indians	J	TL	237	Books for Young Learners	Richard C. Owen
Why Bananas Are Yellow and Bent	Q	F	4391	Take Two Books	Wright Group/ McGraw Hill
Why Bear Sleeps All Winter	L	TL	647	Leveled Readers	Houghton Mifflin Harcourt
Why Bears Have Short Tails	I	TL	250+	Rigby Rocket	Rigby
Why Bears Have Short Tails, A Norwegian Tale	Q	F	1093	Leveled Readers	Houghton Mifflin Harcourt
Why Can't I Fly?	G	F	449	Gelman, Rita	Scholastic
Why Caterpillars Become Butterflies	H	F	198	Gear Up!	Wright Group/McGraw Hill
Why Cats Hunt at Night	H	TL	288	Rigby Rocket	Rigby
Why Cats Wash After Dinner	I	TL	128	Pacific Literacy	Pacific Learning
Why Coyote Howls at Night	K	TL	274	Little Books	Sadlier-Oxford
Why Coyote Howls at Night	Q	TL	250+	Moore, Emily	Farrar, Straus and Giroux
Why Coyote Howls at the Moon	K	TL	250+	Literacy by Design	Rigby
Why Crocodiles Live in Rivers	J	TL	415	Sunshine	Wright Group/McGraw Hill
Why Cry?	I	I	121	Sunshine	Wright Group/McGraw Hill
Why Did the Chicken Cross the Road?	H	F	200+	Reed, Janet	Scholastic
Why Did They Come?	N	I	157	Windows on Literacy	National Geographic
Why Do Birds Sing?	N	I	250+	Why In the World?	Capstone Press
Why Do Elephants Wear Hats?	J	F	115	O'Toole, Mary	Pearson Learning Group
Why Do I Feel Safe?	D	I	61	Questions & Answers	Pearson Learning Group
Why Do I Need to Know When?	G	RF	198	Visions	Wright Group/McGraw Hill
Why Do Worms Come Up When It Rains?	I	I	202	Seedlings	Continental Press
Why Does It Rain?	N	I	1571	On My Own Science	Lerner Publications
Why Does It Work?	Y	I	2160	Independent Readers Science	Houghton Mifflin Harcourt

W

TITLE	LEVEL	GENRE	WORD COUNT	AUTHOR / SERIES	PUBLISHER / DISTRIBUTOR
Why Don't You Get a Horse, Sam Adams?	R	B	250+	Fritz, Jean	G.P. Putnam's Sons
Why Elephants Have Long Noses	G	TL	175	Literacy 2000	Rigby
Why German Immigrants Came to America	S	I	250+	On Deck	Rigby
Why I Like Laura	G	RF	193	Phonics and Friends	Hampton-Brown
Why Irish Immigrants Came to America	S	I	250+	On Deck	Rigby
Why Islands Don't Swim	J	F	250+	Rigby Rocket	Rigby
Why Isn't Pluto a Planet?	N	I	250+	Why In the World?	Capstone Press
Why Italian Immigrants Came to America	S	I	250+	On Deck	Rigby
Why Japanese Immigrants Came to America	S	I	250+	On Deck	Rigby
Why Me?	U	RF	250+	Power Up!	Steck-Vaughn
Why Mexican Immigrants Came to America	S	I	250+	On Deck	Rigby
Why Mosquitoes Buzz in People's Ears	N	TL	250+	Aardema, Verna	Scholastic
Why Night Follows Day	I	TL	169	Gear Up!	Wright Group/McGraw Hill
Why Not?	G	RF	167	Voyages	SRA/McGraw Hill
Why People Move	K	I	250+	People, Spaces & Places	Rand McNally
Why Polar Bears Like Snow . . . and Flamingos Don't	O	I	250+	Navigators Science Series	Benchmark Education
Why Quincy Couldn't Quack	J	F	522	Pair-It Turn and Learn	Steck-Vaughn
Why Rabbits Have Long Ears	L	TL	250+	Literacy 2000	Rigby
Why Rabbit's Tail Is Short	G	TL	296	Leveled Readers	Houghton Mifflin Harcourt
Why the Bear's Tail Is Short	J	TL	431	Sunshine	Wright Group/McGraw Hill
Why the Frog Has Big Eyes	G	TL	132	Green Light Readers	Harcourt
Why the Kangaroo Hops	K	TL	391	Sunshine	Wright Group/McGraw Hill
Why the Leopard Has Spots	L	TL	250+	Pair-It Books	Steck-Vaughn
Why the Moon Is Ivory	N	TL	250+	On Our Way to English	Rigby
Why the Ocean Is Salty	Q	TL	250+	Leonhardt, Alice	Steck-Vaughn
Why the Rooster Crows at Sunrise	K	TL	250+	Sunshine	Wright Group/McGraw Hill
Why the Sea Is Salty	L	TL	250+	Literacy 2000	Rigby
Why the Turtle Does Not Fly: A South Pacific Folktale	K	TL	571	Springboard	Wright Group/McGraw Hill
Why There Are Shooting Stars	K	TL	362	Pacific Literacy	Pacific Learning
Why Vietnamese Immigrants Came to America	S	I	250+	On Deck	Rigby
Why We Have Thanksgiving	F	HF	470	Easy Stories	Norwood House Press
Why We Measure	K	I	178	Spyglass Books	Compass Point Books
Why We Measure	D	I	88	Yellow Umbrella Books	Red Brick Learning
Why We Need Trees	T	I	2072	Vocabulary Readers	Houghton Mifflin Harcourt
Why We Need Trees	T	I	2072	Vocabulary Readers/CA	Houghton Mifflin Harcourt
Why Write?	D	I	47	Moreton, Daniel; Berger, Samantha	Scholastic
Why?	D	I	68	Twig	Wright Group/McGraw Hill
Wibble Wobble, Albatross!	H	I	101	Pacific Literacy	Pacific Learning
Wibble-Wobble	H	RF	263	Storyteller-Night Crickets	Wright Group/McGraw Hill
Wicked Pirates, The	I	F	226	Sunshine	Wright Group/McGraw Hill
Wicked Weather	R	I	250+	Explorer Books-Pathfinder	National Geographic
Wicked Weather	Q	I	250+	Explorer Books-Pioneer	National Geographic
Wide Awake!	H	F	289	Leveled Literacy Intervention/Blue System	Heinemann
Wide Window, The	V	F	250+	Snicket, Lemony	Scholastic
Wide-mouthed Frog, The	E	F	121	Literacy 2000	Rigby
Widget	J	F	346	McFarland, Lyn, Rossiter, and James	Farrar, Straus, and Giroux
Wig for Pig, A	D	F	52	Leveled Readers	Houghton Mifflin Harcourt
Wiggle and Giggle	H	RF	163	Cambridge Reading	Pearson Learning Group
Wigglebottom	G	RF	134	Cambridge Reading	Pearson Learning Group

W

* Collection of short stories
\# Graphic text

TITLE	LEVEL	GENRE	WORD COUNT	AUTHOR / SERIES	PUBLISHER / DISTRIBUTOR
Wiggling Worms at Work	O	I	250+	Pfeffer, Wendy	Scholastic
Wiggly Tooth, The	G	RF	148	Gear Up!	Wright Group/McGraw Hill
Wiggly Worm	G	F	115	Literacy 2000	Rigby
Wiggly, Jiggly, Joggly, Tooth, A	E	RF	61	Little Celebrations	Pearson Learning Group
Wiggly-Jiggly Line, The	I	F	128	Book Bank	Wright Group/McGraw Hill
Wilamina and the Weather Conditions	M	F	250+	Take Two Books	Wright Group/McGraw Hill
Wilbert Took a Walk	H	F	216	Ready Readers	Pearson Learning Group
*Wilbur's Wild Ride and Other Stories	E	RF	164	Story Steps	Rigby
Wild Adaptations	N	I	250+	Bridger, Maggie	Houghton Mifflin Harcourt
Wild Adaptations	P	I	924	Independent Readers Science	Houghton Mifflin Harcourt
Wild and Wooly Mammoths	P	I	250+	Aliki	HarperCollins
Wild Animal, A	J	RF	809	The Fawn	Pioneer Valley
Wild Animals	P	I	250+	Animals Are Amazing	Carus Publishing Company
Wild Animals	A	I	28	Belle River Readers	Belle River Readers, Inc.
Wild Babies	O	I	250+	Simon, Seymour	HarperCollins
Wild Baby Animals	N	I	250+	Little Celebrations	Pearson Learning Group
Wild Bear	A	I	21	Pacific Literacy	Pacific Learning
*Wild Bird and Other Stories of Adventure	O	RF	250+	Belcher, Angie	Pacific Learning
Wild Cat Guide, The	M	I	250+	Lighthouse	Rigby
Wild Cats	Q	I	250+	Leonhardt, Alice	Steck-Vaughn
Wild Cats	N	I	250+	Wonder World	Wright Group/McGraw Hill
Wild Crayons	J	F	270	Story Box	Wright Group/McGraw Hill
Wild Culpepper Cruise, The	O	RF	250+	Paulsen, Gary	Bantam
Wild Easts and the Wild West, The	K	RF	250+	Storyteller-Shooting Stars	Wright Group/McGraw Hill
Wild Girl & Gran	Q	RF	1560	Gregory, Nan	Northern Lights Books for Children
Wild Horses	R	I	250+	Action Packs	Rigby
Wild Horses	M	I	485	Gear Up!	Wright Group/ McGraw Hill
Wild Nature	M	I	340	Gear Up!	Wright Group/ McGraw Hill
Wild Planet	T	I	250+	InfoQuest	Rigby
Wild Ponies	R	I	250+	Explorer Books-Pathfinder	National Geographic
Wild Ponies	P	I	250+	Explorer Books-Pioneer	National Geographic
Wild Rabbits	J	I	405	Sails	Rigby
Wild Race in the Sun, A	S	RF	250+	Sails	Rigby
Wild Ride	N	RF	250+	Girlz Rock!	Mondo
Wild Rides: Amusement Parks Around the World	S	I	250+	Explore More	Wright Group/McGraw Hill
Wild Swans, The	L	TL	754	Tales from Hans Andersen	Wright Group/McGraw Hill
Wild Turkeys	O	I	1435	Early Bird Nature Books	Lerner Publications
Wild Weather	V	I	2411	Leveled Readers Science	Houghton Mifflin Harcourt
Wild Weather	T	I	2277	Reading Street	Pearson
Wild Weather	K	I	187	Rigby Focus	Rigby
Wild Weather, Tall Tales	M	F	321	Vocabulary Readers	Houghton Mifflin Harcourt
Wild Wet Wellington Wind	I	RF	104	Pacific Literacy	Pacific Learning
Wild Wicked Winifred and Horrible Hank	L	F	250+	Popcorn	Sundance
Wild Wicked Winifred and the Pirates	L	F	250+	Popcorn	Sundance
Wild Wicked Winifred and the Sea Serpent	L	F	250+	Popcorn	Sundance
Wild Wicked Winifred and the Treasure Map	L	F	250+	Popcorn	Sundance
Wild Willie and King Kyle, Detectives	N	F	250+	Joosse, Barbara M.	Bantam
Wild Wind, The	H	F	246	Story Box	Wright Group/McGraw Hill
Wild Winds and Thunderclouds	R	I	250+	Explore More	Wright Group/McGraw Hill
Wild World of Sports	S	I	250+	Boldprint	Steck-Vaughn
Wild, Wet and Windy	S	I	250+	WorldScapes	ETA Cuisenaire
Wild, Wild Wolves	M	I	250+	Milton, Joyce	Random House

* Collection of short stories
# Graphic text

W

TITLE	LEVEL	GENRE	WORD COUNT	AUTHOR / SERIES	PUBLISHER / DISTRIBUTOR
Wild, Wooly Child, The	J	F	315	Read Alongs	Rigby
Wilde Street Club and Molly, The	M	RF	965	Sunshine	Wright Group/McGraw Hill
Wilde Street Club and the Duck Man, The	M	RF	1057	Sunshine	Wright Group/McGraw Hill
Wilderness Challenge	U	I	250+	WorldScapes	ETA Cuisenaire
Wilderness Road, 1775, The	V	I	250+	Let Freedom Ring	Capstone Press
Wilderness Road, The	Q	I	250+	On Deck	Rigby
Wilderness Talk	Q	RF	250+	Pair-It Books	Steck-Vaughn
Wildfire!	R	I	1323	Vocabulary Readers	Houghton Mifflin Harcourt
Wildfire!	R	I	1323	Vocabulary Readers/CA	Houghton Mifflin Harcourt
Wildfires	O	I	250+	A True Book	Children's Press
Wildlife	J	I	250+	Independent Readers Science	Houghton Mifflin Harcourt
Wildlife	J	I	145	Independent Readers Social Studies	Houghton Mifflin Harcourt
Wildlife Buffet, A	J	RF	373	Reading Street	Pearson
Wildlife Detectives	T	I	250+	Connectors	Pacific Learning
Wildlife Helpers	G	I	132	Twig	Wright Group/McGraw Hill
Wildlife on Film - Telling a Story	T	I	250+	Connectors	Pacific Learning
Wildlife Photographer Frank Greenway	T	I	250+	iOpeners	Pearson Learning Group
Wildlife Watching	O	I	250+	Wonder World	Wright Group/McGraw Hill
Wilfrid Laurier	X	B	250+	The Canadians	Fitzhenry & Whiteside
Will and Orv	N	HF	1505	On My Own History	Lerner Publications
Will and Squill	K	F	501	Clark, Emma Chichester	Carolrhoda Books
Will It Float?	C	I	43	Gear Up!	Wright Group/McGraw Hill
Will It Rain on the Parade?	H	RF	102	Wonder World	Wright Group/McGraw Hill
Will on a Jet	E	RF	53	Reading Street	Pearson
Will Power	I	RF	250+	Rigby Literacy	Rigby
Will Rogers	O	B	250+	Schott, Jane A.	Carolrhoda Books
Will Smith: The Funny, Funky, and Confident Fresh Prince	R	B	250+	High Five Reading	Red Brick Learning
Will to Survive, The	U	I	250+	Power Up!	Steck-Vaughn
Will We Miss Them? Endangered Species	N	I	250+	Wright, Alexandra	Charlesbridge
Will We See Animals?	E	I	86	Reading Street	Pearson
Will You Play With Me?	D	RF	84	Book Bus	Creative Edge
Will You Play With Me?	E	RF	149	On Our Way to English	Rigby
Will You Play with Us?	D	RF	62	Bookshop	Mondo
Will You Play?	D	F	96	Sun Sprouts	ETA Cuisenaire
Will You Sign Here, John Hancock?	T	B	250+	Fritz, Jean	Scholastic
William Bradford and Plymouth: A Colony Grows	R	I	250+	The Library of the Pilgrims	Rosen Publishing Group
William Henry Harrison	U	B	250+	Profiles of the Presidents	Compass Point Books
William Henry Harrison: Ninth President	R	B	250+	Getting to Know the U.S. Presidents	Children's Press
William Howard Taft	U	B	250+	Profiles of the Presidents	Compass Point Books
William Howard Taft: Twenty-seventh President	R	B	250+	Getting to Know the U.S. Presidents	Children's Press
William Jefferson Clinton	U	B	250+	Profiles of the Presidents	Compass Point Books
William McKinley	U	B	250+	Profiles of the Presidents	Compass Point Books
William McKinley: Twenty-fifth President	R	B	250+	Getting to Know the U.S. Presidents	Children's Press
William Penn	T	B	250+	Amazing Americans	Wright Group/McGraw Hill
William Penn	V	B	2200	Independent Readers Social Studies	Houghton Mifflin Harcourt
William Penn: A Life of Tolerance	O	B	584	Pull Ahead Books	Lerner Publications

W

* Collection of short stories
# Graphic text

TITLE	LEVEL	GENRE	WORD COUNT	AUTHOR / SERIES	PUBLISHER / DISTRIBUTOR
William Penn: Founder of the Pennsylvania Colony	V	B	250+	Let Freedom Ring	Capstone Press
William Problem, The	S	RF	250+	Baker, Barbara	Puffin/Penguin
William Tell	I	TL	127	Jumbled Tumbled Tales & Rhymes	Rigby
William Tell: One Against an Empire	W	TL	4212	Graphic Myths and Legends	Lerner Publications
William, Where Are You?	F	F	239	Gerstein, Mordicai	Crown
William's Journal	N	HF	250+	Early Connections	Benchmark Education
Williams Sisters, The	J	I	318	Leveled Readers	Houghton Mifflin Harcourt
Williams Sisters, The	J	I	318	Leveled Readers/CA	Houghton Mifflin Harcourt
Williams Sisters, The	J	I	318	Leveled Readers/TX	Houghton Mifflin Harcourt
William's Skateboard	G	RF	100	Windmill Books	Wright Group/McGraw Hill
William's Wheelchair Race	J	RF	279	Sunshine	Wright Group/McGraw Hill
Williamsburg	V	I	250+	Cornerstones of Freedom	Children's Press
Williamsburg	U	I	250+	We The People	Compass Point Books
Willie Covan Loved to Dance!	T	B	250+	Bookshop	Mondo
Willie Mays	J	B	380	Leveled Readers	Houghton Mifflin Harcourt
Willie Mays	J	B	380	Leveled Readers/CA	Houghton Mifflin Harcourt
Willie Mays	J	B	380	Leveled Readers/TX	Houghton Mifflin Harcourt
Willie McLean and the Civil War Surrender	P	HF	1997	On My Own History	Lerner Publications
Willie the Slowpoke	G	F	125	First Start	Troll Associates
Willie's Wonderful Pet	I	RF	315	Cebulash, Mel	Scholastic
Williwaw!	V	RF	250+	Bodett, Tom	Alfred A. Knopf
Willow Pattern, The	P	TL	250+	Action Packs	Rigby
Willows and Whirligigs	V	I	250+	Rigby Literacy	Rigby
Willy the Helper	D	RF	79	Little Readers	Houghton Mifflin Harcourt
Willy the Scrub	O	RF	4190	McEwan, Jamie	Darby Creek Publishing
Willy the Wizard	C	F	42	Learn to Read	Creative Teaching Press
Willy's Hats	E	RF	65	Stewart, Josie.; Salem, Lynn	Continental Press
Wilma Mankiller	P	B	250+	Lowery, Linda	Carolrhoda Books
Wilma Rudolph	N	B	204	First Biographies	Capstone Press
Wilma Rudolph	N	B	250+	On My Own Biography	Lerner Publications
Wilma Unlimited: How Wilma Rudolph Became the World's Fastest Woman	Q	B	250+	Krull, Kathleen	Scholastic
Wilma's Wagon	D	RF	48	Ready Readers	Pearson Learning Group
Win a Prize!	F	RF	235	PM Math Readers	Rigby
Wind	E	RF	89	Ready to Read	Pearson Learning Group
Wind	Q	I	250+	Theme Sets	National Geographic
Wind	L	I	430	Vocabulary Readers	Houghton Mifflin Harcourt
Wind	L	I	430	Vocabulary Readers/CA	Houghton Mifflin Harcourt
Wind and Storms	K	I	868	Sunshine	Wright Group/McGraw Hill
Wind and Sun	G	TL	170	Literacy 2000	Rigby
Wind and Sun	I	TL	238	Sunshine	Wright Group/McGraw Hill
*Wind and the Sun and Other Stories, The	J	F	250+	New Way Orange	Steck-Vaughn
Wind and the Sun, The	I	TL	350	Leveled Literacy Intervention/ Blue System	Heinemann
Wind and the Sun, The	K	TL	399	Leveled Readers	Houghton Mifflin Harcourt
Wind and the Sun, The	I	TL	189	Pair-It Turn and Learn	Steck-Vaughn
Wind and the Sun, The: An Aesop Fable	G	TL	234	Rigby Literacy	Rigby
Wind and Water: Two Great Powers	U	I	2567	Independent Readers Social Studies	Houghton Mifflin Harcourt
Wind at Work, The	Q	I	250+	Literacy by Design	Rigby
Wind Blew, The	J	RF	169	Hutchins, Pat	Puffin/Penguin
Wind Blows Strong, The	E	RF	114	Sunshine	Wright Group/McGraw Hill

* Collection of short stories
# Graphic text

W

TITLE	LEVEL	GENRE	WORD COUNT	AUTHOR / SERIES	PUBLISHER / DISTRIBUTOR
Wind Blows, The	B	RF	90	First Stories	Pacific Learning
Wind Blows, The	C	RF	38	Learn to Read	Creative Teaching Press
Wind Eagle, The	K	RF	370	Wonders	Hampton-Brown
Wind in the Door, A	V	F	250+	L'Engle, Madeleine	Bantam
Wind in the Pines	O	I	919	Leveled Readers/TX	Houghton Mifflin Harcourt
Wind Instruments	M	I	391	Vocabulary Readers	Houghton Mifflin Harcourt
Wind Instruments	M	I	391	Vocabulary Readers/CA	Houghton Mifflin Harcourt
Wind Power	V	I	250+	Energy at Work	Capstone Press
Wind Power	J	I	103	Pacific Literacy	Pacific Learning
Wind Power	I	I	116	Windows on Literacy	National Geographic
Wind Surfing	D	RF	224	Sunshine	Wright Group/McGraw Hill
Wind That Would Not Blow, The	M	TL	250+	Kunari, Anna	Hampton-Brown
Wind, The	D	I	82	Big Cat	Pacific Learning
Wind, The	E	I	36	Discovery Links	Newbridge
Wind, The	C	I	46	Gear Up!	Wright Group/McGraw Hill
Wind, The	L	I	445	Leveled Readers	Houghton Mifflin Harcourt
Wind, The	L	I	445	Leveled Readers/CA	Houghton Mifflin Harcourt
Wind, The	L	I	445	Leveled Readers/TX	Houghton Mifflin Harcourt
Wind, The	E	I	64	Pacific Literacy	Pacific Learning
Wind, The	K	I	179	Spyglass Books	Compass Point Books
Wind, The	F	I	84	Voyages	SRA/McGraw Hill
Wind, The	D	RF	34	Wonder World	Wright Group/McGraw Hill
Wind, Water and Ice	R	I	1829	Independent Readers Science	Houghton Mifflin Harcourt
Windmill, The	T	F	250+	Book Blazers	ETA Cuisenaire
Windmills	S	I	783	Independent Readers Science	Houghton Mifflin Harcourt
Window to the Past	O	F	990	Springboard	Wright Group/ McGraw Hill
Window, The	V	RF	250+	Ingold, Jeanette	Harcourt Trade
Windows to the Past	N	F	749	Gear Up!	Wright Group/ McGraw Hill
Windows to the Past	R	I	943	Reading Street	Pearson
Windy	B	I	27	Weather	Lerner Publications
Windy Day, A	E	I	53	Pebble Books	Capstone Press
Windy Day, A	E	I	85	Weather	Lerner Publishing
Windy Ways	G	I	97	Independent Readers Science	Houghton Mifflin Harcourt
Winesburg, Ohio	Z+	RF	250+	Anderson, Sherwood	Random House
Wing High, Goofah	Q	RF	250+	Literacy 2000	Rigby
Wing Nuts: Screwy Haiku	N	F	244	Janeczko, Paul & Lewis, J. Patrick	Little, Brown & Co.
Winged and Toothless: The Adventure of Pteranodon	N	I	250+	Dinosaur World	Picture Window Books
Winged Cat, The: A Tale of Ancient Egypt	U	TL	250+	Lattimore, Deborah Nourse	HarperCollins
Winging It	U	I	250+	iOpeners	Pearson Learning Group
Wingman	O	F	250+	Pinkwater, Daniel	Bantam
Wingman on Ice	Q	RF	250+	Christopher, Matt	Little, Brown & Co.
Wings	B	I	22	Animal Traits	Lerner Publications
Wings	W	I	250+	Boldprint	Steck-Vaughn
Wings	Q	F	250+	Brittain, Bill	HarperTrophy
Wings	F	I	109	Explorations	Eleanor Curtain Publishing
Wings	F	I	109	Explorations	Okapi Educational Materials
Wings	LB	I	14	KinderReaders	Rigby
Wings	M	F	250+	Myers, Christopher	Scholastic
Wings	A	I	24	Rigby Literacy	Rigby
Wings	A	I	20	Rigby StarQuest	Rigby
Wings	C	I	85	Sails	Rigby
Wings	W	TL	250+	Yolen, Jane; Nolan, Dennis	Harcourt Brace

* Collection of short stories
# Graphic text

W

TITLE	LEVEL	GENRE	WORD COUNT	AUTHOR / SERIES	PUBLISHER / DISTRIBUTOR
Wings for a Day	T	F	1842	Leveled Readers	Houghton Mifflin Harcourt
Wings!	D	I	95	Vocabulary Readers	Houghton Mifflin Harcourt
Wings!	D	I	95	Vocabulary Readers/CA	Houghton Mifflin Harcourt
Wings: A Fairy Tale	X	F	250+	Baker, E.D.	Bloomsbury Children's Books
Winking, Blinking, Wiggling, and Waggling	M	I	250+	DK Readers	DK Publishing
Winklepoo the Wicked	M	F	1614	Sunshine	Wright Group/McGraw Hill
Winner, The	J	RF	585	Gear Up!	Wright Group/McGraw Hill
Winner's Guide to Staying Fit, A	S	I	250+	Power Up!	Steck-Vaughn
Winning Combination, A	X	RF	2436	Leveled Readers	Houghton Mifflin Harcourt
Winning Combination, A	X	RF	2436	Leveled Readers/CA	Houghton Mifflin Harcourt
Winning Edge	U	I	250+	The News	Richard C. Owen
Winning Hit, The	G	RF	274	Leveled Readers	Houghton Mifflin Harcourt
Winning Hit, The	G	RF	274	Leveled Readers/CA	Houghton Mifflin Harcourt
Winning Hit, The	G	RF	274	Leveled Readers/TX	Houghton Mifflin Harcourt
Winning Team, A	X	RF	2418	Leveled Readers	Houghton Mifflin Harcourt
Winning Team, A	X	RF	2418	Leveled Readers/CA	Houghton Mifflin Harcourt
Winslow Homer, American Painter	N	I	348	Independent Readers Social Studies	Houghton Mifflin Harcourt
Winston Churchill	V	B	250+	Primary Source Readers	Teacher Created Materials
Winter	C	I	49	Carousel Readers	Pearson Learning Group
Winter	E	I	56	Discovery Links	Newbridge
Winter	C	I	54	Foundations	Wright Group/McGraw Hill
Winter	B	I	79	Leveled Readers	Houghton Mifflin Harcourt
Winter	B	I	79	Leveled Readers/CA	Houghton Mifflin Harcourt
Winter	B	I	79	Leveled Readers/TX	Houghton Mifflin Harcourt
Winter	I	I	240	Pebble Books	Capstone Press
Winter	D	RF	33	Reading Street	Pearson
Winter	E	I	58	Seasons	Lerner Publishing
Winter	H	I	172	Storyteller-Setting Sun	Wright Group/McGraw Hill
Winter Bed, A	E	RF	91	Reading Street	Pearson
Winter Days in the Big Woods	J	HF	250+	Wilder, Laura Ingalls	HarperCollins
Winter Fun	LB	RF	13	Teacher's Choice Series	Pearson Learning Group
Winter Hawk Star	W	RF	250+	Orca Sports	Orca Book Publishers
Winter Holidays	O	RF	1706	Reading Street	Pearson
Winter in Alaska	O	I	347	Vocabulary Readers	Houghton Mifflin Harcourt
Winter Is Here	D	I	55	Weinberger, Kimberly	Scholastic
Winter Is Here	E	I	24	Windows on Literacy	National Geographic
Winter on the Farm	J	HF	250+	Wilder, Laura Ingalls	HarperCollins
Winter on the Ice	L	F	506	PM Plus Story Books	Rigby
Winter Recess	D	RF	87	Emergent Books	Pioneer Valley
Winter Room, The	U	RF	250+	Paulsen, Gary	Bantam
Winter Sleep	C	F	92	Leveled Readers	Houghton Mifflin Harcourt
Winter Sleep	C	F	92	Leveled Readers/CA	Houghton Mifflin Harcourt
Winter Sleeps	F	RF	158	Reading Corners	Pearson Learning Group
Winter Solstice, The	Q	I	250+	Jackson, Ellen	Millbrook Press
Winter Sports: Fun on Ice and Snow	R	I	250+	Explore More	Wright Group/McGraw Hill
Winter Sunshine	N	I	250+	Wonder World	Wright Group/McGraw Hill
Winter Survival	O	I	250+	Literacy Tree	Rigby
Winter Vacation	A	RF	24	Leveled Readers	Houghton Mifflin Harcourt
Winter Vacation	A	F	24	Leveled Readers/CA	Houghton Mifflin Harcourt
Winter Wind, The	H	F	250+	Momentum Literacy Program	Troll Associates
Winter Wind, The	F	F	234	Springboard	Wright Group/McGraw Hill
Winter Wonderland, A	H	RF	230	Literacy by Design	Rigby

* Collection of short stories
# Graphic text

W

TITLE	LEVEL	GENRE	WORD COUNT	AUTHOR / SERIES	PUBLISHER / DISTRIBUTOR
Winter Woollies	K	I	289	Storyteller Nonfiction	Wright Group/McGraw Hill
Winter, Spring, Summer, Fall	F	RF	102	Appleton-Smith, Laura	Flyleaf Publishing
Winterdance: The Fine Madness of Running the Iditarod	W	B	250+	Paulsen, Gary	Harcourt Trade
Winter's Song	H	RF	233	Ready Readers	Pearson Learning Group
Wipeout	Q	RF	250+	West, J.	Stone Arch Books
Wired	U	RF	250+	Orca Currents	Orca Book Publishers
Wired World: A Short History of the Internet	U	I	1527	Leveled Readers Social Studies	Houghton Mifflin Harcourt
Wireless Technology	Z	I	6323	Cool Science	Lerner Publications
Wisconsin	T	I	250+	Hello U.S.A.	Lerner Publications
Wisconsin	R	I	250+	This Land Is Your Land	Compass Point Books
Wise Blackbird, The	I	F	507	Leveled Literacy Intervention/ Blue System	Heinemann
Wise Eyes Club, The	K	RF	537	Springboard	Wright Group/McGraw Hill
Wise Old Turtle, The	K	TL	250+	World Quest Adventures	World Quest Learning
*Wish Fish, The	P	TL	250+	Action Packs	Rigby
Wish Giver, The	T	F	250+	Brittain, Bill	HarperTrophy
Wish on a Unicorn	T	RF	250+	Hesse, Karen	Penguin Group
Wishes Don't Come True	M	RF	250+	Bookshop	Mondo
Wishing for a Horse	D	RF	105	Carousel Readers	Pearson Learning Group
Wishing for Fishing	H	RF	250+	Phonics Readers Plus	Steck-Vaughn
Wishing Shell, The	S	TL	250+	WorldScapes	ETA Cuisenaire
Wishy-Washy Day	E	F	65	Story Basket	Wright Group/McGraw Hill
Witch Hunt: It Happened in Salem Village	Q	I	250+	Krensky, Stephen	Random House
Witch of Blackbird Pond, The	W	HF	250+	Speare, Elizabeth George	Bantam
Witch of Clattering Shaws, The	X	F	250+	Aiken, Joan	Yearling
*Witch of Fourth Street, The	S	HF	250+	Levoy, Myron	Language for Learning Assoc.
Witchcraft of Salem Village, The	U	I	250+	Jackson, Shirley	Random House
Witches Don't Do Backflips	M	F	250+	Dadey, Debbie; Jones, Marcia Thornton	Scholastic
Witches of Worm, The	V	F	250+	Snyder, Zilpha K.	Random House
Witches, The	R	F	250+	Dahl, Roald	Penguin Group
Witch's Cat	P	F	250+	Chew, Ruth	Scholastic
Witch's Haircut, The	G	F	135	Windmill Books	Wright Group/McGraw Hill
With a Dance and a Roar	P	I	663	Leveled Readers	Houghton Mifflin Harcourt
With Courage: Seven Women Who Changed America	T	B	250+	Bookshop	Mondo
With Every Drop of Blood	Y	HF	250+	Collier, James Lincoln and Collier, Christopher	Laurel-Leaf Books
With Help From Abuelo	O	RF	2576	In Step Readers	Rigby
With My Mom and Dad	C	I	63	Early Connections	Benchmark Education
With Open Hands: A Story about Biddy Mason	R	B	8691	Creative Minds Biographies	Carolrhoda Books
Within Reach: My Everest Story	X	B	250+	Pfetzer, Mark & Galvin, Jack	Scholastic
Witness	Z	HF	250+	Hesse, Karen	Scholastic
Wiz	D	F	76	Voyages	SRA/McGraw Hill
Wizard and the Rainbow, The	K	F	250+	Sunshine	Wright Group/McGraw Hill
Wizard and Wart at Sea	J	F	250+	Smith, Janice Lee	HarperTrophy
Wizard Came to Visit, A	K	F	250+	Sunshine	Wright Group/McGraw Hill
Wizard of Earthsea, A	Z	F	250+	LeGuin, Ursula K.	Bantam
Wizard of Oz, The	U	F	250+	Baum, L. Frank	Scholastic
Wizard of Oz, The	L	TL	903	Hunia, Fran	Ladybird Books
Wizard of Sound: A Story About Thomas Edison, The	R	B	8084	Creative Minds Biographies	Carolrhoda Books

W

* Collection of short stories
# Graphic text

TITLE	LEVEL	GENRE	WORD COUNT	AUTHOR / SERIES	PUBLISHER / DISTRIBUTOR
Wizards Don't Need Computers	M	F	250+	Dadey, Debbie; Jones, Marcia Thornton	Scholastic
Wobbly Tooth, The	D	RF	102	Literacy 2000	Rigby
Wobbly Tooth, The	F	RF	74	Oxford Reading Tree	Oxford University Press
Wole Soyinka	X	B	1951	Leveled Readers Social Studies	Houghton Mifflin Harcourt
Wolf and the Kids, The	G	TL	241	Storyworlds	Heinemann Educational Books
Wolf and the Old Woman, The	I	TL	250+	Voyages	SRA/McGraw Hill
Wolf and the Seven Little Kids	L	TL	250+	Hunia, Fran	Ladybird Books
Wolf and the Seven Little Kids, The	J	TL	254	Literacy Tree	Rigby
Wolf Master	S	RF	250+	Storyteller- Whispering Pines	Wright Group/McGraw Hill
Wolf Song	J	RF	130	Books for Young Learners	Richard C. Owen
Wolf Stalker	T	RF	250+	Mysteries in Our National Parks	National Geographic
Wolf Talk	H	I	159	Instant Readers	Harcourt School Publishers
Wolf Who Cried Boy, The	M	F	250+	Hartman, Bob	Scholastic
Wolf, The	S	I	250+	Dahl, Michael	Red Brick Learning
Wolf, The	Z+	RF	250+	Herrick, Steven	Front Street
Wolfgang Amadeus Mozart: Musical Genius	N	B	250+	Rookie Biographies	Children's Press
Wolfman Sam	O	RF	250+	Levy, Elizabeth	HarperTrophy
Wolfmen Don't Hula Dance	M	RF	250+	Dadey, Debbie; Jones, Marcia Thornton	Scholastic
Wolf's Cake	I	F	250+	Sunshine	Wright Group/McGraw Hill
Wolf's Chicken Stew, The	J	F	250+	Leveled Readers Language Support	Houghton Mifflin Harcourt
Wolf's First Deer	M	RF	434	Book Bank	Wright Group/McGraw Hill
Wolverines	P	I	2089	Animal Scavengers	Lerner Publishing
Wolves	P	I	1805	Animal Predators	Lerner Publishing
Wolves	Q	I	250+	Literacy 2000	Rigby
Wolves	I	I	188	Pair-It Books	Steck-Vaughn
Wolves	N	I	250+	PM Animal Facts: Silver	Rigby
Wolves	I	I	233	Sails	Rigby
Wolves	E	I	68	Seedlings	Continental Press
Wolves	U	I	250+	The Untamed World	Steck-Vaughn
Wolves	F	I	132	Twig	Wright Group/McGraw Hill
Wolves	H	I	95	Woodland Animals	Capstone Press
Wolves Have Pups	M	I	250+	Animals and Their Young	Compass Point Books
Wolves of Willoughby Chase, The	V	HF	250+	Aiken, Joan	Bantam
Woman and the Tiny Bird, The	G	TL	198	PM Stars	Rigby
*Woman Hollering Creek and Other Stories	Z	RF	250+	Cisneros, Sandra	Random House
Woman Who Flummoxed the Fairies, The	O	TL	250+	Forest, Heather	Harcourt Trade
Woman Who Fooled the Fairies, The	K	TL	794	Big Cat	Pacific Learning
Woman Who Outshone the Sun, The	M	TL	250+	Martinez, Alejandro Cruz	Children's Press
Women at Work	G	I	112	Foundations	Wright Group/McGraw Hill
Women at Work in the West	Q	I	1428	Leveled Readers	Houghton Mifflin Harcourt
Women at Work in the West	Q	I	1428	Leveled Readers/CA	Houghton Mifflin Harcourt
Women in the Vietnam War	U	I	848	Independent Readers Social Studies	Houghton Mifflin Harcourt
*Women Inventors	O	B	250+	Blashfield, Jean	Red Brick Learning
Women Inventors	P	I	996	Leveled Readers Science	Houghton Mifflin Harcourt
Women of Courage	U	I	250+	Boldprint	Steck-Vaughn
Women of the American Revolution	U	B	250+	Bookshop	Mondo
Women of Valor	U	B	250+	Real Lives	Troll Associates
Women Pioneers in Medicine	T	I	2664	Independent Readers Science	Houghton Mifflin Harcourt
Women Pioneers of Medicine	R	B	2018	Leveled Readers Science	Houghton Mifflin Harcourt

* Collection of short stories
# Graphic text

W

TITLE	LEVEL	GENRE	WORD COUNT	AUTHOR / SERIES	PUBLISHER / DISTRIBUTOR
Women Who Dared	U	B	250+	Navigators Biography Series	Benchmark Education Company
Women Who Made a Difference	O	B	830	Reading Street	Pearson
Women Who Shaped the West	V	B	250+	Cornerstones of Freedom	Children's Press
Women Work for Change	Q	I	250+	Reading Expeditions	National Geographic
Women Writers: Voices from the 1800s	T	I	2535	Independent Readers Social Studies	Houghton Mifflin Harcourt
Women's Baseball League	W	I	2641	Vocabulary Readers	Houghton Mifflin Harcourt
Women's Baseball League	W	I	2641	Vocabulary Readers/CA	Houghton Mifflin Harcourt
Women's Baseball League	W	I	2641	Vocabulary Readers/TX	Houghton Mifflin Harcourt
Women's Movement, The	W	I	2439	Reading Street	Pearson
Women's Right to Vote	V	I	250+	Cornerstones of Freedom	Children's Press
Women's Suffrage Movement, 1848-1920, The	V	I	250+	Let Freedom Ring	Capstone Press
Women's Voting Rights	V	I	250+	Cornerstones of Freedom	Children's Press
Wonder Kid Meets the Evil Lunch Snatcher	M	RF	250+	Duncan, Lois	Little, Brown & Co.
Wonder of Bald Eagles, The	M	I	250+	Soar To Success	Houghton Mifflin Harcourt
Wonder of Our Solar System, The	S	I	250+	Science Readers	Teacher Created Materials
Wonder of Outer Space, The	S	I	250+	Science Readers	Teacher Created Materials
Wonder of the Winds, The	T	I	250+	Connectors	Pacific Learning
Wonder of Wolves, The	M	I	250+	Soar To Success	Houghton Mifflin Harcourt
Wonderer, The	M	RF	250+	Rigby Flying Colors	Rigby
Wonderful Alexander and the Catwings	N	F	250+	LeGuin, Ursula	Scholastic
Wonderful Ears	I	I	1017	Sunshine Science	Wright Group/McGraw Hill
Wonderful Eyes	M	I	1070	Sunshine Science	Wright Group/McGraw Hill
*Wonderful Sky Boat, The: And Other Native American Tales of the Southeast	S	TL	250+	Curry, Jane Louise	Simon & Schuster
*Wonderful Story of Henry Sugar, The: And Six More	U	F	250+	Dahl, Roald	Penguin Group
Wonderful Things	F	RF	98	Early Readers	Compass Point Books
Wonderful Water	C	I	33	Gear Up!	Wright Group/McGraw Hill
Wonderful Water Cycle, The	L	I	250+	On Our Way to English	Rigby
Wonderful Women of Science, The	T	B	2616	Reading Street	Pearson
Wonderful World of Birds, The	M	I	1180	Reading Street	Pearson
Wonderful World of Camouflage, The	U	I	1792	Vocabulary Readers	Houghton Mifflin Harcourt
Wonderful World of Camouflage, The	U	I	1792	Vocabulary Readers/CA	Houghton Mifflin Harcourt
Wonderful Worms	K	I	343	Rigby Flying Colors	Rigby
Wonders of the World	N	I	250+	Sunshine	Wright Group/McGraw Hill
Wonders of the World - Megastructures	T	I	250+	Connectors	Pacific Learning
Won't Take No for an Answer!	U	B	250+	Bookshop	Mondo
Wood	G	I	106	Materials	Lerner Publications
Wood	B	I	26	Twig	Wright Group/McGraw Hill
Wood	E	I	48	Windows on Literacy	National Geographic
Wood and Other Materials	G	I	97	Discovery World	Rigby
Wood Frog	O	I	250+	Life Cycles	Creative Teaching Press
Wood Stork Swamp	N	RF	250+	Orbit Double Takes	Pacific Learning
Woodcutter and the Bear, The: A Play	M	TL	250+	Rigby Literacy	Rigby
Wood-Hoopoe Willie	N	RF	250+	Kroll, Virginia	Charlesbridge
Woodland Desert People	O	I	250+	Literacy by Design	Rigby
Woodlanders Begin, The	M	F	250+	Woodland Mysteries	Wright Group/McGraw Hill
Woodpeckers	I	I	85	Pebble Books	Red Brick Learning
Woodrow Wilson	S	B	250+	Amazing Americans	Wright Group/McGraw Hill
Woodrow Wilson	S	B	3524	History Maker Bios	Lerner Publications
Woodrow Wilson	U	B	250+	Primary Source Readers	Teacher Created Materials
Woodrow Wilson	U	B	250+	Profiles of the Presidents	Compass Point Books

* Collection of short stories
# Graphic text

W

TITLE	LEVEL	GENRE	WORD COUNT	AUTHOR / SERIES	PUBLISHER / DISTRIBUTOR
Woodrow Wilson: Twenty-eighth President	R	B	250+	Getting to Know the U.S. Presidents	Children's Press
Woods, Irons, and Greens	R	I	250+	Wildcats	Wright Group/McGraw Hill
Woodsong	T	B	250+	Paulsen, Gary	Dell
Woody Guthrie	I	B	199	Leveled Readers Social Studies	Houghton Mifflin Harcourt
Woof!	A	F	42	Leveled Literacy Intervention/ Green System	Heinemann
Woof!	C	F	40	Literacy 2000	Rigby
Wool	M	I	660	Leveled Readers	Houghton Mifflin Harcourt
Wool	M	I	660	Leveled Readers/CA	Houghton Mifflin Harcourt
Wool	M	I	660	Leveled Readers/TX	Houghton Mifflin Harcourt
Wool	F	I	91	Sunshine	Wright Group/McGraw Hill
Wool from Sheep	K	I	531	Rigby Flying Colors	Rigby
Wool Keeps Me Warm	K	I	214	Windows on Literacy	National Geographic
Woolly Mammoth	I	I	132	Dinosaur and Prehistoric Animals	Capstone Press
Woolly Mammoths	N	I	1410	On My Own Science	Lerner Publications
Woolly Sally	I	RF	147	Pacific Literacy	Pacific Learning
Woolly, Woolly	E	F	136	Literacy 2000	Rigby
Woosh!	E	RF	124	Story Box	Wright Group/McGraw Hill
Word Eater, The	T	F	250+	Amato, Mary	Holiday House
Word Eater, The	T	F	250+	Dahl, Michael	Stone Arch Books
Word Evidence	S	I	250+	Forensic Crime Solvers	Capstone Press
Word Machine, The	D	F	33	Sunshine	Wright Group/McGraw Hill
Wordful Child, A	O	B	250+	Meet The Author	Richard C. Owen
Words	M	I	578	Pacific Literacy	Pacific Learning
Words	U	RF	250+	Paulsen, Gary	Penguin Group
Words Are Everywhere	E	I	46	Literacy 2000	Rigby
Words by Heart	U	HF	250+	Sebestyen, Ouida	Bantam Doubleday Dell
Words of Promise: A Story about James Weldon Johnson	S	B	8127	Creative Minds Biographies	Lerner Publications
Words of Stone	V	RF	250+	Henkes, Kevin	Penguin Group
Words: A Computer Lesson	F	F	45	Silly Millies	Millbrook Press
Wordsong	K	RF	192	DLM Literature Library	Wright Group/McGraw Hill
Work	Q	I	1746	Early Bird Energy Physics Books	Lerner Publishing
Work	A	I	17	On Our Way to English	Rigby
Work	C	RF	65	TOTTS	Tott Publications
Work Helicopter, The	I	F	250+	PM Plus Story Books	Rigby
Work It Out	Q	I	250+	Orbit Collections	Pacific Learning
Work of Leonardo Da Vinci, The	T	I	1810	Leveled Readers Science	Houghton Mifflin Harcourt
Work Together	A	F	21	Reading Street	Pearson
Work Vehicles	J	I	245	Windows on Literacy	National Geographic
Work We Do, The	K	I	250+	Spyglass Books	Compass Point Books
Worker Bees	E	I	65	Reading Street	Pearson
Workers	LB	F	16	KinderReaders	Rigby
Workers	C	I	41	Time for Kids	Teacher Created Materials
Worker's Tools, A	F	I	93	Discovery World	Rigby
Working	C	I	174	Instant Readers	Harcourt School Publishers
Working	G	I	174	Yellow Umbrella Books	Red Brick Learning
Working at a TV Station	O	I	250+	Working Here	Children's Press
Working at Home	B	I	28	Little Red Readers	Sundance
Working Cotton	N	RF	250+	Williams, Sherley Anne	Harcourt Trade
Working Dogs	L	I	266	Gear Up!	Wright Group/ McGraw Hill
Working for Dad	D	RF	31	Visions	Wright Group/McGraw Hill

* Collection of short stories
# Graphic text

W

TITLE	LEVEL	GENRE	WORD COUNT	AUTHOR / SERIES	PUBLISHER / DISTRIBUTOR
Working in Space	L	I	250+	The Solar System	Capstone Press
Working in the Park	E	RF	118	Leveled Readers	Houghton Mifflin Harcourt
Working in the Park	E	RF	118	Leveled Readers/CA	Houghton Mifflin Harcourt
Working in the Park	E	RF	118	Leveled Readers/TX	Houghton Mifflin Harcourt
Working on Water	L	I	250+	Home Connection Collection	Rigby
Working Then and Now	I	I	207	Then and Now	Lerner Publications
Working Together	C	I	50	Early Connections	Benchmark Education
Working Together	I	I	222	Rigby Focus	Rigby
Working Together	G	I	205	Yellow Umbrella Books	Red Brick Learning
Working with Animals	I	I	250+	Home Connection Collection	Rigby
Working with Electricity and Magnetism	V	I	250+	Navigators Science Series	Benchmark Education
Working with Metal	L	I	299	Rigby Focus	Rigby
Working with Others	M	I	314	Pull Ahead Books	Lerner Publications
Working With Plants	I	I	308	Rigby Flying Colors	Rigby
Working with Wood	P	I	250+	PM Extensions	Rigby
World According to Humphrey, The	S	F	250+	Birney, Betty G.	Puffin Books
World According to Kaley, The	S	RF	8551	Regan, Dian Curtis	Darby Creek Publishing
World Around Us, The	C	I	29	Little Red Readers	Sundance
World at His Fingertips: A Story About Louis Braille, The	R	B	8248	Creative Minds Biographies	Carolrhoda Books
World Beneath the Waves	T	I	250+	Navigators Math Series	Benchmark Education
World Beyond Earth, The Unmanned Explorers and Orbiters	T	I	250+	Connectors	Pacific Learning
World in a Supermarket, The	LB	I	24	Learn to Read	Creative Teaching Press
World in Grandfather's Hands, The	V	RF	250+	Strete, Craig Kee	Clarion
World in Your Kitchen, The	L	I	347	Independent Readers Social Studies	Houghton Mifflin Harcourt
World of Animals, The	U	I	250+	Science Readers	Teacher Created Materials
World of Ants	M	I	582	Vocabulary Readers	Houghton Mifflin Harcourt
World of Ants	M	I	582	Vocabulary Readers/CA	Houghton Mifflin Harcourt
World of Ants	M	I	582	Vocabulary Readers/TX	Houghton Mifflin Harcourt
World of Birds, A	B	I	49	Bookshop	Mondo
World of Birthdays, A	L	I	579	Gear Up!	Wright Group/ McGraw Hill
World of Bread!, The	M	I	357	Reading Street	Pearson
World of Clouds	O	I	901	Vocabulary Readers	Houghton Mifflin Harcourt
World of Clouds	O	I	901	Vocabulary Readers/CA	Houghton Mifflin Harcourt
World of Computers, A	K	I	271	Gear Up!	Wright Group/ McGraw Hill
World of Dogs, The	Q	I	250+	Pair-It Books	Steck-Vaughn
World of Dummies, The	N	I	250+	Pacific Literacy	Pacific Learning
World of Elements and Their Properties, The	Y	I	250+	Science Readers	Teacher Created Materials
World of Fish, A	N	I	974	Rigby Flying Colors	Rigby
World of Food, A	K	I	340	Leveled Readers	Houghton Mifflin Harcourt
World of Food, A	K	I	340	Leveled Readers/CA	Houghton Mifflin Harcourt
World of Food, A	K	I	340	Leveled Readers/TX	Houghton Mifflin Harcourt
World of Fun, A	G	I	176	Instant Readers	Harcourt School Publishers
World of Games, A	P	RF	676	Leveled Readers	Houghton Mifflin Harcourt
World of Genetics, The	Y	I	250+	Science Readers	Teacher Created Materials
World of Homes, A	M	I	732	Rigby Flying Colors	Rigby
World of Imagination, A	R	I	250+	Literacy 2000	Rigby
World of Kites, A	M	I	272	Vocabulary Readers	Houghton Mifflin Harcourt
World of Knowing, A: A Story About Thomas Hopkins Gallaudet	R	B	7226	Creative Minds Biographies	Carolrhoda Books
World of Masks, A	L	I	404	Rigby Flying Colors	Rigby
World of Patterns, A	J	I	250+	On Our Way to English	Rigby

W

* Collection of short stories
# Graphic text

TITLE	LEVEL	GENRE	WORD COUNT	AUTHOR / SERIES	PUBLISHER / DISTRIBUTOR
World of Plants, The	R	I	250+	Science Readers	Teacher Created Materials
World of Robots	T	I	1500	Vocabulary Readers	Houghton Mifflin Harcourt
World of Robots	T	I	1500	Vocabulary Readers/CA	Houghton Mifflin Harcourt
World of Rocks & Minerals, The	U	I	250+	Science Readers	Teacher Created Materials
World of Silence, The	S	I	3382	Take Two Books	Wright Group/McGraw Hill
World of Snow, A	M	RF	250+	Livorse, Kay	Houghton Mifflin Harcourt
World of Sport, A	M	I	250+	Rigby Star Quest	Rigby
World of Treats, A	N	I	250+	InfoQuest	Rigby
World of Trees, The	P	I	1185	Vocabulary Readers	Houghton Mifflin Harcourt
World of Trees, The	P	I	1185	Vocabulary Readers/CA	Houghton Mifflin Harcourt
World of Water, The	O	I	250+	Orbit Chapter Books	Pacific Learning
World Safari	R	I	250+	In Step Readers	Rigby
World Safari	R	I	250+	Literacy by Design	Rigby
World Tour of Cultures, A	O	I	814	Reading Street	Pearson
World War I	W	I	250+	Primary Source Readers	Teacher Created Materials
World War II	W	I	250+	Primary Source Readers	Teacher Created Materials
World War II Spies	X	I	250+	Spies	Capstone Press
World Worth Keeping, A	V	I	250+	Sunshine	Wright Group/McGraw Hill
World's Best Dog-Walker, The	Q	RF	250+	Zollman, Pam	Steck-Vaughn
World's Biggest Baby, The	H	I	239	Ready Readers	Pearson Learning Group
World's Deadliest Poisons, The	X	I	250+	The World's Top 10s	Capstone Press
World's Fastest Animals, The	Q	I	250+	The World's Top 10s	Capstone Press
World's Fastest Boats, The	W	I	250+	Built for Speed	Capstone Press
World's Fastest Cars, The	W	I	250+	Built for Speed	Capstone Press
World's Fastest Military Airplanes, The	W	I	250	Built for Speed	Capstone Press
World's Greatest Juggler, The	E	F	105	Little Readers	Houghton Mifflin Harcourt
World's Greatest Showman, The	Q	B	250+	Power Up!	Steck-Vaughn
World's Greatest Toe Show, The	M	RF	250+	Lamb, Nancy; Singer, Muff	Troll Associates
World's Largest Plants, The: A Book About Trees	M	I	250+	Growing Things	Picture Window Books
World's Longest Toenail, The	L	F	862	Rigby Gigglers	Rigby
World's Most Amazing Survival Stories, The	V	I	250+	The World's Top 10s	Capstone Press
World's Most Dangerous Jobs, The	V	I	250+	The World's Top 10s	Capstone Press
World's Most Dangerous Machines, The	U	I	250+	The World's Top 10s	Capstone Press
World's Most Notorious Crooks, The	W	I	250+	The World's Top 10s	Capstone Press
World's Wildest Roller Coasters, The	W	I	250+	Built for Speed	Capstone Press
Worm Book, The	A	I	36	Bonnell, Kris	Reading Reading Books
Worm Builds	C	F	31	Brand New Readers	Candlewick Press
Worm Farm, The	G	RF	205	Take Two Books	Wright Group/McGraw Hill
Worm Is Hot	D	F	30	Brand New Readers	Candlewick Press
Worm Looks for Lunch	I	F	364	Big Cat	Pacific Learning
Worm Rap	H	F	251	Alphakids	Sundance
Worm Watches	D	F	33	Brand New Readers	Candlewick Press
Worm Work	P	I	250+	Sails	Rigby
Worm, The	C	F	38	Sun Sprouts	ETA Cuisenaire
Worms	D	F	39	Literacy 2000	Rigby
Worms	P	I	250+	Mini Pets	Steck-Vaughn
Worms	N	I	250+	Nature's Friends	Compass Point Books
Worms Eat Our Garbage	G	RF	227	On Our Way to English	Rigby
Worms for Breakfast	I	TL	250+	Little Readers	Houghton Mifflin Harcourt
Worm's Home, A	K	I	281	Independent Readers Science	Houghton Mifflin Harcourt
Worms, Wonderful Worms	L	I	250+	Voyages	SRA/McGraw Hill
Worrisome Wombat, The	M	F	250+	Voyages	SRA/McGraw Hill
Worrywart, The	J	RF	412	InfoTrek	ETA Cuisenaire
Worst Day of My Life, The	L	RF	250+	Cosby, Bill	Scholastic

* Collection of short stories
# Graphic text

W

TITLE	LEVEL	GENRE	WORD COUNT	AUTHOR / SERIES	PUBLISHER / DISTRIBUTOR
Worst House, The	L	RF	250+	Bookweb	Rigby
Worst of the Vikings, The	P	F	250+	High-Fliers	Pacific Learning
Worst Show-and-Tell Ever, The	J	SF	250+	Walsh, Rita	Troll Associates
Worst Team in the World, The	P	RF	250+	High-Fliers	Pacific Learning
Worst Witch at Sea, The	P	F	250+	Murphy, Jill	Candlewick Press
Worst Witch Saves the Day, The	P	F	250+	Murphy, Jill	Candlewick Press
Worst Witch Strikes Again, The	P	F	250+	Murphy, Jill	Candlewick Press
Worst Witch, The	P	F	250+	Murphy, Jill	Puffin/Penguin
Would You Like to Fly?	C	F	52	Twig	Wright Group/McGraw Hill
Would You Snitch?	T	RF	1454	Leveled Readers	Houghton Mifflin Harcourt
Would You Snitch?	T	RF	1454	Leveled Readers/CA	Houghton Mifflin Harcourt
Wow!	D	F	145	Bookshop	Mondo
Wow! Look at This!	B	I	34	Science	Outside the Box
Wow! What a Week!	J	RF	364	Wonders	Hampton-Brown
Wreck Trek	S	I	250+	Belcher, Angie	Pacific Learning
Wrecked! Shipping Disasters	V	I	250+	Story Surfers	ETA Cuisenaire
Wrestling Sturbridge	Z	RF	250+	Wallace, Rich	Random House
Wright 3, The	T	RF	250+	Balliett, Blue	Scholastic
Wright Brothers	L	B	461	Leveled Readers/TX	Houghton Mifflin Harcourt
#Wright Brothers and the Airplane, The	S	B	250	Graphic Library	Capstone Press
Wright Brothers, First Flyers, The	V	B	2700	Independent Readers Science	Houghton Mifflin Harcourt
Wright Brothers, The	M	B	250+	Biography	Benchmark Education
Wright Brothers, The	P	B	250+	Early Biographies	Compass Point Books
Wright Brothers, The	K	B	250+	Famous People in Transportation	Red Brick Learning
Wright Brothers, The	Y	B	250+	Freedman, Russell	Holiday House
Wright Brothers, The	S	B	3396	History Maker Bios	Lerner Publications
Wright Brothers, The	L	B	461	Leveled Readers	Houghton Mifflin Harcourt
Wright Brothers, The	L	B	461	Leveled Readers/CA	Houghton Mifflin Harcourt
Wright Brothers, The	U	B	250+	Sobol, Donald J.	Scholastic
Wringer	U	RF	250+	Spinelli, Jerry	HarperTrophy
Wrinkle in Time, A	W	F	250+	L'Engle, Madeleine	Bantam Doubleday Dell
Wrinkles	C	I	32	Literacy 2000	Rigby
Wrinkly Socks Make Me Giggle	H	RF	146	Wake, Shelley	Kaeden Books
Write It Down!	U	I	250+	iOpeners	Pearson Learning Group
Write Up a Storm with the Polk Street School	M	RF	250+	Giff, Patricia Reilly	Bantam
Write Your Own Adventure Story	U	I	250+	Write Your Own	Compass Point Books
Write Your Own Fantasy Story	U	I	250+	Write Your Own	Compass Point Books
Write Your Own Graphic Novel	U	I	250+	Write Your Own	Compass Point Books
Write Your Own Historical Fiction	U	I	250+	Write Your Own	Compass Point Books
Write Your Own Mystery Story	U	I	250+	Write Your Own	Compass Point Books
Write Your Own Realistic Fiction Story	U	I	250+	Write Your Own	Compass Point Books
Write Your Own Science Fiction Story	U	I	250+	Write Your Own	Compass Point Books
Writer from the Prairie	R	B	1434	Leveled Readers	Houghton Mifflin Harcourt
Writer from the Prairie	R	B	1434	Leveled Readers/CA	Houghton Mifflin Harcourt
Writer from the Prairie	R	B	1434	Leveled Readers/TX	Houghton Mifflin Harcourt
Writer of the Plains: A Story about Willa Cather	Q	B	250+	Streissguth, Tom	Carolrhoda Books
Writer Who Changed America, The	U	B	1976	Leveled Readers	Houghton Mifflin Harcourt
Writer Who Changed America, The	U	B	1976	Leveled Readers/CA	Houghton Mifflin Harcourt
Writer Who Changed America, The	U	B	1976	Leveled Readers/TX	Houghton Mifflin Harcourt
Writers	J	I	264	Vocabulary Readers	Houghton Mifflin Harcourt
Writers	J	I	264	Vocabulary Readers/CA	Houghton Mifflin Harcourt
Writer's Work, A	N	I	481	Wonder World	Wright Group/McGraw Hill
Writers: Then and Now	O	I	250+	Primary Source Readers	Teacher Created Materials
Writing a Biography: Henry Ford	M	I	374	Rigby Flying Colors	Rigby

W

Organized Alphabetically by Title
Storable Database at www.fountasandpinnellleveledbooks.com

* Collection of short stories
# Graphic text

TITLE	LEVEL	GENRE	WORD COUNT	AUTHOR / SERIES	PUBLISHER / DISTRIBUTOR
Writing Bug, The	O	B	250+	Meet The Author	Richard C. Owen
Writing for Freedom: A Story About Lydia Maria Child	R	B	8090	Creative Minds Biographies	Carolrhoda Books
Writing in Ancient China	U	I	250+	On Deck	Rigby
Writing in Ancient Egypt	U	I	250+	On Deck	Rigby
Writing in Ancient India	U	I	250+	On Deck	Rigby
Writing in Ancient Mesopotamia	U	I	250+	On Deck	Rigby
Writing in Ancient Phonecia	U	I	250+	On Deck	Rigby
Writing Places	E	I	30	Chanko, Pamela	Scholastic
Wrong Way Around Magic	N	F	250+	Chew, Ruth	Scholastic
Wrong Way Reggie	J	RF	304	Little Celebrations	Pearson Learning Group
Wrong-Way Rabbit, The	J	F	304	Slater, Teddy	Scholastic
Wuthering Heights	Z	RF	250+	High-Fliers	Pacific Learning
WWW	W	I	250+	Boldprint	Steck-Vaughn
Wyoming	T	I	250+	Hello U.S.A.	Lerner Publications
Wyoming	R	I	250+	This Land Is Your Land	Compass Point Books
Wyoming: Facts and Symbols	O	I	250+	Dubois, Muriel L.	Red Brick Learning

W

TITLE	LEVEL	GENRE	WORD COUNT	AUTHOR / SERIES	PUBLISHER / DISTRIBUTOR
X Games: Action Sports Grab the Spotlight	S	I	250+	High Five Reading	Red Brick Learning
X Marks the Spot	N	I	250+	Home Connection Collection	Rigby
X Marks the Spot	I	RF	309	Pair-It Turn and Learn	Steck-Vaughn
X Ray, The	C	RF	48	Learn to Read	Creative Teaching Press
X-Games, The: Skateboarding's Greatest Event	Q	I	250+	Skateboarding	Capstone Press
X-Rays	X	I	3158	Leveled Readers Science	Houghton Mifflin Harcourt
X-Rays	O	I	250+	Voyages	SRA/McGraw Hill
Xuanzang, Chinese Hero	W	B	3100	Leveled Readers Social Studies	Houghton Mifflin Harcourt
Yabby Tale, A	N	RF	250+	Sunshine	Wright Group/McGraw Hill
Yahoo for You	E	RF	137	Early Readers	Compass Point Books
Yakkity-Yak	C	F	49	Learn to Read	Creative Teaching Press
Yaks	I	I	221	Sails	Rigby
Yang the Eldest and His Odd Jobs	P	RF	250+	Namioka, Lensey	Bantam
Yang the Second and Her Secret Admirer	P	RF	250+	Namioka, Lensey	Bantam
Yang the Third and Her Impossible Family	P	RF	250+	Namioka, Lensey	Bantam
Yang the Youngest and His Terrible Ear	P	RF	250+	Namioka, Lensey	Bantam
Yao Ming	P	B	1945	Amazing Athletes	Lerner Publications
Yao's Wild Ride	Q	HF	250+	Leveled Readers Language Support	Houghton Mifflin Harcourt
Yard for All, A	B	F	55	Reading Street	Pearson
Yard Sale	H	RF	167	Pair-It Turn and Learn	Steck-Vaughn
Yard Sale, The	E	RF	200+	Cherrington, Janelle	Scholastic
Yard Sale, The	I	RF	250+	Little Readers	Houghton Mifflin Harcourt
Yard Sale, The	K	RF	250+	Windows on Literacy	National Geographic
Yasmin and the Flood	F	RF	81	Oxford Reading Tree	Oxford University Press
Yasmin's Box	G	F	170	Cambridge Reading	Pearson Learning Group
Yazhi Laughs	K	RF	320	Gear Up!	Wright Group/McGraw Hill
Year Down Yonder, A	V	HF	250+	Peck, Richard	Penguin Group
Year in Antartica, A	R	I	250+	iOpeners	Pearson Learning Group
Year in the Desert, A	M	I	250+	Yellow Umbrella Books	Red Brick Learning
Year Mom Won the Pennant, The	P	RF	250+	Christopher, Matt	Little, Brown & Co.
Year of Fun, A	A	I	32	Leveled Readers	Houghton Mifflin Harcourt
Year of Fun, A	A	I	32	Leveled Readers/CA	Houghton Mifflin Harcourt
Year of Impossible Goodbyes	W	HF	250+	Choi, Sook Nyui	Yearling
Year of the Dog, The	Q	RF	250+	Lin, Grace	Little, Brown & Co.
Year of the Hangman, The	Y	HF	250+	Blackwood, Gary	Scholastic
Year of the Panda, The	N	RF	250+	Soar To Success	Houghton Mifflin Harcourt
Year of the Rat, The	Q	RF	250+	Lin, Grace	Little, Brown & Co.
Year of the Sawdust Man, The	Y	RF	250+	LaFaye, A.	Simon & Schuster
Year with Mother Bear, A	I	I	164	Storyteller Nonfiction	Wright Group/McGraw Hill
Year, A	H	I	137	The Calendar	Capstone Press
Yearling, The	X	RF	250+	Rawlings, Marjorie Kinnan	Simon & Schuster
Yellow	B	I	26	Colors	Lerner Publications
Yellow	B	I	32	Literacy 2000	Rigby
Yellow Ball	LB	RF	18	Bang, Molly	Morrow
Yellow Bird	F	F	229	Sails	Rigby
Yellow Flowers	C	RF	49	Bonnell, Kris	Reading Reading Books
Yellow Line	Z+	RF	250+	Orca Soundings	Orca Book Publishers
Yellow Overalls	L	F	250+	Literacy 2000	Rigby
Yellow Raft in Blue Water, The	Z+	RF	250+	Dorris, Michael	Henry Holt & Co.
Yellow Yarn Mystery, The	B	F	61	Little Books	Sadlier-Oxford
Yellow: Seeing Yellow All Around Us	K	I	250+	Colors	Capstone Press
Yellowstone 1988: Summer of Fire	W	I	250+	Lauber, Patricia	Scholastic
Yellowstone National Park	O	I	250+	A True Book	Children's Press

XYZ

Organized Alphabetically by Title
Storable Database at www.fountasandpinnellleveledbooks.com

* Collection of short stories
# Graphic text

TITLE	LEVEL	GENRE	WORD COUNT	AUTHOR / SERIES	PUBLISHER / DISTRIBUTOR
Yellowstone, Our First National Park	R	I	1288	Leveled Readers Social Studies	Houghton Mifflin Harcourt
Yellowstone: Our First National Park	N	I	250+	Rosen Real Readers	Rosen Publishing Group
Yemi's Beads	L	RF	250+	Literacy by Design	Rigby
Yen's Story: From China to California	T	HF	250+	Reading Expeditions	National Geographic
Yes Ma'am	H	RF	125	Story Box	Wright Group/McGraw Hill
Yes, I Can	C	RF	30	Teacher's Choice Series	Pearson Learning Group
Yes, I Can!	D	F	45	Ready Readers	Pearson Learning Group
Yes, It Does	D	I	91	Teacher's Choice Series	Pearson Learning Group
Yes, We Can!	B	I	56	On Our Way to English	Rigby
Yikes! Grandma's a Teenager	N	F	250+	The Zack Files	Grossett & Dunlap
Yippy-Day-Yippy-Doo!	E	RF	117	Sunshine	Wright Group/McGraw Hill
Yo Ho! Yo Ho!	I	F	164	Voyages	SRA/McGraw Hill
Yo! Yes?	LB	RF	34	Raschka, Chris	Scholastic
Yoga Class	B	RF	28	Bebop Books	Lee & Low Books Inc.
Yoga Stretches	D	I	65	Gear Up!	Wright Group/McGraw Hill
Yolonda's Genius	V	RF	250+	Fenner, Carol	Aladdin
Yoma Helps a Friend	I	RF	354	InfoTrek	ETA Cuisenaire
Yonder	M	RF	250+	Johnston, Tony	Penguin Group
Yoo Hoo, Moon!	I	F	250+	Blocksma, Mary	Bantam
Yorkshire Terriers	I	I	150	Dogs	Capstone Press
Yoshiko's Surprise	E	RF	81	Seedlings	Continental Press
You	C	I	20	Carousel Earlybirds	Pearson Learning Group
You and Your Teeth	I	I	1009	Sunshine	Wright Group/McGraw Hill
You Are Much Too Small	J	F	250+	Bank Street	Bantam
You Are Special	K	I	250+	Sunshine	Wright Group/McGraw Hill
You Are Unique!	L	I	340	Pair-It Turn and Learn	Steck-Vaughn
*You Be the Detective	Q	RF	250+	Miller, Marvin	Scholastic
*You Be the Detective II	Q	RF	250+	Miller, Marvin	Scholastic
*You Be the Jury	Q	I	250+	Miller, Marvin	Scholastic
*You Be the Jury: Courtroom V	Q	I	250+	Miller, Marvin	Bantam
You Can Always Tell Cathy from Caitlin	K	RF	583	Sunshine	Wright Group/McGraw Hill
You Can Canoe!: A Book of Sporting Activities	O	I	250+	Literacy Tree	Rigby
You Can Cook	M	I	250+	Woo, Lornette	Steck-Vaughn
You Can Do It	F	F	176	Sun Sprouts	ETA Cuisenaire
You Can Do It!	Q	I	250+	Orbit Collections	Pacific Learning
You Can Have a Party Anywhere	J	RF	371	Sails	Rigby
You Can Make a Difference!	M	I	686	Reading Street	Pearson
You Can Make a Memory Scrapbook	J	I	179	How-To Series	Benchmark Education
You Can Make a Pom-pom	G	I	39	Windows on Literacy	National Geographic
You Can Make a Timer	F	I	124	How-To Series	Benchmark Education
You Can Make Skittles	G	I	128	Sunshine	Wright Group/McGraw Hill
You Can Recycle!	K	I	219	Rigby Focus	Rigby
You Can't Catch Me	J	F	250+	Oppenheim, Joanne	Houghton Mifflin Harcourt
You Can't Catch Me!	I	F	244	Cambridge Reading	Pearson Learning Group
You Can't Catch Me!	D	RF	89	Lighthouse	Rigby
You Can't Eat Your Chicken Pox, Amber Brown	N	RF	250+	Danziger, Paula	Scholastic
You Can't See Your Bones with Binoculars	P	I	250+	Ziefert, Harriet	Scholastic
You Can't Taste a Pickle With Your Ear	O	I	250+	Ziefert, Harriet	Scholastic
You Couldn't Pay Me Enough to Do This Job!	S	I	250+	Rigby Literacy	Rigby
You Did It!	G	RF	246	Sunshine	Wright Group/McGraw Hill
You Do Ride Well	H	RF	165	Windmill Books	Rigby
You Don't Know Me	X	RF	250+	Klass, David	Harper Collins
You Don't Look Like Your Mother	L	F	250+	Bookshop	Mondo
You Have Mail: True Stories of Cybercrime	W	I	250+	24/7 Science Behind the Scenes	Scholastic

XYZ

* Collection of short stories
# Graphic text

Storable Database at www.fountasandpinnellleveledbooks.com

TITLE	LEVEL	GENRE	WORD COUNT	AUTHOR / SERIES	PUBLISHER / DISTRIBUTOR
You Look Funny	G	RF	180	First Start	Troll Associates
You Might Fall	H	RF	180	Stepping Stones	Nelson/Michaels Assoc.
You See a Circus I See...	J	RF	250+	Downs, Mike	Charlesbridge
You See with Your Eyes	G	I	218	PM Science Readers	Rigby
You Should Try That with a Rhino	E	F	123	Home Connection Collection	Rigby
You Shouldn't Have to Say Good-bye	T	RF	250+	Hermes, Patricia	Scholastic
You Want Women to Vote, Lizzie Stanton?	W	B	250+	Fritz, Jean	Penguin Group
You'll Roar	H	F	73	Instant Readers	Harcourt School Publishers
You'll Soon Grow into Them Titch	H	RF	191	Hutchins, Pat	Morrow
Young Arthur Ashe: Brave Champion	L	B	250+	First-Start Biography	Troll Associates
Young Cam Jansen and the Baseball Mystery	J	RF	250+	Adler, David A.	Puffin/Penguin
Young Cam Jansen and the Dinosaur Game	J	RF	250+	Adler, David A.	Puffin/Penguin
Young Cam Jansen and the Double Beach Mystery	J	RF	250+	Adler, David A.	Puffin/Penguin
Young Cam Jansen and the Ice Skate Mystery	J	RF	250+	Adler, David A.	Puffin/Penguin
Young Cam Jansen and the Library Mystery	J	RF	250+	Adler, David A.	Puffin/Penguin
Young Cam Jansen and the Lost Tooth	J	RF	250+	Adler, David A.	Puffin/Penguin
Young Cam Jansen and the Missing Cookie	J	RF	250+	Adler, David A.	Puffin/Penguin
Young Cam Jansen and the Pizza Shop Mystery	J	RF	250+	Adler, David A.	Puffin/Penguin
Young Cam Jansen and the Spotted Cat Mystery	J	RF	250+	Adler, David A.	Scholastic
Young Champions: It's All About Attitude	Q	I	250+	High Five Reading	Capstone Press
Young Clara Barton: Battlefield Nurse	L	B	250+	First-Start Biography	Troll Associates
Young Davy Crockett: Frontier Fighter	L	B	250+	First-Start Biography	Troll Associates
Young Eagle and His Horse	Q	HF	1267	Leveled Readers	Houghton Mifflin Harcourt
Young Eagle and His Horse	Q	HF	1267	Leveled Readers/CA	Houghton Mifflin Harcourt
Young Eagle and His Horse	Q	HF	1267	Leveled Readers/TX	Houghton Mifflin Harcourt
Young Frederick Douglass	N	B	250+	First-Start Biography	Scholastic
Young Geographers	O	I	250+	People, Spaces & Places	Rand McNally
Young Helen Keller: Woman of Courage	L	B	250+	First-Start Biography	Troll Associates
Young Heroes of the North and South	Y	B	250+	The Civil War	Carus Publishing
Young Jackie Robinson: Baseball Hero	L	B	250+	First-Start Biography	Troll Associates
Young Jim Thorpe: All-American Athlete	L	B	250+	First-Start Biography	Troll Associates
Young Joan	X	HF	250+	Dana, Barbara	HarperTrophy
Young Land Lords, The	X	RF	250+	Myers, Walter Dean	Penguin Group
Young Man and the Sea, The	S	RF	250+	Philbrick, Rodman	Scholastic
Young Martin Luther King, Jr.	M	B	250+	First-Start Biography	Scholastic
Young Martin's Promise	N	B	250+	Stories of America	Steck-Vaughn
Young Mozart	O	B	250+	Isadora, Rachel	Penguin Group
Young Orville and Wilbur Wright: First to Fly	L	B	250+	First-Start Biography	Troll Associates
Young Reggie Jackson: Hall of Fame Champion	L	B	250+	First-Start Biography	Troll Associates
Young Robin's Hood	R	TL	250+	Bookshop	Mondo
Young Rosa Parks: Civil Rights Heroine	L	B	250+	First-Start Biography	Troll Associates
Young Squanto: The First Thanksgiving	L	B	250+	First-Start Biography	Troll Associates
Young Thurgood Marshall: Fighter for Equality	L	B	250+	First-Start Biography	Troll Associates
Young Tom Edison: Great Inventor	L	B	250+	First-Start Biography	Troll Associates
Young Wolf's First Hunt	M	RF	250+	Shefelman, Janice	Random House
Youngest Giraffe, The	I	RF	250+	PM Plus Story Books	Rigby
Youngest in the Family	F	RF	144	Visions	Wright Group/McGraw Hill
Your Amazing Body!	K	I	293	Reading Street	Pearson
Your Body	J	I	208	Early Connections	Benchmark Education
Your Body in Balance	O	I	250+	Orbit Chapter Books	Pacific Learning
Your Body Up Close	M	I	250+	Rigby Rocket	Rigby
Your Bones	P	I	250+	Your Body	Red Brick Learning
Your Brain	P	I	250+	Your Body	Red Brick Learning

Organized Alphabetically by Title
Storable Database at www.fountasandpinnellleveledbooks.com

* Collection of short stories
\# Graphic text

XYZ

TITLE	LEVEL	GENRE	WORD COUNT	AUTHOR / SERIES	PUBLISHER / DISTRIBUTOR
Your Guide to Pet Care	P	I	1552	Vocabulary Readers	Houghton Mifflin Harcourt
Your Guide to Pet Care	P	I	1552	Vocabulary Readers/CA	Houghton Mifflin Harcourt
Your Heart	L	I	250+	Early Connections	Benchmark Education
Your Heart	P	I	250+	Your Body	Red Brick Learning
Your Heart and Blood	M	I	250+	Rigby Focus	Rigby
Your Heart, Your Blood: The Human Circulatory System	U	I	250+	Explore More	Wright Group/McGraw Hill
Your Lungs	P	I	250+	Your Body	Red Brick Learning
Your Mother Was a Neanderthal	P	F	250+	Scieszka, Jon	Penguin Group
Your Move, J. P.!	R	RF	250+	Lowry, Lois	Random House
Your Muscles	P	I	250+	Your Body	Red Brick Learning
Your Muscles on the Move	T	I	250+	Explore More	Wright Group/McGraw Hill
Your Nervous System	M	I	366	Early Connections	Benchmark Education
Your Senses	H	I	138	Pebble Books	Red Brick Learning
Your Senses Tell You So!	D	I	36	Pair-It Turn and Learn	Steck-Vaughn
Your Stomach	P	I	250+	Your Body	Red Brick Learning
Your Super Computer	P	I	250+	Rigby Focus	Rigby
Your Teeth	J	I	131	Dental Health	Capstone Press
Your Terrific Teeth	I	I	156	Gear Up!	Wright Group/McGraw Hill
You're in Big Trouble, Brad!	K	RF	1345	Real Kids Readers	Millbrook Press
You're My Nikki	M	RF	250+	Eisenberg, Phyllis Rose	Penguin Group
You're Never Too Young to Save the Planet	L	I	250+	Literacy by Design	Rigby
You're on Camera!	T	I	1759	Vocabulary Readers	Houghton Mifflin Harcourt
You're on Camera!	T	I	1759	Vocabulary Readers/CA	Houghton Mifflin Harcourt
You're Out	N	RF	250+	Kroll, Stephen	Avon Camelot
You're So Clever	H	RF	188	Voyages	SRA/McGraw Hill
Yourspace: Questioning New Media	V	I	250+	Media Literacy	Capstone Press
YouTube	T	I	5137	A Great Idea	Norwood House Press
You've Got Cheetah-Mail	M	I	250+	World Quest Adventures	World Quest Learning
Yo-Yo a Go-Go	F	RF	177	Rigby Literacy	Rigby
Yo-Yo Ma: Musical Superstar	Q	B	250+	Leveled Readers Language Support	Houghton Mifflin Harcourt
Yo-Yo Tricks	P	I	250+	Games Around the World	Compass Point Books
Yo-yos	G	RF	62	City Kids	Rigby
Yo-Yo's	O	I	250+	PM Nonfiction-Emerald	Rigby
Yuck Soup	B	F	25	Sunshine	Wright Group/McGraw Hill
Yuck!	K	F	250+	Leveled Readers Language Support	Houghton Mifflin Harcourt
Yucky Reptile Alphabet Book, The	N	I	250+	Pallotta, Jerry	Charlesbridge
Yucky, Mucky Mud	H	F	271	Sun Sprouts	ETA Cuisenaire
Yukadoos	I	F	121	Jellybeans	Rigby
Yum and Yuk	I	F	125	Story Box	Wright Group/McGraw Hill
Yum!	A	I	40	On Our Way to English	Rigby
Yum! Yum!	D	F	84	Bookshop	Mondo
Yum! Yum!	C	F	36	Storyworlds	Heinemann Educational Publishers
Yummy Lunch, A	B	RF	22	Early Emergent	Pioneer Valley
Yummy Snack, A	E	I	114	On Our Way to English	Rigby
Yummy, Tum, Tee	C	F	51	Little Celebrations	Pearson Learning Group
Yummy, Yummy	F	F	115	Grey, Judith	Troll Associates
Yun's Visit	J	RF	250+	On Our Way to English	Rigby
Zac and Chirpy	C	RF	61	PM Photo Stories	Rigby
Zac and Puffing Billy	C	RF	66	PM Photo Stories	Rigby
Zac and the Ducks	C	RF	77	PM Photo Stories	Rigby

XYZ

* Collection of short stories
\# Graphic text

TITLE	LEVEL	GENRE	WORD COUNT	AUTHOR / SERIES	PUBLISHER / DISTRIBUTOR
Zachary and the Pony Express	P	HF	250+	Leveled Readers Language Support	Houghton Mifflin Harcourt
Zachary Taylor	U	B	250+	Profiles of the Presidents	Compass Point Books
Zachary Taylor: Twelfth President	R	B	250+	Getting to Know the U.S. Presidents	Children's Press
Zachary's Ball	N	F	250	Tavares, Matt	Candlewick Press
Zacharys' Plans, The	O	F	250+	Sails	Rigby
Zachary's Ride	R	HF	1780	Leveled Readers	Houghton Mifflin Harcourt
Zack and Nate	H	RF	250+	Early Emergent	Pioneer Valley
Zack's Alligator	K	F	250+	Little Readers	Houghton Mifflin Harcourt
Zack's Alligator	K	F	250+	Mozelle, Shirley	HarperTrophy
Zack's Alligator Goes to School	K	F	250+	Mozelle, Shirley	HarperTrophy
Zack's Halloween Costume	D	RF	103	Early Emergent	Pioneer Valley
Zack's House	D	RF	114	Early Emergent	Pioneer Valley
Zack's Moving Day Surprise	F	RF	122	Developing Books	Pioneer Valley
Zack's Spots	I	F	327	Sails	Rigby
Zac's Train Ride	E	RF	126	PM Photo Stories	Rigby
Zac's Train Set	B	RF	46	PM Photo Stories	Rigby
Zala Runs for Her Life	J	F	250+	PM Story Books-Purple	Rigby
Zamboni's Bath	L	RF	1000	Burns, Vicki Scott	Kaeden Books
Zane's Trace	Z+	RF	250+	Wolf, Allan	Candlewick Press
Zap!	G	F	83	Seedlings	Continental Press
Zap! I'm a Mind Reader	N	SF	250+	The Zack Files	Grossett & Dunlap
Zebras	I	I	122	African Animals	Capstone Press
Zebras	O	I	2484	Early Bird Nature Books	Lerner Publishing
Zebras	O	I	250+	Holmes, Kevin J.	Red Brick Learning
Zebras	N	I	250+	Meadows, Graham; Vial, Claire	Pearson Learning Group
Zebras	U	I	5802	Nature Watch Books	Lerner Publications
Zebras	H	I	78	Seedlings	Continental Press
Zebras Don't Brush Their Teeth!	B	I	54	Evans, Lynette	Scholastic
Zebra's Yellow Van	C	F	31	Ready Readers	Pearson Learning Group
Zebulon Pike: Soldier and Explorer	V	B	250+	Let Freedom Ring	Capstone Press
Zeely	R	RF	250+	Hamilton, Virginia	Macmillan
Zeep's Safety Scare	K	F	250+	InfoTrek	ETA Cuisenaire
Zee's Way	T	RF	250+	Orca Soundings	Orca Book Publishers
Zeke Takes a Bath	J	F	532	Leveled Readers	Houghton Mifflin Harcourt
Zelda and Ivy: One Christmas	K	F	250+	Kvasnosky, Laura McGee	Candlewick Press
Zelda and Ivy: the Runaways	J	F	250+	Kvasnosky, Laura McGee	Candlewick Press
Zemti	L	TL	250+	Books for Young Learners	Richard C. Owen
Zen Shorts	N	F	250+	Muth, Jon J.	Scholastic
Zero	Z+	RF	250+	Tullson, Diane	Fitzhenry & Whiteside
Zeros and Ones	S	I	250+	Wildcats	Wright Group/McGraw Hill
Zero's Slider	M	RF	250+	Christopher, Matt	Little, Brown & Co.
Zeus	W	I	250+	World Mythology	Capstone Press
Ziggy and the Cat	E	RF	72	Windmill Books	Rigby
Zigzag Kayak Trip, The	K	F	467	Springboard	Wright Group/McGraw Hill
Zigzag Movement	F	I	50	The Way Things Move	Red Brick Learning
Zinc Alloy	P	SF	250+	Lemke, Donald	Stone Arch Books
Zinnia, The	B	RF	34	Ray's Readers	Outside the Box
Zip Me Up	E	RF	171	Handprints C, Set 2	Educators Publishing Service
Zippers	C	RF	21	Books for Young Learners	Richard C. Owen
Zipping, Zapping, Zooming Bats	N	I	250+	Soar To Success	Houghton Mifflin Harcourt
Zippity Zinger, The	R	RF	250+	Winkler, Henry and Oliver, Lin	Grosset & Dunlap

XYZ

* Collection of short stories
\# Graphic text

TITLE	LEVEL	GENRE	WORD COUNT	AUTHOR / SERIES	PUBLISHER / DISTRIBUTOR
Zippy Zebra Finds a Friend	F	F	140	Springboard	Wright Group/McGraw Hill
Zippy's Lost Stripes	I	F	327	In Step Readers	Rigby
Zip-Zip, Rattle-Bang!	E	F	141	Story Basket	Wright Group/McGraw Hill
Zithers	G	RF	55	Little Celebrations	Pearson Learning Group
Zlata's Diary	X	B	250+	Filipovic, Zlata	Puffin/Penguin
Zoe and the Lights	I	RF	416	Leveled Readers	Houghton Mifflin Harcourt
Zoe and the Lights	I	RF	416	Leveled Readers/CA	Houghton Mifflin Harcourt
Zoe at the Fancy Dress Ball	J	RF	250+	Literacy 2000	Rigby
Zoe's Birthday Presents	D	RF	83	Emergent	Pioneer Valley
Zombies Don't Play Soccer	M	F	250+	Dadey, Debbie; Jones, Marcia Thornton	Scholastic
Zomo the Rabbit: A Trickster Tale from West Africa	M	TL	250+	McDermott, Gerald	Harcourt Trade
Zoo Animals 1, 2, 3	I	I	208	Counting Books	Capstone Press
Zoo Babies	F	I	51	Little Celebrations	Pearson Learning Group
Zoo Crew, The	I	I	154	Gear Up!	Wright Group/McGraw Hill
Zoo Dinners	B	RF	30	Sails	Rigby
Zoo Food	C	I	58	Reading Corners	Pearson Learning Group
Zoo in Willy's Bed, The	E	RF	81	Gorman, Kate Sturnman	Continental Press
Zoo Keepers	M	I	250+	Community Helpers	Red Brick Learning
Zoo Map	G	I	96	Windows on Literacy	National Geographic
Zoo Overnight	L	RF	250+	Pacific Literacy	Pacific Learning
Zoo Party	H	RF	271	Leveled Readers	Houghton Mifflin Harcourt
Zoo Party	H	RF	271	Leveled Readers/CA	Houghton Mifflin Harcourt
Zoo Party	H	RF	271	Leveled Readers/TX	Houghton Mifflin Harcourt
Zoo Party, A	H	RF	134	Book Bank	Wright Group/McGraw Hill
Zoo Trip!	O	F	250+	Tristars	Richard C. Owen
Zoo Trip, The	E	I	115	Springboard	Wright Group/McGraw Hill
Zoo, A	LB	I	14	Literacy 2000	Rigby
Zoo, The	C	RF	33	Carousel Readers	Pearson Learning Group
Zoo, The	B	I	32	Handprints B	Educators Publishing Service
Zoo, The	B	I	31	Wonder World	Wright Group/McGraw Hill
Zookeepers Sleepers, The	E	F	76	New Reader Series	Bungalo Books
Zoo-Looking	G	RF	149	Bookshop	Mondo
Zoom In!	M	I	250+	Storyteller- Lightning Bolts	Wright Group/ McGraw Hill
Zoom!	A	I	24	Leveled Readers	Houghton Mifflin Harcourt
Zoom!	A	I	24	Leveled Readers/CA	Houghton Mifflin Harcourt
Zoom! Zoom!	C	F	43	Joy Readers	Pearson Learning Group
Zooman Sam	P	RF	250+	Lowry, Lois	Houghton Mifflin Harcourt
Zoomers, The	A	F	28	Kinderstarters	Rigby
Zoos	N	I	1550	Take Two Books	Wright Group/McGraw Hill
Zoos Back to Nature?	W	I	250+	iOpeners	Pearson Learning Group
Zulu Dog	V	RF	250+	Ferreira, Anton	Farrar, Straus and Giroux
Zulu Warriors	T	I	250+	Warriors of History	Capstone Press
Zuni, The	R	I	250+	First Reports	Compass Point Books
Zunid	J	RF	250+	Stepping Stones	Nelson/Michaels Assoc.

* Collection of short stories
# Graphic text

BOOK PUBLISHERS AND DISTRIBUTORS

Some companies publish their own titles, while others distribute series books from a variety of sources. Ordering information on series books is available from the sources on the following page. Trade titles may be ordered from any paperback supplier, many of which offer a flat paperback discount to schools.

Book Publishers

Ace Books
Aladdin
Albert Whitman & Co.
Alfred A. Knopf
Amulet Books
Andre Deutsch
Annick Press
Arte Publico
Atheneum
August House
Avon
Avon Books
Avon Camelot
Ballantine Books
Bantam
Bantam Books
Bantam Doubleday Dell
Barron's Educational
Beech Tree Books
Belle Rivers Readers
Benckmark Education
Berkley Books
Beyond Words
Bloomsbury Children's Books
Blue Sky Press
Bluefish Bay Publishing
Bodley
Books for a Course
Books for Young Readers
Boyds Mills Press
Bradbury/Trumpet
Bridge Water
Bungalo Books
Candlewick Press
Capstone Press
Carolrhoda Books
Carus Publishing

Chariot Victor Publishing
Charlesbridge
Checkerboard
Chelsea House
Children's Press
Chronicle Books
Cinco Puntos Press
Clarion
Collier Books
Compass Point Books
Continental Press
Coward
Crabtree
Creative Arts Book Co.
Creative Edge
Creative Teaching Press
Crestwood House
Cricket Books
Crowell
Crown
Curriculum Press
Cypress
Darby Creek Publishing
David Fickling Publishing
David R. Godine
Dawn
Delacorte
Dell
Dell Yearling
Dial Books
Dial/Penguin
Dillon Press
DK Publishing
Dominie Press
Donovan
Doubleday Books
Douglas & McIntyre
Dover Publications

Dragonfly Books
Dutton
Dutton/Penguin
Eagle Crest Books
EDC Publishing
Educational Insights
Educator's Publishing Service
Eleanor Curtain Publishing
Enslow Publishers, Inc.
ETA/Cuisenaire
Farrar, Straus and Giroux
Fawcett Columbine
Feiwel and Friends
Firefly Books
Fitzhenry & Whiteside
Flyleaf Publishing
Follett
Four Winds
Frances Lincoln
Franklin Watts
Free Spirit Publishing
Front Street
Fulcrum Publishing
G.P. Putnam's Sons
Garrard Publishing Co.
Ginn & Co.
Golden
Gosset & Dunlap
Green Tiger Press
Greenwillow
Grolier Press
Grolier Publishing
Grosset & Dunlap
Grosset & Dunlap/Price Stern Sloane/Penguin
Groundwood Books

Gulf
Hampton-Brown
Harcourt School Publishers
Harcourt Trade
Harper & Row
HarperCollins
HarperPerennial
HarperTrophy
Health Communications
Hearst
Heinemann
Henry Holt & Co.
Herald Press
Heritage House
Holiday House
Houghton Mifflin Harcourt
Hyperion
Hyperion/Madison Press
Ideals Children's Books
Ideals Publications Inc.
Intercultural Center for Research in Education
Just Us Books
Kaeden Books
Kane Press
Kane/Miller Book Publishers
Kar-Ben Publishing
Kids Can Press Ltd.
Kingfisher
Kiva Publishing
Ladybird Books
Language for Learning Assoc.
Laurel-Leaf Books
Learning Works, The
Lee & Low Books Inc.

Lerner Publications
Linnet Books
Literacy Footprints
Little, Brown & Co.
London Town Press
Longman/Bow
Lost Coast Press
Lothian Books
Lothrop
Lothrop, Lee & Shepard
Lowell House
MacAdam/Cage Publishing
Macmillan
Macmillan/McGraw Hill
Magic Attic
Marshall Cavendish
Maryruth Books
McElderry Books
Meadowbrook Press
Merrimak
Milkweed Editions
Millbrook Press
Millmark Education
Mimosa
Modern Curriculum
Mondo
Morrow
Morrow Junior Books
Mulberry Books
National Geographic School Publishing
Nelson/Michaels Assoc.
Newbridge
Northern Lights Books
North-South Books
NorthWord Press
Norwood House Press

Okapi	Pleasant Company	SeaScape Press	Sylvan Dell Publishing	Viking/Penguin
Orca Book Publishers	Pocket Books	SeaStar Books	Teacher Created Materials	Voyager Books
Orchard Books	Prentice-Hall	Secret Passage Press	The Blue Sky Press	W. H. Freeman & Co.
OSI	Puffin Books	Signet Classics	The Broken Rifle Press	W. W. Norton
Outside the Box	Puffin/Penguin	Silver Burdett Press	The Kane Press	Walker & Company
Oxford University Press	Putnam/Penguin	Simon & Schuster	The Lerner Group	Warner Books
Pacific Learning	Rand McNally	Simon & Schuster Trade	The McDonald & Woodward Publishing Co.	WaterBrook Press
Pacific Literacy	Random House	Simon Pulse		Watts
Pantheon	Ransom	Skylark	The Millbrook Press	Weinstein Books
PaperStar	Reading Reading Books	Smithsonian	Thomson Learning	Wendy Lamb
Peachtree	Red Brick Learning	Sourcebooks	Tom Doherty	Whitman
Pearson	Richard C. Owen	Speak	Tor	William Morrow
Pearson Learning Group	Rigby	Square Fish	Tott Publications	Windmill
Peguis	Roaring Book Press	SRA/McGraw Hill	Townsend Press	Winslow Press
Penguin Group	Roberts Rinehart	Steck-Vaughn	Treasure Bay	Wood Lock Educational
Penny Candy Press	Rosen Publishing Group	Step-Up Books	Tricycle Press	World Book
Persea Books	Sadlier-Oxford	Sterling	Troll Associates	World Quest Learning
Peter Smith Publications	Scholastic	Stewart, Tabori & Chang	Tundra Books	Wright Group/McGraw-Hill
Philomel Books	School Zone	Stillwater Publishing	Two-Can Publishing	
Picture Window Books	Schwartz & Wade Books	Stone Arch Books	University of Maine	Yearling
Pinata Books	Scribner	Sunburst	University of New Mexico	
Pioneer Valley	Seal Books	Sundance	Viking	

Series Distributors

Benchmark Education
629 Fifth Avenue
Pelham, NY 10803
Phone 1–877–236–2465
Fax 1–877–732–8273
www.benchmarkeducation.com

Capstone Press
151 Good Counsel Drive
P.O. Box 669
Mankato, MN 56002–0669
Phone 1–800–747–4992
Fax 1–888–262–0705
www.capstone-press.com

Grolier Press
P.O. Box 1795
Danbury, CT 06816
Phone 1–800–621–1115
Fax 1–866–783–3461
www.slpservice@scholasticlibrary.com

Houghton Mifflin Harcourt
6277 Sea Harbor Drive
Orlando, FL 32887
Phone 1–800–225–5425
Fax 1–800–269–5232
www.hmhschool.com

Kaeden Books
P.O. Box 16190
Rocky River, OH 44116
Phone 1–800–890-READ
Fax 1–440–617–1403
www.kaeden.com

Mondo Publishing
980 Avenue of the Americas
New York, NY 10018
Phone 1–888–88MONDO
Fax 1–888–532–4492
www.info@mondopub.com

National Geographic School Publishing
Hampton-Brown
P.O. Box 4002865
Des Moines, IA 50340
Phone 1–888–915–3276
Fax 1–800–840–9807
www.customerservice@NGSP.com

Pearson Learning Group
P.O. Box 2500
Lebanon, IN 46052
Phone 1–800–848–9500
Fax 1–877–260–2530
www.k12cs@custhelp.com

Richard C. Owen Publishers
P.O. Box 585
Katonah, NY 10536
Phone 1–800–262–0787
Fax 1–914–232–3977
www.RCOInfo@rcowen.com

Rigby/Steck-Vaughn
HMH Supplemental Publishers
181 Ballardvale Street
P.O. Box 7050
Wilmington, MA 01877
Phone 1–800–289–4490
Fax 1–800–289–3994
www.greatservice@hmhpub.com

Rosen Classroom Books & Materials
29 East 21st Street
New York, NY 10010
Phone 1–800–237–9932
Fax 1–888–436–4643
www.rosenclassroom.com

Scholastic Inc.
P.O. Box 7502
Jefferson City, MO 65102
Phone 1–800–724–6527
Fax 1–800–560–6815
www.scholastic.com

Sundance Publishing
P.O. Box 740
Northborough, MA 01532
Phone 1–800–343–8204
Fax 1–800–456–2419
www.info@sundancepub.com

Wright Group/McGraw Hill
220 East Danieldale Road
DeSoto, TX 75115
Phone 1–800–648–2970
Fax 1–800–593–4418
www.wrightgroup.com